Émile Durkheim

For Mathieu, Vincent, Sara and Nathan

Émile Durkheim

A Biography

Marcel Fournier

Translated by
David Macey

polity

First published in French as *Émile Durkheim* © Librairie Arthème Fayard, 2007

This English edition © Polity Press, 2013

Ouvrage publié avec le concours du Ministère français de la Culture – Centre national du livre
Published with the assistance of the French Ministry of Culture – National Centre for the Book

Polity Press
65 Bridge Street
Cambridge CB2 1UR, UK

Polity Press
350 Main Street
Malden, MA 02148, USA

ISBN-13: 978-0-7456-4645-9

A catalogue record for this book is available from the British Library

Typeset in 10 on 11pt Times NR
by Servis Filmsetting Ltd, Stockport, Cheshire
Printed and bound in the US by Edwards Brothers, Inc.

The publisher has used its best endeavours to ensure that the URLs for external websites referred to in this book are correct and active at the time of going to press. However, the publisher has no responsibility for the websites and can make no guarantee that a site will remain live or that the content is or will remain appropriate.

Every effort has been made to trace all copyright holders, but if any have been inadvertently overlooked the publisher will be pleased to include any necessary credits in any subsequent reprint or edition.

For further information on Polity, visit our website: www.politybooks.com

Contents

Part IV: Paris and the Sorbonne

Part V: Morality and Religion

Part VI: The Great War

Acknowledgements

After Fayard's publication of my *Marcel Mauss: A Biography* (Fournier 2007[1994]), I published an edition of Émile Durkheim's letters to Mauss (Durkheim 1998) in collaboration with Philippe Besnard. Olivier Bétourné, who at the time was an editor at Fayard, issued an invitation that was also a challenge: 'Now we need a Durkheim.' So here it is!

From the outset, my research was supported by the late Pierre Bourdieu, who supervised the doctoral thesis I wrote at the École pratique des hautes études. He facilitated access to the Fonds Hubert-Mauss, which had been deposited in the Collège de France's archives by the Hubert and Mauss families. The archive, which has now been transferred to the Institut mémoires de l'édition contemporaine in Caen (IMEC) includes all the letters written by Durkheim to his nephew Marcel Mauss. My biography of Durkheim is that of a sociologist who shared Bourdieu's oft-expressed desire to adopt a reflexive approach to the social sciences in his work.

When working on the edition of Émile Durkheim's letters to Mauss, I was also able to benefit from the advice of Philippe Besnard, who is no longer with us. I missed him greatly because, when faced with a difficulty, my first reflex was always to turn spontaneously to that great Durkheim scholar. I would like to pay tribute to the energy and competence he displayed over a period of more than 20 years in his 'relaunch' of Durkheim studies in France.

In order to edit the Durkheim/Mauss correspondence and then to write this book, I had to gain access to a very wide range of information and data, and not least the memories and documents preserved by members of the families concerned, and especially the Durkheim, Mauss and Hubert families. My warmest thanks go, of course, to the late Pierre Mauss, his wife and his nephew Robert, and also to the late Étienne Halphen, the later Marcel Durkheim, Bernard Lyon-Caen and Gérard Hubert. I then had to consult the countless documents that are to be found in a very wide range of institutions and archives: the archives of the Collège de France, obviously, and IMEC-Caen, but also the Archives nationales, the archives of the Alliance israélite universelle, the Consistoire de Paris and the Consistoire de Bordeaux, the departmental archives of the Gironde and Vosges *départements*, the archives of the University of Bordeaux, the Université Paris-Sorbonne, the Musée social, and so on.

My research, which also required many trips back and forth across the Atlantic and the help of research assistants, was made possible by financial assistance from the Social Sciences and Humanities Research Council of Canada (SSHRC).

Throughout my research on Émile Durkheim and his collaborators, I had the support of the many colleagues – both teachers and researchers – who, at one moment or another, passed on documents, gave advice or provided encouragement. My deepest thanks to all of them. I would like to express particular gratitude to the love of my life Yolande Cohen for the support she so generously gave me over 10 years of research and writing, and for the great care with which she read the manuscript. Her knowledge of the history of contemporary France has been more than precious to me.

Introduction

French sociologist, leading figure in the French school of sociology and founding father of sociology: this is how the educated public and specialists in the human and social sciences see Émile Durkheim. The house on the boulevard de Talence in Bordeaux, where he lived for several years, boasts a plaque bearing the legend: 'Émile Durkheim, founder of sociology'. Nothing more and nothing less! Durkheim would appear to have dethroned Auguste Comte, who coined the word *sociologie* – a barbarism derived from the Latin *socius* (society) and the Greek *logos* (discourse).

Myths and Received Ideas

Every science and every discipline has its 'ancestors', pioneers and heroes. From time to time, we celebrate them in order to consolidate our intellectual cohesion and to strengthen our professional identity. Durkheim was more aware of this than most, as he demonstrated how hero worship helps to embody social values and to exemplify collective ideals. Just like Karl Marx and Max Weber – sociology's other two 'founding fathers' – Durkheim is one of the most widely read of the 'classical authors', and familiarity with his books is now part of the universal definition of what a sociologist is. Some find him inspiring and others criticize him, sometimes severely, but they all respect him.

Several myths surround Durkheim: Durkheim-the-prophet, Durkheim-Regent-of-the-Sorbonne, Durkheim-the-friend-of-Jaurès-who-never-became-a-socialist. And in the 'oral tradition' transmitted by lectures, his work is often reduced to just a few received ideas: the objectivist cult of 'facts'; the critique of prenotions and, more generally, common sense; the absolute value attributed to the collective and the supposed negation of individuality that reportedly ensues; the idealization of the collective consciousness, or of a mind that has a bird's-eye viewpoint and that acts independently of the thoughts and actions of social subjects (Karsenti 2006: 3). Durkheim is also associated with the image of the leader of a tightly knit group around the journal *L'Année sociologique* and of a conservative political thinker who is, above all, preoccupied with the social order and moral integration of societies.

The objective of this biography is to debunk the myths that surround the life and career of the founder of sociology in France, and to challenge or qualify received ideas about his work. The intellectual heritage left by Durkheim and his collaborators is rich, and lends itself to different or even contradictory readings, from functionalism to structuralism, from interactionism to ethnomethodology and pragmatic sociology.[1] Which is the 'real' Durkheim?

The approach adopted here, which borrows from biographical techniques and the history of ideas as well as the sociology of science, makes it possible to demonstrate the difficulties that surround the founding of a new discipline and the complexity of the elaboration of a body of work which, by outlining a new theory of the social, brings about a revolution within the human sciences: the repeated defence of the autonomy of sociology (with respect not only to other disciples, and especially psychology, but also to political and religious powers), the systematic elaboration of rules and the adoption of objective methods (including statistics) for studying the social, the condemnation of racial theories, the critique of Eurocentrism and the complete rehabilitation of the humanity of 'the primitive' (or, in other words, cultural relativism) (Mucchielli 1994).

Some Enigmas: New Documents

Not many books have been devoted to the life and work of Émile Durkheim.[2] The only major biography of Durkheim to date is Steven Lukes's magisterial *Émile Durkheim: His Life and Work* (1985), which was originally published in 1973 and which is subtitled *An Historical and Critical Study*. This very well-documented book received a great deal of attention and became a best-seller.

Since then, the opening up of archives and the discovery of manuscripts, administrative reports (reviews, lectures, oral contributions to academic debates) and of notes taken by students have provided new information about Durkheim's life and work, and have led to new analyses and interpretations, as can be seen from the many works that have appeared since the late 1970s.[3] This 'renaissance' in Durkheimian studies has, finally, been marked by major publications: special issues of journals devoted to Durkheim and the French sociological school; the publication of the three volumes of *Textes* edited by Victor Karady for Éditions de Minuit in 1975; the publication of his correspondence with friends and close collaborators; and new translations of a number of his works, including his Latin thesis on Montesquieu, into several languages. My own contribution to the rediscovery of Durkheim was the publication in 1994 of the first big biography of Marcel Mauss (Fournier 2007), and editions of Mauss's political writings (Mauss 1997) and Durkheim's letters to Mauss (Durkheim 1998).

But a life is always mysterious, with its own secret pathways. Not every-thing has been said about the career and work of Durkheim – far from it. His personality and psychological states, his relationship with Judaism, his family life and way of life, his relations with friends and close collabora-tors, his politico-administrative responsibilities, and his political views: all remain enigmatic.

This new biography of Durkheim differs from other studies in a number of respects. First, the description of the life and work of Émile Durkheim and his collaborators is strictly chronological and avoids the usual the-matic approach; second, the emphasis is on the collective dimension of Durkheim's work – hence the idea of a biography that also has something in common with a prosopography; third, the whole of Durkheim's work (and, to a certain extent, that of his collaborators) is discussed, as are the debates surrounding each book or article at the time of its publica-tion; and, finally, a sociological perspective is adopted and Durkheim's life and work are inscribed within the intellectual, institutional and politi-cal context of the years 1850–1920. The book could have been entitled *Durkheim, Mauss & Co*, to borrow an expression from Lucien Febvre. Its goal is therefore to look at both the individual and the collective, the *habitus* and the field, and the *événementiel* and the structural. The reader will understand that, in order to carry out this ambitious programme, my *Durkheim* must, of necessity, be voluminous. A life can be summed up in a few sentences; it takes several hundred pages to tell a life story, if we wish it to be complete.

The Life and Work of Durkheim

Durkheim's life and career can easily be divided into a few main periods:

- childhood and education at the École normale supérieure;
- lycée teacher (Puy, Sens, Saint-Quentin, Troyes) and travels in Germany;
- lecturer and professor of social science and pedagogy in Bordeaux;
- appointed to the Sorbonne, Paris;
- First World War.

These will be the main sections of this book. Although the Bordeaux period seems to have been the most productive, with the publication of the *Division of Labour in Society* (1893), *The Rules of Sociological Method* (1895) and *Suicide* (1897), and the foundation of *L'Année sociologique* in 1896, the Paris-Sorbonne period was more active in terms of his range of intellectual, administrative and political activities, and the First World War period was certainly the most tragic, with the death of several collaborators and also his son André.

In terms of his work, the periodization is more complex. Some describe Durkheim as 'one of the few philosophers and sociologists never to have changed their basic ideas' (Nandan 1980: 13). Others, in contrast, place the emphasis on the discontinuities, changes and even contradictions in the scholar's career. Was there a young Durkheim and an old Durkheim? Was the 'young' Durkheim a materialist and determinist, and was the 'old' Durkheim more idealistic and voluntaristic? And if there was a young Durkheim, what constitutes the early writings?[4] The year 1895 and the transitional period between 1894 and 1896 appear to be particularly significant: in 1894 and 1895, Durkheim gave his first lectures on the sociology of religion in Bordeaux, and in 1895 he had a 'revelation' (Durkheim 1982[1907]: 259) and discovered the essential role played in social life by religion.[5] The rabbi's son had at last found the path that led to the objective sociological study of religion.

Durkheim, Mauss & Co

Durkheim's great strength was his ability to gather together a team of collaborators who helped him to publish *L'Année sociologique* and who formed what is now conventionally known as the French school of sociology: Marcel Mauss, Henri Hubert, Célestin Bouglé, Paul Lapie, Gaston Richard, François Simiand, Maurice Halbwachs, Robert Hertz, and so on. This team stood out from other groups such as the *Revue internationale de sociologie* group because of its academic prestige (École normale supérieure, *agrégations*, doctorates) and its access to posts in higher education and specialist teaching institutions (École pratique des hautes études), but it was far from being homogeneous in intellectual and political terms as certain differences of opinion even led to dissensions – as, for example, with Gaston Richard. The famous psychology/sociology debate was central to discussions between the collaborators.

There is a collective dimension to Durkheim's approach. *L'Année sociologique* was obviously a collective undertaking. But what about the individual books? Who is the author of *The Elementary Forms of Religious Life*? Durkheim or Mauss? The relationship between uncle and nephew was very close – Marcel was Émile's alter ego. 'It is impossible for me extricate myself from the work of the school', said Marcel Mauss (1979[1930]), who set great store by the importance of collective work and collaboration – as opposed to isolation and the pretentious quest for originality (Karady 1979). The nephew made a vital contribution to his uncle's work, even though they were different in many ways, ranging from personality to their lifestyles and political commitments. But their collaboration was like any other: Durkheim was undeniably the intellectual leader – he was the master – but the influences were multiple and reciprocal. Some of the 'disciples' even claimed to be followers of both Bergson and Durkheim.

The ambitious project of *L'Année sociologique* was at the heart of Durkheim's preoccupations. It took an immense effort to mobilize a whole team of collaborators who all had their own research projects and, in many cases, family obligations and political commitments. An overall analysis of the journal is not enough, which is why I discuss each of the 12 volumes here in order to bring out clearly the specific difficulties inherent in this undertaking at various moments in the career of Durkheim and his collaborators.

Many published works, a monumental journal that appeared regularly, access to posts in secondary and higher education: all this aroused both admiration and hatred, as we can see from the reception of every one of Durkheim's books and each issue of *L'Année*. Durkheim was the first to be worried by this. 'Am I just slashing at water with a knife?' he wondered when his *Suicide* appeared. The huge collective effort and the disinterestedness that the publication of each volume of the journal represented were admired, but some people had no qualms about criticizing, often very harshly, the perspective defended by Durkheim and his collaborators, who were accused of having committed every sin in the book: realism, naturalism, positivism, determinism, and so on. In the early 1910s, Durkheim looked like a man with power, or even a man who had to be got rid of; the authors of *La Nouvelle Sorbonne* called him 'the Regent of the Sorbonne' ('Agathon' 1911). At the beginning of the new century, the stars who attracted attention in intellectual and cultural circles, and who aroused curiosity in fashionable milieus, were Gabriel Tarde and Henri Bergson, not Durkheim.

Was he a success or a failure? When it comes to the institutionalization of sociology, can we say, like Victor Karady (1979), that this was a partial failure? Durkheim 'conquered' the citadel of the new Sorbonne, and one of the preconditions for its conquest was the relationship that was established between sociology and the Republic. But, in losing, one can also win; at the very moment when sociology was acquiring a new institutional legitimacy, it was associated with the (new) republican government, and Durkheim, who came in for some sharp criticism, was seen as the Regent of the Sorbonne.

The Specific Intellectual

'We would deem our research not worth the labour of a single hour if its interest were merely speculative', states Durkheim in the preface to the first edition of *The Division of Labour in Society* (1984 [1893]: xxvi). Science can and must, in his view, guide behaviours and help to find solutions to problems. Durkheim kept his distance from political parties and the partisan life, but the 'social question' very quickly became central to his preoccupations. At one point, his ambition was both to found a new science and to go into politics. Sociology would eventually allow him to satisfy his need for both knowledge and action. Durkheim did not publish any major works devoted primarily to political analysis (Nandan 1980), and he was politically active on only two occasions: during the Dreyfus affair and during the First World War. He was also directly caught up in three major events and trends: the occupation of Alsace-Lorraine by

German troops during the Franco-Prussian war (1870–1), the coming of the Third Republic, and the growing number of social conflicts and the development of the socialist movement in Europe.

The ideological side to Durkheim's work did not escape the attention of Paul Nizan (1981[1932]), who described him as a 'watchdog'. It is true that, at that time, (Durkheimian) sociology was accused by communist intellectuals of being a bourgeois science. Durkheim is sometimes seen as a liberal thinker who turned conservative ideas into a systematic socio-logical theory (Nisbet 1967), and sometimes as a conservative theoreti-cian of the social order who rejected socialism (Coser 1960). Steven Lukes (1985[1973]) corrects that impression by demonstrating that Durkheim's political position is deeply reformist. More recently, Durkheim has been described by Jean-Claude Filloux (1977) as a socialist thinker who defended a democratic, or even 'self-management', conception of social-ism: socialism was supposedly the source of his sociological vocation, and he was a 'fellow-traveller'. Durkheim therefore seems to be more 'radical' or 'critical' than he was once thought to be (Gane 1992).

Durkheim's political stance is that of the 'expert intellectual' or, to use Pierre Bourdieu's (1998) expression, the 'specific intellectual', who, while he defends the autonomy of science, also acts, in his areas of competence, as an adviser to the prince or popular educator. But how are we to describe his political position? Several of Durkheim's close collaborators, and espe-cially Marcel Mauss, were very active in the socialist movement. Others, like Célestin Bouglé, deplored what was, in 1900, known as the 'crisis in liberalism'. Durkheim seems, then, to epitomize the golden mean and – why not? – the third way: he attempts to reconcile the contradictory forces of individuality and solidarity, and individualism and socialism (Seidman 1983) because the two great threats to contemporary societies are, in his view, totalitarianism and anarchism. Could it be said of him that he was a liberal socialist?

One of Durkheim's goals was to elaborate a new and scientifically based republican ideology, and to develop a new and positive science of moral-ity and manners. The social and economic problems of the turn of the century, as we can see from the lectures on ethics and even pedagogy that he gave in Bordeaux and then Paris, were amongst his central and constant preoccupations. The context in which Durkheim grew up and lived was that of the Third Republic. It was a Republic of institutions and the law, in which personal power was challenged by the power of institutions, and the marshal's sword by the statesman's rule of law, to use the terminology of Gabriel Hanotaux (1908: 38–41).

The Third Republic was also the *République des professeurs* [teachers' republic].[6] Several teachers were elected to the Assemblée Nationale, but – and this is more important – they were also closely associated with the reform movement instigated by Jules Ferry in the world of education. This movement culminated in the separation of church and state. The three key words of republican ideology were: democracy, *laïcité* [secularism] and science. The political choices that reflected republican values were:

the right of association, freedom of the press, the new divorce law and the civilizing mission. Civic education became part of the school curriculum, and there were campaigns to promote personal hygiene, provident societies and saving. There was, then, something resembling a republican ethos; efforts were made to promote it in schools, with, for example, new classes in civic education, and it was based upon the principle of 'self-government', meaning self-control and personal autonomy. 'It is not enough to be in a republic if one does not have the austerity of republican mores', as Jules Simon liked to repeat (Horne 2002: 50).

Durkheim was, first and foremost, a republican, and the support he lent the Third Republic has been interpreted as a sign of his 'liberalism' (Lehman 1993; Richter 1960). Durkheim did indeed defend the dignity of the individual, individual rights, the freedom of the press and of democratic institutions, and the essential liberal values of tolerance and pluralism. But at the same time he was critical of utilitarian liberalism and laisser-faire economics, and promoted the values of solidarity; in the context of the movement to promote voluntary organizations (the 1901 law), he also defended the role of the emergent professional corporations and criticized the parliamentary system. The 'corporatism' he defended was not, it has to be pointed out, incompatible with republican and democratic traditions. It is therefore not easy to classify Durkheim under one or other of the 'conventional ideological labels' (Hawkins 1995). Durkheim's relationship with liberalism is so complex and so influenced by his sociology that some go so far as to speak of 'a communitarian defence of liberalism' (Cladis 1992).

Fin-de-Siècle Melancholy: A Changing World

Like several of his contemporaries at the turn of the century, Émile Durkheim was aware that 'something is not right'. The problems were certainly social (the falling birth rate) and economic (strikes, etc.), but they were also psychic. Some spoke of an 'over-excitement of the nervous system', and others of 'devitalization and collective degeneration'. The explanation for all this lay in the new living conditions (big cities, noise, restlessness). *Fin-de-siècle* France looked like a 'neurotic community'. One word was on everyone's lips: degeneration. And particular emphasis was placed upon what was called neurasthenia: this is a clinical state characterized by mental hypersensitivity and physical debility, and resulting from great nervous fatigue. Its other symptoms are sadness, indecisiveness, physical lassitude and somatic disturbances (Silverman 1989: 75ff).

Being very sympathetic to the new psychology, Durkheim followed with interest the work of psychiatrists, as well as that of his philosophy and psychology colleagues who were carrying out research into psychopathology. The very first volumes of *L'Année sociologique* reveal a real interest in the work of 'hygienists' and the psychiatrists who were trying to treat the new 'social illnesses'. The index to the journal contains a wide range of entries:

crime and criminality, economy, education, sanctions and responsibilities, religion, women, suicide, city, and so on. But it also includes entries of family, kinship, marriage and sexuality (especially incest and prostitution). Over the following years, other themes took on more and more importance: belief, cult, God, dogma, church, ritual, fetishism, sacrifice, magic, myth, superstition, taboo, totem. Such were the subjects that established Durkheim's programme: the critical study of the social unconscious as objectivation of irrationalism. His sociology is, in a sense, a collective psychology, but the causes of psychic problems are not individual but social, and they lie not just in the 'depths of the soul' but also in 'the basis of collective life'.

'Malaise and 'anxiety': these two words recur constantly in the work of Durkheim, who was interested not only in social problems but also – witness his doctoral thesis, *The Division of Labour in Society* (Durkheim 1984[1893]) – in psychic problems, mental illnesses and neurasthenia. These were, in his view, tensions and frictions that appeared in societies in which the collective consciousness was growing weaker. And then in *Suicide*, he analyses the main types of suicide in contemporary societies, paying very special attention to egotistical and anomic suicide, and speaks, borrowing an expression from Chateaubriand, of the 'disease of the infinite' (Durkheim 2002[1897]: 250). That yearning takes many forms ranging from 'dreams of infinity' to an 'infinity of desires'. There are even 'currents of collective sadness' that run through society and when they are not excessive, they are not, in his view, pathological. Melancholy, in other words, is more frequent in modern societies, but it is not necessarily morbid if it does not take up too much room in our lives. And what is morbid for individuals may not be morbid for societies. 'What would a society be without its neurasthenics?', asks Durkheim.

In praise of melancholy? Melancholy was greatly prized in intellectual and artistic circles. 'Modern man is an animal who is bored', wrote Paul Bourget in 1891. Hypersensitivity, a certain loneliness and sadness: these are the preconditions for creation. For Baudelaire, who is the great poet of melancholy, a great artist is by definition a melancholic artist (Kopp 2005). Can we say that Durkheim was personally predisposed to elaborate a collective psychology of 'a particular type'? There are three things about his life of which we can be certain: his hypersensitivity, his neurasthenic crisis, and his illness during the last days of his life. He himself associated his own 'mental unease' with neurasthenia and melancholy. And Durkheim died of a broken heart or a cancer in 1917. A world changes, a people reverts to barbarism, and a life loses its meaning . . .

It is tempting to describe Durkheim's sociology as an attempt to objectify his own personal problems. 'The man is the work', he said, with his friend Frédéric Rauh in mind (Durkheim 2006[1909]: 31). The work is, however, no more a direct expression of a life than it is a reflection of a society or epoch. The life, the work and society both interpenetrate one another and are far removed from one another. The influences are obvious: they are those of the social trajectory of a child born in Épinal and the son of a rabbi who, after being educated at the École normale supérieure, became a philosopher (the Republic's philosopher), and a professor of pedagogy and social science. He was, in a word, a 'child of his time' (Nye 1983), but he was a child who broke away from his social and intellectual milieu in more than one sense and who pulled off a master stroke: he founded sociology as a science and, basically, brought about a revolution.

Part I

The Young Durkheim

1

A Jewish Education

'Don't forget that I am the son of a rabbi!' David Émile Durkheim was born on 15 April 1858 in Épinal, the capital of the Vosges *département*. The family liked to say that they had been 'rabbis, father and son, for eight generations' (Henri Durkheim, cited in Filloux 1977: 8). It was, said Marcel Mauss, a very long line.[1] Émile's father, Moïse, was a rabbi, as was his father, Israël David, who began his career as a primary school teacher before becoming rabbi of Muntzig (Alsace) in 1805. Israël succeeded his father, Simon Horcheim, who had also married the daughter of a rabbi. Simon Horcheim, who was appointed a rabbi in 1783, was 'famous' and 'well-known for his eloquence'.[2]

Moïse was 11 when his father died in 1816. It can be assumed that he had already begun to study the Talmud under the guidance of his father. At the age of 17 or 18, he left for Frankfurt am Main in Germany, where he attended the Yeshivah run by the city's chief rabbi, Salman Trier. He remained there for seven years, probably from 1820 to 1827. 'I observed his conduct for the seven years during which he pursued his studies in our community', Rabbi Trier was to say of his pupil. Moïse distinguished himself by his 'good conduct' and was 'an interesting young man, remarkable for both his exemplary behaviour and the extent of his knowledge'.[3] The Yeshivah was not a rabbinical school. The institution's only purpose was to teach the Talmud and to watch over the moral and religious education of its pupils. It did not award any qualifications, and did not train them for a career. Moïse returned to France without any qualifications and, in order to make a living, went into business. As he did not have his *baccalauréat*, he could not enrol at the École rabbinique de France in Metz, which opened only in 1830. The list of French rabbis who trained there between 1830 and 1859 (at which point the school moved to Paris) does not include the name of Moïse Durkheim. He in fact studied for several months with Baruch Guggenheim, the chief rabbi of Nancy. The rabbi's opinion of his pupil could not have been more positive: 'Great ability. A great deal of erudition, answering the most difficult Talmudic questions correctly.'[4]

In 1834, Moïse Durkheim, who was already well known in Nancy,[5] was expected to become the rabbi for the *départements* of the Vosges and

Haute-Marne. The members of the Israelite Consistory of the Nancy community enthusiastically supported his appointment because of his 'great
knowledge', 'his disinterested devotion to public affairs whenever his
learning could be of use to the administration' and his 'exemplary conduct
in both moral and religious terms'.[6] Moïse Durkheim then approached
the Consistoire de Paris with a request to be appointed to a more senior
position (*morenou*), and was given 'certificates of ability' from three chief
rabbis.[7] All three recognized his 'talent for Judaic theology, and especially
Talmudic studies', and stressed his 'good morals and punctilious attitude
towards his religious duties as a rabbi'.[8] He was, they went on, a 'doctor
of the law'. In late May 1835, the chief rabbi of Paris declared him fit to
'decide any question in matters religious' and awarded him the title of
rabbi.[9] The new rabbi took up his position in Épinal the following July.
Moïse Durkheim gave his address in French. This in itself was a considerable challenge for the new rabbi, who, coming from a German-speaking
Alsatian family, spoke with a strong accent and was the first rabbi to
be appointed to serve a new community that was still in the process of
establishing itself in a traditionally Catholic area.

The rabbi's stipend was paid by the state.[10] Having been appointed as
rabbi to two *départements* (with a Jewish population of over 1,000), Moïse
Durkheim requested a higher salary, in the region of 1,000 francs. His
request was denied: rabbis were paid a salary of 600 francs. In 1836, Moïse
Durkheim applied to succeed Aaron Worms, the chief rabbi of Metz.
There were four other candidates, including Mayer Lambert, who was
eventually chosen unanimously. The author of several books, including
Catéchisme du culte judaïque and *Éléments du psychologie* (*avec quelques
reflexions sur la liaison entre l'âme et le corps*), Mayer Lambert was head of
the rabbinical school in Metz and the son-in-law of his predecessor Aaron
Worms. This was the beginning of a period in which 'Judaism in Metz,
or rather France more generally, was becoming increasingly emancipated
and beginning to look more modern, while still striving to retain the fine
model profile of the past' (Netter 1938: 365–6).

On 16 August 1837, Moïse Durkheim married Mélanie Isidor in
Charmes (Vosges), a small town some 30 kilometres to the north of Épinal.
He was 32 and his bride, who was born in Charmes in 1820, was 17. She
had lost her mother when she was 5. This was a marriage between religion and trade. Mélanie's father, Joseph Marx Isidorm, was a horse-dealer
in Charmes, where he had lived since 1802.[11] He was highly 'regarded'
there: the *sous-préfet* of Mirecourt said of him that 'of all the Israelites in
Charmes, he made the biggest mark . . . and was best fitted to become an
outstanding *notable* [figure]'.[12] Two of his children, Isaac and Lazare, also
lived in Charmes: one worked as a milliner and the other as a horse-dealer.
According to their marriage contract, the groom contributed the sum of
2,000 francs in cash, and the bride the equivalent of 6,000 francs in *écus*.[13]
When her father died two years later, Mélanie inherited the sum of 12,000
francs.

Moïse and Mélanie set up home in the rue Léopold-Bourg in Épinal.

They were to have five children. The eldest (born in 1845) was, as his name – Désiré – indicates, a long-awaited child: they had been married for more than eight years (his Jewish forename was Israël). He lived for less than one year. He was followed by Rosine (1848), Joseph-Félix (1849) and Céline (1851). Born on 15 April 1858, Émile was the youngest (his Jewish forename was David). There was a big age gap between Émile and his older brother and sisters – seven years between him and his elder sister Rosine. When he was born, his parents were aged, respectively, 53 and 38.

Christophe Charle (1984: 46) speculates that Émile may have been an unwanted child. The baby in the family was, of course, spoiled by his mother and his big sisters, but Émile found himself in the position of the youngest child who had often to put up with being teased by his brother and sisters. Perhaps he was thinking of his own childhood when he remarked at a later date that 'there is something like a chronic impatience on the part of the older ones – a tendency to treat the very young as inferior beings' (Durkheim 1961[1925]: 195). Fortunately, he adds, 'familial feelings suffice in general to prevent excesses'. The respective positions of the brothers is then inverted, the younger becoming better behaved, while the elder put up 'a calm resistance, ignoring all warnings': 'We begged him so often but never succeeded in changing his happy-go-lucky attitude. As a result, he was always naughty and reduced us all to despair.'[14]

Respect for the Law and Devotion to the Book

Épinal is a small town that straggles for three kilometres along the Moselle valley in the Vosges, close to Alsace. It is the capital of the *département*, and its people like to say that it is 'the capital of the Vosges'. In 1866, it had a population of 11,870 and 10 years later, of 14, 894 (Javalet 1969: 28).[15] The town experienced rapid growth when Alsace-Moselle was annexed by Germany. It became a garrison town and a centre for the textile industry (until then, most of the Vosges' textile mills were based in Mulhouse).

Épinal's Jewish community was of recent origin. In 1852, the census recorded the presence of 142 Jews; by 1875, that number had risen to 313.[16] Ten years later, it had risen again, to 349, and in 1910 it reached 452. The group was very much in the minority, and was outnumbered in 1886 by the town's Protestants. Most of Épinal's Jews worked in textiles (fabrics, clothes and the embroidery trade) or the livestock industry.

Until 1864, the synagogue was in the place Léopold (now place Clemenceau); there was a rue des Juifs behind the Stock Exchange and a pont aux Juifs [Jews' Bridge] over the canal des Grands-Moulins. A monumental new synagogue in neo-Romanesque style was built in the rue de l'Ancien-Hospice in the early 1860s. Its construction was financed by subscription from members of the community, with subsidies from the state and the town council. It was opened 'with great pomp' on 24 June 1864 in the presence of the religious, civil and military authorities.[17] The importance of the event escaped no one: it was 'irrefutable proof of the growth of the Jewish population in the big industrial and manufacturing towns' and of the transformation of the status of Jews, who were abandoning their old trades as peddlers, dealers in second-hands goods and sellers of goods on a commission basis in favour of 'devoting themselves' to the manual, industrial and liberal professions. In this way, they were becoming 'citizens who were useful to the country' and honouring the name they bore (Ben-David 1864: 597–8). A few years later, the community decided to extend the synagogue by building a 'schoolroom'; it was in fact a room used for religious instruction. For many years, the community's President was Élie Schwab (1833–97), who was a prosperous draper.

Alsace and Lorraine were the cradles of French Judaism. Their Jewish communities were significant, not only in numerical terms – more than 35,000 members, comprising 80 per cent of France's Jewish population in 1808 – but also because of their religious and communitarian cohesiveness. Being Jewish meant belonging to a minority surrounded by a Catholic majority and a large number of Protestants. Until the Revolution, southern Lorraine had been exclusively Catholic. The arrival of Jews, and of Protestants of Alsatian origin, was a recent phenomenon. Relations between the various religious groups were not always easy. The Jews were subject to abuse and acts of violence in 1789, in 1829–32 and again in 1848. They were hated, and criticized for their commercial activities, so much so that they were described as thieves (Reybel 1904: 88; see Freddy and Weyl 1977). This traditional anti-Semitism often found expression in legends and songs.

In April 1876, the Durkheim family acquired a large house with a small courtyard at 2 rue des Forts, at the corner of the rue de la Préfecture and the rue des Forts in the centre of Épinal. The house consisted of a ground floor built over a cellar, two upper storeys and a loft. It had been partly converted into a dwelling house. The family's living quarters consisted of a dining room, a kitchen, five bedrooms (including one maid's room) and two toilets. One of the bedrooms was used as an office.[18]

In his capacity as chief rabbi of the Vosges and Haute-Marne *départements*, Moïse Durkheim's responsibilities included organizing all the communities in the region. In Épinal, he appointed first M. Flexner, then M. Thibaut Horvilleur (1850–1916) and then M. Klein as his officiating assistant rabbi. Together with abbé Chapellier and pastor Romane, he was also one of the college's three almoners (Javalet 1969: 29). As well as the preparation of lessons and speeches and the organization of services, a rabbi's responsibilities are many and varied: replying to numerous requests (for money or advice), visiting the sick and the bereaved, consistorial meetings, speaking to the authorities on the community's behalf (see Schuhl 1995: 261–3). As an important local figure of acknowledged authority, Moïse Durkheim enjoyed the respect of the administrative authorities and was in constant touch with local politicians. At election time, the Prefect also relied on him to convince his co-religionists to 'vote the right way' (Henri Durkheim, cited in Filloux 1977: 9).

The Durkheim family's tradition was a pious one. Marcel Mauss later recalled that, when he was a child, there were all sorts of stories and legends about his forebears: 'I am not saying that there was a genealogy of saints, but there really was a belief in something of the kind.'[19] Moïse Durkheim belonged to a generation of French rabbis who trained mainly either within their family circles or in the Yeshivas of the Ashkenazi world, most of them German. The tradition to which he belonged was therefore very legalistic – a Lithuanian tradition from Eastern Europe. This was a puritanical and ascetic Judaism, both anti-messianic and anti-mystical. Moïse Durkheim also appears to have taken a great intellectual interest in the rabbinical school of Troyes which was, under Rashi, a major centre for medieval Judaism, characterized by an austere devotion to biblical exegesis and Talmudic jurisprudence. There was therefore little room for the imagination, mysticism, artistic sensibilities or poetry. The emphasis was on erudition, logic, analytic ability and dialectics.[20]

And yet, as Marcel Mauss notes (1969: ii, 381), both Palestinian and diaspora Jews had always had a superstition about the evil eye, and used incantations to protect themselves from spells or the forces of evil; they also believed in the efficaciousness of magic. There was even talk of 'religious biblical magic': Moses' staff had magical powers, and so did curses. There were subterranean forces and a shadowy world of demons: prayer and virtue were a constant source of protection. The Durkheim family owned a 'very precious' book; it was a composite collection of thirty-nine different texts, all dating from the sixteenth century, including ritual prayers and 'a certain number of commentaries, some mystical rather than cabbalistic, on the main services'. Like his ancestors, Moïse Durkheim used it for the Yom Kippur ceremony throughout his fifty years as Épinal's rabbi.[21] Whether or not he was influenced by the teachings of Rashi, Épinal's rabbi's relationship with religion was complex; he certainly continued to respect the tradition, but he was also sympathetic to modernism. He was known for his rigorous morality, but did not necessarily condemn all forms of mysticism. The Durkheim family did not speak Yiddish at home (although they understood it), and Rabbi Moïse did not have a beard. Were these signs of openness and integration?

A 'modernist' or anti-traditionalist current was beginning to emerge within French Judaism at this time. Its goal was to reform the liturgy, or to make a few innovations by doing away with *pioutim* (poetic amplifications between prayers) and introducing organ music. These innovations even became the object of a pastoral letter sent out in the name of the Conférence des grands rabbins de France, dated 25 September 1856 and signed by the chief rabbi of France, Salomon Ulmann. An immediate decision was taken to establish a Commission des conservateurs du Judaïsme, with the avowed aim of rejecting any changes to the ritual. 'I loath ritual changes because they serve no purpose and result in great evils, and especially discord, disunity and encourage irreligiousness', retorted the rabbi of Strasbourg, M. Bloch. The 'Paris' movement found few supporters in either Lorraine or Alsace, or at least not before the war of 1870 (Netter 1938: 423–6).

As Raymond Aron (2003: 12–13) remarks of his grandparents, the Jews of eastern France displayed an 'intransigent patriotism', and never asked themselves the now-fashionable question: 'Jew or French?' When Épinal's synagogue was opened in 1864. M. Sylvain May, a member of the Nancy consistory recalled 'the generosity of the Emperor's liberal government': 'Let us cherish . . . with all the strength of our affection the liberal France which, by adopting us, has elevated us to the status of citizens . . . Let us say it out loud: wherever a free man can worship his God as he sees fit is his fatherland, and France is above all a land of religious freedom, and the *true Jerusalem* that we desire.'[22] Émile Durkheim's parents were Alsatians from a Germanic cultural background, but in Épinal they lived in a world with a Latin culture. They probably spoke French with an accent that betrayed their origins. Indeed, Christian Kiener, a Protestant industrialist from an Alsatian background who became mayor of Épinal in 1867, was accused of using *hachepailler* – in other words, speaking to the enemy in a *Vosgien* German patois.[23] Their mother insisted that both Félix and Émile use their French forename. According to Durkheim's great-niece Mme Claudette Kennedy (cited in Pickering 1994: 36n7), the family insisted that they were French and used the French pronunciation *Durkem*, with a short 'e', rather than the Germanic *Durkheim*. This was also a way of asking people not to write the family name with a 'c' ('Durckheim'), as they did all too often.

At the time, this desire to be integrated went hand in hand with the modernization of tradition. In the mid-nineteenth century, the French Jewish community had to come to terms with a so-called 'regeneration' movement which, in its most radical form, wished to rid Judaism of its 'Asian accoutrements' and to introduce a whole set of administrative, liturgical and religious reforms that went so far as to question the need for circumcision and the Sabbath (which it wanted to move from Saturday to Sunday). Like the *Wissenschaft des Judentum* movement in Germany, it also wanted the Bible to be the object of a scientific study inspired by disciplines such as history, philology, archaeology and anthropology. The journal *Archives israélites de France*, which began publication in 1849, provided a forum for the 'regenerators'. The persistence of regionalism and religious traditionalism combined, however, to block the movement for change. The Jewish community remained divided, reluctant to choose between 'tradition and transformation' (see Berkovitz 1989). A new relationship between Judaism and French citizenship was, however, emerging: it was indeed possible, as can be seen from the example of Adolphe Crémieux (1786–1880), who was something of a model, to choose a secular way of life while still identifying with the Jewish community. Leader of the opposition, and then Minister for Justice, Crémieux was also president of the Consistoire (1843) and president of the Alliance israélite universelle.

The home of Épinal's rabbi was 'austere rather than opulent: the observance of the law was a precept and an example, and there were no distractions from duty' (Davy 1973[1960a]: 18; 1919a: 65). As Émile Durkheim himself was to write (2002[1897]: 114), Judaism 'consists basically of a body of practices minutely governing all the details of life and leaving little room to individual judgement'. Religion's field of action extends far beyond 'man's communication with the divine' and lays down many rules: 'Religion prohibits the Jew from eating certain kinds of meats and lays down that he must dress in a prescribed fashion. It imposes upon him this or that view regarding the nature of men and things, and regarding the origin of the world. Often it regulates legal, moral and economic relationships' (Durkheim 1984[1893]: 118). Religious life, he also remarks, is 'made up entirely of abnegation and altruism' (ibid.: 49); it requires the observation of practices that demand sacrifices both great and small. Offerings must be made, time that could otherwise be devoted to work or leisure activities must be devoted to ritual practices, and all sorts of sacrifices must be made. For several years, Émile's mother Mélanie chaired the Société des secours mutuels des dames israélites.

The education that the young Émile received placed the emphasis on duty and responsibility, inculcating a sense of effort and also scorn for facile success. According to one of his collaborators, he could never 'experience pleasure without feeling some remorse as a result' (Bouglé 1930a: 28). As his nephew Marcel Mauss noted (1969[1925]), this rather strict education helped to 'conceal outbursts of enthusiasm he would have been embarrassed to express'. 'Few people knew him', a fellow student recalled; 'few people knew that his sternness concealed an almost feminine sensitivity or that a heart that loathed facile outpourings was full of tender kindness' (Maurice Holleaux, cited in Davy 1960a: 17). It was not easy to get to know the young Durkheim, who seemed 'somewhat surly'. But beneath 'the brusque exterior', his friends discovered 'an ardent, passionate and generous soul'. He was, according to Sylvain Lévi, a 'real Jewish type'.[24]

Like other young men of his age, David-Émile learned Hebrew, had his bar-mitzvah, regularly attended synagogue on the Sabbath and religious feasts, and became familiar with the Pentateuch and the Talmud; it was his father's intention that he should continue the family tradition by becoming a rabbi. Family legend has it that he was sent to a rabbinical school but rebelled and refused to continue his studies. There was in fact no such school in either Épinal or nearby.[25]

Émile's early experience of Judaism was that of a religion that was not simply a system of ideas, but also a cult or set of ritual acts:

> Anyone who has truly practised a religion knows very well that it is the cult that stimulates the feelings of joy, inner peace, serenity and enthusiasm that, for the faithful, stand as experimental proof of the belief. The cult is not merely a system of signs by which the faith is outwardly expressed: it is the sum total of means by which the faith is created and recreated periodically. (Durkheim 1995[1912]: 420)

Durkheim's experience of Judaism was rooted in 'a small, compact and coherent society with a strong feeling of self-consciousness and unity'. In his study of suicide, he explains the attitude of Jews in terms of 'the hostility surrounding them', which 'created unusually strong feelings of solidarity among them':

> Their need to resist a general hostility, the very impossibility of free com-
> munication with the rest of the community, has forced on them a strict
> union among themselves, Consequently, each community became a small,
> compact and coherent society with a strong feeling of self-consciousness
> and unity. Everyone thought and lived alike; individual divergences were
> made almost impossible by the community of existence and the close and
> constant surveillance of all over each other. (2002[1897]: 114)

Durkheim therefore acquired a 'taste for the collective life'. Referring explicitly to the experience of religious minorities, he once confided to his students that 'there is nothing more agreeable than a collective life if one has had a little experience with it at an early age. There is something in all common activities that warms the heart and fortifies the will . . . There is pleasure in saying "we" rather then "I"' (1961[1925]: 239, 240).

Embroidery: Extra Income

The Durkheim family's financial situation was modest: the rabbi's annual stipend was 800 francs in 1885 (rising to 1,100 francs in 1862 and 1,400 francs in 1874).[26] The situation was untenable, protested Moïse Durkheim as soon as he was appointed rabbi for the two *départements*; the stipend was not enough to meet the needs of the head of a family and quite inap- propriate to his position. He had to 'move around a lot to fulfil his duties as a district rabbi'. He had no housing allowance and was living in a town where 'housing and food were very expensive'.[27] The 'Durkheim affair' (to use the expression employed by the Paris Consistory) went on for several years. In order to supplement her husband's meagre income, his wife opened an embroidery workshop; her small business was also based at 2 rue des Forts. Only a few people worked there, and most of the work was farmed out to women, many of them from the countryside, working in their own homes. Like her father, Mélanie Durkheim had a nose for busi- ness and succeeded in doubling the family's income (Lukes 1985[1973]: 39). This was not to the liking of the Nancy Consistoire, which asked the prefect to investigate an activity to which Rabbi Durkheim 'appeared to be no stranger', even though the royal edict of 1844 stated that the posi- tion of rabbi was incompatible with any industrial and commercial activ- ity.[28] Having investigated the matter, the Prefect told the Consistoire that 'the information supplied to him proved in almost certain terms that M Durkheim had nothing to do with the embroidery business'.[29]

Textiles were a regional speciality. The textile industry was in fact the biggest in the Vosges, which manufactured the famous linen known as '*toile de Vosges*'. The 'Épinal cotton complex' originated in 1872 with the Morel-Winckler cotton mill and the Shupp-Umbert cloth works, and it went on to expand rapidly, with the opening of the David, Trouiller and Adhémar mill in 1874, the Hartmann cloth works in 1876, Julliard and Mégnier in 1878 and the Gestodt-Hiener plant in 1880, followed later by the Gosse cotton mill. At the industrial exposition in 1880, Jules Ferry declared that 'the Vosges is an area that lives not on agitation, but on work' (cited Javalet 1969: 22). The textile industry was, however, still fragile and experienced many crises: fluctuations in the price of cotton, fierce competition after the signing of the 1860 free trade treaty with Britain, and falling raw cotton prices with the outbreak of the American Civil War. In addition, the 1880s saw fires at several mills.

The Durkheim family was, for at least two generations, associated with the embroidery sector and the textile trade. When he married Clara (Clémence) Dreyfus (1856–86), the elder son Félix went to live in Gray (Haute-Saône), where he opened a shop selling cloth, textiles and haberdashery near the place de l'Hôtel-de-Ville. Both the daughters of the house – Rosine and Céline – worked in their mother's workshop. When she married in September 1867, Rosine, who was the eldest child, brought her husband Gerson Mauss (born 1834) into the family business, which now traded as 'Fabrique de broderie à main Mauss-Durkheim' at 5 rue Sadi-Carnot. Gerson was already working in the textile industry when he met Rosine; he was a buyer for a company based in Epsig. His brothers, who lived in Bischwiller, were both involved in the industry. Céline's husband Mirtil Cahen, who was born in Épinal, was a buyer; he also acted as the company's accountant. The couple lived at 18 rue Rualménil, the same street as the president of the Jewish community, Élie Schwab, and the officiating assistant rabbi, Thibaut Horvilleur. The Cahens had three children: Albert (1873), Paul (1882) and Juliette (1882). Albert studied medicine in Paris, and then came back to live in Épinal where he set up in practice in the rue Thiers.

A Humiliating Defeat

Émile Durkheim was 12 when the Franco-Prussian war broke out: 'We were confident of victory. I still remember it well' (Durkheim 1975[1906b]: 188). And then the Germans occupied Épinal: in October 1870, General von Werder entered the town at the head of an army of 15,000 men.

This was defeat, a humiliating defeat, and the people of Épinal remember 1870 as 'the terrible year'. 'Consciousness is not merely an ineffective epiphenomenon; it affects the realities that it clarifies. If, in 1870, we had been aware of our military weakness, we would not have been the people we were' (Durkheim 1969: 579). At the time, Émile was a young adolescent, and this was his first direct encounter with anti-Semitism. Referring to this period, he was to note:

Being Jewish myself, I have been able to observe this at close quarters . . . When a society suffers, it feels a need to find someone to blame; someone on whom it can take out its disappointment. And those who are already seen in a poor light by public opinion are the obvious candidates. The pariahs are used a scapegoats. (1975[1899]: 252–3)

The Treaty of Frankfurt brought the war to an end in May 1871, but Alsace, the north-eastern part of Lorraine, and several *communes* in the Vosges were annexed by Germany for strategic and economic purposes. The occupying troops did not leave Épinal until the end of July 1873: it was a night of delirious joy (Javelet 1969: 18). Those *communes* in the Vosges that had remained in French hands experienced rapid demographic and economic expansion. Thanks to the influx of men and capital, Nancy became the most important city in the east of France. Some Jews, like Rosine Durkheim's two brothers-in-law Michel and Philippe Mauss, 'opted for' France and emigrated from Bischwiller to Elbeuf. They had to pay a high price for their patriotism: even though they were allowed to keep their property in the annexed territories, many of them lost much of their fortunes.

Following the war, the Vosges region was heavily militarized because of its strategic position, and Épinal became a fortified town. Numerous forts were built and major garrisons were established. A narrow-gauge railway line stretching for dozens of kilometres linked the supply depots in the town and the various forts surrounding it. The massive military presence, and the frequent parades and reviews, turned the life of the townspeople upside-down and made a lasting impression on Épinal's youth: their patriotism had been wounded and they wanted to save their honour. A monument erected in 1875 bore the inscription 'Never forget'. Love of the fatherland became a religion, and gave rise to a somewhat chauvinistic patriotism that was intent upon revenge. As a popular song of the day put it, 'We would rather change the position of our hearts than change old Alsace' (cited in Javelet 1969: 32; see Grivel 1997). The left that won the election of 1871 was embodied in one man, Émile Georges (1830–1903), who represented the Vosges in the Assemblée nationale from 1871 to 1876 before becoming Senator for the Vosges. Like Gambetta, he refused to accept defeat (see Grivel 1997). Most Jews were loyal to the left because it could lay claim to the inheritance of the revolution that had emancipated them. In 1875, Ramberviller's Commissioner of Police wrote in a report to the Prefect of the Vosges that 'almost all the Jews are radicals'.[30]

For young thinkers like the philosopher Alfred Espinas and the historian Camille Jullian, the goal became clear: the 'regeneration of our country'. And education and science were the best ways to regenerate it. There was therefore a 'renewal' of interest in some already dated enthusiasms. Ernest Renan sang the praises of Reason and Science in *L'Avenir de la science'* (1848, pub. 1890). Speaking of the postwar period, Durkheim would later say:

All good citizens had the same idea: we must rebuild the country. In order to rebuild it, we first had to educate it. A country that aspires to governing itself needs 'enlightenment' above all else. A democracy would be untrue to itself if it did not have faith in science. The years that followed the war were therefore a fine period of intellectual enthusiasm. The task we assigned ourselves was to build centres of high culture where science had everything it needed, and which it could spread to the nation. (1975[1918a]: 465)

Célestin Bouglé (1938) said much the same: 'It is a curious fact that, in order to prepare for the recovery we need, most [citizens] are counting upon the spirit of truth rather than the spirit of authority.'

Émile Durkheim was one of a generation of young men who, to cite Bouglé (1938), were obsessed with three problems, national recovery, secular emancipation, and social and economic organization, and who worked to 'advance a positive understanding of societies'. As Durkheim himself put it:

The shock produced by events was the stimulus that reanimated men's minds. The country found itself faced with the same question as at the beginning of the century. The organization, or rather the façade, which constituted the imperial system, had just collapsed: it was a matter of making another, or rather of making one which could survive other than by administrative artifice – that is, one that was truly grounded in the nature of things. For that, it was necessary to know what the nature of things was; consequently, the urgent need for a science of societies made itself felt without delay. (1973[1900]: 12)

French society, or so it seemed to the young Émile, was a society in conflict and a society that aspired to unity. It was a society that was asking itself big questions about politics, religion and the working class, and it was eager for answers (Filloux 1977: 10). This was the end of an era in Europe, and the emergence of a new Europe. Did this mean the end of squabbles between nations? Major changes were on the horizon: wars of expansion, economic competition, colonial conquests, imperialism and world politics. Some regretted France's 'absence', and would have liked her to retake her rightful place amongst the family of nations and play a greater role on the world stage (Hanotaux 1908: 48–9)

Education: A Weapon

Émile went on with his studies at the collège d'Épinal. The school had just fewer than 300 pupils. In 1867, only one of its science teachers had a degree in science, and its most proficient French teacher was, at best, a good grammarian who displayed absolutely no enthusiasm, knowledge or culture. Most of the pupils were destined to go into farming or trade. Émile quickly stood out as a 'studious and conscientious'[31] pupil who got excellent marks: he skipped two years, won a distinction in history in the 1873 *concours académique*,[32] then easily passed the *baccalauréat ès lettres* in 1874 and the *baccalauréat ès sciences* the following year (Lukes 1985[1973]: 42; Charle 1985: 65). A rather blurred contemporary photograph shows him leaning his left arm on a school friend's shoulder: he has a high forehead and thinning hair. His fine facial features reveal a feminine sensibility; his hands are delicate and his fingers are long.

While still at the college, the young Durkheim experienced a brief crisis of mysticism, probably between the ages of 13 and 16. This, explains Georges Davy, reflected the influence of an elderly Catholic schoolmistress, and it was as though conversion to Christianity had become a secret obsession (Davy 1919a; Alpert 1939; Lukes 1985[1973]). The decision had been taken: he refused to be 'like his father' or to 'repeat what his father had done'. He wanted to continue his studies and become a teacher.

There was therefore no 'transmissibility', to use Durkheim's own expression. This is one of the characteristics of modern societies: an individual's vocation or choice of profession is not influenced by heredity: 'If the past . . . is no longer transmitted through inheritance by blood, it does not follow that it is wiped out: its remains fixed in the records, the traditions of every kind, and in the habits imparted by education' (Durkheim 1984[1893]: 260). The influence of the social milieu on the genesis of aptitudes and dispositions becomes determinant (ibid.: 255). That is the price that has to be paid for progress, specialization and the division of labour.

Even though he was somewhat embarrassed because 'he would have liked to carry on the family tradition', Rabbi Durkheim did not stand in the way of his son's decision. Having done well at school, he himself, as a young man, had developed a 'definite taste' for secular knowledge and especially the sciences and philosophy. He had reportedly 'planned' to go to Paris, where, 'in order to solve his money problems', he was prepared to 'give private lessons'.[33] That was his modern side (Strenski 1997: 60). But his agreement was conditional: his son was to *work hard* (Lukes 1985[1973]).

Should the young David Émile's decision be seen as a sign of Jewish assimilation in France? The French Jewish community, which first settled in Alsace-Lorraine, was relatively small, with some 86,000 members in 1900, and had very quickly identified with the French Republic in order to ensure its survival and development (see Marrus 1971; Raphaël and Weyl 1980). Émile Durkheim was well aware that his decision was in keeping with a general law: 'religious minorities, in order to protect themselves against the hate to which they are exposed . . . try to surpass in knowledge the populations surrounding them' (Durkheim 2002[1897]: 172). He goes on:

> The Jew, therefore seeks to learn, not in order to replace his collective prejudices by reflective thought, but merely to be better armed for the struggle. For him it is a means on offsetting the unfavourable position imposed upon him by opinion and sometimes by law. And since knowledge by itself has no influence upon a tradition in full vigour, he superim-

poses this intellectual life upon his habitual routine with no effect of the former upon the latter. This is the reason for the complexity he presents. Primitive in certain respects, in others he is an intellectual and a man of culture. He thus combines the advantages of the severe discipline characteristic of small and ancient groups with the benefits of the intense culture enjoyed by great societies. He has all the intelligence of modern man without sharing his despair. (Ibid.: 122–3)

Education as a mark of distinction? Émile Durkheim chose to apply for a place at the École normale supérieure, but in order to prepare for the entrance examination he had to leave Épinal for Paris. Such a big change inevitably created a 'great gap' in his life. His own trajectory was typical of a new phenomenon, which he would later try to explain: young people no longer stayed in the places where they were born, and there were fewer barriers: 'As soon as the children's first growth is over, they often leave to complete their educations away from home; moreover, it is almost the rule that as soon as they are adult, they establish themselves away from their parents and the hearth is deserted' (Durkheim 2002[1897]: 344). There are no more hereditary names, with all the memories they bring back, no more family home, and the family no longer has any traditional reputation. Insofar as it is a 'collective being', the family is dispersed, not to say reduced to nothing. This 'swarming' process is inevitable. Émile could now have his own ambitions and his own interests, but there was a price to be paid. He was lonely: 'Of course, other things being equal, people usually prefer to live where they were born and have been reared. But local patriotisms no longer exist, nor can they' (Durkheim 2002[1897]: 357).

In the autumn of 1876, the young Durkheim enrolled in the '*khâgne*' preparatory class at Louis-le-Grand, which, together with Henri-IV, was one of the best lycées in Paris. The three-year programme comprised two years of rhetoric and one of philosophy. As a pupil, Émile seemed cold and rather boring. He did make some friends, including Frédéric Rauh, a young Jew from the provinces who was, like Durkheim, 'shy, reserved and something quick to take offence'. 'We were in the same class. I can still see him, sitting on the bench immediately below me. Material proximity aside, all sorts of reasons brought us together and we immediately became friends' (Durkheim 2006[1909]: 30). Émile found lodging in the Pension Jauffret. 'Let us be hard' was the institution's motto (see Lapie 1927). This situation made him insecure and anxious. It was difficult in financial terms, as he had only limited resources at his disposal; it was also difficult in social terms: the young provincial was in a new environment, and he found the loneliness hard to cope with. Was he prey to melancholy? In *Suicide* (2002 [1897]: 10), Durkheim tells the story of 'a young girl, daughter of healthy parents, [who] having spent her childhood in the country, has to leave at about the age of fourteen, to finish her education. From that moment she contracts an extreme disgust, a definite desire for solitude and soon an invincible desire to die.' Bored and lonely, the young *lycéen* certainly had a painful experience, but he did not sink into 'extreme depression'. As he admitted to his nephew Marcel Mauss almost 30 years later, he was lonely: 'Twenty-eight years ago, I spent my holidays in complete isolation – apart from the time I spent with you when you were a child – and they were certainly the most fertile period in my life. It was at that time that I corrected the rudder, and I immediately felt that I had the wind in my sails.'[34]

Émile also made friends at the Pension Jauffret, where he met Jean Jaurès. They struck up what was to become a lasting friendship. Speaking of his early days in Paris, Jaurès would write:

> I remember when, as a very young man, I was a newcomer to Paris. One winter evening in the immense city, I was stricken by a sort of social terror. It seemed to me that the thousands and thousands of men who passed each other as though they were strangers, that innumerable crowd of lonely ghosts, were free of all bonds. (1969[1911]: 169)

The young Jaurès's social concerns were already obvious; he was literally terrorized, asking himself, 'How can all these people accept the unequal distribution of wealth and misfortune. By what miracle do these thousands of suffering and dispossessed individuals tolerate all that exists?' (ibid.).

In intellectual terms, Émile Durkheim's experience was one of disappointment. The philosophy he was being taught was a source of irritation:

> From this point onwards, the search for distinction and originality began to have its effect in the classroom. Anyone unusual and new was already at a premium. Thinking along the same lines as they next boy was something to be avoided at all cost. Anyone with an academic ambition tried to create his own system, and not without reason, as that was the way to succeed. The trend was so strong that it even began to affect our teachers. (Durkheim 1975[1895a]: 413)

School itself was another disappointment. Émile was bored with everything: the strict discipline, Latin prose, the formalism and emptiness of the rhetoric he was being taught, the philosophy. He was already more interested in the sciences rather than in literature. And he failed. Unlike his friend Jean Jaurès, he failed to gain admission to the École normale supérieure at the end of his first year and had to go on preparing for the entrance exam. Fortunately, he had the help and encouragement of his philosophy teacher, M. Charpentier, who was, as Durkheim himself was to recognize (1975[1887a]: 51) 'the only light in a grey sky'. And yet he failed again. In the autumn of 1878, he therefore took the statutory examination that would earn him the title of 'non-certified teacher' [*maître auxiliaire*] at the Lycée Louis-le-Grand. He was asked about Charles Rollin's *Traité des études* ('Treatise on pedagogy', 1726). His answers demonstrated that 'he had studied the book, understood its spirit, and had the pedagogical understanding required of a good teacher'. Durkheim accepted the appointment, and undertook to 'dedicate himself to teaching in the public sector for two years'.[35]

It was only at his third attempt in the summer of 1879 that the young man from Épinal was admitted to the École normale supérieure: he was ranked eleventh in the entrance examination. His great determination and his refusal to turn his back on education were to be Émile's salvation. And his future was becoming clear: he knew that he would become a teacher even though he had his doubts about the new mores which, as could be seen from the 1879 *prix d'honneur*, were emerging in the teaching of philosophy.

2

École Normale Supérieure

Émile Durkheim became a student at the École normale supérieure in the autumn of 1879. He had entered a small, closed world: the regime was austere, the discipline was strict and academic standards were both high and demanding. No exceptions were allowed. When Émile enrolled, his father wrote to the director, asking him to be good enough to excuse his son from classes on Saturday. The director replied that 'given that the school was a boarding establishment, all students must submit to the same rules and there could be no exemptions' (Halphen 1987: 7). Rabbi Moïse Durkheim also wanted his son to be given an allowance to cover the cost of his clothing because his stipend was so modest: at the time, he was earning 1,600 francs a year. The administration's answer was negative: 'His father is reasonably well-off' (Charle 1984: 47).[1]

Durkheim's fellow students included Jean Jaurès, Henri Bergson (who would become professor of modern philosophy at the Collège de France),[2] Gustave Belot (who went on to teach philosophy at Louis-le-Grand) – all in the class of 1878 – and Camille Jullian (who would become professor of French antiquities at Bordeaux, the Sorbonne and, in 1905, the Collège de France) from the class of 1877. There were 24 students in Émile's year, including Pierre Janet, Paul Casanova, Edmond Goblot, René Doumic, André Le Breton, Lucien Picard, Maurice Holleaux and Pierre Paris.[3] The class of 1880 included Henri Bernès (who went on to teach at the Lycée Lakanal), Charles Cucuel (professor of Greek literature at Bordeaux), Pierre Imbart de la Tour (professor of medieval history at Bordeaux) and Gaston Richard (professor of social sciences at Bordeaux), while that of 1881 included Henri Berr (founder of the *Revue de synthèse historique*), Georges Radet (professor and dean at Bordeaux) and Frédéric Rauh, whom Émile came to 'know very well': 'I rediscovered an apostle with a lively intellect who wanted to communicate his ideas and to imbue minds with them. He was an apostle, but he was also meditative' (Durkheim 2006[1909]: 30). At the time, Rauh, like Durkheim, enjoyed philosophical discussions. The web of relationships that would both bind together his future colleagues and bring them into conflict was beginning to take shape. He would remain in contact with Jullian, Cucuel, Imbart de la Tour and Radet in Bordeaux, and would see several *normaliens*, including Bergson, elected to the Collège de France.[4] He would become embroiled in polemics with Belot and Bernès, who both took a keen interest in sociology, and would succeed in interesting Gaston Richard in sociology. The small group of friends were all students at the École normale supérieure and, as the saying had it, 'the spirit of the École is primarily an *esprit de corps*'.[5]

Although Émile was close to Jaurès, Lucien Picard, Maurice Holleaux and Frédéric Rauh, his best friend was Victor Hommay. Victor was a young Breton with a gentle expression and a broad smile, and a man of 'extreme, if not a little primitive, simplicity'. He appreciated the 'wild and rather sad beauty' of his native Brittany and was, adds Durkheim, no stranger to the 'joys of melancholy'. Victor and Émile had shared the same experience: they had been late in coming to Paris to complete their studies and had experienced the same 'impression of emptiness and loneliness'. A 'gentle intimacy' gradually developed between the two friends; they lived an 'active life' with 'good chats' and 'heated discussions' within an exceptional environment, and were in constant contact with 'distinguished minds' and 'elite masters'. Such 'happy days'! Émile was to remember them with nostalgia:

> During the three years we spent at the École, we really lived one life: we worked in the same room and studied the same subjects. We even spent our free days together. In the course of our long talks, we drew up so many plans for each other that I can no longer think of them without sadness and bitterness. (Durkheim 1975[1887a]: 423, 421)

The young Durkheim was not over-generous with his friendship; as Xavier Léon would put it, 'one had to deserve it and win it'.[6] He therefore had few friends, but his devotion, attachment and loyalty to them were unfailing. He took the view that there was something sacred about friendship.

The Metaphysician: Formidable in Argument

The student from Épinal was 21. He looked 'considerably older' than his fellow students and had already acquired his characteristically serious demeanour. His friend Maurice Holleaux noted his 'precocious maturity'. Hence, he adds, the nickname 'the Metaphysician' (cited in Davy 1919b: 187). A photograph of the class of 1889 (probably taken in 1887) shows a serious and intense young man. His solemn appearance contrasts with that of his fellow students, who are visibly more relaxed and cheerful. His hair is thinning, and he already has a big, bushy beard and a thin, dark moustache (Davy 1919a: 57; Alpert 1939: 17–18). Few of his friends knew him well. According to Holleaux, what was already a stern exterior concealed an 'almost feminine sensitivity' and 'treasures of kindness'.

Although he may have seemed to be reserved and introverted, Émile did enjoy social life and sought out the company of friends, especially at holiday times. It was his way of imbuing himself with the 'spirit of the community' (Alpert 1939: 22). But philosophical and political discussions were what he enjoyed most. He would often initiate the discussion, and joined in with a 'real passion'. 'I have heard him', recalled Maurice Holleaux, 'spend hours in discussion, with a logical fieriness that amazed his listeners; it would have been impossible for anyone to argue a case more closely, more energetically or more eloquently' (cited in Davy 1919b: 188–9). There were 'good chats' and 'heated discussions' that went on for hours (Durkheim 1975[1887a]: 418). The debates were about the issues of the day: Gambetta's new republican programme, Jules Ferry's reforms, Guesde's 'collectivism'. Émile was, as Henri Bergson recognized (Maire 1935: 54), 'formidable in argument'. He spoke at length, 'with passionate ardour and an imperious decisiveness'. No one who heard him speak once could 'doubt his superiority', said Holleaux: he was already the professor and orator he would be throughout his career. He found the affectations and frivolity of his fellow students irritating, and his simplicity and seriousness was in sharp contrast to their superficial sarcasm. During these discussions, he always focused on higher issues, and concentrated on the principles that were at stake. He saw politics as 'a serious business' and was not interested in personality issues or cliques. According to his friend Holleaux, he always found political scheming 'odious'. The 'main qualities' observed by his teachers in their student were, as well as his easy eloquence, 'a conscience and conviction that gave his style and his words a scintillating quality'.[7]

A 'vocation' was taking shape. Even at the École normale supérieure, and like Jaurès and his other friend Hommay, Émile devoted himself to the study of the 'social question': 'He . . . put the question quite abstractly and philosophically, under the title "The relationship between individualism and socialism"' (Mauss 1962[1928]: 38. The school was beginning to take an interest in social issues: it was certainly still a conservative milieu, with a minority but still very active group of practising Catholics, but it was bubbling with intellectual excitement and, as Marcel Mauss was to note, 'animated by political and moral intentions' (ibid.). These well-intentioned young men shared the conviction that 'salvation would come from the intellect, but that the intellect had to be sustained by positive knowledge and not empty abstractions' (Davy 1973[1960b]: 25). The idea of 'mental reorganization', which they borrowed from Auguste Comte, did not, however, imply any particular political commitment at this time: *normalien* socialism would be for the next generation.

For the moment, *normaliens* were beginning to take an interest in 'moral and social studies'. There was even talk of giving such studies a more important place in the teaching of philosophy. In an article entitled 'Reforming Philosophy Teaching in France', Alfred Fouillée wrote:

Countries which have universal suffrage and egalitarian democracy need, more so than others, to give the young people on whom their future depends a broad philosophical education that includes not only psychology, logic, ethics and metaphysics, but also the philosophy of art, the philosophy of nature, the philosophy of history, natural and written law, political economy and even general politics. . . . The study of society and its laws is of vital importance to those who are called upon to live in society and to influence the direction of society itself through their votes, their influence and their professional activities. (Fouillée 1880)

The greatness and prosperity of France were at stake, Fouillée concluded: 'Our lives have been ruined. Only education can save us from all the evils that are crushing us' (ibid.) Alfred Fouillée had an atypical career as a philosopher and was primarily concerned with ethical questions. In 1883, he published *Critique des systèmes de morale contemporains*; he also took an interest in sociology.[8]

With the Republicans

What were Durkheim's political views? Conservatives and Republicans were vying for control. This was, according to the sceptics who were suspicious of the 'genius' of the 'new reformers', a period of incoherence, trial and error, and uncertainty: 'We are getting nowhere. Nothing gets done, everything is left unfinished, and everything is getting complicated' (Mazade 1880: 943). The most important debate had to do with educational reform. In 1879, the Republicans at last won control of both the Chamber of Deputies and the Senate. Whereas Gambetta was 'the leader of men and the master of hearts', Jules Ferry was 'the man of state and the law' who argued that the marshal's sword should give way to the rule of law, and that institutions with a written constitution, or *the law*, were preferable to personal power (Hanotaux 1908: 38–40). The most active of all the advocates of secular education, he was appointed minister for education, but his attempts to wrest control of teaching from the religious communities brought down the government.

University reform, which was not achieved until 1884, had been central to political debates for more than 10 years. The idea was to create what Victor Duruy called 'an intellectual aristocracy'. At the level of higher education, this raised many issues: it took real dedication to group the scattered faculties together in large university centres, to increase their budgets, to improve lecturers' salaries and give them more autonomy and, finally, to promote the sciences (by, for example, putting the emphasis on teaching the scientific method), and to encourage the development of scientific research, including applied research. Between 1876 and 1879, more than one million francs was invested in reorganizing the salary system, and some 40 new chairs were established. The model was supplied by Germany, though France was home to prestigious figures such as Claude Bernard and Louis Pasteur. Even the law faculties were dreaming of creating 'centres of original research and disinterested science' (Weisz 1983: 79).

The ardent defenders of reform, several of whom were involved in the foundation of the Société de l'enseignement supérieure in 1878, included

Louis Liard, Paul Bert, Ernest Lavisse and the historian Gabriel Monod. Several *normaliens*, like Fustel de Coulanges, held important adminis- trative posts. 'Ultimately', said Jules Lemaître (1895a: 571), 'the *norma- lien* spirit is the university spirit.' These *normaliens* and *professeurs* were attempting to reconcile the professional interests of their academic col- leagues with the political concerns of the republicans. In their speeches and writings, they defined the function, or even mission, of the universi- ties: to create a broader consensus in a society that had been weakened by all kinds of conflicts. They wanted scientific methods to be applied to the study of social problems, and they sought to promote political modera- tion and social integration. Science, in other words, was the only basis for social cohesion. As Jules Ferry said again and again, only the scientific spirit 'can temper and soften the penchant for the absolute, for chimeras, which is the snare of sovereign democracies' and 'readily becomes disorder and anarchy' (cited in Weisz 1983: 128). The university became a symbol of national reconciliation and unity under the auspices of a secular republic.

Did Émile support Jules Ferry's project of constructing a unified secular educational system? He most certainly did. Rejecting the Catholic and monarchist right, Durkheim was on the side of 'political freedom' (freedom to think, to write and to vote):

> Men of my generation recall how great our enthusiasm was when, twenty years ago, we finally saw the fall of the last barriers which restrained our restlessness. But alas! Disenchantment quickly followed. For we soon had to admit that we did not know what to do with this hard-won freedom. Those to whom we owed this freedom used it only to tear each other to pieces. And from that moment on, we felt that wind of sadness and dis- couragement rise over the land which daily grew stronger and eventually finished by disheartening the least resistant spirits. (1973[1898]: 55).

For a while, he idolized Léon Gambetta, and loved him for what he saw as his 'broadmindedness and generosity' (Davy 1919b: 189). On 14 July 1880, he took part with 'real joy' in the first celebration of *la fête nation- ale*, spending the whole day in the streets so as to be part of the wave of popular enthusiasm. Durkheim saw it as something that allowed the community to sustain the cult of its ideal (Davy 1919b: 189–90).

Against Dilettantism

The young *normalien* also had other preoccupations: his studies. And his great fear was that he would fail. His precocious maturity and intellectual superiority quickly made him stand out. The purpose of the École was to train lycée teachers, and possibly university teachers. Some, including Émile Zola, mocked the École normale supérieure for turning out 'stu- dents who could do nothing but supervise schoolchildren'. It was obvious to such critics that 'if we sow teachers, we will not harvest creators'.

The first year at the École normale supérieure was devoted to preparing students for the *licence*, the first of two examinations designed to test their aptitude for teaching. The second of these was the *agrégation*, taken in the third year. The list of texts for commentary included Homer (*The Iliad*), Aeschylus (*Prometheus Unbound*), Herodotus, Demosthenes (*On The Chersonese*) and Plato (*Protagoras*), Terence, Cicero and Seneca, and La Fontaine (*Fables*) and Pascal (*Pensées*) (Paoloetti 1992: 11). Durkheim successfully passed the *licence* examination. He came first and, as, Davy records, astonished his examiners with 'a highly original oral improvisation on the genius of Molière'.

For Émile, the second year went better than the first. 'A year filled with success', notes Maurice Holleaux. He worked freely and gave the impression of being 'in possession of his strength', even though he still had some minor problems with his health. He was, on the other hand, still critical of his teachers. The subjects that interested him were literature and history, and especially philosophy. The dissertation on Stoic ethics amongst the Romans that he wrote for Gérard Boissier, who taught him Latin literature, and the more theoretical lecture on 'the self' [*le moi*] that he prepared for his philosophy teacher Émile Boutroux, who taught a course on Greek philosophy in 1880–1, impressed his teachers, who gave him good marks.

His teachers found him to be a good student and formed a high opinion of him. As Durkheim was about to leave the École, Fustel de Coulanges said of him that he was 'an excellent pupil with a very vigorous mind, at once precise and original' who had demonstrated a 'quite remarkable maturity' and 'a real aptitude for philosophical and above all psychological studies'.[9] The École awarded him the Alphonse-Garnier prize, which was given to 'the most hard-working and deserving student in his class' (Davy 1919b: 185).

The *normalien* took the courses taught by the director, who taught the history of literature, the Latinist Gaston Boissier, the historian Fustel de Coulanges, and the philosophers Léon Ollé-Laprune and Émile Boutroux. With the exception of the courses taught by Fustel de Coulanges and Boutroux, he was disappointed with the teaching he received during his first year: 'great disappointments', remarks Maurice Holleaux. 'It was no more than a fairly wretched rhetoric forced upon students who had had their fill of rhetoric. They had to devote themselves to the most mediocre exercises in an outdated humanism.' Latin prose and Latin or French translations bored him: they were exercises that cost him a great deal of effort, and he did not always do them well. 'I have seen him groaning and sounding off about having to write Latin verse, and getting nothing out of it' (Davy 1919b: 185). Émile was also highly critical of his teachers: he found Bersot superficial and was annoyed by his desire to please and by his fashionable clichés. Gaston Boissier, who taught the second year, was ridiculous, while Léon Ollé-Laprune had no rigour, least of all intellectual rigour (Filloux 1977: 12).[10]

In an article published in 1895, 'L'enseignement de la philosophie et l'agrégation de philosophie' ['The teaching of philosophy and the philosophy *agrégation*'], Durkheim denounced the weaknesses of philosophy teaching and described the teaching methods of his old teacher Léon Ollé-Laprune in scathing terms. Ollé-Laprune was a devout Catholic who had no interest in analytic rigour or rigorous proofs, and who practised the bastard art of combining ideas in the way that an artist combines images and forms with a view to appealing to taste rather than satisfying the mind. In that context, the *agrégation* encouraged 'purely formal talent' and the quest for distinction and originality (Durkheim 1975[1895a]: 416). In more general terms, he criticised French philosophy for what he would call, after he came back from Germany, its over-close relationship with literature: 'When they write, philosophers adopt a delicately crafted style, as though they were writing sonnets' (Durkheim 1975[1887b]: 438).

But not everything was a complete waste of time. He enjoyed the discussions and the dissertations, and read widely. One of the distinctive features of the École normale supérieure was the *conférence* – in other words, an open discussion between students. The student's role was not to listen religiously to his teachers and take notes, but to form an opinion and defend it, while also understanding and discussing the opinions of others. In his first years, Émile Durkheim wrote a dissertation on a phrase from Schiller's *Don Carlos*: 'May you never despise the dreams of your youth.' M. Delacoulonche, who taught literature, read it aloud to his students in admiration. Émile also gave a lecture on the history of the Jews under the Roman Empire, and distinguished himself thanks to his eloquence and intellectual maturity. Written for Ernest Desjardins, who taught him historical geography, it can be seen as the young *normalien*'s way of asserting his identity or of transforming his membership of a community into an object of study. 'Believe only what you see', Desjardins would say as he discussed inscriptions. Émile read the work of Flavius Josephus (*Antiquities of the Jews*) and Philo of Alexandria, as well as Ernest Renan (*L'Histoire des origines du christianisme*; vol. 2: *L'Antéchrist*; vol. 3: *Saint Paul*; vol. 4: *Les Apôtres*) and Louis Halvet (*Le Christianisme et ses origines*). This can be seen as the first indication of Émile's interest in the history of religions (Paoletti 1992: 11).[11]

The Rabbi's son from Épinal was beginning to distance himself from Judaism. It was a 'painful break' (Georges Davy, cited in Lukes 1985[1973]: 44), and it made him feel great remorse, like 'the Jew who for the first time eats pork' (Durkheim 1975[1887c]: 160). He spent his vacations in Épinal, where he found himself amongst 'simple people', as he liked to say (Davy 1919b: 187). The expression does not imply any contempt for simplicity: Durkheim loathed all forms of affectation. But he had distanced himself from his background in both social and religious terms. He would come to find 'provincial life' unbearable. Nothing happened in the provinces and he had few contacts there. 'In small towns', he remarked (Durkheim 1975[1887a]: 421) 'people live on top of one another. They see and observe each other so closely that there is always a danger that everyone will always be offended and wounded.'

In keeping with the École's practice, the second year was devoted to individual projects and gave students greater freedom to choose which lectures they attended. Their only obligation was to attend internal lectures. Throughout the year, Émile read widely and studied a great variety of authors: Cyrano de Bergerac, Saint-Beuve, Madame de Sévigné, Voltaire and Shakespeare, the historians Guizot and Michelet, and the philosophers Kant, Hegel, Leibniz, Cousin and Spinoza. He began to take an interest in political philosophy, reading works by Locke and Mill (*Essays on Religion*) and discovering political economy through Jean-Baptiste Say's *Traité d'économie politique*.

In history, the two teachers who won his admiration and influenced him were Gabriel Monod and Fustel de Coulanges. A *normalien* and history *agrégé* (1865), Gabriel Monod (1844–1912) was director of studies in the sixth section of the École pratique des hautes études; in 1880, he replaced Lavisse and was appointed *maître de conférences* at the École normale supérieure. The author of *Études critiques sur les sources de l'histoire mérovingienne* (1872), *Jules Michelet* (1875) and *Petite Histoire universelle* (1879, in collaboration with G. Dhombres), Monod was very active in historical circles. In 1873, he was co-director, with Gaston Paris, of the *Revue critique d'histoire et de littérature* and, in 1876, co-founder, with Gustave Fagniez, of the *Revue historique*, becoming its sole editor from 1885 onwards (Charle 1985: 137–8).[12] His lectures at the École normale supérieure dealt with early French history from the Carolingian era to the eighteenth century. His lectures were 'solid, conscientious and engaging', and notable for their clarity (Frédéricq 1883: 753–4, cited in Lukes 1985[1973]: 59). His familiarity with the archives allowed him to give precise and colourful details, and subtle descriptions of men and historical periods. Émile Durkheim listened to him with interest and admired him for his rigorous historical methodology.

Normalien, agrégé de lettres (1857) and *docteur ès lettres*, Fustel de Coulanges was appointed director of the École normale supérieure in February 1880. 'The school takes up all my time', he complained.[13] Fustel de Coulanges was the author of *La Cité antique*, which went through seven editions in ten years, and he had just begun to publish a monumental *Histoire des institutions politiques de l'ancienne France* in several volumes (1857–89). His inaugural lecture was entitled 'Changes in land ownership in France from the second to the ninth century'. In his view, 'the way in which land is owned has, at all times and in all countries, been one of the main elements in the state of society and politics (Fustel de Coulanges 1879: 747; see Muchielli 1998: 420). He also published, in 1880, *Étude de la propriété à Sparte*. He can therefore be regarded as one of the pioneers of economic and social history. Rejecting both *événementielle* and strictly political history, his preference was for a sociological history that took institutions into account. 'History is', he declared, 'the science of human societies', adding that it is 'the science of social facts, or in other words sociology itself' (1889: iv–v).

Fustel de Coulanges had a great influence on his students, who would remember warmly a teacher who always rejected dogmatism. 'He was a teacher who encouraged us never to take him at his word, and even dared us to disagree with him . . . he appealed to our individual freedom, and inspired in us a complete confidence in our own strengths. "Teaching must", he would say, "be a way of awakening minds".' Rejecting dilettantism, he valued seriousness, and in his lectures he strove after 'neither eloquence, brilliance nor the picturesque'. His eloquence was that of the scholar who is less concerned with dazzling than with convincing his audience. 'His preferred qualities were sobriety, accuracy and clarity. He loathed flowery languages and purple passages.' He had 'the enthusiasm of faith', but of the scientific faith that is based upon rational proofs (Guirard 1895).

As a historian, Fustel de Coulanges was a great believer in methodological rigour. Indeed, he saw rigour as a moral duty: the history he taught was not only an art, but also a new science. The task of the historian was not to imagine, but to observe texts in detail. Like a chemist who carries out experiments, the historian had to collect, analyse and compare facts, and relate them to one another (Fustel de Coulanges 1888: 32). 'Patriotism is a virtue, and history is a science', he liked to say. Fustel set his students an example of serious-mindedness and strict intellectual discipline; he encouraged them to become involved in controversies, to be careful, to avoid generalizations, and to base their studies of minor subjects on original source-material. He constantly made his students go back to the texts and encouraged them to do all they could to understand them. 'Read the texts', he would tell them. He demanded proof for every claim they made. All this was very much to Durkheim's liking, and he would dedicate one of his first books to Fustel in open recognition of his influence.

For Fustel de Coulanges, history was not just the history of events. It was also the history of institutions and, even though he rejected the term, his work did have a sociological dimension. In his view, history was the science of social facts, and it had to analyse every society as a whole. His attitude towards philosophy was critical, even sceptical. 'To philosophize', he once told Durkheim, 'is to say what one wants' (Durkheim 1975[1910a]: 370). Such comments found an attentive listener in the young *normalien*, but they did not put him off philosophy.

Towards Rationalism

The third year (1881–2) was the year of the *agrégation*. The year was all the more difficult in that Émile once more had health problems that forced him to go home for a few days at the beginning of January. He then had a few spells in the school's infirmary in February. He was seriously ill, recalled his friend Holleaux, with erysipelas and a high fever, and he was not a good patient. Being a 'keen and stubborn worker', Émile had a 'horror of illness and anything that disrupted the life of the mind' (Davy 1919b: 187).

Beginning with the works of Descartes in November 1881, Durkheim read and reread the authors on the syllabus. He also read the works of contemporary commentators and philosophers, such as Liard on Descartes, Fouillée on Plato and Socrates and, of course, the work of his teacher Émile Boutroux, including the manuscripts of the lectures he gave at the École and his thesis 'On the Contingency of the Laws of Nature' (1874).[14] Boutroux's thesis was as follows: science has the capacity to observe, generalize and establish laws, but that does not mean that knowledge can ever be perfect or definitive. Reality is complex. Boutroux was a neo-Kantian with an interest in the philosophy of the sciences; he believed that philosophy must be in direct contact with the realities of nature and life, and that it should be supported by the sciences.

In 1880, Boutroux began to publish an edition of the works of Leibniz, beginning with the *Monadology* and the *New Essays on the Human Understanding*. According to Xavier Léon (1921), there could be no doubt that 'A whole generation owes its philosophical vocation to his teaching at the École normale supérieure, and what a generation it is!' Always generous with his advice, Boutroux introduced his students to the great philosophers of the past. He had his own way, described by Georges Davy (1919b: 187) as 'penetrating and objective', of reconstructing and rethinking systems, and was a demanding teacher who expected a great deal of personal effort from his students.

Boutroux's motto was: 'Laws are facts, not principles.' Like Comte, he held that there are different levels or orders of reality, and that each is relatively autonomous from the others. In his classes, he insisted that every science must be explained in terms of 'its own principles', as Aristotle had demonstrated: psychology had to be explained in terms of psychological principles and biology in terms of biological principles. The superior therefore cannot be reduced to the inferior, and the same applies to social phenomena: 'Humanity is powerful when it deploys the faculty of union' (Boutroux 1874: 167). And good Kantian sociologist that he was, he goes on: 'Ultimately, it is because society is a hierarchy that it can expand man's powers and increase, almost indefinitely, his self-control and control over things. Man is powerful thanks to the society that coordinates his strengths.'

Durkheim became 'imbued' with these ideas, and would later apply them to sociology, having been convinced of the value of this method by his reading of Auguste Comte (Durkheim 1982[1907]: 258–9). The young *normalien*'s intellectual masters were, according to Georges Davy (1919b: 187), Renouvier and Comte, who were both 'positive', rather than Kant (of whom he was suspicious). Durkheim himself never thought of 'attaching any great importance to the question of how [his] thinking was shaped', but he did recognize the importance of the first books he read.

Renan, Taine and Comte were the fashionable authors of the day. The period saw what Émile Boutroux (1908: 684–5) called a 'renewal' in philosophy, thanks to the work of Taine, Ribot and Lachelier, and to the introduction into France of the work of Darwin and Spencer. Indeed, the situation was becoming critical, as the definition of the boundaries of philosophy were challenged. Science and positivism had been in the ascendant ever since the publication of Claude Bernard's *Introduction à l'étude de la médecine expérimentale* in 1865. Claude Bernard taught at the Collège de France, and the triumph of the experimental method and of belief in science did indeed mark the advent of a 'rigorously scientific age'. The world appeared to be determined by, and reducible to, certain laws, and the task of science was to discover those laws. Following the success of the positivist schools, which was at the expense of spiritualism, some spoke of a 'crisis' (Janet 1865; see Fabiani 1988: 124), and feared that philosophy would be replaced by a multiplicity of distinct and autonomous disciplines such as psychology, sociology, and so on.

Émile Durkheim read Ernest Renan's *Dialogues et fragments philosophiques*. He was disappointed, and took an immediate dislike to Renan (1823–92): 'One can be sure of finding in Renan assertions that contradict one another' (Davy 1919b: 186). And what of Taine? Like Renan, Hippolyte Taine (1828–93) was a member of the extended 'positivist' family. He believed in science, and used the natural sciences, including physiology, as a model for constructing the laws of the human past. His ambition was to turn history into a science, and to combine history and psychology; in his view, they had the same object, namely the genesis of man. When did Durkheim read his works? There is no absolute proof that the young Émile was directly influenced by Taine, author of *Histoire de la littérature anglaise* (1864–72) and of *De l'Intelligence* (1870), but he was affected by him, since he identified with the philosophical tradition that Taine introduced and popularized in France – namely, rational empiricism. In the philosophy lectures Durkheim gave at the lycée in Sens shortly after his *agrégation*, he refers several times to Taine, whom he describes as the philosopher who took the most systematic interest in the origins of the idea of a self. The image of Taine that he defends is that of a philosopher who was in close contact with British empiricism and who, 'having an analytic mind, wanted to be synthetic but had no real synthetic genius'. Although 'naturally inclined to take a favourable view of Taine', Durkheim nevertheless criticized him for 'having juxtaposed the two tendencies [empiricism and rationalism] he was trying to reconcile rather than establishing any logical connection between them' (Durkheim 1975[1897]: 175).

Towards the end of 1881, Émile discovered the work of Herbert Spencer, probably via a reading of his *Classification of the Sciences* and *The Data of Ethics*. The following spring, he also read the recently published second French version of *First Principles* (1862). Looking back at the days when he was preparing for his *agrégation*, Henri Bergson recalled: 'There were two sides within the university. One, which was by far the majority, believed that Kant had asked the questions in their definitive form, while the other rallied to Spencer's evolutionism' (cited in Du Bos 1946: 63; Mucchielli 1998: 88). On which side was the young Durkheim? Spencer's evolutionist philosophy was very popular in France and was a major philosophical influence during the period 1870–90. His main works were translated into

French, with *First Principles* (1862) appearing in 1871, the *Principles of Sociology* 1874 and the *Principles of Psychology* in 1874–5. The various volumes of the *Principles of Sociology* were published from 1878 onwards. Thanks to his *Study of Society,* which rapidly became one of the 'most popular' works amongst philosophers, Spencer (1820–1903) was one of those who helped sociology to become a truly empirical science.

Spencer's theory is based upon a few key ideas: society is an organism – in other words, an integrated system of interdependent apparatuses. Evolution reveals a historical direction that moves from the simple to the complex, from homogeneity to heterogeneity, as the division of labour becomes more pronounced and as specialization increases. That is, the parts become both increasingly differentiated and increasingly interdependent. The debate about Spencer's theory was all the more lively in that it is associated with a political philosophy inspired by individualism and liberalism. Its main theses, as formulated by Spencer, are as follows: freedom of competition is the precondition for progress, and non-intervention on the part of the state is the source of social cohesion in differentiated societies. The ideas of differentiation, competition and the struggle for life, seen as the principles governing the evolution of organisms, were central to what was already being called 'social Darwinism' in France (Gautier 1880). The doctrine drew on Darwin and, especially, Spencer, and provided a scientific basis for laisser-faire theories.

That same year, Durkheim also read Auguste Comte's *Cours de philosophie positive,* and Alexis de Tocqueville's *Democracy in America* and *The Old Regime and the Revolution.* He also discovered, finally, Paul Janet's *Philosophie du bonheur* and *Histoire de la science politique,* and Théodule Ribot's studies, *Contemporary English Psychology* and *Contemporary German Psychology,* as well as his work on heredity. The young *normalien* was literally bowled over by Ribot, and read everything by him that he could lay his hands on (Mauss 1969[1939]: 566). He also read the journals of the day, including the *Revue philosophique,* the *Revue des deux mondes* and *La Critique philosophique,* in which were published texts by Janet, Renouvier, Spencer and Wundt, as well as texts on the theory of evolution and reviews of works by authors such as Renan and Espinas. Durkheim developed an enthusiasm for Charles Renouvier (1815–1904), and borrowed several issues of *La Critique philosophique* from the École's library. These included Renouvier's articles, 'Herbert Spencer's principles of psychology', 'The question of certainty' and 'Human freedom from an observational viewpoint'. The 'imprint' left upon the young *normalien* by the author of *La Science de la Morale* (1869) was, according to Georges Davy (1919b: 185), so great that it never faded. It was, above all, a lesson in rigour: 'If you want your mind to mature', he later told René Maublanc, 'make a detailed study of a master, and take apart even the smallest cogs of his system. That is what I did, and my teacher was Renouvier' (Maublanc 1930).

Charles Renouvier, a graduate of the École polytechnique (a *polytechnicien*), did not hold a position at the university. He had a private income and devoted himself exclusively to his work. He was politically active during the 1848 Revolution, and had to retire to the countryside after Louis Napoléon's *coup d'état*. His political views and his hostility towards Victor Cousin, whom he described as France's 'philosophical dictator', ensured that he was not welcome in the university. 'A dangerous man', said some. Renouvier was the author of many essays,[15] and was seen by young philosophers as being avant-garde; Durkheim regarded him as 'the greatest contemporary rationalist' (Durkheim 1983[1955]: 30). Even his enemies respected him as a 'vigorous and penetrating thinker' (Ribot 2000[1877]: 115). His name is identified with the doctrine known as 'criticism', which gives an important role to freedom of thought, critical thinking and reason. We find in Renouvier, who had read William James with great attention, both a philosophy of science ('critique' also means a rejection of positivism and scientific dogmatism), and a philosophy of knowledge centred on the notion of the 'category', which he also calls 'representation'. ('The study of categories,' he liked to say, 'is the key to everything.') His categories, or the first laws of knowledge, are relationship, number, sequence, quality, evolution, causality, finality and personality. In his brief introduction to the thought of Renouvier, Ribot identifies the starting point of his criticism as the 'very simple and common' concept of a thing: 'Things exist, and all things have one feature in common: that of being represented, of revealing themselves.' This analysis of the principles of knowledge is complemented by an investigation into categories or 'the laws of phenomena'. Renouvier's work was not, to Ribot's regret, 'sufficiently widely read and is far from enjoying the success it deserves' in France.

Renouvier also developed a philosophy of history which went against the general trend by calling into question the ideas of necessity and progress, and a science of ethics. As in science, there is no absolute causal determinism, as freedom establishes the limits of determinism. Freedom and constraint combine to give a meaning to history which, far from being linear, is discontinuous. He carefully kept up with the literature on 'morals', and especially the British evolutionists' anthropological studies of man's animal origins. Between 1874 and 1880, he published some 20 articles, most of them on the psychology of primitive man. His criticisms of the evolutionists were harsh, emphasizing their methodological weaknesses and theoretical or empirical contradictions. Renouvier defends the idea that, being a sociable creature, man is a moral being, and that all men have the same (logical) mentality and are equal by nature. 'I not only accept that the logic of primitive man was always the logic we still have; I also insist that he had the same basic ability to apply them, and that the same universal concepts supplied his principles' (Renouvier 1879: 219). Moral sentiments therefore have a social, not an instinctual, basis; as sociology teaches us, it is our being together that spontaneously creates morality. Sociology, he claims, is the science of moral environments, or, in other words, of mores, customs and shared ways of thinking, judging and acting (Renouvier 1874: 278; 1875a: 183). We also find in Renouvier, finally, an embryonic sociology of religion: in the philosopher's view, the formation of religious concepts is dependent upon pre-established moral judgements and moral habits (Renouvier 1875b: 366).

In fact, Renouvier was suspicious of mores and habits. His political motto was: 'Live in accordance with reason rather than habits.' His *Science de la morale* in fact results in a rationalist philosophy of politics: 'The notion of the state is the product of reflection and the will . . . It is therefore morally superior, just as a voluntary association is preferable to spontaneous cooperation, and just as a republic of free agents is superior to a hive of bees' (1908: 286) A republic of free agents was, in Renouvier's view, France's political ideal.

Renouvier was also the author of *Manuel républicain de l'homme et du citoyen* (1848) and, shortly after the events of 1871, became the founder of *La Critique philosophique* (1872). The goal of this journal was not only to talk about philosophy and science, but to defend the republican ideals of justice and equality. In 1879, he published a long article in the journal on the threats facing the Third Republic. He believed that the reason why democracy and socialism were in danger was that the 'revolutionary method', with its violent and authoritarian socialism might provoke a right-wing backlash. The 'social question' must therefore, he concluded, be taken out of the hands of revolutionary socialism, and entrusted to a 'practical sociology'. As a young man, Renouvier had read Saint-Simon with great enthusiasm, and he remained convinced that human beliefs had to be changed completely, and that science and society must be reconstructed so as to promote the interests of humanity. His *Manuel républicain* can be seen as a 'left-wing classic' and as an example of a 'humanist apprehension of collective life' (1981[1848]: 23–4).

Renouvier's influence on republican intellectuals was such that, at the end of the nineteenth century, his doctrine looked like the Third Republic's 'official metaphysics'; the Wise Man, as Henry Michel was to call him, was nothing more and nothing less that the 'conscience of France'. Michel saw him as a saviour who, by going back to Rousseau's primitivist inspiration, gave individualism a solid philosophical basis and who, by rejecting both the radical individualism of the economists and authoritarian socialism, synthesized the two doctrines, borrowing the ideas of freedom and individual independence from the liberals, and those of justice and equality from the socialists. This combination of freedom and justice was, according to Henry Michel, the defining feature of the French conception of the republic (Michel 2003[1890]; see Spitz 2005: ch. 2).

The philosopher could not, according to Renouvier, remain inactive, and must establish the moral and political values of human society, and develop an epistemology of science. He himself wrote a resolutely anti-utilitarian treatise on 'the science of ethics' and suggested that ethics should be studied 'scientifically'. Durkheim took the lesson to heart, and would always remember Renouvier's axiom to the effect that a whole is not equal to the sum of its parts, which was to become the basis of what he called his 'social realism'. 'Renouvierism' was all the more important to Durkheim in that he went on discussing the doctrine with his colleague in Bordeaux Octave Hamelin, a disciple of Renouvier's (Jones 2001). The influence of the man his contemporaries called 'the French Hume' did a great deal to popularize an uncompromising rationalism, and to encourage those who were interested in studying morality scientifically, who had a sense of social justice, who defended the republican educational system and state schools, and who attempted to reconcile the individual and social solidarity in the name of 'personalism'.[16] Renouvier himself defined his doctrine as 'an expression of solidarity': every man should be 'an end for himself and should have the means to pursue that end with the help of others' (Michel 2003[1890]: 649).

Émile Durkheim had only one complaint about the philosophical education he received at the École normale supérieure: it left him with a 'poor understanding of physiological research', which was beginning to be of such importance. It was only after he had taken his *agrégation* that he discovered the work of Charcot.

The *Agrégation*: A Very Testing Experience

The *agrégation* was an unavoidable rite of passage for anyone who wanted to become a *professeur* in a lycée and, eventually, hold a university post. It was, to cite Théodule Ribot (2000[1877]: 120), a 'very difficult' competitive examination. It consisted of a preparatory examination made up of two dissertations – one on a philosophical question and one on a question of the history of philosophy – and three so-called 'definitive' examinations. *Normaliens* had to write a commentary on French, Greek and Latin texts, submit a thesis on a topic dealing with the history of philosophy, and give a talk on a topic chosen from the lycée syllabus. For the 1882 examination, the texts for commentary or translation were Plato's *Timaeus*, Aristotle's *Physics*, Alexander of Aphrodisias's *Treatise on Destiny*, Cicero's *On the Nature of the Gods*, Seneca's *Letters*, Leibniz's *Critique of the Philosophy of Descartes* and Malebranche's *Ethics*. The thesis subjects were (i) Philosophy and the school of Eleus, (ii) The Sophists, (iii) Theories of definition: Plato, Aristotle and Leibniz, (iv) The philosophy of Spinoza, and (v) The ethics of Kant and Fichte.[17]

The two questions in the examination on philosophy and the history of philosophy dealt with 'relations between the imagination and thought', and the modern theory of evolutionism. The first question was particularly difficult because, as Durkheim remarked from the outset, the imagination had, in the seventeenth century, been disparaged ('disorders of the mind', 'disorders of the understanding'), but was now 'extolled at the expense of thought', with great scholars attributing their greatest discoveries to it.

The paradox identified by Durkheim is as follows: the mind is one, whereas the nature of things is characterized by multiplicity. How can this problem be resolved? We must, he replies, referring to Aristotle, find an 'intermediary' with the properties of both unity (that of the mind) and multiplicity (that of the object). And that intermediary is none other than the imagination because this faculty, which is a 'synthetic faculty', 'introduces life and diversity into the understanding'. In other words, Durkheim concludes, it is thanks to the imagination that the encounter between the mind and things can come about. The imagination is the source of thought itself: it is 'the faculty of invention and discovery'.

In the history of philosophy examination, candidates were asked to 'expound and evaluate the modern theory of evolutionism'. Durkheim begins his exposé by picking up the distinction between the reality of things (multiplicity) and the mind (unity): 'The object of science is to allow the mind to understand things, and it must therefore reduce multiplicity to unity.' The basis of evolutionism is no different: in every kingdom, multiplicity is reduced to unity. Durkheim is reformulating Renouvier's systematic critique of English evolutionist theories about man's animal origins: the 'metaphysics of science' known as evolutionism is, in his view, 'premature'. It is premature for two reasons. First, we cannot 'proclaim the homogeneity of things' until each of the sciences has completed its task and has 'reduced every realm to one basic and primary fact'. Second, the principle of continuity, on which evolutionism is based, is a contradiction even in logic and mathematics: 'half can never, by growing continuously, become one'. Durkheim continues the argument: 'An animal cannot, a fortiori, become a man through a process of continuous development, a plant cannot become an animal, a mineral cannot become a plant. One cannot become multiple, and the same cannot become the other.'

According to Durkheim, the principle of unity therefore has only a 'subjective value'. There is no basis for any of this in reality: 'The heterogeneous therefore comes not from the homogeneous, but from the heterogeneous.' The question is therefore not 'how the one becomes the multiple, but how the multiple becomes one'. And in order to answer that question, we must, according to Durkheim, introduce finality, which is the very thing that evolutionism rules out.

The young Durkheim as defender of the imagination? Durkheim the *normalien* criticizing evolutionism? These are, as he himself was to complain (1975[1895a]: 413), academic exercises, and such exercises distract candidates from 'anything to do with positive data and definitive knowledge'. When he became a member of the *agrégation* jury, he was astonished to find that candidates succeeded in discussing, 'with perfect ease', subjects of which they knew nothing, and denounced 'our young philosophers' growing liking for speaking a language which may well be brilliant, but which is extremely vague . . . I could cite brilliant candidates saying things that really do make one believe that philosophy is becoming a form of symbolism and impressionism' (ibid.: 416).

Durkheim had had some difficult in obtaining admission to the École normale supérieure; when he left in July 1882, he obtained below-average results in the philosophy *agrégation*: he was ranked seventh (out of eight candidates). 'M. Durckheim [*sic*] is a serious and logical thinker', noted chairman of the jury Félix Ravaisson, in his report to the minister, adding:

'He must stop using a terminology that is often abstract and obscure.'[18]
The school's director, Fustel de Coulanges, congratulated his student:
'An excellent student with a very vigorous mind, at once precise and
original . . . remarkable maturity. He has a real aptitude for philosophical,
and especially psychological, studies.' Like his other teachers, Fustel de
Coulanges had a 'high opinion' of him, but he did not hide his disappointment: 'His work and merits allowed one to hope that he would gain the
highest marks.'[19] What should have been no more than child's play for this
potential *cacique*[20] ended, as his friend Maurice Holleaux admitted, with a
'semi-failure' (cited in Davy 1919b: 186).

3

'Schopen' at the Lycée

Having successfully passed the *concours*, young *agrégés* had a choice between beginning a career in secondary education and applying for a grant to spend time abroad, which was often an unavoidable 'rite of passage' for anyone who wished to pursue a career in higher education and research.

Émile Durkheim opted to work in a secondary school, He was appointed to teach philosophy [*professeur de philosophie*] at the lycée in Le Puy in October 1882 and, a month later, at the lycée in Sens. Sens was a small town with a population of 13,000 on the Yonne river, some 90 kilometres south-east of Paris. The local paper, *L'Union de l'Yonne* (which was Catholic) announced the arrival of 'M. Durckheim [*sic*], *professeur de philosophie, agrégé*'.[1] Life in a small town was not, he found, unpleasant; he would later say that he had 'the soul of a provincial'.[2] Recalling the time he spent in Sens, he would write: 'I would watch people going past my window from the depths of my armchair. There was a sleepiness in the air; I fought against it but felt it to be very gentle.'[3] His annual salary was 3,200 francs (plus 500 francs for teaching a class in a girls' school). His classes were attended by some 15 students.

He later described the spectacle of what was taught at the lycée as 'dispersed': 'Each person teaches his speciality as if it were an end in itself, although it is only a means to an end to which it should always be related.' The school existed, in other words, in a state of 'anarchic fragmentation'. The minister of the day tried to fight that fragmentation by introducing monthly meetings at which all teachers in a given lycée came together to discuss issues of common concern. That, alas, was no more than an 'empty formality'. Durkheim's colleagues attended the meetings 'with deference', but they all agreed that there was no point to them: 'We were able to state very quickly that we had nothing to say to each other, because we lacked any common objective' (Durkheim 1956: 140).

The young teacher was at the start of his career, and had no idea that his first years would sometimes be very difficult (Durkheim 1975[1887a]). He was somewhat lacking in confidence; his lessons were not always 'adequately prepared' and, 'uncertain of being understood', he 'repeated himself'. Things gradually got better: 'He is certainly improving by the day.' His teaching was, according to his end-of-year report, 'clear, attractive and full of warmth'.[4] He was a well-organized, even systematic, teacher. At the end of every lesson, he would go to the blackboard and write up the titles or themes he had covered to make the structure of his exposé, often loosely interpreted, more obvious to his pupils.

Durkheim was a 'good influence'[5] on his students – or his 'dear friends', as he called them. He hoped to become their guide, but without making them lose their independence. He asked them both to avoid being self-important and to retain a 'very strong vivid of your own identity'. These were, he admitted, 'feelings which appear contradictory, but which strong minds know how to reconcile'. 'Know how to respect natural superiority without losing your self-respect. That is what the future citizens of our democracy must be' (Durkheim 1975[1883]: 417).

The Passion for Knowledge

In order to prepare his classes, Durkheim read the philosophers Seneca, Maine de Biran and Cournot (*Essai sur la connaissance*). He also re-read Fustel de Coulanges (*Histoire des institutions politiques*) and Ribot (*La Psychologie allemande*). But most of the books he borrowed from the school library were by Spencer (*Introduction to Social Science* and *First Principles*). He also borrowed recent (1882 and 1883) issues of the *Revue philosophique*.[6] He covered a wide variety of themes in his lectures: the nature of consciousness; the definition of reason; truth and certainty; methodology in the physical and moral sciences; the history of utilitarianism; domestic ethics, aesthetics; the soul; and the nature and attributes of God.[7] As the syllabus required, he gave 25 lectures in all. Durkheim was preparing his students for a state examination, and he followed the syllabus laid down in 1880: it began with psychology and continued with logic and ethics, ending with metaphysics. There was a logic to this progression, and it was very much inspired by Victor Cousin: what began with consciousness ended with theodicy. Durkheim's brief experience taught him one thing: 'I believe that in a secondary school course it is never a good idea to be innovative except in moderation, and the changes which I am recommending to you can easily be accommodated to tradition' (Durkheim 1978[1888b]: 222).

The philosophy class was, as the saying went 'the class that crowns and completes secondary education'. This was the philosophers' way of reminding people that they were at the top of the hierarchy of knowledge. The tradition that dominated academic philosophy in the nineteenth century was the eclectic and spiritualist philosophy of Victor Cousin (1792–1867), who had been minister of public education and director of the École normale supérieure. Even though he had died several years earlier, the 'famous philosopher' (*dixit* Durkheim) still had great influence. The way he divided up philosophy was, in Durkheim's view, 'like all the simplest ways . . . also the best, and I will adopt it'. The textbook he used was probably Paul Janet's *Traité élémentaire à l'usage des classes*, first published in 1879 and revised in 1883 to bring it into line with the new syllabus introduced in 1880. Janet (1823–99) had studied under Cousin. He was responsible for drawing up the Third Republic's first philosophy syllabuses and, being an 'old spiritualist philosopher', had tried to preserve 'the best of the heritage' (Fabiani 1998: 28). Durkheim was very familiar with the work of Janet, who had been a member of his examination jury at the École normale supérieure.

The syllabus put the emphasis on the importance and specificity of philosophical method: What is philosophy? What is philosophy's object, and what is its method? What is the relationship between science and philosophy? Those were the questions the young teacher asked in his first lessons. 'To philosophize', Durkheim told his students from the outset, 'is to reflect on specific facts in order to reach general conclusions' (Durkheim 2004: 33). He described philosophy as a science, and defined it thus: 'Philosophy is the science of states of consciousness' (ibid.: 35). He therefore discussed science, psychology and even psychophysiology.

One of Cousin's great innovations was to make psychology part of the philosophy syllabus. The author of *Eléments de psychologie* (1864) had developed the so-called 'psychological' model for the study of the faculties of the human mind, and it relied heavily on introspection. Philosophy was, in his view, a basic discipline that did not require the support of either hypotheses or empirical laws. Paul Janet, whose nephew Pierre became an experimental psychologist, opened the debate by giving hypotheses and experimentation a role in animal, physiological and pathological psychology (see Brooks 1993).

The syllabus was no more than a springboard for teachers, who enjoyed a great deal of freedom. At the time when Durkheim was embarking on his career, the idea of the teacher's task was beginning to change: the activity of teaching was no longer described as a rehearsal, but as a performance. A lecture was a 'work of art' in itself, and teaching pupils was a philosophical undertaking in its own right (Fabiani 1998: 61).

Durkheim was close to the tradition of the 'great' Cousin, cautiously departing from it only to the extent that he relied upon the model of the physical sciences. He took the view that the goal of science was to supply explanations, and he defended the use of hypotheses in both philosophy and science. The true philosophical method was experimental and could be broken down into three parts: (1) the observation, classification and generalization of facts; (2) the formulation of hypotheses; and (3) the verification of those hypotheses by means of experimentation. In a word, it is a method that 'takes the middle road between its deductive and empirical counterparts' (Durkheim 2004: 39) and that allows for both the inventive mind and respect for the facts: 'It's the mind that creates and invents, but in doing so it doesn't fail to respect the facts' (2004: 40).

Durkheim therefore takes the side of science; this is a science that strives above all to objectify and satisfy 'a need of the mind' – namely, 'the instinct of curiosity, the passion to know', and its aim, or at least consequence, is 'an improvement in human life' (Durkheim 2004: 41). Before a system of knowledge can merit the name of 'science', it must have an object of its own that is distinct from the objects of other sciences. Its object must be consistent with the law of identity (as in mathematics) or that of causality (as in the physical sciences). And there must, finally, be a method appropriate to the study of that object, namely the experimental method. According to Durkheim, philosophy meets those conditions, and is therefore a science. In the section of his lectures devoted to the theory of knowledge, he raises the question of the philosophy of science and epistemology: are the 'laws of the mind' like the 'laws of things'? Unlike those who succumb to subjectivism, the philosopher defends objectivism and rejects the idealist conception of science in the name of realism. His position is clear and can be summed up in two sentences: 'the external world really does exist. So our doctrine is a realist doctrine' (Durkheim 2004: 85).

Durkheim also attached great importance to the imagination as a source of knowledge, attacking those, like Pascal and Malebranche, who denigrate that faculty and who, like the Cartesians, described it as '*la folle du logis*'.[8] The formulation of new hypotheses does not necessarily rely upon rigorous procedures, and often involves an act of creative imagination. Referring to Newton, he remarks that 'a creative imagination is the *sine qua non* of the inventor' (Durkheim 2004: 126). He takes the example of analogy, which is a widely used and highly effective procedure: 'not everything in analogy has a logical basis – contingency plays an important role in the invention of every hypothesis' (Durkheim 2004: 210). Durkheim goes further still: methodology is not everything. The imagination is also important. It took, he told his pupils, 'the imagination of Galileo to dream that a general law' could be formulated to apply to all pendulums (Durkheim 2004: 127). 'The imagination' was also the subject of a question in the *agrégation* examination.

The Fashion for Pessimism

Because he referred so often to Arthur Schopenhauer (1788–1860), who was at the time the most widely read foreign philosopher in France (Lalande 1960: 24), Durkheim's *lycéens* nicknamed him 'Schopen', which, when pronounced in the French manner, becomes *Chopin*. Renouvier, Guyau, Sully, Prudhomme and Paul Janet all read Schopenhauer. Articles on him appeared in the *Revue des deux mondes*, the *Revue philosphique* and *Critique philosophique*. The first major study of Schopenhauer in France was probably Théodule Ribot's *La Philosophie de Schopenhauer*.[9] Several of the German philosopher's works had been translated into French. *On the Freedom of the Will* (1841) was translated by Salomon Reinach in 1876, and was followed by translations of *On the Basis of Morality* (1842) and *The Fourfold Root of the Principle of Sufficient Reason* (1813) in 1879 and 1882 respectively. The collections known in French as *Aphorismes sur la sagesse dans la vie* and *Pensées et fragments* appeared in 1880 and 1881.

In Paris, 'the pale figure of the world-weary Schopenhauerian' could even be seen in the brasseries. The works of his disciple Eduard von Hartmann, who published *Phenomenology of Moral Consciousness* in 1879, were also widely discussed. As Durkheim himself would learn from his observations of German students, philosophical pessimism was a fashionable fad.[10] At a deeper level, however, it was also a social, or even civilizational, fact, and Durkheim established a connection between 'depressing' theories – he cites Schopenhauer and Hartmann – and periods in which 'collective melancholy' acquires exceptional force. Far from being pleased to see that 'the pessimistic current' was so intense, he viewed it as 'a morbid development' and a sign of 'some disturbance of the social organism' (Durkheim 2002[1897]: 337).

Schopenhauer enjoyed the support of many philosophers, but he also had his enemies. He was, Ferdinand Brunetière reminds us, the butt of many jokes; he was described as 'clownish' and 'pedantic', and his work became synonymous with obscurantism, heaviness and scholastic tedium (see Brunetière 1890).[11] We have here a 'strange' or even 'ludicrous' theory, exclaimed Alfred Fouillée (1881: 127), who regarded the work of this German school as an incoherent jumble of errors and truth, scientific facts, sophisms and obscure pronouncements. He contrasted the German philosophy 'of despair', which saw a final deliverance from the will in the annihilation of all will, all consciousness and all individuality, with a 'philosophy of experience' that put the emphasis on consciousness and mutual union or fraternity.

Durkheim admitted to his young students: 'Today, pessimism is back in vogue . . . In fact, pessimism . . . has become almost popular in many parts of Europe' (Durkheim 2004: 313). At several points, he paused to discuss the work of the 'two great names' associated with the doctrine, namely Schopenhauer and Hartmann. The seventh lecture of the series was called 'Pleasure and Pain', and he dealt with the passions, emotions and inclinations in other lectures, remarking, for example that 'we can even take some pleasure in pain, as when we feel melancholy' (Durkheim 2004: 60). Is it possible, he asks, that pleasure is nothing more than a negative value? That is Schopenhauer's thesis in *The World as Will and Representation* (1819): 'Pain is the more basic fact, and pleasure simply its cessation.' This doctrine has, argues Durkheim, 'some pretty sad consequences', because 'if pleasure is only the absence of pain . . . then life is a sombre affair indeed' (Durkheim 2004: 61). And according to Durkheim, it follows quite logically that the German philosopher's answer to the question 'Is life worth the effort?' must be 'No' (Durkheim 2004: 61). Hartmann (1842–1906) reaches the same conclusions in his *Philosophy of the Unconscious*: 'Life isn't worth the trouble, not because pleasure doesn't exist independent of pain, but because the sum of all pains surpasses the sum of all pleasures' (Durkheim 2004: 61).

In order to refute this thesis, Durkheim puts forward two arguments: (1) not every need is painful, and (2) not all pleasures are associated with need – the announcement of good news, or the pleasures of art and science.

The same applies to the passions. When a passion is too exclusive, too invasive, there is a danger that it may become 'an unhealthy development' (Durkheim 2004: 70) and lead us to 'pursue some object violently'. On the other hand, 'passion is an indispensable condition without which no great things can be accomplished. . . . Consider the passion for glory . . . the passion for work, study, etc.' (2004: 71, 70).

Melancholy at the personal level, pragmatism and the philosophy of the irrational at the intellectual level, pessimism and the view that man is the victim of a thousand torments, suffering as the essence of life and suicide: one could go on drawing comparisons between Schopenhauer and Durkheim, but the influence that the German philosopher might have had on Durkheim should not be overstated, whether it be his notion of will or his philosophy of pessimism (or suffering).[12] Durkheim in fact tended to be critical of the German philosopher, who turns the 'will to live' [*Wille zum leben*] into a sort of universal explanation for a species' instinctual attempts at self-preservation; he very rarely cites his works.[13]

Durkheim takes the view that, while a little melancholy may be a good thing, we can have too much of it: it must not take over our lives, and must be counter-balanced by the opposite tendency (optimism and a liking for joyful expansiveness). He aspires to being 'in harmony with things' and advocates a philosophy of the golden mean.

Faculties of the Soul. Conscious/Unconscious

According to the tradition established by Cousin, 'the first thing we should study is psychology' (Durkheim 2004: 47). Durkheim does not just begin with psychology: he gives it pride of place, devoting more than 30 lectures to it. His 'preliminary matters' (The object and method of philosophy) are followed by four main sections: Sensibility, Intelligence, Aesthetics and Activity. Durkheim deals with a very wide variety of themes: consciousness, reason, the cognitive faculties (imagination, memory, association of ideas), sleep, dreams, madness.

Durkheim was very well versed in the 'new' psychology, which took much of its inspiration from physiology and reduced mind to matter; he cites the work of the German psychologist Wundt, according to whom 'the mind is dependent on the body – that is, the conscious life of the mind has its roots in the unconscious life of the body' (Durkheim 2004: 54). This new psychology had only recently been developed in Germany, England and the United States (Rose 1985; Danziner 1990). Questions that had traditionally been the preserve of philosophy – the theory of knowledge, the faculties of the soul – were becoming objects of experimental and psychometric research. Sensations and perceptions were being studied in laboratories, and quantitative methods were being introduced. Durkheim cites the work of two German schools: the German psychophysical school (Weber, Fechner), which he criticizes, and the psychophysiological school (Wundt): 'Wundt adds that without measurement no science is possible'

(Durkheim 2004: 54). Durkheim saw 'good reason' to be interested in this scholarship, but added that 'it errs' when 'it claims that the only way to study the mind is to study the body'. He had no intention of 'doing away with' psychophysiology, but in his view the two disciplines could collaborate only if they developed independently. The study of 'states of consciousness in and for themselves' (ibid.: 55) required the development of a science of the soul by using the only suitable method, namely 'observation through consciousness'. That method had, he admitted, been criticized, but he rejected the various objections one after another, and especially the objection concerning the relationship between the observed and the observer: 'One can't be simultaneously an actor and a spectator, but one can definitely be an actor and watch oneself act. One can watch oneself in a mirror!' (ibid.: 56).

Durkheim often says that consciousness is everything, and he cannot accept the idea of an unconscious realm. He is also highly critical of Eduard von Hartmann's thesis that 'unconscious phenomena form the foundation of the self and that conscious phenomena are merely the effects of their unconscious counterparts'. If that were the case, we would be 'only instruments of the unconscious' (Durkheim 2004: 87, 88). This view reveals, according to Durkheim, 'the pessimistic tendencies of Hartmann's system. To be happy, we must let ourselves be deceived. If we refuse and stay true to the nature of things, we must resign ourselves to unhappiness' (ibid.: 88).

The 'unconscious' thesis has, according to Durkheim, no solid basis. It confuses unconscious phenomena with habits or tics ('the miller no longer hears the noise of his mill'), and sometimes with passions ('a wounded solider, in the midst of combat, feels his wound only after the battle has ended'). What is described as 'unconscious' is often something we cannot remember, such as a solution or a citation: 'We stop thinking of it consciously, but after a while the citation simply comes to mind' (Durkheim 2004: 87). His final argument is that the 'unconscious' thesis is, quite simply, contradictory: how could we become aware of a psychical phenomenon that is unconscious? Dreams themselves are not expressions of the unconscious, as the 'psychic relaxation of sleep' involves only 'a resting of the will' (ibid.: 130).

Durkheim does, however, have to admit that actions can escape our consciousness, as we can see from hallucinations, when there is perception but no object, and obviously from madness. Consciousness also often appears to have its limitations: we can be conscious of our actions without understanding anything of their causes. And there is no reason for many of our actions, which is a form of freedom: this is known as indifference.

Egoism/Altruism: Society

Psychology, consciousness, reason. The *focus* of such a philosophy is the *self* [*le moi*], and Durkheim dwells on it at length. He begins by identifying the three natural attributes of the self as unity, identity and causality (we provoke actions). He then goes on to describe the self's various inclinations: egoistic inclinations (which have the self as their object), altruistic (other selves) and higher ('certain *ideas* . . . like the *good* or the *beautiful*' (Durkheim 2004: 63, emphasis added). The egoistic inclinations, he goes on, include the instinct for self-preservation, the love of life and the search for well-being (intellectual or physical) as well as 'ambition in all its forms – for love, for grandeur, for wealth, etc.' (ibid.: 64). Altruistic inclinations may be domestic (concerning the family), social (society) or universal (the love of humanity). The perspective introduced by Durkheim is historical: 'It's from love of the family that we learn to love society, and from love of society that we learn to love humanity' (ibid.: 65).

Durkheim therefore looks like an evolutionist, but at the same time he rejects Darwin's evolutionist theory, at least where the development of reason is concerned. He also attacks Spencer, 'the greatest philosophical champion of this doctrine' (2004: 110). At the age of 62, Spencer made a triumphal tour of the United States, where his books *Social Studies* and *The Data of Ethics* were celebrated because they supplied solid justifications for the policy of laisser-faire. His great idea was that of evolution, and he sees it everywhere: the law of organic progress is the law behind all progress. According to Spencer, human evolution goes through a confused sequence of states of consciousness as the nervous system gradually becomes more and more complex and centralized. Durkheim challenges this thesis on the grounds that it cannot be empirically verified, and contends: 'However uncivilized the peoples, none lacks rational principles or possessed them to a lesser degree [than us].' He adds: 'The mind could never have been a *tabula rasa*' (ibid.: 113). His virulent critique of ethnocentrism becomes, not a cultural relativism, but a rational universalism: 'Since reason can't be derived from experience, rational ideas and principles must be innate within us' (ibid.: 114).

On Methodology

Having discussed psychology, Durkheim turns to logic. Logic is a central part of any philosophical training: students have to be taught to master arguments (induction/deduction), to use syllogisms, to be able to root out errors (sophisms) and to arrive at the truth. According to Durkheim, science is a quest for truth and certainty. He therefore pays particular attention to what he calls 'methodologies', meaning both method in general and the methodologies specific to disciplines such as mathematics, physics, the natural sciences, the moral sciences and history.

For Durkheim (2004: 205), a method is a set of procedures that the human mind follows in order to arrive at truth, but those procedures are not necessarily the same for each type of science: 'each type of science has its own method'. He does, however, qualify the importance of method: 'It is clearly an exaggeration to say that methodology is responsible for discoveries. Inventions are a product of genius'. Yet he immediately adds: 'But this does not make methodology any less indispensable to science. Method is to the mind what an instrument is to the hand. To proceed methodically is to act rationally' (ibid.: 206).

His referents are obvious: Claude Bernard, Wundt and Spencer. Durkheim demonstrates his concern for scientificity, the recourse to methods of experimentation and the objective study of the world through the discovery of laws, and he extends his field of interest to the 'new' psychology, anthropology and the moral sciences.[14]

'Man Is a Sociable Animal'

Towards the end of the nineteenth century, the philosophy syllabus began to give greater importance, in relative terms, to ethics as new issues pertaining to civic and social ethics began to emerge. That did not, however, mean that sociology as such was becoming an integral part of the syllabus: at best, it was smuggled in via the analysis of moral issues. Durkheim defines ethics as the science that studies what human beings should do in the various circumstances in which they find themselves, and he makes a distinction between 'general' ethics (which does not concern itself with particular cases) and 'practical' ethics (which seeks to understand how a general ethical law should be applied in particular circumstances).

Durkheim begins with a consideration of theoretical ethics and of the universal and obligatory nature of the moral law, noting that there is 'a significant difference between the law of the savage and that of civilized man' (Durkheim 2004: 232). If, for example, moral law is not the same everywhere, can we conclude that it is not universal? And what is the basis for the obligation to respect the moral law? The explanation cannot, he argues, lie in self-interest or the ethics of natural sentiment (sympathy). Durkheim compares the view of many philosophers – Epicurus, Mill, Spencer, Rousseau, Adam Smith and especially Kant – and finally concludes that the basis of moral law is to be found in the idea of 'finality': 'Act in such a way that you always treat human beings – yourself and others – as an end and not as a means' (Durkheim 2004: 241).

There is also individual ethics (the individual's duty towards himself: his body, his intelligence, his sensibility and his activity), domestic ethics (the duties of the individual in his relations with certain of his fellows, namely those to whom he is bound by a community of origin), civic ethics (the individual's duty towards those of his fellows with whom he shares a territory and certain tastes and interests) and, finally, social ethics (the individual's duties towards other human beings). Durkheim condemns as immoral such behaviours as suicide and self-mutilation; he also introduces and defends values such as the family, marriage and work (which he contrasts with idleness). Durkheim regards society as a large organism (with a central brain issuing commands) and families as its subordinates. The family is, in his view, 'the primary and most natural grouping of individuals' (Durkheim 2004: 255). In social terms, the most important duties are those of justice and charity: these are 'the duties of social life' (ibid.: 265–71).

Given that social ethics presupposes the existence of societies of people who are united by special bonds, Durkheim raises the question of the foundations of society. How could society be 'unnatural', as certain philosophers (Hobbes, Bossuet, Rousseau) think? According to Durkheim, who bases his argument on Frédéric Bastiat (1802–50), economist, politician and author of *L'Harmonie économique*, society is something natural. Following Plato, he argues that man is a sociable animal, adding that, in modern times, sociability finds its expression in the division of labour:

> People join together naturally because no one can be self-sufficient and carry out by himself all the tasks that Europeans consider essential to life. The solution to this problem is the division of labour. Each individual, charged with a specific task, performs it better and more quickly and – by exchanging the fruits of his labour – acquires the goods essential to life . . . This is the advantage offered by the division of labour, and this division is the foundation of society. (2004: 259)

Durkheim then analyses how societies are organized and, more specifically, how governments are constituted. Amongst other questions, he raises that of the functions of government. Rejecting both socialist theory (which denies the rights of individuals and makes citizens the property of the state) and liberal or individualist theory (which sees society as an abstraction: the individual is the only reality), he demonstrates that a government has two functions: it must protect citizens from one another and direct society towards its proper end. There are, however, limits to its actions, which must cease when 'they threaten to undermine the personality of its citizens' (2004: 261).

What duty does the citizen owe to the state? Citizens have four duties, according to Durkheim: obedience to the law, taxes, military service and voting (which is both a right and a duty). 'Of all taxes, the most noble and obligatory is that of blood.' Durkheim wonders if 'someday all nationalities will merge into a universal republic, and concludes: 'It's possible, but for the moment . . . people are divided into rival, frequently conflicting societies.' He also suggests that exemptions from the blood tax might be granted 'to those who devote their lives to the high culture of the mind' (2004: 261–2). He is thinking of those who think they can help to advance the sciences, literature and the arts.

And God . . .

Having discussed ethics, Durkheim moves on, finally, to metaphysics and devotes 12 lectures to that subject. The gradual secularization of the teaching of philosophy meant that religion was now taking up less room on the syllabus. Durkheim deals in turn with various great problems: the immortality of the soul and its relationship with the body, proofs of the existence of God, pantheism, creation and evolution. The strategy he adopts consists in describing existing theses or theories and comparing them, without deciding in favour of one or the other. Creation or evolution? Spiritualism or materialism? Durkheim certainly recognizes that psychological life is dependent on physiology:

> The principle they have in common is the body. . . . This influence is certain and considerable. It's clear, for example, that an illness weakens us psychologically as well as physiologically. It's also clear that thought is more active in the young than in the old. Women live more in the realm of sensibility and less in that of reason; the passions of southerners are more vivid and their will less active than those of others. (2004: 281–2)

He cannot, however, close the debate: 'In our view, the question of the relationship between the soul and the body seems insoluble' (ibid.: 287).

And what about God? Several of the lectures are devoted to describing and criticizing the proofs of the existence of God, both metaphysical and ethical. Durkheim cites both Aquinas and Kant. He discusses the various attributes of God: perfection, omniscience, immortality, and so on. But while we can accept that God created the world, we need not, according to Durkheim, 'try to understand the meaning of this phrase, for it defies both imagination and reason' (Durkheim 2004: 310).

At the very end of his lecture course, Durkheim goes back to the questions of pleasure and pain. The last lecture concludes the discussion of the relationship between God and the world with a consideration of 'providence, evil, optimism and pessimism'. He once more cites Schopenhauer and Hartmann, for whom pain is the 'law of life' (Durkheim 2004: 313). The message he transmits to his students is one of optimism: 'The victory of pleasure over pain isn't impossible, and we mustn't lose hope if there are times when we're not happy. Happiness is an art, and any art can be learned' (ibid.: 314).

The Noble Sadness of Research

Durkheim has no qualms about talking of 'genius' in his lectures; of all the philosophers, Leibniz is, in his view, 'the greatest genius' (Durkheim 2004: 85). At the end of the academic year (August 1883), the young teacher accepted the responsibility of giving a speech on the school's prize-giving day. What he called his 'final lesson' (1975[1883]) was devoted to the role of great men in history. Unlike Renan, who saw great men as humanity's proper end, Durkheim defended the right to culture: 'All individuals, however humble, have a right to aspire to the higher life of the mind' (Fabiani 1998: 25). Nor did he share Renan's suspicion of the democratic ideal that sees the nation as the political expression of the masses, who are ignorant, immoral and undisciplined: 'What makes a nation is not one or two great men born by chance here and there, who can suddenly fail to appear: it is the compact mass of citizens. It is therefore only they who should concern us: it is only their interests that we should consult'. He then adds: 'Still, if only we could produce at the same time men of genius and enlightened masses' (1975[1883]: 413).

To sacrifice genius to the masses would lead to some 'blind love of a sterile equality'. But nor can the masses be sacrificed to genius. The masses have to be raised from their 'self-satisfied mediocrity'. For this, the role of the scholar or the man of letters is to educate the masses, and to remind them that 'humanity was not made to taste easy and vulgar pleasures for ever. It is therefore necessary that an elite be formed to make humanity scorn this inferior life, to tear it from this mortal repose, to urge it to move forward'. Great men such as Bossuet or Pasteur cannot live in 'proud solitude' and must themselves 'return to the masses'. The 'free republic' must raise the average intelligence level (which is already, according to Durkheim, higher in France than elsewhere in Europe). The ultimate lesson Durkheim is trying to teach his pupils is twofold, and apparently contradictory: they must 'respect natural superiority' without losing their independence: 'That is what the future citizens of our democracy must be' (1975[1883]: 413–14).

It seemed to the young teacher that the search for truth was a real 'vocation': 'For myself, I consider truth to have a single reason for and a single mode of existing: that is to be known' (1975[1883]: 417). It is true that the search for the truth is difficult, and may be a source of disappointment and discouragement. There is a danger that the seeker after truth will experience moments of despondency and disgust, and may lose heart. But what does that matter? Sad as it may be, research does bring new joys: 'Everyone has the right to aspire to this noble sadness, which, moreover, is not without charm; for once having tasted it, one no longer desires the other pleasures, which thenceforth are without savour or attraction' (ibid.: 412).[15] 'Noble sadness' is a good description of his relationship with research, and with life in general.

Wishing to be closer to his family, Durkheim requested a transfer, and found himself in February 1884 teaching at the lycée in Saint-Quentin.[16] The young philosopher still had 'a very serious and somewhat cold' appearance; he was 'very serious-minded and very methodical'. His authority, observed André Lalande, was 'natural', and some even changed lycées in order to follow their teacher from Sens to Saint-Quentin. His talent and zeal were quickly noticed (Lalande 1960: 25). He was a 'conscientious, hard working, educated and truly impressive' teacher, who spoke 'loudly and clearly, but not at great length'. His teaching was 'clear and scientific in nature', and, as the rector stressed, 'very detailed, very precise, very clear, but in the scientific rather than the popular sense'. Durkheim displayed such intellectual rigour that he seemed more capable of assimilating than of inventing; all that he needed to be 'extremely successful' was, perhaps, 'a higher degree of finesse, suppleness and tact'. As a teacher, he did not always succeed in matching his teaching to his pupils' abilities: 'There is a danger that his too lofty and sometimes abstract views might sow confusion or doubts in their minds.' His teaching appears to be 'a little abstract and perhaps too advanced for his pupils'.[17]

The young philosopher, who was already 'interested in ethical and economic problems', was insightful and profound; he was a 'man of great moral fibre and with a great capacity for work'.[18] He was, concluded Rector Rollen, a 'teacher with a future', and 'one of our most conscientious young philosophy teachers', added Inspector Jean Lechalier, who lent his support to Durkheim's application for a year's leave: 'He needs the resources of Paris to write his thesis . . . I do not think that the university can refuse him this modest request.'[19]

The *Revue philosophique*: Towards Sociology

Durkheim had been working on his doctoral thesis since 1883. While trying to define its object more clearly (relations between the individual and society rather than the initial topic of relations between individualism and socialism), he drafted a first outline of what was to become *The Division of Labour in Society*. Having learned of Durkheim's plans from Émile Boutroux, Théodule Ribot, creator and editor of the *Revue philosophique*, sounded him out – presumably with a view to recruiting him as a contributor – and sent him some books on social science and sociology to review. While he was in Paris, Durkheim probably attended Ribot's lectures on experimental psychology at the Sorbonne.

A graduate of the École normale supérieure and an *agrégé de philosophie* (1865), Ribot (1839–1916) can be seen as the founder of a 'French science of the soul' that began with Taine and culminated with Pierre Janet. An attentive reader of Darwin, Spencer and especially Galton, he attended Charcot's lectures and had an interest in neurophysiology and pathological psychology. Appointed *chargé de cours* in experimental psychology at the Sorbonne in 1865, he submitted his doctoral thesis in 1872 on psychological heredity, in which the influence of Lamarck could still be felt. Ribot was to introduce contemporary English psychology into France. From 1879 onwards, he introduced the French to the work of the German psychophysiologists Fechner and Wundt (Ribot 1879), and in 1887 he translated Spencer's *Principles of Psychology* in collaboration with Alfred Espinas. He was one of the first in France to adopt the idea of the unconscious, and attempted to demonstrate that consciousness is an epiphenomenon, while at the same time criticizing 'Freudian dogmatism'. In 1888, he published *Les Maladies de la personnalité*, in which he analysed somnambulism, sleep and dreams, split personalities and hallucinations (see James 1995: 219). He put the emphasis on the complex nature of the personality (which is made up of an enormous mass of conscious and subconscious states) and saw it as a product of the nervous system. In his view, 'advances in this psychology were due not to philosophers and not to professional psychologists, but to physiologists and scholars of all kinds' (Durkheim 1975[1887d]; 34).

Ribot advocated a philosophy that broke with the spiritualist tradition, which he condemned harshly – 'a set of opinions based upon common sense and adapted to the religious beliefs of the majority' (Ribot 2000[1877]: 107–23)[20] – and the journal he founded in 1876 was designed to be eclectic (Mauss 1969[1939]). As he himself put it: 'Its characteristic feature will be its openness: no sectarianism' (cited in Fabiani 1998: 34; cf. Thirard 1976). It served, as Xavier Léon put it, an 'admirable purpose' in that it 'obliged the philosophers to keep up with the work of the scientists' and 'allowed the scientists to read the meditations of the philosophers', or, in other words, 'introduced them to one another' (Léon 1893: 2). Ribot was the journal's editorial director until his death in 1916, and his ambition was to paint 'a full and accurate picture of the contemporary trends in philosophy', not only in France but also in other countries: 'A strong desire for information replaced the indifference of the previous generation' (Ribot 2000[1877]: 122).

Between 1885 and 1895, most contributors to the journal were school teachers. The *Revue philosphique* was a specialist journal and helped to 'professionalize' philosophy. It was an immediate success with secondary school teachers: every lycée in France subscribed to it. It had no competitors for almost 40 years, and enjoyed a sort of monopoly.[21]

The journal was innovatory in that it gave a lot of space to the new psychology. Ribot's project was to paint 'a full and accurate picture of contemporary trends in philosophy', and, at the same time, to allow its contributors to describe new development in philosophy. The first issue included a note by Taine on 'the acquisition of language in children and the animal species', and texts by Paul Janet ('Final Causes') and Herbert Spencer ('Outline of a comparative human psychology'). A lot of room – almost one third of the journal – was given over to reviews.

Although it did not ignore questions relating to metaphysics and ethics in the mid-1880s, the monthly *Revue philosophique* did adopt an international perspective (focused mainly on Britain, Germany and Italy), and covered a wide variety of themes: the history of religion (Maurice Vernes), the doctrine of evolution, theories of education, and zoological philosophy (an offshoot of the naturalist philosopher Edmond Perrier). It also attached great importance to work on psychology. Ribot himself published a series of articles on the personality ('The intellectual foundations of the personality' and 'The affective foundations of the personality'), taking an interest in both normal development and in exceptions and morbid cases, such as changes affecting the state of the genital organs (castration, hermaphroditism, sex-changes) and cases of 'contrary sexuality' (an instinctual and violent attraction towards persons of the same sex, together with a pronounced revulsion from the opposite sex).

According to a formula that Célestin Bouglé liked to cite (Bouglé 1935: 13), Ribot complained that all too often, we restrict ourselves to the study of 'adult, white, civilized men'. There were, he pointed out, other types of mentality, and they varied in accordance with their social environments. Ribot was, in other words, reaching out to the sociologists.[22] Early contributors to his journal included Gustave Le Bon[23] and Gabriel Tarde.[24]

In 1877, Gustave Le Bon published his 'Notes on the study of character' and the following year 'Experimental research on variation in the volume of the cranium and applications of the graphic method to the solution of some anthropological problems'. In 1881, he raised the 'question of criminals' from an anthropological point of view. Even though it was restricted to a few articles, Le Bon's involvement with the *Revue philosophique* did lay the foundations for lasting and, it would seem, regular relations with Ribot.[25]

Gabriel Tarde's first articles dealt with ethics: 'The future of ethics' and 'The crisis in ethics'. He then developed an interest in criminology, and especially in Lombroso's *L'Uomo delinquente*, Ferri's *Sociologia criminale* and Garfalo's *La Criminologia*. Italian interest on criminology was so great that there was talk of an Italian school of anthropology. It had great influence in France, where it gave rise to a lively polemic. Was the criminal the last – and now rare – example of the primitive savage? Could criminality be reduced to madness, and could it be explained in terms of anomalies of the brain? Was there such a thing as a born criminal?

Gabriel Tarde opened the polemic with his Italian colleagues Lombroso and Ferri, first in the pages on *La Revue philosophique* and then in his *La Criminalité comparée* (1886). He also contributed to the new journal, *Archives d'anthropologie criminelle,* which had been founded in Lyon in 1885 by Alexandre Lacassagne, a doctor and anthropologist. Tarde become its co-editor from 1894 onwards. He took a rather conservative line on political questions: 'Be revolutionary in the social sciences, but conservative in politics or criminal justice', he writes in *La Philosophie pénale*. In the last chapter of that book, which is devoted to the death penalty, he takes a more moderate view, concluding that we must 'make less use of the death penalty, but not abolish it'.

Tarde also had an interest in socialism: was it, he asked, 'an accidental and probably temporary fever affecting our civilization' or was it 'an irresistible and necessary trend, and a sign of the deluge to come'? He reviewed Paul Janet's book *Les Origines du socialisme contemporain* in the *Revue philosphique*, but was, unlike Janet, inclined to believe that the (French) Revolution had been an accident but that socialism, or at least state socialism, was 'an almost unavoidable necessity'. It was, so to speak, a necessary evil – he spoke of socialism as though it were a disease – but it was, fortunately, a local phenomenon, and he attempted to bring out its paradoxes and contradictions. His main objection to socialism was that 'by greatly demotivating individual self-interest, collectivism dampens the enthusiasm for work'. He concluded that if society was ever to be organized on a socialist basis, 'it would be by force and not choice, by an approved usurpation of power on the part of the state and not thanks to the free attraction of cooperatives or similar associations, and still less thanks to the logical value of the writings of our socialists' (Tarde 1884: 192).[26]

Another of Tarde's articles is entitled simply 'What is Society?' Here, he refuses to define society solely in terms of reciprocity ('mutual assistance'), rights, customs and the social bond ('sharing the same faith, having the same patriotic goal'). Each of those approaches is incomplete: one is economic, another is juridical, while the third is political and religious. He also refuses to identify society with the nation: 'In our day, hundreds of millions of men are being both *denationalized* and increasingly *socialized*' (Tarde 1884: 493).[27]

Any society has, according to Tarde, its 'inexhaustible reserves of routines, its sheep-like and imitative behaviours, and successive generations constantly add to them'. All this belongs to the realm of suggestion and it is, in his view, related to a 'more mysterious phenomenon' that arouses the curiosity of those he calls 'philosophical alienists', namely somnambulism: 'Both the somnambulist and social man are labouring under a delusion: all their ideas have been suggested to them, but they think they are spontaneous' (Tarde 1884: 501). It is not only authority figures that suggest modes of behaviour (one example being a father's authority over his children). *Prestige* also has its effects. There is an element of magnetism in all societies, and they all have their magnetizers. Social life itself looks like a 'cascade of successive and related magnetizations'. Gabriel Tarde defines society in these terms: 'Society is imitation, and imitation is a form of somnambulism' (1894: 506–9). Imitation is to be understood as meaning 'a phenomenon that spreads belief and desire'. Credulity and obedience are a form of imitation, and only the audacity of invention or discovery can escape it. Tarde is convinced that, as he liked to say again and again, imitation is 'the key that opens all doors'.

Socialism, the definition of the social, and criminality were the themes that Gabriel Tarde developed in the mid-1880s. Durkheim dealt with the same themes. Both men attach the same importance to belief. There are similarities between Tarde's sociology and the sociology Durkheim was trying to propound, but they paved the way to differences and then mutual hostility as Tarde began to attack Durkheim. This was the starting point of what Bouglé called the 'famous duel' between the two thinkers whose 'personalities dominated sociology at this time' (Bouglé 1935: 7).

'Something Is Not Right'

The first three reviews that Durkheim published in the *Revue philosophique* all appeared in 1885. They dealt with books by Schäffle, Fouillée and Gumplowicz and reveal his interest in books that combine sociological theory with discussions of political issues. Politics was central to the questions the young philosopher was asking. Like Renan before him, he was asking 'What is a nation?' The increasing number of conflicts, the lack of national unity, the opposition between right and left and the controversies over education were all very disturbing. The elections of October 1885 were a full-scale battle between a resurgent right and a left that proclaimed its loyalty to the institutions of the Republic, which was itself still a recent and fragile idea.

Durkheim had not forgotten the humiliating defeat that had cost France part of its territory and that had, as Georges Davy was to put it, unsettled both minds and institutions. Durkheim was determined to 'play a part in reconstructing a France that been badly wounded by [this] defeat' and to inspire the 'reconstructions that were needed' (Davy 1919b: 183). 'The urgent need for a science of societies' had, in his view, made itself felt in the aftermath of the war of 1870:

> The shock produced by events was the stimulant that reanimated men's minds . . . The organization, or rather the façade [of the imperial system] had just collapsed; it was a matter of remaking another, or rather of making one which could survive other than by administrative artifice – that is, one which was truly grounded in the nature of things. (Durkheim 1973[1900]): 12)

'Something is not right', thought Durkheim, who, having heard what was going on the streets, shared his fellow citizens' fears and vague worries: anarchy, disorganized movements and divided opinions seemed to pose a real threat to national unity. Then there were the displays of *revanchard* patriotism, including Paul Déroulède's decision to found the Ligue des patriotes in 1882 and the premonitory signs of anti-Semitism with the publication of the weekly *L'Antisémite* in 1883. Three years later, Edouard Drumond published *La France juive*.

The rise of individualism had the effect of unleashing unrestrained egoisms. In 1882, Renan warned that this 'inner laxity' posed a threat to France. In a lecture given at the Sorbonne that same year, he attempted to answer the question 'What is a nation?' His answer was 'a daily plebiscite' (Renan 1990[1882]: 19), but the rise of individualism and the centrifugal effect of egoism posed a greater threat than ever.

Everything led Durkheim, who was influenced by his reading of the German theorist Albert Schäffle, to fear the worst: 'If everyone pursued only his personal ends, then society would be done for; torn in all directions, it would soon break apart'. As Schäffle had revealed, 'Individualism reasserts its hold over us once again. Every individual sees of society only the corner in which he lives, and, among all these sparse little worlds there is no longer anything in common' (Durkheim 1978[1885]: 113).

The question of 'national unity' was central to Schäffle's thinking, and he identifies eight kinds of social bond or fabric (origins, territory, interests, opinions, religious beliefs, sociable instincts, historical traditions and language) and shows that the 'homogeneous mass' can be differentiated in many ways. The questions he raises were the same as those that preoccupied Durkheim: under what conditions could the 'vast masses' of 30 or 40 million men who make up modern peoples find equilibrium? How could the man in the street be made to understand the grandeur of the fatherland, or the beauty of sacrifice and disinterestedness? How could he become part of the 'national consciousness'?

Schäffle (1831–1903) began his career as a teacher of political economy before becoming the Austrian monarchy's minister for trade in the Hohenwart government. When the government fell in 1871, he became editor of the *Zeitschrift für die gesamte Staatwissenschaft* . In France, he was best known as the author of *La Quintessence du socialisme*, which had been translated by the anarchist theorist Benoît Malon. As the economist Charles Gide (1887: 85) noted, his work, and that of the German historical school in general, received a rather cold welcome. And yet, as Durkheim (1978[1885]: 110) said of the work of his German colleague:

> There are few readings more highly instructive for a Frenchman. It is by the practice of such patient and laborious studies that we shall fortify our spirit, now too slender, too thin, too fond of simplicity. It is by learning to face the infinite complexity of facts that we free ourselves of those too narrow frameworks in which we had to compartmentalize things. It is perhaps no exaggeration to say that the future work of French sociology depends on this.

The main feature of what was ironically described as a 'sentimentalist' historical school was its emphasis on the observation of the facts as they are (as opposed to overall views and general formulae). Durkheim found a kindred spirit in Schäffle, firstly because of his anti-individualism and awareness of the importance of the social (society as a reality *sui generis* or even a living person), and secondly because of his opposition to economic liberalism and his scepticism about the role of the state in economic and political regulation. Schäffle rejected both individualism and the egoism it unleashed, and despotic socialism. His solution was to revive the old guilds. These were, thought Durkheim, 'ineffective palliatives' (even though he was to adopt the idea himself): 'History teaches us that peoples in which opinion is divided become incapable of any collective effort'. He even criticizes Schäffle for his 'robust faith in reason and the future of humanity'. 'We begin to feel that everything is not so straightforward and that reason does not cure all ills. We have reasoned so much! Moreover, was it not from Germany that we got the idea that unhappiness always increases with consciousness?' (Durkheim 1978[1885]: 114).

Should society be subordinate to the individual, or should the individual be subordinate to society? This 'serious question' preoccupied the 'public consciousness'. Lively debates were going on in political circles and in philosophical journals, which were discussing democracy, guilds, welfare and insurance programmes, the importance of public education as a means of democratizing culture and former citizens, the role of the state and the various forms of socialism.

Philosophy or politics? Psychology or sociology? The young Durkheim initially thought of doing psychological research on quality and quantity.

He abandoned that project to devote himself to work that was, as his friend Xavier Léon put it, 'almost new' in France, because he 'hoped, after the Treaty of Frankfurt, to find an objective basis for the reorganization of national life in a science of societies'. It was that idea that 'guided his tireless activity' (Léon 1917: 750–1). Durkheim was still trying to find his way, and thought at this point of 'dividing his life in two, devoting part of it to purely scientific research, and part to politics'. He chose sociology because 'he wanted to satisfy his need for both knowledge and action' (Halbwachs 1918: 353).

Alfred Fouillée was an essential point of reference for Durkheim. His *La Science sociale contemporaine* had made him an advocate for social science: 'Our century's main task is to establish social science on a positive basis. Once the object of pure curiosity and almost a luxury reserved for a few thinkers, the study of society and its laws will eventually become a pure necessity for everyone in our societies' (Fouillée 1922[1880]: xiii). Having read Rousseau, Mill, Spencer, Schaeffle and Espinas with great attention, Fouillée elaborated on a number of ideas that Durkheim shared concerning, for example, democracy and the role of universal suffrage, seen as 'the things that did most to help the nation become self-aware', and concerning the importance of education (which he called 'intellectual capital') as a way of 'softening antagonisms'. Fouillée was, in Durkheim's opinion, a 'refined dialectician' who distrusted easy answers and tried to combine contradictory doctrines – determinism and freedom, idealism and realism – into 'learned syntheses'. 'He is now trying to reconcile individualism and socialism' (Durkheim 1970[1884]: 177).

In his writings, Fouillée uses notions and elaborates ideas that were to become central to Durkheim's theory: the conception of society as an organism, the idea of the 'mutual dependency of all parts of the social body' and the notions of consensus and the social bond, representation, social or collective consciousness, and mechanical solidarity (which he contrasts with voluntary solidarity). The final chapter of *La Science sociale contemporaine* is devoted to penal justice. Fouillée believed 'evolution to be better than revolutions' and, when it came to social change, recommended prudence (the prudence of a doctor): 'We cannot arbitrarily change everything overnight.' And he appealed to the ideas of fraternity and social justice as forces that could provide a remedy for 'the dispersal of living forces', which might lead to 'real industrial anarchy'.

Given that he recognized the organic character of society, Fouillée should, in all logic, have been a defender of socialism, thought Durkheim. Socialism? 'One of those words that is misused today', replied Fouillée in his defence of liberalism. Socialism was, in his view, 'the logical outcome of applying biology to politics'. According to Durkheim, Fouillée had made the mistake of misreading Schäffle and of accepting that socialism was, by definition, 'despotic, and an enemy of freedom and individual initiative. In a word he confused socialism with administrative hypercentralization (Durkheim 1970[1884] 177). Durkheim is very clear about his differences with Fouillée. According to Fouillée, a spontaneous agreement between individual wills will result in social harmony. But this idea of a 'gentle, enlightened democracy' is, replies Durkheim, no more than a 'seductive dream': 'A society that is not more solidly cemented together would be in danger of being blown away by the first storm' (1970[1884]: 180–3).

Both Fouillée and Durkheim define society in terms of association. According to Fouillée, a society is a voluntary association of men – a contract – and it is self-conscious. 'Society creates itself by conceiving itself and willing itself into existence' (Fouillée 1922[1880]: viii). He criticizes Durkheim, whom he describes as a 'realist', for seeing society as a 'consciousness that speaks in the first person'. The polemic between the two went on until 1910: there was, according to Fouillée, a danger that Durkheim's sociology would lead us to 'a sort of social authoritarianism and a new religion of humanity' (ibid.: ix).[28]

Durkheim's encounters with Fouillée, Schäffle and Gumplowicz allowed him to elaborate what might be called his 'initial problematic': what gives the nation its unity? What role does authoritarianism play in maintaining national unity? If social harmony cannot, as Fouillée believes, result from a 'spontaneous agreement of wills' alone, what can provide the basis for a social consensus? The whole of social life can, if we follow the arguments of Ludwig Gumplowicz (1838–1909), look like a savage struggle for dominance. Even national unity appears to be nothing more than the result of antagonisms between one group and its neighbours. And what of the state? Is it anything more than a 'set of institutions designed to give a minority power over a majority'. If we are to preserve a national unity that is solid and unshakeable, do we need 'an enormous degree of centralization and a government that is oppressive at home and bellicose abroad'? (Durkheim 1970[1884]: 362).

Antagonism or cohesion? 'Optimism is becoming rare', noted Durkheim. Fortunately, there was what the German theorist Schäffle called the 'sense of solidarity'. But can that feeling 'extend to the whole of society?' asks Durkheim. Some see socialism as an alternative, but is it not the enemy of freedom (individual freedom and the freedom of the market)? Can we avoid the 'abyss' of individualism without falling into despotic socialism, or the socialism of Karl Marx? Individualism or socialism: that is the dilemma. Both Fouillée in France and Schäffle in Germany were trying, in their different ways, to reconcile individualism and socialism, and proposed various solutions: a revival of the guilds or a return to authority. Durkheim was perplexed: his faith in reason had been shaken.

The Discovery of Sociology

As Marcel Mauss notes (1962[1928]: 27), Durkheim's analysis gradually convinced him that the answer to these problems would be provided by sociology. Yet, as Mauss himself said, the 'excesses of the last Comtistes' had made sociology look 'ridiculous' in France: it was not exactly fashionable (Durkheim 2002[1897]: xxxiii) and the word itself was 'little known and almost discredited'. Sociology was criticized as 'a very vague and ill-defined science' (1970[1886]: 191). Almost 10 years later, he was to remember the period when he resolved to devote himself to the study of social phenomena:

> The number of people who were interested in these questions was so small that, despite the kind reception given to our first attempts, I could not find the advice and help that I needed after so many hesitant attempts, and to make my research easier. In academic circles, especially, sociology was greatly discredited: not only was the word itself strange to the purists; the thing itself inspired doubts and revulsion in many people. (Durkheim 1975[1895b]: 73)

Was sociology a vague and ill-defined science? Durkheim had two criticisms to make of the sociology of the day. On the one hand, its methodology and findings were not very rigorous, the data was poor and the conclusions were too general. On the other, it was under the illusion that 'practical reforms could be deduced from theory', and the reforms it did propose were 'ambitious and artificial'. It might, in other words, have been designed to arouse the suspicions of both scientists who were convinced of the need for precision and men of action who knew how difficult it would be to reconstruct social reality.

Who was Durkheim thinking of? Was it the followers of Le Play? Frédéric Le Play (1806–82) had just died. An engineer by training, he had turned to the social sciences in an attempt to rouse France from its state of decadence and put it on the road to prosperity. In 1885, he established the first society for social economics in order to promote both the methodical observation of families (his 'great work *Ouvriers européens* [*European workers*] appeared in 1855') and a whole series of reforms. He had also tried to implement a scientific politics. The journal founded by Le Play's close collaborators in 1881 was entitled *La Réforme sociale*. The desire for change was not, however, the expression of any progressive outlook. Le Play was regarded as both a conservative and a supporter of the clergy, and had no qualms about defending the teaching of religion in schools. His vision of society was essentially rural. He was said to be a monarchist who was opposed to universal suffrage. His main works had been published by Mame, which was a Catholic publishing house.

The members of the Le Play school split shortly after his death: the *Réforme sociale* group wanted to go on applying their master's ideas and insights to social problems, while others wanted to continue his scientific work. The latter group, which was led by Edmond Demolins and Abbé Henri de Tourville, broke away to found a new journal called *La Science sociale* in 1886. Tourville developed a new classification or 'nomenclature of social facts' as a guide to fieldwork and the production of future monographs. So much importance was attached to geographical factors that they were seen as the ultimate source of social organizations. It was also believed that a society could be changed if children were so socialized as to accept new values. Convinced that this was the case, Demolins abandoned his research activity to found a model private school known as the École des Roches. Le Play's supporters were not university lecturers, but they were actively involved in education, either at the École libre des sciences politiques or at the Collège libre des sciences sociales. In the mid-1890s, their activities focused on the Société de science sociale and the Musée social (Kalaora and Savoye 1989).

The publication of the work of Tarde and Le Bon had certainly given sociology an 'impetus', but it was far from having the intellectual or institutional status of disciplines such as political economy or even anthropology. Anthropology, and especially racial anthropology, appeared to be more highly developed. The Société d'anthropologie de Paris had been founded in 1859, and a museum and anthropological laboratory had been established at the École pratique des hautes études in 1875. The *Revue d'anthropologie* began publication in 1872, and the École d'anthropologie de Paris was opened in 1875. Its stance was broadly determinist, racial and anti-egalitarian to the extent that it postulated that every physical race corresponded to a different degree of human evolution, mental development and therefore social organization.

The main figure behind this development was Paul Broca (1824–80), a doctor who taught at the Paris medical faculty, and a skilled organizer. Anthropology claimed to be a new and complete human science covering prehistory, linguistics, ethnography, demography and geography. In 1876, he declared that 'anthropology looks at all the facts that might shed some light on the present and past of the human race' (Broca 1876: 6). *L'Homme*, the new journal founded by Gabriel de Mortillet in 1884, adopted the same expansionist programme: the goal of the anthropological sciences was to arrive at a complete understanding of man' (Mortillet 1998[1884]: 51).

Sociology was no more than a subdiscipline that studied 'men's relations with other men and animals'. The first chair in sociology was established in 1885, and was held by Charles Letourneau, who had until then held the chair in the history of civilizations at the École d'anthropologie de Paris. Letourneau's background was in medicine, and he joined the Société d'anthropologie (becoming its secretary-general) because of his interest in the study of religion. His independent wealth allowed him to pursue his work and research without practising medicine, though he continued to take an interest in it, publishing such works as *La Biologie* and *La Physiologie des passions.* He then turned to sociology, and boldly called the publishing programme that he began in 1881 *La Sociologie d'après l'ethnographie* . It included some 12 books, with titles such as *L'Évolution de la morale* and *L'Évolution du mariage et de la propriété*. Dr Letourneau was a prolific and popular author and was, as Mauss put it, about to 'have his hour of scientific fame' (Mauss 1903: 151). His aim was to describe the main manifestations of human activity amongst the main human races, and his method was 'sociology, as defined by ethnography'. In his writings, Letourneau attempted to synthesize the ethnographic data, dealing in turn with animal societies, primitive human societies, ancient Egypt, ancient Greece and Rome, Japan, China and, finally, contemporary societies.

Durkheim was highly critical of Letourneau's methodology. Dissatisified with the French model for both sociology and anthropology, he looked to Germany (and was criticized for doing so), where he had discovered an 'interesting trend' in sociological investigation that was, unfortunately, not well known on the French side of the Rhine. Sociology, which originated in France, increasingly became a 'German science'. He found reading these 'patient and laborious studies' to be 'highly instructive' (Durkheim 1978[1885]: 110).

Durkheim became convinced that sociology, a discipline that was 'born yesterday' and was having difficulty in establishing itself (1970[1886]: 200), was neither a subcategory within psychology nor dependent upon biology: it was an independent science *sui generis* and it had its own object, namely society (1975[1885]: 346). 'Sociology has now left the heroic age. Its right to exist is no longer contested' (1978[1885: 111). The example it now had to follow had been set by Claude Bernard, who had freed physiology from the yoke of physics, chemistry and metaphysics; it must avoid broad generalizations, proceed with caution, base its findings on observation and develop the appropriate methodology. Bernard was also a political point of reference, and some spoke of 'experimental politics' or 'scientific politics'.[29] The goal Durkheim set himself was as follows: 'Let [sociology] be founded and organized and let it outline its program and specify its method' (1978[1885]: 111).

A Research Programme

Durkheim wrote two more reviews for the *Revue philosophique*, which appeared in 1886: one dealt with Guillaume de Greef's *Introduction à la sociologie* and the other with 'a seemingly disparate' series of works by authors as diverse as Alfred Espinas, Gustave Le Bon, Charles Perrier, Albert Régnard and Herbert Spencer. His tone was now more assertive: 'Sociology exists; it is alive and making progress. It has both an object and a methodology' (1970[1886]: 214). His objective was simply to grasp and map out the current state of the main sociological sciences. Although Auguste Comte had done social science 'a great service' by giving it a name and integrating it into the system of the positive sciences, 'brilliant improvisation' could not do everything. It was, Durkheim believed, time to go further and to 'describe the way sociology tends to become both divided and organized'.[30]

In this general survey, Durkheim is already demonstrating his 'social realism' (social institutions such as the law and ethics are things, or even 'living things') and developing a truly sociological problematic. He contrasts it with the utilitarian problematic (which speaks in terms of self-interest) and the psychological approach: 'The sociologist must therefore regard economic facts, the state, ethics, law and religion as so many functions of the social organism' (1970[1886]: 213).

Durkheim's reading of Spencer's *Ecclesiastical Functions* brought him face to face with the 'unknowable' force of religion, made him aware of the 'prodigious complexity of religious phenomena' and led him to take an interest in 'savage peoples'. 'We have,' he admitted, 'some scruples about raising a question we do not feel competent to deal with' (1970[1886]: 190). His review begins by summarizing Spencer's thesis, namely that religion has gradually evolved through various stages as far as monotheism and, following industrialization, the gradual secularization of society. He admires the prodigious erudition and 'very great ingenuity' of the 'eminent' English philosopher, but has no hesitations about criticizing the oversimplification of his thesis (spirit cults as the first form of all religion), and rejects the idea that the end of religious feeling is imminent. He assigns sociology, which must remain distinct from the history of religions, a specific task: analysing the 'social role' of religion. Its role is, in his view, to 'guarantee the equilibrium of society, and to adapt it to the ambient conditions'. Like the law and ethics, it must, that is, have a 'regulatory influence' and act as a social control.

A society is not, in Durkheim's view, a collection or juxtaposition of individuals and, even if individuals and groups do come together, they do not do so for reasons of self-interest or to satisfy primal needs such as the need for an abundance of food. Social life is something more complex: there is, as Espinas had demonstrated with respect to animal societies, 'a need for sociability and for social instincts that are absolutely disinterested' (1970[1886]: 201), and there are also phenomena such as sympathy. Societies, in other words, function on the basis of *solidarity*: solidarity is 'the precondition for social life'. In its absence, societies disperse and are scattered to the four winds.

Solidarity is certainly essential, but so too, Durkheim adds, is *social discipline*. Life in society is based upon commandments and sanctions, and on habits, customs and beliefs. Progress can do nothing to alter that: neither the 'growing omnipotence of free examination' nor the apparent supremacy of rationality has led to the disappearance of customs and prejudices. 'So long as there are men who live together, they will share some faith' (1970[1886]: 197).

In conclusion, Durkheim expressed the hope (i) that the social role of religion would be studied, (ii) that a scientific theory of the state would be elaborated and (iii) that economists would take into account the social aspect of economic questions. He also proposed the idea of a general sociology that would study 'the general properties of social life', and identified a few objects of study: the formation of the collective consciousness, the principle of the division of labour, the role and limits of natural selection and competition, and the law of heredity or of continuity within social evolution.

Durkheim was therefore raising a whole series of problems that would be central to his doctoral thesis: the analogy between the individual organism and society, unity/multiplicity, the differentiation of individuals and social change, the nature of the collective consciousness, and the role of ethics. The questions are still imprecise, the notions vague, and the problems not clearly formulated, but we have here the outline of a new problematic of society and cohesion.

This was a real research programme which, according to Durkheim, required patient investigation, and the analysis of many 'detailed observations'. No more 'confused syntheses' *à la* Auguste Comte! Although some remarkable studies had been carried out (Durkheim cites Gabriel Tarde's work on criminology) and although it was possible to find 'well-prepared raw materials', a lot remained to be done. And it was obvious that one man was not up to the task; if the sciences were to 'make progress', there was, Durkheim admitted (1970[1886]: 214), a need for 'collective work and a collective effort'.

Raising the 'social question', talk of solidarity and the dismissal of both the old liberalism and collectivism – that was politics. Sociology was intimately bound up with both the economic and the socialist movement. Durkheim himself hoped that sociology would be able to 'render invaluable services in the practical domain'. 'Only sociology is in a position to restore the idea of the organic unity of societies.' (Durkheim 1975[1886]: 37). 'Restoration' is not, however, necessarily synonymous with a return to the past.

4

Travels in Germany

Like several of his colleagues, Durkheim was fascinated by the German university model; he admired the 'persevering efforts' that were being made in Germany to 'look the infinite complexity of facts in the face' and to 'take sociological investigations in all directions'. He decided to go to Germany after a meeting with the director of higher education, Louis Liard, during which they discussed republicanism, science and secular ethics. Liard was familiar with Durkheim's first articles, and wanted a young philosopher with an interest in social science to report on how matters stood in Germany (Lenoir 1930: 294). He also hinted that that he would be 'able to offer him a position as *maître de conférence en philosophie* at the beginning of the next academic year'.[1]

Before 'devoting himself body and soul to the celebrated task of university reform and becoming a senior administrator', Liard (1846–1917), a graduate of the École normale supérieure and an *agrégé de philosophie*, had made his name as 'one of the philosophers of his day' thanks to his 'original work'. A disciple of Cournot and Renouvier with a solid background in science – his doctoral thesis of 1874 was on 'geometric definitions and empirical definitions' – he was described as 'one of the first to show by his example how vigorous French philosophy could be when it remained in touch with the sciences'.[2] He began his career as a philosophy teacher at the lycée in Poitiers before becoming a lecturer in philosophy at the Bordeaux faculty of letters (1874–80). He was elected as a town councillor in Bordeaux in 1878, and then became deputy mayor, with responsibility for education and the planned university reforms. After that, he had a career in university administration, becoming rector of the Académie de Caen (1880–84) and director of higher education in 1884.

The task Louis Liard set himself as director of higher education was nothing less than a complete reform of the system. He also wanted to breathe new life into the Sorbonne. 'You will create France's universities', Jules Ferry told him. His model was Germany, even at the architectural level: 'In Germany, a university is not a monument; it is a whole *quartier,* and sometimes even a whole estate, a housing development for science where all services had been centralized and brought together, like organic parts of the same apparatus' (Liard 1890: 42). Liard's goals were to increase the number of students and to improve teaching standards and, in order to do this, to bring all the faculties together in one place. When he paid tribute to the man who was to become both his friend and his superior at the University of Paris, Durkheim would say of him: 'It was he who gave the reconstructed universities their final organizational form . . . The result is a great achievement that will be the glory of the republican government' (Durkheim 1918: 18). It would be said of Liard that he played the leading role in the creation of the modern university. His overall project was ambitious: to reform completely the faculties of letters and science, mainly by increasing their educational resources and implementing a major building programme. He was in favour of establishing just a few major centres: six or seven universities with greater autonomy and whose faculties would be united. The decrees of July and December 1885 gave them legal status and established a General Faculty Council (consisting of the rector, the deans of faculty and elected members of the teaching staff). This was the embryo of the future University Council established by the law of 10 July 1896 (Condette 2006: 256–8).

For young *agrégés* wishing to pursue a career in teaching and research, spending some time abroad was a compulsory rite of passage, or, more accurately, an 'institutional rite'. At the end of the nineteenth century, when it was becoming necessary to reform the French university system, Germany was, because of the superiority (or perceived superiority) of its teaching and research system, a favourite destination: the model provided by German universities appeared to be the only alternative to the sclerotic Napoleonic system. The minister for education sent the most promising *agrégés* to 'study the country and to follow the scientific work that was being done there', as Charles Andler put it (1977[1932]: 230).

Charles Seignobos, Maxime Collignon, Gabriel Séailles, Camille Jullian and Georges Blondel had already been awarded grants to study in Germany (Charle 1994: 28–9). Although they had some criticisms to make, all sang the praises of the German system in one way or another: many chairs had been established, and both teachers and students enjoyed great freedom. There was healthy competition between teachers and it was possible to innovate (new branches of knowledge). Future scholars were being trained in seminars and institutes.

Anthropology and the 'New Psychology'

Durkheim obtained leave of absence (later described in the administration's files as 'leave of absence on health grounds') for the academic year 1885–6. Before going to Germany, he spent the first semester in Paris, where he began the 'first draft' of his doctoral thesis (Mauss 1969[1928]: 27).

For Durkheim, Paris meant hard work and loneliness. At one point, feeling ill and tired, he let it slip in a letter to his friend Victor Hommay, who was teaching in Angers, that he was worried and complained of feeling lonely. Twenty-four hours later, Hommay knocked on his door, having come 'to keep him company and cheer him up'. 'We spent a few good days together, and it reminded us of the happy times we had had at the École normale supérieure' (Durkheim 1975[1887a]: 424). It was to be their last meeting: Victor Hommay was killed in an accident the following July.

Paris also meant new encounters and new friends. Durkheim was now seeing Lucien Herr, whom he appears to have met when he graduated from the École normale supérieure, on a regular basis. Six years older than Durkheim, Herr (1864–1926) was a *normalien* and an *agrégé de philosophie* (1886). The two would meet at the home of the historian Seignobos, and then in the library at the École normale supérieure (Herr would be appointed librarian in 1888). It might be said that this was a decisive encounter: as Marcel Mauss emphasizes, Herr become a 'vigilant friend' to Durkheim, and encouraged him at a time when everyone was discouraging him. Mauss describes the help Herr gave his uncle in these terms:

> The origins of ethics and sociology had a very bad reputation at this time. Herr understood the problem. Durkheim had begun to write in 1882, and until 1884 his work remained philosophical. It was at the beginning of 1885 that he found in the statistical data, and then in the work of the anthropologists – not Spencer, but Tylor and Morgan – the scientific stimulants he needed to elaborate the method he later derived from the way he applied them. (1997[1928]: 741)

Always eager to help any 'original worker', as Mauss put it, Lucien Herr gave Durkheim a lot of bibliographical help. It was Herr who introduced him to the texts of Robertson Smith and Frazer which had been published in the *British Encyclopaedia*. It was Herr who drew his friend's attention to Frazer's famous article 'Totemism' (Mauss 1969[1927]: 524). Durkheim admired the brilliant insights of both authors, who would remain important points of reference throughout his career until the publication of *The Elementary Forms of Religious Life*, and he recognized the quality of their contributions to the comparative science of religions. He would always be grateful to Lucien Herr.

The concept of evolution was central to anthropology, and the evolutionists dominated the discipline, especially in the English-speaking world. Published in 1877, Lewis Henry Morgan's *Ancient Society* identified the different stages or states in the evolution of the human family as savagery, barbarism and civilization. A few years earlier, in 1871, Edward Burnett Tylor, an English theoretician who taught anthropology at Oxford, had published *Primitive Culture*, in which he assigned anthropologists the task of establishing 'at least a crude scale of civilization'. In the late 1880s, the author of the major *Notes and Queries on Anthropology* (1874) was at the peak of his fame and had great influence on all British anthropology. His defence of social anthropology can be summarized in a few theses: humanity always remains the same in psychical terms; the stages of evolution are always the same; a doctrine of survival; and the comparative method.

Although there was some controversy, sociocultural evolution was a 'sort of theoretical orthodoxy' in anthropology. Although the second generation of sociocultural evolutionists, which included Andrew Lang and Robertson Smith, supported the doctrine, they helped to 'reformulate' it in the period between 1880 and 1890 (Stocking 1995: 49). Lang published his *Custom and Myth* in 1884, followed by the two-volume *Myth, Ritual and Religion* in 1887, and Smith published *Kinship and Marriage in Early Arabia* in 1885. Smith, who specialized in the study of the Semitic religions, had already published books on the Old Testament and the prophets of Israel, and was preparing to collect several of his own texts in his major *Lectures on the Religions of the Semites* (1889). There were several good reasons why Durkheim should have taken an interest in the work of Robertson Smith, whose ideas were as follows: religion is the basis of the social order; religion should be defined in social rather than individual terms; the emphasis should be placed on ritual rather than belief; the emotional should be given priority over the intellectual; the concept of the sacred; the centrality of totemism and sacrificial rituals.

And it was in Paris that Durkheim discovered psychophysiology. He read Charcot and attended Théodule Ribot's lecture at the Sorbonne. A 'new experimental psychology' was beginning to emerge at this time.[3] A lot of work was being done on new topics such as suggestion, psychological heredity, hysteria, neurasthenia and madness. There was talk of 'neuroses' and 'nervous illnesses'. In 1885, Freud came to Paris to see Charcot presiding over his world of hysteria. These developments all had an impact on public opinion. This was a period of discoveries and debates, and for the establishment of new institutions. In 1885, Jean Martin Charcot, together with Théodule Ribot, Paul Janet and Charles Richet, founded the Société de psychologie physiologique, which organized the first conference on that theme a few years later: the very expression 'physiological psychology' signalled that psychology was becoming autonomous, distancing itself from philosophy and drawing close to physiology. Its ambitions were, in other words, scientific (Roudinesco 1982: 227; on the history of psychology in France, see also Paicheler 1992).

Jean Martin Charcot (1825–93) was, along with Dr Hippolyte Bernheim from Nancy, one of the pioneers of the new psychology; he was also the founder of modern neurology. He enjoyed an international reputation, and his publications and highly innovative teaching meant that he was known outside medical and scientific circles. His work at the Salpêtrière, where he had been professor of pathological anatomy since 1862, was mainly on illnesses of the nervous system, or the famous 'nervous illnesses', each one of which was associated with a set of internal lesions. Charcot held that the origins of nervous illnesses were physical and organic, and he ascribed their causes to the atrophy or physical degeneracy of the nervous system. In order to treat these various pathologies, he had developed a range of new therapies such as 'galvanization' (the therapeutic use of electric shocks) and 'ferronization' (ingestion of iron).

It was the paper on somnambulism that Charcot read to the Académie des sciences in 1882 that relaunched the debate about hypnosis in France. In the early 1880s, Charcot's close collaborator Charles Richet published two articles on that topic in the *Revue philosophique*, one dealing with 'induced somnambulism' and the other with 'personality and memory in somnambulism'. In 1884, he published a book entitled *L'Homme et l'intelligence*. That same year, Hippolyte Bernheim explained in his *De la suggestion dans l'état hypnotique et dans l'état de veille* that 'sensory hallucinations' are part of everyone's day-to-day life. The subtitle of M. Simon's *Le Monde des rêves* (1888) mapped out the new field: 'Dreams, hallucinations, illusions, artificial paradises, rage, the brain and dreams.' Interest in such phenomena continued to grow. The year 1886 saw the foundation of the *Revue de l'hypnotisme expérimental et thérapeutique*, and the first World Congress on Hypnotism was held in Paris a few years later (1889). That same year, Charcot's pupil Pierre Janet (Paul's nephew) published his *L'Automatisme psychologique*.

Philosophical knowledge was 'swinging towards' psychology. Philosophers no longer studied just the 'highest forms' of human activity, or will power, resolution and free will, but also its 'simplest and most rudimentary forms' (Janet 1889: 1; see James 1995). Did this call into question the notion of creative activity? Even genius could mask something else, namely madness. Cesare Lombroso's *L'Uomo di genio* (1888) was translated into French in 1889.

Criminality and the phenomena of crowd behaviour were also being discussed. The legal implications of suggestion did not escape the philosophers and lawyers, who were beginning to wonder if the claim that the accused had been under hypnosis might be used as an argument for the defence. The most sensational trial was that of a man who, in 1888, confessed under hypnosis that he had murdered a married woman (Silverman 1989: 88). Questions were also being asked about the possible impact of urban life on nervous tensions as the century drew to a close. Wasn't there a danger that the increased availability of news and the accelerated pace of life in the big cities would over-excite the nervous system? In 1890, Richet published a study called 'Mental stress in modern civilization', and Dr Fernand Levillain's *Neurasthénie* appeared the following year, with a preface by Charcot. The origins of neurasthenia might lie, it was thought, in the bustle of the big cities. Degeneracy and devitalization: the pathologies identified by doctors concerned not only the nervous system of individuals, but the social system itself. Both society and the nation were sick.

Of all the philosophers, it was Théodule Ribot who most actively promoted psychological experimentation, even though he did not practise it himself. His work has been described as a 'sieve' (Roudinesco 1986: 231) or melting pot for all the scientific, theoretical and ideological currents of his day. But the man was an admirable 'go-between' who established the foundational link between the physiological and biological fields and that of the new psychology, and played a major role in establishing psychology as an autonomous discipline that was independent of philosophy but dependent upon medicine and clinical psychiatry. Ribot had an unbounded admiration for his teacher Hippolyte Taine (1828–93), whose *De l'intelligence* (1870) gave a whole generation a taste for psychology by outlining a scientific theory of the intellect based on a reading of French alienists and British psychologists.

Ribot's influence on French philosophy was all the more significant in that his *Revue philosophique* published many articles on psychology. In 1889, he was elected to the Collège de France, where he held the first chair in experimental psychology, which had been established for him by Renan. His many books brought him great fame.

'We Have a Lot to Learn From Germany'

When he left for Germany in January 1886, Durkheim was full of enthusiasm. 'When I began the studies, 18 or 20 years ago, that I am still pursuing today', he would say, 'I expected enlightenment to come from Germany' (1975[1902]: 400). He took with him a letter of introduction to Wundt from Théodule Ribot. He had yet to read his work – 'I read Wundt in 1877', he later admitted (Durkheim 1982[1907]: 259) – but he had already met the first psychologist in Germany to have broken almost all links with metaphysics. Wundt enjoyed an international reputation and, as Alfred Binet remarked, 'for a long time [American students] went to Germany, and especially to Wundt's laboratory in Leipzig, and, if they did stop in Paris, it was simply to go to the opera and visit the museums'.[4] As soon as he had crossed the frontier, Durkheim went to Leipzig, where he visited the famous psychophysician's laboratory and witnessed some of the 'rather arid' experimental work that went on there. This was, he thought, an excellent way of 'awakening a love of scientific accuracy in young minds; it breaks the habit of vague generalizations and metaphysical possibilities, and makes them understand the complexity of psychical phenomena' (Durkheim 1975[1887b]: 478). Durkheim was, on the other hand, surprised that Wundt met with 'violent opposition' in his own country: 'When an original mind does manage to shake off the yoke of tradition, he does not find an audience capable of taking an interest in his work' (ibid.: 459).

Born in Neckarau, Wilhelm Wundt (1832–1920) initially studied medicine but, having little interest in practising it, had turned to scientific research and studied psychology with Johannes Müller in Berlin. He established the Psychologisches Institut in Leipzig. It can be regarded as the world's first laboratory for experimental psychology, and trained both Germany's great psychologists and the United States' first generation of experimental psychologists. In Wundt's view, psychology was a science and must be based on experimental methods. His *Grundzüge der physiologischen Psychologie* (1873–4) is regarded as the most important work in the history of modern psychology (Jones 2003).

Wilhelm Wundt was also the author of an *Ethik* (1886) devoted to the empirical study of language, religion, customs and law. His aim was to establish a science of ethics by using a method consisting in the establishment of concrete, objective laws though inductive generalization.

After his stay in Leipzig, Durkheim spent time in Berlin and Marburg. His programme included visits to various universities and libraries to continue his programme of reading, which obviously included Schäffle and Wundt, but also the theoreticians of the 'psychology of peoples' (*Völkerpsychologie*), 'the socialism of the lectern' (*Kathedersozialismus*) and Karl Marx (he was influenced here by Dr Neiglick, a Finnish friend whom he had met in Wundt's laboratory).[5] He also read Schmoller and Wagner, but made no attempt to attend their lectures or to make personal contact with them during his remaining time in Berlin (Durkheim 1982[1907]: 258). Gustav von Schmoller (1838–1917) and Adolf Heinrich Gottheil Wagner (1835–1917) were at the time the leading proponents of professorial socialism, a 'new historical school' for which research was a way of establishing the empirical basis for social development. Schmoller, a professor of political economy at Halle, Strasburg and then Berlin (1882–1913), was to have a huge influence not only on intellectual life (he was the editor of a journal), but also on German social policy in his capacity as co-founder and secretary of the *Verein für Sozialpolitik*. His work comprised vast studies of the history of economic institutions and methodological studies designed to formulate an economic doctrine. The main features of his work, which seemed to gain ground in Germany at the time, were as follows: the emphasis had to be placed on the ethical dimension of economic studies; there was a close link between political economy and jurisprudence (because juridical phenomena are determined by custom); the state should be seen as a 'natural organ' of evolution.

Durkheim would later say that he had no more than a 'very moderate sympathy' for Wagner's work. And the only book by Schmoller that he studied 'carefully and with interest' was his pamphlet *Einige Grundfragen der Rechts- und Volkswirtschaftslehre*. He admitted that Schmoller's 'somewhat indecisive and unsubstantive thought – and especially Wagner's' did not, unlike that of Comte, have a 'profound impact' on him (Durkheim 1980[1913b]: 160).

The reason why Durkheim was fascinated by the work of the economists was that they were establishing a link between political economy and ethics, criticizing the philosophy of natural law, and demonstrating that 'economic phenomena too reveal the influence of extremely flexible elements of ethics' and that 'both rights and duties are the product of contingent historical circumstance' (1975[1887d]: 279). He thought that his reading of the economists would 'provide an answer to the questions that concern me'. Was this anything more than an illusion? Fifteen years later, he would admit that it had served no purpose: 'I spent several years [reading them] and got nothing out of it, other than what can be learned from a negative experience.'[6]

At one point, a very anxious Durkheim even thought of going back to France, fearing that he would not get everything he expected from his time in Germany (Davy 1960a: 19). He was also suffering from homesickness.

'Throughout my stay in Germany my stomach was in knots and, even though I was well looked after, well received and very sympathetic to the German way of life, I was ill at ease at being so far away from home.'[7] A photograph taken in Leipzig in 1886 does show him looking serious and sad. He is standing bolt upright, with a receding hairline and a full beard, draped in a dark overcoat and with one hand on the back of a chair. Behind his glasses, he looks gentle and somewhat melancholic. He was 28. Everything was difficult: he had to master the language and get used to new customs. Just to find out what lectures were on offer in any given faculty, he had to scramble to find the names of the teachers he was looking for 'on bits of paper stuck up next to one another at random' and 'decipher writing that was often illegible'. As he remarked on returning to France: 'Sometimes a little French centralization can be a good thing' (1975[1887b]).

But, as he exclaimed, what a profusion of lectures and chairs! And what capacity for work! In every faculty, there was a 'compact army' of philosophers, whereas in France there was often only one professor. And what an atmosphere! The university was 'so lively' (Durkheim 1975[1887b]).[8] This is how Durkheim describes his first experiences:

> When I first entered a classroom and saw between 150 and 200 students smoking as they waited for their teacher to arrive, I was struck by a feeling of wonder mingled with a little envy. I was looking at students – real students – and it was impossible not to be sad when I thought of the few students who come to hear our philosophy teachers, especially in our provincial faculties, or, which was even worse, of the strange listeners who sometimes turn up out of idle curiosity, or simply because they have an hour to kill. (1975[1887b]: 466)

Durkheim soon lost some of his illusions about German universities. No one really followed most lectures. The system of using *Privatdozenten* (who often had no income apart from the fees their students paid them) created a 'real proletariat' that was 'the only pool from which future teachers are recruited'. The teaching of philosophy was 'very elementary and very general', even though scientific studies were 'increasingly specialized'. The dominant tendency was eclecticism, which was partly explained by 'the absence of any great authority, or of any that was recognized as such'. Kantianism was the only philosophy to have had any lasting influence. Durkheim was also astonished by German student life, and horrified to find that there were student societies devoted solely to 'drinking and making a racket together'. Fortunately, there were also, he observed, study groups in which 'a little science easily coexists with a lot of camaraderie'. He also noted that each German university was a *whole* and inculcated a certain number of 'collective feelings' into its members. This community spirit was, he thought, in keeping with the German 'national temperament'. Durkheim retained an idyllic vision of the life of German students: 'In Germany, everything is done in a group', he told his students at the

Sorbonne. 'People sing together. They take walks together. They play together. They philosophize together, or talk about science and literature . . . The young man is constantly involved in group life. He engages in serious occupations in a group, and he relaxes in a group' (Durkheim 1961[1925]: 234).

Even German professors shared certain of the features of this 'national character'. It seemed to this young academic from abroad that they differed in every respect from their French counterparts. The Germans were serious-minded, had a taste for collective life and long-term projects, whereas the French were more interested in distinction and originality, had a greater sense of their individuality and took only an intermittent and sporadic interest in intellectual work. Durkheim greatly admired his German colleagues, who were so devoted to science and who worked so hard, and he made no secret of where his preferences lay. 'We have a lot to learn from Germany', he concluded. His feelings of admiration faded somewhat when he saw that German teachers had little interest in pedagogy and 'simplified' things in an attempt to reach as many students as possible. Their lectures tended to be 'broad rather than deep, and that was to the detriment of the interests of science'. Durkheim also observed that most of those who attended the lectures only did so because they had to sit an examination. What really caught his attention in Germany was the liveliness and fertile nature of 'moral speculation' (Durkheim 1975[1887b]: 466). It was, he believed, on this branch of science that Germany would leave its 'most lasting mark'.

Towards a Positive Science of Ethics

Durkheim was more convinced than ever of the urgent need to 'import' the moral and social sciences into France: pupils in French lycées had to be offered courses on ethics, and public opinion had to be enlightened. 'We have an even greater need of this than the Germans because we are determined to decide our own future and to govern ourselves.' Durkheim gave philosophy a social and national mission:

> What we need now is to awaken in ourselves a taste for collective life . . . What we need to understand above all is the reason for the existence of national feelings and patriotic faith; we need to know if they are grounded in the nature of things or whether, as the doctrinaires argue, openly or otherwise, they are no more than prejudices and barbaric survivals. (1975[1887b]: 483–5).[9]

On his return from Germany, the grant-holder published his report on philosophy in German universities in the *Revue internationale de l'enseignement* (1975[1887b]). The members of the editorial board included his old teacher Fustel de Coulanges, who was now a member of the Institut de France and a professor in the Paris faculty of letters. Durkheim also wrote a long article on the positive science of ethics in Germany, which appeared in the *Revue philosophique* in 1887. In the young philosopher's view, the 'old philosophy' appeared to be in a state of crisis; this was, he noted, the beginning of its 'dismemberment' (1975[1887d]: 286). The situation was confused because of the conflict that had arisen not within the realm of faith of itself, but between ethics and science. There appeared to be an increasingly urgent need to reconcile moral feelings with the scientific evidence and, as Émile Burnouf (1886) wished as he neared the end of his career, to re-establish philosophy on a positive basis.

Disenchanted with philosophers who were over-inclined to be purely speculative, Durkheim was more interested in the efforts made by specialists from other disciplines (political economy, law and psychology) to establish a positive science of ethics; although he had not forgotten the canonical authors (Kant, Hegel, Spinoza, Fichte, etc.), he was straying away from the beaten path and, like Wundt, the 'hybridizing' disciplines (Ben David and Collins 1966). He was primarily interested in economists, jurists and psychologists, who were, with the exception of Wundt, almost unknown in France. His goal was to popularize their work by exaggerating, to some extent, the importance of their contribution to the positive science of ethics that he wished to establish.

The main virtue of these German scholars was, in Durkheim's view, that they had applied an empirical method and had, like Rudolf von Jhering (1818–92), completely integrated the study of mores [*moeurs*] into ethics. Von Jehring was a professor of law at Göttingen and was involved with the 'historical school' of jurisprudence, which was trying to demonstrate that the law is a product of the collective feelings shared by particular societies, and that laws evolve in the same way as manner or customs. That, thought Durkheim, was the way to make ethics a positive science: 'In ethics, as elsewhere, we must begin by observing.' He was insistent that 'we cannot construct an ethics from scratch and then force it upon things; we must observe things and infer our ethics from them' (1975[1887d]: 278).

Wundt's *Ethik* was a good example: the author set himself the goal of creating a science of ethics by making an empirical study of languages, religion, customs and law. According to Wundt, the empirical method was the only thing that could explain how ethics emerged and developed: the point was no longer to understand 'what *should be* in logical terms, but what *is*' (Durkheim 1975[1887d]: 325). And what do we find if we look beneath the ethics of collective phenomena? We find the collective phenomenon of mores, which can themselves only be the product of other collective phenomena (other mores and, originally, religion).[10]

There is a large element of constraint in social life. There are, in other words, rules or norms, and individuals have to respect them. There are collective ends as well as individual ends. The problem of altruism (and egotism) is central to Wundt's preoccupations: even in the earliest human communities, there appears to have been, in his view, an 'unconscious altruism' or an 'affinity between like and like' which, in its struggle against egoistic tendencies, finds an excellent auxiliary in religion, which quite naturally taught the need for 'disinterestedness and abnegation'. That is the source of ethics, which originally merged with law and religion to form a 'sort of synthesis'. The essential function of ethics is therefore to 'adapt individuals to one another' and, more specifically in Wundt's view, to 'make man feel that he is not a whole, but a part of a whole' (1975[1887d]: 326).

Durkheim paid great attention to Wundt's arguments, even though he did not believe in the existence of a single moral ideal, ever more remote, towards which all religions and all ethics were striving. He rejected the idea of 'one immutable ethics that is valid for all time and all countries'. There was a large element of relativism in his work and he knew that every society has its own ethics. 'There are', he wrote, 'as many ethics as there are social types, and those of lower societies are just as moral as those of cultivated societies.' Imitating the philosophy of law in its attempts to 'deduce an immutable ethics that is valid for all times and all countries from the general nature of man' is therefore out of the question (1975[1887d]: 331).

Durkheim also provides a quick résumé of *Foundations of Law*, by the German moralist Albert Hermann Post. Post's interest was in primitive forms of law, ethics and the family, and his book was 'full of interesting facts and views'. This was another fine example of how German moralists were trying to establish ethics as 'an independent science' or as a 'social science that exists alongside and amongst the other sciences', and to avoid the traps of rationalizing reason. To their great credit, they used 'a truly inductive method' and saw ethical phenomena as 'facts that were both empirical and *sui generis*', and they had 'the courage' to do so (1975[1887d]: 335).

The work of synthesis was a task for the future. Even the task of discovering real laws (that is, 'causal relationships between moral facts and the conditions on which they depend'), leaves a 'lot to be done'. Social facts were, Durkheim repeated, complex. They had to be observed, and many comparisons had to be made. For the moment, or until such time as 'theory can govern practice', it would be wiser to stick to 'the lessons of history'. 'Our moral beliefs', Durkheim concluded, 'are the product of a long process of evolution; they are the result of an interminable sequence of trial and error, efforts and experiments of all kinds.' He was convinced that 'they contain 'more accumulated wisdom than can be found in the brain of the greatest genius' (1975[1887d]: 343).

Individual or State?

The books Durkheim read in Germany inevitably brought him back to questions that had preoccupied him for some years. How can societies sustain themselves and develop? What role is played by self-interest and disinterested feelings? Is society nothing more than a 'vast menagerie of wild beasts'? There was an obvious political dimension to these questions: although it is clearly desirable to avoid economic fatalism, how can we prevent ourselves from lapsing into voluntarism and political idealism? What are we to think of abuses of the rules and of state socialism? Can personal ends be subordinated to collective ends? Is all use of force (*coups d'état*, revolutions) to be systematically condemned in the name of an abstract principle?

Some took the view that economic life was reducible to the sphere of individual interests and the satisfaction of material needs. That utilitarian view was taken by orthodox economics and the economists of the 'Paris group' who, like Paul Leroy-Beaulieu, were opposed to state intervention and preached laisser-faire. In *Le Collectivisme* (1885), Leroy-Beaulieu criticized Schäffle's (collectivist) thesis by showing that there was a danger it would lead to authoritarian despotism. Taking Schäffle's side, Durkheim replied that society could not be reduced to 'the arithmetical sum of its citizens': it was in fact a 'real being which, while it was obviously nothing without the individuals who made it up, still had its own nature and personality'. Expressions that were in common usage actually reflected that reality: we speak of 'social conscience', the 'collective spirit' and the 'body of the nation'.

For others, the solution lay with the state. This was the position of the 'socialists of the lectern', for whom the starting point (of the social economy) is not the individual, but society, which they saw as a whole that could not be reduced to the sum of its parts. Durkheim was much closer to the 'socialists', but criticized them for their belief that moral phenomena could be transformed 'at will', for their 'excessive faith in legislative action' and for their 'predilection for authoritarian methods'.

How could men be 'made to live together'? Was the state the organ that controlled their collective destiny? Durkheim's position – and to this extent he was close to Schäffle – corresponds to a sort of third way that is midway between laisser-faire (political economy), on the one hand, and faith in the state (professorial socialism), on the other. There was no need to choose between economic fatalism and political voluntarism. There was, in Durkheim's view, a place for culture and for morality, as the 'practical function' of ethics was to bring men together. In this context, 'morality' [*la morale*] is to be understood as meaning the collective habits and 'constant ways of behaving' that are common to society as a whole. Morality, he insisted, is a sort of 'crystallization of human behaviour' (1975[1887d]: 275).

This conception of ethics was based upon a theory of social action. Durkheim is critical of all purely philosophical points of view on the grounds that they are too intellectual: life is not reducible to a set of abstract ideas. 'Life means action, not thought', he writes in his discussion of von Jhering's *The End of Law*. But what could the real motivation behind our behaviours be?

Durkheim takes the view that the goal of all action and all human behaviour – collective and individual – is to 'adapt the individual or society to the environment' (1975[1887d]: 289–90). This applies to both ethics and law: their function is 'to maintain society's conditions of existence' and, more specifically, to 'preserve the social order' by bringing constraints to bear on all, but thanks to the strength of public opinion rather than to that of the state. Then there are feelings (honour), propensities (disinterestedness), fashions (which work on the basis of distinction[11]), habits and manners. According to Jhering, consciousness and calculation have a role to play in all this, but Durkheim insists on correcting him by pointing out that their role is less important than we think: 'We so often act without knowing anything of the goal to which we are striving.' Adaptations are often, he goes on in Spinozist vein, 'unconscious'. It might, he suggested, be necessary to 'study the nature of this obscure and diffuse understanding that has a not insignificant influence on the way we lead our lives'.

Durkheim uses the work of German authors who are not sociologists but who could, in his view, 'serve the advancement of sociology' (Durkheim 1975[1902]: 402). To that extent, he was being deliberately subversive. His interest in the study of law, manner and the evolution of societies (from lower to higher societies) is already very obvious and the main themes he will develop in *The Division of Labour in Society* are already present: an evolutionist perspective defined in terms of differentiation and individualization, an organic concept of society, and the notion of the collective consciousness.

Like his reading of the work of the classical economists, Durkheim's stay in Germany was therefore anything but a 'negative experience'. Fifteen years later, he was to acknowledge that:

> Personally, I owe the Germans a great deal. It was in part they who taught me the meaning of social reality, of its complexity, and of its organic development. Thanks to them, I was more able to understand the narrowness of the French school, though I have no intention of underestimating its importance simply because I, like others, recognize its excessive oversimplifications. (1975[1902]: 400)[12]

Back to the Lycée

On returning from Germany on 9 August 1886, Durkheim went to stay with his parents at 2 rue des Forts in Épinal. His father was now over 80, his mother was 66, and a woman servant was living with them. Rosine Durkheim and Gerson Mauss were living at the same address with their two children Marcel and Henri, who were now 14 and 11 respectively.

Émile was at a loss as to what to do: should he go back to teaching in a secondary school, or wait to be appointed *maître de conférences* in a university? 'You led me to expect that this would be possible', he wrote to the director of higher education, Louis Liard, in August 1886. In the event, he found a position at the lycée in Troyes, where he taught philosophy from October 1886 until the summer of 1887. His courses dealt with the relationship between political economy and ethics, and with the doctrine of evolution. He was 'highly considered', and his behaviour was found to be exemplary. He was a 'distinguished, exact and devoted teacher with a real concern for his pupils' and displayed 'extensive knowledge and a truly penetrating mind. He speaks fluently, and in a distinguished and lively fashion, if at times a little too quickly; it is sometimes difficult for his pupils to take notes.'

Only one criticism was made of Durkheim: his lectures, which were always 'very well developed', sometimes 'perhaps went over his students' heads'. It was also feared that he might have too much authority over them and that he encouraged them to be sceptical, as he admitted that 'he could not accept Platonic or Cartesian ideas about the infinite, the absolute or the perfect'.[13]

Part II

The Foundations of Sociology

5

The Bordeaux Years
Pedagogy and the Social Sciences

After almost nine years of service, Durkheim had no intention of remaining in Troyes. He was, said his superiors, 'not lacking in authority and talent'.[1] He could hope for promotion: either to a first-class *lycée* – a wish he expressed in March 1887 – or, better still, to a 'higher post'. A ministerial decree dated 29 July 1887 appointed him a *chargé de cours* [junior lecturer] at the University of Bordeaux, where he succeeded Alfred Espinas. Espinas had recently been promoted to the position of dean of the faculty of letters and had probably arranged for Durkheim's transfer. Durkheim's salary was set at 4,000 francs. 'Durkheim replaced Espinas in Bordeaux', his future collaborator Célestin Bouglé would later say. 'He hoped to launch a positive sociology that would no longer gravitate in the orbit of biology' (Bouglé 1938: 25).

The post was the first of its kind in France, and was established by Eugène Spuller, minister of public education, religion and the arts in the Maurice Rouvier government. It was specifically established for Durkheim at the request of director of higher education Louis Liard, whose aim was 'not to give German universities a monopoly on the social sciences' (Lacroze 1960–1: 61), and to introduce those new disciplines into French universities. Liard devoted all his energies to his great reform of higher education, with consultation after consultation, compromise after compromise and decree after decree. It was a slow and complicated process, and there was a lot of resistance. His plan was to bring the various faculties together – or to federate them, to be more accurate – and to create real universities that would be both 'scientific centres' and 'schools to educate the public' in a number of towns.[2]

The goal was to make the new University 'the centre of speculative life' and its basic role was, as Durkheim himself noted (1918: 469), 'the disinterested promotion of science rather than the search for practical applications'. The new university institutions were designed to be 'free environments', and their role was to bring together all branches of knowledge, and to teach French youth their civic, democratic and social duties. 'It was', admitted Louis Liard (1890), 'very idealistic', especially as he also wanted to decentralize the university system to the four corners of France. These 'centres of attraction' were to include Lyon, Bordeaux and

Montpellier as well as Paris. Those cities had large numbers of students and teachers, the requisite resources and premises, and the widest selection of courses.

Why was Durkheim appointed to Bordeaux? First, because Bordeaux was regarded as one of the main provincial university cities.[3] Second, because teachers often began their university careers in the provinces, and it was, perhaps, easier to be innovatory there than in Paris.

'A Large and Happy City'

Its port made Bordeaux a real geographical crossroads that lay astride the Garonne river. As the main port for the West Indian trade, the city had grown very prosperous in the eighteenth century, importing coffee, sugar, indigo, cocoa and precious woods from both the Americas. The river was full of large sailing ships. 'Money poured in'; this was 'the apotheosis of luxury and the joys of art' (Saunier 1923: 2) The eighteenth century was also a period of major building projects: the town hall was built between 1770 and 1781, followed by the Grand-Théâtre in 1777–80. Designed by Victor Louis, this is one of the most beautiful theatres in Europe; people liked to say that it was 'a masterpiece'.

At the end of the nineteenth century. Bordeaux was still a very busy trading city, and was also gaining increasingly spontaneous recognition for its prestigious vineyards: Médoc, Graves, Sauternes, Saint-Émilion, Pomerol. The urban landscape was being transformed to reflect a new relationship with nature, a new concern with hygiene and a desire to improve security and to enhance its means of communication. The city had had its Parc Bordelais – its answer to Paris's Bois de Boulogne – since 1888. Squares had been created all over the city and there were growing numbers of public fountains. Several markets, including the 'marché des premières mains' in the place des Capucins, had been extended, and vast barracks had been built. A network of new railways lines ran through the Saint-Michel and Sainte-Croix neighbourhoods, and the city was criss-crossed by tramways. The Orléans–Bordeaux railway connected the city to Paris. The journey took about eight hours and, as the adverts announced, passengers enjoyed the luxury of beds, *couchettes* and a restaurant car.

The city was divided into *arrondissements*, and had a population of more than 250,000 people by the end of the nineteenth century. In 1891, it had 18 parishes. In addition to the many Catholic places of worship, including Saint-André Cathedral (a 'huge vessel' 124 metres in length), there were two Protestant churches, one in the rue Notre-Dame and the other in the rue du Hâ, and a synagogue in the rue Labirat. The latter was built after the fire that destroyed the old synagogue built in the rue Causserouge in 1811, or shortly after the city's first consistory had been established. The old synagogue had been known to the city administration as 'The Jews' Temple'. Built on land donated by the city and opened in September 1882, the new synagogue, with its twin towers and three great doors, was one of the largest and most beautiful in France. The architect, Charles Durand, had taken the gamble of using both stone and iron (usually reserved for more utilitarian buildings) and exploiting an eclectic aesthetics that combined medieval art with oriental references, especially in its internal decorations (Jarassé 2002).

Throughout the nineteenth century, Bordeaux's Jewish population was a small minority, amounting to 2 per cent of the total population. In the 1890s, it numbered some 2,100, of whom 40 per cent lived in what was termed a 'voluntary ghetto' around the rue Bouhaut (now rue Sainte-Catherine), which was home to the city's kosher butchers.[4] More than 75 per cent of the city's Jews, even if they were born in Bordeaux, were 'Portuguese' – in other words, of Spanish or Portuguese origin – and were Sephardim. Askhenazis from Germany, Alsace-Lorraine and Poland made up 15 per cent of the Jewish population. The most important families were the Astrucs, the Cardozes, the Gradis, the Lameyras, the Rabas, the Rodrigues-Henriques, the Rogets, the Azevedos and the Lopes-Diaz.

When Émile Durkheim moved to Bordeaux, the chief rabbi was Israël Lévi, an Alsatian who had studied for the rabbinate in Metz and who had only recently been appointed, in 1887. A tireless preacher and a man of action concerned mainly with helping the poor, Israël Lévi also aspired to being a man of science and learning, and published many edifying books on religion and morality, including *Defence of Judaism, or An Examination of Certain Prejudices About Their Beliefs* (1895). Isaac Uhry (1837–1909), head of the boys' school, was also from Alsace. For more than 50 years he was secretary to the consistory and, in a sense, the embodiment of the Jewish community in Bordeaux.

In the mid-nineteenth century, most of the active Jewish population worked in the banking sector, as big retailers and, above all, as small traders and shopkeepers. Many worked as traders or dealers in the textiles industry (haberdashery, silk, second-hand clothes, fashion items, novelties) (Cavignac 1991). Some went to Paris to make their fortune, like Jacob Émile and Isaac Pereire, who founded the Crédit foncier de France bank, or ventured into the railway business and then shipping. Others, like the banker Daniel Osiris Iffla, amassed huge fortunes. Iffla then retired to move in artistic, literary and artistic circles and became an eccentric philanthropist (he bought the Rueil-Malmaison estate in order to donate it to the state, endowed a prize worth 100,000 francs for the most deserving contribution to art, science and history, and built synagogues, including that in the rue Buffault in Paris and the one in Arcachon). Contemporary accounts described, not without a certain malice, the 'Jews of Bordeaux' who, speaking their 'hideous Southern gibberish' and showing an 'unparalleled self-assurance', went up to Paris to become 'masters of the market'. 'Bordeaux had always been', wrote Ernest Feydeau, 'the great breeding-ground that supplied the stock exchange with the sons of Israel' (Feydeau 1873: 165–8; cited in Nahon 2003: 228).

A number of great Jewish families settled in Bordeaux and the Gironde, and bought estates there: the Rothschilds acquired Château-Lafite, while the publisher Michel Lévy bought the Hermitage estate in Gradignan. Taking on responsibilities in Bordeaux's Jewish consistory was not an honour to be refused; Edmond de Rothschild was a delegate member of the central consistory for many years.

'Fatherland and religion' was the motto of a community that felt itself to be fully integrated into the French nation, and which saw education as the means to emancipation but which still preserved its own traditions. In a lecture given to celebrate the centenary of the Revolution in 1889, Chief Rabbi Israél Lévi exhorted his coreligionists: 'Let us love our fellows, but above all let us love our fatherland.' The year 1789 had been the beginning of a new age that saw both the emancipation of the French nation and the enshrinement in law of the rights of man. The centenary of the Revolution was therefore an opportunity for Jews to express their 'gratitude to [their] beloved and generous fatherland'.[5] The chief rabbi of Paris declared: 'The French Revolution restored us our Fatherland', adding that 'the future of humanity is bound up with the grandeur or France'.[6] It was often said that the Jews of Bordeaux represented a 'model of early, successful and recognized integration', but that they were also trying to 'put the future of the Jewish people on a new basis'. Two of the seventeen founders of the Alliance israélite française were from Bordeaux: Rabbi Élie Aristide Astruc and the *polytechnicien* and businessman Jules Carvello, whose sympathies lay with Saint-Simonism.

Bordeaux was a cultural and educational centre: in addition to its lycées, colleges and schools (of hydrography, business and agriculture), there was the 'great and venerable' university, where students were welcomed by Montaigne 'smiling in his tomb' (Hertzog-Cachin 1980: 26). As in every town in France, the government of the Republic had invested generously in public education, opening many primary schools in various neighbourhoods, a girls' lycée in the rue David-Johnston and transferring the School of Fine Arts to the old Benedictine monastery in the Sainte-Croix neighbourhood. The city had its Museum of Fine Arts, founded in 1801 with support from Napoléon: its holdings included works by Van Dyck and Titian. Bordeaux also had its own local artists: Rosa Bonheur and her animal paintings, the symbolist Odilon Redon, and Albert Marquet, with his *Pont de Bordeaux*.

'Considerable efforts' had been devoted to higher education. Witness the observatory built on the Côteau de Floriac in 1885, the new buildings constructed for the faculty of medicine in 1885, and the magnificent and splendidly equipped building on the cours Victor-Hugo constructed for the faculties of letters and science. At first-floor level, the façade was adorned with eight paired Corinthian columns framing three bas-reliefs representing, in the centre, 'Minerva distributing crowns to students' and 'The city of Bordeaux receiving tributes from representatives of the arts and sciences from all periods of history' on either side. The hall housed the tomb of Montaigne, with a statue of him with a neat beard, clad in armour and wearing a helmet, and with a small lion at his feet. The new 'monument' was inaugurated in January 1886, and pride of place was reserved for the arts and sciences section of the monumentally proportioned library. It was tastefully decorated with three frosted-glass cupolas, a vast reading room and a separate room for the teaching staff.

Pedagogy and the Social Sciences

In 1887–8, the faculty of letters had some 120 students, including 20 or so philosophy students (13 degree candidates and 6 candidates for the *agré-gation*).[7] Its move into the new building had caught the attention of the general public and had been given a sympathetic welcome. There was even talk of establishing an archaeological museum. Public lectures, which had been temporarily suspended, were reorganized, and were now given in the new lecture theatre. New staff were appointed. M. Jullian was appointed to the chair in Greek and Latin antiquities, with additional responsibility for the new course of public lectures on the history of the southwest. A very active man, Jullian produced editions of the works of Fustel de Coulanges, and then of Montesquieu's *L'Esprit des lois*, and rapidly became 'one of those teachers who are spreading the reputation of our faculty through-out the world of scholarship'. For his part, M. Paris, a former student at the École d'Athènes, taught Greek language and literature; he was subse-quently appointed to the new tenured chair in archaeology and the history of art.

Until Durkheim's arrival, Octave Hamelin and Alfred Espinas had shared joint responsibility for teaching philosophy. Hamelin prepared stu-dents for the *agrégation*, while Espinas taught a course on 'intelligence' and a degree-level course on the origins of Cartesianism. He also taught two courses on pedagogy: one, for women training to become primary school-mistresses, on physical, aesthetic and intellectual education in primary schools, and one, for philosophy students, on the history of education ('Humanism and its vicissitudes'). They were a great success with their students. The 'experiment' overcame their 'reservations' about pedagogy, and proved that the subject did have its place in the university.

Education was, argued republicans, the best way of creating harmony and social consensus, and in order to do that the teaching profession required a united leadership. The teaching corps had, declared Henri Marion in 1890, 'enormous potential. What could it not do if it could be given a soul! . . . and is this soul anything other than a common doc-trine?' (cited in Weisz 1983: 280).[8] The faculties of letters began to teach pedagogy in 1882 and 1883. In the provinces, the first courses on peda-gogy were established by town councils and were designed with primary school teachers in mind. The state then took over financial responsibility for them, and a change of policy prioritized the training of teachers for secondary schools. In 1892, there was a chair in educational science at the Sorbonne and six of the most important faculties (including Bordeaux, Lyon, Montpellier, Nancy and Toulouse) were teaching pedagogy (Weisz 1979: 86).

Durkheim's course on pedagogy was the only university course established by the ministry to be officially described as such.[9] The usual term was 'Science of education', which was the title of the courses taught in Bordeaux by Alfred Espinas from 1884 to 1887. It was widely believed that institutions of higher education were, as M. Stapfer, dean of the faculty of letters put it, '*écoles normales* that were open to all' and that their mission was to 'train good teachers' (Stapfer 1887).

When Durkheim was appointed *chargé de cours* (official documents still sometimes referred to him as 'Durckheim'), he was officially described as teaching 'social science'. The lawyers challenged this description, arguing that the law school might be the right place for a course in social science. Durkheim took the view that 'where' it was taught was of little importance: 'The boundaries which separate the various parts of the university are not so sharply drawn that certain courses may not be equally well placed in one or another curriculum' (Durkheim 1978[1888a]: 68). The debate left him somewhat indifferent: 'The important thing is not that this class take place here or there, but that it be produced at all and that it survive' (Durkheim 1978[1888b]: 227). Some 10 years later, he would recall that although 'the social nature of their studies seems to predispose them to devoting considerable resources to our science' 'legal minds' were for a long time 'hostile to sociology' and, more generally, 'modern ideas' (Durkheim 1975[1895b]: 106). The resistance was, however, gradually overcome.

But why entrust the new course to a philosopher? All this was a provisional arrangement, explained Dean Espinas: 'For some time, this subject will have close affinities with philosophy. Sociology's principles and methods will become as well defined as those of philosophy.' Émile Durkheim was, the dean noted with admiration, the first to 'take up the challenge' (Espinas 1888). Bordeaux was very pleased to have him. The young professor already had the reputation of being a 'distinguished mind and a great worker' (Lacroze 1960–1961: 61). Writing to Alfred Espinas in September, he informed the Dean that he intended to deal with 'social solidarity' in his social science course. 'That,' exclaimed the Dean in a speech given in November 1888 to mark the beginning of the new academic year, 'is a major event, to judge by the emotion it has provoked'. This victory was pregnant with meaning: 'It is probable that the role of sociology – given that we have to call it by its name – will be of growing importance to our studies as a whole' (Espinas 1888).

Why not call it a course on 'sociology'? Some took the view that the new science was still in its infancy: it had no object of its own and no new methodology, and there was no clear line of demarcation between it and the moral and political sciences. In his inaugural lecture, Durkheim himself said that the 'whole of Spencer's work' was 'a sort of bird's eye view of societies' (Durkheim 1978[1888a]: 57). His own course was definitely on sociology: 'A happy conjunction of circumstances . . . set up on our behalf a regular course on sociology . . . allowed us to devote ourselves early on the study of social science and even to make it our professional concern. Thus we have been able to move on from these over-general problems and tackle a certain number of specific problems' (Durkheim 1982[1895]: 49).

A Good Marriage

When he arrived in Bordeaux, Durkheim was 29, and a newly married man. At 3pm on 17 October 1887, he married Louise Julie Dreyfus at the *mairie* of the tenth arrondissement in Paris. The witnesses were, on Émile's side, his uncle Maurice Lyon, described as a 'man of independent means', and his brother Félix, described as a 'merchant'; on Louise's side were her uncles Salomon and Moyse Dreyfus. The religious ceremony took place the next day in the great La Victoire synagogue, and the couple were blessed by Zadoc Kahn, the Chief Rabbi of Paris. Louise Dreyfus was just 21 and, as the marriage certificate indicates, did not work. She was the youngest of three children – her sister Lucie was born in 1862, and her brother Jules Armand in 1863 – and the family lived at 162 rue du Faubourg-Saint-Martin. Her father, Henry Dreyfus, was born in 1833, and came from Wissembourg in Alsace. The son of a shopkeeper, he went to Paris, with his brothers Salomon and Moyse, to work in a foundry. By 1860, he and his brothers were able to set up a small firm specializing in the manufacture of pipes for the sugar refineries and distilleries based on the quai d'Austerlitz. The family was living on the quai d'Austerlitz when Louise was born. Business was booming (Charle 1984). Salomon, who was the elder of the two brothers, was 58 when Louise married, and described himself as a builder residing at 55 boulevard de Strasbourg; Moyse was 58, and an engineer. His address – 7 rue de Monceau – was at the time very prestigious; according to Proust, only millionaires could afford to live there (Assouline 1997: 23). Their mother Rosalie Lévy (b. 1834) had worked as a primary schoolteacher until the birth of her first child.

How did Émile meet his future wife? The most likely hypothesis is that they met through family and/or professional connections at either a religious festival or a wedding.[10] The wedding united two very different families: one was Parisian and wealthy, the other provincial and in possession of symbolic capital and, in the case of Émile, a lot of academic capital. It was a good marriage. Louise was, according to contemporary witnesses, an ideal wife, an 'admirable partner', highly educated, and with a dowry of 100,000 francs. Durkheim's more modest contribution amounted to 38,000 francs from his parents and what little savings he had. When he went to Paris – to sit on a jury *d'agrégation*, for example – he stayed with his in-laws in the faubourg Saint-Martin.

'What Has To Be Done Has To Be Done'

Durkheim's teaching and research express his interest in sexual relations, marriage and the family. Marriage was, in his view, a social institution with 'something mysterious' about it, and extra-marital sexual intercourse was, as he would say on several occasions, 'immoral'. He viewed the sexual act as 'a grave, solemn and religious act' (Durkheim 1979[1911b]: 141). The sexual act had always, he thought, awakened feelings that were 'mysterious, 'disturbing' and 'disconcerting'. The act itself was both repulsive and attractive: on the one hand, it was 'the immodest act *par excellence*' and was immoral; on the other, it bound human beings together, and had an 'associative, and therefore moralizing, power'. The 'basic immorality' of the sexual act had, he thought, to do with its 'exceptional intensity': 'each of the two personalities in contact is engulfed by the other. On no occasion is the abandoning . . . so complete' (ibid.: 146).' He even speaks of a 'desecration' that leads to 'a communion of the most intimate kind possible between two conscious beings . . . the two persons united become one', and of a 'fusion' that produces a 'new personality, enveloping and embracing the other two individual' (ibid.: 147).

The young couple set up home at 179 boulevard de Talence, and led the 'respectable and peaceful life' that was, in Durkheim's view, 'the best guarantee of morality and life'. They were never apart for a moment. Émile was convinced that 'a hermetically closed . . . family was very much drawn in upon itself. As a result, it obviously brought together, in close unity, husband and wife acting like parents, and their children' (1980[1901c]: 256).

The boulevard de Talences divided Bordeaux from Talence, and going from one to the other was almost like going from the town to the countryside. There were fields and vineyards nearby, but the area was becoming industrialized and there were already some large factories: the Roussel chemical plant, the Wolff brewery and the Gironde *blanchisserie* [laundry]). The city was changing and the development of its means of communications would, as Durkheim could foresee, 'make it possible to spread housing over a wider surface rather than crowding everything into narrow limits' (Durkheim 1969[1901]: 310) Cities certainly had their 'disadvantages' (dubious hygiene) and 'evils' (higher mortality rates), but he believed that they would be done away with 'by scientific progress'. Cities, in his view, led to concentration, over-excitement and, therefore, civilization.

The following year, Louise gave birth to their first child – a daughter – on 8 September 1888. The birth took place not in Bordeaux but in the Parisian suburb of Saint-Cloud and, as Etienne Halphen notes, at the end of the university vacation, rather as though Émile had 'arranged' for things to happen that way. Durkheim would never, he adds, allow a purely family matter to interfere with his teaching (Halphen 1998: 18. Étienne Halphen is Émile's grandson).They called their daughter Marie. It is hard to think of a more 'Christian' name, but it was common in Jewish families at the time, and could be seen as an indication of their desire to distance themselves from Judaism and to become integrated. Her middle name was Bella. Their whole lives were devoted to their family and to academic life. There were no – or very few – trips to the theatre, even though this was something that Émile enjoyed doing. There were occasional days on the beach, and short excursions by train to Biarritz or Guéthary on the Basque coast.

Louise was said to be 'highly educated' (even though what she studied and where she went to school is not on record), but she did not work. This division of labour was, in Durkheim's view, quite natural. He did not believe in going back to some 'primeval homogeneity': 'labour [is] increasingly divided up . . . between the sexes' (Durkheim 1984[1893]: 18–21), and that differentiation was, he argued, the source of conjugal solidarity.

Louise became a close collaborator, and ensured that her husband enjoyed what Mauss called 'the best possible working conditions' until the very end (Mauss 1927: 526). She agreed to 'devote the whole of her own life to her husband's austere and scholarly life, and did so with joy' (Davy 1991a: 65). She was, said Mauss, a saint, but also a woman who enjoyed life. She was kind-hearted, devoting herself to her husband and to making the difficult and austere scientific life he had chosen comfortable, easy and cheerful (Bourgin 1938: 217–18). Their nephew Henri, who lived with them, describes the atmosphere in the home of Émile and Louise: '[My uncle] was always in his study, but he worked everywhere else as well; he worked wherever he was. His wife was extraordinarily devoted to him, and respected his work; her main complaint was that he was always so tired. His answer to all her entreaties was "What has to be done has to be done"' (cited in Filloux 1977: 34).

The birth of their daughter Marie brought a 'breath of fresh air' into a life devoted entirely to academic work and into a family life that was 'more than austere', as Marcel Mauss once put it (1997[1938]). When his elder brother Félix died, Émile took in his nephew Henri Edmond. In the autumn of 1890, a second nephew – Marcel Mauss, the son of Rosine (née Durkheim) and Gerson Mauss – also came to Bordeaux, to study philosophy at the university. Émile found himself taking on more and more responsibilities: husband, father and, before long, guardian. Like his father before him, he was a strict father and, to the indignation of his sisters, was quite capable of leaving his children to cry rather than picking them up, recalled Marcel Mauss, who used him as an example to show that 'man is an animal who educates and trains his offspring'.

The essay 'Childhood' (published in 1911) shows that Émile was probably amazed at the child's 'power of movement, of growth and development': 'What eagerness greets every novelty!', exclaimed a father who was able to observe a whole range of emotions in his children: tears and laughter, cuddly submissiveness and stubborn resistance, tenderness and anger (Durkheim 1979[1911a]: 151).

But in Durkheim's view, a parent should never forget the 'double nature' of the child he is bringing up: weakness and fragility on the one hand, movement on the other. He advised educators to remember how weak a child is, and to look at the progress he is making. The second truism was the importance of taking into account the need for movement: the educator must avoid 'extinguishing the flame' or choking 'the keen and joyous impulses of a young life' (Durkheim 1979[1911]: 152). And should 'beware of the fatigue which nullifies all effort, both its own as well as its tutor's'. He thought it desirable to establish a system of pedagogy that could 'make special allowances for all the child's pleasure, such as varied activity, free movement and unhindered development' (ibid.: 152–3].

Émile was, however, always a man who believed in the need for discipline and rules: 'The child must learn to regulate and coordinate his actions . . . learn to control himself . . . contain and master himself and formulate his own principles'. Education therefore consists in 'veritable metamorphosis': even though a child is a 'sort of anarchist, ignorant of all rules . . . it is easy to make the child acquire habits'. As a father, he would experience some disappointments but he would also have what he himself called 'some nice surprises' (Durkheim 1979[1911]: 153–4).

Louise and Émile had only two children. Durkheim himself would analyse this 'inadequate birth rate', which he saw as a 'collective illness': 'A society cannot be healthy unless it has enough living elements.' Demographers had already observed that 'there is a lack of families of an average density [three children]. Too many families are content to have one or two children, and that is what makes the state of our population so precarious.' The explanation for all this, Durkheim explains, lies in 'the weakening of the feeling of collective solidarity' and the rise of the 'spirit of individuation'. Something that had happened in the 'domestic realm' was making us less willing to 'have large families':

> We now have a very different vision of family life. The abstract personality of family society is no longer the object of the same feelings; it is not the family that we love, but the individual personalities who make it up and, first and foremost, our children. It is in their interest not to have too many children. If we are to be able to raise them carefully, our attentions must not be divided amongst too many heads. Our desire to leave them wealthy encourages the same tendency. (1969[1900a]: 237–40)

Tragedy now struck the Durkheim family. In 1886, Émile's brother Félix lost his wife Clara (née Clémence), who had just turned 30. The family had gone to live in Gray (Haute Saône), where Félix had opened a shop selling fabrics and haberdashery. Less than two years later, in December 1888, Félix too died. He was not yet 40 and his death left the 7-year-old Henri-Edmond an orphan. The boy was brought up first by his maternal uncle Edmond Dreyfus, and then his paternal uncle Émile Durkheim. He went to secondary school in Rouen, where he was a boarder, before moving in 1898 to Bordeaux, where he attended the Lycée Michel-Montaigne.

New Colleagues

The young couple settled into life in Bordeaux with no difficulty. The new *maître de conférences* [lecturer] fitted easily into his new academic environment, and 'gave it new life': he was 'a fine, upstanding man (excellent relations with colleagues, likeable and reserved character)'.[11]

Several of his old acquaintances from the École normale were now

teaching in the faculty of letters: Camille Jullian (Greek and Latin antiquities), Maurice Holleaux (ancient history; he left Bordeaux for Lyon the
following year), Imbart de La Tour (history), Cuceul (Greek literature)
and Radet (ancient history). Some of his colleagues rapidly became known
as experts in their own fields: the archaeologist Pierrre Paris; Maxime
Colllignon and Camille Jullian, who specialized in Graeco-Latin antiquities; the historian-archaeologist Maurice Denis; and Stapfer, who taught
French literature. Couat, a specialist in Greek literature and dean of the
faculty until 1887, had just left Bordeaux to take up the post of rector of
the Académie de Lille; in 1892 he returned to Bordeaux as rector. In the
late 1880s, the teaching staff also included M. de Thevernet (foreign literature) and M. Luchaire (geography), not to mention other lecturers, including Ouvré (Greek language), de la Ville de Mirmont (Latin literature),
Hamelin (philosophy). The philosophers still remembered Alfred Fouillée
and Louis Liard (who held the title of honorary professor). During his first
years in Bordeaux, Émile became friendly with Octave Hamelin, a liberal
Protestant who taught the history of philosophy. Both men soon stood out
because of 'their pedagogic zeal and scientific ardour'.[12]

When Durkheim arrived, the University of Bordeaux was becoming,
as René Worms noted (1917: 562), 'a very lively centre for sociological
studies'. The teaching staff also included Léon Duguit, Fernand Faure
and Henri Saint-Marc in the faculty of law. Although he did not really
enjoy socializing, Durkheim did frequent the salon held by Léon Duguit,
a lawyer of his own age who organized 'so-called sociological chats' at
his home (Didry 1990: 7). Duguit's *agrégation* was in public and constitutional law, and he had published a short pamphlet entitled *Quelques mots
sur la famille primitive* (1883). He was interested in political economy and,
like his colleague Fernard Faure, who was appointed to a chair in political
economy in Paris in 1892 before going into politics, was in favour of teaching sociology in law faculties. In 'Constitutional law and sociology', an
article published in 1889 in the *Revue internationale de l'enseignement* (the
editor was by Louis Liard), Duguit let it be known that he believed that
law faculties should be turned into institutions providing vocational training, intellectual culture and scientific research. He was critical of deductive
methods, which he thought 'dangerous', and defended the observational
method – in his view, the only 'scientific' method. He also argued that
research should focus on the discovery of scientific laws – defined as constant relations between observable facts – and supported the thesis that
social phenomena were governed by a general determinism (Favre 1989:
185). Duguit also had some ideas about society, which he regarded as an
organism: 'Society itself is a living being, an organized being.' He pursued
the same line of arguments in two later articles published in the *Revue
internationale de sociologie*. He was therefore one of Durkheim's allies,
but he reduced sociology to economics and law. Durkheim did, however,
persuade him to come round to his point of view, and in 1891, Duguit gave
a seminar on sociology for a small group of advanced students (Duguit
1893).[13]

Léon Duguit (1859–1928) was the son of a lawyer from Libourne, and was only 30 at this time. He became the 'archetypal grand bourgeois jurist of the *fin de siècle*', and succeeded in combining an academic career with an involvement in social and political life as a charity administrator and a member of the Bordeaux city council from 1908 to 1912. A gourmet who enjoyed fashionable life, he was 'at home' for friends and acquaintances several times a week in the superb house he had had built in the middle of extensive grounds. The historian Camille Jullian and the physicist Pierre Duhem were regular guests. Duguit's academic and professional career was exemplary. He performed brilliantly at law school, and then went into higher education, taking his *agrégation* in 1882. He was appointed to a post in the law faculty in Caen, but was quickly transferred to Bordeaux, where he enjoyed a brilliant career, becoming associate dean in 1910 and dean in 1919. He was the author of books on public law: *L'Etat, le droit objectif et la loi positive* (1901), *L'Etat, les gouvernants et les agents* (1903), and of a major *Traité de droit constitutionnel* (first edition 1911).

Henri Saint-Marc, who taught law, was one of the first teachers in higher education to take an interest in and collaborate on studies in sociology.[14] An *agrégé* and professor of political economy in the law faculty at Bordeaux, Saint-Marc was a member of the editorial committee of the *Revue d'économie politique*; he explored his interests further with a small group of friends and colleagues, including Espinas, Fernand Faure, Duguit, Durkheim and Samazeuilh. In 1882–93, he introduced a new *cours libre* on statistics at Bordeaux.[15]

In Bordeaux, interest in the social question led to the foundation of a Union de la paix sociale in 1890, when Ernest Fournier de Flaix gave a public lecture entitled 'The social economy: methods and progress' in the Salle philomathique. The social economy he described was heavily influenced by Le Play. The three main ideas were association, cooperation and fraternity, and the objective of the social economy was to preserve social harmony by instilling respect for the social order, and social duty. Change required reforms, including limitations on the hours men, women and children could be required to work (Fournier de Flaix 1890).

Durkheim was not fond of salons, which he described as a rather superficial form of sociability. Such things could be compared to games and art, which 'diverges from [the realm of] moral life since it departs from reality' (Durkheim 1961[1925]: 271). The new professor led a studious life that consisted mainly of preparing lectures, writing articles and reviews and joining in discussions with colleagues. The couple spent their holidays either with Émile's parents in Épinal, or in Switzerland.

Alfred Espinas: 'The First to be Drawn to Sociology'

Alfred Espinas (1844–1922) was an *agrégé de philosophie* (1871) with a doctorate in letters, and had been teaching in the faculty of letters for some 10 years. One of his areas of interest was pedagogy: his book, *L'Idée générale de la pédagogie*, was published in 1884. He taught a course of pedagogy, and gave public lectures to large audiences. In 1887, he was appointed dean of the faculty of letters and remained in that post until 1890. In 1891, he visited England and Scotland to study the workings of the university extension movement. Everyone in the university had great respect for his work. When he left Bordeaux in 1893, Dean Stapfer said of him: 'This great scholar is a good man. His conscientiousness is that of a true scientist' (Stapfer 1894). He was also a 'stubbornly independent thinker' who took refuge in 'a sort of gruff isolation' (Bourgin 1938: 90).

Espinas's thesis on animal societies (1877) caused a scandal. He recalled: 'Four years later, M. Janet forced me to suppress the historical introduction to my thesis because I refused to remove the name of Auguste Comte' (Espinas 1901: 449). In his thesis, he examined the various kinds of association – from parasitism to mutualism – that can be observed in the animal kingdom, and even goes so far as to speak of 'lasting voluntary reunions; and conjugal fidelity'. It begins: 'The idea of society is that of permanent competition between separate living beings.' It deals in turn with association (the law of all life), the family, conjugal society and small tribes. In his conclusion, Espinas speaks of 'the laws governing social facts in the animal kingdom' and of the 'morality of animals'. This was, he admitted, a 'rudimentary' morality, but it was a morality, with a certain form of altruism, if not pure kindness and abnegation, and a kind of collective consciousness. Human beings had no monopoly on virtue!

When the second edition of *Des Sociétés animales* was published in 1878, Espinas added a long introduction of more than 150 pages entitled 'Introduction to the history of sociology in general'. He once more defends his approach:

> I believe that we can be of better service to civilization by showing that humanity is the final stage in an earlier development, that its starting point is a summit, than by leaving humanity alone in the world and allowing it to rule over a nature that is devoid of intelligence and feeling. (Espinas 1878: 155)

He attempts to convince his readers that the study of animals – both animal and human – comes with the remit of sociology. What is the relationship between the individual and the group? How can the individuality of the parts be reconciled with the whole? What sort of being is society?

Espinas is convinced that the experimental method and its 'admirable techniques' – he is citing Claude Bernard – can be applied to the object known as 'society'. He also believes that social science can be a guide to practice – and can answer such questions as 'Should the state play a more important role, or a lesser role? – but only after it has 'carefully' examined the facts and the laws that govern them; and that requires 'lengthy' research and 'long' discussions.

This is, Espinas admits, a point of view or doctrine that 'might offend some'. 'New tendencies' always meet with resistance, and sociology was still rejected in the name of moral conscience, either for metaphysical and religious reasons (the idea of Providence, or the idea that acts of God can influence society), or because of hostility to positivism. Espinas is trying to overcome prejudices, and to defend science's main findings: association or 'grouping together' is the general law of all life. Society is a 'natural being', or in other words a moral organism as well as a natural organism. Social life presupposes representation, and therefore consciousness. The social order is based upon consensus and the division of labour. The basis for humanity's gradual progress is evolution (and not revolution or dramatic turns of events) and the inevitability of progress.

Alfred Espinas has been described as a devout Lamarckian: he introduces into sociology the idea of a collective consciousness by likening society to a living organism. He did not, however, pursue that line of investigation. He did some research on psychology and studied the sense of colour and space, and also sleep and hysteria. He was interested in the history of ideas and doctrines, and devoted a lot of effort to map 'the state of European thought' by publishing a study, 'Experimental philosophy in Italy' (1880), and then translating Spencer's *Principles of Psychology* (1887) with the help of Théodule Ribot. In France, he was seen as a 'disciple' of Spencer, but was in fact representative of an uninterrupted French tradition from Comte onwards. He took his inspiration from 'the development of the evolutionist hypothesis' and was to 'help to redefine the general problems of sociology' (Durkheim 1975[1895b]: 90).

In 1882, Espinas published an article on sociological studies in France in the *Revue philosophique.* 'The moment has come for enlightened minds that are capable of virile work to rely upon precise data to justify their doctrines, and such data will soon be available on all points that matter to men of good will' (Espinas 1882: 366). Espinas was one of those thinkers who, in the aftermath of the Franco-Prussian war, set themselves the goal of 'regenerating' their country by putting politics on a scientific footing. In the preface to his *Histoire des doctrines politiques*, which he was writing at this time and which would be published in 1891, he describes the debate over social science, 'which will go on for a long time':

> Some see every society as no more than an encounter between the individualities that make it up: the individual or moral personality is both the starting point and the end point of all political, and therefore economic, relations: the individual enters society of his own free will, and rules it as he sees fit. Others believe that, on the contrary, society is an organism or living being, and that individuals play the role of that organism's cells, both in the sphere of rights, and in that of the interests that are, of necessity, subordinated to and sacrificed for the sake of the whole. (Espinas 1891: 13)

Individualism or socialism? Espinas raises the question in order immediately to reject both doctrines, at least in their absolute or radical form, on the grounds that they are 'agents of dissolution rather than ways to organize and promote peace'. They are 'unrealistic dreams and, besides, they are not productive from the economic point of view' (ibid.: 15). Espinas is particularly harsh on the revolutionary socialism of Karl Marx and dismisses his abstract arguments, naivety, retrograde aberrations and anarchism. Being a man of good will who takes his inspiration from the teachings of the social sciences, he argues the case for economic doctrines that are 'wisely subordinate to higher interests', meaning the love of justice, the fatherland and humanity, and, while he defends the idea of nationality, he believes it possible that 'states may accede to some form of economic unity and then political unity'. They will, he writes in his conclusion, be the 'future United States of Europe' (ibid.: 349).

Durkheim was very familiar with the work of Alfred Espinas, and cites him in his earliest writings. He regards him as a precursor and recognizes that he was 'the first to be drawn to sociology, and to define its positive nature and essential spirit' (Durkheim 1975[1895b]: 90). Durkheim felt a close kinship with Espinas, who was rather like an elder brother to him. They shared the same conception of 'social realism': 'It came to me directly from Comte, Spencer and Espinas' (Durkheim 1982[1907]: 259). That would not, however, prevent him from developing a critical attitude towards his colleague's theses.

The Bordeaux School

The friendship Durkheim struck up with Octave Hamelin was even more important. Born in 1856, Hamelin was educated at the Lycée Henri-IV and obtained his *licence-ès-lettres* [BA] in 1872; he taught at lycées in Foix and Pau before going to Bordeaux in 1884 to take up a chair that had been turned down by Henri Bergson. It took him a long time to write his thesis, *Essai sur les éléments principaux de la représentation*, and it was not until April 1907 that he defended it before a jury in Paris. The delay was due to his complete devotion to his teaching and his students. Durkheim speaks of his 'exclusive dedication' to teaching: 'he sacrificed his whole life to his students' (Durkheim 1975[1907c]: 428; see Némedi and Pickering 1995).

When Émile arrived in Bordeaux, Hamelin was teaching a final year course on the history of philosophy. He was a rather modest man who tended to hold honours in contempt, and his defining characteristic was his serious-mindednesss. That character trait was obviously to Durkheim's liking: 'He was a pure rationalist with an austere love of righteous reason, and the enemy of all dilettantism. In his view, thinking was the only serious thing in life. He combined 'the rigour of reason and a firmness of will' with 'a truly feminine tenderness and sensitivity' (Durkheim 1975[1911]: 433). And, just like Durkheim, he was a meticulous teacher who wrote out all his lectures in full. As Durkheim noted, Hamelin wrote them with the same care that he put into everything he did, but he wrote them as *lectures*, as though he were 'thinking as he stood before a future audience'. Hence the formulas and the expository techniques that no teacher can do without: frequent summaries, clear links between one lecture and the next, clearly marked divisions.

Octave Hamelin was a disciple of Charles Renouvier, the author of *Science de la morale* (1869). He was also a neo-critical philosopher identified with the *Année philosophique* group which, under the editorship of Edouard Pillion, was trying to develop a neo-Kantian theory of knowledge. Hamelin's *Eléments principaux de la représentation* was the product of 30 years of meditation and research. His major contribution was without doubt his theory of knowledge which, rejecting all forms of intuition and all transcendental reason, claimed to rely solely upon 'clear, precise and clearly-defined concepts'. Hamelin's ambition was to develop a system of categories based on the central idea that any representation is, like the world itself, a *relationship*. 'The simplest law of things,' he liked to say, 'is a relationship.' 'The world is a hierarchy of relationships.' The method he developed consisted in synthesizing antithetical notions in order to elaborate new ones such as time, number, space, causality, finality, and so on. His completely idealist philosophy constructs a priori categories; and while it is guided by experience, it claims to rise above all empiricism and positive sciences: 'The theory of knowledge is one thing, and psychology is another.' He frequently lectured on 'the main elements of representation'.

Durkheim had great admiration for his friend, who had 'his own way' of being a historian of philosophy: he combined the dogmatic method with the historical method by transforming both. The first studies doctrines from a strictly dogmatic point of view, 'as bodies of abstract propositions that exist outside such considerations as time and space, as though they were products of pure understanding'; the second takes into consideration society, time and the personality of authors'. 'No one was more concerned [than Hamelin] to give each [philosophical] system its local colour, and to reconstruct its internal economy, as conceived by its author. No one made a greater effort to situate them in historical terms' (Durkheim 1977[1911]: 434–7) The interesting feature of Hamelin's approach is that it contextualizes a given author's conceptions or solutions by looking at their historical context and above all attempts to see the 'resistance' that conception meets with, 'the difficulties with which it had to contend, the ways in which it strove to overcome them, the ways in which it felt its way, and even its failures'. Resistance, trial and error, failure and triumph: such, in Hamelin's view, was the history of ideas. Viewed in this way, the 'history of philosophy became', concluded Durkheim, 'a way of teaching philosophy' (ibid.: 435).

The new friends had many things in common. They were republican intellectuals who wanted to popularize an uncompromising rationalism; they wished to encourage the study of science and ethics. They had a sense of social justice, defended the republican education system and wanted to reconcile individualism and social solidarity. In 1894, they were joined by Louis-Georges Rodier, who was born in Bordeaux in 1864. Louis-Georges studied philosophy and law, and attended the lectures given by Hamelin and Espinas. The influence of Hamelin's teaching was to have

Table 5.1   Courses given by Durkheim at Bordeaux, 1887–1902[16]

	Public lectures on social science	Lectures on pedagogy
1887–88	Social solidarity	Not specified (moral education)[17]
1888–89	(1) The family, origins, main types (2) Ethics and morality in Kant's moral philosophy	Commentary on authors Educating the intellect
1889–90	Suicide	History of pedagogy Moral education
1890–91	Physiology of law and morals (the family)	French pedagogy (C18th–19th) and morals (the family) Intellectual education
1891–92	The Family (from the patriarchal family onwards)	Education and pedagogy in Antiquity Practical pedagogy
1892–93	Sociology of crime	Pedagogy in the 19th century Psychology applied to education
1893–94	Sociology of crime (cont'd) Punishment; responsibility; procedure	Psychology applied to education
	Tutorials for candidates for the *agrégation de philosophie*	
1894–95	Religion	Lectures on psychology
	Tutorials for candidates for the *agrégation de philosophie*	
1895–96	History of socialism (the family)	Lectures on psychology: the emotions, activity
	Tutorials for candidates for the *agrégation de philosophie*	
1896–97	General physics of morals and law	Lectures on psychology
	Tutorials for candidates for the *agrégation de philosophie*	
1897–98	General physics of morals and law	Lectures on psychology
	Tutorials for candidates for the *agrégation de philosophie*	
1898–99	General physics of morals and law (theory of obligation, sanctions and morality)	Moral education
	Tutorials for candidates for the *agrégation de philosophie*	
1899–1900	General physics of morals and law (punishment, responsibility) (Civic and professional morality; Domestic organization and domestic morality)	Moral education

Table 5.1   (*cont.*)

	Public lectures on social science	Lectures on pedagogy
	Tutorials for candidates for the *agrégation de philosophie*	
1900–01	Elementary forms of religion	Intellectual education
	Tutorials for candidates for the *agrégation de philosophie*	
1901–02	History of sociological doctrines	Psychology applied to education
	Tutorials for candidates for the *agrégation de philosophie*	

a lifelong influence on the form and direction taken by his philosophical activity.[18] Rodier obtained his philosophy *agrégation* in 1886, and then taught philosophy in lycées in Rochefort and Tarbes before defending his doctoral thesis, 'The physics of Strato of Lampsacus', in 1892. He was then appointed *maître de conférences* at the faculty of letters in Toulouse before returning to the town where he was born. Rodier was a historian of Greek philosophy with a specialist interest in Aristotle – in 1900 he published an edition of *De Anima*, with commentary – and Plato. Like Durkheim, he also taught pedagogy. Durkheim, Hamelin and Rodier: the team quickly became known as 'the Bordeaux school', and their 'reputation very quickly spread far beyond the Académie de Bordeaux'. They were all still under the age of 40, were of different religious confessions – Jewish, Protestant and Catholic – and soon went in very different directions; but they were all devotees of 'the cult of reason' and they shared a hostility towards philosophies of life and action, which they criticized on the grounds that they 'befuddled the mind'. In the last decade of the nineteenth century, philosophy in Bordeaux 'shone with an incomparable brightness' (Lacroze 1960–1: 617–18).

Classes and Lectures

The University of Bordeaux had asked Durkheim to teach 'social science and pedagogy', but he decided on his arrival there to separate the two topics, and to give public lectures on social science and a series of lectures on pedagogy. The course on pedagogy was at first given from 5 p.m. to 6 p.m. on Tuesdays and 4 p.m. to 5 p.m. on Thursdays, but was then transferred to Thursdays at 10–11 a.m. and 4–5 p.m. It was addressed to a restricted audience of primary school teachers (men and women), and then to degree and *agrégation* candidates. The lecture on social science was taught from 3.45 p.m. to 4.45 p.m. on Fridays and then moved to 4.15–5.15 p.m. on Saturdays. The fact that it was given on the day of the Sabbath did not appear to pose any problems for Durkheim. He had in fact little or no contact with the Jewish community in Bordeaux. In

March 1895, he was invited by Chief Rabbi Israël Lévi to give a lecture on Judaism, but it is unlikely that he gave it (Birnbaum 1971: 19).

The first two courses began at the beginning of November, and the third – on social science – at the beginning of December. Abandoning the seminar format he had experienced in Germany, Durkheim opted for the more traditional format of the lecture, which maintained the hierarchical relationship between teacher and students.

Opening Lecture on the Social Sciences

One Saturday in December 1887, the new and very nervous professor began to address his audience in a lecture theatre in the faculty of letters:

> Charged with the task of teaching a science born only yesterday, one which can as yet claim but a small number of principles to be definitively established, it would be rash on my part not to be awed by the difficulties of my task. Moreover, I make this avowal without difficulty or timidity. Indeed, I believe that there is room in our universities, beside those chairs from which established science and acquired truths are taught, for other courses in which the professor in part creates the science even as he is teaching it; in which his listeners are almost as much collaborators as pupils; in which they join him in searching, in feeling the way, and sometimes even in wandering astray. (Durkheim 1978[1888a]: 43)

Those were the first words of Durkheim's opening lecture on social science, which was devoted to sociology's 'initial problem': social solidarity. 'What are the bonds that unite men?'[19] The question, which had been nagging at him for some time, was to be the subject of his doctoral thesis.

There was everything to play for: there was still a lot of resistance to the idea of teaching sociology at university. Durkheim devotes his opening lecture to defending the title of his new course: his explicit intention is to help establish a new, positive science of society, or in other words not to ask 'what we must do' but to 'study that which exists'.

Durkheim begins by describing his approach. Having given a rapid expository account of the history of social science in the nineteenth century (Comte, Spencer, Espinas, German specialists such as Schäffle and Wagner), the new professor spells out his objectives: 'I shall show you the progress which has been made and that which remains to be accomplished' (1978[1888a]: 44). An account of his recent reading allows him to reformulate the ideas that are so dear to him and that will provide the framework for his sociological problematic: the idea of social laws and of the interdependence of social facts ('Social facts can only really be explained by other social facts'), the concept of society as a whole or organism, the notion of 'society's consciousness', the critique of linear and teleological evolutionism, the idea of social constraint (which restricts individual freedom at all times and in all places), and the sense of the complexity of things.

All the elements of a new problematic are here. Durkheim's lecture is in a sense sociology's birth certificate: sociology 'has a clearly defined object, and a method for studying it. The object consists of social facts. The method is observation and indirect experimentation, or, in other words, the comparative method'. The day of 'very synthetic minds' was over. 'We are entering into what Comte would have called the era of specialization.' Science was dividing and subdividing, and looking at 'increasingly determinate problems'; it was also becoming 'more objective, more impersonal, and, consequently, accessible to a variety of talents' (1978[1888a]: 62).

Durkheim explicitly avoids, or, to be more accurate and as he himself admits, 'it is better to do without[,] the facile pleasure of sketching in broad outline the plan of an entire science waiting to be created' (1978[1888a: 64). He adopts a more modest approach and lists the benefits in a few areas of research: the study of ideas and shared feelings (social psychology, the science of ethics and law, political economy). According to Durkheim, there is only one way to prove that movement is possible: 'Walk!' The only way to defend social science is therefore to 'continue the work that has begun', to take all the time that is needed, to proceed with caution, and to restrict the field of research as much as possible (to, for example, the study of the social functions of institutions).

The call went out to 'all workers of good will' (Durkheim 1978[1888a]: 62). Durkheim was to make the same appeal the following year: 'Let us proceed as quickly as possible and . . . let us unite our efforts and work in common' (Durkheim 1978[1888b: 228]). He had every intention of turning his classroom into a research laboratory as well as a place for transmitting knowledge. He could have paraphrased Zola's answer to Jules Huret's question about literary evolution: 'The future belongs to he, or they, who can understand the soul of modern society' (Zola, cited in Mitterrand 2002: 16).

By adopting this attitude, Durkheim made it clear that he was not one of those teachers or intellectual guides who come along to 'reveal a doctrine' or to 'offer ready-made solutions that will cure our modern societies of the ills that may affect them'. The task he sets himself is at once more modest and more ambitious: he believes that he can make himself useful by providing an introduction to social science for students from various disciplines (philosophy, history and law) and, at the level of the population as a whole, by educating public opinion. He declares that sociology's first duty is to educate: '[our science] can have a salutary influence on practice', especially in a country where 'the collective spirit has been weakened in us'. It is important to react in view of the exaggerated opinion everyone has of their 'sense of self' and the illusion that everyone has their own power:

> Our society must regain awareness of its organic unity. The individual must develop a sense for this social mass which envelops and penetrates him; he must sense it always near and active. And this sentiment must always rule his contact . . . I believe that sociology, more than any other

science, is in a position to restore these ideas. It is sociology which will make the individual understand what society is, how it completes him, and how little he really is when reduced to his own forces alone. It will teach him that he is not an empire embedded in another empire but the organ of an organism. It will show him all that is beautiful in conscientiously performing his role as an organ. It will make him feel that there is no diminution in being integrated with others and in depending on them, in not belonging quite entirely to himself. (Durkheim 1978[1888a]: 69)

Sociology therefore implies a political vision of change that is based upon solidarity, but it is quite different from collectivism. Durkheim makes that point clear when he describes the programme of his German counterpart Schäffle in the *Revue d'économie politique*: 'Its aim is not just to improve a situation of workers a little. It sets itself the higher goal of opposing, in a general way, the dispersive tendencies generated by the practice of individualism' (Durkheim 1975[1888]: 379).

He rejects collectivism, but is in favour of socialism. The philosopher-sociologist has a research programme, but it is also a political project. His ambition is to 'spread' his ideas amongst the 'lower strata' of the population, but only on condition, he is quick to point out, that those ideas are scientifically elaborated within the university. That is his 'principal concern', and 'I could know no greater joy than to achieve some measure of success in this attempt' (Durkheim 1978[1888a]: 70).

Pedagogy: A Practical Theory

Sociology infiltrated the university via pedagogy, a discipline with little scientific legitimacy, no noble past and no real institutional status. Its only legitimacy was 'social': the project for a scientific pedagogy was seen as a precondition for the rationalization of the educational system. Courses on pedagogy, which were established as part of a major educational reform, were designed the give future teachers a 'professional education' (Dumesnil 1888: 539). Every week, Durkheim had to devote some of his time to 'advancing' pedagogy, a discipline that was 'more practical than sociology, but basically less essential even though it is of primordial public interest' (Mauss 1969[1925]: 486). Pedagogy was neither a science nor an art, but a 'methodical and well-documented way of thinking' that was designed to inform the practice of teaching. As Durkheim would later say, it was something 'intermediate' between science and art. 'When I described it as a practical theory, I was trying to capture its intermediate nature' (Durkheim 1956[1922]: 102).

Durkheim quickly proved himself to be competent in this new field. He attached the greatest importance to his lectures on pedagogy, not only as a scholar but also as a citizen. He was certainly, as Paul Fauconnet wrote, 'hostile to reformist agitation, which disturbs without improving, above all to negative reforms, which destroy without replacing, he had, however, a feeling and a taste for action' (in Durkheim 1956: 39). Well aware that he was speaking to educators, he tried to give his lectures an 'immediately practical' character, and his choice of topics reflected the problems they regularly encountered in their work. It is true, as he himself admitted, that he scarcely had time to pursue purely speculative research.

Some 15 students attended his lectures on a regular basis. They formed a sympathetic group, full of energy and enthusiasm. 'A fairly large number of them were students and educated individuals', remarked Durkheim. But according to the Inspector-General's report, they did experience some difficulties: the students did not in fact appear to be very assiduous and it was only with 'great difficulty' that they succeeded in writing essays. Durkheim was still convinced of 'the interest and effectiveness of his influence on them'. His elocution was 'confident and flowing', and his public lectures were 'excellent, very good'. The young *chargé de cours* succeeded in having 'a significant impact on the primary school teachers (both men and women), and his lectures were very helpful to them'.[20]

It was not until later that teaching became a burden. Durkheim's activities became fragmented and unfocused. He found that he was forced 'to break off his favourite studies – those in which he felt he had sole responsibility and was ahead of anyone else – to concentrate on less urgent and less grandiose tasks'. That did not, however, prevent him from doing his job 'honourably and conscientiously', and Marcel Mauss speaks of his 'real devotion'. He brought to the teaching of pedagogy 'the same wit, the same originality and the same personal input – in as positive a manner as he did everything' (Mauss 1969[1925]: 486).

There is no record of the content of Durkheim's first lecture course on pedagogy. In the second year, he restricted himself to critical analysis, and then embarked upon a new project: educating the mind (or intellectual education). This was obviously a topic that was of interest to the teacher of philosophy: he returned to it in 1890–1, and on several other occasions (1900–1, 1905–6, 1910–11). The lectures were, according to Mauss, 'at times powerfully original', but 'less complete or thorough than some other courses'. This was because Durkheim had not yet developed his theory about the social origins of *reason* and had not really had 'time to think about how science could be articulated with practice' (Mauss 1969[1926]: 486). Durkheim himself was not entirely satisfied and 'found it difficult to reach an acceptable level of formulation in this work', as Paul Fauconnet put it (in Durkheim 1956[1922]: 46).

The course on pedagogy was like a vast building project, and Durkheim allowed himself several years to reach his objective. His goal was to study in turn the ways in which various subjects were taught: mathematics and the categories of number and form; physics and the notion of reality; geography and the notion of a planetary environment; history and the notions of historical duration and development. The list is incomplete, as Durkheim would also deal in following years with the use of languages to teach logic. And while he did discuss educating the mind (1889–90) and 'intellectual education' (1890–1), he also touched upon various other topics, including the general development of the memory, the culture of perceptions, various types of representation and culture of the main faculties (attention, judgement and reasoning), the evolution of the intellect in children, the disciplines, history, and so on (Halbwachs 1977[1938]: xi).

Durkheim also dealt directly with the issue of moral education in these lectures, especially during the 1889–90 academic year, but then abandoned that topic and did not return to it for another nine years. At roughly the same time – 1890–1 – he devoted his lectures on sociology to the physiology (or general physics) of morals and law. He dealt with the issues of professional ethics (relations with professional bodies), civic ethics (relations with the state), and men's general duties towards one another (respect for life, property and honour). He then abandoned that topic too for a few years, but returned to it in 1895–6 in his course on ethics. At this point, he wrote up his lectures, but then rewrote them and introduced some major changes in 1898–1900. No version of the first series of lectures has survived, but some of the content was reworked for those sections of *The Division of Labour in Society* that deal with sanctions and regulatory power. While it was only later that Durkheim developed his civic and professional ethics, in these lectures he was already discussing the anomic state of societies and the need for professional organization.

Durkheim quickly added, finally, a historical dimension to his lecture of pedagogy: 'The history of pedagogy' (1889–90) and 'French pedagogy in the eighteenth and nineteenth centuries' (1890–1). The series of lectures continued until 1904, and dealt with both the history of pedagogic doctrines and the history of secondary education in France. It was, said Marcel Mauss, 'a discontinuous history because it did not at once paint a picture of the development of educational institutions and of pedagogic ideas' (Mauss 1969[1925]: 478; see also Mauss 1969[1937]). As with his other lectures, Durkheim put in a lot of effort. He was a conscientious teacher, and a good one. He did not simply want to acquit himself of a task that had been forced on him; it was one part of the human sciences (and one of their essential practical applications) and it was, in his view, worth putting all his efforts into it. He also felt that it was what was expected of him by his superior Louis Liard, who wanted those who were preparing for a career in secondary education to know where their duty lay and to understand the issues surrounding teaching and pedagogy.

An Overwhelming Task

Academic life had its joys, but Durkheim had few illusions. As he puts it in *The Division of Labour in Society* (1984[1893]: 187): 'Thought is undoubtedly a source of happiness, one that can be very acute. On the other hand, how many joys are disturbed by it! For one problem solved, how many questions are raised to which there is no answer! For one doubt cleared up, how many mysteries do we perceive that disconcert us!' And then there was boredom, 'that torment of the cultivated mind'.

Frightened of the scale of his task, the newly appointed lecturer worked from morning to night. In his 'great eagerness' to make a success of his lectures, he wrote them out in their entirety, even taking the pains to write them in complete sentences. 'An overwhelming task', said his nephew:

> Each lecture was perfectly formed. These were no notes. These were complete lectures and classes. Each lecture followed on from the last, and every part was so articulated as to form a sustained argument. Every phrase was carefully thought out. Each page involved making count-less drafts covered in hieroglyphs, and Durkheim would unhesitatingly throw them into the wastepaper basket until he felt that he had arranged his facts and ideas into a logical order . . . It was a new task, and the task was overwhelming. Week after week, and with astonishing and crushing regularity, he had to come up with new intellectual material that was not only worked up with a view to telling the truth but also designed for a very broad audience. Durkheim never faltered. (Mauss 1969[1925]: 483–5)

The uncertainty was also a source of anxiety. The young teacher was 'basically on his own, with no support'.

Durkheim had some problems during his first year. The audience for his lectures on social science was at first 'quite large', but then 'thinned out a lot'. What was going on? 'It is not surprising', noted Inspector Zeller, 'that [Durkheim] has not yet succeeded, despite his detailed studies and dem-onstrations of good will.' Teaching a new subject was 'very difficult', and the new lecturer appeared not to have mastered his subject, even though he seemed to 'have made a conscientious study' of the books in his field. It was, according to the Inspector-General, only a matter of time and experi-ence: Durkheim would learn to 'introduce greater clarity, accuracy and soundness into his interesting classes'.[21]

The rector did not take the same harsh view of a colleague who was just beginning his career in higher education, and was very pleased to find that his new recruit 'had a distinguished mind, an original style, and is very familiar with a field of study of which we know little here in Bordeaux'. Durkheim was, he concluded, a teacher who would have a 'good influence on the faculty'.[22]

The situation changed in his second year, when Durkheim enjoyed 'great success'. Even some of the staff from the law faculty attended his lectures on social science, which had been renamed 'sociology'. There were a few student philosophers from the faculty of letters, but also 'jurists, law students, a few colleagues; this was quite a demanding audience', noted Mauss (1969[1925]: 484). Not to mention 'all the stray members of the public who pack into the lecture theatres of our big provincial universi-ties'. Durkheim succeeded, 'with huge effort, in simultaneously teaching two official courses that were both difficult for a young lecturer: one on pedagogy, and another on social science'. And what was more, he satisfied 'both the schoolteachers and those who were curious about sociology' thanks to 'the force and novelty of his teaching'. Already seen as a 'master', this 'young and highly valued young scholar' was, according to the rector, a 'zealous teacher who has a very great influence on his students . . . No lecturer works harder or gives more of himself', so much so that he was in danger of damaging his health.[23]

Durkheim's reputation as 'an admirable lecturer' was spreading. It was not just that his lectures 'could not have been clearer', remarked someone who heard him lecture in Bordeaux (Lacroze 1961–1: 63): 'He was deeply attached to his profession, and fearlessly accepted the constraints of his profession, even when they distracted him from his research.' Durkheim spoke clearly and introduced concrete data, such as the official statistics on suicide; he was very eloquent, but remained rigorous and attempted to convince rather than to persuade, appealing 'not so much to the emotions as to reason' (Delprat 1900: 357). Durkheim was a 'wonderful teacher' and attempted to be both a 'seeker after the scientific truth and an effective teacher'. Meeting such contradictory demands was, noted his nephew, 'very hard' (Mauss 1969[1925: 484–5).[24]

Durkheim's students included Marcel Mauss, Charles Lalo, Paul Hourticq, Abel Aubin, André Darbon, Albert Léon,[25] Georges Grenier, Gustave Périsson, Léon Duguit, Marcel Cachin,[26] and Alfred Alengry.[27] His audience also included Nikolaï Roussanov (1859–1939), a 30-year-old Russian student who attended Durkheim's lectures from October 1888 to the summer of 1890: 'His lectures were rich because of the data – ethnographic, historical, and statistical – on which his theories were based.' An active member of the populist movement, and subsequently of the Social Revolutionary Party, Roussanov had fled from the Tsarist regime and spent several years in France. In 1895, he published a major article on *The Division of Labour in Society*.[28]

Some of Durkheim's students later took a more active interest in sociology. Marcel Mauss is the obvious example, but Charles Lalo,[29] Paul Hourticq[30] and Abel Aubin all displayed the same interest.[31] They were all from relatively modest petit-bourgeois backgrounds and were awarded grants to go to university; their academic careers were not always linear. They all attended Durkheim's lectures between 1890 and 1898, saw the publications of *The Rules of Sociological Method* and *Suicide,* and, as Mauss puts it, 'came under the master's sway, admired his erudition, and praised his loyalty and genius' (Mauss 1969[1925]: 484–5).

Religion: A Sociological Phenomenon

Having already published his report on German philosophy and his article on the science of ethics in Germany, the new *maître de conférences* published another review in *La Revue philosophique* in 1887. His seventh contribution to Théodule Ribot's journal in under three years was a review of *L'Irréligion de l'avenir* (1975[1887]),[32] which was subtitled 'A sociological study'. Its author was Jean-Marie Guyau (1854–88), a prolific philosopher who had enjoyed early success. He had already published two books on ethical and religious issues: *Morale anglaise* and *Esquisse d'une morale sans obligation ni sanction* (1884).[33]

It was, exclaimed Durkheim, 'a fine book' and 'an important step forward in the scientific study of religions'. What was more, it adopted a sociological approach: 'Religion is wholly, or for the most part, a sociological phenomenon . . . and in order to study it we must first take up a sociological position. . . . That is what is new about this book' (Durkheim 1975[1897]: 160).

There was nothing new about Durkheim's interest in religion, and he had expressed a wish in the previous year's 'Etudes récentes en science sociale' to study it as a 'social phenomenon'. To no avail. Religion was still seen merely to do with 'individual consciousness' and as a 'product of the individual imagination'. Once the almost exclusive preserve of theologians, religion was now a 'territory within the science of man – anthropology'.

His reading of Guyau made one thing clear to Durkheim: everything to do with religion is a matter of obligation and involves sanctions. A religion is a set of prescriptions, and they are obligatory. He refers to his own experience: 'The Christian who for the first time eats a normal meal on Good Friday, and the Jew who for the first time eats pork, both experience a remorse that it is impossible to distinguish from moral remorse' (Durkheim 1975[1897]: 161). If there is one point of view that Durkheim refuses to accept, it is pure 'intellectualism', and he criticizes Guyau for adopting the viewpoint of 'cultivated minds' and ignoring what 'most people' think. All this was pure speculation or reflexive thought: 'The life of the psyche has as its goal action: it must adapt to the surrounding physical or social environment' (ibid.: 164). There are two sides or levels to Durkheim's argument: on the one hand, a theory of society that makes allowance for the obligatory nature of life in society and for social obligations, and, on the other, a theory of action that reveals the practical, even non-reflexive, nature of human action (in ordinary life, at least).

Guyau predicts the end of religion and the victory of science, and describes 'religious anomie' as the ideal of all religions, rather as though the purpose of religion was to abolish religion. What does he mean by 'anomie'? Being a Hellenist, Guyau was familiar with the word, which means iniquity, injustice or disorder, but he gives it a different meaning that has no negative connotations: anomie is the result of an inevitable process: the gradual individualization of moral rules, and of criteria for behaviour and belief. It means, in other words, that the individual is set free by the suppression of all dogmatic faiths. In his earlier *Esquisse d'une morale sans obligation ni sanction*, Guyau had advocated moral anomie as a moral ideal: morale anomie meant that there were no set or universal rules.

Durkheim, for his part, refused to take such a simplistic view: 'It is not with the aid of logic that we shall stamp out faith' (1975 [1897]: 164). Men would always share a religious faith.

Forms of Sociability: The Family

During the 1888–9 academic year, Durkheim's course on social science (now described as a course of sociology) abandoned the great theme of solidarity, even though it meant so much to him, in favour of more specific topics such as the family. His first course of lectures on the family was entitled 'The physiology of law and morals'. 'It is a little crude', he said when he rewrote it in its entirety and then made it available to his collaborators.[34] Durkheim was now more confident, as he no longer had to introduce or defend his discipline: sociology was no longer 'something foreign' to his students. Once the initial results of his research had been published, he felt ready to deal with 'more particular' problems. His first lecture was published in the *Annuaire de la faculté des lettres de Bordeaux* under the title: 'The family: origins and main types'.

At the same time, Durkheim was also teaching a course on Kant's ethics and philosophy of law. There was nothing new about the association between the family and ethics, but the reference to ethnography and sociology was new. To that extent, the young philosophy lecturer might be said to be adopting an approach similar to that of the doctor-anthropologist Charles Letourneau, whose *Évolution de la morale* and *Évolution du mariage et de la famille* were published in 1887 and 1888 respectively. Durkheim was very familiar with Letourneau's work, and cited him in his lectures. It represented, he would say a few years later, 'a considerable amount of work'. He was also critical of it. It was 'hasty work': Letourneau provided catalogues of facts and lists of documents, but his analysis was either non-existent or fanciful. The main problem was that of sources: 'A sociologist who bases his work exclusively or mainly on travellers' tales is in danger of being accused of being fanciful' (Durkheim 1975[1895b]: 78).

Distrustful of such documentary evidence, Durkheim warned his students against the a priori and prejudices that inform the observations of travellers, and even against the statements of those they observed, insisting that they should adopt a critical approach to source material. They should 'discard these narrative accounts and descriptions. They may have literary intent, or even moral authority, but they are not the sort of material which science can usefully employ.' He illustrates his argument thus: 'A traveller visits some country. He comes into contact with a certain number of families in which he observes . . . a fairly large number of facts regarding conjugal devotion and filial piety'. He concludes from this that the family is quite strongly unified. Can we accept a conclusion grounded in this way? To do so would be to expose ourselves to 'serious errors' (Durkheim 1978[1888b]: 212). His first methodological rule states that we must avoid individual observations, and look only at 'those ways of acting which have been consolidated by habit of by what we call custom, law, and mores' (ibid.: 214).

Why was Durkheim interested in the family? Because it was, he said, 'the simplest group of all, the one whose history is most ancient' (Durkheim 1978[1888b]: 207). It was as though he was already carrying out research on 'origins' and 'elementary forms'. The family was also an institution that was in crisis, and that worried the young sociologist, who believed, as he told Georges Davy, in 'the need for it' and its 'benign influence'. He was afraid of anything that might disrupt or undermine the family. He regarded the family as the classic moral focus where all the basic virtues were learned: 'respect for duty, the taste of justice, and the habit of altruism'. The family was already one of his 'favourite' objects of study (Davy 1919: 198b).

It was obviously not easy to discuss the question of the family, 'which is so close to us'. Having recently become a father, Durkheim was well aware of that. 'We cannot keep our emotions from impinging'. He therefore advised researchers to adopt an attitude of 'perfect sincerity' and to rid their minds of any prejudices, 'both optimistic and pessimistic'. He himself approached his research only with a 'profound sense of the complexity' of the subject (Durkheim 1978[1888b]: 218–19).

The objective Durkheim set himself in his lectures and in his research on the family was to establish and classify the main types of family, and he intended to do this 'preparatory work' in the first year. His ambition, however, was to find the causes that determined the appearance of these different types in order to explain 'the contemporary European family'. Although his perspective was evolutionist and took as its starting point 'the families of previous ages', there was no question of establishing a hierarchy of forms. For Durkheim, historical relativism was a matter of principle: 'What is good for one is, therefore, not necessarily good for another. . . . Today's family is neither more nor less perfect than that of yesterday; it is different because circumstances are different' (Durkheim 1978[1888b]: 219).

The approach adopted by Durkheim, who was already well informed about the work that had been done in this area, was to 'collect a large body of facts' (1978[1888b]: 212), including figures and statistical data. Much of his 'Introduction to the sociology of the family' deals with questions of methodology, the comparative method and sources of information (ethnography, history and demography). He advises his students: 'Do not rest content with giving your students a general idea' (ibid.: 222). He gives the example of suicide: 'A few well-chosen statistics on the relationship of this morbid phenomenon with civil status . . . will be infinitely more instructive than the traditional dissertation on the legitimacy or illegitimacy of suicide' (ibid.: 222).

Durkheim establishes – 'with certainty' – a distinction between 'two grand social types of which all societies, past and present, are but variations' (1978[1888b] 205): on the one hand, 'unorganized, amorphous' societies, which 'range from the primitive horde of related individuals to the city', and, on the other, 'states, properly so called, which begin with the city and end with the great nations of the present day' (ibid.: 206). Durkheim uses the words 'inferior' and 'superior' to describe these types of society, but does not organize them into a hierarchy. Each type of society has a corresponding and 'very different' form of solidarity or sociability. *Mechanical solidarity* is due to a 'similarity of consciousnesses' and a community of ideas and feelings, whereas *organic solidarity* is a product of the differentiation of functions and the division of labour (ibid.: 206). The simultaneous increase in the size and density of societies is, in Durkheim's view, the great difference between modern nations and those of the past: 'the intensity of the struggle grows with the number of combatants' and 'the division of labour . . . becomes the primary condition of social equilibrium' (ibid.: 207). We have here elements of the problematic that Durkheim was to develop in his thesis on the division of labour in society, which, according to information subsequently supplied by Marcel Mauss, he was rewriting at this time. He had drawn up an outline plan in 1884, and had already written a first draft in 1886 (Mauss 1962[1928]: 32–3).

Marriage and Inheritance

In the following year, Durkheim did not deal with the question of the family, but returned to 'The physiology of law and morals (the family)' in 1890–1, and 'The family (from the patriarchal family onwards)' in 1891–2. It was not until much later that he wrote anything more than a few book reviews on the subject. But, as Mauss noted, the family was, together with ethics, Durkheim's 'favourite work' (Mauss 1969[1925]: 480). Speaking of his 'as yet unpublished' lecture on the family, Émile explained that it provided him with an opportunity to 'apply [his] methodology' (Durkheim 1975[1895c]: 70).

In 1892, Louise gave birth to a second son, André, in the tenth arrondissement in Paris. His second name was Armand (after his maternal uncle). He had no Jewish forename. We do not know if he was circumcised in accordance with the Jewish tradition. This was the archetypal conjugal family: husband, wife and two children. This would be the new reality that Durkheim discussed at the very end of his lecture course in April 1892. The previous lecture dealt with the paternal family, or the domestic institution of the Germanic peoples (as opposed to the patriarchal Roman family). Durkheim's approach was based on evolution: a long process of evolution led, in the case of the most civilized peoples of modern Europe, to the *conjugal family*: husband, wife and children who were minors and unmarried. The great change was, in Durkheim's view, the collapse of 'the old familial communism' (1978[1888b]: 233). Then there was the ever-increasing intervention of the state into the internal life of the family: orphaned minors could be taken into care, courts could strip fathers of their rights, and marriage was subject to regulations (Durkheim 1978[1892]).

This was a phenomenon of *contraction*: 'The family must necessarily contract as the social milieu, with which every individual is in direct relationship, extends further' (1978[1892]: 232). Durkheim was quite happy to speak of a general law which had already been observed in biology: the increase in individualization is proportional to the expansion of the social environment – from the village, the city state and the nation to our vast modern societies – in which we are all dependent upon one another.

As the family changes, domestic solidarity changes too: the ties that bind individuals to the family are now more personal (father, mother, etc.) than economic (things or domestic property). 'Things cease, to an ever greater extent, to act as a cement for domestic society' (Durkheim 1978 [1892]: 234). How can we 'get out of this crisis'? asks Durkheim. We must begin by finding a remedy for one social injustice that is becoming increasingly intolerable, or even irreconcilable with our modern societies' conditions of existence: the transmission of inherited wealth. A combination of factors is undermining the right of inheritance, even in its testamentary form, and this is one way of making individuals more equal. Social inequalities are, in other words, now justifiable only if they are determined by the personal value of the individual rather than by some external cause such as hereditary wealth.

What should we leave to our children? According to Durkheim, who had recently become a father, the possibility of passing on the fruits of one's labour by hereditary means has become 'our prime motive for doing anything'. He is not suggesting that the pursuit of personal goals is all that matters: 'The individual is not an end sufficient unto himself. When he looks for purpose within himself, he falls into the state of moral misery which leads him to suicide' (1978[1892]: 236). Durkheim had already given one lecture on suicide, and he believed in the virtues of the family: 'What binds us to our work is the fact that it is our means of enriching the domestic patrimony, of increasing the well-being of our children. If this prospect were withdrawn, this extraordinarily powerful and moral stimulant would be taken away as well' (ibid.). But is that 'stimulant' enough? It was not, according to Durkheim for those 'civil servants, soldiers, and scholars who give the state a purely recompensed life of labour' (ibid.: 270n). Their work brings them only 'honour and respect', and those qualities cannot be passed on in hereditary fashion. This was, to some extent, the position Durkheim found himself in: he was one of those 'workers' who 'can no longer transmit to their children the fruits of their labour' (1978[1892]: 235).

What remains when neither self-interest, economic interest, conjugal love nor love of one's family can provide a real incentive? It is, Durkheim believes, possible to set oneself higher goals and to discover a 'social interest' that is neither too remote nor too impersonal. He is thinking here of occupational groups.

> In my view, only [the occupational group] can succeed the family in the economic and moral functions, which the family is becoming more and

more incapable of fulfilling. To extricate ourselves from the state of crisis which we are passing through, the suppression of the role of hereditary transmissions is not enough. Men must gradually be bound to professional life and must establish strong groups of this kind. (Durkheim 1978[1892]: 238)

Domestic solidarity must, in other words, give way to the broader solidarity of the occupational group. This was, said Mauss, one of Durkheim's 'most general and most profound ideas' – first elaborated as early as 1889, it was 'one of the ideas he held most dear' (1969[1925]: 502).

Durkheim ends his final lecture with an outright condemnation of cohabitation or *union libre* (which the anarcho-syndicalist groups were defending at his time), which he defines as a conjugal association in which there are no obligations, and which therefore 'disturbs the public order'. A society that tolerates cohabitation is, in his view, 'an immoral society'. 'And that is why children reared in such conditions present such great numbers of moral flaws. It is because they have not been reared in a moral environment' (1978[1892]: 239). He expresses the hope that the 'legislator' would examine the problem and rule that marriage is the only form of union.

On the one hand, marriage, the family and kinship; on the other, the right to inherit, professional solidarity and cohabitation. Durkheim's study of the family takes him not only to the heart of scientific debates that were central to anthropology; it also involves him in political controversy. The very fact of taking on marriage and inheritance, which are society's central institutions, as objects of study is in itself an assault on the status quo. While Durkheim may seem to be 'open to change' when it comes to the question of inheritance, his views on the marriage question remain somewhat 'conservative'.

What were his views on the education of children? He was not only a theorist: at home, he was also a practical pedagogue. His son André was not sent to school, and spent the first 10 years of his life at home. A few hours of work a day gave little André 'the elementary knowledge it takes so long to acquire in our classrooms'. Durkheim himself taught his son Latin at a very early age, and gave him lessons in algebra and geometry. Those lessons awakened in his son 'such a lively curiosity that he looked for them as real objects of curiosity' (Durkheim 1975[1917]: 446).

'Happiness Is Such a Relative Thing'

Durkheim had already developed a great interest in the question of suicide. He discussed it in his lectures, and then devoted an article and an entire course to the subject in 1889–90. He appears to have been greatly affected by the recent death of his friend Victor Hommay. Hommay's death was accidental, but it could have been suicide, even though there are no grounds for thinking that he was contemplating taking his own life.[35] The number of suicides had been rising steadily for some 10 years, with the annual average rising from 5,276 cases in 1871–5 to more than 8,000 in 1886. The murder rate was rising too. 'How strange!' exclaimed Edmond Villey. But was there any cause to be surprised? he asked himself. In his view, the explanation lay in the demise of spiritual beliefs: the here and now was the only thing that mattered, and everyone wanted at all cost to enjoy things that the vast majority could not afford (Villey 1888).[36]

The article Durkheim published in the *Revue philosophique* was enigmatically entitled 'Suicide and the birth rate', and subtitled 'A study in moral statistics'. For the first time, Durkheim now undertook a statistical analysis of the data supplied by various studies (Morselli in Italy; Bertillon, Legoyt and Yvernès in France). He was, as Mauss later noted (1997[1928]: 742), gradually turning away from philosophy and had found the data and studies that would provide 'the raw materials he needed to elaborate the method that was to emerge from its applications'.

When it came to the management of social problems ranging from depopulation to public health and even 'the worker question', statistics, and especially population statistics, were becoming more and more indispensable. In 1879, the Ville de Paris opened a Bureau de statistique municipale and appointed Louis Adolphe Bertillon as its director. The first *Annuaire statistique de la ville de Paris* was published in 1882. It included a systematic comparison of the death rates, birth rates and marriage rates for Paris and for France as a whole. The Société statistique de Paris, founded in 1880, experienced a 'new lease' of life under the chairmanship of Émile Cheysson in the 1880s: public lectures were organized and an annual prize was awarded.[37] The society's plans included the establishment of a central commission on statistics. The Conseil supérieur des statistiques was established in 1885. One of its goals was to improve the collection of statistical data about the population. Its members included, as well as Émile Cheysson, statisticians who had actively promoted their discipline, such as Émile Levasseur, Maurice Block, who was the author of *Un Traité théorique et pratique de statistique* (1878), Toussaint Loua and Jacques Bertillon.[38]

There was a new interest in statistics on both the left and the right. As the socialist Auguste Chirac put it, 'words confuse; figures shed light' (1905: 8).[39] The declining population was a problem that preoccupied everyone. Although it was generally agreed that the decline was a fact, there was no consensus as to its causes, or how to remedy the problem. Did the explanation lie in a fall in the number of births or a fall in infant mortality? Was the birth rate falling faster amongst married or unmarried women? Which social groups were 'responsible' for the falling birth rate? Most analyses ended by discussing the decline of civilization, the rise of individualism and egoism, and the declining influence of religion. The new statistical discipline of demography was making an increasingly indispensable contribution to the elaboration of family policy measures: scientific analyses made it possible to rationalize and justify the actions of the legislators. The new experts were to succeed in making the birth rate the most important question on the politico-administrative agenda (Lenoir 2003).

There is no obvious correlation between the family and suicide, but some themes are more closely related than it might seem. For Durkheim, both the suicide rate and the birth rate were indicators of 'social happiness'. This was a fragile happiness that could not, in his view, be guaranteed solely by wealth or increased resources (which led to an increase in consumer goods), and it could at any moment be easily destroyed by social disturbances. There were therefore healthy societies and sick societies, and Durkheim had no hesitations about saying so. The great difficulty lay in 'establishing a society's degree of happiness with any accuracy'. It was, he thought, easier to make 'a comparative estimate of its state of health or illness'. The increase in the number of 'abnormal acts' such as suicides was, in his view, an expression of 'social discontent', and a sign that 'society's organic conditions had been seriously disturbed'.

What of rising or falling birth rates? Could a very low birth rate be seen as 'causing damage to society' or as a 'social evil'? Some did take that view: public opinion, on both the left and the right of the political spectrum, was worried about the (temporary) fall in the birth rate observed in France at this time. According to the founder of the Alliance pour l'accroissement de la population française [Society for the growth of the French population], it was a sign that France had become decadent. Many books were published on this issue, addressed not only to specialists but also to the general public. In 1896, Georges Rossignol, who taught at the lycée in Bordeaux, published a book entitled *D'un pays de célibataires et de fils uniques* ['On a country of bachelors and only sons']. It was an immediate bestseller.

The approach adopted by Durkheim consisted in establishing, with figures to hand, a correlation between the rise in the number of suicides, on the one hand, and changes in the birth rate on the other: 'These two social facts vary in inverse proportion to each other' (Durkheim 1992[1888]: 184).[40] A law had been established, but it had yet to be interpreted: if the variations in the two phenomena were proportional, the cause must be social or moral. Those causes were, in Durkheim's view, the decline of domesticity and loneliness, or, in other words, 'regression in terms of domestic feelings'. 'Domestic solidarity' explained everything: 'Where families are smaller, weaker, less fertile, individuals, being less close to each other, leave gaps between them through which there blows the icy blast of egoism, chilling the heart and breaking the spirit' (1992[1888]: 195).

'Domestic society', or in other words the family, has, according to Durkheim 'beneficial properties', and they are not restricted to the economic advantages it has to offer. It provides access to what he calls 'the pleasures of a shared life'. 'Utilitarian calculation' does not explain everything; there are also such things as 'social feelings'. Durkheim organizes his study of social life around an opposition between 'material wealth' and 'the joys of collective life', which broadly corresponds to an opposition between egoism and altruism. 'Social interest' or altruism finds its political expression in attachment to the group.

The Critique of Economics

Durkheim was corresponding with his German colleague Schäffle who, ever since the publication of Benôit Malon's *Quintessence du socialisme*, had always been identified in France with collectivism. That impression was mistaken, and Durkheim set out to correct it. At the beginning of 1888, he published a 'sort of programme' (in 11 points) in the *Revue d'économie politique*. It had been sent to him in confidence by Schäffle, and it summarized his economic doctrine (Durkheim 1975[1888]: 378).

This was Durkheim's first and only contribution to the journal, which was founded in 1887. Its editorial secretary Léon Duguit was a colleague who taught in the faculty of law at Bordeaux. Its real editor was in fact Charles Gide, who taught in the Montpellier faculty of law and who was very active in the cooperative movement. Gide was his own man. He saw his journal as 'a weapon in the battle against liberalism', and wanted to use it to promote the very different doctrines of interventionism, socialism and solidarism. He succeeded in winning the support of his friend Léon Walras of the Académie de Lausanne. Everyone on the journal had a strong feeling that France was going through a difficult period.

Political economy was undergoing a revival. New journals were appearing both in Europe and in the United States, where *The Economic Journal* began publication in 1891, followed by the *Journal of Political Economy* in 1893. There was even a weekly *L'Économiste français* (1873), which brought fame to its founder Paul Leroy-Beaulieu, author of a five-volume *Traité théorique et pratique d'économie politique*.[41] The discussions, which could be highly animated, had to do with the individualist nature of *homo oeconomicus*.

Why did Durkheim agree to contribute to the *Revue d'économie politique*? For two reasons: first, he and Duguit knew each other well and, second, the journal might have been designed with him in mind. It was 'freely open to all doctrines' and 'welcomed all studies of the science without any discrimination, the only proviso being that they had to be inspired only by the scientific spirit'.[42] The first volumes carried articles on wages in the nineteenth century, the value of money, the notion of value in Bastiat, socialism in the United States, and reviews of books by authors as diverse as Walras and Spencer. Third, although it was not associated with any particular school – it had 'neither a flag nor a master' – the *Revue d'économie politique* attached great importance to the work of the new German school (variously described as 'historical' or 'socialist') that Durkheim had discovered during his stay in Germany. Since 1880, the new school's intellectual leader had been Gustav von Schmoller, professor in Strasbourg from 1872 to 1882 before moving to Berlin, and also editor of what had come to be known as *Schmoller's Jahrbuch*.

In his first editorial column, Charles Gide made no secret of his sympathy for the new school. Its emergence was, in his view, 'one of the great events of our age' (Gide 1887: 85).[43] He clearly explained the differences between the new school and the 'old school', which was also known as the 'classical, orthodox or dogmatic school', or the Manchester school (a school which, although increasingly theoretical and deductive, laid claim to being an 'economic science'). The first difference was methodological: the schools differed, in the same way that bird's eye views or general formulations differed from the observation of the facts themselves. They also have different conceptions of the economy: the old school believes in a 'natural order' that is established by certain basic laws – the laws of the market, and of supply and demand – and describes those laws as timeless and universal. The new school regards economic facts as historical phenomena; they are therefore contingent products of the social environment. The slogan of the new historical school was: 'Everything is relative, and only the relative is absolute.' The schools also had different views of the role of the state: the classical school was opposed to state intervention, while the historical school held that state intervention could be effective, and that it was necessary if the fate of the working classes was to be improved and if the era of social justice was to be ushered in. From that point of view, the state could take on important economic functions (the postal service, roads), act in a regulatory capacity (regulating markets, including the stock market) and promote education and culture.

Those who published in the *Revue d'économie politique* were disassociating themselves from (classical) economics; they were also distancing themselves from the most important French economic journal of the day: the *Journal des économistes*, which celebrated its 50th anniversary in 1891. Its editor-in-chief Gustave de Molinari was an ultraliberal and a supporter of social Darwinism, and he had serious reservations about the 'new authoritarian school' (or 'socialism of the lectern'). In his view, such an approach was simply dangerous.

The *Revue d'économie politique* published Schäffle's work for two reasons. It wanted to draw attention to the German school, which had so far been given a 'cool reception' in France, even though some economists already regarded its views as 'productive', and its 'methodology' as 'reliable'. It also wanted to 'establish scientific relations' between French and German universities. Durkheim had more than one reason to be interested in Schäffle, whom he regarded as a sociologist working in the tradition of Comte and Spencer. Schäffle was critical of the Marxist theory of value and of the idea of revolution, and was in favour of 'social reform, defined in a positive sense'. He did not rule out state intervention when it was needed, but had no illusions about legislators' ability to influence reality, which often proved to be less easy and less profound than one might think. When he spoke of 'socialism', he did not mean state socialism. Schäffle proposed 'the legally binding union of many branches of industrial production into "solidarist" guilds as a way of paving the way for an (authoritarian) socialism'. Durkheim took up this idea, and seemed inclined to set himself the same goal as his German colleague: 'His objective is not to make small improvements to the situation of the workers. He sets himself the higher goal of resisting, in general terms, the centrifugal tendencies that are born of the practice of individualism' (Durkheim 1975[1888]: 379).

Was Durkheim a sentimentalist? In his short introductory text, he simply corrects certain misunderstandings: Schäffle was neither a collectivist nor an authoritarian. The misunderstanding had arisen because the German economist used the ambiguous expression 'authoritarian socialism' to describe an organized form of socialism in which 'industrial forces are grouped together around action centres that regulate competition between them'. This certainly implied a degree of authority, but only to the extent that it was needed to coordinate the action centres and to subordinate some to others. This is far removed from despotic power, and we should, rather, be speaking of the 'nerve centres of an organism'. This is equally far removed from any holism: in the life of any society, authority is an expression of 'the free initiatives of individuals' and collective life is, Durkheim insists, 'the resultant of individual activities'.

Schäffle was very pleased with the work of his young French colleague, and made a point of thanking him: 'You have revealed the real meaning of my doctrine.'

Long Live the (French) Revolution!

In 1899, the Exposition universelle was held in Paris; it was also the centenary of the French Revolution. An important commemorative event, the Exposition celebrated both the triumph of French democracy and the rise of the new industrial order. Two superb metal structures were built: the Galerie des Machines and the Eiffel Tower. Their architecture and the choice of materials became symbols of both the Third Republic and the 'new world', made possible by technological innovation and scientific rationalism. Built entirely from iron girders and panes of glass, the gallery looked like a vast hangar. Ordinary machines were exhibited as though they were valuable objects or museum pieces. The tower was, in accordance with Gustave Eiffel's plans, designed to be a synthesis of new materials and new engineering and building techniques. It soared into the sky like some giant crucifix, and looked like 'the new church of technological progress' (Vogüe 1889: 190–1; cf Harris 1995: 10; Silverman 1977). It was said to be a metaphor for the liberal credo of progress, love of labour and respect for freedom, and a tribute to human audacity. The architecture and the materials used to build these monuments were associated with youth, virility, productivity and democracy. A new age was dawning with 'art nouveau', the 'new psychology' and the 'new woman'.

When the Exposition was first planned, no thought was given to 'the social question'. Just two years before it opened, Émile Cheysson, an engineer and follower of Le Play, was given responsibility for the 'social economics' section, which was designed to reveal the social side of the industrial world. Reformists like Cheysson had no intention of overlooking the social cost of industrialization, but they also wanted to give the Republic an image of social and political harmony. Their goal was both to promote a progressive discourse (a prefiguration of 'welfare' policies), and to defend the revolutionary heritage of the Republic and a more scientific approach to the analysis of industrial society. The 'social economy' section on the esplanade des Invalides consisted of two main exhibitions devoted to working-class culture: the 'Cité sociale' was a huge workers' village (with four full-scale models of low-cost houses), while the 'social economics gallery' featured recent experiments in social welfare. This gallery, which was more traditional, was a veritable 'museum of documents', with displays of brochures, books, diagrams and wall charts.

Visitors could obtain information on profit-sharing schemes, mutual benefit organizations, gymnastic associations and workers' clubs. The 1889 Exposition celebrated both community life and the neopaternalism of employers, and promoted a liberal vision of social welfare in which the state had no role to play. Lectures and conferences were organized to encourage exchanges of views and to mobilize public opinion. This gave new impetus to the social reform movement and led to several initiatives, such as the foundation of the Société française d'habitations à bon marché [French social housing society] and, a few years later, of a musée social. The great exhibition provided a major platform for the social economy movement, and gave it greater legitimacy. This was why, Cheysson concluded, the nineteenth century really was 'the century of social questions': an answer to these questions had yet to be found, but their importance had at last been understood (Cheysson, cited in Horne 2002: 78; cf Cheysson 1889).

Durkheim wrote 'The principles of 1789 and sociology' for the *Revue internationale de l'enseignement*, which published it the following year (Durkheim 1973[1890]). It was a review of Thomas Ferneuil's book *Les Principes de 1789 et la science sociale*, and Durkheim knew the author: 'Ferneuil' was the pseudonym of Fernand Samazeuilh, who was his colleague at Bordeaux.

An extract from Ferneuil's book was published in the *Revue d'économie politique* under the title 'Socialisme et individualisme' (Ferneuil 1889). 'It is a mistake to believe,' he wrote, 'that socialism rejects individual freedom.' Such an idea was unlikely to leave Durkheim indifferent and, what was more, the author discussed the work of Schäffle at some length. Ferneuil accepted the German economist's argument that the socialist movement was 'irresistible', but he contended that, although it was a 'long-term historical process', it was already under way, as contemporary society had germinated 'many seeds that outline the essential features of the socialism of the future'. Ferneuil rejected the idea of violent revolution on the grounds that it would destroy all individual freedom; there was a danger that it would lead only to despotism, and that outcome would be intolerable. He was in favour of socialism, provided that it could be adapted to modern society. The lesson Ferneuil drew from this was sociological, and it explained why he was so hostile to Marxism: any profound change required time, patience and education. It in fact required a great deal of education, both intellectual and moral (civic culture, the defence of the general interest, and a sense of duty). The only defensible socialism was, in other words, a 'positive socialism that had learned the lessons of experience', and the sociologist's role was to 'help it achieve its goals'. Ferneuil opposed revolution in the name of evolution and reform (universal personal insurance, the establishment of shareholder groups, the recognition of trade associations and unions, the formation of guilds) which, far from delaying the advent of socialism, would pave the way for it. The eventual transition to socialism would then, as Schäffle himself put it, be no more than a matter of taking 'a few steps'.

The year 1789 was, in effect, synonymous with Revolution. What was the meaning of 'revolutionary religion'? Was it a 'pathological phenomenon' or, on the contrary, 'a necessary transformation of our social conscience' (Durkheim 1973[1890]: 41)? According to Durkheim, the Revolution was not only an object of faith, but also a 'scientific object' (ibid.: 34). The principles of 1789 were 'a sort of breviary of sociology', but they were also 'an expression of the state of mind of an age and of a society' and 'the conscious outcome of an entire unconscious process' (ibid.: 35, 36).

These principles are, to a large extent, a product of the way the 'men of 1789' saw the social body. The individual was seen as 'an autonomous power which depends only upon itself' (Durkheim 1973 [1890]: 40), and there were no intermediate bodies – such as associations – between individual and state. This was, according to Ferneuil, a mistaken view, and the Revolution lost its way because it failed to see the need for corporatist groupings. What is left of those principles? Durkheim wondered. There remains, of course, a 'general spirit' from which, he added, the majority of French moralists and economists still take their inspiration. They take as their starting point an abstract concept of the individual, rather as though there were no tradition and no past, and as though everyone is motivated purely by self-interest. According to that view, prejudices, mores and customs are nothing more than 'a remnant of barbarism' (ibid.).

That, retorted Durkheim, was the result of a methodological error: man is not just 'an individual and egoistic being' (Durkheim 1973[1890]: 39). He belongs to a time and a place, and shares the same prejudices and beliefs as his fellow citizens. Durkheim denounces the 'intransigent individualism' that the economists have turned into a real *orthodoxy*. It took some courage for Ferneuil to denounce this orthodoxy, as 'there is therein a way of looking at and experiencing social matters that our exclusively literary education has strongly impressed on our intellects' (Durkheim 1973[1890]: 40). Durkheim was well aware of the fact that he was swimming against the current, that the conception of collective life he was defending might be accused of being 'a German import', and that he himself ran the risk of 'being accused of state socialism and treated as an enemy of freedom' (ibid.: 41).

No matter! European society still had to solve the problem it had been trying to deal with for the past 100 years: namely, 'adapting the traditional structure of society to the new and unconscious aspirations which have afflicted them for a century'. Convoking 'a council of sociologists', as some had suggested, would not provide a solution, as the question had more to do with 'political 'art' than sociology: 'The practical difficulties can be definitely solved only by practice, by everyday experience. This is not a sociologist's advice – it will be the societies themselves which will find the solution.' Sociology did have a contribution to make, but it was a more modest one: sociology, 'like any science, studies what is and what has been, seeks laws, but is not interested in the future' (Durkheim 1973[1890]: 42).

A Young German Author: Ferdinand Tönnies

In 1889, Émile Durkheim wrote two reviews for the *Revue philosophique*, one dealing with *Gemeinschaft und Gesellschaft* by the unknown German author, Ferdinand Tönnies (1855–1936).[44] It was from this youthful work (the author was 34), which was to become one of sociology's founding texts, that Durkheim derived the idea that there were two types of groupings, or two forms of social life: *Gemeinschaft* and *Gesellschaft*. This was to become a classic sociological dichotomy, and the basis for discussions of the similarities and differences between traditional and modern societies.

Insofar as it represents a type of social life, *Gemeinschaft* is, according to Tönnies, characterized by complete unity (which precludes any distinction between parts of society) and a consensus based upon resemblances (consanguinity, neighbouring, shared memories). Property is held in common, and both trade and contracts are unknown. *Gemeinschaft* therefore means community (and communism). *Gesellschaft* is completely different; the term describes life in the big modern cities of the age of commerce, industry, free trade and cosmopolitanism. It also describes the age of individualism. According to Tönnies, the whole of history is reducible to the transition from one of these forms of social life to the other; one replaces the other in the same way that science replaces tradition, and that customs give way to 'opinions freely reflected upon' (Durkheim 1978[1889]: 119). The explanation for this transition lies in demographic shifts, or, in other words, in the growing size of the population. Durkheim would adopt this explanatory principle in his doctoral thesis.

There is also a political dimension to Tönnies's book: 'Communism is the regime of *Gemeinschaft*, just as socialism is the regime of *Gesellschaft*.' The transition from one form or social life or regime is not, in Tönnies's view, evidence of progress. He has a somewhat pessimistic view of history. This process will lead to 'the rupture of all social relations and the decomposition of the social body'. Socialism is 'the beginning of a more or less proximate end' (Durkheim 1978[1889]: 120).

While he does not share Tönnies's pessimism, Durkheim does accept his central thesis: 'Like the author, I believe that there are two great types of society, and the terms he uses to describe them indicate their nature rather well' (Durkheim 1978[1889]: 121). He also accepts his German colleague's general description of *community*. He does not, however, accept that a *Gesellschaft* is simply a 'mechanical aggregate': the surviving elements of collective life are not simply an effect of 'the action of the state'. On the contrary, he believes:

> The life of great social agglomerations is every bit as natural as that of small aggregates. It is neither less organic nor less self-contained. Aside from purely individual activities, there is in our contemporary societies a truly collective activity which is just as natural as that of the less extensive societies of former times; it constitutes another type. (1978[1889]: 121)

But how can we prove that this is the case? Unlike Tönnies, we would have to 'observe the facts', 'proceed inductively' and look at the law and social mores in order to study the forms of social life, 'but we would need an entire book to prove this' (1978[1889]: 121). Durkheim is obviously thinking here of the book he was working on, and which Tönnies would review on publication (Tönnies cited by Michael Schmid in Besnard et al. 1993).

Jean-Jacques Rousseau: Sociologist

As Marcel Mauss notes, Durkheim attached 'some importance' to his work on the history of doctrines. 'His lectures on the founders of sociology meant a lot to him. In his view, these tributes to the philosophers who came before him recognized the nobility of our science in proven areas.' Durkheim had a detailed knowledge of Condorcet, for whom he had 'great admiration'. He was also especially proud of the lecture he gave on Hobbes.[45] One of his projects was to 'publish most of his lectures and to collect them in a volume entitled "The Origins of Sociology"'. The project never came to anything.

It was only in his last year in Bordeaux (1901–2) that Durkheim lectured on the history of doctrines. This was a sociology course entitled 'The history of sociological doctrines'. Durkheim obviously talked about the authors of these doctrines with the students he prepared for the *agrégation*. He also discussed them in his lectures on pedagogy, in which he talked a lot about the history of educational theories or doctrines and considered various authors (most of them French), including Rabelais, Montaigne, Port-Royal and the Jansenists, and Fénelon.[46]

And he obviously discussed Rousseau, who was one of his favourite authors, and devoted several lectures to him, beginning either in 1889–90 or the following academic year. It is not, however, easy to determine precisely when these lectures were given. It was only from 1908 onwards, when he was at the Sorbonne, that Durkheim taught a lecture course that was actually entitled 'History of educational doctrines'. The only other possible indication comes from a letter written to his nephew: 'My course on Rousseau is coming along' (Durkheim 1998: 63).[47]

One certainly feels, on reading Durkheim, that the work of Rousseau was both an important source of inspiration and a subject for debate. In his lectures, he concentrates not, as one might have expected, on Rousseau the educationalist or the Rousseau who wrote *Émile,* but on the social philosopher and the author of *The Social Contract.* He returned later to Rousseau's work on education. The goal of his lectures was to give a detailed account of the writer's social philosophy or 'what we might call sociology'. Arguing against those who try to portray him as 'the father of anarchy and individualism and of laissser-faire in pedagogy',[48] Durkheim attempts to demonstrate the extent to which Rousseau understood the social nature of man and of the reality of society. He was, remarks Mauss (1969[1925]: 483), quite proud of 'having discovered Rousseau's socio-logical spirit'. Durkheim sets out to prove, text in hand, that Rousseau had a 'keen sense' of the need for, and power of, education, and that he understood the social nature and reality of society. The educator's mission was, in his view, to 'put the child in harmony with the environment' and to 'shape the social man'.

Durkheim divided his lectures into four sections: 'The state of nature'; 'Origin of societies'; 'The social contract and the constitution of the body politics'; 'Of the sovereign in general, of law in general, and of political laws in particular.'

The state of nature? What appeals to Durkheim about Rousseau's approach is that he is careful not to make the same mistake as 'those who, in reasoning about the state of nature, make use of ideas drawn from society', and his insistence on ridding himself of prejudices – both true and false – drawn from society. What is more, Rousseau's concept of a state of nature is not, as has sometimes been thought, a 'figment of sentimental reverie [*rêverie sentimentaliste*[49]]' but a 'methodological device'. But how can we succeed in understanding this natural man? The ways or methods suggested by Rousseau include the observation of animals (which provide examples of what mental life could mean if we ignore all social influences) and the observation of savages (with some reservations).

What, then, is the famous state of nature of which Jean-Jacques Rousseau speaks? The most important terms that Durkheim uses to discuss it are 'equilibrium' (between needs and resources, and between man and his environment) and 'harmony' (man has all that he desires because he desires only what he has). Rousseau describes natural man as ' "wandering through the forest, without occupation, without speech, without a home, without war and without ties, with no need of his fellow men and no wish to harm them, perhaps not even recognizing any of them individually' (Durkheim 1960[1918]: 74). Natural man is not unsocial, but asocial, and neither moral nor immoral, but amoral. He lives in what Rousseau calls a state of innocence, and Durkheim concludes: 'Morality could come into being only with society' (ibid.: 75).

What is the origin of societies? If there is one question that preoccupies Durkheim, it is that of origins. What, according to Rousseau, are the pre-conditions for the emergence of societies? The causes that he identifies are external and have to do with the natural environment: years in which the crops fail, there are long, harsh winters and hot summers. Hence the need for changes in man's relationship with nature – a 'new industry' – and in relations between men (mutual aid, the beginnings of language). These changes lead, according to Rousseau, to the formation of the 'first flocks of human beings'. As they become accustomed to living in groups, they develop new ideas about interhuman relations (civic duties, etc.), and an embryonic morality develops. This leads to the development of agriculture and the other arts, the appearance of an early division of labour (metal-working on the one hand and ploughing and cultivation of the soil on the other), and the sharing out of the land as property rights develop. This paves the way for all kinds of inequalities: the powerful versus the power-less, the rich versus the poor. Finally, laws and governments are created.

Durkheim makes no attempt to conceal his admiration for Rousseau's 'dialectical ingenuity': 'He starts with the individual and, without ascrib-ing to him the slightest social inclination . . . undertakes to explain how a being so fundamentally indifferent to any kind of life in common came to form societies.' Rousseau's solution is, he accepts, 'fraught with con-tradictions': the original balance is 'unstable', but 'though social life does not exist in the beginning, its germs are present. They are embryonic, but if favourable circumstances arise, they cannot fail to develop' (Durkheim 1960[1918]: 80).

There is one other thing about Rousseau's study of the origins of society that is of great interest to Durkheim: society is more than the sum of its parts, 'a moral entity having specific qualities distinct from those of the individual beings which compose it'. This 'remarkable passage' proves, for Durkheim, that Rousseau 'was keenly aware of the specificity of the social order': 'It is a new world superimposed on the purely psychological world . . . Society is nothing if not a single definite body distinct from its parts' (Durkheim 1960[1918]: 83).

Given that society does not exist in nature, are we to conclude that it is unnatural? Is it 'a corruption of nature, the consequence of some sort of fall and degeneration' (Durkheim 1960[1918]: 85)? Rousseau certainly regards society as 'a monstrosity' and as a product of 'an interdependence of human beings [that] is contrary to nature. Such is the meaning of the famous statement: "Man is born free, and everywhere he is in chains"' (ibid.: 86, 87). Durkheim is, however, careful not to impute to Rousseau 'the radical pessimism that has been attributed to him'. On the contrary, 'the germ of social existence is inherent in the state of nature' . . . What dis-tinguishes [man] most from the animal is "the ability to perfect himself"' (ibid.: 90).

The establishment of the body politic. How can society be organized so as to ensure us the greatest possible happiness and perfectibility? This is, according to Durkheim, the question that *The Social Contract* attempts to answer, and it is what Rousseau calls *'the great problem in politics'*. Both Rousseau and Durkheim therefore raise the question of forms of govern-ment, regimes and legislation. Durkheim pays great attention to the way Rousseau analyses the constitution of society 'once the state of nature has become impossible' and when society becomes 'the only environment in which man can live'. Men are obviously still dependent upon one another, but a 'new force [is] born of the combination of individuals into societies'. It is an impersonal force, and it is, *mutatis mutandis*, similar to the forces of nature insofar as it is 'superior to all individuals', but it must be 'based on nature'. Does this mean that might is right? According to Rousseau, that principle can never provide the basis for a society. 'A society is an organized body in which each part is dependent upon the whole and vice versa', whereas a mob subjected to a chief is '"an aggregation, but not an association"' (Durkheim 1960[1918]: 94–8).

The distinction between 'aggregation' and 'association' is important to Durkheim. If there is such a thing as an association, it must be 'a form of association which will defend and protect with the whole common force the person and goods of each association, and in which each, while uniting with all, may still obey himself alone, and remain as free as before'. According to Rousseau, 'such an association can result only from a contract by which each member alienates himself, with all his rights, to the community. By this contract, each individual vanishes into a common, general will, which is the basis of the society' (Durkheim 1960[1918]: 98).

'Impersonal force', 'the general will', 'a moral and collective body' and 'common interest': all these expressions spoke directly to Durkheim at a time when he is attempting to base sociology on the idea that 'Collective utility has a certain character of its own. It is defined, not with respect to the individual . . . but with respect to society as an organic unit' (ibid.: 106). And he is interested in Rousseau's concept of the general will or the common interest because it once more reveals the 'two antithetical tendencies' within Rousseau's doctrine: 'On the one hand, society as a mere instrument for the use of the individual; on the other, the individual as dependent upon society, which far transcends the multitude of individuals' (Durkheim 1960[1918]: 108).

The general will remains a superficial idea, and 'we must look beneath, into the less conscious areas, and examine the people's habits, trends, customs'. Durkheim attaches great importance to those chapters of *The Social Contract* that deal with laws. They obviously refer to political civil and criminal law, but also to other kinds of law, namely 'customs, manners, and above all public opinion, which to his mind is the keystone of the social system' (Durkheim 1960[1918]: 122). Durkheim adopts this formula as his own, and notes approvingly: 'It is quite interesting that he should place diffuse custom and written law side by side.'

Durkheim dwells at length on the question of the classification of forms of government. He also addresses the same question in his reading of Montesquieu's *The Spirit of the Laws* – to which he would devote his *thèse complémentaire* or 'Latin thesis' (Durkheim 1960[1892]). He compares the ways Montesquieu and Rousseau classify governments. Monarchy, aristocracy or democracy? As Durkheim shows, Montesquieu and Rousseau reach different conclusions. The former prefers monarchy and the latter aristocracy – by which he means 'a society in which the government is composed of a minority chosen on the basis of age and experience, or by election' (Durkheim 1960[1918]: 127). Rousseau's ideal government would be democratic, but that ideal is out of reach: '"Were there a people of gods, their government would be democratic. So perfect a government is not for men"' (ibid.: 126).

Whatever form a government takes, it seems that 'clever constitutional mechanisms' will not in themselves guarantee social cohesion. Here, Durkheim agrees with Rousseau that a 'certain intellectual communion' is also required (1960[1918]: 132). That communion existed when every society had its own religion, and when that religion was the basis of its social order. In modern societies, it is what might be called a civil religion with a civil creed that proclaims the sanctity of the social contract and laws, and forbids all intolerance. That rejection of intolerance also applies to religion: the state cannot tolerate any religion that does not tolerate other religions.

Durkheim ends his lecture course by summarizing Rousseau's argument: we move from the state of nature, which is 'a kind of peaceful anarchy in which individuals, independent of each other and without ties between them, depend only upon the abstract force of nature', to the civil state, in which individuals 'are dependent upon a new force, which is superimposed on the natural forces but has the same generality and necessity, namely, the general will' (1960[1918]: 135). Man spontaneously submits not to natural forces, but to the general will. Durkheim detects a 'weakness' in Rousseau's argument. While Rousseau obviously agrees that collective life does not go against the natural order of things, he does not really demonstrate how it is possible: 'So unstable is its foundation in the nature of things that it cannot but appear to us as a tottering structure whose delicate balance can be established and maintained only by an almost miraculous conjuncture of circumstances' (ibid.: 137–8).

What does Durkheim retain from his reading of *The Social Contract*? First, a dualistic conception of man, with nature on the one hand and the social on the other. Second, the idea that the 'true basis' of society is not an aggregation but an association, and that that association is born of a 'common will' (a soul that is 'one and indivisible'). And finally, Durkheim finds an ally in Rousseau because he defends the specificity of the social realm and describes society as a 'moral being' with its own qualities that are distinct from those of the particular beings that make it up. At the same time, although he uncovers a contradiction – society is both a rational being and an organism – he congratulates Rousseau because he abandons neither the 'individualist principle' nor the 'social-ist principle'. He also congratulates himself on having demolished the widely accepted interpretation of Rousseau's doctrines that makes him the ancestor of individualism and anarchy. Durkheim and Rousseau differ over one point: in Durkheim's view, the existence of society precedes that of the individual. The same basic idea can be found in Aristotle (whom Durkheim regards as a distant precursor because of his sharp sense of the reality of social being).

A Nephew's Education

In the autumn of 1890, Marcel Mauss, the elder son of Rosine Durkheim and Gerson Mauss, joined his uncle in Bordeaux, where he wanted to study philosophy. He was just 18, and less than 15 years younger than his uncle. He mother Rosine (born in 1848) was Émile's elder sister. When she married Gerson Mauss (born in 1834), she and her husband took over the family business, which now traded under the name '*Broderie à la main, Durkheim-Mauss*'. The couple had two children, both boys: Marcel was born in 1872, and Henry in 1876. The younger brother took the traditional path and went into the family business. Marcel did brilliantly in his classical studies at the industrial school and then the college in Épinal, and passed his baccalauréat 'with honours' in July 1890.

Over the summer, he discussed philosophy and sociology with Durkheim, who was on holiday in Épinal, and asked his advice on what he should read. Durkheim advised him to read *La Psychologie anglaise contemporaine* and *La Psychologie allemande contemporaine* by the philosopher Théodule Ribot. Marcel literally devoured Ribot's 'little books' and was 'won over', just as Émile had been 10 years earlier. He then resolved to study philosophy at university, and to follow in his uncle's footsteps by taking an interest in sociology. His family had no objections. It is true that Émile Durkheim enjoyed great prestige in the eyes of his family: they admired him and consulted him for advice.

Why did Marcel opt to go to university rather than follow his uncle by going to the École normale supérieure? He had every intention of taking the *agrégation* but refused to apply to the École because, as his uncle reminded him, he loathed the idea of being a boarder. Durkheim did not insist: he himself had found the academic competition difficult, and had developed a fear of failure. And he had been disappointed by the education he had received at the École. It was too literary, dilettantish and superficial. For several years, he gave tutorials to *agrégation* candidates, and was prepared to help his nephew.

Mauss enjoyed a certain freedom in Bordeaux. He initially lived in lodgings at 2 rue du Cours and then at 21 rue de Talence, which was near his uncle's home. He enrolled in the faculty of letters to study for a degree in philosophy, but also followed lectures in the faculty of law for a year. At university, he was, like the other students, subject only to a 'voluntary discipline', as Durkheim himself put it. 'He chose what seemed to him to be the most useful courses, and attended lectures only when he wished to'. This was in keeping with the university's cherished principle of academic freedom (Durkheim 1918). He graduated in philosophy and letters in July 1892. The following academic year (1892–3), he enrolled as an *étudiant libre* at Bordeaux, but then went to Paris and enrolled at the Sorbonne for the year 1893–4, before returning to Bordeaux as an *étudiant libre* in 1894–5.[50]

Marcel obviously attended his uncle's lectures, and described him as 'the most reliable and agreeable of orators'. Given his intellectual power and moral ideals, his uncle quickly became both his master and his model. Émile himself accepted his responsibilities, and wrote to his nephew: 'She [your mother] asked me to educate you. I educated you in accordance with my ideal. She must accept the consequences of what she wanted. She can regret it if she wishes, but she will not be able to hold it against you.'[51]

The philosophical training Marcel Mauss received at Bordeaux was sympathetic to psychology and sociology. Two of Durkheim's colleagues also had a profound influence on the young scholar: Alfred Espinas and Octave Hamelin. In 1893–4, Espinas taught a course entitled 'The higher forms of the human will' and another called 'Greek philosophy up to Socrates'. In another of his courses, Espinas discusses the question of technique and technology that would become the subject of his *Origines de la technologie* (1897). Mauss's ties with another professor of philosophy were even closer, as Octave Hamelin was his uncle's friend. The authors and topics dealt with by Hamelin in his lectures and classes were Aristotle, Kant, Spinoza and Leibniz. Even when he was in Paris, Mauss remained in close contact with his teacher and put him up when he came to the capital.

The intellectual world in which Marcel Mauss found himself was at the crossroads between various disciplines (philosophy, psychology, biology and sociology). The theory of knowledge, the theory of evolution and the theory of science were the new issues that divided researchers in all these disciplines. Sociology, which was beginning to look like a family business, was fully involved in all these debates.

Both Bordeaux and Paris were in a state of intellectual turmoil. Students were discussing Marx's *Capital* at meetings of the Cercle d'études sociales, and some of the most brilliant of them were converting to socialism, especially in its Marxist or Guesdiste forms. In 1893, Jaurès himself came to Bordeaux, at the invitation of the students and the Parti ouvrier français, to give a lecture in which he took the opportunity to praise the work of Durkheim. The two men, who had been at École normale supérieure together, met and had discussions.

Marcel Mauss was engaged in politics as a student and, unlike his uncle, became an activist and a 'party man'. While he was studying philosophy in the faculty of letters, he made the acquaintance of another Marcel. Marcel Cachin, who was a few years older than Mauss, had come to Bordeaux to study philosophy in 1890. The young Breton joined the socialist students' group, took part in their activities and then, in March 1892, joined the Parti ouvrier français. An ardent supporter of Guesde, Cachin became, as Mauss put it, a sort of 'unpaid full-timer' and devoted all his time to political activism.[52] Mauss also became involved with Groupe des étudiants socialistes and joined the Parti ouvrier français, probably to annoy his uncle who refused to become involved in party politics and loathed the 'idea of submitting to a disciplined party, and especially an international party'.

6

The Individual and Society The Social Bond

The Doctoral Thesis

During the period between 1890 and 1895, the trade union movement became more influential as it became more radical. It adopted the principle of the general strike. The number of labour exchanges increased, while Fernand Pelloutier's influence led to the establishment of the Confédération générale du travail in 1895. At the same time, the socialist movement made some important breakthroughs with the founding of the newspaper *La Petite République*, the drawing up of a minimal programme and the election of Jean Jaurès to the Chambre des députés in January 1893. In June of that year, a further 50 socialist *députés* were elected. This caused a major upheaval: socialism was acquiring 'the parliamentary consistency of a resolute group'. The political balance was shifting and the rules of the game were changing. The ruling majority was insulted and outraged, and the government was accused of all sorts of crimes, while the newly elected socialists were criticized for their excessive passion, their provocative violence and their aggressive brutality. Jules Guesde was waging an active propaganda campaign, mainly in the industrial areas of the north, and his Parti ouvrier français grew rapidly as its membership rose from 2,000 in 1890 to more than 10,000 in 1893.

More so than ever before, political debate centred on the 'social question'. The theory of 'laisser-faire, laisser-passer' had been demolished in both Catholic and Protestant circles. Ever since the late 1870s, Albert de Mun, who together with René de La Tour du Pin had founded a movement of workers' circles that was becoming a real 'army of God', had been travelling throughout France to argue the case for 'a social overhaul of society' based upon a revival of Catholic guilds and professional associations, and for a rejection of the law of self-interest. When he was elected to the Chambre des députés, this great and powerful orator argued the case for pro-worker legislation and, in 1892, championed the law on women's work. The encyclical *Rerum novarum* (1891) earned Leo XIII the nickname 'the workers' Pope', and laid the foundations for a social Catholicism. This gave rise to many initiatives ranging from the founding of newspapers and magazines to the establishment of trade unions, youth groups and cooperatives.

In 1894, Marc Sangnier founded *Le Sillon* in an attempt to reconcile the doctrine of the church with democratic republican values. Influenced by the 'social gospel' movements that were emerging in the United States and Britain, Protestants were talking of social Protestantism or even Christian socialism. Jules Siegfried (1836–1922), whose wife was the daughter of an eminent Protestant pastor, became the spokesman and symbol of that movement in reformist republican circles. He was behind the idea of the Musée social, which opened in 1894, with Robert Pinot, deputy director of Sciences Po [political science college], as its first director. Its board of directors included several of Le Play's supporters, including Émile Cheysson.

Things were beginning to get out of hand. On 9 December 1893, a bomb was thrown into the Chambre des députés. Brutally repressive measures – *les lois scélérates* – were introduced and many arrests followed. Sadi Carnot was assassinated in June 1894, and the Trial of the Thirty began in August. Auguste Vaillant, perpetrator of the bomb in the Chambre, was sentenced to death on 11 January 1894 and guillotined on 5 February. The anarchist Caserio then assassinated the President of the Republic in order to avenge his death. The anarchist movement was very active at this time, and enjoyed a certain prestige amongst a younger generation of intellectuals and artists described by Maurice Barrès in his novel *Les Déracinés* ['The uprooted', 1897] as a sort of 'intellectual proletariat' who had been sensitized to the critique of bourgeois society by their loss of status.

Attempts were being made to replace love of the fatherland with a cult of individualism. Faith in reason, science and progress was losing ground. Even Émile Zola, who had been promoting the cause of positivism for 30 years, felt that his convictions had been 'shaken' and was asking: 'Who will give me a new ideal?' (cited in Mitterrand 2002: 62). The literary avant-garde was drawing closer to the political avant-garde. The new journals – such as *La Revue blanche*, *Les Entretiens littéraires* and *L'Art social* – were devoting more space to ideological questions. Individual or collectivity? Spontaneity or constraint (or plots)? Nostalgia for the past or hope for a coming renaissance? Art for art's sake, or commitment? The new function of those who were coming to be known as 'intellectuals' was, as Bernard Lazare argued in *La Révolte*, to *act*, not by using guns, knives or dynamite, but by using their pens and taking 'intellectual action' (Charle 1990: 105f).

Others, finally, were worried by the rising crime rate and thought that society was being 'swamped', as they put it at the time. This was, it was believed, a sign that France was in a state of moral crisis, or moral decadence. A study of *La France criminelle* was published in 1889. Its author was Henri Joly, an orthodox follower of Le Play who taught a course on criminal and penitentiary science in the Paris faculty of law. He attempted to demonstrate, with maps to support his case, that this moral decadence was bound up with the deracination of modern man, who was forced to live in the anonymity and loneliness of the big cities.

Writing his thesis caused Durkheim great anxiety. The subjects were new, the method was new and the facts he was studying had scarcely been analysed before. He sometimes had to force himself, day after day, to write the simplest passage. As his superiors observed, he led a 'very serious' life: he was 'fully preoccupied with his work, and lives only for science.'[1] He published no articles or reviews in 1891 or 1892, but was still a member of the *jury d'agrégation*. He continued to have a very heavy teaching load; in addition to the course on the family, which he had prepared three years earlier and which dealt with the patriarchal family, he was preparing four new courses, one on criminal sociology and three on pedagogy: 'Education and pedagogy in the ancient world', 'Pedagogy in the eighteenth century' and 'Psychology applied to education'. Some 40 people, including a few women and some dedicated laymen, attended his public lectures, which were said to be 'quite remarkable'. This was the first time that Durkheim had used the words 'sociology' and 'psychology' in a course description. With a display of 'conviction and authority', he succeeded in 'teaching the most difficult of the sciences thanks to his deep understanding of the subject and his precocious maturity'. He was, concluded the rector, 'worthy of being appointed to a professorial chair'. As we have already seen, 1892 was also marked by a happy event, but it also gave him greater responsibilities at home: the birth of André.

Durkheim submitted the manuscript of his doctoral thesis on 24 March 1892 (Borlandi 1994a), and the manuscript of his Latin thesis in November of the same year.[2] The viva did not take place until a year later. The Latin thesis was published in Bordeaux in 1892, and the doctoral thesis was published by Alcan in Paris the following year. Durkheim was granted leave from his University to be in Paris from 1 March 1893 to 11 March to defend his thesis in a public oral examination.

Montesquieu and Political Science

Durkheim devoted his complementary thesis to Montesquieu and dedi-cated it to the memory of Fustel de Coulanges, who had taught him at the École normale supérieure. As the title – *Quid Secundatus Politicae Scientiae Instituendae Contulerit* [*Montesquieu's Contribution to the Rise of Social Science*] – indicates, it did indeed deal with 'political science', but Durkheim is really talking about what had come to be known as 'sociol-ogy' – 'a rather barbarous name to tell the truth' (Durkheim 1960[1892]: 1).

The choice of Montesquieu may seem surprising. The idea came from Émile Boutroux, who had been Durkheim's teacher at the École. Durkheim may also have been influenced by Paul Janet's *Histoire de la science poli-tique dans ses rapports avec la morale*. Janet, who was on the jury, was one of the best commentators on Montesquieu's social and political theory. Durkheim cites his work and makes it clear that, on his advice, he was trying not so much to expose Montesquieu's 'errors' as to demonstrate his 'strength of mind'. It also has to be said that the author of the *Lettres persanes* came from Bordeaux. There are two fine statues in the faculty of law there: one of Cujas and one of Montesquieu. In devoting his thesis to his famous fellow citizen, Durkheim was pointing out that, far from being 'foreign to our ways and to the French mind . . . this science came into being in France' (Durkheim 1960[1892]: 1). Indeed, it was born in Bordeaux! 'The very impetus of our present concern with social problems came from our eighteenth-century philosophers.' The choice of this 'brilliant precursor', to use Georges Davy's expression (ibid.: 154), therefore seemed 'natural': it was Montesquieu who established the principles of the new science of sociology. He took a very early interest in history and political philosophy, and between 1728 and 1731 he travelled throughout Europe (and especially England) in order to gather documentation for his study of the political organization of different countries.

Montesquieu's *The Spirit of the Laws* (1748) was a considerable success, and his achievement seemed all the more remarkable to the young philosopher-sociologist in that his only information about faraway peoples came from a few travellers' tales and he had no statistical data on the various 'events of life' that he was studying (deaths, marriages, murder) (Durkheim 1960[1892]: 2). In *The Spirit of the Laws*, societies are classified on the basis of their form of government, which may be either republican (democratic or aristocratic), monarchic or despotic. The classification also takes into account the size of the population, and the relative distribution and cohesion of its elements. Montesquieu in fact establishes a causal relationship between, on the one hand, geographical and morphological features – climate, geography and the size and distribution of the population, life style – and, on the other, forms of government: despotism is to democracy what a large country with an extreme climate is to a small country with a cold climate and poor soil. This is what Pierre Bourdieu (1980) was to call 'the Montesquieu effect'.

Irrespective of the political positions defended by Montesquieu, his comments on the republic took on a new meaning in a France that aspired to being a republic. And we do find in *The Spirit of the Laws* elements of what might be called a republican ethos: a love of laws and of the fatherland that requires the public interest to take precedence over self-interest; the power of education; a love of democracy and equality; frugality in domestic or personal spending. In such a political context, every citizen has an immense debt that can never be repaid, and his sole ambition is therefore to render 'greater services to [the] homeland than other citizens'. His 'desire to possess' is restricted to 'that which is necessary for [his] family' and he gives any surplus to the state. 'Good democracies', in other words, encourage 'frugality in domestic life', and this establishes a basis for public spending (Montesquieu 1989[1748]: 43). Law, democracy, equality, education, public spending: all these themes can be found in Montesquieu, and could not fail to be of interest to anyone who took an interest in political science at the end of the nineteenth century.

Montesquieu's other great virtue is that he establishes what Durkheim calls 'the conditions necessary for the establishment of social science' (1960[1892]: 3). The first chapter of his Latin thesis deals with questions of methodology: a science must, first of all, have an object; it must not be purely descriptive and must also offer an interpretation; there is a way, finally, of doing science – an ethos, one might say – which consists in avoiding haste, trying to understand past and present reality before looking to the future (and establishing a new political order), examining things carefully and calmly and disregarding one's own loves and hates, keeping one's distance from debates, or, in a word, elaborating a method. That is the difference between science and *art* (the art of politics), prophecy and literature, but Durkheim immediately adds: 'This does not mean that science is useless in the conduct of human life. Quite the contrary. The sharper the distinction between the science and art, the more useful science can be to art' (Durkheim 1960[1892]: 7). Durkheim is, however, aware of the difficulties inherent in any attempt to study society as though it was an object. The 'things' under observation vary greatly and change rapidly, causes and effects are closely interwoven, and it is impossible to carry out experiments on human societies. It is, on the other hand, difficult to find any other method. There is no alternative but to proceed by trial and error and, as in psychology, there will inevitably be 'much groping' (Durkheim 1960[1892]: 13). There is no choice: 'The only way to discover the laws of nature is to study nature itself. Moreover, it is not enough to observe nature. She must be questioned, hounded, put to the test in a thousand and one ways' (Durkheim 1960[1892]: 50).

As Durkheim admits, a Latin thesis is not the place to examine all these questions in depth. Montesquieu's contribution to social science (or political science, to be more accurate) is important not only because he defines a specific object of study (laws, morality, religion) and defends the use of the inductive method and comparative analysis, but also because he is the first to define basic principles and to elaborate key notions (*type* and *law*). Montesquieu's great strength – and his great achievement – is his ability to take into account every aspect of the life – morality, religion, the family, marriage, education, crime and punishment – of different societies, and to find the 'reasons' for their differences in the 'conditions of collective life' rather than in the human mind. The nature of a society is determined by the nature and organization of its constituent elements, and how those elements generate social facts.

The author of *The Spirit of the Laws* has, therefore, Durkheim notes, an instinctive understanding of a certain number of things. He understands, for example, that these elements are all so interrelated that they cannot be understood individually, each one separated from the others. As the example of a monarchy shows, society itself is a sort of living being whose elements, each in its own way, serve certain functions. The contemporary relevance of Montesquieu is that he describes various 'forms of social life', various types of social bond and various forms of consensus or social solidarity. This is, in Durkheim's view, a good starting point (for sociology). His Latin thesis provides him with a sort of pretext for exploring a whole series of issues or methodological and epistemological questions that were to be central to his later work: rationalism versus empiricism, rationality versus non-rationality, individualism versus holism, the nature of causality, the distinction between the normal and the pathological, determinism versus contingency or freedom. His explorations lead him to conclude that social matters are not, as a rule, the result of deliberate decisions.

Durkheim's approach is often interrogative and open. Human societies leave him perplexed, as it is difficult to decide what the 'normal state' of a society might be. His enthusiasm for Montesquieu is not unqualified. The doctoral candidate often displays the enormous confidence of a teacher who is giving his student good and bad marks: Montesquieu can be 'hasty and superficial' (1960[1892]: 19), and his assumptions are sometimes 'erroneous' (1960[1892]: 62). He demonstrates perspicacity, but he can also be wrong. Durkheim's explicit aim is to judge what part Montesquieu played in laying down the principles of social science. *The Spirit of the Laws* has, in his view, certain flaws, and he points them out: efficient causes are confused with final causes, the use of the deductive and inductive approaches is ambiguous, and the distinction between 'science' and practice or 'art' is unclear. Durkheim also criticizes Montesquieu for overlooking the idea of progress and failing to take the evolution of societies into account. He fails, that is, to see that 'the nature of a society depends upon the form of the societies preceding it' (1960[1892]: 59). The question of change is, of course, central to Durkheim's doctoral thesis: how do we move from one form of society to another or, more specifically, from one type of solidarity to another?

Latin thesis, doctoral thesis. Durkheim's reading of *The Spirit of the Laws* allows him to open the debate about the new science of sociology. His thesis on Montesquieu could have been a purely academic exercise: it is important because he both gives a sociological interpretation of the author and uses his reading of *The Spirit of the Laws* to introduce his own ideas about methodology in the social sciences (see Watts Miller 1993, 1997).

The Division of Labour?

La Division du travail social ['The division of social labour']: the title of Durkheim's doctoral thesis may seem enigmatic – it does not deal with 'social labour', or with the way tasks are apportioned within industry, which is what the 'division of labour' is usually understood to mean. Its object is 'the division of labour as social phenomenon' or 'the division of labour in society'.[3] We all have different functions, observes Durkheim: poets dream, scientists do research, workers spend their lives making pinheads, ploughmen follow the plough, and shopkeepers stand behind their counters. Why the specialization?

In the preface to the first edition of his thesis, Durkheim recalls that 'the starting point for our study has been that of the connection between the individual personality and social solidarity. How does it come about that the individual, whilst becoming more autonomous, depends ever more closely upon society?' (Durkheim 1984[1893]: xxx). Even in the introduction to his thesis, Durkheim poses the problem of the division of labour in moral terms: is the division of labour 'also a moral rule for human conduct?' (ibid.: 3). His main concern is to 'constitute the science of morality', or in other words 'to treat the facts of moral life according to the methods of the positive sciences' (ibid.: iv). As he admits, it is by no means universally agreed that observing moral facts, classifying them and seeking out the laws that explain them is the appropriate way of going about things: 'The objection will be raised regarding the existence of freedom' (ibid.: xxv). When he asserts that moral facts are facts like any others, and that they can be studied in the same way that natural facts can be studied, he is going against collective feelings and received ideas. He is attacking what might be called the traditional philosophical conception of ethics, which tries to deduce moral principles from a priori principles. Such principles are obstacles that hinder the development of disciplines such as psychology and sociology, and the young philosopher is well aware of it. He resolves to go off the beaten track and to explore two other paths that are less well signposted: political economy on the one hand, and the history of law and criminology on the other. The lawyers were already interested in both disciplines, and the novelty of Durkheim's approach is that he looks at them through the prism of ethnography.

But why the division of labour, which would appear to have very little to do with morality? Durkheim is interested in it for several reasons. The question concerned him as a scholar (the division of intellectual labour), as a husband (the sexual division of labour) and as a citizen (the division of labour in society). For the scholar, the (over-)specialization to be observed in the various domains of knowledge seems to pose a serious problem. What has become of 'the perfect man' [*l'honnête homme*]? Durkheim argues the need for the quest for perfection, both in terms of general culture and in terms of education and science: 'The time lies far behind us when philosophy constituted the sole science'; 'that general culture, once so highly extolled, no longer impresses us save as flabby, lax form of discipline'. So, there can be no more dilettantism! 'We perceive perfection in the competent man . . . one who has a well-defined job to which he devotes himself.' His maxim for modern times appears to be: '*Equip yourself to fulfil usefully a specific function.*' Durkheim appears, then, to be arguing the case for even greater functional specialization (1984[1893]: 2–4).

As a young husband, Durkheim was becoming aware of the respective rights and duties of husband and wife, and discovering the division of domestic and sexual labour: 'At first limited to the sexual functions alone, [the sexual division of labour] gradually extended to many other functions. The woman had long withdrawn from warfare and public affairs, and had centred her existence entirely round the family. Since then her role has become even more specialized.' Even her gentleness which is now a distinctively female characteristic, 'does not appear to have been characteristic of her'. The sexual division of labour now appears to be clearer than ever, with 'one sex having taken over the affective, the other the intellectual function' (Durkheim 1984[1893]: 20). While art and letters are beginning to become 'matters that occupy women', men appear to be devoting themselves more especially to science. These differences are not, in Durkheim's view, purely functional; they are also morphological. The conclusion is obvious: the sources of conjugal solidarity are to be found in the division of sexual labour, which was 'an event of prime importance in the evolution of the sentiments . . . because it has made possible perhaps the strongest of all disinterested tendencies' (ibid.: 18).

This is, as Durkheim himself admits, a somewhat hasty analysis: he is using these different examples to show that the division of labour creates solidarity. Taking the argument one stage further, he then puts forward a general hypothesis about contemporary societies: the division of labour '[fulfils] the function of integrating the body social and of ensuring its unity' (Durkheim 1984[1893]: 23). Not everything can be reduced to its strictly economic function (increased productivity, the intellectual and material development of society). There is also a moral dimension. The division of labour has a moral function because it creates a 'feeling of solidarity' between individuals.

No matter whether the discussion concerns the distribution of property, social and economic inequalities or the class struggle, Durkheim is well aware that the burning question of the day – the 'social question' – is that of the division of labour. How can we guarantee solidarity in a society that is based upon the division of labour? There are two answers to that question. On the one hand, there are the economists who, following Adam Smith, try to demonstrate that the division of labour provides many 'economic services' (increased productivity, the material development of societies). Gustave de Molinari, the editor in chief of the *Journal des économistes* and author of *La Morale économique* (1888) goes so far as to speak of 'the pacification of relations between capital and labour'. On the other hand, there are the socialists, who take a critical view of the division of labour on the grounds that a fully developed division of labour would hand power to the big factory owners. The division of labour is simply another name for the exploitation, or even the assassination, of the people.

Rather like Germany's so-called 'socialists of the lectern', Durkheim dismisses both these arguments, and opens his thesis with a critique of the purely economic conception of the causes and functions of the division of labour. He is determined to shatter the narrow vision of the economists – utilitarianism – and to outline a sociological approach to economic questions. In his view, economics is a subfield of sociology. The supporters of the classical 'laisser-faire, laisser-passer', school were to become his bête noire.

Durkheim's main interlocutor (or adversary) is Herbert Spencer, one of the authors most widely read by philosophers in France.[4] Spencer's main arguments are: (1) that the social role of the individual increases as civilizations progresses, and (2) that social harmony (or what he calls industrial solidarity) is essentially a product of the division of labour. From the utilitarian point of view, we have individuals who, being independent and isolated, are motivated by the profits they can make from trade. The division of labour results – almost automatically, one might say – from the individual pursuit of self-interest.

Durkheim is keen to distance himself from Spencer: 'Our conclusions are in contradiction to his, more than echoing them' (Durkheim 1984[1893]: 141). He prefers to speak of 'organized society' rather than industrial society, and is highly critical of the utilitarian thesis that social solidarity is nothing more than 'a spontaneous agreement between individual interests', and that 'society [is] no more than the establishment of relationships between individuals exchanging the products of their labour' (ibid.: 152).

Durkheim's approach is in more than one respect similar to that of the German economist Gustav von Schmoller, who, in 1889 and 1890, published in the *Revue d'économie politique* three long articles on the division of labour viewed in historical terms. Schmoller's articles are well documented, drawing on both historical and geographical material and anthropological data – and his evolutionist perspective is quite similar to Spencer's, as he examines the transition that takes us from primitive peoples to civilized peoples, and from the homogeneous to the heterogeneous. At the economic level, the great historico-social process can be divided into three phases: the domestic or family economy, the urban regional and national economy and, finally, the world or global economy. Schmoller rejects the monocausal approach, and takes into account a multiplicity of factors: the development of means of transport, the increase in population density, the development of cities, the establishment of markets, and politico-administrative innovations. His study looks at both the causes and the effects of the division of labour. The division of labour does not simply create differences (between individuals who become increasingly independent); it also creates *communities* by encouraging the *socialization* of individuals and by making the social organism 'more closely united' (Schmoller 1889: 238). This is, in his view, a precondition for progress and civilization, including the high intellectual culture, the moral, aesthetic and economic culture, and the development of the feelings of solidarity that bind together whole peoples. Things that appear to be contradictory – difference and community, individualism and solidarity – come together. Durkheim had great respect for his German colleague, and cites him several times in his thesis. Their many differences of opinion would, however, also lead them to disagree with one another.

Durkheim, for his part, makes a distinction between mechanical and organic solidarity, introduces the notion of collective consciousness and anomie, and outlines a sociological theory of social change. His study is divided into two main parts. Book I looks at the function of the division of labour, and Book II at its causes and conditions: 'We shall first investigate the function of the division of labour, that is, the social need to which it corresponds' (Durkheim 1984[1893]: 6). The organicist metaphor is obvious: it is as though society were a living organism made up of various organs, each with its own function.

Crime and Punishment. Types of Solidarity

Durkheim is faced with a methodological problem. While social solidarity is a moral phenomenon, it can neither be observed nor quantified with any accuracy. Durkheim's solution is to choose an indictor – a 'visible symbol' – that allows the object to be grasped. His indicator is the law, which codifies in writing imperative rules governing how we behave in social life: 'Thus we may be sure to find reflected in the law all the essential varieties of social solidarity' (Durkheim 1984[1893]: 25). We must compare this social bond to others, and 'to do this it is essential to begin by classifying the different species of social solidarity' (ibid.: 24).

This helps to explain Durkheim's interest in the sociology of crime and legal history. His lectures of 1892–3 and 1893–4 dealt with a theme that seems to have little to do with the subject of his thesis: crime. What he is really interested in is the theory of sanctions. He studies the relationship between crime and punishment, and makes a distinction between legal and moral sanctions, and the restitutory and repressive sanctions that are central to his thesis. He said that he was rather 'pleased' with his lecture on responsibility: 'It was hard, but I think it paid off.'[5] The interest in the sociology of crime and in the ethnography of criminal law was a recent phenomenon in Europe. The history of law was gradually beginning to incorporate ethnographic studies of, for example, archaic forms of punishment and responsibility, or punishment and the function of penal law into a sociological perspective

In 1893, Durkheim published a review of Gaston Richard's essay *L'Origine de l'idée de droit*. It was, he wrote, 'a vigorous effort to open up a new pathway in legal ethics and legal philosophy', and revealed 'a remarkable dialectical ingenuity' (Durkheim 1975[1893b]: 239–41). Richard demonstrated that the philosophy of law cannot be divorced from sociology: the law is part of a social relationship, implies compromises on both sides, and further implies a spirit of understanding and harmony. Durkheim had found an ally. He is, on the other hand, also critical of his future collaborator because he prioritizes a system of concepts (the ideas of arbitration, punishment and debt) over 'things', or, in other words, rules: ['the idea of the law] dimly reflects the juridical life itself, it does not create it; in just the same way as our idea of the world is only a reflection of the world in which we live' (ibid.). We have, in reality, *laws*, or in other words an indeterminate number of laws.

In his thesis, Durkheim's starting point is reality, or, in other words, rules, crimes and punishment. He discusses all manner of crimes (and the associated punishments); incest, offences against sexual honour, crimes against religion, mores or authority, plots and rebellions, fraud, theft and murder. Punishments are emotional reactions that both expiate the crime and defend the group: they are all the more severe when the crimes offend 'strong states' of the collective consciousness. It is the group and not the individual that cries vengeance, as one can see from vendettas.

Durkheim leaves aside the usual distinctions made by jurists (between, for example, public and private law) in order to make a more sociological distinction that takes into account the various punishments and sanctions that are associated with the legal rules: there are, on the one hand, *repressive* sanctions (punishment is inflicted on the criminal), which are represented by penal law and, on the other, the *restitutory* sanctions ('*restoration of the "status quo ante"*' (Durkheim 1984[1893]: 68) represented by civil law, commercial law, administrative law or constitutional law.

His general hypothesis is that penal law (crime + repressive sanctions) – and, more generally, repression – decline in importance as mechanical solidarity becomes less important, and this change is part of a broader trend leading to the increased complexity of society, the development of the administration, specialization and individual autonomy, of a greater respect for justice, equality of opportunity and individual dignity. A new form of solidarity is emerging, and it results not from similarities, but from the growing division of labour. This is organic solidarity. Mechanical solidarity is to so-called lower or primitive societies what organic solidarity is to so-called higher societies: one functions on the basis of similarity, and the other on the basis of complementarity.

Mechanical solidarity is a characteristic of so-called lower societies. Durkheim looks in turn at the Hebrews, the Kabyles and North American Indians, as well as the ancient Germans, the Romans, the Gauls and the ancient Celts. His sources range from the Pentateuch to the work of Fustel de Coulanges, Morgan, Fison and Howitt and, of course, Spencer.

The adoption of such a relativist position indicates that the Rabbi's son is distancing himself from Judaism. The Pentateuch is, in his view, 'a summary of . . . traditions of all kinds' (Durkheim 1984[1893]: 36). And while he carefully analyses the four final books, he does so in order to demonstrate that Hebrew law is essentially repressive, and that this is characteristic of lower societies (ibid.: 92–3). He also reveals the social dimension of dietary prohibitions: 'There are no grounds for a society to prohibit the eating of a particular kind of meat . . . But once an abhorrence of this food has become an integral part of the common consciousness it cannot disappear without healthy bonds becoming loosened, and of this the healthy individual consciousness is vaguely aware' (ibid.: 62).

The comparative method therefore allows him to relativize things somewhat. Durkheim describes so-called lower societies, which function on the basis of mechanical solidarity (solidarity by similarities), in the following terms: they are, in morphological terms, segmentary societies (which are clan- and then territorially based), with small populations and little interdependence between their members. In cultural or psychical terms, they have a high level of collective or shared consciousness, which leaves little room for the personal consciousness.

Durkheim identifies the *horde* as the ideal-type of lower society, and finds an almost pure model amongst the Indians of North America: the sexes are equal, affairs are managed collectively, and kinship is relatively unorganized. The horde then becomes an element of a group as clans are established and as clan-based segmentary societies develop. Such groups and societies function on a consensual basis: 'the collective personality is the sole existing one' (1984[1893]: 130). They are also societies in which religion pervades the whole of juridical life, and the whole of social life: 'At this time, religion includes everything, extends to everything' (ibid.: 90). Durkheim is aware that his study has its limitations – there is no scientific notion of religion and the comparative method has its weaknesses – but he already attaches great importance to religion which, in his view, is central to the collective consciousness.

We have, then, *mechanical solidarity* when there exists 'a solidarity *sui generis* which, deriving from resemblances, binds the individual directly to society' (Durkheim 1984[1893]: 61). The conformity of all individual consciences is therefore the principle that explains social cohesion. The similarities between individuals are so great that there is little or no room for originality or, obviously, dissidence. This does not mean that there is no such thing as an individual consciousness, but it does mean that it is bound up with the common consciousness and merges into it. The bond of solidarity between the two types of consciousness is such that the weakening of the collective consciousness can, according to Durkheim, 'depress us' and trigger feelings of trouble and discontent in individuals.

Lower societies are also societies whose primitive organization is based on the family and in which the common consciousness is 'something other than itself . . . [and is] made up entirely of altruism'. Altruism is the very basis of life in society; 'Everywhere that societies exist there is altruism, because there is solidarity' (Durkheim 1984[1883]: 145). It is the 'fundamental basis' of all societies (ibid.: 173); living together implies sociability, strong and lasting bonds, and mutual sacrifices. 'Every society is a moral society' and Durkheim even speaks, referring to lower societies, of 'communism': 'Where the collective personality is the sole existing one, property itself is inevitably collective' (ibid.: 130). It is not, however, his intention either to paint primitive humanity in 'the gloomiest colours' or to reinvent 'paradise lost' (ibid.: 144).

Arguing that sociability is the distinguishing characteristic of human beings – who are sociable animals first and rational animals second – Durkheim elaborates a theory of sociability based upon the distinction between two forms of sociability: association and coordination. He suggests that society must make allowance for collective emotions, and goes so far as to claim that 'every strong state of the consciousness is a source of life'. Hence the emotional behaviour of large gatherings. Society reacts 'passionately', as we can see from acts of revenge and the punishments that are inflicted for violating certain rules: 'A representation is . . . a force that stirs up around us a whole whirlwind of organic and psychological phenomena'; it acts as a 'nervous current', and 'sparks off the beginnings of illusions and may even effect the maturative functions'. This may well be more obvious in 'less cultivated societies' but it does not necessarily mean that they are irrational (Durkheim 1984[1893]: 53–5).

Long Live Cooperation! Make Room for 'Individual Acts of Dissent!'

What happens when the community becomes less important and when individuals become increasingly diverse, as they do in 'higher-type' societies? There are no more shared beliefs. We move, explains Durkheim, from mere association to cooperation. We have only to 'cast an eye over our legal codes [the civil code, contractual law and procedural law] to confirm the much diminished position occupied in them by repressive law in comparison with co-operative law' (Durkheim 1984[1983]: 101). Rules lose their penal nature, with some exceptions such as the prohibition of adultery and bigamy, or – in the religious context – heresy. This relaxation corresponds to the general tendency for the collective to 'regress' and for social bonds to break down.

The only important change identified by Durkheim concerns the individual: 'The sole collective sentiments that have gained in intensity are those that relate, not to social matters, but to the individual' (Durkheim 1984[1893]: 117). Society's respect for the individual promotes the 'worship of the dignity of the human person', and 'the individual becomes the object of a sort of religion' (ibid.: 122).

And yet this dissolution is not complete, as societies still have a deep sense of their own identity and unity. What is happening? The progress of history takes us from mechanical solidarity to *organic* solidarity, and that form of solidarity is a product of the division of labour. Such is the paradox of advanced or organized societies: there is a greater diversity of individuals and a greater division of functions – everyone has their own sphere of action, and therefore their own personality, and everyone has their own opinions, beliefs and aspirations – but social bonds still exist, even though they may be weaker than they once were. Durkheim describes as 'organic' the solidarity that results from the division of labour because of the analogy with what we observe in the higher animals: each organ is autonomous, but the organism is a whole.

One of the preconditions for its coherence is cooperation, and cooperation is a product of the division of labour. Its classical legal expression is the contract. But if cooperation is to be harmonious, it is not enough for individuals to be bound together by contracts or to relate to one another. There must also be regulation: the rights and duties of all have to be defined. The idea of regulation (or regulatory action) is one of the *idées forces* of *The Division of Labour in Society*. In contemporary societies, the state has, according to Durkheim, an increasingly important regulatory role to play in the administration of justice, education, health and public welfare, and the organization of transport, communications and statistical services. The growing importance of the coordinating organ is therefore, in his view, a normal phenomenon. Its importance grows as the division of labour becomes more pronounced.

A Certain Way of Being Happy

Having analysed the functions of the division of labour, Durkheim begins the second part of his study by raising the question of its origins. From the outset, he is very critical of the widespread theory that claims that the origins of the division of labour are to be found in the quest for happiness. Nothing could be less certain, he adds. And, turning for support to physiological studies of pain, he adds that 'our capacity for happiness is very restricted' (Durkheim 1984[1893]: 181).

Durkheim has his own idea of what happiness means. 'Harmony', 'balance' and 'moderation' are the words he normally uses to defend (true) pleasure, which is to be found between two extremes, or is, in other words, the happy medium. 'Health consists in a moderate degree of activity' (Durkheim 1984[1893]:183). Not even aesthetic activity escapes this law (of limitation): 'Too much artistic sensibility is a sign of sickness that cannot be generalized without danger to society' (Durkheim 1984[1893]: 185).

Everything is, of course, relative. Our happiness is not quite the same as that of our forefathers. At any moment in history our yearning for science, art and material well-being corresponds to what Durkheim calls 'a maximum limit that cannot be exceeded with impunity' (1984[1893]: 183). The same applies to work. Finding pleasure in 'regular and persistent labour' (ibid.: 186) is a new phenomenon. Durkheim then takes the analysis further and sees morality in very relativist terms: 'Every people has its moral code that is determined by the conditions under which it is living' (ibid.: 184).

What applies to pleasure also applies to pain; every period knows its own form of sorrow. And if we compare the contemporary period with others, it is by no means certain that we are better off: 'If we are sensitive to more pleasures, we are also sensitive to more sorrows. . . . In fact, very highly strung nervous systems live in pain and even end up by becoming attached to it' (Durkheim 1984[1893]: 187).

In order to demonstrate that the problem is growing worse, Durkheim tries to find an objective way of quantifying unhappiness. His index of unhappiness is the number of suicides, or the incidence of 'true suicide, the suicide of sadness'. The frequency of this type of suicide is, he observes, 'geographically distributed according to the level of civilization' (Durkheim 1984[1893]: 191). It is more common in the central region of Europe than in the south, in towns than in the countryside, amongst the liberal professions than amongst farmers, and amongst men than amongst women. Does this reflect a prejudice against women? Woman is, according to Durkheim, 'less concerned than man in the civilizing process' and 'recalls certain characteristics to be found in primitive natures' (ibid.: 192).

The 'upward trend' in suicide numbers is a widespread phenomenon that can 'be observed everywhere', and the 'mounting tide of self-inflicted deaths' is an indication that 'the general happiness of society is on the decrease' (Durkheim 1984[1893]: 193). But all this is relative, and is counterbalanced by the quest for greater variety and novelty. Being in favour of the happy medium, Durkheim is suspicious of the thirst for novelty when it reaches 'an exceptional level of intensity'. 'Nothing already existing satisfies them; they yearn for the impossible.' There is, in a word, a danger that we will become 'incorrigibly dissatisfied' (ibid.: 198). Life is, in Durkheim's view, a combination of change and continuity, novelty and regularity.

The Struggle for Survival

Neither the quest for happiness nor the attractions of the new can really explain the growing division of labour. The reasons for its growth are to be found, according to Durkheim, in morphological changes: individuals are growing closer together and are in more active contact with one another. This is the book's central thesis: the growth of the division of labour reflects the 'gradual condensation' of societies, or, in other words, the increase in their moral or dynamic density, which can result from the concentration of the population, the development of towns or the increase in the number and rapidity of means of communication and transport. This is, one might say, 'the social world's law of gravitation'. All these changes coincide with the disappearance of 'the segmentary type' or of 'the complete fusion of the segments' (families, clans, etc.) which, in traditional society, enmeshed individuals and bound them closely to their domestic environment and traditions.

Why do we specialize? Durkheim looks at various hypotheses: the influence of external conditions (such as climatic conditions), the different abilities of individuals (which often appear to be hereditary), the impact of age and gender, but finally invokes the explanatory principle of 'the struggle for existence': 'The division of labour is therefore one result of the struggle for existence: but it is a gentle dénouement' (Durkheim 1984[1893]: 213). There are, of course, winners and losers in this struggle: the owner of a small company becomes a foreman, and the small shopkeeper becomes an employee. None of this is inevitable: there are what Durkheim calls pathological situations, as when there are too many civil servants, too many priests or too many soldiers.

Specialization was not the only solution possible but, on the whole, it works to everyone's advantage. Because we are in pursuit of different goals, we do each other no harm. Soldiers want military glory, priests want moral authority, statesmen want power, industrialists want wealth, and scholars want scientific fame: 'If we specialize it is not so as to produce more, but to enable us to live in the new conditions of existence created for us' (Durkheim 1984[1893]: 217).

Need and Desire

What are these 'new conditions'? In Durkheim's view, one word sums up the transformations that characterize the transition to modernity: *mobility*, by which he means geographical mobility, social mobility as well as the mobility of capital and labour. The undermining of traditions coincides both with greater population shifts and with the hybridization of populations. In order to make his point, Durkheim, who had himself experienced exile – he left his family and region of origin to seek his fortune elsewhere – turns to the statistical data on migratory movements into the big cities of Europe, population movements with France between 1876 and 1881, and the distribution of age groups in the towns and the countryside. The city described by Durkheim is a city of young people and novelties, and it is undeniably a centre for progress. And it is oriented towards the future. Everything changes rapidly: beliefs, tastes, passions and fashions. Big cities encourage the free expansion of individual variations. They are also, he notes, anonymous places: we are all strangers who know nothing of each other and who are indifferent to each other. They are also places where there is less surveillance and where what others think counts for less. The slackening of social controls gives individuals greater freedom and allows them to cast off the 'collective yoke'.

We travel more frequently, establish more contacts, and conduct our business at a distance. We escape the confines of our local environment, and look to the outside world. Morals become more relaxed, religious observance declines and there is greater tolerance (cohabitation, adultery): all these factors help to undermine the collective consciousness. Geographical mobility increases, and so does social mobility as progress helps us shrug off the yoke of heredity, and destroys class and caste systems. In this new context, 'hereditary' professions become less common, and individuals can create their own lives and 'rise' from the humble to the most noble professions. We make the transition from a society in which things are innate to one in which they are acquired – and this includes individuals' property. People free themselves from the 'yoke of the organism' and become differentiated, acquiring personalities of their own. They are no longer tightly chained to their past, enjoy greater freedom and are better equipped to adapt to new circumstances.

One thing is certain: we begin to specialize. The day of the wise man, the man of parts and the dilettante is over. We work more, have more intense social lives, and our faculties become over-excited. Should this give us cause for worry? The city was already being described as one of the agents of nervous pathology. In a little book entitled *La Neurasthénie* (1891), Dr Fernand Levillain contended that the source of neurasthenia was to be found in the big cities. The tendency to apply the discovery of nervous pathologies to society and the nation peaked with the translation of the best-selling *Dégénérescence* in 1894. Its author, Max Nordau, was a doctor of German origin who had studied with Charcot; he deplored the artistic decadence of *fin-de-siècle* France and saw aesthetes as the victims of neuropathology. He also extends his analysis of the artist to the nation as a whole: artistic decadence was the symptom of a national degeneracy caused by the over-excitement and fatigue that came from living in an urban environment in which we are bombarded with sensations and speed. Nordau even goes so far as to speak of 'collective neurasthenia'. If we accept his argument, the conclusion is obvious: artistic decadence is a symptom of a national decline and a national decadence. With its rising rates of crime and suicide, France is described as '*La Grande Dégénérée*' ['The Great Degenerate'].

Durkheim is convinced that the 'hyperactivity of general life is wearisome, tensing up our nervous system,' and that this general level of stimulation also raises cultural standards. It does not, however, lead to greater happiness or greater morality. It is an inevitable process: 'Men go forward because they must' (Durkheim 1984[1893]: 276).

Freedom and determinism, individual and society: Durkheim is torn between the need to recognize the importance of individual spontaneity, on the one hand, and the need to defend the authority of the group, on the other. He regards sociology as the science of relations between individual and society, but does not regard social facts as mere extensions of psychical facts. He tends in fact to take the opposite view: psychical facts are to a large extent only the 'prolongation' of social facts within the individual consciousness (Durkheim 1984[1893]: 286–7). Society is the determinant factor: 'This is why, although society is nothing without individuals, each one of them is much more a product of society than he is the author' (ibid.: 288n).

Is this a determinist view of history? Not entirely: for Durkheim, man is not 'a mere inactive spectator of his own history' (Durkheim 1984[1893]: 279), especially as we move from a world of instincts and need to one of consciousness and desire. We no longer live in a world of 'obscure' images in which we proceed by 'vague trial and error', but in a world of clear ideas and in which our aspirations teach us the direction in which we should be moving. Culture becomes more intense and more varied, the intellect develops and sensibilities become more acute. Society moves in the direction of a universalism that affects every area of social life from religion to the rules of law and morality. Rationality becomes universal.

Civilization is therefore the most advanced stage of evolution. And civilization is, it must be added, all the more rational and logical in that it becomes 'a desirable object – in short, an ideal' (Durkheim 1984[1893]: 278). An ideal is an 'anticipated representation of a result that is desired', but it remains 'proximate'. There is no end to progress, and the ideal is never exhausted. Durkheim's vision of history tends, therefore, to be optimistic, provided that we avoid excess, as 'a certain refinement of civilization' demonstrates civilization's 'unhealthy character' through its anxiety and restlessness' (ibid.: 279).

Illness, discontent and uncertainty. There are several mentions of psychical problems, nervous illnesses and neurasthenia in *The Division of Labour* and Durkheim speaks of the inner conflicts that arise when the collective consciousness is weakened. He never mentions the work of Freud, but the introduction of the notion of a collective consciousness and the use of various metaphors (nervous currents, waves that circulate between individuals, latent energies) mean that the sociology he is outlining is a truly collective psychology that seeks to find causes not only at the individual level, but also at the social level, and not only in the depths of the soul, but also in the bedrock of collective life.

Anomie

Durkheim is not unaware of the fact that the division of labour has been, and is, the object of critiques. If it goes too far, there is indeed a danger that it will have a 'dissolving influence' and will, as Auguste Comte feared, become a threat to social cohesion or a source of disintegration. Borrowing the expression 'Division means dispersion' from his colleague Alfred Espinas (Durkheim 1984[1893]: 295), Durkheim devotes the final part of his book to abnormal or exceptional forms of the division of labour. These include industrial and commercial crises (he takes as his index the number of bankruptcies, which rose by 70 per cent between 1845 and 1869), the antagonism between labour and capital, and the fragmentation of science. He makes a point of saying that the facts are serious. Durkheim is therefore somewhat ambivalent: on the one hand, he takes an optimistic view of the development of the division of labour, but on the other he makes a very gloomy diagnosis when he identifies its abnormal forms.

The unity of an organized society does not, in Durkheim's view, depend solely upon a consensus or the division of labour; there must also be 'a regulatory system sufficiently developed to determine the mutual relationships between functions' (Durkheim 1984[1893]: 301). The alternative is anarchy, as we can see from the state of science. The same is true of the industrial world: 'The relationships between capital and labour have up to now remained in the same legal state of indeterminacy' (ibid.: 303). This indeterminacy or absence of rules is what Durkheim calls *anomie*.

Regulation is normally such that it is effectively spontaneous: exchanges 'regulate themselves'. That is in the order of things. It is when there is no longer any contiguity between organisms and when 'the producer can no longer keep the whole market within his purview' that problems begin to arise. The extension of the market (which is no longer segmented and becomes a single at the level of society as a whole, or even at a world level), on the one hand, and the emergence of large-scale industry, on the other, transforms the relationship between employers and workers. This occasions 'greater fatigue to the nervous system' and 'causes the needs of the workers to increase'. All the preconditions for conflict are there, not only because all these transformations have been accomplished with extreme rapidity but also because 'the conflicting interests have not yet had time to strike an equilibrium' (Durkheim 1984[1893]: 304–6).

Durkheim makes no secret of his indignation about the conditions that are forced upon factory workers. They are treated as though they were machines, and this has the effect of 'diminishing the individual' (1984[1893]: 306). What can be done to remedy this 'evil'? Durkheim suggests that work should be reorganized in such a way that each worker remains in close contact with his colleagues and collaborators, and that the worker has a new purpose or goal that lets him know that his activity 'has a meaning' (ibid.: 308). A social environment must, in other words, be created to give work a meaning.

Durkheim does not, however, associate these conflicts of interest with 'class war'. Class struggle is, in his view, an indication that the situation is morbid or abnormal. He concentrates on two issues: social inequalities and fair social relations (including fair wages). These questions were being widely discussed, and divided intellectual and political circles at the time. Durkheim rapidly evokes Marx and his famous comment about how the division of labour 'causes the pores of the working-day to contract' (Durkheim 1984[1893]: 327). His interlocutors include Marxists and socialists, but he wishes to take a more balanced view than them. The growth of the division of labour certainly goes hand in hand with an ever-increasing inequality, but the economic and social situation is not as catastrophic as these theoreticians suggest. Things have improved: employment in the public sector is open to all, social mobility is possible, and there is an increasingly widespread belief that there should be more equality between citizens.

Durkheim does not believe that we can do away with all these inequalities. From his point of view, de facto inequalities are justifiable, but on two conditions: first, they must be expressions of natural inequalities, and, second, there must be 'equality in the external conditions of the struggle' (Durkheim 1984[1893]: 316). All must have equal opportunities. There is, finally, one other important condition: 'contractual solidarity': 'The contract is not fully agreed unless the services exchanged are equivalent in social value' (Durkheim 1984[1893]: 317). Work must, in other words, be 'rewarded on a fair basis' (cf Bouglé 1903: 107).

A Celebration of Work

The Division of Labour in Society is at once a eulogy of specialization and a celebration of work. It is not simply that we work more, but that work has become 'a permanent occupation, a habit and even a necessity' (Durkheim 1984[1893]: 328). (Modern) man is, that is, defined by the work he does and the way he specializes. We have moved from parochialism to corporatism.

Specialization, which is a precondition for social cohesion and balance, therefore becomes a real duty. This is, according to Durkheim, a moral question, and morality is not to be defined as freedom, but as a state of dependence: 'What is moral is everything that is a source of solidarity' (Durkheim 1984[1893]: 331). Morality consists in solidarity with the group, and there is a moral dimension to the division of labour because it allows the individual to feel 'the salutary pressure of society that moderates his egoism, making of him a moral creature. This is what constitutes the moral value of the division of labour. Through it the individual is once more made aware of his dependent state *vis à vis* society' (ibid.: 333).

Durkheim's great fear is that the 'loosening' he has observed will be exacerbated. The remedy lies in neither a return to the past nor a flight into the future. The priority has to be putting an end to anomie, and in order to do that we must react by establishing a new discipline. Our first duty is to elaborate a new morality based upon 'the worship of the dignity of the human person' (insofar as the individual is an autonomous source of action), respect for justice in social relationships and a recognition of the central importance of work. Given that 'we may predict that . . . the day will come when the whole of our social and political organization will have an exclusively, or almost exclusively, professional basis' (Durkheim 1984[1893]: 139), that morality will be work-based. In an organized society, work or the fulfilment of a function becomes a duty.

The Utopia of a World Society

The great value that Durkheim is defending is therefore altruism, and the ideal he is trying to promote is that of *fraternity*. His cherished dream is an end to wars, the establishment of peaceful relations between societies that will allow men to work for a common purpose. This ideal means that we must look for mechanisms that can 'moderate' the egoism of both individuals and groups. There is such a thing as the regulatory action of societies on individuals, and of societies upon one another. So why not a single human society? Durkheim does not have many illusions. The formation of one single human society is, in his view 'for ever ruled out'. What is possible is 'the formation of larger societies', as we can see from Europe: 'We have already seen that there is tending to form, above European peoples, a European society that has even now some feeling of its own identity and the beginnings of an organization' (Durkheim 1984[1893]: 337).

The Oral Examination

Durkheim defended his thesis at the Sorbonne on 3 March 1893. He was 34. 'Tall, thin, blonde' and 'already bald',[6] he had difficulty in concealing the fact that he was nervous, had spent a long time preparing for his oral examination, and was trying to anticipate the objections that might be raised. There was a lot at stake. Who could fail to be surprised that a philosopher should be interested in the division of labour, or that he should subtitle his thesis 'A study of the higher societies'? Durkheim himself felt that his study might offend 'certain received ideas'. He also knew that this would be a 'fairly difficult ordeal' because of 'the important privileges that are attached to success': he would need his doctorate if he was to be appointed a university lecturer (Durkheim (1973a[1918]: 479).

The oral examination was a society event, but there was also a theatrical side to it. The candidate wore a morning coat. The dean chaired the session and asked questions, as did the other six members of the jury. The jury consisted of Paul Janet, Charles Waddington, Henri Marion, Émile Boutroux, Victor Brochard and Gabriel Séailles.[7] Marion was the *rapporteur*, and had read the manuscript before it was printed. All the members of the jury taught in the Paris faculty of letters and some already knew the candidate. Durkheim dedicated his thesis to Émile Boutroux, his teacher at the École normale supérieure.

Although Durkheim's thesis did not create the same scandal as, for example, Alfred Espinas's thesis on animal societies, it did encounter a lot of resistance, observed Célestin Bouglé (1930a), who was at the time a student at the École normale supérieure. The members of the jury had not been won over to Durkheim's ideas by any means. Even Émile Boutroux could not accept 'without grimacing' this 'deterministic' demonstration, which looked like a 'return to the spirit of Taine'. At one point during the viva, an exasperated Paul Janet thumped the table and invoked the name of God. Durkheim was visibly ill at ease: as the dean observed, his voice was 'nervous and shook with emotion'. He gradually became more confident: 'His voice, which was weak and soft to begin with, rose, swelled and became capable of filling a vast vessel', and his eloquence at times became dramatic.[8]

Even the word 'sociology' grated because, as M. Perreur underlined in his report to the rector, it was 'too closely related to "socialism", which covers so many enormities . . . so much stupidity and such violence; but it is, nonetheless, the name of an embryonic science that is trying to decipher the enigma so as to ensure that the dreadful sphinx does not devour us.' The political dimension of the thesis therefore did not escape its first readers. 'This is', M. Perreur went on, 'a science that has yet to be of any use to anyone. Does that make the socialist politicians blush?' Those with an interest in sociology were already following Durkheim's work attentively. The audience in the lecture theatre included René Worms, the editorial director of the new *Revue internationale de sociologie*; he too was fighting to ensure that the new science kept 'the impartial and reserved attitude of science' in the midst of all these rivalries (Worms 1903a: 1).

Durkheim was first asked about his Latin thesis on Montesquieu. A somewhat irritated Paul Janet observed that it was 'ill-mannered to base the new sociology on contempt for earlier work'. Montesquieu did not, he argued, found political science, as he came after Aristotle.' For his part, Victor Brochard mentioned both Spinoza and Hobbes. Émile's reply to both objections was that something changed with Montesquieu: sociology took on a 'particularly methodological character'.[9]

The members of the jury in fact disagreed not so much with the candidate's interpretation as with 'the personal views he introduced, which were ingenious and daring, but at times dubious'. They were perplexed. The impenitent Durkheim therefore had to defend them 'vigorously'; he succeeded in sounding convincing and made a strong impression of them thanks to 'the clarity of his ideas, the confidence with which he spoke, and the strength of his convictions, which he demonstrated throughout'. 'This was an original and powerful mind', they remarked in the course of their deliberations. Their unanimous verdict was positive: this was 'an in-depth study of the texts' that gave an interpretation of Montesquieu's doctrine which was 'almost beyond criticism'. All the members of the jury paid tribute to 'the excellence of the methodology, and the clarity of the exposition'. 'If the Latin thesis had been the main thesis, it would have been enough to guarantee him an outstanding doctorate.' The candidate was congratulated for 'the care and the scientific spirit' he had shown in his study.[10]

M. Marion then invited Durkheim to summarize his thesis about the division of labour in society. 'The social self [*moi*] has never asserted itself more energetically than it does today. The nineteenth century has seen the development of both the individual and socialism. Choosing between these two tendencies is not very scientific. But how can extreme individualism coexist with solidarity?' This opened up the debate. Durkheim emphasized the 'purely scientific nature' of his approach. But in the eyes of the jury, there was no doubt about it: the candidate aspired to 'being a moralist'. From the outset, Marion cleverly criticized the candidate for not overlooking morality: 'Your thesis is not sophisticated enough to have an effect on morality. It is a thesis on the physics of morals.' Durkheim was forced to explain why he placed so much importance on morality, for both historical and polemical reasons: 'Certain moralists are attacking sociology. We have to make them see sense.'[11]

Paul Janet picked up his colleague's objections: 'Why do you describe your book as a book on ethics? Should the division of labour be seen as a duty or not? You confuse "function" with "duty".' Durkheim replied that 'the modern consciousness regards its professional specialization as a duty. The division of labour is the individual's only solution, other than death or emigration.' He added: 'To be a man today means consenting to be an organ of society.'[12] M. Waddington's contribution to the debate was somewhat bitter in its eloquence, and also very critical: 'You are telling us nothing new; we are dealing with the lowest levels of ethics . . . Are you ignoring the issue of freedom, and do you not believe in duty in general?' A visibly annoyed Durkheim replied: 'That is not my subject. Why are you asking me questions that my thesis does not raise?' He made the same reply several times more before the end of the session. Throughout, he demonstrated, 'with a somewhat impatient presence of mind, a simple and sincere eloquence'.

Émile Boutroux, for his part, dropped the problem of morality and raised a methodological issue: 'What certainty-value does your work have?' He had a problem with the approach adopted by Durkheim: he had trapped himself into 'discussing signs of realities rather than actual realities'. Nor was Boutroux convinced that the law of the division of labour (which is directly proportional to the size and density of the population) that Durkheim had discovered was 'the only solution to the problem that has been raised'. 'My law is not the only possible law', replied the candidate, 'but it is an inescapable finding. There are others, and they are secondary but attenuated.' In his report, Marion remarked of the methodology used that 'it was nonetheless original'.

The question of formal morality had by no means been ignored. Séailles and Brochard returned to this point at the end of the viva: 'Is your main argument against formal moralities that none of them can explain charity?' asked Brochard. Durkheim immediately replied: 'I do not see the distinction you are making, and I do define charity: man's attachment to something other than himself. The relationship between solidarity and charity is that between motion and force.' And he concluded: 'I am a scientist: I study motion.'

Durkheim defended his new theories, 'which were closely articulated', 'with a rare distinction'. 'Both the faculty and the audience were struck by his intellectual self-confidence, the breadth of his knowledge and the authority with which he spoke.' The viva actually began to look like a joust in which Durkheim seemed to be the equal of his judges, even sometimes getting the better of them. 'Our candidate's abilities as an orator are not illusory. His answers – and this is very unusual – are good answers that never lead to prevarications, or capitulation for reasons of cowardice or caution.' Intrigued by the novelty of the subject matter and stimulated by the candidate's unusual talent, the members of the jury became quite taken with him. 'If they had not all showered him with praise', he might have seemed like an enemy.[13] He succeeded in making a good impression on the audience as well as on the jury; there was more than one outbreak of sustained applause.

'One of the most remarkable of oral examinations, and one the most completely satisfying.'[14] 'Durkheim's thesis is remarkable and remarkably well defended. Immense success, perhaps the greatest since Bergson', Xavier Léon wrote to Élie Halévy in 1893 (Léon and Halévy 1993: 200). It was, according to René Worms, an event: 'The candidate has for some years enjoyed an honourable reputation amongst that section of the philosophical audience that has an interest in social studies' (Worms 1893: 359). The French thesis was judged to be 'even more remarkable' than the Latin thesis, and was recognized as 'a major work'. The jury admired the 'solidity' of his arguments and the 'novelty' of his overall conceptions. The subject matter was certainly difficult and the thesis itself was not, they admitted, 'very easy reading': 'It took some considerable effort to read it, but the effort was worth it.'[15]

For Durkheim, this was recognition for several years' work: he had been recognized as 'one of the best doctoral candidates' and 'one of the most distinguished' to have been honoured for a long time. It was also a victory: as the *rapporteur* observed, his thesis was, whatever objections one might have to it, the 'cornerstone of the new building' known as sociology. Fifteen years after Espinas's 'remarkable' thesis on animal societies, sociology had made its 'triumphal entry' into the Sorbonne. 'We expected a great deal of this thesis, and we were not disappointed' (Worms 1893: 359). For those who were listening, the new doctor had become 'the most authoritative representative' of the young discipline and had supplanted Charles Gide and Gabriel Tarde. 'This one will be a master', exclaimed one observer.[16]

As Perreur suggested in his concluding remarks, Durkheim could therefore hope to have a brilliant career: 'Should the new doctor's desire or destiny ever bring him to Paris, it would not, I think, be over-optimistic to predict that he will have a most important position'. In Bordeaux, Durkheim's success was a cause for celebration: 'The dazzling success of Durkheim's theses and the value of his teaching make him worthy of the title of professor.'[17] *La Petite Gironde* described the author as one of the most hard-working and distinguished members of the University of Bordeaux. This was, it was recognized, a great event for the social sciences: sociology's legitimacy had been recognized by the Sorbonne.

Durkheim for his part, wished to leave Bordeaux. His first choice was the Sorbonne, but, as he realized, he had little chance of success given that Alfred Espinas was determined to apply. Émile Egger had recently been appointed to a post in Paris, which meant that there was an opening in Nancy.[18] Durkheim immediately wrote to Louis Liard, the director of higher education, to express his interest:

> The reason why Nancy has attractions that no other provincial city can offer is that, being from Lorraine, I would be close to my family. What is more, I would be in my home environment, and that is not a negligible factor when one is planning for what will no doubt be a long career. I would not, it is true, only be teaching sociology; but it would, I hope, be easy to do so on a part-time or intermittent basis and, therefore, not to abandon my favourite studies.[19]

There was no reply. Durkheim had his doctorate, but he stayed in Bordeaux.

A Few Misunderstandings

Durkheim wrote a long preface for the first edition, which was published by Alcan in 1893 (the print-run was probably of between 1,000 and 1,500 copies).[20] He wanted to reply to the objections raised by the members of his thesis jury, and especially those relating to the question of morality.

Duty or function? Solidarity or charity? The members of the jury, who were the first to read his thesis, were not easily convinced. In the first part of his introduction, Durkheim tries to reassert that his book is indeed about morality, that it takes moral facts as its object, and that the question he is trying to answer is: does the division of labour have a moral value?

He is less interested in traditional discussions of moral doctrines than in the study of 'moral facts' or the multitude of particular precepts, no matter whether they are part of a written code or to do with popular consciousness. He had been criticized for dealing only with the 'lower regions of morality' and for being interested in *practical* rather than *theoretical* morality, and therefore had to supply a definition of 'the facts of moral life'. In order to do so, he analyses a great number of situations which correspond to this practical morality: the cult of the dead, the 'refined modesty' of the cultivated classes, respect for the elderly, paternity, the taboo on inflicting pain on animals, dietary restrictions (such as the Jewish prohibition on eating pork) and philanthropy. Turning to the issue of philanthropy, Durkheim wonders, in somewhat ironic terms, if it might not be useless, or even harmful, given that it might prolong the lives of 'cretins, idiots, lunatics and incurables of all kinds' (1975[1893a]: 264–5). One could be tempted to say that such generosity might do more harm than good, but the cautious Durkheim limits himself to saying that 'its benefits are very dubious.'

There is no question of basing morality on utility, be it individual or collective. There is always something 'obscure' or 'conjectural' about morality. If there is any rationality involved, it can only be (very) limited. Durkheim defined a moral fact as 'any rule of conduct associated with a sanction' (1975[1893a]: 278). A moral fact therefore has two distinguishing characteristics: it is obligatory and diffuse (unlike the law, which is formal). Given that any sanction is a social thing, it follows that 'morality is a branch of sociology'. Not everything in life is a matter of obligation: there is such a thing as contingency, and there is also room for the imagination. This is the world of non-necessary acts or 'gratuitous actions' ranging from gifts and caresses to the refinements of modern urbanity and heroic sacrifices. Outside our working hours, we expend energy 'for the pleasure of doing so, for the joy of being free. This, in a word, is the realm of *luxury* and art'. And despite what we may think, life is, he argues, full of these inventions, and that is what gives it its charm

Morality may well be timeless, but it is also relative and specific to one period and one type of society. 'The question is no different from the questions that biologists ask themselves,' remarks Durkheim, picking up his distinction between the normal and the pathological: 'A moral fact is normal for a given social type', when we observe it in the average society of that type (1975[1893a]: xxxvi). Morality is a social issue: the prohibitions on killing an emblematic animal in a totemic society, or on infanticide in our European societies, are typical examples. It is also a historical example, as we can see from the example of freedom of thought.

In the final part of his introduction, Durkheim also attempts to clear up a few misunderstandings. The first misunderstanding concerns the philosophy/science opposition. Even though he is not opposed to philosophy, Durkheim sees his own work as scientific, and intends to submit it to the criterion of verification. He cites at length a *Manuel de philosophie*, whose author Paul Janet was a member of his thesis jury: 'Any science must, in a word, be based upon facts. And the facts that help to found morality are generally accepted values.' Durkheim is quite clear: 'Moral facts are phenomena like any others . . . It should thus be possible to observe, describe and classify them, as well as seek out the laws that explain them' (Durkheim 1984[1893]: xxv). His intention is to use the methodology of the positive sciences to describe the facts of moral life.

Durkheim states on several occasions that his approach is scientific: it is based on detailed observations and quantitative methods, avoids personal judgments and subjective impressions, and carries out real experiments in the form of methodical comparisons: 'We have attempted to satisfy this, the condition of all science' (Durkheim 1984[1893]: xxix). His thesis is a first attempt to do so, and may therefore have its imperfections, and he is aware that the task will be difficult and complex.

The second misunderstanding concerns the status of the observer: is he neutral or committed? Durkheim accepts that, if it is to become scientific, the study of moral facts must follow the example set by the other sciences, which strive to set aside the observer's personal feelings in order to look at the facts themselves. He has, on the other hand, no intention of being a neutral or resigned spectator: 'Yet because what we propose to study is above all reality, it does not follow that we should give up the idea of improving it. We would esteem our research not worth the labour of a single hour if its interest were merely speculative' (1984[1893]: xxvi). Sociology is therefore in favour of change, and allows us both to resolve practical problems and to offer suggestions that may improve things. That requires, however, a very cautious approach: '[Science] imparts to us a prudently conservative disposition of mind . . . A fact does not change in a trice, even when this may be desirable' (Durkheim 1984[1893]: xxviii).

Controversy

The book's publication caused a real sensation. It was read and discussed by students who were looking for new ideals. Some were frustrated by it, and others were simply outraged. Célestin Bouglé recalled how one student – Henri Vaugois – walked down the corridors of the Sorbonne denouncing the formulae adopted by Durkheim, such as: 'Man must be taught to play his role as an organ.'[21] Others, who were obsessed with the problem of rebuilding the nation, of secular emancipation and social and economic organization, found Durkheim's theses very attractive: the need to establish new social relations, the defence of specialization, equality of conditions and competition between individuals, reconstitution of professional groups. Some discovered that they had a vocation for sociology, and wanted to work under Durkheim's supervision and to promote a scientific understanding of sociology. One of the first to join what was to become known as the 'Bordeaux school' was Célestin Bouglé (1870–1940), a young *normalien* born in Saint-Brieuc (Côtes-du-Nord). Having passed his *aggrégation*, he obtained a travel grant and left for Germany in August 1893, and attended lectures given by Simmel, von Jhering, Wagner and Lazarus. When he went back to France, he turned to sociology, though not without some hesitations.

Although it was a 'very serious study' that seemed to be 'ill-suited to popularization', *The Division of Labour in Society* sold relatively well. Durkheim was obviously pleased: at the end of May 1894, only 500 of the 1,330 copies remained unsold.[22] When, in July 1893, the book was submitted to the economic and social sciences section of the Comité des travaux historiques et scientifiques in the hope that it would subscribe to purchase further copies, the response was positive. The *rapporteur* Octave Gérard, who was deputy rector of the University of Paris, emphasized the 'great value' of the book, and its importance 'in both philosophical and social terms'. Such a study deserved, he concluded, 'to be encouraged by a subscription to put it in libraries, and to make it available to the readers to whom it is addressed.'[23]

The book 'caused quite a stir' in the small world of philosophy, as Georges Sorel (1895) put it. It was, exclaimed Léon Brunschvicg and Élie Halévy (1893), 'an admirable thesis', but they also foresaw that the audacity and originality of Durkheim's book meant that it would encounter a lot of hostility. Both men were contributors to the *Revue de métaphysique et de morale*, and made no secret of their objections to it: introducing 'sociological positivism' into the domain of morality was, in their view, quite unacceptable. In the review of 'the year in philosophy 1893', Brunschvicg and Halévy also discussed Gabriel Tarde's *Transformations du droit*. Durkheim was once more contrasted with Tarde, and the comparison was not to Durkheim's advantage: he was criticized for his reliance on mechanistic explanations and a sociological method that ignored psychological factors. Such a sociology, in their view, soon ceased to be either a science or an ethics. Gabriel Tarde, in contrast, saw the 'end of the social' as the individual. They concluded: 'The only thing that is real is individual initiative and, therefore, free associations of individuals.' The very notion of 'collective happiness' looked to them like a form of idolatry.

Durkheim obviously had his supporters, including his friend Lucien Herr, who, although still enamoured of metaphysics and not strictly speaking a sociologist, defended and promoted his book. Herr admired the book because it displayed a rare understanding of the social realities of the day: 'The research has been carried out with a concern for the truth, a scorn of verbosity and with an intensity of conviction which, when taken to this degree, are not vulgar' (Herr 1893: 581). He would later say that 'Durkheim's magisterial thesis made a very strong impression on me'.

Lévy-Bruhl and Durkheim had a lot in common: born one year apart (in 1857 and 1858 respectively) into Jewish families from the east of France, they both studied at the École normale supérieure, were *agrégés de philosophie*, and had spent time in Germany.[24] Their in-laws were vaguely related. Both became members of the *jury d'agrégation* in 1892, and shared an interest in social and political questions. Lévy-Bruhl had written on responsibility, solidarity and socialism, and was impressed by the strength of his colleague's convictions. He played an important role in Durkheim's career, and was so close to him that he was seen as his disciple when he published his *La Morale et la science des moeurs* in 1903.

As Marcel Mauss recounts (1962[1928]: 34), Durkheim was soon being criticised for his 'collectivism' by 'touchy moralists and classic or Christian economists': it was 'due to conflicts of this kind [that] he was excluded from professorships in Paris'. His opponents included 'competitors' like René Worms,[25] Alfred Fouillée (1895a)[26] and Gabriel Tarde (1983), who, irritated by the author's sociological 'imperialism', denounced his 'social realism'.[27] Tarde's review marked the beginning of a debate that quickly became a real quarrel between the two men, with one arguing the case for individualism, and the other that for collectivism. Tarde published what appeared to be a flattering review of *The Division of Labour,* describing it as a 'remarkable and profound study' and noting that Durkheim's 'understanding of collective psychology was evident on every page'.

The portrait of Durkheim that he painted was not, on the other hand, very flattering: 'M. Durkheim [is] a stubborn dreamer. He is a quiet extremist, an imperturbable logician, a deeper thinker rather than a fair one, and is so specious that he deceives himself and is convinced that his *a priori* constructs are observed truths' (Tarde 1895[1893]: 182). Tarde disagreed totally with Durkheim's basic thesis, and had three general criticisms to make: the study of social evolution focused solely on international relations (wars, massacres and annexations); the division of labour resulted not from the growing size and density of the population, but from creativity and genetic accident. He also queried the dichotomy between the two forms of solidarity, and cast doubt upon the division of labour's tendency to promote socialization and moralization.

Although they shared Durkheim's worries about the weakening of the social bond, the reformist economists on *La Revue d'économie politique* had, for their part, certain reservations and described as 'utopian' Durkheim's demand for complete equality of opportunity, which would, in their view – and as Saint-Marc (1893) insisted – lead to the abolition of private property. The German economist Gustav von Schmoller criticized Durkheim on the grounds that, because of his moral ideals, his outline of the problems arising from the division of labour was over-hasty.[28] The members of the German historical school and the 'professorial socialists' who had inspired Durkheim criticized him for defending radical and socialist ideas to the detriment of any serious historical research. Could it be that Durkheim was, without realizing it himself, a socialist? Although he criticized him for his anti-economic reductionism, which implied that the goal of society was not the production of goods, Paul Barth, another German colleague, was kinder to Durkheim, whom he regarded not so much as a social reformer as a philosopher of history, and praised him for having discovered 'social life'.[29]

A Message to Socialists: 'Be Clear and United'

Paris was still in a state of shock provoked by the terrorist activity of the anarchists. The anarchist movement was very active, and enjoyed a certain prestige amongst the younger generation of intellectuals and artists. There was a lot of turmoil in the Latin Quarter. The influence of small groups like the Étudiants socialistes révolutionnaires internationalistes grew when a student at the École des Beaux-Arts was found guilty of 'affronting public decency'. Demonstrations degenerated into pitched battles when the police intervened, and the temperature was rising. The socialist students organized meeting after meeting, lecture after lecture, and published lots of leaflets. More than 1,500 young people attended Jean Jaurès's lecture, 'Idealism and materialism in the conception of history'. Even the École normale supérieure was affected, when the '*littéraires*' of 1894, including Charles Péguy, rallied to socialism. When he evoked this period, Péguy recalled with delight the attractions of socialism at this time: 'A young socialism, a new socialism, a socialism that was serious, and somewhat childish – but that is all part of being young – a young man's socialism had been born' (Leroy 1981: 54).

What did Durkheim think of these disturbances and of socialism? He had known Jaurès since their days at the École normale supérieure, and it is said that in 1885–6 he turned the future socialist leader away from the 'political formalism and shallow philosophy of the radicals'. He was obviously interested in socialist ideas, and had mastered their 'very sources' (Saint-Simon and Marx) at a very early age. He did, however, have his reservations and, as Mauss points out, made no secret of his principled opposition to 'its violent nature, its class character – more or less purely working-men's – and therefore its political and even politician-like tone'. 'Durkheim was profoundly opposed to all wars of class or nation. He desired change only for the benefit of the whole of society and not for one of its parts – even if the latter had numbers and forces. He considered political revolutions as superficial, costly and more dramatic than serious' (Mauss 1962[1928]: 34).

Durkheim 'sympathized', as Mauss put it, with the socialists, socialism and Jaurès, but never became involved. Some years later, when his nephew once more tried to convert him, he told him: 'Preaching serves no purpose. I am ready to join socialism when it changes its formulae, or in other words when it is no longer an exclusively class-based party.'[30]

The Division of Labour in Society was published in 1893, and Durkheim published a 'Note on the definition of socialism' in the *Revue philosophique* that same year. His intention was to discuss an eminently political question in scientific terms. He was very familiar with the socialist movement. His short 'Note' is an indication of a distant sympathy. The article is part of polemical exchange with Gustave Belot, a former fellow student at the École normale supérieure who tried to supply a definition of socialism in the pages of the review (Belot 1893). Durkheim made it clear from the outset that, unlike Belot, he was not interested in the idea (of socialism), but in the thing itself, and that his intention was to adopt a scientific approach so as to identify 'tendencies' – a common spirit – that could be found in all the socialist doctrines he was familiar with.

Durkheim dismissed all the various 'socialist sects': some identified socialism with the negation of private property, others with the subordination of the individual to the collective, and still others with involvement with the suffering classes. That, however, was not the important point. According to Durkheim, the one thing that all forms of socialism had in common was a critique of the current state of economic affairs and a call for its transformation in either the short or the long term. The central problem was that of regulation: given that society was in a state of 'dispersion', how could the state 'introduce a higher morality into it'? What role could the state play as a 'central regulatory organ'? How, in other words, could the untamed nature of the market in a capitalist society be attenuated in such a way as to subordinate egoistic ends to social ends, and to introduce a 'higher morality' and greater fairness?

The definition he proposes reduces socialism to 'a tendency that causes economic functions to move, either abruptly or progressively, from the dispersed state in which they exist, to an organized state' (Durkheim 1986[1893]: 118). He is convinced that 'the more history advances the more social functions that were originally dispersed become organized and "socialized"' (ibid.: 120).

Turning back the clock and going back to earlier social forms is therefore out of the question. That, he believes, is the error of collectivism, which is often described as a return to primitive communism, or in other words to an earlier historical phase characterized by highly dispersed social activity. He is careful to point out that Marx himself does not share this simplistic view.

Durkheim's comments are political but not partisan.[31] He is telling the various socialist groups to 'stop quarrelling, and be clear'. Doctrinal clarity and unity are the only things that can strengthen the socialist movement, with which he sympathizes because 'the significance of this movement can no longer be denied, at least as regards its essentials' (Durkheim 1986[1893]: 119). The message is addressed to his friend (Jaurès) and to his nephew.

7

An Object, a Method and Some Rules

As he wrote his doctoral thesis, Durkheim became convinced that 'science presupposes the entire freedom of the mind' (1984[1893]: xxix). He was, however, well aware that a new science always finds obstacles in its path, and that 'there is no science which at its beginnings has not encountered similar resistances' (Durkheim 1982[1895]: 74). The 'resistance' is all the greater when man or morality becomes an object of science.

A great deal was expected of sociology as it would, or so it was believed, help to restore social peace. Durkheim himself had few illusions as to its possible contribution in that domain, and admitted that: 'Sociology, at its present stage, is hardly capable of guiding us effectively towards the solution of these practical problems' (Durkheim 1984[1893]: 278.) He had now set himself a goal, and had found a way of achieving it: he could use the methodology of the positive sciences. His new passion was for science, but not for science in its current form: 'Besides this present-day science, consisting of what has already been acquired, there is another, which is concrete and living, which is in part still unaware of itself and still seeking its way' (Durkheim 1984[1893]: 299).

A Position in Paris? The 'Espinas Affair'

Durkheim had little cause to be worried about his professional future. For the moment, the University of Bordeaux 'made use of his services liberally', as M. Perreur remarked in his report, adding that 'not all elite men come to Paris.'[1] Durkheim had now obtained his doctorate, and the Council of the faculty of letters in Bordeaux unanimously resolved to offer him the position of *professeur adjoint* [assistant professor] and to increase his salary to 5,000 francs. There was a real hope that 'granting him tenure would keep him at the University of Bordeaux on a permanent basis. His was, the rector accepted, a 'mind of great value'; he expressed himself 'with conviction and authority' in his lectures. His work was still held in very high regard: 'No teacher works harder, or at greater cost to himself. Even M. Durkheim's health has been compromised.' The only criticism made of him was that he 'still takes too little interest in the academic questions in which a teacher in higher education should not lose interest. Being an eminent scholar is not enough; a teacher must also be an active member of the corporation he has been invited to join.'[2]

Durkheim still dreamed, however, of going to Paris. 'As a stay in Paris is, for all sorts of reasons, greatly sought after, it is', he admitted, 'very unusual for anyone to begin his career there' (Durkheim 1918). Even though he had proved himself both as a teacher and a scholar, he feared, as he told his nephew, that he would be forced to stay in Bordeaux because of the 'Espinas affair'. When he learned that a new course on the history of social economics was to be established at the Paris faculty of letters, the newly qualified doctor was eager to apply for it.

Although students were now taking a growing interest in the social sciences, they were not taught on a regular basis in the Paris faculty of letters. Some teachers were worried about this, including Ernest Lavisse, professor of modern history in the faculty, and recently elected to the Académie française. Already worried about educational issues, he was wondering how to protect young people against both 'blind passion' and 'indifference, ignorance and inertia'. In his view, teaching them about social problems and the solutions to them that were being put forward was a matter of great urgency, and that implied teaching them about new research methods.

The members of the faculty council were divided amongst themselves. The philosopher Paul Janet, on the one hand, suggested that a course on experimental psychology should be introduced. The suggestion was tailor-made for his nephew, the psychologist Pierre Janet, who was better placed than anyone else for such a position. Émile Boutroux, on the other hand, was more in favour of putting sociology on the philosophy syllabus. It was, in his view, 'a branch of new studies that is now being widely discussed in the world of political and current affairs'. Was he thinking of his former pupil Émile? Charles Waddington, who was on the point of taking retirement, was hostile to sociology because its scientific nature had not, in his view, been proven. The discussion went no further. The council unanimously voted to establish a second lectureship in Latin.

Shortly after this, Comte Aldebert de Chambrun let it be known that he was prepared to make an annual endowment of 5,000 francs to establish a chair in social economics. Chambrun, whose wife had inherited the Baccarat glassmaking business, was an eccentric and enigmatic figure, but he had had an impressive career. He ran the family business, but at the same time pursued a political career in the Assemblée nationale and then the Senate. He then left political life in order to devote himself to his passion for music and the arts, and became a patron of the arts. He had given major endowments to the Société d'économie sociale (which represented the Le Play tendency) and financed the establishment of a chair in social economics at the École libre des sciences politiques. He was 'converted' to social economics, probably in 1891 – to his mind it was the same thing as sociology – and met Jules Siegfried and Émile Cheysson, who persuaded him to devote his philanthropic activities to social reform and the study of social questions. They even suggested to him that he should play a part in establishing a 'social museum' in Paris.

How could the university reject even a modest endowment? The members of the law faculty did not know what to make of the suggestion: what *was* social economics? If it was another name for sociology, should it be taught in a faculty of letters or a faculty of law? The lawyers could not agree on an answer to that question, but they certainly took an interest in the social sciences, and especially the political sciences. They also took the view that teaching political science, or the 'science of state', which had hitherto been the responsibility of the École libre des sciences politiques, should come within the remit of the faculties of law. At the time, public law was developing so rapidly that it aspired to having a monopoly on political science as a whole (Favre 1989: 72).

In 1893, Fernand Faure submitted a request to the faculty council asking for a chair in social science to be established. His request was rejected by a majority of professors on the grounds that the subject was insufficiently scientific to be taught in an approved university faculty. Faure then wrote a pamphlet entitled *La Sociologie dans les facultés de droit de France*. Taking his lead from Comte, he attempted to demonstrate the need for a general science that could coordinate all the other specialized social sciences and supply a number of basic notions (cited in Weisz 1979: 90).

The law faculty did not want to see the faculty of letters making a 'conquest' by getting approval for a course on sociology. They had to act quickly. The council unanimously supported a motion from its dean, Calmet de Santerre, calling for the establishment of a sociology course dominated by legal issues. That, in the dean's view, guaranteed that it would be safe and 'purely scientific in character'.[3] Disagreements rapidly emerged, with some of the staff severely criticizing their dean, accusing him of acting *ultra vires* and asking for the request to be adjourned for further discussion. The lawyers were always very suspicious of sociology, and took a poor view of its reformist and collectivist overtones.[4] There appeared to be no obvious solution. A few months later, the faculty of letters withdrew its request for a course on sociology and resigned itself, for the moment, to teaching one on the history of social economics. The law faculty's request was also duly postponed for further debate. There were no winners.

So much for social economics! The faculty's professors obviously could not allow the Comte de Chambrun to force his choice of professor on them (anxious to find a professor who was neither a Jaurès-style revolutionary nor a Leroy-Beaulieu-style reactionary, he had suggested three names, including those of Jules Siegfried and Émile Cheysson). What were Durkheim's chances? It all depended on the content and orientation of the new course: 'If we understand social economics to mean theoretical sociology, the post should obviously go to a man like Durkheim. If the emphasis has to be on the history of doctrines, then Espinas becomes the ideal candidate'.[5] Espinas had published *Histoire des doctrines économiques* in 1891, and had edited, in collaboration with Challey, an anthology: *Extraits des principes économistes des dix-huitième et dix-neuvième siècles*. In June 1893, he was made a Chevalier de la Légion d'honneur.

Durkheim went to visit Lavisse in Paris. 'I become more aware by the day that, especially at a time when passions are aroused, our mores are not conducive to the scientific study of these questions, even though everyone senses the need to do so.'[6] He adopted a very cautious attitude, and was unwilling to submit his application unless the new course was sociologically based.

The faculty then made what Durkheim himself called a 'sudden about-turn', and the Chambrun foundation was behind its change of heart. Espinas was standing as a candidate for the new post and was, it seemed, in a position to win the support of the Sorbonne. 'He argued', explained Durkheim, 'that the Chambrun endowment meant that the new course would not really be on sociology, and that he was therefore prepared to teach at the Sorbonne, which he would not have done, he says, if it had been a sociology course. That was his way of recognizing that I am more competent to teach it.'[7] Durkheim therefore backed down in favour of his colleague, who was duly appointed. He had 'briefly entertained' the hope of going to Paris to continue the 'experiment' he had been pursuing in Bordeaux for almost seven years. 'I cannot', he said, 'abandon that hope without a certain sadness.'[8] After this failure, Durkheim wrote in a letter to his parents, probably in January 1894:

> I am quite prepared to stay in Bordeaux for as long as they want me to. That does not frighten me at all. My decision is taken, and I will stand by it. I have said all I had to say to demonstrate how useful a sociology course would be in Paris. But it was obviously not the right moment. It is quite clear to me that they find my doctrines somewhat disturbing. All I can do is let this period pass. We will see where I am going as time goes by, and if we do not, that is too bad!

Durkheim was still bitter, and when he learned that even though Alfred Espinas had 'sworn to him by all he held dear that he would not have stood against him if it had been a purely sociological course', he was, as Durkheim had guessed he would do, teaching 'some sort of sociology'. Durkheim was furious and bitterly attacked Espinas for his lack of both generosity and honesty. His behaviour had been dishonest and under-hand, 'quite apart from the fact that it was petty-minded'.[9]

Espinas, who was the only candidate, was unanimously elected and gave his inaugural lecture at the end of March. He introduced his own theory of action and his critique of socialist theorists, especially Marx. The response was at best lukewarm. The new professor's analyses were, according to Dick May, 'a little too conservative, and caused consternation amongst the audience, and especially the collectivist and catholic groups'.[10] Some groups of collectivist students were so dissatisfied that they threatened to disrupt Espinas's lectures, and wanted him to be replaced by Durkheim who was following the situation from a distance. He was well informed and somewhat amused. To the administration's surprise, Espinas, who had 'enjoyed such great prestige in Bordeaux', drew only a small audience of between 12 and 45 students, depending on the lecture's topic. Inspector Perreur wondered if 'the young Israelite, Durkheim, who was so unhappy at seeing M. Espinas being chosen in preference to him' might not have attracted a bigger audience.[11] Things settled down, and Espinas went on with his critique of socialist doctrines.

Sociology and Psychology

'Nothing new' was happening in Bordeaux. Durkheim's course on the sociology of crime came to an end in the spring of 1894. It dealt with punishment and responsibility, but the sections dealing with procedure had to be postponed indefinitely. About 30 students attended his lectures. He had also taken on a new responsibility, and was taking tutorials for the *agrégation* candidates, and he 'derived great profit' from 'dealing with all the big questions'.[12] He expected to have eight or nine students, including his nephew, attending his classes in the autumn. One of his topics was to be 'certainty'.

His teaching load for the following year included a new course on religion and a lecture on psychology. In December 1894, Durkheim was appointed *professeur adjoint* of philosophy (sociology). He was given a very positive evaluation, but it did include one small insidious comment: 'An unusually vigorous mind, and a clear speaker who shows exceptional dedication to his work; whatever one may think of his doctrines, one has to admire the philosopher, the scholar and the orator.'[13]

While he was completing his articles on 'Method', which would appear in the *Revue philosophique* from March 1894 onwards, Durkheim was also lecturing on sociology and psychology: 'Teaching sociology is', he wrote to his nephew, 'a very good way of doing philosophy, and even psychology. At the moment, I am standing in for both a philosopher and a psychologist.'[14] And he strongly urged Mauss to go on studying psychology (including the association of ideas or the will).

Psychology was beginning to play an increasingly important role in the European intellectual and scientific world. Indeed, it appeared to be the science that held the 'key to the human world', as Célestin Bouglé (1935: 1) put it, adding: 'France loved psychology and excelled at it.' The English philosophical journal *Mind* first began to appear in 1892. Subtitled *A Quarterly Review of Psychology and Philosophy*, it regularly discussed books on sociology in French, including those by Durkheim. In 1893, the Americans James McKeen and James Mark Baldwin founded *Psychological Review,* which devoted a lot of space to psychophysiology. The first issues included articles by William James and John Dewey. In Italy, finally, the *Rivista italiana de filosofia* put the problems of psychology on the agenda and in 1893 published articles on psychology as an experimental science and on the psychology of suggestion.

Durkheim lectured on psychology for three years. The discipline was, in his view, essential to any understanding how the senses in children – memory, imagination, language, abstract thought, feelings, character and will power – were shaped and developed. Durkheim cited books on psychology, described the results of Binet and Henry's research into the natural suggestibility of children (their findings would be published in the *Année philosophique* in 1894), and discussed the work of Guyau, Ribot and Johann Friedrich Herbart, a German philosopher and the author of *Handbuch zur Psychologie*, whose work was little known in France.

Herbart was a 'difficult' author, but Durkheim admired his scientific mind: his main contribution, he was to say, was to have replaced the idea of 'faculty' with that of 'representation', which paved the way for the scientific study of psychological phenomena. Durkheim was, therefore, very familiar with current work in psychology, and used it in his lectures on pedagogy.[15] But he never tired of saying that the important thing was to take into account the social environment, society and the historical context. From his point of view, the science of education had to be a sociological science.

An Observer in Paris

Having been awarded his *licence ès lettres*, Mauss was now ready to take the *agrégation* in philosophy. He had a so-called *bourse* [grant] *d'agrégation* for the academic year 1893–4 and went to Paris, where he shared an apartment with his cousin Albert Cahen. The following year, he went back to Bordeaux, where he could count on his uncle and his philosophy teachers for advice. Having been a member of the *agrégation* jury since 1887 and having taught tutorials for candidates, Durkheim was very familiar with the workings of the examination system, and would criticize certain of its weak points in an article published in the *Revue philosophique* in 1895 (Durkheim 1975[1895a]). He put a lot of effort into helping his students prepare for the examination and, as Mauss was to recall, never failed to study what they called 'the set author'.

Mauss wrote several dissertations that were marked and annotated by his uncle in 1894. Durkheim's intention was to follow his nephew's progress in what he hoped would be a 'regular' exchange of letters. He was also somewhat annoyed that Marcel Mauss was so far away from him in Paris: 'If, as has to be feared, I have to remain in Bordeaux, I wonder if it might not be better to have you by my side for the year while you prepare for the *agrégation*.'[16] It all depended on what was to be gained from living in Paris. Durkheim wanted Marcel to keep him 'up to date with what [he was] doing', but he also wanted to let him know what was going on in Paris – 'It is in my interest to be well-informed' – and asked him to tell him 'what is being said [about me]'. 'Even rumours have their importance.'

Marcel Mauss was acting as an observer for his uncle, who also asked him to do various commissions, such as going to Alcan to look for a book he needed to prepare his lectures on religion.

Durkheim gave his nephew a lot of detailed advice. In his first letter to him, dated 10 December 1893, he wrote: 'No useless erudition: that is the best way of showing that your own erudition is serious. Cite only the important texts, the crucial one. Don't overburden your essays with quotations; put them in the footnotes.' In his next letter, he identified some of his nephew's weaknesses:

> You haven't succeeded in outlining the approach you are going to take at the beginning of the lesson in such a way as to reassure your listeners and make it easier for them to pay attention, without necessarily saying everything in advance and in a confused way, even if does mean having to repeat yourself later . . . You are not doing enough to evaporate your erudition so as to leave only a useful, non-pedantic residue whilst still giving the impression that your work is serious. That is what you have to work on.[17]

Returning an essay Mauss had shown him, he again criticized him by pointing out other failings at the formal level: 'The sentence-construction is a little too careless.' 'Too many parenthetical clauses – parentheses, appositions – in your sentences.' He then gave him some encouragement: 'Your dissertation seemed fine to me, and it gave me great pleasure on a first reading.' 'Your dissertation is good. This is, perhaps, the best thing you have done for me. It abounds in good insights. Take heart, and settle down to the task.'

At a deeper level, Durkheim was worried about what he saw as Marcel's 'lack of accuracy and regularity' and his 'lack of will power', and tried above all to instil in him a sense of discipline and method. 'Work steadily, without over-doing things . . . plan every day, with a limited but well-filled programme of study. But, I beg you, apply yourself to sticking more closely to the syllabus . . . That is a question of method.'[18]

Durkheim also gave Mauss advice on what he should read, and whom he should meet. He suggested on several occasions that he should work with Victor Brochard, who was now a *chargé de cours* in philosophy at the faculty of letters. The 'new environment' his nephew was discovering was the Sorbonne, where he followed courses and lectures as he prepared to sit the *concours* [examination]. Together with his new friends, Mauss formed what he called a *syndicat*: his friends – 'those good *ouvriéristes*' Edgar Milhaud, Abel Rey and Paul Fauconnet. They venerated the same masters – Émile Boutroux, Gabriel Séailles and Victor Brochard – all of whom taught philosophy at the Paris faculty of letters. They also followed Théodule Ribot's lectures at the Collège de France, and regarded him as a 'model of clarity, justice and fairness'.[19] Such enthusiasm was not to his uncle's liking; he criticized Mauss for his choices and warned him against certain 'excessive enthusiasms', especially where Théodule Ribot's lectures were concerned. 'His lectures are an excellent example to you in methodological terms, but I do not think he is very inventive or very productive.'[20]

Durkheim sometimes showed his displeasure: 'You have done nothing new this year.' He criticized his nephew for wasting his time in the new environment of Paris, and was severely critical of both the form and the content of his work. Durkheim set more store on good 'sound work' than on 'purely formal talent', the quest for 'distinction and originality' or 'brilliance'.

Durkheim had more than one reason to be worried. In Paris, Mauss was trying to make the best of things, and was once more moving in political and socialist circles. Together with Edgar Milhaud (1872–1964) and his brother Albert, Mauss was running the Ligue démocratique des écoles (founded in 1893), and was actively involved with the Groupe des étudiants collectivistes. When he told his uncle about his recent encounters and 'discoveries', Durkheim advised him to be cautious: 'As for the Ligue démocratique des écoles, find out what it is before you join. It does not mean much to me. And do you know what is going on in the Cercle d'études sociales, which is part of the Association? Or in the Cercle des étudiants socialistes? Keep me informed about all that.'[21]

René Worms: A Tireless Organizer

Things were changing. Without going so far as to say that sociology was becoming fashionable, it does seem that, as Marcel Bernès (1894: 194) observed, sociological studies were beginning to 'find some favour with the enlightened public'. The Librairie Alcan was publishing a lot of books on the subject, and the Bibliothèque sociologique internationale had just been launched. The abundance of publications was a sign of 'the somewhat tumultuous effervescence of a science in the making'. Sociology was, in other words, 'really flourishing', noted Marcel Bernès (1895b: 186), who began to give a lecture course on sociology at the faculty of letters in Montpellier in 1893.

The word 'sociology' had therefore entered current usage. But people were asking just what this science was. Its defenders' main concern was to define its domain, object and methods. In effect, 1894 was what Paul Lapie called a 'year of reflection'. Sociologists were reflecting and asking themselves: 'How are social facts to be defined, and how are they to be explained?' (Lapie 1895: 309). The theme of the congress of the new Institut international de sociologie, to be held in 1895, was 'What is sociology?' Who could answer that question? wondered Bernès. His answer to his own question was that, with the exception of Gabriel Tarde, no one was better qualified to answer it than the 'learned professor' of sociology in Bordeaux. According to Bernès, the future of sociology in France depended upon three people: Tarde, Worms and Durkheim.

Gabriel Tarde had certainly enjoyed great fame from 1890 onwards, thanks to his *Lois de l'imitation* (which had been translated into Russian and English) and *La Philosophie pénale*. But did René Worms have the same importance?[22] He was, it is true, a tireless organizer. He founded the journal *La Revue internationale de sociologie* in 1893, and established the Institut international de sociologie and the Société de sociologie de Paris. He was often surrounded by controversy. There was ironic talk of his ability to assimilate everything and of his 'inexhaustible fecundity'. Durkheim himself had a poor opinion of 'this young man', and explained to Mauss: 'What puts me off this journal is Worms's reputation for being a clown, and the fact that I cannot contribute to a journal whose editor has no specific qualifications ... And I did tell Espinas that the Sorbonne failed his thesis. That is not a humiliation that is inflicted on everyone.'[23]

René Worms defended his doctoral thesis 'Organisme et société' at the Sorbonne in 1896. It was described as 'respectable', and was given a rather cold welcome. Alfred Espinas called it 'a useful textbook'. Obviously annoyed with the 'vague' nature of the concepts of 'organism' and 'society' and with Worms's misplaced biological metaphors, Émile Boutroux criticized the 'extreme effrontery' of an argument that came down to the syllogism, 'Organism = society; society = organism. Organism and society are therefore one and the same thing.' He demolished Worms's pretentions: 'You are too quick to relate specious concepts to rudimentary observations', and concluded 'real science is more cautious and more patient'. The jury had, in short, a lot of reservations: 'While the edifice has been built, one can see that it is fragile.' This was a 'theory that thinks it is based upon an experimental method, but it does not apply to any observable case'.[24]

The planned new *Revue internationale de sociologie* was not very well received by the philosophers either, who had their doubts about such a 'generalist' journal that was ready to open its pages to moralists, biologists and jurists and which was prepared to publish 'mere historical curiosities' and 'very curious articles' alongside scientific texts. It was criticized for its 'lack of direction': the journal 'liberally' accepted 'all sorts of material and ideas' from all sides.[25] Without mentioning it by name, Durkheim said of the *Revue internationale* that its publication was 'premature': 'There is not in fact enough truly sociological literature in Europe to sustain a periodical journal.' Perhaps he felt that he was being left behind. The initiative was still, in his view, 'an interesting event that was symptomatic of the contemporary state of mind' (Durkheim 1975[1895b]).

The journal's 'original desire' was, Worms would later say (1903a: 2), to be 'an open forum to which all opinions and all doctrines' could have access, and the authors of articles were requested to display both 'scientific probity' and 'the appropriate language. The issue dated May–June 1893 included Léon Duguit's 'A sociology seminar', Louis Gumplovicz's 'The ancient populations of Hungary', and Gabriel Tarde's 'Monads and social science'. The 1894 issue contained Tarde on 'logical states' and a translation of extracts from Simmel's *Über soziale Differenzierung* ['Social differentiation']. The journal appeared on a monthly basis, and kept its readers informed about new lectures and publications. As the title indicates, it was meant to be international in scope, and very quickly became associated with new journals in other countries, including the *American Journal of Sociology*. One of its columns, entitled 'Le mouvement social' was open to foreign colleagues and allowed them to describe the situation in their respective countries (Belgium, Italy, the United States, Brazil).

The conception of science defended by Worms was positivist: 'A fact is always a fact', he wrote in the first issue. The journal's goal was 'to apply only the strict procedures of science' and to 'bring together social facts in order to discover the laws that govern them.' There was, on the other hand, no specific theoretical line: 'We appeal to all men of good will, and intend to open up our columns to all the sciences' (Worms 1903a: 2). His journal was deliberately eclectic and tried to attract young philosophers, including Élie Halévy, who declined the invitation and contributed only to the *Revue de métaphysique et de morale*. Worms eventually found supporters in legal circles: the editorial secretary was Alfred Lambert, a lawyer at the Paris Court of Appeal. Just over one-fifth of the contributors were lawyers. Lawyers aside, Worms gathered around him a number of Russian intellectuals who had found refuge in Paris. They formed the most active and most visible group within the Institut international de sociologie, and included Eugène de Roberty, Maxim Kovalevsky, Jacques Novicow and Paul de Lilienfeld. Worms's strategy was to establish an international network, with Ward in the United States, Simmel and Tönnies in Germany, and Tylor in England.

Worms also forged, finally, a sort of alliance with certain anthropologists, including Léonce Manouvrier (1850–1927), professor of physiological anthropology at the École d'anthropologie de Paris, and Charles Letourneau. In 1895, the latter was elected vice-president of the Institut international de sociologie. The first congresses organized by the institute in Paris in 1894 and 1895 were a great success.[26] They were somewhat fashionable gatherings that attracted a very varied audience made up of students, teachers and intellectual dilettantes.

In response to demands from the institute's Parisian members, who wanted to meet more frequently, Worms founded the Société de sociologie de Paris, which held its first meeting on 11 December 1895. He was its 'soul', and its first president was Gabriel Tarde. The participants were enthusiastic and the discussions were lively, but most of its members were 'amateurs'. There were also diplomats and military men who wanted to acquire some knowledge of sociology for their foreign missions, and who hoped to bring back sociological reports from their travels. A few women also attended, including Lydie Martial, president of the Union de pensée féminine.[27]

There was one absence (later described as conspicuous): Durkheim. Perhaps he did not wish to be identified with Alfred Fouillée, Charles Letourneau and Gabriel Tarde. Relations between Durkheim and Worms were never very cordial.

Allies Amongst the Philosophers?

Durkheim was the first to rejoice at the fact that the word 'sociology' was gradually entering 'common usage' and that the idea had become of interest to 'educated young people', but he also warned against excessive impatience and premature projects, such as the suggestion that special chairs in sociology should be created in all the universities. Now that his thesis had been published, could he hope to become sociology's representative in France? Several commentators thought so. He had acquired greater intellectual maturity. He had already defined his main interest (the social role and historical development of ethics) and had identified a whole range of empirical interests (changes in the social structure, and the corresponding changes in institutions, practices and beliefs). And he had developed a method: asking functional questions from an evolutionist perspective.

In an article published in Italy, Durkheim painted a 'general picture' of the research that had been carried out in France for the benefit of his foreign readers. In his view, France brought together 'the conditions most conducive to the progress of sociology': (1) an awareness that social phenomena are complex, and (2) a rationalist state of mind that could 'shed some light on their obscurity'. People were no longer afraid of sociology. All the more reason, in his view, to clarify what was at stake because 'there is a danger that all this activity will go in a dangerous direction if it does not have a method to guide it' (1975[1895b]: 75).

Although he was a professor of philosophy and was preparing students for the philosophy *agrégation*, Durkheim did not restrict himself to the subject. He intervened in domains that appeared to have little to do with his actual qualifications (political economy, law, history, anthropology and psychology), and dealt with somewhat unconventional problems such as the division of labour, suicide, the family and religion. And yet his work was still grounded in philosophy, and his articles appeared in philosophical journals.

From the mid-1890s onwards, philosophical life revolved around two journals: the *Revue philosophique* and the new *Revue de métaphysique et de morale*. Durkheim was, as we have seen, given a warm reception by the *Revue philosophique,* and published the vast majority (70 per cent) of his articles and reviews in it between 1885 and 1895. Although it did not abandon philosophy – far from it – the *Revue philosophique* was characterized by its openness to other disciplines (law, linguistics, history and sociology) and its exceptional interest in psychology (including psychophysiology). It published articles on cognition, pain, perception, movement, consciousness (and the unconscious), attention, association, the emotions, the imagination, colour, suggestion and sleep. Alfred Binet was one of its most prolific contributors. The German psychologist Wundt also took pride of place with some 15 articles. The journal's special interest in psychopathology was, finally, reflected in the themes or problems dealt with by its contributors: hallucinations, hypnotism, hysteria, mental illness, nervous illness, nervous disorders and paranoia.

Sociology, with some 60 texts, came a long way behind psychology. Social questions, social problems, socialism, anarchy, the social contract, social economics, population and the city all came under the 'sociology' rubric. If texts on criminology (more than 40), economics, politics and the state are also taken into account, we get some idea of the importance the *Revue philosophique* attached to the social sciences. Its most active sociological contributors were Alfred Fouillée (21 articles), Gabriel Tarde (17) and Eugène de Roberty (11). Durkheim (written 'Durckheim' in the index) contributed 7 articles. The journal also published several texts by foreign researchers, such as Spencer, Tönnies, Simmel, Gumplowicz, De Greef and Lester Ward.

For over a decade, the *Revue philosophique* had a quasi-monopoly on philosophical publications. The appearance of the *Revue de métaphysique et de morale* in January 1893 then transformed the picture and allowed new alliances and rivalries to emerge. The goal of the new journal was to meet the needs of philosophers and to refocus the debate, or, in other words, to limit its frame of reference, by placing more emphasis on philosophical doctrines in the strict sense of the term. It wanted, that is, to avoid the *Revue philosophique*'s extreme eclecticism.

Did the journal have room for sociology, and for the kind of sociology Durkheim was advocating? 'Managing' relations with sociology was all the more delicate in view of the ties of friendship that existed between its editor Xavier Léon and Durkheim, and in that the generation of young people mobilized by the journal included some of the latter's collaborators. Xavier Léon (1868–1935) was the main driving force behind the new journal. At the time, he was only 24.[28] His closest collaborators were Élie Halévy (1870–1937) and Léon Brunschvicg (1869–1944), both of whom were educated at the Lycée Condorcet, were *normaliens* and *agrégés de philosophie*.[29] Élie Halévy, Xavier's friend, was the real co-founder of the new journal, which he described as being 'rationalist and moral'. The journal's sworn enemies were the spirit of 'religiosity' – in other words, Catholic intolerance on the one hand and, on the other, the positivist philosophy that dominated the republic's educational system.

The journal soon had to position itself with respect to the *Revue philosophique*; the two were addressed to the same academic audience and were in competition. There was no question of the new journal's adopting its rival's policy of 'absolute eclecticism' in admitting articles.[30] Xavier Léon, for his part, had reservations about what he called 'the specialized cast of mind' that reduced metaphysics to physiological or experimental psychology, and ethics to sociology. 'We would like to do something different here', said the journal's promoters.[31]

While the *Revue de métaphysique et de morale* wanted to stand out from the *Revue philosophique* in more than one sense, the journals' editorial practices were, in the long term, quite similar, and both journals displayed a real openness. A good number of philosophers published in both on an alternating basis. From the outset, Xavier Léon, who was the journal's secretary, opened its pages to debates about sociology. In 1893, it published a discussion about law between Gabriel Tarde (who greeted the appearance of the new journal with enthusiasm and sent it his *Les Transformations du droit* [1894] for review[32]) and R. Berthelot, and a piece by Marcel Bernès on 'La méthode et les principes de la philosophie du droit' ['Method and principles of the philosophy of law']. Two new columns, edited by Paul Lapie and then François Simiand, were established to cover 'Practical questions' and 'The year in sociology'. The former in fact dealt with moral philosophy, and was designed to give philosophers a platform that would allow them to discuss civil society, the fatherland and justice or duty. It dealt with a wide range of topics, from a progressive inheritance tax to the major theme of 'science, morality and religion', the emancipation of women, and the idea of arbitration and freedom in economics.

Durkheim was often mentioned in the first issues of the journal. Thanks to his 'remarkable thesis' on *The Division of Labour in Society*, Durkheim, who was identified with the 'observational school', had become an unavoidable point of reference for anyone interested in the development of a science of ethics. Gustave Belot had no hesitation about speaking of a 'new sociology' that was both 'objective' and 'scientific'. Its main ideas were, in his view, as follows: consciousness and finality must be ignored in favour of the unconscious and 'mechanism'; the social consciousness was quite independent of individuals. He did not, however, completely agree with Durkheim: while sociology did provide ethics with certain essential data, 'it is no more ethics than physiology is medicine or hygienics' (Belot 1894: 458). The ethics defended by Durkheim's former colleague had to ward off both relativism and the criterion of truth. Belot was quite prepared to subordinate the individual to society (which lays down rules), but only to the extent that society was subordinated to the individual (as a moral agent).

In general terms, the *Revue de métaphysique et de morale*, which also published articles by Bergson on 'perception and matter' and by Schopenhauer, was somewhat suspicious of Durkheim. His position on the teaching of philosophy, which he made known in an 'interesting study' published in *La Revue philosophique*, was a source of annoyance to some. Teachers felt that they were being 'indirectly' targeted, and failed to understand that he was not trying to reduce their discipline to the logic of the sciences even though he was suggesting that what they taught should be 'purely sociological and practical'. It was, the editorial board concluded, 'dangerous to have M. Durkheim as an ally'.[33]

Célestin Bouglé and the Younger Generation

The target audience of the new *Revue de métaphysique et de morale* was the 'younger generation'. Xavier Léon's 'burning desire' was to 'get young unknowns to work on books by other people'[34] and he wanted nothing to do with a philosophy that was 'confined to state-financed chairs'. The two leitmotifs were: deal with ideas and not facts; reject both positivism and mysticism, mere facts and superstitions, and make way for reason. Three of the young people whom Léon and Halévy wanted to 'exploit' were associated with Durkheim's project and the foundation of sociology: Célestin Bouglé, Paul Lapie and Dominique Parodi.

Bouglé played the role of go-between. As Halbwachs was to say, he 'quickly felt a strong affinity' with the men behind the *Revue de métaphysique et de morale* and, even though he took the side of the sociologists, he retained 'some sympathy for metaphysical psychology'. Bouglé had met Élie Halévy at the École normale supérieure, and they became very close friends. Halévy introduced Bouglé to Xavier Léon and invited him to do their journal 'a favour' by, for example, writing some reviews.[35] Célestin Bouglé quickly became an 'excellent editorial adviser', and was largely responsible for the journal's new openness towards the social sciences.

Élie Halévy also recruited their mutual friend Dominique Parodi, whom he had known at the Lycée Condorcet and at the École normale supérieure. Parodi did not want to be identified with 'the sociologists', even though he admitted in ironic terms to 'believing more and more in sociology'.[36] An *agrégé de philosophie*, he taught in various provincial lycées (including that in Bordeaux) before being transferred to Paris, where he taught in turn at the Lycée Charlemagne, Michelet and Condorcet.

It was at Bouglé's insistence that Paul Lapie (1869–1927) agreed to write reviews for the *Revue de métaphysique et de morale*. Lapie edited the 'year in sociology' column for two years, though not without a certain reluctance because, while he believed that it was 'possible to establish a science of societies', he did not feel that he was qualified to evaluate the work of contemporary sociologists.[37] He finally agreed. Lapie's growing interest in sociology reflected, it seems, Célestin Bouglé's influence (and especially that of his articles on the social sciences in Germany), as well as his own 'Tunisian experience'. During his stay in Tunisia, he attempted to do 'practical sociology by observing what was going on around him'.[38] His plan was to 'gather detailed observations about the morals, institutions and law of both Israelites and Muslims' by interviewing the chief rabbi and teachers at the Muslim university.

Célestin Bouglé and Paul Lapie felt that they had a 'vocation' for sociology. Bouglé's decision to turn to the 'social sciences' was made when a government grant allowed him to spend a year studying in Germany. He acted as an emissary for the *Revue de métaphysique et de morale* by soliciting contributions from German scholars, including Georg Simmel. As soon as he arrived in Berlin in March 1894, the young Bouglé was keen to attend Simmel's lectures, and actually met him. This proved to be a decisive meeting, and Bouglé felt that he had a great deal in common with Simmel. He also translated Simmel's article, 'Le problème de la sociologie', which appeared in the second issue of the journal.[39]

The question raised by Simmel's article is as follows: should all individual events be reduced to the historical state, needs and activities of the whole? According to the professor at the University of Berlin, sociology had to change direction if it was to become a 'real sociology' that studied only that which is 'specifically social', namely the form and forms of association. 'Society in the broad sense exists', he added, 'wherever there is reciprocal interaction between individuals' (Simmel 1894: 499). Émile Durkheim also thought of republishing the article in the first issue of the *Année sociologique*. Much to Simmel's disappointment, that never happened: 'I was sad to hear that because I thought that that little article was the most promising thing I had done.'[40] Simmel attracted envy. In 1894, in its second issue, the *Revue internationale de sociologie* published his article on 'social differentiation'.[41] The *Revue de métaphysique et de morale* also published Simmel's 'On relations between theoretical thought and practical issues' in March 1896; once again, the translation was by Célestin Bouglé.

Bouglé's 'vocation' for sociology was revealed to him in somewhat negative terms: he proved to have 'no talent for metaphysics'. Ultimately, he chose to turn to 'collecting facts rather than metaphysics'. 'Fortunately, there is such a thing as good, positivist sociology.'[42] On his return from Germany in January 1896, Célestin Bouglé devoted a series of articles to a description and critical assessment of 'trends in the social science in Germany', just as Durkheim had done 10 years earlier (Bouglé 1894a; 1894b; 1895). They dealt mainly with Simmel, Wagner, Jhering and Lazarus, whose lectures he had attended. They were published in the *Revue de métaphysique et de morale*.

Bouglé's study of the work of his German colleagues suggested a few general ideas, and he drew a number of conclusions. The idea that modern society is characterized by a growing differentiation and by an increase in the number of social circles to which we belong derived from Simmel and his *Einleitung in die Moralwissenschaft* ['Introduction to the science of ethics']. He also agreed with Simmel about the need to develop a science of norms rather than a normative science, and accepted that the precise methodologies of the physical sciences could not be applied to 'psychological things'.

Having read Wagner's *Principes de l'économie politique*, Bouglé flung himself into the 'battle over methodology', and reformulated the methodological, theoretical and political questions that Durkheim had raised in his analyses of the work of the German historical school: the relationship between induction and deduction, the establishment of laws, statistics in the social sciences, the dichotomy between theory and practice, relations between psychology and sociology, and the errors of individualism and socialism. He criticized, finally, the idea of a sociology that aspired to 'embrace all aspects of social life' and concluded that, when it came to the social sciences, specialization is a 'scientific duty'.

The idea of specialization reappears in the conclusion to his third article, which deals with Rudolf von Jhering: 'If we wish to understand the social fabric scientifically, we must separate out its various threads.' He concluded that this was the way to elaborate a specifically social science. Sociology's problem was that it was currently having difficulty in 'establishing itself as something "specific"'. Before it could achieve that status, it required a 'specific explanatory principle' (Bouglé 1895: 476). Bouglé was sceptical about the very idea of 'absolute objectivity', and defended the recourse to subjective observation or even autobiography. He was struck by the formula 'social phenomena must be described as things', but he was not convinced by it.

The publication of Bouglé's articles on the social sciences was a 'considerable success', as Xavier Léon put it.[43] Their success convinced Xavier Léon that he should work together with his young colleague: 'I am counting a great deal on your activity to speak to our readers about sociologists and sociology.'[44] Bouglé's articles were republished in book form as *Les Sciences sociales en Allemagne* (Bouglé 1912[1896]), which was very well received and enjoyed great success.[45] Bouglé sent a copy to Émile Durkheim, some of whose works (and especially *The Division of Labour*) are cited, albeit briefly in most cases. Durkheim replied immediately, thanked him and congratulated him: 'I read it with great interest, or rather reread it, as I followed your articles in the *Revue de métaphysique*.' Durkheim felt somewhat uncomfortable about 'replying by letter', but he wanted to be able to express his thoughts better so as to 'reduce the distance' that separated – or might separate – him from his young colleague. He stressed two points. First, the dichotomy between sociology and psychology: 'I have never said that there is nothing psychological about sociology, and I readily accept your formula . . . namely that it is a psychology, but that it is distinct from individual psychology. I have never thought otherwise.' Second, the definition of social facts as things: 'In what sense does that hypostasize them?' In Durkheim's view, both points were essential. And they were, he admitted, the points to which he attached the most importance. And, sensing a 'sharp sense of the specificity of social facts' in Bouglé, he asked 'Why are we not in agreement?'[46] His question marked the beginning of a long discussion.

Some Good Reasons for Writing *The Rules*

Between May and August 1894, Durkheim published a series of four articles under the general title of 'The rules of sociological method' in the *Revue philosophique*. He probably wrote them after submitting his Latin thesis on Montesquieu, in other words between December 1892 and April–May 1894. The four articles on 'The method', to use Durkheim's own description of his work, were republished, with some 70 minor corrections and the addition of a preface, as *Les Règles de la méthode sociologique* [*The Rules of Sociological Method*], which was published in Alcan's 'Bibliothèque de la philosophie contemporaine' in 1895.

Why attempt to define the rules of a discipline? It was first of all a matter of temperament. In philosophical terms, Durkheim was a rationalist: every proof had to be argued in order to make explicit the presuppositions and implications inherent in any stance he took. He also wanted to reply to and convince hostile and sceptical minds; being convinced of the importance of the social sciences in a time of social crisis, he was afraid that his critics would be dangerously irresponsible. He also had a plan, and wanted to establish a school and recruit a team of competent and dynamic researchers who would all adopt the same approach. A 'little book', *The Rules* has all the characteristics of a manifesto or even, as some put it, a catechism (that of the 'Church of St Durkheim'[47]) or a breviary (of sociology) (Durkheim 1957[1894]: xliii).

The truth was rather more prosaic, as Durkheim himself admitted. Thanks to a 'happy conjunction of circumstances', the faculty of letters at Bordeaux had set up on his behalf a 'regular course in sociology' that 'allowed us to devote ourselves early to the study of social science' and to work out a method adapted to the specific nature of social phenomena: 'It is the results of our work which we wish to set down here and submit to debate' (Durkheim 1982[1895]: 49). When the second edition was published, he again stated that the book was a summary of 'an individual practice that is inevitably restricted' (ibid.: 35). On several occasions, he explicitly refers to his study of solidarity and the division of labour or to his lectures (on, for instance, the family). His work had allowed him to discuss various social problems and to carry out 'experiments' that demonstrated the soundness of his analytic principles.

Why rules? Quite simply because sociologists – with the exception of August Comte – have hitherto 'scarcely occupied themselves with the task of studying and defining the method that they apply to the study of social facts' (Durkheim 1982[1895]: 48). Or, as he puts it in *The Division of Labour in Society*, what applies to science also applies to life in society: we cannot do without rules, and methodological rules are to science what the rules governing behaviour are to morality. Every science is a sort of 'independent world', has its own method, and tries to coordinate the approach of its practitioners. Durkheim also deplores the fact that there is no coordinated dialogue between disciplines and especially between the 'young' moral sciences (psychology, law, anthropology, statistics, economics, history).

Is it fair to criticize Durkheim because he did not have a background in the natural sciences and for his inability to improve his mathematical skills to any significant extent? Is it fair to criticize him for his failure to notice the extraordinary scientific revolution that was establishing links between logic, mathematics and physics (Schmauss 1994: 28–31; Berthelot 1995: 23)? Durkheim was writing at a time when scientific thought had reached a turning point. Biology, which had just adopted the experimental method, was becoming a standard point of reference for philosophers. Biological analogies, inductive logic and causalism were the main characteristics of the (scientific) state of mind in the period 1880–1900.

Durkheim had a good understanding of science, but it was that of a philosopher. He regarded himself as a rationalist, and described Descartes as the founder of science. In *Rules*, he recommends Copernicus' approach as exemplary, borrows the idea of *praenotiones* from Bacon (1982[1895]: 62) and, while he adopts a positivist conception of science, is not afraid to criticize Auguste Comte. He takes as his model the physicist, or the vivisectionist who has no time for sentiment and scruples.

Durkheim makes a point of saying again and again that science has as its objects facts and not ideas. If it is to establish itself as a science, sociology must therefore shrug off its ideological character. 'In our present state of knowledge we do not know exactly what the state is, nor sovereignty, political freedom, democracy, socialism, communism, etc. . . . Yet the words that express them recur continually in the discussions of sociologists' (1982[1895]: 65–6). As we can see from ethics or political economy, their science is not very different from that of medieval doctors. Even, 'the celebrated law of supply and demand', for instance, 'has never been established inductively as an expression of economic reality' (Durkheim 1982[1895]: 68).

Durkheim wants to introduce a 'reform' or even a revolution identical in every respect to the revolution that has turned psychology upside down over the past 30 years as psychologists abandoned the introspective approach, and moved from the 'subjective' to the 'objective stage'. The introduction of the experimental method (or experimental reasoning) had already led to the creation of laboratories in France, Germany and the United States. Journals were describing and discussing their findings. When *Rules* appeared in 1895, Binet and Beaunis had just convinced the publisher Alcan to launch a new journal called *L'Année psychologique*, and Binet had published his *Introduction à la psychologie expérimentale* with the same house.

First of all, the (social) facts must be defined. Durkheim uses concrete examples, often drawn from his own experience, to demonstrate the objective and external nature of social reality. Parents teach their children to eat, drink and sleep at regular intervals, and to observe cleanliness, calm and obedience. They force them to be mindful of others, and to respect customs and conventions. In a word, parents 'shape' the child in their own image. Education sets out to create a social being: 'all education consists of a continual effort to impose upon the child ways of seeing, thinking and acting which he himself would not have arrived at spontaneously' (1982[1895]: 53).

Nationality, language, the monetary system, professional practice, the rules of law and 'what is customary in my country and in my social class' (modes of dress, and ways of eating, drinking and sleeping) are, according to Durkheim, 'ways of acting, thinking and feeling which possess the remarkable property of existing outside the consciousness of the individual' (1982[1895]: 51) – not to mention 'social currents' ('waves of enthusiasm, indignation and pity'). And when he wonders if his definition is complete, the author of *The Division of Labour in Society* extends it to 'collective ways of being', or to social facts of a morphological nature (the distribution of the population over the earth's surface, the extent and nature of the network of communications, the design of dwellings). There is no way of escaping them, as they are the 'substratum of collective life' (ibid.: 57).

Pressure, constraint and coercion: these are the terms that Durkheim uses to describe 'social' and the way in which the group or society acts upon the individual. He then adds the criterion of generality: a phenomenon is collective in the sense that, because it is obligatory, it applies to all members of a society. The substratum of representations, beliefs and collective actions is not the individual, but society (be it political society or partial groups such as religious confessions or occupational corporations). Here, Durkheim runs the risk of infuriating 'those who zealously uphold out-and-out individualism' (1982[1895]: 52), and he knows it. He devotes considerable effort to demonstrating that there are two categories of facts, and that 'the social fact exists separately from its individual effects' (ibid.: 55). The social dimension of reality is not, however, always an observable given; we need, as Durkheim admits, the 'help of certain methodological devices' such as statistics – birth, marriage and suicide rates – in order to identify currents of opinion, social currents and even – why not? – the state of the collective soul.

We cannot, in other words, do without a (scientific) method and a certain number of rules. Durkheim makes a distinction between five types of rule, depending on whether they relate (1) to the observation of social facts; (2) to the distinction between the normal and the pathological; (3) to the constitution of social types; (4) to the explanation of social facts; or (5) to the demonstration of proof. The first and most basic rule is 'consider social facts as things'. The corollary rules are as follows: 'systematically discard all preconceptions' (Durkheim 1982[1895]: 72); 'distinguish between the normal and the pathological'; explain the social facts; and apply the test of truth. The first and most basic rule is to regard social facts as things: 'When the sociologist undertakes to investigate any order of social facts, he must strive to consider them from a viewpoint where they present themselves in isolation from their individual manifestations' (ibid.: 72).

Durkheim explicitly takes the side of Descartes and adopts his famous 'method of doubt' (1982[1895]: 72). A science certainly starts out from sensation or vulgar knowledge, but the scientist must 'free himself from those fallacious notions which hold sway over the mind of the ordinary person' (ibid.: 73). Everyone 'knows', or thinks they know, what the family, cleanliness or morality is. But we must, he hammers home with great energy, distrust our feelings and presuppositions: 'Feeling is an object for scientific study, not the criterion of scientific truth' (ibid.: 74).

The Normal and the Pathological

Is crime an evil or an illness? Durkheim demonstrates, with statistics to prove his point, that criminality has been increasing everywhere since the beginning of the nineteenth century. He formulates a proposition that was to annoy more than one reader of *The Rules* by contending that crime has to be considered as something normal, or even something that is inevitable and useful to society. He goes so far as to assert that '[the criminal] plays a normal rule in social life' (Durkheim 1982[1895] 102). He would be accused of being an apologist for crime, but he qualifies his initial statement and takes many oratorical precautions to make it clear that, while crime is one of the 'phenomena of normal sociology' (ibid.: 98), it does not follow that 'the criminal is a person normally constituted from the biological and psychological viewpoints' (ibid.: 106 n8).

As in medicine, the whole question centres on the distinction between the normal and the pathological. When it comes to social, political or even religious questions, the diagnosis is usually a matter of opinion of subjective assumptions. What are we to think of the weakening of religious beliefs? What are we to say about capitalism or the development of the powers of the state? Politicians and ideologues usually fall back on cursory observation and defend their views 'by dint of syllogisms' (Durkheim 1982[1895]: 97).

In order to avoid such errors, Durkheim suggests that the criterion of normality should be the generality of the phenomena concerned in a given type of society at a given moment in its evolution. Basically, everything is relative. 'What is normal for the savage is not always so for the civilized person and vice versa' (Durkheim 1982[1895]: 92). Similarly, the 'weakening of traditional beliefs' is 'utterly normal' and 'relates to the nature of the social environment' (ibid.: 106 n8). Durkheim then remarks that: 'Nothing is good indefinitely and without limits' (ibid.: 101.

The political conclusion is inescapable: we have to abandon the dream of an ideal world or a perfect society. A 'society of saints' living in 'an exemplary and perfect cloister' is nothing more than illusion. Durkheim therefore invites us not to 'pursue desperately an end which recedes as we move forward', but to 'work steadily and persistently to maintain the normal state, to re-establish it if it is disturbed, and to rediscover the conditions of normality if they happen to change' (1982[1895]: 104). Under these conditions, the duty of the statesman is similar to that of a doctor: rather than propelling societies violently towards an ideal, he should simply prevent the outbreak of diseases, and try to cure them. Because it can tell the difference between health and sickness, sociology, like science, can therefore claim to have a practical efficacy. Durkheim insists on defending the rights of reason against the claims of ideology.

The Explanation for Social Lies in Society

Durkheim is aware that sociology is not 'sufficiently advanced'. But he is certain of one thing: the nature of a society depends upon the character and number of the elements that make it up, and upon the way they are combined. Societies range, therefore, from the less elaborate groupings (a single-segment society), to those whose composition is more complex (polysegmentary societies). The approach recommended by Durkheim consists in systematically identifying the various combinations that generate a finite range of types of human society. In just a few lines, he traces a broad fresco of the history of lower societies, from small groups, through tribes (e.g. Iroquois, Australians, Kabyles), to confederations and the city-state.

The establishment of social species and their classification represents only one step towards the development of a truly explanatory sociology. As in *The Division of Labour in Society,* Durkheim attacks the utilitarian conception of social science that claims that any institution can be explained in terms of its utility, and insists that we must divorce the search for the efficient cause that produces the social fact from the function it fulfils. He understands 'function' as meaning the correspondence that exists between the fact under consideration and the general needs of the social organism, without seeking to know if it is intentional or not. Durkheim also criticizes the first explanation of social facts that suggests itself to sociologists on the grounds that it is 'exclusively psychological' (Durkheim 1982[1895]: 162) in that it reduces everything to human nature and to individual factors or feelings.

In Durkheim's view, sociology is not 'a corollary of psychology' (Durkheim 1982[1895]: 127). We have to look at society and not individuals because 'it is in the nature of society itself that we must seek the explanation of social life' (ibid.: 128). He once more attacks explanations that associate social phenomena with psychical states such as feelings of religiosity, sexual jealousy, familial piety and paternal love. He also criticizes all attempts to reduce religious institutions to man's feeling of fear in the face of a greater force, or that reduce systems of juridical and moral rules to the feelings of sympathy that are experienced by individuals. Even organo-psychic factors such as race or ethnicity do not have the influence that is ascribed to them: 'We know of no social phenomenon which is unquestionably dependent on race' (ibid.: 132).

All these explanations make reference to 'vague' and 'malleable' states and predispositions, and 'cannot therefore fail to miss completely all that is specific, i.e. social, about them' (Durkheim 1982[1895]: 131). Durkheim now formulates a rule that will become central in methodological terms: 'The determining cause of a social fact must be sought among antecedent social facts' (Durkheim 1982[1895]: 134). And, given that the first social fact is association, social phenomena vary in accordance with forms of association – that is, 'how the constituent elements in a society are grouped' (ibid.: 135). The analysis must, in other words, begin with the 'internal social environment' which, while it is certainly made up of individuals, is also made up of things (material objects, the products of social activity, law, customs, literary and artistic monuments) which, although they have no motive power, do have a certain influence on the evolution of society.

The principle of causality is, in Durkheim's view, basic to science: '*To the same effect there always corresponds the same cause*' (1982[1895]: 150). A sociological explanation must, like any scientific explanation, establish relationships of causality. Now the only method that meets that requirement and that is adequate to the sociological object is the so-called method of concomitant variations, which he describes at some length in the last chapter of his book. The idea of concomitance is of central importance: given that sociology cannot carry out experiments in the true sense of the word, it must find a comparative method that makes it possible to prove that one (social) phenomenon is the cause of another. The 'demonstration of proof' consists first in establishing series of facts and examining them in such a way as to bring out significant quantitative relations, or what we would now call correlations, between them.

He takes, for example, the curve that represents a suicide trend over a sufficiently extended period of time, and observes the variations that are exhibited by phenomena corresponding to differences between provinces, classes, rural and urban environments, sex, age, civil status, and so on. Was he already thinking of the book he would devote to this theme? The study of relations between these variables makes it possible to establish 'real laws'. 'As soon as we have proved that in a certain number of cases two phenomena vary with each other, we may be certain that we are confronted with a law' (1982[1895]: 153).

Durkheim is not necessarily intent upon accumulating 'documents'; if they are well chosen and studied closely, 'a few facts suffice' (1982[1895] 153). He is especially critical of ethnography and the 'confused and cursory observations of travellers', and prefers comparative history, meaning not just the 'comparative history of the great European countries', but one that goes 'even further back' (ibid.: 157). Comparative sociology is, in his view, synonymous with sociology itself.

Sociology, as defined by Durkheim, aspires primarily to being independent and emancipated from philosophy: 'We must abandon generalities and enter into the detailed examination of facts.' It must also be independent of political doctrines and all parties: 'Sociology thus understood will be neither individualist, communist nor socialist' (Durkheim 1982[1895]: 160). It will simply be objective, specialized and in direct contact with things. Passion, in other words, is the antithesis of science. Durkheim hopes that sociology will 'speak authoritatively enough to quell passions and dispel prejudices' (ibid.: 163). This does not, however, lead him to conclude that it must 'profess no interest in practical questions'; on the contrary, such questions are 'our constant preoccupation' (ibid.: 160). He then goes on to add: 'We believe, on the contrary, that the time has come for sociology to renounce worldly successes, so to speak, and take on the esoteric character which befits all science. Thus it will gain in dignity what it will perhaps lose in popularity' (ibid.: 163). The book's conclusion is an invitation to work: 'From this very moment onwards, we must work' (ibid.).

For or Against?

The first reactions to *The Rules of Sociological Method* were not slow in appearing. Georges Sorel, Gabriel Tarde and Lucien Herr responded as soon as Durkheim's articles appeared in the *Revue philosophique*, even before they were published in book form. When the book was published by Alcan in 1895, there were many more responses.

In February 1895, Georges Sorel[48] published two articles in the new socialist journal *Le Devenir social*, the international journal of economics, history and politics founded by Alfred Bonnet, which published texts by Engels, Kautsky, Plekhanov, Vandervelde, Labriola and Lafargue. The journal devoted a lot of space to sociology, which it regarded as 'a completely distinct discipline'. From 1896, Marcel Mauss was a contributor to the journal, in which science and politics were so closely intertwined that Hubert Bourgin spoke of its 'socialo-sociology'.

Sorel hailed the publication of Durkheim's books as proof that sociology had finally got away from dilettantism. Durkheim was, he added, a metaphysician of 'rare subtlety' and a scholar who was 'fully armed for battle.' The Durkheim who interested Sorel was, for political reasons, not so much the author of the *Rules* as that of *The Division of Labour in Society*. He saw him as a 'first-rate enemy' of socialism (which he tended to define as a form of collectivism). He did not, however, despair of Durkheim, even inviting him to take sides:

> The author has taken his research as far as it is possible to go without becoming a socialist . . . Perhaps he will eventually cross the frontier that keeps us apart. That would be a happy event for social philosophy, and I would be the first to acclaim him as a master. No scholar is better prepared to introduce Marx's theories into higher education. He is the only French sociologist with an adequate philosophical training and a critical mind that is sufficiently developed to understand the scientific laws behind historical changes, and the material conditions for future developments. (Sorel 1895a)

In a second article published that year, which dealt with the penal theories of Durkheim and Tarde, Sorel defended the courage and scientific rigour of the *Rules* and contrasted them with the moralistic and sentimental pretensions of the theorist of imitation. Before Durkheim, 'sociology was nothing more than a collection of declarations made in a barbarous and obscure language, a variant on that deliquescent jokeology that our contemporaries so easily mistake for science.' With Durkheim, it had become something very different: the professor from Bordeaux was trying to get out of the rut in which his predecessors had become bogged down' (Sorel 1895b; cited in Paoletti 1995: 268).

As he would later recall, it might have been predicted that the principles formulated by Durkheim would certainly not be accepted by all those sociologists. René Worms, for instance, thought them to be 'overstated', and criticized Durkheim for taking 'objectivist tendencies' beyond what was required by science (Worms 1917: 563). The *Revue internationale de sociologie* solicited two contributions from Durkheim, but its stance towards him was always distant and critical. The journal had, it is true, chosen Tarde over Durkheim. Durkheim or Tarde? It was this conflict that caught

James H. Tuft's attention in his article 'Recent sociological tendencies in France', which appeared in the first volume of the *American Journal of Sociology* in 1896.[49]

One of the first reactions to the appearance of the four articles on the rules of sociological method came, as Durkheim must have expected, from Gabriel Tarde, who is mentioned only once in a footnote but who was at the time the most famous sociologist in France. No fewer than four articles, written in 1894 and early 1895, contain an attack on the *Rules*. He is even harsher on it than he was on *The Division of Labour in Society*: 'These annoying tendencies are even more pronounced in his new book. The author takes to new extremes his talent for mistaking his mental constructs for objective findings' (Tarde 1895a: 199).

In a second attack, Tarde, who was director of the ministry of justice's statistical service, begins by attacking Durkheim's 'new idea' that crime is a normal phenomenon. When so defined, crime is, in Durkheim's view, 'a factor in public health, an integrative element in any healthy society' (1982[1895]: 98). But Tarde's real disagreement with Durkheim is more serious, and had to do with the conception of science itself. 'I cannot admit, with my subtle contradictor, and it is not my least disagreement with him, that science, or what he calls science, cold product of abstract reason, alien by hypothesis to every inspiration of the conscience and heart, has the supreme authority over conduct which it legitimately exercises over thought' (Tarde 1895b: 161).

Tarde then challenges Durkheim's conception of the 'social fact' for two reasons: he defines it in terms of constraint, and in terms of its autonomy from its individual manifestations. In a lecture given to the first international congress of sociology in October 1894, he raises his tone and speaks of 'M. Durkheim's ontological phantasmagoria', adding: 'I have, I admit, great difficulty in understanding how there can still be such a thing as society if we take individuals out of the equation. Are we going back to the realism of the Middle Ages?' (Tarde 1895c: viii).

As he prepared his reply, which would appear in the May 1895 issue of the *Revue philosophique*, a visibly annoyed Durkheim wrote to Tarde: 'As you will see from this note, I judge to be false, like you, many of the propositions you attribute to me. I would be happy if these explanations could do something to reduce the distance that separates us, but the end of your article leads me to believe that we profoundly disagree over this essential point.'[50]

The two men had their differences, but that did not prevent them from respecting one another: 'Militant as I may be, I am enough of a philosopher to understand that it is important for viewpoints other than mine to be represented in this science and, while I struggle against it, I acknowledge the utility of the resistance I am fighting against.' A few days later, on 31 March, Durkheim wrote again to Tarde:

I have long been worried about these invasive would-be sociologists . . . I believe that the only way to stop them is to have no mercy on these self-styled sociologists, who are compromising a science that is already too easy to understand. The problem is that everyone believes themselves to be competent in these matters, and that allows clever men to deceive the public. I am pleased to see that you too sense this danger.[51]

His remarks should not, perhaps, be taken at face value. These letters reveal a Durkheim who is being 'a little malicious and almost crafty'. He subsequently wrote to Gabriel Tarde on several occasions to ask to borrow statistical books from the criminal justice administration, to allow Marcel Mauss to consult the files on individual suicides, and to help his students to draw a map of suicides in France by *arrondissement* over a five-year period. The last request was 'all the more comical' in that the map would help to refute Tarde's theses about 'imitation'. When he described 'the current state of sociology in France' for the benefit of his Italian colleagues, Durkheim was at first kind to Gabriel Tarde, noting that there was something 'interesting' and 'fruitful' about his colleague's approach because, by privileging a sociological approach, he rejected finalist and utilitarian explanations along the lines of 'it serves some purpose'. The tone then changes. Durkheim challenges the vital role Tarde gives to imitation – which he regards as 'a mistake'. Imitation is at best, in his view, 'a secondary factor in social evolution'. He has a lot of criticisms to make of Tarde: the discussion is muddled, and the proofs are inadequate. He criticizes him, finally, for concentrating on the accidental, chance or, in a word, the irrational, and making it 'impossible to use any methodical controls'. The verdict was harsh: Tarde had no scientific rigour, and what he was doing was the very opposite of science (Durkheim 1975[1895b]: 78).

Lucien Lévy-Bruhl defends the same point of view in the bibliographical survey of 'sociological questions' he published in the *Revue bleue* in 1895. Comparing the work of Durkheim with that of Tarde and other authors, he detects a clear-cut distinction between two kinds of sociology. There is, on the one hand, the sociology of scholars 'who proceed methodically to the study of facts and the search for laws', and, on the other, that of the 'free thinkers' who 'gratify the public with their thoughts – which may or may not be new or ingenious – on sociological questions'. Durkheim is, predictably, on the side of 'scientificity and academic seriousness', and Tarde on that of 'amateurism and fickle psychologism'. Lévy-Bruhl certainly admires Tarde's 'extremely rich imagination' (he regards him as a poet), but his preference goes to the methodological rigour of Durkheim, who makes it possible to 'divorce sociology from everything that is not sociology . . . and to drive away the chatterers, the muddleheads and the show-offs who are attracted to this new science, and who will quickly discredit it' (Lévy-Bruhl 1895).

Émile Durkheim obviously read his colleague's article 'with great interest'. They had served together on the *agrégation* jury, and met when Durkheim was in Paris. Their wives knew each other. Even though he was sorry that Lévy-Bruhl had not discussed his book 'in greater detail' – 'that would have been to everyone's benefit' – he was 'very grateful' to him for having understood 'the general spirit of [my] method' and especially for having said that it 'erected a barrier between the serious workers and the would-be sociologists and dilettantes'. As for Lévy-Bruhl's warnings to sociology, he judges them 'most timely': 'The vogue it is enjoying is indeed the worst of all threats to it. The time has come for it to be more suspicious of its friends than of its enemies. Its enemies can only give it a hard time, which is all to the good, whilst its friends will quickly bring it into disrepute.'[52]

Durkheim's article on method had been published in *La Revue philosophique*, and it was Marcel Bernès (whom Durkheim addressed as 'our colleague') who opened the debate in its pages. He was less harsh than Tarde. His main objection was to Durkheim's projected 'purely objective science'. This was, he thought, 'a philosophical postulate that had been prematurely imposed upon sociology'. He was also critical of Durkheim's emphasis on constraint and the objective nature of social facts, and did not believe there was any need to establish methodological rules: 'In sociology, it is impossible to reduce an intellectual trend to a few general rules.' He went on: 'Very precise rules have even less to do with the real conditions of research here than they do elsewhere.' To conclude, he summarizes his criticisms: 'Let me say that basically all my objections come down to this: this conception is too exclusively, and too stubbornly, objectivist' (Bernès 1895d: 375).[53] And in his view, objectivism was not applicable to social facts.

Bernès wanted to play the role of moderator in this debate, and he adopted a more conciliatory position in the *Revue de métaphysique et de morale*: 'The study of the present must be both objective and subjective . . . The natural centre for the study of the social present is therefore a collective or sociological psychology' (Bernès 1895c: 166). The same issue of the *Revue* also carried a more detailed – and more critical – review of the *Rules*. Paul Lapie devoted a few lines of his survey of 'The year in sociology' to Durkheim's book. He begins by attacking the organicism he detects in several authors and criticizes both Tarde and Durkheim for their use of organico-social analogies. He then recalls that sociology is a young science, and suggests that it should not 'go too fast'. 'The terms "nation", "race" and "society" are too complex to be defined by a science that is still in its infancy.' And what about the history of humanity? The sociologists' mistake is to 'want to find historical laws before they understand the universal laws of humanity', rather as though they wanted to do for the history of man what Laplace has done for the history of the world. Unfortunately, he adds, 'no Newton has appeared in their ranks'. Although he is influenced by Tarde, he criticizes some of 'his rather crude logical errors', and is very critical of the way Durkheim divorces the individual from the collective: 'Is there no place for individual initiatives in sociology?' In his view, 'social science must be completely psychological', and 'social facts are a variety of psychological facts' (Lapie 1895: 321–3). To his astonishment, Durkheim is the only one to reject that theory. It is of course legitimate to try to make a distinction between sociology and psychology, but it is, in his view, as impossible to divorce one from the other as it is to divorce physics from mechanics. Paul Lapie obviously had little in common with Durkheim.

An even harsher review of the *Rules* appeared in the *Revue de métaphysique et de morale* the following year. Charles Andler was a philosopher by training, but had turned to German studies after his unfortunate experience of the *agrégation*. He spoke on behalf of the philosophers in order to denounce the 'so-called science known as sociology', which he saw as nothing more than a fashionable trend: 'No one has ever seen "the collective mind" speak or guide the pens of secretaries in deliberative assemblies' (Andler 1896: 254). He took the same ironic view of the externality of social facts, 'great shades that are not individual beings walk among us, hover over all human societies and govern them. Acts are performed within us, but not by us' (Andler 1896: 245). Charles Andler is scathing: 'Durkheim's assertions belong to the realm of the unthinkable, and have not been proven, and his social realism is nothing more than a form of mysticism, or the very thing he likes to criticize his enemies for.'

The publication of the *Rules* sometimes made Durkheim's relationships with his friends difficult, as they preferred to distance themselves from him even though they still admired him. Lucien Herr was typical. In the review of Durkheim's book that he published in the *Revue universitaire*, he began by expressing his admiration for Durkheim's sincerity, character and intellectual abilities, and congratulated him on his critique of contemporary society and desire to make sociology a scientific discipline (Herr 1894: 487–8). His tone changes when he begins to discuss the question of the divorce between the individual and society, as he is greatly irritated by the idea of a reality that is external and superior to individuals, of the coercive power of signs and symbols, and the notion that a whole community can feel the same emotions. It is as though the horrible 'phantom of the old realist metaphysics' were still there. A furious Herr claims that he does not understand, and regards as non-scientific, anything that is constructed on this basis. In short, he refuses to lend Durkheim his support. There was what Mauss would call 'a momentary difference of opinion' between Durkheim and Herr, and it was only with the publication of *Suicide* that 'the two men were reconciled'.

When Durkheim's book was submitted to the 'economic and social science' section of the Comité des travaux historiques et scientifiques with a request for a subscription, *rapporteur* J. Martha may well have been puzzled by what seemed to him to be 'over-general and rather vague' rules, but he congratulated the author on having expounded them 'stylishly'. His opinion of the book was favourable: 'At a time when we are thinking of establishing chairs in sociology and when every professor will have to develop his own method, this little book, incomplete as it may be, might be of particular interest.'[54]

The Analytic Mind and the Sense of Complexity

Sociology had now reached what might be called a 'decisive period' in its development. Marcel Bernès (who was now devoting his new course in Montpellier to general sociology) hoped, for his part, that now that it had taken its first tentative steps, it would be able to 'develop a more reliable method that [would] allow it to discover new truths' (Bernès 1895c: 148).[55] A more reliable method: not everyone was convinced by *The Rules of Sociological Method*. Far from it, and the issue of methodology was to become even more heated.

Shortly after publishing his articles on method, Durkheim agreed to write an account of 'the current state of sociology in France' for the Italian journal *La Riforma sociale* (Durkheim 1975[1895b]). He took a harsh view of sociological research in his own country: it had no methodology, it was poorly informed, and its findings were too general. His main targets were Charles Letourneau and Gabriel Tarde: being an erudite anthropologist or having a lot of factual information about crime was not enough. Methodology and scientific rigour were what was required.

Durkheim transposed the polemic on to the European stage, and his criticisms were incisive. His aim was clear: he wanted to introduce his Italian audience to his own conception of sociological research and to remind it that his goal was to get beyond the 'lower stage' of sociology and to elevate it to 'the rank of a truly objective science' (Durkheim 1975[1895b]: 96). He repeats the message of the *Rules*: 'social facts are things'. Sociology's first task is to elaborate a scientific method and to concern itself with objectivity, rigour and accuracy. Its method must be sociological: 'a social fact cannot be explained except by another social fact' (1982[1895]: 162). Durkheim is prepared to admit that 'individual consciousnesses are not all there is to society', but immediately adds: 'Rather than remaining external to one another, those consciousnesses are closely related and merge into one another. This mutual penetration of actions and reactions . . . gives rise to a new order of facts whose properties are independent of the elements that make them up' (1975[1895b]: 102). There is therefore something resembling a 'social realm'.

A lot of work remains to be done, Durkheim admits: the most important advances have yet to be made. But sociology is, fortunately 'making progress', and the present state of mind signals, in his view, a very important change of direction: 'Everyone understands that social reality is not such a simple thing.' Durkheim tells his Italian readers of his deep-seated conviction that France, thanks to a national spirit that is deeply imbued with clarity and profoundly rationalist – that is, Cartesian – is fertile ground for the development of sociology, but only on condition that it recognizes, as Germany tends to do more spontaneously, the complexity of social phenomena. Sociology is, in other words, possible only when two things coexist: the analytic mind, and a sense of complexity.

Émile Durkheim concludes by reasserting that there is no room in politics for either simplism or mysticism. Dismissing both anarchic individualism ('which was for a long time our credo') and authoritarian and violent socialism, he defends a 'practical doctrine' which, because it is based on the objective study of social facts, can avoid partisan conclusions and allow itself to be guided not by 'the passion that sees only one aspect of things, but by the science that tries to understand and study them in their entirety' (1975[1895b]: 107–8). Once it has become scientific, sociology will, he believes, be able to shed some light on a world in which there are still many dark, shadowy areas.

8

1895

The Revelation

'The Year of Ethics'

The wave of terrorist attacks between 1892 and 1894 had a major emotional impact on writers and artists, who responded to the atrocities by publishing atypical works characterized by verbal violence, mockery and a sense of panic and parodic intent. Even Paul Claudel, who was passing through Paris on his way from the United States to China, expressed his revolt in anarchic terms. André Gide published his novel *Paludes* (1895), which seemed to speak for an irreverent but powerless younger generation that was torn between a sinful freedom and a suffocatingly puritanical virtue. Toulouse-Lautrec preached the gospel of 'Nothing to be done, nothing' in magnificent lithographs with zany captions that were inserted into the supplement to the *Revue blanche.* Alfred Jarry published *César-Antéchrist* and finished writing his *Ubu roi* (first performed in December 1896). Some advocated nihilism, while others made a cult of incoherence without concerning themselves too much about morality, when they were not mocking 'good morals' and provoking scandals. In May 1895, Paul Adam published a long plea ('Critique des moeurs') in support of Oscar Wilde, who had just been sentenced to two years' hard labour for homosexuality (Bourrelier 2007: 480–8).

For sociology, 1894 was, it has been said, a 'year of reflection', as its supporters paused to think about their object and method. The following year, 1895, was, according to Paul Lapie, who edited 'the year in sociology' column in the *Revue de métaphysique et de morale*, going to be the year of social ethics: 'Yesterday, we defined science; today, we are constructing a social ethics'. The debates had to do with social duty, equality, freedom, charity, justice, the role of the state and even happiness. Questions were also being asked about the workings of the ideal society and the legitimacy of political power. Could (social) science really provide the basis for an ethics, wondered the young Lapie? His answer was that, even though it was a young discipline that was still 'vague and provisional', sociology could have an influence on a vulgar morality that was based upon instincts rather than principles. He contrasted that morality with a rational ethics that was neither utilitarian nor sentimental, and argued that it could, with the help of sociology, help to forge an alliance between art and science, and between consciousness and experience (Lapie 1895: 321).

A Movement

In the mid-1890s, sociology was surrounded by real excitement, both in France and other countries. Journals were launched, centres and schools were founded, and a lot was published about the social and human sciences.[1] Sociology appeared to be becoming a real movement. In France, 1895 (which also saw the birth of the new science of psychoanalysis)[2] alone saw the publication of Durkheim's *Rules of Sociological Method*, Gabriel Tarde's *La Logique sociale* and Gustave Le Bon's *Psychologie des foules*. Then there was Jean Izolet's thesis, *La Cité moderne et la métaphysique de la sociologie*, which he defended at the Sorbonne against a backdrop of noisy protests.[3]

There were also several initiatives at the institutional level, with the establishment of the Comité de défense et de progrès social[4] and the Collège libre de sciences sociales, and the opening of the Musée social, a private foundation with a social purpose. The Collège libre de science sociales, which had premises at 8 rue de Tournon, offered courses designed in 'an essentially practical spirit', as well as lectures on political doctrines and on history and sociology (including one on the sociology of Catholicism, another on Comte, and a third on the economic and moral doctrines of Le Play). It also offered courses on methodology designed to apply the methods of the exact sciences (general methodology, research monographs, statistics and demography) to social phenomena.

The Musée social was founded in 1895 with a generous donation from the Comte de Chambrun. The idea behind it, as Léon Bourgeois explained when he opened the Musée, was to depoliticize the observation of social facts, and to introduce into politics the serenity and good faith without which there could be no real science.[5] That was, in his view, the best way of helping to build a 'social peace'. The following year, he published a little book entitled *Solidarité*. Léon Bourgeois was a moderate radical and an advocate of 'solidarism', a social doctrine which, borrowing the metaphor of the social organism, stressed the value of interdependence between generations, individuals and groups. The doctrine extolled the virtue of individual and group initiatives while recommending, in the name of social justice, a degree of state interventionism to protect the common good and the general interest.

Social science, social peace and collaboration between labour and capital: these ideas, which might be termed 'social liberalism', guided the Musée's activities. The goals of this 'social laboratory for modern France' (Horne, 2002) were to consolidate voluntary social networks, to act as a sort of 'think-tank' devoted to social reform, and to collect data (including statistics) on contemporary social issues (agriculture, workers' associations and cooperatives, social welfare provision). The Musée had a well-endowed library, and organized various educational and research activities: its public lectures were very well attended. Its first two fact-finding missions, led by Le Play's disciple Paul de Rousiers and Georges Blondel, respectively, looked at trade unionism in England and the agrarian crisis in Germany.

The Musée social was therefore associated with the social reform movement. It argued the case for a stronger voluntary sector based upon mutualism and corporatism, and its founders believed that the best way to protect individual freedoms was to guarantee a minimal level of social welfare thanks to a combination of private initiatives, associations and government intervention at either the state or the municipal level. That perspective appealed to many reformists, regardless of their religious or political affiliations. The defence of individual freedoms went hand in hand with a critique of the excesses of industrial capitalism. The Comte de Chambrun spoke of 'free socialism', but many of those who worked with the Musée social tended to be strongly opposed to socialism. In 1895, Cheysson, Jacques Picot[6] and Anatole Leroy-Beaulieu embarked on a virulently anti-socialist campaign targeted mainly at state socialism and what they called 'state idolatry'. These reformists also shared the idea that social science or sociology would inevitably unmask the socialist or idealist ideal: because it led to differentiation and individualism, the progress of humanity would in the long term destroy socialism (Horne 2002).

What did Durkheim think of all this fuss as he watched it from the south-west of France? When he was asked by the Italian journal *La Riforma sociale* to describe the state of sociology in France, he made no mention of René Worms and his *Revue internationale de sociologie*, of the Musée social or of Le Play's disciples. The three main groups that he identified were the anthropologist-ethnographers (including Letourneau), the criminologists (Lacassagne, Tarde) and the academics (Espinas, Fouillée, Gaston Richard). He himself identified with the latter group, which he regarded as the most serious. It was made up of philosophers trained at the École normale supérieure, which is where the 'professorial elite' was trained. Being the leader of 'a school that was on the point of taking shape', Durkheim, who was going through a difficult period in his life, had to defend sociology on several fronts, prepare new courses (including one on religion), as well as recruiting new supporters and future collaborators. He was also becoming involved in a very lively polemic that divided philosophy teachers: the reform of their specialism.

New Courses

In 1894–5, Émile Durkheim began to teach a new course on religion, followed by another new course on the history of socialism in 1896–6. He then taught his course on the physics of morals and law for three years. He was still teaching his psychology course (the theme for 1895–6 was

'Emotions. Activity'), and would devote several lectures to Jean-Jacques Rousseau in 1897–8.

Some 30 students followed his sociology course in 1894 and 1895. Durkheim was the first to rejoice at the fact that 'educated young people' were taking an interest in social science, and even predicted that those young people who were still at university would 'become increasingly interested in the study of these problems'. Young people, he observed, were losing interest in traditional political issues such as the freedom of the press, relations between church and state, and between the executive and the legislative, which left them 'cold and indifferent'. What did fascinate them was 'anything to do with the internal organization of society and its moral structure, namely the family, property, and so on. Students are, in other words, losing interest in political science and becoming interested in sociology.' This was, he exclaimed, nothing less than 'a real revolution'. He was, on the other hand, still worried: 'There is a danger that all this activity will lead in a dangerous direction if it is not guided by a method' (Durkheim 1975[1895b]: 74–5).

It was said of his teaching at Bordeaux that it had a 'magisterial power'. The professor's 'great authority', strength of conviction and eloquence were impressive. His superiors spoke very highly of him: 'A tireless worker'; 'Character, conduct and social habits. Relations with his superiors, the authorities and the public: excellent'; 'Wisdom and judgement. Confidence: remarkable'; 'Punctiliousness and zeal: highly praiseworthy.' The answer to the question 'Does his teaching display the seriousness and depth essential to a faculty course?' was a clear 'Absolutely' and 'Certainly'. The general comments from the university's administrators were full of praise: 'A most distinguished professor, rigorous mind. I would like to see M. Durkheim stay in Bordeaux for as long as possible and would like to create a permanent position that will keep him here.' And the following year: 'M. Durkheim displays an unusual intellectual rigour, is an eloquent speaker and shows an exceptional dedication to work. Whatever one thinks of his doctrines, one has to admire him as a learned philosopher and as an orator.' In April 1895, he was awarded the title of Officier de l'instruction publique.

Given that Durkheim displayed such 'eloquence, erudition and profundity', the dean was astonished that Durkheim had not already been given tenure. 'In the meantime . . . M. Durkheim, *professeur-adjoint*, certainly deserves the maximum salary of 5,500 francs payable to non-tenured teachers.' The rector immediately corrected him: the dean's comment was 'probably pointless' because 'the chair in sociology will soon be established'.[7]

Reforming the Teaching of Philosophy

The debate about philosophy teaching was launched in 1894 by Fernand Vendérem's series of articles, 'Une classe à supprimer' ['One class to be suppressed'], in the *Revue bleue.* The tone was provocative. Vendérem wrote that the teaching of philosophy was 'Empty and boring'. It went 'over the heads of the students': on average, 5 students in a class of 50 understood what they were being told. In his view, the syllabus was too crowded, the teachers were too specialized, and the students were ill-prepared. Having made his diagnosis, Vendérem asked teachers to 'give their opinion'. Alongside the 'serious' articles from professors at the Sorbonne and the École normale supérieure – Émile Boutroux, Paul Janet, Gorges Monod and Henri Marion – there were 'humorous contributions' from eccentric columnists.[8]

This was, as Paul Janet put it, 'a burning issue'. Rumour had it that philosophy was about to disappear almost completely from the lycée syllabus. Some teachers were quite simply asking for the subject to be abolished; more serious critics – such as Léon Marillier at the École pratique des hautes études – were calling for reform, suggesting that the historical part of the syllabus should be abolished, and that the teaching of science and philosophy should be more closely linked. In a response entitled 'The teaching of philosophy and French democracy', Alfred Fouillée added a political dimension to the debate: given the dangers that threatened democracy (utilitarianism, the positivist spirit, intellectual and moral scepticism, intolerance) and the need to fight intellectual and moral anarchy, he suggested that the philosophy syllabus should be reorganized to get rid of the superfluities, to do away with the study of philosophical authors, and to place more emphasis on ethics, and especially social ethics. 'Let it be clearly understood', he concluded, 'that the state cannot and must not lose interest in the teaching of moral and social philosophy' (Fouillée 1894).

As a member of the *agrégation* jury, Durkheim was very familiar with the workings of the *concours*. Far from satisfied with the minor improvements that had been proposed, which would do nothing to change the traditional organization of philosophy classes in any real sense, he hurled himself into the fray with an article entitled simply 'The teaching of philosophy and the *agrégation de philosophie*', published in the *Revue philosophique* in February 1895.[9]

This was a 'crisis' and 'the most serious fears for the future' were, Durkheim admitted, legitimate: they were faced with a real 'pedagogic danger'. He began by suggesting that a degree of hindsight and an analysis of the historical antecedents would make it easier to identify the real issues. It was not true to say that everything began with Victor Cousin, but it was true that Cousin did assign to philosophy, which had until then played only 'a humble role', a 'social and educational function of the greatest importance'. It was, that is, destined to give France a new moral unity. Cousin wanted, in other words, to found a new religion. Such a project gave philosophy the mission of inculcating cardinal virtues and of transmitting a 'sort of credo' from generation to generation. In Durkheim's view, this was not just ambiguous – 'the idea of a rational dogma is irrational' (1975[1895a]: 409–10). It had also ceased to have an effect: the teaching of philosophy was no longer anything more than a 'gymnastics' designed to make minds more flexible. The study of the great doctrines and problems was no more than a pretext.

Far from becoming more relaxed, the new mores that Durkheim had deplored when he was a lycée student 15 years earlier had become more rigid, and the tendency to celebrate 'purely formal talent' and the quest for distinction and originality were becoming more pronounced. He complained that examinations discouraged students from taking an interest in anything to do with 'positive data and definitive knowledge'. Students were becoming 'clever conjurors' who thought they had no need for any documentation and turned simple questions about psychology and logic into 'meditations on transcendental metaphysics'.

Durkheim also found that the essays he was marking displayed 'vagueness at the linguistic level' and a 'corresponding vagueness at the level of ideas'. He was afraid that philosophy was becoming 'a form of symbolism and impressionism', and his fears were all the more justified in that, as students became more interested in mysticism, 'the path lay open to all sorts of fantasies'. Unfortunately, 'brilliance' was preferred to 'solidity'. Durkheim even spoke in alarmist terms: the situation was dangerous because, he asserted, philosophy was turning into an 'anarchic dilettantism'. Philosophy had lost sight of its collective goals, was preaching individualism and was becoming 'an art form' (Durkheim 1975[1895a]: 416–18). All this prefigured 'the reign to do what you please'.

Abolishing the teaching of philosophy was obviously out of the question. Like any institution, the philosophy class could 'serve different purposes at different times'. In his view, the goal of philosophy was now to transmit a culture that was both social and scientific. Social culture was the more important of the two. The younger generations had to be prepared for collective life in the very particular context that he described as a 'state of discontent and anxiety'. Society had been transformed, and the organization of society was no longer based solely upon automatisms, habits and traditions, but also – and above all – on reflexivity and rationality.

Dealing with social questions in the classroom was not, Durkheim admitted, an easy matter. Either teachers were obliged to teach a single doctrine, or they had to be given the freedom to teach the doctrine of their choice. This was a battle between state doctrine and anarchy. Dismissing both solutions, Durkheim suggested that 'young people should be equipped with all the knowledge they need to be able one day to examine these doctrines intelligently and reach their own informed opinion' (Durkheim 1975[1895a]: 412). Neither passions nor feelings should be allowed to dominate public debates; students had to be encouraged to think calmly and to develop a sense of how complex things were. And the only way to teach them to do that was to 'accustom young people to seeing human and social things as objects of science, or in other words as natural things that are neither mysterious nor sacrosanct', and to give them some 'understanding of man', mainly by teaching them psychology.

Instincts, habits, the personality, the emotions, and language: all these aspects of the 'human person' should also be on the syllabus, insisted Durkheim, who wanted sociology to be taught in schools and morality to be its prime object; the family, property, honour, contracts, charity, responsibility, crime and punishment: all were possible topics for discussion.

Turning to scientific culture, Durkheim now set the teaching of philosophy a second goal: 'Get pupils to think about the nature of the methods and basic notions they use.' Its goal was, in other words, to 'train minds' and to transmit a solid 'scientific culture'. Studying philosophy, in Durkheim's view, did not simply mean discussing immortality, the existence of God or freedom and determinism; it also meant thinking about what was meant by a law, a classification or a mathematical argument. He was not proposing a new syllabus. The changes would come from within, by training a new generation of teachers to teach science on the basis of practical experience.

Durkheim sought to make himself clear. He did not want to make a 'fetish' of science; he merely wanted 'the scientific spirit to have a greater presence'. He had no intention of 'speaking ill of the humanities', but he did point out that there had been enough study of languages and literary masterpieces. 'We now need not so much delicate minds who can enjoy beautiful things and express themselves appropriately, as solid thinkers who can, without bothering about the storms that threaten us, look resolutely to the future and see the goal towards which we must march (Durkheim 1975[1895a]: 432–3). He therefore criticizes forms of philosophy that are nothing more than 'abstract literature' and ridicules 'talent' (of teachers) that has not been trained by 'strict discipline'. His accusations are so serious that he feels obliged, at the very end of his article, to beg forgiveness for having been so harsh, and to remind his readers that he does believe in the 'good' that philosophy teaching can do.

Durkheim's comments provoked an almost immediate response from philosophers, who criticized him for wanting to reduce the subject to the logic of the sciences and for seeing the teaching of philosophy in lycées as 'a purely sociological and practical subject'. Their annoyance was all the greater in that his criticisms of students' 'ill-advised essays' implied that their teachers were incompetent. Because he was seen as philosophy's gravedigger and as a critic of 'doctrinaire sentimentalists', Durkheim was easily categorized as a latter-day positivist and a reductionist dogmatist by both the *Revue de métaphysique et de morale* and the *Revue philosophique.*

While it praised Durkheim for his 'righteous and vigorous thinking', the *Revue philosophique* also criticized his 'careless attitude': there was a danger that such statements would play into the hands of those who were opposed to the teaching of philosophy in the lycées. Marcel Bernès, who was the journal's spokesman on sociological issues, criticized him for this 'extreme scientific realism', and accused him of wanting to see science play a greater role and of suggesting that secondary education should be even more specialized than it already was. For his own part, Bernès was in favour of striking a balance: the humanities should remain a basic part of the general syllabus, but more emphasis should be placed on the teaching of ethics, and candidates for the *agrégation* should receive a 'serious scientific education' (Bernès 1895a).[10]

The *Revue de métaphysique et de morale* published a number of commentaries. Durkheim complained that his remarks had been misinterpreted and, fearing that these comments would lead to 'misunderstandings', demanded a right to reply.

> The main point I would like to take up relates to the gratuitous accusation that my article is an attack on 'the masters of contemporary philosophy'. Nothing could be further from the truth. I was simply criticizing a relatively recent trend, or at least its extreme manifestations . . . I did not attack any doctrine or any thinker.

Although it noted this correction, the editorial board maintained its stance, claiming the right to 'remain true to itself': 'In our view, the content of philosophy cannot be of the same nature as the content of science, as the positivists would have it.' An attempt was being made to contrast the 'common ground' of things with another 'common ground', namely that of ideas. The *Revue de métaphysique et de morale* was, in other words, siding with 'the spirit of critical reflection' as opposed to the 'spirit of positive science' (which was supposedly 'the flavour of the century').[11]

A Discovery: The Vital Role of Religion

'Can social facts be understood without religion?' asked Paul Lapie in the *Revue de métaphysique et de morale* (Lapie 1895: 337).[12] Religion, which had until then been the concern of a few scholars and men of erudition, became at the turn of the century a topic of public debate. Everyone was talking about religion. Émile Zola had stirred up a controversy with *Lourdes*, a novel about that place of pilgrimage, followed two years later by *Rome*, which dealt with the Eternal City: his aim was to announce the 'collapse of the old Catholicism' and the victory of reason. One of his characters, Pierre Froment, states: 'Science remains the only possible truth.' Early in 1895, the literary critique Ferdinand Brunetière visited the Vatican, and published a eulogy to Pope Leo XIII in the *Revue des deux mondes* on his return. He attacked science's claims to be able to replace religion as the basis for an ethics, and concluded: 'Science has for the moment, and for a long time to come, lost the argument.' The mystery remained intact. The reply came from chemist and politician Marcellin Berthelot, who published an article on science and morality in the new *Revue de Paris* in February 1895. It was not, in his view, religion (and its dogmas) that had changed, but science. Brunetière replied that science had lost some of its prestige, while religion had regained some of its old prestige.

If there was one question that seemed 'essential', it was that of the relationship between morality and religion. 'The task of our century', wrote the philosopher Alphonse Darlu (1985: 244), 'has been to secularize religious ideas.' By placing itself under the aegis of political liberalism, the Third Republic had indeed tried to 'set minds free' and had adopted important measures designed to do precisely that: freedom of the press and freedom of assembly in 1881, secularism in state schools in 1882–6, and the freedom to form trade unions in 1884. Other measures were introduced at the beginning of the twentieth century: freedom of association was recognized in 1901, and freedom of worship was once more guaranteed by the separation of church and state in 1905. There was an obvious desire to complete the secularization of society, which had been under way since the Revolution, and to found a 'new France'. Jules Ferry himself intervened to justify the establishment of a chair in the history of religions at the Collège de France, even though there was a danger that it would be seen as a politically motivated decision: 'The true history of man', he proclaimed, 'is the history of religion.'

Protestants, many of them liberal, played a central role in this process. Convinced that only they truly understood the scriptures, they were also less reluctant than Catholics to embark upon the study of religions. The positivist Émile Littré (1879) admitted from the outset: 'It is greatly to Protestantism's credit that it has never objected to method taking precedence over dogma. The same cannot be said of Catholicism' (see Cabanel 1994). Three Protestant historians stood out: Maurice Vernes, Albert Réville and his son Jean. The son of a pastor, a specialist in the history of Israel and a philo-Semite, Maurice Vernes (1845–1923) was actively involved in the campaign to promote the history of religions and had, as early as 1880, founded the *Revue de l'histoire des religions*, with financial support from Émile Guimet, a rich industrialist from Lyon and a connoisseur of Asian art. Vernes studied in Strasbourg, and was one of the first to teach at the faculty of Protestant theology in Paris, which was established in 1877. He was one of the 'young' teachers at the fifth section of the École pratique des hautes études, where he taught the 'history of the Semite peoples'. Albert Réville (1826–1906) and his son Jean (1854–1908) were the driving forces behind the fifth section ('religious sciences'), where they acted as, respectively, president and secretary in the 1880s. Both were subsequently elected to the chair in the history of religions at the Collège de France. The architects of the reforms in primary education included, finally, the trio made up of Ferdinand Buisson, Félix Pécaut and Jules Steeg. A Protestant of Swiss origins, Buisson became involved in the 'battle over sacred history' at a very early stage; as early as 1869, he suggested that sacred history should be replaced by a history of humanity, arguing that the Bible should be replaced in primary schools by what Renouvier termed the 'Book of Man'.

Catholic circles were seriously worried, and feared that the neutrality that teachers were required to observe in the classroom would do away with all reference to God in schools, and that theology would disappear from the universities. In France, as in other countries, the idea that the history of religions should be a subject for historical research, and that the discipline should be taught at the Collège de France, seemed 'dangerous and misplaced' (Loisy 1932: 96).[13] The new discipline, which taught that there was no such thing as papal infallibility and that orthodoxy was a chimera, made the Catholic Church all the more nervous in that Ernest Renan – the former seminarian turned philosopher and specialist in the Semitic languages, who had died in 1892 – had popularized the idea that religions, and especially Catholicism, should be studied on a scientific and not a confessional basis. His *Vie de Jésus* (1863) was a great success.

Jews also became involved in the move to elaborate a 'science of Judaism'. In 1879, Baron James de Rothschild founded a society of Jewish studies [Société des études juives] to encourage studies of Judaism, and the following year he financed the new *Revue d'études juives*, whose goals were scientific rather than propagandist. For those who were identified as 'Israelites', the 'Jewish question' was complex in more than one sense, as it raised religious as well as ethnic and racial issues. Even though Zionism found it difficult to put down roots in France, where it appealed mainly to recent emigrants from Europe, plans to establish a Jewish state called into question the Jewish community's desire for integration (Abitol 1989: 19). There were two conflicting visions of Judaism; for some, it was primarily a religion, but for others the Jews were a people or ethnic group. Those who specialized in the history of religions could not ignore this debate: was this a religion or a race? wondered Ernest Renan.

The 'modernist' movement was slow to take off in France, and became mainly an issue for historians. The history of religions or religious science was a young discipline, but it had captured a few strongholds by the end of the nineteenth century: a chair in the history of religions was established at the Collège de France in 1879, the *Revue de l'histoire des religions* began publication in 1880 and the fifth section of the École pratique des hautes études opened a few years later. Some anthropologists were beginning to investigate the origins of religion, and had begun to adopt a comparative and evolutionist approach. André Lefebvre published *La Religion* in 1892. The task was not easy, as the study of the cults and myths of so-called primitive people met with sharp resistance: ethnocentrism, etc.

It was in this very lively intellectual and political context that Durkheim became aware of the importance of religion in the life of societies. It was by his own admission 'only in 1895 that I had a clear view of the capital role played by religion in social life'. Although he had already written on the subject, he went on:

> It was in that year that, for the first time, I found a means of tackling sociologically the study of religion. It was a revelation to me. That lecture course on 1895 marks a watershed in my thinking, so much so that all my previous research had to be started all over again so as to be harmonized with the new views. The *Ethik* of Wundt, which I had read eight years previously, played no part in this change of direction. It was due entirely to the studies of religious history which I had just embarked upon, and

in particular to the works of Robertson Smith and his school. (Durkheim 1982[1907]: 259–60)

There is something surprising, even astonishing, about Durkheim's 'revelation'. Had there been a change in his personal attitude towards religion and Judaism? In March 1895, he received a letter from Israël Lévi, the chief rabbi of Bordeaux, inviting him to give a lecture on Judaism. There are no grounds for believing that he accepted the invitation (Birnbaum 1971: 17). It seems that the famous lectures of 1894–5 on 'The origins of religion' were written with his nephew in mind. 'We did the research together. We were both trying to make the best use of my strengths', said Mauss (1979[1930]: 214). Little is known about these unpublished lectures, except that Durkheim did not begin by asking what the religious idea and religious feelings were, but by studying the various religions that have existed and that still exist. 'We compared them. We identified their common characteristics, and were thus able to determine objectively what the religious phenomenon consists in. Our analysis concentrated on what we had defined in this way.' When he began to study religion, Durkheim therefore used the method he had already used to study crime and punishment in the study of responsibility that he had undertaken for his thesis.

The 'Religious Sciences' Section. Sylvain Lévi

'We did the research together': Mauss's choice of direction was clearly influenced by his uncle. It was on his uncle's advice that he turned to the study of the history of religions after his *agrégation*. Marcel was at first unsure of what to do: he thought seriously of making a career in secondary teaching, but he also considered taking up a position at the University of Algiers. Writing a doctoral thesis on Leo the Hebrew and Spinoza was a further possibility. Discussing his choice of profession, Mauss remarks: 'During my student years, I hesitated between quantitative studies [in collaboration with Durkheim], suicide, the history of cities and human settlements . . . studying law [three years] and studying the sociology of religions'. He adds: 'It was because of my interest in philosophy and at the suggestion of Durkheim that I took the conscious decision to specialize in the study of religious phenomena, and I have always devoted myself almost exclusively to that' (1979[1930]: 214). Rather than going immediately into teaching, Marcel therefore decided to complete his education and enrolled at the École pratique des hautes études, where he signed up for the fourth (historical sciences and philology) and fifth (religious sciences) sections.

The École pratique des hautes études, together with the Collège de France, was one of the first institutions to open its doors to the 'new religious sciences'.[14] The fifth section (religious sciences) was established in 1866 by the new director of higher education Louis Liard. Its establishment and installation at the Sorbonne took place in an atmosphere of controversy, going hand in hand with the closure of the Sorbonne's faculty of Catholic theology. Sacred history had at last been secularized, as Maurice Vernes put it. Christianity was obviously studied there, but so too were Greece and Rome, the Semitic religions, and Egypt, India and the Far East.

Ever since its foundation, the fifth section had, like the other sections, always taken a scientific stance and, while it was neither anti-religious nor irreligious, it was resolutely secular. Complete intellectual freedom, tolerance and an impartial passion for the truth were the goals and values shared by all its staff, who made an effort to divorce the history of religions from both apologetics and theology and to pursue what the Dutch historian Chantepie de la Saussaye called 'the impartial and free search for the truth'. The representation of different confessions within the teaching staff was still an issue, but the tensions that existed inside the school never became overtly conflictual. Religions were studied with 'the same freedom and the same independence of mind' as the other disciplines (Lévi 1932: 143). The balance between the various religious confessions was, however, still precarious.

Mauss's choice of subject was decisive for both nephew and uncle, as Durkheim was to find supporters and collaborators amongst Mauss's teachers and friends. Mauss was interested in both the study of religions (the ancient religions of India and primitive religion) and the study of languages (comparative Indo-European linguistics, Sanskrit and Hebrew). At the École pratique, he discovered 'guides', some of whom would, like Antoine Meillet, Léon Marillier, and Isräel and Sylvain Lévi, become both friends and colleagues.

Meillet (1866–1937) was a philologist, linguist and historian, and a former student of Ferdinand de Saussure's. It was he who introduced Mauss – his junior by six years – to the comparative method, and a solid friendship was to develop between teacher and pupil (Mauss 1969[1936]: 548). Marillier (1863–1901) was an *agrégé de philosophie* with an interest in biology and physiology, and had done work placements in the faculty of medicine's laboratories and in mental hospitals. He taught in the religious sciences section, where he gave lectures on religious psychology and, from 1890 onwards, on the religions of non-civilized peoples. He was the joint editor of the *Revue d'histoire des religions,* and his motto was 'Convictions should be based upon the facts and only the facts' (Marillier 1901: 181). Isräel Lévi (1865–1939), a man of scrupulous rigour and exceptional intellectual honesty, helped Mauss to improve his knowledge of Hebrew and introduced him to the study of 'the origins of rabbinical prayer'.

Marcel's most important encounter was with Sylvain Lévi, whom he met just before the beginning of the 1895 academic year. The unchallenged doyen of oriental studies, Lévi (1963–35) was at the time a professor at the Collège de France and was about to publish his *Doctrine du sacrifice dans les Brahmanas* (1896). Sylvain (as Mauss called him) immediately became Mauss's 'second uncle', and a strong filial relationship soon developed between the two. It later developed into a firm friendship (Mauss

1969[1935]: 545). Durkheim came into contact with Lévi thanks to Mauss, and the two men became friends. The Indianist had a major influence on both uncle and nephew, and introduced them to what might be called 'methodological ritualism' (Strenski 1997).

The broad outlines of Mauss's intellectual project were beginning to emerge: philosophy, philology and the study of primitive religions. It coincided with a central strand in his uncle's work. The fourth section had a decisive influence on the birth of sociology in two senses. In intellectual terms, it prioritized the study of the religions of so-called primitive peoples, and in social terms it led to the creation of a multidisciplinary research environment that welcomed the new discipline. Many of the team who would subsequently work on *L'Année sociologique* were directly associated with the École pratique des hautes études, including Henri Hubert, Antoine Meillet and Robert Hertz.

Marriage or Cohabitation?

For Durkheim, the period 1895–6 was, in terms of publications, the 'least productive' in his entire career: he published only four texts. In addition to his contribution to *La Riforma sociale* and his lengthy discussion of the teaching of philosophy in the *Revue philosophique*, he discussed Westermarck's book on the origins of marriage (1975[1895c]), and drafted a response to Tarde's criticism of his comments on the normality of crime. He was, however, far from inactive. In the spring of 1895, he began to write a new book on suicide, and he was planning to launch a new sociological journal. He was also preparing a new lecture course on socialism.

The themes of free love, group marriage, sexual communism, prostitution and polygamy were beginning to attract the attention of scholars as well as the general public. The danger was – and Durkheim was more aware of it than ever – that self-styled sociologists' eagerness for success would try to 'provide immediate responses to the demands and preoccupations of the mob'. Durkheim preferred empirical observations to generalizations, and the qualities he looked for in researchers were an abundance of information, an honest attitude towards their research, independence of judgement, and circumspection. He saw himself as someone who had 'direct practical knowledge of the facts' and who carried out 'specialist research' (1975[1895c]).

In his hands, the method became a formidable weapon. And it was in the name of 'method' that he criticized the Finnish ethnologist Edvard Westermarck's work on the origins of marriage. He had several criticisms to make: Westermarck looked only at the ethnographic facts and took no account of historical facts; he explained social facts in psychological terms; and his definition of marriage was 'arbitrary'. Westermarck's most serious mistake was, in Durkheim's view, that he made no distinction between 'two sorts of sexual association that are so different that they affect the moral consciousnesses of societies in completely different ways'.

On the one hand, there was 'legal and regularized marriage' and, on the other, free love or, if one prefers, he goes on, cohabitation. In Durkheim's view, marriage was defined by the law, rights and duties, sanctions, and was approved by public morality. There was none of this in cohabitation: 'The fact that lovers have been together for their entire lives does not make them a married couple' (Durkheim 1975[1895c]: 79). The defining characteristic of marriage is therefore not the duration of the sexual relationship, but the fact that it is regulated: it is a social institution. Mere sexual intercourse is dismissed as the bestiality of the animal kingdom: 'There is no such thing as marriage in the animal kingdom, except perhaps in a metaphorical sense' (ibid.: 80).[15]

Durkheim also challenges the thesis that something resembling 'group marriage' (defined solely by promiscuity) is to be found in primitive societies. What does, in his view, characterize the primitive state is the absence of all regulation, or 'real sexual anomie'. Marriage therefore simply cannot be regarded as a 'primitive institution'; to argue that it is means reverting to the biblical conception of the family, which holds that marriage has been in existence throughout the history of humanity.

Researching the elementary forms of marriage and the family is therefore a difficult task. The 'distant past' has gone, but it has left 'traces'. Durkheim was critical of 'facile Darwinism', but he did believe in social evolution: there was a 'huge difference' between 'primitive humanity's' family and the present state of the family. Every form of social organization, or every social type, has a corresponding family organization. Durkheim was familiar with the work of [Lewis Henry] Morgan, who had analysed the diversity of kinship nomenclatures in 139 tribes, and he was also struck by the great diversity and extreme complexity of the forms taken by the social organization of the family. Durkheim would return to this issue in the long essay entitled 'La prohibition de l'inceste et ses origines' ['Incest: the nature and origins of the taboo'], which he published in the first volume of *L'Année sociologique* in 1898 (Durkheim 1963[1898]).

Crime and Mental Health

Some saw the rising crime rate and the increase in the number of suicides as symptoms of 'degeneracy', and were therefore outraged when Durkheim dared to describe crime as 'normal' in the *Rules*. In his article 'Crime and social health', which was written in March 1895, he insists on correcting some misunderstandings, and replies to Gabriel Tarde's article in the previous issue of the *Revue philosophique*. He was obviously furious: 'Most of the propositions which my eminent critic attributes to me are not mine' (Durkheim 1978[1985]: 181). 'I did not say', he protests, 'that the rise in criminality, documented by our statistics, was normal'. On the contrary, it was a 'sad spectacle' (ibid.: 182). He goes on: 'I did not say that, if certain crimes become rare, the penalties which they incur would necessarily be raised' (ibid.: 183). 'Nowhere did I say that crime and genius were merely two aspects of a single mental state' (ibid.: 184). At one point, he loses his temper: 'All this part of M. Tarde's discussion is beyond me' (ibid.)

In his own defence, Durkheim reiterates the propositions that he really wanted to establish: (1) crime is 'normal' 'because it is linked to the fundamental conditions of all social life'; (2) 'I said that the existence of crime had a *generally* indirect and *sometimes* direct utility'; (3) morality is a social function; it must, therefore, 'have only a limited degree of vitality' (for example, if our respect for human life were to surpass a certain intensity, we would not put up with even the idea of war; 'and yet in the present state of international relations, we must be able to make war'; 'too much pity for the suffering of animals . . . becomes an obstacle to the progress of science') (1978[1985]: 186). He then replies to Tarde's accusation that he has confused 'normal' and 'average' types, adding that it is 'my ingenious critic' who has perpetrated 'this strange confusion' (ibid.: 187). He goes on to explain that a society 'comprised solely of average individuals would essentially be abnormal. For there is no society which does not include multitudes of individual anomalies, and so universal a fact is not without a reason for existing. It is, therefore, socially normal that there be in every society psychologically abnormal individuals' (ibid.: 187). And while he insists that there is a deep dividing line between the social and the psychic, he concludes that 'the normal state of societies implies the sickness of individuals; a certain incidence of mortality, like a certain incidence of crime, is indispensable to the collective health' (ibid.: 188).

Durkheim and Tarde disagreed completely, and 'the source of the differences between us . . . arises, above all, from the fact that I believe in science and M. Tarde doesn't' (1978[1985]: 188). His theory placed 'sensation, instinct, passion, all the base and darker aspects of ourselves' 'above reason'; Durkheim opposed them in the name of science, which was not 'an intellectual amusement' and must be of 'practical utility' (ibid.). He also informs his readers that 'in a book I am preparing on suicide will be found a refutation of [Tarde's] thesis' (ibid.: 181). He had already made this point in his letter to Tarde.

Relations between the two sociologists were very hostile, and Durkheim was very critical of Tarde. As he remarked to his Italian colleague Cesare Lombroso (who was also attacked by Tarde on the grounds that he denied the existence of free will): 'It is at last beginning to be noticed that Tarde's work is purely literary and is not scientific. He is an amateur and not a scholar. And he therefore feels threatened by anyone who tries to turn sociology into a real science.'[16]

Suicide: The First Draft

There was nothing new about Durkheim's interest in suicide. One of the first articles he published was on suicide and the birth rate (Durkheim 1888). Suicide was also the theme of the series of public lectures he gave in Bordeaux in 1889–90, and both the lectures on the family given in 1892 and the doctoral thesis, *The Division of Labour in Society*, contain several references to suicide. As soon as he found an idea or a piece of data, he made a note of it and then went on with what he was doing. His mode of reading was 'fairly random' (Borlandi 2000: 31), and depended on the lectures he was giving (suicide in 1892–3, and the sociology of crime in 1893–4).

Most of Book I of *Suicide* and the first four chapters of Book II were, in all probability, written between the spring and autumn of 1895. At this point, Durkheim was only one third of the way through his work. It is unlikely that he began a final draft before 1895, first because it was only when he became head of the criminal statistics office in 1894 that Gabriel Tarde was able to grant him access to the files on suicides, and, second, because it was only in the summer and autumn of 1895 that his two research assistants (Ferrand, and then Marcel Mauss) consulted the data held by the ministry for justice. Ferrand (whom Durkheim thanks at the end of the introduction to *Suicide*), was in Paris in June–July 1895 to collect data on the distribution of suicide rates in France by *département* between 1887 and 1891. And it was in November that Mauss, who by then had his *agrégation*, went to Tarde's office and carried on sifting through the individual files on suicides recorded in France between 1889 and 1891. The files were made available given to him by Gabriel Tarde, and it took him many hours to work through them.[17] We get some idea of the scale of his task if we recall the number of variables involved: age, sex, matrimonial status, Paris and the provinces, presence of children, etc. Given the richness of the data he was collecting, the task probably took Mauss three to four months. This data made it possible to map out the pattern of suicides in France by *arrondissement* for the period 1887–91.

Durkheim also asked his nephew to provide documentation by analysing journal articles on suicide in England and Spain, and on 'suicide in the German army'. He advised him to collect 'only statistical information that appeared to be of interest', and above all not to 'take too much time over it. I'm only asking you to do this research so as to be on the safe side.'[18]

The International Exhibition of 1895: Popularizing Sociology

With the help of his nephew, Durkheim presented the findings of his research to the International Exhibition held in Bordeaux in May–November 1895. This was the 13th exhibition organized by the Société philomathique de Bordeaux, and was international in the sense that many countries were represented, and in that a 'palais des Colonies' was built, featuring an 'African village'. The organizers wanted to highlight the importance of electricity, the region's wines and spirits, and the social sciences. The decorative arts were a further attraction.

It was a major event, with more than 9,500 exhibitors and representatives from some 30 countries. It was held on the great place des Quinconces, with the palais des Colonies on one side, the workers' exhibition on the other, and the social sciences section beneath the central dome. The social sciences section included exhibits dealing with company benefit schemes, welfare, housing and the press. It included a 'curious and precious' collection of documents – graphs, reports and statistics – contributed by both local organizations (charities, welfare associations and bodies mediating between labour and capital) and 'the authors of theoretical studies and plans for practical reforms' (Bénard 1899: 409). The exhibition was a great success with the public.

Durkheim's contribution was the map of suicides in France drawn with the help of his nephew. 'A curious map', observed the dean of the faculty of letters.[19] Durkheim also exhibited another artefact – in a 'striking form', adds his nephew. It was 'a phylogenetic outline of the various structures taken, first by the politico-familial organization and then by the more purely familial domestic sub-group' (Mauss 1969[1925]: 481). It was, in a word, a genealogy of the family in which Durkheim schematically outlined the contents of his lectures on the family for a popular audience.

Little is known about Durkheim's role in the organization of the exhibition (in which some of his colleagues, including M. Paris – who took responsibility for the fine arts section – were also involved), except that he was mandated by the commission responsible for the social sciences section to coordinate the work of the exhibitors, including those from abroad (Bosc 1999). Despite his differences with Lombroso, Durkheim was eager to give the sociology of crime a prominent role, and asked his Italian colleague for help: 'We all feel that the exhibition would be seriously incomplete if your school was not prominently represented.' The documents Durkheim wished to obtain were 'diagrams, maps and graphics that might give the public some idea of the state of the research and the methods used'.[20] Durkheim was pleased with his honourable colleague's 'prompt response', and later praised him for the services he had rendered to science by adapting the methods of the positive sciences to the study of moral phenomena and by drawing attention to the archaic features of the penal regime.

Even though there was a 'distance', and even 'major differences of opinion', between himself and Tarde, Durkheim agreed to display the two volumes of statistics he had been sent by his colleague. Their 'disagreements over doctrine' by no means implied any lack of mutual respect: 'For my part, I do not need to tell you of my deference towards your work and yourself', he wrote to his colleague, adding: 'And besides, militant as I may be, I am enough of a philosopher to understand the importance of representing viewpoints other than mine and, although I fight it, I quite understand that the resistance I am fighting has its uses.'[21] A few days later, he admitted to Tarde that he was 'worried that sociology might be invaded by charlatans'. He saw this as a threat: 'The disease is spreading remarkably quickly. I think that the only thing to be done is to show no complacency towards these self-styled sociologists, who are compromising a science that is already too easily compromised.'[22] He said that he was glad that Tarde shared his opinion. Was he implying that the 'amateurish'

Tarde was a would-be sociologist? Or was he being hypocritical? It has to be recalled that Tarde had allowed Marcel Mauss to go to the ministry for justice to consult its 'unpublished documents' on suicides in France.

A History of Socialism

The most significant events of 1895 were the conquest of Madagascar and the founding of the Conféderation générale du travail. In political terms, the year saw the election of the radical Léon Bourgeois as a replacement for Alexandre Ribot, who had been accused of corruption. Bourgeois's presidency lasted for only six months, and he tried in vain to implement his plan to introduce an income tax, organizing pension schemes for workers and a bill on associations that was designed to pave the way for the separation of church and state.

Although they were not well organized, the socialists were active, making a lot of noise, and their newspapers, pamphlets and almanacs were everywhere. The main groupings were as follows. Jules Guesde's Parti ouvrier français was a centralized class party that aspired to being 'conscious and organized', while Jean Allemane's Parti ouvrier socialiste révolutionnaire (whose members included Lucien Herr and Charles Andler) was anti-militarist and anti-parliamentarian. Then there was Edouard Vaillant's Comité révolutionnaire central, and the so-called independent socialists Benoît Malon, Jean Jaurès and Alexandre Millerand. The independents, who clustered around journals such as *La Revue socialiste* and *La Petite République*, were reformists who were opposed to violence, and in favour of both universal suffrage and parliamentary action. On 25 September 1893, Jean Jaurès had declared in *La Dépêche*: 'We are not the destroyers of individual property. On the contrary: we want to restore it' – much to the astonishment of all those who believed that collectivism meant replacing individual property with collective property. He was surprised to see independent socialists posing as the champions of freedom and individual property. 'Where are we going when socialists defend the rights of small landowners?', asked the economist Charles Gide (1894), who saw this change of heart as an unfortunate concession, if not political opportunism. Others said it was eyewash. In 1896, the economist Charles Say published a book entitled *Contre le socialisme*. He could not have made himself clearer.

It was in 1892 that Jean Jaurès 'converted' to socialism and, according to Charles Andler, it was Lucien Herr who convinced him to make the decision. A graduate of the École normale supérieure (1878) and an *agrégé de philosophie* (1881), Jaurès had been elected a *député* for the Tarn constituency in 1885, when he stood on the 'Union républicaine' platform. At that time, he described himself as a republican and a democrat. In 1892, he stood in a by-election as a socialist republican candidate for Guesde's Parti ouvrier français, but soon distanced himself from Guesde, alienated by his verbal intransigence and by his narrow interpretation of Marx.

Opposed to dogmatism and sectarianism, Jaurès felt close to the independent socialists, and that allowed him to support socialism while retaining
his freedom of opinion. He developed a theory that there was a continuity
between republicanism and socialism, and rejected the idea of insurrection
or revolutionary violence. That point of view was shared by the intellectuals grouped around the socialist leader, such as Lucien Herr and Charles
Andler, who were convinced that Marxism was in a state of decay. They
were spokesmen for what was called the 'socialism of the intellectuals'.

Some, like Émile Zola, chose to remain silent in the face of these debates
and never-ending splits. Durkheim found it impossible to ignore what was
going on around him. In 1895, he resumed teaching at the faculty and
taught throughout the academic year 1895–6. The theme of his public lectures was political: socialism or, more specifically, the history of socialism.
This may seem a surprising theme for a lecture course on philosophy, but
other teachers of philosophy or history who took an interest in the social
sciences were also discussing the issues of socialism and social solidarity.[23]
Even the Société de sociologie de Paris was debating 'The sociological view
of political economy and socialism'. Both René Worms and Gabriel Tarde
attended the debate and accepted the need for sociologists to regard the
demands of the socialists as 'one of the most characteristic features of the
contemporary age'.[24] In a word, everyone – from activists to professors, in
the salons and in the streets – was talking about socialism.

As a student at the École normale supérieure, Durkheim had devoted his
attention to an examination of the social question, even though, as Mauss
recalled, 'creating the foundations of a science had of course absorbed his
energies'. But he did not lose sight of his point of departure: social problems continued to underpin his interests. The conclusion to his doctoral
thesis had moral, political and economic implications, as would his study
of suicide. Both demonstrated the importance of professional groups 'if
the individual is not to be alone in the face of the state and live in a kind of
alternation between anarchy and servitude' (Mauss 1962[1928]: 33). The
idea 'impressed great minds', as is obvious from the writings of Georges
Sorel.

In Paris, Marcel Mauss was very active. He had just left the Parti ouvrier
to join the Parti ouvrier socialiste révolutionnaie (POSR). Led by Jean
Allemane, a typographer and Communard who had been elected a *député*
for Paris, the party declared itself to be atheist, republican, communist and
internationalist. It preached the doctrine of class struggle, was in favour of a
general strike and was suspicious of parliamentary action. It was, in a sense,
an ouvrierist sect within the socialist movement. Marcel Mauss was at this
time one of those students who wanted to 'develop a socialist consciousness
amongst students and teachers', as Hubert Lagardelle's slogan had it. His
friends, most of whom were at the École normale supérieure, shared the
same political ideals. They wanted both to pursue their studies and have an
academic career and to make a political contribution by their writing and
becoming involved in extra-curricular activities (Charle 1995: 152).

Durkheim observed his nephew's political activities from afar and with

a certain apprehension, but did 'sympathize' with the socialists and socialism. He and his friend Jaurès were in agreement over a number of points.
Both recognized the importance of morality and collective and national
values; they rejected violence at all cost and played down the importance
of the principle of class struggle. Both refused to see *Das Kapital* as 'an
entirely scientific work' (Birnbaum 1971: 18). And yet, while Durkheim
was sympathetic to socialism, he remained 'uncommitted [and] never gave
himself to it'. Like any fellow-traveller, he felt a need 'to justify himself in
his own eyes, in those of his students, and one day in the eyes of the world'
(Mauss 1962[1928]: 35). Mauss had frequent discussions with his uncle,
who did not always approve of his political activism, and it might even be
said that the lectures on 'the history of socialism' were a way of pursuing
these discussions.

Durkheim therefore owed it to himself to clarify certain issues. He had
not gone back to studying socialism, but that was for lack of time rather
than of conviction. A series of events now forced him to 'take sides', as
Mauss put it. Jules Guesde's supporters had a solid foothold in Bordeaux,
and there were intense debates between them and the supporters of Jaurès,
who often travelled to the city to defend his ideas and who saw Durkheim
when he was there. Durkheim was also annoyed by the way his thesis, *The
Division of Labour*, had been criticized for its 'collectivism'. Such criticisms
had, he thought, denied him a chair in Paris. But what caused him most
concern was seeing that his most brilliant students, including his nephew,
were being seduced by Guesdiste and Marxist socialism.

The lectures were, according to Mauss, a great success, and attracted a
large audience. Durkheim displayed 'eloquence, erudition and profundity'
in equal measure.[25] The first lectures dealt with Saint-Simon and the Saint-
Simonians. The other two, which he was still preparing, dealt with Fourier
and Proudhon (he owned copies of their books and had studied them),
and with Lassalle, Marx and German socialism, with which he was already
familiar. Durkheim confined himself 'to the works of the masters, to their
thought, rather than to their personal lives' (Mauss 1962[1928]: 35).

Durkheim's research was, as his nephew emphasizes, 'unbiased'. He
looked at socialism, or socialist doctrine, 'from a purely scientific point
of view, as a fact which the scholar should look upon coldly' (Mauss
1962[1928]: 33). He was looking at a sociological problem. He was trying
to explain an ideology, and in order to do so he had to analyse the social
facts that had forced men like Saint-Simon, Fourier, Owen and Marx
to outline new principles for moral, political and social action. 'Tireless
worker' that he was, Durkheim carefully wrote his lectures, dividing the
course into 14 lectures and a conclusion. It was 'a model of the application
of sociological and historic method to the analysis of the causes of an idea'
(Mauss 1962[1928]: 34)

Durkheim did not regard socialism as a 'scientific doctrine'. Indeed,
it was the complete antithesis of a scientific doctrine: 'Entirely oriented
toward the future, it is above all a plan for the reconstruction of societies,
a programme for a collective life which does not exist as yet . . . It is an

ideal' (Durkheim 1962[1928]: 39). On the other hand, he did accept that the doctrine of socialism had inspired scientific activity and did borrow from the sciences. Its history was entwined with the history of the social sciences, but there was still a long way to go. The social sciences were still much too young to serve as a basis for practical doctrines. Durkheim was quite clear: science will not be hurried, and the scientist's attitude towards such problems must be reserved and circumspect.

There could, in other words, be no such thing as 'scientific socialism': 'Socialism is not a science, a sociology in miniature – it is a cry of grief, sometimes of anger, uttered by men who feel most keenly our collective *malaise*' (Durkheim 1962[1928]: 41). Durkheim is especially harsh on Marx, and criticizes him for not using the requisite statistical data in *Das Kapital* and for failing to make the historical comparisons needed to settle the countless questions he raises. He also mocks Marx's attempts to elaborate a theory of value in just a few lines.

Durkheim is interested in studying socialism as a social fact, and in analysing its conditions of possibility: 'If it is not a product of science, it is an object of science . . . we do have to know what it is, where it came from, and where it is going'. Investigating the origins of socialism would reveal the origins of our 'profound uneasiness', of which socialist doctrines were no more than 'symptoms and episodic superficialities'. He did not want 'to subject it to dialectical discussion, but rather to fathom its history'. He begins by rejecting subjective notions and 'the definitions most commonly given to socialism' on the grounds that they are inconsistent and contradictory. His method is based upon the principle: 'Instead of questioning ourselves, we will question things' (Durkheim 1962[1928]: 42, 44, 51).

Durkheim begins by adopting a botanist's approach to political doctrines: he observes, compares and classifies. Insofar as it is a doctrine concerned with 'social things', socialism is not a speculative and scientific doctrine, but a doctrine with reformist aims and, more specifically, one that aims to transform the state of the economy, and that relates commercial and industrial functions to society's directive and conscious functions. His final definition of socialism is as follows: 'We denote as socialist every doctrine which demands the connection of all economic functions, or of certain among them, to the directing and conscious centres of society' (1962[1928]: 54). He speaks of 'connection' not 'subordination' because some socialist systems can lead to anarchy. These 'directing and conscious centres' are embodied in the state, which is, in Durkheim's view, a real *social brain* connected to countless secondary organs by a whole chain of channels of communication. Socialism is therefore not about wages or the class struggle; it is primarily a plan for the reconstruction of society, and usually leads to more surveillance and greater regulation of social life. And while there are two types of socialism – working-class socialism or socialism from below, and state socialism or socialism from above – they are variations on a theme. There is a family resemblance between them, as both advocate democracy, freedom in conjugal relations, legal equality between the sexes, a more altruistic morality, and simplified juridical forms. Durkheim's definition of socialism would leave neither Jaurès nor Guesde indifferent.

In Durkheim's view, socialism (which he distinguishes from communism, seeing that as 'retrograde') is possible only when certain social conditions have been met. It appeared at a 'specific moment' in history – in the eighteenth century – and in the industrialized countries. As can be seen from the example of France, these conditions include the growing importance in public opinion of the economy, the secularization of the state (which thus becomes a profane power), the increased centralization of society and the emergence of large-scale industry.

One of the questions that preoccupies Durkheim has to do with the role of the French Revolution. And the thesis he defends is that elaborated by Jaurès in his *Histoire socialiste de la Révolution française*: the events of 1789 are one of the essential causes of modern socialism. The revolution contains, according to Durkheim, two major 'seeds' of socialism – namely, resentment against social inequalities and a political conception that gives the state a more important role.

But for Durkheim 'socialism' means primarily Saint-Simon, to whom he devotes no fewer than seven lectures. He was the 'first socialist Messiah' (Mauss 1962[1928]: 35). 'Before studying the doctrine, let us look at the man,' writes Durkheim (1962[1928]: 119), who was literally fascinated by the career, character and way of life of this exceptional thinker. He makes no secret of his admiration for Saint-Simon, who, before even Comte, began to study the progress of human societies, and to see both man and science as scientific objects. He also recognizes the greatness of Saint-Simon's doctrine and his desire 'to reorganize European societies by giving them science and industry as bases' (Durkheim 1962[1928]: 123). The great thing about him is that he succeeds in synthesizing all the tendencies of his day: positive philosophy, positive sociology, and socialism. 'Saint-Simon, founder of positivism and sociology' was the title of the previously unpublished article by Durkheim published in the *Revue philosophique* in 1925 to mark the centenary of 'the illustrious founder of socialism'.

Durkheim dwells at some length on what Saint-Simon has to say about the industrial system, which he describes as the characteristic feature of European society. Its cornerstones are industrial capacity and the authority of scientists. It is obvious, according to Saint-Simon, that its 'reorganization' cannot be accomplished in just one country: 'The industrial regime . . . cannot remain strictly national' and implies the creation of a 'vaster society', in other words a European union (Durkheim 1962[1928]: 228, 229).

Durkheim is also aware of the weakness and ambiguity of the doctrine of Saint-Simon, who, towards the end of his life, placed the emphasis on religion. 'Such a doctrine', in Durkheim's view, 'could only end in a mystical sensualism, in an apotheosis of comfort, in the sanction of excess' (Durkheim 1962[1928]: 279). In the last of his lectures, Durkheim looks at the Saint-Simonian school and at Bazard in particular. Bazard argues for the transformation of property rights and for the abolition of the right of inheritance. He also begins to look at the role of religion, which Bazard saw as nothing other than an expression of the collective thinking of a people, or even of humanity. He found one of Bazard's formulae especially appealing: 'everything social is religious' and vice versa (ibid.: 272).

In conclusion, Durkheim draws an analogy between the period in which Saint-Simon elaborated his system, and his own period. Both are characterized by three ideas or trends which, while they appear to be contradictory, emerge at the same time: the idea of extending the methodology of the positive sciences to the social sciences, the idea of a religious revival, and the socialist idea. All three trends reflect what he calls an 'abnormal' state and an 'unsettled collective organization'. Hence the need for a restraint, or for the presence of moral agents. The 'social question' is not a question of money or power; it is a moral question. Saint-Simon shows the way forward: 'discover through science the moral restraint which can regulate economic life, and by this regulation control selfishness and thus gratify needs' (Durkheim 1962[1928]: 284–5).

At the end of April 1896, Durkheim interrupted his course of lectures in order to 'devote [himself] fully' to the book on suicide that he was preparing.[26] He went back to what Mauss called 'pure science' and his intention was to devote his energies to the projected *L'Année sociologique*. He had intended the 1896–7 lecture course to be on Fourier and Proudhon, whose works he had studied and which he owned. The third year was to have been devoted to Lassalle, Marx and German socialism. There was now a change of plan: the lectures for 1896–7, and for the three following years, would be on 'the physics of morals and law'.[27] The history of socialism 'remained incomplete. [Durkheim] always regretted his inability to continue or resume it' (Mauss 1962[1928]: 35).

Sociology and Democracy: Andler versus Durkheim

What can sociology tell us about democracy, asked Célestin Bouglé, who regarded democracy as a 'contemporary trend that seems to have something durable or even universal about it' (Bouglé 1896a: 121). Bouglé's article appeared in the *Revue de métaphysique et de morale* in 1896. Sociologists had, he wrote, answered the question in two very different ways. Some, like Gustave Le Bon, believed that all gatherings were 'impulsive, excessive, changeable, irritable and intolerant', and concluded that men were 'intellectually inferior' when gathered together. The characteristic features of all collective deliberations were credulity, over-simplification and poor arguments: as numbers rose, standards fell. Others, like Spencer and Tarde, saw the democratic movement as something essential. Spencer argued that industrialization would lead to equality between citizens, while Tarde held that imitation was the explanation for democracy ('Equality is the daughter of resemblance, and resemblance is the daughter of imitation'). Durkheim, according to Bouglé, also took that view: 'Societies were automatically becoming more democratic, simply because their volume and density were increasing' (ibid.: 121). In other words, and no matter what point of view one adopts (the transition from militarism to individualism, from the age of custom to the age of fashion, or from mechanical solidarity to organic solidarity), the evolution of societies always demands the same thing: namely, 'equal freedom' and all that it implied, including discussions, joint deliberations and the power of crowds.

Were 'the people' unable to understand what was happening, or was the will of the people omnipotent? For or against the people? Could the people be made to be happy? Both theses could be supported by the facts. Not wishing to divorce popular sovereignty from freedom, Bouglé ended his article with a series of questions, but was unable to find a satisfactory answer.

The reaction was not slow in coming, but it was directed at Durkheim rather than at Bouglé. In the following issue of the *Revue de métaphysique et de morale*, Charles Andler vehemently denounced the 'so-called science' known as sociology as an 'illusion, a 'mistake' and 'a very childish method' (Andler 1896: 249). Dealing first with the questions of political or democratic 'self-government', of referendums, the role of civil servants, and bureaucracy, he argued that the issues involved were clearly political: given that the outcome of 'talking assemblies' could only be conventional or 'mediocre', and given that the direction of public affairs was inevitably entrusted to 'the mediocrity of collective thinking', it followed that democracy meant the rule of mediocrity. Such was the doctrine implicit in sociology, and he rejected it. Andler argued that collaboration was the 'precondition for progress'. 'The mystical virtues that were attributed to association simply reflected the fact that everyone profits from and is strengthened by collective achievements.' The best example was that of science.

Democracy was still, according to Andler, an ideal, or a cause that had made 'little progress' and was 'still fragile'. The evolution of societies did not, as the sociologists claimed, lead inevitably to democracy. The classic counter-example was the nineteenth century: the century of industry had been marked by 'unprecedented revivals of the military spirit'. The 'inevitable triumph' of democracy could, in his view, only be guaranteed by 'an overwhelming majority of men acting in a limited period of time', or in other words by demographic changes, which might also encourage social mobility and allow 'men from humble backgrounds to achieve positions of power or wealth'. The 'problem of democracy' was therefore, he concluded, a 'very complex aggregate of questions relating to economic, military and political history, positive and ideal law, demographic statistics and general civilization'. Only a collective effort on the part of specialist sciences could resolve them. Sociology was powerless to deal with them on its own.

Should Durkheim respond, given that he was under direct attack? As he told Célestin Bouglé, he thought it would be 'useful' to do so, but he did not want to respond in person as he was short of time. He was therefore delighted to learn that Bouglé was willing to respond on his behalf, even though he and his young colleague 'might disagree over certain points':

> These attacks on me are an attack on sociology, and it is sociology that must be defended. It also seems to me that, as you say yourself, we are in agreement about the main question raised in such wretched terms by Andler's article, namely the heterogeneity of psychical facts and social facts (whatever the relationship between the two may be). That is the important point, and that is also where the solution to the practical problem you raise lies. A collective consciousness is the only true judge of collective things . . . The specificity of social facts, which you have grasped, seems to me to be one of the points on which we can agree.[28]

Durkheim believed that it was 'all the more useful' not to remain silent given that:

> [S]ociology has for some time been compromised by charlatans who have exploited its rapid rise to fame. As a result, it is falling out of favour, and those who find it embarrassing will take advantage of that. And it does embarrass the little churches that have their faith, their priests and their faithful. We have to distance ourselves from those who want to discredit it in order to defuse potentially justifiable criticisms.[29]

Having discussed the matter with Durkheim, Bouglé agreed to 'fight for the honour of sociology'. His reply (Bouglé 1896b) was stinging: he gave Charles Andler a few lessons in the history of scientific disciplines, and accused him of misreading – or not reading – the authors he was attacking, especially when he criticized certain contemporary sociologists for their rejection of all individual psychology and even of history. Andler was making sociologists say the opposite of what they were actually saying, argued Bouglé, and he produced the textual evidence to support his claims. Of course, Durkheim rejected psychology, but it was a mistake to accuse him of hypostasis, he wrote, citing *The Rules of Sociological Method* at some length. Even the most 'psychological' of sociologists accepted that sociology did have its exclusive preserve. The specificity or 'substance' of sociology was, according to Bouglé, largely inspired by Simmel. Sociology could be defined as the study of various forms of association (subordination, cooperation, hierarchy, equality, division) and their implications (both intellectual and affective, and, by extension, all sorts of economic, legal, religious and moral phenomena).[30]

The *Revue de métaphysique et de morale* immediately granted Charles Andler the 'right to reply to objections' in the same issue (Andler 1896). He set out to correct 'the gross inaccuracies – so gross that a philologist could see them' – by making five points, with textual evidence (primarily the *Rules*) to support his claims: (1) sociology's main theses, and not just those of Durkheim, took 'little account of psychology'; (2) there were similarities between Durkheim and Tarde in that one spoke of a 'collective soul', and the other of a 'public heart'; (3) there was in Durkheim's work a 'substantialist mythology of the social spirit', and his notion of a *thing* could not be more vague; (4) hypostasis was a natural feature of all sciences; the problem is not that Durkheim objectified notions, but that he objectified false notions; (5) when it came to the specific case of societies' evolution towards democracy, the sociological theoreticians, including Durkheim, were mistaken: 'They have created a sociology that ignores history.' In Andler's view, the debate was closed: the 'errors' and 'confused ideas' were not of his making. Incisive and aggressive as ever, he praised Durkheim for only one thing: his 'warlike ardour'.

The polemic inspired nothing but a 'kind of horror (a religious horror, if you like)' in the journal's co-editor Élie Halévy.[31] As soon as Bouglé's response was published, Durkheim made a point of thanking him for 'the care with which you have defended both myself and sociology over certain essential points'. 'I am', he added, 'very grateful to you.'[32] When Andler's 'additional note' appeared, he thought of 'intervening very briefly', but said that he was convinced that he had 'nothing to add' to what Bouglé had said. This was, he concluded, a debate that had 'reached its natural end', and there was therefore no point in prolonging it. He was, however, so annoyed by Andler's attack that he changed his mind and wrote to the journal's secretary Xavier Léon to tell him that he wanted to add some factual corrections and to disassociate himself from the 'absurd proposition' that had been attributed him without 'reopening the controversy'.[33] His reply, which was immediately published in the journal, was only a few lines long: 'I wish to make it clear that I completely reject the ideas M. Andler ascribes to me, especially in his last note. He is able to attribute them to me only by distorting a few isolated words, whereas I took great care to warn the reader against such distortions.'[34]

A Moral Crisis?

This was a slack period and a critical phase. The years 1895–6 seem to have been a period of transition and uncertainty. Durkheim was the object of frequent and harsh criticism, even from close colleagues like Lucien Herr and Charles Andler. In July 1896, the planned *Année sociologique* seemed doomed to failure, and there seemed to be little prospect of recruiting young *agrégés* such as Bouglé and Lapie. Was Durkheim beginning to have doubts about his own project?

Did he still have his eye on Paris? There was once again talk of establishing a chair in 'ethics as a positive science' at the Collège de France. In March 1896, Senator Lavertujon laid a request before the senate committee, which passed it on to the minister for public education. The philosophers were both intrigued and worried by the suggestion.[35] As in 1893, the *Revue de métaphysique et de morale* suggested that the chair should simply be described as a 'chair in ethics'. If it were so designated, it was unlikely that Durkheim would be elected.

On the personal and family level, 1896 was, as has already been said, a difficult year for both Durkheim and his nephew Marcel. Émile's father had resigned from his position at the end of 1894. He was 88. His flock had been 'complaining about his inability to fulfil his mission' (Grivel 2005). He had been in post for more than 60 years, which was quite exceptional. His successor was another Alsatian, Rabbi Moïse Schuhl (1845–1911), who had been the chief rabbi of Vesoul since 1888. Moïse Durkheim died in February 1896 at the age of 91. The oldest rabbi in France was, as *L'Univers israélite* noted, 'an excellent pastor' and highly respected.[36] The rabbi of Épinal's funeral took place 'with great pomp'. The service was held in the synagogue, and was attended by representatives of the local political, religious and military authorities, and by a large and emotional crowd. Rabbi Schuhl gave a funeral oration praising the late lamented rabbi and recalling his 'virtues and pastoral services'. The community had lost its 'respected guide'.

Émile's mother Mélanie was now 76. In financial terms, she was comfortably off: she could count on her share of the inheritance and on an annual income of 2,800 francs from renting out the house at 2 rue des Forts.[37]

At the beginning of the summer, Marcel's father Gerson Mauss died at the age of 62 while on a trip to Paris for an appointment with a doctor specializing in heart disease. His son Marcel was 24. 'A modest man who did what he had to do with a keen sense of duty, a very upright man who loved justice and who left his son a fine inheritance of honour and loyalty', said Épinal's new rabbi, Moïse Schuhl, who also recalled the memory of the 'respected and greatly mourned' Rabbi Durkheim.[38] The two deaths – which Sylvain Lévy called 'a double blow'[39] – shook the whole family badly. Durkheim already had responsibility for the education of two of his nephews – including Henri Durkheim, who came to live with him in Bordeaux after the death of his father Félix – and he now became head of the family. It was with him that his elder sister Rosine discussed the options that were available to her son Marcel. Although he had a *bourse d'agrégation* the previous year (1895–6), Marcel still had to rely on his family – in other words, his mother – for financial help. To save money, he was sharing an apartment with his cousins – an arrangement that was not without its drawbacks. When times were difficult, he would ask his uncle to speak to his mother on his behalf. Rosine, who was still living in Épinal, now became the real centre of the family. She was, according to those around her, a 'strong woman' who ran the family business energetically, and who kept a careful eye on the careers of both her son and her brother Émile.

A deeply affected Durkheim was distraught at the very time when he was so busy writing *Suicide*. This was what Philippe Besnard (1987: 134) calls the 'most anomic period' in his life in both personal and professional terms. He had lost his father and his work had been subject to harsh criticism. He was finding it difficult to launch his new journal, and was still reeling from the way his scientific horizons had suddenly broadened. There seemed to be a new line of demarcation in his intellectual life: religion as an object for sociological study.

He had discovered the crucial role of religion in 1985. Moïse Durkheim died in 1896. Is it possible to establish a link between the two events? Could the 'return of the religious repressed' have something to do with the death of Durkheim's father, who was the last in a long line of rabbis? According to that hypothesis, Émile could not have taken religion as an object for sociological study and could not have objectified his own religious beliefs so long as the figure of the father, a strong and noble hieratic figure identified with the law, was present.[40] The time gap suggests that the hypothesis is mistaken, unless we assume that Durkheim foresaw his father's death 15 months in advance. And besides, while this return of the repressed does coincide with the 'return to the primitive' in his anthropological works, it is hard to understand why Durkheim was still arguing against the exploitation of anthropological material in 1895.[41] Durkheim's interest in religion did not, finally, date from 1895, even though his nephew's decision to enrol in the 'religious sciences' section at the École pratique can only have revived it.

If Moïse Durkheim's death did have an influence on his son's work, it is more likely to have been on *Suicide*, as it occurred just as Durkheim was halfway through writing it. The anomie theorized by Durkheim in his book might correspond to the anomie he experience in 1896. But if there was a 'road to Damascus', its impact is perceptible only in the longer period between *The Division of Labour in Society*, *Suicide* and *The Elementary Forms of Religious Life*. As in his lectures on socialism in 1896, Durkheim ceased to prioritize the economic dimension of social life after writing *Suicide* and now focused his attention on the religious dimension. One thing is certain: he had had enough of the political economy that had, as he told Célestin Bouglé, cost him 15 years of his life. 'I hope that reading the economists does you more good than it did me. When I began 15 years ago, I too thought that I would find an answer to the questions that preoccupied me in political economy. I spent several years on it, and got nothing out of it, or only what one can learn from a negative experience.'[42]

Part III

A Journal and a Team

9

Converts

From Suicide to *L'Année sociologique*

Now that his lecture course on socialism had come to an end, Émile Durkheim returned, in May 1896, to writing his book on suicide:

> I hope that, when it is published, people will have a better understanding of the reality of what I am calling a social fact, which has been challenged; because what I am studying is suicide as a social trend, or the suicide rate within social groups, quite independently of its individual manifestations (this obviously involves a process of abstraction, but there is no other way for a science to isolate its object).[1]

He devoted the whole of the following summer and autumn to his book, working on it full time. He did not work on any other publications that year. He sometimes complained that his various commitments and the book ('I'm still working on it') left him little free time, but he was confident. As he put it: 'The book is coming along. I've now written 300 pages; that leaves 100 to go. It will definitely be in octavo selling for 7.5 francs. The 400 pages of manuscript are very closely written. That will come to 500 or 600 pages of copy.'[2] His calculations were accurate. Émile had the eye of an editor.

The Nephew's 'Personal Work'

Durkheim relied on his nephew in Paris to carry out the final bibliographical and documentary research, and to produce the statistical tables. Marcel consulted his teacher Sylvain Lévi for information about suicide amongst Hindus, and Lévi quickly provided data about the position of Brahmins, Buddhist and Jains with regard to suicide. Mauss also worked in libraries, studying journal articles and books, and checking the bibliographical references. His uncle was very impatient, and sometimes displeased: 'It has taken you two days to annotate 12 pages, and there are 100 pages. Do the sums. And you are embellishing the footnotes; you're playing about rather than just proving the essential references.' He was also annoyed about the statistical tables: 'Are they ready or not? If they are not ready this week, send them to me immediately. I'll do them here.' In anger, he then added: 'You've made a real mess of it.'[3] He ended his letter without the usual '*Je t'embrasse*'. In *Suicide*, Durkheim speaks of 'our work', but he never mentions that his nephew was his collaborator.

Durkheim asked Marcel to do things for him, but he also urged him not to neglect his 'personal work', and even criticized his 'rather lazy tendency to read endlessly, and with no specific purpose in mind'. 'You know', he told him, 'that that is your problem. Don't let it become a habit. Always bear in mind that you have to finish things.'[4] Marcel Mauss published his first two scientific texts in 1896. They were book reviews for the *Revue de l'histoire des religions*, a prestigious periodical devoted to the science of religions that also took an interest in ethnology. Léon Marillier, who was one of Mauss's teachers at the École pratique, was one of the co-editors.

The first review was on a book on mythology in Guinea by Adolf Bastian, a doctor who was one of the pioneers of ethnographic research and the driving force behind an important ethnological society in Germany. Mauss's criticisms were devastating: the book was poorly organized, had no overall argument, provided only a limited amount of new knowledge and was full of mistakes. He then turned his attention to a book on 'religion and the origins of penal law' by Steinmetz (Mauss 1969[1897]). His critical notice was very well documented. 'This will become a standard point of reference', exclaimed an enthusiastic Durkheim, who showered his nephew with praise and warnings: 'The only thing that worries me is that, as always, you pack too much in . . . You don't have to say everything at once . . . so try not to cram too much in.' Durkheim's view was that Marcel seemed to have a natural tendency to do this, and that it was a 'beginner's failing'.[5] He advised him to avoid generalizations and to stick to a few specific points, such as totemism and religious thought. When he read a revised version of the article, he added a few comments on the theory that – wrongly, in his view – reduced all sacrifices to communion and said that he would be willing to pursue the discussion with his nephew when he had seen the final version.[6]

Mauss offers a sociological explanation for primitive punishment (vendetta), and argues that the origins of private vengeance are religious; punishment therefore has a social dimension. This analysis extends that made by Durkheim in *The Division of Labour in Society*, where he argues that vendetta was 'the primitive form of punishment' and that 'penal law was essentially religious in origin' (Durkheim 1984[1893]: 49). On reading the first version of Mauss's article, Durkheim was 'struck by the similarities between some of [your] conclusions and my own'.[7] In other words, he liked the text: 'I see that your erudition has grown out of all proportion, and yet you are still in control of it. All that – and the form too – is beginning to smack of maturity.' The 'old' teacher did, on the other hand, insist on pointing out some weaknesses, including 'a certain complacency concerning inaccuracies'. He also commented: 'The fact that you are a polyglot does not mean that you have to use a lot of different languages.' Durkheim was all the more pleased with Mauss's work in that reading him and chatting with him made him 'more fully aware of what I myself am thinking'. He added: 'That is the greatest favour you could do me.'[8]

Writing this article allowed Mauss to identify a whole set of themes and problems that he would later take as his objects of study: sacrifice, magical power (or *mana*) and, more generally, the sacred. It is also obvious that the nephew was already more convinced than his uncle that the science of religions was of interest to ethnology, which, because it was the 'study of social phenomena amongst primitive peoples' had the advantage of studying 'simpler phenomena' that were 'closer to their origins' and 'related to one another in a more immediate way'. Mauss also raised, finally, the great questions that would dominate Durkheim's subsequent work: How can social facts be explained? What is the relationship between psychology and sociology? How can functional analysis be reconciled with an evolutionist approach? His insights seemed so important and original to Émile that, two years later, he himself summarized this 'very well-documented' article on Steinmetz in *L'Année sociologique* (Durkheim 1969[1898]: 129). Mauss was also congratulated by Gabriel Tarde, the head of the ministry of justice's statistical service, who wrote to tell him that this was a 'very interesting' study, and that 'penetrating insights of the critic' were as precious as the 'precision of the scholar and the extent of his knowledge'.[9]

In the autumn of 1896, Mauss – who was once more immersed in religion thanks to the lectures given by Sylvain Lévi and his collaborator Alfred Foucher on the ancient religions of India and Léon Marillier's lectures on primitive religions – met Henri Hubert. It would prove to be a decisive encounter. Born in Paris, Hubert had a degree in history, and was a *normalien* and *agrégé d'histoire* (1895). His contemporaries at ENS included his friend Marcel Drouin[10] and two future collaborators on *L'Année sociologique*: Demangeon and Martonne. Having been awarded a grant by the University of Paris, Hubert travelled in Germany and Italy and enrolled at the École pratique des hautes études, where he studied Hebrew and the history of religions: on the one hand, he was interested in Byzantinism and, on the other, in the Semitic languages. Born into a wealthy family, Hubert had a passion for art (he both drew and painted, and later became a collector) and, being a man of independent means, intended to devote himself to the study of the religions of Assyria and Asia Minor; he would later specialize in archaeology.

Like his friend Mauss, Henri Hubert became one of Sylvain Lévi's 'protégés'. 'From day one, he was one of our own and a very close friend.'[11] Mauss liked to recall that he and Hubert were 'Siamese brothers' and 'working twins'. They were both born in 1872 and discovered that they had the same intellectual interests, which laid the foundations for an exceptionally strong friendship. They were both active contributors to the *Revue de l'histoire des religions*, which was run by teachers from the religious studies section. Marcel drew his friend Henri into 'the sociologists' camp' and introduced him to his uncle. Hubert was 'one of the first' to support Durkheim and 'became one his most fervent disciples, but also one of the most independent'.[12] The history of *L'Année sociologique* was, in other words, to be the history of a family and a group of friends.

Promotion At Last

At the end of June 1896, or nine years after he joined the University of Bordeaux as a *chargé de cours* and three years after submitting his thesis, Durkheim was given a major promotion when a chair in social science was established. It was a promotion in two senses: he was given tenure (and the increase in salary that went with it; he was now earning 6,000 francs per year) and the chair was in 'social science', without further qualification. The reference to 'pedagogy' was dropped. Durkheim had more than one reason to rejoice. 'Basically, I am very glad to have obtained tenure', he told his nephew. 'The sense of security has great charm.'[13] The *Revue internationale de sociologie* stressed the importance of the event: 'This is the first chair in the social sciences to be established in a French university'. *L'Univers israélite* also informed its readers of the 'news'.[14]

When he returned from holiday in the autumn, Durkheim put the final touches to the definitive version of his manuscript on suicide. Having to teach a course on the 'general physics of morals and law' held him up a little. The course was in two parts: the 'objective' part with juridical moral rules and the main penal sanctions, and the 'subjective' part with the subject's experience of 'moral obligation' (the notion of responsibility and the moral conscience). Durkheim wanted the lectures to be as 'secret' as possible (they were not advertised in the faculty of law), and he even spoke in very 'abstract' terms in his first lectures in order to discourage students from attending. He still drew an audience of 30 or so and, unusually for him, devoted only two days a week to preparing his lectures.

'I will go on like this until my book is finished', he told Mauss. The rewriting was going well. 'I think I have 320 pages of the final transcript done.' He was rather pleased with 'the work' he had done, but the idea that the end was in sight made him rather sad: 'I am almost afraid of reaching the point when I will have to take my leave of a task that has given me so much pleasure.'

At the beginning of 1897, Durkheim was making the final corrections: 'My manuscript is finished, and I have only one more chapter to reread.'[15] In March, he went to Paris to give it to Félix Alcan in person. He would have liked to have had the opportunity to talk to him about his plans for a journal, but the publisher was preoccupied with the preparations for his daughter's wedding, and was not available. Émile arrived in Paris on the evening of Sunday 14 March, and had a 'chat' with his nephew about the journal, and about Mauss's plan to apply for a position at the Institut Thiers. His uncle did not understand him:

I don't really see you ending your student career in a fairly second-rate internship after having done everything possible to avoid doing such a thing . . . You only go to the Institut Thiers when that way of life suits you, or when you have no other way of remaining usefully in Paris for a few more years, and not when you are in your position [i.e. that of a] young man who is doing so well.[16]

Durkheim advised him to wait until the autumn and to try to obtain a travel grant to go to England and Holland if that was what he wanted to do.

In Praise of Taine

When he published his book on suicide, Durkheim was involved in a 'symposium' on the work of Taine. His contribution (Durkheim 1975[1897]) appeared in *La Revue blanche*. One might have expected him to lend his support to the naturalists, but here he was supporting the symbolists and the cultural avant-garde. Was this a matter of elective affinities, political sympathy or networking? The *Revue blanche* (which was originally based in Liège) was launched in the early 1890s by three brothers of Polish-Jewish origin: Alexandre, Thadée and Louis-Alfred Natanson. Alexandre, the eldest, was very wealthy and had recruited Lucien Muhlfed (who acted as editorial secretary and managing editor until March 1898). Léon Blum (who contributed book reviews), Tristan Bernard and Pierre Louÿs were all actively involved. The *Revue blanche* was a cultural journal that covered the fields of literature, drama, art and music (Debussy was a contributor). Early issues contained texts by Verlaine and Mallarmé, who were the leading lights of the symbolist generation. Also involved were painters such as Vuillard, Bonnard, Vallottin and Toulouse-Lautrec, who designed its poster and cover pages and contributed drawings. The young writers associated with the journal included Paul Claudel, André Gide, Alfred Jarry and Guillaume Apollinaire.

Following the anarchist bomb attacks of early 1894, the *Revue blanche* became associated with the protest movement inspired by the repression, and published very vehement unsigned notes. The author Félix Fénéon was arrested, taken to court during the notorious 'Trial of the thirty', and acquitted. The journal then began to publish columns devoted to political and social issues; it also organized a series of symposiums. One of the first looked into the history of the Commune. The symposium on Taine was part of this series. It was coordinated by Léon Belugo (1865–1934), a close friend of Théodule Ribot (whose lectures he attended at the Collège de France and oversaw their publication), a great admirer of Taine and an advocate of positivist philosophy. He used his column to sing the praises of the psychology of Ribot, the sociology of Durkheim and Tarde, and the metaphysics of Bergson and Nietzsche. The symposium on Taine (who had died a few years earlier in 1893) consisted of contributions from 13 eminent specialists, including Maurice Barrès (who described Taine as 'one of the great events in our mental life'), Gabriel Monod (who admired

Taine as a philosopher and advocate for positivism but was critical of his historical writings), Gabriel Tarde (a critical admirer of Taine's naturalist interpretation of social facts), Émile Boutroux (who had his reservations) and Durkheim. The symposium's findings were published in the issue dated 15 August 1897.

In his response, Durkheim identifies himself with the philosophical tradition of Spinoza, which Taine had introduced into France. He describes Taine's philosophical position or 'posture' as 'rationalist empiricism' because it aspired to being the 'intermediary between two extremes' and because, while it 'worshipped' facts (hence the emphasis on experimentation and observation), it also attempted to explain them. 'Although it shares empiricism's concern with the realm of science, while it opens up the whole world to free enquiry and insists that it is possible to explain things, [rationalist empiricism] completely rejects summary and simplistic explanations.' He also argues that Taine's position satisfies the contradictory impulses that are 'the classic driving force behind intellectual development: the feeling that everything is obscure, and faith in the efficacy of the human mind' (Durkheim 1975[1897]: 174). On the one hand, there is 'darkness' and, on the other, the 'light' that is gradually shed by a science, but, given the 'enormous complexity of things', the progress of science will inevitably be 'slow and laborious'. In Durkheim's view, positivism is meaningful only if it is rationalist. In his eulogy to Taine, he advocates, finally, 'studying morality from a scientific point of view'. The main preoccupations of such a study would be the observation and explanation of the facts: 'It is true that this science does not yet exist; all the more reason to work on it as a matter of urgency' (ibid.: 176).

Because of its political stance, the *Revue blanche* was close to the socialists, and then the Dreyfusards. The Natanson brothers who had founded the journal were staunch supporters of the Dreyfusards and put its resources at their disposal. The journal initially had only a small circulation, but at the height of the Dreyfus Affair, it was selling 10,000 copies. There were several links between the *Revue blanche* and the *Année sociologique* group. At the time of the Dreyfus Affair, Lucien Herr and Léon Blum were the obvious intermediaries. When it began publication in 1898, Durkheim's journal was favourably reviewed in the *Revue blanche*. In the 1900s, Marcel Drouin – Mauss and Hubert's friend – and François Simiand both wrote columns for the *Revue blanche*.

Suicide, or 'Rationalist Empiricism'

Suicide, which was simply subtitled 'a study in sociology', was published by Alcan in March 1897, with a print-run of around 1,000 copies (or 1,500 at the very most) (P. Besnard 2000: 195). It was more than 450 pages long and included some 30 statistical tables and several plates (maps): 'Suicides and alcoholism', 'Suicides in France by *arrondissement*', 'Suicides in

Central Europe', 'Suicides and the size of families', 'Suicides and wealth', etc.

Sociology was a young discipline, and the publication of *Suicide* was therefore a major event. Durkheim had produced a broad empirical study and had learned, without any previous training, to handle social statistics. His aim was to apply the principles laid down in *The Rules of Sociological Method*, even though there are only a few references to that book.

By taking suicide as his object, Durkheim set out to study the most individual and private act possible from a sociological point of view. He was also making a clinical diagnosis of the state of health of contemporary societies and 'civilized' peoples. Some questions, already well known to statisticians, medical hygienists and alienists, were still of contemporary relevance. Does conjugal life protect men from certain misfortunes, including suicide? Is suicide a form of madness? Is there a link between the rising suicide rate and societies' intellectual progress? Some were even asking themselves whether World Fairs really were 'happy events'. Others, including some in the Jewish community, wondered whether religion was a protective factor, given that most religions forbid suicide (Cahen 1892). And in the background, there was the more general issue of whether or not depopulation,[17] the growing incidence of psychopathological illnesses, alcoholism and the rise in the suicide rate were symptoms of the degeneracy of nations and the decadence of countries.

There was no shortage of data. As Émile Levasseur noted (1894: 824–5), scholars had an 'enormous mass of demographic material' on a whole range of phenomena (birth rates, marriage rates, death rates). He concluded that demography was 'a real social barometer'. With *Suicide,* Durkheim was therefore venturing into the territory of specialists in social statistics, and he adopted a resolutely quantitative approach. This was a bold move for a philosopher. Some of his data came from a variety of secondary sources, including official statistical publications and studies of suicide in general. Other data was supplied by specialists like Dr Legoupils, who provided him with information about three small communes in the Pont-L'Évêque *arrondissement*. Durkheim also made extensive use of the nineteenth-century literature on 'alienism' and especially of the work of Alexandre Brierre de Boismont (1797–1881), founder of the *Annales médico-psychologiques.* Boismont was interested in hallucinatory phenomena and the psychopathological effects of alcoholism, but suicide was his favourite subject. In 1865, he published his *Du Suicide et de la folie suicide*, which included a great deal of statistical data. Brierre de Boismont was one of the few alienists of his generation to study the statistical data on voluntary death (J. Besnard 2000). Durkheim also cites the confessions made to Brierre de Boismont by patients, and the stories and case-studies relayed by other doctors such as Esquirol (mental illness) and Falret (hypochondria and suicide).

The issues raised by Durkheim are important: the mechanisms of integration and social regulation, racism, and even freedom. Yet his book appeared to have no theoretical ambitions, and claimed to be empirical and based on the facts. The style is sober and almost neutral. The book is austere, and includes many maps and statistical tables. In the very first lines of the introduction, he writes: 'Only comparison offers explanation. A scientific investigation can thus be achieved only if it deals with comparable facts' (Durkheim 2002[1897]: xxxix).

His concern for methodology is evident throughout. The sociologist's first task – and here Durkheim remains true to *The Rules* – is to 'determine the order of facts to be studied under the name of suicides' (Durkheim 2002[1897]: xl) and therefore to define what is meant by suicide. One basic question immediately arises: what about intent and motive? Durkheim immediately rules out any discussion of motives: 'Intent is too intimate a thing to be more than approximately interpreted by another. It even escapes self-observation. How often we mistake the true reason for our acts! We constantly explain acts due to petty feelings or blind routine by generous passions or lofty considerations' (ibid.: xli). Durkheim finally adopts the following definition of suicide: 'The term suicide is applied to any death which is the direct or indirect result of a positive or negative act accomplished by the victim himself' (ibid.: xl).

How can such an individual fact be the object of sociology? In order to justify his claim to be making an objective study of suicide, Durkheim even includes statistical tables in his introduction: 'Stability of suicide in the principal European countries (1841–1872)', and 'Rates of suicides per million inhabitants in the different European countries (1866–1878)'. On the basis of these observations, he establishes a 'numerical datum': '*the rate of mortality through suicide, characteristic of the society under consideration*' (2002[1897]: xlv). The suicide rate is therefore a social phenomenon that is typically both stable (over long periods in a given society) and variable (from one society to another). Durkheim concludes from this: 'In short, these statistical data express the suicidal tendency with which each society is collectively afflicted . . . Each society is predisposed to contribute a definite quota of voluntary deaths' (ibid.: l). It is these rates that define suicide as a social fact.

The goal Durkheim sets himself is limited: he is not attempting to 'make as nearly complete an inventory as possible of all the conditions affecting the origin of individual suicides', but simply to 'examine those on which the definite fact that we have called the social suicide-rate depends'(Durkheim 2002[1897]: l). *Suicide* is divided into three main parts: (I) 'Extra-social factors'; (II) 'Social causes and social types; and (III) 'General nature of suicide as a social phenomenon'. Durkheim puts forward his own hypotheses only when he has refuted, in Part I, the theses defended by the alienists and that 'circulate' amongst the general public: madness and various psychopathological states, alcoholism, heredity and even the climate and seasonal temperatures. His intention is to demonstrate, with statistics to support his argument, that extra-social factors have little or no effect on the suicide rate.

In Praise of Neurasthenia

Suicide was so closely associated with mental illness and madness that Brierre de Boismont used to say of the alienists that 'they see madmen everywhere'. Does 'suicidal insanity exist?' asks Durkheim. He answers his own question: we cannot accept the thesis that 'every suicide is a madman'. He refutes that thesis by making two points: suicide is neither 'a distinct form of insanity' (2002[1897]: 8) (this is the 'monomaniac suicide' thesis), nor 'an event involved in one of several varieties of insanity' (ibid.: 4) He then dwells at some length on melancholy suicide, which is in his view, 'that which may appear hardest [of all the suicides] to detect of those observed among the sane' (ibid.: 12). Melancholy is characterized by a general state of extreme depression, exaggerated sadness, a pronounced taste for solitude and sometimes hallucinations.

The notions of neurosis or nervous illness, including hysteria, enjoyed great popularity at the end of the nineteenth century (J. Besnard 2000; Goldstein 1987). They were regarded as 'intermediary stages ['*demi-folies*'] between mental alienation properly so-called and perfect equilibrium of intelligence' (Durkheim 2002[1897]: 14). Neurasthenia (a generic term applied to various anomalies) was seen as a sort of elementary insanity; it was also regarded as the psychological type most commonly found among suicides. In other words, and as Durkheim accepts, neurasthenia does predispose individuals to commit suicide: it is characterized by hypersensitivity to pain, nervous irritability, and an unstable balance between ideas and emotions. The neurasthenic suffers if he is thrown into active life, but can withdraw to lead a more contemplative existence or create a 'special environment' (ibid.: 15). We can therefore understand why neurasthenia is the psychological type most commonly found among suicides, but it does not necessarily lead to suicide: 'The social suicide-rate therefore bears no definite relation to insanity, nor, inductively considered, to the tendency to the various forms of neurasthenia' (ibid.: 24).[18]

Is Durkheim singing the praises of neurasthenia? He accepts that the neurasthenic, with his 'delicate organism', 'has the capacity to taste fully the rarest pleasures of thought'. His excessive sensitivity may disqualify him from action, but does qualify him for intellectual functions. In 'mobile' and civilized societies, he therefore has 'a useful role to play' because he is 'superlatively the instrument of progress . . . a highly fertile source of innovation' (Durkheim 2002[1897]: 24). Speaking of egoistic suicide, he again makes the point: 'Today neurasthenia is rather considered a mark of distinction than a weakness. In our refined societies, enamoured of things intellectual, nervous members constitute almost a nobility' (ibid.: 137). These societies are very complex and depend for their existence upon almost constant change. It is therefore no paradox that 'neurasthenics have most reason for existence precisely when they are the most numerous' (ibid.: 24). A society without neurasthenics is inconceivable: they have a role to play.

Alcoholism and Heredity. The Critique of Racism

'For some time it has been the custom to attribute almost all the ills of our civilization . . . [to] alcoholism. Rightly or wrongly, the progress of insanity, pauperism and criminality have already been attributed to it.' Surely the same could be said of the increase in the number of suicides. Durkheim's reply to this argument is: 'Facts are unanswerable. Let us test them' (2002[1897]: 25). And having compared the various French *départements* and European countries, he demonstrates that there is no necessary correlation between the abuse of 'spiritous liquors' and the suicide-rate (ibid.: 29 n37).

Durkheim also refutes the theses of 'writers on suicide' ['*suicidographes*'], who claim that suicide results from a genetic flaw, and that each race has 'a characteristic suicide-rate of its own' (Durkheim 2002[1897]: 30). But what is a race? Is measuring the size and shape of skulls enough to determine human types? Everyone was talking about race, about the cephalic index and the distinction between the dolichocephalic (tall and blonde) and the brachycephalic,[19] but no one, Durkheim remarks with irony, seems to know what they are talking about. The race question brings us face to face with 'anthropological uncertainty': 'the word "race" no longer corresponds to anything definite . . . Thus conceived, race becomes almost identical with nationality' (ibid.: 33). What was at stake in this debate was political as well as scientific. As Alfred Fouillée feared (1895b: 365), a new form of pan-Germanism was emerging: 'Woe betide anyone with a dark skin.'

A sceptical Durkheim accepts that organic dispositions such as human types may influence the suicide rate, but the statistical data that he analyses does not allow him to verify the hypothesis of a correlation between the main human types in Europe – the Germanic, the Celto-Roman and the Slav – and suicide. There are great variations within nations of the same race, and the factor that explains differences between races is usually not the blood that runs through their veins, but the civilizations in which people are brought up. Durkheim looks in some detail at the case of France, but finds no decisive proof to support explanations that invoke 'the obscure operations of race'. He simply notes that, in both moral and anthropological terms, France can be divided into two parts: the North, which is the 'centre of French civilization', with its increased 'circulation of persons, ideas and things' and the Midi, where 'the provincial spirit and local traditionalism have remained much stronger' (2002[1897]: 41–2). He adds: 'The same remark applies to Italy too' (ibid.: 42 n13).

Durkheim then goes on to discuss the influence of heredity, but seems rather puzzled by the theory that the tendency to kill oneself can be directly transmitted from parents to their children. Having studied the facts, he reaches the inescapable conclusion that the variation of suicide with age and sex proves that 'no organic-psychic state can possibly be its determining cause' (Durkheim 2002[1897]: 51). According to Durkheim, contagion has greater influence than heredity. Fragile individuals are 'very accessible to suggestion' and 'susceptible to hypnosis' (ibid.: 45). The phenomenon of contagion can become so widespread that it is possible to speak of 'epidemics' of suicide. Durkheim also speaks (ibid.: 48) of a hereditary 'germ', but implies that it will germinate only when the physical or material conditions are right.

Finally, Durkheim looks at 'cosmic factors', including climate and seasonal temperatures, which had attracted the notice of some specialists. His answer is clear: there is no correlation between the temperate climate and suicidal tendencies. And although seasonal temperatures do seem to have an influence, they do not intervene in autumn or winter (dark times of the year that are conducive to depression), as is usually believed, but in summer. Does this mean that heat acts as a 'stimulant to suicide' (ibid.: 62)? Durkheim compares the number of suicides in France, Italy and Prussia with the average temperature in each season or month in each country. He then introduces another variable – the average length of the day in France – and establishes that 'the suicides naturally grow more numerous as the day lengthens'. He correlates the number of suicides with the time of day and reaches the conclusion that 'daytime is richer in suicides than night' (ibid.: 67). Such daily variations, he concludes, have nothing to do with changes in temperature, but they do relate to the changing pattern of activity; there are two climactic periods. 'Day favours suicide because it is the time of most active existence, when human relations cross and recross, when social life is most intense.' But at midday, there is a period of calm and 'suicide pauses momentarily' (ibid.: 68).

These factors are, in Durkheim's view, social. If the monthly distribution of suicides in the towns is compared with that in the countryside, the 'greater intensity' of social life appears to explain everything (2002[1897]: 72). Durkheim even constructs an indicator for the intensity of social life: the volume of communications and intersocial relations, as measured by 'the seasonal receipts of our great railroad lines' (ibid.: 71). The technological dimension appears to be important. The conclusion is inescapable: the physical environment has 'no effect on the progression of suicide' (ibid.: 73). It depends on social conditions. Which leaves us with the question of 'how collective life can have this effect' (ibid.).[20]

Imitation

Before going on to analyse the social causes of suicides, Durkheim refutes Gabriel Tarde's popular thesis that everything to do with social life is a question of imitation. If that is the case, imitation should be a factor that explains suicide. Durkheim first demonstrates, not without a certain humour, that the word itself is used to describe a number of very different realities: the 'levelling' of the 'consciousness of different individuals', reflecting the influence of the group or crowd, the adoption of 'ways of thought or action which surround us' and 'ape-like imitation for its own sake' (Durkheim 2002[1897]: 75, 76).

Without actually citing Gustave Le Bon, Durkheim looks first at what happens in a crowd. We observe the emergence of 'similar states of consciousness' and 'a fusion of a number of states within one another, distinct from them: this is the collective state' (2002[1897]: 77). Yet this is only 'a conjectural and approximate description' (ibid.: 81); we have 'only a vague idea' of how collective feelings arise. These questions are 'too complex to be solved solely by introspection . . . Manifold experiments and observations would be required'. As it is, 'our explanations are often mere metaphors' (ibid.: 81 n10).

Why do we accept a shared opinion? Why do we follow a fashion or custom? How do we come to accept a new idea? Is it a matter of spontaneity or constraint? We do what others do either because we sympathize with friends, because we respect someone, because we are forced to do so, or because we are afraid of what other people might think. But such behaviours are never, Durkheim insists, reducible to 'reproduction', or 'repetition'. They are not something we do mechanically, or automatically. This is not a matter of imitation because an 'intellectual operation', either explicit or implicit, intrudes between the representation and the execution of the act. These are forms of 'reasonable, deliberate behaviour' (Durkheim 2002[1897]: 79) and not automatic reflexes. They result from 'judgments and reasonings' (ibid.: 80).

Durkheim does not deny that suicide can spread by contagion: it does so in the army and in prisons. Contagion does not, however, explain everything.[21] Being a good loser, he nonetheless accepts the need to 'verify by decisive experience the reality of the wonderful power ascribed to imitation' (Durkheim 2002[1897]: 84). The decisive evidence comes from the map of suicides in France by *arrondissement* for the period 1887–91. According to the 'imitation' thesis, suicide should spread outwards from centres such as regional capitals or big towns thanks to a process of contagion or propagation. Durkheim's findings are 'most unexpected' (ibid.: 86) because his maps are not based upon *départements*, as is usually the case, but upon the far smaller *arrondissements*. The 'configuration' he observes on studying his maps does not reveal the influence of imitation (concentric circles grouped around certain centres). These observations apply not only to France, but also to other European countries such as Germany.

What about the influence of newspapers? Some claim that they have a very great influence and suggest that they should be prohibited from making any mention of suicide or murder. While Durkheim has no difficulty in accepting that they are a 'powerful diffusive instrument' (2002[1897]: 90), it seems to him difficult to determine their effect upon public opinion or to measure the extent of their influence. He does not, on the other hand, accept that reading newspapers can be a determining factor because, to restrict the argument to France, it cannot be 'supposed that . . . fewer newspapers are read south rather than north of the Loire' (ibid.: 91). There is, in other words, no correlation between the readership of newspapers and the suicide rate. Durkheim does, however, accept that the way in which the newspapers talk about suicide may have an influence: when society is morally decadent, 'its state of uncertainty inspires in it an indulgence for immoral acts' and there is therefore a danger that example becomes 'truly dangerous' (ibid.: 93).

One conclusion is inescapable: the virtues ascribed to imitation are 'imaginary'; the influence of imitation alone cannot 'reach and modify the heart of society' (Durkheim 2002[1897]: 93). Durkheim is all the more critical of Tarde's thesis in that his hypothesis 'has never even begun to receive experimental proof . . . [S]ociology can only claim to be treated as a science when those who pursue it are forbidden to dogmatize . . . so patently eluding the regular requirements of proof' (ibid.: 94). His study of suicide is designed to meet those requirements.

The Taste for Free Enquiry and the Taste for Learning

Book II, 'Social causes and social types', opens with a chapter on methodology. Durkheim is faced with a complex problem because he does not have the data he needs to classify suicides of sane persons 'in terms of their morphological types or characteristics' (2002[1897]: 98). The available data deal with only a very small number of cases, and are usually insufficient, if not suspect. It is therefore impossible to work backwards from the effects (different types of suicide) to their causes. He must 'reverse the order of study' (ibid.) – in other words, begin with the causes (which are social) and work backwards to the effects. This approach is all the more justified given that the object of his study is the social rate of suicide: 'If one wants to know the several tributaries of suicide as a collective phenomenon one must regard it in its collective form, that is, through statistical data, from the start. The social rate must be taken directly as the object of analysis' (ibid.: 100).

Durkheim is primarily interested in determining causes. But how can one reach these causes? The usual initial explanations refer to motives such as family trouble, remorse, drunkenness, etc. Most European countries provide statistical tables under such rubrics as 'presumptive motives of suicides', but official establishments of facts are 'often defective' (Durkheim 2002[1897]: 100) because 'human volition is the most complex of all phenomena'. 'We therefore make it a rule not to employ in our studies such uncertain and uninstructive data' (ibid.: 101). Disregarding 'the individual as such, his motives and his ideas', Durkheim therefore looks at 'various social environments (religious confessions, family, political society, occupational groups, etc.) (ibid.: 104). Do not suicide rates vary according to these different environments, he wonders? His analysis deals with the three main types of suicide: egoistic, altruistic and anomic suicide (to which he adds fatalistic suicide).

Durkheim begins with egoistical suicide, and establishes that its incidence is inversely proportional to (1) the degree of integration of religious society, (2) the degree of integration of domestic society and (3) the degree of integration of political society. His general conclusion is as follows: 'Suicide varies inversely with the degree of integration of the social groups of which the individual forms a part' (2002[1897]: 167).

He takes no rhetorical precautions: 'First let us see how the different religious confessions affect suicide' (2002[1897]: 105). Using statistics to support his argument, Durkheim compares the suicide rates for the various religious confessions in France and in different European countries. He first takes a look at the map of European suicides: it is less developed in Catholic countries (Spain, Portugal, Italy) than in Protestant countries (Prussia, Saxony, Denmark). After comparing the German states and the Swiss cantons, he reaches the same conclusion: 'Confessional influence is . . . so great as to dominate all others' (ibid.: 108).

Having established the facts, Durkheim looks for an explanation. Is this an effect of status, he wonders? Do minorities have no choice other than to exercise severe control over themselves, subject themselves to an especially rigorous discipline and practice greater morality? While he does not completely reject that explanation, the solution to the enigma lies, he believes, in the nature of religious systems. No religion unites men by 'a temporal bond of unity', for example 'an exchange and reciprocity of services', but by 'an identical body of doctrine' and 'a collective credo' (2002[1897]: 113). Even though Protestantism and Catholicism have similar precepts and forbid suicide, there is, Durkheim believes, one essential difference between them: except in England, the Protestant religion is less hierarchical and 'permits free inquiry to a far greater degree'. Freedom of enquiry is a source of divergences, or even schisms: 'the Protestant is far more the author of his faith' (ibid.: 112).[22] The Protestant Church allows individuals much greater intellectual freedom and is much less highly integrated than the Catholic Church. Does this make it superior?

The same explanation applies, Durkheim immediately adds, to 'the slight tendency of the Jews to suicide': in a context characterized by general animosity, intolerance and ostracism, the Jewish minority has little choice but to become 'a small, compact and coherent society' and that leaves little room for individual divergences. Indeed, 'Judaism . . . consists basically of a body of practices minutely governing all the details of life and leaving little free room to individual judgment' (2002[1897]: 114).

While the degree to which the various religions tolerate freedom of enquiry therefore appears to be determinant, it has to be admitted, Durkheim goes on, that broader cultural transformations, such as the undermining of traditional beliefs and the spread of education, also have an influence. Freedom of enquiry can therefore be contrasted with the 'yoke of tradition', and 'enlightened consciousness, of which knowledge is only the highest form', with 'irrational practices' and 'collective and customary prejudices'. Durkheim therefore attempts to establish a link between the taste for education and religious confession, and between education and suicide. 'Do the facts confirm this twofold hypothesis?' (2002[1897]: 116). The analysis is delicate because it assumes that Protestant peoples have a greater taste for education than Catholic peoples, and in that respect Catholic France lags behind Protestant Germany.

Durkheim takes as his index of the 'desire for knowledge' not the level of higher education or scientific productivity (at this level, France and Germany are not very different), but the level of primary instruction. The facts speak for themselves: levels of school attendance are higher in Protestant countries than in Catholic countries, and in Germany illiteracy rates are higher in Catholic regions. The correlation between illiteracy (as measured by rates in Italy and Germany) and suicide is obvious: suicide is 'exceptionally frequent in the highest classes of society' (2002[1897]: 120) – the liberal professions in France, the corps of public officials in Prussia – and it is more common amongst men than women, who (with the exception of Negro women in the United States) are, as a rule, less well educated and more 'traditional' than their husbands.

There is only one exception – described by Durkheim as 'one case . . . in which our law might seem not to be verified' (2002[1897]: 121). His core-ligionists are both 'well instructed and very disinclined to suicide'. This is, he thinks, explained by Jews' status as a religious minority. Jews seek to learn because 'in order to protect themselves better against the hate to which they are exposed [they] try to surpass in knowledge the populations surrounding them' (ibid.: 122). This is a general rule: it is a minority's way of 'offsetting the unfavourable position imposed [upon it] by opinion and sometimes by law' (ibid.: 123). In this case, knowledge and tradition are superimposed. This creates a very complex physiognomy, a mixture of primitive traits and refinement, of strong discipline and intense culture: the Jew 'has all the intelligence of modern man without sharing his despair' (ibid.). The apparent exception does not, concludes Durkheim, invalidate the law.

The first part of his analysis leads Durkheim to an initial general conclusion: 'Suicide increases with knowledge' (2002[1897]: 123). It is therefore very tempting to blame knowledge for the rising suicide rate because it leads to a loss of cohesion. But, far from seeing knowledge as 'the source of the evil' or as 'an enemy', Durkheim, describes it as 'the only remedy we have' (ibid.: 124). What are we to do now that established beliefs have been carried away and that 'the social instinct is blunted'? Durkheim's answer is this: 'intelligence is the only guide left [to] us' (ibid.).

Religion therefore has a moderating influence or 'prophylactic effect upon suicide'. Not because of the very nature of its dogmas and rituals or its punishments and proscriptions, but simply because it is a force for social cohesion and a support for 'a sufficiently intense collective life' (2002[1897]: 125).

In Praise of Marriage and Large Families

What applies to religion should, Durkheim goes on, apply to other societies such as the family and political society. His initial data appear to invalidate that hypothesis: unmarried people commit suicide less than married ones. Could it be that unmarried people have an easier life and are spared a lot of burdens and responsibilities? Durkheim borrows an 'ingenious calculation' (2002[1897]: 127) from the demographer Louis-Adolphe Bertillon that allows him to correct this methodological error. He manages in this way to separate out the influence of marital status from that of age. He then presents the findings of his own research, or what he calls 'our' research, given that it was carried out by his nephew, who classified the ministry of justice's statistics on some 25,000 suicides in France over a period of three years (1889, 1890 and 1891) on the basis of age, sex and marital status. In order to make the meaning of his figures clearer, he devises a 'coefficient of preservation' (or aggravation). A reading of the tables he has established then allows him to reach the following conclusions: early marriage has an aggravating influence, especially on men. From the age of 20 onwards, marriage has a preserving influence, again especially on men; this influence is also felt by widowers, but to a lesser degree. Married people, he concludes, enjoy a certain 'immunity'.

What is the explanation for this immunity? Durkheim rules out one thesis – the 'matrimonial selection' thesis, which describes married people as 'the elite of the population' and the unmarried as 'the human dregs of the country' (2002[1897]: 137) – and contends that the determining factor is the influence of the family environment, defined sometimes as the married couple, or conjugal group, sometimes as the family group proper – parents and children. Durkheim makes a clear distinction between these two societies: the former springs from a contract and elective affinity, and the latter from a natural phenomenon (consanguinity). Parents are 'functionaries of the family association' (2002[1897]: 156). Durkheim's statistics, which are somewhat 'surprising', allow him to show that the immunity of married men has little to do with conjugal society, and to challenge the received idea that women have more to gain from marriage than men and that being widowed is, especially for women, 'a hopelessly disadvantaged condition' (ibid.: 154).

The essential factor that determines the immunity of married people is not marriage but the family, and their immunity increases as the density (or volume) of the family increases. The 'density' factor is all the more important in that it too is determined by the intensity of collective feelings: shared memories are more intense, and impressions and opinions circulate more rapidly and more continuously. Durkheim observes that, between 1821 and 1861, there was 'a tendency for the family to break up and disperse more and more' (2002[1897]: 158). This was the hypothesis formulated in his 1888 article in the *Revue philosophique*. Rejecting the widespread view which, ever since Malthus, holds that restrictions on the size of families are 'necessary to general well-being', Durkheim argues that dense families, are 'an indispensable staff of daily life', or the best of investments. When the family is small, 'domestic life languishes' (ibid.: 159, 160).

The Beneficial Effects of Revolutions and Wars

Public opinion believes that revolutions, wars and 'great political upheavals' (Durkheim 2002[1897]: 161) lead to an increase in the number of suicides. On the contrary, states Durkheim, such crises, like the war of 1870–1, have an influence only because they 'rouse collective sentiments' (ibid.: 166). This influence appears to be greater in the towns than in the country – the urban population is 'more sensitive, impressionable and also better informed on current events' (ibid.) – and the explanation is that such commotions lead to greater social integration because they give birth to more intense collective feelings, towards, for example, the political party, patriotism and faith in the nation. Faced with danger, 'men . . . close ranks and confront the common danger, the individual thinks less of himself and more of the common cause' (ibid.: 167).

Durkheim uses the word 'egoism' to describe a state of 'excessive individualism' in which 'the individual ego asserts itself to excess in the face of the social ego and at its expense' (2002[1897]: 168). But why should excessive individualism encourage what he calls 'egoistic suicide'? What Durkheim regards as the 'good society' is characterized by its 'attachment to a common cause', a 'lofty goal', a 'constant interchange of ideas and feelings' and 'something like a mutual moral support' (ibid.). It is, in other words, an integrated society. In his study of suicide, Durkheim defines the three dimensions of integration: common ideas and beliefs (religious society), a system of interaction (domestic society) and common goals (political society) (see Besnard 1987: 99).

Any society, be it a nation, a church or a party, functions on the basis of belief, and when the social bond is loosened, doubts and anxieties begin to arise as people ask themselves 'to what purpose?' Durkheim now reiterates his thesis that 'man is double . . . because social man superimposes himself upon physical man' (2002[1897]: 171). It is society that awakens in him a supra-physical life (art, morality, religion, political faith, science), that gives rise to feelings of sympathy and solidarity, and gives him a *raison d'être*. We are society's 'handiwork', and we therefore catch its diseases. Collective mood swings and currents of depression and disenchantment reflect the loosening of social bonds; Durkheim calls this social unease 'a sort of collective asthenia' (ibid.: 172). Conditions are now ripe for the appearance of 'metaphysical and religious systems . . . which . . . attempt to prove to men the senselessness of life and that it is self-deception to believe that it has purpose' (ibid.). Although he does not mention him by name, Durkheim is referring here to Schopenhauer. Even depression and melancholia are expressions of an exaggerated individualism – there is a collective dimension to them: men effect 'communication through sadness when [they] no longer have anything else with which to achieve it' (ibid.: 173).

Everything else is a matter of 'incidental causes': the individual is 'a ready prey to suicide' (2002[1897]: 173). The less the individual is involved in society, the greater his chances of survival, as we can see from the example of children and old people. The same is true of women, adds Durkheim. Because her sensibility is more 'rudimentary', woman 'lives outside of community existence more than man'. He gives the example of the old unmarried woman 'with a few devotional practices and some animals to care for'. Her life is 'full', and she 'thus finds ready protection against suicide'. Being 'a more complex social being', man is hard beset in this respect; his 'moral balance' is more easily disturbed (ibid.: 174).

The Altruism of Lower Societies

While the absence of integration creates problems, so too does extreme integration: people kill themselves when they are too highly integrated into society. Always an advocate of moderation, Durkheim remarks that 'in the order of existence, no good is measureless' (2002[1897]: 175)

Despite the widespread view to the contrary, suicides do occur in so-called lower or primitive societies. It may not be egoistic suicide, but there are lots of cases in these societies, where it exists 'in an endemic state' (2002[1897]: 176). Durkheim cites historians and anthropologists and many accounts of a vast range of societies from China to North America, from India to Polynesia, and from Fiji to the New Hebrides. Old men commit suicide; women commit suicide when their husbands die; servants or clients do the same when their chiefs die. Such suicides are committed out of a sense of duty or honour in societies that function on the basis of mechanical solidarity, and which take little notice of individual personalities: everyone shares the same way of life, 'everything is common to all, ideas, feelings, occupations', and 'collective supervision is constant'. 'The whole . . . is a compact, continuous mass.' These are not egoistic suicides because 'the ego is not even its own property'. Such extreme altruism with respect to the group or society is, according to Durkheim, 'a moral characteristic of primitive man.' He describes this form of suicide as 'altruistic' (ibid.: 179, 180, 181).[23]

Altruistic suicides certainly exist in more recent civilizations and contemporary societies – Christian martyrs, soldiers who would rather die than suffer humiliation, the men of the Revolution who were carried away by a collective enthusiasm – but they are exceptions. And yet the army is now a special environment where altruistic suicide is chronic. Throughout Europe, the suicide rate amongst soldiers (average age between 20 and 30) is much higher than amongst civilians of the same age. This is astonishing, given that the army is composed of people who represent 'the flower of the country' (Durkheim 2002[1897]: 187), of carefully selected young men who enjoy an intense collective life and have an *esprit de corps*. Why should this be the case? Is it because they are unmarried? Is it the result of alcoholism? Disgust with the service? The many privations of living in barracks?

Durkheim rejects these 'simplistic' explanations one by one and then turns to the specificity of the situation and the military spirit: a sort of impersonality, an aptitude for abnegation and a lack of individualism.

The army is a sort of lower society, 'a massive, compact group providing a rigid setting for the individual' (2002[1897]: 193). Durkheim even describes 'military morality' as 'a survival of primitive morality'. Then there are the phenomena of propagation: the tendency to self-destruction spreads 'like a trail of gunpowder' (ibid.: 198, 199). Although this type of suicide is 'altruistic', it should not be regarded as a moral act. Nor, for that matter, should egoistic suicide be seen as a moral act. Both are 'merely the exaggerated or deflected form of a virtue'; egoism presupposes 'the sentiment of individual autonomy' and altruism the love of others (ibid.: 200).

The Scourge of the Age: Anomie

The second axis of the analysis proposed by Durkheim is that of regulation. If every society is, from the 'integration' point of view, 'something attracting the sentiments and activities of individuals', it is also, from the 'regulation' point of view, 'a power controlling them' (Durkheim 2002[1897]: 201). In the chapter entitled 'Anomic suicide', Durkheim sets out to establish the relationship between regulative action and the social suicide rate: the weaker the regulative action, the higher the suicide rate. This type of suicide occurs when the hold of the group is weakened and when the individual finds himself alone with his desires and passions. Durkheim therefore looks at two types of anomic situation: economic anomie and domestic anomie.

Some conjunctures have beneficial effects, and others do not. Adopting a macrosociological point of view, Durkheim looks at the 'aggravating effect' of economic crises. That they have such an effect is more than a well-known fact; it is a law, he concludes, on the basis of a few case-studies: the financial crisis of 1873–4 in Vienna, the Paris stock exchange crash of 1882, and the 'serious disturbances' (as measured by the annual number of bankruptcies) that occurred between 1845 and 1869. And yet explanations that relate the increase in the number of suicides to the increase in poverty and to the fact that life becomes more difficult seem to be too simplistic and contradicted by the facts. During periods of 'fortunate crises' (such as situations in which comfort, as measured by the price of the most necessary foods, increases, as it did between 1848 and 1881), of 'collective renaissance' (as in Italy after 1870, where wages rose after the unification and industrialization of the country), or even during 'favourable events' (such as world expositions), the number of suicides does not decrease (Durkheim 2002[1897]: 203, 204, 205); instead, there is an abnormal increase. Durkheim therefore concludes that 'economic distress' does not explain everything. Both financial crises and 'crises of prosperity' have the same effects because they are 'disturbances of the collective order' (ibid.: 206). They upset the balance, and give rise to situations of economic anomie.

Before reaching this conclusion, Durkheim puts forward some 'preliminary considerations' that help to clarify what he understands by happiness (which rests, in his view, on the balance between needs and means). When the individual is alone in the face of his destiny, there are no limits: 'Our capacity for feeling is in itself an insatiable and bottomless abyss'. This can only be a 'source of torment' in itself. Durkheim is strongly opposed to modish philosophies that encourage 'unlimited desires' and that claim that man's 'goal is infinity' (2002[1897]: 208).

Durkheim's recipe for happiness is simple: 'the passions first must be limited' (by the regulative and moderating influence of society or one of its organs). He also speaks of 'contentment': while striving to give beauty to his life, each person must be 'in harmony with his situation'. This contentment is the only source of 'the feeling of calm, active happiness, the pleasure in existing and living which characterizes health for societies as well as for individuals'. Such contentment ensures that 'the hierarchy of functions is . . . just'. This is a matter of regulation, but it also reflects the state of public opinion. At every moment in history, a society has a 'dim perception' of what things are worth, of the respective value of 'different social services, the relative reward due to each, and the consequent degree of comfort appropriate on the average to workers in each occupation' (2002[1897]: 209–11).

In society – and elsewhere in the world, adds Durkheim – there are ties of interdependence between beings, and there are also regulatory mechanisms that exercise constraints and apply 'brakes'. In the case of man, the constraint is 'moral, that is social': he 'escapes the body's yoke, but is subject to that of society' (2002[1897]: 213). Unfortunately, the 'brakes' do not always work. In crises, both painful and fortunate, and periods of rapid transformation, the suicide curve suddenly rises. Whether they are economic disasters (bankruptcy, outstanding debts), or 'fortunate' crises, involving 'an abrupt growth of power and wealth', these changes are so rapid that the balance of social forces becomes unstable, and the situation becomes indeterminate: 'The limits are unknown between the possible and the impossible, what is just and what is unjust' (ibid.).

Demands and expectations become unreasonable, and resignation gives way to envy. Public opinion is disoriented. There are no limits and no discipline. Ambitions are unbounded and desires know no limits. There is constant turmoil and no recognized way of classifying things. As in *The Division of Labour in Society*, Durkheim describes this state of non-regulation as 'anomie'. Passions are unleashed, the (class) struggle becomes violent and painful and, Durkheim adds as though it were self-evident, the desire to live is weakened. To prove his point, he gives the example of poor countries, which enjoy a 'remarkable immunity': 'Poverty protects against suicide because it is a restraint in itself' and 'Not without reason, have so many religions dwelt on the advantages and moral value of poverty' (2002[1897]: 214).

Crises, disasters and rapid transformations are certainly acute situations, but they are intermittent. The problem – and here Durkheim becomes alarmist – is that anomie has become chronic in the world of trade and industry. There had been no regulation of industrial relations for 100 years: neither religion, the state nor professional corporations were able to exercise such influence. Durkheim's tone now becomes dramatic: thanks to the development of industry, the expansion of the market and the effervescence that ensues, desires know no bounds, to the extent that anomie now affects the whole of society and seems almost to be 'normal'. People are feverishly impatient and envious, subject to wild imaginings and ephemeral pleasures, and in pursuit of goals they can never attain.

It is not surprising, Durkheim concludes, that such a (moral) state should lead to exhaustion and disenchantment. And when that moral state coincides with an economic disaster, the situation is inevitably 'fertile in suicides'. 'The very lack of organization throws the door open to every sort of adventure' (2002[1897]: 217). That industrial and commercial functions and 'the possessors of most comfort' are 'most stricken by the state of anomie' and 'furnish the greatest number of suicides' is a sign of the times. Durkheim describes this last type of suicide as 'anomic suicide', but he emphasizes that it is not unrelated to egoistic suicide: both spring from 'society's insufficient presence in individuals' (ibid.: 219).

The Dangers of Divorce

The divorced might be described as being 'at risk'. As early as 1882, the demographer Bertillon had established a correlation between the number of suicides and the number of divorces. Durkheim tests this hypothesis by looking at various European countries, and at various *départements* and cantons in France and Switzerland, but finds Bertillon's explanation – namely, divorce affects 'incompatible married couples' and 'people of irregular lives' – unconvincing. The cause lies not in organic predispositions or psychopathic flaws, but in the intrinsic nature of divorce itself. Durkheim makes two points: amongst divorced persons of both sexes, suicide is three or four times more likely than it is amongst married persons, and it is also more common – in certain countries even twice as common – than amongst widowed persons. This cannot simply be the outcome of a 'change of moral and material regimen': divorce is usually a 'deliverance' for both sexes (2002[1897]: 224).

Convinced that this must be related to 'some quality of the matrimonial society' (2002[1897]: 225), Durkheim compares national and *départemental* (Seine/the provinces) suicide rates, depending on whether or not divorce is permitted, and concludes that in countries where divorce is not so common, married persons are less likely than single persons to commit suicide. This is the case in Italy, a Catholic country in which there are few divorces, and in the French provinces. The 'origin of the evil' is not so much the family ('the family spirit') as the nature of marriage (2002[1897]: 228). 'Conjugal quarrels' do not explain everything, as they affect both partners. The problem is not social integration, but the conjugal bond. In order to verify his hypothesis, Durkheim looks at the situation of married women and concludes: 'The coefficient of preservation of married women rises proportionately to the fall of that of husbands, or in proportion as divorces are more frequent and vice versa' (ibid.: 229). Where there are more divorces, in other words, marriage favours wives more than husbands, and vice versa.

It may seem paradoxical that marriage should favour one sex and disadvantage the other. His analysis of this phenomenon leads Durkheim to raise the issue of love, which he regards as 'a far more mental than organic fact' (2002[1897]: 233). This is not simply a matter of 'generic desire' or 'natural proclivity'; in addition there are 'aesthetic and moral feelings', 'intellectual elements', 'physical desire' – in other words, 'various inclinations' that require social regulation. Durkheim sees marriage, and especially monogamous marriage, as a mechanism that regulates relations between the sexes. Because it forces a man 'to attach himself forever to the same woman' (ibid.), the institution of marriage regulates the life of passion by 'closing the horizon'. Marriage is a salutary discipline and it certainly involves obligations, but it also had its advantages: 'though his enjoyment is restricted, it is assured' (ibid.: 234). The 'humdrum existence of the ordinary bachelor' is very different. Durkheim eloquently describes the life of this unfortunate Don Juan: new hopes, a trail of weariness and disillusionment, a state of disturbance, agitation and discontent, the 'uncertainty of the future', indeterminateness, constant change mobility, and – not least – a lower coefficient of preservation against suicide (ibid.).

Divorce reflects the state of society's mores, and as it becomes more frequent, there is a possibility that the conjugal bond will be broken. The weakening of matrimonial regulation means that, for a married man, 'moral calmness and tranquillity' are replaced by 'uneasiness': 'the future is less certain' (2002[1897]: 235).

The married man's vulnerability means that from this point of view he resembles more closely the unmarried man. Divorce does not have the same negative effect upon women. Why not? At this point, Durkheim forgets about the rules of sociological method and introduces a biological explanation: the difference between men and women is the difference between the mental and the instinctive. Woman's sexual needs have 'less of a mental character' and are therefore 'naturally limited': 'regulation therefore is a restraint to her without any great advantages' (2002[1897]: 236).[24] Man's situation is very different: he needs marriage but 'custom . . . grants him certain privileges which allow him in some measure to lessen the strictness of the regime' (ibid.: 235).

We have, then, an 'antagonism of the sexes': one needs restraint and the other liberty. It is not, however, enough to believe that 'man is naturally a wicked and egoistic being whose role in a household is to make his companion suffer' (2002[1897]: 238). Once again, Durkheim swims against the tide: despite the current idea that marriage protects women from 'masculine caprice', the conjugal bond is a sacrifice for women and not men. Men, and not women, have good reason to renounce freedom: it is a 'source of torment to him' (ibid.: 239).

Durkheim is well aware that the times have changed and that public opinion is changing too. And yet he fears any modification of the law. The passions must be restrained to prevent 'the taste for anomie' from gaining ground.

A Fourth Type of Suicide: Fatalistic Suicide

In a long footnote, Durkheim remarks that 'there is a type of suicide the opposite of anomic suicide, just as egoistic and altruistic suicides are opposites'. It is, one might say, that excessive regulation is the opposite of 'oppressive discipline'. The example he gives is of 'very young husbands' and 'the married woman who is childless'. Their futures are 'pitilessly blocked', and their passions 'violently choked'. He then gives the historical example of suicide amongst slaves, which is said to have been frequent. These are exceptional cases, and have to do with 'excessive physical or moral despotism'. The rule is inflexible and there is no appeal against it. Hence the term 'fatalistic suicide' (2002[1897]: 239 n25).

A World of Emotions

We can represent Durkheim's argument in diagrammatic form if we draw two intersecting axes for social integration (+ and –) and social regulation (+ and –) (see Besnard 1987). A lack of integration corresponds to egoism, and excess integration to fatalism. Egoism, altruism, anomie and fatalism: Durkheim's aim is to trace the various tendencies which generate suicide 'from their social origins to their individual manifestations' (Durkheim 2002[1897]: 240) by looking not at individual factors such as temperament or special circumstances (which would be impossible), but the social and general causes that give suicides their special or collective mark. This can, he admits, be done 'only approximately', yet this research is far from being useless to the extent that it helps us to grasp the multiple meanings of suicide.

Egoistic suicide is characterized by apathy, and Durkheim identifies its two main forms. The first or 'lofty' form is melancholic (the ideal type is the hero of Lamartine's *Raphäel*), and the second or 'more common-place' form is typified by a 'sceptical, disillusioned matter-of-factness' and languor and indifference. The individual becomes detached from the outside world, and retreats from it into himself. Self-absorption and isolation are the characteristic features of the 'morbid joy' (to use Lamartine's expression) known as melancholy (Durkheim 2002[1897]: 242–3). All this results from 'over-individuation': 'a mind that questions everything . . . risks questioning itself and being engulfed in doubt' (ibid.: 244, 245). Having identified this form of egoistic suicide, Durkheim then defines a second or more 'Epicurean' form: here, the suicide 'knows his own egoism' and 'assigns himself the single task of satisfying his personal needs'.

This is the case of 'voluptuaries' who, having had an easy existence, 'kill themselves with ironic tranquillity' (ibid.: 245, 246).

Turning to altruistic suicide, which does not involve depression but, rather, 'a certain expenditure of energy' since its source is a violent emotion, Durkheim identifies three psychological forms, defined, respectively, by 'a serene conviction derived from the feeling of duty accomplished (the energy is controlled by reason and the will and the suicide 'kills himself at the command of his conscience'), a 'burst of faith and enthusiasm' (the religious fervour of the fanatic), and 'perfect tranquillity' (2002[1897]: 246).

Turning, finally, to anomic suicide, Durkheim identifies its main emotional characteristics as irritation and exasperated weariness, and 'violent recriminations against life in general, sometimes . . . against a particular person'. Such suicides are sometimes preceded by a murder: 'a man kills himself after having killed someone else'. The reasons for the suicide may vary: a man may, for instance, be 'abruptly cast down below his accustomed status', while others become 'caught up in a palpably hopeless pursuit, which only irritates rather than appeases their desires' (2002[1897]: 248, 249). Durkheim also describes the cases of Goethe's Werther and Chateaubriand's René, who is the insatiate type: 'Is it my fault if everywhere I find limits, if everything once experienced has no value for me?' (ibid.: 250).

The egoistic suicide and the anomic suicide have something in common: they both suffer from 'the disease of the infinite' (2002 [1897]: 250). But whereas we find 'reflective intelligence' in one, we find 'over-excited' emotion in the other. The former is lost in the infinity of dreams, the latter in the infinity of desires. Durkheim admits that these features are not found in their pure state, but in various combinations: ego-anomic suicide (a mixture of agitation and apathy, of action and reverie), anomic-altruistic suicide (exasperated effervescence), and ego-altruistic suicide (melancholy tempered with moral fortitude). In some cases, the individual 'may play both roles' (that of the egoist and that of the victim of agitation), while others may 'live a twofold, contradictory existence: individualists so far as the real world is concerned, they are immoderate altruists in everything that concerns [an] ideal objective' (ibid.: 251, 253).

At the end of Part II of *Suicide*, Durkheim asks himself if there is some relation between the nature of suicide and the kind of death chosen: strangulation and hanging, drowning, firearms, leaping from a high spot, poison or asphyxiation. A study of statistical data (distribution of suicides by country and by month) obliges him to answer his own question in the negative. Hanging, for instance, is not a 'natural expression' of suicide from melancholia (2002[1897]: 256). The methods used vary from country to country: 'each people has its favourite sort of death' (ibid.: 254). Other factors must also be taken into consideration, including the 'line of least resistance' (ibid.: 256), which is determined by the state of industrial technology (railroads become more general, electricity becomes commoner, etc.), the most widespread forms of architecture (buildings are higher in towns), scientific knowledge, or even cultural factors relating to conceptions of human dignity (some forms of death or more noble or more vulgar than others).

The Cult of the Individual

The third and final part of *Suicide* is entitled 'General nature of suicide as a social phenomenon'. Durkheim now attempts to 'define the reality to which this [social rate of suicide] corresponds. He begins by reviewing the main findings of his research: individual peculiarities (poverty, sickness, disappointments) do not explain the social rate of suicide, and nor does the biological constitution of an individual's physical environment. If, on the other hand, we look at society, we find ourselves 'face to face with real laws'. Durkheim therefore reaches the inescapable conclusion that: 'the social suicide rate can be explained only sociologically . . . There is, therefore, for each people a collective force of a definite amount of energy, impelling men to self-destruction' (2002[1897]: 263).

Durkheim is aware that his suggestion that social facts should be seen as objective facts flies in the face of common sense; 'If there is such a science as sociology, it can only be the study of a world hitherto unknown' (2002[1897]: 274). He attempts to reply to the objections even before they have been formulated, and to clarify certain points. There is no doubt in his mind: society is made up of individuals, but the way they combine forms 'a psychical entity of a new kind' and is 'productive of special effects' (ibid.: 275). He therefore makes a clear distinction between individual life and social life, but immediately admits that both are psychical in nature, as both are made up of representations: 'We see no objection to calling sociology a variety of psychology, if we carefully add that social psychology has its own laws which are not those of individual psychology' (ibid.: 276). He gives the example of religion, which is not an expression of 'feelings of fear or reverence inspired in conscious persons', but 'the system of symbols by means of which society becomes conscious of itself; it is the characteristic way of thinking of collective existence' (ibid.: 276, 277). The gods are only the hypostatic form of society. The idea that the social and the individual are heterogeneous also applies to law, fashion, morality and political institutions.

Durkheim is once more criticizing Gabriel Tarde, whose theses are a refutation of the whole of contemporary psychology (which is, in his view, a depth psychology), and forcefully and clearly reiterating his theory of energy and currents (in the sense in which one speaks of electric currents). Every society is shot through with various currents (languid melancholy, active renunciation, exasperated lassitude) that 'penetrate' individuals. 'All sorts of currents come, go, circulate everywhere, cross and mingle in a thousand different ways . . . Today, a breath of sadness and discouragement . . . tomorrow one of joyous confidence. . . Yesterday cosmopolitanism was the rage, today patriotism has the floor'. All these 'eddies, all these fluxes and refluxes' affect individual consciousnesses with greater or lesser force and intensity (2002[1897]: 279). There is always a gap between these collective feelings and the fluctuating feelings of what Durkheim calls the 'ordinary man', who, being hesitant and ready to compromise, tries to escape certain obligations, such as paying taxes or doing his military service. We all have a 'distinct personality' and we therefore lead a 'sort of double existence' and have a 'double impulse': 'we are drawn in a social direction and tend to follow the inclination of our own natures' (ibid.: 283). These are antagonistic forces: the pressure of society (which is always the stronger) and the resistance of the individual.

A society's moral ideal is thus a combination of egoism, altruism and anomie. These three currents of opinion coexist, and when they temper one another, they create a state of equilibrium within the individual and thus protect him from suicide. The individual is, depending on his disposition, to a greater or lesser extent subject to the influence of these currents. But there is, Durkheim points out, a 'natural kinship' between collective feelings and individual dispositions: society creates individuals in its own image, and while hypercivilization leads to egoism and anomie, it also refines the nervous system.

What freedom is left to the individual? Durkheim initially refuses to address this question (on the grounds that it is metaphysical) but adds in a footnote that 'this theory of statistics does not deny men every sort of freedom' (2002[1897]: 289 n20). We can either fight and swim against these currents or be swept away by them. The fact that the environment can be considered a determinant factor does not mean that man, or even the criminal or suicide, has no free will or that he is not responsible for his own actions.

There is, according to Durkheim, no reason to regard suicide as a crime. To support his claim, he turns to history and comparative law. In all societies, with the possible exception of those primitive societies in which there is a certain complacency towards suicide, and ignoring a few exceptional cases of retrogression (Greece and Italy), suicide is the object of general reprobation and, as we progress through history, the prohibition becomes more radical. Christianity plays a central role by introducing a new conception of the human personality, which now becomes the most sacred thing of all: 'man is a god to mankind' (2002[1897]: 331). The cult of man, which is very different from egoistic individualism, is therefore a real 'religion of humanity' (ibid.: 302). Now that the human personality has become 'something sacred' (ibid.: 303), we can understand that suicide, while not the same as homicide, is regarded as a form of sacrilege and an immoral act.

The Case for Decentralization

What should the modern attitude to suicide be? Before answering that question, Durkheim raises the issue of the normal and the abnormal (or the pathological). Well aware that his position has been seen as 'subversive', he sums up his argument thus: 'If it is normal that there should be crimes, it is normal that they should be punished' (2002[1897]: 330).

Although it is difficult to prove that suicide is a universal phenomenon, Durkheim has demonstrated that it is widespread among the peoples of Europe: 'Suicide is . . . an element of their normal constitution, and even, probably, of any social constitution' (2002[1897]: 330]. Everything is connected: altruism and lower societies go together; individualism and egoism are similar and stimulate one another, and the morality of progress and perfection and anomie are inseparable. Does this imply that we have to conclude that here is an element of exaggeration or excess in suicidogenic currents? Even excesses have their uses, replies Durkheim, who sings the praises of intellectual individualism because it is a precondition for the abandoning of traditions and the emergence of new beliefs. If a society is to be able to deal with a variety of situations, there must be room for everything: there must be room for criticism and free enquiry and for authoritarianism (the army), for joy and melancholy, and for optimism and pessimism: 'the spirit of renunciation, the love of progress, the taste for individuation have their place in every kind of society' (ibid.: 334).

But what are we to conclude from the 'enormous aggravation' or 'rising flood of voluntary deaths' over the past century? Is this the 'ransom-money of civilization'? That is unlikely: there is something abnormal about 'the special conditions under which it occurs in our day'. There is a 'morbid effervescence, the grievous repercussions of which each one of us feels'. In Durkheim's view, so grave and rapid an alteration 'must be morbid' because 'a society cannot change its structure so suddenly' (2002[1897]: 334–6). The work of centuries cannot be remade in a few years. It takes time: real changes are the result of slow, almost imperceptible, modifications. Even though he is in no position to be specific, Durkheim makes so bold as to claim that 'while able to uproot the institutions of the past', this morbid disturbance has 'put nothing in their place'. Europe, in other words, finds itself in a 'state of crisis and perturbation' (ibid.: 336). And the crisis is all the more disturbing in that the collective sadness or melancholy that is usually a submerged current has reached a degree of morbid intensity and has become the basis for 'complete theories of life'. The appearance of 'discouraging theories' – Schopenhauer, Hartmann – clearly demonstrates that 'the current of pessimism has reached a degree of abnormal intensity'. According to Durkheim, the same applies to other forms of negativity, such as anarchism, aestheticism, mysticism and revolutionary socialism: 'even if they do not despair of the future, [they] have in common with the pessimist a single sentiment of hatred and disgust for the existing order, a single craving to destroy or to escape from reality' (ibid.: 337).

There is, concludes Durkheim, something morbid about all this, and the rise in the number of suicides (meaning, of course, egoistic and anomic suicides) must therefore be seen as pathological. Durkheim is being alarmist, perhaps too much so.[25] The phenomenon is becoming a threat, but by what means can it be overcome? Some authors have recommended the re-establishment of the penalties formerly in use. Durkheim, who finds 'our present indulgence towards suicide' to be 'excessive', tends to agree with them, but also argues that severe punishment is impossible because it would not be tolerated by public opinion: up to a point, the act is either 'approved or tolerated'. Legislation can do little to prevent an act that is not really seen as immoral. The only solution is to 'act directly on the current of pessimism, to lead it back to its normal bed' (2002[1897]: 339). Consciences must be relieved from its influence, and recover their 'moral equilibrium'. That, however, is easier said than done. Even education, which seems to some to be the surest means of obtaining this result, may prove ineffective: 'This is to ascribe to education a power it lacks. It is only the image and reflection of society. It imitates and reproduces the latter in abbreviated form; it does not create it.' Durkheim adds: 'Education . . . can be reformed only if society itself is reformed' (ibid.: 340).

The message is clear: society must provide the solution, but society is 'weak and disturbed'. The only remedy for the ill is therefore 'to restore enough consistency to social groups for them to obtain a firmer grip on the individual, and for him to feel bound to them' (2002[1897]: 341). We cannot rely on the state or political society to develop this sentiment of solidarity. Political society is 'too far removed from the individual to affect him uninterruptedly and with sufficient force' (ibid.). The state is 'a cumbersome machine, made only for general and clear-cut tasks' (ibid.: 347). Even 'the idea of country' cannot 'become the guiding motive of action', except in exceptional circumstances (such as a great national or political crisis) (ibid.: 341). It has been suggested that either religion or the family can resolve the problem, but Durkheim argues that it is too late for that. Religion no longer has any real influence on individual minds, and is no longer an agent of socialization. On the contrary, it 'offends our dearest sentiments' because 'the history of the human mind is the very history of the progress of free thought' (ibid.: 342). In Durkheim's view, the only viable religions are those that permit 'more freedom to the right of criticism, to individual initiative' (ibid.: 343). Unless, of course, we revert to the most archaic religions!

What about the family? In Durkheim's view, 'changes have . . . occurred in the constitution of the family which no longer allow it to have the same preservative influence as formerly'. The family is no longer 'a compact mass, indivisible and endowed with a quality of permanence.' It is no longer a 'house' with ancestors, a name and a reputation and its 'duration is now brief' (2002[1897]: 344). Barely formed, it begins to disperse and break up: in most cases, the family has been reduced to the married couple alone and households of a single person are increasingly common.

The influence of institutions such as religion and the family appears to be secondary. If there is a 'genuine remedy', it lies, Durkheim believes, in 'societies', or in other words the occupational group (2002[1897]: 345). He takes up the idea formulated in the conclusion to *The Division of Labour in Society*. Because it forms a 'collective personality', the corporation brings together people. Durkheim is well aware that the old, narrowly local corporation had a bad name for being a 'state within a state'; 'It must be organized on wholly different bases from those of today'. 'Hours of work . . . health . . . wages . . . social insurance and assistance . . . disputes constantly arising between the branches of the same occupation. . . . all these things can be taken care of by corporations. If they were, 'the social fabric, the meshes of which are so dangerously relaxed, would tighten' (ibid.: 347, 348).

Durkheim speaks of the need for social renewal, and sees the corporation as a remedy for anomie because it can establish limits, impose discipline, moderate the passions, regulate relations between the weak and the strong, if not production itself. Whilst it has a role to play in distributive justice, it cannot, however, take over the state's 'important functions'. Only the state can speak in the name of 'general utility' and 'organic equilibrium', but its action can be useful 'only if a whole system of secondary organs exists to diversify the action' (Durkheim 2002[1897]: 351).

Given that the state has become 'inflated and hypertrophied', Durkheim argues the case for decentralization, but does not believe that it can be implemented at the local or regional level. It is too late for that: 'the general life of the country [has been] unified' and, while we may regret it, 'local patriotisms no longer exist' and it is 'impossible to artificially resuscitate a particularist spirit which no longer has any foundation'. All that we can do is 'to lighten somewhat the functioning of the machinery of government' (2002[1897]: 357). The only thing that 'would make possible the multiplication of the centres of communal life without weakening national unity is occupational decentralization' (ibid.: 358). This has been understood by the growing numbers of authors and statesmen who wish to make the occupational group 'the base of our political organization' by dividing the electoral college not by sections of territory, but by corporations. Durkheim seems somewhat perplexed about this. It may well be possible to decree that representatives shall be elected by corporation, but that would be pointless unless we begin by organizing the corporation in such a way as to make it 'a definite institution, a collective personality' and 'a moral individuality' (ibid.).

Durkheim is looking for a practical solution. His cure for the collective malady is neither an artificial return to the past nor a utopian flight into the future: 'We must seek in the past the germs of a new life which it contained, and hasten their development' (2002[1897]: 359). He refuses, on the other hand, to give a precise definition of the future 'occupational organization'. It will, he suggests, take a 'special study', and we must be wary of programmes that are 'too definite': these are 'imaginative flights, too far from the complexity of facts to be of much practical value'. Social reality is 'not neat enough' and 'too little understood'. His advice is as follows: remain in 'direct contact with things', identify the evil and the remedy and, rather than drawing up fine plans that anticipate everything, 'set resolutely to work' (ibid.).

'Stabbing at Water'

'A fine volume', exclaimed Gustave Belot (1898: 653). In Bordeaux, there was talk of a 'remarkable book', but there were also fears that a 'teacher of this value' would leave the university.[26] Even before it was published, Durkheim was worried about its possible reception: 'Will it make converts? I don't know; even though it seems to me that I have made more ground than I have lost, I am sceptical. I fear that I will fall between two stools: the specialists do not think me specialist enough, and philosophers and scholars like their science to be more entertaining. But the important thing is to say what you have to say, and let the rest of them get on with it.'[27]

Durkheim's goal was to make converts, gain ground and convince people. He was eager to see how his future collaborators would react. Paul Lapie allowed himself to be convinced, but had some reservations. He had read Durkheim's book 'with great pleasure', he wrote to Célestin Bouglé.[28] 'I find in it a high level of awareness and a very skilful interpretation of the facts. Basically, it is not far removed from social psychology.' He was especially pleased to see that Durkheim had 'been inspired by their correspondence' and was 'willing to make concessions'. He even had the impression that he 'won the argument': 'I am well aware that he insists that we know nothing of social man's motives, but whether or not his egoism, altruism and anomie are, to a greater or lesser degree, conscious, they are still psychological causes.' Even though he had some reservations – Durkheim's critique of the theses he rejected was incomplete, and what he described as a 'new' statistical method was in fact quite old – Lapie greatly admired a book, which 'makes one think' and which, unusually, contained both 'some interesting general ideas' and 'meticulous observations'. His reaction did not displease Durkheim, who told Bouglé: 'The outcome is that we are, insofar as that is possible, in complete agreement about the litigious question, and I am very pleased about that.'[29]

Dominique Parodi also read *Suicide* with 'great interest': 'At last we have a real book on sociology that gets beyond the eternal questions of methodology.' He was highly amused by the 'bitter-sweet (more bitter than sweet) polemic' between Durkheim and Tarde, but was sorry that Durkheim had still not succeeded in 'defining the relationship between the psychological and the social'. Nor was he entirely satisfied with Durkheim's interpretations of his statistical data. He found some of them 'very strange'. He did, however, admit that the statistics collected by the author displayed 'some truly remarkable regularities'. He added, not without irony: 'I really am beginning to believe more and more in sociology.' And he suggested a slogan: 'Advance, sociologists: work towards a new science and effectively establish it.'[30]

Célestin Bouglé had much more serious reservations, and even criticized Durkheim for displaying a certain 'scientific narrow-mindedness'.[31] He passed his comments on to Durkheim, who kindly replied:

> There is a lot of truth in what you say. It might have been more politic not to present things in that way. But what do you expect? I do tend to be blunt about these things. That's the way I am. And if you want to pursue your ideas to their logical conclusion, it seems to me to be impossible not to formulate things the way I have.

For Durkheim, 'pursuing ideas to their logical conclusion' meant dealing directly with the question of the relationship between the social and the individual and stating quite clearly that sociology cannot begin by analysing the individual consciousness and that 'we have to look at social facts from the outside'. Isn't there some interest, he asks, in showing that morality is in a sense something that exists outside individuals? This is a very 'simple' suggestion but 'we automatically jib at the idea'.[32]

Durkheim sent a copy of his book to his young colleague, but reassured him that it was 'a keepsake and token of friendship and not something to work on'. Later in his letter, he does, however, discuss at length how to organize the work for the next issue of *L'Année sociologique*. While he did not want to force Bouglé to do so, Durkheim said that he would like him to do some 'extra work' by reviewing his book in the *Revue philosophique*. He attached great importance to the journal which, he said, 'partly serves as a sociology journal', and had discussed the possibility of a review with its director Ribot, who had originally thought of asking Gaston Richard to review it. Bouglé's initial response was to say 'no'. Durkheim had, for other (obvious) reasons, refused to allow the journal to approach Gabriel Tarde. He now began to pressurize Bouglé: 'Do you want me to challenge you on some pretext or other? Would you be willing to take on the task? Only if it fits in with your plans, obviously.'[33]

Durkheim understood perfectly well that Bouglé had 'doubts' about reviewing *Suicide*. When Bouglé suggested the name of Gustave Belot, he was more than dubious:

> He is at least as incompetent as you, but he has the added disadvantage of having no sense of his incompetence and ignorance . . . It is intolerable that someone should spend his life dogmatizing about social matters when he has never come into contact with them. And besides, his verbose, formal dialectics are not to my liking.[34]

Gustave Belot published a review of *Suicide* in June 1898. In the event, it was his future collaborator Paul Fauconnet who reviewed it in the April issue. Fauconnet emphasized the originality of Durkheim's work, which he described as 'both scientific and sociological'. 'This monograph on suicide is an attempt to raise a specific problem and to give a sociological answer based on the observation of all the known facts.' He adds: '*Suicide* has to be seen as a new exposition and illustration of the *Rules of Sociological Method* laid down by M. Durkheim.' The method produces results and shows that 'an inductive sociology is possible'. Fauconnet was obviously aware that the book would inevitably provoke objections because there was a danger that its author would be accused of dogmatism. But he warned the objectors: 'A few dialectical arguments are not enough; you will either have to come up with new facts or a new interpretation of the statistics' (Fauconnet 1898: 428).[35]

Another future contributor to *L'Année sociologique* reviewed Durkheim's book for the *Revue de métaphysique et de morale*: François Simiand, who edited the 'Année sociologique 1897' column (Simiand 1898). His criticisms were incisive and focused on methodological issues: there is no critique of the geographical and historical value of the statistics; the findings are established on a base that is too narrow, and so on. He also regrets the fact that Durkheim wastes his time by devoting an entire chapter to refuting Tarde's theory of imitation. But, above, all, he is critical of the conception of social facts outlined in the book: 'Sociology can be put on a scientific footing at much less cost.' Why, he asks, the insistence that collective tendencies are 'forces that are as real as cosmic forces'? He rejects, in other words, what he calls Durkheim's 'sociological realism'.

Although Durkheim had been apprehensive about their possible reaction, the philosophers were interested in – and even impressed by – his statistically based argument. A short review published in the November 1897 supplement to the *Revue de métaphysique et de morale* spoke of his 'slow, patient research' and 'complete scientific honesty'. 'We have here', wrote the anonymous reviewer, 'a book which, had it been known earlier, would probably have spared the reader of the *Rules of Sociological Method* some unfortunate misunderstandings.'[36] Lucien Herr, who was 'still helping Durkheim to prepare his lectures at Bordeaux' by giving him 'a lot of bibliographical help' (Mauss 1997[1928]: 742), seems to have had the same reaction: while they had had 'some differences of opinion' when the *Rules of Sociological Method* appeared, the publication of *Suicide* had reconciled them. Even though he was critical of Durkheim's general thesis ('he describes as "social" causes that are originally no more than individual causes'), Pillon, the director of *La Revue philosophique*, pointed to 'some excellent pages' and said of the book that it was 'full of interesting observations and views'. *Suicide* therefore allowed Durkheim to regain some credit amongst philosophers.

Outside the circle of philosophy and the human sciences, Durkheim's book made little impact. In the medical press, the silence was almost total, even from psychiatrists who were interested in suicide.[37] This did not mean that the psychiatrists were not interested in sociology. On the contrary, there had never before been so much talk of sociology in those circles. 'Alas!' remarked Durkheim. 'The meaning they give to the word is extraordinary. There isn't a chairman of a charitable society or the director of a night shelter who doesn't believe he is doing social science. One of them came to ask me for a copy of my book *Suicide* on those grounds.'[38]

There were also a few reviews in political and literary journals. The *Revue socialiste* was fairly sympathetic to Durkheim's sociology, but its regular contributor Pierre Deloire (1897) criticized him for relying so much on statistics and studying only the 'external manifestations' of social sentiments. He was also critical of the book's political aspects, and of the corporatist solution outlined by Durkheim. He was also sorry that he did not criticize the way most employers 'constantly stole surplus-time.' The 'man of letters' Émile Faguet (1907[1898]) published a fairly sympathetic review of the book in the *Revue bleue*, but in his view individualism was the only factor that could explain suicide, and he saw only one means of combating it: voluntary association.

When *Suicide* was submitted as part of a grant application to the social and economic sciences section of the Comité des travaux historiques et scientifiques, the task of writing the report was entrusted to A. de Foville, who was a contributor to the *Revue internationale de sociologie*. The Leplaysian made no secret of his dissatisfaction: 'Despite all his talent and all his work, the author has not succeeded in drawing the obvious conclusions.' He also criticized Durkheim for his style, which was not simple enough: 'The prose of sociologists is not always exempt from a certain pedantry.' De Foville did, however, praise Durkheim – a 'distinguished mind' – and his overall evaluation was quite positive: 'a remarkable monograph', 'rich and reliable documentation', 'subtle analyses'. There was, in his view, no doubt that the book should be in the main libraries of the big university centres.[39]

An all-out attack was expected from Durkheim's sociological enemies, and especially Gabriel Tarde. *Suicide* was indeed to a large extent what Philippe Besnard (2000) calls 'an anti-Tarde book'. The confrontation was more than predictable. Tarde let Durkheim know that he intended to 'take him to task again', even though he said he was tired of 'having to cross swords with him'. 'To my great regret', he stated, Durkheim appears to have little inclination to 'reply', taking the view that 'the debate had gone on long enough'.[40]

In July and August 1987, Tarde wrote a response provisionally entitled 'Contre Durkheim à propos de son *Suicide*'. It consists of disjointed notes and is sometimes repetitive. It is, in other words, a draft. The tone is polemical, as it is a reply to the man who wanted to 'pulverize' Tarde's ideas. Tarde certainly acknowledges the author's 'fine talent for exposition' and is astounded to see that 'so much research has been devoted to such a 'sad and profound' subject. But he quickly moves from praise to irony: 'D. is my pupil without realizing it . . . Durkheim is a psychologist despite himself and without realizing it' (Tarde 2000: 219–55). Then come the personal attacks: pedantry, a liking for metaphors, pure mythology, authoritarian dogmatism, bizarre ideas. On several occasions, Tarde accuses his colleague of 'failing to understand' what he had written about imitation.

Tarde makes a few highly pertinent comments on *Suicide* and, for example, the contagion model. His most telling criticism has to do with suicides in the army: why is suicide so common in the army, and unheard of in monasteries? He is, finally, surprised by Durkheim's proposed analysis of political crises (which, if they overthrow institutions, cannot be factors that promote integration) and mocks the penchant for symmetry that leads him to make a distinction between 'too much and too little' when it comes to integration.

Tarde repeats his main arguments against Durkheim's sociology. He begins by criticizing him for putting the individual 'under the yoke of society' and for making society something 'external and superior', or even a 'divine personality'. The social rate, the social environment and the collective state are, in his view, 'so many nebulous divinities that come to Durkheim's rescue when he gets into difficulty' (Tarde 2000: 231). He then challenges the famous distinction between the normal and the pathological. He thinks that there is something morbid about suicide and, for that matter, crime. He cannot understand how anyone can make 'such a heavy dose of sadness and melancholy an essential ingredient of healthy life'. He is also astonished that anyone can sing the praises of neurasthenia.

Finally, Tarde turns to the question of 'remedies'. He recognizes the importance of professional groups, but does not see 'professional decentralization' as a solution, especially if there is no simultaneous reorganization of the family, which he defends on the grounds that it is the 'basis for everything': 'The family is the mirror of the people, and family education is the mirror of national life.' He also criticizes Durkheim for his adoption of a socialist position: the struggle against anomie will inevitably lead to the 'organization of labour taken to extremes' or even 'civil regimentation'. 'Durkheim leaves us no choice but the choice between the tyranny or rules . . . that damages our freedom, and the suicide that does away with our existence' (Tarde 2000: 244). But when it comes to anomie in contemporary societies, Tarde does not reject the notion of 'the hyper-excitation of desires and hopes'; because of its 'greater social and moral density', urban society is 'more hyper-excited, and more stimulating in terms of hopes and wishes, and more ambitious when it comes to love'. That, he concludes, provides a 'very simple explanation for the regularities' to be observed in the yearly figures for divorce and suicide. Why, he asks, does this regularity suggest such 'bizarre ideas' to Durkheim (ibid.: 225)?

Tarde decided not to publish his response. It is true that suicide was a 'domain' with which he was not familiar – his speciality was comparative criminality – and that handling statistical data was not his strong point. It is also true that his son Paul was studying in Bordeaux, and that one of his examinations would be marked by Durkheim.[41] It is also possible that, with one eye on the Collège de France, he was reluctant to indulge in further confrontation with Durkheim, who was also a potential candidate for a chair. There was therefore no further discussion.

The 'Tardean' response to Durkheim came from abroad, and through the intermediary of authors who had links with Tarde. The Italian statistician Augusto Bosco was the first to respond in a fairly critical review of the book in the *Rivista italiana di sociologia* (Bosco 1897). Durkheim had been too quick to deny the influence of race. His interpretation of seasonal variations in the suicide rate was ingenious but erroneous, and he failed to take into account the problems inherent in recording them, while his analysis of suicide amongst soldiers was weak. The evidence was, in a word, 'far from successful'. The same points were made by Gustavo Tosti in a review entitled 'Suicide in the light of recent studies' in the *American Journal of Sociology* (Tosti 1898c) and in a short review in *Psychological Review* (Tosti 1898b). If Durkheim's book on suicide was designed to demonstrate the positive nature of his conception of society, it was, according to Tosti, 'a complete failure'.

Tosti was an amateur sociologist of Italian origin who lived in New York. He corresponded with Tarde, and had published a laudatory article on him in *Political Science Quarterly*. Tosti began by singing Durkheim's praises and describes his book as 'the most complete analysis ever attempted' to understand the life of modern societies since Wagner and Morselli. He also said that he agreed with Durkheim that social facts were not identical with the sum of their constituent elements (individuals). He then set out his objections, criticizing Durkheim for overlooking the law of intercerebral action (imitation): the great weakness of his approach was that it could not explain how 'social forces . . . are incorporated into individuals' (Tosti 1898b: 426). Durkheim did not understand, he went on, that 'a compound is explained both by the character of its elements and by the law which governs their combining together' (Tosti 1898c).

The comment infuriated Durkheim, who immediately wrote a letter to the editor of the *American Journal of Sociology* pointing out: 'I have made it a rule to profit from the criticisms that may be made of my work, without replying directly to them, save when the ideas discussed in relation to myself are so foreign to me that I must disavow them in order to prevent substantial errors from gaining credence.'[42] Tosti's article 'forces me . . . to emerge from my reserve' (Durkheim 1982[1898]: 251). In this short text, which appeared in the May issue, Durkheim cites several passages from *Suicide* to prove that he does acknowledge the importance of individual factors: 'I do not deny in any way that individual natures are the components of the social fact. What must be ascertained is whether as they combine together to produce the social fact, they are not transformed by the very fact of their combination. Is the synthesis purely mechanical, or chemical? This is the heart of the question' (ibid.: 252). Gustave Tosti replied in the July 1898 issue. He was furious with the man he calls 'the Maître of the University of Bordeaux' for accusing him of 'superficiality' and 'carelessness' and for saying that his argument was based upon 'substantial errors'. His article was entitled 'The delusions of Durkheim's sociological objectivism' (Tosti 1898a). He reproduces long quotations from *Suicide* and concludes that they 'speak for themselves'. And then he lets the cat out of the bag: he criticizes Durkheim because he denies the law of imitation of intercerebral interaction; were Durkheim to be right, his own theory would be nothing more than a verbal construct.

The Italian economist Vilfredo Pareto also reviewed *Suicide* in the new journal *Zeitschrift für Sozialwissenschaft* (1898). Pareto, who, like Durkheim, adopted the 'experimental method' viewpoint, emphasized the interest of the book but was quite harsh on it, pointing out that the argument was far from rigorous, that it contained countless errors, and that the statistics were relatively old. When, for instance, Durkheim looks at the regularity of suicide rates, he chooses the years to suit his argument, and when he looks at suicide among soldiers, his proof is purely a priori. 'Metaphysical abstractions!' he exclaims.

At the University of Bordeaux, they rejoiced at Durkheim's success: 'M. Durkheim tireless pursues his fine work', commented the rector. 'He published a remarkable book on suicide this year . . . His lectures are still as rich, as dense, and as original.' He then adds, on a slightly worried note: 'It is to be hoped for the sake of the University of Bordeaux that a teacher of this value will remain here as long as possible.'[43]

10

L'Année *sociologique*

Birth of a Team

Durkheim spoke to his Italian readers of 'a movement with nothing superficial about it'. A movement? A new school? As we have seen from his analysis of Saint-Simonism, Durkheim was well aware that establishing a new school of thought always involves the recruitment of supporters, a group of teachers to systematize its doctrine, and a journal or review for propaganda purposes.

A Crop of Journals

In the nineteenth century, the journal was to intellectual and scientific life what the salon was to fashionable life. The years 1880–90 and 1890–1900 saw the emergence of 'the greatest crop' of specialized societies and journals ever recorded: more than 200 new learned reviews and journals began publication between 1892 and 1900. The same period saw the launch of several literary and social science journals, some of which took up an avant-garde position, as we can see from the role played by the *Revue de métaphysique et de morale* in philosophy (Charle 2004: 186–7). The 'Année' ['The Year in . . .] formula was fashionable in intellectual and scientific circles: *L'Année artistique* (1878), *L'Année médicale* (1878), *L'Année archéologique* (1879), *L'Année épigraphique* (1888), *L'Année cartographie* (1890), *L'Année philosophique* and *L'Année psychologique*. Edited by Pillon, *L'Année philosophique* resumed publication in 1891; first published in 1868 and 1869, it had been replaced by *La Critique philosophique* between 1872 and 1889. Appearing on an annual basis, it carried both articles and a substantial bibliographical section edited by Renouvier that surveyed the previous year's philosophical literature for France.

The first volume of *L'Année psychologique*, which was also published by Alcan, was launched in 1895. Edited by Alfred Binet and H. Beaumis, and described as the publication of the Sorbonne's laboratory of physiological psychology (Binet was the laboratory's director and Beaumis an honorary professor in the Nancy faculty of medicine), it was to serve as Durkheim's model. Each volume comprised three parts: (1) previously unpublished articles and memoirs describing the greater part of the laboratory's work;

(2) reviews of the year's most important publications (books and articles from both France and other countries; (3) bibliographical tables listing publications in a wide variety of fields (physiology of the nervous system, mental pathology, pedagogy, criminality, child psychology) that might be of interest to psychologists. A fourth 'miscellaneous' section dealt with new observations, experiments and instruments that might be of use to psychology.

The anthropologists (as they were known at the time) were also very active. There was a Société d'anthropologie in Paris, and the *Revue d'anthropologie* and the *Revue d'ethnographie* had successfully merged to form the bi-monthly *L'Anthropologie*, which was edited by M. Boule and R. Verneau. Some of those who were to work on the *Année sociologique* – Henri Hubert and Henri Beuchat – were contributors. The disciple also acquired a new public showcase when the new palaeontology and anthropology galleries opened at the Muséum national d'histoire naturelle in 1898.

The initial issue of the first major sociology journal, the *American Journal of Sociology*, appeared in 1896. For 30 years it was to be edited by Albion W. Small (University of Chicago). Sociology was at this time an ill-defined discipline that attracted people, often from very different backgrounds, who thought that it would be useful to apply formal knowledge to social problems (Abbott 1999: 81). According to its editor, the *American Journal of Sociology* aspired to being not an abstract or theoretical journal, but a lively practical one that combined theory with action. Albion Small himself wrote a short article on 'studies and social agitation' for the first issue, which published several pieces on American issues of the day, including the anti-trust laws and the programme for municipal reforms. The articles on Christian sociology and English Christian Socialism were a clear indication of the religious commitment of both the editor (who was to become a pastor) and the early contributors. As well as these concrete articles, there were more abstract contributions dealing with methodological issues, including G. Vincent on 'the field of sociology', W. Thomas on 'the goal and method of the psychology of peoples', articles by L.F. Ward and a series of 'contributions to social philosophy'. Small defined sociology's goal as 'the synthesis of the individual social sciences'.

The first issues of the *American Journal of Sociology* also revealed it to be very sympathetic to European sociology. It published two articles by Georg Simmel ('Superiority and subordination as subject-matter of sociology' and 'The persistence of social groups'), an article on Le Play's school of thought '(Introduction to the observation of social facts according to the Le Play method of monographs on families'), two pieces on the status of sociology in Germany and France,[1] and a short introduction to the famous debate about the role of sociology in law faculties. The 'reviews' and 'notes and abstracts' sections, finally, carried several reviews of books published in France and Italy. The *American Journal* was, in organizational terms, very different from the future *Année sociologique*. Published by a university press and edited by colleagues and friends working in the same department, it was an institutional journal and, for the next 10 years, had the support of an emerging academic and professional movement that would result in the establishment of the American Sociological Association.

In France, the appearance of the new American journal was given an enthusiastic welcome as its ideas were similar to 'those that tend to be dominant in France and Germany'. The *Revue de métaphysique et de morale*'s reviewer was, on the other hand, surprised to find that the *Journal* had 'such a broad conception' of sociology, that it dealt with such a wide range of topics, and that so much space was given over to 'Christian tendencies'. The reviewer also regretted the fact that, while it had published several articles on major practical and methodological issues, it published so little on sociology in the strict sense of the term:

> The study of social phenomena in no way depends upon some prior science, nor does it need such a science to demonstrate the excellence of its methods. None of the sociological journals published to date seems to have taken upon itself to prove, 'by walking', that there are phenomena whose proper study is sociology.[2]

Émile Durkheim and his future collaborators obviously got the message.

Plans for a Journal: Negotiations

The idea for a new sociology journal came not from Durkheim himself, but from his future collaborator Célestin Bouglé who, on his return from Germany, suggested launching an international journal to promote sociology. After talking to his friend Paul Fauconnet, he 'urged Durkheim to set up *L'Année sociologique*'.[3] 'We begged him to be its editor', he added. Durkheim himself admitted that this was the case: 'It was you who provoked me.'[4] Durkheim and Bouglé met in Paris in April 1896. And Durkheim made his initial approach to his editor Félix Alcan the following month.

Born into an old Jewish family from Metz, Alcan was a *normalien* with a gift for music. He had an extensive knowledge of music, and was interested in the arts and the social sciences. He realized his ambition of opening a major intellectual bookshop in 1875. Within the space of a few years, the shop at 104 boulevard Saint-Germain had become a major publishing house, producing books on both the social sciences and the human sciences. The launch of both the *Revue historique* (Gabriel Monod) and the *Revue philosophique* (Théodule Ribot) in 1876 gave him great credibility and he went on to publish other major journals and to develop several collections. Durkheim's first two books were published in the 'Bibliothèque de philosophie contemporaine' collection, which was launched in 1880.

Durkheim told Bouglé about his first dealings with Alcan in a letter dated 16 May 1896. The publisher was not keen on the *Année* formula.

'*L'Année philosophique* would not survive without its ministerial subsidy. *L'Année psychologique* is Binet's property.' But Alcan's answer was not 'a definite no'. There was hope and, what was more important, there was a proposal on the table: 'Split the *Année philosophique* in two', so there would be an 'Année philosophique et sociologique', which would be 'published in one volume *for the moment*'. Durkheim was not exactly overjoyed with this 'arrangement' and suspected that the *Année philosophique*'s editor Pillon would reject it.[5]

When Élie Halévy asked how things stood with the plan for a new journal in June, the latter replied: 'The "*Année sociologique*" has gone under.' At the end of November, it was the turn of Paul Lapie, who was teaching in Tunis, to ask Bouglé about how things were going: 'Do you have any plans for the *Année sociologique*?' Lapie wanted to know what his friend intended the journal to be: 'A research tool, or an inventory of discoveries?'[6] Bouglé was, in other words, one of the driving forces behind the project. He was only 26.

Before a real team could be formed, a lot of people had to be convinced that the *Année* was a viable proposition, and it was not until early 1897 that the project got under way. Durkheim exchanged a lot of letters with his future collaborators, who came from three distinct groups. One (Gaston Richard) was a colleague. The second group consisted of three *agrégés de philosophie* from the class of 1893 (Célestin Bouglé and his friends Paul Lapie and Dominique Parodi), and the third of friends of Durkheim's nephew. Mauss, who was still in Paris, became what he himself called a 'recruiting agent', and succeeded in interesting five of his friends in the project: Paul Fauconnet, Henri Hubert, Emmanuel Lévy, Albert Milhaud and François Simiand.

For 10 years, Gaston Richard was 'one of Durkheim's most devoted and most gifted assistants' (Essetier 1930: 364–5), but we do not know how or when he took on that role.[7] Émile and Gaston were much the same age and shared the same interests in morality, law, criminality and the evolution of societies. They were also both critical of the work that was being done on criminal anthropology and ethnographic sociology. In 1892, Richard published his 'Essai sur l'origine de droit' – Durkheim called it 'a fine effort' – and then published two essays on questions that were of great interest to his colleague – one on criminality, the other on ethnographic sociology and history – in the *Revue philosophique*. In his discussion of homicide in Europe, Richard (1895) demonstrated that 'the determinant influence of race is not apparent anywhere', and recalled that social life is characterized by constraint (and therefore inhibition) and implies internalization. It was a Durkheimian formula.

Making Converts

The *Année sociologique* project entered a decisive phase when Durkheim succeeded in persuading Félix Alcan to publish it. He discussed the possibility that colleagues such as Sylvain Lévy, Séailles and especially Théodule Ribot might be interested in contributing. He was afraid that the editor of the *Revue philosophique* (who was not keen on the *Année* formula either) would 'not look favourably on what we are doing', and therefore advised Marcel Mauss not to 'turn him against our project; otherwise he might see it as a competitor'.[8] Durkheim was also eager to win the support of his nephew's friends, including Emmanuel Lévy (1871–1943), who had just successfully defended his doctoral thesis in law (1896) and been appointed to a post as *chargé de cours* in the Lyon faculty of law. 'Tell him I would be very happy to have him as a collaborator . . . I could not replace him.'[9] Albert Milhaud (born in 1871, *agrégé d'histoire* 1894) was more of a problem: 'Can we make use of him and, if so, what for?', asked a rather puzzled Durkheim. As for Milhaud's brother Edgar – 'the philosopher' as Durkheim called him – there was no point, he thought, as he was in Germany, where he spent long months collecting data on trade-unionism, the cooperative movement and sociology. Finally, the uncle asked his nephew to ask some of his teachers at the École pratique to contribute feature articles: 'You should sound them out about this.'

Durkheim made repeated approaches to Célestin Bouglé:

> First of all, I have never seen the difference between the formula you have accepted and the one I put forward. Let me say once more that I never dreamed of saying that one can be a sociologist without having a background in psychology, or that sociology was anything other than a psychology. What I did say was that collective psychology cannot simply be deduced from individual psychology because a new factor – association – has intervened and has transformed the psychic raw material. That factor is the source of all the differences and of everything that is new. A phenomenon of individual psych. has as its substratum an individual consciousness, and a phenomenon of collective psych. has as its substratum a group of individual minds [*consciences*].[10]

Durkheim hoped that his *Suicide*, which dealt with this question, would 'clear up any misunderstandings'. He also hoped that future collaborators would 'bring out what we have in common', and saw the coming *Année sociologique* as 'an interesting event' because, 'for the first time, a group of sociologists will be seen to set themselves the same task and work together towards the same goal'. That did not mean, he added, that 'everyone has exactly the same formula'. Durkheim assured Bouglé that 'the preface will not embarrass anyone'. Bouglé was happy to commit himself to such a collective undertaking. His stay in Germany had allowed him to discover research institutes and to realize that similar collectively based intellectual organizations could be useful to sociology in France (Bouglé 1930b: 35).

Everyone was beginning to 'get down to work', and not least Durkheim, who had already approached Simmel, who had promised to send him an article of 40–50 pages entitled 'Die Selbsterhaltung der Gesellschaft'. He laid down rules for the reviews (such as 'do not go back to anything before 1896') and was coordinating the work of his future collaborators by assigning them sections or parts (the moral part of the 'legal and moral sociology' section and the 'general sociology' section, for example, were assigned to Célestin Bouglé and Paul Lapie), suggesting books for review and asking for suggestions. 'Tell me which ones you want, and I will keep my eyes open.' 'Let us hope', he wrote to Bouglé in December 1896, 'that it all works.'

The Durkheim family moved from 179 boulevard de Talence to no 218 at the beginning of April 1897; moving house is always a major upheaval. The new house was big: more than 200 square metres, with a huge garden surrounded by a wrought-iron fence to the rear. It took Émile some 30 minutes to get to the university unless he took the omnibus (on rails, but horse-drawn), or, later, the tram. *L'Année sociologique*'s letterhead gave 218 boulevard de Talence as the journal's editorial address.

Durkheim's intention was to 'devote myself almost completely' to the new project. The most important thing was, obviously, to recruit collaborators. He thought he had won the support of Emmanuel Lévy, but was worried because he had not had 'the slightest answer' from him. 'He is an element that would be very useful to the combination.' He had also acted on Marcel Mauss's suggestion, and was hoping to make contact with François Simiand, whose cooperation seemed to him to be decisive: 'I would like to have a direct answer from him before I go to talk to Alcan.'[11]

Was Durkheim prepared to make concessions? He taught a course on psychology in 1896–7. He continued his discussions with Célestin Bouglé and Paul Lapie in an attempt to overcome their last objections to his theory of the difference between sociology and psychology. He insisted that his young collaborators had to agree about 'the need to do sociology *sociologically* – in other words, not to reduce that science to something it was not'. Lapie challenged this position: sociology might well be independent of the sciences of mind, but not to such an extent as to make it a 'self-sufficient science': its links with the other sciences had to be asserted.[12] Durkheim replied immediately: 'I do not see sociology as anything other than a psychology, but it is a *psychology sui generis*.' And he added that he insisted that 'the emphasis has to be on the *sui generis*'. Lapie replied on his own behalf and that of Bouglé: 'In that sense, we are in agreement.'

Durkheim and Lapie met at the beginning of May, but Lapie found their conversation 'long and quite confused'. The young collaborator was shy, and his protests at what appeared to him to be some 'dubious' statements were muted: 'I am not qualified to discuss these matters with a gentleman who is so well-documented and so sure about what he is saying', he said in an attempt to justify himself. What surprised him most was the importance Durkheim attached to religion: 'Basically, he explains everything in terms of religion at the moment. The taboo on marrying relatives is religious; punishment is religious; everything is religious.'[13]

Durkheim appeared to have strong views about the question of the relationship between psychology and sociology. He was, Lapie pointed out, 'much less of a psychologist when he speaks than when he writes'. 'We must', Durkheim told his young collaborator, 'do sociology sociologically, and then see if the facts we have observed can be reduced to psychological or other laws.' He was, however, rather vague about the second stage of this search for laws. 'He leaves that very unclear', remarked Lapie. But he did allow himself to be persuaded: he found Durkheim 'charming', and agreed to 'work on the *Année*'.

On the other hand, he completely disagreed with Durkheim as to how the future journal should be organized. Its organization seemed to him to be 'somewhat artificial', 'unclear' and full of gaps and uncertainties: 'It seems to me that the way the future *Année's* bibliography has been divided up is not very systematic. There is something to satisfy everyone. Wouldn't we do better the follow the natural divisions of science?' Lapie did not dare to make suggestions to Durkheim himself, but did confide in his friend Célestin Bouglé. When it came to the moral sociology section, which was his responsibility, Lapie was puzzled. What were the section's limits? How could juridical sociology be divorced from moral sociology? While he hoped that Durkheim would define his area more clearly, he was afraid that he would not find many books in this area, and that he would have nothing to contribute. He was still not enthusiastic: 'I'm not convinced that I will be able to write four lines.'[14]

Célestin Bouglé had been given responsibility for the 'general sociology' section, but his discussions were not restricted to the choice of books for review. They also raised issues of general strategy, and especially relations with other journals, and with their collaborators. There was a great deal of work to be done and many contacts to be set up with bookshops and publishers. A circular had to be sent to them. Durkheim wanted to reassure them that 'the project is commercially viable, and therefore serious'. Most publishers agreed to cooperate. 'We are beginning to make ourselves known. There is no difficulty in having the books delivered', he told Bouglé. He also complained that there was going to be a lot of work; in the space of two months, he had written 'something like 150 letters'.[15]

It was from the outset a team with a definite leader, but Durkheim wanted it to work in a spirit of cooperation and mutual aid. 'The most important thing is that the *Année sociologique* must be a mutual-aid society for its members.'[16] Durkheim consulted his colleagues, made suggestions as to how the work should be organized and which books should be reviewed, but he was in charge. It was he who coordinated the work, laid down the rules, commissioned the articles, distributed the tasks and sent books to the contributors. 'Everyone is getting down to work. I am beginning to see the meaning of the individual articles. Let's hope that everything works.'[17]

A few months later, Durkheim said that he was impressed by everyone's devotion. 'It's true that that also puts me under an obligation', he added.[18] Bouglé and Lapie were 'full of ardour' and wrote him letters that were 'full of devotion and very zealous'. Gaston Richard and Emmanuel Lévy had already set to work. Marcel Mauss had both general and specialist (religious sociology) skills, and it was obvious from the outset that his would be a major role. His workload would be 'heavy', as his uncle put it, and his section was to be 'one of the most important'. Durkheim gave him some freedom to choose which books to review and he was, in a sense, 'left to his own devices'. His freedom was short-lived. In May 1897, Durkheim wrote to tell him: 'Yours is the only section I haven't looked at so far. It's time we got down to it.' He then asked Marcel to draw up a list of the books that were, in his view, most important and 'of most use to sociology'. Visibly annoyed at seeing that his nephew had not 'set to work', he lost his temper: 'None of our collaborators is so late.' He advised him to 'get on with it'.

'Let Us Set to Work with a Good Heart'

'I've got down to work too. Everything is coming along.' By June 1897, Durkheim already had a good idea of what the first volume of *L'Année sociologique* would look like: 'I think it will be interesting.' He had a lot of work to do. There were books to be ordered and distributed, and journals to go through (fortunately there were 'not very many of them'). Simmel's article had to be translated (several passages were awkward), and a title had to be found for it (Durkheim's first suggestion was 'How social forms sustain themselves'). And lots of letters had to be written to publishers. 'You have no idea how much trouble this *Année sociologique* is causing me. It is a source of tribulations to me', he told his nephew.[19] He was completely 'overwhelmed', especially as he was also 'drowning in work': there were exam scripts to be marked, and reviews to be written (one of Gaston Richard's *Le Socialisme et les sciences sociales*, and one on Antonio Labriola's *Essais sur la conception matérialiste de l'histoire*). 'I am very tired', he told Bouglé.[20]

Durkheim was satisfied with his collaborators' work and was feeling fairly confident. 'You have all shown such devotion that it would be very surprising if we can't do something good.'[21] 'We can produce an interesting and useful *Année sociologique* for 1898. The more progress I make, the more I feel that our work will be good, and everyone seems to feel the same. Let us set to work with a good heart.'[22] Durkheim quite often went to Paris to talk to his publisher Alcan, to see his nephew Marcel, Henri Hubert and Célestin Bouglé, and to recruit potential collaborators, including Henri Muffang, a colleague of Bouglé's at the lycée in Saint-Brieuc, Dominique Parodi and his nephew's friend Paul Fauconnet.

The geographical distances involved meant that communications were not always easy. Durkheim was in Bordeaux, Mauss in England, Muffang in Brittany, and Emmanuel Lévi in Toulouse. In 1897, Paul Fauconnet was appointed to a teaching post in philosophy at the lycée in Roanne, while Paul Lapie found a position at the lycée in Pau. Lapie wanted to work in higher education. His friend Célestin Bouglé shared the same ambition, and was even thinking of applying to Bordeaux. Durkheim was very pleased to hear that, and said that he would be happy to speak to the Rector on his behalf: 'I'm sure we can do good work together.'[23] Durkheim was now acting both as team-leader and 'patron', as Clark (1973) puts it.

Each of his collaborators had his own research and publishing programme. Bouglé had just published an article entitled 'What is sociology?' and was working on his doctoral thesis on equality. Mauss was abroad. He first went to Holland, where he met Caland, and was hoping to finish an article on Spinoza. He then went to England. Hubert was writing his first articles, including some reviews, for the *Revue archéologique* and the *Revue historique*, and was preparing to write a thesis on the Syrian goddess. François Simiand was at the Fondation Thiers (1896–99), and was writing on 'The English mechanics' strike and trade-unionism' for the *Manuel général de l'instruction publique* (February and March 1898). Paul Lapie, who was now back from Tunis, published a long text on 'Deductive morality' in the *Revue de métaphysique et de morale* in 1897.

Organizing the various sections of *L'Année psychologique* was still proving problematic. 'It is giving me a lot of trouble', admitted Durkheim.[24] For the moment, 'being complete' and covering every branch of sociology was, however, out of the question. 'It would not be a good idea to be complete from the outset', he told Bouglé. 'We have to leave enough room for future developments.' When there were not enough books to make up a separate section, as was the case with aesthetic sociology, they were included in the 'miscellaneous' category. There were also contingent factors: 'aesthetics' was supposed to be the responsibility of a certain [Henri] Ouvré, but he, noted Durkheim, 'was definitely more interested in writing novels'.

Durkheim regularly consulted his collaborators, giving them advice and making suggestions, which were often specific: shorten the article, cut the repetitions, and so on. 'I'm getting involved in the smallest details', he told Bouglé. He made certain cuts himself. He was generous with his encouragement and congratulations: 'Very lively, very interesting analysis.' 'Clear and interesting exposition.'

Not everything was simple: the books he ordered did not always turn up, and there were delays and misunderstandings. When his nephew was very late in giving him his list of books, he lost his temper: 'It's a real disappointment to me.' And he added: 'I had a moment of discouragement.' He complained that his nephew was not taking the work seriously: 'Our undertaking is, where you are concerned, an impossible undertaking.' He then calmed down and adopted a more conciliatory tone: 'Try to get a sense of what is useful and feasible.' Taking 'religious sociology' – which his nephew 'knew better' than him – as an example, he showed him how 'useful' the journal could be for sociologists and for people interested in sociology: it could familiarize them with the problems raised by the discipline, 'bring together those books that can advance the questions' and finally 'extract the whole residue' – in other words, show what seems to come out of the books being compared.

Although he was outlining a method (which he himself used when reviewing books on law), Durkheim was careful not to be too directive: 'There are no absolutes in any of the above.' The most important thing was, in his view, to 'interest the public'; otherwise, the sociologists would say that all this has nothing to do with them. And, well aware of the fact that it could be done, he concluded: 'Try to see what is important, what is feasible. And do it. Don't get bogged down in details and minutiae . . . Don't ignore something good because something else looks better. That won't work.'[25] A few days later, he repeated the same advice: 'I stress that we should not be perfect from the outset. We have to leave room for future developments.' Although he would have liked to paint a 'picture of what is being done in sociology', Durkheim was enough of a realist to know that they had to 'concentrate on what is important, productive or useful'. And, comparing his project for a journal with the *Année biologique*, he concluded: 'We are even less interested in current developments. Our goal is not so much to paint a picture of an existing science as to help to constitute a science in the making.'[26]

Durkheim also believed that 'the sight of a group of workers with a common purpose and working towards the same goal will be a spectacle of considerable interest'.[27] A common purpose? Durkheim wanted *L'Année sociologique* to be 'generally homogeneous, but that homogeneity should not detract from each contributor's independence'.[28] His discussions with Bouglé had reassured him that this would be the case, but he still complained to his nephew: 'I thought Bouglé had come over to my side, but he still hasn't made his mind up.'[29]

At one point, Durkheim thought that he was going to 'lose' his nephew, and reminded him that he was counting on his support because his work on religion was so important to him:

> You are one of the lynchpins of the combination and you are very important, not only because you are in Paris, but also because I foresee and hope that the *Année sociologique* will elaborate a theory which, despite its objectivist tendencies, will be the complete antithesis of historical materialism, which is so crude and so simplistic, and which will make religion, and not the economy, the matrix for social facts.

That was the 'line' that would characterize the new journal. A few months later, the uncle reminded his nephew that 'Basically, the sociological importance of the religious phenomenon is the culmination of everything I have done.'[30] Mauss took on the major responsibility of editing the 'religious sociology' section. The uncle was quite optimistic about the journal's impact: 'It could have a considerable moral effect.' And he concluded: The main thing is to do something, and to do it well.'[31]

Durkheim's goal was to publish the first volume of the *Année* in March 1898 at the latest. At the beginning of July 1897, his plan was to receive the manuscripts in late November or early December, and to get them to the printer in January 1898.

A Moment of Discouragement

'My proofs [of *Suicide*], my lectures, *L'Année sociologique*: that's enough for one man', Durkheim told his nephew. He was 'an indefatigable worker', noted his admiring dean in June 1897. He was 'giving as much of himself' as ever, and was now seen in academic circles as 'the leader of a school and a theoretician, rather than as a man for practical details'. A remarkably eloquent speaker, 'clear and decisive', remarked Dean Stapfer.

At the end of the academic year, Durkheim also began to write up his lectures on Rousseau. His teaching load for 1897–8 was the same as the previous year, with a course on sociology ('General physics of morals and law') and one on psychology. He also had to conduct tutorials for candidates for the *agrégation*. The students who followed Durkheim's lectures between 1897 and 1890 once more included Abel Aubin (an *étudiant libre*), Jean-Paul Hourticq and Charles Lalo. All three were candidates for the *agrégation*. The blind Albert Léon was still attending his lectures.

Durkheim was beginning to find teaching 'a burden'. His work no longer had any focus. He had to abandon his preferred studies for the sake of 'less urgent, less important work', and had to devote part of his time to promoting a discipline (pedagogy) that seemed to him to be 'more practical' but 'less essential' than sociology. He complained to his nephew: 'The time is coming when I will not get much out of teaching, which remains a heavy burden.'[32] And a few days later, he admitted: 'I am a little tired.'

He then received an 'unexpected letter' from Théodule Ribot informing him that 'a group of politicians [want] to have a chair in social philosophy' established at the Collège de France for Jean Izoulet, the author of *La Cité moderne* who taught philosophy at the Lycée Condorcet. What was to be done? Durkeim was well aware of the prestige of the Collège, which had been founded to meet 'new needs' and to encourage 'a taste for science and a love of positive knowledge' (Durkheim 1975[1918b]). He was, on the other hand, surprised to be approached by his colleague, who suggested that he should do something. He was uncertain what to do. 'I have no objections to the establishment of a chair; if it is established, it is my duty to apply for it.' But he could not hide his disappointment: 'If the course I was asked to try out here had not been a success, no one would have dreamed of establishing a chair at the Collège de France.'[33]

A few days later, Émile wrote: 'I had cheerfully come to terms with the possibility that Izoulet might be appointed. I have never aspired to administrative success. But I would have liked to have some influence on current developments. I now realize that there is no hope of that.' He had no illusions about the chair, but he insisted on drawing attention to 'the loss of face' he would suffer if he were deemed to be unworthy to finish the work he had begun.[34] He wrote to director of higher education Louis Liard to let him know, for the record, of his great desire to be appointed to the post, 'if it is established and if you deem me worthy of it, Monsieur le Ministre'. Reminding Liard that, just 10 years ago, he had been tasked with introducing teaching on social science into the university, he added that 'public opinion will not agree that I am unworthy of it because someone else will be appointed to continue in Paris an experiment I was tasked with attempting here'.[35] He would have liked to give his family, and especially his in-laws, the impression that 'all this business leaves me cold'.[36] Nothing could have been further from the truth.

Durkheim was also 'deeply disappointed' with the reception given to his *Suicide*.

> I thought that my *Suicide* would clear up the ambiguities and determine an agreement. I now see that that will not be the case. I still sense the same misgivings in what people write to me . . . This one challenges one thing, and that one challenges another. I am beginning to see that I am powerless against prevailing opinion. . . . My only ambition is to see to it that my work is not sterile. I do not want to be praised for my talent or my style, but I do want to feel that all the trouble I have taken has served some purpose.[37]

There was no longer anything to spur him on. 'Under these conditions, what is the point of *L'Année sociologique*? It is already causing me sleepless nights, but where is it getting me?' He had no alternative but to 'concentrate on teaching' and give up working on the family in order to concentrate on the history of doctrines: 'That will fill the void in my professional life.' He tried to convince himself that 'that is what I am going to do' in an attempt to give some meaning to his life. He expressly asked Mauss not to talk to the other collaborators about 'his plans'.

Giving up the idea of publishing the first volume of *L'Année sociologique* was, on the other hand, out of the question. 'But I have more or less decided to give up when it is published. I can't do any more.' Durkheim, who thought he had 'developed a lot' and had 'reached maturity', was beginning to have self-doubts, and the 'stubborn resistance' he had encountered made him feel guilty about having dragged his nephew into all this: 'One day, I will tell you about the dream in which I saw you abandon me. Perhaps you would do well to abandon me while there is still time . . . Think well before you commit yourself completely.'[38] Although he was 'very tired' and 'very annoyed', Durkheim was determined not to 'give in' and, apologizing for his 'intellectual megalomania', cheered up: 'This *Année* does not look too bad, and it could be so good and so useful. I still feel great affection for it.' He was anything but a dilettante, and he now began to 'work a lot' in order to 'forget myself' and not 'see the time slipping by'. He was soon 'up to his neck in work'. Even when he did have a moment's rest and could spend an afternoon in the country, he took 'some exam scripts to mark' with him.

Far from contemplating abandoning his uncle, Marcel Mauss reassured him and gave him many signs of affection and encouragement. 'It's true that there don't need to be many of us', replied Durkheim: 'The fact that there are two of us is enough to make us stand out.'[39] But the work was, as he complained to Paul Lapie, 'tedious': it took up a lot of time and was 'monotonous'. And it was not very interesting: 'There is nothing sociological or personal about it.'[40] Other collaborators such as Emmanuel Lévy and Albert Milhaud shared that view and found 'nothing that is really sociological' in the books they had to analyse.

At the beginning of April, the uncle went to Paris to visit Victor Brochard, who was professor of philosophy at the Sorbonne, 'out of curiosity and friendship'. And he also saw Marcel Mauss, Célstin Bouglé and his nephew's friend Paul Fauconnet, who he wanted to recruit for *L'Année* in order to 'relieve himself of some of the burden'. Shortly after his return to Épinal, he left for a holiday in Adelboden (Switzerland). He was back in Épinal by the end of August, and had every intention of staying there until the end of September. He told all his collaborators to try to be ready by the beginning of November. The goal was to publish in February.[41]

'We Will Do Better Another Time'

By the end of October, 'all the work on the *Année* is well advanced'. Durkheim had almost finished his own manuscript. And he had just received Simmel's text. 'The work is interesting', he wrote to Célestin Bouglé. 'Like all these very general articles, it has the flaw of being a whole sociology in 50 printed pages because it touches upon so many things. But it is lively, pleasant to read and quite in keeping with the general tone of the *Année*.' He thanked his young colleague for 'being kind enough to offer to help [him] with the translation'.[42]

And then he changed his mind: the text was too long, and the title was untranslatable: 'I had thought of "The main types of organization that allow social groups to preserve their unity".' He asked Bouglé to help him 'condense' it. When Bouglé sent his corrections to Simmel, the latter did not hide his disappointment. Durkheim went back to 'struggle' with the translation, which had been revised and corrected by Simmel: 'I'm doing everything I can to lighten it a little.' The translation was fairly 'personal', and Durkheim had no qualms about cutting some passages (including the paragraph on honour).

The Dreyfus Affair complicated relations between Simmel and Durkheim still further. Durkheim asked the author to cut a passage that might have disastrous implications for him and the journal: 'They'll describe me as a Zionist.' Simmel agreed to the cut, but did not inform Durkheim that he was Jewish himself (even though he and his family had converted to Protestantism). His German colleague's silence 'somewhat surprised' Durkheim.[43]

It seemed that all the collaborators would meet their deadlines. Durkheim was almost ready to send the manuscript to the printer; all that remained for him to do was write the preface. A few days later, he realized that, 'unfortunately, the manuscript is still not complete'. Why the delay? There had been 'silences' and delays from Albert Milhaud and Emmanuel Lévy, whose loyalties were still uncertain.[44] The main problem, however, was 'the nephew's indisposition', though Durkheim did concede that Marcel's task was a 'heavy' one. The uncle chivvied the nephew – 'stick to the limits I set you' – and advised him not to strive after perfection: 'We will do better another time.' He also reminded him of his own work ethic:

> You also have to train yourself to get all your pleasure from work, and not think of anything else. That has to be an absolute rule. Everything else is contingent, and you should not attach any importance to it. I apply that rule to myself, and I feel quite detached from all the things that used to fascinate me.[45]

The thing about his nephew that annoyed and disappointed him was his idleness and especially his 'fine theory of blessed tranquillity' and his happy-go-lucky attitude. 'Think hard about all that', he told Marcel, even though he did not believe that his nephew would be willing to change his ways.

The manuscript was sent to the printer at the end of December: 900 pages. Durkheim was afraid that the publisher would find it 'too voluminous'. This gave him a 'moment's respite': 'It's the first for a very long time, and I am enjoying it.'[46] The publisher was 'very satisfied' and told Durkheim that the *Année* was 'a very interesting ensemble'. That obviously delighted Durkheim, who was busy writing the preface. He also consulted his close collaborators, including Mauss, Bouglé and Simiand, asking them for their opinion about what he should add and what he should cut. He asked them to tell him if they were in 'complete agreement about the ideas expressed in it'.

It would soon be time to correct the proofs, but Durkheim was already working on other things. He had begun to write the article on 'Individual and collective representations' (1974[1898]) that he had promised to the *Revue de métaphysique et de morale*, and had accepted Ribot's invitation to write an article about 'the moral ideal' for the *Revue philosophique*. That project did not come to anything. He was also following with great attention the work that Marcel Mauss and Henri Hubert were doing on sacrifice, and offered his close collaboration: 'It would give me great pleasure to work with you . . . I am enchanted with the idea of working with you.' At the same time, he was anxious to 'let everyone work on their own initiative and to intervene only very indirectly'. He was generous with his encouragement: that was 'a very important piece of work'. And he advised his nephew to devote himself completely to it, even if it meant putting his thesis to one side: 'Let's not rush things. And arriving at the Sorbonne with a certain authority is no bad thing either.'

Durkheim was already thinking about the second volume of *L'Année sociologique*, and he also said that he intended to publish Hubert and Mauss's memoir on sacrifice and his two lectures on the definition of religion at the same time. That would, he believed, 'set a very high standard': 'That way, people will see that religion is not up in the air; your work is proof of that. And they will see that this work relates to a very general conception that may have very many applications.' He concluded: 'The *Année* will have less variety, but that does not matter.'[47] Durkheim said the same to Henri Hubert: 'Next year in *L'Année sociologique*, I am thinking of stressing the idea I talked to you about, namely that the religious fact is the source of all the rest, that it contains them in an embryonic state. That is all the more important in that religion is regarded as something extra-sociological.' If he had one hope, it was that this 'small example' would have a 'certain import'.[48]

Durkheim was not necessarily looking to expand his team of collaborators, but he did agree to meet a friend of Henri Hubert's who had been at the École normale supérieure with him. Emmanuel de Martonne (1873–1955) was an *agrégé d'histoire* with an interest in geography.[49] As he wrote to Hubert, Durkheim thought it unlikely that Martonne would ever become 'one of ours'. He was disappointed by his conversation with Martonne, who admitted from the outset that he 'did not [know] what sociology was'. His very tone surprised Durkheim: 'I ask myself why, under these conditions, he agreed to make contact with me, even on a temporary basis.'[50] He was also irritated by the young *agrégé*'s attitude and warned him about his 'good opinion of himself'. He did not want him to join the journal 'out of the goodness of his soul and condescension'. He in fact took an active dislike to the young man: 'I bent over backwards not to break off relations on the spot . . . I do not see how we can use him.'[51] Two things were, he reminded Hubert, indispensable if what he called 'our joint undertaking' was to work: 'a common faith' and 'great mutual trust'. As Durkheim had realized from their first conversation, the problem with Martonne was that he 'was not of our faith'.[52] He never contributed to the journal.

The team that worked on the first volume of *L'Année sociologique* was far from homogeneous. Indeed, Henri Muffang, a supporter of the anthroposociological school was invited to review works by members of his own school even though it had aroused the 'suspicions' of Durkheim. Henri Hubert was astonished: 'Who is this Muffang? He wrote an imbecilic review of Lapouge's book. It was worse than stupid.'[53] Muffang also contributed to the *Revue internationale de sociologie*, publishing an article on 'Schoolboys and peasants in Saint-Brieuc' in 1897. The following year, he translated and introduced O. Ammon's 'History of an idea: anthroposociology' for the same journal. Muffang was quite favourably disposed to socioanthropology and described its task as 'revealing the importance of ethnic factors in the evolution of historical civilizations'. He described the *Essai sur l'inégalité des races humaines* as Gobineau's 'masterpiece'. He did not take offence when anthroposociology was criticized for its 'over-vague generalizations', and suggested that local councils should allow the systematic collection of anthropological statistics in schools and barracks'. That was, he believed, the only way to 'dispel misunderstandings' and 'make discoveries' (Muffang 1898). As might have been predicted, Muffang did not remain with *L'Année sociologique* for very long.

Publication

February 1898: it was time to correct the first, and then the second, proofs. The printer was not dragging his feet. On the contrary, he was 'working very fast', and at a speed that surprised Durkheim: 'I'm all on edge . . . we have to keep up with him.' The spelling of names and the titles of books had to be checked, and the reviews had to be copy-edited. Durkheim scarcely had time to 'catch his breath'. He was busy with the lay-out and drawing up a list, at Alcan's request, of the journals and individuals who should be sent review copies. He was already thinking of exchanges with other scholarly journals (*Revue d'histoire des religions*, *American Journal of Sociology*, etc.) and wondering who could 'review us' for the *Revue philosophique*.[54] By the end of February, the first volume of *L'Année sociologique* was in print. Durkheim made no secret of his worries: 'There is every reason to fear that we are not meeting existing needs . . . I have the feeling that I have done everything that is humanly possible to ensure that it is good, so too bad if it is not a success.' As he himself noted, this was not the 'best time to launch it': the Dreyfus affair began in early 1898.

Durkheim spells out the new journal's goals clearly in the preface. While it is obviously intended to provide a 'complete picture' of sociology and its various currents, it also aims to keep sociologists 'regularly informed of the investigations being performed in the special science: history of law, customs, religion, moral statistics, and so on' (Durkheim 1980[1898–9]: 47). Its goal was, in other words, to provide an 'inventory' of all such resources' by 'indicating what profit sociology can reap' from them. The era of self-justification and approximations was over: 'However underdeveloped our science may be, it has produced sufficient results to warrant its right to exist' (ibid.: 50). The new journal's audience was 'the sociological audience', and that audience was 'very wide, too fashionable but very important' (Mauss 1898: 232).

It was an ambitious project, but Durkheim describes it with a certain modesty and stresses the difficulty of the undertaking and the inevitable trial and error involved. He defines the journal's task as a 'preliminary investigation' designed to 'hasten the progress' of sociology (Durkheim 1980[1898–9]: 47). It was also designed to demonstrate that the special sciences (history, statistics, etc.) complement one another. The need to do so was all the greater because 'there are still too many sociologists who pontificate daily about the law, ethics, and religion with haphazard information or even mere insights from natural philosophy, seemingly unaware that a considerable number of documents on such points have been assembled by historical and ethnographic schools in Germany and England' (ibid.). As for new material, the answer is obvious: such studies must have a definite objective and 'be done methodically'. He loathed the abuse of generalities and fantasy above all else, and the emphasis was therefore on 'studies dealing with more restricted subjects and arising from the [specialized] branches of sociology' (Durkheim 1980[1898–9]: 49).

L'Année sociologique was a collective undertaking and a joint project.

Durkheim describes his first collaborators as 'workers' brought together by an 'instinctive meeting of minds'. He insists that it is not a personal adventure: 'Science, since it is objective, is essentially an impersonal matter and can develop only from collective effort.' His most sincere wish was that 'our attempt [would be] welcomed with interest by all those who are committed to helping sociology grow out of its philosophical phase and take its rightful place among the sciences' (Durkheim 1980[1898–9]: 51). The publication of *L'Année sociologique* marked, in other words, the birth of the new scientific discipline of sociology, or what Paul Fauconnet called 'the Goddess Sociology'. It also allowed a new group of researchers to acquire a greater visibility.

Methodical Work

The journal was divided into two parts, the first devoted to new work [*mémoires originaux*] and the second (which was larger) to reviews, analyses and book listings.

Durkheim was the main contributor. In the first volume, he published a long essay, edited several subsections (on the family, marriage, punishment and social organization) and contributed almost 70 pages of analyses and reviews. The other main contributors were Marcel Mauss (more than 95 pages, including some 15 written in collaboration with Henri Hubert), Gaston Richard (65 pages), François Simiand (55) and Célestin Bouglé (49), followed by, in decreasing order of importance, Henri Hubert, Paul Lapie, Henri Muffang, Albert Milhaud, Emmanuel Lévy, Paul Fauconnet and Dominique Parodi. The most active of their number also edited one or another of the five main sections (the sixth was 'miscellaneous'). With the exception of Mauss, each of them also wrote a short introduction or preface to their section. The sections and editors were as shown in table 10.1.

The largest two sections were devoted to religious sociology and juridic and moral sociology, which accounted for 25 per cent of the pages devoted to reviews respectively, followed by economic sociology (16.5 per cent), criminal sociology (14.5 per cent) and general sociology (11 per cent). The pattern remained much the same for the second volume, except that economic sociology took up more room (20.5 per cent) and criminal sociology less (8.5 per cent).

This was the intellectual world that Durkheim had created over the previous 10 years or so. A variety of disciplines were represented: history, law, anthropology, political economy, criminology and demography. The research programme was focused on a few main themes, such as the family, religion, morality, crime and punishment. Methodological issues took precedence. Even though no section or subsection was devoted to them, they were everywhere. Durkheim and his collaborators were obviously intent upon their conception of sociology, its object and its method. The journal's intended audience was one of informed readers.

Table 10.1 *L'Année Sociologique*: section editors

Section 1	General sociology	Célestin Bouglé
Section 2	Religious sociology	Marcel Mauss, with the assistance of Henri Hubert for the 'Myths' subsection
Section 3	Juridic and moral sociology	Paul Lapie. Three subsections edited by Durkheim, one by Emmanuel Lévy (Property law), and one (Miscellaneous) by Durkheim with Mauss and Lévy
Section 4	Criminal sociology	Gaston Richard
Section 5	Economic sociology	François Simiand (subsections in collaboration with Albert Milhaud)
Section 6	Miscellaneous	Anthroposociology (Muffang) Sociogeography (Durkheim) Demography (Fauconnet and Parodi)

A considerable number of texts, books and articles in a wide range of languages were analysed or reviewed. Most were written in French, but some were in English, German or Italian. The first problem facing any learned journal is the choice of texts to be published or reviewed. The journal covered a vast domain, and its frontiers were ill-defined. How, wondered Durkheim, was one to choose. In his view, some journals and books were automatically ruled out, including the *Revue internationale de sociologie*: 'I don't think we would get much out of that.' Differences of opinion, theoretical and otherwise, did not, on the other hand, prevent him from recognizing the importance of the contribution of authors such as the German sociologist Simmel (one article and one review), the American sociologist Giddings, the Italian criminologist Ferri, or Gabriel Tarde. *L'Année*'s choice of authors and books defined the contours of sociology as a discipline. Indeed, in Durkheim's view, the lack of documentation meant that sociology needed the help of other disciplines, and especially history. It had a lot to give in return. Durkheim believed that the two disciplines 'naturally tend to blend with each other': 'Once subject to comparison, history does not become distinctly different from sociology.' And he happily cited his teacher Fustel de Coulanges, 'who liked to repeat that true sociology is history' (Durkheim 1980[1898–9]: 48, 49).

'Methodical' analysis meant developing a new method of analysis. 'Playing the role of the sort of judge who passes sentence and rates talent' was no longer enough. The author and the critic were not on different sides; they were collaborators: 'Our role must be to extract the objective materials from the works we are studying, namely suggestive phenomena and promising views . . . for however slight a book's substantive value, it is a corresponding gain for science' (Durkheim 1980[1898–9]: 51).

A New Research Programme

The specialist research areas that were of most interest to Durkheim and his collaborators were juridic and moral sociology, and religious sociology. Durkheim himself devoted a lot of energy to the former, and reviewed more than 15 books on the family, morality, punishment and social organization. They dealt with primitive or ancient societies, totemism, taboo, the clan and kinship. All this was not far removed from religion, and to some extent the 'moral sociology' section overlapped with 'religious sociology'.

That religious sociology was the second most important section is clear testimony both to that area's importance to the Durkheimians, and to Marcel Mauss's role in the team. The way in which the section was divided up gives the impression that the section dealt with a wealth of objects and phenomena: primitive religion, domestic cults, beliefs and practices pertaining to the dead, popular cults, rituals, myths, and so on. A short subsection is devoted to 'the great religions in general'. The approach is obviously comparative and allows for reviews of studies dealing with several different religions, different historical periods and different regions, countries or continents. The whole scientific work in which Mauss had been steeped since his studies of the history of religions and his trip to Holland is there: Caland and his studies of ancient India, Steinmetz and his analysis of punishment in primitive societies, Max Müller, the English school of anthropology. Most of these studies dealt with so-called primitive societies. As Mauss put it in his review of the first volume of *L'Année sociologique*: 'Sociologists must attach the greatest importance to the study of the elementary social structures of so-called non-civilised societies . . . Any social fact must first be studied by looking at its crudest aspects' (Mauss 1898: 232).

L'Année sociologique pooled information, discussed a wide variety of books and organized the intellectual division of labour around a number of 'fields'. As a result, it resembled what Terry N. Clark (1968c) calls a 'research centre'. The journal's editorial director agreed to work as a member of a team, and to take into consideration – or even allow himself to be influenced by – his younger collaborators. He had, for instance, no hesitations about recognizing the 'originality' of Mauss's study, 'Religion and the origins of penal law' (1969[1897]) or about acknowledging his debt to it.[55]

The journal provided Durkheim and his collaborators with a showcase, as the reviews highlighted the work of the members of the new team. Some used short reviews as a form of self-advertisement. The practice of reviewing one another's books did not, on the other hand, lead to complacency, as we can see from Gaston Richard's review (1898b) of *Suicide*. Not only did Richard criticize Durkheim for his holism; he also rejected the individual/collective action dichotomy on the grounds that both were 'facts in all social life'. And astonishing as it may seem, he also defended the notion of imitation, which was not, he argued, the same thing as fashion: 'No one commits suicide unless he is more of an imitator than the average man, because imitation is a psychic reflex whose intensity is proportional to the weakness of the will.' Richard nonetheless defended Durkheim over one central issue, namely the normality of criminality and punishment.[56] It took a lot of courage to be so critical of the editorial director of the new *Année sociologique*.

Differences of Opinion

It is true that the various members of the team still had their differences of opinion, especially when it came to the relationship between individual and society. The debate sparked by Durkheim's first books was far from closed. Three years after the publication of *The Rules of Sociological Method*, sociology's great problem was still that of its specificity, and therefore of its relationship with other disciplines, and especially biology and psychology. 'What might a sociology in the true sense be?', asked Bouglé in a popularizing article for the *Revue de Paris* (Bouglé 1897).[57] According to Bouglé, 'social phenomena are, at bottom, psychological phenomena because they result from the interaction between individual minds [*consciences*]'. He then immediately adds that they are a special kind of psychological phenomena, and that 'minds' must be understood as meaning a relationship rather than 'individual minds'. And the reason why Franklin H. Giddings's *Principles of Sociology* caught his attention is that the American sociologist had succeeded in developing a sociology based upon the idea that all social facts are the products of interaction between individuals and of communications between consciousnesses.

The *Année* team was, in other words, trying to get beyond the individual/ society dichotomy while still recognizing the role of the individual. Bouglé's point of view was shared by Paul Lapie, who suggested in his review of Labriola's book *Materialismo storico* that historical materialism should give way to a 'psychological naturalism': 'Sociology is to psychology what the science of the complex is to the science of the simple . . . social facts may well have properties that are different from those of individual facts, but it is still the case that the explanation for them lies in those facts' (Lapie: 1898a: 277).

And what of the boundary between science and politics? Political preoccupations appear to be absent from the pages of *L'Année sociologique*: there was no section or subsection devoted to politics, and no general considerations as to the social or political role of sociology. And yet politics was everywhere in its discussions of the links between sociology and morality, and its analyses of books on socialism, trade unions and professional corporations, property law and depopulation.

There were many references to historical materialism, which had become 'fashionable'. 'The materialist conception of history was in fashion', Lapie noted, 'as one can see from every page of *L'Année sociologique*.' Lapie himself wrote a long critical analysis of Antonio Labriola's book: historical materialism had lost its *nom de guerre* and 'fortunately', he concluded, had calmed down and become 'circumspect' (1898a: 270).The *Année*'s collaborators all had the same criticisms to make of historical materialism and challenged the dominant role it gave to the economy. Its mistake, in Bouglé's view, was to see the economy as the 'one key to the whole of social evolution' and to regard 'superstructures' as epiphenomena. Moral forces and ideas should also be taken into account. Gaston Richard devoted large sections of his *Le Socialisme et la science sociale* to a harsh critique of Marxism.

There were, however, obvious differences of political opinion between the *Année*'s collaborators. Not all of them believed that socialism and social science were incompatible – far from it. François Simiand, for instance, feared that Richard's critique of Marxism – it was '30 years out of date' – would lead to a rejection of socialism in its entirety. He believed that socialism would always be reborn in new forms 'so long as one fact – poverty – remains constant, and that one feeling – the desire to abolish poverty – influences a few men' (Simiand 1898: 486).

Paul Lapie, for his part, had serious reservations about the sociologist's political role: impartiality was, in his view, the essential precondition for scientific research, and a clear distinction had to be made between judgement and observation. And while he accepted that theory could not be divorced from practice, he argued that the relationship between the two should be one of succession and not identity: 'practice follows theory'. Lapie was confident that, if sociological truths could be discovered, they would soon be transformed into practical rules and would 'make it possible to attain the ideal defined by consciousness'. Gaston Richard was rather sceptical about sociological predictions, on the grounds that they would be a 'sort of divination or vague intuition about the societies of the future'; he defended the idea of an applied sociology with more modest ambitions. 'Sociology cannot be the art of destroying and remaking the social order on a rational level, and must simply be the art of preventing problems and supplying a remedy for the ills that might arise in the life of a determinate group' (Richard 1898a: 392).

A lot of hope was being invested in the social sciences. In his review of *Suicide*, Richard (1898b) spoke openly of how 'informed observers of the great crisis we are going through base their hopes on social sciences'. On the other hand, he regretted the fact that 'parties (and sometimes individuals) are trying to use social science.' His position was clear: '[sociology] serves no one.' And he added: 'M. Durkheim is proof of that: he dismisses both the socialists and the economists with a certificate of incompetence.'

Durkheim's book therefore had a 'practical import': 'Statistics on morality make it possible to analyse the sufferings of society and they reveal its disorders to anyone who can read them.'

Why Simmel?

The first of the two original works published in *L'Année* was entitled 'The persistence of social groups'. The journal published the text even though Durkheim found its author – the German sociologist Georg Simmel – profoundly irritating. Even Célestin Bouglé, who knew Simmel's work well, complained that it was too 'abstract' and feared that it would breed 'contempt for facts' (Bouglé 1898). Was Durkheim aware of Simmel's remarks to the effect that the 'plasticity' of Jews was a precondition for their survival (Simmel 1898: 71)? Did the journal need to exploit the fame of a German colleague who also had an article published in the *American Journal of Sociology*? The *Revue de métaphysique et de morale* had already published Simmel's 'The problem of sociology' in 1894, and his 'Sur quelques relations entre la pensée théorique avec les intérêts pratiques' in 1896.

Simmel and Durkheim did have one thing in common. As Bouglé noted, they both wanted 'to prove that a sociology *strictu senso* had the right to exist'. According to Simmel, society was 'a unity *sui generis* and distinct from its individual elements': a society existed when men 'influenced one another' and when they formed 'a permanent or temporary unit'. This critique of the 'individualist conception' obviously appealed to Durkheim. Simmel was also convinced that sociology was not a philosophy of history but a 'special social science' based upon the identification of 'social forms'. He spoke ironically of the unenviable privileges of an emerging science like sociology, which was in danger of becoming a 'temporary refuge for all the problems that are now being debated' and of attracting all those he called 'stateless'. 'For a long time, it seemed that the word sociological had magical powers: it was the key to all the enigmas of history, and of practice, morality, aesthetics, and so on. That was because everything that happens in society was seen as sociology's object' (Simmel 1898: 73).

Simmel called on sociologists to be bold. Sociology was a real hotch-potch: it had to take sides and rid itself of the 'confused mass of problems' that clung to it. Such views were bound to appeal to Durkheim and his collaborators.

Incest and the Separation of the Sexes

The other new work [*mémoire original*] was by Durkheim himself, entitled 'Incest: the nature and origin of the taboo' (Durkheim 1963[1898]). This was part of his programme of research on the family, kinship and marriage, which touched upon the more general issues of the separation of the sexes and sexual relations. Durkheim gave a clear indication of the direction his research was taking: it was going back to the beginning and making systematic use of work in anthropology. He was also preoccupied with the study of representations and interested in anything to do with religion.

Durkheim applies the 'back to the beginning' method to incest: 'In order to understand a practice or an institution, a judicial or moral role, it is necessary to trace it as nearly back as possible to its origins; for between the form it now takes and what it has been, there is a rigorous relationship' (Durkheim 1963[1898]: 13). The taboo on incest is, in the form of exogamy, widespread and present in most societies, past and present. Durkheim was aware that Abraham's wife was his half-sister, and he also knew that incest was acceptable to some peoples, though they were the exception to the rule. This was a delicate issue, as marriage between blood relations was still seen as prejudicial to the species. Incestuous unions would, it was believed, 'weaken the race' (ibid.: 61). Incest was a controversial issue in anthropology, and involved discussions of the origins of exogamy, and the study of primitive forms of the family and of the meaning of the clan system. Durkheim joined in the controversy, challenging both Morgan's theory about the clan system, and Spencer's, MacLennan's and Westermarck's theories about incest and exogamy.

Public opinion held that exogamy was a product of the rejection of marriage between blood relatives, which, it was believed would 'increase the tendency to nervous disorders and to undersized persons' (Durkheim 1963[1898]: 62). Durkheim was sceptical about this: 'The era of the discussions raised on this problem is far from being closed' (ibid.: 64). While it was 'wise not to contract [consanguineous marriages] except with prudence . . . we are, of course, very far from always knowing clearly the reasons that make us act' (ibid.: 62).

Durkheim adopts the 'horror of blood' thesis. But in order to explain the horror of blood, he rejects all reference to instincts and places the emphasis on a sociological approach that begins with exogamy, totemism and taboo (viewed as a set of ritual prohibitions on all contact). He establishes a homology between the elite/vulgar, sacred/profane and male/female dichotomies: 'The two sexes must avoid each other with the same care as the profane flees from the sacred, and the sacred from the profane' (1963[1898]: 71). From puberty onwards, women are 'invested by universal beliefs with an isolating power of some sort' (ibid.: 72) (they have to fast and are hermetically isolated), and they become an object of horror when they are menstruating. The feeling of horror takes on a religious dimension and leads to a 'chronic' separation of the sexes: women must not eat at the same table as men, men and women have different occupations, and religious life is dualistic – 'the woman found herself to a large extent excluded from religion' (ibid.: 78). Men and women live in different worlds and speak different languages. Everything that escapes the gaze of men heightens what Durkheim calls 'feminine mysteries', and those mysteries are all the deeper in that an 'occult property [is] attributed to the feminine organism in general' and to menstrual blood in particular (ibid.: 81).

'Simple hygienic preoccupations' are not enough to explain this horror: 'all blood is terrible and all sorts of taboos are instituted to prevent contact with it' (1963[1898]: 83). Woman is the object of a particular repulsion because 'in a rather chronic manner [she] is the theatre of these bloody demonstrations': 'the woman, so to speak, passes a part of her life in blood' (ibid.: 85, 90). This may also explain, Durkheim speculates, 'the prudery concerning the sexual parts of the body' (ibid.: 86).

Durkheim uses expressions such as 'absurd prejudices' (1963[1898]: 97) to describe the primitive mind and members of lower societies. While men obviously have good reason to behave as they do, we 'must be on guard against literally accepting the popular explanations that men devise to account for the customs that they follow. It is known how these theories are constructed; it is not required that they be adequate or objective, but merely that they justify the practice' (ibid.: 92). The scientist's first duty is to observe the facts themselves, or in this case to study the ritual prohibitions that apply in different societies and at different times.

How does this apply to contemporary morality? Incest is obviously strictly regulated, but the nature of exogamy has evolved alongside that of the family; the list of those who are prohibited from marrying one another has fallen. Relatives are prohibited from marrying, not because of 'any unhealthy consequences that these unions might have', but because 'they would be subversive to the domestic order' (Durkheim 1963[1898]: 98). Were such unions permitted, they would lead to disorder and debauchery. Durkheim normally distrusts public opinion, but finds that this belief is perfectly justified and endorses 'the obscure feeling of the populace': 'If incest were permitted, the family would no longer be the family, just as marriage would no longer be marriage' (ibid.: 99). His argument is based upon the distinction between kinship functions and conjugal functions, and between family life and sexual relationships, or between duty, obligations, love-as-respect, the strict joys of the family, the religious nature of the home, and spontaneity, elective affinities, spontaneity, freedom and boundless imagination. Instinct desire and the 'mutual attraction of the sexes' represent 'a danger for morality' (ibid.: 102) because they are unregulated.

Dichotomies such as duty/passion and sacred/profane are, according to Durkheim, the basis of the moral order because the alternative is chaos. Hence the need for separate *spheres*: on the one hand, the clan or family (the focus or morality and the centre of religious life) and, on the other, sexual relationships (the world of freedom). The difference between the sexes reflects the duality of social life: there are 'two societies' within society. Durkheim argues the case for the separation of men and women: 'the mystery . . . is one of the most powerful stimuli of amorous intrigue,' and such intrigue is part of the 'relaxations of existence' (1963[1898]: 113).

'A Good Piece of Work Botched'

Only one copy of the first volume of *L'Année* was given to each collaborator, which meant that they could not easily send copies to friends or colleagues. Durkheim complained about the situation. He sent copies to a few academics, including Bréal and Liard, in the hope that they would take out subscriptions. He also saw to it that colleagues or friends reviewed the first volume for specialist journals: Salomon Reinach for *L'Anthropologie* and Belot for the *Revue philosophique*.

Durkheim's article certainly sparked some lively discussions, as we can see from Reinach's review (Reinach 1899),[58] but on the whole it was well received both in France and abroad. Gustave Belot was pleased because he had been afraid that Durkheim would try to 'establish a doctrine and turn his *Année sociologique* into the manifesto of a school'. Now the goal Durkheim had set himself was to 'provide an insight into the wealth of material that is available' in order to save sociologists from the temptation to 'pontificate' (Belot 1898: 650). Imperfect as it may have been, the enterprise seemed to him to be 'very useful'.

On the other side of the Channel, where the work of Durkheim and his young collaborators was being followed with interest, *Folk-Lore* also emphasized the interest of the first volume of *L'Année sociologique*: 'We wish well to the new venture; and we gladly hail the rise of a French critical and constructive school of enquirers into the savage customs.' The editorial director's contribution put forward an 'ingenious theory' and it was 'a very stimulating essay'.[59] In the United States, the *American Journal of Sociology*, which was edited by Albion W. Small, announced the appearance of the new French journal and briefly described the contents of the first issue. Small had no doubts about the importance and interest of the articles, but was less enthusiastic about the reviews: 'It does not seem to me that the reviewers always have a point of view which presents the most just estimate of the literature.'[60] It is true that Small always kept his distance from the *Année* and that he preferred the *Revue internationale de sociologie*.

'Everyone seems to recognize the importance and usefulness of our journal', wrote Durkheim. 'It seems to be going well so far.'[61] The journal covered its costs in less than three months; of the 1,100 copies printed, only 380 remained unsold.[62] Durkheim therefore had every reason to be relatively satisfied with the team's work: 'I really don't think we could have done better in our first year.'[63] He and his collaborators were aware that the first volume had its faults: there were typographical errors, some of the choices as to which books to review had been arbitrary, and some of the studies were too detailed. Marcel Mauss admitted that it was 'a difficult goal' to achieve. 'We cannot dream of being complete. There will be more fumbles over the next few years' (Mauss 1898: 232). Henri Hubert, for his part, was rather harsh: 'The main problem with the *Année* is that a good piece of work has been botched. That's sad.'[64] Hubert was, however, the most 'selfless' member of the team. That worried Durkheim, but it also pleased him:

I am very touched, my dear friend, by the way you speak of your devotion and even, to use you own expression, your devotion to the *Année*. I hope that the first volume, which you should now have in your hands, has not diminished your ardour too much. It seems to be that it would have been difficult to do better to begin with, but that it will be possible to do better in the future, if God and those who buy it grant us life. That is the only cloud in the sky.[65]

Although he had been harsh on Durkheim when *Suicide* was published, François Simiand congratulated him on the publication of the *Année*, and expressed the hope that it would not be an ephemeral project, and that sociology would one day take 'its place among the sciences':

> What is, perhaps more than anything else, significant about this work is that a group of men, each devoted to a different discipline, should have come together feeling the same need for positive research, and united to improve, by a sustained and substantial critique, the present state of sociology, and to apply a truly sociological method to all branches of sociology. (1898: 653)

Simiand was hailing the birth of a team, and he was already part of it.

11

The Dreyfus Affair and the Defence of Human Rights

The scientist has the duty of developing his critical sense, of submitting his judgment to no authority other than reason; he must school himself to have an open mind. (Durkheim (1957[1950]: 5)

'Let us speak first of matters French', Émile Durkheim wrote to his nephew Marcel.[1] It was February 1898. Émile was in Bordeaux, Marcel in Oxford. On 13 January, Émile Zola had published a 'cry from [the] soul' in *L'Aurore*: 'I have only one passion – the passion for enlightenment – and I speak in the name of a humanity that has suffered so much and that has the right to be happy.' Zola restated his belief loud and clear: Dreyfus was innocent, and his accusers were liars; Esterhazy was guilty, and his acquittal was a crime. Who had not heard his repeated '*J'accuse, j'accuse, j'accuse*'? 'I know of nothing more beautiful that the architectural structure of this accusation', wrote Charles Péguy. In all, 300,000 copies of *L'Aurore's* issue of 13 January were sold; this was three times its normal print-run (Mitterrand 2002: 377–9). All day long, hoarse-voiced newspaper sellers cried '*J'accuse*' as they ran through the streets of Paris with great bundles of *L'Aurore* under their arms. The protests were becoming more and more vocal. 'The shock was so great that Paris almost keeled over', said Péguy (1902: 537–8).

'A Terrible Storm'

Public opinion was up in arms, and tempers were flaring. In various towns, including Bordeaux, thousands of people demonstrated in the streets to the cry of: 'Death to the Jews, Death to Zola, Death to Dreyfus.' The whole of Lorraine was affected. There were demonstrations in Épinal, Nancy and Bar-le-Duc. Windows were broken, and Zola and the Jews were insulted. Anti-Semitic tracts were circulating. There were attacks on 'the Jews' and 'the Jews on the Stock Exchange', who were symbolized by Rothschild. It was said of the Jews of Bordeaux that, 'even though they are scattered, they still form a distinct nation, a people apart'.[2] The walls were covered with posters telling the people of Bordeaux not to buy from Jewish shops. The Jewish community was obviously alarmed but rarely reacted. When it did so, its protests were muted. In March 1898, the Consistoire israélite de la Gironde demanded the removal of the anti-Semitic posters that had been plastered all over the town. The community became more anxious when Captain Dreyfus was brought before the court martial in Rennes and when more 'hostile demonstrations' were held. In an attempt to prevent 'more serious disturbances', the Consistoire asked for 'all measures to be taken to protect our coreligionists'.[3] 'French Jews avoided the subject', wrote Léon Blum (1982[1935]: 42). 'They no longer talked about the affair among themselves . . . A great misfortune had befallen Israel. They put up with it without saying a word, waiting for time and silence to erase its effects.' It is true that, in times of adversity, French Jews tended to place themselves under the protection of the ideals of the French Revolution, and proved to be more French than the French. When Jews did join in the debate, it was often not so much a matter of solidarity with one of their own as of a passion for justice and humanism.

In Épinal, the small Jewish community was exasperated by this 'terrible storm'; it was impossible to talk of anything other than this 'wretched affair'.[4] Émile's sister Rosine Mauss was frightened, and refused to leave the house. Every bench, she complained to her son Marcel, had been daubed with the slogan 'Death to the Jews'. Jewish shops were covered with posters overnight; boys launched fireships on the Moselle carrying similar placards, and the same shouts were heard in the streets. Rosine Mauss was all the more alarmed because she was afraid that her elder son's involvement with the Dreyfusards would 'damage his career'. She wanted to 'go to Alsace to get some peace' and wished that her sons Henri and Marcel could 'find positions abroad'.[5]

The Jewish community slowly began to realize what was at stake. 'I would like to ask for your opinion about a serious question: the Dreyfus question', Élie Halévy wrote to his friend Célestin Bouglé in November 1987. 'Until Sunday, I refused to believe in the possibility of his innocence.'[6] *Le Figaro* had just published a statement from the president of the senate, August Scheurer-Kestner, who was demanding a retrial, now that new evidence had come to light. Two days later, Halévy went a little further: 'I still think it possible that Dreyfus may have been involved; I think it likely that he is innocent.' He then added: 'It has become impossible for me to doubt Captain Dreyfus's innocence.'[7]

On 22 December 1894, a court martial had found Captain Alfred Dreyfus, a graduate of the École polytechnique and Jew from Alsace who had opted for French nationality, guilty of high treason and had sentenced him to be deported to Devil's Island (French Guyana) for life. The whole case rested upon a handwritten, unsigned note that had reached the hands of the military attaché in Paris and that had been found in a wastepaper basket. Dreyfus was deported in February 1895. Only his brother Mathieu and a few loyal friends, including the three Reinach brothers, the philosopher Lucien Lévy-Bruhl (who was Dreyfus's cousin by marriage – he had been a defence witness in 1894) and the writer Bernard Lazare, were convinced of his innocence and were trying to prove it. In 1897, the little 'Dreyfusard phalange' was growing in size, and the question became as much an intellectual and moral issue as a political and social one. Was the accused guilty or innocent? As he admitted to Henri Hubert, Durkheim was 'convinced that Dreyfus was innocent', but he was reluctant to speak out and to protest at the court's judgment. As he put it: 'Personal feelings do not justify public protests.' He also believed that 'the protests should be confined to the question of form: was he found guilty without being able to defend himself against the charges brought against him? I have learned from experience that one encounters much less resistance when one takes care to make that distinction clear.'[8]

'The situation is very serious', Émile wrote to his nephew, but he was thinking less of the wave of anti-Semitism (which was, in his view, no more than a 'superficial manifestation') than of 'the deep moral crisis': 'There has never been such moral disorder in France.' He feared that there would be a reaction against 'all sorts of principles that were, we thought, firmly established'. He was not very optimistic, but he refused to 'lose heart' or 'give up the fight': 'On the contrary, one of the good things about this situation is that it has revived a taste for battle that had been somnolent for so long. There is something to be done because there is a new struggle to be waged, and if we have the will to do so, we will quickly gain ground.' He concluded: 'The main thing is that the elements that have coalesced must remain united, and that there must be no disarray.'[9] He expressed the same fears in September: 'The intellectuals' group must not break up. We must learn the lessons of this crisis and do all we can to prevent it from happening again . . . Let this be a lesson to us.'[10]

The Intellectuals Mobilize

'We have the feeling that we are at a low ebb', remarked Maurice Halbwachs, who was a student at the École normale supérieure at the time.[11] Élie Halévy, who was trying to get his friend Xavier Léon, the editor of the *Revue de morale et de métaphysique*, to do something, felt the same: 'Complete apathy in the face of a very powerful clerical organiza-tion.'[12] Durkheim's close collaborators Célestin Bouglé and Paul Lapie were also alarmed: 'This is illegal – and probably iniquitous.'[13] For a moment, Dreyfus's supporters had lost heart, but they were recovering their strength and confidence. They were, as Élie Halévy put it, going from apathy to over-excitement. The day after the publication of Zola's 'J'accuse', a petition calling for a retrial was circulating. Within a few days, it had been signed by several hundred so-called 'intellectuals', most of them writers, artists, poets and academics. Teachers were, Durkheim would later write, all the more willing to play the 'intellectual' role in that public opinion held them 'in high regard'. Witness their presence in politi-cal gatherings and government advisory bodies: 'Whenever the country goes through a political or moral crisis, teachers in higher education play a role, and it is often a very important one' (Durkheim 1975[1918a]).

The signatories included Anatole France, Émile Duclaux, Claude Monet, Jules Renard, Octave Mirbeau, Marcel Proust, Théodore Monod, Félix Fénéon and Léon Blum (for *La Revue blanche*), and Alfred Bonnet, secretary of *Le Devenir social*. *L'Aurore*'s editor-in-chief Georges Clemenceau saluted them on 18 January: 'It has to be said that the intellectuals were the first to mobilize, and that does them honour' (cited in Julliard and Winock 1996: 372). Émile Durkheim's name was on the first list of those who protested against the 'violation of legal norms' during the 1894 trial and the 'mystery surrounding the Esterhazy affair', and who were calling for a retrial. The list also included the names of his friend Lucien Herr and his close collaborators Célestin Bouglé, Paul Lapie and François Simiand. The names of Henri Hubert and Paul Fauconnet appeared on the second and fifth lists, together with that of their friend Marcel Drouin. Émile Durkheim's name appeared once more on the seventh list. A few colleagues from Bordeaux (O. Hamelin and G. Rodier from philosophy, H. Ouvré) and a few students from philosophy (G.-L. Duchêne) and law (H. Delafargue from the Association générale des étudiants) signed the petition. It was, as Octave Hamelin wrote to Marcel Mauss, a 'terrible business'.[14] It was only later that Mauss, who was abroad, signed the petition (eleventh list); he also supported a second protest in which the signatories denounced the irregularities that had occurred during Dreyfus's trial in 1894, expressed their surprise that Lieutenant-Colonel Picquart's quarters had been searched, and demanded the preservation of 'citizens' legal guarantees against all arbitrary use of power'. The signatories included teachers from the École pratique's religious sciences section (Albert Réville, Maurice Vernes), and from the École d'anthropologie (Charles Letourneau, André Lefebvre), the sociologist Eugène de Roberty, the Bouguin brothers (Hubert and George), and Charles Péguy from the École normale supérieure. They represented nothing more than what Élie Halévy called a 'stubborn minority', but they did succeed in 'making their voices heard, despite the hostility of the military, the priests, the bourgeois, the courts, the lawyers and the mob'.[15] Sylvain Lévi did not sign the petition, but he did write an open letter defending Captain Dreyfus to the Ligue des droits de l'homme; he also joined the committee of the Alliance israélite universelle. He later told Marcel Mauss:

> My optimism over this issue is unshakeable, and I will predict to anyone that Dreyfus will be acquitted. But that fact that something is badly amiss has been, if not revealed, at least brought to light, and we have seen our country's uninformed fanaticism, bad faith and lack of understanding! My brain is so obsessed with it that I can think of nothing else, and I have done nothing – nothing – for two months.[16]

Zola himself was charged with slander. His trial opened on Monday 7 February, and at the end of the month he received the maximum sentence of one year in prison and fine of 3,000 francs. The anti-Dreyfusards were delighted. There were street demonstrations in several towns, including Bordeaux. Jews were hunted down, shop windows were broken, and effigies of Dreyfus were burned. 'An astonishing civil war', observed Daniel Halévy. It was waged 'without any brutality and without a drop of blood being spilled, but with such intellectual passion that men died of exhaustion, sadness, pain and anger' (Halévy 1932: 170).

Durkheim and Zola did not know one another, but their positions were the same: naturalism was to literature what sociology was to the human sciences. Durkheim described his own position as 'sociological naturalism'. Both men took the same objective view of social reality. Zola observed it with his own eyes, taking notes and discovering photography, while Durkheim collected and constructed statistical data, and analysed travellers' tales and the observations of anthropologists. Both defended the idea of experimentation (as defined by Claude Bernard) and positivism. Zola argued the case for an 'experimental novel' that facilitated the observation of the main cultural trends. The author of *Germinal* and *La Bête humaine* was on the side of the little man, of the people whose poverty he had observed. Deeply concerned with the question of solidarity and the association of capital and labour, he made no secret of his socialist sympathies but remained resolutely independent of all political parties. This surprised a lot of people: 'How is it that the man who demanded justice in an individual case fails to recognize that universal injustice is a daily occurrence?' asked Charles Péguy (1902: 552). Émile Zola knew full well that polemic, or even scandal, could help to overcome conformism or the conspiracy of silence: 'If we do not make any noise, we are doing nothing. We have to be discussed, ill-treated and roused by our enemies' seething anger . . . [Paris] will only listen to roars and cannon fire. Woe to the man who lacks courage' (cited in Charle 2004: 209).

In Durkheim's view, the important thing was the 'unity' of the opposition: there must be no disunity. As Élie Halévy remarked, the Dreyfusards were, by definition, a heterogeneous group: 'Israelite bankers have allied themselves with anarchist agitators, and Protestant pastors with naturalist writers, to demand a new trial.'[17] Durkheim put forward the idea of a 'permanent league for the respect of legality', and wrote to Henri Hubert:

I would be very sorry if the permanent organization had such a limited and specific goal as the one you describe: a league demanding a new trial. The cause is too general and too serious to be disfigured in that way. You will not rouse the crowd with an issue such as that. Why not say out loud that the goal we are pursuing is at once general and specific? If I had any say in the matter, I would vote for a title like: League for the Respect of Legality and the Defence of the Nation's Honour. That would catch out the so-called nationalists.[18]

Hubert was very active in the pro-Dreyfus movement. Durkheim urged his young collaborator to speak to Lucien Herr and to ask him to speak

to Émile Duclaux, the biologist-director of the Institut Pasteur. Durkheim
met Duclaux in March 1898, but found to his regret that he was not 'a man
of action'. The goal of a permanent organization should, in his view, be
to 'demonstrate that we have not abdicated, to counter the effects of this
moral condemnation, and to prepare for the future: 'We shall see what
comes of it.'[19]

The Ligue pour la défense des droits de l'homme et du citoyen was
founded on 20 February on the initiative of Ludovic Trarieux, a senator
and former minister for justice. Its goals were: (1) to use propaganda to
enshrine the principles of the Revolution in both law and institutions;
(2) to give advice and counselling to anyone whose freedom had been
threatened or whose rights had been violated. The most important of the
intellectuals mobilized by the Zola trial attended its first meeting: Émile
Duclaux from the Institut Pasteur, Louis Havet, teacher at the Collège de
France, Jean Psichiari, director of studies at the École pratique des hautes
études, Edouard Grimaux, chemistry teacher at the École polytechnique,
Dr Héricourt, director of the faculty of medicine's laboratory, and Paul
Meyer, Arthur Giry and Paul Violet, all of whom taught at the École des
chartes. Charles Seignobos (1854–1942), a *normalien* and *agrégé d'histoire*,
who had been teaching modern history at the Sorbonne since 1898, and
who was both a Protestant and a republican, also became a member of the
league's central committee.

Élie Halévy, who was passing through Paris, wrote to Célestin Bouglé
to ask: 'Are you going to join? . . . Do you think you can recruit other
members?'[20] Durkheim, who was a member of the league *avant la letter*,
urged Bouglé to let Duclaux know that he and his close friends would join.
Bouglé, who had recently been appointed to a post in Montpellier (he was
appointed *maître de conférences de philosophie* in the faculty of letters on
30 December 1897), joined the league. His friend Élie Halévy congratulated him on being such 'an ardent defender of the republic'. Durkheim
was quite pleased with the league's 'programme', and told Hubert that it
was 'in keeping with what [he] wanted': 'We must not abdicate, especially
not in the face of public opinion.' He believed that 'individual propaganda' was the best way to get results, and said he was confident he could
get signatures from his colleagues: 'Those who sign may perhaps expose
themselves to some ill will, and may be refused promotion; but we can ask
people to take such risks, and I am still not convinced that they are real.
You know that the university administration is on our side.'[21]

The Stapfer Affair: 'The Sickening Spectacle of So Much Cowardice'

Durkheim became first secretary of the league's Bordeaux section, and set
about trying to recruit people to the new organization. 'But it's so hard!'
he exclaimed. His first approaches to colleagues in Bordeaux were difficult. 'I have obtained five signatures here so far. The distressing thing is

the cowardice you come up against. It really is wretched.'[22] Durkheim did what he could and resigned himself to the fact that he could do no more. He felt more isolated than ever. 'I feel as though I am living in internal exile. So I have almost completely withdrawn from the life of the faculty. The spectacle of what I see there is too painful.'[23] His colleague André Le Breton (1860–1931), who had been with him at the École normale supérieure and who had joined the faculty in 1893, was an anti-Dreyfusard and a member of the Ligue de la patrie française. The 'sickening spectacle of so much cowardice' was too much for Durkheim and his 'feeling of loneliness' became 'unbearable'. In a moment of moral and intellectual depression, he confided in Célestin Bouglé that he had just lived through the 'saddest winter'. 'In these conditions, you eventually retreat into yourself, and do not have the heart to do anything.' Despite everything, he tried to remain optimistic and was anxious to do more.[24]

Durkheim's involvement caused him problems in Bordeaux. He and his colleague Waitz were accused by the daily *Le Nouvelliste* of 'approaching students to ask them to sign', and he and his friends and colleagues Octave Rodier and Octave Hamelin were described as 'the leading lights in the union'. 'Nothing could be further from the truth', declared Durkheim,[25] but he did admit to having met two students who had come to ask him for advice on 21 January. He explained his views on the Dreyfus affair (irregularities during the trial), but refused to give them any advice as to how they should behave. As he told *Le Nouvelliste*, he did not believe that students should be involved in such things.

A student delegation went to *Le Nouvelliste* to protest and to state that none of their teachers had asked them to sign a petition in support of Zola. 'None of that matters', Durkheim concluded,[26] but he was annoyed by all the talk of a *'syndicat'*: 'We have absolutely no knowledge of any *syndicat*, and when it comes to a matter of conscience, we will take orders from no one.'[27]

All this may well have been 'of no importance', but the position Durkheim and his friends had adopted isolated him from his colleagues. He had thought of introducing a course on the science of religions and of bringing his nephew to Bordeaux, but that was now out of the question. 'I would have had to have the ear of the faculty, and my colleagues must have no reason to suspect me of acting out of nepotism.'[28] Marcel was already opposed to the idea because, being the 'enemy of other injustices and other favours', he did not want there to be any 'hint of nepotism or cliquishness, which might have been justified'.[29] Nor could Durkheim argue the case for the introduction of a course on oriental antiquities, which might have led to the appointment of Isidore Lévy: 'Personally, I think I would do better to abstain from voting, and to justify my abstention orally . . . If I voted for I. Lévy, who would only get the votes of a few friends, it might do him more harm than good.' He did not, he concluded, want to 'make Semitism the answer to Foucart's nepotism'.[30] At the beginning of April, Durkheim went to Paris to talk to Alcan, and took the opportunity to see 'as many people as possible', including Jaurès. On the morning of

3 April, he spent two hours discussing 'the events' with Salomon Reinach, who had asked to see him.

> I am beginning to get a clearer picture of things. The duplicity is even worse than I could have believed. The day will come when those who refused to follow us for fear of public opinion will blush at their own cowardice; and Lavisse will regret his prevarications . . . Putting everything off until after the elections looks to me like putting one's head in the sand.[31]

In June 1898, Durkheim noted that, while support for Dreyfus was growing in the provinces, the same 'fear of public opinion' meant that people would not express their feeling aloud. He was impatiently waiting for the league to 'act', and regretted the fact that its president, Ludovic Trarieux, was not 'a more energetic man'.[32]

Durkheim intervened once more in July 1898, but this time in the daily *Le Temps* and in relation to the Stapfer affair. Paul Stapfer, who was dean of the faculty of letters at Bordeaux, gave the funeral oration for Rector Auguste Couat before an impressive crowd and a large number of personalities. The dean, who was both a Protestant and a Dreyfusard, made a fairly obvious allusion to the Dreyfus affair when he stated: 'A just man has died.' In paying tribute to his colleague (fidelity to duty, moral delicacy, conscience, modest veracity, courage, simplicity, love of justice, etc.), he referred, without saying too much about it, to 'the atrocious patriotic suffering' that had troubled the last years of his life: 'He was a man who believed in justice and logic, and he was truly horrified by the sectarian violence, the confusion and the way all ideas were being swept away by the wind of furious unreason.'

His words provoked 'a certain emotion'. On 24 July, the professorial board of the faculty of letters issued a statement to the press insisting that the dean had spoken in a purely personal capacity. And, as *Le Temps* reported, delegations from the various faculties went to the main barracks in the town to demonstrate their support for the army. So far as the faculty of letters was concerned, the report was inaccurate, and Durkheim immediately wrote to *Le Temps* to point out that the professorial board's statement was simply intended to spare the embarrassment of those who did not share the dean's views, adding, however, that 'several of us do share his views'.[33] He also wrote to *L'Aurore* to ask it to rectify its error. 'In general terms', he wrote, 'the kernel of the little army that is fighting at our side was not formed in the University.' The newspaper praised the letter's signatory for his courage at a time when 'anyone who dares to speak the truth is sacked, suspended and prosecuted'. It thanked him for having spoken 'in the name of the truth' and for setting 'a fine example'.

Seven professors, including Le Breton, reacted to this by writing to *Le Temps* and *Le Nouvelliste* to condemn Durkheim's actions and to make it clear that the faculty of letters unanimously condemned the dean's inappropriate remarks. The Stapfer affair caused such a scandal that Léon

Bourgeois (1851–1925), minister for public instruction, suspended the dean for six months. When his period of suspension was over, he resigned in order to 'regain his freedom'. A former lawyer and prefect, Bourgeois, who had been elected as a Radical *député* and who served as prime minister from November 1895 to April 1896, returned to his previous position in June 1898. When he attended the prize-winning ceremony for the winners of the *concours général*, a 'vociferous and noisy gang' of students, *normaliens* and young people from the Latin Quarter gathered outside the Sorbonne to boo the minister, who was 'guilty of suspending Bordeaux's Dreyfusard dean'. Teachers and students applauded and encouraged them from the first and second floor windows (Bourin 1938: 182–3).

For his part, Durkheim was astonished that 'such simple letters' could lead to such disturbances: 'What a strange phenomenon of popular psychology!' he exclaimed. He expected to receive a reprimand from the minister for what *Le Temps* ironically described as a 'heroic' gesture. If he professed the same views, the newspaper went on, he should share his dean's 'disgrace'.[34] He asked his nephew to reassure the family: 'Make them understand that my future does not depend upon any government.'[35]

In the last assessment of Durkheim's work that he wrote before resigning from his post, Dean Stapfer could not prevent himself from admiring his colleague's behaviour: 'One of those professors who does the faculty the greatest honour thanks to his activities in the service of the common good, justice and truth as well as our students.' His comments once more annoyed Rector Bizot, who had just replaced Auguste Couat: 'I do not know what M. Stapfer means when he states that M. Durkehim is a servant of the common good, justice and truth.' For his own part, he preferred to speak only of what was 'real': 'M. Durkheim has a lot of talent, an original and very vigorous mind, albeit a little woolly, some theories of his own, doctrines that make students think and reflect, and a loud and rousing voice.'[36]

Durkheim was very disappointed by the attitude of his colleagues, who were too easily 'intimidated by some ministerial statement': 'It is all so sickening!' When he felt that he had been betrayed by his colleague the historian Camille Jullian (who did not support him during this affair), he could not hide a 'sorrow that cast a shadow over the whole of the first half of his holidays'. Refusing to 'condemn' a colleague to whom he was by no means 'indifferent', he took refuge in silence and tried to understand: he could clearly see the 'strength of the resistance' of 'clerical Boulangism, anti-Semitism and anti-Protestantism', and was well aware of the potential impact of an *esprit de corps* or lack of information. And yet, he told Jullian, *'for any liberal thinker, the question of legality should have taken precedence over everything else'*.[37] Durkheim did not want to break off relations with Jullian over this, but told him that they could no longer 'enjoy the same freedom or the same trust as before'. Durkheim was aware of the 'unfortunate effects' that the stance he had adopted might have on his career: 'I can now count on the hostility of the administration, for anything that depends upon the arbitrary whim of a minister, such as promotion and so forth. As far as a position in Paris is concerned, it is difficult to say in advance how it might be affected by this incident.' It was, he told his nephew, a mistake to think of its 'unfortunate effects', serious as they may be. 'We have to do what we can without worrying about the consequences, especially when our material existence is not at stake.'[38]

The circulation of the petition and the founding of the league were greeted with hostility and derision. Maurice Barrès spoke with contempt of 'these intellectual aristocrats' who made 'a point of showing that they do not think in the same way as hoi polloi', adding that 'nothing could be worse than these gangs of semi-intellectuals . . . these self-proclaimed intellectuals are the inevitable waste products of society's attempts to produce an elite' (Barrès 1898: 1). Openly and ferociously anti-Dreyfusard, the writer from Lorraine who had theorized 'the cult of the self' immediately joined the Ligue de la patrie française when it was founded on 31 December 1898. 'I am', retorted Lucien Herr, 'one of the intellectuals whose protests amuse you so much' (Herr 1898: 241).

Ferdinand Brunetière also laughed at the petition that was 'being circulated amongst the intellectuals' (cited in Julliard and Winock 1996: 373). Born into a bourgeois family from Toulouse in 1848, Brunetière became the secretary to the *Revue des Deux Mondes* in 1877 before becoming its editor in 1893. Under his editorship, the 'venerable and influential institution', which had 25,000 subscribers, became the voice of the Catholic right (Charle 2004: 171). The man who had twice failed the École normale supérieure's entrance examination became a specialist on seventeenth- and eighteenth-century literature and published several books on French literature., Elected to the Académie française in 1894, Brunetière was a respected literary critic, praised for his erudition and feared because of his harsh intransigence.

Brunetière was also a polemicist with a taste for provocation. After a visit to the Vatican in November 1894, during which he was granted a private audience with the Pope, the devout Catholic caused a scandal by proclaiming that the idea that there was a link between progress and science was an illusion, especially in moral terms. It was, he concluded, proof that science was 'bankrupt'. Science's defenders were quick to respond. Marcellin Berthelot published an article entitled 'Science and morality' in the *Revue de Paris*, a new journal founded in 1894 that was to the left of the *Revue des Deux Mondes*. Its editorial secretary was Lucien Herr, the librarian at the École normale supérieure.[39] Berthelot's article was an attack on religious dogmas, which had led to no discoveries and done nothing to improve humanity's condition, and then took the side of science which had 'transformed material and moral living conditions.' Émile Zola, who was working on his novel *Rome*, now joined in the debate with a speech made at a dinner organized by the Union de la jeunesse républicaine in Saint-Mandé: 'Science is all-powerful, and faith trembles before it . . . Science never stops, and constantly allows truth to triumph over error. To say that it is bankrupt because it cannot explain everything all at once is stupid' (Mitterrand 2002: 144). Zola insisted that the power of 'sovereign reason' would defeat Catholicism old and new. Such inflexible philosophical and moral positions meant that ideological differences were becoming insurmountable.

In Defence of Individualism

When the Dreyfus affair took off, Brunetière attacked Zola, describing him as a 'parvenu' who, without any proof, thought he had the right to 'crudely insult the courts and the army'. His 'J'accuse' letter was, in Brunetière's view, nothing more than a monument to stupidity and impudence. What did Zola think he was doing, and what gave him the competence and authority to say anything, fumed Brunetière, who saw the affair simply as a 'question of military justice'. The article he published in the *Revue des Deux Mondes* on 15 March was entitled 'After the trial'. It raised three questions: the causes of anti-Semitism, the role of the army (in preserving security, prosperity and democracy) and the pretensions of intellectuals who thought they were in possession of the truth and had the right to talk about things that were not within their competence. He described intellectuals as 'democracy's worst enemies' on the grounds that they were the defenders of individualism, if not anarchy. Intellectualism, individualism and self-infatuation went hand in hand, concluded Brunetière, who regarded individualism as 'the great sickness of modern times'; the only way to protect 'the social bond' was to rely upon institutions such as the church and the army.

The 'intellectuals' – Émile Duclaux, the philosopher Victor Basch, Frédéric Paulhan and Alphonse Darlu – reacted immediately. Outraged by Brunetière's remarks – he described him as 'a well-known hack' – Durkheim decided that he should reply too. First, he wrote to his nephew Marcel: 'When ideas like this become the norm in France, we have to fight them.' It was a question of duty: 'We would suffer too much if we did not do so . . . I am not going to rush into the fray, but I will do what I can to prevent the movement of intellectual and moral reaction that is clearly taking shape.'[40] He had to find the time and the energy to write the article that he provisionally called 'On the individualism of intellectuals'. His intention was to show that 'not only is individualism not anarchical, but it henceforth is the only system of beliefs which can ensure the moral unity of the country' (Durkheim 1973[1898]: 50). What he termed individualism had inherited the positive content of Christianity and stemmed 'not from egoism but from sympathy for all that is human, a broader pity for all sufferings, for all human miseries' (Durkheim 1973[1898]: 49–50).'These are', his letter to Mauss concluded, 'things that I have already said.'

Durkheim was unsure to which journal he should offer his article. His first thought was to send it to the *Revue de Paris*. He knew well both its editor Ernest Lavisse and its editorial secretary Lucien Herr. Lavisse (1842–1922) had been a professor at the Sorbonne since 1888, and had advised Louis Liard on his university reforms in 1896; Durkheim had met him a few years earlier in 1895, when he went to Bordeaux to sit in on the lectures of all the teachers in the faculty of letters. Lavisse was, however, a moderate – a 'Dreyfusien' rather than a Dreyfusard – and his main concern was to prevent the nation from tearing itself apart. He was calling for 'reconciliation and peace', and rejected the view that the army and justice were on different sides. He refused to allow his journal to become actively involved in the battle over Dreyfus.[41] 'Given that the *Revue de Paris* won't take it, the only alternative that I can see is the *Revue bleue*', Durkheim wrote to Célestin Bouglé.[42]

The article, now entitled 'Individualism and the intellectuals', appeared in July 1898 in the rather more academic *Revue bleue*, which described itself as a 'political and literary journal'. It had begun life by publishing transcripts of important lectures given at the Sorbonne and the Collège de France, but had then turned into a more general journal publishing extracts from literary works, literary criticism, reports on current events and symposia. It was published on a weekly basis. In April 1898, it had published a rather favourable review of Durkheim's *Suicide* by Émile Faguet, who taught at the faculty of letters in Paris.

Durkheim begins by taking the side of the so-called 'intellectuals' (he uses inverted commas) who, 'refuse to bend their logic before the word of any army general' and 'place their reason above authority' (Durkheim 1973[1898]: 43), but adds a footnote making it clear 'that this convenient word has in no way the impertinent sense that has so maliciously been attributed to it'. He then gives his own definition: 'The intellectual is not a man who has a monopoly on intelligence; there is no social function for which intelligence is not necessary' (ibid.: 231 n2). The defining feature of the intellectual is that his profession (the arts and sciences) means that intelligence is 'both the means and the end'; he therefore uses it to 'enrich it with new knowledge, ideas or sensations'.

Durkheim makes only one brief allusion to the affair: 'Let us . . . leave aside . . . the sad spectacles we have witnessed.' He also refuses to dwell on 'arguments over circumstances', and concentrates on what is really at stake: the rights of the individual (which intellectuals should always defend). It is this defence of individualism that has triggered a 'veritable crusade' (Durkheim 1973[1898] 44, 43), He takes the side of the scientists and writers who, in addressing 'a problem of practical ethics', have refused 'to concur in a judgment whose legality appeared to them suspect', not 'because, in their capacity as chemists or philologists, as philosophers or historians, they attributed to themselves some sort of special privilege . . . but because, being men, they intend to exercise all their human rights' (ibid.: 50).

But what, he asks, do we mean by individualism? Durkheim's first objective is to get rid of a number of ambiguities. First, individualism is being confused with utilitarianism (or utilitarian egoism). Second, a false distinction is being made between individualism and the rights of the community. It is 'an easy game' to criticize utilitarianism, a simplistic doctrine deriving from 'crass commercialism' and which is 'quietly dying a natural death' (Durkheim 1973[1898]: 44) for want of adherents. He has never been so harsh on Spencer and the economists: individualism does not, he argues, mean 'private interest' (class interest, passions, money) or the 'egoistic cult of the self' (ibid.: 45). On the contrary, it refers to 'the human person' (ibid.: 46), defined as an individual with rights. 'After all, individualism thus extended is the glorification not of the self but of the individual in general' (ibid.: 48). There is something intransigent about this doctrine: 'the individual is placed in the ranks of sacrosanct objects' (ibid.: 46). This individualism has been professed for more than a century by most philosophers from Kant to Rousseau. Its political expression is the Declaration of the Rights of Man, and it has 'penetrated our institutions and our mores [and] has blended with our whole life'. It has become 'a religion in which man is at once the worshipper and the god'. And it is intransigent: 'There is no political reason which can excuse an attack upon the individual when the rights of the individual are above those of the state' (ibid.: 46–7).

This 'religion of humanity' functions like any other religion: it has its worshippers (to whom it speaks in the imperative mode) and its object of worship (the human person). It has a dogma (the autonomy of reason) and even its rites (free enquiry). Durkheim is well aware of the objections that this sociological analysis might encounter: such liberalism leads to anarchy (both intellectual and moral) and is a threat to social harmony. He is prepared to admit that individualism goes hand in hand with a 'certain intellectualism', that it encourages free thinking, but not that it results in 'an absurd infatuation with oneself'. Far from being 'anarchical', 'it henceforth is the only system of beliefs which can ensure the moral unity of the country'. It is a central element in a (civil) religion that needs no 'temples or priests' and no 'exterior apparatus' (Durkheim 1973[1898]: 50, 51).

Durkheim then returns to his theme of harmony through consensus: any society requires 'a certain intellectual and moral community' (Durkheim 1973[1898]: 50). What happens when a society becomes more voluminous, expands over vaster territories, and when individual variations (between opinions and sentiments) become more pronounced? The only thing they now have in common is, according to Durkheim, the idea of the human person: 'That is how man has become a god for man and why he cannot create other gods without lying to himself.' Durkheim extends his argument by demonstrating that the individualistic ethic is not 'the antagonist of Christian morality'. On the contrary, one derives from the other: 'The originality of Christianity [consists] precisely in a remarkable development of the individualistic spirit' (ibid.: 53, 52).

If there is one country in which 'the individualistic cause' is a truly national cause, it is, in Durkheim's view, France, which is the land of (political) freedom. It cannot be disavowed 'without disavowing ourselves, without diminishing ourselves in the eyes of the world, without committing a terrible moral suicide'. Individualism is 'our historical *raison d'être*' (Durkheim 1973[1898]: 54): 'It is a matter of completing, extending, and organizing individualism':

Let us therefore make use of our liberties to seek out what we must do and to do it, to smooth the functioning of the social machine, still so harsh on individuals, to place within their reach all possible means of developing their abilities without hindrance, to work finally to make a reality of the famous precept: to each according to his labour. (ibid.: 55–6)

Durkheim's reaction to the crisis affecting France is a call to 'use reflection' to get out of our 'present difficulties'. Meditating upon politics in the Holy Scriptures will not help to organize economic life or to introduce 'greater justice in contractual relations'. He appeals to all those who believe 'in the necessity of the moral transformations accomplished in the past century': 'Today, the urgent task is to save our moral patrimony.' Believing that they could exploit the weaknesses (improvisation, dilettantism) of adversaries who are 'neither apostles who let their anger or enthusiasm overflow nor scholars who bring us the product of their research', but 'men of letters seduced by an interesting theme', he was confident that victory was possible: reason must and would prevail (Durkheim 1973[1898]: 56, 57).

Durkheim therefore joined in the fray in the name of a humanist universalism and moral demands. He deplored, as he would say shortly afterwards, the 'lengthy abstention' shown by intellectuals and the moral 'indifference' displayed by scholars and artists during the first 20 years of the Third Republic. It took a 'great impersonal cause' to make scholars 'leave their laboratories, the learned to leave their libraries to draw nearer the masses, to involve themselves in life' and, in a word, to become intellectuals (Durkheim 1973[1898]: 59).

The lesson that Durkheim drew from this experience of 'moral agitation' was: 'Writers and scholars are citizens. It is therefore obvious that they have a strict duty to participate in public life' (Durkheim 1973[1898]: 58). He does not mean that they should become actively involved in political life or try to get themselves elected to parliament: 'a sociologist has a very good chance of making a very incomplete statesman' (ibid.). Their action should be exerted through books, seminars and popular education: 'Above all, we must be *advisers, educators*'; that, he thinks, is the best way to gain the confidence of the people: 'The lecturer of today must not be suspected to be the candidate of tomorrow' (ibid.: 59).

'Action! Action!'

'Draw closer to the masses'? Go to the people? Durkheim's young collaborators took a much more radical stance on this issue. François Simiand, who was actively involved in the debate, described himself as a 'violent and intransigent Dreyfusard', and took part in the pro-Dreyfus demonstration at the Longchamp racecourse in 1899. In 1900–1, he was editing the *Revue blanche*'s 'political and social notes' column, and published many short articles dealing with the issue of the moment. The *Revue blanche* was one of the first journals to support Dreyfus; in February, it published a 'protest' against the illegal actions of the military bureaucracy and anti-Semitism. One of the first to sign the protest of the 'intellectuals' was the young poet Fernand Gregh, who regularly published in the *Revue blanche*. In November 1898, Simiand published a short article entitled 'Intellectuals and democracy' in *La Volonté* under the pseudonym 'François Deveillans'. It was an open letter to Gregh, and congratulated the poet for having left his 'ivory tower' and taking 'the side of justice and freedom'. But he also criticized him for the way he had 'gone to the people'. The very expression 'going to the people' annoyed him because it implied the idea of an 'intellectual aristocracy'. In Simiand's view, it was not up to the people to understand art: it was up to art to understand the people. There was, he added, too great a tendency to believe in the initiative and power of individuals rather than in mass spontaneity and mass action. 'The will of the people will decide', he concluded, and it was 'the duty of intellectuals' to organize and interpret the will of the people' (cited in Mergy 2001: 'Appendix N').

More of the *Année sociologique*'s collaborators now became involved. Paul Lapie published an article on 'Penal justice' in the *Revue de métaphysique et de morale* (Lapie 1898b). 'How', he asked, could order 'fail to take precedence in a country where the executive believed itself to be superior to the judiciary?' Célestin Bouglé, for his part, published an article on 'Individualism and sociology' in the *Revue bleue*. He too criticized Brunetière. He contrasted the doctrine of the classic economists (the economic liberalism of laisser-faire), which viewed individualism as an *end*, with what he described as the new sociological doctrine of individualism as a *means*. According to this view, the dignity, freedom and duties of the individual lay at the heart of social policy. The only individualism that counted was, in his view, the individualism that 'required the collectivity to intervene, and men to control themselves'. Such individualism was 'both democratic and rationalist.' An active and very popular speaker, Bouglé gave a lot of lectures, and collected them in a short book entitled *Pour la démocratie française* (1900a). He dealt with a wide variety of themes and topics, ranging from 'The French tradition', 'The philosophy of anti-Semitism', 'The army and democracy', and 'Intellectual and manual workers' to 'Civilization and democracy'. He warned his audiences against ideas that might become 'oppressive or place restrictions on the moral personality of individuals'. They included the ideas of nationality, race and class. He contrasted the idea of nationality or the nationalist conception with the true French tradition, which he described as individualistic and emancipatory. In a lecture dealing specifically with anti-Semitism, Bouglé criticized the philosophy of race, which had become, in his view, a weapon in the hands of the leaders of anti-Semitism.[43]

A powerless and miserable Mauss was observing 'things in France' from Oxford. 'The moral fog hanging over France makes me forget the country's attractions', he wrote to Henri Hubert.[44] He was indignant, and his feelings turned from disgust to revolt. Mauss returned to France in July, just as Zola was fleeing the country for England. His name appeared, together with those of the signatories to various petitions, including several publishers (Stock, Armand Colin and Charpentier, amongst others) in the *Livre d'hommage des lettres françaises à Émile Zola*.

Émile Zola left France for England on 18 July 1898 to avoid being sent to prison, and thus became a 'political refugee'. The author of 'J'accuse' would not return to France until June 1899, the same month in which the *Livre d'hommage* was published in Paris and Brussels. Durkheim was less optimistic than he had been about this 'sorry situation': 'I am not at all hopeful: you cannot destroy a collective state as strong as this one is proving itself to be with good logical arguments'. 'We will not divert a collective current as strong as the one we are fighting against with juridical solutions.'[45] On the other hand, there was enough that was artificial about this state that it might be possible to make it change its mind if they tried hard enough. 'That is why we have to fight to hold the positions we have captured, refuse to give ground, and prevent him from being exiled.'[46]

Like Zola, who told Péguy how miserable he was (Péguy 1902: 538), Durkheim was disappointed with the 'dubious' position of the socialists, with the exception, he was quick to point out, of Jaurès. As Hubert Lagardelle observed in *Le Mouvement socialiste* (1899: 155), the real problem was that socialists were confused and unsure about what to do. He described the Dreyfus affair as 'a murky business' and concluded that 'it was not a ground on which the proletariat can fight'. But when Zola went on trial, he did join in the debate: 'It is impossible to abstain.' There were, in his view, two good reasons why the socialist party should join in the fight: the defence of human rights and individual freedoms, and anti-militarism.

Durkheim reportedly went to see his friend Jaurès in Paris at the request of Dreyfus's brother Mathieu in a bid to try to convince him that the affair was a crime against justice and an act of lese-majesty, and to invite him to join in the 'quest for justice' (Weil 1898: 12; cited in Mergy 2001: 201). But even when Jaurès did mobilize his troops, the other socialist groups still had their doubts. Charles Rappoport refused to sign any petition supporting either Dreyfus or Zola on the grounds that he 'did not see that a proletariat unjustly condemned to poverty had any interest in an affair concerning a wealthy captain who had wrongly been found guilty of treason'. He initially viewed the affair as 'a banal injustice of the kind that is so commonplace in capitalist society' and as an injustice that was of little importance because it concerned a member of the bourgeoisie, 'roused the powers of money for its own purposes and stirred up the self-interested passions of the Semites' (Rappoport 1991: 166).

There was a dramatic development at the end of August when Lieutenant-Colonel Henry, who had been charged together with Dreyfus and found guilty of fraud, committed suicide. For the anti-Dreyfusards, this was 'the beginning of the rout'. In the autumn, Durkheim went to Paris and spent an afternoon with Jean Jaurès, who did not tell him 'anything of great importance'. He was feeling optimistic: 'Nothing can prevent the inevitable', he wrote to Célestin Bouglé; 'but in view of the circumstances we must try to keep together the group we established. And if we succeed in doing so, the miserable year we have just had will not have been wasted.'[47] The public prosecutor had recently called for a new trial, and the court of appeal found that the request was admissible. By late November, Durkheim was elated to see that 'things are going better than we could have hoped for . . . It is true that our attitude is completely revolutionary. But whose fault is that? This revolt was quite in keeping with the logic of events. The only thing that surprises me is that it did not begin earlier.'[48] Émile Zola was equally optimistic, and wrote to Eugène Fasquelle from exile in London: 'I am beginning to believe not only that an innocent man will be saved, but that the guilty will be punished.'[49]

With a few years of hindsight, Mauss would see this 'agitation, this exasperation' as a sign of the 'conquering militaristic and nationalistic madness' that had taken hold of several European democracies. It was, he thought, a 'nationalistic delirium' (Mauss 1900b; in 1997: 32). On his return to Paris, Mauss became a regular visitor to the Bellais bookshop, which Charles Péguy had bought in 1898. Situated on the corner of the rue Cujas and the rue Victor-Hugo, the bookshop became the headquarters of the Dreyfusards in the Latin Quarter. Péguy was the 'military 'leader' of justice and truth, the little army of socialist students and *normaliens* who defended the Sorbonne's Dreyfusard professors (Ferdinand Buisson, Alphonse Aulard and Charles Seignobos) against the anti-Semite gangs (Bredin 1983: 263). It took all Herr's influence to persuade Mauss to 'follow Péguy', who had, it is true, some interest in sociology. He reviewed *Suicide* for the *Revue socialiste* and wrote a 'First dialogue on the harmonious society', which he titled 'Marcel'. In it, he described the work of the sociologists, who were doing their best to survey the opinions of citizens. The alliance between Mauss and Péguy was to be short-lived: 'He is a dangerous madman', exclaimed Mauss.[50] It was in the bookshop that Mauss met Lucien Herr who, more active than ever, was trying to organize young people. He was a friend of Marcel's uncle's, and Mauss was more than willing to see him as 'a constant adviser one could listen to'. The two men shared the same political ideas: 'Our socialism brought us together', said Mauss. They did everything together and became friends. Hubert, who was an assistant librarian at the École normale supérieure in 1893–4, also became a 'real devotee' of Herr's, and regarded him as 'a model of moral probity for himself and others, a model of selfless work, team work and selflessness'.

The Dreyfus affair politicized all the young *normaliens* of the day. In January 1899, the young Maurice Halbwachs, who would subsequently become a member of Durkheim's team, went to hear Jaurès 'slate Brunetière' in a lecture given in the library at the École normale supérieure. He also began to frequent the Bellais bookshop, where he met Charles Péguy. Péguy explained the goals of the bookshop: 'It is time to think of winning over the popular universities.' Halbwachs's friend had told him about Célestin Bouglé and his thesis concerning 'egalitarian ideas', which was at the time the object of 'impassioned discussions'. Halbwachs thus discovered sociology while he was still a student at the École normale supérieure. He read Durkheim's articles on sociological method, and became convinced that sociology would become 'the truly living branch of philosophy'. He therefore turned to the new discipline. 'This science will establish itself. It is, perhaps, *the* science, or at least the point where knowledge and life meet.'[51] One of the articles that had the greatest influence on the young Halbwachs was Durkheim's 'Individualism and the intellectuals.'

'Individual and Collective Representations'

Durkheim finished writing his article 'Représentations individuelles et représentations collectives' ['Individual and collective representations'] (1974[1898]) towards the end of February 1898. He was in a hurry to finish it because he wanted to 'begin [his] review [for *L'Année sociologique*] immediately'. He also had to devote three days a week to his lectures on the family. 'While they are very general, I have never found these lectures to be of no use to me.'

> How can I write this book the way I dream of writing it? If only I could find some nice little job in Paris that would leave me some free time! That is what I need. It won't be long before I don't get much out of teaching, but it is still a heavy burden. If I could find some corner in Paris where I could work in peace, and learn all the things I do not know . . . that really would be ideal. But it is very difficult to find somewhere like that.[52]

It was, he told Mauss, 'an article on metaphysics for the journal of that name'. He then corrected himself: 'No, it is about psychology, not metaphysics'.[53] It was indeed an article on sociology: almost all the authors cited – Huxley, Maudsley, Wundt, Pierre Janet, as well as the American William James, author of the *Principles of Psychology* – and Durkheim discusses in detail studies of the association of ideas and memory. He stresses that, over the past 10 years, there has been a major new development in psychology. A truly psychological – and experimentally based – psychology has rejected both introspectionism and psychophysiology (or biological naturalism) of earlier times in favour of a 'psychological naturalism' that potentially offers a positive understanding of intellectual phenomena (or what is known as spirituality). Mental life has been shown to be a vast, profound and complex system of *sui generis* realities made up of a large number of superimposed layers. Durkheim defends the new school of psychology against introspectionism, psychophysiology and psychoanalysis because he is also trying to defend his own conception of sociology, which he describes as 'sociological naturalism'. His favourite argumentative technique is analogy, which he considers to be central to science. His goal is to demonstrate that individual and collective representations are comparable, and that 'both maintain the same relations with their respective substrata', but that they are also two worlds (and two sciences) that retain their 'relative independence' (Durkheim 1974[1898]: 2).

The whole debate revolves around the status of consciousness. Consciousness is not, Durkheim argues, a mere epiphenomenon: 'The agent endowed with reason does not behave like a thing of which the activity can be reduced to a system of reflexes. He hesitates, feels his way, deliberates, and by that distinguishing mark he is recognized' (Durkheim 1974[1898]: 3). He is prepared to admit, following Wundt, that the 'field of the mind's activity is . . . very limited . . . Our direction is guided . . . [by] the habits which we have contracted, the prejudices . . . in a word, all that constitutes our moral character' (ibid.: 6). And besides, mental states are closely bound up with 'nerve currents' and muscular movement' (ibid.: 7, 8); it is as though it was 'the organism that leads the man' (ibid.: 6). Durkheim cites studies of hypnosis and Pierre Janet's work on psychological automatism to demonstrate that there such things as non-conscious psychical states: 'Our judgments are influenced at any moment by unconscious judgements; we see only what our prejudices permit us to see and yet we are unaware of them'. 'We are always to a certain extent', he adds, 'in a state of distraction . . . We imagine that we hate someone when in fact we love him.' There is therefore, he concludes, 'an interior world of the mind [that] is still, to a great extent, unexplored' (ibid.: 21, 22).

Then why not speak of 'unconsciousness'? William James suggests that the term should be avoided because there is no proof that there is such a thing as an 'unconscious'. Durkheim, who regards the notion of an unconscious representation and 'consciousness without the ego' as 'basically equivalent', also rejects that idea: 'It is no easier for us to imagine a representation without the thinking subject than to imagine a representation without consciousness' (1974[1898]: 23 n1). He accepts the idea that the state of the brain affects all intellectual phenomena, but rejects that of a 'cerebral map' that allows every intellectual function to be localized: that has more in common with fiction than fact.

Durkheim then turns from psychology to sociology. There are, he argues, analogies between the 'social realm' and the 'psychic realm', and the relationship between social facts and individuals is analogous to that between mental facts and the brain cells. While he repeats this thesis that social facts are external to and exist independently of individuals, Durkheim also makes it more clear than ever before that society has as its substratum 'the mass of associated individuals' (1974[1898]: 24): 'The system which they form by uniting together, and which varies according to their geographical disposition and the nature and number of their channels of communication, is the basis from which social life is raised. . . . [R]epresentations . . . arise from the relations between the individuals thus combined.' Collective representations are products of 'the action and reaction between the individual minds that form the society [but] do not derive directly from the latter and consequently surpass them' (ibid.: 24–5). Durkheim admits that the theory that 'all social facts without exception impose themselves from without upon the individual' is open to dispute, but insists that it must be recognized that religious beliefs, the rules of morality and 'the innumerable precepts of law' are 'expressly obligatory': 'these ways of thinking and acting are not the work of the individual but come from a moral power above him' (ibid.: 25).' Collective representations do not derive from individuals *qua* individuals but from associations of individuals. Individual characteristics combine, as in a real 'chemical synthesis' and, 'since this synthesis is the work of the whole, its sphere is the whole'. It is the 'aggregate in its totality' that 'thinks, wishes, feels' (ibid.: 26). Durkheim is harshly critical of individualist sociology which, like materialist metaphysics, tries to explain the complex in terms of the simple, the superior in terms of the inferior, and the whole in terms of the parts. In his view, the opposite view (idealist metaphysics) is just as untenable. The whole has to be explained in terms of the whole, the complex in terms of the complex, and social facts have to be explained in social terms: 'This the only path that a science can follow' (ibid.: 29). An association consists of its parts, but it forms a synthesis that is (partly) independent of its constituent elements. Collective life is therefore at once dependent upon and distinct from its substratum. And it should not be forgotten that there is 'a moral power above' the individual (ibid.: 25). Society is not an epiphenomenon.

The same is true of collective representations which, being partly autonomous, have their own life and influence one another. They give rise to new syntheses, as we have seen from the development of religion, which produces a 'luxuriant growth of myths and legends, theogonic and cosmological systems . . . which is not directly related to the particular features of the social morphology. Thus it is that the social nature of religion has been so often misunderstood' (1974[1898]: 31).

Durkheim would like to see sociology undergo a transformation similar to that undergone by psychology. If it made way for what he calls a 'sociological naturalism', it would be possible to see social phenomena as fact *sui generis*. He also makes a point of replying to those who accuse him of endorsing 'materialism': they are mistaken because social life is, in his view, characterized by its '*hyperspirituality*' in the same way that spirituality is 'the distinctive property of the individual representational life' (Durkheim 1974[1898]: 34). He hopes to open up a new world for science. That would make it possible to discover laws with a hitherto unsuspected force. And he adds in a footnote (ibid.: 32 n1): 'A special branch of sociology, which does not yet exist, should be devoted to research into the laws of collective ideation.'

Some of the *Année*'s contributors, not least Célestin Bouglé, were delighted with the position adopted by Durkheim: 'sociological naturalism' did not mean that psychology was not part of sociology; it implied the elaboration of a 'special and truly collective psychology' (Bouglé 1899c: 155).

In the late 1890s, just as he was preparing the second volume of *L'Année sociologique*, Durkheim introduced certain qualifications, and redefined his research programme by focusing on the world of collective representations (which was, he now accepted, an autonomous part of social life) and religion.

The Republic versus the Army

Although he was swamped with work – 'I've not had one completely free afternoon since November' – Durkheim was still actively following the Dreyfus affair. He agreed to sign a petition (an 'Appeal to the nation') and to respond to various surveys on militarism, anti-Semitism and the teaching of sociology in secondary schools. Newspapers and journals were publishing more and more 'surveys' about a very wide range of topics, most of them to do with current events: anti-Semitism, the role of women in modern sport, Tolstoy and art, marriage and divorce. The surveys were a way of gauging public opinion, but they also had the effect of conferring an 'intellectual status' on writers and academics.

That Durkheim was invited to sign petitions or asked about his opinion of current events is testimony to the fact that he was now recognized as an authority within his own field, and helped to give him greater visibility in intellectual and political circles. It was at the request of Ernest Lavisse that he signed the 'Appeal to the nation', which was published in *Le Temps* on 23 January 1899. He also tried to find a dozen or so signatories within his 'circle of action' of colleagues at the university. 'I think that this eminently moderate formula will even win the support of those who have so far remained quite uncommitted.'[54] The signatures meant that he no longer felt so alone: 'These are people I could talk to about the affair and engage in discussion', he wrote to Mauss.[55] In early February, he also gave a 'brilliant' lecture to the 'Patronage laïque de Nansouty', in which he spoke eloquently of his 'devotion to the cause of education' and belief that 'the three parts of the education system are inseparable'.[56]

Durkheim also devoted a little time to the Ligue des droits, and succeeded in organizing a Bordeaux branch: 'It was a little difficult because the *bordelais* temperament is so indolent. But we've got it off the ground at last.' In December 1898, the branch had some 60 members; three months later, it had between 180 and 190. But there was no possibility of organizing a lecture in Bordeaux. Durkheim thought it would be better to wait: 'We can really put our backs into it now that a retrial has been announced and before the court martial is convened.'[57] And although Jaurès was 'fairly confident' and everyone was 'full of hope', he still had his doubts: would 'the pressure of common sense' be enough to overcome the hair-splitting of jurisprudence'? At least, he concluded, 'they were sufficiently well-armed to go on waging a struggle which everyone is, of course, resolved to continue'.[58]

In May 1899, Durkheim contributed to *L'Humanité nouvelle*'s symposium on 'War and militarism'. War, he observed, was being celebrated and militarism was once more on the rise. There was, he went on, nothing normal about this. The army and military power had become sacred, and were beyond criticism. 'The mere act of submitting it to the critique of reason produces the effect of committing an impiety' (Durkheim 1986[1889]: 212), and Durkheim found this unacceptable. He quite understood that an apologia for warfare could be 'an historical necessity', and accepted that war may even be of some use to the extent that, at least in theory, 'nothing real exists without some useful effect' (ibid.), but he also believed that 'war is increasingly destined to lose ground' and that 'a violent courage, namely a disdain for one's life', was a thing of the past. Scientists, engineers, doctors and industrialists had to be convinced that there were other values, namely 'a quieter form of endurance, a less strident form of energy that is calmer and likewise more sustained . . . we must be trained in a different school' (ibid.: 211–12).

In France, 'transitory circumstances' had given rise to a 'veritable cult of superstition' centred upon memories of 1870 and a desire to avenge that defeat. He noted that 'doubtless in this fetichistic approach much is mere words', but he was still worried by the 'tumultuous manifestations of this so-called nationalism' because 'the army has . . . acquired a prestige beyond all bounds, whose danger we are at last beginning to see'. This was not 'a serious form of nationalism', but it did mean that French society was faced with a serious problem, or an 'inner contradiction' between its 'historic role' and its 'reason for existence' and between the need to proclaim the rights of free enquiry and the supremacy of civil power and 'granting such preponderance to the military power [and] the intellectual servitude that this comprises'. There would inevitably be a 'violent collision' between these 'opposing principles', and 'it is this conflict that we are witnessing at the present time' (Durkheim 1986[1899]: 212).

What was the answer to 'the moral divorce from which we are suffering'? Durkheim saw only one solution: education. A 'great nation' must obviously be strong in order to be respected, but it could be better occupied than in continually burnishing its weapons. It could pursue other goals such as a recognition of rights, respect for the law and love of liberty, and a fairer distributive justice. To sum up, the Republic rather than the army. Durkheim accepted that the roots of militarism were weak, but thought that 'the mentors of youth' could cause republicanism to penetrate more deeply into the very being of the people. It was time to do away with the 'legend of the soldier', who, a stranger to the passions and beliefs of his contemporaries, remains ignorant of all that happens around him.

When, in 1899, the Dreyfusard Henri Dagan undertook his 'inquiry into anti-Semitism', his goal was educational. It was designed to 'inform the public of the intellectual attitudes of cultured people in connection with one aspect of the social conflict' (Dagan 1899: vii). Everyone would, he believed, find it instructive and profitable.[59] The questions raised by Dagan were as follows: (1) What is the origin of anti-Semitic agitation? (2) What is its religious, ethnic or economic nature? (3) Which categories of people are involved in this agitation? Why do wage-earners and the unemployed take no interest in the movement? (4) What measures are the anti-Semites proposing? (5) What will its social effects be? (6) What is likely to happen?

The questions were addressed primarily to scholars, many of them academics, who were known for their competence in one or another domain. The major figures interviewed included writers, amongst them Zola, who admitted that he was not qualified to take part in a survey of this kind: 'I will simply give you some retrospective impressions and observations' (Dagan 1899: 18).[60] Several related the rise of anti-Semitism to the economic situation, and argued that it was a revolt against the dominance of high finance. Cesare Lombroso and Charles Gide were more pessimistic, and warned that anti-Semitic measures would be dangerous: the expulsion of the Jews had, for example, ruined Spain. According to Zola, the answer was obvious: it was Drumont's fault.

Durkheim adopted a prudent stance: 'To discuss anti-semitism properly . . . would involve a certain amount of research, which I have not done. So I can only give you an impression' (cited in Pickering and Martins 1994: 177). His close collaborators were just as concerned about anti-Semitism. At the beginning of January 1899, Célestin Bouglé published an article on the philosophy of anti-Semitism and the notion of race, in which he drew a distinction between 'ideas imported from Germany' and ideas that were 'the very soul of France' (Bouglé 1899b: 158). Durkheim drew a similar distinction between foreign (German and Russian) and French anti-Semitism: the former was 'chronic, traditional' and the latter 'acute' and 'brought about by chance circumstances'. France was experiencing an acute crisis that drew upon violent, destructive passions very similar to those seen in the east of the country in 1848 and 1870. Referring to the war of 1870, Durkheim spoke of his own experience: 'As I am of Jewish origin myself, I was able to observe it on that occasion at close quarters. It was the Jews who were blamed for the defeats' (cited in Pickering and Martins 1994: 177–8).

Durkheim's conclusion was as follows: 'Our present anti-Semitism is the consequence and superficial symptom of a state of social malaise.' He quickly developed the scapegoat thesis:[61]

When a society is ailing it feels the need to find someone to blame for this ill, someone on whom it can take out its disappointments; and those who are already out of favour with public opinion are tailor-made for the role. It is the pariahs who serve as expiatory victims. What bears out this interpretation is the nature of the reception reserved for the outcome of the Dreyfus trial in 1864 . . . so now at last everyone knew whom to blame for the economic crisis and the moral anguish from which they were suffering! It was the Jews who were the source of the ill. (1975[1899]: 253)

There were also 'secondary factors', such as 'certain defects of the Jewish race'. Durkheim immediately corrects himself: 'The shortcomings of the Jew are offset by undeniable qualities and, though better races there may be, there are some which are worse. Moreover, Jews lose their ethnic characteristics extremely fast. Two more generations, and the process is complete.' Durkheim used himself as an example: he was of Jewish origin, but had assimilated. And in the meantime, he had experienced anti-Semitism (and its main cause was moral).

While a 'serious moral disorder' was the explanation for anti-Semitism, the only cure was to 'put an end to it'. That was not, he admitted, an easy task: 'This is not achieved in the space of a day.' But there were things that must be done immediately: 'All incitement to hatred by one citizen against another should . . . be severely curbed.' Mass education was the other answer: Durkheim was convinced that 'all men of good sense' should be called upon to 'join forces to ensure victory over public madness' (1975[1899]: 254).

12

A Failure?

At the height of the Dreyfus affair, the members of the small team working on *L'Année sociologique* were busy preparing the second volume of the journal and writing lots of reviews. 'Let's get down to preparing the next *Année*', Durkheim wrote to his nephew. 'I want it to be good. Once we have been in existence for two years, we can relax a little, if we want to go on. And if we do go under, let's at least have done some good work first.' He added: 'I don't want to overlook anything this year.'[1] He was still worried by the possibility of failure: 'There is every reason to fear that we are not meeting existing needs . . . I have the feeling that we have done everything possible to ensure that it is good, so too bad if it's not a success.'[2] He was all the more worried in that he had little idea of what people thought of the journal. He asked his nephew, who was his informant in Paris, to 'keep me with up to date with what people are saying about the *Année*'.[3] 'People' included his collaborators. He was afraid of failing, and tired and depressed: 'I feel that I am losing some of my taste for action, and my ambitions – all my ambitions – are fading. Everything that has happened over the last six months has made me very sad and has sapped my strength. I would like some rest.'[4]

But there was little time for rest: publishers and editors once more had to be approached with requests for review copies. If need be, books had to be bought and subscriptions to journals had to be taken out if the publishers refused to supply copies on an exchange basis. The journal had a bit of money. Rather than trying to 'expand', Durkheim was still cautious: 'We have to develop gradually.' In his view, the principle that should guide their choice was, as he again told his nephew, 'review only those books that are of interest to sociology, either directly or indirectly'.[5] He gave Henri Hubert the same advice: 'We are a sociology journal . . . We must therefore feature only work that might be of use to sociologists. The demarcation line is, by definition, uncertain; but with experience, we will have no difficulty in establishing it.'[6]

At the beginning of May 1898, Durkheim expressed some satisfaction at the way his collaborators were working: 'I am now confident that Volume II will be better than Volume I.'[7] He was also delighted that François Simiand had taken sole responsibility for the economic history section.

An Essay on Sacrifice

Marcel Mauss and Henri Hubert were, in the meantime, working on their first great collaborative project: a long article on the 'nature and function of sacrifice', due to appear in the second volume of *L'Année sociologique*. Durkheim wanted to lend them a hand by writing an article of his own for the same issue, 'Concerning the definition of religious phenomena':

> After having thought about it a lot, I think it preferable to publish my paper on religion together with yours. Because that is the only way to demonstrate in general terms that religion is something sociological . . . So it would not be a bad idea to show how, in general terms and in what sense, there is such a thing as a sociology of religion . . . My article will simply emphasize the social character of religious phenomena and show how private manifestations of religion are not central to it.[8]

Completing the study on sacrifice proved to be difficult. In intellectual terms, it was an ambitious project. The fact that Marcel Mauss was abroad for much of 1898 did not make things any easier. His friend Henri Hubert, for his part, had just found a position as an *attaché libre* at the Musée des antiquités nationales, where Salomon Reinach was curator. At first, everything was done by post. Hubert and Mauss drafted and redrafted outlines, exchanged files, discussed various questions at length in their letters, and revised preliminary versions. Durkheim, on the other hand, was so fascinated by the work that he found it difficult to be just an outside observer. 'Over the last few months, I have been thinking quite a lot about the question of sacrifice . . . The more I think about it, the more I am convinced that it is a fundamental notion that has played a vital role in the evolution of both mores and ideas.'[9] He was therefore 'very keen' to see the article completed: '[this essay] does more than anything else to show what we dream of doing, and who knows if there will be a third *Année*.'[10] He also wrote to Hubert: 'I am very pleased to see that our second volume will start with your study.'[11] Durkheim enjoyed the 'long chats' he had with his young collaborator on his visits to Paris. Even though they 'started out from different points', they were both 'in immediate agreement'. As Hubert put it: 'With a little good will, we eventually came to an understanding.'[12]

Although he was afraid of 'even seeming to be in control or looking like a manager', Durkheim found that working with Marcel and Henri was a 'delight'. The man his nephew described as 'impatient' and 'fearful' kept a close eye on everything, followed the progress of their work from Bordeaux, and gave his nephew lots of advice and encouragement: 'The first draft does not need to be written carefully.' 'I am begging you on bended knee not to drown. Don't lapse into pointless erudition, I beg you.' Durkheim also advised Henri Hubert not to try to be exhaustive: 'There is no such thing as all the facts. All we can do, and all we must do, is think about those facts . . . that are the most significant possible.'[13]

The uncle made no secret of the fact that he was worried: 'Are you sure you can complete it?' He was worried about his nephew's lack of ambition, as he seemed prepared to spend his life in a lycée giving the same lessons year after year. Durkheim could have 'got used to that life', but suspected that it would not suit his nephew: 'You would make a mediocre *professeur de lycée* now.'[14] He thought that 'a post in higher education where [he] could work without too many worries would suit [him] much better.' He feared that his nephew, who was interested only in peace and quiet, or even bliss, would 'end up in Nirvana, or, in other words, would become mindless'.[15] The uncle tried to shake up his nephew because he was afraid for his future: 'React, please. Be a young man and not a retiree before your time. Do a lot, so that people can be proud of you.' And he set him a goal: 'There is only one thing you really have to do: finish your thesis. You must. It is a matter of dignity, and you owe us that.' He concluded: 'You will do what you can. But honour will be saved.'[16]

Durkheim wanted his nephew to return from England – arguing that he had 'got all that he could out of it' – in order to finish the article. He wanted him to spend July in Bordeaux, where he could give him a bedroom next to his study – and then to go to Épinal where, together with Hubert, they could both 'add the final touches'. Durkheim was convinced that the idea was 'interesting' and that all they had to do was 'pad it out with enough facts to show that you know what you are talking about.' In his letters, he set out what he saw as 'the broad outlines of [their] work': a historical account and critique of the theories (including Frazer's), a definition of sacrifice, and an argument (a study of its essential characteristics – i.e. the 'sacred and taboo' aspects of sacrifice). He even went into detail by making a distinction between, for example, 'communion' sacrifice and penal sacrifice. In his long letter, he added that communion sacrifice was 'an alliance, contract and convention', and that its purpose was 'to sustain the life' of the group: the very fact of gathering together meant that 'the group's self-awareness is heightened because it feels stronger and in better health'. Durkheim ended his letter thus: 'Tell me if I've understood what you are thinking; if I have, this outline seems to be the obvious one . . . So let's set to work. You will make a god job of it, I'm sure of that. And the whole *Année sociologique* will be well on its way.'[17]

When he learned that his nephew intended to stay in Oxford for another two weeks, Durkheim, who was suspicious of Marcel's 'usual and deplorable erring ways', lost his temper: 'Pack your bags and leave.' Marcel's mother Rosine was also bringing pressure to bear by threatening to cut off his allowance. She was, said Émile, afraid that her son would become 'bogged down over there'. Durkheim was ready to help her, and once more told his nephew: 'Giving up so easily is not allowed at your age . . . Rather than indulging in your vices, why don't we agree to fight them together?'[18] A few days later, he wrote to him again: 'I am very grateful to you for what you have done, and now feel that I owe you something. But I am not so sure about your will power: I am fighting that weakness with all my strength.'[19] The uncle found his nephew's sloppiness quite unacceptable: 'I will never accept that. Don't count on it. I'll never be able to watch you lazing about without doing anything and, taking on never-ending tasks without purpose, without any deadlines . . . You cannot be a man unless you have a taste for noble concerns.' Reassured by Marcel's replies, Durkheim went back to the underling issues. Because he wanted to be 'of use' to Mauss and Hubert, he planned to be in Épinal at the end of August and to work with his collaborators: 'You'll see how quickly the three of us can work. I'd be very surprised if the three of us couldn't do something good together.'[20] Even though he found the outline 'a little dense', he was convinced that Marcel and Henri could 'do something very good and that would do [them] proud'. The comparative method meant bringing together facts that were often disparate and chosen from different regions and eras, without thereby denying their specificity. Mauss wanted to 'do something that was as non-superficial as possible', and was afraid that it would be 'written up too quickly'.[21] Well aware that they were short of time and space, Hubert suggested to his friend that they should 'stick to facts they already knew well'. And in a letter to Durkheim, he clearly indicated where the limitations of their work lay: 'We do not claim to be writing an exhaustive, scientific study; we are putting forward a hypothesis constructed on the basis of a certain number of facts.'[22]

A Working Holiday

At the end of July 1898, Durkheim went to Villars-sur-Ollon in Switzerland for a holiday. The weather was glorious, the air was soft and the Grand Hotel was comfortable. He went for long walks in the morning and the late afternoon. 'I've not yet found the time to do anything, not even to attend to the letters I have to write. I am being conscientiously lazy.' He added: 'All this will give me a rest from all that fuss and bother. There are naturally a few coreligionists in the establishment. You can tell from the copies of *L'Aurore* and *Le Siècle* that they are accepted here.' Durkheim could not completely forget the political situation and the Dreyfus affair: 'There are both sickening and comforting sides to what is happening. All this cowardice is enough to make me throw up.' He concluded; 'Me and my hobbyhorse again. It really is an obsession. There is no getting away from it.'[23]

Even on holiday, Durkheim found it hard to relax. 'Wandering around and resting when you are working for the common cause depresses me . . . so, I'm anxious to get back . . . I'm also anxious to get back to work; that is the only thing that takes my mind off what is going on.'[24] And just as he was about to leave at the end of August, he again wrote: 'I am anxious to be with you. Your work preys on my mind, both because it fascinates me and because I would like to be able to help you.'[25] While he begged his nephew to 'finish', he also reminded him of what was at stake in the article: the critique of Frazer, etc. Just as he was about to leave, he went back to the question of definitions. He wrote fast: 'I'm gasping for breath!' What

Durkheim called 'conversation by letter' still did not advance things. It would be better to see each other, and to talk. The uncle dreamed of 'complete communion', which was the precondition for 'real collective work'.[26]

Forced to meet his deadline, Mauss finally joined his uncle in Épinal at the end of the summer. Durkheim was just back from his holiday in Switzerland and was 'very happy' to lend his nephew a hand. 'It won't take long', he hoped. Once the outline had been settled, the corrections did not in fact take long, but this meant that Hubert was left out.

A month later, neither 'Sacrifice' nor the reviews were in print. The publication date was put back until December. Durkheim went to Paris to work with Marcel and Henri in October, and again in November. He gave them yet more advice on how to write the reviews. 'A good review must leave some lasting impression, some notion, or some fact.' 'What you should do is look either for the ideas that emerge from the book, or for facts that might suggest ideas or views with a general import.'[27] The uncle was very satisfied with his nephew's work: 'All the reviews are very interesting; much more so than last year. They are also better written.' Durkheim was optimistic: 'Either I am very much mistaken, or volume two of the *Année* is a great improvement on the first volume. Your section, in particular, is of great interest (you see how you can deceive me).'[28]

Back in Bordeaux, Durkheim was already 'very busy' and preoccupied with the beginning of the new academic year. 'My Fridays and Saturdays are not my own, and I don't even have all my Thursdays free', he wrote to Marcel. He also had new family responsibilities: his nephew Henri, Félix's son, had just moved to Bordeaux, where he had enrolled at the Lycée Montaigne for the second part of the *baccalauréat* (philosophy). He was living with his uncle who, since the death of his father, had been acting as his guardian; in the evening, he would go with him to meetings of the Ligue des droits de l'homme. He did not sit his exam in Bordeaux, but in Toulouse, in accordance with the wishes of his uncle Émile, who wanted to avoid any hint of nepotism. In 1900–1, Henri enrolled in the faculty of law for his first year. The following year, he went with his uncle to Paris, where he took his law degree. During the summer, young Henri went back to Épinal, where he taught his uncle to ride a bicycle – *la petite reine* ['the little queen'], as it was known at the time. The uncle went for a ride every day. He liked to ride along the right bank of the Moselle to Archettes, and to return via Arches on the left bank. It was a trip he made with 'great pleasure,' with his nephew Henri by his side.[29] The latter always enjoyed a close relationship with his uncle, whose stern appearance never failed to astonish Henri's friends.

At the beginning of December, Durkheim sent a summary of the second volume of the *Année* to his publisher Alcan. He told Célestin Bouglé:

> The manuscript of this year's *Année* has been difficult to finish and has given me a lot of trouble. Everyone has been very devoted, but some people were ill and some of the calculations were wrong. So there has been some delay and some bother. On the other hand, I think that, as a

whole, it will be much better, much richer in content and more interesting. We can't pack in anything more.

Durkheim was also grateful for what Bouglé had done for the journal: 'I'm in indebted again. More so than ever!'[30]

Durkheim suggested that Hubert and Mauss's article should be called 'Essay on the nature and function of sacrifice'. He emphasized the word 'function' and asked his collaborators if they agreed to this addition. They had still not finished the essay: Durkheim had yet to see the rest of it, and was very upset. He wrote to Hubert to ask him if really they should not 'give up on the idea'.[31] He even suggested that, if need be, their text could be replaced by an article by Steinmetz, and said that he would translate it. His nephew's carelessness and delays were a constant source of annoyance, and Durkheim had had visions of himself finishing correcting the proofs during his Easter vacation. He went to Paris – 'by express train', he pointed out – to 'transcribe the final corrections on the spot'. He also took the opportunity to go to see Salomon Reinach, whose father Joseph had just died. Reinach had published an article entitled 'The prohibition of incest' in the journal *L'Anthropologie*. Reinach was favourably disposed to the *Année*, but this 'active mind' was still, in Durkheim's view, that of 'a philologist . . . very remote from us'.[32]

The finishing touches to 'sacrifice' had to be added in late January to late February 1899. At the time, Mauss was in Bordeaux with his uncle, who wanted to make some last-minute changes: 'I have tried to get inside your minds. If I've distorted your argument, I have done so quite unintentionally. But it's only a matter of detail'.[33] He was quite pleased with the results. 'I think your work will do you honour. In any case, I am glad I suggested that you should write this. It sets a good example.'[34] The third and final proofs were ready in March. Free at last, Durkheim exclaimed: 'I've been busy with the 1898 *Année* for a year, and your work [on sacrifice] has been my main concern over the last eight months. It is time I moved on to other things.'[35]

A Specialist Journal

When the second volume appeared, Durkheim was obviously pleased with the 'very favourable response' to its predecessor: 'We were quite well understood.' Alive to the few criticisms that had been made of it – it either had too much content or not enough – he made it clear that he had every intention of carrying out the necessary improvements.

The team and the division of labour remained much the same for the second volume, the only real difference being that Henri Hubert now played a bigger role, with an article co-authored with Mauss and a lot of signed reviews. The team had lost one collaborator (Albert Milhaud) but been joined by a newcomer. Born in 1865, Marcel Foucault was one of the Bordeaux contingent. He had studied in Bordeaux and had followed

Durkheim's lectures. His *agrégation* was in philosophy, but his main interest was in the question of statistical methodology. His involvement with the *Année* was sporadic as he contributed to only two volumes (the second and the seventh). Isidore Lévy also contributed to the second volume, and coedited the 'miscellaneous studies of the great religions' subsection with Mauss and Hubert.[36] His involvement with the *Année* was, like Foucault's, limited, as he contributed only to volumes 2 and 3 and, some years later, volumes 6, 7 and 8.

In his preface, Durkheim stresses that the journal's goal was to introduce 'a sense of novelty' (Durkheim 1980[1898–9]: 52) into sociology by bringing it into contact with other disciplines, and especially history: 'There is then a task to be attempted that is urgent and truly sociological: we must try to make out of all such special sciences a like number of branches of sociology' (ibid.: 53).[37] The question of the relationship between sociology and psychology still preoccupied the *Année*'s collaborators, but their interest in it was less obsessive than it had been. The specialist nature of the journal was now more pronounced – and would become increasingly so – than in the previous volume: 'the time has come for [sociology] to depart from such generalities and to become specialized' (ibid.: 52). Durkheim wanted to make a clear distinction between sociology and philosophy and insisted that it was not 'a metaphysical branch of the social sciences . . . Our principal goal is to counter by being precise, as a way of interpreting and of practicing sociology' (ibid.). The journal now abandoned expressions such as 'philosophical sociology' 'biological sociology' and 'psychological sociology' in favour of 'social philosophy', 'sociology and psychology' and 'sociology and history'. The use of the word 'method' became more frequent, and was applied to general sociology, religious sociology and criminal sociology, not forgetting the issues around statistical methodology raised in the 'miscellaneous' section.

Durkheim stressed the 'very special' nature of the works analysed in the journal, and contrasts literature and erudition with science and method. The approach adopted by Durkheim and his young colleagues was designed to be methodical, and expresses a desire for a rational organization of knowledge. A lot of books were reviewed, and it was difficult to classify them. The second volume introduced several changes, the most important being a 'completely new' section on 'social morphology'. Durkheim himself edited this section, which incorporated the old subsections dealing with sociogeography and demographic questions: 'Social life rests upon a substratum determinate in both size and form' (Durkheim 1982[1899]: 241).

Durkheim was, in other words, hostile to the new school of geography that went by the name of 'political geography', attempted to establish political geography as science and sought to make it 'the most basic of all the social sciences', on the grounds that – according to the school's founder, the German geographer Friedrich Ratzel – the geographical factor had a preponderant influence on social evolution as a whole. In the second volume of the *Année*, Durkheim published a long review of

Ratzel's *Politische Geographie* (1897; Durkheim 1969[1899]). While he was obviously pleased to see what had been very different disciplines coming closer together, he criticized his German colleague because his conception of social morphology was so vague, and because his comparisons were lacking in methodological rigour. But these were, he admitted, 'imperfections inherent in any emergent science'. He invited his German colleague, whom he regarded as a sociologist, to contribute an article entitled 'Soil, society and state' to the third volume of *L'Année sociologique.*

Some sections, such as 'general sociology', which was edited by Célestin Bouglé and Dominique Parodi, underwent few modifications, though the first rubric was now devoted to methodology. Others, in contrast, including 'religious sociology' and 'economic sociology', were subject to several changes. Marcel Mauss and Henri Hubert, editors of the former, introduced some new subsections or rubrics (magic, witchcraft, superstitions), and expanded others (ritual, myths, legends and popular beliefs). Simiand introduced a historical perspective into the 'economic sociology' section, and identified several periods (the economy of primitive peoples, Antiquity and the Middle Ages, the modern economy, and the Western economy). The 'anthroposociology' section of 'miscellaneous' was once more edited by Muffang, but now also included collective ethology and statistical methodology.

There was one minor innovation: the introduction of an alphabetical index of topics made it immediately obvious to the reader that little importance was attached to philosophical concepts (consciousness, justice) other than that of the individual (individualization, individualism and individuality). Sociology's objects of study included crime, the economy, education, religion, women, the city. Political economy had not been completely dropped (social classes, corporations, trade-unionism, labour, value were all still discussed), but it was obvious that more interest was now being taken in the family, marriage, kinship and anything to do with sexuality (incest, prostitution, modesty). Durkheim himself either edited or coedited several subsections ('morals and habitat', sexual morality, women, the family, marriage). This change of emphasis was not specific to *L'Année sociologique.* In May 1899, the eminently serious *American Journal of Sociology* published an article by W.I. Thomas called 'Sex in primitive morality'.

Religious Sociology Takes Priority: The Study of the Sacred

It was now obvious that anything to do with religion was central to the journal's concerns: beliefs, worship, gods, dogmas, churches, fetishes, the immortality of the soul, initiation, magic, death, mysteries, occultism, penitence, prayer, rituals, sacrifice, superstitions, taboo, totemism. With some 100 pages of reviews, 'Religious sociology' was now, together with 'Economic sociology' and 'Moral and juridic sociology', one of the biggest sections.

Durkheim explained to any readers who might have been surprised by the priority given by the *Année* to religious sociology: 'Religion holds within it, from the very beginning, but in a muddled sort of way, all the elements that have given rise to the various manifestations of collective life' (Durkheim 1980[1898–9]: 54). He gave many examples: science is born of myths, the visual arts of cult ceremonies, law and morality of religious practices, and philosophy of religious beliefs. With the possible exception of economic organization, everything – from kinship to punishment, and from the gift to the contract – was bound up with religion. The importance that Durkheim now attached to the study of religion was to have an immediate impact on his teaching: in 1900–1, his sociology lectures looked at 'elementary forms of religion'. He had already come up with an idea for the title of the book he was to write a few years later. Durkheim felt obliged to defend the 'procedure' or method he and his collaborators had adopted. It consisted in trying to identify origins, and elementary or primitive forms of the phenomenon under discussion: 'In order to be able, with some chance of success, to tell what the society of tomorrow will be, it is indispensable to have studied the social patterns of the most remote past. To understand the present, one must depart from it' (ibid.: 55). He wished, however, to avoid possible misunderstandings: 'But, of course, the important role we thus attribute to religious sociology in no way implies that religion must play, in contemporary societies, the same role as formerly . . . Precisely because religion is a primitive phenomenon, it ought to give way more and more to the new social structures it has engendered (ibid.: 55 n1).

Given that religious sociology deals with religious facts, it must, logically, begin by defining them. Durkheim sets about that task in an article simply entitled 'Concerning the definition of religious phenomena' (1994[1899]) and, following the methodological rules he has established, he begins by leaving aside 'the more or less vague idea that each of us has about religion'. He dwells at some length on the more popular definition, which refers to the idea of God. That definition does not hold because there are religions that escape it. The essential dogmas of Buddhism, for example, make no reference to any divinity; nor does Jainism or, in a sense, Brahmanism. They are atheist religions. The idea of a divinity is, he concludes, only a 'secondary aspect of religious life' (ibid.: 84).

Religion is characterized, rather, by the presence of structures or rituals that operate mechanically, if not automatically, and which, like sacrifice, act by themselves or by virtue of some power of their own. Durkheim cites Berdaigne's study of the Vedic religion '"Sacrifice exercises a direct influence upon the celestial phenomena"' (Durkheim 1994[1899]: 86). Berdaigne had taught Sylvain Lévi, and his *Religion védique* had been required reading for Mauss when he began his studies in the sixth section.

There are, then, cults or practices that function by themselves. We can therefore understand, Durkheim goes on, the primordial importance accorded to 'the material part of the ceremonies' by almost all cults. This is 'religious formalism' (in the sense in which one can speak of judicial

formalism): 'the formulae pronounced contain with them the source of
their effectiveness' (Durkheim 1994[1899]: 87). The distinction between the
sacred and the profane, which is basic to all organized religion, does not
imply the idea of God, which is a later development. The notion of divinity plays a role in the religious life of people, one that is 'analogous to that
of the idea of the ego in the psychic life of the individual: it is a principle
of grouping and unification' (ibid.: 87). For Durkheim, the most important part of the definition of religion is therefore ritual, which consists in
'clearly defined ways of behaviour' (ibid.: 87, 88): 'Ritual is an element of
all religion, which is no less essential than faith' (ibid.: 91). This does not
mean that Durkheim overlooks representations or beliefs – that is, myths
and dogmas. He speaks, on the one hand, of a practical discipline and,
on the other, of inescapable beliefs. The two are closely related: practices are expressions of beliefs, and beliefs are interpretations of practices.
Durkheim's definition takes both aspects into account: 'phenomena held
to be religious consist in obligatory beliefs, connected with clearly defined
practices which are related to given objects of those beliefs' (ibid.: 93).

This perspective means, according to Durkheim, that the science of religions can become a 'truly sociological science': if religious practices and
beliefs are obligatory, and if everything obligatory is social in origin, religion is essentially a social phenomenon. Obligation implies a command
and consequently an authority which commands. The rules the individual
is obliged to follow are defined by the group, by society, 'the only thinking being which is greater than man', and a 'synthesis of individuals':
'The state of perpetual dependence in which we find ourselves in the face
of society inspires in us a feeling of religious awe' (1994[1899]: 93). And
the powers before which the believer prostrates himself are social forces.
They are the products of collective sentiments. What are those sentiments?
Durkheim's reply to that question is this: 'These are the questions that
the science of religions must consider; and to deal with them we have to
observe the conditions of collective existence' (ibid.: 94).

The task Durkheim sets the scientist is to resolve the apparently incomprehensible mystery of religion, and to find an explanation for something
that seems strange to us. He must, in other words, discover the laws of
'collective conceptualization' and 'the appropriate laws of social mentality'. Religion is not 'some great hallucination and phantasmagoria'.
Humanity has not been duped. Religion does consist of representations,
and they are 'not the handiwork of the individual reason but that of the
collective mind'. Society is a reality *sui generis*, with its own way of being
and its own way of thinking: 'It has its passions, its habits and its needs,
which are not those of the individual' (1994[1899]: 95).

We are now, Durkheim continues, in a better position to understand
the distinction between sacred and profane things, which is found in all
religions. The distinction between the two is the same as that between
collective representations (collective states of all kinds, traditions, shared
emotions) and individual representations (individual impressions). We
have, on the one hand, a plurality of brains and minds that act upon one

another and react and, on the other, a single brain and a single mind. This duality is a symbolic expression of the duality of the individual and the social, of psychology (the science of individual mentalities) and sociology (the science of collective mentalities). This is why the socialization of the individual involves an initiation into sacred things, as we can see from the bar-mitzvah. Durkheim is aware that not everyone will agree with him here. Are there not such things as beliefs and practices that result from individual spontaneity? Are there not such things as 'free meditation' and individual ways of practising a religion? There is, Durkheim concedes, such a thing as a 'free, private, optional religion' and 'private belief . . . derived from public belief': the individual is not a passive witness; he pictures religion in is own way and personalizes it; 'Owing to the force of circumstances, there are in every church almost as many heterodox as orthodox, and unorthodox opinions multiply and become more obvious in proportion to the growth of individual thought' (1994[1899]: 96, 97). A personal religion is not more than the subjective aspect of a public religion. The same is true, Durkheim remarks, of all aspects of social life: 'There are no forms of collective activity which do not become personalized in this way. Each of us has his personal moral code, his personal approach' (ibid.: 97). He insists, however, that these individual manifestations are products of social institutions.

When Gaston Richard asked him a few questions about the article he had just published, Durkheim replied in a letter: (1) 'Nothing could be vaguer or more diffuse than religiosity. Everything to do with religious phenomena is confused.' (2) Given that myths 'represent things as sacred things', their origins are religious, no matter what Lang thinks. (3) No matter whether we look at 'Judaism, Buddhism, Christianity or even Mahometanism', there is no religion that is ultimately a human artefact (he was reluctant to say more about Islam, as he had so little information). He added: 'There are a certain number of elementary notions (I am not saying that they are simple in logical terms) that have dominated the entire history of humanity's evolution).' In this short letter, Durkheim suggests that religion is to society what sensation is to the individual: 'Society sees its own life and that of the objects to which it relates as sacred things. It tinges them with religiosity. Why? That is a topic for a big debate!'[38] A few years later, Richard was to remark that the 'basic ideas of the *Elementary Forms of the Religious Life* had taken shape in the author's mind long before this'.[39]

Durkheim's article was immediately followed by Hubert and Mauss's longer essay on sacrifice. Their analysis deals with only two religions – Hinduism and Judaism – but uses the comparative method to try to reach 'conclusions that are sufficiently general' (Hubert and Mauss 1964[1899]: 8). It is a well-documented piece of research based on a reading of written texts – the Vedas, Brahmanas and Sutras in the case of Vedic ritual, and the Pentateuch in the case of Judaism – collections of hymns, methodological and theological commentaries, and manuals. The reading of the Sanskrit and Hebrew texts is supplemented by a study of texts from classical and Christian antiquity. But there is no reliance on ethnographic data: 'Generally distorted through over-hasty observation or falsified by the exactness of our languages, the facts recorded by ethnographers have value only if they are compared with more precise and more complete documents' (ibid.).

The authors follow Durkheim's advice and begin by defining the facts they describe as 'sacrifice'. The emphasis is on consecration: '*Sacrifice is a religious act which, through the consecration of a victim, modifies the condition of the moral person who accomplishes it or that of certain objects with which he is concerned*' (Hubert and Mauss 1964[1899]: 13). Their goal is to 'disentangle the simple and elementary forms of an institution' (ibid.: 7). What is a sacrificial ritual? It is, according to Hubert and Mauss, a way of 'establishing a means of communication between the sacred and profane worlds through the mediation of a victim, that is, of a thing that in the course of the ceremony is destroyed' (ibid.: 97). Their detailed and rigorous study is designed to uncover the general schema or grammar of sacrifice: the 'entry' or prelude, the drama or destruction of the victim, and a conclusion or 'exit'. They also identify the various elements that make up a sacrifice: the thing to be sacrificed, the sacrificer, the place and instruments, and the sequence of events.

The object of their study is 'the sacred', and they wish to supply a 'clear example of the workings of the idea of the sacred' (Mauss 1979[1930]: 218) and to reveal the social dimension and function of religion: 'Religious notions exist because they are believed; they have an objective existence, like social facts. Sacrifice functions with reference to sacred things, and sacred things are social things.' When they reassess their earlier work, Hubert and Mauss went still further:

> In our view, anything that, in the eyes of the group and its members, describes their society, is seen as sacred. When the gods, each at their appointed time, come out of the temple and become profane, we see things that are human but social – the fatherland, property, work, the human personality – enter the temple one by one. (Hubert and Mauss 1969[1906]: 16–17)

'Sacrifice' outlines a whole research programme in which Hubert and Mauss outline a sociological analysis of a set of social beliefs and practices that are not religious: it deals in turn with contract, redemption, penalties, gifts, abnegation and ideas relating to the soul and immortality, and thus 'indicates the importance of sacrifice for sociology' (Hubert and Mauss 1964[1899]: 103).

Sidney E. Hartland reviewed every volume of *L'Année sociologique* for the British journal *Folk-Lore*, and praised the journal for its 'high standards'. He enthusiastically described Durkheim's article as 'a thoughtful methodological dissertation.' He was also full of praise for Hubert and Mauss's 'Sacrifice', and called it 'a brilliant and suggestive essay' (Hartland 1900). He did not, on the other hand, believe that a theory of sacrifice could be based upon a study of just Hinduism and Judaism. But it is still true to say that many were impressed by the authors' deep understanding of the ancient texts and by their vast erudition (Bochard 1899). Some, however, were sceptical: 'A curious and powerful study', exclaimed Belot (1905). Writing in *L'Anthropologie*, René Verneau (1900) described it as 'A tiresome reading of some arid questions.'

A Failure?

Durkheim was, as always, worried: 'It is a funny thing, but I have yet to see any indication that this volume is in circulation; not a word, not even a request for a copy . . . and a few letters from authors.' He was therefore under the impression that the *Année* was 'not circulating'. 'My God! It would be extraordinary, given that it is better, if it were to sell less well.'[40] Annoyed but not surprised at 'receiving almost no news', he went on to complain: 'Perhaps I am mistaken, but I get the impression that, even though I am much more satisfied with it than with the first, our second volume is having less success.'[41] He then quickly revised his opinion: 'Our second *Année* has had a much more favourable welcome than the first', he wrote to Célestin Bouglé. 'And it does seem to me to be much better.' Dominique Parodi felt the same: the second volume seemed to him to be 'much better than the first, and excellent'. He congratulated himself on having contributed to it, and was especially pleased to see that 'the notion of sociology is becoming clearer and clearer'.[42]

Durkheim regretted, on the other hand, that 'sociology was not visible enough' in Mauss and Hubert's article. 'Sacrifice is too important a social fact for a comparative study not to be sociological. Think of this institution's influence on ideas and mores. But before we can study its influence, we have to establish the notion of an institution.' Durkheim himself intended to return to this question in the third volume: 'My next memoir will be this subject: what a general sociology can be.'[43]

Its competitor, the *Revue internationale de sociologie*, praised *L'Année sociologique* for its 'innovatory' analysis of works on sociology, but also had one criticism: the reviews were too short. The two journals still had their differences. The *Revue internationale* refused to accept the idea of a collective consciousness: 'We should not go so far as to say that "society" has its own way of thinking.' Nor did it accept that 'exceptional importance' should be given to religious phenomena: if something had to be prioritized – which the journal doubted – it should be economic phenomena (Bochard 1899). The historians, and especially historians of religion, had come under direct attack, and could not remain silent. Durkheim and Mauss had accused them of being Eurocentric, Christo-centric and intellectualist (if not spiritualist). Jean Réville (1909: 223) tried to warn against the 'exaggerations of the sociologists' who, because they prioritize the study of non-civilized religions, 'see totems and taboos everywhere'.[44]

French anthropologists, for their part, appeared to take no notice of the publication of *L'Année sociologique*. It was only after Mauss and Hubert's essay had been published that René Verneau, who was one of editors-in-chief of *L'Anthropologie*, but who described himself as a 'layman', devoted a short review to it. The new journal received more attention (and admiration) on the other side of the Channel, where Sidney Hartland (1890: 96) praised it for its 'high level', and truly scientific spirit. He admired its sophistication and the sure judgement of its reviews. Solid results could, he concluded, be expected of it. In the United States, the *American Journal of Sociology* insisted that *L'Année* had done sociology a 'great service' – 'indispensable work' – but its editor was still critical of the quality of its reviews.

What was already being called 'the French school of sociology' was beginning to emerge. The first translation of one of Durkheim's books appeared in 1899, when F.A. Logamson translated *The Rules of Sociological Method* into Russian. The book had attracted great interest ever since its publication into French, and there had been many commentaries, including critical ones.

Bouglé on Equality

In 1899, Célestin Bouglé defended his doctoral thesis on the social origins of egalitarianism at the Sorbonne, and this was a major event for everyone associated with the *Année*. Later that year, Alcan published his thesis as *Les Idées égalitaires;* it was subtitled 'A sociological study'. As was the custom at this time, the candidate also submitted a Latin thesis on Cournot: *Quid e Cournoti disciplina ad scientias sociologicas promovendas sumere liceat.* The jury consisted of Henry Michel, Alfred Croiset, Émile Boutroux and Georges Séailles. Michel had taught Bouglé at the Lycée Henri-IV, and Bouglé had dedicated his first book on the social sciences in Germany to his old teacher. A few years later, he wrote an article (Bouglé 1905b) on Michel's *Une Doctrine idéaliste de la démocratie*.[45]

What are the social preconditions for the emergence and spread of egalitarian ideas? Such was the central question posed in Bouglé's thesis. In his opinion, egalitarian thought was articulated around the values of humanity and individuality, took account of both differences and similarities, and attached great importance to rights. It was, in practice, closely associated with the democratic ideal and found its conditions of possibility in Western societies characterized by (1) a sharp increase in social density and number of social contacts; (2) increased 'social complexity' and increasingly divided social loyalties (to social groups or circles); and (3) a high enough level of social unification and state power to guarantee that all are equal in the eyes of the law. There are therefore several concurrent reasons, rather than just one, for the rise of egalitarianism.

The notion of density derives from the work of Durkheim, and that of social complexity from Simmel. This is therefore sociology, and not a study in the history of ideas: ideas do not rule the world. Bouglé demonstrates the limitations of 'ideological explanations', which lead only to the 'worship of a mystery'. It is not, on the other hand, for sociology to decree that one idea is better than another. Bouglé is obviously in favour of egalitarianism, but he refuses to use science to defend his personal convictions (Bouglé 1899a: 78–80).

During the oral examination [*soutenance*], discussion centred mainly on rationality's causal role in the emergence of social phenomena. Alfred Croiset was critical: 'You seriously underestimate the importance of the essential intermediary between the sociological causes of egalitarian ideas and their success: rationalism.' Boutroux also had his criticisms: 'The egalitarian idea comes from the human soul, and not from social forms.'[46]

Bouglé immediately sent a copy of his book to Durkheim, and dedicated it to him 'with affection'. Durkheim did not have time to read it – he kept it for the Easter vacation – but made no secret of the pleasure he felt on seeing one of his close collaborators 'discussing collective representations, not as combinations of concepts that have nothing to do with anything, but as products of determinate social states. That is, I believe, the only way of doing collective psychology, and the method is still so unknown and so little practised for your work not to be of interest and value.'[47] As he later told Bouglé, he did, however, have some doubts: 'The speed with which you polished off your work worries me a little.'[48] A month later, Durkheim, who had spent a working holiday divided between Paris and Épinal correcting 600 pages of second proofs of the *Année,* had just begun – 'Hmm', he added in parentheses – to read Bouglé's essay, but he had read the first lecture with great pleasure: 'You add a certain charm to sociology. I have often been criticized for being somewhat brutal about putting my ideas forward. You, on the other hand, are more gently persuasive. And I am very pleased when you do this for the ideas we share. And those are the most important points.'[49]

Another month went by. Durkheim now wrote to his collaborator to tell him that he had read all of his book. He was pleased to be able to report that his fears had been groundless: Bouglé had put together a 'very respectable' number of facts. And his methodology was excellent. 'You relate ideas and social trends to a definite social state, leave nothing up in the air, and show that they are part of the real, that they come from the real and go back to the real. All this is very new.' He then added: 'But you will probably have some big battles to fight at the Sorbonne, especially with your old teacher Michel, who does the very opposite in his history of the idea of the state.'[50]

Durkheim criticized Bouglé, finally, for his reluctance to defend his own ideas. 'What I criticize you for is the sort of discretion that means that you dare not take your own ideas to heart.' He took as an example egalitarianism, which Bouglé appeared to reduce 'to the basic principle of fairness: to each according to their needs'. He asked:

Is there not a more radical egalitarianism, which takes no account of this latter equality but which is no more than one form of it? And isn't there something shocking when the inequality of conditions becomes too pronounced; I am well aware that this hyper-egalitarianism is challenged more, but that trend does exist, and I do not think it is without foundation.

Durkheim had one other polite objection to make:

> You say that the moral consciousness is also in a position to praise or condemn the egalitarian tendency, even though you have shown that this tendency is bound up with our social state as a whole. But if our whole social state implies egalitarianism, what can our poor moral consciousness do about it? Protests cannot, at all events, be anything more than platonic, unless they lead to collective suicide.

The methodological principle defended by Durkheim is this: 'Anything that is necessary to life, or anything that derives from the basic [non-accidental] conditions of life cannot be bad.' That, he added, was what he would have 'quibbled over' if he had been a member of the thesis jury; he then quickly ended the discussion.[51]

Rigour and extreme caution at the methodological level: such were the qualities of what Dominique Parodi (1900) described as a 'remarkable book', which had made 'the most precious contribution to date to elaborating a sociology in the true sense of the word'. This was his way of saying that it was 'a truly scientific work'. The days of 'fumbling, sterile discussions of methodology and dazzling but vague declarations' were over. Sociology had now reached 'the stage of modest research and fruitful work'. In his long review of his friend's book, Parodi demonstrated that its 'considerable import' lay in the conception of sociology to be found in it. It was, in other words, close to Durkheim, but at the same time different. Bouglé obviously defended the specificity of sociology, but he also elaborated a methodology that could never be objective and which used 'psychological deduction' to reintroduce into sociology the 'psychological intermediaries' known as feelings and ideas.[52]

In 1900, Bouglé left Montpellier for Toulouse, where his new course on public lectures dealt with the theme of 'Scientific morality and the egalitarian ideal'. He also taught a course on the theory of action, and prepared students for the *agrégation*. The following year, his lectures were on 'Specialization and competition: an examination of their moral and pedagogic implications'. He also gave lectures on 'The analysis of the feeling of freedom' to degree students. Paul Fauconnet, meanwhile, was working on his doctoral thesis, which he intended to devote to the question of responsibility. That was a question of interest to Durkheim. Fauconnet had been appointed to the Lycée Louis-le Grand and returned to Paris, but only for a year. The following year, he was awarded a travel grant to go to Germany before returning to Paris with a study grant that would allow him to work on his doctorate during the 1899–1900 academic year.

The Next Volume of *L'Année sociologique*

The publication of the second volume of *l'Année sociologique* indicated that it was a going concern. The editorial board still had a lot of work to do: journals and books had to be obtained from publishers and sent out to contributors. 'I have written 200 letters to publishers', Durkheim told Hubert, 'not to mention the postal orders I have sent off. It may not be much of a task in itself, but it becomes something of a burden on top of everything else.'[53] 'You have to fight to get [books] from the publishers', he complained, adding that he was prepared to 'buy everything we need without counting the cost'.[54]

Durkheim now gave his collaborators greater freedom to choose which books to review. 'Start out from the principle that you cannot analyse more than 30 or so books of any consequence, and then choose the ones that best fit into the framework of the *Année*.'[55] He obviously had to keep up the morale of his troops, ensure that everyone contributed something and, insofar as it was possible to do so, expand the pool of contributors. 'Can we still count on your friend Parodi?' he asked Bouglé.[56] He also thought that one of his students, who had passed his *agrégation* a year earlier, might be able to help Bouglé. Emmanuel Lévy's collaboration was also a problem: 'He is certainly willing, but he still hasn't completed the lighter task I asked him to do, and it has been three years now.'[57]

Durkheim then persuaded two other researchers – F. Sigel and Joe T. Stickney – to contribute, albeit on a very limited basis. Little is known about Sigel, other than the fact that he was a professor at the University of Warsaw. His contribution was restricted to a few reviews in the third volume. Stickney was a friend of Mauss and Hubert.[58] He coedited the 'political organization' subsection of the journal with Durkheim. His contribution to *L'Année* was, as Hubert (1905) put it, 'sporadic but useful'. He joined the team and shared their ideas, 'perhaps out of friendship rather than for rational reasons'.

Marcel Mauss's prolonged silences and lack of commitment were a constant source of annoyance to his uncle, who made no effort to conceal the fact that his happy-go-lucky attitude caused him 'pain and worry': 'You've given me some bad moments this past week.' Over a period of more than two months, he asked Mauss on several occasions to send the latest volume and galley proofs of *L'Année sociologique* to Steinmetz, who was 'unhappy' and wanted them 'immediately'. 'This has been a nasty surprise.' Mauss's carelessness seemed all the more 'unspeakable' in that Steinmetz was supposed to contribute to the next volume.

Durkheim also wanted to know what his nephew was doing. 'Where are you?' he would regularly ask him. 'When you keep quiet, it means you are hiding something from me.'[59] When Marcel did try to explain, his excuses were 'vague and contradictory', especially when he avoided revealing how his thesis was coming along. 'You really have to get on with your thesis.' 'It would in every respect be wise on your part to tell me the truth, if you don't mind me saying so.'[60] Things soon calmed down. 'I've run out of patience', Durkheim wrote, but he tried to make the best of it. 'I've given up protesting about your apathy all the time. I'll just have to put up with it; that way, it won't cause me any more heartache.'[61] Durkheim often 'cleaned up' the drafts his nephew sent him – in other words, he copied them out and abridged them: 'Devoting my time to helping you gives me great pleasure.'[62] The uncle was also irritated by his nephew's 'improbable optimism', and his belief that the 'job' would be finished soon, if not within the next 24 hours. He also thought that Marcel was over-ambitious: 'You do not have to revolutionize science in a single essay. Don't be in such a rush to express ideas that seem to me to be insufficiently mature.' Then came the congratulations and the encouragement: 'So, take heart; if we work well, keep our heads and don't try to do too much, we'll get there in the end.' Durkheim finally sent the manuscript to Alcan at the beginning of February. 'It's good', he told his nephew, except for Steinmetz's essay, which was 'long and appalling.' 'I thought of rejecting it, he admitted to Bouglé, 'but that would have made the *Année* another enemy.'[63] Not knowing quite what to do, Durkheim consulted his colleague Octave Hamelin, and finally agreed to publish: 'But it will stick out like a sore thumb.'[64]

Ratzel, Richard and Steinmetz: Three Articles

The third volume of *L'Année* differed from its predecessors in that more space was devoted to articles. It continued three original articles: two ('Land, society and state' and 'Classifications of social types') by foreign researchers: Friedrich Ratzel was German, Sebald Rudolf Steinmetz was Dutch (he studied under Ratzel in Leipzig). The third author (of 'Social crises and criminality') was Gaston Richard, a regular contributor to *L'Année*. It was 'the best', said Durkheim, who concluded: 'We will only be satisfied with the articles that we write ourselves. That must be our goal.'[65]

The overall organization remained the same. There were six main sections, of which moral and juridic sociology (133 pages) and religious sociology (125 pages) were the largest. Less space was given to the other sections: 63 pages for economic sociology, 43 for general sociology and 38 for criminal sociology. Some modifications and changes were introduced, as each section editor tried to introduce new rubrics. 'Civilization and progress' and 'Individual personality and collective personality' were, for instance, added to the 'general sociology' section, while 'responsibility' was added to 'general sociology', and 'traditions and beliefs' to 'religious sociology.' The final 'miscellaneous' section, which consisted of some 20 pages of reviews, still included the 'anthroposociological' section[66] (with a note adding 'with the same reservations as in previous years'), but also a new 'aesthetic sociology' section edited by Hubert and Parodi. Durkheim believed that it was a good idea to introduce the new section. 'I have always thought of doing so', he told Hubert, 'And now is the time to try it out.'[67] Hubert was the most 'artistic' of all the *Année*'s contributors, being both an amateur painter (he also drew) and a collector. Marcel Mauss described the 'miscellaneous' section as 'general and insignificant', and rued the fact that 'the role of aesthetic phenomena [has been] overlooked' (Mauss 1927),[68] and that the field of aesthetic sociology was so broadly and badly defined: it included everything from primitive art to literature and music, and also covered games. The section's stance was clearly anthropological. There was one other innovation: the subject index was now complemented by an author index (of those whose works were analysed or appeared in the bibliographies).

The first article, 'Land, society and state' (Ratzel 1900), was very short, at only 15 pages. Friedrich Ratzel (1844–1904), who began his career by studying biology and pharmacy, was a German geographer influenced by the work of Darwin and his German disciple Ernst Haeckel. He was the founder of the new school of anthropogeography, whose goal was to analyse the distribution of men across the surface of the globe and to determine 'the possible influence of the land on man'. He was also the inventor of the concept of *Lebensraum* ('living space'), and in his *Das Meer als Quelle der Völkergrösse* (1900) [*The Sea as Source of National Power*] he argued the need for Germany to expand its navy. He was, of course, a fervent nationalist.

In his study, Ratzel criticized sociologists for describing societies without taking into account the spatial factor of land. In his view, the first need of any population was a territory to provide both homes and food. The ways in which those needs were met by their territories had a direct influence on the societies that lived in them. Ratzel therefore classified peoples on the basis of their attachment to their territory. Small nomadic peoples (Gypsies, Eskimos) were at the bottom of the hierarchy, and 'the civilized and sedentary peoples whose symbol is the town' at the very top. The influence of territory was determinant: 'It rules the destiny of peoples with a blind brutality. A people must live on the land granted it by fate, die there and live by its law. This is what feeds the political egoism that makes land the main objective of public life' (Ratzel 1900: 12–13). According to Ratzel, land was the main factor behind human progress: 'The gradual expansion of the territory of states is an essential characteristic of historical progress and, at the same time, a powerful motor behind progress' (ibid.: 14). And when its territory shrank, it was usually 'the beginning of the end' for the community concerned.'

The *Année*'s publication of an article like this was an indication that sociology should attach great importance to social morphology. Durkheim published a review of Ratzel's recent *Anthropogeographie* in the same volume, and congratulated him on his wish to 'drag geography out of the isolation in which it languished, to bring it closer to sociology, and to turn it into a truly social science' (Durkheim 1969[1900b]: 236). But while Ratzel's approach was 'suggestive', it also had its weaknesses. Durkheim was sceptical about an approach that attempted to use one science to explain a whole set of heterogeneous phenomena. Geographical factors could not explain everything, and geography was, in Durkheim's view, less important than it used to be: 'The truths of science are now independent of all local situations. Thanks to easier communications, the fashions, tastes and mores of different regions are becoming more and more homogeneous' (ibid.: 237). People now found it increasingly easy to transform the land in order to meet their needs, and it was no longer the land that explained man, but rather the converse. Durkheim's remarks can be seen as a radical critique of any theory of territorial expansion that serves the interest of one nation.

The second article was by Gaston Richard, a long-standing contributor to the *Année* (but not a member of what might be called its 'general staff'). His 'Les crises sociales et les conditions de la criminalité' ['Social crises and the preconditions for criminality'] picked up the main arguments of *Suicide* and, like Durkheim, Richard criticized the criminologists of the Italian school: it is not organic factors that determine homicide rates but, as the statistical data show, the social environment. We can therefore legitimately conclude, in Richard's view, that 'the cause of criminality lies in crises or violent transformations of moral, religious and political discipline, beneficial and inevitable as those transformations may be' (Richard 1900a: 32). His thesis is that when a society is in a 'normal state', or a state of slow, harmonious and regular development, it spontaneously and consciously organizes resistance to criminal tendencies, but when it is in a 'state of crisis', it determines the appearance of criminality (ibid.: 16). 'To what type of crisis should we attribute the rise in criminality? The economic crisis or the political crisis?' Richard's answer is that the two are closely related. Rejecting the economic determinism of Labriola and Marx, he traces its origin back to an ethical-religious crisis and to the rapid disintegration of collective beliefs and habits.

The last article, 'Classification des types sociaux et catalogue des peuples' ['Classifying social types and cataloguing peoples'], by Sebald Rudolf Steinmetz (1862–1940), was much longer, and ran to more than 100 pages. This was a question of great interest to Durkheim, who had already established a classification of social types. Steinmetz outlined something different; he wanted to know if it was possible to differentiate between social groups on the basis of objective criteria, as had already been done in chemistry and biology. Such a classification would, in his view, mark a definite break with 'abstract and philosophical sociology'. Abstract deductions would give way to a mass of classified facts. Steinmetz's damning comments on the dilettantes who had nothing to do with real science but who were still 'the leading lights' in France (Steinmetz 1900: 67) was unlikely to appeal to Durkheim.

Steinmetz discusses the various attempts that had been made to classify social types, including Durkheim's. He criticizes him on the grounds that his classification is based upon only one criterion, namely degrees of segmentation, and argues that segmentation is not the most essential characteristic of societies. 'I fear that this division of societies into simple and poly-segmentary groups, will never have any impact on the educated public, or even on sociologists' (Steinmetz 1900: 67). Steinmetz tended to favour the approach adopted by the naturalist Sutherland, who classified peoples on the basis of their general level of intelligence: savagery, barbarism, civilization and culture.[69] According to Steinmetz, the great advantage of this classification is that it takes the general level of intelligence as its criterion: 'There is no circumstance that is more important to human society, culture and man.'

Irrespective of whether or not his classification is accepted, Steinmetz concludes his article with a call for the mobilization of researchers and outlines a programme of work for historians and ethnographers: they should systematically record the most important social characteristics of all peoples (economic life, government, social composition, family organization, property ownership, demographic situation, intellectual and religious phase). His idea is to establish a universal database to which the whole scientific community can contribute.

Durkheim was, quite understandably, reluctant to publish the article: 'This rehash is not much of a meal for the *Année*. But what can we do?'[70] He was harshly critical of Steinmetz's approach: 'It does not seem to us very scientific to classify societies according to their level of civilization, as Spencer and even Steinmetz have done' (Durkheim 1978[1901]: 263 n3).

With hindsight, Durkheim identified the publication of this article with a 'real crisis' (one of several that had hit the journal since the publication of 'Sacrifice') that was linked to the problems that the *Année* had with articles.[71] Both Steinmeitz's and Ratzel's articles were given a very cool reception. Writing in the new *Revue de synthèse historique*, with which some contributors to the *Année* were associated, Edmond Goblot (1900) was disappointed with Steinmetz's proposed classification: 'True, it is no more than a programme. But the programme lacks clarity.' Richard's 'fine article' was the only one that inspired any enthusiasm: it was closely argued, and displayed a broad and reliable erudition. A careful reader of *L'Année sociologique*, Gustave Belot (1901) was equally sceptical about Steinmetz's classification. The essay, he said, was 'not much better than those he criticizes'. As for Ratzel (who revived the old sociological theory of 'climates' that made social man dependent upon his physical environment), his thesis was 'fragile': 'The fact remains that it is always man who makes all the difference . . . Which is why geography tends to become social, and why sociology does not become geographical' (Belot 1901: 664). Belot was not convinced by Gaston Richard's argument either. In his view, the real reason for criminality was not degeneracy (dissolute habits and feelings), but parasitism. He was, in other words, still very 'suspicious' of (Durkheimian) sociology.

A Discovery: Spencer and Gillen

Durkheim wrote almost 60 reviews for the third volume of the *Année*. This involved a considerable amount of work – more than that done by any other contributor. Several dealt with the issues of social organization, marriage and the family, birth rates and descent. His aim was to publicize and criticize what he saw as important or useful books – such as Franz Boas's study of the secret societies of the Kwakiutl Indians and Thorsten Veblen's article 'The beginnings of ownership' – and to reiterate some of his own theses, including those on individualism. He also discussed social problems and contemporary issues such as the alarming decline in the French birth rate: in his view, this was anything but a transient phenomenon, and the reasons for it were neither organic nor economic, but moral.

The book that really drew attention was, of course, *The Native Tribes of Central Australia*, by Baldwin Spencer and F.J. Gillen (1899), which brought together 'an enormous amount of facts' and was therefore 'infinitely precious'. This was, it was said, 'one of the most important books on ethnography and descriptive sociology' to deal with the tribes of Central Australia. One of the authors was an Australian zoologist of English origin, the other an Australian-born Irishman who had been head of a transcontinental telegraph station for 20 years. Both had observed native ceremonies at length and had interviewed informants; as Gillen remarked to Spencer, it would all have been of no value if he had not lived with the natives and won their trust (see Stocking 1995: 95). Spencer and Gillen, together with Alfred C. Haddon, the Reverend Lorimer Fison and Alfred William Howitt, were members of a new generation of researchers who abandoned the library to work in the field and make 'definitive studies' (Mauss 1969[1902]: 460).

The Native Tribes was, Hartland remarked (1899: 23), an extraordinary book about the strange institution known as totemism. He believed that it embodied many hopes, and even the hope that the history of humanity could be reconstructed with greater accuracy than even before. This was something that previous generations could never have expected to see. The publication of *The Native Tribes* had been eagerly awaited by everyone who was working directly on totemism and marked, according to Henri Hubert (1902: 403), 'an important date in the history of anthropological and sociological studies' because it brought together a mass of detailed documents on tribes that were on the point of extinction and because of the unexpected facts that it revealed. It was, exclaimed Durkheim 'a discovery'.

Durkheim and Mauss agreed to 'share the Spencer and Gillen' in a review that was at once admiring and critical. Durkheim's attention was initially caught by some 'interesting facts' and especially those relating to totemic sacrifices. 'This time, there are no doubts as to their widespread existence in this special environment.'[72] Mauss dealt with the sections dealing with religious phenomena and especially totemism and initiation ceremonies (Mauss 1969[1900]). He also reviewed James Frazer's 'The origins of totemism' in the same volume of the *Année*.

Durkheim, for his part, chose to discuss the sections devoted to social and family organization (territorial groups, matrimonial classes and totemic groups). 'We can see how complex the organization of these tribes is. And they are, I believe, complicated because of the overlap between different systems corresponding to different stages of social evolution.' He also identified other 'very useful pieces of information' and 'interesting facts' about the family and sexual relations. The text showed that there was once such a thing as 'group marriage' (a thesis defended by Morgan and challenged by Durkheim) and supplied one example of the exceptional transgression of the rules of exogamy. 'There is an obligation to come into contact with the thing from which one must, in normal circumstances, abstain' (1969[1900c]). This was, Durkheim concluded, a book 'rich in raw materials', and it would be of vital importance when he came to write his essay 'Sur le totémisme'. The *Année*'s review section was once more described as 'admirable' (Fouillée 1899: 674), even by its competitors, but the reader's attention was often drawn not so much by the reviews – the 'rest of the journal' – as by the articles. And if there was one thing that annoyed A. Bochard, a contributor to the *Revue internationale de sociologie*, it was that 'far too much room' was, perhaps, given to the comparative history of religions (Bochard 1900: 915). He appeared to take the view that a sociology journal should not attach such importance to so-called primitive peoples.[73]

Election to the Collège de France: Gabriel Tarde or Henri Bergson?

In the summer of 1899, it was rumoured that a chair in modern philosophy was about to be established at the Collège de France and that Gabriel Tarde was the likely candidate. Émile was not especially keen on keeping up with the latest Parisian gossip, but he did ask his nephew to keep him informed about what '[he] should be aware of'. He would have liked to 'remain above all that', but such wheeling and dealing saddened him. He also wanted something to happen: 'I am a little tired at the moment, intellectually depressed, even: I think I need something of a stimulus.'[74] Although he was usually an anxious man, he showed astonishingly little 'impatience' about knowing the results of the procedure and wanted, he said, to 'keep out of it'. Perhaps he was aware that he had little hope of being chosen. 'I do not have to put myself forward for a chair in philosophy, and I see no reason why Tarde should not be appointed.'[75] Durkheim knew that 'they won't even think of getting me out of here [Bordeaux] until he [Tarde] has been fixed up'. Putting himself forward as a candidate for a chair in modern philosophy was out of the question; as he explained to Xavier Léon, he was not 'a philosopher in the professional sense of the word'. But he deeply regretted the fact that sociology was still being confused with philosophy. It was in the interest of both disciplines to 'remain distinct': 'Many good minds still do not really understand what either should be'.[76]

The main candidates were Gabriel Tarde and Henri Bergson, who were both major figures in intellectual circles and straddled the divide between philosophy, psychology and sociology.

Tarde's *Les Lois de l'imitation* [*The Laws of Imitation*] had made him famous (it had been translated into both Russian and English, and he had recently published two books with Alcan: *Les Lois sociales* (1898) and *Les Transformations du pouvoir* (1899). He was a very active member of the Société de sociologie de Paris, and had given a lecture on *'l'esprit de groupe'* ['group spirit'] in the autumn of 1899.[77] Although Tarde worked on his own, he had outlined an 'Outline for an individual sociological survey'. The plan was for to ask informants to write 'personal monographs' based on personal information and interviews with 'friends and acquaintances'. The possible subjects, which he described as 'easy to write', included 'Hereditary professions in modern society', and he suggested that members of the society should choose it because of its 'relative simplicity'.

Henri Bergson already had 'a very great influence on contemporary speculation', and his work was 'highly esteemed by anyone interested in philosophy' (Parodi 1901: 236).[78] Even Georges Sorel became 'one of his most subtle and most supportive interpreters' and played, it was later said, the role of the 'leader of a sort of Bergsonian left, or even far left'.[79] Bergson published *Essai sur les données immédiates de la conscience*, his first book, in 1889 (see Bergson 1910[1889]). It was the thesis he had recently defended. The book was, as Xavier Léon put it, 'a huge success'. Théodule Ribot remarked: 'They tell me at the Sorbonne that Boutroux's star is beginning to fade and that this young conceptual juggler, Bergson, is the rising star.' His second book, *Matière et mémoire*, appeared in 1896 (see Bergson 1911[1896]) and was also hailed as a masterpiece. Bergsonism was beginning to look more and more like anti-rationalism. There was an obvious resemblance between Bergsonism and fin-de-siècle aestheticism, and Bergson was emerging as symbolism's official philosopher; he was seen as an ally of Verlaine, Mallarmé and the advocates of free verse. Symbolism was to mysticism what Parnassianism was to positivism: one was internalized in the object, while the other described objects. Intuition, *durée* and freedom were the watchwords of a philosophy that fascinated writers and artists. They contrasted intuition with reason, synthesis with analysis, and preferred a philosophy of freedom to positive science. The distinguishing features of this fashionable philosophy were its anti-intellectualism, its anti-Cartesianism, its mysticism and its doctrine of vitalism. In 1898, Bergson had been considered for a position at the Sorbonne, but was rejected in favour of the 'obscure but conformist' Georges Séailles, who enjoyed the backing of Émile Boutroux. For the first semester of 1897–8, he replaced Charles Lévesque at the Collège de France – 'with great success', it was said – and then became *maître de conferences* at the École normale supérieure. Charles Péguy, who had now become a Catholic and a nationalist, and who was still very active on the literary and political scene (he founded the *Cahiers de la quinzaine* in 1900), was a great fan, and religiously attended Bergson's lectures: 'We listened to his every word.'

When the professors of the Collège de France met on 7 January 1900, the task of describing the two candidates' qualifications fell to Théodule

Ribot. On the one hand, there was Bergson – a metaphysician, but a metaphysician who always combined speculation with positive research, as in his work on memory disturbances, and 'a subtle and vigorous mind who already has many enthusiastic disciples amongst the young'. On the other, there was an 'autodidact' whose considerable body of work was 'the exclusive product of his own reading and reflection, one of the most original minds of our time, and a man who is highly respected in other countries'. Despite his handicaps (he had no academic qualifications), Tarde was the winner.[80] He was also a candidate for election to the late Paul Janet's seat in the Académie des sciences morales et politiques.

On 17 May, Bergson was elected to a chair in Greek and Latin philosophy at the Collège and retained that position unto 1904, when he was elected to another chair. This made him famous. He attracted a very wide audience of essayists, poets and a lot of 'fashionable people'. It was said that 'his words dripped with poetry'. A rivalry between the Sorbonne and the Collège de France was beginning to develop. On the one hand, a sclerotic university with its 'Germanic' scholarship and professors who were old before their time; on the other, youth, charm, open-mindedness and the mystical spirit (Azouvi 2007: 60).

When he heard that Tarde had been elected, Émile Durkheim remarked to his nephew: 'The incident is closed . . . I am very happy with the outcome, as it relieves me of the chore of putting in an application just for the sake of it.' Only one thing mattered to him: that Tarde had not 'espoused sociology *coram populo* with the Collège de France given that he is now an *officier d'État*; that would have set a bad example' (cited in Azouvi 2007: 60). Shortly afterwards, he commented: 'So that's Tarde fixed up. I'm very pleased for him.'[81]

Gabriel Tarde gave his inaugural lecture on 8 March 1900.[82] The first part dealt with 'how scientific activity and philosophical effervescence can be of mutual benefit'. The title of his chair seemed to him to be 'infinitely wide-ranging and somewhat embarrassing' because it was impossible to discuss modern philosophy without talking about modern science. His intention was to give his teaching of philosophy 'a sociological direction and tone': 'Could anything be more essentially modern in philosophy than a consideration of social matters?' On the other hand, he was opposed to 'objectivism' in the social sciences, meaning that he rejected the importation of the methods that had been forced upon the natural sciences and the desire to 'look at their objects from the outside'. Although no names were mentioned, this was clearly an attack upon his colleague Durkheim: 'Sociology', he insisted, 'is steeped in social life. It sees it from the inside, and is one of its agents.' Far from being a disadvantage, this was a 'privilege that many sociologists fail to recognize'. He added: 'Psychology helps us to understand social life.'

In conclusion, the newly appointed professor briefly indicated that the following year's lectures would be on 'social psychology'. His decision obviously delighted his colleagues on the *Revue internationale de sociologie*: 'We note that the choice of professor and subject-matter marks a further step towards the gradual transformation of the Collège de France into a truly official faculty of social sciences, and that the *Revue* was the first to recommend that change some years ago.'[83]

Once he had been elected, Gabriel Tarde agreed to publish an article in the *Revue de métaphysique et de morale* that he had written 20 years earlier: 'L'action des faits futurs' (Tarde 1901a). This was an exercise in the epistemology and philosophy of the sciences, but it was also Tarde's way of saying that he had written a reply to the *Rules of Sociological Method* before Durkheim's book had even been published. It was a critique of both historical explanations ('we would do better to address the men of the twentieth century than our prehistoric ancestors') and of the notion of normal development.

In 1901, the Collège de France's new professor published three studies in social psychology under the title *L'Opinion et la foule*. In the foreword, he summarily rejected the 'chimerical sense' in which social psychology was often understood; it consisted in the view that some collective spirit or social consciousness existed outside or above individual minds. The 'mysterious conception' he was attacking was Durkheim's. In an article published in the *Revue philosophique* that same year – 'La réalité sociale' – Tarde was 'very kind' to Durkheim, and congratulated him on having 'come much closer to a psychological conception of social facts' since the launch of *L'Année sociologique.*

Durkheim's response was not slow in coming. He wrote a letter to the journal's editor Théodule Ribot expressing his surprise that his thought had been subjected to such an 'inexact interpretation'. In order to dispel any misunderstandings, he restated his position: there was a clear distinction between individual psychology and sociology, and social life was a system of representations or mental states that were *sui generis*: 'Indeed, it has been at all times my own view. I have repeated a number of times that to place sociology outside individual psychology was simply to say that it constituted a *special psychology*, having its own subject matter and a distinctive method' (Durkheim 1982[1901]: 253).

Abel Aubin, a young contributor to the *Année sociologique*, described the exchange in his review of Tarde's article. He recalled that Durkheim had immediately protested that he had been misunderstood: 'He completely denies what M. Tarde accepts, namely that the phenomena of individual consciousness provide an immediate explanation for social phenomena.' That was, he concluded, the 'only really important issue in the discussion'. While all the journal's contributors were, in his view, involved in developing an objective and specific sociology, it was far from certain that they all agreed as to what the essence of social reality might be. They could work together only because they shared the conviction that 'social facts are things, and are subject to laws that cannot be deduced from individual psychology' (Aubin 1903: 133).

The debate was still not over. François Simiand published a short and very critical review of Tarde's latest book, *Psychologie économique*, in the *Année*, complaining that Tarde was not qualified to discuss economic issues and that there was no coherent plan to the book. It was, in a word, 'unreliable' and not based upon any objective data (Simiand 1903b: 460–1). But another contributor – Gaston Richard – gave the book a fairly positive review in the *Revue philosophique* and described it as 'fine and deserving of praise'. He even expressed a certain admiration for this 'aristocrat and redoubtable enemy of democracy', who, without supporting any of the classic socialist schools, had done 'more than anyone else to condemn economic policies based upon competition and to recommend association through cooperation' (Richard 1902a).[84] Which was one way of saying that relations between Gabriel Tarde and the Durkheimians always were very ambivalent.

13

Summed Up in One Word
Solidarity

At the turn of the new century, Alfred Dreyfus was newly convicted, then released. The amnesty law was promulgated at the end of December 1900.[1] '*Vive Dreyfus!*' Charles Péguy exclaimed in the *Cahiers de la Quinzaine*. The legislative elections of 1902 were won by the Bloc des gauches [coalition of the left], and Émile Combes formed his radical government. In October, 50,000 people followed the funeral cortège of Émile Zola across working-class Paris to the Cimetière Montmartre, where the author of *Germinal* was laid to rest.

Paris 1900: A New Consciousness

Paris celebrated the dawn of the new century by hosting the great Exposition universelle, which was held in the spring of 1900. It was designed to provide 'a picture of the progress made by the human mind' over the previous 100 years. For the French republic, it was a way of bringing the nineteenth century to a 'dignified close' and of displaying its 'desire to remain in the forefront of civilization'. France wanted to display its industrial, scientific and cultural strength. This was to be the 'triumph of the French genius' (Halley 1901: 204–5; see also Schroeder-Gudehus and Rasmussen 1993). The 1889 Exposition had been a celebration of machines and iron; this was a eulogy to the magic of electricity, with its Palace of Electricity, thousands of multi-coloured lights on the water tower, the electric railway and the long moving walkway. For the last third of the nineteenth century, the development of electrical power was, indeed, as the German sociologist Tönnies noted (1903: 657), 'a most significant event'.

The focal point of the Exposition, which was held on the Champs-Elysées and the Esplanade des Invalides – now linked by the Pont Alexandre-III – was the monumental arch of the Porte Binet (named after the architect René Binet). Surmounted by a gigantic statue of *La Parisienne* and flanked by two slender minarets, this was democracy's arc de triomphe and greeted Western civilization's entry into the ages of the masses (Prochasson 1999: 101). The Grand Palais and the Petit Palais, both in the rococo style, were the Exposition's main permanent structures, and became temples of art exhibiting both applied and fine art.

The Exposition was a celebration of both design and domesticity. The Pavillon de l'art nouveau was designed to celebrate France's new *style moderne*. It featured a model house whose décor and furniture made it the 'quintessence of French modern design'; it was also a celebration of a domesticity that expressed a dream world and a haven for modern life (Silverman 1989: 284–314). Two artists took pride of place: the glassmaker and ceramicist Émile Gallé, with his famous vases, and the sculptor Auguste Rodin, whose works (*Les Portes de l'Enfer, La Pensée*) were displayed in a dedicated pavilion. Gallé was one of the major figures in the art nouveau movement. A supporter of 'industrial art' – art by all and for all – he argued that art must support the 'struggle for justice', and had been quick to support Dreyfus (Tillier 2004). Rodin, for his part, had grasped one of the main themes of this *fin de siècle*: the reaction against positivism and the emergence of a new world-view based upon the primacy of the self and the celebration of the irrational. His work looked to Georg Simmel (1912) like 'the expression of the modern spirit'. There was indeed a new consciousness that found expression in a rejection of Enlightenment rationalism and in the work of Henri Bergson. An active participant in the great international conferences on psychology and philosophy, Bergson emerged as one of the Exposition's emblematic figures.[2]

The many exhibits and educational displays attracted a huge audience. New communication technologies made it possible to 'travel without moving' and to visit a village in Laos or Switzerland, a street in Algiers or a mosque in Tunis. A panorama recreated a journey from Peking to Moscow on the Trans-Siberian Express. The event's organizers had abandoned the idea of the exhibition as museum in favour of that of the exhibition as festival. The general idea was to create a great 'feast' by trying at all cost to astonish and to fire the imagination (Deshairs 1900: 355). The Exposition had 84,000 exhibitors and attracted more than 50 million visitors.

Its educational aims were clear: the Exposition was designed to be a window on to the world at large. It was seen as the 'triumph of human solidarity'. The benefit of an event such as this, it was thought, was that it brought together men of all races, all nationalities, all provinces, all classes and all parties: 'The separatist idea of race has been abolished, and the unity of humanity is more obvious than ever.' The Exposition was, in other words, 'essentially democratic'. A new equation had been written by the central figures of the republican France of the new century, which aspired to be modern and resolutely progressive: these figures included the industrialist, the republican and the free-thinker (Coste 1900).

Great Scientific Events

The Exposition was the setting for many international scientific events which were, as Waldeck-Rousseau put it, designed to 'draw up a balance sheet of scientific progress, and to give all peoples access to the modern archives of social progress'. In terms of the human sciences, the two most important conferences were the Congrès international de philosophie at the beginning of August and the IVth Congrès international de psychologie at the end of the same month. A Congrès international de sociologie also took place in September, but at René Worms's Institut international de sociologie at the Sorbonne rather than in the exhibition grounds. The Congrès international de philosophie was organized around four main themes: metaphysics and general philosophy, logic and the philosophy of the sciences, ethics, and the history of philosophy (Lalande 1900). Ethics was much more than a 'theme': it was the subject of several debates and brought the conference to a magnificent close when Ferdinand Buisson argued the case for a secular ethics in the final session.

Durkheim was due to speak at the Congrès international de philosophie at the invitation of his friend Xavier Léon, the editorial director of The *Revue de métaphysique et de morale*, who acted as secretary-general to the conference. But being full preoccupied with preparations for the third volume of the *Année*, he scarcely had time to think about the topic he wished to discuss. He had suggested 'Patriotism and cosmopolitanism'[3] as a subject, but never wrote the paper. Neither he nor any of his close associates took part in the conference. Sociology was not, however, completely unrepresented, as both Georg Simmel[4] and Ferdinand Tönnies spoke, with the latter giving a paper on 'Religion from the point of view of the theory of knowledge.'

The Congrès international de psychologie was chaired by Théodule Ribot and attracted an audience of almost 450 people. More than 150 papers were delivered, dealing with topics ranging from the anatomy and physiology of the nervous system, morbid psychology (aphasia and amnesia), the psychology of sleep, to hypnotism and suggestion. There were also many papers on social and criminal psychology. One of the sessions was devoted to the comparative study of animal psychology and anthropology and ethnology. Speakers included both Henri Bergson and Gabriel Tarde. Bergson presented a 'Note on the consciousness of individual effort', while Tarde chaired the session on 'Social and criminal psychology', defining both its object and its methodology in his address.

The *Année* group shunned philosophical and psychological circles, but did attend other scientific congresses. Henri Hubert, a contributor to both the *Revue archéologique* and *L'Anthropologie*, was treasurer to the organizing committee of the Congrès international d'anthropologie et d'archéologie préhistorique, which convened in mid-August. He gave a paper to the session on archaeology entitled 'The discovery of a chariot burial in Nanterre', while François Simiand addressed the Congrès international de l'enseignement des sciences sociales on 'teaching in primary schools'.[5] Others opted to take part in political events: Marcel Mauss, for instance, attended the Congrès international des coopératives socialistes, and Émile Durkheim the Congrès d'éducation sociale.

Cooperation, Solidarity and Social Education

The Exposition universelle was an excellent public platform for activists from various political movements. They were all eager to publicize their activities and to give them an international dimension. Some events were held in Paris, but outside the framework of the fair itself. The Congrès international des étudiants et anciens étudiants socialistes, which was run by François Simiand and Charles Péguy, was held, for instance, in the premises of the Hôtel des sociétés savantes on 20–22 September. Participants included the Groupe des étudiants collectivistes de Paris, *Le Mouvement socialiste*, several foreign students groups and some teachers. The conference was addressed by Jean Jaurès, who put forward a motion in favour of anti-militarist propaganda (Boucher 1900: 674).

For his part, Mauss attended the first Congrès international des coopératives socialistes (7–10 July), which brought together more than 30 Parisian cooperatives and delegations from Belgium, Spain, Hungary and Italy. Jean Jaurès (who had been converted to cooperation by Mauss) was once more present (Boucher 1900: 121). Mauss addressed it several times in his capacity as a delegate from the Coopérative socialiste. He presented the report on procedural questions and spoke in favour of two motions: one on the foundation of an international bank of workers' cooperatives, and the other on the international organization of an insurance scheme (fire, accidents, life and sickness). This was, he concluded, an excellent way of 'building up a real arsenal of socialist capital in the midst of bourgeois capital'.[6]

The social question was the focus of a lot of activity at the Palais de l'économie sociale. More than 5,000 exhibitors crowded into it, almost half of them from abroad – mainly from the United States, Italy, Russia, Germany or Belgium. Every institution working in the field of social economics was represented: welfare schemes for working-class children, trade unions, cooperatives, provident societies, health insurance schemes, etc. There were even eight full-scale 'workers' houses', but they were built in the parc de Vincennes on the other side of Paris. Between May and August, an uninterrupted sequence of conferences were held one after the other in the Palais de l'économie sociale: five on cooperation, one on legal protection for workers, one on agricultural unions, one on social education, and three international women's congresses (two of them feminist). All these activities took place under the banner of solidarity. When the exhibition opened on 1 May, the minister for trade and industry Alexandre Millerand reminded his audience that 'science has revealed the secret behind the material and moral grandeur of societies, and it can be summed up in one word: solidarity'. At the prize-giving held on 18 August, the president of the republic, Émile Loubet, said the same thing: 'The 1900 Exposition has been the most brilliant expression of solidarity. The solidarity to which we owe so much . . . will give us a clearer vision of the goal to which all free minds and generous hearts aspire: a reduction in poverty of all kinds, and the realization of fraternity' (Gide 1903: 268).

The great Congrès international d'éducation sociale (26–30 September) took solidarity as its main theme. Participants included politicians, administrators and academics, and there were some 50 delegates from other countries (Weisz 1976). The goal of the conference was to define in scientific terms the preconditions for universal voluntary associations and to find ways of popularizing such ideas. Social education, in other words, meant teaching everyone to be a useful and conscious member of society.[7] Solidarity theories enjoyed immense popularity at the beginning of the new century. As Bouglé (1923[1904]: 266) put it, 'the word "solidarity" comes up again and again in all today's moral and social discussions'.

The task of opening the debates fell to Léon Bourgeois, a very eloquent politician with something of the preacher about him who had been elected as a Radical deputy in 1887 and who became president of the chamber of deputies in 1902. He had succeeded in popularizing the word 'solidarity'. It was the title of a book he had published in 1896, which had been reprinted many times. His initial idea was as follows: social life is not characterized by competition alone ('the law of the strongest'), but also by association and the existence of groups. The vitality of a group depended upon its degree of integration and the amount of support (or consent) that it received. We are not just 'beasts of prey'; we are also 'herd animals'. His 'little book' *Essai d'une philosophie de la solidarité* (1902) made a 'huge impact, and many saw it as inaugurating a real social philosophy that went by the name of solidarism (which, in political terms, was closely associated with radicalism[8]). This political doctrine was the perfect expression of the 'republican movement': it represented 'a specifically republican attempt, at the turn of the century, to reconcile the notions of justice and freedom', and to demonstrate that, whatever the liberals might think, equality of opportunity was compatible with freedom. Although it refused to choose between socialism and 'liberal' economism, which appeared to be mutually exclusive, it attempted to synthesize the two (Spitz 2005: 180). Solidarism represented an attempt to find a 'third way': this new synthesis borrowed the idea of greater differentiation and liberation (which gave individuals both freedom and mobility) from liberalism, and the idea of growing interdependence (which implied the need for some form of central regulation) from socialism.

Léon Bourgeois was one of the theorists of solidarism, and its main spokesman. He succeeded in bringing the idea of solidarism 'down to earth' and spelled out its practical implications on the political platform: free education at every level, restrictions to working hours, a guaranteed minimum standard of living for all, a ban on monopolies and trusts, and progressive taxation. In his lecture, Bourgeois summed up these ideas in a few proposals. He placed great emphasis on the idea of debt, arguing that the exchange of services meant that everyone had a debt to society, based on an exchange of services. This was what he called the 'social debt': 'This debt must be repaid.' He defined social solidarity as the repayment of that debt, and the recognition of one's social duty. Debt and duty were both facets of solidarity. The idea that men were interdependent implied that

morality would no longer be restricted to conscience and personal responsibility and freedom; it implied the idea of collective responsibility: 'We are
not completely free because we are all in debt' (Bourgeois 1906[1900]: 96).[9]
A lively discussion ensued. Many objected to the idea of a quasi-contract:
how could the individual's personal account be reckoned? And how could
we calculate what everyone owed?

The Social Role of Universities: Open Universities

Durkheim attended the Congrès international d'éducation sociale. He was
in Paris between 29 and 31 July, and took the opportunity to see some
close associates, including Célestin Bouglé, whom he arranged to meet for
lunch at the Soufflot on Monday 30 July. He did not, it seems, take part in
the various activities associated with the conference (Weisz 1976: 378; on
his involvement, see Lukes 1985[1973]: 350–1), but he did read a paper to
the session devoted to the use of the education system to promote solidarist ideas. Other academics, including the historian Charles Seignobos, the
economist Charles Gide and Ferdinand Buisson, were also present, as was
Alexandre Millerand, the minister for trade. Durkheim chose to address
the congress on the topic of 'The role of the universities in social education
in France' (Durkheim 1976[1900]). He began by summing up the current
state of affairs, and then went on to make some proposals of his own. For
the last 30 years, or ever since the war of 1870, the universities had, he
argued, shown little interest in their social role. Priority had been given
to developing 'very productive teaching methods', turning the universities
into 'centres of scientific life', and recruiting a teaching corps that could
transmit a love of and respect for science to the younger generation. In
Durkheim's view, there had been a price to pay for all this: the universities
had become introverted, teaching had become esoteric, and moral education had ceased to be one of their tasks. 'Academics stopped listening to
the noise from outside, but as a result they became somewhat cut off from
the society around them.'

The time had come for the universities to break out of this 'isolation'; if
they really wanted to demonstrate their social utility, they had to be 'more
involved in public life'. This was, he exclaimed, a 'new task' and, thinking
of the Dreyfus affair, he recalled that famous scientists had recently left
their laboratories and lent their scientific authority to a 'real ministry'.
He wanted academics' involvement in public life to go beyond 'individual
initiatives', which were usually doomed to failure, and to take the form
of organized activity within the framework of what he called 'impersonal
institutions that would last'.

Turning to the social role of the universities, Durkheim had several suggestions to make. First of all, sociology allowed them to have a truly moral
influence. The universities could no longer restrict themselves to intellectual and scientific education; they must also provide their students with the
wherewithal to become aware of and think about the issue of beliefs and

moral rules. He feared that 'intense intellectual development might lead to moral scepticism'. There was an answer to that problem. The teaching of sociology should have a role to play 'in all the universities, and it should be a major role'. Sociology made it possible to demonstrate that 'beliefs and moral rules are social formations', and that solidarity is society's very condition of existence and 'the essential law of humanity'.

While he regretted the fact that there was only one chair in sociology – his own in Bordeaux – Durkheim stressed the importance of his '13 years of this kind of teaching', which had allowed him, 'in complete security', to have a 'favourable influence' not only upon minds but also upon the will: 'Sociology is a powerful instrument of moral education . . . It sheds light upon and guides our actions simply because it allows us to understand in detail the origins and ends of moral facts' (Durkheim 1976[1900]: 184). He got his message across, and the congress adopted a resolution recommending that all universities should offer courses on sociology.

But given that morality was primarily a matter of practice rather than theory, there had to be other ways of influencing students at the level of their lived experience. Durkheim suggested that associations similar to those he had seen during his study trip to Germany should be established. This was his second suggestion. He was not thinking of large-scale associations bringing together all the students in a given university (at the time, such associations appeared to have little success), but of small associations organized around disciplines (science, literature or morality) or even leisure activities such as chess. This was one way of ensuring that students did not become isolated and of making them feel that they had some support and supervision. 'Basically, this is a way of giving French youth a taste for collective life and of encouraging the habit of acting together.' Given the way individuals were 'dispersed', this was, in his view, an 'urgent issue'.

His third suggestion was that morality should be taught at every level, even in primary schools. Durkheim recalled that '30 years ago, we embarked upon a task. We wanted to give the country a system of moral education that was rationalist.' The 'old morality of our fathers' was a thing of the past. It was time to do away with religious symbols and what were now 'archaic conceptions', and to make way for 'a new morality'. This required a great deal of thought and reorganization, but Durkheim was reluctant to go into further detail in his lecture. 'Ultimately, we have to outline the main features of the ideal to which we aspire, even though we cannot perceive it with any clarity.' He suggested that a course on pedagogy should be designed specifically for teachers in the primary sector.

Durkheim observed, finally, that 'something new was coming into being' and that it could produce a 'tumultuous life'. Witness the rapid development, within the space of barely a year, of the people's universities. His nephew Marcel and other young contributors to the *Année* were giving lectures at the new socialist school. This was a real people's university where evening classes were taught. 'Everyone feels the urgent need to train the minds of the working classes in order to enable them to fulfil their destinies.' That, in his view, was the task of a people's university, provided that its teaching was well organized. Durkheim was in fact highly critical of what was being taught at this new institution: its main failing was 'the lack of any unified vision'. He suggested that the system of lectures on a wide variety of topics should be replaced by a series of lectures that followed on logically from one to another, or in other words by a curriculum. Teaching should be concentrated on specific objects appropriate to their 'special audience'. He was thinking here of the history of industrial organization, industrial law and political economy. He was not suggesting that literary and artistic culture was pointless, but merely that it was 'less essential'. The message got through: the conference adopted a resolution recommending that the people's universities should offer courses on social economics (trade unions, cooperatives, employers' associations, etc.).

Durkheim believed that the universities had a duty to channel the political, moral and philosophical currents within public opinion, to do more to make contact with the nation's 'masses', and even to give the popular masses a 'clear awareness of their usefulness'. He therefore suggested that they themselves should organize the people's universities, which would thus become their annexes or outposts. Durkheim therefore regarded the real universities as educational establishments in the broadest of senses: they should play a role in 'moral life' by helping to shape 'the French moral consciousness'. They could obviously promote the arts and sciences, which had a universal import, but they must also be open to all tendencies within public opinion and welcome 'every major manifestation of the collective mentality'. This was, he concluded, a way of demonstrating that they were not a 'sort of luxury' and that they did have some 'purpose'.

Sociology: 'An Essentially French Science'

It was during the great Exposition universelle that Durkheim published an essay entitled 'Sociology in France in the nineteenth century' in the 19–26 May 1900 issue of *La Revue bleue* (Durkheim 1973[1900]). His object was not only to show the journal's educated readers what sociology consisted of in France, but also to demonstrate to them that it was an 'essentially French science'.

The article takes the form of a lecture on the history of sociology. Durkheim insists from the outset that the discipline's origins cannot, as some claim, be traced back to Plato and Aristotle. That is a mistake. The application of reflection to a given order of facts is not, in Durkheim's view, enough to give rise to a science: before it can become a science, it must elaborate the notion of a law (the central element in scientific thought) and adopt the appropriate methods.[10] All this is a relatively recent development within the history of humanity. Sociology appears 'only at a late moment of scientific evolution' because it encounters 'quite special resistances'. Social issues were for a long time the object, not of science in the true sense, but of 'indecisive speculations', and not of 'systematic analysis' but of 'literary description' (Durkheim 1973[1900]: 5).

It is not easy to change things. The preconditions for change include, in Durkheim's view, 'the disruption of the old social system' at the end of the eighteenth century. This challenged intellectuals to 'seek out a remedy for the evils from which society suffered': 'What is certain is that from the day when the revolutionary tempest had passed, the notion of sociology (*la science sociale*) was formed as if by magic' (Durkheim 1973[1900]: 5, 6).

The history of sociology in France outlined by Durkheim has its precursors (Montesquieu and Condorcet) and then its founding fathers (Saint-Simon and Auguste Comte). There followed, to Durkheim's astonishment, a 'stagnancy' or 'a long period of drowsiness' (Durkheim 1973[1900]: 11). The only sociological contribution was Cournot's *Essay on the Foundation of our Knowledge*. It was only after the war of 1870 that the 'reawakening' took place (ibid.: 12). The organization of the imperial system had collapsed, and 'the urgent need for a science of society made itself felt without delay'. Conceptions of social reality remained, however, 'general and schematic'. It was', suggests Durkheim, 'time to deal more directly with the facts' (ibid.: 14). This was of course his own ambition. He cites his own work which, while 'only concerned with judicial or moral rules', opened up 'what Comte would have called the era of specialization' (ibid.: 15).

The establishment of methodological rules (which Durkheim briefly describes) is the essential stage. The *Année sociologique*'s editorial director has no qualms about describing his methodology as 'naturalistic' (meaning that it implies a serious mental attitude towards the natural sciences), but immediately adds that this 'naturalism' is 'essentially sociological' (Durkheim 1973[1900]: 18) given that the social realm has its own uniqueness. The elements that characterize the scientific approach in sociology are the patient observation of facts, the adoption of a positive method and the establishment of laws.

In Durkheim's view, any attempt to resist this development is a 'sort of scientific reaction'. He cites the example of Gabriel Tarde: his conception of sociology is not scientific, but 'a very particular form of speculation in which imagination plays the preponderant role'. Tarde's speculations imply a belief in the contingent, and attach great importance to 'the unintelligible accident' and 'individual inventions' (Durkheim 1973[1900]: 18, 19). The article is, in other words, an all-out attack on the Collège de France's newly elected professor.

Durkheim's answer to the question 'what contribution has France made to the birth of sociology?' may seem somewhat chauvinistic: the French contribution has been essential because sociology was born in France and remains 'an essentially French science' (Durkheim 1973[1900]: 3) (and not, as some suggest, a German science). He is convinced that 'everything predestines our country to play an important role' in the development of sociology. Two causes are likely to favour its progress in France: the weakening of traditionalism in both religious and political terms, and the rationalist state of mind: 'We are and we remain . . . the country of Descartes', and 'we have the irresistible need to bring things back to definite notions'. The 'cult of distinct ideas' is 'the very root of the French spirit as well as the basis of all science' (ibid.: 22).

And yet nothing is simple. Durkheim even speaks of 'danger' and describes the period France is passing through as 'particularly critical': 'Because so much is expected of our science, it will be discredited if it does not live up to its promises' (1973[1900]: 22). There is a danger that there will be 'an intellectual lull'. We must, he concludes, make haste. As Célestin Bouglé (1900b: 153–4) put it, this was 'the decisive moment'.

'Ardent Proselytism'

The social and political situation was alarming, even explosive. There were social conflicts and strikes, while poverty and destitution were widespread. There were women and children working in factories, and then there were the problems of vagrancy, alcoholism, delinquency and suicide. The crisis affecting France and Europe in the nineteenth century obviously had a lot to do with industrialization and its effects on all traditional social structures but, as Durkheim never tired of saying, it also had its effects on morality and solidarity.

Marx died in 1883, and Engels in 1895. Marxism, often in a schematic form, had become an inescapable point of reference for the new socialist leaders and provided the basis for their ideology and programmes. The socialist movement was at its height and theoretical debates were intense, but there were also deep divisions. In France, the main division was that between Jules Guesde, the spokesman for revolutionary socialism who had founded France's first socialist party (the Fédération des travailleurs socialistes de France, better known as the Parti ouvrier [Workers' Party]), and Jean Jaurès, whose preference was for the democratic Marx rather than the revolutionary Marx. Even though the collectivization of the means of production was his ideal, Jaurès rejected the idea of the dictatorship of the proletariat and the idea that an active minority should seize power, and believed that the revolution in France would come about through parliamentary action. There appeared to be only two alternatives: revolution or parliamentary action.

Several of the contributors to *L'Année sociologique* were committed to political action, and their rallying point was still the Société nouvelle de librairie et d'édition, which had been founded by Lucien Herr at the time of the Dreyfus affair. They included Marcel Mauss, but also Henri Hubert and François Simiand, now more zealous than ever. The board of directors included Léon Blum, Hubert Bourgin and Mario Roques. Charles Péguy, who often attended its meetings, was accorded the title of 'publishing delegate. His presence was short-lived: the break was sudden, and couched in terms that were as 'unpleasant as they were unforeseeable', as Mauss put it (1997[1928]: 742).

The Société nouvelle was active on many different fronts: it published many books, including a translation of the *Communist Manifesto* with an introduction by Charles Andler, and the journal *Le Mouvement sociale*, and it organized an École socialiste. Its publishing activities were designed to complement its agitational work (Andler 1977[1932]: 162). The bi-monthly *Mouvement socialiste* was founded in 1899 by Hubert Lagardelle (1875–1958) and its managing editor was Jean Longuet (1876–1938), a grandson of Karl Marx and nephew of Paul Lafargue. Its goal was to 'provide an accurate picture of the socialist movement as a whole' without lapsing into either dogmatic oversimplifications or exclusivity.[11] The front page of the first issue featured an article by Jaurès on 'social-ist unity'. In 1899, it published Mauss's first major political article, enti-tled simply 'L'action socialiste' (Mauss 1997[1899]). Mauss thought of himself as both a revolutionary and a republican. He rejected violence in favour of 'conscious, rational and humanitarian action' and was, in other words, concerned mainly with freedom, justice and rights. Waiting for 'the Revolution' was pointless: he wanted to 'live the socialist life now, and create it from scratch'. His article was a plea for party unity.

Mauss persuaded his friends François Simiand and Paul Fauconnet to contribute to the new journal. All three wanted to 'base socialism on soci-ology', wanted socialist action to be rationalist and held that it should be 'inspired by actual facts, as explained by a scientific method of explo-ration' (Andler 1977[1932]: 163). All three were enthusiastic supporters of the École socialiste, which was founded by Lucien Herr and Charles Andler in December 1899 – on the eve of the Japy Congress. Four lecture courses were offered, either at the end of the working day or in the evening: the history of socialist doctrines, the organization of socialist parties, eco-nomic organization (cooperation, trade unions and socialism at the local level), and social legislation. The goal was 'to educate, and then prepare for action'. In pedagogic terms, 'ceremonial lectures' were rejected in favour of 'simple chats', informal lessons and discussions, some led by Hubert Bourgin, another contributor to *L'Année sociologique*. Marcel Mauss suc-ceeded in recruiting other friends (Emmanuel Lévy) and students, includ-ing Robert Hertz, who gave a talk on Saint-Simon and the Fabians. To begin with, the École enjoyed only limited success. A few years later – in 1904, it would seem – Durkheim himself agreed to give a lecture on 'Sociology and socialism'. Social education, a people's university – some of the contributors to the *Année* and Durkheim appeared to be on the same wavelength. Marcel thought that his uncle was a first-class commentator on contemporary developments.

In June 1899, Alexandre Millerand joined Pierre Waldeck-Rousseau's Union républicaine government, and thus provoked a crisis amongst socialists. The 'ministerial question' led to conflict between the two main branches of the socialist movement, one fairly liberal and the other more collectivist. The faction led by Jaurès supported the government, while that led by Guesde and Vaillant rejected any form of participation. The Japy 'socialist union' congress was held a few months later in December 1899, and was attended by more than 700 delegates (Guesdists, Allemanistes, Blanquists and independents). Mauss attended in his capacity as a delegate from the Montpellier 'collectivist students' group. Together with his friends from the Société nouvelle de librairie et d'édition, he had just founded the socialist unity group, and believed that 'union, if not unity, is possible'.

The Japy Congress was, as might have been expected, stormy, and the socialist movement's hard-won unity proved to be fragile. A compromise resolution condemned the acceptance of ministerial positions, but approved of it in exceptional circumstances. The delegates left with 'the enthusiastic strains of the *Internationale* and the *Carmagnole* ringing in their ears' (Unger 2005: 111). But the conflict between what Lagardelle (1900) called Guesde's 'dogmatic anti-ministerialism' and Jaurès's 'dogmatic ministerialism' was not over. 'The irritation caused by the Millerand case became', he wrote, 'an unbearable tiredness'. Disappointed with the congress, Charles Péguy broke with official socialism and finally quarrelled with Lucien Herr and Marcel Mauss, both of whom were beside themselves with rage. It had been a 'deplorable congress', Durkheim wrote to his nephew; he wanted to talk to him to 'open his eyes'.[12]

A split was now inevitable. It came during the national congress, held in December 1900, when the Parti ouvrier's delegates walked out of the Salle Wagram. Although he was saddened by the split, Mauss refused to be demoralized. 'Socialism is more alive than ever', he wrote. He asked socialist militants to 'work energetically on propaganda' (1900c: 130). Paul Fauconnet wrote to Durkheim to tell him how much the split had saddened him. As he admitted to Mauss, Durkheim found it difficult to explain this:

> The socialism of socialists like Guesde and *tutti quanti* is the worst thing of all. Those people are wretched politicians, just like the first opportunist who comes along, perhaps even worse. A split was quite desirable. Class socialism, which reduces the social question to the worker question, is socialism for the uneducated and for people who are filled with hate. We can understand it and support it to a reasonable extent, but we cannot accept the principle behind it. And recent events only go to show how mean-spirited it is. The workers are perfectly amenable to other ideas, but they have been blinded by these people.[13]

Durkheim attended a banquet in Bordeaux at which all parties were represented, although the socialists were in the majority. He gave a speech, and said all that he had to say. He was delighted to receive a sympathetic hearing, but was sickened by the tone and comments of the next speaker: 'Oh, what a wretch! Bah! Sycophancy! And all the things he left out!' Durkheim was convinced that 'there is a lot to be done, and good things to be done.' In a letter to his nephew, which he asked him to pass on to Paul Fauconnet, he added: 'We have to help Jaurès and his friends to become more self-aware and to put an end to an ambiguity that just helps to perpetuate bourgeois traditionalism. I am prepared to do everything I can to do that.'[14]

G. Bizos, the rector of the Académie de Bordeaux, was worried about 'Professor Durckheim's' (*sic*) presence at a 'political banquet', and wrote to the minister for education, enclosing a copy of *La France du Sud-Ouest* containing an analysis of his speech:

> I take the view that, no matter what teachers at the University of Bordeaux say at these political gatherings, they never do any good because they make their discourse more and more palpable to the population and especially to students to whom they should be preaching peace and unity, and encourage them to follow suit and to take part in demonstrations led by a few hot-headed outsiders, beneath rival banners and in mutually hostile groups.[15]

Durkheim refused to be intimidated, and gave another lecture in Lot-et-Garonne in December. In his assessment of Durkheim's teaching, Dean Bizos could not hide his annoyance at his colleague's 'ardent and militant proselytism': 'A highly original and very vigorous theoretician. M. Durkheim [plays] the role of an oracle for his students, and they listen to him with a sort of fervour'.[16] 'Strikingly powerful and dialectical elocution', noted Watz, the newly appointed dean. The authority conferred upon Durkheim by his publications gave him cause for both admiration and annoyance. 'A powerful originality', an 'individuality that is out of the ordinary', noted his superiors, but they were also critical of the over-confidence expressed in his opinions and doctrines, even though he was, they accepted, capable of taking account of the opinion of others. 'In Bordeaux, [M. Durkheim] plays the role of an oracle who is listened to with a sort of fervour, no matter whether he is talking about sociology, politics or militant [philosophy?].'[17] 'An uncompromising and rigorous thinker, a rigid logician, quite absolute and systematic.'[18] The rector went so far as to speak of the 'mission' of a man he described as a *maître*, who had 'considerable influence' on his students which extended beyond the lecture room and guided them through life and society. The effects of the Stapfer affair continued to make themselves felt. Was there still room for such a striking personality in Bordeaux?

An organizer for the league and a public speaker: Durkheim had never been so politically active. In late 1899, he, Dean Stapfer and other colleagues were involved in founding the Association amicale des membres de l'enseignement public de l'académie de Bordeaux. Mauss reacted to his uncle's new activism by making one more attempt to persuade him to join the socialist party. 'There is no point in preaching', replied his uncle: 'I will be ready to join when it has expanded its formulae, or in other words when it has ceased to be an exclusively class party. And I hope that the merger of particular groups and little churches will naturally lead to that result. A lot of us would join if those conditions were met.'[19] He also expressed a wish to see Jaurès during his coming visit to Paris.

Notes Critiques: Sciences Sociales

When, in 1899, the Société nouvelle de librairie et d'édition decided to begin publishing a bibliographical bulletin entitled *Notes critiques: Sciences sociales*, François Simiand was appointed editorial secretary. Durkheim was approached and spontaneously agreed to lend his 'support'. 'As you no doubt know, I have the backing of Durkheim', Simiand wrote to Mauss.[20] He also turned to his friends Henri Hubert, Marcel Mauss and Paul Fauconnet.

François Simiand had been at Lucien Herr's side during the Dreyfus battle and, being an admirer of Jaurès, he now joined in the battle for socialism because it seemed to him that 'the socialist order' was the only thing that could guarantee social progress. As he was both a sociologist and a socialist, it was said of him that he was 'both a man of science and a man with a mission' (Bourgin 1938).[21] Simiand combined the qualities of an expert with those of a socialist militant: his economic sociology was also a critique of economic science. In addition, he had an interest in practical solutions and a taste for administration, and was quite happy to take on practical tasks (such as publishing the Bibliothèque socialiste collection of propagandist works).

The *Notes* began publication in 1900 and, like *L'Année sociologique*, consisted of several sections: general sociology, ethnography and folklore, religious sciences, science of law and mores, economic sciences and miscellaneous studies.[22] Durkheim, who was overwhelmed with work as the editorial director of *L'Année*, immediately thought of merging the two journals, which were doing similar bibliographical work. *Notes critiques* continued publication until 1906, and continued to have close links with the *Année* as many new contributors (Hubert Bourgin, Maurice Halbwachs, Henri Beuchat and Louis Gernet) wrote for both journals. In all, 22 authors wrote for them both. Some were recruited to the *Année* after having published analyses in *Notes critiques*, and most of the new recruits were students of Mauss and Hubert at the École pratique des hautes études. *Notes critiques* differed from the *Année* in several respects. Its periodicity was different (between 20 and 5 numbers per year), and it included a second section devoted to problems of a practical and political nature. It thus allowed Dreyfusard intellectuals and socialist militants to use the social sciences to defend their political ideals (Mergy 1998).[23]

Émile Durkheim's first contribution to *Notes critiques* was published in 1901 (see 1980[1901/2]). It was a short analysis of Georg Simmel's *Philosophie des Geldes* ['Philosophy of money'], which he also reviewed for *L'Année sociologique* the following year.[24] The book contained, he noted, 'many fine, ingenious and sometimes suggestive ideas, a quite stimulating mixture of historical and ethnographic facts (which are, however, introduced without any detail or guarantees) and observations culled from the most mundane aspects of everyday life)'. Durkheim also had 'major reservations' about it, and criticized Simmel for trying to turn philosophy into a sort of speculative exercise in which the proofs did not need to be as rigorous as possible and in which the author's imagination had 'the last word'. He also regarded Simmel's theory about the nature and function of money as 'very unsatisfactory' and criticized his notion of money on the grounds that it confused legal tender with fiduciary money (paper money). These were, Durkheim concluded, two different institutions, and their essence could not be determined 'by the same criterion'.

Durkheim also sent reviews of two other books to *Notes critiques* in 1901. These looked at *Les Grandes Routes des peuples* by Le Play's disciple Edmond Demolins, and Edouard Lambert's *La Tradition romaine sur la succession des formes de testament devant l'histoire contemporaine*. Lambert, a professor in the faculty of law in Lyon was a friend of Emmanuel Lévy and Paul Huvelin, and Durkheim would later ask him to contribute to *L'Année*.

Between 1901 and 1904, Durkheim published eight reviews in *Notes critiques*. This was a relatively minor contribution compared with those made by Marcel Mauss and Henri Hubert over the same period.[25] Most of his reviews were republished, in a revised and usually expanded form, in *L'Année sociologique*. The only review to appear only in *Notes critiques* was of Arthur Bauer's *Les Classes sociales* (Durkheim 1998[1902]).[26] Durkheim praised the author's cleverness but criticized the 'arbitrary nature' of his thesis that sociology, because it was a science of social facts, should be regarded as the 'science of classes', and that society as a whole should be seen as 'the integral system of classes'. His conclusion was unambiguous: 'Over and above the life of each organ, there is such a thing as the general life of society. There are phenomena that are not localized in any occupational group, that are found in all groups, and these are of course the most essential of all social facts: examples include morality, religion, all shared ideas, and so on.'

Liberalism in Crisis? In Search of a Third Way

Far from forming a homogeneous group, the *Année sociologique*'s early contributors belonged, as we have seen, to different circles or subgroups. On the one hand, there were the 'researchers' (Mauss, Hubert and Simiand) and, on the other, the 'teachers' (Bouglé, Lapie, Parodi, Richard and Fauconnet). Their professional status was to a large extent reflected in their mode of involvement in political life: on the one hand, there were those who were active in parties, associations or union organizations, and, on the other, those who wrote articles for learned journals (many of them philosophical) and published essays; on the one hand, the socialists and those who were fighting for equality, and, on the other, the 'liberals' and those who defended the values of justice, democracy and freedom. Although the two groups related to politics in different ways and adopted different political positions, they were not entirely mutually exclusive. Both adopted a distant or critical stance with respect to political doctrines, with the socialists rejecting the dogmatism of the Marxists and the 'liberals' distancing themselves from any form of ultra-liberalism. It was as though they were trying to meet one another halfway. Was there a 'third way'? Célestin Bouglé was one of the *Année*'s most politically active contributors. He belonged to a generation of intellectuals who saw science and knowledge as a prelude to action and who were trying to 'demonstrate that theoretical truths could be put to practical use in both politics and pedagogy'. His lifelong concern was, as Édouard Herriot put it, to 'unite thought and action'.[27] He was also an excellent orator – one of the finest, it was said, ever to have emerged from the École normale supérieure. He was talented enough to be able to address a variety of audiences ranging from lycée students to the members of feminist clubs, workers and trade-unionists.

Always tempted by politics, Bouglé stood as a 'radical' candidate in the elections of 1902. His decision to do so puzzled his friend Élie Halévy but, after due reflection, he gave him his encouragement: 'I believe that your honesty can work miracles and will make you more skilful than the skilled politicians.'[28] Bouglé was not successful in the legislative elections of 27 April and 11 May 1902. Hotly contested, the elections were won by the left coalition, with the socialists winning some 50 seats, and the radicals more than 200.

'Look at the century we live in', cried a worried Bouglé, who feared for the country's social unity after the three great 'unexpected shocks' that had shaken France: the anarchist outrages (and the way the press covered them), the Dreyfus affair and the divisions it had caused, and the expansion of religious (Catholic) groups, which had their own militias and which were 'infiltrating' everywhere. The country faced the prospect of divisions and dislocations. In Bouglé's view, a minimal level of obedience to and respect for the law was essential, but there was also a need for citizens to display some mutual understanding. He was particularly worried by the 'various fractions of public opinion' that were demanding the restriction or surveillance of various freedoms, including the freedom of the press, the freedom of association, the freedom to teach and academic freedom in general. In both political and educational terms, Bouglé was essentially an 'individualist': freedom was his basic principle, but he believed in a freedom that was guided, controlled and disciplined. He put his 'faith', in other words, in 'democracy' and held that the individual should have a major role. While he argued against Jaurès in a famous debate staged in Toulouse, he still admired the socialist leader and was greatly influenced by him. He refused, however, to describe himself as a socialist in the Marxist sense of the term. Victor Basch (1863–1944), his colleague and fellow activist in the Ligue de défense des droits de l'homme, described him as a democrat who was as devoted to social justice as he was to freedom'.[29]

The situation of liberalism in France was all the more fragile and complicated in that, as Gaston Richard demonstrated (1902b), this political doctrine often implied a certain sympathy for England and similar societies.[30] 'La crise du libéralisme' was the title of Bouglé's article in the *Revue de métaphysique et de morale*. But in his view, it was not so much economic liberalism (a doctrine that was 'dead and buried' given that no government ruled out the idea of economic intervention) as 'intellectual liberalism' that was in crisis (Bouglé 1902: 699).

His friends Paul Lapie and Dominique Parodi also hurled themselves into the fray, but they were acting in the name of academic freedom. The main issue was whether or not clerics should be banned from teaching. The question of secularism was already central to the debate. Lapie's answer introduced certain qualifications: he wanted the republic's serv- ants to receive a 'republican education'. But 'imposing a new orthodoxy on minds' was out of the question: pedagogic methods should be 'crit- ical' and not dogmatic; they should encourage reflection and destroy prejudices.

In an article entitled 'Liberté et égalité', Dominique Parodi, who taught philosophy at the lycée in Bordeaux, argued that schools should be neutral (meaning that both pupils and students should enjoy 'complete freedom of religious and philosophical thought and practice'), and that schools should teach a free and fertile diversity of doctrines, the only limitations being those imposed by scientific methods and findings' (Parodi 1902: 781). In his view, the universities were the real home of liberal teaching: there should be no state doctrine, teachers should not be required to make any declaration of faith, all opinions should be open to discussion, and students should enjoy freedom of choice (ibid.: 782–3).

If Bouglé, Parodi, Lapie and Richard appeared to be 'liberals', it was in Lapie's sense of the term: before a regime could be said to be liberal, 'the freedom of citizens must not be restricted by the capricious author- ity of one or more individuals, but by the rational authority of a law that enjoyed unanimous support' (Lapie 1899b).[31] They were, therefore, the defenders of freedom and, it must be added, of social justice.[32]

The great contemporary issue for all academics was that of educational reform. Should anyone be allowed to teach whatever they liked? Should private institutions be allowed to 'take away the freedom of the individu- als they incorporate'? And while the unanimity of associations of teachers was as undesirable as the eccentricity of individuals, should one go so far as to restrict freedoms by adopting 'antiliberal measures'? Should we be for or against the state? According to Bouglé, it was difficult to decide 'objectively' between these two positions. Although he was unable to reach any 'definite conclusion', he warned against 'blind passions' and invited his fellow citizens to 'lower their tone and raise the level of discussion': 'these are the mores we expect of a free country' (Bouglé 1902a: 651–2). The slogan of intellectual liberalism should be 'Let men speak, let them think and let them enlighten one another through universal discussions' (ibid.: 635).

It was, Bouglé believed, dangerous to restrict either intellectual freedom or the activities of certain associations. This was Durkheim's 'counter- weight' thesis, and Bouglé cites the preface to the second edition of *The Division of Labour* (Durkheim 1984[1893]: liv): 'A society made up of an extremely large mass of unorganized individuals, which an overgrown state attempts to limit and restrain, constitutes a veritable sociological monstrosity' (Bouglé 1902a: 649).

Leaving everything in 'the big, rough hands' of the state was therefore out of the question. Indeed, in Bouglé's view it was foolish to expect the state to 'rebuild our moral unity': 'Asking the state to reunite souls is tantamount to giving the state a mitre and cross, or transforming it into a church. It would probably lead to the restoration of a new clericalism that would speak in the name of reason, science and freedom, but that might be no less dogmatic or intolerant than the old' (Bouglé 1902a: 651).

Like Durkheim, Célestin Bouglé was opposed to anti-state ultra-liberalism, but he was also critical of a state that all too often tended to be over-oppressive and bureaucratic. He argued that public actions should be decentralized to a certain extent, but he also emphasized the virtues of representative democracy. He took the view that modern societies were unified societies, but also thought that associative life, which implied, amongst other things, the development of intermediary bodies, was indispensable. He therefore agreed with Durkheim when the latter argued that professional groups were tailor-made to bring about the moral reorganization of society, provided, he added, that the nation did not become a 'mosaic of professions'. He therefore refused to accept that parliamentary democracy should be replaced by economic democracy.

Bouglé took the view – and here he remained true to Durkheim's teachings – that there was no contradiction between the assertion of individuality and state intervention, or between the defence of individual rights and the solidity of the social body. In his view, the central idea of republicanism was that the individual liberation went hand in hand with state intervention (1923[1904]: 275). He was in favour of what might be called a 'personalist' individualism (see Spitz 2005: 358–63). He was always more concerned with human rights than with any phobia about the state.

Bouglé always had a 'sense of balance', rejected simplifications and denounced all forms of demagogy. His radicalism, which might be more accurately described as 'reformist socialism', led him to recognize both the power of individualism (which should not be confused with the cult of the ego) and the need for solidarity. 'In a word, we can state that, as production becomes more and more collective, our morality becomes more and more individualist' (Bouglé 1932[1904]: 280). In political terms, he was a Radical Socialist who was at once close to and far removed from Léon Bourgeois. Because he was trying to find a synthesis of competition and solidarity, Bouglé shared the idea that solidarism was a specifically republican attempt to reconcile the notions of justice and freedom.

The Sickness and the Remedy: A Greater Role for Professional Groups

Was the contradiction between socialism and liberalism insurmountable? Solidarism represented an attempt to synthesize the two great political doctrines, and looked like a 'third way', similar to what might now be called liberal communitarianism or even liberal socialism. Durkheim intervened in the great debates about educational reform and other topics that dominated political life in France at the beginning of the twentieth century. The lectures he was giving in Bordeaux at the turn of the century were on morality: domestic morality on the one hand, and professional and civic morality on the other. In his lectures on professional ethics, he returned to the theme of professional groups and, in an extension of his earlier argument, he refers to the analysis made in *The Division of Labour in Society* and places the emphasis on the 'real decentralization of the moral life' that results from the division of labour: 'the differentiation of function amounts to a kind of moral polymorphism' (Durkheim 1957[1950]: 7). The strength of these 'decentralized' moralities depends, however, on the consistency and organization of the professional groups concerned: frequent and intimate contacts between individuals, exchanges of ideas and feelings, and the sharing of so many things all help to shape a current of opinion specific to the group in question. Durkheim outlines an analysis of the moral diversity of such groups. At one extreme, there are professions that are, either directly or indirectly, involved with the state (the army, the teaching profession, the legal profession, the administration, which are all well organized), and, at the other extreme, economic professions (industrialists, the retail sector, etc.) that are not organized at all.

As Durkheim had demonstrated in his doctoral thesis, the problem is that the economic professions are not organized: there is unfair competition between industrialists, and relations between employers and workers are poorly regulated. In this area of social life, in which there is no professional morality, everything therefore works on an 'economistic' basis: a balance will, supposedly, be found between different economic interests. Durkheim therefore reverts to the idea of the 'crisis in European societies'. The lack of any moral regulation of economic life in what have become essentially industrial societies results in 'real anarchy'. The decline in public morality (as the values of selflessness, abnegation and sacrifice disappear) and the lack of any discipline that can restrain egoism create, he concludes, a 'moral vacuum'. There is only 'one remedy' for the sickness, he insists: professional groups must be given more 'consistence'. Durkheim has a very clear idea of what the good life and the good society are. Anarchy, with its 'everlasting wranglings and endless friction' is 'painful' because 'though we may like a fight, we also love the joys of peace'. We would therefore do better 'taking shelter under the roof of a collectivity' and to enjoy the 'pleasure of mixing with [our] fellows' and 'the pleasure of communing together' (Durkheim 1957[1950]: 24, 25).

Durkheim's lectures on professional morality pursue the argument outlined in the preface to the second edition of *The Division of Labour in Society* (which appeared in 1902 and was translated into English in 1908). He had, he states, no intention of modifying the book's 'original structure': 'A book has an individuality that it ought to retain' (Durkheim

1984[1893]: xxxi) He introduces only one modification: 'We have confined ourselves to eliminating from the original Introduction some thirty pages, which now appear to us to be of no value' (ibid.: lvii n1).

Durkheim attached a particular importance to the new preface, which is quite simply entitled 'Some remarks on professional groups'. He wishes to bring out more clearly an idea that 'remained somewhat obscure' in the first edition, namely 'the role that professional groups are called upon to fulfil at the present time in the social organization of peoples'. He admits to having touched only 'obliquely' on this problem 'because we were intending . . . to make it the object of a special study'. He was, to his regret, diverted from that project by 'other preoccupations'. The purpose of the new preface is therefore to demonstrate 'the urgency and importance of the problem' (1984[1893]: xxxi).

The preface reiterates some of the conclusions he had reached in *Suicide* (where a strong corporate organization was described 'as a means of curing the malaise whose existence is demonstrated by the increase in suicide' (1984[1893]: lv). Several people had remarked that 'the remedy we propounded did not match up to the extent of the evil.' His critics had, he insists, 'misunderstood the true nature of the corporation'. He therefore felt a need to introduce certain clarifications.

He begins by going back to one of the main points made in his study of suicide. 'The state of legal and moral anomie in which economic life exists at the present time' (1984[1893]: xxxi–xxxiii) results in incessant conflicts and disorders of all kinds. It exists in a state of anarchy in which there can be no stable equilibrium. Hence 'the continually recurring conflicts and disorders of which the economic world affords so sorry a spectacle'. Durkheim even speaks of 'a state of war, either latent or acute' (ibid.: xxxii). The situation is especially serious because of the exponential development of economic functions over the past 200 years: 'Our societies are, or tend to be, essentially industrial' (ibid.: xxxiii). Nothing is regulated and economic discipline has been undermined, and that explains the general feeling of demoralization and the declining standards of public morality.

In Durkheim's view, 'men's passions are only stayed by a moral presence they respect' (1984[1893] xxxii–xxxiii). There is therefore no contradiction between the authority of rules and the freedom of the individual: on the contrary, freedom 'is itself the product of a set of rules', a 'rule' being defined as '*an obligatory manner of acting*' (ibid.: xxxiii, xxxiv) which, because it is not subject to individual arbitrariness, is prescribed by a 'moral entity which is above . . . private individuals [and] constituted by the collectivity'. Such rules 'rest upon a climate of opinion', and 'all opinion is a collective matter, the result of being worked out collectively' (ibid.: xxxv). The absence of rules, or anomie, is a sickness, and it damages society, which needs cohesion and stability if it is to survive. Individuals are also affected by these 'conflicts and disorders' because 'it is not good for a man to live, so to speak, on a war footing among his immediate companions' (ibid.: xlviii).

The group (or 'collective life') is, in Durkheim's view, the only source of morality. But which group can regulate morality today? It cannot be either society as a whole or the state, as morality depends upon the regulation of economic life – in other words, a set of very special and increasingly specialized activities that are outside their control. The task should rather, he believes, be entrusted to corporations or professional groups that are in fairly close contact with the world of work. Durkheim is well aware that the plan he outlines, which consists in turning the various economic professions into a real 'public institution', is all the more difficult to implement in that it 'clashes with a certain number of prejudices' (1984[1893]: xxxvi).

Far from seeing the corporation as a temporary organization, Durkheim describes it as an enduring institution that has played, and that can still play, a major role in contemporary societies: 'What we particularly see in the professional grouping is a moral force capable of curbing individual egoism, nurturing among workers a more invigorated feeling of their common solidarity, and preventing the law of the strongest from being applied too brutally in industrial and commercial relationships' (1984[1893]: xxxix). Durkheim wishes to make himself clearly understood: his goal is not to revive an institution from the past, but to transform it in order to adapt it to modern societies. That is a task for the statesman and not the sociologist: 'We do not have to set out in detail what that reform should be.' He does, however, establish some general principles: (1) the framework of the professional group should be related to that of economic life; whereas its framework was once municipal, it must now become national or even international; (2) the 'corporations of the future' must be assigned 'greater and more complex functions, because of their increased scope' (purely professional functions, but also functions of mutual assistance, educational activities and aesthetic activities such as concerts and dramatic performances).

Durkheim goes so far as to suppose that the corporation will become 'the foundation, or one of the essential foundations, of our political organization' (1984[1893]: liii). The corporation or guild was an elementary division of collective life in the Middle Ages; there is no reason why it should not be 'the elementary division of the state, the basic political unit'. He goes on: 'Society, instead of remaining what it is today – a conglomerate of land masses juxtaposed together – would become a vast system of national corporations' (ibid.). He therefore suggests that electoral colleges should be constituted by professions and not by territorial constituencies: 'In this way political assemblies would more accurately reflect the diversity of social interests and their interconnections. They would more exactly epitomise social life as a whole.'[33] This would mean acknowledging that the organized profession or corporation should become 'the essential organ of public life' (1984[1893] liv).

While he adds a footnote indicating that territorial constituencies will not disappear completely – 'material proximity will always constitute a link between men' (1984[1893]: lix n37) – they will 'fade into the background'. Durkheim is arguing the case for 'secondary' or intermediary groups that are 'close enough to the individual to attract him strongly into their activities and, in doing so, to absorb him into the mainstream of social life' (ibid.: liv). Reliance upon such groups can, he believes, provide a corrective to the 'veritable sociological monstrosity' of a society 'made up of a mass of unorganized individuals' and restrained by an 'overgrown state'.

The revived corporation would not, however, be beyond the control of the state, as Durkheim makes clear in his lectures on professional morality,[34] and again in his lectures of ethics. It must remain in 'immediate and constant contact with the state'. Because every national corporation is of such importance, the state cannot take no interest in the rules that govern it. A corporation would have powers (over, for instance, collective labour contracts), but they would obviously be sanctioned by the state. Society, on the other hand, should not be seen as a collection of independent professional federations. Durkheim is therefore keen to stress that his 'corporatism' does not mean that the state will be absorbed by professional groups. Everything suggests that history is moving in the opposite direction. The whole question revolves around the nature of the state (Durkheim 1975[1909c]: 217–20).[35]

Nor does Durkheim believe that the corporation is a 'cure-all which can serve any purpose' because the crisis society is suffering does not stem from 'one single, unique cause' (1984[1893]: lv). It cannot guarantee equality of opportunity or any just distribution of social status, 'yet if corporate reform does not remove the need for other reforms, it is the *sine qua non* of their effectiveness'. Reform must begin with the creation of 'the body needed for the creation of the new law'. What law is he referring to? It cannot be defined 'except in ever approximate and uncertain terms'. Durkheim therefore ends the preface to the second edition of his thesis by inviting his colleagues and fellow citizens to 'set to work immediately on constituting the moral forces which alone can give that law substance and shape' (ibid.: lvii).

Bouglé too was interested in the question of social differentiation – hence his work on castes. In 1902, he published a note on 'differentiation and progress' in the *Revue de synthèse historique* and began to write an article on 'Theories of the division of labour', which was published in *L'Année sociologique* the following year. He adopted a Durkheimian perspective but, when it came to the effects of the division of labour, he cited Marx to the effect that 'the subdivision of labour is the murderer of the people'.

The second edition of *The Division of Labour in Society* did not escape the attention of the American sociologist Albion W. Small, who rejected Durkheim's new argument that the development of morality depended on the expansion of the corporative sector. Small argued (1902) that more light should be thrown on sectional interests, as corporations were the 'creatures of interest'. The idea that professional groups should be given a greater role gave rise to a lot of misunderstandings, as it was confused with a defence of corporatism. When Durkheim's lecture, 'Professional morality' was published in 1937, Mauss was at pains to emphasize its importance 'in this age of soviets, corporations of all sorts and of all kinds of corporatism . . . of such savage revolutions and reactions'. Durkheim had, he insisted, 'outlined the practical solution, which was at once moral, juridical and economic'.

14

L'Année *in Crisis*

L'Année and *Notes critiques*: **A Planned Merger**

Now that the third volume had been put to bed, Durkheim once more felt discouraged. It was a very heavy task, perhaps too heavy:

> I don't see how I can go on with the *Année*. It takes up all my time. I have no regrets about that; but I have to give up all my time if I am to go on. I have been able to continue with it because I've been teaching a general lecture course. But I have reached the end of my tether. I have to teach a new course next year, and that will take time . . . If I am to take on a new *Année*, there is a danger that I would never complete it.

He could not both teach and edit the journal without taking a period of leave, and he refused to do that.

Durkheim was also worried on behalf of his collaborators and his nephew: 'As for you, it will take time. I cannot take up four or five months of your time every year.'[1] He told him the same thing a few days later: 'I cannot agree to you spending five or six months working on this. And apart from this, you've done nothing serious since August.'[2] Durkheim's prime concern was to fulfil his 'professional duties': 'I cannot take on commitments I will find impossible to meet.' Then there were his 'duties as a father', which he had 'shamefully neglected for the past three years': 'I cannot do anything about my children's education.'[3]

There was, as Paul Lapie put it, a 'crisis at the *Année sociologique*'. Durkheim himself wrote to his close collaborators Célestin Bouglé, Paul Fauconnet and François Simiand, and asked Mauss to speak directly to his friend Henri Hubert about the situation: 'Make sure to tell everyone that I will happily do everything possible to keep our group together, so far as that is possible.'[4] Mauss suggested to him that they should reorganize the journal, and made two proposals: appoint editorial assistants and decentralize the work. He also thought that they should recruit new collaborators. Durkheim liked the idea of editorial assistance: 'With friends as devoted as you all are, we would get along well and could share the task.' But the solution seemed unrealistic: 'Given the distances involved, it's impossible.' He was thinking of the question of ordering books, distributing them to contributors and the physical organization of the manuscript. 'All that could be easily be done if I was in Paris and had your help. But not by post.'[5] As for the idea of greater decentralization, which was designed to relieve him of some of his responsibilities by making each contributor responsible for his own section and bibliography, that was just 'childish'. He added: 'The *Année* is a whole, and that is its great merit. So someone has to look after everything.'[6]

For the moment, Durkheim saw only one solution: the *Année* and *Notes critiques* should merge. Most of the *Année*'s contributors, including Durkheim, published reviews in the *Notes* on a regular basis. Only Bouglé, Parodi and Lapie did not contribute to it. Paul Lapie was well aware that the *Année* burdened all its contributors with 'extra work' and that it 'absorbed Durkheim'. He therefore tended to be in favour of a merger, but he had one reservation: *Notes critiques* had the obvious advantage of 'being short and appearing more frequently than the *Année*', but the downside was that it was 'political rather than scientific'.[7]

Nothing came of the merger project for the moment. Durkheim said that he was 'ready to do anything within my power to keep the *Année* alive; I would be an ungrateful wretch if I did not.' He was thinking of an alternative solution: shared editorial responsibility: 'So I do not need two scribes, but I do need a co-editor.'[8] He did not believe that he should cease to do his share of reviewing – 'in some respects', he wrote, 'it would be more helpful if I dealt with these issues' – but he agreed that some reorganization was required to deal with practical issues such as relations with the publisher, ordering books, the overall plan for the next volume, preparing the manuscript, correcting proofs, translations and the index. The publisher wanted to reduce the number of pages, and it had even been suggested that the 'original articles' should be dropped. 'It seems to me that that could be done.' He then put the ball in his colleagues' court: 'See what you think is possible in the circumstances.'[9]

Durkheim was grateful when Hubert said that he was prepared to 'lighten the load' by sending out the circulars and writing letters to publishers: 'My thanks and apologies for the tasks I have burdened you with.'[10] He wrote to him again a few months later: 'I am very touched by your desire to defend my time and my freedom of mind, even if it means arguing against me.'[11] He was worried all the same: 'My mind will be at rest as we prepare the next volume of the *Année* over the summer months only when I feel that the *Année* is coming along, or, in other words, only when I know that we have enough copy and when I know how it is going to be organized.' He admitted that he was a born fighter.

Hubert's help lightened his burden considerably. Durkheim even said that he himself was prepared to 'gradually step aside', allow his collaborator to 'take more and more initiatives and responsibilities' and 'let him do things as he saw fit'.[12] Even though he would not admit it, he was literally exhausted. And a few weeks later, he did admit that: 'I have suffered quite a violent neurasthenic crisis, but it was acute rather than serious.' At the beginning of August, he went to Houlgate for a few days' rest. Although he was well known for his 'usual sobriety', he ate a lot and slept for 12 hours a night. He recovered quite quickly: 'The feeling that my brain was empty has now passed; it is just that my legs still feel weak and that there is no strength in my muscles.' Hoping that he would recover when he got to Épinal, he concluded his letter with the words: 'Just now, the transformation has been surprising.'[13] When his nephew expressed concern, he reassured him: 'I am better and growing stronger by the day ... The speed with which I am recovering shows that it was nothing serious.'[14]

'We Go On'

When Durkheim sent him a few books, Paul Lapie concluded: 'At least there will be a fourth volume of *L'Année sociologique*.'[15] The necessary things had to be done: sell more copies of the third volume; persuade Louis Liard to buy more copies on a subscription basis; order books. Time was passing: 'We have already lost time, and now we are losing more time, and I am beginning to fear that vol. IV will be just like its elders.' 'Our delay is unpleasant', added Durkheim, who was afraid that they would 'make the same mistakes' with the next volume.[16]

Durkheim asked Auguste Bosco to contribute an article on sociology and statistics, but Bosco let him down (the journal did, however, publish a review of his 'Législation et statistiques comparés de quelques infractions à la loi pénale'). Durkheim had no choice but to try to 'fill the gap' immediately. He thought of writing 'an article of some 20 pages' himself, but he also thought of his nephew and of François Simiand, who might be willing to 'publish 20 or so pages of his thesis'.[17] 'Had quite a long chat with Durkheim', Mauss wrote to Hubert. 'We've agreed that I will write an article on how the world is divided into clans (a contribution to the study of collective representations): 30 or so pages. He is writing an article on the Aruntas. Simiand is writing one on value, as revealed by the price of coal.'[18] Now that he had been awarded his doctorate, Célestin Bouglé had begun to write an article on the 'caste regime'. He was having some difficulties and was 'groping his way', observed Durkheim, who wrote to his nephew asking him to help Bouglé without 'frightening him': otherwise there was a danger that he would lapse into 'that formalism for which he still has some inclination'.[19] Durkheim reminded him of the 'principles' on which their reviews must be based: 'We are much less interested in judging authors than in identifying facts and ideas, and helping to define the issues involved.' But, as had been the case with the other volumes, the *Année's* contributors were faced with the problem of how to classify the books they were reviewing. There had to be some readjustments, and a great deal of flexibility was required. Durkheim discussed the organization of the 'religious sociology' section, which he and Mauss edited, with Hubert. He made it clear that he wanted to introduce a 'Religious representations' rubric. As far the introduction of a section on 'magic', he warned his colleague to add a word of explanation: 'It would be a good idea to say that you do not intend to make a radical distinction between religion and magic, and that you have your reasons.'[20]

The 'miscellaneous' section still included the 'aesthetic sociology' component, but Durkheim needed time to define the section's goals more clearly:

> I have some reservations about expanding it, because we do not exactly have good intentions towards it. For my own part, I have never thought of it as anything but an extra. If we are going to deal with 'aesthetic sociology', good intentions and the ability to do so are not enough, and nor is the vague conviction that aesthetic phenomena are social facts. We also have to have some idea of how to approach them if we are to be able to discuss them in sociological terms. And we will all have to work on that together.[21]

Durkheim also wanted to introduce a new section: 'Do you have any objections to "technology"? Or "material instruments of civilization"?', he asked Hubert.[22] Lack of space meant that 'anthroposociology' might have to be cut. 'I have decided to drop anthropology. We only have 576 pages to play with. So I have told Muffang that I will no longer have anything to send him. Which means that we have no one who is qualified to deal with those issues . . . I will add a note to that effect in the *Année*.'[23]

Back to Religion, Back to Basics

As he was planning the next volume of the *Année sociologique*, Durkheim's teaching took a new direction. The theme of his sociology lectures for the academic year 1900–1 in Bordeaux was 'elementary forms of religion'. This return to both religion and its 'primitive' origins reveals Durkheim's interest in what was to become, 12 years later, the subject of his next book:

> This year, I have had to rehash my old course on the elementary forms of religion without, it's true, succeeding in learning anything new – or almost nothing – for lack of time. But I have come around to asking myself whether it might not be worth taking a new look at the ambiguity of religion, in the sense defined by [Robertson] Smith, and at whether there might not be two spheres which, while there is a continuity and contiguity between them, are still distinct.[24]

It was, amongst other things, the question of magic that led him to see things in this light, and he discussed the issue with Henri Hubert.

Now that he was back from England, Marcel Mauss had to face up to the problem of his professional future. When, at the end of January 1900, he received, via a telegram addressed to his uncle, an invitation from the minister to chair the 'philosophy degree' delegation for the coming academic year,' Durkheim was not very enthusiastic. 'I hardly need to point out that you should think of your thesis before you think about anything else.'[25] He was, on the other hand, willing to go along with his nephew's decision: 'The decision has to be yours. And so I have to regard your decision as the right one.'[26] Marcel once more turned down the invitation. Unable to conceal his satisfaction, Durkheim wrote to him immediately: 'I am neither surprised not distressed by your resolve . . . I think we are going to do some good work.'[27] The uncle was eager to help his nephew and to work with him. He sent him all the files he had accumulated for his general bibliography. 'This is for my own purposes. I would like to get down to some work I have been thinking about for a long time.'[28] He was referring to his study of primitive forms of classification.

In the event, Mauss did not find himself teaching either in a lycée or at the university. A year later, he accepted Sylvain Lévy's invitation to replace Alfred Fouillée, who had been appointed director of the École française de l'Extrême-Orient for a year, and to teach a course on the history of religions at the École pratique des hautes études. He taught two seminars in 1900–1: one on the history of religions in India, and the other on the analysis of the various systems of Hindu philosophy. Marcel thought that this was a great honour. Durkheim did not really approve, but found it difficult to object: 'I am not sufficiently confident in my ability to find you a post, even when you have your doctorate, to be able to give you the advice to disappoint the people who have, in the circumstances, taken an interest in you, by saying no to them.' What worried him was the nature of the teaching involved – he thought that Mauss would be teaching philosophy – and above all the danger that his 'work' (his thesis) would 'never get beyond the planning stage'. He therefore advised him to 'take advantage of any spare time he could find to get on with [his] work'.[29] He was pleased to learn that the course Mauss was teaching was a success: 'I congratulate you and I congratulate us now that you have a fairly steady job.' Uncle and nephew were now researching the same field – the study of religions – and had adopted the same comparative method.

Durkheim himself was no longer teaching moral education in his course on pedagogy, but was discussing intellectual education; his topic for the following year was the application of psychology to education. His lectures on sociology and pedagogy were attended by some 30 students. He was still taking tutorials for students studying for the *agrégation*. His superiors regarded him as 'a speculative thinker' rather than an administrator, and praised his 'great self-possession', his 'vigour and authority' and his 'powerful and vigorous elocution'. He was 'a forceful personality' and a 'master', noted the rector in late April 1900, adding: 'M. Durkheim is an original thinker, a scholarly and vigorous writer, and a zealous teacher who has a very great influence on his disciples. He is also inspired by an ardent and militant proselytism.' He was viewed as 'a very constructive thinker who works synthetically rather than analytically'; M. Durkheim was 'uncompromising, a rigid logician who is strong-minded, absolute and systematic'. The same criticism was made the following year: 'ardent proselytism'. 'He sees his teaching as a sort of apostolic mission', wrote Dean Bizos, 'that must continue outside the faculty, and reach his students in their lives and in society.'[30]

The Role of Sociology in Secondary Education

The debate – or *'enquête'* [inquiry], to use the fashionable expression – about the role of sociology in secondary education was opened by the *Revue internationale de sociologie*. Given what Alfred Fouillée called the 'rise of the social sciences', referring to the growing number of sociological studies and their 'popularity' with both scholars and the public, some thought that sociology should become part of the philosophy curriculum. That would, according to the journal's director René Worms, give young men 'an overview of human knowledge'. Ever since it had been founded, the journal has campaigned for the promotion of the discipline in universities. What not continue the trend? If, as Worms asserted, 'in today's climate no questions are more important and more widely debated than social questions', why not put sociology on the curriculum of the more senior classes in secondary schools? The debate began at a time when secondary education as a whole was already the subject of a broad political debate inaugurated by a commission of inquiry into the question.

Responses to the survey were published between October 1899 and February 1900. The first were from Alfred Fouillée, Alfred Espinas, Gabriel Tarde, Émile Durkheim and Alexis Bertrand, who taught philosophy at the Lyon faculty of letters. Almost all the respondents were contributors to the *Revue internationale de sociologie*. Durkheim was one of the few 'outsiders' at the journal, as René Worms put it, and it is surprising that he agreed to take part in the survey. René Worms was one of his critics, reproaching him for his methodological 'excesses' and especially for his adoption of a purely mechanist approach. Durkheim's reply was brief.

Everyone was agreed that 'sociology should be taught in higher education', but they were cautious when it came to secondary education. This was for two reasons: first, the discipline was still too young and, second, the curriculum was already over-loaded. 'It is a little too soon', declared Gabriel Tarde, adding: 'It would be dangerous to ossify it too soon, or to officially recognize and immobilize a scientific organism that is still in its adolescence' (Tarde 1899: 678).

Most of the respondents, however, took the view that secondary schools could not ignore sociology completely – which raised the issue of how it should be taught. There were two conflicting answers: some wanted part of the curriculum to be devoted specifically to sociology, while others thought that it should be an integral part of a broader curriculum. Alfred Fouillée defended the first position, suggesting that sociology should be taught by philosophy teachers and that six or seven lessons should be devoted to the nature of society, the preconditions for progress, nations and the psychologies of peoples, property ownership, moral, juridical and criminal sociology (including the study of problems such as alcoholism, depopulation and juvenile criminality) and political psychology (including the advantages and disadvantages of democracy). One further lesson on religious sociology (the origins of religion, etc.) should be added to complete the picture (Fouillée 1899: 679). Marcel Bernès, who taught philosophy at the Lycée Louis-le-Grand, argued that there should not be a separate sociology curriculum. That would be 'pointless': 'Secondary education comprises and includes a sociological culture.' It would, he argued, be better to be very 'discreet'; otherwise there was a danger of giving the impression of 'a real revolution in teaching' (Bernès 1900: 8).

In his reply, Durkheim (1899: 679) identified with those who feared that sociology's role in the curriculum would be 'too narrowly defined and therefore too restricted'. He thought that sociology should, rather, be 'an integral part of the philosophy syllabus', and that philosophy teachers had already acquired enough of a 'sociological culture' to be able to deal with all the domains to which their pupils should be introduced. The main thing was, he went on, 'to make them think about the nature of society, the family and the state, about their main juridical and moral obligations, and about the way various social phenomena came into being.' It seemed that it was possible to do that, and he cited his own course on 'The general physics of law and mores', in which all these issues were discussed in sociological terms. He saw no need for any reform, except in the sense that teachers should be reminded of the need 'not to ignore the sociological point of view'. The preamble to the course should, in his view, mention the issue of 'relations between psychology and sociology', and similar reminders should be given whenever the issues of instinct, personality, language or art arose. He identified, finally, one major gap: pupils know nothing about the 'evolution of religion': A few lessons on the history of religions could replace the customary lessons on the history of philosophy, which serve little purpose.

A New Spirit

Five years after its publications, *The Rules of Sociological Method* was still the subject of 'lively controversies'. Sociology was, Durkheim noted (1975[1902]: 400) with regret, enjoying 'almost too much popularity'. He was obviously delighted to see that there was so much interest in what had once been a discredited discipline – he spoke of 'an intellectual movement that will leave its mark on the history of ideas' – but he was also afraid that the enthusiasm it had inspired would be dissipated unless it developed a specific methodology. Célestin Bouglé (1899) made the same point: 'Everyone is talking about it, but few people know what it is.' Sociology was now more fashionable than ever, and there was a lot of interest in it, even on the part of philosophers.[31] Discussions about sociology were, however, and as Jankélévitch remarked (1902: 501), not about questions of detail, but basic issues of methodology and principles. Was sociology a science? Could it claim that it would one day be a science?

Although resistance seemed to have 'gradually weakened', Durkheim still had to be a vocal defender of sociology as both a science and a specialism. He published an article called 'Sociology in France in the nineteenth century' in the *Revue bleue* (1973[1900]) and another, 'La sociologie et son domaine scientifique' ['The realm of sociology as a science'], in the *Rivista italiana di sociologia* (Durkheim 1981[1900]). He also wrote a new preface for *Rules of Sociological Method*, which was published by Alcan in 1901. In Bordeaux, he devoted that year's lectures to the 'history of sociological doctrines'. His young associates, Marcel Mauss and Paul Fauconnet, took up the torch with a text defending (Durkheimian) sociology in the *Grande Encyclopédie* (Mauss and Fauconnet 1901).

Durkheim agreed to take part in the *Rivista italiana di sociologia*'s survey on 'the specific function of sociology and its role in the contemporary scientific movement' because, as he told Bouglé, it gave him an international platform that allowed him to restate his doctrinal position and to attack his 'opponents', and especially Georg Simmel: 'The article on, or rather against, "the sociology of forms" that I told you about appeared in this month's *Rivista italiana di sociologia*. They wanted to carry out a sort of survey about conceptions of sociology, given that opinions are divided; and this is the point of view I adopted.'[32] Durkheim was harshly critical of Simmel's methodology, which gave rise to 'fantastic constructions and a useless mythology'. Sociology could no longer be 'tied to metaphysical ideology' or 'imaginary constructions'. The break between Durkheim and Simmel was now complete.

It was, Durkheim repeated, a matter of great urgency. Sociology was in danger of being reduced to 'an incoherent collection of disparate disciplines' (Durkheim 1981[1900]: 1055) and of remaining vague and ill-defined. He was trying to convince his Italian colleagues that it was time to concentrate on methodology and to develop a 'greater awareness' of sociology's object: the time had come for sociology to become a science. Being a sociologist meant correlating facts and establishing laws. This was what he meant by the 'new spirit'. The very use of the term 'sociology' was, according to Durkheim, 'the signal for a far-reaching reform' in the social and human sciences (which had until now had their sources in literature and erudition). There had been a change of direction: sociology no longer looked at 'events on the surface of social life' but at 'the deeper wellsprings of social life, the intimate sources, the impersonal and hidden forces which motivate persons and the collectivity' (ibid.: 1069).

Addressing his Italian colleagues, Durkheim restated the positions he had been defending ever since he wrote the *Rules*. The domain of sociology was, he reminded them, the group (either simple or complex), which he defined as the 'combination of persons and things which are necessarily registered in space' (1981[1900]: 1059), and as 'the substratum on which social life rests' (ibid.: 1057), as well as the group in action and the workings of social life. Durkheim categorically rejected all explanations that referred to the nature of individuals. His answer to those who claimed that society was simply made up of individuals was that they were wrong: social facts had a specific character, that of an external constraint, such as the 'imperative' element we see in systems of religious, moral and juridical belief. Durkheim demonstrates that individual opposition (rebellion, destruction) to 'social realities' or 'moral and other forces' was 'childish' and inevitably met with 'strong resistance' (ibid.: 1063) on the part of society or the group. He gives other examples of resistance: innovatory boldness at the level of language, individual attempts to rebel against customs, and the conflict between innovation and the organization of the economy.

There was, however, a new element in Durkheim's argument: there was room for the individual and for innovation. He accepts that while social life (in the form of, for instance, beliefs) 'enters into' individuals, it does not do so without 'undergoing variations': when we assimilate collective institutions, we imprint them with 'our individual character' to a greater or lesser extent. He then adds: 'Each one of us, up to a point, formulates his own religious faith, his own cult, his own morality, his own ways of doing things. There is no social uniformity which does not admit a whole range of individual gradations' (1981[1900]: 1065). He immediately adds, however, that the field of possible variations is 'restricted', and that its limits vary from one field of activity to another: there is less freedom in the domain of religion, where innovation and reforms are rejected on the grounds that they are heretical and sacrilegious, than in the economic field.

Durkheim dwells for a moment on the process of the individualization of social facts, which he describes as 'a process that moves from outside to inside' (Durkheim 1981[1900]: 1065). Education is one example, as it inculcates moral rules, practices of civility and opinions into individuals. Constraint, (moral) authority, superiority: Durkheim even speaks of something divine, but refuses to refer to the transcendental: 'the domain of sciences does not go beyond the empirical universe. Science is not even concerned with knowing whether another reality exists' (ibid.: 1063).

Durkheim convincingly argues that a sociological science must demonstrate the existence of a 'social realm' (in the sense that there are individual, biological and mineral realms). He describes it as a whole world, 'immense and unexplored', 'unknowns which must be conquered and bent to human intelligence' (1981[1900: 1066–7). While he is enthusiastic about this prospect, Durkheim appeals for moderation and warns those who want to venture into it that reality is complex, and that this world will not be easily conquered. Célestin Bouglé (1925[1899]: 56) was more positive: this was 'judgment day', and the wheat had to be sorted from the chaff if a 'scientific sociology' was to emerge.

A 'Provisional' Method

Durkheim wrote a new 10-page preface for the second edition of *The Rules of Sociological Method*; it was also published in the *Revue de synthèse historique* under the title 'De la méthode objective en sociologie'. This was his first contribution to Henri Berr's new journal, and was followed by a short review of Georges Palante's *Précis de sociologie* the following year (Durkheim 1902). The first issue of the *Revue de synthèse historique* appeared in July 1900 and in introducing its 'programme' (which some regarded as 'vast' and 'over-ambitious'), Berr (1900) made it very clear that, given his prejudice in favour of 'good methodology', the journal would discuss sociology, and especially 'positive' sociology – in other words, a sociology that applied 'a specific, experimental and comparative method to the concrete facts of history'. The sociology in question was obviously that of Durkheim and his associates. The new journal claimed to welcome 'a range of interventions', but the sociology section was the responsibility of contributors to *L'Année sociologique* because, wrote Berr, 'they were willing to take charge of it'.

When Berr founded his journal, he brought enough pressure to bear to 'convince Durkheim to join him', and Durkheim told Bouglé: 'It goes without saying that we will be regular contributors to the *Revue* where sociology is concerned.' Contributors to the new journal included Durkheim himself, Marcel Mauss, Henri Hubert, Célestin Bouglé, Paul Fauconnet, Gaston Richard and François Simiand. In exchange, the review regularly published reviews of the *Année sociologique*. Goblot's reviews were invariably positive and praised the *Année* for its full bibliographies, its extensive analyses and the prodigious amount of work that went into it. Each volume, in short, illustrated 'an illuminating method and a brilliant self-awareness' (Goblot 1901).

Durkheim did not forget the unfair attacks that had been made on him by his enemies when he wrote his preface to the second edition of *The Rules* in 1900. He therefore tried to dispel certain misunderstandings, to reply to certain criticisms and to give 'fresh clarification of certain points'. He also tried to correct the dogmatic impression that the *Rules* may have given:

> It is . . . very apparent that our postulates are destined to be revised in the future. Summarising, as they do, an individual practice that is inevitably restricted, they must necessarily evolve as wider and deeper experience of social reality is gained. Furthermore, as regards methods, not one can ever be used that is not provisional, for they change as science progresses. (1982[1900]: 34–5)

Durkheim reiterates the central propositions of *The Rules*: 'social facts must be treated as things', 'social phenomena [are] external to individuals', 'social facts [are] manners of acting or thinking . . . capable of exercising a direct influence on the consciousness of individuals' (1982[1900]: 35, 38, 43). The 'state of mind' defended by Durkheim is that of a physicist, chemist or physiologist: the sociologist is 'penetrating into the unknown' and will make 'discoveries which will surprise and disconcert him' (ibid.: 37). His answer to those who complacently claim to have an answer to even the most obscure questions is that we need to be more modest or even to plead ignorance: 'In the present state of the discipline, we do not really know the nature of the principal social institutions, such as the state or the family, property rights or contract, punishment and responsibility' (ibid.: 38).

Turning to relations between the individual and society, Durkheim refuses to argue in terms of certainties, and is very cautious. While he is prepared to admit that there may be similarities between the mentality of a group and that of an individual, he immediately adds that there are also marked differences between the two: collective representations (such as myths, legends, religious conceptions and moral beliefs) are not simply expressions of individual reality. There is, in a word, such a thing as 'social thought' or 'collective thought', and it has a 'coercive influence' on individual minds [*consciences*]. Social life belongs to the realm of constraint. There are therefore such things as what Durkheim calls 'institutions', namely 'all the beliefs and modes of behaviour instituted by the collectivity' (1982[1900]: 45).

Borrowing a phrase from the article that Fauconnet and Mauss were writing, he concludes that sociology is, quite simply, the science of institutions, their genesis and their functioning (1982[1900]: 45). It does not follow, he adds in a footnote, that 'social conformity' leads to the disappearance of individuality: 'Each of us creates to a certain extent *his own* morality, *his own* religion, *his own* techniques. Every type of social conformity carries with it a full gamut of individual variations' (ibid.: 47 n6).

Although he is reluctant to go back to all the controversies stirred up by his book, he does identify a clear dividing line between those who accept 'our' basic principle, namely that of 'the objective reality of social facts', and those who do not. The paramountcy of that principle is, in his view, the hallmark of the 'sociological tradition'. There is no denying that sociology had made 'great progress', but it is also true that there is a lot of work still to be done if the road to science is to be unblocked. Durkheim defines his goal as overcoming the 'deplorable prejudice' that stands in the way of science, namely the 'anthropocentric postulate' that gives man the impression of having 'unlimited power over the social order' and that inclines him to deny the existence of collective forms (1982[1900]: 46). Durkheim is convinced that 'the cause of a sociology that is objective, specific and methodical has continually gained ground', and that the founding of the *Année sociologique* has contributed to its success by imparting 'a feeling of what sociology must and can become'. He pays tribute to the 'enthusiasm and devotion' of his colleagues: 'It is thanks to them that this demonstration by facts could be attempted and can continue' (1982[1900]: 35).

Marcel Mauss and Paul Fauconnet published an article on sociology in the *Grande Encyclopédie* that same year. When they were asked to write it, Durkheim had his doubts, as he was not really convinced that such an article would be 'of any use'. Did anyone read this publication, he asked himself? He was also afraid that 'it would distract both of them from the work that must be [their] main goal: 'waste as little time as possible' was his advice. But he did draw up a plan of work and offered to help on an anonymous basis: 'My name will, of course, not appear.' He was especially interested in the section on the history of sociology: 'Neither of you is ready to write that part. So that is a job I could do: origins of sociology, Saint-Simon, Comte, Spencer', he wrote to Mauss. According to the plan, he had outlines, the second part – which dealt with 'dogma' – would consist of two sections: one devoted to the object of sociology and the other to method. He suggested that Fauconnet should write the first, and his nephew the second. He advised them both to 'do only what you can'.

Durkheim was interested in the project, and in the end he encouraged his colleagues: 'It only means writing 15 or so pages each, that is by no means impossible.'[33] He admitted that his outline had been 'somewhat improvised' but that, 'on reflection, I cannot think of an alternative'.[34] He did, however, agree that his colleagues were free to come up with an alternative, and that they could, for example, deal with method before defining the object of sociology.

At the beginning of June, Durkheim was worrying that 'nothing has been done yet'. He was also worried about the *Année sociologique*: 'This delay will cause others for the *Année*.'[35] He then suggested that all three of them should work in Épinal in late August. Autumn came, and the article was still not finished: 'I blame myself for having allowed you to commit yourselves to this plan, or rather for not having stood up to you more.'[36]

The final version of the article (Fauconnet and Mauss 1901) had little to say about the history of the human sciences, and contained only a few references to Comte, Mill, Tylor and Spencer. Fauconnet and Mauss take social reality as their starting point, and give many concrete examples: industrial production, the division of labour, credit, marriage, religion, suicide, crime: social phenomena are distinct from those studied by, for example, psychology. They are institutions – in other words, 'sets of instituted acts or ideas that individuals find before them and to which they are, to a greater or lesser extent, obliged to conform'. These 'acts or ideas' could just as easily be prejudices, political constitutions or juridical organizations. Such things are sociology's specific object.

Having defined sociology's object, Mauss and Fauconnet go back to Durkheim's discussion of sociological explanations: the explanation for a social fact is always another social fact. There is a clear difference between sociology and philosophy, or any other doctrine which seeks to find the explanation for social phenomena in the nature of individuals. Sociology studies not essences, but phenomena, and not religion, but religions that have their own history and that relate to clearly defined human groups. Mauss and Fauconnet also avoid prioritizing morphological or economic phenomena. In some cases, it is morphology that is determinant; in others, it is representations. The explanation must, in other words, be circular without begging the question. Even so, they give the psychic dimension of social life a determinant role: 'Collective life is a set of representations.'

Mauss and Fauconnet obviously wish to play down Durkheim's so-called dogmatism: the rules of sociological method cannot be formulated in definitive terms. The scientific approach is simply defined by a number of principles, such as definition, observation and systematization, the testing of hypotheses, and so on. The authors scoff at dialectical discussions and encyclopaedic erudition, and have no time for either the 'abdications of empiricism' or 'hasty generalizations'. The characteristics of the new ethos of the social sciences researcher are, in their view, as follows: it ignores personal feelings and opinions, is severely critical of its sources, adopts a comparative approach and rejects the notion of absolute truth. Such are the preconditions for scientific progress.

Célestin Bouglé reviewed Fauconnet and Mauss's text in the *Année sociologique* (Bouglé 1902b) at Durkheim's request ('Just a few lines will be enough'). He emphasizes that, in the author's view, sociological explanations cannot do without psychology: 'The "interaction" between minds [*consciences*] produces psychic phenomena of a new kind. They can evolve of their own accord, modify one another and form a definite system – and they are therefore worthy of study in their own right and with a specific method.' The perspective could not have been more Durkheimian in terms of the definition of both sociology's object and its method. 'The ideas that inspired this article', notes Bouglé (1902b: 135), 'are those from which the *Année* takes its inspiration.'

Although he was often accused of being too much of a psychologist, Bouglé therefore unhesitatingly lends his support to the 'programme of the Bordeaux school', as formulated by Mauss and Fauconnet. He no longer defends the introspective method: we must, he asserts, 'observe social realities from "the outside"'. Let us make contact with the detailed facts. 'We need more special analyses; that is the way to arrive at a better understanding of social reality' (Bouglé 1902b: 135). Such was the leitmotiv of the *Année,* which demonstrates 'what sociology can and must be'.

Bouglé takes up the defence of the school, whose 'uncontested leader is now Durkheim'. Its great strength is that it brings together the raw materials needed to 'reconstruct sociology' and to prove that an 'objective sociology' is possible. Gaston Richard, for his part, added that 'we can celebrate the victory of the new science', and that its victory was as complete in the domain of practice as it was in the domain of theory' (Richard 1901a: 201; 1901b: 675).[37]

This was a real offensive – and, one might almost say, an orchestrated offensive – in a context in which controversy was still lively. Doing something was not enough: Durkheim and his colleagues had to state and restate what they were doing. In 1903, Durkheim published another article, 'Sociology and the social sciences' (with Paul Fauconnet) in the *Revue philosophique* (Durkheim 1982[1903]: 175–208]).

L'Année, Volume IV

'Are things going to begin the way they did before?' Durkheim wrote to his nephew in November 1900, enclosing a postcard for him to send back with a note of 'the date when [he] will have finished the *Année*'.[38] Marcel was, it was true, very involved in politics, publishing articles in *Le Mouvement socialiste* and giving lectures on the cooperative movement (which was rapidly expanding) at the École socialiste. In March 1900, he was involved in establishing a small cooperative – the Nouvelle coopérative socialiste – called simply 'La boulangerie' ['The bakery']. Durkheim's nephew was rather pleased about his activism. 'I am well. I am writing a lot. I am acting quite decisively.'[39]

All this annoyed Durkheim, who was 'very busy' and trying to finish his reviews as soon as possible. At the beginning of December, he became even more insistent: 'The only things that are missing are you and a review from E[mmanuel] Lévy.' Lévy was listed as one of the contributors to the fourth volume (which covered the year 1899–1900), was still coeditor of the 'law' subsections and even published a few reviews. Henri Muffang's was the only name to have disappeared, having been squeezed out of the journal. This was the end of the 'anthropobiology' section. The *Année sociologique* had recruited two new contributors, both *agrégés*. Abel Aubin was taken on as an assistant to Célestin Bouglé (general sociology) and Paul Fauconnet (juridic and moral sociology); Hubert Bourgin was taken on to assist François Simiand with the economic sociology section and, more specifically, the 'regime of cooperation' and 'trusts' rubrics. Their initial contributions were restricted to a few reviews. Abel Aubin had attended Durkheim's lecture in Bordeaux, where he had studied for his *agrégation*, which he was awarded in 1898. Since then, he had been teaching philosophy in the lycée in Châteauroux. He was experiencing 'administrative difficulties' because teaching morality was 'controversial'. 'But the ideas he is teaching are the ideas that I taught him', retorted a prickly Durkheim, who feared that 'this incident might pose a threat to our freedom to teach'.[40]

Born in Nevers in 1874, Henri Bourgin was educated at the lycée in Nevers, and then at the Lycée Janson in Paris. He was awarded his *licence ès lettres* in 1893, entered the École normale supérieure in 1895, and passed the *agrégation* three years later. Very active in politics (he contributed to *Le Mouvement socialiste*, was involved with the Société nouvelle de librairie et d'édition, and had published a little book on Proudhon), he was close to François Simiand, who introduced him to both economic sociology and Durkheim. He was teaching at the lycée in Beauvais when he began to contribute to the *Année*.

When, as Durkheim had expected, Bosco let him down, a solution to the 'article problem' had to be found quickly. Durkheim himself wrote an article entitled 'Two laws of penal evolution' (1978[1901]): 'I had to fill a gap in a hurry and as best I could', he later told François Simiand.[41] He also asked Célestin Bouglé to publish part of his study of the caste regime. Bouglé had recently been appointed to a post in Montpellier, and was lecturing on that topic in the faculty of letters. He also published an article on the same subject in the *Revue philosophique*. Durkheim was following his work attentively, and was happy to give him books, to pass on his old lecture notes on the family and to make suggestions about, for instance, the relationship between clans and castes. 'These notes may be too short, but if they are of any use to you, so much the better. That would give me great pleasure.'[42] The third memoir was by Joseph Charmont, who taught in the law faculty at Montpellier (his inaugural lecture on civil law was on 'The socialization of the law') and who was therefore one of Bouglé's colleagues. His article was called 'The causes of the disappearance of corporate property'. It was said to be 'a little too succinct' to demonstrate the topic's 'real interest'.[43]

Pragmatology; or, The Science of Acts

A few changes were now made to the journal. When they started it, Durkheim and his colleagues 'thought it prudent not to adopt at once an overly systematic classification' because they were aware that such a vast subject-matter could not be 'organized all at once and in an a priori manner' (1980[1901a]: 403). They tried, rather, to learn the lessons of their joint experiment as they went along.

As Durkheim reminded his readers, one of the *Année*'s main tasks was 'precisely to work progressively to determine the natural boundaries of sociology. This is, in fact, the best way to assign definite themes to be investigated, and in just that way to free our science from the vague generalizations which have delayed its progress' (1980[1901a]: 403–4). The issue of classification was, in his view, 'important'. 'That is how sociology is organized. Introducing some order into this shapeless mass is no small task. Perhaps that will be part of the *Année*'s legacy. We will gradually get closer to a rational classification.'[44]

The changes affected both the relative balance between the sections and the internal organization of their rubrics.[45] 'Religious sociology' (more than 150 pages) was now the biggest section; 'ritual' and 'religious representations' (myths, dogma, etc.) were treated in separate rubrics. The second largest section, with just over 120 pages, was now 'juridic and moral sociology', and it had undergone a few modifications. The ideas of 'civilization and progress' were dropped from the general sociology section and replaced by 'social evolution'. A new 'anthropology and sociology' section, under the editorship of Hubert and Mauss, was also introduced. It was harshly critical of works dealing with 'raceology', including Georges Vacher de Lapouge's *L'Aryen. Son rôle social*.

The desire to extend the field of criminal sociology expanded that section from 38 to 50 pages, and it now included 'moral statistics'. More space was devoted to 'domestic and conjugal life', 'sexual morality' and 'immorality'. The section also covered the 'repressive system' and 'madness as social fact.' Durkheim was keen to expand the criminal sociology section because it made it possible to bring together two facets of collective morality: positive morality, or morality in the true sense of the word, and negative morality or criminality: 'Violating a rule is one way of putting it into practice.'

These 'improvements' to the way that the books reviewed were classi-fied meant that the object of other sections had to be redefined. Anything to do with history and comparative ethnography now came under 'moral and juridic sociology'. This led to the creation of a new section dealing with 'the functioning of juridic and moral rules', and it included both honest and immoral acts. Durkheim was even tempted to introduce the neologism of *pragmatology*; 'Since all these investigations necessarily have to do with subject matter involving deeds committed by human beings – for social institutions live and function only through the behaviour of citizens, functionaries, etcetera – we had thought to call the science dealing with this subject *pragmatology*, in order to give it a definite sense of unity' (1980[1901a]: 405). He then rejected the idea on the grounds that 'any neologism that is not pre-tested and validated through use has little chance of succeeding'.

The Position of Women; or, The Gender of Words

Durkheim wrote more than 60 reviews for the fourth volume of the *Année*. Several of them dealt with the family and marriage, law (as relating to the family, inheritance law, and wills in France), population and the birth rate. Durkheim was obviously preoccupied with the situation of women: these texts deal with sex, family and inheritance law, the situation of widows ('Women find it easier to do without men than men to do without women'), relations between the sexes, civil and occupational status (the low percentage of married women running companies) and the respect accorded to women in the Middle Ages and by modern peoples.[46]

One of Durkheim's reviews deals with James Frazer's 'highly qualified' defence of the thesis that the origins of gender are to be found in language. The question of gender must, in Durkheim's view, be 'related to the set of beliefs and practices that provide the basis for exogamy.' If, as he believes, 'any group that lives a different life and that has a certain individuality tends to develop a language of its own', the same must apply to the sexes: 'The outcome is that words are given a sort of gender.' In his response to Jacques Lourbet's *Le Problème des sexes*, Durkheim explicitly deals with the question of equality. Good sociologist that he is, he takes the view that 'the equality of the two sexes will be achieved only if the woman blends herself more and more into external life; but then how will the family be transformed? Some profound changes are necessary and we cannot defer those desired changes which must be anticipated' (1980[1901a]: 305).

Birth of the Prison

Durkheim's contribution to the fourth volume of the *Année* was consider-able, as he also wrote an article entitled 'Penal evolution'. This gave him the opportunity to come back to a problem that had interested him ever since he wrote his doctoral thesis. His analysis of the repressive system was, he apologized, somewhat schematic, but it allowed him to identify two great laws. The first can be formulated as follows: '*The intensity of punishment is greater as societies belong to a less advanced type – and as centralized power has a more absolute power*' (1978[1901]: 153). The second demonstrates that: '*Punishments consisting in privation of freedom – and freedom alone – for lengths of time varying according to the gravity of the crime, tend more and more to become the normal type of repression*' (ibid.: 164). Death is not always the ultimate punishment, and there is a long list of horrible punishments ranging from burning at the stake to crucifixion, from being trampled to death by an elephant, to having boiling oil poured into the ears or mouth, or being torn to pieces by dogs in a public square. Even though punishments did become milder with the passage of time, Durkheim makes it clear that primitive societies have no monopoly on atrocities or barbarity. The type of society (lower or advanced) is not the only explanatory factor; the type of 'governmental power' is just as important. It may, to a greater or lesser extent, be centralized or absolute: 'The apogee of absolute monarchy also marks the apogee of repression' (ibid.: 163).

Durkheim also demonstrates that the privation of freedom, and therefore detention, are relatively recent measures and that it is only in Christian societies that they become significant. One of the preconditions for their existence is the transition from collective responsibility to individual responsibility, together with the existence of public establishments that are spacious enough to be used as prisons, initially for purposes of prevention.

Because detention is a milder form of punishment, it is tempting to explain this development in terms of a relaxation of customs and a rejection of violence. But Durkheim suggests that it is, rather, the changing pattern of crime that leads to changes in punishment: as we move from crimes against collective things (such as public authority, traditions and religion) to crimes against individuals (murder, wounding), and from religious to human criminality, the form of repression changes and average punishments become milder. Morality itself loses its religious quality, as do 'collective things' (1978[1901]: 177); as they become 'human realities', they are secularized. A moral shift has occurred. 'Collective feelings' have changed and collective coercion 'is eased . . . and becomes less exclusive of free inquiry' (ibid.: 178). Durkheim speaks of a 'new mentality' which means that we no longer react to crime with 'indignant stupefaction' but with 'calmer, more reflective emotion' (ibid.: 179). The reason why penal law is now in crisis is, he believes, that penal institutions no longer correspond to the 'new aspirations of moral consciousness' (ibid.: 180). If we wish to arrest the evil, we must create new institutions rather than 'galvanize' the old ones' (1980[1901]: 446).

The climate was such that some associated the increase in juvenile criminality with secular education and recent pedagogical reforms. As Durkheim notes in his review of Alfred Fouillée's *La France au point de vue moral*, 'the present malaise is related essentially to a disintegration of our moral beliefs'. France is experiencing a moral crisis because 'the goals to which our fathers were attached have lost their authority and their appeal' (1980[1901]: 407). As a result, there is a 'real void in our moral consciousness'. Durkheim is sceptical about Fouillée's suggestion that various legislative measures should be adopted (legislation against the increase in alcoholism, strengthening of repressive legislation). He is just as cautious when it comes to the role of education: 'properly directed, it cannot but have its effective uses', but only if 'the masters be shown to what new ideal they are to attach themselves and to attach the hearts of the children' (1980[1901]: 407–8).

The 'clarity' of Durkheim's 'very penetrating' argument may have impressed his readers, but were they convinced by it? Gustave Belot once more expresses certain reservations in the *Revue philosophique* (Belot 1901). He regrets the fact that sociology, which he described as 'fairly obscure and fairly complex', has become embroiled in 'false problems'. While he is well aware that he will be told that science makes progress by offending common sense, he refuses to compare sociology's situation to that of the physical sciences, and therefore criticizes 'the most distinguished of our sociologists' (including, of course, Durkheim) for wanting to apply scientific methods to sociology: 'Society means us, and we see society from within. The relationship between common sense and social facts is a constant and reciprocal relationship of cause and effect.' He therefore feels a 'quite legitimate distrust' of Durkheim and his associates.

Bibliographic Work: A New Crisis

Others, however, took the view that the *Année sociologique*'s services to sociology were 'indispensable'. Philosophers were glad that the journal was in the hands of an editor who was 'an essentially rationalist thinker'. At the philosophical level, its most important contribution came not from the articles but from the analyses or reviews.[47]

L'Année provided 'services', 'the most noteworthy being that it shows that some of those working in sociology are more interested in coming together in order to cooperate rather than in standing out or making a name for themselves', remarked Durkheim to Bouglé.[48] He was, however, far from satisfied: 'The *Année* is not what it should be.' What worried him most was seeing his young colleagues 'devoting themselves to a purely bibliographical work.' He added: 'We have to be productive. I will never tire of telling you that.' He himself had given up all hope of writing anything that year: 'Even if I produce nothing myself, that does not matter. You are the ones who matter.'[49] He was actually distressed to see his editors 'spending a lot of time on bibliographical work': 'I feel responsible for all that, and that causes me a lot of pain. I cannot tell you how painful I find it. The fact that you are wasting your energy is itself unpleasant, but the fact that I have to take some responsibility for that is unbearable. If only the results were comforting!'[50]

Well aware of the limitations of the *Année sociologique's* current formula, Durkheim was the first to want to 'modify the way we conceive it'. 'If we go on without any change of direction, we really will be seen as just another bookseller's catalogue, not by everyone but by a lot of people. We must take a step forward if we really want to do something useful.'[51]

Mauss made some suggestions as to how the journal should be reorganized: 'Drop Parodi, condense Bouglé and alter the division of labour between Simiand and Bourgin.' Durkheim could not conceal the fact that he felt 'tired and discouraged', but he was all the more sceptical about his nephew's suggestions in that the conditions were not right: Emmanuel Lévy had to make an 'effective' contribution and, more important, Marcel, who was already very busy, must be 'ready to take a leading role' and have time to 'take more care over his reviews'. Durkheim was also aware that all – or almost all – his colleagues were 'distracted by all sorts of occupations on all sides'. That they all lived in different places merely 'added to the difficulties'.

Durkheim was already thinking about the next volume: 'Volume V is under way; let's go ahead with it and try to do as best we can.' In order to do that, he thought, they had only to 'change direction, and do more personal work by concentrating on what really is of sociological interest'.[52] He was also afraid that his nephew's 'new commitments' at the École pratique would mean that he would be 'of absolutely no use for vol. V unless we resign ourselves to an indefinite delay in publishing'. He reminded Hubert that the problem with Mauss was 'the ease with which he deludes himself into thinking that he can do so much'.[53] He was therefore afraid that Hubert would have 'everything on his plate' and would be in danger of having 'too great a burden of extra work.' Even so, he still gave the journal all his attention and kept a close eye on the preparation of the manuscript. When he realized that the next volume of the *Année* would be 'too copious', he dropped a lot of the short reviews. This was, he explained to Hubert, a way of introducing a 'slight change' of direction:

> When we started, the important thing was to make the specialists aware that we were knowledgeable, to make sociologists aware that they knew nothing and to let the public know what it could legitimately ask of sociologists. As a result, our first concern was to produce bibliographies that were as complete as possible. We obviously must not stop doing that, but we also have to think of something else; and we cannot do that unless we are primarily a good bibliographical index.

Durkheim knew that he and his colleagues could not 'wrestle with every category of specialists' in each of the journal's four main sections. When it came to the science of religions, law or political economy, it was impossible to be 'as well informed' as the specialist journals. The point was to 'show clearly that we are not just a collection of special bibliographical journals . . . We must be first and foremost a sociological journal'. In order to prove that they were, Durkheim suggested that they should restrict their efforts to questions on which they felt they were 'in a position to shed some sociological light'. This implied making choices: 'Let's not spread ourselves too thin: our domain is vast enough as it is. So we should include in our bibliographies only books that we feel are able to advance or shed light on this or that sociological problem.' He suggested to Henri Hubert that he should discuss this change of direction to his friends: 'I think that this is a stage in our onward march, and that this is what we must do now that we have a greater awareness of who we are.'[54]

When Hubert asked him about how much space should be devoted to archaeology, Durkheim was unsure what to say, as this was one of his colleagues' specialized areas. 'The sociological interest of the question is the sole criterion on which our choices must be based.' He then qualified his answer: 'There is probably nothing in history or archaeology that is not sociological, but we cannot demonstrate that yet.' He wanted the journal to concentrate more on 'trying to teach', and to 'take the reader by the hand and bring him around to our point of view'. Hence the need to 'dot the i's' and, whenever possible, 'preface the reviews with a preamble explaining the state of the question'.[55]

Durkheim was also planning to write an article on totemism. He asked Mauss to pass on his notes: 'Perhaps we could turn everything into one article.'[56] Writing 'a major article on totemism' was, on the other hand, out of the question. 'I am really tired,' he added.[57] He did not, however, abandon the project and, two months later, he was satisfied with what he had done: 'My article on the Aruntas is virtually ready. I am pleased with what I've found. My theory about Australian classes does seem to be confirmed by everything I have seen. This is the first time in a long time that I have done something with pleasure.' He later added: 'My work on Spencer and Gillen is growing longer.' His hostility to James Frazer, whom he found 'detestable', acted as a stimulus. Frazer had already published several texts on this question, including 'The origin of totemism' (1899), which would subsequently become one of the four volumes he published under the title *Totemism and Exogamy* in 1910. Durkheim remarked of his English colleague's theory that: 'It does not hold up.'[58]

While he was writing his article, Durkheim put the final touches to the new preface to his doctoral thesis, which he sent to his publisher, Alcan, in May 1901. 'The old text remains intact, apart from the fact that 24 pages have simply been cut. Other than that, nothing has been changed. On the other hand, the new preface is longer and that makes up for the cuts.'[59] 'As for the book itself', he confided to Hubert, 'it is of interest only to beginners, and I am republishing it for beginners.'[60] Émile was tired, and used his summer holiday to rest and look after himself in Plombières (Vosges) from 13 to 24 August. He then spent the period 24 August to 15 September with his family in Épinal, ending his holiday in Paris, where he met his associates.

The uncle was still worried about his nephew's attitude towards the *Année*, and was afraid that he wanted to 'drop everything'. He therefore remained vigilant, and repeated his advice about reviews to Mauss: 'Reviewing a book is not the same thing as correcting an essay.' Two points seemed to him to be essential: '(1) Show the general value of the book . . . (2) Retain anything that can be kept, or expound an idea suggested by the book.'[61]

Durkheim wanted the manuscript for the next volume of the *Année* to be ready for the printer in the new year. This was a strategic issue: 'If I am to convince Alcan to go on, I must be able to give him the manuscript without any delay', he told Mauss. A month later, he again wrote to Mauss: 'I beg you, do not start the way you've started every year.' He was even prepared to 'lend him a hand' and to write up the reviews on the basis of his rough drafts: 'Don't hesitate to make use of me.' His nephew's 'delays' were all the more annoying in that they were in his view simply 'a waste of time'.[62] When it came to his nephew's unacceptable delays, Durkheim could not hide his displeasure from his closest friend Henri Hubert: 'There is no cure for the illness: we are dealing with an incurable. I don't know that I can do more than I am already doing to help to improve matters; I am constantly reminding him of where his duty lies and trying to get him to do some of the work; but I am not sure that I will always be able to lend him a hand.'

And then it was the new year. At the beginning of January 1902, Durkheim again wrote to Mauss: 'I'm in a hurry to get this finished with.' He then lost his temper: 'You will be the death of me . . . Keeping the *Année* waiting for ever is just not acceptable.'[63] He had to wait until the beginning of February before he could send off the manuscript. He insisted that his nephew should learn his lesson immediately: 'Remember that you were the last to be ready . . . even though you had help . . . I ask myself what you will be like in the future.' To add to his worries, Mauss had a lecture course to prepare.

No sooner was the next volume of the *Année sociologique* in press than Durkheim was planning future issues. They were to include an article on magic by Hubert and Mauss. 'It seems to me that there is a lot of talk about magic', he wrote. Hubert agreed: 'The time is ripe', he told Durkheim, who asked his nephew to meet his friend to 'talk about the question together'. He was, however, worried about Hubert's state of health – he was complaining about being 'over-worked' – and did not make too much of an issue of it: 'Hubert must not do too much work for the *Année*', he told Marcel. A few days later, he told him not to 'overdo it', as Hubert was displaying symptoms of 'fatigue and discouragement'.[64] Durkheim was also unhappy about his own state of health. He was still finding his editorial role a heavy burden:

> Do you think that I will have to restrict myself to this bibliographical work for another five years? For one reason or another, it takes up my whole year. I can only save scraps of time. I have to stand in for this one,

and then for that one. It's childish to think that you can run the *Année*
and work at the same time.

It was the same old story a few months later. 'So it's time we all stopped
talking about it and got on with things. If we go on with the *Année* this
way, that's my whole life taken up, just with odd jobs.'[65] Under these conditions, Durkheim did not see how he could complete his planned study
of the family. The same applied to his young colleagues, who were also
'paralysed by this bibliographical work'. 'My own view is that we have to
be productive, that we will make any impact only to the extent that we are
productive.'[66] The hardest thing of all was that, every year, the *Année* had
problems with articles. They may have been a 'useful' way of launching the
Année, but they had become a 'real worry' and Durkheim wanted to be rid
of them, especially as he was convinced that he had established a 'client-
base' of between 500 and 550 readers, according to his estimates, who
would remain 'loyal'. If that was the case, the *Année* could, he was convinced, 'have a comfortable life'. And he would be freed from his 'biggest
worry'.

The journal's financial position was still precarious: the first four
volumes had made a loss (of some 885 francs). Sales were stagnant (610,
511, 499 and 560 copies respectively) and were directly related to the date
of publication. Alcan was prepared to go on, but only on certain conditions: the number of pages had to be reduced, and Durkheim would have
to bear the cost of any overrun and corrections. Durkheim felt 'morally'
obliged not to look for another publisher 'before [he] had reached the final
limits of the sacrifices [he] was prepared to make'.[67] He also said that he
would like Hubert, Mauss, Simiand and Fauconnet to meet to 'talk about
the issue' and then let him know what they 'all felt'.

The time had come for Durkheim to sign a new five-year contract
with Alcan. He was 'strongly in favour of separating what must be separated'. The analyses (or reviews) should appear at regular intervals, and
the studies or articles should appear in a series called *Études sociologiques*,
'when the material comes in (roughly one volume per year)'. Durkheim
was thinking here of his colleagues' work, namely Mauss's thesis and
the article on magic he was supposed to be writing with Hubert, and
studies by Paul Huvelin,[68] Simiand and Fauconnet. This was the so-called
'two-part' solution. Durkheim looked at several options, and found what
seemed, 'at first sight', to be an attractive alternative: *Notes critiques*
should concentrate on the bibliographical work, and the *Année* should
be exclusively devoted to articles. Perhaps there should also be a change
of title. He asked his nephew to think about this, and consulted Henri
Hubert, Célestin Bouglé and François Simiand by post: 'Let me have
your opinion as soon as possible.'[69] Several of his colleagues reacted negatively, and there were a lot of objections. There were, as Durkheim himself
observed, 'differences of opinion', and they were 'clear'. There were two
schools of thought. Some (Bouglé and Simiand) argued against the 'two-
part solution', mainly because of the effect it would have on sales, whilst

others (Fauconnet, Hubert and Mauss) welcomed the idea, but could not agree as to how to implement it. They were, on the other hand, agreed about one thing: no matter whether they were published in a separate collection or in the *Année*, the memoir must, as Durkheim noted, be 'our work or the work of people who are in complete agreement with us'. The goal he had set himself was to 'make the *Année* a collection that requires only one thing of its contributors: scientific honesty'. He had never dared to 'hope for the moral homogeneity that had been established between its contributors'. 'In what has been published, the only things of value have come from us.'[70]

Durkheim thought that 'the original reasons for keeping the memoirs in the *Année* are no longer valid'. 'We are now known to the audience we wish to reach', he told Simiand. He was still convinced that 'the *Année* will have to be transformed one day or another', but given the cool reception to that suggestion by several contributors, it seemed wiser to abandon the idea: 'The present system is the one thing we all agree about. It also has the advantage of experience. I am reluctant to change it for purely personal reasons . . . The status quo is better than a hasty change that has not been fully thought through.'[71]

Durkheim insisted on consulting his close collaborators: he wanted to preserve the spirit of cooperation at all cost. When François Simiand sent his 'affectionate greetings' for the New Year and expressed his gratitude, Durkheim replied immediately: 'Nothing gives me greater pleasure than the idea that you like the work we are doing together. But do not talk to me about gratitude. I owe you all more than you owe me in every respect. And that, as it happens, is the precondition for all good cooperation and the feelings that implies.'[72] Durkheim continued to consult widely. He went to Paris in March and wanted to see his colleagues before going to Alcan. They all preferred a 'joint meeting' to the 'individual meetings' he had expected. This was one of the *Année*'s few group meetings. No one changed his position.

Durkheim agreed to describe both proposals – the two-part solution and the status quo – the next day and to tell the publisher: 'We cannot reach a decision.' Alcan was frightened that the two-part solution would be 'commercially dangerous'; he preferred the status quo, but suggested some minor changes. Durkheim agreed in principle, but made no definite commitment. 'I did not want to say yes before we had all examined the question together.' His own view was that they should commit themselves for only one year. 'That gives us time to think', he told Simiand. Durkheim's attitude was one of 'see what happens, and think'. As he explained to Simiand:

> I do not think that we can wait for a new generation of pupils to replace us in order to ensure that the bibliographical work goes on. I think that that is our only possible starting point but, little by little, we will have to move on to something else. We have actually to do sociology, rather than perpetually gathering material. But as the years go by, we've become

used to this bibliographical work and have got out of the habit of being productive.[73]

As for the articles, Durkheim agreed to stick with the present arrangement, with the proviso that a 'long-term programme' had to be established. They would therefore have to stop 'going begging every year and being dependent on the good will of others'; they would also have to find a way of ensuring that the articles were not 'written at the last moment'. He outlined a programme: nothing in volume VI (unless Bouglé had something to offer), magic in volume VII, and his own articles on marriage or the family for the following volumes. He also wrote to François Simiand to ask him if he and Bourgin would be able to write something for volumes VIII and IX. That would, he concluded, be one way of 'no longer living from year to year'.[74]

The group also discussed changing publishers and going to Armand Colin. Henri Hubert acted as the go-between and tried to get 'formal assurances'. Durkheim was 'not at all keen to remain with Alcan', but admitted to Hubert that they had to 'make an honest exit'. That was not easy, as Alcan did not want to break with the *Année* at all. Durkheim was wary of changing publishers as it meant 'giving up what they had for an uncertain future'.[75] He therefore felt 'no desire to change, as there is no need to': most of the journal's 'regular customers' were, he believed, customers of Alcan.[76]

Durkheim did not stop working; he was already planning an article about 'the division of the world into clans (a contribution to the study of collective representations)'. The title, which he described as 'approximate and provisional', was 'Primitive classifications of things'.[77] He invited Mauss to co-author it, and said that he would like his nephew to 'think as much as possible about [this] article'. He hoped that he would come to Bordeaux to work with him from the end of June to the end of July and to write a first draft. 'I will take care of the final version', he added.[78] He also advised his nephew to 'discuss the topic' in his lectures at the École pratique. He even asked him to send him his lecture notes, and to 'carefully keep on one side the files containing the facts that we will have to use.' His goal was to produce an article of some 60 pages.

Once the crisis was over, the journal's position was 'broadly the same as it always was'. But one major change was in store for the whole *Année* team: Durkheim might be going to Paris. He hoped to leave Bordeaux, as there had been talk of his being appointed to the Sorbonne in February 1901. Durkheim wrote a few letters to his colleagues (Boutroux and Brochard), who were both 'obviously very much in favour', but he did not have too many illusions: 'There are internal tactical issues that make success impossible for the moment.' He had at least the consolation of knowing that he was to be promoted with a salary of 8,000 francs. As he wrote to his nephew, 'In the meantime, that's something more definite.'[79]

An Impending Death: Mélanie Durkheim

At the end of June 1901, Émile Durkheim had to rush to Épinal: his mother, who was now over 80, was ill. He spoke of his 'painful worries' to Henri Hubert: 'My mother has suddenly grown weaker, and her condition appears to be getting worse.' He left Bordeaux and went directly to Épinal, travelling via Paris but without stopping there. 'It is not that there is any immediate danger, or so they think, but if I want to see her before she succumbs to total mental depression, I have to hurry.'[80] 'A distressing situation', he wrote to Octave Hamelin, as it meant that he could not be in Bordeaux for the degree examinations and had to ask his friend to take his place on the board for the orals. Mélanie Durkheim was close to death, and had already fallen into a deep coma. 'Her condition is deteriorating, but no one can say when the inevitable end will come.' Durhkeim described his mother's condition in detail: 'She is perfectly calm and is in no pain; her heart is beating and she is still breathing, but there are no other signs of life.' His only hope was 'that it will all end peacefully'.[81] The doctor reassures him that it would. In the midst of all these 'great sorrows', he received news that filled him with 'great joy': his colleague Marcel Foucault had successfully defended his doctoral thesis. He would subsequently publish his *La Psycho-physique* in Alcan's 'Bibliothèque de philosophie contemporaine'.

Mélanie Durkheim died on 20 June 1901. In his eulogy, Moïse Schuhl, the rabbi of Épinal, recalled that she had been the 'devoted wife' of the 'venerated rabbi and founder of Épinal's Israelite community', and that both Moïse and Mélanie Durkheim had inculcated 'a sense of righteousness and honour' into their children and had been given in return 'the satisfaction of being surrounded by the love, profound respect and tender solicitude of their children and their children's children'. The rabbi described Mélanie as 'an intelligent, active mother who sacrificed the best years of her life in order to guarantee her children a future', and as a woman who was known for her great kindness to 'widows, orphans and the unfortunate poor'. Her greatest joy was that she was 'cherished by her children'. Moïse Schuhl gave as an example the attitude of her son Émile:

> When I saw her son, mature in his learning and one of the leading lights in the French literature and science, become a child once more as he pushed the wheelchair she was forced to use in recent weeks to go for a walk and or to take the air, that picture seemed to me to exemplify the acts of extreme and almost naive acts of filial piety described in the Talmud . . . and that illustrious rabbis performed for their mothers.[82]

Rabbi Schuhl had already pointed out that Émile Durkheim had attended service in the synagogue; he saw the presence of a university professor and a 'very enlightened man' in the congregation as a sign of the vitality of the Jewish religion. That did not please Durkheim, who had made the 'sacrifice' of going to the synagogue at his mother's insistence.[83]

A few days later, Émile wrote again to his friend (he had already informed him of his mother's death) to tell him that he would have to extend his stay in Épinal so as to respect the 'old customs' his mother had always respected (seven-day period of mourning without leaving the house) and so as to avoid 'creating a scandal'. He was also worried about the 'moral state' of his sisters and feared that 'such a sudden departure' would distress them still further. It had been a difficult ordeal for all of them.

> We had some difficult moments. My poor mother did not suffer, but we all did, and it lasted for no less than 36 hours. We had in fact known for three days that it was all over. Our nerves were in such shreds that the final crisis was less difficult to bear than one might have feared, especially for my sisters.

He added: 'Yes, you have a good idea of what our mother meant to us. But I refuse to accept that the ties that bound me to the past can be broken for ever. They have to be replaced. That, basically, is why I am extending my stay.'[84] The tone sounded detached, but the modesty of his words does not disguise Durkheim's feelings. He had turned a page. At the time of her death, his mother's estate was worth over 200,000 francs. There was the house, but most of the money was invested in moveable property. The activities of the family embroidery business had done rather more than 'supplement the income' of the Rabbi of Épinal.[85]

The Inner Sanctum: Henri Hubert and Marcel Mauss at the École Pratique

The deaths of two professors at the École pratique des hautes études in the spring and autumn of 1901 threw the life of the sixth section into confusion. August Sabatier, who held the chair of Christian literature passed away in April, and Léon Marillier, professor of the history of the religions of non-civilized peoples, died in tragic circumstances in October. Both Marcel Mauss and his friend Henri Hubert were qualified to apply for chairs. Which of them was more likely to succeed was a different matter. The death of Auguste Sabatier created the first vacancy. Marcel Mauss thought of applying, but only if the chair was renamed. His friend Hubert took the same view. Neither was guaranteed success. They analysed the situation together and talked strategy with Sylvain Lévi, who believed that 'something could be done for Hubert'. Hubert therefore asked Ernest Lavisse and Émile Durkheim for references. Durkheim had no hesitations about supporting his close colleague, for whom he had 'high esteem': 'He is one of the few historians who, without losing any of his concern for accuracy and detail, has succeeded in transcending the strictly historical point of view and who feels the need to explore new lines of research.'[86] Henri Hubert appeared to stand little chance, and the vote was very close: Hubert emerged victorious from the third round. As Durkheim pointed out, this was also a victory for sociology: 'From the general point of view, it is not uninteresting that sociology has found its way into the École des hautes études. Once again, sociology may not have the starring role, but it is there in the choice and in the man. That is reason enough to celebrate.'[87]

The chair in the history of the religions of non-civilized peoples was another possibility. Mauss looked like his old teacher's obvious heir. He knew his work and his books, and he was a regular contributor to the *Revue de l'histoire des religions*, which published three reviews by him in 1901. His election did not, however, look like a foregone conclusion, and there were other candidates. Durkheim went to Paris to talk to Sylvain Lévi about how they should proceed. If necessary, he was also prepared to approach professors at the École, including Albert Réville, who chaired the fifth section. He advised his nephew to publicize his work and to 'distribute' copies of his article on sacrifice, his articles on Steinmetz and the *Grande Encyclopédie* essay on sociology. He also suggested that he should attend a reception being organized by Hartwig Durembourg, professor of Islamic studies and of the religions of Arabia. 'It is obvious that you must do all you can to demonstrate the value of your work. You must do all you can to overcome your reserve and discretion beyond all conceivable limits.' Durkheim also gave Mauss specific advice on how to behave when he went to see Albert Réville: '

> Be careful. He is an old man, so don't say anything that might upset or surprise him. You can try to convince him. The main thing is not to give him any excuse to take against you. Let him take the lead. Do not press him too far. You're there to let him get to know you, not to preach him a sermon. There is no point in trying to get him to understand what you are doing or the methods you are using. If he asks you about that, keep your answers as simple and as measured as you can.[88]

The section's chairman refused to make any 'prior declaration', seemed have a moment's doubt and even suggested to Mauss that he should not apply. On the other hand, he made no secret of his sympathy for Mauss.[89] Even though he was aware that 'his position as Mauss's uncle meant that he should keep his distance', Durkheim intervened directly. He also approached Louis Liard through the intermediary of Victor Brochard, who taught philosophy at the Sorbonne, arguing that 'doing away with this course' (the history of the religions of non-civilized peoples) would mean doing away with most of the École's courses on the comparative science of religions because religious ethnography was, together with folklore, the starting point for this kind of research.

> Doing away with a course like that in a school of religious science seems to me to be like blocking up one of the few openings that lets some light into a dark house. I in fact think it impossible to understand more

complex religious phenomena if you do not first have some notion of simpler phenomena. This is an essential foundation course.[90]

There was also, he added, 'a more personal reason': 'One of the goals we are pursuing is to succeed in making the science of religions a branch of sociology. And it is really only the primitive religions, which are simpler, that can be described from that point of view.'[91] When it came to strategy, the uncle was unsure what advice to give his nephew, and simply told him to follow the advice of Sylvain Lévi: 'There may be customs and ways of going about things that I know nothing about. Let him be your guide.' Should Marcel go to see Liard? A sceptical Durkheim was all the more unconvinced in that his was a temporary appointment: '[Liard] would tell you to get lost. For an administrator, "temporary" means "permanent" in the long term.' And if Mauss did go to see him, his uncle advised caution: 'Do not give the impression that you want him to commit himself. Let him know how you see your work, and the real nature of your studies. Don't make it look as though you want to move heaven and earth, avoid using big words, and don't get carried away, whatever you do.'[92]

Durkheim was quite optimistic. 'I am very pleased with the way things have turned out. In my view, we can only wait for the outcome.' He even suggested to his nephew that he should be thinking about what his lectures would be on: 'Choose something you already have worked on . . . This time, you have to show what you are made of.'[93] The section's council eventually decided that the course on the religions of non-civilised peoples should stay. In the meeting Sylvain Lévi and Israël Lévi sprang to Mauss's defence and pointed out that, over the past few years, he had developed an interest in ethnography. Mauss was elected unopposed. Sylvain Lévi immediately wrote to Durkheim to say that he was 'glad to have been able to help Marcel find a proper position, and in a place for which he was made'. He added: 'I have no doubts about his genius, but I do have some doubts about his assiduity' (cited in Mauss 1969[1935]: 539). Durkheim too was 'very pleased' to see that his nephew had 'this time found a position that fits him like a glove'. All he had to do now was devote himself to it completely. 'And it is because I wanted you to feel free to devote yourself to it properly that I am so keen not to let the *Année* drag on too long. Please, hurry up and get it over with so that you can make a real effort with the other thing. You will have to rid yourself of this commitment without too much delay.'[94]

Durkheim therefore had more than one reason to celebrate at the end of 1901: Célestin Bouglé had been appointed professor of social philosophy in the faculty of letters in Toulouse; Gaston Richard had been awarded the Crouzet prize, and Emmanuel Lévy had been awarded his *agrégation* in law. Marcel Mauss gave his inaugural lecture in January 1902. Durkheim was astonished when his nephew told him about this: 'I knew nothing about this, and thought it had been put back to a later date.' He warned him to be careful about writing up his lecture, which was to be published in the *Revue de l'histoire des religions*:

Be careful what you say about Marillier. Don't think you can get away with obviously contradictory things by saying on the one hand that he is your master and that you are his little student – which you can do easily enough – and then telling him some harsh truths on the other. Once you have observed all the conventions, you have to show that you are going to do something new, but without describing yourself as the hero who will civilize and transform everything.

Durkheim invited his nephew to send him the text if he had 'any doubts'.[95]

In his inaugural lecture, Mauss sang the praises of his predecessor Léon Marillier, whom he described as a philosopher. He began by making it clear that he would not be following in his footsteps, and then described the broad outlines of his own work. The title of his lecture ('The history of the religions of non-civilized religions) was a source of annoyance to him, as it implied a whole set of prejudices: non-civilized people were, it was believed, 'savages' or 'big children', and their customs (cannibalism, tattooing, totemism, magic, etc.) seemed bizarre. They were said to be naive and devoid of any intelligence. Mauss's position was clear: 'There is no such thing as a non-civilized people, but only peoples of different civilizations' (Mauss 1969[1902]: 229). He announced that his lectures would provide his students with an introduction to bibliographic research (ethnographic studies of magic amongst the Melanesians being one example) and would introduce them to the study of elementary forms of prayer in Australia and Melanesia. He was trying to establish a link between what he was teaching and the doctoral thesis he planned to write. He made a point of reminding his listeners that his programme was characterized by 'its methodological caution': it would deal with facts (both religious and social) rather than grand general theories.

'A Huge Amount of Work'

The fifth volume of *L'Année sociologique* (1900–1) appeared at the beginning of February 2002. The team had now been expanded by the arrival of two new contributors: Antoine Meillet and Claude Maître; Marcel Mauss, now in post at the École pratique des hautes études, was the 'go-between'.

Antoine Meillet was an important recruit. He was a philologist, a linguist and a historian, who had studied with Ferdinand de Saussure before replacing him at the École pratique (fifth section: historical and philological sciences.) He had published a *Note sur la difficulté générale de la grammaire comparée* in 1900.[96] His sympathy for sociology and his decision to join the *Année* may seem surprising, as he was neither a pupil nor a disciple of Durkheim's. He had just published two articles on 'Les Lois du langage' in the *Revue internationale de sociologie*. Marcel Mauss, his junior by six years, knew him very well: he had attended his lecture at the École pratique in 1899–1900 and again in 1900–1, and had great admiration for this 'prodigious scholar', who was seen by his students as a 'sort of magus'.

Meillet introduced Mauss to the comparative method, and the teacher and his student had developed a strong friendship based upon trust and openness. Claude Maître (born 1876, École normale supérieure 1895, *agrégé de philosophie* 1895) had studied under Mauss, who was his elder by six years, and had been attending his lectures at the École pratique for several years. His contribution to the *Année* was restricted to this volume and was limited to Henri Hubert's 'aesthetic sociology' rubric. He was also a contributor to *Notes critiques*.

Reviews were still distributed across six main sections; the seventh 'miscellaneous' section was precisely that. 'Religious sociology', edited by Hubert and Mauss, was still the largest (130 pages, or 27 per cent of all reviews), followed by juridic and moral sociology' (23 per cent), 'economic sociology' and 'general sociology' (12.5 per cent), 'criminal sociology and moral statistics' (7.5 per cent), 'miscellaneous' (6 per cent) and 'social morphology' (3.5 per cent). The small 'miscellaneous' section now comprised four rubrics, two of which ('language' and 'war', edited by Antoine Meillet and Paul Fauconnet respectively) were new. 'Aesthetic sociology' and 'technology' were still the responsibility of Henri Hubert, who paid particular attention to prehistory and ethnography even though, to his regret, books on these topics often devoted little place to aesthetics. It should not be forgotten, he wrote, that 'there are arts that still give aesthetic pleasure'.

It is to be noted, finally, that the 'general sociology' section now devoted a great deal of space to the question of group mentalities, to anything to do with the study of races and, more generally, collective ethology. If there was one question that preoccupied everyone, it was that of 'national character'. Alfred Fouillée had published *Psychologie du peuple français* and was working on 'Esquisse des peuples européens', while Émile Boutmy had published two *Essais de psychologie politique*, one on the English and the other on Americans. Most of these studies did not extend beyond stereotypes: Italians displayed a precocious sexuality and terrible jealousy; the French were characterized by their excitability, credulity and scepticism; the English by their taste for reflection and premeditated action; and the Americans by their love of individual initiative and freedom. The psychology of peoples, group psychology, collective psychology – as Durkheim wrote to Bouglé:

> The terminological uncertainty concealed an intellectual confusion. In sociology, everything has to do with group or collective psychology. In that sense studying moral beliefs and practices is still a form of collective psychology, and when we look at crowds or at some sect or other, we are studying social mentalities.

He even suggested adopting the expression 'social ethology'. 'There really is such a thing as social ethology, just as there is such a thing as individual ethology, and the question is worth raising.' Paul Lapie took up the invitation, began to write on political ethology, and suggested that the psychological method should be subordinated to the sociological method.[97]

For volume V of the *Année*, Durkheim, as before, wrote some 60 reviews. Questions of marriage (including so-called group marriage), the family, kinship, exogamy and sexual morality were now central preoccupations, and he devoted two long articles to J. Kohler's studies of Papuan law (Durkheim 1969[1902a]) and the Marshall Islands. And, as always, he carefully followed the work of his American colleagues A.W. Small, C.A. Ellwood and Lester F. Ward and their publications in the *American Journal of Sociology*.

Two recent books were of particular interest to Durkheim: Charles Seignobos's *La Méthode historique appliquée aux sciences sociales* and Georg Simmel's *Philosophie des Geldes* (which he had already reviewed in *Notes critiques* the previous year). Siegnobos's book would also become the object of a controversy begun by François Simiand in the pages of the *Revue de synthèse historique*. Durkheim found Simmel's book to be 'laborious' but 'suggestive' reading (1980[1901/2]: 97). It contained 'a number of ingenious ideas [and] pungent views' but Durkheim had little time for 'this bastard type of speculation, whereby reality is expressed in necessarily subjective terms, as in art, but abstract as in science' (1980 [1901/2]: 98). He was critical of Simmel's position, which suggested that 'philosophy is not like the sciences (in the true sense of this word), subject to the usual requirements of proof; it appears to work in the field of that which cannot be demonstrated' (1980[1901/2]: 90). It was, in other words, all very 'subjective'.

From the Aruntas to the Price of Coal

'A huge amount of work', exclaimed Edmond Goblot (1903: 239), noting that Durkheim had once more 'taken on most of the burden'. As well as writing a large number of reviews, Durkheim was the author of one of the two articles published in the fifth volume: this was his essay on totemism (Durkheim 1969[1902b]). The other was by François Simiand, and dealt with the price of coal in the nineteenth century. On the one hand, a study of an institution specific to so-called primitive societies; on the other, an analysis of the market for an energy source characteristic of contemporary industrial societies. But there was a common thread: both articles raised methodological questions pertaining to sociological method.

A thesis? 'That would be putting it a little too strongly', admitted Durkheim.[98] He was referring to his own essay on totemism, which was based on *The Native Tribes in Central Australia* by Baldwin Spencer and his associate F.J. Gillen. He and his nephew had reviewed the book in the previous volume of *L'Année*. These 'competent observers' must, in his view, take the credit for having studied the working of a 'real' totem religion amongst the Aruntas of central Australia. Their concrete observations of a living people had proved Robertson Smith's theory about the primitive sacrificial and totemic meal. To the surprise of some readers, they had also demonstrated the role that totemism played in the regulation of marriage. In Durkheim's view, their 'discovery' was all the more important in that it had implications for every domain within sociology: kinship, marriage, sexual morality, social organization, and so on. The question was whether or not 'the facts they have observed bear out the interpretation they offer us'. His analysis is based on a very loose reading of Spencer and Gillen's book.

The Aruntas are presented here as the most primitive savages known to humanity. It is, retorts Durkheim, a mistake to see them as 'backward representatives of early humanity'. On the contrary, they have a 'long historical past' and have evolved; hence the complexity of their social organization, which has changed but still displays more primitive elements. 'We therefore find amongst the Aruntas both the most distant past, which has survived, and the future that lies in store' (1969[1902b]: 351). Durkheim uses these tribes as a 'prototype': the interesting thing about the Aruntas is that they have a totemic system, but not the twin taboos that are usually associated with totemism: exogamy, or the prohibition of marriage between individuals bearing the same totem, and the prohibition on killing and eating the totemic plant or animal. Hence the question: what are the characteristics of totemic religion? Durkheim challenges the analysis of James Frazer, who describes totemism as a 'sort of economic enterprise' based upon reciprocity. Drawing on Spencer and Gillen, he argued: 'The environment in which the Aruntas live is completely imbued with religiosity, and the origins of that religiosity are essentially totemic.' The totemic animal was 'sacred', and eating it gave rise to a 'real sacramental communion'.

First rule: exogamy (which implies sexual morality). Durkheim is careful not to reject the thesis – which had often been demonstrated and which was now universally accepted – that totemism can coexist with exogamy. Amongst the Aruntas, everything was decided not at the level of clans, but at the level of what he calls *phratries*, which can be divided into *classes*. This division of the tribe into two great phratries (which are exogamous) appears to be widespread in Australia and very common in America. In a sense, this gives us the 'primal clan'. In order to prove beyond doubt his 'phratry-totem' thesis, he analyses the organization of *intichiuma* ceremonies (the head of the local community has both civil and religious functions), and the way in which the cult instruments known as *churingas* (with emblematic drawings of the totem) and popular traditions (the way ancestors are divided into totemic groups) are passed on.

The Aruntas do, however, have a legend about primitive endogamy. What is the explanation for myths? asks Durkheim They are 'systems of representations' and were largely invented by the popular imagination 'to make existing practices intellectually comprehensible'. The Aruntas' legends are therefore 'dubious' and 'suspect', and their myths are based upon errors that can easily be explained in terms of the 'innate simplicity' of the human mind, which is inclined to believe that the part exists prior to the whole, and that the individual exists prior to society. Hence the need for what he calls a 'defiantly critical' interpretation of traditions: they are 'intellectual constructs'.

Before endogamy gives way to exogamy, and before the clan (which was originally exogamic) could cease to exist, 'a great transformation, even a revolution' must have taken place in its social framework. Durkheim's hypothesis is that it had to do with the system of descent (which, in the case of the Aruntas, is now paternal but which was once uterine or maternal, as in almost all Australian societies). Durkheim cites several facts in order to demonstrate that there was once a matriarchy: the Aruntas' traditions and myths reveal 'traces' of a *class* mode of organization in a strongly united society with a strong sense of solidarity.

Having demonstrated his thesis with respect to matrimonial taboos, Durkheim immediately moves on to alimentary taboos. He congratulates Spencer and Gillen on having made a 'major contribution' to religious and juridic sociology. They have, he says, improved our understanding of the primitive organization of societies that practice totemism, revealed not only the negative side of totemism (prohibitions), but also its positive side (positive benefits), and studied the processes whereby more general and more unified systems of beliefs are elaborated (the transition from the religion of clans to that of tribes). It is now possible, he concludes, to see 'how totemism relates to the religious systems that come after it'.

Simiand's article (2002) on the price of coal in France created problems at the editorial and printing stages as it included a lot of graphs. This worried the École normale supérieure's librarian Lucien Herr. 'Let's hope that [Simiand] has time to knock it into shape and to say clearly everything that he has to say', he said to Durkheim. Herr was prepared to help Simiand with the editing. Durkheim also offered to help: 'I do not need to tell you that if I can be of any use, I am at your service.' When he read his colleague's manuscript – 'quickly', he apologized – he was more than satisfied:

> Your work does the *Année* great honour and will attract attention. The section on method seemed excellent to me. The analysis of such complex statistical data may be a little concise and dense, but the conclusion explains it well . . . I cannot tell you what pleasure it gives me to see one of you making a positive contribution to the *Année*, especially when the contribution is as important as this.[99]

'It must have taken you a lot of effort.'[100]

In his article, Simiand deliberately restricts himself to one product (coal), one society (France) and one period (the nineteenth century). Given that he is dealing with the price of things that are bought and sold, he immediately rules out 'qualitative observations that are vague and often personal' in favour of 'quantitative findings that are precise and objective': 'The objective study of prices begins with the observation of prices.' He describes his method as 'experimental'. His goal is to base his study on the data given in *La Statistique de l'industrie minérale*, to explain it and to ensure that both his observations and the explanation are scientific. Questions of method are a major concern for Simiand, who discusses at length the value of the statistics he is using. He then asserts that the determination of prices is 'social', but that the phenomenon is still social because it is a matter of 'opinion'.

'Scholarly Cooperation'; or, What 'Speaking Durkheim's Language' Means

Gustave Belot's long review of the fifth volume of *L'Année sociologique* concentrates mainly on the articles by François Simiand and Émile Durkheim. He is, he says, impressed by Simiand's 'considerable amount of work', and praises his 'very exhaustive monograph', his 'painstaking accumulation of statistical data', 'interesting graphs' and 'extensive interpretive discussion' (Belot 1903). He does not, on the other hand, see 'any methodological innovations of any great note' in either his empiricism or his sociologism. Edmond Goblot (1903), for his part, was delighted to encounter 'a scholar who scrupulously collects facts and, with an unusually analytic mind and acute insight, tries to extract laws from them'. He was, he admitted, 'unhappy about attacking' Simiand, but concluded: 'He has not convinced me.'

Gustave Belot was unsparing in his praise of Durkheim, and spoke of the extent of his erudition, the rigour of his thought, the clarity of his method and, above all, his serious commitment to science. In his view, the problem with the article had to do with method and, more specifically, the principles behind Durkheim's sociological explanations, and he challenged his major thesis that 'in social life, what is obligatory comes before what is optional, and freedom is by definition won by overcoming primary prescriptions and prohibitions'. This was not, as he himself said, the first time he had disagreed with his colleague.

Belot (1903) was also complimentary about Durkheim's growing number of 'faithful' co-workers and their 'painstaking work', and described what they had accomplished as 'useful' in methodological terms. He refused to describe the researchers Durkheim had gathered around him as 'disciples', but spoke, rather, of a 'working group', and of a 'scholarly cooperation' in which they all displayed 'real independence' as well as the 'same desire to do scientific work', and in which everyone made his own contribution. The division of labour coexisted, in other words, with specific skills. He observed, finally, that the 'obvious differences of opinion' that had been visible when the journal began publication had faded, and had given way to a great 'theoretical homogeneity'. This was not a body of work 'set in stone for all time. It is alive and still developing, and is determined by both its internal principles and the scientific environment.'[101]

Edmond Goblot also praised the 'hard-working and eminent workers' who had gathered around Durkheim and taken their inspiration from him. We now have, he added, 'a real school in which there are well-defined tendencies, especially when it comes to method'. Like his philosopher-colleague, Goblot adopted a cautious attitude towards Durkheim's essay on totemism and refrained from 'evaluating the value of his conclusions' because he had yet to read Spencer and Gillen: 'new sources of information' were needed before any light could be shed on the question.

The *Revue de métaphysique et de morale*, in contrast, was more aggressive towards the *Année*. Élie Halévy sarcastically remarked: 'Everyone who writes for it speaks M. Durkheim's language.' Durkheim objected to the tone of his comments, and immediately wrote to the journal's editor, Xavier Léon, to express his surprise:

> I do not stand on ceremony when it comes to discussions – even lively ones; but I am sorry that you did not entrust this little task to someone who had the minimal sympathy (I am not saying that he has to sympathize with the way they are interpreted) for these studies without which no critic can have an adequate understanding of the things he is talking about.

It annoyed him that the author of the review spoke of '[his] sociologism' and '[his] method', and described them as 'impedimenta that [his] collaborators should overcome'. Such language was, he complained, unfair and inopportune. He also criticized the author for having 'personalized his criticisms of a body of work that is essentially collective and impersonal, and which I try to keep as impersonal as possible'. Durkheim therefore made it clear to the journal's editor (whom he knew and who would become a friend) that he had not written to him because his pride had been hurt, but to point out that it was inappropriate to publish such aggressive criticisms of an author who contributed to the journal. 'Why', he asked ironically, 'do you bother with my sociologism if it bothers you so much?'[102] Xavier Léon immediately wrote back to him to say that it had been 'an editorial mistake', and to submit his forthcoming inaugural lecture to the Sorbonne, 'Pedagogy and sociology' (1956[1903]), for publication in the journal. Durkheim was quite willing to 'forget this little incident' and readily accepted his friend's invitation.[103]

Many people had reservations about Durkheim's article because, as Salomon Reinach pointed out, the issue of totemism was not simple: 'When we enter the "maze" of exogamous marriage, we are no longer dealing with literature or history, but with algebra. It requires a real effort to understand or comprehend it' (Reinach 1903a: 667). The director of the Musée de Saint-Germain took great interest in work on this question, arguing that 'it is not very scientific to say that exogamy is a characteristic feature of totemism'. Although he praised Durkheim's talent for 'detailed analysis' and his 'critical and philosophical mind', he was nevertheless sorry to see that he had taken no account of the reservations he had expressed.

The English anthropologist Andrew Lang, an important specialist on totemism, was very harsh on Durkheim and demolished his thesis about the subdivision of the primal horde into phratries. Durkheim counterattacked with a lengthy review of Lang's *Social Origins* in the journal *Folk-Lore* (Durkheim 1975[1903d]). His criticisms were harsh: Lang had outlined a theory of exogamy that was at once 'conjectural' and unclear (according to Lang, the explanation lay either in the weakness of women, which could be passed on to the opposite sex by contagion, or in male sexual jealousy). What was worse, he overlooked the essential feature of exogamy and therefore totemism – namely, 'the religious nature of sexual relations and of the prohibition on exogamy'. 'All this is purely imaginary and, while one at times admires its ingenuity, it is not based upon any positive proof.' Claiming that he was acting in self-defence, Lang was given the right to reply and launched his own 'direct' attack. Durkheim had, he claimed, refuted his own theory about the nature of the totem, namely the argument that a clan could change its totem (Lang 1904). Durkheim then asked the journal to be so 'hospitable' as to allow him to make a few observations. His response was a straight denial: despite Lang's claims, he was still of the same opinion: it was always possible to change totems and names, but only in determinate conditions, and never thanks to legislative measures or by decree. He ended his article with a categorical: 'I now regard the debate as closed' (Durkheim 1975[1904b]).[104]

Part IV

Paris and the Sorbonne

15

At the Sorbonne

The new century began very auspiciously for Durkheim and the whole *Année sociologique* team. A Russian translation of *The Division of Labour in Society* was published in 1900. The second edition of *The Rules of Sociological Method* appeared in 1901, followed by the second edition of *The Division of Labour* in 1902 (with a print-run of 1,000). In 1902, Durkheim was a candidate for a chair at the Sorbonne. Some major articles on totemism and the matrimonial organization of Australian societies, primitive systems of classification, and magic had been published. The *Année* team had been expanded by the arrival of Antoine Meillet and a number of young contributors, and the journal had weathered another crisis. Durkheim and his associates appeared to have consolidated their position in academic circles and the intellectual field. Some had positions in Bordeaux, Toulouse and Lyon, and Mauss and Hubert were teaching at the École pratique. The group controlled one journal, and had access to several others not only in philosophy, but also in the various human sciences (including the *Revue de synthèse historique*, the *Revue de l'histoire des religions* and *L'Anthropologie*). Its network of contacts in intellectual and political circles was both wide and diversified. What was more important still, a new generation seemed poised to continue to take over its work. But although Durkheim was winning converts and new supporters, he was also making more enemies, and they were becoming more vocal. While *Suicide* had provoked some negative responses because it added a social dimension to a psychological problem, he encountered even more serious opposition when he began to objectify such central objects as religion, morality and knowledge. This caused a general outcry. Some criticized him for his total lack of respect for religious beliefs, while others were outraged because he 'relativized' all knowledge by giving it a social basis. In addition, he was also accused of wanting to bury the great culture of the humanities. Sociology's victory was therefore anything but a foregone conclusion.

'At a Standstill'

Durkheim's emergence had done little to change the sociological 'landscape'. His main enemies – Worms, Tarde and Le Bon – were still very active. The secretary of the Institut international de sociologie was still editing the *Revue internationale de sociologie* and organizing international conferences. The 1903 conference was due to be held in Paris under the chairmanship of Lester F. Ward from the University of Chicago; its theme was the relationship between sociology and psychology. Worms had begun to write his ambitious *Philosophie des sciences sociales.* The first two volumes appeared in 1903 and 1904, and dealt, respectively, with the object and method of the social sciences. Gabriel Tarde, who was closely associated with the *Revue internationale de sociologie*, published *L'Opinion publique et la foule* in 1901, followed by the two-volume *Psychologie économique* in 1902. The polemic between Durkheim and Tarde was still ongoing, but both men would agree to take part in a public debate. In 1902, Gustave Le Bon published his *Psychologie de l'éducation* and became editor of Flammarion's highly successful 'Bibliothèque de philosophie scientifique'. The first book he published was Henri Poincaré's *La Science et l'hypothèse*.[1] He was also the organizer of a 'Wednesday lunch' attended by leading figures in political, academic and artistic circles. Le Bon was an excellent scientific popularizer, but never held an academic position. He made no secret of his contempt for 'our poor French universities' and succeeded in alienating a number of professors, including Ernest Lavisse and the Indianist Sylvain Lévi (he had challenged the value of his work). Academics had many reasons to dislike Le Bon,[2] and so too did Durkheim and the *Année sociologique* group. Georges Bourgin, for instance, said, of Le Bon that he was a perfect example of the 'bad, facile and imperious sociology that prevails in non-scientific circles' (1913: 303–10). Over the previous 20 years, there had been what Durkheim (1982[1903]: 181) called a 'veritable flowering' of sociological literature.' Once 'intermittent and sparse', it had become 'continuous', but this was not necessarily a cause for celebration: 'the impression is conveyed of marking time'. He goes so far as to describe the situation as 'alarming' because 'any division of labour, or indeed, any continuity in research, becomes impossible, and consequently so does any progress' (1982[1903]: 194).

Sociology was, in other words, a discipline that had little or no institutional presence when compared with other social science disciplines such as social economics or political economy (which were now taught in the faculties of law and teacher training colleges),[3] or even anthropology (the École d'anthropologie de Paris was relatively well organized and offered courses on research methods[4]). There was no chair in sociology, and no training in research methods. The discipline still depended for its dynamism on the action of more or less isolated individuals and on institutions that were to a greater or lesser extent marginal: the École libre des sciences politiques,[5] the École des hautes études sociales (which replaced the Collège libre des sciences sociales in 1900).[6] There was also the Musée social. This was not, strictly speaking, a teaching institution but it did have a library, offered some public lectures and had a programme of 'missions and surveys'. The Le Play network was still quietly active and centred on the journal *La Science sociale* (founded in 1886 after splitting from *La Réforme sociale*; its full title was *La Science sociale d'après la méthode Le Play*). This was controlled by the Abbé de Tourville[7] and his friend Edmond Demolins, who founded the private École des Roches in 1900: it was now undergoing a rapid expansion. The other core members of the group were Paul des Rousiers, Robert Pinot and Prosper Prieur.[8]

The most active institution was, of course, the École des hautes études sociales, which was made up of four distinct schools: the École de morale et de pédagogie, the École sociale, the École de journalisme and the newly established École d'art (which had three sections: aesthetics and visual arts, music, and theatre). The École taught a wide number of courses, ranging from 'Social and moral theories of the church' and 'The repression of begging and nomadism' to 'People's universities' and 'Practical social questions' (the latter was taught by Paul Bureau). Every year, it organized a very popular series of lectures on specific themes such as solidarity, with professors from the Sorbonne (Émile Boutroux, Alfred Croiset and Georges Dumas) and politicians (Léon Bourgeois) as guest speakers. At this time, the École probably offered more sociology and sociology-related courses than any other institution in Paris: Comte's sociology, ethnic and sociological method, general sociology. The teaching staff in the sociology section included Vidal de la Blache (geography), Maxim Kovalevsky (ethnography), the Italian Enrico Ferri (criminology) and Léonce Manouvrier (anthropology). In 1902–3, papers on the history of social doctrines were given by Wilfredo Pareto, amongst others. The Institut international de sociologie was especially well represented, and the school advertised its programme of lectures in the pages of the *Revue internationale de sociologie*.

The school's secretary-general and main driving force was the extraordinarily dynamic Dick May (whose real name was Jeanne Weill).[9] She succeeded in recruiting Émile Boutroux and Émile Duclaux to serve as the school's honorary presidents, and Dean Alfred Croiset as chair of its board of governors. Émile Durkheim and his colleague Célestin Bouglé agreed to take part in some of the school's activities.

'An Outstanding Candidate'

When Ferdinand Buisson, professor of educational science, was elected to the National Assembly as a Radical Socialist *député*, his post at the Sorbonne fell vacant. The name of Émile Durkheim was immediately mentioned as a possible candidate.

An *agrégé d'histoire*, Ferdinand Buisson was a former director of primary education (1879–96), a founding member of the Ligue des droits de l'homme (he became its president in 1913), and a Dreyfusard. When he became director of primary education in 1897, he took on the responsibility of reforming the Third Republic's primary sector. He described its reform as

> one of the most moving sociological experiments recorded by history. It was the reform of a country, of the only country in the world until then to try to found a democracy on the principle of respect for one authority – reason – which implied the existence of both freedom and equality, with all its short- and long-term implications, both political and economic, both moral and social.[10]

A Protestant by upbringing, Buisson was an anti-clerical free-thinker, but he did not believe that God was dead; he wanted to secularize religion while retaining the religious feeling. Buisson had surrounded himself with a group of liberal Protestants (Steeg, Pécail, Albert Réville) who contributed to the *Dictionnaire de pédagogie et d'instruction primaire* (1882, reprinted 1911). The *Dictionary*'s guiding principle was freedom: psychology was given a major role, the principle of duty was identified with the moral law, while both utilitarianism and the morality of self-interest were rejected. Buisson was the author of articles on secularism, including one entitled 'Neutralité scolaire'. Non-denominational neutrality did not, in his view, mean either indifference or impartiality; secularism had a political dimension because it allowed education to be based upon republican principles. Buisson wanted schools to teach a morality that was neither dogmatic nor doctrinal. Although he was not a sociologist, he was sympathetic to sociology. He became a member of the Société de sociologie de Paris, and agreed – 'with humility', he said – to take over from Léon Bourgeois as the learned society's president. Émile Durkheim was a contributor to the second edition of the *Dictionnaire de pédagogie*.

Buisson wrote a letter to Durkheim expressing his 'admiration' for him, and Durkheim therefore assumed that he would support his application. He could not, however, weigh up the advantages and disadvantages of changing jobs: 'They cancel each other out. Leaving Bordeaux in order to teach pedagogy does not appeal to me. Hence my attitude.'[11] Replacing Buisson was certainly 'rather tempting', but not at any cost. As Durkheim told Célestin Bouglé, who had come to visit him in Bordeaux, he was afraid that teaching a new course would 'take up all his time' and 'prevent [him] from working'. He did want the job, not for the 'honour of going to Paris, but to do some useful work there'. He added: 'I don't think they attach too much importance to sociology.'[12]

Durkheim also had other things to worry about. His sister Rosine, Marcel Mauss's mother, was having problems with her health ('exhaustion – in other words, neurasthenia' – was the doctor's diagnosis).[13] And his nephew had 'disappointed' him. He was in danger of losing the sum of 20,000 francs that he had 'invested' in the socialist cooperative La Boulangerie. This was a delicate situation, as it was family money that Mauss had invested. He tried to explain himself to his uncle:

I know better than anyone else that I was gambling a large sum of money and how much I was committed. I was well aware of what I was doing . . . even now, I feel under an obligation to do all I reasonably can to support a collective enterprise that I helped to found . . . Given the way things are going, there is still some hope that this sacrifice will one day become an investment. But I have no illusions.[14]

When Mauss told him of his misfortunes, Durkheim was deeply distressed: 'The pain you have caused me makes it quite impossible for me to work.' In a long letter, he criticized his nephew for his thoughtlessness, and explained to him that he had 'seriously betrayed two people'. First of all, he had betrayed himself: 'You used a sum of money that *did not belong to you.*' He had also betrayed his mother by hurting and upsetting her. He concluded: 'You have failed to carry out two essential duties as a result of your taste for moral grandstanding, and you have made everything worse by acting in secrecy.'[15] Durkheim advised his nephew to tell his mother 'the plain truth', offered to 'advance him the funds' and gave him all the details of the transaction. But he then hesitated, as he was not used to this kind of arrangement: 'There are purely commercial questions here that I do not feel competent to deal with.' He had between 18 and 20,000 francs in cash, and was ready to lend Mauss that sum: 'I can offer you this loan without compromising the interests of my children.'

Durkheim was very displeased and certainly did not want Marcel to forget this incident: 'Let this business be a lesson to you, let it teach you to have more modest ambitions, and to better understand what you are doing before you commit yourself to something. You aim too high and try to do too many things.' On the other hand, he was also worried that the incident might distract Marcel from his work: 'Put it out of your mind for the moment. . . Back to work.'[16]

Once that issue had been settled, Durkheim went to back to the mountain of things he had to deal with, starting with his application to the Sorbonne. The rumour mill was already hard at work. It was said that a certain Lyon, who was already well known for his 'Machiavellian plans' would be a candidate. Durkheim found that funny: 'It was noticed some time ago that he had an interest in pedagogy.' Frédéric Rauh then wrote to his old friend Émile to inform him of his intentions. A *normalien, agrégé de philosophie* (1885) and *docteur ès lettres*, Rauh was three years younger than Durkheim. The two men had known each other well since their days at the lycée and the École normale supérieure. Rauh had taught for a number of years (1888–1900) at the faculty of letters in Toulouse before going to Paris to take up a post as *maître de conférences* in 1900, and had just published *La Psychologie appliqué à l'éducation* (1900). A Jew, he had been an ardent Dreyfusard. He had run an open university in Toulouse, and then in Paris, and was said to have socialist sympathies. But Rauh stood little chance, as Buisson wanted nothing to do with him. There were some 10 other candidates.

'Do you see me throwing myself into the fray?', Durkheim asked Célestin Bouglé. He went on: 'No, my dear friend, I will not be a candidate. The fight would be demeaning, and there is nothing serious to be gained from it.' He even suggested that his colleague should apply for the post, 'if you feel like it': 'It is obvious that it would be infinitely better if this post went to a sociologist . . . And besides, the greater part of pedagogy is sociological.'

In Paris, Mauss acted as go-between and went to see Victor Brochard. When Henri Delacroix heard that Durkheim might be taking over from Buisson, he immediately wrote to Mauss: 'Is this true? I do hope so.' He then asked the question that everyone was asking: 'Who will they send to Bordeaux to replace Durkheim?'[17] Mauss also went to see Lévy-Bruhl. 'Do not overstate my wish to come under these conditions', Durkheim told his nephew. 'No, the idea of teaching pedagogy does not really [appeal?] to me. Basically, I always thought that the only outcome of all this would be to remind people of my existence.'[18] He said the same to Brochard and Lévi-Bruhl: taking over from Buisson was out of the question unless he could 'devote an hour to sociology'. He found Brochard's attitude off-putting, as he did not seem very enthusiastic even though he was doing all he could to get him to come to Paris.[19] Durkheim was anything but self-confident: how could a specialist in sociology apply for a chair in education? He feared that he would not be up to the task, unless he taught nothing but moral education. And he did not wish to give the impression that he was trying to 'insinuate himself into Paris' (Lukes 1985[1973]: 365).

Durkheim saw himself as a 'poor politician' who was not very good at the art of selling himself. Was he afraid of 'personal failure?' His nephew thought so. In an attempt to justify his failure to do anything so far, Durkheim once more told him that he did not know 'if it would suit him': 'I must not let anything distract me from my main goal.' He added: 'In my view, all this had just been about deciding where I could be of most use, and about what use could best be made of me (while causing the least pain).'

'Torn in several directions', he did not know what to do. 'This is a serious matter', he added. He was reluctant to write to Buisson in person: 'He would brush me off, and I would be no better off than I am now.' In the end, he did write to him 'to ensure that we will not be trapped by the description of the chair, if we do succeed'. He reminded him that the course on pedagogy he had been teaching at Bordeaux since 1887 was 'based on sociology, and that the two things could not be divorced', and asked him if a similar course would be suitable. His intention was to teach a course on moral science (the physics of morals and law) as well as to lecture on pedagogy. Durkheim uses 'we' to emphasize that there was a collective dimension to his decision, and that it also concerned his associates:

> I am doing this because it seems to me that I owe it to you all, because I do not wish to disappoint the expressions of good will that I have received, and because not everyone would understand that there are serious reasons why I am not applying. But I am very apprehensive, and I will not hide that from you. Because I know that I am no good outside

my own realm and in uncomfortable situations. I told you at Easter that my future prospects did not fill me with joy, even if it did mean teaching sociology. So you can imagine how I feel about teaching education.[20]

Pedagogy was a discipline whose scientific status was still ill-defined. It was not a science, Durkheim later told his new students at the Sorbonne: 'Educational theory essentially is the most methodical and best-documented thinking available, put at the service of teaching' (Durkheim 1961[1925]: 2). Durkheim also wrote to Émile Boutroux – 'for the sake of propriety', he said. He asked his nephew to go to see the faculty's secretary and to ask if 14 June was the 'closing date' for applications. He anxiously awaited his reply: 'Send me a telegram as soon as you can.' He was at last planning a trip to Paris. 'There is no reason to let anyone know the real reasons for my trip', he told Mauss. At the beginning of June, he made a quick visit to Paris – a 'round trip of 36 hours' – to see Ferdinand Buisson.

When she heard that Durkheim might be coming to Paris, Dick May was delighted: there was, she said, 'a gap', adding that it was not her job to fill it. Durkheim did not like her attitude. 'She's got some chutzpah', he remarked to Mauss.[21] He expressed the same annoyance when May expressed the wish that 'some of us [on the *Année*] could join the Collège des sciences sociales'. 'She's a sly one! And it is so humiliating to see Boutroux tagging along behind her.'[22]

A few days before the faculty board met, Durkheim was still unsure what to do, but then the situation suddenly shifted. Victor Brochard had not so far been very enthusiastic about Durkheim's application, but underwent a change of heart after a visit from Lucien Lévy-Bruhl, who had been the first to suggest to Durkheim that he should apply. Durkheim now decided to 'try for it', but was no more enthusiastic than before: 'I ask myself if I am doing the right thing . . . You can see that I am in a lousy state of mind', he told Bouglé.[23] For the past three weeks, he had been 'obsessionally debating whether or not he should apply for Buisson's old position'. It was only 'at the last moment' that he made his decision.[24]

On 24 June, the faculty board met under the chairmanship of Dean Alfred Croiset, a specialist in Greek language and literature. Émile Boutroux, Victor Brochard and Ferdinand Buisson gave their opinions. Boutroux's contribution provoked an 'incident' and a reaction from Alphonse Aulard, professor of the history of the French Revolution. Durkheim tried to find out more about what had happened: 'Why is Aulard criticizing Boutroux for trying to damage my case, and why should Boutroux's [crude] language lead Aulard to vote against me?'[25] Durkheim was elected as Buisson's replacement by a very large majority and was appointed *chargé de cours*. In professional terms, the distinction between *chargés de cours* (and *maîtres de conférence*) and tenured professors (tenure being the 'crowning achievement' of anyone's career) was, as Durkheim himself noted (1975[1918b]: 25–6), based upon age, scientific authority and salary: *chargés de cours* and *maîtres de conférences* were younger and just starting out on their careers. According to the official decree of 24 July, Durkheim was appointed for a period of one year, from 1 October 1902 until 31 October 1903. His salary was 9,000 francs.

Dean Alfred Croiset immediately wrote to Rector Octave Gréard to inform him of the decision: 'Durkheim proved to be the outstanding candidate because of his considerable body of work, the power and soundness of his teaching, and the originality of his method. M. Durkheim is a first-class sociologist, but isn't pedagogy a province of sociology?'[26] The faculty's decision was rapidly endorsed by the university council: 'His name and works are known to everyone and mean that I do not have to justify the faculty's choice at any length', noted the dean of the faculty of letters.

So, as in Bordeaux, sociology was not immediately recognized at the Sorbonne: it slipped in 'through the narrow gate of educational theory', as Maurice Halbwachs (1977[1938]: xi) put it. Durkheim's new colleague Michel Henry sent him an 'unctuous letter' to offer his support: 'Many friends have been expecting you for a long time. I am one of their number.' Durkheim was all the more astonished by this display of friendship in that his colleague had always kept his silence, especially where the *Année sociologique* was concerned. A *chargé de cours* who taught the history of political doctrines at the Sorbonne since 1896, Henry was in fact quite hostile to sociology, as is obvious from his correspondence with Célestin Bouglé, who wrote his thesis under his supervision. Émile sister's was especially pleased, but 'like all joys, [hers] was marred by the fear that overwork might undermine his health'. 'Let us hope', she wrote to her son, 'that his disciples will help him to smooth away the difficulties, and that everything will turn out well in the end.'[27] His close associates Hubert and Fauconnet did not immediately write to offer their congratulations. Worried at having no news from them, Durkheim tried to put his mind at ease: 'They've done a fine job. There is no need for such formalities between us.'[28] François Simiand wrote to 'cheer him up'. 'It is only natural', replied Durkheim, 'that I should feel some regrets about leaving the course I started here and which, it seemed to me, I could never give up in order to go on with it in Paris.' 'It has been a difficult moment', he added. He dreamed of 'a less concentrated emotional and intellectual life', but he was, he told Simiand, 'somewhat worried about teaching something that is not my subject . . . But I will worry about that tomorrow.'[29]

Camille Jullian, a colleague from Bordeaux, sent his 'friendly congratulations'. Durkheim wrote back: 'You can see from my example that everything turns out well in the end, because I found it more difficult than you did to find somewhere in Paris; you will soon be joining me here. I have no doubts on that score.'[30] One of the first concerns of the Sorbonne's new professor was 'to make an effort to try to get' his friend Octave Hamelin to Paris, even though he did not have a doctorate: 'No, you cannot end your career in Bordeaux. You must think about it and get ready to come to Paris.'[31] Durkheim realized that going to Paris was a promotion: 'A position in Paris is, for various reasons, much sought after; it is very much the exception for someone to begin their career there.' The University of Paris was 'more strictly selective' than other universities: academics had to begin their teaching careers in the provinces and 'prove themselves as teacher and scholars' before 'being called to Paris' (Durkheim 1975[1918b]: 27).

Now that 'the deed was done', Durkheim felt he was in a 'very good state of mind'.

> The ease with which it has all gone through and the expressions of support all cheer me up; at the same time I am beginning to think that, if I had reconciled myself to spending the rest of my life in Bordeaux, it would have been a life of excessive concentration. I am still afraid that I will not be accepted, and that I will not be in the incomparable moral situation I am in here, but I will worry about that tomorrow.

He added in a postscript: 'Now that the deed is done, I realize that, without wishing to, we have played a good trick on those who wanted to keep me away.'[32] The difficult moment was over, and Durkheim could dream of a 'less concentrated intellectual and emotional life than the one I have been leading until now'.[33]

A Painful Change

Durkheim and his family did not move to Paris until 1 August. Their new home was at 260 rue Saint-Jacques in the Val-de-Grâce district of the 5th *arrondissement*, and only a few minutes' walk from the École normale supérieure. The fifth-floor apartment, which had small balconies, was in a stone-built block between the rue des Feuillantines and the rue des Ursulines, close to the Institut des sourds-muets (founded by the abbé de l'Epée) and the church of Saint-Jacques-du-Haut-Pas (later renamed Saint-Jacques-de-Compostelle). In the main courtyard of the Institut, there was a magnificent elm some 45 metres high, planted, it was said, in the sixteenth century. The apartment had once belonged to Durkheim's old teacher Émile Boutroux, who had been appointed director of the Thiers Foundation. 'I did everything I could to avoid this', said Durkheim, 'but force of circumstances prevailed.'[34] Most of faculty's teaching staff lived in apartments close to the Sorbonne, in either the 5th or the 6th *arrondissement*.

In terms of his son's education, Durkheim had moved to Paris at just the right moment. In 1902, the 10-year-old André was enrolled at the Lycée Montaigne in the rue Auguste-Comte. The school was next to the École coloniale, in the 6th *arrondissement*, adjacent to the Luxembourg gardens. 'He spent two blessed years in this cheerful establishment, which was a real nest of laughing, playful children', his father later recalled (Durkheim 1975[1917]: 446–7). André immediately found himself at the 'top of his class', and collected a 'rich crop of prizes' the following spring. He made steady progress 'with an even step, with the smiling confidence and good grace that were a feature of his physiognomy', and had the 'good luck' to encounter 'excellent teachers' whom he was to remember with gratitude. One of them, Augustin Monod, had been in the same class as Durkheim at the École normale supérieure: a combination of authority, kindness and almost motherly attention gave him a real moral influence over his pupils.

It was at the lycée that André discovered an early vocation for philosophy. 'It is not as though he was a metaphysician by temperament. Of course he enjoyed beautiful speculations, when they were more than just conceptual games, but it was man, the classic object of philosophical reflection, that really drew him to the study of philosophy and that interested him.' His 'natural taste for facts and things that were concrete' led him to 'distrust vague generalities'. André very quickly showed a 'marked interest' in the research his father was pursuing, and the 'intellectual intimacy' between the two of them 'could not have been closer.' As Émile had hoped, André was on his way to becoming his 'workmate'. André's sister Marie probably remained at home, and it was her mother Louise who 'took charge of her primary education' (Mauss 1969[1927]: 523), just as she had done for her son.

Paris was far from being unfamiliar to Durkheim. He had family there and especially the two nephews who had been his wards: Marcel Mauss and Henri Durkheim. Marcel was very close to his cousin André, and regarded him as both a brother and a son. A year after the Durkheims came to Paris, Marcel gave up his apartment in the rue des Gobelins, and moved into a sixth-floor apartment at 31 rue Saint-Jacques in order to be closer to his uncle. Henri Durkheim had already begun his law studies in Bordeaux. When his uncle moved to Paris, he followed him and studied for his law degree at the University of Paris's faculty of law. Having first completed a training course, Henri Durkheim then embarked upon a career as a magistrate, first in Nantes and then in Versailles.

Paris also brought Durkheim into close contact with the Dreyfus family and his brother-in-law Jules Dreyfus, whom he saw regularly. He was also in contact with the 'extended' family of the *Année*'s contributors: Henri Hubert, Paul Fauconnet, François Simiand and all the others. The new professor was no stranger to the academic circles in which he was now moving at the Sorbonne. Victor Brochard and Gabriel Séailles, who both taught there, had been on the jury that examined his doctoral thesis 10 years earlier. His academic environment was relatively homogeneous in terms of both social and educational background: the vast majority (almost 80 per cent) of faculty members had studied at the École normale supérieure (Charle 1985: 1–12).[35]

Émile already knew Lucien Lévy-Bruhl very well. He had just been appointed to the chair left vacant by Boutroux, and was director of studies in philosophy. Durkheim also knew Ferdinand Brunot, who was from the Vosges region and who had been a member of his class at the École normale supérieure; he was now professor of the history of the French language. Michel Diehl (1859–1944), *chargé de cours* in Byzantine history, and Pierre Puech (1860–1940), *maître de conférences* in Greek language and literature, had been in the year above him at the École normale supérieure. Léon Collignon (1849–1917), *agrégé de lettres*, professor of archaeology and in charge of the Musée d'art antique, had been teaching a course at Bordeaux on Greek antiquities from 1866 to 1879, which was before Durkheim was appointed, but he also had ties (on his mother's side) with the Moselle region, and with Lorraine (he had attended the lycée in Metz). Another of Durkheim's colleagues was also from Moselle. Émile Haumant, who was a year younger than Durkheim, had followed a different career path, having studied at the Écoles des chartes, the École pratique des hautes études and the École des langues orientales, before qualifying as an *agrégé d'histoire* and *docteur ès lettres*. A specialist in Russian language and literature, he too joined the Sorbonne as a *maître de conférences* in 1902.

Émile also had several Jewish friends in Paris, some of them very active in the Alliance israélite universelle. They included the publisher Félix Alcan, Sylvain Lévi, Salomon Reinach, Xavier Léon (editor of the *Revue de métaphysique et de morale*), and Lucien Lévy-Bruhl and Frédéric Rauh, who taught at the École normale supérieure. Durkheim later described how he would go to see Rauh at home. He would find him surrounded by his family and the 'two charming daughters' who were 'his pride and joy': 'calm, gentle, radiant happiness' (Durkheim 2006[1909]).[36] The circles in which Durkheim was moving did not constitute a 'network' as such, and were far from being homogeneous in either religious or political terms. Durkheim himself was non-practising and, in all probability, agnostic. He still retained, however, a deep respect for Judaism and, as he grew older, he developed the *habitus* of a rabbi. A photograph taken in 1900 shows him sitting in a rocking chair and surrounded by his wife, daughter and sons, dressed in dark clothes, bearded and wearing the cap he wore indoors. On the other hand, Judaism was far from being a guarantee of friendship or closeness, as can be seen in the strained relations that Durkheim had with both Henri Bergson and René Worms (who was active in the Consistoire de Paris for some years).[37]

When it came to politics, the staff of course had their differences of opinion (some were Radicals, and others Radical Socialists, or socialists), but two-thirds of those who taught at the Sorbonne between 1879 and 1908 were, like Durkheim, Dreyfusards, including Charles Andler, François Aulard, Gustave Bloch, Ferdinand Brunot, Léon Collignon, Ernest Lavisse, Lucien Lévy-Bruhl, Frédéric Rauh and Gabriel Séailles.[38] Several were either active socialists or socialist sympathizers, and were active in the Ligue des droits de l'homme.

The social circles in which Émile moved now that he was in Paris were expanding, and included relatives, collaborators, old friends and new colleagues. Colleagues and friends such as Gustave Lanson, Henri Berr and, in particular, his friend Xavier Léon invited him to the *soirées* they organized, and at which academics mingled with politicians (such as Millerand, Henri Poincaré and Painlevé). Émile, tall and slim with shining eyes, moved through these gatherings, stopping to chat or exchange a few words with this person or that. It was, said Bougin, 'a way of pursuing his mission without any affectation' (1938: 223–4).

When he moved into his new apartment, Durkheim 'almost immediately found [himself] in a poor moral state that gave [him] – and everyone around him – some bad moments'. He was at a low ebb. He found two explanations for his 'mental malaise', one physical and the other moral. The holidays he had spent by the sea and the lack of rest had left him 'over-excited': 'My nerves were all on edge.' The moral explanation was that he had had to leave Bordeaux. He felt that 'he had lost a certain moral standing' because he had renounced, 'for no absolutely imperious reason, the austere life he used to live with [Hamelin]'. It was certainly a dull existence, but it meant a lot to him and it would not let him go: 'So it is not surprising that the change has been painful.' He admitted that he had not been 'strong' during his ordeal: 'It is true that I did not do brilliantly.' And he concluded: 'Now that I've drawn up a new life-plan – for at least four years – I am back on my feet' (Bourgin 1938: 223–4).

Durkheim did not, it is true, attach any great importance to having local roots or to the feeling of 'belonging' to a place or territory. As he explained to his students at the Sorbonne:

> The links that bind each one of us to a particular spot in an area where we live are incalculably frail and can be broken with the greatest ease. We are here one day and elsewhere the next. We feel as much at home in one province as another, or at least, the special affinities of a regional origin are quite secondary and no longer have any great influence on our life. (1957[1950]: 102)

People were no longer greatly interested in 'the way of life immediately surrounding us', or in 'events that happen in my own *commune* or *département*' (ibid.: 102–3).

> What matters far more to us, according to the functions we have to fulfil, is what goes on at scientific conferences, what is being said in the great centres of production; the news events in the world of art in the big cities of France or abroad have an interest that is very different for the painter or sculptor from, say, municipal affairs. We might say the same of the manufacturer. (ibid.: 103)

Durkheim had lived in Épinal, Paris, Sens, Bordeaux and was now back in Paris, but had never taken much interest in the things that were going on around him: 'I can even live my every-day life and know nothing of them at all' (ibid.).

It is obvious from his choice of reading matter that Durkheim was interested in the urban question, and that he saw the trend for the population to become concentrated in the cities as 'one of the most general of the laws that govern the development of societies'. The effects of this concentration were not all harmful, and while some saw cities as 'the great destroyers of human lives', they could also be 'centres of civilization'.[39]

Durkheim was no less attached to the region in which he had grown up. He loved going there at holiday times, when he would stay in a small, separate apartment on the first floor of his parent's home at 2 rue des Forts.

He spent his holidays studying, and when he did take a break from work, he would visit his sisters Rosine and Céline, or go for long walks, often in the company of his nephew Marcel. This was his way of recovering his strength: 'The pine woods and a little altitude are excellent for the highly-strung; I come back to life here, and I happily go for strolls.' 'It is true that the reasons for my fondness for this region are probably the same reasons that make you an unrepentant Breton. And I notice that, as we grow older, we become more attached to the place where we were born.'[40]

The New Sorbonne

Durkheim could easily walk to the Sorbonne, which stood at the corner of the rue Saint-Jacques and the rue des Écoles, in under 10 minutes. The new buildings were designed by the architect Henri Paul Nénot (prix de Rome), and construction had begun in 1885. Rather than transforming the old buildings, it might, Durkheim remarked, have been possible to adopt 'a radical and rational plan', 'sweep away the past' and 'establish the restored university outside the city walls, in the countryside' (Durkheim 1975[1918b]: 19). He was, however, aware that such a plan would have upset some 'traditions that deserved respect': the intellectual and academic life of Paris had centred on the left bank of the Seine, and on what was known as 'the land of study' or 'the Latin land', since the twelfth century. With the exception of the church, the old buildings had been demolished, and the new buildings had all been built around the same centre: the Sorbonne.

The Sorbonne became what the rector called a 'factory' covering a vast rectangle of 21,000 square metres, mostly taken up by the faculty of science and its laboratories. The plan was to use the physical organization of space to encourage a 'new spirit'. It was a sort of compromise between the German and French models. There were 'amphitheatres' for public lectures, and smaller 'lecture rooms' that brought 'hard-working young people' closer to their teachers; this allowed them to work on the scientific examination of texts and the evaluation of documentary material' (Gréard 1893: 17–18). The latter exercise was more 'esoteric' and took the form of 'tutorials' that implied a closer collaboration between students and teachers. Students gave talks and produced critical commentaries that were then criticized by their teachers. This was, according to Dean Alfred Croiset, 'another new feature of the modern Sorbonne' (Croiset 1918: 39). The lectures and tutorials (which were mainly for degree and *agrégation* students) were designed to bring students into contact with 'experienced teachers' who could reconcile 'the need for specialization, which is indispensable for the scholar, and for the general culture without which no man can be a well-rounded individual.' 'I think I can say', observed the dean, 'that we work hard at the Sorbonne, and that we work well . . . There are very few idlers. They would feel out of place here. The atmosphere we breathe is one of work and energy' (Croiset 1906: 115).

The new Sorbonne was officially opened in 1895, but the building work went on until 1903. One side of the building housed the university's central services: the rector's office, the reception rooms, the board room and the committee rooms. Two spaces quickly acquired symbolic power: the great amphitheatre and the library. The great 'amphi', Durkheim remarked, was 'shared by the whole university. It can hold an audience of more than 3,000. It may be the largest lecture theatre in the world.' An allegorical painting by Puvis de Chavannes, widely regarded as his masterpiece, hung on the wall behind the rostrum. Durkheim was very impressed by the fact there were so many fine works of art everywhere in the Sorbonne: 'One could write a book about art in the Sorbonne' (Durkheim 1975[1918b]: 21).[41]

A broad staircase with a wrought-iron handrail led to the library on the first floor; above it hung a large fresco entitled *The song of the muses awakens the human soul*. To the left and the right, there were two smaller frescoes; *Science* (a reflective woman with her hand on her chin) and *The Dream* (a very melancholy woman). The library was shared by the faculties of letters and sciences, becoming, with its thousands of books and many periodicals, a 'very rich and much-appreciated tool' (Croiset 1918: 47) for the faculty of letters. The great reading room, which was 75 metres long, could seat 300 people.

The University of Paris consisted of the faculty of letters, the faculty of sciences, the faculty of law, the faculty of medicine, the École supérieure de pharmacie and the faculty of Protestant theology (which ceased to be part of the university in 1904). The teaching staff numbered almost 250 (tenured professors, *chargés de cours* and *maîtres de conférences*), including the mathematician Henri Poincaré, the physicists Paul Janet and Pierre Curie (who, with his wife Marie, won the Nobel prize in 1903 for their work on radium), and Dr Richet, a specialist on the nervous system.

In terms of the courses it offered, the University of Paris was very different from American universities, with their great diversity and many different degree-awarding institutions (undergraduate faculties, technical schools, professional schools, etc.). It is not that the University of Paris had no interest in the applied sciences (it awarded a diploma in chemical engineering, and taught both the theory and practice of aviation), but its basic role was, rather, to promote a 'disinterested culture'. It was primarily what Durkheim (1975[1918b]: 22) called a 'centre for speculative life', and he emphasized that the main feature of the way that French universities were organized was that they were a collection or federation of faculties and schools which retained their individuality and autonomy within the university.

The University of Paris had almost 12,000 students, almost all of them male. 'An enormous mass of young men', said Durkheim, who insisted that the university should, like its German counterparts, do more to promote the 'moral welfare' of these newcomers: there should be a general student association, as well as school- or faculty-based associations, and associations based on nationality and gender (in the case of women students). The faculty of letters had 1,830 students, most of them studying, as we can see from the statistics for 1902–3, for first degrees or for qualifications that would allow them to teach in secondary schools. There were very few – about 80 – 'French ladies', as they were known at this time, most of whom attended lectures but had no other teaching. Public lectures attracted large audiences and were often attended by foreign students (almost 400, including many women; the largest contingents were from Russia, Germany and the United States). They came to Paris, remarked Durkheim (1975[1918]: 30), 'purely to complete their education, and not to train for specific careers in France'. In 1903 and 1904, philosophy had, respectively, 148 and 68 students enrolled in degree and *aggrégation* courses; only four 'ladies' were taking a degree in philosophy. The 'new' University of Paris was therefore, as Durkheim put it, 'the product of a powerful concentration of intellectual forces; it is once again a centre of international life'. 'It has become a state institution, an apparatus of public life, but it remains in control of its individual destinies. It is very young and very old; it combines the glories of its past with the vigour of its youth' (ibid.: 32–3).

Durkheim knew well the man who had been appointed to the university council and who became vice-rector of the Académie de Paris: Louis Liard had 'protected him since the beginning of his academic career'. He was a man who had had a very distinguished administrative career. For more than 20 years, he had devoted 'tireless enthusiasm and passionate energy to the reorganization and development of higher education'. The universities were, it was said, his creation. It was not without a certain pride that he told the first meeting of the university council: 'I believe I know which spirit was meant to inspire the law that established the universities. It was the spirit of science and independence, and I will take my inspiration from it.' He added that one of his main concerns, day-to-day issues aside, was the issue of training teachers for the secondary education sector: 'The University of Paris is a womb for teachers.'[42] That he should have taken a great interest in Durkheim's work on the science of education throughout his period of office is therefore understandable. He also made no secret of his desire to reorganize the École normale supérieure and to make it part of the university, while preserving its individuality and autonomy.

The faculty of letters had a teaching staff of 50, half of them with professorial status, and awarded two qualifications: a degree (letters, philosophy, history and modern languages),[43] and a doctorate. The faculty's main fields were: philosophy (Boutroux, Brochard, Egger, Séailles and Lévy-Bruhl); history (Aulard, Lavisse and Langlois) and geography (Vidal de La Blache); and languages and literature (Latin, Greek, English and German). Most of the philosophy course was devoted to the history of philosophy (ancient and modern). In 1902–3, course titles included: 'The ethics of the Epicureans and the Stoics' (Victor Brochard), 'The origins of philosophy in the eighteenth century' (Lucien Lévy-Bruhl), 'History of Greek philosophy' (V. Delbos). Even Albert Espinas, professor of the history of social economics, lectured on 'Ancient social philosophy' and 'Voltaire and Rousseau'. Various specialist courses were also taught:

history of art, archaeology, Sanskrit and comparative grammar, history of economic doctrines, experimental psychology (Georges Dumas), the pedagogy of the historical sciences, and, of course, educational science taught by Buisson – whose final lecture was called 'Educating the social sense' – and now Durkheim. There was a lot of academic interest in psychology.[44]

Alfred Espinas's course on social economics was the only social science course offered by the faculty of letters. Teaching the social sciences was effectively the prerogative of the faculty of law; social science was a comparative subject or, at doctoral level, a special subject. There were courses on the political sciences, and especially economic science: political economy, comparative social economics, the history of economic doctrines and statistics. Durkheim's arrival changed everything.

A Successor in Bordeaux

The Sorbonne was not the only faculty of letters in which philosophy, psychology and pedagogy existed side by side. Educational science or pedagogy was also part of the philosophy syllabus in Dijon, Lille, Lyon, Poitiers, Rennes, Toulouse and, of course, Bordeaux. Philosophy lecturers also taught additional classes – open to all students – on pedagogy in secondary schools, and were often responsible for training primary school inspectors. In addition to Durkheim, two of those associated with *L'Année sociologique* taught or lectured on pedagogy at university level. Célestin Bouglé gave public lectures on 'Competition and cooperation' at Toulouse, while Paul Lapie taught a course on pedagogy at Aix-en-Provence, where he had been appointed *chargé de cours* in 1902. In April 1902, Lapie defended his doctoral thesis, 'La logique de la volonté', at the Sorbonne; it was published later that year by Alcan. As the editors of the *Revue de la métaphysique et de la morale* noted, an attempt was obviously being made to bring both philosophy and the sociological method to bear on educational reform.[45]

In Bordeaux, Gaston Richard replaced Durkheim as *chargé de cours* in 1903. As the rector observed, 'Taking over from M. Durkheim is a very heavy responsibility. Thanks to his unceasing labours, M. Richard had not been crushed by it. He is a modest man, but an upright one.'[46] He was required both to teach a course on sociology ('Moral solidarity, as revealed by crime statistics' in the first semester, and 'August Comte on social dynamics' in the second) and to lecture on pedagogy ('Educability and its limitations' in the first semester, and 'Locke and the English school on the theory of education' in the second). He also gave first-year lectures on 'Kant and education', 'Civic education', 'Comte' and 'The education of women'. Some 30 or so students attended his lectures. The new lecturer, with his serious and rather sad demeanour, was described as 'an excellent teacher, hard-working, conscientious, skilful and thoughtful'. In 1903, Richard published a textbook entitled *Notions élémentaires de sociologie* that quickly went through two editions. He regularly wrote long reviews for the *Revue philosophique,* and was promoted to the rank of professor of social sciences in 1906.

Octave Hamelin eventually took the decision to go to Paris in order to pursue his career at the École normale supérieure, and this raised the question of his successor. Émile Durkheim immediately told him: 'Lapie will probably be a candidate.' The name of Marcel Foucault had also been mentioned, but Durkheim thought that he should apply not to Bordeaux, but to Aix, where 'he stands every chance of being granted tenure'.[47] He could, that is, take the place of Lapie, who was now teaching the history of philosophy in Bordeaux, where he worked alongside Gaston Richard. Paul Lapie lectured on 'The principles of Descartes', and also on Kant and Schopenhauer (1904–5) and Spinoza (1905–6). In 1905, he was appointed to the so-called 'Durkheim chair' as *chargé de cours de sciences sociales.* He was also interested in education and gave a lecture on that topic at the École normale supérieure in which he placed great emphasis on the scientific mission of the primary schoolteacher, who must, he argued, devote his leisure time to the pursuit of scientific truth. He also suggested that teachers in primary schools should study the local archives in order to reconstruct the history of the *communes* in which they worked, write psychological reports on the children in their classes, and make short sociological studies of their families. As well as contributing to both the *Revue de métaphysique et de morale* and the *Année sociologique*, Lapie published his lecture, 'La mission scientifique de l'instituteur', in the *Revue pédagogique* in 1904, followed by 'La hiérarchie des professions' in the *Revue de Paris* in 1905. The dean of the faculty of letters, Georges Radet, was rather pleased to have him at Bordeaux, and described him as 'a man of experience and talent' who stood out from the crowd because of 'the authority of his words and his activity as a writer'. His superiors' assessments of his work were excellent: 'a noble, mature mind'; 'rigour and action'. He was considered 'one of the best teachers in the faculty; the best and most devoted of teachers'.

Durkheim was very pleased with his friend Hamelin's decision: 'This way, we can be sure of growing old together, to the extent that I've been told I will be staying in Paris.' He also tried to convince him that he had made the right decision: 'You could not do anything else. There are general reasons that demand your presence in Paris. It is not possible to leave philosophy in the hands of those who compromise it. Right-minded people must organize the resistance.' Realizing that coming to Paris would cause him a 'period of disruption', he also tried to reassure him: 'You will find this change of life pleasant. No doubt your life will be less peaceful than it was in Bordeaux, but your environment will give you the strength to put up with that.' He concluded: 'No one would have understood if you had said "No".' In 1905–6, Paul Hamelin taught a course on Aristotle and took tutorials for degree students. Georges Radet, dean of the faculty of letters in Bordeaux, was far from happy with Hamelin's decision: 'The departure of M. Hamelin, like that of M. Durkheim last year, deprives us of a teacher with rare qualities; he will be missed both by his colleagues – he was an outstanding colleague – and by his students, on whom he had such a powerful and beneficial influence.'[48]

Hamelin's arrival in Paris coincided with a reform designed to make the École normale superieure part of the University of Paris. This had the effect of bringing new tenured professors into the faculty of letters, including Charles Andler, Gabriel Monod, Pierre Girard, Émile Bourgeois, Frédéric Rauh and Mario Rocques. The reform also provoked a sharp emotional reaction, as many former *normaliens* feared that its goal was to 'destroy the École [normale]', and to 'turn the house of Taine, Pasteur and Fustel de Coulanges into an institute of education'. The university was accused of being 'jealous' and 'greedy'. Dean Croiset replied:

> The real home of higher education is in universities that offer a wide range of different courses, many of them open to the public, and where students have a wide range of choice . . . The École normale supérieure must seek from the University of Paris the scientific help it was already asking for on a more regular basis. [This change was] in accordance with the nature of things, and in line with the developments that have allowed our university to make progress over the last twenty years. (Croiset 1906: 116–17)

The Inaugural Lecture

'Gentlemen. This is a very great honour for me . . .' Durkheim gave his inaugural lecture on educational science at the Sorbonne on 4 December 1902 (Durkheim 1956[1903]: 113).[49] An inaugural lecture is an important event, as it allows the new professor to define his programme of research and teaching. For Durkheim it was a way of 'identifying and specifying the idea that has dominated and will dominate all my teaching'. His very choice of title – 'Pedagogy and sociology' – made his intentions clear: 'As a sociologist, it is above all as a sociologist that I shall speak to you of education' (ibid.: 114). 'I am now going to uncle Émile's inaugural lecture', Marcel Mauss wrote to his mother. 'It will surely be a very great, very fine success.'[50]

Durkheim felt 'singularly frightened' by the difficulties of his new task, and, even though he had been teaching pedagogy at the University of Bordeaux for the past 15 years, he claimed not to have the 'distinctive competence' of his predecessor Ferdinand Buisson. He begins by paying a glowing tribute to 'the man of high reason and of firm will to whom France owes so much for the improvement of her primary education'. He even speaks of 'one of the greatest and most fortunate revolutions which have ever been produced in the history of our national education': 'The schools multiplied and materially transformed, rational methods substituted for the old routines of bygone times, a new impetus given to pedagogical reflection' (1956[1903]: 113). Durkheim intended to expound, however, a different view of the complex issue of education, as he had already done in

Bordeaux: 'I regard as the prime postulate of all pedagogical speculation that education is an eminently social thing in its origins as in its function, and that, therefore, pedagogy depends on sociology more closely than on any other science' (ibid.: 114).

This set the tone. Durkheim was swimming against the current of modern pedagogy, which viewed education as 'an eminently individual thing', which relied upon psychology and which assumed that there is '*one* human nature' (1956[1903]: 115). He disagreed completely: 'Unfortunately, this conception of education stands in absolute contradiction to all that history teaches us: there is not a people, indeed, among whom it has ever been put into practice' (ibid.: 116). The history of education is a history of variations: it varies from one period and one country to another, from one caste to another, and from one social class or profession to another: 'There is, so to speak, no society in which different pedagogical systems do not coexist and function side by side.' Homogeneity is a characteristic of 'prehistoric societies'; as we can see from 'all civilized countries', the trend is for greater diversification and specialization' and for 'special educations' (ibid.: 117). Durkheim accepts that 'this special culture' does not necessarily bring us any closer to 'human perfection' and that it may even lead to the atrophy of some natural predispositions: there are men who devote themselves exclusively to intellectual life and 'who do nothing but think'. All the energies of activity have been 'converted into reflection', but these 'incomplete natures' are 'the indispensable agents of scientific progress' (ibid.: 118, 119).

Durkheim's second point is that the 'common education which generally passes for the true education' (1956[1903]: 119) is subject to prodigious historical and geographical variations because 'systems of education . . . are so obviously tied up with given social systems that they are inseparable from them': education was 'ascetic' in the Middle Ages, 'liberal' in the Renaissance, 'literary' in the seventeenth century, and has now become 'scientific': for a long time, science and the critical thinking that modern society values so highly were regarded with suspicion. Scales of values change as societies change: where courage was once the prime virtue, modern societies value thought and reflection, and the societies of the future may attach the same value to sophisticated taste and an artistic sensibility. Such variations reflect the changing nature of 'human needs', which are themselves defined by social conditions. The paradox is that, while we readily accept that this was the case in the ancient societies of Greece and Rome, we are reluctant to agree that the same applies to our societies. This is all the more surprising in that education is now, in European societies, 'a true public service' (1956[1903]: 121) that comes more and more directly under the control of the state and pursues essentially collective ends. The explanation for this rejection of relativism lies, according to Durkheim, in the social structure of modern societies, namely the extreme division of labour, racial diversity and geographical scale. What do all these individuals have in common, 'except their human quality in general'? 'In societies so differentiated, there can hardly be any collective type other than the generic type of man' (1956[1903]: 122).

A society cannot survive unless there is a social consensus and an adequate level of homogeneity, and 'education perpetuates and reinforces this homogeneity . . . It consists, in one or another of its aspects, of a systematic socialization of the younger generation' (1956[1903]: 124). The individual being must give way to the social being', and a 'new man' must be added to 'the egoistic and asocial being that has just been born' (ibid.: 125). Here, Durkheim is reiterating his thesis about the duality of human nature: individual human beings experience subjective mental states, but social beings have religious beliefs, moral convictions and practices, national traditions and collective views of all kinds. The purpose of education is produce such social beings (which are not defined by the 'primitive' nature of human beings). Obedience to authority, respect for discipline, devotion and sacrifice are therefore not spontaneous and have nothing to do with congenital dispositions; they are products of society and are transmitted through education, which is not what happens with animals. In order to make himself perfectly clear, Durkheim takes the example of a ceremony that is found in many societies: the initiation ceremony that marks a young man's transition to adulthood and that confers upon him the status of man and citizen. As he puts it in the review of his own lecture that he published in the *Année sociologique* (1979[1904]: 127): 'Education is indeed an eminently social matter . . . It is education, therefore, which creates within us all that lies outside the realm of pure sensations; our will and our understanding are fashioned in its image.'

Durkheim acknowledges that the science of individuals can be of use to pedagogy, but argues that 'psychology by itself is an inadequate resource for the pedagogue'. We obviously have 'general aptitudes' (an aptitude for sacrifice, a 'certain tendency to know', and 'there is in us . . . a primary impersonality which prepares for disinterestedness' (1956[1903]: 128). If, however, we wish to determine the ends that education should follow, we cannot do without sociology: 'The better we understand society, the better shall we be able to account for all that happens in that social microcosm that the school is' (ibid.: 131). The end of pedagogy, and pedagogic methods are all determined both by the social structure of society and the great social currents that permeate it: education is an 'expression' of collective ideas and feelings. Durkheim gives the example of the pedagogic methods used in the seventeenth and eighteenth centuries: they are 'a reflection of the aspirations of their time' (ibid.: 132), while respect for inner liberty, and love of the child are expressions of 'our modern individualism'. School discipline, in other words, displays the same basic features as civic [*de la cité*] discipline, and educational institutions are 'an abbreviated form of social institutions proper' (1979[1904]: 127).

In conclusion, Durkheim attempts to convince his audience that, in France, the sociological point of view is 'indicated in a particularly urgent fashion because it has no feeling of 'moral and moral security' (1956[1903]: 133). The profound transformations which contemporary societies are undergoing necessitate 'corresponding transformations in the national education'. But no one knows what changes are necessary, and public opinion is undecided. The situation is all the more difficult in that 'it is no longer a matter of putting verified ideas into practice, but of finding ideas to guide us' (ibid.: 134). If we are to find these ideas, 'looking inside ourselves' is not enough; we need to understand society and its needs: 'I do not believe that I am following a mere prejudice or yielding to an immoderate love for a science which I have cultivated all my life, in saying that never was a sociological approach more necessary for the educator.' Durkheim assigns sociology a mission: it must provide 'a body of guiding ideas that may be the core of our practice, and that . . . give a meaning to our practice' (ibid.).

Pedagogy was therefore an integral part of Durkheim's teaching in both Paris and Bordeaux, and the three viewpoints he adopts are those of classical pedagogy: moral education, child psychology and the history of pedagogic doctrines. There was, remarked Maurice Halbwachs, 'scarcely a province in this area which he did not explore' (1977[1938]: xi). In 1908–9 and 1910–11, his lecture course was devoted to 'Rousseau on educational theory' (1979[1919], but his main concern was with the history of secondary education in France.

'A Huge Success'

Durkheim's promotion to a chair in Paris confirmed, as the *Revue de métaphysique et de morale* noted, his 'growing influence' as the leader of a school. The *American Journal of Sociology* also published a summary of his lecture.[51] Elsewhere, the fact that he would be able to 'apply sociological method to educational reform' was given an enthusiastic welcome.[52] His work on pedagogy – public lectures, lectures for primary schoolteachers, lecture for students at the École normale supérieure – was to take up one-third, and often two-thirds, of the time he devoted to teaching.

'My duties have been defined', Durkheim told Octave Hamelin in October 1902. His duties included, in his first year at the Sorbonne, teaching a course on 'Renaissance education' and giving a series of public lectures on 'Moral education.' 'Ah, what I've been told about these public lectures does little to reconcile me to giving them', he grumbled.[53] He was also required to give tutorials for students preparing for the *agrégation* in philosophy; 'That will be the heaviest part of my task.' He taught the same courses the following year, the only difference being that his lectures entitled 'Pedagogy at the start of the twentieth century' were on authors such as Pestalozzi and Herbart, and that the course on moral education dealt with moral education in primary schools. As soon as he arrived in Paris, Durkheim was, together with Gabriel Séailles, responsible for marking the degree examinations: 'They tell me I will be getting 80 scripts. One of the unhappy privileges of being in Paris.' The speed at which examinations (for the *baccalauréat* for example) went ahead seemed simply 'unbelievable': 'It's like working in heavy industry.'[54]

Mauss found his uncle's 'wild success' at the Sorbonne disturbing, and wrote to Henri Hubert: 'Uncle has begun his lectures: enormous crowds, but the wrong audience . . . He is taking a lot of trouble over something that is not worthy of him. We must keep going with the *Année* at all costs.'[55] He said the same thing at the end of 1902: 'The lectures [on moral education] are sincere, very successful and I believe, without any exaggeration, that they are having a huge influence on the Sorbonne's young students.' There was even a suggestion that Dick May, through the intermediary of Alcan and Dean Croiset, was going to ask Durkheim to become Director of the École des hautes études sociales.[56] The new professor's audience at the Sorbonne extended far beyond the circle of students and their lecturers and he was now talking to the general public: in March 1903, he gave an important lecture on 'Clan religion (totemism)' to the Société des amis de l'Université de Paris.

Durkheim's intention was to continue the work he had begun at Bordeaux, and the issues of morality (or, to be more specific, a science of morals) and moral education were still his major preoccupations. He did, however, introduce two changes: he was now placing less emphasis on psychology and, from 1904 to 1905 onwards, he began his major course of lectures on the history of secondary education in France. In 1906–7, he also went back to the topic of religion and, more specifically, the origins of religion, but only for one year. The following year's lectures were on the evolution of marriage and the family. He found life in Paris and his workload as a teacher and examiner so 'absorbing' that he was forced to abandon the practice he had adopted at Bordeaux. Abandoning his old practice, he no longer wrote out his lectures in full, and often relied upon rough notes and summaries.

Lectures took place between 9 o'clock in the morning and 7 o'clock in the evening, from Monday to Saturday inclusive. Émile Durkheim's lectures were normally given in the late afternoon from 5 o'clock onwards on Tuesdays and Thursdays, but his course on 'Secondary education in France' was taught from 5 o'clock onwards on Saturdays at the Musée pédagogique in the rue Gay-Lussac. He was also available to students on Sunday mornings. Teaching at the university was, in other words, a full-time occupation, and there was no distinction between the working week and days of rest. Durkheim's public or general lectures were given in the Descartes, Guizot or Turgot lecture theatres, and his tutorials in either room C or room G. The Descartes theatre could hold more than 200 students, and was adorned with a painting of two women by Édouard Toudouze: one, with her chin resting on her hand, symbolized philosophy, and the other, theology. Durkheim had had some 'very good students' in Bordeaux, but, as Mauss said more than once, it was only in Paris that 'the full effects of his personal efforts' were really felt. He now had a larger audience, and his students were better informed (Mauss 1969[1925]: 485). His audience grew steadily, and his students were fascinated by the intellectual passion, eloquence and logical skill of their new professor. He was, exclaimed Georges Davy (1919b: 194), 'an admirable professor': 'His students regarded him not only as the 'master of sociology', but also as

Table 15.1 Courses taught in Paris: 1902–1916[57]

1902–3	Moral education Lectures on Renaissance pedagogy Tutorials for philosophy *agrégation* candidates
1903–4	Teaching morality in schools Major pedagogic theories of the nineteenth century Tutorials for philosophy *agrégation* candidates
1904–5	Teaching morality in schools Public lecture: History of secondary education in France.* Tutorials for philosophy *agrégation* candidates
1905–6	Intellectual education in primary schools. Formation and development of secondary education in France* Tutorials for philosophy *agrégation* candidates Critical analysis of texts on educational science
1906–7	Public lecture: Origins of religion Science of education. Formation and development of secondary education in France* Moral education in schools
1907–8	Evolution of marriage and the family Formation and development of secondary education in France* Teaching morality in schools
1908–9	Sociology. Morality Science of education. Formation and development of secondary education in France* Science of education. history of pedagogic doctrines
1909–10	Sociology. Morality (contd.) Science of education. Formation and development of secondary education in France* Science of education. History of pedagogic doctrines
1910–11	Sociology. Morality (contd: social and individual morality) Science of education. Secondary education in France* Science of education. Intellectual education
1911–12	Sociology. Theory of sanctions Moral education in schools Formation and development of secondary education in France*
1912–13	Durkheim on leave[58] Formation and development of secondary education in France*
1913–14	Sociology. Pragmatism and sociology Science of education. Teaching morality in schools Tutorials for degree candidates
1914–15	Sociology. Morality Science of education. History of pedagogic doctrines Tutorials for degree candidates

Table 15.1 (*cont.*)

1915–16   Social philosophy of Saint-Simon[59]
Major pedagogic doctrines of 18th and 19th centuries
Tutorials for degree candidates
* Lectures given at École normale supérieure

a professor with a logical and systematic mind whose every lecture was the best of models'. His future collaborator described his 'distinguished professor' as 'an original thinker' and a 'peerless orator'. 'He was a man of passion and conviction. His faith lent an enthusiastic and imperative tone to his thoughts and words. It is tempting to say that he was inspired, and those who heard him did have the impression that they had before them the prophet of some new religion.' He gave the appearance of being a cold man, but he spoke warmly.

Serious and stern, with a cold mechanical voice: this was the less flattering portrait painted by Gilbert Maire, a young devotee of Bergson's and therefore an adversary (1935: 140). Maire described him as a 'sort of automaton' who was always 'preaching a new Reformation'. Hubert Bourgin (1938: 217) was to remember the Sorbonne's new professor as 'a secular priest'. 'His entire physical being and moral personality were testimony to the fact that he was a priest rather than a scholar. He was a hieratic figure. His mission was a religious one.' In Durkheim's view, every teacher should be on the same mission. He was aware that any pedagogic relationship has to be based upon the teacher's moral ascendancy over his pupils, and that there are two preconditions for that moral ascendancy. The teacher must have 'will', and must not hesitate, shift or go back on his decisions. And he must feel that he effectively possesses this authority. Durkheim speaks of the teacher's 'inner faith': 'He must believe not in himself, no doubt, not in the superior qualities of his intelligence or of his soul, but in his task and in the importance of his task' (1956: 89). The example he gives is that of a priest with a high idea of his calling who 'speaks in the name of a god in whom he believes, to whom he feels closer that the crowd of the uninitiated'. The teacher finds himself in a similar position: 'He too is the agent of a great moral person who surpasses him: it is society . . . the teacher is the interpreter of the great moral ideas of his time and of his country'. There must be not 'pride, no vanity, no pedantry' in his authority: 'it is made up entirely of the respect which he has for his functions' (ibid.: 89). As they walked past Notre-Dame, Durkheim reportedly said to Célestin Bouglé: 'I should be speaking from a *chaire* like that', playing on the word's two meanings ['professorial chair' and 'pulpit'].

Everyone who attended Durkheim's lectures or who met him was, like Hubert Bourgin, impressed by the master's physical appearance:

Professor [Durkheim] was tall and pale, wearing a grey morning coat, with a huge head and dark eyes. As he stood on the lecture theatre's rostrum, students – both men and women – crowded on to the benches to hear him. He would pick up his lecture at the point where he had left off and went on with it after giving a brief résumé. Without using rhetorical or artistic affectation, but employing a tightly knit dialectic, and making lots of references, he went on with his argument – and there was always an argument – about marriage, the family, morality or education. His severity never lightened. Although his voice was always slightly husky as he made his most important points, it was not without a certain charm; one had the impression of falling under a sort of spell. (Bourgin 1938: 222)

His future collaborator also remembered how Durkheim received him in his study:

It was a vast, bare space devoid of any affectation or concern for art. His long, thin body was wrapped in a loose dressing gown – a padded cassock – that seemed to swallow up his bony, muscular frame, which was the fragile support for his thought. His pale, ascetic face emerged from it: a high, bald forehead, a short beard, a thick moustache, the prominent nose of a rabbi but a cold, hard face, magnificently lit up by his deep eyes, and intense, gentle power that demanded respect, attention and even submission, and that required the same very bare simplicity that you could see before you, sovereign, imperious and inspiring trust.

Hubert Bourgin's first encounter with Durkheim left him with the impression of an upright man who walked in straight lines without ever taking his eyes off his goal, of 'a man who observed the rules and conventions', and who could adapt his appearance to the conditions and circumstances in which he was working. He was a man of erudition who 'draped and wrapped himself in his dressing gown to read, meditate, speculate and write'. The young philosopher discovered the great intellectual qualities of the editorial director of the *Année sociologique*: 'Long periods of intense thought, a rare talent for abstraction, a hard, steady, assiduous worker who paid attention to both details and the broader perspective, a stubborn, heroic dedication to the task in hand, and an extremely rigorous method applied to an object strictly determined by him.'

Durkheim's 'inner flame' and 'the professor's great ardour' were the qualities that struck those who met him. 'We were quite inspired as we came out of his lectures', recalled Mme Lahy-Hollebecque. 'He was somewhat scrawny and wore a tight-fitting frock coat, but his face lit up as he spoke; he had a beautiful voice and we were all excited by him' (cited in Bossu 1976–84: ii/148). At such times, Durkheim appeared to be possessed by 'the demon of oratorical inspiration'. Like a man speaking to a crowd, he appeared to achieve communion with it. He himself describes such a speaker: 'His language becomes high-flown in a way that would be ridiculous in ordinary circumstances; his gestures take on an overbearing quality . . . The passionate energies he arouses re-echo in turn within him, and they increase his dynamism. It is then no longer a mere individual who speaks but a group incarnated and personified' (1995[1912]: 212)

Xavier Léon, editor of the *Revue de métaphysique et de morale*, painted a similar portrait of his friend Émile:

> The explanation for his influence does not lie simply in the dominating power of his philosophical thought, or the many fields that his work has opened up to the curiosity and activity of his disciples; it lies in the face and body of this ascetic, the glittering light of a gaze that is deeply buried in the eye-sockets, and the metallic tone and accent of the voice expressing a burning faith which inspired this heir to the prophets to shape and carry the convictions of his listeners. (Léon 1917: 749)

Durkheim said of Wundt that he was 'a model of clarity and elegance', and those words could equally apply to Durkheim himself. His students regarded him as one of the heroes of human thought, and as a new Aristotle, Descartes, Spinoza or Kant (Maublanc 1930: 298).

Durkheim was a man who never tolerated complacency and never compromised either his principles or his conscience (Léon 1917: 749). Gabriel Séailles, professor of the history of philosophy at the Sorbonne, described his colleague as:

> a man who was harsh on himself and others, but his harshness simply reflected the demanding nature of a lofty conscience that would not allow him to tell complacent lies. One approached him with a feeling of respect; the more one got to know him, the more one loved him as one discovered the qualities that were not on open display: the candour, the bravery and the generosity. He excelled at inspiring vocations. He really could win over the best minds.[60]

Durkheim's 'great austerity' was impressive, and his sternness intimidated even those who were close to him. 'He looked terrifying', said Georges Davy. 'Uncle Émile was tall and thin and wore a *pince-nez* like Dr Cahen', recalled Mme Cahen (cited in Bossu 1976–84: ii/149). 'When you first met him, he seemed cold and glacial, but when you got to know him, he was "a great guy". Even so, I never dared to say a word in his presence.'

Academic Work Is Serious Work

As soon as he was in post, Durkheim was recruited to serve on thesis juries. The first jury met in 1903 to examine Charles Ribéry's thesis, 'The classification of characters and pedagogy'. It resulted in some sharp exchanges, and Durkheim had a lot of questions:

> I will ask first why you have employed the deductive method. I am aware that . . . you cover yourself by invoking the authority of J.S. Mill . . . But

your argument does not seem to me to be sufficient. It seems to me, on the contrary, that in a science such as that of ethology, that is, in what one might call the science of individuals, the method needed is that which begins from observation . . . You say that emotion is altruistic. I shall ask you now, therefore, how do you manage to deduce altruism from emotion? . . . I will ask you now why you did not think of making habit one of the principal elements in your classification.

When Ribéry gave vague or fanciful answers (he said that 'woman is more altruistic than man'), Durkheim's astonishment grew. Ribéry provoked the same reaction when he chose examples from literature or history: 'So far as historical persons are concerned, we in general do not know them except as transformed by legend. And as to persons taken from literature, in any case imaginary beings, they can prove nothing at all.' Durkheim then moved on to other questions but remained just as aggressive (1975[1903a]).

The Sorbonne's new professor could also be generous with his praise, as when he examined Glotz's thesis, *Solidarity of the Family in the Criminal Law of Ancient Greece* (1975[1904a]). On reading it, he was pleased to find both that 'between history and sociology there is no watertight division' and that the candidate displayed 'a mistrust of easy, so-called rational solutions in the explanation of social facts . . . In order to understand ancient institutions, it is necessary, however difficult it may be for us, to attempt to reproduce the ancient way of thinking.' Hence the need for comparative studies. Durkheim did, however, criticize Glotz for not always being 'sufficiently prudent in the comparisons you make', but then added: 'The reproach I am now making is one I have myself sometimes deserved.'

Over the next few years, Durkheim was to be a member of other juries at the Sorbonne, examining L. Gockler's *The Pedagogy of Herbart* (1975[1905c]), Hubert Bourguin on Fourier, Louis-Germain Lévy's *Family Solidarity and Totemism amongst the Hebrews*, and G. Aslan's *The Ethics of Guyau*. The topics overlapped in one way or another with his own research interests: the family, law, totemism, pedagogy, socialism and ethics. Being an academic was, in his view, a serious matter and it required definite intellectual qualities. His criteria for assessing the value of a thesis were his own, and they never changed: sound erudition, a critical attitude towards sources, impartiality and independence of mind.

In June 1903, Émile Durkheim was elected to the economic and social sciences section of the Comité des travaux historiques et scientifiques. The goal of the committee, which was set up in 1834, was to promote historical research via the agency of learned societies and to encourage the publication of previously unpublished documents on the history of France. When it was reorganized by Jules Ferry in 1883, five different sections were created, including one for economic and social sciences; its goal was to encourage contemporary studies, and especially those that abandoned the 'theoretical dissertation' model in favour of scholarship and a concentration of facts (such as statistics).

The new section's chairman was Émile Levasseur and its assistant secretary was H. Harmand, a lawyer at the Paris bar. Its members included Émile Boutmy, Paul Leroy-Beaulieu and Léon Say. Several were also members of the Académie des sciences morales et politiques or professors at the École libre des sciences politiques. The committee's members had various institutional affiliations, and some were also members or chairmen of learned societies such as the Société de statistiques de Paris, the Société d'économie sociale and the Société de législation comparée (Durkheim 2003: 3–4). Durkheim was very familiar with the way the committee worked: it had given his books a positive evaluation, and had subscribed to them.

At 45, Émile was the youngest member of the committee; the average age of his colleagues was 64, and most were either *chevaliers* or *officiers* of the Légion d'honneur. Many of them did not attend meetings. Durkheim attended his first meeting on 15 July 1903. Those present included Alphonse Aulard, a colleague at the Paris faculty of letters, Émile Cheysson, inspector-general at the Ponts et chaussées, and Gabriel Tarde, professor at the Collège de France. The discussion centred on what appeared to be the section's three 'missions': organizing the next annual congress of learned societies, finalizing a proposal for a series of monographs on the *communes* of France, and assessing those books for which 'requests for subscriptions' had been received.[61]

At his first meeting, Durkheim was invited to comment on Lucien Lévy-Bruhl's *La Morale et la science des moeurs*, which had been published by Alcan. Durkheim described the author's main ideas in the report he presented at the next meeting: Lévy-Bruhl argued the case for a science of morals on the grounds that it was a branch of sociology and the only discipline that could provide a 'rational basis for the art of ethics'. Durkheim obviously shared his colleague's views, and praised him for his 'truly dialectical insights' and 'unusual lucidity'. He expressed the hope that the book would be widely distributed to lycées so as to allow teachers to make their classes more concrete and lively. Durkheim was, in other words, sympathetic to the author's aims.[62]

Subsequent meetings were devoted to a discussion of the proposed series of monographs on the *communes*. It was Cheysson who defined the terms of the discussion. A commission was set up, and Durkheim was elected to it. Gabriel Tarde took part in the discussions. Everyone agreed that a monograph on the economic and social sciences was not the same thing as a historical monograph, and that it should begin with a topographical description of the *commune* in question.

It was not until the following March that Durkheim reported on more books. Three of his reports were negative, and one positive. He was a harsh critic. He described Spencer's *Faits et commentaires* as a collection of 'notes' that had little scientific value and that was addressed to 'society men rather than scholars'. The Italian Eugenio Rignano's essay, *Un socialisme en harmonie avec la doctrine libérale*, contained 'no really new ideas' and was at times 'facile'. Ludovic Dumas' *L'Absolu, forme pathologique et normale des sentiments* (which dealt with stubbornness, fanaticism, asceticism and modesty) seemed to him to be a product of 'insufficiently scientific work'. The book's utility was therefore, he concluded, 'artificial'. Its methodology was that of a sophisticated, moralist whose insight was often subtle, but not that of a scientist. Victor Basch's *L'Individualisme anarchique*, in contrast, deserved the honour of a subscription because it was 'well documented, suggestive and sometimes brilliantly written', even though some its historical assertions were 'open to challenge'. Durkheim was concerned to defend not so much his conception of sociology as his conception of intellectual work, or his research ethos: method as opposed to intuition, and serious work as opposed to fashionable facileness. Such were the qualities of a good scholarly book (see Fabiani 2003).

16

Le Grand Manitou and the Totem-Taboo Clan

Now that both uncle and nephew were living in the rue Saint-Jacques, and Henri Hubert in the rue Claude-Bernard, there was no need to write letters. Conditions seemed to be ripe for doing 'some good work', publishing a better *Année sociologique* and, at last, establishing sociology. Holding editorial meetings, however, was out of the question. The journal still functioned on the basis of 'No conferences, no meetings and no slogans', said Davy in an attempt to correct the widespread impression that Durkheim was 'the apostle of tyranny'. 'Everyone liked to go and see him, both to take his advice and to feel the affectionate interest he took in all of us' (Davy 1919b: 195). Durkheim certainly had an 'extraordinary ascendancy' over his associates, and especially the younger ones, but he also respected everyone's freedom.

The Debate with Gabriel Tarde: Sociology and Social Science

Astonishing as it may seem, Durkheim agreed to take part in a debate with Gabriel Tarde at the beginning of the 1903 academic year. The topic was his article 'Sociology and the social sciences'. The debate took place at the École des hautes études sociales in Paris, and was chaired by Alfred Croiset. Durkheim had just agreed to take part in the school's activities, and his name appeared alongside that of Tarde in the lecture programme for the autumn of 1903. They both taught on the 'general introduction' course (relations between sociology, the various social sciences and their auxiliary disciplines). Relations between the two men were tense. Tarde's latest book, *Psychologie économique*, had been savagely criticized by François Simiand in the *Année sociologique*; he described Tarde's views as 'ingenious', but his book was 'fanciful' (Simiand 1903).[1] Durkheim and Tarde were complete opposites. When Tarde implied in his article 'La réalité social' (Tarde 1901b) that Durkheim had drawn much 'closer to the psychological conception of social facts' since the launch of the *Année sociologique*, an obviously angry Durkheim wrote to the *Revue philosophique*'s editor Théodule Ribot to dispel 'the misunderstandings that have accumulated' (1982[1901]: 254). He had not changed his opinion: 'Social life is a system of representations and mental states, provided that it is clearly understood that these representations are *sui generis*' (ibid.: 253).

Durkheim was the first to speak and he began with a provocative question: 'Must sociology go on being nothing more than a form of philosophical speculation that embraces social life in a synthetic formula?' Sociology was obviously the 'daughter of philosophical thought' and its 'logical culmination', but there could, in his view, be no question of 'studying social facts in the abstract' or of restricting sociology's field of research to the study of a single problem such as the discovery of the general law of sociality. He defended a more cautious and modest position based upon two points: (1) 'Social reality is essentially complex' and (2) 'Sociology is not a unified science.' Durkheim urged researchers to look at the concrete facts, which were, he repeated 'complex': 'Even the most primitive societies are extremely complex.' He recommended a 'special research' approach, adding that it demanded precision, objectivity and specialization (Durkheim 1975[1904e]: 160–1).

'Should we be speaking of social science or the social sciences?' Gabriel Tarde asked in his turn. He agreed with Durkheim that sociology was 'the science – and not the philosophy – of social facts' and that it was based upon the comparative method, but argued that the trend was for the social sciences to take the place of social science. He criticized Durkheim's belief that 'scientific progress requires a growing division of labour and means that the social sciences must be divorced from one another'. He once more argued the need for an 'interpsychology' or 'inter-mind psychology'. The evolution of the social sciences was, he believed, leading in that direction: 'All the social sciences that started out from an objectivist point of view have become psychologized' (Tarde 1975[1904]: 162–4).

In the discussion that followed, Durkheim and Tarde 'very heatedly' defended their respective theses. Tarde accepted the importance of general laws established by the comparative method, but still defended what he called the 'social microscopy' method. In reply, Durkheim once more argued that 'if it ignores the social sciences, general sociology cannot be anything other than a synthesis of the findings of specific social sciences'. Turning to Tarde, he then added: 'Given the current state of our knowledge, we are unable to say what the elementary social fact is. We know too little, and in the circumstances the idea of an elementary social fact can only be arbitrary.' In reply, Tarde challenged Durkheim's idea that it was only when they were fully constituted that the sciences could formulate laws, and that the social sciences owed their progress to the comparative method. He then asked his colleague if he believed that there was such a thing as a 'social reality' other than 'individuals and individual actions of facts'. Well aware of Durkheim's position, he concluded: 'Individual actions and reactions are all that exists. Everything else is nothing more than a metaphysical entity, a form of mysticism.' The debate was going nowhere and turning into a dialogue of the deaf. 'You are confusing two different questions', retorted Durkheim, who refused to continue the discussion, on the grounds that he had 'nothing to say about a problem he had not dealt with and that had nothing to do with the debate'.

A summary of both papers and of the ensuing discussion was published in the *Revue internationale de sociologie*. The issue of relations between the two disciplines was obviously of great concern to the journal's editor René Worms. The 5th congress of the Institut international de sociologie was due to open in Paris in July 1903, and interdisciplinarity was its central concern. The theme of the conference was 'Relations between sociology and psychology'. Lester F. Ward, who had come from Washington for the occasion, gave the opening address; the preliminary report was drawn up by Gabriel Tarde and delivered by his son.[2]

This was Gabriel Tarde's last public appearance. The newly elected member of the Institut (Académie des sciences morales et politiques) died suddenly on 12 May 1904 after a short illness whose 'fatal outcome' could not have been predicted. He 'was still working, his influence was at its height and his thought was at its most productive'. The *Revue philosophique* emphasized the importance of Tarde's contribution to the revolution in social psychology: although his ideas might seem paradoxical, they stood out because of 'their richness' and the 'ingenuity of his broadest conceptions'.[3] 'A brilliant mind, full of ingenious ideas and resources, and an inexhaustible source of new views', commented the *Revue internationale de sociologie*, which had lost 'one of its most long-standing and brilliant contributors'.[4]

Durkheim published a review of Tarde's last article, 'Interpsychology', which had appeared in June 1903, in volume X of the *Année sociologique* (1980[1906c]), He recalled that, towards the end of his life, Tarde 'liked to replace the expression "collective psychology" with "interpsychology"': 'It is already clear how arbitrary and confused this notion is.' According to Durkheim, not everything was a product of imitation, whose action depended, as Tarde himself recognized, on other social factors. He once more criticized his old enemy's over-simplistic arguments and mocked his methodology, which consisted in simply 'compiling a few freely annotated anecdotes' (1980[1906c]: 72).

'It Is Not We Who Think, but the World That Thinks In Us'

Far from being discouraged, Durkheim still hoped to convince his philosopher-colleagues. Together with Paul Fauconnet, he wrote a long article, 'Sociology and the social sciences', published in the *Revue philosophique* in 1903 (1982[1903]). He began writing it in April 1902, at a time when he was very busy. He was working on his essay, 'Primitive forms of classification.' 'Unfortunately, it will mean a lot of work', he wrote to Mauss, adding: 'You cannot turn bits of articles into one article. Hence the difficulties. But I think I can see how to do it.'[5] Fauconnet and Durkheim were coeditors of the *Anné sociologique*'s 'Juridic and moral sociology' rubric, and Fauconnet was currently teaching philosophy at the Lycée Louis-le-

Grand. As their title indicated, Durkheim and Fauconnet were concerned about the relationship between sociology and the other social and historical sciences (the history of religions, statistics, economic science, etc.). There were two possibilities: 'either sociology has the same subject matter as those sciences termed historical or social and is then merged with them; or it is a distinct science, possessing its own individual character' (ibid.: 175). Rather than becoming involved in an abstract debate, Durkheim and Fauconnet chose to discuss what sociology 'is becoming as it develops' (ibid.: 176). There were three strands to their argument.

The first concerned tradition. Ever since the time of Comte, the 'founder', and his successor Spencer, 'sociology [had never been] conceived to be anything save a speculative, complete entity, closely linked to general philosophy' (1982[1903]: 176). It was now necessary, argued Durkheim and Fauconnet, to break with that tradition. Their second point had to do with change: there had to be a radical change in the way research was organized: 'For progress to be accomplished, the science must resolve itself into an increasingly large number of specific questions, so as to render possible co-operation between different minds and different generations' (ibid.: 181). Scientific progress, that is, implies a division of labour, and this applies to sociology too. In the absence of that division of labour, there is a danger that it will become a general social science or 'a very special kind of speculation, halfway between philosophy and literature' (ibid.: 188).[6] Durkheim and Fauconnet then make a critique of contemporary sociologists such as Simmel, Giddings, Ward and Tarde.

Thirdly, Durkheim and Fauconnet are not suggesting that the Comtean heritage should be dismissed, or that the idea of a positive science of societies has to be abandoned. On the contrary, they argue the need to go beyond it: the idea must be applied to 'the totality, without exception, of social facts' (1982[1903]: 194), which implies that the so-called special social sciences (history, political economy, etc.) must follow the example of sociology and 'take on a sociological character'. This does not really imply a 'veritable evolution', since this 'spontaneous development' (ibid.: 195–6) is already under way as specialists begin 'to turn to sociology of their own accord'. The authors cite the examples of Germany (Schmoller in political economy, Herman Post and Steinmetz in anthropology) and England (Lang, Robertson Smith and Frazer on the study of religion). They then put forward a general proposition, which they borrow from Hermann Post: 'It is not we who think, but the world that thinks in us.' History, in other words, is governed by impersonal forces, and the decisive actions are those of the masses, and not of brilliant individuals. Morals, customs and the spirit of peoples are 'the work of the peoples themselves'. The same applies to art and literature, and even 'literary monuments' such as the Bible or the Homeric poems 'ascribed to an obscure and indeterminate multitude of anonymous collaborators' (ibid.: 201).

Even so, 'what remains to be done is still 'considerable' (1982[1903]: 202): 'the principle of interdependence of social facts', which is 'admitted in theory' must be 'put into practice' (ibid.: 205). The idea or project is 'a body of distinct but solidly linked sciences, with each possessing a sense of that solidarity'. This will, the authors hope, 'become the subject of a renewed, rejuvenated social philosophy, one which will be positive and progressive, like the very sciences whose crowning glory it will be' (ibid.: 206).

In 1902, Durkheim took part in the *Mercure de France*'s symposium on German influences on French philosophy (Durkheim 1975[1902]). He admitted that personally, he owed the Germans a great deal; they allowed him to understand the complexity of social reality, and to gain a better understanding of how narrow the French school's conceptions were. He was, on the other hand, somewhat disappointed by the German contribution to the social sciences; it was certainly 'greater than ours', but did not provide 'any new impetus'. 'Germany has not been able to come up with new formulae.' Whereas sociology was 'almost too fashionable' in France, it had almost no representatives in Germany. This astonished Durkheim, who had expected 'enlightenment' from Germany. He saw this as a sign of a 'certain lack of curiosity, a sort of introversion', and of an 'intellectual plethora' that was 'an obstacle to further progress'.

English Converts?

The *Année sociologique* carefully followed the work of foreign colleagues, and especially those in England, Germany and the United States. Its reviews were often critical, especially where the work of American sociologists such as Giddings, Small and Ward were concerned; the *American Journal of Sociology*, which was edited by Small, had in a sense taken the side of René Worms and his *Revue internationale de sociologie*.

So what of England? In June 1904, the new Sociological Society, which had been founded the previous year, invited Durkheim to a meeting to defend his ideas before its members. Sociology appeared to be 'underdeveloped' in England: the first chair in sociology was not established until 1907 and went to Leonard Hobhouse, a former journalist and editor of the *Manchester Guardian*. Most of the new learned society's members did not hold university positions: they were writers or journalists, many of them with links to the socialist or liberal movements. They tended to be concerned with practical issues, and wanted to orient sociology towards practical applications. They were familiar with the work of Durkheim and his associates but, thanks to the Scottish sociologist Patrick Geddes and his collaborator V.V. Branford, who was very active in the society, Le Play was the dominant influence. The society was also very interested in the work of the Institut international de sociologie and its director René Worms.

The society had three sections. The first was devoted to eugenics (one of its first invited speakers was Francis Galton in 1903), and the second to 'civics'; the third was concerned with theoretical and methodological studies. It was one of the conveners of the third section, Hobhouse, who invited Durkheim to speak about his 'theses'. Durkheim accepted the invitation and drafted a three-page summary of the article he and Fauconnet had just published. The article, together with one by Branford, was sent to various specialists, including philosophers, historians, sociologists and economists in different European countries.

The meeting was held before a very diverse audience at the London School of Economics and Political Science on 20 June 1904. A few German historians had come to London to take part in the discussion. The meeting was chaired by the philosopher Bernard Bosanquet, who read Durkheim's paper, which had been written in English. Branford then read his paper. A very lively discussion ensued. Both were then published, together with comments from the specialists who had organized the event: Fouillée, Bernès, Worms and Maxim Kovalevsky (France), F. Cossenti (from the journal *La scienza sociale*) and A. Loria (Italy), and Paul Barth, Ferdinand Tönnies and Steinmetz (Germany). As the deadline was tight, the American sociologists were unable to respond. The discussion had a considerable impact.[7]

'The first postulate of a science of society', declared Durkheim, 'is that human phenomena are part of nature.' Speaking to his English colleagues, Durkheim described himself as heir to both Comte and Spencer, but stressed that, unlike them, he preferred the observation of detailed facts to far-reaching speculation, and argued the case for the social sciences on the grounds that sociology must become a body of specific disciplines. While he emphasized that various attempts had been made to reorganize the social sciences on a sociological basis without any reference to a philosophical synthesis, he also warned against what he called 'dangerous tendencies towards isolation'.

Durkheim's goal was clear: to ensure that sociology was sufficiently specialized to become a 'real positive science'. The 'trend' was moving in that direction and simply had to be consciously organized. Given the current situation, there were still many 'obvious deficiencies': a failure to recognize that social phenomena were interdependent, too many facile and simplistic explanations; and there was still a tendency to explain social phenomena in terms of only one (economic or religious) factor. Specialist sciences overlapped; energy was being wasted; and broad sectors of society were being left unexplored. Having made his diagnosis, the solution was, he argued, simple: there should be greater cooperation between the specialist sciences, and they should all adopt a sociological point of view. He was, in other words, arguing the case for both diversity and unity.

It was then Victor Branford's turn to speak. He took the view that the urgent problems sociology had to deal with were methodological and historical. He too defended the idea of specialization within sociology, and insisted, finally, that social theory and practice were interdependent. Branford was close to the Le Play school, and might therefore have been expected to be critical of Durkheim's theses. He did not in fact contradict his French colleague, merely adding a footnote alluding discreetly to their differences of opinion. Much of the discussion centred on the scientific status of sociology. Many of the participants were critical of Durkheim. He was criticized for clinging to the old positivism (of Comte), for defending the 'unity of nature' thesis, and for regarding social phenomena as natural phenomena. He was also criticized – paradoxically, one might say – for according too much importance to Spencer (who had died a few months earlier), and it is true that his sociology was to a large extent a hostile response to Spencer's work. Finally, he was also criticized for making no allowance for synthetic disciplines such as the philosophy of the social sciences. His obvious desire to 'annex' history also came in for criticism.

Durkheim would have liked to defend himself against these attacks, but doing so would have meant writing 'a major essay', and his 'total lack of leisure' prevented him from doing that. He therefore wrote a short reply and sent it to the secretary of the society; it was published alongside his paper in *Sociological Papers* (Galton et al. 1905: 257). He was, he said, 'especially concerned to combat the conception – still too widely accepted – which makes sociology a branch of philosophy, in which questions are only considered in their most schematic aspect, and are attacked without specialized competence.' He therefore urged, above all, 'the need for systematic specialization'. In his reply, he insisted on the need for a 'synthetic science': 'It belongs to this science to disengage from the different specialist disciplines certain general conclusions . . . which will stimulate and inspire the specialist, which will guide and illuminate his researches, and which will lead to ever-fresh discoveries; resulting, in turn, to further progress of philosophical thought, and so on, indefinitely' (ibid.). He agreed that he had 'somewhat neglected' this aspect of the question, but added: 'I have purposed, for more than two years past, to develop this idea in an essay which would be the sequel and complement of the one summarised for the Sociological Society.' The project had been 'postponed' for lack of time: 'I do not know when it will be possible to put it into practice' (ibid.)

A Great Debate: Historical Method and Social Science

One contributor to the debate at the Sociological Society argued that historians needed psychology more than they needed sociology. Durkheim always defended the idea that 'history cannot be a science without rising above the individual', and that when it did so, 'it ceases to be itself and becomes a branch of sociology' (1980[1903d]: 71). Reviewing a special issue of the *Rivista italiana di sociologia* devoted to 'History as social science', Durkheim reasserted his position and agreed with the philosopher Benedetto Croce when he argued that all sciences began with concrete facts but then 'elevated' themselves to the general, in order to 'constitute types and laws'. If history limited itself to 'the study of each national individuality taken in itself', it was 'no more than a narration that enabled societies to remember their past' and 'the eminent form of collective memory'. There were therefore two different conceptions of history:

history as science, and history as art. Far from excluding each other, they 'mutually presuppose[d] one another', but that was no reason to 'confound them' (ibid.). The question of relations between history and sociology was a major concern for Fustel de Coulange's old student.

Charles Seignobos's *La Méthode historique appliquée aux sciences sociales* was published in 1901, and attempted to show that the social sciences were dependent upon the historical method: social facts were their object, and they therefore had to rely upon documentary evidence. He made a distinction between the statistical sciences (including demography), the sciences of economic life and the history of economic doctrines, but made no reference to sociology. Seignobos was also the author, with Charles Victor Langlois, of the important *Introduction aux méthodes historiques* (1897).[8] As an advocate of narrative or factual [*événementielle*] history, Seignobos attached great importance to documents, and defined history as 'the science of past human facts'. It was, however, the 'science of things that only happened once'. History was, in his view, an imperfect form of knowledge that could make no claim to being objective: 'The very nature of its documents means that history is by definition a subjective science' (Langlois and Seignobos 1898: 47).

Durkheim had little time for his new colleague's position (though they were, at least in political terms, close: Seignobos was from a republican family and had been a Dreyfusard). He criticized him both for his attempt to reduce the social sciences to history and for his purely conjectural and subjective conception of history itself. Durkheim refused to abandon his project for an objective science of societies: 'If it is incontestable that social life is made up exclusively of representations, it in no way follows that an objective science cannot be made of them' (1980[1902]: 69). He feared that Seignobos 'means to relegate us to the literary fantasies of the purely introspective method'. He was also critical of his colleague's claim that sociology was no longer 'in fashion'. Such a claim was 'particularly paradoxical at a time when one could well complain of the excessive vogue the word enjoys and of the abuse that is constantly being made of it' (ibid.: 68).

François Simiand revived the polemic in his lecture, 'Historical method and social science', which he gave to the members of the Société d'histoire moderne et contemporaine in January 1903. The young man whom Charles Péguy described as having 'a thin, cold smile'[9] was hard on his former comrade, and triggered a 'violent discussion' that might even be described as a polemic. Now that he had become a follower of Bergson, Péguy disagreed completely with Simiand: in his view, history was an art form. Henri Berr promptly published Simiand's article (Simiand 1903a) in two parts in his *Revue de synthèse historique*, which devoted a lot of space to history. Like Simiand, he argued the case for a synthetic history. 'The dust of facts is nothing', he wrote in the programme outlined in the journal's first issue (Berr 1900: 7). 'As the old tradition teaches us, science can only be the science of generalities.'

Simiand was highly critical of Seignobos and Langlois's *Introduction aux études historiques*, and opened the debate by contrasting 'traditional' history or 'historicizing history' with the 'new' social science, whose conceptions upset 'a number of intellectual habits'. As the 'main points' of the debate came down, in his view, to objections to 'the historical spirit' and to the idea of a positive science of social facts, he challenged each of the five propositions made by Langlois and Seignobos: the psychological, and therefore subjective, nature of social facts (which led, he argued, to a confusion between 'psychological' and 'subjective'); their refusal to use abstractions (state, church, the textile industry, etc.) and their emphasis on collective and individual actors; the role of contingency and the notion of causality; the relevance of documents to scientific observation. Like Durkheim, Simiand argued that 'the social element is not simply a juxtaposition and complication of individual elements', but readily agreed that 'it is only with the individual consciousness that social phenomena have any existence'. Simiand's criticism of historians was that they worshipped three idols: chronology, events and the individual (and contingency). In his view, the usual spirit and methods of history were 'in complete disagreement' with the method used in social science: while sociologists looked for laws and facts, historians observed coincidences and dwelt at length on reasons and circumstances that explained them. Sociology was a science, and history was a narrative or description.

The two points of view were 'irreconcilable', admitted Paul Mantoux in the *Revue de synthèse historique* (1903), to which he was a regular contributor. His reply to Simiand was an attempt to promote an understanding or compromise between two disciplines that could be 'of use to one another'. A historian by training, Mantoux paid tribute to Durkheim and praised him for having 'taken social science from the metaphysical era to the positive era' by looking not only at concepts, but also at 'humble facts' in his work of suicide and the division of labour. Mantoux believed that it was possible for history and sociology to work together, provided that they avoided 'preconceived methods' and 'established specific rules of method through practice'. Paul Mantoux was close to the Dreyfusards and especially Marcel Mauss, and, like Mauss, was a militant socialist. François Simiand gave Mantoux's important book *La Révolution industrielle au XVIIIe siècle* a very favourable review in the *Année sociologique*: it was, he said a 'remarkable work' (Simiand 1907: 550).[10]

'*Adorons le totem, le grand manitou*'

Durkheim's enemies at the Sorbonne saw him as the head of a new church or, more specifically, a clan. Célestin Bouglé jokingly described his followers as the 'taboo-totem' clan, alluding to the close relationship between uncle and nephew.[11] Durkheim's students at the École normale supérieure even composed a song in his honour:

Adorons le totem, le grand manitou
Que le maître Durkheim prêche parmi nous[12]

Durkheim had just published his article on totemism in the fifth volume of *L'Année sociologique*. 'Too much is too much', complained Élie Halévy, who suggested to his friend Célestin that the *Année* would do well to develop an interest in 'something other than totem and taboo'.[13]

Durkheim recruited two new contributors to work on volume VI of the *Année*, one older than him, Charles Fossey, and one younger, Paul Huvelin. Fossey had been teaching a *cours libre* on Babylonian religion at the École pratique, where his colleagues included Henri Hubert and Marcel Mauss.[14] He was awarded a doctorate for his thesis, 'Assyrian magic' (1902), and was now writing *Manuel d'assyriologie* (1904). In 1906, he was elected to the Collège de France, where his chair was in Assyrian philology and archaeology. Fossey's contributions to the *Année* were restricted to volumes VI and VII.

Paul Huvelin was a friend of Emmanuel Lévy's, and his colleague at the Lyon faculty of law. Born in Mirebeau in 1873, he was awarded a law doctorate for his thesis on the laws governing markets and fairs (1897), which he published as *Les Courriers des foires de Champagne* in 1898. His authority as a jurist and historian of law was, said Mauss, 'unchallengeable . . . and extremely useful' (1969[1925]: 478).[15]

Another of Mauss's and Hubert's friends made a very modest contribution to volume VI of the *Année*. Joe Stickney's sole contribution was a review of Florenz's *Nihondi, Zeitalter der Götter* in the religious sociology section. Stickney was a young American who had come to pursue his studies under the supervision of Sylvain Lévi at the École pratique. His thesis was 'Gnomic poetry in Greece, compared with gnomic poetry in India.' He also published, in 1903, *Les Sentences dans la poésie grecque d'Homère à Euripide*, which Hubert (1904b) reviewed in the *Année*.

René Chaillié also published his first reviews in volume VI. Born in 1870, he was two years younger than Mauss, and had been one of his first and most faithful students, attending his lectures from 1901 to 1904. Chaillé was awarded a diploma by the École pratique in 1902, and contributed to volumes VI, IX and X of the *Année*.

A new balance had now been struck between the two main sections, and 'religious sociology' and 'juridic and moral sociology' were of equal length (129 pages). 'Criminal sociology and moral statistics', 'general sociology' and 'economic sociology' now took up between 90 and 100 pages each. The 'miscellaneous' and 'social morphology' sections remained marginal (some 20 pages each). Several minor changes were made to the sections: new rubrics were introduced, and some of the old ones were consolidated and expanded. The changes were small and did not amount to a full reorganization: the 'war' rubric, for instance, was removed, making room for 'socialism' (Paul Fauconnet). There were also some new rubrics: 'suicide' (in the 'criminal sociology and moral statistics' section); 'history of sociology' (in 'general sociology'); and 'linguistics' and 'socialism' (in the 'miscellaneous' section). The changes were intended to provide a better fit between the rubrics and the publications under review, and to provide an outlet for new preoccupations and sensibilities.

Some of the section editors added a few indications as to the direction their work was taking. In his introductory notes to the 'juridic systems' and 'social organization' sections, Durkheim once more pointed out that juridical phenomena did not exist in isolation: *juridical practices*, together with other practices, gave rise to *institutions* and, finally, to a society's *juridical system*. Some readers might have wondered what linguistics and socialism were doing in a sociology journal. The arrival of Antoine Meillet was enough to justify replacing the 'language' rubric with 'linguistics'. He himself argued that linguistics in the strict sense (grammar, philology, and so on) did not come within the remit of such a journal, but language did have 'an eminently social character: languages are spoken by populations, and populations create languages through their specific social organizations and in specific circumstances' (Meillet 1903: 572–773). Paul Fauconnet explained the inclusion of a new rubric dealing with 'socialism': socialism comprised 'a whole range of contemporary facts' ranging from economic transformations and the development of new institutions to the political action of the working class. These were, he added, facts that should be studied from a 'purely scientific point of view' and without any practical preoccupation. The goal was to 'advance the sociological theory of socialism.'

Durkheim wrote some 50 reviews for the rubrics he edited ('juridic systems', 'domestic and conjugal life', 'population' and 'urban groups'). He discussed the kinship system, marriage and family law, the execution of wills in the Middle Ages, the dowry system in France, the influence of urban conurbations, and the debates that had taken place at the Tenth International Congress on Hygiene and Demography. His contribution to the 'marriage and sexual morality, position of women' rubric dealt with the more familiar topics of sexual taboos and incest, as well as the issue of the inferior status of women.[16] He sometimes used his reviews to correct misinterpretations of his own work and to reveal errors 'only to give an impression that we cannot acquiesce by keeping silent' (1980[1903f]: 98). His review of Steinmetz's study of 'hereditary social traits', for instance, allowed him to comment on the way this contributor to the *Année* had interpreted his *Suicide*: 'We are afraid that he has read our book somewhat rapidly' (ibid.).

Durkheim also used the *Année* to pursue some of the polemics in which he had become involved. One such polemic concerned the mutual repulsion between the sexes, which lead to their separation and, in some cases, to a real antagonism that put them on a war footing. He discusses (Durkheim 1975[1903c]), for instance, Ernest Crawley's *The Mystic Rose. A Study of Primitive Marriage*, which challenged his thesis about the sacred nature of blood in his study of incest: 'The religious nature of woman appears to be closely related to a number of manifestations of the lives of women, which are essentially characterized by blood: puberty, menstruation and childbirth . . . To deny that blood plays an important role in religious life is to fly in the face of the evidence.' And when, rejecting the ideas of group marriage and compulsory promiscuity, Crawley argues that 'man was initially characterized by an intransigent individualism, whereas socialism [which he confuses with primitive communism] is a product of history', Durkheim demonstrates his methodological weaknesses and shows that his argument is 'open to challenge and out of date'. 'It is true to say that individualism already existed at this stage of evolution. But only in embryonic form.' Durkheim also reviewed a study written by E. Esmein of sexual customs in Greek mythology: the frequency of extra-marital sexual relations, the custom that prescribed a husband's loan of his wife or daughter to a special guest, and the practice of incest. Durkheim points out the errors: 'We have no knowledge of these primitive peoples, no matter how grotesque [they] seem in practising this custom with such tolerance' (1980[1903a]: 262).[17]

Durkheim also took an interest into contemporary issues such as the investigation of paternity in France (1980[1903b] and divorce in Switzerland and Germany. His interest in divorce was already apparent in *Suicide*. Three factors appear to encourage the propensity to divorce: greater tolerance (divorce by mutual consent), mixed marriages and the 'extreme fragility' of precocious marriages: 'in an important number of cases, the real cause of divorce is quite simply the desire to marry again' (1980[1903c]: 424).[18] Perhaps legislators should take that into account and either oblige couples to wait longer before marrying, or forbid early marriages. He was to write an article entitled 'Divorce by mutual consent' for the *Revue bleue* a few years later: there were, he wrote, 'reasons to fear' that it would have a 'very dangerous influence on marriage and its normal functioning' (1978[1906]: 241).

A New Research Programme: Categories of Thought

As he explained to François Simiand, Durkheim wished to retain the 'articles' format for the *Année*:

> This last principle seems to me to be quite excellent. I do not need to tell you how much it cost me to publish certain things. I did so because, in theory, I did not dare to hope for the verbal homogeneity that has been established between us . . . and because I dream only of making the *Année* a collection for which scientific honesty is the only criterion for admission. I also did it because it was impossible to do otherwise. But it is clear that, limited as it may be, this eclecticism damages the overall impression.

As for the articles that had already been published in the *Année*, he added: 'The only ones that have any value are by us.'[19] This was the journal's new *leitmotiv*. Both the articles published in volume VI were by members of the team: a study of primitive classification by Durkheim and Mauss (1963[1903]) and an essay of recent theories of the division of labour by Bouglé (1903).

A number of philosophers were interested in what Ribot called 'the progress of the mind': knowledge was a philosophical theme, if not *the* philosophical theme of the moment. Ribot's *L'Évolution des idées générales* (1897) dealt with the question of the relationship between thought and language, and analysed various cognitive processes (abstraction, generalization and classification). Ribot made a study of about 100 people – men and women – from various professions or occupations in an attempt to capture 'the instanteous work of the mind (conscious or unconscious)'.[20] Paul Lapie (1904) made a similar empirical study of his students at the École normale supérieure des instituteurs in Aix-en-Provence. He described it as an 'experiment' on 'intellectual activity'. 'When does thought begin to stir?', he asked.[21]

Durkheim and his colleagues were also interested in dissecting the 'work' of the mind. When he began to draft his essay on the problem of classifications, Durkheim gave his nephew some general suggestions 'My work suggests that there is a question here, that this way of thinking evolved, and that we need to ask how.' In order to clear up any 'misunderstandings', he then went on: 'There should be an introduction to explain that the goal of the study is to show how the notions of genus and species came into being. The mental operation we call classification did not spring full-formed from the human brain. Something must have led men to classify beings in this way. Genera are not natural phenomena. They are constructs.'[22]

Durkheim took responsibility for this part of the article in the full knowledge that it would be 'difficult but interesting'. The 'historical and descriptive part' would take up the bulk of the work. 'In order to resolve the problem, we will have to go back in time, to the most elementary classifications of things that we can find.' Then there should be a short conclusion demonstrating the 'social character' of classification and defending the thesis that 'hierarchy is a reflection of social classification'. 'This will be a nice example of a real social psychology, or at least the beginnings of one', he believed. He also suggested that the early classifications of the Greek philosophers might be a good line of research, 'to see if it gives anything'.[23]

Mauss's contribution to the essay was essential, and he was later to say: 'I supplied all the facts' (1979[1930]: 210). The final version, which had more than 200 footnotes, brought together a mass of ethnographic data on all kinds of Australian and American tribes. In the last section, the comparative examination of classificatory systems was to include Chinese divinatory systems (astrology and horoscopes) and references to Greek and Brahmanic mythology. Mauss was very familiar with all this material: he had read, reread and, in most cases, criticized the work of Bastian, Barth, Caland, Curr, Cushing, De Groot, Frazer, Gillen, Haddon, Lang, Power, Spencer and Usener. Durkheim and Mauss set out to analyse 'the most rudimentary classifications made by mankind' (1963[1903]: 9), namely those elaborated by Australian tribes, and to demonstrate that they correspond to their social organization (phratries, matrimonial classes, clans): the classification of things reproduces the classification of men. They emphasize the 'sociocentrism' of their analysis: 'Society was not simply a model which classificatory thought followed; it was its own divisions which served as divisions for the system of classification. The first logical categories were social categories; the first classes of things were classes of men' (1963[1903]: 82).

Durkheim and Mauss had opened up a whole new domain for the sociology of knowledge: as they had hoped, it was indeed possible, to 'analyse other basic functions or notions of the human understanding', such as the ideas of space, time, cause and substance, and various forms of reasoning. Such was the *Année sociologique*'s new 'programme'. The general intention was to establish a relationship of interdependence and interpenetration between very different realms of social facts, such as social organization and collective representations. That task was never completed. 'Primitive classifications', Mauss would later argue, should have become a new rubric in the *Année* devoted to collective representations: 'A study of folk tales, cosmologies in general, science and of notions to do with the soul, time, space, causality and law (to list them in no particular order) should certainly have been undertaken; the general relationship between groups and their environment, and their mentality, should also have been the object of an even more general study'. 'Unfortunately', added Mauss, the journal could not give such facts the 'space they deserved', because 'the state of science does not yet allow collective representations to be studied as such'. He reminded his readers that he and Durkheim had been forced to choose to 'study only the religious aspect of collective representations'. 'To a certain extent, the very nature of the facts justifies our choice. Most of these notions were shaped by religion, or were originally profoundly religious' (Mauss and Hubert 1903: 225–6).

The essay on primitive classification represented, according to Mauss, one of the most 'philosophical' efforts ever made by any 'school' (Mauss 1979[1903]: 218.) The philosophers were delighted – 'the school of which M. Durkheim is the unchallenged leader reveals the growth of its influence year by year' – and congratulated the *Année*'s 'scholarly and hardworking editors' on 'their important and precious publication'. The bibliographical section was, in their view, 'always remarkable'. There was only one critical comment: the 'religious sociology' section was 'devoted completely to primitive forms of religious life' and ignored so-called 'modern' religions.[24] The *Revue de métaphysique et de morale* was anxious to correct the image of the *Année* and its editor that it had given the previous year, and was even prepared to lend its 'unreserved' support to the positions that Durkheim and his associates were defending in sociology: 'In today's France, Durkheim is the man who appears to have the outstanding qualities of intelligence and character required to make this attempt to persuade people to think systematically.' The journal was quite happy to learn that Durkheim intended to devote several years to the study of totemic institutions, and that Mauss planned to specialize in the sociology of religions. Its support was, however, lukewarm, and the publication of the essay on primitive classification was all it took for the 'old prejudices to emerge once more'.

Durkheim and Mauss had gone too far by writing an 'essay on general philosophy' and attempting to prove that 'the methods of scientific thought are real social institutions'. The reaction from the philosophers was immediate, and ranged from astonishment to virulent criticism. 'A very curious and very characteristic contribution', noted Gustave Belot in the *Revue philosophique* (Belot 1904). He acknowledged that it was 'a remarkably suggestive contribution to the study of the primitive mentality', but added that it did raise problems: 'The concern that dominates their sociology is an attempt to find the origins of the psychological in the social, rather than the other way around.'

Most objections came from the *Revue de métaphysique et de morale*. It complained, first of all, that Durkheim and Mauss were literally obsessed with their theory of totemism, which was still challenged by other theories, and which was far from able to explain all the facts that had been observed. Some of their 'few facts' might even 'explode' their theoretical framework. As to the social origins of primitive peoples' philosophy of nature, the journal challenged their theory by pointing out its weaknesses. It was more inclined to look to individual psychology for an explanation for primitive classifications. Durkheim had not succeeded in proving his 'initial thesis' that classificatory techniques could not be 'innate or established by individual forces alone'. 'We find it difficult to believe that sociology can replace metaphysics when it comes to resolving this kind of question', replied the philosophers, who believed that 'individual human beings have an '"innate" ability to divide and classify'. Rather than saying, like Durkheim, that 'men gathered together and saw themselves as a group', we should be saying that men 'formed groups'. And they were far from convinced that 'in order to study social categories, we must believe that the earliest logical categories were social categories'. Why should religious beliefs not be 'at least in part, the product of feelings born of and developed by the consciousness of the individual'?

Even philosophers who claimed, like Alfred Fouillée, to be sympathetic to sociology refused to regard logic as a 'social thing'. Durkheim retorted that 'classifications express society', and that logical functions, just like moral functions, vary from one society to another: 'Collective understanding varies like the other mental functions of the society' (1980[1907b]: 143). Edmond Goblot (1904), finally, could not conceal his surprise. This was, he exclaimed in the *Revue de synthèse historique*, 'a curious theory that is completely new and original'. Could the origins of the logical realm lie in the social realm? 'I am wary of challenging this theory . . . The authors have opened up a new field of research.' He cautiously restricted himself to one comment: 'Despite the abundance of interesting facts, clever insights and penetrating analyses, a great deal remains to be done if we are to trace the origins of the human mind's classificatory and generalizing functions back to certain features of the structure of primitive societies.' The reaction from the anthropologists was similar. 'A fine article', exclaimed Salomon Reinach (1903b) on reading the essay. He congratulated his colleagues on having raised 'a problem of vital importance', but added: 'Opinions about the solution they propose will no doubt vary.' Whereas other scholars postulated that the logical relationship between things supplied the basis for relations between men, the position of Durkheim and Mauss seemed to him to be 'bold' because they inverted that thesis by arguing that 'social relations are the cause, and logical relations are the effect'. This should, he argued, be described as *sociocentrism*. Surely, would not primitive men have had at least an obscure idea of classification before social relations could be established? It was also the more difficult to answer such a question in that the basic data was not available. Durkheim and Mauss were, he concluded, 'scholars and researchers who . . . by trying to pierce the darkness, become lost in it'.

'An acute and learned paper', wrote E. Sidney Hartland in his long and detailed review in the journal *Folk-Lore* (Hartland 1903). It was, he concluded, 'a fine example of sociology's ability to shed light on the study of the genesis of logical operations'. He made only one general remark to the effect that the value of its conclusions depended upon the prevalence of totemism in the earliest stages of society. As a whole, the volume was, in a word, 'Excellent'.

The Division of Labour in Society, Revised and Updated

Célestin's Bouglé's 'Théories récentes sur la division du travail' (1903) looked at first sight like a 'sort of report' on the 'main recent findings' of the social sciences. It was a very broad survey ranging from Karl Marx to Durkheim and from Adam Smith to Spencer, not forgetting many contemporary authors (Schmoller, Veblen, Bauer, Goblot and Tarde). Bouglé was obviously writing from a Durkheimian perspective: the analysis did not deal with the role of individuals in industry, but with the mode of their involvement in society. The 'driving force behind evolution' was social morphology – in other words, the volume and density of the population. The division of labour had positive effects, both on the emancipation of individuals and on the cohesion of society, but only on certain conditions.[25] 'In moral terms', he wrote, '[the division of labour] stimulates both life and progress.'[26]

Certain inflexions reveal, however, the differences between Durkheim and Bouglé. They concern the specific contribution made by Durkheim's disciple. First of all, Bouglé rejects the purely social approach and introduces a historical dimension by identifying the great economic phases of history as follows: domestic economy (self-sufficiency), urban economy (guilds with restricted numbers of customers), national economy (industry and trade, anonymous customers), world economy (the market expands almost to infinity, and the variety of available products is endless). The transition from the domestic economy to the urban economy is characterized by the emergence of professions (or trades), and that from the urban economy to the national economy by the fragmentation of the labour process. This development therefore leads to an expansion of the market, to the growth of the distance between producers and consumers, and to the specialization and fragmentation of labour. Bouglé also believes that high-volume, dense and mobile populations have a beneficial effect in that they are 'the most free' from the tyranny of the collective consciousness; great nations and big towns also 'do most to stimulate' professional innovations.

Bouglé now has to address the questions that everyone – socialist militants in particular – was asking: do the workers own their own tools, and is the division of labour 'the mother of classes' (1925: 78)? Bouglé accepts that specialization may have a 'dispersant effect' on the social organization as a whole, but also makes it clear that he disagrees with the Marxists for at least two reasons. First, he refuses to take into consideration only the technical aspect of the division of labour, and looks also at all its social (economic, political and juridical) aspects – in other words, human relations. Second, class distinctions do not simply reproduce the earlier distinction between trades, as other factors also come into play (religious prestige, political influence and economic power). The growth of the division of labour is, in Bouglé's view, bound up not only with social differentiation, but also with what he calls 'social complication' (ibid.: 79) – that is, individualization and the increase in the number of social circles.

Bouglé attempts, finally, to demonstrate that 'sociology does not preclude psychology' (1925: 92). He is therefore unwilling to let himself become trapped into a theory of evolution that limits the role of intermediary factors such as subjective feelings and desires. He takes the logic of distinction as an example: 'The desire to make oneself stand out and the desire to fit in and to retain or improve one's status are probably the most powerful incitement to consume' (1925: 91). This is what he calls the law of 'social capillarity: the inferior do all they can to look like their superiors, and the superior do all they can to get away from their inferiors' (ibid.).

In his conclusion, Bouglé defends interdisciplinarity, which can, he argues, 'remedy the disadvantages of the division of scientific literature' (1925: 94). He refuses, on the other hand, to take a triumphalist stance (which would imply a desire to 'rule' the other social sciences), and suggests, rather, 'assimilating their conquests'. And while he hopes that sociology can be of some use, provided that its ambitions are modest: it can 'expand our horizons', enlighten minds, and have 'wider influences'. There is therefore no suggestion that sociology should 'replace' ethics (ibid.).

Disagreements?

Despite their basic disagreements with Durkheim, the editors of the *Revue de métaphysique et de morale* agreed with him about one thing: this was the attitude to adopt if one wished to defend the interests of the social sciences: 'Just as materialism can help to advance the physical senses, even though it is untenable in metaphysical terms, so "sociologism", which it would be difficult to defend on logical grounds, can lead to a fanatical belief in sociology, and that can encourage studies pertaining to the phenomena of collective life.' Disagreements, they added, were only to be expected. 'After a while, the rigour of the discipline will cease to appeal to all its disciples: there will be expulsions and desertions. But no system is immune to that law.' Who were the authors thinking of? Durkheim was, they conceded, capable of a 'praiseworthy liberalism', the best example being Célestin Bouglé's recent essay on recent theories of the division of labour: 'There are different tendencies.'

Of all the *Année*'s contributors, it was Gaston Richard who had the least compunction about making public some of his differences with Durkheim. In an article in which he discussed the study of religions, Richard (1902) raised the issue of the ever-present latent conflict between (Christian) theology and objective sociology.[27] He was not obviously opposed to the idea of a comparative science of religions, but he was critical of Durkheim's position: 'The sociologist must be careful not to see the collective consciousness as an entity and to give it a creative potential of its own. Sociological method requires us to see it, rather, as a system of inter-psychological relations and to refrain from saying "we" while denying the importance of "I".' He was telling sociologists that they had to respect certain limits: 'From a religious point of view, it is legitimate for the sociologist to show us the correlation between religions and social types, but he strays away from his own territory when he claims, in the name of science, to take sides against a religion, or against the Christian conception of the religious life.'

Richard also noted that those he called the 'sociologists of Comte's school' had an 'aversion to liberal institutions' and, more generally, to liberalism as an economic and political doctrine. Was this an allusion to Durkheim? Sociology was, in Richard's view, intimately bound up with the idea of consensus and also with that of altruism, which it saw as the criterion for 'normality in political institutions'. He was therefore not surprised to see it taking the side of liberalism's 'happy rival', namely state socialism.

Richard, amongst others, did not want to 'create a gulf' between sociology and the psychological study of social bonds, and he warned his colleagues against the 'chimera of absolute sociality': 'It is in sociology's interest to avoid any compromising solidarity with the enemies of private and public freedoms. No other science comes up against so many prejudices or demands absolute freedom of enquiry to such an extent. And we know only too well what happens to scientific freedom when political and religious freedom are eclipsed.' Richard's *Notions élémentaires de sociologie* was published by Delagrave in 1903. A short book of some 100 pages, it was written with secondary school teachers in mind and was an immediate success: it was reprinted three times in less than a year. While he identifies observation as a sociological method, he distances himself from Durkheim in several respects. First, he took the view that sociology should work from the known to the unknown, and that it should therefore take the study of Western society as its starting point. He then argued, rather like Le Play, that the family is of primordial importance, and rejected the idea that the economy or religion was the matrix of social facts. And when

it came to ethics, he refused to play down the role of the individual consciousness: 'Morality is sociality transformed by a self-conscious personal
reaction.' The book was 'rich in ideas and facts', noted Paul Lapie (2005),
who immediately went on to challenge his colleague's 'personal ideas'. 'He
might tell us why he regards as inadequate more widespread theories such
as historical materialism, or the theory that regards religion as the matrix
for social facts.' And why, he asked, did religious phenomena play such
an important role in his book. 'A book that is full of substance', remarked
Frédéric Rauh, who then objected that it did not place sufficient emphasis
on the originality of the collective consciousness. He added, with a hint of
irony, that 'R[ichard] should be read in conjunction with M. Durkheim'
(Rauh 1904: 119).

   In the same year, 1903, Gaston Richard's *L'Idée d'évolution dans la
nature et dans l'histoire* was published in Alcan's 'Bibliothèque de philosophie contemporaine' series. It was an attack on evolutionist philosophy, and especially that of Spencer, and argued that it should give way
to a so-called 'genetic' method that could be reconciled with the idea of
contingency. The book left the *Année* team puzzled. In his review of it,
Dominique Parodi (1904b) argued that the interpretation of evolutionism was narrow, that the author's perspective placed too much emphasis
on 'contingence', and that the book was confused. He did, on the other
hand, emphasize that it abounded in ideas and contained a wide range of
information. Paul Lapie took the same view, but was astonished to find an
ally in Richard: 'In what is often a confused way, he has some interesting
things to say about sociology: "Sociology is either a social psychology,
or it is nothing." I did not know that he was on our side in the *Année*.'[28]
Richard's position was paradoxical: he was both a dissident and, in certain
respects, an ally. Conditions were ripe for either exclusion or a schism.

17

The Next Generation

'Morality is on the Agenda'

Everyone was talking about morality in debate after debate and publication after publication. There was now, as Émile Boutroux stated at the opening of the École de morale (a section of the École des hautes études sociales), a 'desire to see morality become a living reality and an active force, and not simply a system of abstract truths.' It was a desire for nothing less than a 'moral upheaval'. 'Morality is on the agenda', exclaimed Durkheim, who worried about this inflated speculation over moral issues: every philosopher was trying to establish his own theory of morality.

As Alfred Fouillée demonstrated in his *La France au point de vue moral*, there was undeniably a 'malaise' and it had to do, in Durkheim's view, with a 'disintegration of our moral beliefs': 'The goals to which our fathers were attached have lost their authority and appeal', and this had created 'a real void in our moral consciousness'. Durkheim accepted Fouillée's diagnosis, but was somewhat sceptical about his proposed remedy (legal proceedings), and asked: what 'new ideal are we . . . to attach to the hearts of the children?' (Durkheim 1980[1901b]: 407, 408).

France was in the midst of what Durkheim called a 'revolution in pedagogy': the great parliamentary inquiry of 1899 had allowed everyone to express their views. The entire organization of secondary education – the role of Latin and Greek, length of studies, discipline, organization of the *baccalauréat* – had been called into question. As the historian Charles Victor Langlois noted (1900: 382), this 'crisis' (which led to the reforms of 1902) reflected the declining popularity of state education and the growing prosperity of the private 'congregational' schools. Paul Lapie was also worried by the 'growing competition' from the congregationists: the number of children attending state lycées and colleges had fallen from 98,900 in 1887 to 86,300 in 1898 (Lapie 1901: 798). In his view, this called for an immediate response, and his *Pour la raison* (1902b) was an attempt to defend republican morality.[1]

Secularism [*laïcité*] was now the great issue of the day: 'We decided to give children in our state-sponsored schools a purely secular moral education' (Durkheim 1961[1925]: 3). This was a difficult and complex task, as religion and morality have always been closely associated throughout the history of all civilizations. The question was hotly debated in Parliament and on village squares as the schoolteacher and the priest came into conflict. On one side, there were those Bouglé called 'the supporters of religious beliefs', who denied that a neutral educational system could have any real effect on minds; on the other were the 'supporters of secular education', led by Ferdinand Buisson, who were trying to find 'a sort a substitute for religiously based morality by teaching morality in the schools'.

The great 'masters' of the Sorbonne – Octave Gréard, Louis Liard and Ernest Lavisse – shared the same concerns. There was, in other words, an 'intellectual movement' – 'one of the most interesting of our times', according to Georges Cantecor (1904: 225) – that wanted to develop 'a new, and "scientific" form of morality'. Victor Brochard, professor of the history of ancient philosophy at the Sorbonne, summed it up well: 'In our day, an attempt is being made on all sides and in all countries to establish a moral doctrine that is both intellectually satisfying and scientific in nature (1901: 12). Contrasting 'traditional' morality with 'modern' morality, he defended the idea of a 'rational morality' that must, he argued, be 'divorced from theology'. He wanted 'to bring morality down from heaven to earth and, in a sense, to secularize it. That which belongs to religion should be left to religion.' S. Jankélévitch (1905), who had recently begun to contribute to the *Revue de synthèse historique*, reached the same conclusion. 'We are now witnessing the completion of the positivist programme', he observed in his description of this attempt to apply to social facts the research method that had been applied to the study of physical-mathematic, and then chemical and biological, phenomena. He cited the 'efforts' of Durkheim and his students as one example. Although he did not reject the view that 'any moral fact is a social fact', he did worry about the dangers implicit in a science of morals: it could lead to 'an almost absolute social and moral relativism'. It would be preferable, in his view, to turn to what some called 'moral experience', which was, by definition, deeply individual. Far from being unanimously accepted, the idea of a 'purely rationalist moral education' gave rise to 'contradictory passions'.

Lévy-Bruhl on Morality and the Science of Morals

If there was one book that gave rise to what Jankélévitch called 'some lively debates', it was Lucien Lévy-Bruhl's *La Morale et la science des moeurs* [*Morality and the Science of Morals*], which was published by Alcan in 1903. Lévy-Bruhl was close to Durkheim, now his colleague at the Sorbonne, and had, when it was published, praised the *Rules of Sociological Method*: 'Being in complete agreement with the spirit of this work, I am happy to acknowledge here my debt to its author' (Lévy-Bruhl 1903: 14 n1). While he was, according to Mauss (1997[1939]),[2] still 'more of a philosopher than a sociologist', the *Année* group was more than willing to accept that Lévy-Bruhl was 'in agreement' with Durkheim on all the essential methodological issues (Fauconnet 1904: 83). His book was part of a campaign to storm 'a citadel', and the siege was under way. His decision to support sociology, and Durkheimian sociology in particular, was a major event.

Lévy-Bruhl saw sociology as the only truly rational way of speculating about moral issues. The main ideas expounded in his book were as follows: the traditional conception of moral science is obsolete; moral facts are social facts, and an object for scientific study; the establishment of a moral science will lead to that of a rational art capable of governing moral behaviour. Progress in the direction of such a science would be slow and difficult because 'morality is marked by religious characteristics that make it immune to truly scientific thought, or, in other words, free thought'. It was 'masked by a veneer of beliefs and symbols' that made it 'something sacred'; it was therefore difficult to discuss it in scientific and positive terms. Lévy-Bruhl attacked these prejudices, demonstrating that what are now, like biology, established sciences had to fight the same prejudices in order to define nature as an objective reality that is subject to laws.

The problematic adopted by Lévy-Bruhl is sociological: a society has a morality in the same way that it has a language, a religion and a legal system. Morality is a social institution and a manifestation of collective life; the task of sociology is to study it, and to take a society's system of morals, and the practices associated with it, as an object of study. Lévy-Bruhl also contends that morality is a rational art: as it develops, the science of morals will become able to modify moral reality: the reforms it is proposing are not those of utopians, and the caution it urges to adopt is not the caution of conservatives.

For minds prepared to accept 'something new', Lévy-Bruhl's book was a 'precious guide' that could allow them to 'contract certain mental habits', and to apply them to, for example relativism. Fauconnet praised it highly, and 'fully agreed with the ideas that are its raison d'être'. Lévy-Bruhl's book was, he concluded, 'a work of propaganda and vulgarization in the best sense of the word' (Fauconnet 1904: 82).

Durkheim and Lévy-Bruhl were thinking along similar lines, and Durkheim said so himself when he reviewed his colleague's book in the *Année sociologique*: 'One will find in this work, analysed and demonstrated with rare dialectical vigour, the very idea that is basic to everything that we are doing here, namely that there is a positive science of moral acts, and that it is on this science that the moralists' practical speculations must rely' (1980[1904c]: 127). Durkheim agreed with Lévy-Bruhl that 'theoretical' morality, as opposed to practical morality, is not a science of social facts; at best, it 'echoes the time' (ibid.: 128) and is a reflection of practices. The moral conscience is, in other words, 'a product of history', and there is no such thing as a natural morality grounded in the human constitution as such, but only 'the diverse moral standards that have been effectively in use in different societies'. The goal of a *science of customs* is to identify 'moral institutions' (maxims, beliefs, customs, and so on), to discover what they consist in and what factors determine them. And given that 'the conditions on which each moral standard depends at each moment in time are social' (ibid.: 129), it is obvious that the science of customs is part of sociology. As he puts it in his review of the British anthropologist Edward Westermarck's *Origins and Development of the Moral Ideas*, Durkheim's intention is to 'study scientifically' moral facts 'in the light of history and comparative ethnography' (1980[1907e]: 150).

Like Lévy-Bruhl, Durkheim is convinced that this science is the only thing that can provide 'a rational basis for practical applications'. And yet, 'science arrives only very slowly at results that are always partial' (1980[1904c]: 128). Like the clinician, the scientist 'decides upon the course of action that in the present state of his knowledge appears most reasonable. Rational moral art will do likewise.' Neither Kantian nor utilitarian theories can show us 'the goals to which one must aspire, the path that one must follow in the concrete circumstances of life' (ibid.: 130). Durkheim uses the examples of divorce and socialism to illustrate this indeterminacy. As it is impossible to know what to do about such things, the theorist must work by trial and error: there is no perfect method. Durkheim is well aware that Lévy-Bruhl's book will not satisfy 'spirits devoted to the absolute, for whom tentative assurances, relative to science, cannot suffice'. Lévy-Bruhl's book enjoyed some success, as a second edition appeared in 1904, followed by a new revised and expanded edition, with a new preface, in 1907. The relationship between Lévy-Bruhl and Durkheim and his associates was to be complex, being based on a combination of complicity and critical distance.[3]

Lectures on Moral Education

Morality was a central topic in the lectures Durkheim was giving at the Sorbonne on both pedagogy and sociology. He was not, it has to be noted, the only person to discuss morality in the Sorbonne's lecture theatres. Gabriel Séailles was giving lectures on 'the moral ideal', and Victor Brochard on the 'ethics of the Epicureans and Stoics', while Lucien Lévy-Bruhl had recently published his *La Morale et la science des moeurs*. And one of the set topics for degree and *agrégation* students in 1902 was 'morality and politics'. As can be seen from their teaching and research, several of the *Année sociologique*'s contributors shared the same concern. In Bordeaux, Gaston Richard was teaching a course on 'the moral doctrine of Auguste Comte'. In Toulouse, Célestin Bouglé, who was not too sure how to go about 'teaching morality', was conducting a survey of second-, third- and fourth-year students in *lycées* and colleges.

Moral education was the subject of the lectures Durkheim gave on taking up his position at the Sorbonne. They were a continuation of those he had given in Bordeaux. Judging by the few bibliographical references to be found in his lecture notes, he probably first lectured on this topic in 1898–9 (Besnard 1993). These lectures, which were written out in full, were in a sense a draft for the lectures he later gave in Paris. As Fauconnet notes, the course of moral education was an exercise in popularization (in Durkheim 1956). Durkheim's audience consisted of primary schoolteachers, and the lectures were a way of translating the findings of the new science of morals so as to make them comprehensible to young minds.

The lectures were also what Bouglé described as a way of helping the secular school system's new teachers to 'perform their duty to the nation'. The approach adopted by the sociologist-pedagogue was not just inductive or descriptive; as Mauss noted (1969[1925]), it was also 'normative' and designed to 'give young teachers a better understanding of [pedagogic] practice, to help them apply their strengths more effectively and to hasten the reforms he hinted at so gently'. In his lectures, Durkheim demonstrated that so-called civilized societies attached greater importance to justice, and spoke of the rights of the individual and of the sacred nature of the 'human personality'. He also defended the idea that there had to be a move towards 'purely rational education' and 'entirely rational moral education'. There must, in other words, be no 'references to any principles borrowed from revealed religions'. This was not just a matter of personal conviction. It was also a contemporary issue: new times required a new morality because individual liberation was both a precondition for the liberation of individual thought and its corollary.

Durkheim was aware that moral issues had 'the unfortunate effect of arousing passionate argument' and therefore tried to introduce a 'modicum of scientific attitude' in order to avoid 'arousing passions and . . . giving offence to legitimate feelings' (1961[1925] 3, 4). (Moral) education was primarily a thing or fact. Durkheim was aware that describing morality as a 'natural phenomenon' was blasphemous and might cause a scandal

Durkheim's lectures on moral education were in two parts, one dealing with 'theoretical morality' (duty, good and autonomy), and the other (which was symmetrical with the first) divided into three sections devoted, respectively, to the spirit of discipline, the spirit of abnegation and the autonomy of the will. The end of one lecture almost always overlapped with the beginning of the next, with Durkheim summing up or rephrasing what he had already said for the benefit of his audience. He often used concrete examples. For Durkheim, lecturing on pedagogy was a form of research that fed into his work on sociology. Sociology, as Maurice Halbwachs (1977[1938]) puts it, was a form of pedagogy: education was a form of socialization, or 'the most powerful instrument a society possesses for fashioning its members in its own image' (ibid.: xii). Pedagogy was not restricted to the pupil–teacher relationship; it was part of a specific social environment: namely, the school environment that has such a profound influence on children.

There had long been two conflicting views as to what pedagogy meant. One was that education was 'systematic training' by the imposition of an external discipline; the other that it was 'leading children out' by inspiring individuals to create their own lives. The schoolmen and their Jesuit successors took the former view: education was primarily a matter of turning the child into an 'obedient subject'. Both Rabelais and Montaigne had rebelled against this conception of education, which placed the emphasis on memory, emulation and discipline, in the name of liberty and life. At the beginning of the twentieth century, the battle between 'authoritarian pedagogy' and 'liberal education' was still raging.

The sociology Durkheim defended may seem to be hostile to the 'desire for freedom' that was so obvious in educational circles. The idea of reducing education to the socialization of the next generation was alarming to believers in liberalism and individualism. But, according to Durkheim, the 'three essential elements of morality' were the spirit of discipline, attachment to social groups and the autonomy of the will.

Discipline

The idea of discipline is, not surprisingly, of great importance to Durkheim. He associates it with the moderation of desires and self-control which, from his point of view, relate to a whole set of values characteristic of civilization (which he contrasts with primitive humanity). How, he asks, can the child's desires and passions be held in check? External checks can be opposed to the child's desires and passions, and we can accustom him to 'self-control and moderation', and make him feel that 'he should not yield without reservation to his inclinations' and that 'there is always a limit beyond which he ought not to go' (Durkheim 1961[1925]: 142). He identifies two ways of accustoming children to regularity: force of habit and suggestion. But education must not, he insists, become a form of servitude; on the contrary, the freedom of the child must be protected from the omnipotence of education (ibid.: 143).

For anyone concerned with moral education, there is more than one reason for attaching such importance to schooling: school is the best place and instrument for inculcating the spirit of discipline. Durkheim was a serious-minded man who loved work and regular habits. He was a 'scientist', but, behind the scientist, there was always the 'moralist' or, as Célestin Bouglé put it, 'a man for whom duty was the ultimate reality'. He was also a man of great generosity with a sense of duty and of his responsibilities to others. As is very obvious from his lectures, he would not tolerate either laziness or irregularity, and he was quick to criticize the undisciplined and the anarchistic. His emphasis on work and effort does not mean that games and relaxation are unimportant – Durkheim concedes (1961[1925]: 273) that 'we cannot work all the time' – provided that our leisure activities are neither crude nor purely material. He is not suggesting that a school should be a military camp, or that a class should be a regiment. He recommends firmness, but not harshness or cruelty. At this point, the sociologist's personal views overlap with his theoretical (and political) views.[4]

'How do we go about it?' asks Durkheim (1961[1925]: 21). He contrasts the introspective approach, which is very limited and too subjective, with an objective approach based upon observation, which demonstrates that the one thing that all moral actions have in common is that they conform to rules or norms: 'there are clear-cut and specific ways of acting required of us . . . Law and the mores prescribe our conduct' (ibid.: 26). The rules prescribing chastity and prohibiting incest, for instance, are concrete forms that determine social behaviours ranging from relations between husband and wife to the way parents behave towards their children, and relations between things and people.

It is therefore obvious to Durkheim that morality is based upon habit. Morality is synonymous with regularity. The idea of regularity is also closely associated with that of *authority*: 'all rules command' (1961[1925]: 30). Durkheim then goes on: 'The moral rule consists entirely in a commandment and in nothing else . . . when it speaks, all other considerations must be subordinated' (ibid.: 30–1). The preference for regularity and respect for authority are one and the same, or aspects of the more complex state of mind that he describes as 'the spirit of discipline'. Durkheim regards discipline as a salutary constraint that helps men to develop a taste for measure and moderation and a sense of 'social limits' that protects them from 'the disease of the infinite'.

Lack of regulation, the unleashing of the passions and disenchantment are all part of the same sequence; 'an inability to restrict one's self with determinate limits' inevitably leads to sadness, discouragement and torment, and it is also a 'sign of disease' (1961[1925]: 38). Too much is too much, even when it comes to art, which must never come to play an excessive part in the life of a people; if it does, 'its days are numbered' (ibid.: 39). It is all a question of balance. The same obviously applies to children, who can, according to Durkheim, be taught to moderate their desires and limit their appetites as soon as they are old enough to attend school. Self-control may take different forms in different countries, different eras and different age cohorts, but it is always 'the condition of happiness and moral health' (ibid.: 44). Durkheim realizes that this thesis will meet with some objections, and his answer to his detractors is that the taste for moderation that he is recommending does not imply resignation or immobility, and that he is not demanding blind or slavish obedience. 'Rules' and 'liberty' are not antithetical terms; on the contrary, 'liberty is the fruit of regulation' (ibid.: 54).

The spirit of association and attachment to the group

The issues at stake in education are, in Durkheim's view, all the higher in that, in modern societies, there is no longer any society mediating between the family and the state: the provinces, *communes* and corporations or guilds of old have all been abolished, or exist only in fragmentary form. France therefore has a 'superstitious horror' of all particularist associations, and prioritizes the defence of the republic against all forms of communitarianism: 'the weakness of the spirit of association is one of the characteristics of our national temperament. We have a marked inclination towards a fierce individualism' (1961[1925]: 234). In Durkheim's view, 'this state of affairs constitutes a serious crisis' (ibid.: 233). What can be done to remedy it? In *The Division of Labour in Society*, Durkheim argued that the solution lay in professional corporations. Speaking to his students at the Sorbonne, he takes a more pessimistic view: reviving corporations is no easy undertaking because is implies that the spirit of association must be revived. He now argues that education may provide the solution: 'We have through the school the means of training the child in a collective life different from home life' (1973[1925]: 235).

From a sociological point of view, the second element in morality seems obvious, as attachment to the group is indeed the very basis of social life. The goals that individuals pursue are obviously personal, but Durkheim insists that they are also impersonal or supra-individual. He completely rejects utilitarianism: individuals do not belong to a group or to society because it is in their interest to do so or because they get something in return, and society is not just an aggregate of individuals. Indeed, the opposite is true: every society has its own 'collective personality' as well as a collective consciousness.

Durkheim's intention is simply to demonstrate that the individual is, to a large extent, a product of society: language is a social phenomenon, religion is a social institution, science is a product of society, and the sources of morality are to be found in society. There can be no civilization without society. Without society, man would 'fall to the level of animals' (1961[1925]: 72). 'Family, fatherland and humanity': that is what we are. For Durkheim, commitment to the group is 'the duty par excellence', and he is highly critical of absolute egoism, which he regards as a feature of 'calamitous times' (ibid.: 72).

What about love of the fatherland or nationalism? For Durkheim, 'the school is the only moral agent through which the child is able systematically to learn to know and love his country' (1961[1925]: 79). Should cosmopolitanism therefore be subordinated to nationalism? Yes and no. 'Yes' because human goals are more elevated than national goals, and 'no' because 'mankind' is not 'a social organism having its own consciousness, its own individuality, and its own organization'. In comparison, 'the state is actually the most highly organized form of human organization in existence' (ibid.: 76). This situation is unlikely to change: 'There is nothing to justify the supposition that there will ever emerge a state embracing the whole of humanity.' The only way to overcome this contradiction is for the state to commit itself 'to the goal of realizing among its own people the general interests of humanity' (ibid.: 77).

There is therefore such a thing as a 'good' nationalism, and it is centrifugal, peaceful and concerned with the domains of science, art and industry. It rejects war and aggression, and promotes peace and cooperation between peoples. Devotion, the spirit of sacrifice and solidarity are not, as Renan would have it, absurdities. They are grounded in our nature: 'We have been able to find altruism in the child beginning with the first years of his life' (1961[1925]: 222). Durkheim asks how the child can be encouraged to develop these altruistic and disinterested feelings, and how we can 'give the child the clearest possible idea of the social groups to which he belongs' (ibid.: 228). He concludes that the best way to develop this 'social sense' is to make use of the school environment, as it brings together groups of young people of the same age: 'Common ideas, common feelings, common responsibilities – we have enough here to nurture the collective life of the class' (ibid.: 246).[5] The discipline of history can obviously be pressed into service here: it can give the child an adequate idea of what society is and of how it relates to individuals, and bring him into direct contact with its 'collective spirit' (ibid.: 278).

Morality consists, according to Durkheim (1961[1925]: 96), in a combination of an imperative law and a splendid ideal to which we aspire (group loyalty, and the spirit of devotion and sacrifice). The two facets of morality are closely linked, and they are also the twin axes of the sociological analysis of suicide, namely regulation and integration. Depending on where the emphasis falls, it is, Durkheim suggests (ibid.: 100), possible to identify two different temperaments or types: on the one hand, the disciplined man of 'substantial intellect and strong will' and, on the other, the sociable man who likes to attach himself and to devote himself. This distinction makes it possible to identify two types of society, one working on the basis of rules and order, and the other on the basis of the spirit of sacrifice and devotion.

The autonomy of the will

The discipline that applies rules and administers punishment is not the only element in morality; there is therefore 'faith in a common ideal', such as the new ideas of justice and solidarity: 'It is necessary to involve individuals in the pursuit of great collective ideals to which they can devote themselves' (1961[1925]: 102), and Durkheim is convinced that the school can 'bring children to cherish them' (ibid.: 103). But that in itself is not enough: 'We must have knowledge, as clear and complete an awareness as possible of the reasons for our conduct. This consciousness confers on our behaviour the autonomy that the public consciousness from now on requires of every genuinely and completely moral being' (ibid.: 120). Despite its importance, Durkheim in fact spends very little time discussing the 'autonomy of the will', whose roots lie in knowledge and in the 'science of morals'.

The third element in morality is therefore 'knowledge of morality' and this is, for Durkheim, the differential characteristic of secular morality. The role of the educator is not to preach or inculcate morality, but to explain it. The (secular) teacher must be aware of his mission: his task is 'not to repeat to [the child] . . . a certain number of very general maxims valid eternally and everywhere; but to make him understand his country and his times, to make him feel his responsibilities . . . and thus to prepare him to take his part in the collective tasks awaiting him' (1961[1925]: 123–4). Morality therefore cannot be taught as a separate subject, or at more or less short intervals during the week: 'it is implicated in every moment': 'It must be mingled in the whole of school life' (ibid.: 125).

Even such specialized subjects as the sciences or art can have a 'moral interest' and play a role in moral education. If we wish to combat the 'oversimplified' rationalism that is so typical of French culture, children must be given a sense of the complexity of things. This can only be done by teaching elementary science (and especially the physical and natural sciences). Art too can be an instrument of moral education, but matters are more complicated here, as 'the domain of art is not that of reality' (1961[1925]: 269). Art belongs to the realm of the imagination and play.[6]

Durkheim then goes further and argues that children must be taught *things*. He is very critical of the academic tradition that places the emphasis on the acquisition of an encyclopedic culture, and places the emphasis on the inculcation of a number of basic skills, or, to be more accurate, key ideas, such as *our* idea of the physical world, *our* idea of life, and *our* idea of man. These are, he adds, *collective ideas* that have evolved over time and that are now heavily dependent on developments in the physical and moral sciences.

This is far removed from the humanist conception which, like Montaigne, defends the (purely formal) virtues of a literary education. This is neither the first nor the last of Durkheim's attacks on the arts.

A Role for Magic

The seventh volume of the *Année soiologique* appeared in 1904, and contained only one article: Mauss and Hubert's 'General theory of magic', which ran to almost 150 pages. It had been expected for some time. Ever since he had been appointed to the École pratique, Mauss had devoted one of his lecture courses to magic in Melanesia. 'What is magic? And what is religion?' he asked himself. His goal was to study the 'human origins' of religion.[7] In 1903–4, his lecture course was 'The general theory of magic and its relationship with religion'; in 1904–5, it was 'Analysis of basic notions about magic'. In 1905, he published a long essay, 'The origin of magical powers in Australian societies', in the *Annuaire de l'École pratique des hautes études*. For his part, in the same year's *Annuaire*, Hubert published a study, 'The representation of time in religion and magic'. 'General theory of magic' was the product of close collaboration between the two friends, who still worked under the watchful eye of Durkheim. Hubert wished that they had been able to collaborate 'more closely', and even criticized Durkheim for interfering with his nephew's work: 'I believe that our collaborative work would have been better without Durkheim's revisions, as they seem to me to exaggerate the flaws in his own work.'[8]

The approach adopted by Hubert and Mauss was similar to that recommended in their essay on sacrifice: critical study of documents, comparisons between a limited number of societies, and parallels between magic in primitive societies and differentiated societies. The essay is in three parts: a definition of magic; elements of magic; analysis and explanation. The central issue is that of the distinction between magical rites and religious rituals, given that both are a matter of belief and opinion. Hubert and Mauss use the social conditions in which the rituals are performed as a criterion (agents, places, organization); they also demonstrate that magic, which has something in common with science and technologies, is primarily 'an art of doing things', a practical art, or, to be more accurate, a 'practical idea'. The essay is a contribution to the study of collective representations as well as to the sociology of religion: 'We shall find magical origins in those early forms of collective representations which have since become the basis for individual understanding' (Mauss 2001[1904]: 178). The authors identify the central notion of a 'force-milieu', which they refer to as *mana*. The notion, which could also be observed in Amerindian societies, had been brought to their attention by Dr Codrington's *The Melanesians, Their Anthropology and Folklore* (1890). *Mana* belongs to the same realm as the sacred: '*mana* is power, *par excellence*, the genuine effectiveness of things' (ibid.: 137). In his 'Origine des pouvoirs magiques', Mauss had clearly demonstrated that the special power or *mana* of the magician can exist only on the basis of a social consensus – in other words, public opinion. Everything works on the basis of collective belief. Mauss's study is an implicit critique of the theses of Frazer, who makes the mistake of establishing a sharp contrast between magic and religion, and of regarding the former as the 'first form of human thought' and 'the first stage in human evolution', the others being religion and science. In their essay, Hubert and Mauss make a renewed attack, with a close analysis of the work of the British school of anthropology in general and Frazer in particular. In the second edition of his *Golden Bough* – the 'Bible of the anthropological school' – Frazer reduces magical practice to the sophisms that come naturally to the human mind: association of ideas, analogical reasoning, and mistaken applications of the principle of causality. His thesis is, argue Hubert and Mauss, 'too intellectualist'. They also criticize him for overlooking the ritual dimension of religious and magical phenomena (Hubert 1901).

For their young colleague Paul Huvelin, Mauss and Hubert's article marked a 'decisive stage' in the study of magic, which was entering its 'scientific stage' (Huvelin 1907: 1). While no one denied the existence of the notion of *mana*, its use was to become the subject of much controversy. Huvelin, for example, criticized Hubert and Mauss for giving their notion of *mana* a 'universal dimension'. Robert Hertz, another young contributor to the *Année*, remarked that the work of Hubert and Mauss went beyond the framework of the history of religions, and made 'a truly positive and experimental contribution to a new theory of knowledge' by showing that concepts were 'collective representations' (Hertz 1909: 219). Always attentive to the importance of the *Année*'s potential contribution, Hartland, writing in the journal *Folk-Lore* was just as enthusiastic, though he was sorry that the authors had taken no note of his own position. He was easily convinced by Mauss and Hubert's well-constructed argument: 'The rationalism of primitive man is incredible' (Hartland 1904).

It comes as no surprise to see that rationalist philosophers reacted badly to the essay and saw Hubert and Mauss's analysis as 'an inverted counterpart to Kant's argument': 'In this theory, the role that collective Unreason plays with respect to individual experiences is the role that [Kant] ascribed to an impersonal Reason' (Belot 1905). Writing in the *Revue philosophique*, Gustave Belot mocked the author's 'collective mind', and claimed that, when they worked together, 'they probably both argue their case less successfully than they would have done if they had worked on their own'. Belot emphasized the quality of their research (a rich collection of facts and solid documentation), but added that their analysis left 'a rather confused impression' (Belot 1905). Reviewing the ninth volume of the *Année* as a whole, the *Revue de métaphysique et de morale* was once more impressed by the quality of the reviews: 'Praise would be superfluous, and it goes without saying that they are an essential tool for anyone who is interested in the problems studied here.' The reviewer was not, however, convinced by Hubert and Mauss's analysis: 'We will not criticize Mauss and Hubert for defending their thesis, but we do criticize them for defining it so badly. Their study is very rich but obscure.'[9]

An Essential Tool

The name of Claude Maître did not figure in the list of contributors to the seventh volume of the *Année*, while those of Paul Hourtiq and Charles Lalo were added, but there were few other changes. Both Hourtiq and Lalo had been taught by Durkheim, and were identified with the 'Bordeaux school'. Lalo had just become a philosophy teacher in Bayonne, and helped Mauss with the 'aesthetic sociology' rubric, while Hourticq helped Durkheim and Bouglé with 'political organization'. The name of Marcel Foucault also appeared for the second and last time. Foucault had studied with Durkheim in Bordeaux and his doctoral thesis, on 'Psycho-physics' (1906), had recently been published by Alcan in the Bibliothèque de philosophie contemporaine series, which only published work by Durkheim and his *Année* associates. In 1906, Foucault was appointed *maître de conférences* at Montpellier University. He worked with Gaston Richard on the 'methodology of moral statistics' rubric.

'Religious sociology' was once more the largest section, with more than 170 pages (33 per cent of the 'analyses' section). 'The two of us have more or less taken over the whole of the *Année*', Mauss wrote to his friend Hubert.[10] There was only one small change of any note: a new rubric simply entitled 'education' was added to the 'aesthetics', 'linguistics' and 'technology' rubrics in the 'miscellaneous' section. It was edited by Durkheim (who reviewed his own lecture-article, 'Pedagogy and sociology'). The reviews once more attracted praise: the *Revue de métaphysique et de morale* called it 'work that needed to be done'. Henri Berr, writing in the *Revue de synthèse historique*, described it as 'a precious collection of information' for the journal's readers, and 'a wonderful way of making progress' for its editors. The range of books reviewed was once more wide and covered a number of languages: English (Boas, Lang, Ross, Small and Ward), Italian (Bosco and Rossi), and German (Simmel and Sombart). Books on philosophy were also reviewed. Mauss, for instance, devoted a long and detailed review to William James's *Varieties of Religious Experience*. The journal's critical spirit was as lively as ever, as its enemies found out to their cost. Bouglé sneered at the 'generalities' to be found in both the *Annales de l'Institut international de sociologie* and the American sociologist Lester Ward's new *Pure Sociology*. While Durkheim was fascinated by Georg Simmel's 'subtlety of mind', he made no secret of his irritation with his German colleague's methodological weaknesses (no proof, arguments consisting of only a few words) and conceptual vagueness: 'The concepts he uses . . . become excessively elastic as he develops his argument' (Durkheim 1969[1904b]: 475–6; 1904a: 477–8).

Unlike his contributors, who specialized in one or another domain of sociology or the social sciences, Durkheim acted as a general coordinator rather than as a specialist, and reviewed books on moral and political sociology, criminal sociology and moral statistics, and social morphology. The issues that concerned him were morality, law and various forms of social organization. He was harsh as he had always been on books that made no critical analysis of their source material and made 'hasty' analyses of institutions such as exogamy: 'Comparative sociology does not just mean putting together all sorts of raw materials in something of a hurry' (Durkheim 1975[1904d]: 147).

Durkheim took an interest in anything to do with kinship, the family, marriage and relations between men and women, and wrote several reviews discussing the theses of various authors at some length. What, he asked, are we to think of Charles Letourneau's *La Condition des femmes*, and of the claim that 'the present mental inferiority of women' was the product of history and, more specifically, of 'men's age-old enslavement of women'? (1975[1904c]: 147) He was somewhat sceptical about his colleague's analysis and speculated as to what the future held in store for women. Letourneau wanted to see greater equality between the sexes, in education, marriage, the family and society in general. 'Will equal rights be enough to do away ipso facto with a hereditary inequality?' asked Durkheim. He answered his own question: 'The problem seems to me to be more complex. Legal equality must result from mental evolution rather than coming before it' (ibid.).

He was also interested in marriage and, more specifically, the nuptial ceremony. Durkheim was not displeased to find in Gaudefroy-Demombynes's study of nuptial ceremonies in Algeria a thesis that he had defended on a number of occasions: the religious nature of sexual relations, even in relatively advanced peoples (Durkheim 1975[1904c]). Max Bauer's study of sexual life in ancient Germany was of interest to him for more than one reason, as the author dealt with the central issue of the origins of the sentiments of modesty and mutual continence that still dominated what Durkheim called 'sexual relations' (1980[1904a]: 301). Durkheim also discusses Bauer's thesis that the radical separation between free love and love within marriage coincided with the bourgeoisie's entry into political life: 'It is quite certain that in order to protect their wives and daughters, the bourgeoisie felt the need to control debauchery. From there came the institution of the house of prostitution.' Prostitution, in other words, 'constituted a truly public service' (ibid.: 302).

A paradox in Glasson's *Histoire du droit et des institutions de la France à l'époque monarchique* also caught Durkheim's attention. Because the moral importance of women's role grew as domestic life developed, the matrimonial bond became more constricting and the family became more concentrated, and this led to 'the legal subordination of the wife to her husband (1980[1904b]: 209). Turning to modern society, Durkheim notes that the modern conception of the family is characterized not only by the preponderant position of wedlock and the conjugal association, but also by something that is very new, namely the 'progressive secularization of the marriage ceremony'. On the one hand, sexual relations are still religious; on the other, the secularization of the marriage contract is institutionalized (ibid.: 210).

Henri Berr: A Critical Eye

Was religion the matrix for social facts? The amount of space taken up by the *Année*'s 'religious sociology' section is an indication of how important religion was to Durkheim and his associates. Mauss's lectures at the École pratique were devoted to the elementary forms of prayer and to relations between the family and religion and then turned to the subject of magic. In an explanatory note in the *Année*, Mauss (1969[1904a]: 94) described religions as 'religious phenomena that are, to a greater or lesser extent, elaborated into the systems that we call religions, which have a historically defined existence within specific periods and specific human groups'. As an advocate of a 'strict inductive discipline', he believed that it was possible to 'identify increasingly elementary religious phenomena'. Sociology needed history and ethnography because, he argued in conclusion, an understanding of the past would lead to 'a better understanding of the present that would help humanity become aware of where its future lay'.

Henri Hubert, Mauss's co-editor on the 'religious sociology' section, and Isidore Lévy now embarked upon the major project of translating into French Pierre-Daniel Chantepie de la Saussaye's handbook on the history of religions. Chantepie de la Saussaye was an eminent Dutch specialist, and the translation of his book was a major event: the decision to do so meant taking the side of the scientists. Henri Hubert contributed an introduction of some 40 pages. It was, exclaimed Mauss, a 'real manifesto . . . a persuasive defence of sociology's right to study all manifestations of religious life' (Mauss 1904: 177).[11] Jean Réville, director of studies at the École pratique, had the same reaction: 'This Introduction is a manifesto, couched in very moderate terms, on behalf of the new school to which M. Hubert belongs, and which was founded in France by M. Durkheim' (Réville 1905: 75).[12] In Hubert's view, sociology was, it is true, no longer the 'humble servant of theology': it was a science and was therefore justified in ridding its domain of 'the unknowable' so as to 'demonstrate, insofar as possible, that religious practices and beliefs are products of human dreams'. Religious facts were the object of sociology, and there were two kinds of religious facts: movements (rituals) and representations (notions about gods and demons, purity and impurity, myths and dogmas).

Hubert's perspective is clearly Durkheimian. Rejecting any notion of individualism, he regards religious facts as social facts, and emphasizes the influence of the system of human relations into which individuals are inserted: 'Thought is the product not of some notion of an individual personality, but of the feeling of being part of a group. The individual is self-conscious only to the extent that he relates to his fellows. It is not the individual who projects his soul into society; it is society that gives him his soul.' The collective nature of religious phenomena is obvious: laws and beliefs have the power to constrain, crowd behaviour does exist, and religious societies are socially organized into hierarchies. It is the notion of the sacred that dominates religious belief, and it does so to a greater extent than anything else. It is the idea of the sacred that dominates religious belief, which Hubert defines as 'the administration of the sacred' (Hubert 1904a: xlvii). Hubert's introduction was published just as the seventh volume of the *Année sociologique* became available in bookshops.

Some found that the combination of a long 'Introduction' from Hubert and a solid analysis of magic from Hubert and Mauss was too much. In a lengthy article entitled 'Developments in the sociology of religion', Henri Berr (1906), editor of the *Revue de synthèse historique*, congratulated Mauss and Hubert on 'the precision and cautious meticulousness' of their analysis of magic, but expressed annoyance at the way contributors to the *Année* submitted to a 'strict discipline, even though they freely submit to it', and at their total abnegation (indeed, 'some of the most gifted amongst them have so far published nothing').[13] What really irritated him was not so much the huge importance the 'school' accorded to the sociology of religion, as its 'prejudice and obsession with doctrine': 'This unified doctrine is both their strength and their weakness'. When the journal claimed that both knowledge and religion were social phenomena, it was going too far! The 'real problem' or 'mistake' was to believe that, like the notion of the sacred, 'representations have always been collective'. Berr therefore criticizes Durkheim and his associates Hubert and Mauss for the 'sociological prejudice' that leads them 'at times, to force the sociological interpretation'. Their mistake or error was to 'see the social everywhere': 'Worse still, they do not make any distinction between the human and collective, and the social.' Berr also criticizes them for going back to the beginning, ascribing too much importance to totemism and giving that phenomenon a universal import. 'Even in the beginning, everything that is religious is not necessarily social' (Berr 1906: 43).

Paradoxical as it may seem, Berr both claims that 'the Durkheim school is right, and more than right, to see society as a reality *sui generis*' and also asks them to make allowances for individual initiative and imitation. The allusion to Gabriel Tarde is transparent. Berr appears, then, to be arguing the case for both a social psychology (the study of needs and their representations) and sociology (a comparative study of institutions), and to be trying to strike a balance between Durkheim and Tarde. He also suggests that historical facts belong to one of two distinct domains: that of contingency (of the variable or the unpredictable, which are individual in origin), and that of necessity (which is the domain of sociology). Berr recommends Durkheim's method when it comes to the domain of necessity, but criticizes him for claiming that individuals have no historical role. When Berr published his *La Synthèse en histoire*, Durkheim reviewed it for the *Année* and protested: 'We have acknowledged that historical personages have been factors in history.' Their influence should not, however, be overstated: 'The individual himself is a product of necessary causes' (Durkheim 1980[1913a]: 89)

Henri Berr sent Mauss the issue of the *Revue de synthèse* in which he said what he thought of his work with Mauss: 'The praise greatly outweighs the reservations. When you read it, you will see how much I value your contributions.'[14] The *Revue de synthèse historique* in fact distanced itself from the Durkheim group and, in keeping with its eclectic spirit, gave more coverage to its competitors, such as Worms and contributors to the *Revue internationale de sociologie*, and to Le Play's followers. Célestin Bouglé then took a swipe at Berr because of his eclecticism and his attempts to reconcile Spencer, Tarde and Durkheim: his conceptual distinctions were laboured; these were old controversies (Bouglé 1905a: 165).

The Dreyfus Affair: 'A Strict Duty to Participate in Public Life'

Education, morality and professional groups: the issues raised by Durkheim in his lectures had obvious political implications. So too did several of the reviews he wrote for the *Année* and *Notes critiques* (which was intended for an audience of activists), as they dealt with the position of women, divorce and social classes. He also made a few public interventions and contributed, in 1904, to the *Revue bleue*'s symposium, 'The intellectual elite and democracy'.

The *Revue bleue* described Durkheim as the 'master sociologist', and summarized his position thus: 'Social science must be built up slowly and on the basis of a mass of detailed observations. But precisely because it is objective and definitive, it can provide men of action with a lot of useful inspiration.' True to his principles, Durkheim argued that the role of the scholar was to act as an educator, and not to worry about getting into parliament. He had not, in other words, forgotten the Dreyfus affair, which had posed 'a great grave question of principle' (1973[1904]: 59). In response, 'the scholars were seen to leave their laboratories, the learned to leave their libraries to draw nearer the masses, to involve themselves in life'. There was a lesson to be learned from this: 'Experience has proved that they know how to make themselves heard' (ibid.).

Durkheim raises the question of the role of the intellectual elite, and of sociologists in particular. He had already discussed the issue of the scientist's duty: 'The scientist has the duty of developing his critical sense, of submitting his judgment to no authority other than reason; he must school himself to have an open mind.' That was the difference between the scientist and the priest or soldier, for whom 'passive obedience, within prescribed limits, [is] obligatory' (1957[1950]: 5). The scientist must keep 'an open mind' but he was also an intellectual; like the writer, he is a citizen and therefore has 'a strict duty to participate in public life' (1973[1904]: 58). What form did that duty take? Durkheim was not suggesting that 'men of thought and imagination' were predestined to 'a properly political career'. The task of the historian or sociologist was 'to contemplate societies' and 'a sociologist has every chance of making a very incomplete statesman'. The same is true of the great physiologist, who is 'generally a very mediocre clinician'. It is therefore difficult to become a deputy or senator without ceasing to be a writer or scholar: 'these two types of function imply so different an orientation of mind and will' (ibid.: 59).

Durkheim does not rule out the possibility that intellectuals might be represented in 'deliberative societies' as they are well informed and 'more qualified than anyone else to defend before the public powers the interests of the arts and sciences'. There is, on the other hand, no need for them to be numerous in parliament. Their political action should be exerted indirectly, 'through books, seminars and popular education' (1973[1904] 58, 59): 'Above all, we must be *advisors, educators*. It is our function to help our contemporaries know themselves in their ideas and in their feelings, far more than to govern them.' They must also defend the autonomy of academics: 'The lecturer of today must not be suspected to be the candidate of tomorrow.'

Durkheim's political position is therefore that of the 'specific intellectual' (Bourdieu 1998). He obviously intervenes publicly into the domains in which he is competent, both to enlighten political leaders and to educate the population as a whole, but his main concern must be to defend the autonomy of science. The Dreyfus affair, according to Durkheim, had proved two things: scientists and artists were not as indifferent to matters of public interest as might have been believed, and intellectuals could make themselves understood to 'the mob'. His dearest wish was to see that the 'moral agitation' that France had recently experienced did not 'die down'. The previous four years had left him quite optimistic, and he was glad to see that 'a lasting current of collective activity of considerable intensity' still existed. He did not, on the other hand, believe that anti-clericalism was enough: 'I hope to see society soon attach itself to more objective ends.' His short article ends with a call for mobilization: 'Our hour of repose has not struck. There is too much to do' (1973[1904]: 60). Two years later, Captain Dreyfus was rehabilitated, and was made a chevalier de la Légion d'honneur in a ceremony at the École militaire.

L'Humanité. A Waste of Time?

The first issue of *L'Humanité* – a 'newspaper of ideas and news' – appeared on 18 April 1904. It was founded by Jean Jaurès, the great parliamentary spokesman for socialism; Lucien Lévy-Bruhl, Lucien Herr and Léon Blum had helped him raise the funds needed to launch it. In his first article, which was entitled simply 'Our goal', Jaurès justified the paper's title by identifying socialism with the blossoming of humanity. Its watchwords were accuracy, truth, loyalty and freedom. Given its team of seven *normaliens* and eight *agrégés* Aristide Briand was prompted to quip: 'This is not *L'Humanité*; this is the humanities!'

Several activists from the Groupe d'unité socialiste were in key positions, including Lucien Herr and Charles Andler (foreign policy), Albert Thomas (the trade union movement) and Edgar Milhaud (economic issues). Léon Blum wrote for its literary pages. Mauss and Philippe Landrieu coedited the 'cooperatives' rubric. Mauss had a press card and regularly visited the editorial offices, where he met Jaurès, for whom he had great admiration. Between June and December, Mauss wrote some 10 articles on the cooperative movement, enthusiastically defending the 'cause' of consumers' cooperatives, which could, he believed, help to bring about 'practical socialism' or socialism in the here and now (Mauss 1997[1904]).

Mauss had not been discouraged by the unfortunate Boulangerie affair; he still had 'boundless ambition' and was involved in 'all sorts of undertakings', to the great displeasure of his uncle, who blamed Lucien Herr for having persuaded his nephew to 'accept a role' on *L'Humanité*.[15] 'You have reached a critical point', his uncle wrote to him. 'Are you going to give up your legitimate scientific ambitions – by putting them off year after year – and get involved in tasks that require qualities and failings that you do not have?' When he spoke of Mauss's 'scientific ambitions', Durkheim was thinking of the 'qualifications' – a doctorate – that would allow his nephew to find a 'more useful teaching post' and 'more interesting students'.

When Mauss decided, not without some hesitations, to go to Budapest to cover an international cooperative congress, Durkheim was rather more than bewildered: 'It is up to you to decide what use that will be. Of course going away will do you good. But don't tell me that you can make up for lost time. You never do. You will be late again.'[16] Durkheim was also worried about Robert Hertz: 'It is to be hoped that we do not lose this brilliant mind to politics! That's the danger. But he has enough scientific fibre to resist temptation.'[17]

Holidays at Last! A New Position?

When they were not being swept away by the whirlwind of politics, the members of the *Année* team worked on their doctorates, pursued their research and published articles and books. They also travelled and fulfilled family commitments.

The theses came first. In 1904, François Simiand defended his thesis, *Le Salaire des ouvriers des mines en charbon en France*, for a doctorate in law and economic and political sciences at the Sorbonne. He had amassed statistical data based on annual series (number of days worked, average monetary wages, yearly physical output, retail price per ton of coal) and then developed an interpretative schema. His action theory demonstrated that the actions of both workers and employers were determined by different tendencies: the tendency to go on making the same amount without making more effort, and the tendency to make more money by making less effort. Simiand demonstrated the existence of statistical patterns and supplied a socioeconomic explanation that gave a central role to collective representations. Collective representations provided the link between the data available to actors, their decisions and their observable behaviours.[18] Simiand's plan for a positive economics was ambitious, as he wanted to find a sociological explanation for the great transformation affecting what he called 'complex exchange economies'.

In 1905, it was the turn of Simiand's close friend Hubert Bourgin to defend his doctoral thesis on Fourier at the Sorbonne. Once again, sociology seemed to be synonymous with socialism. Durkheim, who was a member of the jury, praised the candidate's work for its 'sureness, impartiality and honesty', but still thought that it had its flaws: 'What is lacking, in the study of the doctrine, is a positive basis in the facts . . . M. Bourgin might have been able to study and describe the chief currents of contemporary ideas to which Fourier's thought belonged.' The candidate replied that 'the current of ideas cannot at present be known in a scientific manner'. Durkheim could not accept that, and gave a few examples, including 'the socialist messianism' that one finds in Saint-Simon as well as Fourier, and the 'proletarian sentiment' in Fourier (1975[1905c]).

Durkheim's collaborators were also moving around the country. Paul Fauconnet was having difficulty with his thesis, which was on 'responsibility'. After being on leave for three years, he had found a position in the autumn of 1903 teaching philosophy at a college in Saint-Germain-en-Laye. Durkheim had written in person to the rector of the Académie de Paris to tell him how highly he thought of his collaborator: 'I know of few more lucid minds or sounder men.' 'Everyone feels the same about him', he added. He went on: 'Leaving aside his serious family problems, it is in the interests of science to find a way to keep him in Paris for the moment.' By 'interests of science', Durkheim meant his thesis: 'He would find it difficult to go on with it in a small town, where he will certainly not find the resources he needs.'[19] Fauconnet succeeded in discussing the questions that interested him in the classroom. They included solidarity, mutual aid societies, the organization of pension funds in Germany, and old age, sickness and accident assurance. In the autumn of 1905, Fauconnet left Saint-Germain to take up a post in the provinces at the lycée in Cherbourg. In the meantime, Henri Hubert's dream had finally come true. He spent 1902 and 1903 travelling around the world, visiting the United States (New York, where he was the guest of the Potters,[20] Washington and New Orleans), Japan, China and Indochina. He attended the first Congress of Far Eastern Studies in Hanoi, and read a paper entitled 'The pre-history of Indochina'. Marcel Mauss was also travelling, but for political reasons. In 1905, he covered the Cooperative congresses in London and Budapest.

Relations between uncle and nephew were becoming strained, despite (or because of) the fact that they were living so close to one another. Marcel's prevarications, silences and evasiveness were beginning to irritate Durkheim: 'Don't you think that you ought to explain to me why the *Année* isn't finished?' He did not approve of the life his nephew was leading, or of his political activism. He was so worried that, one evening, he went directly to his nephew's apartment after giving his lecture: 'You were out . . . I really do not know what is becoming of you or what you are thinking. You cause me such sadness!'[21]

Marcel was now 30, and still single. His mother Rosine wanted only one thing for her son: a good marriage. She feared that he would become an 'old bachelor'.[22] There was in fact a woman in Marcel's life, and he loved her. It was Émile who, despite himself, he claimed, took it upon himself to tell his sister that Marcel was 'sharing his life' with a woman. The news made her both angry and sad. Durkheim went on holiday in August, travelling first to Höchenschwand in Switzerland and then to Épinal. 'I am still enjoying my holiday', he wrote to his friend Hamelin. 'For the last six weeks, I have enjoyed a moral calm that I have not known for two years.' He even described his travels as 'therapy'. 'Why do we put ourselves through this hell just to write a lecture course? My mind is getting lazy, my dear friend. Is it age or fatigue? I don't think so. But I am very reluctant to get back to work. I have to fight harder and harder against my taste for idle daydreaming and absolute relaxation.'[23]

Writing from his hotel in Switzerland, Durkheim sent a 'personal note' to his nephew in order to explain himself. Why had he betrayed his 'secret'? 'I never thought that you would hold it against me. If I'm guilty of anything, it's of waiting so long.' He did, however, add that, if it was his fault that 'the news got out', he had not really meant to betray Marcel's secret: 'All I did was make her a little more acutely aware of something she already knew about. She knew almost everything, and told me that her fears often kept her awake at night.'

When Marcel decided to break off the relationship, his uncle was pleased and advised him not to make a tragedy of it: 'Put it all out of your mind for the moment. Recover the peace of mind that will allow you to take a saner view of what you have to do.' He added: 'For my own part, I am glad to hear that you have been rescued from a situation that would have cost you everything – and I do mean everything – without your realizing it.' And he was delighted that he would once more be able to see his nephew 'without any ulterior motives': 'You know that I need you. I need you too, and I missed you.'

The possibility of a chair at the Collège de France was raised again in the autumn of 1904. 'Your letter suggests that I should wait for the outcome of the discussions in your apartment', he wrote to his nephew. When Gabriel Tarde died, Henri Bergson was elected to the chair of social philosophy, and Durkheim hoped that his old chair in ancient philosophy would convert to a chair in sociology. He could count upon the support of some professors at the Collège, including Pierre Janet, a fellow student at the École nomale and, since 1902, professor of experimental and comparative psychology. At the suggestion of both Janet and Bergson, Durkheim embarked upon the traditional round of visits to the Collège's professors. At the beginning of November, he went to call on Paul Leroy-Beaulieu, the economist and founder, in 1873, of *L'Économiste français*. 'They fear he will attack me', wrote Durkheim, immediately adding: 'No fears on that score: [Leroy-Beaulieu] knows me well, thinks highly of me and finds the idea of renaming the chair interesting.' But he had no illusions: 'I've done what I can . . . I've tried not to overlook anything. But the outcome is not in doubt, so there is no point in wasting time . . . I do not even know if I will be a candidate', he wrote to his nephew. He wanted people to think that he was 'non-existent'. He thought he 'stood less chance than Jullian of having the chair renamed.'[24] His worst fear was that he would be defeated, and that it would be the 'story of Berr' all over again. Henri Berr, who taught at the Lycée Henri-IV, had just been refused a chair at the Collège. The historians and literary specialists eventually succeeded in establishing a chair in the history of national antiquities. Camille Jullian, a former colleague of Durkheim's at Bordeaux, and two years his junior, was elected, taking up his new post in April 1905.

The death in 1904 of Henry Michel, who had been professor of the history of political doctrines for five years, meant that there was now a vacant chair at the Sorbonne. Xavier Léon, editor of the *Revue de métaphysique et de morale,* advised his associate Élie Halévy to apply. Michel had chaired the jury that examined his thesis, *The Revolution and the Doctrine of Utility* (and his Latin thesis on the idea of association). Halévy had sworn to 'say no' to any offer of a chair at the Sorbonne and, true to his word, he turned it down and put forward the name of his friend Bouglé, 'an excellent candidate, more popular [than me] with the staff, and certain to be more popular with the students'.[25] Henry Michel had taught Bouglé at the lycée and had been a member of the jury that examined his thesis in 1899. Was Bouglé about to succeed him at the Sorbonne?

A New Generation: Georges Bourgin, Maurice Halbwachs, Robert Hertz, and Others

The manuscript of volume VIII of the *Année sociologique* went off to the printer in mid-April: 'It is vital not to waste time . . . I'm in a hurry to have this volume finished, and to get on with the next', Durkheim wrote to Henri Hubert.[26] It appeared in June 1905.

The arrival of several new contributors led to the expansion of the *Année*'s team. Together with some of the stalwarts, Georges Bourgin, Maurice Halbwachs, Robert Hertz and Antoine Vacher become coeditors of various rubrics, while Henri Beuchat, Antoine Bianconi and Jean Reynier contributed their first reviews.

Georges Bourgin was Hubert's brother. Born in 1879, he had had a very different educational and professional career. Awarded a degree in law and letters, and diplomas from the École des chartes and then the École pratique des hautes études, he was appointed a member of the École française de Rome in 1903, spent nine months in Italy, and began to take a professional interest in history. On his return to France in 1904, he was recruited by the Archives nationales and spent the rest of his career there. Georges Bourgin was primarily a historian of the Commune, and was author of a major study, *Le Régime de l'industrie en France de 1814 à 1830* (three volumes), and also of *Le Socialisme français de 1789 à 1848*.

Maurice Halbwachs was born in 1877 in Reims, where his father taught German; he attended the Lycée Michelet and the Lycée Henri-IV (where he was taught by Henri Bergson), before entering the École normale supérieure in 1898. Having passed his *agrégation de philosophie* in 1901, he began his teaching career at lycées in Constantine and Montpellier. He took a period of leave from 1902 to 1908, spending a year in Göttingen (1903) before resuming his law studies and writing a doctoral thesis in 1909. He then went back to teaching in secondary schools in Reims (1908) and Tours (1909–14), and it was only on the eve of the First World War that he found a position in higher education in Strasbourg. When he began to contribute to the *Année sociologique*, he was also writing reviews for Simiand's *Notes critiques*. In 1905, he, Simiand and Herz all became involved in the new *Revue syndicaliste*, recently launched by Albert Thomas with the financial backing of Lucien Herr, Lucien Lévy-Bruhl and Léon Blum. He also published an article in the *Revue philosophique* that year: 'Needs and tendencies in the social economy'.

As Marcel Mauss later put it (Mauss 1997[1928]: 742), it was the École normale supérieure's librarian Lucien Herr who 'recommended Durkheim to the best in the school'. 'The best' included Hertz, Bianconi, Reynier and, later, Gelly and Maxime David. Robert Hertz, who was born in Saint-Cloud in 1881, had been one of Durkheim's students, and later became a friend. He was educated at the Lycée Janson-de-Sailly before transferring to Henri-IV in 1898 to prepare for the École normale supérieure's entrance examinations. He was admitted to the École normale supérieure two years later, which was when he met Durkheim, who was struck by the extent and precocity of Hertz's knowledge, his mental strength and maturity, and his extraordinary modesty (Durkheim 1975[1916]: 439). A graduate of the École normale supérieure and an *agrégé de lettres*, Hertz passed the *agrégation de philosophie* in 1904, much to Durkheim's delight. Durkheim did not know Hertz well at this time, but admitted that he had taken a liking to him.[27] The young Hertz had been a socialist ever since his days at the École normale supérieure, and was 'inspired by the loftiest social virtues': he wanted to 'found socialism', which he understood to mean both a method of study, and a solution to social problems that was based upon positive science' (Alphandéry 1919: 336). Durkheim spoke admiringly of the young *normalien*'s 'thirst for justice': 'he had long been drawn to social questions' (Durkheim 1975[1916]: 440). Hertz became an active member of the École socialiste, whose membership included several contributors to the *Année*.

Once Hertz had passed his *agrégation*, he chose to concentrate on 'issues where morality overlaps with religion'. He was interested in the 'dark and sinister sides of human mentality', and intrigued by crime, sin, punishment and forgiveness. How and why could society wash away sin and crime? How and why could society forget? In 1905–6, Hertz obtained a grant to study in London, where he attended Sarck's lecture on the origins and development of moral ideas. He also met Hartland at the Folklore Society, Tylor in Oxford and, in Cambridge, James Frazer (who admitted to him that he had never read Durkheim's essay on the prohibition of incest).

Durkheim was very keen for Robert Hertz to contribute to the *Année*, and wrote to Mauss: 'You haven't written back to say how much help Hertz might give us. Do you think he would agree to do a little work for us, and give you some help with "general sociology" at the same time?'[28] His wish was granted, and it was for the 'general sociology' section that Hertz wrote his first reviews. The young collaborator, who had a 'rigorous and keen mind' and 'an unusually noble character', quickly became a friend. Master and pupil developed a 'very close relationship' characterized by 'shared feelings, mutual affection and complete trust' (Durkheim 1975[1916]: 440).

On returning from London, Robert Hertz agreed – for 'moral reasons', according to Durkheim – to accept a position teaching in a lycée in Douai (which he ironically described as 'the Athens of the North' [i.e. the *département* of Nord]): he took the view that 'all citizens had a duty to fulfil a specific function in society, and to have a particular task'. After a year's experience, he returned to Paris to 'begin his scientific production'. 'At last!' exclaimed Durkheim (1975[1916]: 441). It is true that, as Hertz himself admitted, he had felt the 'pressure of the collective opinion' of Durkheim, Mauss and other members of the *Année* team, who did not approve of his 'virtuous and truly disinterested resolve' to teach philosophy and advised him to 'work in Paris' and to 'advance science'. Durkheim himself took an authoritarian stance and forced him to finish the article on funerary rites, which he had begun in England, for the *Année*. 'That was the last straw.'[29] His plans for both his career and his thesis were, however, still 'ill-defined'. Under Durkheim's influence, he now outlined his research programme more carefully. His research included work on collective representations of death and religious polarities, and his thesis (which he never completed) dealt with sin and expiation in primitive societies.

Antoine Vacher was born in 1873, studied at the École normale supérieure (1895) and was an *agrégé d'histoire* (1900). He began his academic career as a *maître de conférences* (1895), and defended his doctoral thesis a few years later in 1980. His contributions to the *Année sociologique* were restricted to volumes VIII and IX. His interests included human geography and social morphology, with special reference to urban conurbations.

Born in 1878, Henri Beuchet was 'one of Mauss's first students and associates'; he had attended his lectures on 'The elementary forms of prayer' in 1902–3, and had taken an active part in the discussions about ethnographic texts on Melanesia. He was also a protégé of Léon de Rosny, who also taught at the École pratique and who specialized in the religions of the Far East and Amerindia. Under his influence, Beuchat developed an interest in the American continent, and especially in the peoples of New Mexico and Sonora. He also became secretary and treasurer of the *Revue des études américaines* although he had no academic qualifications. He was an autodidact and had done various jobs (including, for instance, working as a typesetter in a print shop). When he began to work with Mauss in 1903, he was embarking on an illustrated book on Mexican art, coauthored with M. Le Souëf. Mauss said of his student: 'Beuchat knows an infinite number of things, and he knows them very well' (Mauss 1969[1925]). Having seen his technical skills, Mauss gave him the task of compiling the table of contents and index for the *Année sociologique*. Beuchat wrote reviews for volumes VIII, IX and X, and also contributed to *Notes critiques.*

Antoine Bianconi was born in Digne in 1882 and was educated in Lyon and then at the Lycée Henri-IV in Paris before attending the École normale supérieure and taking his *agrégation de philosophie* in 1906. He planned to write a thesis on mental organization in West African societies, and to produce an ethnographic bibliography on the African colonies, as well as a study of 'the idea of grace in St Augustine'. He was editorial secretary for the *Revue du mois*, and taught in Valenciennes. The *Année*'s young contributor had led a busy life, and Mauss said of him that he had such 'a passion for teaching' that there was a danger he would be 'distracted from his work of pure science' (Mauss 1969[1925]: 493).

Jean Reynier, born in 1881, was a *normalien* (1903) with a diploma from the École pratique des hautes études, where he had attended Sylvain Lévi's lectures. He took the *agrégation de philosophie* in 1908. He planned to do research on mixed moral-religious phenomena, and to write his thesis on Christian asceticism. This developed into an interest in Hindu asceticism, which he went to India in order to study (Mauss 1969[1925]: 495). He also went on to teach philosophy in secondary schools and, like Bianconi and Hertz, devoted himself to it with great passion.

The new recruits were allotted tasks as follows: Georges Bourgin joined his brother Hubert on the 'economic sociology' section; Maurice

Halbwachs was assigned to 'criminal sociology and moral statistics' with Durkheim and Fauconnet, and to 'social morphology'; Robert Hertz worked on the 'general sociology' rubrics of 'social philosophy' and 'psychology of peoples'; and Vacher was assigned to 'social morphology'.

When volume VIII appeared, Durkheim hoped to be able to 'count upon more support' from his new associates, and especially from Robert Hertz, who would, he hoped, 'take on more than religious sociology'. When Mauss told his uncle that Hertz had the impression that he 'was wasting his time', Durkheim was 'angry': 'What makes him think that? Find out so that other people can learn from his experience.'[30]

The number of pages devoted to reviews fell from 536 in volume VII to 493 in volume VIII. 'Religious sociology' was still the biggest section (almost 150 pages, or 30 per cent of the total), with 'criminal sociology and moral statistics' (23.5 per cent) a poor second.[31] Short introductory notes were once more used to signal the introduction of new rubrics or to explain the journal's orientation. Mauss, for instance, added a 'note on totemism' to defend the idea that a discussion of totemism was a discussion of religion: 'We conclude that totemism is the most widespread religious system in social organizations based upon exogamic clans' (Mauss 1969[1905]: 162).

The *Année* remained loyal to its 'enemies' in the sense that it went on publishing hostile reviews of their work. The young Robert Hertz was dispatched to the front to open hostilities, with attacks on Georg Simmel (flawed methodology, studies of empty and indeterminate forms), the Le Play school (inadequate methodology, a monographic approach that raises serious objections: 'We need general surveys, and statistical averages') and Edmond Demolins' thesis about the superiority of the Anglo-Saxons ('an axiom unworthy of discussion'), René Worms and the *Annales de l'Institut international de sociologie* ('a collection of unrelated essays'). Hertz (1905) was scathing about anyone who attempted to replace the 'objective method' with the 'psychological method', which has more in common with an 'impressionist method'.

Durkheim wrote some 30 reviews. This was fewer than usual, and five were written in collaboration with Paul Fauconnet. His interest in marriage – its religious nature, reflected in the theory of the 'danger' of sexual intercourse, as amongst the Jews of ancient times (1980[1905]: 270) – divorce (by mutual consent, as in Japan) and the position of women was undiminished, and it is true that he also contributed an article on 'the matrimonial organization of Australian societies' (Durkheim 1969[1905]) to this volume.

From Matrimonial Organization to the Butchery Trade

Two articles were published in volume VIII of the *Année*. As well as one by Durkheim on 'matrimonial organization', there was Hubert Bourgin's 'Essai sur une forme d'industrie. L'Industrie de la boucherie à Paris au

XIXe siècle' ['A form of industry: butchery in Paris in the 19th century']: it was, on the one hand, a very general institution and, on the other hand, a very distinctive industry; on the one hand, a very 'primitive' society, on the other, contemporary France. Durkheim's article on matrimonial organization was a continuation of the study of totemism that he had published in volume V. Spencer and Gillen had just published their *Northern Tribes of Central Australia* (1904) and any book by Spencer and Gillen was, in Durkheim's view, 'a stroke of luck for a sociologist' because of the authors' descriptions of crucial facts, and their analysis of essential institutions. All this made it possible to make progress with certain questions that had long been controversial: which totem does the child belong to – the mother's, or the father's? How does the distribution of the population into classes affect the regulation of marriage? There were several reasons for Durkheim's interest in Spencer and Gillen's book: their work shed 'new light' on the matrimonial organization of Australian societies, and their observations challenged the 'survival' theory that he had advanced in his article on totemism: 'We attempted to show that the explanation for some of the specific features of the Arunta organization appears to be change in the mode of filiation, which was originally uterine, but then became paternal.' 'A survival or vestige of an earlier system would therefore explain everything' (Durkheim 1969[1905]: 495).

Who was mistaken? Durkheim attempts to demonstrate that his 'explanatory' hypothesis is, on a comparative basis, confirmed by the facts: 'We now believe that we can regard it as definitely established that the Arunta organization is not primitive.' He argues that such a 'convergence of proofs' means that all this is obvious. The thesis that uterine filiation is earlier than paternal filiation is beyond dispute. Durkheim's analysis seems fragile, even tentative, but it does open up several lines for further research: the discovery that 'primitive thought' has a rational power, the study of marriage as an exchange of women between clans in accordance with definite rules, the study of the interplay between the transmission of the totem (filiation) and the material fact of generation (or engendering). His argument is so complex that his skilful juggling with the categories of 'class' and 'phratry' made it seem that he was discussing a mathematical problem This was 'further proof that these classes and phratries are not just social categories; they are also logical categories which are, of course, subject to a special logic, which may well be different from ours, but which still has definite rules' (1969[1905]: 510).

In his article on butchery, Hubert Bourgin attempts to establish statistical series relating to various aspects of the trade in Paris over a period of 100 years (1800–1900): the number of butchers, the number of employers and employees, the number and size of businesses. Bourgin analyses a large quantity of documents (which he uses critically), and elaborates indices (number of butchers in relation to population of *arrondissements*) as well as statistics. His article runs to more than 100 pages and includes some 15 statistical tables and several graphs (based on techniques developed by Simiand) illustrating the process of historical change.

Bourgin was aware of the 'limited nature' of his study. His main concerns were with methodology: establishing statistical series and deciphering their meaning. He wanted to demonstrate the complexity of the questions he was dealing with, and criticized both hasty generalizations and all-too-common subjective judgements. A few facts were enough to refute such subjective judgements: 'Science advances by combining fragmentary truths that are acquired with difficulty: there is no other way (Bourgin 1905: 111).

Bourgin's analysis of his data leads him to draw some general conclusions: the growth of the population is not a 'sufficient cause' behind the growth of the butchery trade; its growth is independent of economic development as a whole, but the consumption of meat has a 'causal effect' on it. He clearly identifies, finally, the effects of specialization – the emergence of unprecedently large businesses, greater differentiation – on changes in the trade. The analysis is deliberately modest.[32]

Writing in the *American Journal of Sociology*, Albion W. Small (1906) had his doubts about what he saw as the 'poor' sociological value of Bourgin's monograph. He was interested in Durkheim's article, but that was because, being familiar with his work, he could 'relate it to his general methodology'. And he was still critical of the *Année*'s bibliographical work; it certainly provided a 'useful service', but the views held on sociological research held by Durkheim and his collaborators did not help to define 'their relationship with other scholars working in the same field.'

18

The Evolution of Educational Thought; *or, Triadic Culture*

Émile Durkheim began his major lecture course on the history of secondary education in France at the start of the 1904–5 academic year. The lectures took place late on Saturday afternoon in the premises of the Musée pédagogique in the rue Gay-Lussac. He had been invited to teach this new course by Louis Liard, the rector of the university. It was intended for future *agrégés*, was regarded as 'an essential part of their educational training', and was part of what was described as a 'practical course' that began in their first year at university: 'The teachers of the future will acquire the ability to understand the history of the career they are about to take up, and will have the opportunity to think about how it must change if it is to be better adapted to modern life', explained Dean Croiset, adding: 'It is to be hoped that the memory of M. Durkheim's lectures . . . will help to bring about the convergence of energies that are all too often paralysed and dissipated because they are divorced from one another.'[1] The dean was pleased that the new course was being taught by Durkheim because 'he has thought about the historical conditions that have determined the form of the course he is teaching'.

Durkheim himself was convinced of the importance of introducing the teachers of the future to the 'great problems' raised by the courses for which they would be responsible and of inculcating a real 'educational culture' into them. Any attempt to do so was likely to encounter a lot of resistance, and Durkheim's aim was to demonstrate that 'educational theory is nothing more than reflection applied as methodically as possible to educational matters' (Durkheim 1977[1938]: 4). Education could no longer be an exception; as in other spheres of action, science and reflection must 'illuminate practice'. There was, on the other hand, no reason to be excited. Given the present state of the human sciences, Durkheim recommended modesty, prudence, circumspection and, above all, a methodical approach.

Durkheim made no secret of the 'great difficulties' inherent in his project, attractive as it may have been. Because of the greater division of educational labour, secondary education was 'a much more complex organism' (1977[1938]: 6) than primary education. He had been interested in this topic for a long time, and it was only because he had been 'deflected by other concerns' (ibid.: 3) that he had not dealt with it earlier.

'Circumstances' now lent themselves to such a project. The reforms implemented by the government in 1902 looked, as the historian Victor Langlois (1900) put it, like something that could 'save France' and 'save the greatness of France'. If France was to 'remain the country with the highest intellectual culture', there was 'no time to lose'. One solution, and it seemed to Langlois to be 'the simplest, the most elegant and the most radical' solution, depended upon teacher training: the teachers of the future needed a new philosophy of education. Durkheim's close associate Paul Lapie was also arguing that 'teaching and educational methods should be adapted in the light of scientific progress' and that education should be 'more in keeping with the demands of pedagogy' (Lapie 1901: 798).[2]

Educational reform was at the heart of the republican project. The situation was such that Durkheim spoke openly of a 'very serious crisis' and 'an acute state of crisis'. This was especially true of secondary education: attempts were being made to introduce a new system that appeared to be 'full of youth and enthusiasm' but which had little sense of where it was going. There was no clearly defined ideal and no sense of the goals the lycées were meant to be pursuing. 'What about the glorious past of humanism?' people were asking. Hence the intellectual confusion of a generation torn between 'a past that is dying and a future yet undetermined'. Durkheim found that lycée teachers tended to be sceptical, disenchanted or uneasy because 'no new faith has yet come to replace that which has disappeared'. This worried Durkheim, who was convinced that 'a teaching body without a pedagogical faith is a body without a soul' (1956[1906]: 143, 144). Durkheim was clear about what needed to be done. Given all the fluctuations that there had been in the curriculum, it was, as he put it in a later lecture, 'time to put an end to these wanderings . . . and to confront the problem with courage' (1977[1938]: 308). Finding a solution would not be easy, but there was clearly 'pressing need' to study the history of secondary education. His intention was, therefore, to proceed methodically in order to learn a few lessons from the past.

Knowing and Understanding Our Educational Machine

Durkheim gave his first lecture at the beginning of November.[3] In a preliminary session, Louis Liard, rector of the university, Ernest Lavisse, professor of modern history and director of the École normale supérieure, and Charles Langlois, director of the Musée pédagogique, informed the students of the measures that had been implemented to 'organize their professional training'. Durkheim's lectures on the history of secondary education in France were intended for those studying for the *agrégation*. 'I'm going right away to uncle Émile's first lecture', Mauss wrote to his mother. 'I am certain that it will be a very great, very fine success.'[4]

The lectures on the history of secondary education were, in Mauss's view, Durkheim's most important contribution to the science of education. Durkheim wanted to avoid becoming involved in the political debate over the issue; he wanted, rather, not without some anxiety, to explain to the teachers of the future how 'the institution they were about to enter was the product of centuries of history', by using, Mauss emphasized, the same 'historical and sociological method'. His intention was 'to help them understand educational practice by tracing its history to date (Mauss 1969[1925]: 487–8). This was, Halbwachs would later say, 'a good example and a fine model of what a study of teaching institutions in their historical context' could be in the hands of a 'great sociologist' (Halbwachs 1969[1938]: xi).

This was, as Mauss noted, 'a difficult task', as the lectures were intended for 'a demanding audience'. The burden was all the heavier in that it fell upon 'the shoulders of a scholar who was also preoccupied with many other things'. Durkheim happily agreed to make such a 'considerable effort', and did so 'enthusiastically, conscientiously and efficiently'. He was, as always, very anxious to make a success of his lectures and was therefore 'very happy' when he found that he had done so (Mauss 1969[1925]). Marcel worried on his behalf:

> Uncle goes on with his lectures. He packs out an enormous room. A bad audience, for the most part. Perhaps he is stirring up some unexpected enthusiasm. He is becoming tired, and he is tired. I am very worried. I fear for the *Année*. Except when he is on holiday, he gets so carried away that it takes up all his time.[5]

Pedagogy was a discipline that had 'fallen into disrepute', and that was, thanks to 'an old French prejudice', regarded as 'an inferior mode of speculation'. Could Durkheim 'revive' it, as he wished to do? He had no intention of teaching his students 'the techniques of their profession': teaching was a profession that could only be learned in the classroom. His goal was not 'to teach future practitioners a certain number of techniques and recipes for success, but to make them fully aware of the nature of their function'. He wanted, in a word, to make them think about 'things educational'. Durkheim therefore had no hesitations about arguing the need for reflection, which he described as a factor for change; reflection made it possible, he believed, to resist routine, to introduce a degree of suppleness and flexibility that made it easier to adapt to different and changing circumstances. He had 'a feeling and taste for action', and was able to give his classes 'an immediately practical character' (Fauconnet 1956[1922]: 39).

This openness to reflection and science seemed all the more important to Durkheim in that the teaching profession was in a state of 'intellectual confusion'. It was trapped between 'a past that is dying and a future yet undetermined'. He set himself a 'mission': he would use educational science to develop a new ideal, a 'new faith' and eventually a 'new life'.

The Reformist and the Scholar. A New Faith

If France wished to emerge from this 'era of trouble and uncertainty', it could not count only on the efficacy of decrees and regulations. 'As long as men's minds are full of indecision, there is no administrative decree that can put an end to it. One does not decree the ideal; it must be understood, liked, desired by all those who have the duty of realizing it.' It was not enough to 'train future teachers in the practice of their profession'; above all, it was necessary to 'produce in them an energetic effort of reflection, which they should pursue throughout their careers, but which must begin here at the University' (Durkheim 1956[1906]: 143). In methodological terms, Durkheim is critical of 'revolutionary spirits' who dreamed of building 'from the ground up an entirely new scholastic system'. The 'enthusiasms of iconoclasts' were 'chimerical and even dangerous'; it was neither possible nor desirable for the present organization to 'collapse in an instant'. Durkheim did not believe either in creations *ex nihilo* or in the social or the physical order: 'The future cannot be evoked from nothing; we can build it only with the materials that the past has bequeathed to us' (1956: 110). Even the reformers who wish to 'envisage the future with a minimum of risks' and who are sympathetic to 'reforming tendencies' tend to be under an illusion because 'it is not possible for the ideal of tomorrow to be entirely original' (1956[1906]: 151). The ideal of tomorrow contains much of the ideal of yesterday, and 'our mentality is not going to change completely overnight'. Hence the need to proceed with caution because 'a new ideal always appears in a state of natural antagonism to the old ideal . . . although, in fact, it is only its consequence and its development' (ibid.). The fate of humanism is one example of what happens when we make the mistake of throwing everything overboard: we 'must know how to preserve whatever part of it should be retained' (ibid.). When it comes to the past, Durkheim takes the view that we are its 'heirs', and that we must be aware of the close kinship that exists between past and present.

Durkheim therefore invited his students to abandon 'ideological constructions and fruitless dreams' (1956[1906]: 143), and to take part in a serious attempt to reflect and to reorganize. This is the teaching profession's first duty. Durkheim sees himself as a reformist: the best way to realize a new pedagogic ideal is 'to use the established organization . . . to shape it to the new ends which it is to serve. How many reforms . . . can be accomplished, without its being necessary to change existing curricula drastically!' A new spirit is all that is required, 'but one acts efficaciously on things only to the degree that one knows their nature'. It is therefore necessary to begin with an understanding of what the school system is, what the conceptions are that underlie it, the needs that it answers and the causes that have created it. Hence the need for a scientific and objective study of the educational system.

Durkheim therefore insists on the need to understand the 'objective nature' (1956[1906]: 147) of the scholastic machine and to analyse the currents of opinion that produced it, and the social needs or aspirations that brought it into existence. A whole research programme – consisting of different theories of education – is needed to analyse the projects for reform and plans for reconstruction that inspired it. A parallel must then be established between those theories and currents of opinion, and society's various needs and aspirations. That is not, however, enough. We must also understand these currents of opinion, and decide whether to accept them or reject them. Are they bound up with 'the normal evolution of our society'? The only way to answer that question is to reconstruct their history. Various schools of educational theory and pedagogic doctrines can then be seen as historic facts that can be compared, classified and interpreted. They are then not so much 'sources of inspiration [as] documents on the spirit of the time' (ibid.: 153).

In his lectures, Durkheim obviously adopts an 'exclusively scientific' stance, but this is not in order to devote himself to 'pure research': 'it is to arrive at practical results'. His intention is not to preach: 'I shall remain, here, a man of science. Only, I think that the science of human affairs can serve to guide human behaviour usefully. To behave well, says an old adage, one must know oneself well' (1956[1906]: 152). Durkheim's goal is to raise the problem of secondary education as a whole. He expresses the hope that his students will understand 'the interest and novelty of the enterprise' and will give him their 'active cooperation . . . without which I could do no useful work' (ibid.: 153).

Turning to History; or, The Quest for Origins

As Maurice Halbwachs notes (1977[1938]: xi), there is something 'special' about Durkheim's lectures on the history of education: 'Durkheim has furnished us with a model example of what can be made of a study of educational institutions carried out within an historical framework by a great sociologist.' Durkheim paints 'a large bold fresco' of the progress of the human mind over ten centuries of history. 'Only Durkheim was capable of this', concludes an admiring Halbwachs (1977[1938]: xiii–xiv).

Did Durkheim see himself as a historian? His answer to those who ask if history can be of any practical use is 'I believe . . . that it is only by carefully studying the past that we can come to anticipate the future and to understand the present' (Durkheim 1977[1938]: 9). A study of the history of education is a sound basis for the study of educational theory. His answer to the objection that students should be looking at 'the man of our times' is that 'in each one of us, in differing degrees, is contained the person we were yesterday' (ibid.: 11). This is 'the unconscious part of ourselves', and it has been 'relegated to the shadows' (ibid.: 12). History therefore has many virtues: it warns us against the mistakes that were made in the past and, above all, teaches us to be relativists: every society has its educational system, and it is because society changes that educational systems change.

In order to study the contemporary pedagogic ideal, we must 'transport ourselves to the other end of the historical time-scale' (Durkheim

1977[1938]: 12), and begin by studying the ideals of the earliest European societies, or 'the educational ideology most remote in time from our own, the one which was the first to be elaborated in European culture' (ibid.). The contemporary situation is 'where we must end, not where we must begin' (ibid.). Such is the 'spirit' in which he undertakes his study, but he is also aware of its limitations: he is not proposing to make an erudite archaeological study of the educational system, but a historical study that will be of great pedagogic value. Whilst he is convinced that such a study will be of practical use, he never forgets that a history of secondary education also has its intellectual interest. Retracing the history of educational theories in France is also a way of studying the history of the 'French mind' and of describing 'our national temperament' in all its singularity. There is a close link between the history of educational theory and collective ethology.

A Theory of Change

Durkheim divides his lectures into two main periods: before and after the Renaissance. The Renaissance was a period of 'crisis' (growth), but it was, in Durkheim's view, by no means the only great period of innovation. He sets out, rather, to demonstrate that history, and especially the history of education, is an uninterrupted series of rebirths. Even the Middle Ages, in his view, was not a 'dark age' but a period of great mobility (at least for monks and the teachers in the first universities), overlapping influences and innovations, including educational innovations. When Durkheim speaks of 'progress', he makes it clear that, far from progressing in a straight line, history makes 'turnings and detours; advances are followed by recessions' (1977[1938]: 167). Durkheim's historical analysis concentrates on major social transformations but does not completely overlook the role of individuals. There are, he admits, 'accidental' individuals such as Charlemagne, Erasmus and Rabelais. But as a sociologist, he has no illusions about 'individual genius' and does not believe that innovations can be explained in terms of miracles: that is nothing more than 'historical mythology'. Educational theories and achievements are 'expressions' of great 'currents of opinion' and of 'the deepest states of the social consciousness'. Every change that occurs within education has 'deep roots'; every change is the result and symptom of the social transformation that explains it. 'In order for a people to feel at any particular moment in time the need to change its educational system, it is necessary that new ideas and needs have emerged for which the former system is no longer adequate' (ibid.: 166).

History is punctuated by what Durkheim calls 'creative periods', characterized, in civilizational terms, by great effervescence or intellectual excitement. The preconditions for their emergence are the availability of a 'supply of energy', personal mobility (nomadism and cosmopolitanism) and the establishment of a centre (such as Paris). Durkheim's approach is multidimensional and the factors that he identifies – in, for instance, his account of the Renaissance – are various: (1) economic transformations that follow from the increase in the number of large trading centres and the opening up of 'new worlds' (the trade route to India, discovery of the New World), an increase in wellbeing and the accumulation of great fortunes; (2) social changes that bring all social classes closer together; (3) political changes and the 'increase in individualization and differentiation' that leads to the emergence of the great European nationalities; and (4) cultural changes and shifts of opinion: decisive and transitional periods are often characterized by contradictory currents of opinion.

Studying the history of education therefore means elaborating a sociology of knowledge, as changes in education correspond to the 'mental development' of peoples and the intellectual structure of countries. It also means elaborating a sociology of culture: education gives individuals talents and inculcates a number of particular habits, but it also inculcates a *habitus* (of our moral being) – in other words, a 'general disposition of the mind and the will'. Becoming a man means developing a specific way of feeling and thinking which acts upon 'the deepest recesses of the soul' (1977[1938]: 29). The school is not just a place, but also – and above all – a 'moral environment' (ibid.: 30).

The 'Essential Characteristics' of the Education System

Durkheim pays particular attention to the education system as well as to pedagogic ideals and theories. He turns to history in order to identify what he calls the 'essential characteristics' of the way education is organized in France. Education was, in its earliest stages, linked to the church and was seemingly an 'annex' of religion. Faith and culture were one and the same thing. Far from seeing the church as a reactionary force, Durkheim stresses the importance of its contributions and, more generally, those of Christianity (the idea of the unity of science and truth). At a later stage, there is a contradiction between the religious element (Christian doctrine) and the profane or secular element (ancient civilization or pagan culture): 'From their origins [French] schools carried within themselves the germ of that great struggle between the sacred and the profane, the secular and the religious' (1977[1938]: 26). Secularity is therefore something 'congenital': the French educational system has always carried the 'germ' of secularity (which will eventually become dominant). There is also, finally, a tension between the diversity of the educational system and its unity, as it becomes both more unified and separate.

Durkheim identifies two other main characteristics of the French educational system: a hierarchical three-level structure (primary, secondary and university), with secondary education as the centre or 'cornerstone', and a dichotomy between the two great branches of knowledge – namely, the humanities (knowledge relating to man) and the natural sciences (knowledge relating to things). Durkheim's analysis makes it possible to bring out both the singularity and the complexity of this way of organizing education.

The Three Great Ages of Education

Durkheim's periodization is based mainly on changes in the educational ideal and in the curriculum (as different disciplines come to the fore). He identifies three main periods: a preliminary or introductory period that he calls the age of grammar, and two principal periods described as the *logical* or *scholastic age* and the *humanistic age*, which are followed by the new phase, the *realist age*. Each of these periods corresponds, roughly speaking, to a historical period: the 'age of grammar' refers to the Carolingian Renaissance (ninth to eleventh centuries), the 'logical' or humanistic age to the second Renaissance (twelfth to sixteenth centuries), and the 'realist age' to the French Revolution.

A preliminary period: the age of grammar

During this period, education was encyclopedic, sympathetic to the natural sciences (geometry, arithmetic, astronomy), and characterized by an 'extreme formalism' in that it privileged certain disciplines relating to 'forms' of thought and expression. Its goal was 'to get humanity to reflect upon its own nature, to understand itself and to be conscious of itself' (1977[1938]: 49). Grammar thus became the object of a cult, and the main focus of both teaching activity and literary activity. The study of languages such as Latin – 'a language of mystery' (ibid.: 56) – was important because 'language is an . . . integrated element in human thought': 'the study of language is . . . to study thought itself' (ibid.: 57). The study of grammar is 'an early form of the study of language. It is a preliminary way in which the mind can reflect upon its own nature' (ibid.: 59). And given that the mind is a microcosm, it is also, to some extent, a way of understanding the world. Durkheim criticizes this form of education for the extreme formalism that leads it to take as its subject matter a system that is so far removed from reality, but he immediately adds that, far from being sterile, it contained 'fertile seeds' and was 'the womb of logic' (ibid.: 63).

The great period or the age of logic (or 'scholasticism')

This 'second Renaissance' was, Durkheim notes, characterized by 'a veritable intellectual effervescence amongst all the peoples of knowledge' (1977[1938]: 65). The only explanation for this is that fresh circumstances meant that 'new inspiration was being breathed over the whole of Europe': the death of Charlemagne had led to the collapse of the Carolingian Empire, the consolidation of the Capetian monarchy and the establishment of Paris as the capital of the kingdom. This was a period of 'painful anguish and general anxiety' and of 'a thousand urgent problems', characterized by numerous conflicts and, finally, great religious mobilization. The Crusades encouraged both mobility and cosmopolitanism. Overexcitation and nomadism (ibid.: 67) were the two factors that, together with the creation of a new educational organization – the University of Paris – gave a new impetus to education.

These were 'impersonal causes' but when combined with 'individual accidents' they explain the changes that occurred in education when Abelard won his reputation in the famous philosophical controversy over *universals*. This occasioned the first great clash between faith and reason. The great achievement of scholasticism was, according to Durkheim, that 'It confronted dogma with reason, even though it refused to deny the truth of dogma' (1977[1938]: 73). Abelard emerges as the representative figure of this period of effervescence because, more so than anyone else, he personified the 'painful disharmony' (ibid.: 73) between faith and reason. His name is closely associated with the innovatory, or even revolutionary, change that led to the foundation of the University of Paris, 'the institution which most faithfully and representatively reflected this period' (ibid.: 75).

Durkheim devoted nine lectures to the university, analysing its genesis, its organization and the workings of its faculties. The university was innovatory for several reasons. It was independent of the church (its teachers were laymen and led a secular life); its teachers banded together, enjoyed a monopoly and formed a corporation; it was organized into faculties, with the faculty of arts as its central core; it established colleges and introduced a boarding system; it established new diplomas (the degree) and new curricula that placed great emphasis upon dialectics and disputation. At the organizational level, the development of the university involved both a process of relative autonomization and a process of differentiation.

An educational system is, in Durkheim's opinion, certainly a *body* (schools, an organization) but it is also, and above all, a *spirit* (methods and curricula). He discusses the medieval university's teaching methods at some length. They centred on textual commentary and exegesis. Teachers simply commented on books dealing with the sciences, and the curriculum was organized around a list of authors rather than problems. Hence the 'cult of the book'. Durkheim has serious reservations about this form of teaching which, unlike the methods used in his day, involved no direct contact with reality and no training in the sciences: the methodical and systematic confrontation of opinions took precedence over the systematic confrontation of facts. He describes this period as 'the age of dialectic' because teaching was designed to train students in the practice of dialectic: they were taught the skills of disputation rather than of reasoning. This implied, in Durkheim's view, a very partial and incomplete conception of education: 'the premium on brilliance . . . encouraged people to vie with one another in empty subtleties' (1977[1938]: 142), and dialectic degenerated into pointless wordplay, while the 'object lesson' degenerated into 'empty verbal exercises' (ibid.: 143). And because man was regarded purely as an intellect, other aspects of his 'multiple and varied' humanity (differences between arts and literatures, moralities and religions) were overlooked.

Humanism and erudition

The second part of Durkheim's lecture course dealt with the period stretching from the Renaissance to the present day. Educational institutions were hit by a 'violent crisis', and conflicting currents of opinion emerged. Durkheim identifies two such currents in the sixteenth century: the encyclopedic current associated with Rabelais, and the humanist current associated with Erasmus. On the one hand, a rejection of all regulations and a desire to transcend the average human condition, and a preference for science as positive knowledge when it comes to understanding both nature and man. On the other, a similar enthusiasm for scientific activity, but also a cult of literature (and especially great works of literature) and the ancient languages, and a desire to develop the child's ability to discourse (rhetoric), to teach him to express himself (stylistic exercises and compositions) and to 'mould his taste'. This development represented an intellectual and moral revolution, and Durkheim identifies the reasons for the change as the increase in wealth and wellbeing, communication between the wealthy and the aristocracy, the emergence of 'circles' and salons in which women played a central role, the recourse to letter-writing as a means of communication, the emergence of what he describes as 'polite' society (elegance, sensitivity, affectation), and the formation of a society of wits who were both elegant and educated.

Durkheim is very critical of this concept of education, which appears to him to be 'essentially aristocratic in nature' (1977[1938]: 205). It was 'an education for a life of luxury' and a 'totally inadequate preparation for life' (ibid.: 207). It cultivates only literary and aesthetic qualities, and can easily result in dilettantism. Durkheim is suspicious of this over-indulgent aesthetic culture, which exists in a world of fictions and images, and distracts us from action and the real world. He also regrets the fact that education, as defined by Erasmus, was based not upon a sense of duty and discipline, but upon emulation, and a system of prizes and competitions. The taste for fame and the thirst for glory were the main reasons for doing anything. Although they are very different, there are similarities between these two views of education: the enfeeblement of moral feeling, and an aristocratic and aesthetic conception that turns erudition and knowledge into something disinterested that is of no practical use ('knowledge for its own sake'). It loses sight of the 'immediate necessities of life', remarks Durkheim, who is very critical of this aristocratic conception. Even Montaigne, who preferred 'a well-constructed head to a well-filled one' (ibid.: 223), comes in for criticism because he is so profoundly indifferent to science and sees it merely as 'an accumulation of pieces of information' (ibid.: 222) that are of no practical or educational value. The problem is serious because although society and the economy are changing, education is not and has nothing to do with serious life. The change came not from the university, but from a new teaching corporation that was to destroy its monopoly and to succeed in gaining a sort of hegemony over the educational system: the Jesuits.

The Jesuits and classical culture

Does Durkheim defend the Jesuits? Their arrival marked a 'setback' for the trend towards the secularization of education and was met with 'strong resistance' on the part of the state, the clergy, the university and parliament. Their 'extraordinary success' had to do with the fact that the teaching they offered was appreciated and was in keeping with the taste and needs of the day. 'Let us embark upon an analysis of the facts', exclaims Durkheim (1977[1938]: 241], and then begins to make a detailed analysis of how the curricula of the *ratio studorium* were organized: the exclusion of French in favour of the ancient languages (including Latin and Greek), an increase in the number of written assignments, the emphasis on ancient literature, the pre-eminence of the oratory in literature, the introduction of a tutorial system (constant and personal contact between pupil and teacher) and of a system of permanent competition and emulation (prizes). They avoided the Moderns and took refuge in Antiquity, and created an academic environment 'foreign to the spirit of the age' (ibid.: 246). Anachronistic as it may seem, this system was to some extent in keeping with the times. A change in academic discipline is not, in Durkheim's view, possible unless there has been a great change in society's moral constitution: the moral organization of the school must reflect that of civil society. And the great change was the trend for individualization: the individual was becoming considerably more important in society, and was becoming a person. School discipline therefore had to take 'personal dignity' into account, and it has to be admitted that there was nothing 'arbitrary' about the Jesuits' innovations (ibid.: 264). Durkheim is, however, critical of the 'spirit of extremism' in which they made them: there was too much supervision, and an immoderate use was made of competition: this was 'a highly sophisticated piece of machinery designed to master the pupil's will' (ibid.: 266).

The realist age

The final stage in the development of education, and therefore in the mental development of Europe, is the phase of realism, which triumphs with the French Revolution. The educational achievements of the Revolution are characterized, on the one hand, by the 'encyclopedic viewpoint' (teaching all disciplines) and, on the other, by their practical and vocational preoccupations. The traditional system was completely over-thrown. Everything – from the organization of methods to the teaching staff – was new. And while a predominant role was given to disciplines relating to things and to nature (drawing, natural history, mathematics, physics and chemistry), the moral and social sciences that made it possible to study human nature also became part of the curriculum. The new theory of education was described as 'realist' because it was designed to put the pupil in touch with reality, with things and with nature; it was also scientific (and therefore very different from the literary culture of the humanists). Durkheim speaks (1977[1938]: 292) of the 'veritable about-turn' that came about with Saint-Simon, Comte and the positivist philosophy of the nineteenth century. Economic and political interests took precedence over religious interests. The goal was not simply to produce good Christians, but also good citizens (by training children to fulfil specific social functions).

Towards a New Curriculum: Studying Man and Studying Nature

The nineteenth century was 'not very rich in innovations', but it did provoke a 'backlash which, albeit falteringly, occupied the greater part of the nineteenth century . . . a backlash . . . which proved so difficult to resist and overcome. In this endeavour, our finest intellectual forces were engaged throughout this period' (1977[1938]: 305).[6] As a result, the system was in a state of 'extraordinary instability' and 'the programmes [were] in a perpetual state of flux ' Durkheim speaks of 'an evil which has been chronic for the whole century and which is apparently the product of impersonal forces' (ibid.: 307). It was time to cure the evil and 'to put an end to these wanderings' (ibid.: 308). Durkheim asks his students to leave the past behind, and to enter the future.

Durkheim has no intention of challenging the purpose of secondary education ('to arouse and develop a capacity for thinking without trying to tie it down to any one particular vocation'), but warns that there must be no return to any formalist theory of education: 'it is impossible to exercise a capacity for thinking in the void: it has to be directed towards particular objects of thought' (1977[1938]: 320). The mind therefore has to be brought face to face with reality, with things and solid objects. These can be divided into two categories: man or the world of consciousness, and nature or the 'physical world' (ibid.: 319). Durkheim's lecture ends with two conclusions, one dealing with 'education and the world of persons', and the other with 'education and the world of nature'.

He begins (1977[1938]: 323) by asking: 'How in schools are we to teach those things that have to do with man?' We cannot fall back on the old humanism, which relied upon the twin postulates that human nature is universally and eternally the same, and that 'the excellence of the classical writers, but especially of the Latin writers, constitutes the best possible academy in which to study the world of human nature'. This assumption is unfounded: 'far from being immutable . . . humanity . . . is infinite in its variety, with regard to both time and place' (ibid.: 323, 324). There is therefore no 'one single moral system'; there are as many different moral systems as there are types of society. How should the idiosyncratic, the accidental, the contingent and the ephemeral be dealt with in the classroom? Durkheim takes the view that the study of the infinite variety of human nature can be 'of immense educational value', provided that 'difference' does not imply a hierarchy of superior and inferior: 'In the myths, legends and skills of even the most primitive peoples there are involved highly complex mental processes, which sometimes shed more light on the mechanisms of the human mind than the more self-conscious intellectual operations on which the positive sciences are based' (ibid.: 328). Durkheim describes man and human nature to his students in terms that make generous allowance for diversity, flexibility and creativity.

He also reminds his students that willpower is not everything: 'We contain within us hidden depths where unknown powers slumber . . . there live in us, as it were, other men than those with whom we are familiar' (1973[1938]: 330). He emphasizes the importance of the findings of modern psychology, 'which reveal the existence of an unconscious psychic life beyond that of consciousness'. 'We must treat ourselves as an unknown quantity, whose nature and characters we must seek to grasp by examining (as is the case with external things) the objective phenomena which express it.' He gives the example of 'the choice of a vocation', 'which is often made at random, though it ought to be guided by objective considerations based on observation' (ibid.: 331).

The whole question of education revolves around the issue of which disciplines can give young people an idea of this diversity. Durkheim thinks first of all of the psychological and social sciences but decides that their 'rudimentary state' makes them unsuitable for this purpose. There is therefore no other choice but to turn to history – but not just any history. History must mean 'the history of several peoples', selected with discrimination: it is 'essential to take the pupil out of his own country, to acquaint him with men other than those to whose ways he is accustomed' (1977[1938]: 331–2). The history of Greece and Italy should certainly be taught, but so should that of 'lower forms of humanity.' Durkheim wants teachers to be familiar with peoples other than those of Greece and Rome. Historical education must also, finally, include the teaching of the relevant literatures. 'Let us then continue the work of the Humanists', proclaims Durkheim, before immediately adding: 'but transforming it and revitalizing it with new ideas' (ibid.: 332). The point is to show man as he is, 'with his almost limitless capacity for change, in the extreme complexity of his nature'.

Durkheim cannot avoid the great debate that brings the champion of literary studies into conflict with the defenders of science and which, to his regret, is 'far too vulnerable to personal preferences' for either 'aesthetic subtlety' or 'scientific precision' (1977[1938]: 334). He himself is less concerned with the 'means' (or discipline) than with the 'ultimate aim' of training the mind. Rejecting all forms of 'formal gymnastics' or 'training in the void', he reasserts the need to bring young people into contact with 'things', by which he means both 'human things' and the physical world. He is very familiar with the arguments that have been put forward to defend the teaching of the natural sciences: professional and utilitarian requirements (for engineers, those working in industry, shopkeepers, and so on) and the recognition that some scientific education is necessary if a man is not to be 'regarded as being intellectually incomplete' (ibid.: 336). But in Durkheim's view, it is important to teach science not only because it is efficacious (and gives us greater control over the world of things) or useful (and leads to an increase in material prosperity), but because, at a deeper level, 'it has the capacity of exerting a moral influence'. He puts forward several arguments in defence of science, first demonstrating that an understanding of nature gives some idea of man's position in the universe and thus inculcates 'a certain way of conceiving the universe' (ibid.: 336, 337). Secular education can therefore take the place of religious education. Durkheim gives two examples: the idea of determinism (which he contrasts with that of 'the arbitrary whim of fate' and that of 'a benevolent personal Providence'), and the idea that the human species is an animal species 'with an organic substratum' (ibid.: 338, 339). He then argues that young people must understand the processes of scientific thought because the sciences imply a way of thinking and reasoning (deductive reasoning in mathematics, the experimental method and inductive reasoning). Teaching science, in other words, is an 'invaluable tool in the development of logical thinking', and 'it is only by living the scientific life that we can acquire an understanding of this logic' (ibid.: 341, 340). He then adds that scientific method 'can only be really understood by the pupils if they see it in action'. In short, 'a sound scientific education seems to be an indispensable condition of all truly human education' (ibid.: 342, 342).

Durkheim is therefore less interested in contrasting the old humanist teaching with the new learning than in demonstrating that they complement one another. He ends his lecture course by describing his own educational ideals: 'Our goal must not be to turn each one of our pupils into a perfect polymath, but to render, in each one of them, the faculty of reason comprehensive' (1977[1938]: 348). We must remain Cartesians in the sense that 'we must fashion rationalists . . . but they must be rationalists of a new kind' who can see the irreducible complexity of things and the infinite richness of reality. The development of the 'whole man' thus implies a triadic culture: linguistic, scientific and historical.

Cartesianism; or, The National Temperament

Is Durkheim a nationalist? He regards Cartesianism as something that is specifically French, even as a 'national heritage'. The goal of education can thus be defined as using history and literature to introduce young people to a 'particular civilization: our own'. Durkheim speaks of 'we

Frenchmen', and describes France as a society or 'race' with a mentality of its own, and as a 'civilization'. He gives a few examples of the main characteristics of 'our national temperament' (1977[1938]: 276), including a taste for clarity and precision ('Our children must . . . be trained to think lucidly, for this is the essential attribute of our race; it is our national quality and the qualities of our language and our style are simply a consequence of this'); the love of order, as seen on the political level, the French being an 'essentially organising people' (centralization, unity of the nation, the general necessity of habit); and the pronounced taste for 'generalized and impersonal types' in literature (Andromaque, Célimène, Harpagon) and universalism – which can be contrasted here with relativism (ibid.: 272). There is therefore a tendency to ignore variations and diversity in favour of invariables and universals, and to set great store by intellectual cosmopolitanism.

Yet while he speaks with pride of the 'national genius', Durkheim has no qualms about denouncing certain features of the French character, which he regards as 'constitutional flaws': the urge for simplification, the 'mathematical mentality which inculcates in us a kind of natural tendency to deny reality to anything which is too complex to be contained within the meagre categories of our understanding' (1977[1938]: 275) and an abstract individualism. The French are too concerned with order: hence the excessive centralization, the emphasis upon moral and political unity and the loathing for anything unexpected or irregular. One of Durkheim's ambitions is to modify 'the French humour', and to encourage a new taste for a free and varied life, with all the irregularities that implies. In educational terms, Durkheim does not simply argue the case for discipline (and the respect for authority that this implies); he also displays a certain suppleness, and argues that allowance should be made for respect for the individual, autonomy and, indeed, freedom. He recommends, in other words, the golden mean.

As Mauss remarks (1969[1925]: 487), Durkheim is trying to 'to persuade young teachers to make better use of their strengths and to adopt the reforms he is hinting at'. Those who attended Durkheim's lectures and who went on to work in teaching or to play an administrative role in the government or the university would 'always remember these lessons' and would be able to introduce reforms based upon 'an objective understanding of social facts' (Bouglé 1938: 35).

19

Church, State and Fatherland

The Church is a Monster

The Chambre des députés first debated the bill proposing the separation of church and state on 21 March 1905. Every *député* recognized the importance of the debate; it was said to be 'the most serious debate our Assemblies have had since the Revolution'. But there was a vast gulf between right and left. The right accused the left of wanting to 'destroy Catholicism in this country', and asked: 'Do you want to annihilate religion?' Some *députés* feared that the *communes* and the state would take over the churches and religious buildings, and that priests would be reduced to begging for a living. Some on the left denounced 'religious interference in politics' as 'odious'. The socialist Gabriel Deville begged his fellow *députés*: 'In the name of the interests of the Republic, gentlemen, separate church and state as soon as possible.' A few days later, another socialist *député* intervened to say: 'Over the past 100 years, we have secularized marriage, the family, education and teaching; it is now time to go ahead with the secularization of the state.' Both sides were convinced they were right, and very few *députés* changed their views. The debates were stormy, and the outcome of the vote reflected the composition of the Chamber: 341 voted for the bill, and 233 against.

In March and May 1905, Durkheim took part in a debate on the separation of church and state organized by the Union pour la vérité, which had been founded a year earlier (Durkheim 1975[1904–5]).[1] The Union was liberal, elitist and concerned with ethical issues. It had a modest membership of, at most, 1,000 people. Economists, historians, sociologists, philosophers, lawyers, trade-unionists and businessmen were invited to exchange views on contemporary issues such as the separation of church and state, developments in education, and internationalism. The meetings were organized by Paul Desjardins (1859–1904), a *normalien* and *agrégé de lettres* who taught in a lycée; he was also a critic who wrote for the *Journal des débats* and a member of the Ligue des droits de l'homme. One of his goals was to reconcile Catholics and free thinkers, and he was said to be an agnostic.[2] Summaries of the Union's debates were published in *Les Libres entretiens*.

The 'free debate' was about one specific clause in the bill: the transfer of the powers of parish councils to voluntary associations. Ferdinand Buisson, president of the Assocation nationale des libres-penseurs de France, who had chaired the committee that drafted the bill, asked Durkheim if there was, from a sociological point of view, 'any justification for the bishops' distrust of associations'. In reply, Durkheim gave what he called his 'impression'. 'I think that the bishops' fears are groundless. To the extent that it will give laymen greater autonomy, the law will get the Catholic Church out of the abnormal situation in which it finds itself.' He added: 'From a sociological point of view, the church is a monster.'

His statement caused a stir in the audience, and Desjardin asked Durkheim to explain what he meant. Durkheim tried to be more specific: 'It is unnatural for such a vast and extensive association, which itself brought together such complex moral groups . . . to be subject to such absolute intellectual and moral homogeneity.' He thought the law would have a positive effect to the extent that it would 'unleash within this body differential causes that have been muzzled for centuries' and would lead to a 'natural diversity'.

Durkheim them turned to Buisson and asked: 'If two churches both describe themselves as Catholic, it would be against the spirit of the law for the courts to pronounce in favour of one of them. Suppose that both churches have a claim to the same building, then what happens?' In his reply, Buisson hid behind the letter of the law: 'The dispute would be settled by the courts.' His answer inevitably provoked the question: 'How would the court reach its decision?' A lawyer in the audience tried to clarify the issue: 'The court would resolve the issue in the same way that it resolves other issues: on the basis of the facts in the case, in accordance with general legal principles and in accordance with the rules of equity.'

In Durkheim's view, the debate revealed two positions; on the one hand, a defence of the 'monarchic nature' of the church and, on the other, the democratization of the church. 'When one looks at the top end of the church hierarchy, it seems that it must remain for ever military and monarchic. When we look at it from below, it appears that separation must be the start of a trend towards dispersal and decentralization.' Hence the question: 'How can these contradictory principles be reconciled?' When Abbé Hemmer, who was in the audience, replied: 'There is no need for either principle to prevail. They will cancel one another out', Durkheim intervened once again: 'The rule of even moderate public opinion is the essence of any democratic constitution. Something will change in the church, assuming that the separation takes place in conditions that stir up public opinion amongst the faithful.' In answer to those who believed that it was possible to reconcile the 'democratic spirit' and the 'monarchic spirit' inside the church and that there was room for 'initiatives', Durkheim simply rephrased his answer: 'It seems that separation will breathe new life into the church. There is a unitarian and authoritarian tendency, and then there is another one. How will the two sides behave with respect to one another?' This was, replied Abbé Hemmer 'a pleasing observation': in apologetics, he added, it was the basis for one of the proofs of the divinity of the church (Hemmer 1905: 4). The church might not, in other words, be as monstrous as Durkheim thought.

Patriotism or Internationalism? A Critique of Marxism

In March 1905, Durkheim agreed to take part in another open debate, on internationalism (1975[1905b]). The socialist movement was undergoing a process of restructuring at this time, and 'unity' was the great issue of the day. The Socialist Party emerged reunited after the great congress of April 1905, calling itself Section française de l'Internationale ouvrière (SFIO). Was the country gradually moving towards socialism, and was the 'true republic' beginning to emerge, asked foreign observers, including two professors at the Collège libre des sciences sociales in Paris and the Université in Brussels (Hamon and Hamon 1905: 128). Several members of the *Année* team enthusiastically joined the new party – Mauss was one of the first to do so. Durkheim was still a great admirer of Jaurès, but joining the party was out of the question. Some of his associates, who had political ambitions, took the same stance. Durkheim asked them to remain 'free spirits' despite their commitments.

The left's response to the rise of nationalism, which had been given a new impetus by the monarchist movement's defence of 'integral nationalism' and by the appearance of *Action française* (which published articles by Charles Maurras, Léon Daudet and Jacques Bainville), was internationalism. Did this mean giving the right a monopoly on nationalism? And where, some asked, was the workers' 'fatherland'?

People, state, nationality, nation, fatherland: none of these words, Paul Desjardins admitted, had anything more than 'an approximate meaning'. Hence the confusion. He was therefore only too happy to ask the sociologist Émile Durkheim what they meant, and to invite him to take part in a new debate. Durkheim replied: 'What is important is not to distinguish between words, but to succeed in distinguishing the things covered by the words.' Which human groups resemble one another? And which human groups do not? As for the words themselves, he was quite happy to drop 'those words used in common usage' and to introduce 'brand new ones'. Unfortunately, 'this cannot always be done'.

Durkheim then attempted to identify the four most important human groups. The first was political society (the 'highest and most individualized one. If we so desire, we can designate political society by the term "State".' The second was 'nationality': that is, a group of men who do not constitute a political society and yet nevertheless form a unity. Examples included Poland and Finland. The third was the nation: in other words, a group that was, like France, both a state and a nationality. The fourth was the fatherland [*la patrie*], or a political society, insofar as its members feel themselves attached to it by a 'bond of sentiment'. Durkheim did not give an example of a fatherland, but did mention Finland, which 'belongs to the Russian state'; 'but is there any Russian patriotism to be found amongst the Finns?'

In order to get the view of a geographer, Desjardins then turned to Vidal de la Blache, professor at the Sorbonne and author of a recent *Tableau de la géographie en France* (1903). The reply cited the specific examples of Switzerland and Belgium. Both were nations with observable differences in terms of race, customs and languages; they were also, Vidal added, societies cemented together by 'economic facts', namely colossal developments in industry and the need for new outlets. The same obviously applied to Europe as a whole: 'Economic interests are an element more than ever today in the formation of a nation.' In his response, Durkheim agreed that he would not dream of excluding this. But he did have one objection: the German state is a nation, but German nationality extends beyond the framework of the German state.

The Le Playsian Paul Bureau and the philosopher Frédéric Rauh then joined in the debate. What about Hungary and Austria? What about the Germans in Brazil, or French Canadians in Canada? Was the fatherland the same thing as the state? As more and more people joined in, the debate became bogged down. Two, and then three, types of patriotism were identified. Desjardins intervened in an attempt to focus the debate on the example of France, which was, according to Durkheim, a nationality organized into a state and therefore 'properly and fully a nation'. In an attempt to get his meaning across, Durkheim asked: 'Do you not feel three different realities: (1) the Russian state, (2) Polish nationality, (3) the French nation?' Vidal de la Bache replied with another question: 'French civilization, which you put forward in order to define France as a nation – is it distinguishable from Latin civilization as a whole?' In Durkheim's view, there was an obvious difference, and he mentioned three distinctive facts: the French Revolution, a centralized educational system, and early centralization.

It was clearly not easy to agree upon words and their definitions. Why not, asked Paul Bureau, speak of peoples rather than nationalities? Durkheim was uncertain about how to respond: '"People" is something different; we need that word to designate those in a state who have no share in its government'. The chairman of the debate once more intervened to restore some focus: 'Finally, we must tackle the definition of *fatherland*.' The philosopher André Lalande suggested that they should look first at the feelings of belonging that bind individuals to groups, make a distinction between territorial groupings, and also between different forms of patriotism (local, regional and national). Durkheim replied to his old pupil: 'We cannot classify all possible groupings and the particular attachment of men to each one of these groupings.' 'True patriotism means attachment to a nation that is also a state, to a country that is a state.' When someone gave as an example the patriotism of the Boers or of the dispersed Jews, Durkheim replied: 'That is the patriotism of nationalities' (1975[1905a: 178–86]).

Internationalism was the subject of another debate, but this time the focus was on 'class struggle'. Durkheim agreed to take part and, perhaps surprisingly, to discuss the issue with Hubert Lagardelle, editor of *Le Mouvement socialiste*. Lagardelle had been close to Marcel Mauss but their relationship became difficult when Lagardelle, who had grown disappointed with Millerand, drifted away from Jaurès and the Société d'édition et de librairie. The break was consummated when, in 1904, the journal took a different direction in order to accommodate the new Marxist currents bound up with the rise of revolutionary syndicalism. The socialist perspective defended by Lagardelle was, as Desjardins put it in his introduction, resolutely 'revolutionary and anti-patriotic'. The class struggle, 'non-solidarity' and the need to eliminate the parasitic classes implied both destruction and creativity. In Lagardelle's view, the idea of property, the family and the fatherland were 'completely alien to the labour movement. We represent a movement of barbarians and we are, in a word, antagonistic to bourgeois society.'

Paul Desjardins opened the debate by asking: 'Can "class consciousness" do as much to stimulate devoted energies as the patriotism you claim it has replaced?' Always willing to talk about 'class struggle', Hubert Lagardelle was the first to speak: 'I am very familiar with this, as are all socialists. The idea of "class struggle" is essential. It is the mother of socialism. Class struggle is the explanation for socialism.' Durkheim did not share that view and began by dismissing the idea of the 'need for destruction'; this idea, which was a relatively new addition to the socialist vocabulary, seemed to him to be mistaken, 'contrary to everything [he] knew about the facts', and an 'enormity'. He put forward three arguments: (1) the development of large-scale industry was 'normal' (why attempt to destroy this industrial system when it was simply a matter of 'harmonizing' juridical and moral institutions?); (2) the worker was not just a producer or *homo economicus*; (3) the idea of destruction was a 'childish dream'. 'This is not the way to recreate collective life; if we destroyed our social organization, it would take hundreds of years to build a new one.' He went on: 'In the meantime, there would be a new Middle Ages . . . a New Dark Age.' Rather than 'hastening that period, we must use all our intelligence to ward it off, or, should that prove impossible, to shorten it and make it less dark' (Durkheim 1970[1906]: 286–7). Lagardelle was not at all moved by Durkheim's arguments: 'Working-class socialism is a movement created only by the working class. No intellectual has any part to play in it. The workers do not have to justify themselves to an intellectual like M. Durkheim. An intellectual cannot understand their arguments; and he is not there to get them through their exams.' 'That is not the point', retorted Durkheim. Turning to the question of patriotism, Lagardelle dismissed it as a bourgeois position, as the workers regarded themselves as being 'outside the fatherland'. 'That conviction may scandalize you, but it is a fact.' Durkheim interrupted him: 'All illnesses are facts', which provoked some laughter in the audience.

Durkheim was annoyed by the attitude of Lagardelle, who hid behind 'the feelings of the vast majority of militant workers' but refused to quantify those 'feelings'. 'Come now, you cannot abdicate your reason! You cannot approve of a violent movement simply because it is violent. I know that one cannot always make rational judgements, and that action requires a certain partisan spirit. But we are gathered together here in this room to judge our feelings, to think about them, and not to surrender blindly to them.' And when Lagardelle replied that 'the ideas [he was] expounding were the products of a major mass movement', Durkheim became sarcastic: 'We know. You are a mass, you are a force. So? Is that your only justification?' 'No', replied Lagardelle, who now went back to Durkheim's three arguments. He once more defended the idea that 'capitalist production bears within it the forces that will destroy the capitalist regime and transform society'.

This was a short-term view, replied Durkheim, who went on to give the revolutionary militant a few lessons in history: (1) major economic changes (the transition from manufacture to large-scale industry) were not a purely nineteenth-century phenomenon: there were seventeenth- and eighteenth-century precedents (the transition from the crafts of the Middle Ages to the large-scale manufacturing of the eighteenth century); (2) socialism began with the French Revolution and there was nothing new about the ideas Lagardelle was defending. And when Largardelle described his ideas – the negation of the principle of individual property, resistance to the arbitrary power of employers, and the right of the working class to regulate its own labour – as 'specifically working class', Durkheim objected: 'Which is of course why, even though I am no proletarian, I have in many respects come up with the same ideas in my study . . . Of course these ideas take on a class complexion . . . But they are indeed the same ideas, with different nuances' (1970[1906]: 291). They were, he argued, members of the same society, breathed the same 'moral atmosphere' and were therefore 'imbued with the same ideas.'

The hour was getting late and there seemed to be no agreement in sight. 'You are a prisoner of the Marxist materialist formula', declared Durkheim, who was sorry to find that Lagardelle's ideas were no more than 'articles of faith' that required no proof. At risk of repeating himself, he once more criticized the idea of the need for destruction. 'This is a notion that I cannot understand . . . I cannot even conceive of that.' Durkheim obviously did not believe in 'revolution' or 'miraculous socialism'. In his view, socialism, far from 'going against the nature of our societies', was in keeping with 'the general trend of their normal evolution': there was no need to 'throw them into upheaval' in order to establish socialism. He concluded: 'It seems to me that history illustrates this conception' (1970[1906]: 290–2). Durkheim was therefore a socialist, though the word required some qualification.

Durkheim took part in one more free debate that year. It was on the similar topic, 'Patriotism and internationalism of the social classes', and participants included Paul Bureau, the philosophers Belot and Rauh, and the historian Seignobos. Like his colleagues, Durkheim accepted that 'the workers are internationalists, and the employers are not' and that 'one is even astonished at the passivity manifested by the employers to the threat of wars. On the contrary, the resistance to them is very strong among the workers . . . Most businessmen and industrialists are in favour of peace, but they do nothing to avoid war'. Their different attitudes had, in his view, less to do with the effects of economic causes than with 'the moral environments in which they are at work' (1986[1906]: 214).

Did they simply have different interests, asked Paul Bureau. Durkheim replied with a question: 'What indeed can the worker lose in a war?' 'His life!' came the answer from the floor. 'The employer too', he replied. 'Reasons of an economic nature' were not enough, in his view, to explain working-class resistance: 'To show resistance one must disdain what people may say. One must not be afraid to upset certain received ideas' (1986[1906]: 215). When a certain Mme Campain claimed that the workers had replaced their religious faith with a faith in the future, Durkheim disagreed completely: 'The worker has no sense of the real future, he lives outside time, in the ideal world. If he had the misfortune to think overmuch about the future, his situation would be frightful' (ibid.: 216). Loss of belief in God was not an adequate explanation for their faith in internationalism; one had to look at how the new morality was being shaped. Belot asked whether positive morality was destined to become 'the morality of the people' as Comte believed. The same theory could be found in Saint-Simon, replied Durkheim, who concluded with the enigmatic words: 'I understand this well, but within the system there is something else' (ibid.).

Durkheim returned to the issue of war in the public lecture he gave at the École de la Paix in 1906. This was a private institution founded in 1905 by Horace Thivet in order to spread pacifism. The list of lecturers for 1906 also included the name of Gustave Belot ('Freedom') and Jean Izoulet ('The elite and the crowd'). Durkheim's lecture was entitled 'The feeling of honour.'[3] Was war also a question or honour, or of morality?

Morality Without God? Rebelling Against Tradition

In 1905, *La Revue* (formerly known as *La Revue des revues*) organized a symposium on the theme 'Morality without God: an attempt to find a collective solution', and Durkheim agreed to take part. His comments were brief. He described himself as a man who regarded morality 'quite simply as the vital element in collective discipline', and as 'a human creation, fashioned by men and for men'. He went on: 'I do not mean that we can construct it in the silence of the study and by dint of pure understanding alone . . . It is a set of rules of conduct, of practical imperatives which have grown up historically under the influence of specific social necessities' (1975[1905a]: 335). Morality, in other words, 'belongs to the realm of life, not to speculation.'

Durkheim once more argues that it is possible to develop a science of morality in the sense that there can be a science of the phenomena of the physical world, and that it is both possible and legitimate to use history

and statistics 'to discover which causes have given rise to the moral precepts which we practise'. Rather than relying on 'vague syntheses', it is
possible to 'weigh up one by one the principal maxims of morality in order
to determine their conditions, to see what social states they result from,
and what social ends they serve. It is to the development of such a science
that I have devoted myself for twenty years or so' (1975[1905a]: 336).

This does not, however, make it possible to say what morality will
become. The science of morality, as defined by Durkheim, teaches us two
things: morality must change, so as to fit in with the new conditions of
social life, which are constantly changing, and 'a knowledge of the present
and the past is the only means available for predicting the future with the
least margin of error'. Durkheim outlines a methodology: 'It is by analogy
with the past that it is possible to conjecture – one can do no more than
that – what the change will be.' He then parries the objection that his
science of morality is still in its infancy, and argues that it is nonetheless
able even now to 'provide all the pointers required for elementary teaching' whereby children must be taught why they must be attached to their
family, to their country and to mankind. He was confident of this because
this method is being applied today in primary schools and in lycées by a
number of my former pupils: 'it seem that this has not produced any bad
results' (1975[1905a]: 337).

In the winter of 1905–6, Durkheim was once more invited by the École
des hautes études sociales to address a very general audience on the theme
of 'morality, religion and society'. According to André Lalande, he went
much further than that by trying to demonstrate on practical and historical grounds that 'God is society' and that society, when seen in positive
terms, can provide morality with all the supports provided by the revealed
religions. Durkheim began by listing the attributes of God (a friendly but
terrible force, a mysterious force that transcends us and constitutes the
source of our union, the eternal who outlives human generations), in order
to demonstrate that society possesses all these attributes. The function of
religious rituals is to 'make us stronger'.

Durkheim then went on to describe the evolution of religion, which
takes us from the 'ethnic gods' of barbarous peoples to the 'one God' of
civilized peoples. Could this expansion of social life have 'expanded the
conception of God and given birth to monotheism'? And what of 'the
positivist cult of humanity'? That cult had been 'imperfectly realized', but
it expressed a profound and authentically religious truth, as it meant not
that God had disappeared into humanity, but that humanity had discovered God within itself, and adored God with equal fervour as a result
(Durkheim 1975[1906a]: 11).[4]

The reference to Auguste Comte is more than explicit: according to
Lalande, Durkheim's talk was 'a speech by one of humanity's great
priests'. Durkheim obviously did not attend 'the little church in the rue
Monsieur-Le-Prince', but Lucien Lévy-Bruhl, who had published a book
on the philosophy of August Comte in 1901, was not the only one to see
him as 'Comte's real heir'.

In February 1906, Durkheim once more addressed members of the Société française de philosophie on the need for a science of morals, given 'the confused state of moral ideas'. There was, in his view, only one solution: work methodically, begin with the facts, and arrive at a provisional definition. Durkheim understood 'morality' to mean any 'system of rules of conduct' with the following 'distinctive features': obligation (or what Kant called the notion of duty) and desirability (the notion of good). These notions were, he added, somewhat contradictory, but they could also be found in the idea of the *sacred*: the sacred being is both a being that is prohibited, and a being that is loved and sought after (Durkheim 1974[1906a]).

The initial conclusion is obvious: morality begins when the individual becomes a member of a group, no matter how restricted it may be. That group might be a family, a guild or corporation, political society, the fatherland or an international grouping.[5] There must, then, be a group or a 'collective subject' that is greater than the sum total of the individuals who make it up. Durkheim is aware of the analogy between his argument and that of Kant: his 'society' is an equivalent to Kant's 'God': We must choose between God and society – 'that choice leaves me indifferent, as I simply regard the divinity as society transfigured and conceived in symbolic terms'. His conception revolves around three postulates: (1) society is a 'good thing, and desirable to the individual'; (2) society has a moral authority, hence the obligatory nature of rules of conduct; (3) insofar as they are collective feelings, the nature of 'moral things' is *sacred*. 'It would seem that in presuming to think of it and study it with the procedures of *profane* science we are profaning morality itself and threatening its dignity' (1974[1906a]: 49). Hence the great reluctance to hand 'moral reality' over to 'men's disputes.' Society is therefore the 'pre-eminent goal of all moral activity'. That is why society has a moral authority and demands respect. This, Durkheim believes, is the source of moral rules. But is this true in any empirical sense? Answering such a question would, he argues, require an exhaustive study of all the particular rules that combine to make up our morality. 'I have followed this method in my teaching.' And he adds: 'In the course of my research, I have yet to encounter a single moral rule that is not the product of determinate social factors.' The fact is, in his view, undeniable: the morality of a society or people is 'a function of its social organization'. In other words, 'Every society has, roughly speaking, the morality it requires' (ibid.). Durkheim once more uses the example of moral individualism or the cult of the self, which is, in today's society, 'the product of society': it is society that made from man the God that it serves.

Does this conception of morality preclude the possibility of passing judgement upon it? Are we doomed to follow public opinion without ever being able to rebel against it? This was a criticism that was often directed against Durkheim. His answer to that objection is that the science of the real gives us the ability to 'modify and control the real. The science of moral opinion give us the ability to judge opinion and, if need be, to rectify it' (1974[1906a]: 61). Take, for example, the hypothetical example of the 'temporary upheaval' in which a society loses sight of the sacred rights of the individual; one could, he believes, restore them authoritatively by recalling that respect for those rights is part of the structure of our great European societies. By the same criterion, in the face of new ideas, the science of morals can demonstrate that such ideas 'relate to changes that have occurred in our collective conditions of existence'.

Durkheim even goes so far as to say that, when moral ideas are 'outdated', rebellion (against moral opinion) is justified. This is, of course, a difficult moral dilemma. If one thing is certain, it is that 'we cannot aspire to any morality other than that demanded by our social state'. All this is a matter of reason, and we must always rely upon what we know. What, he asks in conclusion, are we to do when science is not sufficiently advanced to be our guide? 'We must do the best we can' because, when we have to act we are left with no other choice but to have recourse to 'summary, hurried science, and to rely upon our sensibility to remedy its shortcomings'.

Durkheim hoped that he had gone some way towards making his concept of moral facts more comprehensible. His goal was the same as it had been throughout the previous 20 years of research: to provide an 'empirical description of moral facts', while respecting their specificity – in other words, their religiosity. When he read Durkheim's text, Élie Halévy could not resist joking: 'Durkheim was admirably enthusiastic, even fanatical, I would say.' He added: 'He interested me, and clarified many things about his doctrine that were still obscure to me – but he did not convert me to the theory that anything within us that transcends the level of purely biological and material existence, must be regarded as social, and no more than social.'[6]

The discussion continued on 23 March and brought Durkheim face to face with his philosopher-colleagues Parodi, Brunschvicg, Darlu, Jacob, Malapert and Rauh. They raised a lot of objections. Many of Durkheim's answers reiterated his old themes; he also clarified some points and, to a certain extent, qualified them. When Dominique Parodi asked if the state of society was more important than the state of public opinion, Durkheim replied that understanding the state of opinion was less important than understanding the state of society. And when someone asked what morality modern French society needed, he replied that the only thing that could be done was to analyse that society: increased concentration and unification, improved means of communication, the absorption of local life into general life, the rise of big industry, the emergence of the spirit of individualism. Public opinion, confused aspirations, passions and prejudices must obviously be taken into consideration, but the important thing was to 'get in touch with reality'.

Durkheim was an unlikely rebel, but his listeners were shocked by his comments on rebellion. Alphonse Darlu saw any rebellion against the moral tradition as 'the individual's revolt against the community, the revolt of individual feelings against collective feelings'. Durkheim himself took the view that the principle behind revolt was the same as that behind conformism: both had to do with 'the *real* nature of society'. And when he appealed to reason, he meant that reason, or the science of moral facts, should be methodically applied to moral reality. 'All my efforts have been devoted to extricating morality from the sentimental subjectivism in which it is still trapped' (1974[1906b]).

When Darlu claimed to see 'infinitely more things in the consciousness of any individual than in the most complex and most perfect society', Durkheim retorted: 'It seems to be that the opposite is obvious.' 'It is in and thanks to society that science and art find their full existence.' The same was true of morality: 'The moral life of society, with all its complementary and contradictory aspirations, is so much richer and complex!' Turning to the question of the 'ideal man', he then demonstrated that 'the man we are trying to be is the man of our times and our environment ... It is a rather gross illusion to believe that we gave birth to him in our innermost consciousness and of our own free will' (1974[1906b]: 74).

As might have been expected, those present could not agree about the sacred nature of moral facts. Durkheim therefore tried to clarify his remarks: although he obviously believed that morality would no longer be morality if there was nothing religious about it, he was, he insisted, trying to describe the sacred 'in secular terms'. 'That is, in fact, the distinctive mark of my attitude' (1974[1906b]: 69). All his efforts were devoted to translating the religiosity of morality into 'rational language': 'I do say that there is such a thing as the sacred, but my secular thinking still remains fully independent.' The paradoxical claim that dependence (upon society) was the path to (individual) liberation did not go unchallenged. In reply to a question from Léon Brunschvicg, Durkheim clearly stated that the individual submits to society, and that submission is the precondition for his liberation; 'there is no contradiction there'. Asked about the moral authority of the community, he replied that most of our mental life is a product of society; our individual reason is what the collective and impersonal reason known as science makes it, and science is an eminently social thing. Our aesthetic faculties and the sophistication of our tastes are determined by art, and art too is a social thing. Our ability to control things is part of our greatness, but we owe it to society. It is society that sets us free from nature. It is therefore only natural that we should see society as a superior psychic being. 'The believer bows before his God', and we are right to feel the same about the community (1974[1906b]: 73).

This would be the case even if society were not 'ideally perfect' in the sense that not even God is perfect (he created a world full of imperfection and ugliness). Durkheim knew only too well that people spoke disdainfully of society: 'Then it is seen only as a bourgeois administration with the gendarme to protect it', but society was 'the most rich and complex moral reality that we have ever had a chance of observing' (1974[1906b]: 74).

Durkheim was primarily interested in the moral reality that existed outside the minds of philosophers. How could that morality be discovered? This was a delicate question, but not an insoluble one. It is possible to study moral maxims and ideals; there are lots of them and they are easily accessible. It is also possible to study the law, literary works and the conceptions of philosophers. It is possible to decipher all these things, and then 'go further in our analysis of the communal consciousness to that substratum where these obscure and only half-conscious currents are elaborated' (1974[1906b]: 77). These were, Durkheim admitted, 'clumsy methods . . . but this is a difficulty that faces all science at the outset. We have first of all to cut broad avenues that may bring in some light to this virgin forest of moral and, more generally, social facts' (ibid.). The final objection concerned what Frédéric Rauh called 'subjective representations of morality'. Durkheim did not deny their existence: 'Every individual has, to a certain extent, his own morality . . . Each one of us has his own moral life' (ibid.: 78). There was therefore such a thing as 'an inner moral life', but, at least for the moment, Durkheim deliberately left aside this field of research.

When G. Aslan defended his thesis, 'The ethics of Guyau', one member of the jury, Gabriel Seailles, raised the question once more concerning the 'individual or society': 'In order to have a social individual, you need society, and society needs individuals.' Durkheim insisted that his point of view did not imply the negation of the individual: 'It is impossible to explain the whole of the individual by the social, but nor can one succeed in explaining the social by the individual. The social as such must be explained by the social. The sociological point of view thus implies that the two terms "individual" and "society" are postulated from the beginning as inseparable' (cited in Lukes 1985[1973]: 638).

Marriage and Divorce

Men of letters, lawyers and statesmen all appeared to be ready to 'pronounce . . . without hesitation in favour of the most drastic and revolutionary solution as if it were self-evident' (Durkheim 1978[1906]: 240). Durkheim is referring to 'divorce by mutual consent', which was the subject of an article he published in the *Revue bleue* in 1906. He wrote: 'Anyone who tries to resist so universal a current risks passing for a reactionary', but tried to defend himself against that charge: 'Yet, to whatever extent one can know oneself, I do not feel that I am a reactionary' (ibid.). He added: 'There is no institution, even among those which pass for being the most sacred, which I consider to be above question. I believe that the moral world is just as properly the object of the disputes of men as the physical' (ibid.).

The proposed reform of the divorce laws caused Durkheim an 'uneasiness', and his article is an attempt to explain why. He did not set out to challenge the principle of divorce (which allowed a couple to separate if their relationship had become intolerable) or to deny that they had the right, in certain conditions, to 'escape from their marriage'. He was mainly worried about the institution of matrimony itself: 'There are . . . reasons to fear that divorce by mutual consent would have a very dangerous influence on marriage and its normal functioning.' An attempt to remedy 'individual evils' might, that is, constitute 'a grave social malady whose repercussions the individual would bear' (1978[1906]: 241).

The law had been relaxed, and it was becoming easier to obtain a divorce. Attitudes were changing. And yet studies had shown that the change in the law did not appear to have had a negative effect on marriage rates, the birth rate or even the crime rate.[7] Durkheim took the view that 'it is very certain that a marriage that can no longer fulfil its function has outlived its purpose' (1980[1906d]: 430). The fact that the courts were making divorce easier – and that public opinion agreed that it should be made easier – did not, however, mean that there was anything natural about this trend. The real question was: 'Is it normal that husband and wife can sever by a single willful act the marriage bond?' (1980[1906d] 429–30). Marriage, in other words, is not simply a by-product of the wishes of the parties concerned, and is something more than a contract between two individuals: it is a social institution.

Durkheim also raises the question of the subjective issues involved:

> If only the feelings the spouses think they have for each other were indeed like the ones they experience in reality. But it is common knowledge how frequent the errors are. It happens all the time that we love the one we think we hate, we perceive the ties that bind us to one another only at the moment when they are severed . . . The idea they entertain of their relationship is therefore a very bad criterion for judging the true state of those relations. (1980[1906d]: 430–1)

Durkheim remained convinced that a rising divorce rate posed a threat to the institution of marriage, and warned statesmen that they should be neither too rigid nor too flexible. The same year also saw the publication of Auguste Rol's *L'Évolution du divorce*, which was reviewed by Durkheim in the next volume of the *Année*. Like Valensi, Rol argued that the divorce law should conform 'to the nature of things and to the requirements of the public conscience' (Durkheim 1980[1907d]: 283). One of those 'requirements' was the secular morality that had replaced 'outmoded religious beliefs', and which looked upon marriage only as a contract. Durkheim's response to this argument was forceful:

> It is in no way demonstrated that the marriage bond ought to lose its former holy character simply because such sanctity ceases to exist in the mind in the form of religious symbols. The institution of marriage has in itself a moral validity and has a social function, the implications of which go beyond the concerns of the individual. (Ibid.: 283–4)

Worries and Annoyance

Durkheim's lectures at the Sorbonne came to an end in late June 1905, and he settled down to work on the tenth volume of the *Année*. 'That is how

I am filling my time', he wrote to his nephew. Two first-year *normaliens* came to tell him of their interest in his discipline: 'I did nothing to persuade them – on the contrary – but they have both decided to do sociology. I asked them to think hard before taking that decision. But they have made up their minds.' The two young men were Maxime David and, in all probability, Jean Rey. David seemed to Durkheim to be 'serious-minded', and Rey was 'quite resolved to do some serious work'. Durkheim already had something in mind for them: David could do something on marriage in Australia, and Rey could use the archives of the Bureau des statistiques criminelles to do some work on suicide, 'the way we did for *Suicide*'.[8]

Maxime David had attended Durkheim's lectures at the Sorbonne, and later, under his supervision, wrote a dissertation entitled 'Group marriage in Australia'. David had also attended Mauss's lectures and was awarded a postgraduate diploma from the École pratique des hautes études in the same year that he was awarded his *agrégation en philosphie* (1907). He was teaching philosophy in a secondary school, had an interest in philology, history and sociology, and had contributed to two volumes of the *Année*. Jean Rey was a member of the École normale supérieure's class of 1904, and was also awarded his *agrégation de philosophie* in 1907. He later contributed to the *Année*'s criminal sociology and moral statistics section (volumes XI and XII).

It was examination time: 'I have finished the exams', Durkheim wrote to Mauss. 'I am not tired, but it is time I knocked off.'[9] He was thinking of going to Switzerland for the holidays again, and left for Klosters. At first, the weather was so bad that he thought of 'running away' to Épinal. He still had a number of problems on his mind: his health, his nephew's 'situation', and the 'situation' of the journal *L'Humanité*. First and foremost was his health: 'I am, I think, coming home in a good state', he wrote to his friend Hamelin: 'I feel quite strong, and I am walking well. There is one area in which I have made no progress, and that worries me somewhat. I thought in July that my verbal memory was failing, and it has still not improved.'[10]

Then there was the 'sexual affair' Marcel had got himself into and which, in his view, was no one else's business. When Durkheim learned that a woman was 'sharing' his nephew's life, the uncle was angry: 'Think of your own happiness! You are living in a make-believe set-up because there has, in moral terms, been a divorce (since there is a moral divorce when serious things take place that cannot be forgiven), in a family you have broken up, and you spoil everything you touch.'[11] 'No one approves of what you are doing', he added, before accusing his nephew of being 'morally reckless'. Everyone was indeed worried about Marcel. Durkheim was trying to protect his sister Rosine, Marcel's mother: 'I do not think that knowing the truth would do her any good, so I am doing all I can to keep her in the dark.'

Émile took offence at his nephew's 'constant criticisms' of 'our close-knit family': 'In any case, you take advantage of it, because that is what lets you devote yourself to your favourite studies without having to worry about money.' He could not understand his nephew's willingness to 'break the ties that mean most [to you] in order to preserve the ties that keep [you] prisoner'. If this continued, he would 'shorten his mother's life' and cause his uncle pain. 'It hurts me to see the state you are in; it hurts me to see you in pain, and to see that you are spineless.' He begged him: 'I wait with impatience you hear that you have come to your senses. For my sake, go back to being what you used to be for me. Please.'[12]

Marcel was away in England at the time. Émile thought that this would be a good time for his nephew to 'finally make up your mind': 'Get a grip on yourself while you are on you own. Being alone will do you a world of good.' But when he learned that his nephew was about to 'meet that woman over there', he felt that he had been shamefully deceived: 'I will never forgive you as long as I live.' Yet he still refused to believe what was happening.[13] A few weeks later, when he realized that his nephew 'was not brave enough, or man enough, to put up with the self-imposed solitude he had so sincerely agreed to', he concluded: 'Obviously. It's over.' He then told Mauss that their relationship could not go on. 'When you get back, we will make the necessary arrangements. We will go on with our scientific work together, but there has to be an end to the life we used to share, as that is the way you want it to be. Just say to yourself that I am suffering as a result.'

In the autumn of 1905, Durkheim was complaining to Henri Hubert about the constant delays. Bibliographical problems could be handled by post, though not without difficulty, but what really 'tortured' Durkheim was the work his nephew was supposed to be doing on the Eskimos. He had agreed to coauthor a paper on that topic with Henri Beuchat, but there was still no sign of it.

Now that he was back in Paris, Durkheim tried to find out what his nephew and collaborator was up to, and was growing worried: 'I still haven't seen anything', he wrote at the end of July. 'I would have gone away with my mind at rest if I had seen some of this work.'[14] A few months later, he asked his nephew: 'So when am I going to see this manuscript? I should have had a draft at Easter, and here we are in September!'[15] At the beginning of September, Durkheim went in person to Mauss's apartment, where he found Beuchat's manuscript, but not his nephew's: 'No sign of yours . . . Where is the manuscript?' He was afraid that Mauss had lost it and was, he said, 'more worried than ever'.

By late December, Durkheim was very angry: it looked as though he would have to give up his New Year's Day holiday if he wanted to get the ninth volume of the *Année* finished. It was obviously Mauss's fault: 'You have spoiled the coming year for me', he wrote to him. 'If this year is like the last, I give up and it will be your fault.' A few months later, he wrote: 'The end of the *Année* grows closer by the day, as it is now physically impossible to start work on volume X on time. You will have to take full responsibility for that.'[16] The situation became more complicated when Paul Fauconnet accepted the position of philosophy teacher at the lycée in Cherbourg: 'Fauconnet's departure deprives me of a precious supporter.'[17] To make matters worse, Durkheim had just experienced 'a period of fatigue, during which I had some definite symptoms'. The symptoms themselves were 'of no importance', but 'according to the doctor they are a warning that must be taken seriously'. Although he had 'very recently . . . recovered his health', he was, 'unfortunately' still forced to look after himself (showers and walks), and that left him with little free time, now that he had to teach two lecture courses a week.

Fauconnet was away, Hubert was suffering from fatigue,[18] and Mauss was 'distracted' by his political – and other – activities. Durkheim was having health problems, and his teaching was taking up more and more of his time. Editing the journal was becoming 'a very heavy task'. 'The task gets heavier', he told Hubert, 'and I no longer have the strength to face up to it.' He said the same thing to Mauss: 'If I do not get some help, I will have to give up. So it is obvious that we will not get beyond volume X. Perhaps it would be better to give up now.' He then made a definite threat: 'If they want me to do it one last time, I might try to get some help. It is obviously no longer possible in these conditions.'[19]

Durkheim still believed that 'we have done some useful work' and that 'the continued existence of our group is of great moral importance', but he was 'losing heart' and was acutely aware that he was not getting any younger:

> I feel that I am in my prime and I can, I believe, still do something, especially if you all help. But in order to do that I cannot devote at least four months of the year to bibliographies and reviews. The 10 years I have spent working with you have had a very useful influence. We have restored sociology's image; but we cannot spend for ever on this preparatory work. We have to do more than get on with things; we have to force ourselves to finish this.

All the *Année*'s contributors were in the same position, but the situation was 'more acute' for Durkheim. 'I was 48 a few weeks ago. What does not get done in the next 10 years will never get done. We have to come to terms with that and look at the situation like men.' He concluded: 'The time has come for us to force ourselves to work.'[20]

A Generation Goes Astray: Bouglé Stands For Election; Mauss Goes To Russia

When a general election was called for May 1906, Célestin Bouglé was tempted to stand again as a candidate for Toulouse. He was fascinated by political and social issues. Alcan had just published his *De la Démocratie devant la science*, which was subtitled 'Critical studies of heredity, competition and differentiation.' Its aims were obviously scientific – the book was designed to refute the main arguments of social Darwinism and to challenge Spencer's thesis that unfettered competition was a pre-condition for progress – but they were also political. Bouglé's political philosophy was based on a recognition of the need for both competition and cooperation, but he also argued the case for state intervention. The primary role of the state was to correct hereditary inequalities and to guarantee universal access to material preconditions for autonomy, and therefore education. It was a militant book, and each of its arguments represented a 'tactic'. They were elements of a political programme: inheritance laws, labour regulation (health and safety, accident-prevention), mutual insurance against accidents and social welfare schemes. But was Bouglé really cut out to be a politician? His friend Halévy, who hoped that he 'would live to see a liberal republican regime', tried to 'put him away from politics': 'I can't really see you going into politics . . . There is nothing specific to be done in France.' A few days later, he advised him to leave France: 'Go to America.'[21]

Célestin Bouglé did not listen to his friend's advice, and stood for election. Halévy joked that he was now 'a monsieur preparing his election campaign'. He found it 'amusing' that his friend might become a *député*, and 'almost' began to believe that he might be elected. Bouglé was defeated, but the left did win the election. The Radical Socialists, the Radicals and their allies formed a majority government with 360 seats. The united socialists increased their share of the seats from 41 to 54, and the independents now had 20 deputies, including Millerand and Viviani.

Halévy once more advised Bouglé: 'Finish your book on castes, and go to America.' Bouglé still dreamed of establishing 'a French solidarist party'. Halévy told him that he was 'more utopian than Jaurès'. He then asked his friend: 'How far back does a sociologist have to stand to see social phenomena? Can the Durkheim school teach me that?'[22] Most of the *Année*'s contributors were faced with the same dilemma: how could they defend a socialist ideal without sacrificing their lives as scholars? Heavily influenced by (Durkheimian) sociology, that ideal was neither revolutionary nor Marxist, and implied that there should always be a critical distance between research and political activity.

A year after its foundation, *L'Humanité* was facing a major crisis due to falling sales. It needed to raise new capital. Marcel Mauss asked Durkheim to speak to his wife's uncle Moyse Dreyfus (1837–1911), a company director and partner of his brothers Henry and Salomon. 'I know nothing about *L'Humanité* or the people around it', replied Durkheim. 'All that I know comes from you, and you admit that you do not know very much.' He was obviously exasperated. 'There is something ridiculous about putting me – and a relative – forward as the designated saviour.' Durkheim was unwilling to take such a step unless his friend Jaurès asked him to 'intervene'. 'In that case, I would simply have to act as an intermediary. I would acquit myself of that role with pleasure, and as best I could.'[23] He would not take the decision without being approached by Jaurès. He did, however, write to his uncle Moyse to 'explain the paper's situation' and to tell him that it would 'greatly to be regretted if the paper had to fold before the elections', without asking for anything. Uncle Moyse was 'obviously willing to help', but before going any further Durkheim wanted to know 'if help was needed, and if so, how much' and suggested that his nephew should ask

Jaurès himself. 'If the answer is "yes", we will see what needs to be done and how we should go about doing it.'[24]

New funds were eventually raised from working-class, union and cooperative organizations, and one generous citizen. The paper was saved, but had to cut its staff. Mauss was no longer part of the team, but was free to go on contributing on an unpaid basis. He decided to leave *L'Humanité*. His friends approved of his decision. Lucien Herr advised him to get back to work with a vengeance, to finish his thesis quickly and to finally give the general public a real sense of his 'scientific worth'. He added: 'The day you are elected to the Collège de France, you will be able to go back to your active life without sacrificing your life as a scholar . . . In this society, you know that high academic and scientific qualifications give what we do an authority and a value it would not necessarily have without them.'[25]

Marcel then did a U-turn, declared himself to be 'absolutely devoted' to Jaurès and agreed to join the board of directors responsible for publishing *L'Humanité* in his capacity as a spokesman for the SFIO. His uncle was furious: his nephew had 'distorted the truth', and he had been the last to be told of his decision: 'I do not need to tell you how much that hurt me.' He was also very disappointed that Marcel was being so inconsistent: 'On the one hand, you tell me that you are sick and tired of politics . . . On the other, you contradict yourself by saying you have all sorts of plans . . . There is nothing here to suggest any change of lifestyle.' He went on: 'You have *absolutely no modesty*. You don't shrink from any task, not even those you are completely unqualified to take on.'[26] He then became even more insistent: 'You have reached a turning point. You have to decide if you are going to abandon your legitimate scientific ambitions – by putting them off year by year – and continue to get involved in things that require both *strengths* and *weaknesses* that you do not have.'[27]

The following July, Marcel agreed to go to Moscow and St Petersburg, 'on behalf of *L'Humanité*' and at the request of Jaurés. His 'mission' was to pass on the advice of Jaurés, who was, he later said, recommending 'strength and prudence' (Mauss 1997[1921]: 435). The socialist leader was currently leading a unitary campaign in support of the Russian Revolution and feared that the Tsar was planning a *coup d'état*. Mauss also received a commission from the ministry for public instruction to pursue his ethnographic research in Russia.

As soon as Mauss reached St Petersburg, the Tsar dissolved the Duma. Mauss's journey had been wasted. He visited a few ethnographic museums in Russia, and travelled back via Warsaw and Berlin, where he visited other museums. A disappointed Mauss got back to Paris in August. Durkheim was on holiday in Val-André (Côtes-du-Nord), and wrote to his friend Hamelin: 'My nephew is back from Russia after having drawn a blank, and is completely disgusted with the people and things he saw there. It is to be hoped that his experience will take him back to what I see as his real work.'[28] Mauss insisted that he wanted to publish an article on what was happening in Russia in the *Revue de Paris*. His uncle did all he could to discourage him:

You have just spent a fortnight in Russia. You do not speak the language. And you want to write an article on Russia! You are familiar enough with scientific method to know that that is not a sensible idea. You would do well to realize that silence is your best course of action; we understand nothing about what is happening at home, and you want to try to understand something about a very obscure state of affairs, when you have urgent tasks to deal with.[29]

Paul Fauconnet was of the same opinion, and spoke of the 'bad habits of our generation or, rather, our little group'. For the benefit of his friend, he added: 'You cannot be both an ethnographer and a journalist.'[30]

A Ninth *Année*: 'The Life of Collectivites is Not as Simple as That of Birds'

The manuscript of volume IX was sent to the printers towards mid-May 1906. The proofs now had to be corrected. Durkheim was once more annoyed that Marcel was taking too long over his set. He proposed a new 'solution': they would publish, still on a yearly basis, what he called *Annales de la sociologie*. 'Each volume could contain, in addition to the articles we publish, a bibliography, but no reviews.' The next volume would not adopt that format. 'We will stay with the present formula for volume X of the *Année*, and use the time to get ourselves organized.'[31] Contributors to volume IX of the *Année sociologique* included Mauss's faithful students René Chaillié and Henri Beuchat (who compiled the index), and two of Mauss and Hubert's younger students from the École pratique's fifth section (Antoine Bianconi and Jean Reynier). There were also two new recruits: Philippe de Félice and Georges Gelly, both students at the École pratiques des hautes études. Félice, who had a postgraduate diploma from the École (1880), was putting the finishing touches to his *L'Autre Monde. Mythes et légendes du purgatoire de Saint-Patrice* (1906), and would later become the curator of the Bibliothèque du protestantisme. Georges Gelly (1882–1917) was a graduate of the École normale supérieure and an *agrégé de grammaire* (1905). A philosopher and a philologist, he was interested in aesthetic and literary history, and the relationship between myths, fables and the novel. He began his research with classical antiquity before moving on to the Anglo-Saxon and Celtic Middle Ages (Mauss 1969[1925]: 495).

There were few major changes to the way the journal was organized. 'Religious sociology' was still the largest section: at more than 150 pages, it accounted for 25 per cent of the 600 pages devoted to reviews. 'Juridic sociology' and 'economic sociology' accounted for 16 and 15 per cent of the total respectively.[32]

Some of the works analysed were by authors close to the journal. Henri Hubert said of Salomon Reinach that he gave sociology 'almost the same meaning as we do'. Durkheim himself reviewed Albert Bayet's *La Morale scientifique*, remarking that he had 'read us with sympathy' and presented his own book 'as a practical application of the principles by which we are inspired here', only to add that 'on many essential points we cannot accept the interpretation he seems to give to our thought' (1980[1906a]:135). The *Année* could still be cutting, as was apparent from Robert Hertz's comments of Edmond Demolins's *Classification sociale*: 'a premature undertaking'. Durkheim wrote some 30 reviews for the ninth volume: this appeared to be his new cruising speed. He once more reviewed Théodule Ribot, an author he knew well and who had just published *Logique des sentiments* (1980[1906b]). Nor had he forgotten Gabriel Tarde. One of Tarde's last texts was on 'interpsychology', and Durkheim was scathing. The notion of interpsychology was 'arbitrary and confused', and Tarde had simply compiled 'a few freely annotated anecdotes' (1980[1906c]: 72).

The ninth volume of the *Année* (1904–5) contained two major articles, both dealing with the topic of 'variation': Antoine Meillet's 'Comment les mots changent de sens' ['How words change their meaning'], and Marcel Mauss's 'Essai sur les variations saisonnières des sociétés eskimos' ['Seasonal variations of the Eskimo'], written in collaboration with Henri Beuchat. Meillet edited the 'Language' rubric, which was still marginal, as it included at most some 10 reviews and notices. He regarded language as a social fact: 'The existence of human societies is the first precondition for the existence of language. It is one of human societies' indispensable tools, and they use it constantly . . . Language is therefore an eminently social fact' (Meillet 1906: 1–2). While he recognized the autonomy of language and the specificity of linguistic facts, Meillet wished to correct the anomaly that led sociology to ignore linguistics. His study was restricted to a group of linguistic facts in which the influence of society was obvious: changes in the meaning of words. His thesis was as follows: the fact that men who speak the same language are divided into different classes has an influence on the meaning of words. His teacher Bréal had said precisely the same thing when he took the word 'operation' to demonstrate how the meaning of a word can vary from one professional group to another: surgeons, soldiers and mathematicians all use it to mean different things.

Social heterogeneity is therefore a factor that explains change. This is true not only of professional groups, but of all sets of individuals bound together by special ties: men and women, dominant and dominated. All societies are characterized by contradictory tendencies: the tendency to become more uniform, which reflects the influence of society as a whole, and the tendency to become more differentiated, which reflects the influence of particular groups (which use the special languages known as slang). It is therefore conceivable that general languages will give way to special languages, and vice versa. Meillet gives many examples to illustrate the phenomenon of social distinction: the differentiation of the elements that make up society is its primary cause.

Marcel Mauss had persuaded Henri Beuchat to work with him on his study of seasonal variations in Eskimo societies: 'I had thought only of collaborating with Beuchat', but 'the poor devil', as Hubert called him, was 'worn out by his money problems'.[33] In the event, Mauss had to 'rework everything' and write the whole article himself, except for the final section. Beuchat, who was an excellent draughtsman, drew the plans of the houses and the maps. The article was given a very Durkheimian subtitle: 'A study in social morphology' (Mauss and Beuchat 1906). It gave Mauss an opportunity to pursue his work on primitive forms of classification and to demonstrate that 'the mentality of inferior tribes is a direct reflection of their anatomical constitution'. The methodological issue was, in other words, to establish a correlation between, on the one hand, social life in all its forms (morality, religious, legal structures) and, on the other, their material substratum or morphology (volume, density and make-up of the population). For this study, Mauss abandoned the usual comparative method (which Durkheim also used) and referred only to Eskimo societies. He described his decision to do so as a 'crucial experiment' that would prove his hypothesis that social life goes through 'successive and regular phases of increased and decreased intensity, rest and activity, and expenditure and reparation'. Eskimos spent the summer living in scattered groups, with families living in tents, and the summer in tightly-knit groups living in houses. Adaptation to environmental constraints (hunting caribou and walruses) was not enough to explain these seasonal variations. The two seasons also differed in other respects (religion, family, property regimes, political organization, etc.): winter was characterized by individualism, isolation and moral and religious poverty, and summer by collectivism, moral and religious unity, and the communal sharing of property and food in feasts.

Mauss found the same 'curious alternation' in other societies (the Kwakiutl of the Pacific coast) and in the rural areas of Western societies: torpor during the winter and great animation during the summer ('the time for festivals, major projects and great debauchery'). One might even speak, he concluded of a 'general law': collective life, and its 'violent' effect on minds [*consciences*], was only possible if group members could, to some extent, get away from it' (Mauss and Beuchat 1906).

The question of the rhythms of collective life had preoccupied Durkheim when he was writing *Suicide*, and was also of interest to Henri Hubert who, in his study of time in magic and religion, tried to explain the origins of the calendar. Although he was sympathetic to the *Année*, E. Sidney Hartland thought that Mauss's argument was 'weak' (unsupported by the facts) and remarked that, while it was possible that these variations corresponded to some general law, it was by no means obvious that they resulted from morphological changes: 'The life of communities is not as simple as that of birds' (Hartland 1907: 100).

Promotion At Last

The faculty board met in the Sorbonne on 16 June 1906. There were three candidates for promotion: Émile Durkheim (*chargé de cours*), Célestin

Bouglé (*professeur* in the faculty of letters, University of Toulouse) and M. Malapert (*professeur de philosophie,* Lycée Louis-le-Grand). Boutroux and Séailles briefly described the 'qualifications' of the 'competitors' and described their colleague Durkheim as 'the outstanding candidate by far'. The result of the vote came as no surprise: Durkheim was the winner with 25 votes: no one voted against him.[34] Durkheim's appointment as *chargé de cours* was extended until 31 November 1906 and his annual salary was raised to 9,000 francs. He would be promoted to his chair on 1 November 1906.

Durkheim was closely identified with the 'new Sorbonne'. News of his appointment was greeted with enthusiasm, but also with a lot of virulent criticism. Charles Péguy devoted two articles to Durkheim in the *Cahiers de la quinzaine,* one on the situation of history and sociology in modern time, and the other on the treatment of intellectuals in the modern world. He compared Durkheim to one of Joan of Arc's inquisitors; he rejected the idea of a godless world, which looked to him like a form of regression. It implied a new governmental catechism that would be taught by gendarmes acting under the benevolent eye of the police. In his view, official freedom of thought was quite simply the opposite of true freedom.

V

Morality and Religion

20

A Tenth Anniversary

The 'strength' of Durkheim's doctrine stemmed, as Goblet d'Alviella remarked (1913), from his ability to recruit supporters inside the university system and to gather some 30 collaborators around the *Année sociologique*, most of them with 'official positions in higher education'. The end of the 1900s did mark a turning point, as the *Année* consolidated its position in the academic field. Meillet was teaching at the Collège de France, and Mauss had applied for a chair there. Paul Huvelin was a candidate for a position in the Paris faculty of law. Célestin Bouglé was teaching at the Sorbonne, and Paul Fauconnet was working in Toulouse, while Paul Lapie had been promoted to a tenured chair in Bordeaux. *L'Année sociologique* was celebrating its tenth anniversary. The claim that sociology had been 'institutionalized' (Clark 1968a) has some validity in that a combination of social circumstances had allowed the discipline to become a professional activity in its own right and to acquire greater social legitimacy. But at the very time when (Durkheimian) sociology was becoming part of the academic landscape, Durkheim and his associates were the target of growing criticism and a lot of misunderstandings. Philosophy was 'in crisis' and the future of philosophical thought looked uncertain. Durkheim was both an essential point of reference and open to criticism. On the one hand, he enjoyed the respect of philosophers, who still regarded him as 'one of their own' and recognized the 'philosophical dignity' of his work (Boutroux 1908);[1] on the other, he was, as Xavier Léon put it, 'one of the men you must insult in order to become a philosopher'.[2] Léon's comment is an indication of how much Durkheim was hated by his philosopher-colleagues.

Intuition versus Method

Henri Bergson's *L'Évolution créatrice* was published in May 1907, and the initial print-run sold out within weeks. The book was a sensation and had a huge impact that extended far beyond academic circles. Bergson's lectures at the Collège de France were drawing bigger and bigger crowds. For those who saw his philosophy as a celebration of the dark forces of instinct and intuition, his success was a 'nightmare'.

What became known as 'Bergsonism' marked the revival of philosophy. Neither the left nor the right was spared the impact of this new trend, and the social sciences did not escape unscathed. Georges Sorel praised Bergson's book in a series of articles in *Le Mouvement socialiste*; in his *Reflections on Violence* (1999[1908]), he drew heavily upon Bergson's work in his elaboration of his theory of (revolutionary) myths . In Sorel's view, the rightful place of Bergson's theory lay 'in the social sciences', and the theoretician of revolutionary syndicalism transposed the philosopher's theories of creative freedom and *élan vital* into the study of social movements.

The *Année*'s young contributors Maurice Halbwachs and Robert Hertz were also fascinated by Bergson. Halbwachs had been taught by him at Henri-IV, and then at the École normale supérieure, while Hertz had attended his lectures at the Collège de France in 1901–2. Both had been won over. Hertz regarded Bergson as 'one of the most daring philosophers of the contemporary period'; he was an 'inventor', and his philosophy was 'subtle and bold' (see Hertz 2002). Bergson's thought also appears to have made a great impression on François Simiand, who thought that the notion of duration (*la durée*) was similar to that of an *élan* that derived its strength from its capacity for transformation and innovation (Bouglé 1936). Henri Hubert also read Bergson, citing him in his 'Étude sommaire du temps dans la religion et la magie' (1905); he then distanced himself from him.[3]

The Sorbonne was proudly republican and rationalist, and most of its professors took a dim view of the philosophy of *élan vital*. Durkheim cherished 'an undying hatred' for the philosopher who had once been his fellow student at the École normale supérieure. As Mauss (1969[1933]) was to point out, Bergson did acknowledge, in *The Two Sources of Morality and Religion* (1963[1932]), 'the contribution made to these sources by the sociologists, including Durkheim and others', but relegated the facts they studied to the domain of the 'closed' and the 'congealed'; understanding all that was 'open, vital, and truly psychical and creative' was the preserve of philosophy and psychology. Bergson did not actually take a stand against the 'positivist Sorbonne', but he did have right-wing sympathies, and the struggle against positivism was one of the right's favourite themes. On the other hand, he is said to have been in favour of establishing a chair in sociology at the Collège de France and he did praise Durkheim (Mossé-Bastide, cited in Fabiani 1998: 113).

Enemies and Competitors

Gabriel Tarde was now dead, but there had been few other changes in the small world of sociology. René Worms, for example, was still very active. He had recently published a three-volume *Philosophie des sciences sociales* (1903–5), was lecturing on the history of sociology at the École des hautes études sociales and, from 1910 onwards, would teach a course on 'Specific social sciences and general sociology' in the faculty of law. He was still the editor of the *Revue internationale de sociologie* – which had scarcely changed and which remained, according to Bouglé, 'too general'. He was the driving force behind the Institut international de sociologie and organized the monthly meetings of the Société française de sociologie. The society now had almost 300 members, and continued to attract a wide audience of lawyers, doctors, civil servants, army officers, journalists and industrialists. There were also a few female members, including Mme Lydie Martial, who wanted women to be represented on its committee. The society was very proud to have politicians such as Léon Bourgeois, Ferdinand Buisson and Joseph-Paul Boncour as members. Its discussions were 'very instructive' and enjoyed great popularity but, as Bouglé (1907b: 193) emphasized, there was never any objective approach to the topics under discussion. René Worms did not escape the criticisms of the *Année sociologique*'s contributors, especially when he recycled Durkheim's ideas about religion without acknowledging his sources.[4]

Worms could still count on the same group of contributors to the *Revue internationale de sociologie:* Levasseur and Fouillée (France), G. De Greef (Belgium), Simmel and Tönnies (Germany), and Ward and Giddings (United States). Worms owed part of his 'success' to his ability to poach some of Durkheim's colleagues, critics and even associates and to persuade them to become involved in other projects: Charles Andler, Marcel Bernès, Ferdinand Buisson, Léon Duguit, Alfred Espinas and Henri Hauser. There had been only one major change at the *Revue* itself: the recruitment of René Maunier, a *diplomé* of the École pratique, where he attended Mauss's lectures between 1907 and 1911, and a graduate of the Paris law faculty. He had been elected to the Société de sociologie de Paris and was now its journal's editorial secretary. He also contributed many reviews and articles, including a series on 'Religious life and economic life' in which he often referred to Durkheim's work.[5]

Gustave Le Bon, for his part, published *Évolution de la matière* in 1905, followed by *Évolution des forces* in 1907. He was a regular contributor to the journal *L'Opinion*, which hosted a weekly Wednesday lunch in a well-known restaurant. Regular guests included Paul Painlevé, a professor in the Paris faculty of science, and they were joined by a few women, including Anna de Noailles. Le Bon became the guru of Marie Bonaparte, a great friend of Sigmund Freud and one of the founders of the French psychoanalytic movement.

The Le Playsians of *La Science sociale* had founded a Société internationale de science sociale,[6] held monthly meetings and ran the somewhat eccentric educational establishment known as the École des Roches, which had been founded some ten years earlier by Edmond Demolins. As the core group expanded, it came to include Paul Bureau (1865–1923), Gabriel d'Alazumba (1869–1934), Philippe Champault (1852–1915) and Paul Descamps (1873–1946). Methodological issues were now more important than ever before. The famous nomenclature established for the observation of working-class families by the abbé de Tourville was a frequent topic for discussion, and many proposals for modifying it were put forward, mainly by Paul Bureau, Joseph Durieu, Philippe Champault, Léon Géri[7] and Paul Decamps (whose *Cours de méthode de science sociale* was published in 1913). The death of the abbé de Tourville in 1902, followed by that of Demolins in 1907, considerably weakened the dynamism of the group. The conflict between the Le Playsians and the Durkheimians then became less pronounced, as can be seen from Bureau's subsequent career. He later argued that too much importance had been given to 'material elements' (the environment and work) and began to place more emphasis on ideological and psycho-social factors, or what he called 'representations of life'. Like his colleague Joseph Wilbois, he subsequently recognized the importance of the work of Durkheim and his associates, and believed that, before long, sociologists would no longer be working in isolation (Kalaora and Savoie 1989: 212).[8]

Arnold Van Gennep's decision to launch a new journal entitled *Revue des études éthnographiques et sociologiques* in 1907 was the only new initiative.[9] Relations between Van Gennep, Durkheim and the *Année sociologique* were especially complex in that their scientific preoccupations were similar. After attending Léon Marrillier's lectures at the École pratique des hautes études, Van Gennep knew where his 'vocation' lay. He devoted himself to general studies of religious phenomena, and worked closely with the *Revue de l'histoire des religions*, for which he wrote many reviews. During a stay in England, he developed close contacts with Frazer,[10] the British anthropologists and, especially, Andrew Lang, whom he admired for his research into 'very minor details' (Van Gennep 1912). In 1903, he submitted a dissertation on 'Taboo and totemism' to the École Pratique and, subsequently, published *Mythes et légendes en Australie* (1906) and *Rites de passage* (1909). Antoine Meillet described these as 'major works that revealed a rare ability to understand the mental state of half-civilized populations'.[11] Marcel Mauss, in contrast, gave them harsh reviews, and criticized the author for 'wandering through history and the whole of ethnography rather than restricting his study to a few specific and typical facts' (Mauss 1969[1910]: 555).

Durkheim's Collaborators

Health, marriage, family and (obviously) career were the main concerns of Durkheim and his associates. Now that Durkheim was out of the running, his associates had some chance of being elected to the Collège de France. Antoine Meillet and Charles Fossey were indeed chosen in 1906. Meillet had been a regular contributor to the *Année* since volume V and Fossey was an occasional contributor, with four reviews in volumes VI and VII. Meillet was appointed to a chair in comparative grammar, and Fossey to a chair in Assyrian philology and archaeology.[12] Was there hope for Marcel Mauss too? Lucien Herr thought so.

The death of Albert Réville, a professor at the college (and president of the religious sciences department at the École pratique), at the beginning of 1907 gave Mauss his first opportunity. Mauss was 35, and had just become assistant director of the École pratique. He could count on the support of his old teacher Sylvain Lévi and the newly elected Meillet and Fossey. His friends urged him to put his name forward. Mauss would have preferred to remain in the shadows and make way for his elders. He was not prepared to exploit personal connections to get himself elected as a successor to Albert Réville's son Jean (1854–1908). Jean Réville was secretary of the religious sciences department, and very active in the academic world. He was editor of the *Revue de l'histoire des religions*, and an organizer of scientific congresses. His main rival was Georges Foucart, an Egyptologist and professor of the history and religions of the Ancient East at the University of Aix-Marseille. His father, Paul Foucart, was a professor at the Collège de France. It was he who put forward his son's application. This was going to be a 'battle between the heirs'.

Jean Réville was elected in the second round of voting at the meeting of 17 February 1907, when the votes cast for Mauss and Vernes in the first round were transferred to him. Mauss was the runner-up by a considerable margin. 'High praise', said his mother, who was anxious to see Marcel 'put some order into his life, work and finances'.[13] For his own part, Mauss, who was very interested in museology, in fact hoped to be appointed Director of the Musée du Trocadéro, but that post eventually went to René Verneau. He was not finding it easy to escape from what his mother called the 'mousetrap' of the École pratique. Célestin Bouglé, for his part, had every reason to hope that he would be able to leave Toulouse for Paris when a post at the Sorbonne fell vacant at the end of November; a *chargé de cours* in the history of social economics was required to cover for Alfred Espinas while he was on study leave. There were two other candidates: Henri Hauser, from the University of Dijon, and Marcel Marion from the University of Bordeaux. Espinas quickly pronounced himself in favour of Hauser, who had, he said, 'for some years been producing insightful studies of the economic theories of the sixteenth and seventeenth centuries in relation to contemporary economic phenomena'.[14]

The faculty board met on 2 November. Espinas compared the qualifications of the two main candidates: 'M. Hauser is obviously not a philosopher . . . But Bouglé is not a historian, and his enthusiasm for sociology has, to date, distracted his attention away from economics and its history. He is a logician, a sociologist and a politician with a remarkable gift for oratory.' The choice was between an economic historian who was not a philosopher, and 'a philosopher, polemicist and a politician' who was neither an economist nor a historian.

Émile Durkheim then spoke and gave, not his own opinion, but that of his colleague Victor Brochard, who had been unable to attend the meeting and had expressed his views in writing: 'Bouglé is a philosopher-sociologist who must be given the post for which he is equipped.' He recalled, with a certain irony, that Espinas had been the obvious candidate for the same reasons, and that Bouglé's appointment would be in keeping with the wishes of the comte de Chambrun who, when he endowed the chair, had definitely taken the view that it should be 'have to do with sociological studies'. Most of the faculty's historians took the same view.

Brochard put forward three further arguments. First, many students were interested – 'passionately so' – in sociology. Second, Durkheim was in a difficult position as he had to 'divide his energies between sociology and pedagogy, and no longer had the assistance of Henry Michel'. Finally, the faculty needed a philosopher or a sociologist who could both explicate the work of political writers and economists, and prepare students for the *agrégation*. There were, that is, good reasons for supporting Bouglé's application: he was 'young, full of enthusiasm, and a very talented orator'.

Durkheim pointed out that, given that this was a course on the 'history of doctrines', the candidate required 'the ability to analyse ideas and a knowledge of the philosophical doctrines that lay at the root of all the great economic theories'. The die was almost cast. Bouglé received 25 votes, as opposed to the 4 cast for Hauser. Marion and Milhaud both received 1 vote. On 26 November, Bouglé was appointed *chargé de cours* (the position was endowed by the comtesse de Chambrun and the Université de Paris) and was required to teach the history of social economics for the academic year 1907–8. Bouglé's public lectures were on 'Social forms and economies' in 1907–8, and on 'Economic materialism and French socialists up to 1848' the following year. He also gave a major public lecture on 'The economic philosophy of the labour movement' to the Société des amis de l'université de Paris, and published an article on 'Marxism and sociology' in the *Revue de métaphysique et de morale*.

Lucien Lévy-Bruhl, who was sympathetic to Durkheim's sociology, was appointed to the chair in modern philosophy the same year. Victor Brochard, who had the support of Durkheim, was appointed to teach a course in German language and literature.[15] Things were changing in the faculty. Louis-Georges Rodier, an old colleague of Durkheim's at Bordeaux, moved to Paris to replace Victor Brochard as professor of the history of ancient philosophy when he died on 25 November 1907, just as the academic year was about to begin. Rodier had taught at Bordeaux since 1894, first as a *chargé de cours* and then as a professor. Had it not been for Octave Hamelin's accidental death, the whole of the 'Bordeaux school' would now have been in Paris.

The chair in social philosophy at Toulouse was still vacant, and Durkheim, Bouglé and Lévi-Bruhl orchestrated a strong campaign to have Paul Fauconnet appointed. The only problem was that he did not have a doctorate. He therefore took a year's sabbatical and spent the time in Paris, writing his thesis on responsibility. Durkheim admitted that there was a problem and explained in the reference he wrote that the reason why Fauconnet had not completed his thesis was that he had 'serious domestic and material problems that all too often left him without the free time and peace of mind that he needed'. There was, he emphasized, also another reason: his collaborator was devoting 'most of his time' to *L'Année socio-*

logique. 'This periodical would not appear were it not for the abnegation of its contributors, who have had to sacrifice much of their personal
work to devote themselves to a publication that does not publish their
names. If, as we are ready to admit, it has been of some use, is it not fair
to take this into account?' He reminded the director that 'for the past 10
years, Fauconnet has looked at every relevant book on penal law, criminal responsibility and civil responsibility'. His contributions were often
'equivalent to a fascicule of between 40 and 50 pages'.

Durkheim 'dared' to support his associate's application because the
post required a specialist in social philosophy: 'Now that sociology is a
compulsory part of the degree programme, would it not be desirable for
it to be taught by truly competent teachers?' It was no longer possible for
it to be taught by 'philosophers who describe social phenomena intui-
tively'. Anyone teaching such a course should have 'become familiar with
a whole culture', or should, in other words, 'have the requisite historical
or statistical knowledge'. Paul Fauconnet met those requirements. 'Ten
years of special studies have given him a very good preparation for teaching a course such as this, and I am convinced that he will be of service.'
Durkheim emphasized that Fauconnet was 'not without some publications': he had contributed to the *Revue philosophique*, had coauthored an
article on 'Sociology and social science' (which had been translated into
English and Spanish), had written an article on sociology with Mauss for
the *Grande Encyclopédie*, and had contributed to the *Année*. Durkheim
ended his letter to director of higher education, Charles Bayet, by apologizing for 'having taken the liberty' to write to him'.[16] Paul Fauconnet was
appointed.

The appointments of Célestin Bouglé and Paul Fauconnet were major
events that consolidated the Durkheim group's position in France. In June
1907, Paul Huvelin, who was teaching in the Lyon law faculty, applied for
the position of professor of Roman law in the Paris faculty of law. Émile
Durkheim once more wrote to Bayet to 'explain briefly and in purely scientific terms' why his associate, whom he had 'come to value', was more
interesting than he might seem. He was referring to Paul Huvelin's 'special
competence' in Roman law: 'He is wonderfully qualified to examine
Roman law in the light of comparative law, would do so carefully and
could therefore add new interest to the subject.' He stressed the value of
Huvelin's 'active involvement' with *L'Année sociologique* over a period of
many years: 'He is one of the young generation of jurists who are trying
to develop new lines of research, not without encountering some resistance from those around them.'[17] Durkheim's support was not enough to
overcome the 'resistance', and Huvelin did not get the position at the
Sorbonne.

Durkheimian sociology was gradually taking root in the provincial universities. Bordeaux was still one of its strongholds, as Paul Lapie and
Gaston Richard were teaching there. Lapie had become the tenured professor of philosophy in 1907, and was organizing a survey designed to
refute the argument that state schools were 'the mother of all vices' and a

'breeding ground for criminals'.[18] He was also completing his *La Femme dans la famille*, which was published in 1908.

Younger collaborators like Charles Lalo and Maurice Halbwachs, who both had a background in philosophy, were at the start of their teaching careers. Lalo was awarded his doctorate for his *Esquisse d'une esthétique musicale scientifique* (Paris: Alcan, 1908) and was appointed a professor of philosophy in Limoges the following year. In the same year, he also published a study of Aristotle in the 'Les philosophes' collection. Halbwachs was teaching philosophy at the lycée in Tours, and his first book – a study of Leibniz – was published in the same collection (1928[1907]). Why Leibniz? Halbwachs described the German philosopher as a researcher who, throughout his very active life, took an interest in everything from politics to war and military inventions, from the customs of savages to the Jesuit missions to China. He was also a believer in science.

Teaching and Thesis Examiners: The Facts!

In his lectures, Durkheim concentrated mainly on the same themes, but his interest in religion once more became apparent in the academic year 1906–7. In 1907–8, he reverted to the theme of the evolution of marriage and the family. For the next three years (1908–11), he lectured on morality, as in previous years. His lectures on pedagogy were called 'Teaching morality in schools,' 'The history of pedagogic doctrines', and 'The formation and development of secondary education in France'.

As we have already seen, he was often invited to take part in examining theses.[19] The vivas gave Durkheim an opportunity to discuss some basic issues and to defend his own ideas. His general approach was to look at the coherence of the author's argument, but he also demanded a great deal of documentation and even data. He accepted, for instance, that Louis-Germain Lévy had made 'an attempt to interpret these texts as impartially as possible', but criticized him for his tendency 'to believe that the Jewish people was a people apart' (see Lukes 1985[1973]: 627). Durkheim's many criticisms of Lévy's thesis concentrated not only on its form – 'its design is defective; the texts are grouped in a somewhat artificial fashion' (ibid.) – but also on its content, and especially on his rejection of the idea of totemism – 'totemism . . . was not part of your subject' (ibid.: 628). He was far from convinced by Lévy's claim that totemism was not found in Hebraic societies.[20]

Durkheim praised Mendousse's thesis 'From animal training to education' because the first part was 'very rich', but was somewhat critical of the second part because the subject was 'very general' and 'a somewhat lengthy dissertation', of the type written at school. It was, in other words, 'academic'. And when Mendousse attempted to summarize the entire history of pedagogy, he became sarcastic: 'The history of pedagogy has certainly not come to an end; these studies do not go far enough for one to be able to come to such summary conclusions' (Lukes 1985[1973]:

647). Durkheim suggested, finally, that a clearer distinction should be made between training and education; 'This is the significance of social life: for the creature of instinct it is necessary to substitute a being who does violence to these instincts . . . Training inculcates habits, education inculcates rules . . . It is in the specific nature of man to follow rules. One knows how difficult it is to inculcate in the child a feeling for a rule' (ibid.: 648, 649).

When he examined Revault d'Allonne's study of the Monodist group or sect, Durkheim focuses on the issue of data, and wondered 'how many Monodist churches there have been, and what was their geographical distribution' (Lukes 1985[1973]: 639). And while he praised Cramaussel's thesis for 'the sincerity of the observations', he immediately went on to ask for 'several clarifications relating to the method followed. How have the observations been made? Are the data transcribed immediately or on the basis of more or less distorting memories?' (ibid.: 641). His main criticism was that the author 'has observed only four children, so that, sometimes, a generalization rests on one sole fact' (ibid.). His final complaint was that 'Your whole theory is based on an impressionistic interpretation of the child's smile' (ibid.: 642).

Examining Maurice Pradines, Durkheim began by remarking: 'You have remarkable facility in handling concepts, and your book bears witness to an undeniable power of meditation' (Lukes 1985[1973]: 645), but he was surprised to hear that the author had 'really "lived" it' . . . What about the control of the facts? I have looked in vain throughout the whole book for a single instance taken either from common experience or personal experience. But let us leave this point: you are not a scientist, but a dialectician. I do not scorn dialectics, but I want people to understand themselves, and also that they should make themselves understood' (ibid.: 646).

Disciplinary Conflicts

Durkheim was leading a busy life: never before had he been so active in public affairs. He was involved in what might be called academic and disciplinary debates about sociology's relationship with disciplines such as ethnology, history, political economy and geography. There was also the issue of the *agrégation*.

The debate about the boundaries between disciplines was far from closed. In 1906, the Comité des travaux historiques et scientifiques (Section des sciences économiques et sociales) discussed the relationship between ethnology and sociology (see Lukes 1982: 209–10), while the Union pour la vérité debated 'Teaching law'. In 1908, Durkheim chaired a discussion at the Sorbonne for the Congrès des sociétés savantes concerning relations between sociology and geography. In April of that year, he debated the question of 'Political economy and the social sciences' with the Société d'économie politique (ibid.: 229–235), and then a discussion on 'History and sociology' at the Société française de philosophie. In 1909, his essay on 'Sociology and the social sciences' was published in the collective *De la méthode dans les sciences* (see Durkheim 1978[1909]). Then there was the endless debate on 'the science of morality', and his important reply to Simon Deploige's comment on the influence of Germany sociology (see Lukes 1982: 257–60).

Ethnology

The issue of whether or not ethnology should be subordinate to sociology led to a debate between René Worms and Émile Durkheim. In Worms's view, the two disciplines were as different as gathering together building materials and constructing a building, analysis and synthesis, and the study of barbarian or savages societies and of civilized societies. 'Ethnography had', in his view, 'done a great deal for sociology' (when it came, for instance, to understanding the family), but 'it was more important to examine the great civilized societies of the West' which, because they were more complex, gave the investigator 'richer material'. Ethnographic data could no longer be modern sociology's 'main source of information'.

The following year, Durkheim contributed to the symposium on sociology organized by *Les Documents du progrès*, a journal with socialist leanings (see Lukes 1982: 245–7).[21] The first question was: 'Is it possible to draw conclusions, on the basis of the development so far accomplished with sociological studies, with respect to the future discovery of laws of development and causal relations in social life?' In Durkheim's view, the answer was so obvious that he wasted little time on it: 'Naturally I believe that the present movement in sociology opens up vistas for the future discovery of the laws of social evolution, for I cannot but have faith in the usefulness of the task to which, with so many others, I have devoted my life' (ibid.: 245).

The second question was: 'By what method will sociology be able to attain that result?' Durkheim's reply was succinct: 'It must be historical and objective.' He went on: 'Historical: the purpose of sociology is . . . to understand present-day social institutions.' But in order to understand an institution, 'we must first know its composition', we must 'follow its genesis'. 'In the order of social realities history thus plays a role analogous to that played by the microscope in the order of physical realities.' Objectivity meant that 'the sociologist must take on the state of mind of the physicists, chemists and biologists when they venture into a territory hitherto unexplored', and abandon the 'usual representations'. Such representations were 'so many idols, as Bacon said, from which we must free ourselves'. Dismissing both explanations that referred to human nature, and individual psychology, Durkheim once more asserted that: 'In social life, everything consists of representations, ideas and sentiments' (in Lukes 1982: 245, 246, 247).

Political economy

This was a subject in which Durkheim had been very interested when he began his career. But it must 'serve as a focus and to some extent as the mother of the other sociological sciences' (Lukes 1982: 229). The debate took place at the Société d'économie politique, and was chaired by the economist Paul Leroy-Beaulieu. M. Limousin opened the discussion in aggressive terms: only political economy had sufficient data to formulate laws (the division of labour and specialization, the law of supply and demand, the law of capital), and sociology was a science that did not yet exist. In an attempt to avoid confrontation, Durkheim admitted that the question was 'difficult'. But were the facts dealt with by political economy and those that were the object of the other social sciences 'very different in nature'? One might think so, replied Durkheim, citing the examples of ethics and law, which are 'essentially questions of opinion'. The same was not true, it might be argued, of wealth, which consisted of 'things which are apparently essentially objective and seemingly independent of opinion' (ibid.: 230). This was, Durkheim went on, because the theory of economic materialism makes economic life 'the substructure of all social life', and exerted a 'veritable hegemony' over the other sociological disciplines. Economic facts could, however, be considered from a different viewpoint. They too were a matter of opinion: 'The value of things . . . depends not only upon their objective properties, but also on the opinion one forms of them' (ibid.: 231). Durkheim then gave the examples of wine and meat (pork); when they were proscribed by religious opinion, they lost their exchange-value. The same was true of 'a particular material' or a precious stone; their value was determined by fluctuations in opinion. The same could be said of rates of pay: the 'minimum amount of resources needed for a man to live' was the basic standard used to determine them, but it too was fixed by public opinion. Economic science therefore dealt with facts that were in some respect 'matters of opinion'. Durkheim was, however, prepared to grant political economy 'a sort of primacy' because economic factors had a profound effect on the morphology of population (distribution, density) and therefore upon 'the various states of opinion' (ibid.: 232). The discussion was ill-tempered. Durkheim was immediately taken to task by someone who described himself as 'something of an economist and a lawyer' and who was, he said, 'somewhat shocked' by what he had just heard. To claim that law was a matter of opinion was to make it 'a pure concept of the mind, essentially fluctuating and fanciful' (ibid.): 'But it is always the law of supply and demand, completely independent of opinion, which regulates the price of things, just as it determines all values' (ibid.: 233).

Durkheim was unable to make sense of this view, and could only assume that 'opinion' had been understood in the derogatory sense, or as synonymous with 'mindless prejudices' or 'fanciful feelings.' He wished to correct that impression: the speaker had forgotten that 'opinion is also the end result of the experience of peoples over the centuries' (Lukes 1982: 233). A moral rule was not just the 'result of the dialectical constructs of the jurist and the moralist' but also 'the fruit of peoples' experience over the centuries'. Both opinion and morality changed, and they did so 'legitimately'. As for economic matters, Durkheim emphasized that they too derived 'some *part* of their reality from opinion'. He then added that 'opinion itself has its laws which do not depend upon opinion' (ibid.: 234).

Leroy-Beaulieu summed up the discussion by reiterating the idea that 'political economy is at the present time the only social science of a really positive character', and criticized Durkheim for having 'exaggerated the influence of opinion'. Referring to the law of the division of labour and that of supply and demand, he concluded that the great economic laws were 'immutable', and that 'political economy occupies the first place among the social sciences' (Lukes 1982: 235).

Law

The law was still one of Durkheim's main concerns, and he knew only too well that law faculties were careful to keep sociology under their control. When asked to take part in the Union de la vérité's debate on the possible need for law reform, he therefore had no hesitation in stating that the teaching of law was too formal, and that students needed to be taught that the law was 'a system of living realities, or in other words social realities'. Teaching law should therefore be a task for sociology, but 'unfortunately sociology is not sufficiently advanced'. He therefore suggested that the 'closely related' discipline of history should take on that task and give young people 'a sense of what historical evolution is'. Providing 'a summary and schematic view of history in general' was pointless. It was more relevant to understand a people, such as the Roman people, because law evolved a lot in Rome (Durkheim 1975[1907a]: 243–5).

History

The debate about history and sociology that took place at the Société française de philosophie on 28 May 1908 was a continuation of the one initiated by François Simiand a few years earlier. The theme was 'The unknown and the unconscious in history' and the session took the form of a discussion or, rather, a confrontation between Durkheim and his colleague Charles Seignobos. The philosopher André Lalande acted as chairman, and the debate also involved Célestin Bouglé and the historians Gustave Bloch and Paul Lacombe.[22]

Seignobos opened the discussion, and a somewhat 'embarrassed' Durkheim intervened to say that he was not sure that he had 'mastered his thought' and would like to know if Seignobos admitted 'the reality of the unconscious' (Lukes 1982: 211). He then criticized him for acknowledging only 'conscious causes, those which men themselves attribute to events and actions of which they are the agents' when 'everybody knows how full the consciousness is of illusions' (ibid.: 212]). 'We must penetrate much more deeply into reality in order to understand it' (ibid.: 215). Seignobos tried to unsettle his colleague by attacking the notion of a 'collective consciousness': 'Fustel de Coulanges abominated the very notion of the "collective consciousness" . . . 'I would like indeed to know where is located the place where the collectivity thinks consciously' (ibid.: 211). Durkheim avoided the question:

> The ideas of Fustel de Coulanges about the collective consciousness are completely irrelevant here . . . I have no need to tackle here the question of the collective consciousness, which goes far beyond the subject with which we are dealing. All I would say is that, if we admit the existence of a collective consciousness, we have not dreamed it up with the aim of explaining the unconscious. (Ibid.)

Dismissing the introspective method, Durkheim agreed that, in psychology, 'every causal relationship is unconscious' (ibid.: 212). Without making explicit reference to psychoanalysis, he went on: 'In psychology one seeks to study the unconscious, and is successful without in doing so building constructs in the sky' (ibid.: 216). The same was true of social facts, 'whose causes elude even more plainly the consciousness of the individual'. He then gave the example of religious prohibitions: 'I am aware of no case in which the participants perceived the precise causes' (ibid.: 213). When Seignobos remarked 'That's an exaggeration. There are cases in which the witnesses are not mistaken,' he qualified his statement somewhat: 'I am not saying that these interpretations are bereft of interest. When a sick person believes he has a temperature, his view, whether it is right or wrong, is an interesting fact that the doctor must take into consideration' (ibid.: 217).The confusion arose because Seignobos was, in Durkheim's view, confusing the (historically) unknown and the unconscious: 'In reality, what is conscious is also very obscure. So I will say that the conscious and the unconscious are equally obscure' (ibid.: 218). Durkheim also contended that the distinction between conscious and unconscious causes was not based upon some a priori criterion: it is 'the fruit of historical research'. 'The unconscious is often explained by the conscious, and vice versa. The unconscious is often only a lesser state of consciousness. In short, there is no particular problem posed in order to acquire knowledge of the unconscious' (ibid.: 227).

Durkheim steered the discussion towards methodological issues, and the question of comparisons between series of phenomena and the establishment of laws. Seignobos was sceptical: 'Comparison in history in the end is reduced to analogy'. Lacombe now intervened, and took the side of Durkheim: 'Without comparison, there is no certainty' (Lukes 1982: 220). It was, he argued, pointless to 'compare large masses of facts and events with each other. We should begin by analysing and comparing fragments' (ibid.: 224). And when Seignobos admitted to having 'little faith in the possibility of reconstituting in this way the psychology of individuals or of groups', Lacombe asked him: 'What in the world then impels you to write history?' On being told, 'My purpose, very simply, is to explain . . . by what chain of facts we have arrived at the present state', Lacombe replied: 'But behind the facts what we are always looking for is Man . . . the purpose is always to succeed in revealing the psychological mechanisms of actions and events' (ibid.: 226).

Durkheim claimed to 'be in agreement with Bloch' when he argued the need to be more careful about making general statements about history, and the need to make a distinction between historical events and permanent social functions: there was, on the one hand, 'an indefinite mountain of facts', and, on the other, 'the functions, the institutions, the ways, fixed and organized, of thinking and acting'. He expressed his admiration for 'historians who can live comfortably amid this pile of disordered events'. He himself was happier with institutions: instead of being 'overwhelmed by the extreme diversity of the given facts', he noted the existence of 'a very small number of distinct types'. 'Up to now I have only been able to carry this out for types of family' (Lukes 1982: 224).

As the debate drew to a close, Lalande tried to establish a consensus, and noted that the historian and the sociologist were in agreement, 'insofar as they both admit that individuals can never be considered in isolation'. 'Let us say', Durkheim interrupted, 'that Seignobos, like myself, admits that a society changes individuals.' Seignobos immediately replied: 'Agreed, but only on condition that the society is conceived of solely as the totality of individuals.' When Durkheim insisted that 'the composing of the assembled whole changes each one of the elements to be assembled together', Seignobos responded: 'I admit that tautology' (Lukes 1982: 228).

Sociology and the social sciences

Durkheim once more agreed to defend sociology and to explain his vision of the discipline to the general public by contributing to the collective *De la méthode dans les sciences* published by Alcan in 1909. He began by briefly tracing the history of a discipline which, 'born only yesterday, is merely in the process of being constituted' (Durkheim 1978[1909]: 71). Its aim was to study societies 'simply to *know them* and to *understand them*'. The domain of social facts is so complex – historical events are 'chaotic, capricious, disconcerting' – that it was only at the beginning of the nineteenth century that 'a new conception was definitively brought to light' and that institutions began to be seen not as a product of the will of princes and statesmen, but as 'the necessary result of determinate causes'. Durkheim was aware that this conception implied 'a sort of fatalism' (ibid.: 74–5), and he himself had often been criticized for his way of seeing things. He still praised the natural sciences (which adopted the 'determinist postulate'): 'What changes we have introduced into the universe', he went on enthusiastically:

It will be the same way in the social realm . . . it is sociology which by discovering the laws of social reality will permit us to direct historical evolution with greater reflection than in the past; for we can change nature,
whether moral or physical, only by conforming to its laws . . . At the same
time that they proclaim the necessity of things, the sciences place in our
hands the means to dominate that necessity. (ibid.: 75)

Sociological determinism and free will were therefore not irreconcilable. Here, Durkheim qualifies the 'passively conservative' attitude he
had defended in *The Division of Labour in Society*: 'Sociology in no way
imposes upon man a passively conservative attitude . . . It only turns us
away from ill-conceived and sterile enterprises inspired by the belief that
we are able to change the social order as we wish, without taking into
account customs, traditions, and the mental constitution of man and of
societies' (1978[1909]: 75–6).

For Durkheim, it was self-evident that sociology had an object of its
own, as distinct from that of psychology: 'Individual consciousnesses,
by associating themselves in a stable way, reveal, through their relationships, a new life', namely religions, institutions and beliefs (1978[1909]:76).
Civilization presupposed cooperation between members of society, and
was possible only if the results obtained by one generation were transmitted to the next. Sociology was, he repeated, a science. Durkheim explains
that the comparative method is the sociological method's classic tool, as
it turns to statistics in order to demonstrate that they are an essential tool
when studying morality (homicide, divorce . . .). In conclusion, he recalled
his initial advice: the sociologist 'must begin by making a *tabula rasa* of
the notions . . . which he may have formed in the course of his life'. Social
life fostered the 'natural illusion' that such ideas help us to understand
social phenomena, but sociology must not be 'a simple illustration of
ready-made and deceptive truisms'; it must fashion discoveries and 'upset
accepted notions': 'We know nothing at all of these social phenomena
amid which we move' (ibid.: 86, 87).

Another Crisis at the *Année*. Magic, Death and Castes

Durkheim still found planning a volume of the *Année* an ordeal, and the
fact that there had been little improvement in his relationship with his
nephew did nothing to make things easier. 'I have to make a new attempt',
he wrote to Mauss in late 1906, 'to get you to do what I am begging you
to do.'[23] He wanted Mauss to go to the library to borrow or look at books
for him. He made the same request at the end of March 1907. He was 'in
a great hurry' because he wanted to get the manuscript to Alcan 'immediately'. Mauss had not changed his habits and was slow in getting down
to work. His uncle made no secret of his 'annoyance'. 'You still have the
Wundt to do, what you call five or six bits and pieces, and all the journals.' 'The Wundt' was a reference to the major review of the German

psychologist's study of myths and religion that Mauss was supposed to be writing. This signalled another crisis. Marcel Mauss thought of 'refusing to contribute' to the *Année*, which his mother thought would be more sensible than to continue to 'commit himself without keeping his word'. His nephew's behaviour was becoming so impossible that Durkheim lost his temper and then lapsed into silence: 'I suspect that my silence leaves you in no doubt as to how I feel about your behaviour towards me. But in order to ensure that there are no misunderstandings, I wanted to tell you again how I feel.'[24] Marcel Mauss had moved out of the rue Saint-Jacques and was now living at 3 rue de Cluny. From 1907 to 1911, he had had a room above Durkheim's apartment in the rue Saint-Jacques, and probably used it as a study. It also meant that his uncle could make sure that he was working.

The various members of the *Année* team were now very much in demand and were finding it difficult to meet the demands of a journal that, as Fauconnet complained, took up a lot of their time: 'You say that Durkheim must produce something. That is not enough: we all have to produce something.' He reminded Bouglé that he had an 'urgent duty' to finish his thesis. Durkheim had new plans for the journal and intended to keep the articles and the reviews separate. Bouglé and Fauconnet agreed with him. Fauconnet thought that Mauss would 'come round' to the idea. Simiand was the only one to have doubts, and the others hoped that Durkheim would succeed in convincing him. Bouglé suggested a new title: *Le Mouvement sociologique*. 'Durkheim must obviously remain in charge', insisted Fauconnet. There was no suggestion of his giving up the editorship, but he would have liked to be 'relieved of some of the work'. Fauconnet therefore suggested that Bouglé should be Durkheim's assistant, 'at least for a while'. 'You can take on that responsibility for the moment.'[25] Bouglé described the journal's situation thus: 'Basically, what staff does the *Année* still have, apart from the librarian? One home-nurse, one fanatic and one mental patient (that's me).'[26] 'I have visions of you saving the *Année sociologique* (or rather the Sociological Olympiad) from certain death simply by being at the centre of operations', replied Halévy.[27]

The situation became more complicated when Bouglé had problems with what he called 'the totem-taboo clan' or the 'United Sociological Party'. He had sent the manuscript of his book on castes to Durkheim, who had passed it on to Mauss and asked for his comments. Durkheim himself had a lot of criticisms to make: there were gaps in Bouglé's knowledge of Indian sects, his knowledge of Indian literature was inadequate, and he described India as a society 'that had never known anything other than castes and an anti-individualist civilization'. He suggested some modifications: a 'special chapter' should be added to place more emphasis on the religious aspects of the institution of castes. 'Castes are by definition religious', he pointed out. Durkheim was, in a word, asking Bouglé to change the entire structure of his book, and to replace his juridico-economic model with a politico-religious model.

Mauss returned the manuscript to Bouglé, with detailed comments on intercalated sheets of paper. He also wrote him a long letter explaining that Durkheim had not had time to look at it. He apologized for 'having taken so long to read it properly. I had to look at it in my spare moments.'[28] Mauss made the same points as Durkheim, but added a whole series of detailed comments of his own. This was, as Durkheim remarked, 'a letter which, at my insistence, made a lot of demands'. He refused to publish the book in his new 'Travaux sociologiques' collection: 'I am not prepared to give it my seal of approval.'[29]

At first, Bouglé refused to take any notice of these criticisms. 'When *Castes* is published, the totem-taboo clan will pull me to pieces', he told his friend Halévy. He then changed his mind: 'I have started to correct, or at least tone down, *Castes*; that way, Mauss's oracular pronouncements will not have been in vain.'[30] *Castes* was the first book to appear in the 'Travaux sociologiques' collection; the *American Journal of Sociology* greeted its publication as a major event (Loos 1909).[31]

Volume X of the *Année* appeared in 1907, and it was the last to adhere to the original formula of articles and reviews. The three articles dealt, respectively, with castes in India, magic and law, and representations of death. Their themes were a clear indication that the *Année*'s contributors – both young (Huvelin and Hertz) and not so young (Bouglé) – were still interested in the sociology of religion and law, and that they were also very interested in ethnography, history and comparative studies.

Bouglé used his book as the basis for an article on 'law and castes' in India, and attempted to 'identify some general tendencies in Hindu law and to demonstrate how they relate to the caste system' (Bouglé 1907a). Hindu law was hallmarked with the 'stamp of religion', with its binary oppositions between pollution and purification, profane and sacred, and its many taboos. In more general terms, caste was 'a religious matter'. Bouglé's study dealt specifically with the code of Manu, often regarded as 'the Indian code', with its many varied prescriptions and its emphasis upon repressive, rather than restitutive, law. Bouglé was trying to show that 'the law is an expression of the typical characteristics of a given society' and, more specifically, to verify, with respect to Hindu law and the caste system, Durkheim's hypothesis that simple societies with a strong central government usually have a highly developed collective consciousness and a repressive system that can be described as 'barbarous'. Matters were not in fact that simple, as India is characterized by the absence of any notion of a state; there are countless groups, and a caste system with little internal differentiation and a high degree of unanimity. But we also find intense collective sentiments and a widespread respect for the caste system. The paradox was, Bouglé concluded, that 'Hindus were united only by the worship of what divided them'.

Huvelin's article was called 'Magic and individual law'. The title was enigmatic, as there is no obvious connection between magic and law. The article was an extract from the book Huvelin was writing: *Les Obligations dans le très ancien droit romain*. It did discuss the magical origins of the art of law, but only in a limited way, and it demonstrated that the origins of punishments for crimes against individual property, and especially theft within the family, were magical (curses and so on) rather than religious. The article was quite explicitly an extension of Mauss and Hubert's work on magic: 'We know from this decisive demonstration that the facts we describe as "magical" are social things in the same way that what we call religious phenomena are also social facts' (Huvelin 1907a: 1).[32] In conclusion, Huvelin identifies elements of a theory of magic, as applied to the law: the law is 'a rule governing social life . . . based upon a shared belief', and 'is, in its earliest forms, indistinguishable from religion'. At the same time, he also makes a distinction between magic and religion: 'In the legal domain, a magical ritual is nothing more than a religious ritual that is diverted from its usual goal, and used to make an individual wish or belief come true.' 'Magician' is synonymous with individualist, anarchist and sorcerer, and always has to do with the realm of the anti-social. The form of a magical rite is religious, but its goals are anti-religious.

The third article was by Robert Hertz, entitled 'Contribution to a study of the collective representation of death'. Hertz was dealing here with what Durkheim was to call the dark sides of life. Death is, he wrote, 'an organic event', but it was 'the complex set of beliefs, emotions and acts that give it its characteristics'. 'For the social consciousness, death therefore has a determinate meaning, and is the object of collective representations' (Hertz 1907: 48–9). The purpose of his study, which looks at societies that are 'less advanced than ours' (and especially Indonesian peoples), is to analyse beliefs pertaining to death and funerary practices (such as 'double burials', in which there is a time-gap between death, permanent burial and the final ceremony). Hertz is concerned with the impurity of the corpse, and takes into account the temporal dimension: 'It take some time to banish death from the world of the living.' Society therefore projects 'its own ways of thinking and feeling' on to the world.

The general conclusion is as follows: 'For the collective consciousness, death in normal circumstances means the temporary exclusion of the individual from the human community, and this has the effect of taking the individual from the visible society of the living and into the invisible society of ancestors.' Insofar as it is a social phenomenon, death consists in 'the twofold and painful work of mental disintegration and synthesis'. It is only when that work has been done that society, now restored to peace, 'can triumph over death' (Hertz 1907: 136–7).

A New Balance

'Moral and juridic sociology' now became the largest section of the *Année*, with 30.8 per cent of the 500 pages of reviews, followed by 'religious sociology' (29.5 per cent) and 'economic sociology' (25 per cent). A balance had therefore been struck between the journal's main interests. The 'general sociology' section was much smaller (7 per cent), while both the 'social morphology' and 'miscellaneous' sections were still marginal (4.85 and

2.5 per cent respectively). Durkheim and Mauss were still the most active contributors in terms of the number of reviews published, but Durkheim wrote only 20 or so. Disappointed with the very general level of recent books on morality, and above all frustrated that people spoke of the science of moral facts as though it did not exist, Durkheim attempted to reply to his contradictors 'with impartiality' and asked them to spell out clearly how his method gave rise to 'errors' in practice. He was able to call upon 'some years of experience' to defend the idea of a positive science of morals, which some still saw as a form of 'desecration'.

Durkheim could not remain 'indifferent' to the criticisms of Alfred Fouillée and Gustave Belot, as their objective was 'to argue with sociology over the study of moral facts' (1980[1907b]: 137).[33] He noted first that the pages devoted to him written by Fouillée contained 'grave mistakes in the interpretation of our thought': 'We are accused of denying human thought all value judgements' (ibid.: 139). 'Not at all', he retorts, contrasting 'thoughtless prejudices' with the 'thoughtful, enlightened, methodical judgements that the science of moral facts . . . is intended to make possible'. He points to the example of the *Division of Labour* and his assessment of 'the moral ideal of the gentleman', which can be regarded as 'about to be outdated' (ibid.: 139 n1). 'The explanation of an ethical maxim does not justify it . . . but the explanation points the way towards the justification.' Durkheim is harshly critical of 'the methods used by the philosophers when they speculate on morals' because he wishes to 'cut loose from all hidebound views when faced with sentiment and prejudice'. Fouillée had always been interested in sociology but saw 'no need "for long studies of history . . . [or] comparative religion"' (ibid.: 141). Durkheim once more contrasts the philosopher's simplistic explanations with the 'new methods' that are required to explain the complexity of moral facts. He points out that introspection alone is not enough and that we must turn to history and ethnography in order to explore the 'baffling problems' posed by the right to property and the idea that 'mere words' makes wishes binding (ibid.: 142). Durkheim's hypothesis is that 'morality, at each moment in time, depends on the social circumstance'. It does not follow, he is quick to add, that 'all social life is necessarily, entirely expressible in sociological terms'. He admits that moral beliefs become 'individualized and diversified', but insists that 'the social aspect is the principal part' (ibid.: 143, 144).

Durkheim also reviewed *The Origin and Development of the Moral Ideas* (1906), by the Finnish ethnologist Edvard Westermarck (Durkheim 1980[1907e]) and the Scottish anthropologist Andrew Lang's *Secret of the Totem*. Although he praises Westermarck's 'immense learning' and describes his book as 'a gigantic work', Durkheim points out their 'essential divergences' over both method and theory. His main criticism is that Westermarck attempts to explain morality in terms of 'the most general and permanent inclinations of human nature' (ibid.: 151). There is therefore 'one and the same morality, implanted within man's congenital nature'. Westermarck has, in other words, simply rediscovered 'the old

philosophy of natural law' conception, and amassed an 'enormous accumulation of facts' (ibid.: 159).[34] The polemic continues in the review of the
'aggressive and quarrelsome' Andrew Lang (Durkheim 1907). Durkheim
complains that his colleague enjoys 'torturing texts and finding contradictory passages' in the work of his opponents.

The *Année* still carried reviews of works by its contributors, and in some
cases they reviewed their own books. But as Henri Hubert (1907) noted
when he apologized for reviewing his friend Mauss's work on magic in
Australian societies, 'we prefer to talk about other people rather than
about ourselves'. The foreign researchers reviewed in volume X of the
Année included Simmel, Pareto, Alfred Weber, Sombart and Tönnies. The
reviews were harsh, as can be seen from Bouglé's comments on Simmel's
study of fashion[35] and the very brief remarks by Halbwachs about Pareto's
Manuel di economia politica: 'the *nec plus ultra* in political economy'.[36]

A Predictable Exclusion

There were few changes to the team that worked on volume X, but
Antoine Vacher, who had contributed only four reviews to the previous
two volumes, ceased to be a member. There were no new contributors, but
the younger associates – Georges Bourguin, Maurice Halbwachs, Philippe
de Felice, Antoine Bianconi and Robert Hertz – who had been working
on it for the last two or three years, gave the journal a new dynamism.
The 'old hands' were delighted about this. 'I am very pleased that our
young sociologists are working on the bibliography', Fauconnet admitted
to Mauss. 'It will be a useful piece of work if it is well done.'[37]

Gaston Richard was still in Bordeaux and had become professor of
social sciences in 1906, but his position on the team looked increasingly
precarious. The 'criminal sociology' section, which he had been editing so
far, did not appear in volume X, as it had been incorporated into the larger
'moral and juridic sociology' section, which was now subtitled 'studies
of the genesis of juridic and moral rules'. Responsibility for the different
sections was now shared by some 10 people, including Durkheim and
Fauconnet. Gaston Richard was still editing three of them: 'criminality
by age and gender', 'special forms of criminality', and the 'penitentiary
system.'

Volume X included Durkheim's review of Gaston Richard's article 'Les
lois de la solidarité morale', which had been published in the November
1905 issue of the *Revue philosophique*, and it was harsh. Durkheim did
not understand why Richard opposed '"that positive conception . . . that
identifies morality with an entirely automatic type of society"'. He had
no objections to the thesis that 'the more advanced we become, the more
the personal factor becomes an essential element in the pursuit of good
conduct . . . Richard has made his point ahead of time.' However, it did
not follow that 'ethical standards become less and less a group matter':
'There are two very different issues involved here, and we fear that the

author has confused the problems they raise.' He also had reservations about some of Richard's other proposals, and especially his rejection of the thesis that taboo is a primitive and universal religious phenomenon: 'We confess not to know any religion in which the notion of the taboo is not to be found, and we cannot even imagine how this may be the case' (1980[1907c]: 150).

Another Ordeal: The Death of Octave Hamelin

In August 1907, Mauss was in Zermatt, and the Durkheims were staying at the Hôtel Bellevue in Kandersteg. Durkheim urged his nephew to be 'very careful'. For his own part, he was more than 'delighted with this area: it is certainly the most beautiful that I have visited'. The glaciers, waterfalls, lakes and pine forests provided 'a huge variety of impressions'. He took advantage of them to 'walk quite a lot', and went on many excursions, some long but most 'short and very pleasant'. He was more than happy: everything was fine and the holiday was, he believed, doing him 'some good'.[38] As usual, he went back to Épinal at the end of August. Octave Hamelin died in an accident at the beginning of September. He was a friend. 'He died devoting himself to others', said Durkheim. Hamelin was swept out to sea while trying to save two people from drowning off a beach in the Landes, where he had a house in the country. Mauss spoke to Henri Hubert of his sadness: 'The country has lost an exceptional man, and I have lost a friend who was devoted to the point of being biased.'[39]

Hamelin had been a colleague of Durkheim's at Bordeaux and had, at his friend's urging, recently accepted a post at the École normale supérieure in Paris before becoming a *chargé de cours* at the Sorbonne. He had just submitted his doctoral thesis – the 'fruit of 25 years of meditation': *Les Eléments principaux de la représentation*. Durkheim wrote an obituary for the daily *Le Temps* describing him as a man who, although not well known to the public, was a 'very great figure': 'A very major loss to philosophy' (Durkheim 1975[1907b]). Durkheim described Hamelin as a man who had devoted his life to teaching: 'He sacrificed his whole life to his students.' He was 'a pure rationalist, an austere lover of righteous reason, and an enemy of all dilettantism.' These were the qualities Durkheim prized, both in himself and in others. He concluded: 'This great thinker was at the same time an upright man. He also had a tender heart.' There were many reasons to mourn the death of Hamelin: a great intellect, a strong will, and a feminine tenderness and sensitivity. Durkheim had lost 'a friend who can never be replaced'.

Immediately after Hamelin's death, Durkheim, out of a sense of both duty and friendship, made a point of putting together all the notes he had left behind so as to 'allow the scientific public to benefit from them'. The notes were for *Le Système de Descartes*, and Durkheim edited them with all the care that was to be expected from a professor. The book was published in 1911. Some years later, Durkheim would edit Octave Hamelin's *Lettres d'Epicure* for the *Revue de métaphysique et de morale.*

'I Certainly Owe a Great Deal to the Germans'

Durkheim became the target of virulent criticism from Belgium when he least expected it. Simon Deploige, an abbot (and subsequently a Monsignor), who taught at the Catholic University of Louvain, published an article on the 'Genesis of Durkheim's system' in the *Revue néo-scolastique.* He spoke of Durkheim's 'social realism', and alluded to the French sociologist's 'disguised borrowings' from 'certain German writers'. Annoyed at these accusations, Durkheim reacted energetically and wrote a letter to the journal's director on 20 October 1907:

> As for all these German works of which Monsieur Deploige speaks, it was I who made them known in France; it was I who showed how, although they were not the work of sociologists, they could none the less serve the advancement of sociology. Indeed, I rather exaggerated rather than played down the importance of their contribution. (Cited in Lukes 1982: 258)

In a postscript, he remarked that his Belgian colleague's article contained 'some grave and indisputable errors': 'I certainly owe a great deal to the Germans, as I do to Comte and others. But the real influence that Germany has exerted upon me is very different from what he asserts' (ibid.).

Cut to the quick, Deploige replied in a latter dated 24 October: 'I have simply tried to determine the origin of the ideas that are jumbled together in Durkheim's system', without 'challenging his honesty as a writer'. He added:

> While he [Durkheim] sometimes names the authors he disagrees with, he usually fails to name those he follows. I cannot give any positive proof of this, as we are talking about omissions . . . This does not mean that he has deliberately tried to deceive: I say nothing about his intentions, of which he may not be aware. The only thing that I do say is in fact that the German raw materials that have gone into his construct do not always have a manufacturer's label.

He also reminded Durkheim that Ribot, Espinas and Fouillée had introduced the French public to the work of Lazarus and Schäffle before he did. He criticized him for having claimed in his article in *Revue bleue* on the history of sociology in France (Durkheim 1973[1900]) that sociology was an essentially French science – 'no mention of what he owes to the Germans' – and for being contemptuous and scornful of the work of his French compatriots (Tarde, Le Play, Letourneau and Lapouge). Referring to the 'errors' in his article, he asked Durkheim to 'explain what he meant'.

Durkheim agreed to give examples of Deploige's 'errors' in a letter dated 8 November: (1) he had never read Simmel's *Einleitung in die Moralwissenschaft* and only knew his *Philosophie des Geldes*; (2) he had read the work of Schmoller and Wagner but, contrary to Deploige's claims, had 'never sought to follow their teachings, nor even to have personal contact with them' during the time he spent in Germany; (3) the notion of 'social realism' came to him directly not from Schäffle, but from Comte, Spencer and Espinas, who 'only learnt German very late on . . . and did not know of Schäffle when he wrote his *Sociétés animales*'; (4) the distinction between sociology and psychology did not come from Wundt, but from Boutroux, his 'mentor' at the École normale supérieure; (5) the idea that religion is the matrix of moral and juridical ideas was not inspired by Wundt (he read his *Ethik* in 1887) but from his studies of religious history and his reading of Robertson Smith and his school, which inspired his 'change of direction': 'it was a revelation to me' (see Lukes 1982: 258–60). At this point, Durkheim broke off and refused to give 'other examples of errors or inaccuracies': 'It is true that I lay no claim whatsoever to some impossible originality. I am indeed convinced that my ideas have their roots in those of my predecessors; and it is precisely because of this that I have some confidence in their fruitfulness.' He added:

> I certainly have a debt to Germany, but I owe much more to its historians than to its economists and – something which Monsieur Deploige does not seem to suspect – I owe at least as much to England . . . I would not dream of attributing too great an importance to the question of knowing how my thinking has been formed. (Ibid.: 260)

Simon Deploige used his right of reply to counter-attack, and accused Durkheim of having made errors, and having forgotten certain things: 'Until proof to the contrary is forthcoming, the fact remains that there are some stones from France in this building, and a lot of German bricks.' Deploige mocked the information Durkheim had supplied about his lack of contact with Schmoller, his limited sympathy for Wagner and Espinas's poor knowledge of German. At best, 'these minor details may have some documentary value for an anecdotal history of an individual', but not for an objective history of the formation of a system of ideas'. The same was true of Wundt's 'suggestion' (as to the importance of religion), which had 'slumbered inside his brain for eight years': Durkheim was apparently suggesting that the idea had 'lain for eight years in a state of virtuality, in the obscure realms of the subconscious', emerging into 'the bright light of consciousness' after Robertson Smith's intervention. This information was, in Deploige's view, at best 'useful documentation for a psychologist writing a study of M. Durkheim's psychology'. Durkheim's most serious problem was his inability to 'stand back from his own work and to look at it, like us, coldly and from the outside, like a thing'. The sociologist's attitude towards his own work was in other words, that of a believer. 'What has happened to M. Durkheim suggests that the man still believes in something. If it is not Jehovah, it is himself or his work.'[40]

Durkheim at 50: The *Légion d'honneur* and a Banquet

At the beginning of January 1907, Durkheim received a telegram from Rector Louis Liard himself 'confirming the news' that he had been made a Chevalier in the Légion d'honneur. Durkheim replied immediately: 'I already owe you a lot, and I will not forget that, and will therefore take every opportunity to show my gratitude through my devotion.'[41] His nomination was officially put forward by the minister for public instruction and fine arts on 13 January, and the order's insignia was conferred on him in March 1907 by his colleague Victor Brochard, who was an officer in the Légion d'honneur and a member of the Institute.[42] That same year, Durkheim refused to allow his name to be put forward for the Institut, despite all the pressure brought to bear by Liard, Ribot and Lévy-Bruhl. He was 50 and was, he said, flattered, but he preferred to make way for an older professor: he could not tolerate the idea that he might be standing in the way of someone who was nearing the end of his career and his life (Davy 1960b: 18).[43]

The *Année* team secretly organized a 'communal banquet' to mark the journal's tenth anniversary. There was also talk of 'organizing a *Festschrift* for Durkheim's fiftieth birthday' in 1908. It was to include contributions from Mauss, Hubert, Simiand, Bouglé and Fauconnet. The latter wondered if other friends, such as Aubi, Hourticq, Lapie and Richard – should be asked to contribute, even if it meant that it would not be very sociological. Who should be asked to contribute was something of a problem, and there was one other difficulty: 'The book must be worthy of the master, without offending anyone.'[44] The book never materialized, but the banquet did take place in the presence of Jaurès, who 'outshone all the professor-doctors, scholars, intellectuals and selected *normaliens*' (Bourgin 1938: 192).

When Gustave Lanson refused to let himself be considered for the position the following year (arguing that he 'never had been, was not and never would be a candidate for the position of director'), Liard and Ernest Lavisse put forward Durkheim's name for the position of director of the École normale supérieure. Lavisse was the 'first-line' candidate, elected with 14 out of 15 votes, and Durkheim the 'second-line' candidate (14 out of 15 votes). 'We are happy to pay tribute to the talent and services rendered by M. Durkheim', declared Liard.[45] This was his way of announcing that the philosopher-sociologist-pedagogue would soon be director of the prestigious institution in the rue d'Ulm.

The son was following in his father's footsteps. André Durkheim was in his last year at school and preparing to take the École normale supérieure's entrance exam. He was accepted at the end of 1909, and was ranked 12th in his class. 'He was not yet 18', his father would point out.

He discovered an interest in linguistics in his second year; if there was one form of human activity in which he had a 'sort of early curiosity', it was the phenomenon of language: 'He sensed that the mechanism of language and that of thought are inseparable, that we cannot understand one without understanding the other, and that a philosopher who was also a linguist could attempt to give new insights into many traditional problems' (Durkheim 1975[1917]: 447). André was also attending the lectures given at the Collège de France by Antoine Meillet, a contributor to the *Année* and a friend of his uncle Marcel: 'André Durkheim should have been his disciple' (Mauss 1969[1936]). This introduction to linguistics confirmed his sense of vocation.

André was a brilliant student; according to his father's detailed account, he was 'well ahead of his fellow degree students after a very competitive examination'. He took his *diplôme d'études supérieures en philosophie* the following year. He was given an 'exceptionally high mark' for his dissertation on 'the notion of the phenomenon in Leibniz'. Émile was immensely proud of the academic success of his son, who now only had 'to get through the last stage of his career as a *normalien*: the *agrégation*' (Durkheim 1975[1917]: 447).

Durkheim still took a critical view of 'the somewhat archaic nature of our system of examinations and *concours*'. Both the oral and the written parts of the *agrégation* forced candidates to 'improvise answers to questions they have not had time to think about'. Success depended not on the candidate's knowledge or ability to think, but on his 'formal talent'. Like some of his colleagues, Durkheim wanted to see changes, but not just any changes. Given that candidates would spend their careers teaching in schools, there should be more emphasis upon general culture as opposed to early specialization. In conclusion, he wrote: 'My main concern is to make [the examination] less superficial' (1975[1909d]: 434–6).[46]

21

'Change the World'

The early years of the twentieth century were a period of widespread social and political unrest. In March 1906, a methane explosion in the Courrières coal mines near Lens (Pas-de-Calais) resulted in more than 1,100 deaths. The miners accused the company of negligence and called a major strike. In October, the congress of the CGT adopted the Amiens Charter, which resulted in the adoption of a revolutionary syndicalism that asserted its independence from all political parties. The emphasis was now on direct action in all its forms, including acts of sabotage and either limited or general strikes. Some, like Georges Sorel, whose *Reflections on Violence* (1999[1908]) was a best seller, called for a general strike. The issue of violence was a central part of the debate. There were more strikes in the spring of 1907. On 8 March, electricians led by the CGT plunged Paris into darkness; on 11 March, the CGT brought workers in the capital's food industry out on strike. In June, the strike movement spread to the wine-producing areas of Languedoc, where there was a crisis of over-production. In Montpellier, 700,000 people took to the streets, and the army refused to open fire on the strikers. The movement's leader, Marcellin Albert, began to look like 'the redeemer'.

A Durkheimian Stance: The *Cahiers du socialiste*

The 'events in the Midi' and the mobilization of the wine-growers were, in Robert Hertz's view, 'terribly symptomatic'. On the one hand, there were people who were 'playing at revolution' and who were willing to die 'for the sacred cause of the vine'; on the other, there was a 'government of clowns and cynics, who claimed to be defending the social order and to respect the very law they are constantly breaking', and who laughed and cracked jokes in parliament. The government was led by Prime Minister Clemenceau, Joseph Caillaux and Aristide Briand (who became minister for justice in December while still remaining minister for religion). 'All this is merely a general expression of the state of French society, the loosening of all bonds, the lack of any shared faith, the lack of respect, and the jokes, the egotism and the sloppiness', complained Hertz. 'What is the alternative?, he asked. The general atmosphere was undermining the workers' attempts to organize, and he had no faith in either the unions or the voluntary sector (which had in his view fragmented into individual groups defending their corporate interests). 'In practical terms, I am in favour of unity and a follower of Jaurès but, like a lot of other people, I am "very anxious and disturbed".' He added: 'So you see, I am a resolute Durkheimian.'[1]

Notes critiques had ceased publication. The political activities of the *Année* group now centred on the Hertz's Groupe d'études socialistes. Hertz wanted to reform the old Librairie group along the lines of the Fabian Society and started the *Cahiers du socialiste* because he had a 'taste for action' and wanted to use Durkheim's sociology to promote the socialist cause.

Robert Hertz was eager to have the support of Marcel Mauss – in order to 'benefit from your long experience and natural wisdom'.[2] Like Paul Fauconnet, who thought the project 'sensible' but was not, 'for the moment, keen on being directly involved',[3] Mauss was happy simply to follow and encourage the activities of his close associate and friend. His involvement was restricted to occasional contributions to the group's debates. Mauss, who appeared to have calmed down a lot, kept his distance from his friends' activities, including the *Revue syndicaliste*, which had been founded by Albert Thomas with the financial backing of Lucien Herr, Lucien Lévy-Bruhl and Léon Blum, and to which Hertz, Simiand and Halbwachs all contributed. Although he was still a member of *L'Humanité*'s board of directors, he was less closely involved with the paper than before. He also agreed to give talks on cooperation at the École socialiste and lectures in the open universities.

François Simiand also supported the new initiative, even though he was at first somewhat sceptical about it and feared that, given its semi-scientific nature, it would attract only 'incompetents and non-professionals'.[4] The group's first meeting was held at his home. The socialism it wanted to construct was what Hubert Bourgin called a 'positive socialism'. A new, expanded and greatly improved edition of Simiand's *Le Salaire des ouvriers des mines de charbon* was published in 1907.[5] Simiand also edited, with Georges Renard,[6] the collective *Le Socialisme à l'œuvre. Ce qu'on a fait. Ce qu'on peut faire* (1907), which quickly became a standard work. It argued the case for a 'modern' socialism, was vehemently opposed to revolutionary socialism and sceptical about Marxism, rejected utopianism and was interested in practical achievements. Cooperation and municipal socialism were seen as the main instruments for bringing about the transformation of society.

The goal of the *Cahiers* was to employ discussions and publications to make a useful contribution to a 'policy of reform' by opposing sterile dogmatism in the name of reason and bringing doctrine into line with the current state of the social sciences. 'Socialists have never been in such need of detailed knowledge and clear ideas about all the problems the country has to face. Many activists expect us to provide that knowledge and those ideas. We would be guilty if we failed to meet those expectations.'[7] There were restrictions on the number of members – around 40 – and recruitment was selective. Its membership included several members of the *Année* clan: Simiand, Gernet, Halbwachs, Marcel Granet and Henri Lévy-Bruhl.[8] The initiative had the support of Jaurès. As well as organizing monthly dinners, the group held discussions on a variety of topics. Simiand spoke on strikes in the public sector, Halbwachs on working-class housing, and Gernet on the problem of alcohol. Other topics included consumer cooperatives, home-working and industrial hygiene. The group also published a series of brochures entitled *Les Cahiers du socialiste*. One of the first titles in the series was Maurice Halbwachs's *La Politique foncière des municipalités*. In it, he concluded by expressing the hope that socialist municipalities would quickly be able to develop a land policy that was both 'coherent and fair.'[9]

In 1908, Halbwachs also agreed to write some articles on the subject of rents for *L'Humanité*. Having failed to obtain a position in the law faculty, he went back to teaching in a lycée in 1908. He was also completing his doctoral thesis, which would be published in 1909 under the title *Les Expropriations et les prix des terrains à Paris, 1860–1900*. It represented a genuine sociology of the market and of housing conditions in the city and was, as critics noted, written from a Durkheimian perspective.[10]

Halbwachs went to Berlin to pursue his research during the academic year 1910–11, but he was deported for political reasons. He had written an article for *L'Humanité* describing the Prussian government's brutal repression of a strike. He then travelled to Vienna before returning to Paris. It had been an action-packed year.

Although Durkheim did not play any part in the activities of the socialist group, he was more active than ever before on the public stage between 1907 and 1909 and was involved in many discussions. In 1907, he contributed to the *Mercure de France* symposium on the 'religious question', and gave a lecture entitled 'Pacifism and patriotism' to the Société française de philosophie at the end of December 1907 (Durkheim 1973[1908]). He also took part in the *Libres entretiens* debate organized by the Union de la vérité on 'Reforming legal institutions and the teaching of law', and on 19 January and 16 February 1908, on the subject of the status of civil servants. On 15 April 1908, he took part in *La Revue*'s symposium on parliamentary impotence, and then contributed to the discussion organized by the Société française de philosophie on science and religion.

Pacifism and Patriotism

'War on war' was the new anti-militarist slogan adopted by the Socialist International at its Stuttgart Congress of 1907; the French delegation was led by Jean Jaurès, Guesde, Vaillant and Hervé.[11] In Morocco, France was pursuing a policy of penetration, and French troops occupied Oujda in 1907. Some, and not least the socialist leader, thought that if the fighting continued, both peoples would be 'swept away, like a naval squadron in a cyclone'. 'Capitalism leads to wars: that is its very essence', wrote Jaurès. Marcel Mauss, for his part, was both a pacifist and an internationalist: 'In my view, we will not have peace unless, sooner or later, we build an ever-expanding International', he had declared a few years earlier.[12]

In late December 1907, Émile Durkheim and Théodore Ruyssen debated the issue of pacifism and patriotism in front of an audience from the Société française de philosophie. Dominique Parodi was also involved. Durkheim unambiguously rejected both anti-patriotism and nationalism. Anti-patriotism seemed to him to be a 'real absurdity': 'We would not exist without an organized society, and the most highly organized form of society is the fatherland [la patrie].' 'What kind of fatherland should we be looking for?' he asked the audience: a national fatherland, a European fatherland, or a human fatherland? Should we defend the independence of our current (national) fatherland, or hasten the advent of the broader fatherland of Europe or 'the civilized world' (in which case our fatherland would be 'no more than a province')?

His colleague Ruyssen also believed in the need for ever-greater units, but was unsure as to how national patriotisms could be reconciled with a European or world patriotism. In Durkheim's view, the emergence of a greater fatherland did not pose a threat to peace: 'Keeping the peace would cease to be just a moral aspiration and would become a legal obligation because there would be an organized society with an obligation to ensure that it was respected.' But what was internationalism? Did it mean arbitration and negotiated agreements between nations, or federations of nations? Durkheim believed that the historical trend was irreversible: 'Small fatherlands will merge into larger ones: that is in the nature of things.' Pacifism was something that emerges when that trend is 'peaceful, and not the result of violence and war'. Parodi, who had learned a lot from teaching at open universities, worried that it would be difficult to give working-class people any sense of the extent of the fatherland's 'living strength'. Indeed. It would be all the more difficult to do so given that social classes came into conflict *within* nations. Durkheim was well aware of the strength of 'passionate prejudices', but believed that it was possible to explain the fatherland's *raison d'être* to workers. As for the idea of an 'international proletariat', it was, he believed, based upon a misunderstanding: 'Even an expanded class is not, and cannot be, a fatherland; it is no more than a fragment of a fatherland.' While he was critical of internationalism, which he described as 'violent, aggressive and anti-patriotic', he was, on the whole, optimistic: internationalism was a recent phenomenon, and there was therefore 'room for hope'. What really annoyed him was the 'nationalist talk' that was being heard too often, and which held that French culture was superior to others, 'sometimes on revolutionary grounds'. If the only way to be patriotic was to claim that France was better than other countries, 'there was no hope'. People had to be taught to 'love the fatherland in the abstract'.

'We Are All Civil Servants of Society'

Did civil servants have the right to form trade unions, or even to affiliate
to the CGT? How should the country react when primary school teachers
demanded that right? Like the socialist movement, the trade-union movement was expanding, spreading its influence, and becoming more radical.
Under the leadership of Fernand Pelloutier, the CGT, which had been
founded in 1895, had adopted the famous Amiens Charter in 1906. This
was the 'bible' of anarcho-syndicalism: unions must not be subordinate to
political parties and must prepare for revolution on their own by means
of strikes, including general strikes, anti-militarism and even acts of sabotage. This conception of syndicalism undermined the SFIO by depriving it
of the support of the unions. Strikes became more frequent, and the issue
of civil service unions (which had been banned under the law of 1848) was
becoming increasingly important. Civil service unions were now formed
and tolerated. In April 1906, Prime Minister Georges Clemenceau put
forward a bill: civil servants would be allowed to form associations to
defend their professional interests, but not to form unions. Affiliation to
the CGT was out of the question, as it made 'apologias for sabotage' and
'encouraged hatred among citizens', as Clemenceau put it. At the beginning of April, Élie Nègre, secretary of the teachers' union, denounced
the attitude of the government, and demanded the right to form a union.
He was immediately sacked. His dismissal notice was signed by Aristide
Briand, minister for public instruction and a former socialist activist. Jean
Jaurès attacked his friend-turned-enemy in parliament.

The debate about civil servants' unions was heated and aroused a lot
of passion. Maxime Leroy published a book entitled *Les Transformations
de la puissance publique: les syndicats des fonctionnaires*. The *Revue de
métaphysique et de morale* asked Célestin Bouglé, who was at last 'rid of
Castes', to write an article on unions and the public sector for its 'practical issues' rubric. Bouglé had stood unsuccessfully in the elections of
1906, was a contributor to the *Dépêche de Toulouse* and published political essays, including *Syndicalisme et démocratie: Impressions et réflexions*
(1908), in which he defended syndicalism, provided that it was moderate.

Durkheim took part in two debates organized by the Union de la vérité:
'le fonctionnaire citoyen' ['the public-spirited civil servant'] (19 January
1908) and 'Le syndicat des fonctionnaires' ['the civil service union'] (16
February 1908) The first debate was chaired by Paul Desjardins. It opened
with a clash between Durkheim and Henry Berthélemy, a professor of law,
who made a distinction between direct and indirect agents. The former
had power and issued orders, like a station-master, while the latter performed 'tasks' (like a postman). Judges came into a separate category,
added Berthélemy, because their position required them to be independent. Durkheim took the view that it was impossible to classify people
in this way; any civil servant, even a rural postman, had 'some public
authority' and was therefore both an 'agent of authority' and 'a private
man and citizen.' Was this a watertight division? Durkheim admitted that

it was, 'unfortunately, impossible to make that radical distinction'. It was not easy for anyone to 'shed completely their civil-servant status' in their private lives. Hence the moral dilemmas that were so difficult to resolve. The principle, on the other hand, was there: 'The character or authority that the civil servant has because of his position must not extend beyond it.' His professional authority must not be used to promote either 'personal ideas' or a confessional or religious party.

When Berthélemy argued that a professor was 'free in his academic capacity', Durkheim replied: 'Not at all. I believe that not even teachers in the higher education sector can be said to have that absolute freedom . . . I take the view that a teacher who, even outside the classroom, tries to exert a political influence over his students often puts himself in a delicate position' (Durkheim 1975[1908b]: 192–3). The same applied to the relationship between an engineer and his subordinates. That did not mean that the teacher or engineer was not completely free to express his view in a newspaper or on a public platform. But when Paul Desjardins suggested that the distinction he was making should be enshrined in law, Durkheim sounded a note of caution: these situations were 'too fluid' to be regulated by the law. There might, at most, be a need for 'a good disciplinary tribune', but even that was a 'major question'.

The debate was attended by the independent socialist *député* Alexandre Millerand (who, in 1908, was reappointed minister for public works and the postal service in Clemenceau's government). When he took the floor, the tone of the debate changed, as he was a skilled orator who could provoke both applause and laughter. Like Durkheim, Millerand accepted that it would be difficult to resolve such a problem through legislation. He also agreed about the need for a disciplinary tribune, but rejected the idea of legislation to solve the problem of how to reconcile the duties of the civil servant with the rights of the citizen. That would be like 'trying to square the circle'. Millerand saw, finally, little difference between strikes in the public sector and strikes in industry, and even suggested that relations between civil servants and the state should be modelled on those between employers and employees. An outraged Durkheim raised some 'serious objections', but admitted that 'everyone was, to some extent, a civil servant of society'. The issue of whether or not civil servants should join a union or, more generally, be involved in politics was problematic. 'I know many civil servants who are asking themselves this question, and they are unable to give a clear answer.' Millerand rejected the idea that civil servants could be 'systematically opposed' to the government or, for example, say in public that it was failing in all its duties. An astonished Durkheim found his position 'insane'. He then tried to make a distinction between the teacher (who had a professional duty not 'to spread ideas that had nothing to do with his subject') and the citizen (who had the right to 'express his views' on political issues 'in suitable terms'). His reaction caused a stir and provoked some laughter. He then challenged Millerand directly: 'You will sacrifice much more serious moral interests to temporary political interests.' When Millerand replied that 'making no mention of the teacher's position is just more hypocrisy', there were more protests from the floor.

Paul Desjardins, who was chairing the debate, intervened to restore order and invited Durkheim to close the discussion by explaining what he meant when he said: 'We are all civil servants of society.' It is a way of saying', replied Durkheim, 'that we are all servants of the public interest, some of us directly, and some of us indirectly. There are *public* civil servants on the one hand, and *private* (or economic) civil servants on the other.' He even thought that this distinction was of 'practical relevance', as it allowed the problem of trade unions in the public sector to be seen in different terms: the private sector should be modelled on the public sector, and not (as Millerand had suggested) vice versa. He therefore argued that the model of the private company should not be extended to the public sector; that idea seemed to him to be 'retrograde'. The progressive move would be to give employees the guarantees and security enjoyed by public employees and not to 'introduce into the public sector the anarchy that all too often prevails in the economic realm.'

The Union de la vérité organized another debate about the delicate issue of unionism in the public sector on 16 February. Paul Desjardins was once more in the chair. Participants included Ferdinand Buisson, a former professor at the Sorbonne and a close friend of Desjardins, the economist Charles Gide, Célestin Bouglé and a number of trade unionists. Some of the speakers, including Buisson, argued that civil servants had no right of association. Durkheim began by asking the supporters of trade unionism why they believed that 'a union would be an effective way of correcting the vices of the administration'. He accepted that 'civil servants' complaints are often justified', and that a union would be more than an association to 'give them satisfaction'. But did that justify 'losing sight of the general interest of the country'? He feared that the unionization of the civil service would 'disrupt the most essential public services' (Durkheim 1975[1908b]: 204). Realizing that this might make him sound like a conservative, he then tried to justify himself: 'I believe that the trade-union movement is going against the general direction of our historical evolution. It may look revolutionary, but there is something reactionary about it.'

Returning to the idea that 'we are all civil servants of society', he recalled that, ever since the nineteenth century, unions had made it possible to 'introduce some order into the anarchy' and to 'emphasize the social nature of economic functions'. But why attempt to force such a form of organization onto 'the most eminently social functions'? He feared that the cure would be worse than the illness: there was a danger that the defence of the particular interests of civil servants would 'disrupt the normal workings of social life'.

Célestin Bouglé then intervened to say that he 'tended to agree' with Durkheim, but added that, while civil servants might like the word 'union', the general public did not. 'In the last analysis, it will be public opinion that decides the issue . . . The vast majority of the population refuses to listen.' He therefore appealed for moderation (Durkheim 1975[1908b]: 204).

In Durkheim's view, authority and hierarchy were essential elements of administrative life: 'There must be command structures.' That did not rule out the possibility of major reforms such as electing staff representatives or even introducing cooperation into the administrative system, to the extent that it was legitimate to do so. Being convinced that the administration needed to have the support of professional groups, he suggested reforms and the creation of a professional association of civil servants: 'I would establish it on a legal and statutory basis' (Durkheim 1975[1908b]: 217). His position was therefore based upon the idea of a happy medium: professional associations but no unions; administrative regulation but no legislation.

La Revue's symposium in April 1908 on 'parliamentary impotence' signalled the rise of a new anti-parliamentarianism, and it was further exacerbated by the increase in allowances, despite the fact that so many *députés* did not actually attend parliament. In his reply (1975[1908a]), Durkheim was critical of parliamentarians, and accused them of 'legislative sterility'. He argued that not even electoral reform would do anything to remedy or improve the situation because 'the sickness went much deeper'. He went on: 'It has to do mainly with the mental disarray and extreme intellectual confusion in which we find ourselves. The most varied and contradictory conceptions clash, confuse minds and frustrate one another. The powerlessness of legislators thus reflects the country's uncertainties.' He added, more bluntly, that 'mere constitutional tricks' would not be enough. Beneath the political, there lay the social, and it consisted essentially of representations. Durkheim therefore played down the importance of political or parliamentary action, or what Mauss called the 'narrow and abstract sphere of pure politics', and emphasized the importance of other forms of actions involving intermediary groupings, including professional associations.

Divorce. The Woman Question

Durkheim returned to the issue of divorce in a debate organized by the Union de la vérité in 1909. Again, he stated that divorce was not just about what individuals wanted, and that 'more thought should be given to the broader interests of society' (Durkheim 1975[1909a]). He believed that 'rule' and 'discipline' were not just 'empty words' and 'expressed moral realities that man cannot do without': 'I believe that it is in the nature of man for his desires and passions to be kept within certain limits; that there are external moral forces that restrain him, and that force upon him a moral duty to be moderate and to rein in his desires.' If that were not the case, unruly and exacerbated appetites would take over and lead to suffering. Happiness was synonymous with discipline. And marriage was a form of discipline: it 'disciplined sexual life' and put 'a brake on the sexual appetite'. In order to demonstrate that, far from being a nuisance or problem, that brake enhanced the ability to face up the 'difficulties of life', he repeated the conclusions of his study of suicide: 'There are more suicides when divorce is easier and more commonplace. This is a law of moral statistics, and there are no known exceptions to the rule' (ibid.: 212). The law applied, however, more to men than to women, whose sexual instincts were, he repeated, 'already contained and moderated'. Matrimonial discipline or regulation was 'useful, even indispensable', because it was 'good for the individual's health'.

Marriage was much more than a mere union between individuals: it was a social institution. 'Marriage is the basis of the family.' And the 'moral influence of marriage on the whole of our lives is still of primordial importance. That is its true function.' Not everything could be decided by the 'capriciousness of individual desires' (Durkheim 1975[1909a]: 214). When Fabry disagreed with Durkheim's suggestion that marriage should be indissoluble, he immediately corrected that mistaken interpretation: 'Oh, forgive me! I do accept the need for divorce. I mean that marriage should be indissoluble in a relative sense; I think that absolute indissolubility is impossible.' Fabry was puzzled: 'You mean that a divorce should be granted by the magistrates only with great difficulty?' Durkheim now tried to make himself more clear: 'What I would suggest is that, when a magistrate looks at particular cases, he should take into account not only the desires expressed by the parties concerned, but should think more about the broad social issues that are involved in all matters of this kind, as that is his responsibility' (ibid.: 215).

When Marianne Weber published a book describing the situation of women throughout history – based upon secondary sources – Durkheim reviewed it at some length in the *Année sociologique* (Durkheim 1980[1910b]).The author, a German feminist, was the wife of Max Weber. She set out to find, through historical research, a solution to the problem of the legal position in both the family and society. Her book was, Durkheim accepted 'an 'in-depth inquiry', but it lacked 'a disposition to organize facts' (ibid.: 285). While there was a dominant view that 'a woman's place in the family' determines her 'place in society', it was, unfortunately, 'simplistic' (ibid.: 286). Durkheim also challenged the author's main premise that 'the patriarchal family has brought about the woman's complete subservience' (ibid.: 288). The situation was more complex than she suggested. Over time, 'husband and wife have become closer', and the 'feeling of respect' directed towards women has become more pronounced.

As for the proposed remedy, Durkheim was puzzled. The 'prudently conservative' Weber was certainly not suggesting that marriage should be suppressed 'because it shackles the wife to the husband and puts her in a state of dependency', but, while she accepted that 'the formalities of a wedding were indispensable', she argued that, 'in the name of personal morality', it should be 'possible for the marriage to be broken simply at the wishes . . . of the parties concerned' ((Durkheim 1980[1910b]: 287). This, Durkheim contended, posed a threat to the 'organic unity of the family and of marriage' (ibid.: 288) and would diminish woman's status. The feelings of respect directed towards women originated in the religious respect inspired by hearth and home, and this would cease to be the case if family life became nothing more than a 'precarious cohabitation'. It would be difficult for such a religion to survive. Woman's status would be diminished as result: what was a gain in one respect (greater rights, a role in civil life) would be a loss in another. Such important losses demonstrated only one thing: 'The problem is less simple than is commonly believed' (ibid.: 289).

The woman question was also of great interest to two of the *Année*'s contributors. Paul Lapie published his *La Femme dans la famille* in 1908, and it was followed a year later by Gaston Richard's *La Femme dans l'histoire*. Both books appeared in the 'Bibliothèque biologique et sociologique des femmes' collection, which had recently been launched by Éditions Drouin in a bid to make public the vast panorama of knowledge about women that had been accumulated in the domains of biology, sociology and pedagogy. Only four books were published in the collection.

The new collection's editor was Édouard Toulouse (1865–1947), a psychiatrist who had written a thesis on 'Senile melancholy in women' and a book called *Les Causes de la folie* (1896), and who had for some years been in charge of the women's ward at the Villejuif asylum.[13] He was one of the pioneers of sexology in France, and an advocate of birth control for prophylactic purposes. He was also a feminist fellow-traveller, a supporter of women's right to vote, an advocate of coeducation in schools, and of women's right to work.

Toulouse was an essayist and a very active popularizer who described himself as a sociologist, but he refused to make any distinction between sociology and biology: 'Social facts are biological facts.' He therefore took a very different view from Durkheim, even though he admired the statistical analysis that had gone into *Suicide*. When that book was published, he suggested to Durkheim that he should conduct a more clinical analysis by interviewing both the friends and relatives of suicide victims, as well as those who had attempted suicide. But, as is apparent from the reviews of three volumes of the *Année sociologique* that he published in the *Revue scientifique*, he was also critical of Durkheim's sociology on the grounds that it was too theoretical, dogmatic and speculative, and too obsessed with definitional and methodological issues. In his view, direct observation was the only 'truly scientific' method. The best way to study social facts was to look at them from the inside, not from the outside. Toulouse published the work of two of the *Année*'s team in his collection, but they – and especially Richard – were its most heterodox members.

In his book *La Femme dans la famille*, Lapie contended that, as could be seen in a variety of societies, work was a constituent element of the dignity of women. The position and recognition that women enjoyed in any given society were, in his view, broadly determined by the value-judgements of men. The various changes that had taken place in contemporary society (state involvement in family matters, the emergence of large-scale industry) had completely disrupted the old cohesion of the family: women were leaving the family 'temple' and working outside the home. This was not, he insisted, an argument in favour of confining women to the domestic sphere. He predicted that all housework would eventually be out-sourced, and that childcare would become the responsibility of employees of the state. He also proposed reforms to family law that would turn marriage into a real contract, with the rules established by both partners: choice of family home and of family name, division of labour, and management of the household budget. Paul Lapie rejected both traditional marriage, free love, the Napoleonic code (which defended men's superiority over women) and feminist demands in favour of what might be termed a third way (Lapie 1908: 105).

Gaston Richard was more critical of feminism, which he regarded as 'an expression of sentimentality that cannot and must not enter the terminology of the human sciences' (1909: 429). A great defender of the role of mothers, Richard also advocated women's right to work. Turning to relations between men and women, he divided history into three important phases: matriarchy, patriarchy and modern individualism. Discussing the contemporary period, he showed that the emancipation of women (admission to university), went hand in hand with the spread of democracy and, more specifically, the development of individual rights. He also observed that progress in the direction of female individualism had been more rapid in England than in France or Spain; the explanation for the difference was at once religious (Protestantism gave women's souls a taste for moral independence) and political (decentralization excluded fewer women from public life). The short appendix to Richard's book rejected Durkheim's theses about the role played by blood in the prohibition of incest.

Durkheim could not let this pass without comment, and reviewed the book in the *Année* (Durkheim 1980[1910a]). He made no attempt to conceal his annoyance with the erroneous statement made by his (former) associate and criticized his historical analysis for its 'simplicity' (ibid.: 289). It was with 'the greatest surprise' that he read Richard's claim that '"the taboo is a Polynesian institution: the totem is an Amerindian institution"', but simply remarked that 'The taboo . . . has nothing inherently Polynesian about it: it is universal' (ibid.: 290).

When Richard published his *La Sociologie générale et les lois sociologiques* in 1912, Durkheim once more insisted on correcting him: 'He declares that, in our view, all general sociology is an impossibility. Such an affirmation is fundamentally erroneous . . . All we did was to deny the possibility of a synthesis that would not rely on a sufficiently profound analysis' (Durkheim 1980[1913c]: 85–6). He then attacked the 'scientific Phariseeism' that postponed indefinitely 'the time for useful generalizations'. He was in favour of generalizations based upon 'clear-cut investigations' and 'extensive and varied scientific experiments', but rejected those consisting of 'a few summary and schematic views based on a rapid inventory of a few arbitrarily chosen facts' (ibid.: 86).[14]

The Origins of Religion

The issue of religion had been widely discussed ever since the separation of church and state in 1905. The future of religion – or the 'universal crisis' in religion – was debated in journals, newspapers and salons, as were such specialized or esoteric topics as totemism and the rites and customs of Australian aborigines. As more and more books were published on so-called 'primitive' religions, the question of the origins of religion aroused as much passion as Darwin's discovery of the evolution of species a few decades earlier.

Durkheim's enemies at the Sorbonne regarded him as a sort of *grand manitou* who, ever since his major article on totemism had been published in the *Année*, had reduced everything to totemism. He was also criticized for his complete lack of respect for religious beliefs. Because of his positivism, students mocked him for being 'a crummy Comte' (Azouvi 2007). In 1906–7, Durkheim's public lectures at the Sorbonne were, for the first time, devoted to the origins of religion. His other courses, as we have already seen, were on the history of secondary education (these were given at the École normale supérieure) and moral education in schools.

In a letter to his friend Xavier Léon, Durkheim announced that he planned to write a new book: 'You know that I have begun to write my book on the elementary forms of religious practice and thought.'[15] He was willing to 'give something' to the *Revue de métaphysique et de morale*, but could not think of 'anything suitable for separate publication, apart from an introduction that has yet to be written'. He hoped to write the introduction in September: 'It will be a short exposition in which I will explain the book's purpose, from the viewpoint of both the genesis and nature of religious thought and, in more general terms, the genesis and nature of thought.' He went into more detail: 'As the book progresses, I hope to reveal some of the social elements that have helped to constitute certain of our categories (causality, the notion of force, the notion of personality). I have long been preoccupied with this question, but although I dare not deal with it directly for the moment, I do think it will be possible to approach it by looking at religious thought.'

Durkheim was 'very happy' to give Xavier Léon the preface for the *Revue*, in order to 'repay a debt', but was afraid that it might look like a 'special offer' designed to attract more readers. And when his friend invited him to speak at an international congress on philosophy in Heidelberg, Durkheim replied that although he was 'quite convinced that it was not in his interest to refuse to attend international gatherings', he did not want to go 'empty-handed'. He informed Léon that François Simiand would be attending: 'Simiand suggests that he should go and speak in the name of all of us, and he will acquit himself admirably of that task.'[16]

Durkheim also told Xavier Léon that the *Revue philosophique*'s editor Théodule Ribot had asked him for an article, and informed him that he was going to let him have 'part of the book that can easily stand alone because it is from the beginning: it is a critical look at the classic theories'. Paul

Fontana's summary of the lectures on religion appeared in three instalments in the *Revue philosophique* in 1907 (issues 5, 7 and 12). Durkheim was described as a professor with great authority: 'We know that he is the leader of a school that is trying to apply the objective method to the study of social phenomena, and to turn sociology into a real science.' Whether one agreed or disagreed with him, it was, in other words, impossible to ignore Durkheim. In his lectures, Durkheim went back to the earlier research that would eventually result in his masterful *Elementary Forms of Religious Life*. He was aware of how difficult the task would be: given that science had become 'something secular', it could not, he remarked from the outset, 'be applied to sacred things without profaning them' (Durkheim 1975[1907d]: 69). He was interested in two things: defining religion, and identifying the 'simplest and most primitive' religion known to humanity.

He first required a definition (which would inevitably be no more than provisional), but was not content with 'vulgar notions' that were, by definition, 'vague, incomplete and confused'. He established two principles: we must first rid ourselves of the notions we have acquired thanks to our education, and then establish the common features of all the religions of the past. He began by rejecting two 'scholarly definitions'. One explained religion by referring to the idea of the supernatural, or the idea that there was something mysterious about it (Spencer and Muller), and the other (Tylor) invoked the idea of God or, more specifically, of supernatural beings. If that were the case, what was the status of Buddhism, which was no more than an ethics? Rather than defining religion as a whole, Durkheim began by defining religious phenomena – in other words, the constituent elements of religion – and established that religious phenomena were 'based upon' a form of classification that divided things into two categories: the sacred and the profane. But what was the sacred? The sacred is defined in 'absolute opposition' to the profane. The distinction is such that it takes the form of a series of prohibitions of contact (direct contact, eye contact, verbal contact).

Durkheim begins by formulating two propositions: 'Religious beliefs are beliefs that have sacred things as their object', and 'There is no religion without a church.' He then gives the following definition of religion: 'A system of beliefs and practices relating to sacred things – the beliefs and practices shared by a given community.' Religion was therefore, in his view, a 'social phenomenon'.

But 'what is the most primitive form of religion?' Durkheim asks. He now joined in the debate about the origins of religious life that divided his English colleagues. Some supported the animist thesis, and others the naturist thesis. The supporters of the former, led by Tylor, contended that religion initially took the form of the worship of spiritual beings. Primitive man was in a sense a 'prisoner of the imaginary world' he had created. Durkheim admitted that this theory had been 'of great service' in that it revealed the fact that the soul was 'a very complex product of history, mythology and religion'. He was, however, also critical of Tylor's theory because he could not accept that the source of religion was to be found in dreams: dreams were such a 'habitual' phenomena that primitive man can scarcely have worried himself about finding an explanation for them. He added: 'The less civilized we are, the less we dream' (1975[1907d]: 74). The alternative theory was that the first objects of worship were material things or nature (naturism): the first gods were 'personifications of natural forces'. And according to Max Müller, it was language that allowed them to be personified.

Durkheim's project was ambitious. He wanted to 'explain the religious evolution of humanity and understand the nature of religion in general'. Having ruled out both the available theories, he turned to observation in a bid to 'look for the most primitive religion known to us', namely totemism. He was not interested in the conceptions of so-called primitive peoples because he wished to see what was archaic about them, but because he wished to 'understand the nature of religion in general'. The 'lowest' human societies that Durkheim set out to study were characterized, at the level of their social organization, by the fact that they were divided into clans and that each clan had both a name and a totem (such as the 'wolf clan'). He then rapidly traced the history of the debate about totemism. Each clan used its totem as an insignia, an emblem and a symbol. There was, however, more to the totem than that: it was the 'centre of a real religion' that had its sacred objects, its prohibition, its myths and its ceremonies. Rather than reducing totemism to the idolatrous worship of animals or plants, Durkheim extended it to mean 'a system of ideas and beliefs that encompasses all that exists, a complete representation of the universe'. More specifically, it was the coming together of the cults of a tribe's various clans that established totemism as a religion.

The questions Durkheim was trying to answer, and which would become central to *Elementary Forms*, were as follows: 'How does religious sentiment come into being?' and 'What gives birth to religion?' In his view, this was the same as asking about the birth of totemism. Durkheim then advanced the hypothesis he intended to defend: 'Religion was from the outset a social fact.' In order to do this, he identified the totemic principle as 'a nameless and impersonal force', a 'something' or a 'fluid' such as *mana, orinda* or *manitou*. 'Such a conception already contains the embryo of later conceptions of divinity.' Durkheim then puts forward his main thesis: as the god and the clan are one and the same, the totemic divinity was nothing but 'society itself, but in sublimated, hypostasized form' (1975[1907d]: 94).

Durkheim's thesis was to prove highly controversial. He was convinced that society has 'everything required to awaken religious feelings in individuals': the ability to impose rules, and a helpful and 'uplifting' force (examples might include 'great national currents'). 'Society is constantly creating the sacred', he declared. And, as Mauss demonstrated in his essay of 'seasonal variations', the life of societies alternates between phases of concentration (heightened passions and paroxysms) and phases of dispersal, as can be seen in Australian societies. There is a world of sacred things, and a world of profane things. The 'roots' of religious feelings lie in society, but such feelings exist 'only within individuals', and individuals therefore feel that the power of religion is 'immanent with them'. As religious things have both a moral and a material aspect, religion is both 'a moral discipline and a technique' and a set of beliefs and rituals. Durkheim analyses various religious beliefs pertaining to the soul, spirits, genies and demons, and then both the positive and negative rituals that constitute systems of prohibition. One ceremony is of particular interest to him: *intichiuma*.

In his lectures, Durkheim defended certain ideas that were dear to him: religion does not mean that man is the dupe of some 'illusion', and human cults are not 'aberrations'. Religion acts as the 'predecessor' of philosophy and science. 'The divinity is nothing other than society itself.' Durkheim believes in the 'profound moral efficacy' of rituals (which determine the belief in the physical efficacy of something 'illusory'). There is even something eternal about religion: 'it will be indispensable so long as there are men, or in other words societies', he asserts, giving the French Revolution as an example. And he concludes: 'When this need for a cult is no longer felt, both society and individuals are going through a serious crisis, as any living being must feel the need to live a more intense and broader life, and to renew life' (1975[1907d]: 122).

The End of Religion?

In 1907, Durkheim responded to the *Mercure de France*'s symposium on 'the religious question'. He took the view that 'we are witnessing the dissolution of the religious form' established in medieval Europe, and that its dissolution began in the sixteenth century:

> So long as religion, and especially the Catholic religion, retained its full authority, it was immune to criticism and to science; the fact that the scientific spirit has seized hold of it and questions it with the same freedom that is used to question natural phenomena tends to prove that it has lost the ascendancy that once protected it from profane thought.

Are we therefore to conclude that 'religious thought has reached the end of its career'? Durkheim refuses to play at being a prophet, as our present state of knowledge does not allow us to predict what the religious forms of the future will be. We simply have to assume that 'they will be even more permeated with rationality than the most rational of today's religions, and that the social bond, which has always been the soul of religions, will assert itself more directly and more expressly than in the past, and without concealing itself behind myths and symbols' (1975[1907b]: 169–70). This argument would be expanded in the opening chapter of *The Elementary Forms of Religious Life*.

In November 1908, Durkheim took part in another discussion on science and religion. The debate was organized by the Société française de philosophie and brought him face to face with his old teacher and colleague Émile Boutroux, and the philosopher and mathematician Édouard Le Roy.[17] Durkheim began by asking why we wanted to 'protect religion from science?' The explanation was, in his view, simple: there was a fear that, if religion was subjected to reason, it would be rejected in the name of reason. And yet 'science cannot bring about the disappearance of the reality to which it is applied'. Religion was 'a fact', but there was a stubborn prejudice that saw the sacred as 'something irrational and mysterious that eludes science'. Durkheim contended that, 'in reality, we constantly see the sacred come into being before our very eyes'. He gave the examples of progress and democracy, which look like sacred ideas to those who believe in them.

Being convinced that religion would not vanish into science when it became an object for science. Durkheim was astonished to see a believer refusing to raise the problem in those terms. There was every reason to argue that religion had had two very different functions at different points of history. Its practical function was to 'help men to live, and to adapt to their conditions of existence'. Its intellectual function was to supply a 'form of speculative thought', 'a way of representing the world', or a sort of 'pre-scientific science'. It seemed obvious to him that its second function was 'increasingly redundant': 'The most recent religions are not cosmogonies, but moral disciplines.' 'This regression [had] continued uninterrupted throughout history.' He refused, on the other hand, to be too absolute or too assertive: 'I am not claiming that the religions of the future will lose their speculative character in any absolute sense.' But one thing was certain: the practical function of religion was still 'intact'. 'In this domain, science cannot replace religion in any way.' In response to Le Roy's claim that the scientific explanation of a religious fact 'dissolved it as such', Durkheim argued that the existence of rites and religions could be both explained and justified in historical terms: 'It can be shown that it was good and necessary for rites to exist. The crude practices of the Australian have as much human meaning as those of the most idealistic religions' (Durkheim 1975[1908c]: 141–6).

The Sociology of Religion and the Theory of Knowledge

Durkheim finally responded to Xavier Léon's invitation and sent him an article for the *Revue de métaphysique et de morale*. The first two sections of the article consisted of the 'Introduction' to *Elementary Forms*, which would not be published until 1912. Durkheim was thus in a position to publish the introduction to his study before he had even finished writing it. The main purpose of the introduction was to define 'our object of study', namely 'the simplest and most primitive religion that is known at present' (Durkheim 1995[1912]: 1). His description of it would have 'all the care and precision that an ethnographer or an historian would bring to the task'.

But, as a sociologist, he also intended to ask other questions: his study of a very archaic religion 'will not be for the sheer pleasure of recounting the bizarre and the eccentric'. It would, on the contrary, 'help us to comprehend the religious nature of man, that is, to reveal a fundamental and permanent aspect of humanity' (ibid.).

Durkheim was aware of the objections that would be raised. Why go back to the beginning of history in order to understand humanity as it is at present? How could 'the crude cults of Australian tribes' help us to understand 'higher' forms of religious thought such as Christianity? He was well aware that ethnography and religious history had been criticized on the grounds that they were 'a means of making war against religion'. His own position was quite clear: 'such could not possibly be a sociologist's point of view. Indeed, it is a fundamental postulate of sociology that a human institution cannot rest upon error and falsehood.' There are no religions that are false: 'All are true after their own fashion. All fulfil given conditions of human existence, though in different ways' (1995[1912]: 2).

Durkheim accepted that it was possible to rank religions hierarchically: some were 'richer in ideas and feeling', and were of 'greater complexity and higher ideal content', but 'all are equally religions'. His hypothesis was that 'the most bizarre or barbarous rites and the strangest myths translate some human need and some aspect of life, whether social or individual'. It was all the more essential to adopt this approach in that 'the reasons the faithful settle for in justifying those rites and myths may be mistaken, and most often are; but the true reasons exist nonetheless, and it is the business of science to uncover them' (1995[1912]: 2). In methodological terms, the recourse to history is essential as we cannot understand the most recent religions without understanding their evolution: explaining anything human means 'going back to its simplest and most primitive form' (ibid.: 3). Citing Descartes, Durkheim added: 'The first link takes precedence in the chain of scientific truths'. The 'first link' is not a 'logical concept', but a 'concrete reality that historical and ethnographic observation alone can reveal to us' (ibid.). Primitive religions also have the advantage of being simple, and this makes it easier to identify their constituent elements, and to understand them. Turning to the observations of ethnologists, Durkheim describes them as 'veritable revelations that have breathed new life into the study of human institutions' (ibid.: 6), as can be seen from the study of kinship. They are comparable with biology's 'discovery of unicellular creatures'.

Durkheim's choice of title for the article – 'The sociology of religion and the theory of knowledge' – intended to show his colleagues that his study was of interest not only to the science of religions, but also to the theory of knowledge: 'There is no religion that is not both a cosmology and a speculation about the divine.' Religion began by serving as science and philosophy. Durkheim is fascinated by the 'fundamental notions' that dominate our intellectual life, by what are conventionally known as 'the categories of the understanding' ('notions of time, space, class, number, cause, substance, personality, etc.'). Such notions are 'like solid frames that confine thought' (1995[1912]: 8–9).

Durkheim's starting point is the conviction that the 'principal categories' are 'born in and from religion; they are a product of religious thought'. But if religion is 'an eminently social thing', and if religious representations are 'collective representations that express collective realities' (1995[1912]: 9), the problem of knowledge, which is central to philosophy, must be 'framed in new terms' (ibid.: 12). Durkheim dismisses both the main theses about the theory of knowledge – namely, the apriorist thesis (that categories do not derive from experience and are logically prior to experience) and the empiricist thesis (that categories are constructed by the individual) – and is convinced that 'if the social origin of the categories is accepted, a new stance becomes possible, one that should enable us, I believe, to avoid these opposite difficulties' (ibid.: 14). Durkheim once more asserts that, because the categories are 'essentially collective representations', they 'translate states of the collectivity': they are 'the product of an immense cooperation that extends not only through space but also through time' (ibid.: 15).

Durkheim now reiterates his thesis about human duality – man is both an individual being and a social being – to demonstrate that it is the social nature of man that makes the categories of the understanding necessary: before society can exist, there must be a 'minimum moral consensus but also a minimum logical consensus'; 'That is why . . . we feel that we are not fully free . . . Outside us, it is opinion that judges us' (1995[1912]: 16). The categories are 'ingenious instruments of thought, which human groups have painstakingly forged over centuries, and in which they have amassed the best of their intellectual capital' (ibid.: 18). Durkheim is therefore opening up a whole new field of knowledge: if we wish to study the history of human mentality, we must develop a 'whole science' which can 'advance only slowly and by collective labour'. His own role will, he insists, be a modest one: 'the present is an attempt to make certain fragmentary contributions to that science' (ibid.).

In the third part of the article (which was not included in the introduction to *Elementary Forms*), Durkheim specifically addresses his philosopher colleagues and deals with sociology's contributions to psychology and philosophy. He attempts to clear up certain misunderstandings: sociology is not indifferent to anything to do with man, is not hostile to philosophy, and is not a narrow empiricism. This reproach in 'unjustified', as the study of religious phenomena that he is outlining will 'throw some light on the religious nature of man, and the science of morals must end in explaining the moral consciousness' (1982[1909]: 236). Durkheim reassures the philosophers: the 'metaphysical problems' that have wracked them will not 'be allowed to fall into oblivion'. He also warns them that these problems must 'take new forms', and that sociology, more than any other science, can contribute to this renewal' (ibid.: 237). For philosophers, sociology is therefore 'the most useful of all preparatory studies' (ibid.: 238).

Given that the study of collective representations must begin with a study of categories, it should be obvious to Durkheim's readers that sociology is destined to become 'the central concern of philosophical speculation'. Durkheim is convinced that sociology, which has finally escaped the tutelage of philosophy is destined to 'provide philosophy with the indispensable foundations which it at present lacks'. Sociological reflection will therefore 'take upon an extension, in a natural progression, in the form of philosophical thinking'. He concludes that, 'to do this, a whole series of investigations must be undertaken' (1982[1909]: 239).

Mauss's *La Prière*. A Chair at the Collège de France?

It was probably in 1907 or 1908 that Marcel Mauss began to write his doctoral thesis on prayer. Fortunately, he now had some respite from writing reviews: from volume X onwards, the *Année* was published only once every three years. Mauss was, however, 'making slow progress'.[18] His friends expressed the hope that he 'would soon finish *Prayer* once and for all'.

Mauss's plans comprised three stages: definition (and rejection of pre-notions), observation (and critical reading of documents), and explanation. The provisional definition of prayer given at the beginning of his study was as follows: 'Prayer is an oral religious ritual that is directly addressed to sacred things' (1969[1909]: 414).[19] He wished to use the sacred/profane distinction to get away from the modern notion of prayer, and to avoid seeing things through the prism of Christianity. Mauss adopted an historical approach – from collective religion to individual religion – and focused his attention on 'elementary oral ritual', such as that found in Australian societies. His argument is based upon a study of *intichiumas*, and his manuscript ends with a description of the *intichiuma* ceremony of the caterpillar clan in Alice Springs. *Intichiumas* are melodic and rhythmic formulae, sometimes reduced to a monotone cry, that the Arunta of Australia sing together as they dance during their ceremonies. The whole ceremony is bound up with the cult of the totem, as the formulae include an appeal to the divine totem animal. All this was obviously also of interest to his uncle Émile.

Mauss circulated his text, and then decided to have the first two fascicules (one quarter of the book) printed by Alcan. He then retrieved them from the printer on the advice of Sylvain Lévi as he had learned that the German missionary Carl Strehlow had some new documentation. It consisted of a series of fascicules entitled *Die Aranda und Loritja-Stämme in Zentral-Australien.* The first two were published in 1907 and 1908 respectively. Mauss made contact with Strehlow, who passed them on to him, and he reviewed them in volume XI of the *Année* (in collaboration with Durkheim) and in volume XII. The data was on the totem cult of the Arunta and the Loritja and brought together a great deal of material, including 1,500 lines of Arunta poetry. Mauss was 'impatient' to have it, especially as it challenged the theses of Spencer and Gillen and provided new material confirming 'the hypotheses we have often advanced here': some peculiar features of the Aruntas' social organization were not typical of primitive totemism, and were 'curious and late anomalies', and the idea of uterine descent preceded that of descent through the paternal line. This was, according to Durkheim and Mauss, a book which, while it might not have the 'revolutionary impact' ascribed to it, was 'highly instructive'. Strehlow had one great advantage in that he spoke the Arunta language; but he also had one weakness: he had not been initiated into the clan and, because he was a missionary, certain practices had presumably not been described to him, or had been concealed from him. Mauss at last had something definite to work on. But the thesis never moved beyond the planning stage.

In the same year, Mauss also published a long critical note on Wundt's theory of art and myths in the *Revue philosophique* (Mauss 1969[1908]). It was a clear expression of his hostility towards his German colleague's collective psychology [*Völkerpsychologie*], but he also described Wundt as 'one of the last encyclopaedic minds'. Wundt held that it was possible to abstract facts – language, myths, art and morality – from their 'natural ambiance', or, in other words, their social context. Mauss commented: 'It is quite arbitrary to imagine a mental life that exists independently of its organization.' Turning to art, Mauss criticized Wundt for 'failing to get away from pure psychology and to relate art to its social conditions of existence' (ibid.: 205; see Fournier 1987).

Mauss had long intended to collect the 'little things' he had written with his friend Henri Hubert for 'a sort of *Mélanges* of religious history'. Both men had written a number of articles but had 'scattered them to the four winds', as Hubert put it.[20] Neither man had a book to his name. Sylvain Lévi was urging them to publish something. The two friends wanted to reply to the criticisms that had been directed at their work, and at the same time to celebrate their few 'victories': they had identified the notion of the sacred as the central religious phenomenon, made a distinction between positive and negative rituals (as they made clear, the distinction came from Durkheim), and had studied the origins of human understanding ('we began this study with and after Durkheim'). The main problem that concerned them was also central to Durkheim's work: the relationship between individual and society. 'What is the attitude of the individual towards social phenomena?' 'What role does society play in shaping the consciousness of the individual?' (Hubert and Mauss 1969[1906]) Their answer was that magic, sacrifice, myth and prayer all revealed the power of tradition or suggestion. Hubert and Mauss were, in other words, sociologists and intended to go on being sociologists. They wished to defend the comparative method, which consisted in studying the institutions and representations of different societies. Their goal was to discover the general phenomena of social life, but to put things on a solid footing by beginning with the study of particular institutions such as sacrifice, magic and forms of classification. And as they themselves put it, the facts took priority over faith.

Mélanges was published in Alcan's 'Travaux de *L'Année sociologique*' series, which was edited by Durkheim. It was the second book to appear in the collection, the first being Célestin Bouglé's study of castes. Durkheim oversaw its publication with some apprehension. As always, he was worried about how long it was taking, and once more wrote to his sister Rosine to complain that Mauss was holding things up. Mauss, especially, seemed to be terrified of him. Louis Gernet described seeing Mauss 'with Hubert, carrying their manuscript but not daring to venture into Durkheim's office to give him it' (cited in Davidovitch 1966: 19). Georges Davy told a similar story: as he was having a beer with Mauss in a nearby café, he saw Durkheim in the courtyard of the Sorbonne. A nervous Mauss said to him: 'Quick, hide me. My uncle's coming' (cited in Clark 1973: 182).

Mauss had good reason to be nervous. After a first rapid and superficial reading of the preface, a tired Durkheim lost his temper:

> Your preface causes me a lot of pain. The beginning, in particular, seems to me to be *perfectly ridiculous*. The tone is that of someone who has lost all self-respect. It contains everything that could discredit you. And rightly so. You are you own master, and you have the right to publish it if you wish to do so. But not in the 'Travaux de *L'Année*'. I will not take the responsibility.

He added: 'You speak as though everyone was watching you and was interested in your every thought. I don't think this will do you any good, and I think there is a danger that it will damage the pair of you – and especially you.' His uncle was almost convinced that Mauss should cut the whole preface, but suggested that he should show the text to Sylvain Lévi: 'His opinion might be worth more than mine.'[21]

On the other hand, Durkheim was also afraid that Hubert and Mauss's book would lose 'part of its significance if it is divorced from the *Année* and the whole movement to which it relates . . . In itself, it is no more than a collection of articles; it becomes meaningful only in the context of the collective and anonymous body of work of which it is part.'[22] Durkheim was also annoyed to find that his nephew had relied on the same data on the *intichiuma* that he himself intended to use in his own book: 'Is it really necessary to spread the idea, and in the very terms that I normally use to express myself? Give some thought to the way you go about things; I know very well that is a matter of carelessness.'[23] Durkheim and Mauss were, then, using the same ethnographic data – one for his book, and the other for his thesis – and were both fascinated by the Arunta, the best-known tribe in Australia. The tribe was a 'rare example, an exceptionally rich and suggestive source of information', and 'of great scientific importance': 'We find amongst the Arunta both a survival of the most distant past and a foretaste of the future' (Durkheim 1985[1902]). Mauss had chosen these tribes for his 'fieldwork' for the same reasons: they displayed 'signs of primitiveness' but could not themselves be regarded as primitive (Mauss 1969[1909]: 358–9).

The book appeared in 1909, and marked what Robert Hertz (1909: 219) called 'a milestone in the science of religions'. Some, however, saw the association with Durkheim as a flaw: 'Unfortunately, the whole book is inspired by the spirit of materialism. The very name of Durkheim, behind which the authors take refuge, sounds an alarm that says "this is wrong"' (Relle 1910). Mauss and Durkheim were criticized for their 'overly socio-logical theory', and their 'over-ambitious approach' which, Alfred Loisy (1909: 406) complained, 'encroached upon the domain of the philosophy of knowledge by demonstrating that intellectual categories are social'.

For Mauss, its publication was all the more important because he could once more set his sights on a chair at the Collège de France following the death in 1909 of Jean Réville (who had replaced his father two years earlier). 'You really do have an unexpected opportunity to provide the perfect setting for your life, your work and your teaching', Paul Fauconnet wrote to him.[24] Mauss applied for the post. When he began his campaign in June, he was in a good position, and it seemed likely that he would be appointed'. But as more candidates emerged, the competition intensified. They included Georges Foucart, whose father Paul was already a profes-sor at the Collège and who had just published *La Méthode comparative dans l'histoire des religions*; and Maurice Vernes and Jules Toutain, who were both colleagues of Mauss at the École pratique des hautes études. The situation became more complicated in the autumn, when Alfred Loisy joined the race. Loisy, a priest and Dreyufsard who was identified with the 'modernist current' within the history of religion, had been excommuni-cated by the Vatican in 1908. His candidature took on a political-religious dimension that blurred the classic faultlines that divided the Collège's teaching staff. Mauss was assured of the support of his former teachers and friends Sylvain Lèvi, Charles Fossey and Antoine Meillet. He could also count on the votes of Georges Renard, the former editor of *La Revue socialiste*, and Maurice Croiset. Croiset was one of the *Année*'s reviewers and, as Durkheim had predicted, spoke well of Mauss's recent *Mélanges*. There was, on the other hand, a great deal of hostility to sociology, and especially Durkheimian sociology, particularly on the part of professor of social philosophy Jean Izoulet, who had stated that to teach Durkheimian sociology to future primary school teachers was a 'threat to the nation'. It was therefore not easy for Mauss to expand his electoral base and to become, as Salomon Reinach had hoped for him, 'the church's candidate standing against someone who had been excommunicated'.

The battle was hard fought. Alfred Loisy won in the fifth round of voting, thanks to the support of Bergson and others. There were a lot of people at Sylvain Lévi's home that evening, and many were upset. Even Alfred Espinas was outraged. Loisy's victory provoked strong reactions, especially in right-wing Catholic circles. In Fauconnet's view, the election of Loisy was a 'mistake': 'You were the only man for the chair. In scientific terms, appointing Loisy is a mistake. The Collège does not understand what the history of religions is.'[25] 'The future belongs to you; you will have your revenge', Abel Rey wrote to Mauss.[26]

Émile; or, 'The Sense of the Real'

Durkheim had already devoted lectures to Rousseau when he was teaching at Bordeaux. He said at the time that he was quite prepared to adopt Rousseau's view that the basic rule of education was freedom, provided that the 'yoke of necessity' was also taken into account. This was, he noted, a 'little-known' aspect of Rousseau's doctrine: he certainly spoke of freedom, but also said that freedom must be restricted or contained. The ideal – and the precondition for 'true happiness' – was, according to Rousseau (as revised and updated by Durkheim), 'adaptation to the environment', 'a balance between needs and means', and an equilibrium between power and will. It was clear to anyone who heard his lectures that the work of Rousseau was at once a major source of inspiration for Durkheim and a topic for discussion. In his study of Rousseau's *Social Contract*, he gave a detailed account of the author's social philosophy, of 'what we might call his sociology'. Which elements of it did he retain? First, a dualist conception of man, with nature on the one hand, and society on the other. And second, the idea that the 'real basis' of society is not 'aggregation' but *association*, and that association gives birth to a 'common will' (a soul that is 'one and indivisible'). Durkheim finds both a precursor and an ally in Rousseau, who describes society as 'a moral entity having specific qualities distinct from those of the individual beings which compose it' (Durkheim 1960[1918]: 82).

If Durkheim is particularly interested in Jean-Jacques Rousseau, it is because he asks the same question that he himself is trying to answer: 'How can society be organized in such a way as to make us better and happier?' (1960b [1918]: 91). What, in other words, is the best political organization? To his great credit, Rousseau understood that habits, trends and customs are 'the real constitution of the state' (ibid.: 109). The coercive power of a sovereign cannot in itself preserve the social order: minds must be so shaped that nothing resists it. Similarly, if the authority of the legislator is to be respected, there must already be a certain social spirit. Religion was once the cement that held society together, or 'the basis of the social order' (ibid.: 132). Rousseau therefore suggests the idea of a 'civil religion' consisting of nothing more than the few principles that are needed to give morality its authority, and Durkheim takes up that idea.

Durkheim twice taught a course on Rousseau's theory of education at the Sorbonne, probably in 1908–9 and 1909–10. His lectures allowed him to demonstrate once more 'how far Rousseau was aware of the social nature of man and of the reality of society', as Xavier Léon puts in his introductory note to 'Rousseau on educational theory' (Durkheim 1979[1919]: 163n).

The *Revue de métaphysique et de morale* published Durkheim's lecture notes in 1918. Their interest was, Xavier Léon wrote in his introductory note, 'self-evident', as they were 'well thought out and organized' and 'quite conclusive' (Durkheim 1979[1919]: 163): 'This is not a partially prepared work: it is complete.' At the beginning of his career, Durkheim 'painstakingly wrote out every sentence in full', but now that he was at the height of his powers, he abandoned that 'time-consuming task' and made do 'with indicating the theme of each sentence, certain thereby that in its every detail he was master of his thought'. He now spoke without notes, with only 'an extremely brief résumé' in front of him, consisting of headings. The style is stenographic: some sentences have no verbs, and some nouns no articles. He did, however, have all the texts he referred to hand, 'meticulously marked and annotated'. He took great pains 'to make sure his students knew the original text'.

There are four lectures on Rousseau's educational theory. The first is dedicated to the method and principles of Rousseau's pedagogy, the second to education and nature, the third to 'education by things', and the fourth to relations between master and pupil and the application of his theory to moral education.

Pedagogic method

Rousseau is not interested in 'chance conditions', and sets aside 'the accidental, the variable' in order to 'get at the essential, the rock upon which human reality rests' (1979[1919]: 166). 'Is man naturally good?' Does everything degenerate in the hands of man? Durkheim cites texts that appear to confirm this thesis and speak of 'denaturing'. The educational consequences are obvious: laisser-faire. This is the 'thesis frequently attributed to Rousseau. And yet few people had a more acute sense of the need for education: 'Education transforms nature, it denatures it' (ibid.: 167). If, however, 'the child is man in the *natural state*', as Rousseau believes, it is obvious that 'the child's nature must be respected' (ibid.: 168, 169). The 'novelty' of Rousseau's theory of education is, without doubt, its 'psychological character' and its preoccupation with the study of children. Convinced that pedagogy must be based upon 'the objective study of a given reality', Durkheim finds in Rousseau an ally because he refers to 'the given fact, placed beyond the realm of fantasy' (1979[1919]: 170). This, thought Durkheim, signalled an incipient science.

Education and nature

'What does nature teach us about education?' According to Rousseau, it teaches us to accept the rule of freedom. Durkheim accepts this: '*No swaddling clothes*. No reins.' But there is also such a thing as 'the yoke of necessity': man must feel that 'he is under the sway of a moral force comparable in strength to a physical force' (1979[1919]: 171). This introduces the idea of limitations; that force is 'necessary and inescapable, it limits and stops him'. This is a 'little known aspect of Rousseau's doctrine', and Durkheim wishes to emphasize its importance. Rousseau certainly defends 'true freedom: doing what one can' (ibid.: 174), but he argues that the 'notion of limitation' is also essential. Freedom is therefore limited or contained. Durkheim turns Rousseau's views into his own: there can be no freedom without constraints.

Education by things

Durkheim now raises the central issue of obedience: he believes that discipline is indispensable. We know that Rousseau rules out giving orders, and that he regarded all form of emulation as 'artificial'. The principles of education should be no order, no obedience, no commands and no punishment. According to Durkheim, Rousseau did not, however, completely reject the idea of discipline and set great store by 'self-control'. This is another little known aspect of his doctrine. There is such a thing as 'the power of things': 'Limitation. Desires which are restricted.' Things act from necessity, and 'it is from them alone that . . . early education must emanate' (1979[1919]: 178.). This is 'a great innovation' (ibid.: 182). The role of the teacher would appear, then, to be limited to doing nothing but without allowing the pupil to get away with anything. He must, in other words, remain in the background, and keep an eye on his pupil but take no direct action. The approach recommended by Rousseau involves neither commands nor prohibitions, but it does involve a degree of stage-management: 'Tutor must conceal his action so that pupil is not aware of it' (ibid.: 189). If the tutor wishes to make his authority felt, he should not give orders, but allow things to speak: 'Not the tutor who thinks; but things through him' (ibid.: 181).[27]

Moral education

Must the child remain in ignorance of the moral world? The idea that there should be no authority in either education or social life leaves Durkheim puzzled, as he believes that there can be a morality in the absence of authority. And yet he does find some value in Rousseau's conception of education, namely 'negative education'. 'This negative morality also has a positive value' (1979[1919]: 191). Durkheim gives an example: 'Never hurt anybody' (ibid.: 187). This gives rise to a conception of social life: 'men not doing wrong to each other, or encroaching; respecting limits'. Rousseau concludes that 'the noblest virtues are negative'. As Durkheim explains, the action of things is 'positive. It pre-forms. It imprints upon the mind certain specific attitudes that will crop up again and again.' 'Things are instructive because addressed to the imagination' (ibid.: 187, 188). Contact with nature can be useful, and science can contribute to moral education by inculcating a 'feeling of necessity, of the *resistance of things*. Superior to will.' This is a sort of pre-moral education, and Durkheim would take this idea up again in his lectures on moral education. Hence the importance of early education (from birth to the age of 12), as this is when we acquire a 'sense of the real'.

Is this 'impossible in practical terms'? There are two aspects to moral life: rights and duties. Rousseau suggests that rights must come first, and that education should begin not with the idea of freedom, but with that of property or the idea of property (1979[1918]: 190). This can be taught by the 'lesson of things', which teaches the child to respect the property of others. Hence the sequence: contract, first obligation, first social tie. 'This is our introduction to the moral world.'

Change the World

Durkheim went back to lecturing on morality in 1908–9.[28] As always, he prepared his lectures very carefully and summarized those that had gone before to ensure that his students understood what he was saying. He often cited authors such as Kant, and sometimes Spencer and Renouvier. He did not miss the opportunity to provide statistical data (homicide and mortality rates for France from 1855 to 1860, statistics on suicides) or to talk about totemism, with ethnographic documents at hand to support his argument. These must have caught the imagination of his students, as they discovered exotic societies with bizarre rituals and curious myths. 'These are not', Durkheim reminded them, 'mere superstitions.' In a sense, the professor used his classroom to 'put to the test' the themes he intended to develop in the book he was writing on the elementary forms of religious life, and often used the formulae that had become so dear to him, including 'hypostasized society' and 'divinization of society'.

The plan for his proposed study of morality was in three parts: the study of (sanctioned) moral rules, relating both to determinate groups (the family or domestic group, professional groups, political society) and to moral agents' relations with others (respect for people and things) and themselves (individual morality); the study of sanctions (including classifications of the main sanctions and the study of morality); the study of the genesis and workings of the individual's moral conscience. The themes he developed in his lectures were those he dealt with in the articles and books he was preparing: the moral ideal, professional morality and the fatherland.

The moral ideal

Durkheim once more stresses various distinctions, such as that between practical morality (duties) and theoretical morality (questions raised in scholastic terms), between the morality that exists 'within us' (the moral conscience) and the moral opinions of the group or shared morality, and between morality as object (rules) and the study of that object (the science of rules). He also goes back to his definition of moral rules: they are 'sanctioned rules for behaviour', and may be either positive or negative. He gives several examples: respect for life,[29] the sense of honour and various moral precepts. He then dwells at some length on a dimension of morality that was of growing interest to him: the moral ideal (which is shaped within supra-individual groups and preserved in things). The moral ideal is a 'force that shapes wills', and the ideal 'a set of real forces.' In order to get his point across, the professor analysed various situations or periods of unrest in which individuals had been swept away by collective waves of emotion (the French Revolution, the war of 1870, the Dreyfus Affair, the Socialist Party), and described the different mechanisms that created ideals: attachment to objects (emblems), places (shrines), days and dates (birthdays, national days), words or party slogans, and even men (Ablélard, Voltaire, Napoleon). A shortage of public festivities, he believed, was an indication that 'we haven't established a new ideal'. It is 'only in creative periods' that individuals actually experience these moral ideals.

Professional ethics

One of Durkheim's lectures was on a topic close to his heart: the occupational group as 'an agent of professional morality' (1975[1909c]). It was self-evident to him that 'when the professional group is strong, its morality will be strong.' This was true of personnel in all administrations (judges, priests, soldiers, teachers), and of lawyers. The same was not true of the economic domain: unions were not occupational groups, and there was no 'feeling of professional duty' in the economic professions. 'We find there a certain state of amorality.' Durkheim wishes to see a strengthening of the sense of professional duty, and hopes that 'corporations' will develop a sentimental life of their own by organizing meetings and festivals. The guild or corporation must be reborn, but in a new form. These 'new forms' refer to the national, rather than the 'parish', dimension, as exemplified by the teaching profession.

This raised the issue of relations between occupational groups and the state. The state could not ignore occupational groups, especially as there was a danger that it might be absorbed into them. But before going on to discuss the state (his remarks do not appear in the lecture notes), Durkheim talked to his students about civic morality and the fatherland.

The fatherland

Is the fatherland 'a necessary precondition for a moral life?' asked Durkheim in a debate about patriotism (1975[1909b]). He understood 'fatherland' to mean 'a social group that can impose certain obligations that are defined by its members'.[30] A fatherland is a 'relatively autonomous' society (with borders) and a 'collective personality'. 'The border therefore marks the limits of the collective personality' (ibid.: 221).

Durkheim refuses to liken the fatherland to a 'cultural community', as chauvinist patriotism so often does. It is based, rather, upon 'shared historical memories', but that does not imply national exclusivism – which Durkheim views as a hateful idea. He then looks at the question of the decline of fatherlands and the transition to 'bigger' fatherlands. These new entities are certainly bigger, but they are also more 'individuated'. Durkheim actually sees that as a precondition for peace: 'As our [national] personalities become accentuated, international relations become more peaceful.' He notes that various tendencies are encouraging nationalities to grow closer together and to commune as international associations and arbitration tribunals are established, and then speaks of a hypothetical 'European fatherland', but he finds the idea of 'one fatherland' 'inconceivable.' 'The self [*le moi*] posits its existence by opposing other selves. A personality that exists alone is unthinkable. Human affairs shift between unity and diversity' (ibid.: 224).

Research and reform

'The sense of the unknown. The confession of ignorance': such, according to Durkheim, must be the state of mind into which one must put oneself in order to tackle questions of ethics. 'The object is created by science.' It is impossible, he reminded his students, to construct the notion of ethics except 'by observation and inductively'. There is, therefore, 'material to observe' here. The same holds to a certain degree for the collective consciousness as for radioactivity, light or electricity. 'Giving a clear notion of collective consciousness lies at the end of science, not at its point of departure' (Durkheim 1975[1909e]).[31]

Finally, Durkheim defended in his lessons the utility of the studies he was undertaking: 'Studies are needed to know what ethics is.' It was enough to assert that one of the conditions of a moral fact has changed, to conclude that 'this fact must change'. Durkheim gives the example of inheritance, with which he was very familiar. He believed that the scholar can 'make use of science to modify the world', and he spoke freely of emancipation and the possibility of 'changing the world'. 'From the day that men began to reflect on moral reality, they began to free themselves.' However, in the absence of a science of morality, Durkheim was aware of the risks even when he called for reforms: 'There can never be absolute assurance in prediction. Each time we act, moreover, we are at risk' (Durkheim 1975[1909e]: 312).

A Science of Morality. Sociability or Rationality?

Durkheim took part in five debates organized by the Société française de philosophie in 1908 and 1909. Three of them were about morality, and the other two about 'science and religion' and 'the notion of equality'. The first, which took place in March 1908, was on 'positive morality', and also involved Gustave Belot, who had just published three articles entitled 'The search for positive morality' in the *Revue de métaphysique et de morale*. Belot had for some years been carefully following the work of his old classmate at the École normale supérieure, but still profoundly disagreed with the editor of the *Année* and his collaborators.

Belot began by distancing himself from sociology, which reduced the social world to 'the free play of needs and interests, to the automatism of tradition and routine' (in Durkheim 1979[1908]: 52). He preferred to assign to morality 'the task of rationalizing and spiritualizing society, of turning it into a veritable co-operative venture of free minds' (ibid.: 53.) Durkheim responded by questioning Belot's notion of rationality and his suggestion that 'the more reflective and reasonable conduct is, the more moral it will be'. It was far from certain that reflection was 'a necessary factor in morality': 'Never at any moment in history has the individual been capable of rethinking the morality of his time as a whole . . . the overwhelming majority of people are content to accept passively the reigning morality as it is' (ibid.: 55). Belot, who admitted that he had 'never wished to adopt the purely sociological point of view' (ibid.: 57), could not accept that. He wished to go beyond 'purely external descriptive observation to discover the social finality which generates all moralities', and believed that he had found in that finality 'the dynamic and rational principle of their creation and continual development'.

In an attempt to clarify the terms of the debate, Durkheim then asked a question about methodology: 'How can the principle of a new moral orientation be created from even the complete systematization of moral data?' (ibid.: 58). When he failed to get a direct answer, he went straight to the heart of the debate. What was the essential factor in morality: sociability or rationality? Belot refused to answer the question directly; he attempted to describe the two as complementing one another, and then observed that 'in social reality a moment almost always comes when individual *consciences* rebel against the collective imperatives, conceive new imperatives and create new *working hypotheses*.' Sociological observation itself 'shows this individualism in action and in continual rebirth' (ibid.: 60). There were also 'isolated movements of *conscience*' and 'spontaneous rational effort'. The difference between the two men now became more obvious, as Belot criticized the idea of the 'pure passivity of the agent, [and the] absence of all initiative and reflection which organizes', and Durkheim accepted that reflection might be an element in morality but insisted that it was not 'the necessary condition of it' (ibid.: 61). They also took different views of the role of observation. Durkheim asked his colleague about the nature of the work on which he based his hypotheses and suggested that they were founded solely upon 'a few facts'. Cut to the quick, Belot counter-attacked: 'Did you not believe yourself that you could define the religious fact in 28 pages?' Durkheim replied immediately: 'An argument *ad hominem* does not constitute a scientific argument, even if it is well founded.' He went on to point out that he had simply been trying to provide 'an initial provisional definition . . . which does not serve as a conclusion to research but on the contrary merely precedes and prepares the way for it' (ibid.: 63). And to close the debate, he turned upon an interlocutor who had become an adversary: 'I cannot help but find that something else is needed to provide the beginnings of a proof . . . besides the three or four fine studies contained in your book.'

Durkheim reviewed Belot's articles on 'positive morality' in volume X of the *Année sociologique* (1980[1907a]). In reply to his detractor, who saw his science of morality as nothing more than 'purely erudite research, incapable of affecting the practice of moral art', he argued that 'as the science is more advanced and more apt . . . it is able to explain social action' (ibid.: 144, 145), and concluded that 'to ratiocinate about ethics, it is first of all necessary to know what it is; and . . . to know what it is, it is necessary to observe it' (ibid.: 149).[32]

The second debate, again organized by the Société française de philosophie, took place in May 1909 and was about 'the effectiveness of moral doctrines' (Durkheim 1979[1909]). The discussion involved Delvolvé and Édouard Le Roy, as well as Dominique Parodi and Célestin Bouglé, both of whom were involved with the *Année*. Why are there such things as duties, and what is the rationale for discipline? These were, as Durkheim knew, far from being secondary issues. Children did not understand enough about them. Durkheim explained that the 'chief aim' of his course on educational theory was 'to show students how they can give their teaching this essential unity' (1979[1909]: 129).

'Moral education' was not, he insisted, to be confused with 'the teaching of morality': the inculcation of 'habits to be formed' was part and parcel of education, but the teaching of morality had quite a different aim: 'bringing about comprehension'. The teacher 'does not address himself directly to the will, but to the understanding' (1979[1909]: 130). From primary school onwards, the French educational system represented the first attempt not 'to teach morality in a secular way, but quite simply to teach it'. Previously, it was not taught at all: 'It was inculcated by the catechism . . . Children were drilled in it.' The decision to introduce this reform was not the result of 'some wild fantasy': 'circumstances forced us to do so.' 'Regret it as we may, we cannot prevent the spirit of free inquiry from raising questions of morality too'. A schoolchild must learn something about morality, and 'we must therefore arm his intelligence with solid reasons'; otherwise, the child will 'believe that it is governments and the ruling classes who have invented morality in order to bring the people to heel more effectively' (ibid.).

Why not appeal to religion or to God? Durkheim rejected that suggestion. When Bouglé intervened to argue that, despite their differences, both Delvolvé and Durkheim saw the need to appeal to some kind of reality that underlay morality ('for the former . . . nature or the divine; for the latter, society'), Durkheim immediately denied that was any similarity: 'There is as a wide a gulf between the views of Delvolvé and my own as there is between agnosticism and rationalism' (1979[1909: 138).

Bouglé also worried that people were now 'critical and were not inclined to be conformist'. He asked how society could 'be shown to be sacred' (1979[1909]: 137). Durkheim replied that appealing to some 'skilful artifice' was out of the question, as was appealing to 'some sort of *obscurantism*' in order to make people feel that society had a moral power 'superior to the individual'. Even anarchists could be convinced of this: there were 'curable anarchists' : 'It is even an eminently soluble question of moral education to find out what makes up the spirit of anarchy, anti-social attitudes and impatience with rules' (ibid.: 138).

At the end of December 1909, Durkheim spoke once more to an audience from the Société française de philosophie about the 'notion of social equality' (Durkheim 1979[1910]). Parodi had contended that it was a self-evident truth that 'morality has continued to become more and more rational with the passing of time' (1979[1910]: 65), but his assertion seemed to Durkheim to be 'highly contestable': 'Every moral system has its own rationality . . . All of them are natural and consequently rational, like the rest of nature (1979[1910]: 66). Parodi's remarks signalled 'a serious misunderstanding of moral reality, which consists not in a system of concepts . . . but in a system of forces . . . mental, moral forces, forces which derive all their power from action, *representations* and from states of *consciousness*'. Such forces had 'the property of either inhibiting or provoking movement (1979[1910]: 65, 66). Durkheim did, however, accept that there were differences between the morality of today and that of times gone by: 'Our morality is more impersonal, more abstract, freer from the contingencies of time and space. We conceive of it as valid for all mankind' (1979[1910: 66).[33]

Was anyone listening? One thing was certain: his position in the debate about morality and religion was now central. Everyone was waiting for his great book, *The Elementary Forms of Religious Life*.

22

Regent of the Sorbonne

'A Time for Specific Knowledge and Accurate Methods'

The University of Paris underwent a complete transformation at the beginning of the twentieth century. A rebuilding programme, the establishment of new chairs and new endowments were all signs that the Sorbonne was facing fresh challenges, including developments in the sciences, relations between business and the university, and the growing importance of philanthropy. The faculty of science had the second largest budget (the faculty of medicine had the largest), and there were many new developments in that area. A radium laboratory had been built for Marie Curie, and a former seminary in the rue Notre-Dame-des-Champs had been acquired to house the new departments of applied mechanics and aviation. Although it was experiencing 'serious disturbances' (there were demonstrations by law students in December 1909),[1] the university aspired to play an international role. It welcomed Andrew Carnegie in 1909 and, in April 1910, former US President Theodore Roosevelt was invited to give a public lecture (in English), entitled 'The education of citizens and the republic'. The lecture was given in the Richelieu theatre; it aroused an 'extraordinary amount of interest' and made a 'considerable impact'. It was said to be 'a great lesson in social philosophy from a professor of great authority'.[2] In his eulogy of Andrew Carnegie, Rector Liard recalled great names from the Sorbonne's past: Ampère, Laennec, Berthelot, Pasteur and the Curies. He concluded that 'The discoveries of science were the seeds of modern industry and all its progeny.'[3] He said the same thing a few years later when he paid tribute to Ernest Solvay: 'The seeds of the power [of Solvay's company] were a scientific discovery . . . Solvay is a very fine example of a man for modern times.'[4] Solvay & Co. donated 500,000 francs to establish a chair in applied chemistry. The rector's leitmotivs were love of science, love of the fatherland and love of humanity.

There were new developments in the human sciences too: a major endowment from the Marquise Arconati-Visconti (née Peyrat) financed the building of the geography institute. A donation from M. Pathé made it possible to build the Musée de la Parole (the future Archives de la parole) and to equip it fully (recording equipment, collections), while a gift from the Société des établissements Gaumont provided the equipment for making and projecting films.

The faculty of letters was a 'complex organization' with a variety of functions. It oversaw and evaluated secondary schools, trained teachers for the secondary and higher sectors of education (awarding degrees, postgraduate diplomas and doctorates, and training candidates for the *agrégation*), and organized centres of scholarship. It also had the equivalent of an 'outreach' function, publicizing research findings and maintaining relations with foreign scholars and universities in order to 'raise the general level of human civilization and spread the fame and influence of France'. All this teaching, research and dissemination was inspired by the 'scientific spirit', meaning respect for the truth, sustained research and a refusal to be influenced by prejudice. In the universities, it was 'time for specific knowledge and accurate methods'.[5]

The dean of the faculty of letters, Alfred Croiset, was a great believer in scientific method and rationalism, and openly attacked the detestable 'intellectual fashion' for appealing to the 'irrational forces of the soul' and intuition. Such a fashion could, he feared, lead to 'absurdity and madness'.[6] The 'battle of the Sorbonne', which had already broken out, was exacerbated in 1910 when the government ruled that some school certificates were equivalent to the *baccalauréat*, thereby allowing their holders the right to enrol in the faculty of science.

The faculty of letters had a teaching staff of almost 80, including 36 tenured professors. Things had changed in recent years: the teaching staff had had to take on new 'tasks' that took up a lot of time and threatened to 'seriously slow down their research activity or bring it to a halt'. They complained about this, and demanded 'more free time to pursue productive research', arguing that their students would be 'the first to benefit from it'. For the moment, neither the faculty's buildings nor its equipment was adequate for its new needs: 'The faculty is suffocating for lack of space.'[7]

In 1912–13, the faculty of letters had more than 3,200 students of whom more than 1,200 (532 men and 693 women) were from abroad, although most were not studying for any specific qualifications. 'A modern Tower of Babel', grumbled 'Agathon' in *L'Esprit de la Nouvelle Sorbonne*, as he denounced the policy of the university: the 'cosmopolitan crowd' of 'bizarre auditors' who spoke all sorts of languages was so large that special measures were required to reserve the front seats in the lecture theatres for regular students. 'It might be more useful to think about the French students who want to improve themselves and to learn'.[8]

The appointment of more lecturers and senior lecturers resulted in an influx of new blood. André Lalande (1867–1963) had been taught by Durkheim at the lycée in Sens, had studied at the École normale supérieure and the École pratique des hautes études (fourth section) and was now both an *agrégé de philosophie* and a *docteur ès lettres*. After teaching in secondary schools for only a few years, he became a *chargé de cours* at the Sorbonne in 1904, and was promoted to the rank of professor in 1909. The same year saw the deaths of Victor Egger (who had been a professor of philosophy and psychology since 1894) and Frédéric Rauh (who, at the age of 48, had been appointed professor of philosophy only four months earlier),[9] and the arrival of Henri Delacroix and Léon Brunschvicg.[10]

Célestin Bouglé, in the meantime, found himself in a complex situation in administrative terms. What Fauconnet called the 'Bouglé affair' began in 1912, when Alfred Espinas, who had been on leave for the previous five years, began to think of retiring. His chair had been endowed by the Comte de Chambrun, and the university had to find a new source of funding.[11] The university council eventually found a solution after interventions from Rector Liard, Dean Croiset and Durkheim himself. It was pointed out that Bouglé, a *chargé de cours* teaching social economics, was 'a very distinguished teacher' but had to face 'very onerous family outgoings'. Durkheim argued that his colleague and collaborator should receive an allowance in addition to his salary of 8,000 francs. The council resolved to renew Bouglé's appointment until January 1916.[12] Durkheim's collaborators, and especially Paul Fauconnet, were delighted with the decision. Bouglé had been appointed to a post in Paris but retained his tenure in Toulouse for a further four years: the chair would be 'kept waiting for him'.[13]

Now that Durkheim, Bouglé and Lévy-Bruhl (who was teaching a course on Schopenhauer) were in post, sociology's position within the university was being consolidated, especially given that the *Année sociologique* also had supporters in the faculty of letters. The 30 or so philosophy professors in French universities had a wide range of interests (the history of philosophy, ethics, education, psychology, and the sciences), and by the 1910s at least eight of them had also developed an interest in sociology. The subjects proposed for the oral part of the *agrégation de philosophie* for 1912 were a further indication of the philosophical interest in sociology, as they included 'history and sociology', and 'can the nation be seen as a moral reality?' Auguste Comte's *Discours sur l'esprit positif* was on the syllabus for the University of Paris's *diplôme d'études supérieures*. Had it not been for the 'treachery' of Gaston Richard,[14] the Durkheim group's grip on sociology in the faculties of letters would have been very strong.[15]

Generational Conflict: *Les Jeunes Gens d'aujourd'hui*

Durkheim, it would seem, was coming under attack from a younger generation. He himself quite accepted that 'every generation has its own spirit, its own way of thinking and feeling, its own needs and its special aspirations'. This was 'a fact . . . whose causes are as yet not well known, but an indisputable fact, nonetheless'. Linguistic changes, changes in fashion, and changes in aesthetic appreciation and in philosophical views are typical examples: 'A cosmopolitan generation is succeeded by a very nationalistic generation, or vice versa. Optimism follows pessimism. Anarchism follows religious dogmatism, and so on' (Durkheim 1961[1925]: 248–9).

Henri Massis (aged 27) and Alfred de Tarde (the 33–year-old son of

Gabriel), who wrote under the pseudonym 'Agathon', published a series of articles in the daily *L'Opinion* in 1910, and republished them in book form as *Les Jeunes Gens d'aujourd'hui* in 1913. The articles were based on the findings of their 'informal' survey of the opinions of young men aged between 18 and 25. Their subjects were from the *grandes écoles*, the lycées and the universities and were chosen because they were 'the most representative of their group'. A younger generation was coming into conflict with an older or 'sacrificed' generation that had been marked by the defeat of 1870 and by the Dreyfus affair. They were optimistic, had a 'taste for action' and preferred 'the good life' to 'good ideas'. They wanted to be up to date, were enthusiastic about sport, which was becoming more widely practised, and were eager to travel. The days of 'the legendary Bohemianism of the Latin Quarter' were over. Tarde and Massis described this new generation as unsentimental, albeit without revolutionary ambitions, and as 'a new elite, the yeast that would leaven the shapeless masses'.

Agathon's book could be seen as an attempt to harness the confused feelings of intellectual youth to the cause of a right-wing nationalism, and to recapture the cultural ferment of the *fin du siècle* and its waves of political agitation. Henri Bergson admired the serious-mindedness of these young people, their boldness and the sense of responsibility with which they approached life: 'I believe that we are witnessing a major and profound change in the minds of modern youth.' He believed that he was seeing a 'sort of moral rebirth in France', and concluded: 'The way modern youth is developing looks to me like a kind of miracle' (cited in Agathon 1995[1913]: 270–2). It is true that Bergson, the defender of intuitive knowledge, was the very embodiment of the world that was coming into being. A philosopher whose 'ideas profoundly influenced the way the present generation thinks' was becoming, despite himself, the hero of the artistic avant-garde, which included Debussy in music, Marinetti and the Italian futurists, and the cubists. More than 500 members of the general public, led by *'les snobinettes'*, would crowd into the lecture theatre to hear 'the famous professor'. When Bergson left for a lecture tour of the United States, people asked themselves what could replace his 'five-o'clocks'. 'Will our beautiful socialites go to the Sorbonne to see the sociologist Durkheim . . . or Monsieur Dumas?'[16]

An establishment which had, like the Sorbonne, rejected the man they described as 'the most important contemporary philosopher', could not be a real teaching institution. Massis and Tarde worried that many young people were not interested in going to the Sorbonne. Far from being a crisis in education, this was a 'moral crisis.' What was on offer at the Sorbonne? 'An empty science that takes only the needs of the intelligence into account, a pedantic materialism and a sceptical form of investigation which both damages and demeans us.' Young people were changing: the positivist ideal was in decline, and Catholicism was once more in the ascendancy thanks to authors such as Paul Claudel, Charles Péguy and Francis Jammes, and thanks too to the influence of Jacques Maritain, a teacher at the Institut catholique who had recently converted to Catholicism.

The two writers also published, still under the same pseudonym, a tract entitled *L'Esprit de la nouvelle Sorbonne*. It was subtitled 'The crisis in classical culture' and 'The crisis in French'. They attacked the various reforms that had been introduced over the previous 10 years, beginning with the Sorbonne's 'annexation' of the École normale supérieure in 1904. Talk of a 'new spirit' was a reference to the emphasis on science, as opposed to the intellect and classical culture. The differences between the two were as great as those between precision and elegance, mediocrity and elitism, utilitarian preoccupations and dilettantism, and philology and the French spirit. They attacked the new Sorbonne for its adulation of Germanic science, especially in history and philology.

Agathon's criticisms were directly mainly at 'new trends' in the teaching of the arts and philosophy. Their criticisms were harsh: 'At the Sorbonne, the writing is bad enough but the reading is even worse.' This was a crisis: French was in a poor state. The *agrégation* juries were unanimous: students had an increasingly poor sense of form; their dissertations were careless or badly planned, and marred by their poor spelling and infelicities of expression. The problem appeared to be all the more serious in that these formal defects went hand in hand with intellectual weaknesses. The Sorbonne and its professors were to blame: they had abandoned the cultural techniques appropriate to the 'French genius' and, in the teaching of literature, had introduced new methods borrowed from the natural sciences. 'Method! That is our teachers' favourite word.' 'Handbooks on pure methodology' were the first things they gave their students to read: Seignobos and Langlois's *Introduction aux études historiques* for history students and Durkheim's *Rules of Sociological Method* for sociology students. The latter was described as 'a little book on metaphysics which determines in advance all the preconditions for any future sociology' (Agathon 1995[1913]: 34). General culture and reflection had been abandoned in favour of specialized knowledge and the accumulation of data. The system was based upon index cards and bibliographies. 'They are obsessed with index cards!' complained Agathon: 'Your marks at the Sorbonne depend on how many index cards you have.' Students compiled information. 'Patience has replaced brilliance.' The little rooms where students gathered to read and discuss the authors on the syllabus used to be called *studies*, but they were now called *laboratories*. That was a sign of the times.

The absence of any strong moral culture was even more worrying. The target here was history as well as sociology, which, by demonstrating that pubic opinion was fickle, encouraged students to be sceptical. Agathon borrowed an epigraph from Durkheim: 'Crime is a factor in social health.' This 'gloomy' sociological determinism was all the more pernicious in that it paralysed activity and killed off individual initiatives (the only sources of progress). The authors' main criticism of the 'new' way of teaching philosophy was that it 'systematically neglected general culture'. 'In 1910, not one lecture was given on philosophy. There were only specialisms.' The specialisms in question were the 'kind of social catechism' taught by Durkheim ('a narrow-minded sociologist, a scornful enemy of all philosophy'), 'Lévy-Bruhl's studies of savages, George Davy's studies of the insane', André Lalande's dissertations on scientific methodology, and Delbos's lectures on psychology, not forgetting the lecture on the history of economic doctrines from Célestin Bouglé ('Durkheim's lieutenant'). In short, 'there is now not a single philosopher at the Sorbonne'. Philosophy was no longer at home at the Sorbonne, and had crossed the rue Saint-Jacques to the Collège de France (where Bergson was teaching).

Émile Durkheim became a target for anyone who wished to attack the new Sorbonne. Massis and Tarde believed that they had 'reasons to fear him'. Louis Liard had made him the academic equivalent of a *préfet de police*, by appointing him first to the council of the University of Paris and then to the consultative committee. This allowed him to 'control all appointments in higher education'. Massis and Tarde described him as 'the regent of the Sorbonne, the all-powerful master' who was both 'dogmatic and authoritarian'. As for the teachers in the philosophy section, they had been reduced to the status of 'mere functionaries' who 'followed his orders and were under his iron rule'.

According to Agathon, Durkheim's 'intellectual despotism' was exercised through the intermediary of his 'own domain' of educational theory and sociology. 'Pedagogy was the "great creation" (or should we say "great idea") of the new Sorbonne.' Durkheim's lectures on pedagogy were the only ones that *agrégation* students had to attend, and this, Agathon implied, allowed him to use his position for political ends. As for sociology, it was the 'keystone of the new Sorbonne': it had acquired 'a kind of supremacy', and its ambition was to rule over 'the various human sciences, and the particular techniques of human activity known as ethics, pedagogy and politics'.

One of the reasons why Durkheim came in for such criticism was, perhaps, that one of the authors of *L'Esprit de la nouvelle Sorbonne* was the son of Gabriel Tarde, who used the same arguments that his father had used when he attacked the *Rules of Sociological Method* for its 'pseudo-scientific mysticism' and 'gloomy determinism'. Durkheim's sociology was, he claimed, characterized by its horror of anything individual, and its reasoned contempt for all psychology: the individual consciousness was not the source of anything, and social facts were nothing but a form of coercion. It was a sociology that denied the existence of individual creativity and inventiveness, and that described knowledge as 'the product of the *polis* [*la cité*]'. The attack was also directed against Durkheim's colleague Lanson, who was allegedly imbued with the same collective fanaticism and the same distrust of individuals. Such were the foundations of the Sorbonne's sociology, which described any masterpiece as a 'collective product'.[17]

The 'great social being' was a 'fundamental given' for the Sorbonne's young philosophers. Such a perspective could only strengthen the dominant tendencies in the faculty of letters: authoritarian fanaticism, contempt for individuality, the cult of specialization, and a horror of any real philosophical culture (Agathon 1911: 105).[18] 'How', ask Massis and Tarde, 'can a man who worships only this vague being, which is as monstrous and tyrannical as the God of the Jews, be a real educator?' (ibid.: 112). The way the question is formulated, and the reference to 'the God of the Jews', may reveal a form of anti-Semitism. Massis and Tarde see the sociological method as a 'vehicle for despotism'. The philosophy of the Sorbonne has a taste for domination, they conclude, and its ideal is moral subservience and dogmatism. This frontal attack was very similar in tone to that of Charles Péguy on sociology and its 'all-powerful master'. The author of *Notre Jeunesse* complained: 'There is a Sorbonne that is too fond of the sound of its own voice to be an honest Sorbonne. The Sorbonne has once more lapsed into scholasticism, this time in the name of sociology.' Péguy had once been close to Mauss, but now described him as 'a filing cabinet'.[19]

Reactions were not slow in coming. Émile Faguet, professor of French poetry at the Sorbonne, literary critic and contributor to various journals, had come under personal attack, but laughed at what he called a 'miraculous generation' of young men who were pure, ardent, brave, in love with life and devoted to the fatherland, and joked that it 'should delight us and make our coming departure less melancholic' (cited in Becker 1995).[20] Gabriel Séailles, professor of the history of philosophy, also spoke ironically of 'these young men in a hurry [who] celebrate their own heroism before they have had the opportunity to prove their worth' (ibid.). Marcel Mauss was very annoyed, and reacted immediately, attacking the 'tendentious, specious and mendacious' survey that had been carried out by 'these new Agathons'.[21] Even those sociologists who were not especially close to Durkheim were outraged by Agathon's 'excessive criticisms'. Arthur Bauer, who contributed to the *Revue internationale de sociologie*, defended the use of index cards and the resort to history as a way of understanding literary texts; he also rushed to defend 'Sorbonne sociology', which did not deserve 'all the anathemas directed against it'.[22]

Regent of the Sorbonne?

On 28 February 1910, Émile Durkheim attended the council meeting at the University of Paris. He had recently been elected to represent the faculty of letters, and his colleague Gustave Lanson had just been re-elected.[23] Rector Louis Liard welcomed the new members in a speech praising their 'competence, concern for the general interest, and authority'. The university council was chaired by the rector (or, rather, the deputy rector[24]) and had two categories of members. Faculty deans, the director of the École supérieure de pharmacie and the director and deputy director of the École normale supérieure were all *ex officio* members; in addition, each school or faculty elected two members. As the deans and directors were elected and then officially appointed by the minister, the council in fact consisted of elected members, with the exception of the deputy rector who was, as Durkheim (1975[1918b]: 23) put it, 'torn between two functions' that were, in theory, contradictory: as a government appointee he was the state's representative within the university and therefore responsible for the application of its laws and general rules, but he was also the university's representative and defender of its interests.

The university council was 'the central body that recorded and controlled every aspect of academic life'.'[25] Durkheim said of the university that it was 'much more than the mere juxtaposition of the faculties and schools that made it up. It is a quite natural whole.' The purpose of council was, he added, 'to serve the university as a whole'. The council had many different responsibilities. It administered the university's shared resources, drew up the budget and controlled expenditure, and was responsible for the general organization of courses. 'The [council] represents the general interests of the university as a whole, as opposed to the potential individual interests of the faculties and schools. It is also its responsibility to guarantee respect for order and general discipline throughout the university' (Durkheim 1975[1918b]: 23). The main feature of the 'new' University was its independence. Given that the science it cultivated and taught 'could not exist unless it was free', the institution had to enjoy a 'broad autonomy at the levels of its faculties, schools and council'.

The council met once a month from 10 a.m. to noon in the magnificent room reserved for its meetings. Its agenda could be very varied. There was the budget and 'current affairs' of all kinds ranging from heating and lighting to the acquisition and building of new premises. The council dealt with everything: tenders for the supply of coal, financial support for the widow of Charlois, the astronomer at the Nice observatory who had recently been murdered, the organization of delegations to various academic events in other countries. The discussions were often technical, and the decisions purely administrative, but they could be heated.

The council also dealt with a wide range of academic and administrative issues: the appointment of deans and professors, the establishment of chairs, the authorization of *cours libres* [open lectures],[26] dispensations from enrolment fees, and the many prizes (Fondation Arconati-Visconti, A. Colin, Fonds Marillier) and grants (the 'Curie grants', Rothschild, Commercy and Albert Khan prizes) that were awarded for travel and staff exchanges with foreign universities. An Institut français was being established in Saint Petersburg. The many disciplinary issues that arose (theft, cheating in examinations) meant that the council often had to sit as a court, listen to witnesses, pass judgement and impose sentences (exclusion, withdrawal of the right to sit examinations[27]). Durkheim regularly attended meetings, but remained fairly quiet to begin with; he later refused to take on onerous responsibilities such as serving as secretary to the council – a position normally held by a professor from the faculty of letters. He did, on the other hand, take an interest in links with foreign universities, student exchanges and promoting France's cultural influence abroad. This was one of the rector's priorities. In the second year of his mandate, Durkheim agreed to sit, first as *rapporteur* and then as chair, on the committee that awarded travel grants and grants for study in foreign universities. It was his responsibility to describe and justify the committee's choice of candidates to council: 'I am convinced that these young men will benefit from having grants.'[28]

During the second year of his mandate, Durkheim took on new responsibilities in the autumn. He agreed to chair the committee that had been set up to discuss Charles Henry's proposal to establish a laboratory for general psychobiology at the École des hautes études. The committee made its recommendation a few months later: 'It would be advisable to postpone the establishment of the proposed laboratory until such time as general psychobiology has done more to prove its worth.'[29] The council agreed unanimously.

The council served as a kind of forum for the discussion of the university's main strategies, and gave members the opportunity to hear the opinions of colleagues or to defend their own interests when, for example, the issue of tenure arose. Was it, for instance, wise to follow the usual – and simple – procedure of asking the opinion of a scholar nominated by the professor who was seeking tenure? The debate took place in public, and one *député* called for an inquiry while the budget was being discussed in July 1911. There had been a proposal to set up a an advisory committee on skills, much to the annoyance of the professors, who wanted to defend the principle of the independence of their faculties and who refused to allow appointments to be made on the arbitrary decision of the minister. 'This is an important issue', remarked Professor Larnaude, and 'opinions varied', as Rector Liard put it.

The discussion took up two meetings. Some council members, including Gustave Lanson, were in favour of maintaining the status quo and of consulting specialists on an informal basis. Others feared that, as 'members of the consultative committee are not qualified to judge all candidates', consultation should apply only 'in case of doubt'. 'When there is any doubt, the minister should consult those members of the university who are best qualified to judge the respective qualifications of the candidates.' 'That is the wisest course', agreed Rector Liard, who also believed that account should also be taken of 'the mood amongst *députés*' when the budget was adopted', and that 'minimal concessions' should be made to the malcontents. Durkheim objected that 'the proposed solution will not get rid of the malcontents' because, given that the opinions of those consulted had not been made pubic, they could always argue that the decision had been taken without their consent. 'We must accept that', replied Liard. The proposal was adopted unanimously, with three abstentions.

Was Durkheim truly the 'regent of the Sorbonne'? He had agreed to sit on the university council for the sake of his friendship with Louis Liard and because he had a sense or responsibility, but he was not really suited to the role. Power within the university was a very relative concept, as was obvious from the way that members of staff were appointed and promoted. The decision-making process was bottom-up, and in most cases the council did no more than ratify the decisions of the faculties and schools, which therefore had – along with their teaching staff – a great deal of power. A seat on council was often a stepping stone towards an administrative position. Like Ernest Lavisse before him, Gustave Lanson was appointed associate dean of the faculty of letters (1910–13) and then director of the École normale supérieure (1919–23). Was there any reason why Durkheim should not, in turn, become director of the school?

Moving House. Commitments on All Sides

A member of the university council; teaching responsibilities; revisions to the final draft of *The Elementary Forms* (publication of which was predicted for 1912); editor of volumes XI and XII of the *Année* (which appeared in 1910 and 1913 respectively): Durkheim was a busy man. And the sixth edition of *The Rules of Sociological Method* came out in 1912.

Durkheim's lectures at the Sorbonne in 1911–12 were, as they had been for the past three years, on moral education and secondary education. As before, the lectures on moral education were given late on Thursday afternoon in the Guizot theatre and those on secondary education late on Saturday afternoon at the École normale supérieure. There was only one change: he had reverted to his old theme of the theory of punishment in the lectures he gave in the Guizot theatre late on Tuesday afternoons. He also dealt with the question of responsibility, to which Paul Fauconnet intended to devote his doctoral thesis.

Were fewer people attending his lectures? As Massis and Tarde had hinted in *Les Jeunes Gens d'aujourd'hui*, the Sorbonne's philosophy students were 'losing interest in the sociological methods of the Durkheims and the Lévy-Bruhls and choosing Catholics like Victor Delbos as their intellectual masters'. The number of Catholic students at the École normale supérieure had risen from 3 or 4 in 1905 to about 40 (one-third of the total) in 1912 (Prochasson and Rasmussen 1996: 41).[30]

Durkheim was being asked to sit on doctoral juries: In December 1910 for Joseph Segond's thesis, 'Prayer: a study in religious psychology', and in 1912 for E. Terraillon's 'Honour: Sentiment and Moral Principle'. Like Mauss, Durkheim could be strict about methodological questions, especially if the thesis was about a problem he knew well, such as magic. He criticized Segond's definition of religion on the grounds that it was 'traditional' and 'very debatable' in the sense that it was 'too personal' (Durkheim 1975[1910]). He made similar comments on Taraillon's thesis: 'The subject is a fine one . . . But . . . it would have been best to have given at the outset a definition of honour. In the absence of this, honour is often confused with the causes on which it may depend' (1975[1912]).

'What a year for hard work!' exclaimed Paul Fauconet, who was hoping to finish his doctoral thesis on responsibility.[31] Publishing the journal meant a lot of work for all its contributors. As usual, Mauss complained about this: 'I've been working on the *Année* for most of the year. It's pure poison, worse than the 'flu.'[32] His mother Rosine was worried, sad and upset. She wanted only two things: to see him finish his thesis and 'lead a more regular life and start a family'.[33] Even when he was on holiday at the Hôtel Mont-Blanc and looking at 'the very beautiful view', Durkheim was thinking of getting back to work and, as usual, wrote to his nephew in an attempt to encourage him to do the same.

Both uncle and nephew moved out of the rue Saint-Jacques in 1911. Durkheim moved to 4 avenue d'Orléans in the 14th *arrondissement*, and Mauss to 17 rue Malebranche (then to 39 rue de Saxe in 1912). Louise and Émile did not buy their new apartment, even though they were in a financial position to do so, as she had inherited a large sum of money when her father Moyse Dreyfus died in the spring of 1911.[34] The avenue d'Orléans, which was 1,200 metres long, was the main street in the *arrondissement*. Planted with trees, it was an extension of the main road (route nationale 20) linking Paris and Toulouse. Their apartment was very close to the place Denfert-Rochereau and its *'lion de Belfort'*, which symbolized the defence of the nation. It was also close to the Paris-Denfert railway station at the intersection of the boulevard d'Italie, the boulevard Raspail and the boulevard Arago. The station was the line's terminus until 1895, when the underground railway was extended to the Luxembourg. Known as 'le Petit Montrouge', this was one of Paris's oldest suburbs. Durkheim's colleague Ferdinand Brunot, who once lived at 3 avenue d'Orléans, was elected mayor of the 14th *arrondissement* in 1914.

Everyone now had more and more professional, social and family commitments, and there were appointments, promotions, political activities and marriages. Célestin Bouglé had four children and Paul Fauconnet went on to have three. Henri Hubert became engaged, and was married in August 1914.[35]

Bouglé was now in post at the Sorbonne, where he taught his main course on the social economics of positivism. His other courses were on Jean-Jacques Rousseau's *Social Contract* and research on political economy and the science of morality. He had also developed an interest in Proudhon, and in 1910 had published an article, 'Proudhon as sociologist', in the *Revue de métaphysique et morale*; he would later use this as the basis for his book *Sociologie de Proudhon*, which was published by Alcan two years later (see Logue 2003). In the same year, he published an article on Rousseau and socialism; he also gave a series of six lectures entitled 'Stages in the development of the French labour movement in the nineteenth century' at the University of London, and a lecture on religion and morality in Mulhouse. In addition, Bouglé was very active in the Ligue des droits de l'homme, becoming one of its vice-presidents in 1911. His friend Élie Halévy called him 'the musketeer of politics, philosophy and sociology'; he was, as Maurice Halbwachs (1941) put it, 'inspired by a deep-seated impetus'.

Was Proudhon a sociologist? Bouglé thought so, and detected similarities between his message and that of Durkheim: both were trying to 'force collective reason to sanctify personal rights' (Bouglé 1912: 329). He found in Proudhon 'a sort of solidarism *avant la lettre*' because he believed in the human importance of associations of all kinds (including economic associations). Bouglé rejected many of socialism's basic theses, but remained sympathetic to French socialism because it retained the liberal dimension he had discovered in Proudhon.

Henri Hubert was now dividing his time between the École pratique des hautes études and the Musée Saint-Germain, where he still worked under Salomon Reinach, author of the best-selling *Orpheus*. Hubert was promoted to the rank of deputy curator in 1910, and devoted all his efforts to expanding the museum and creating and organizing new rooms. As well as contributing to the *Année sociologique*, Hubert published articles and reviews in journals such as *L'Anthropologie*, the *Revue archéologique* and the *Revue celtique*. The 'archaeological notes' he contributed to the latter were the first of his many writings on the Celts. Active in both national and international learned societies, Hubert helped to found the Institut français d'anthropologie in 1911. Its backers included René Verneau, professor of anthropology at the Musée d'histoire naturelle and editor-in-chief of the journal *L'Anthropologie*. The aim of the institute was to bring together specialists (in limited numbers, it was made clear) from all branches of the human sciences so as to allow them to 'exchange ideas, shed light on one another, and synthesize their findings' (Verneau 1911: 110).[36] When the institute opened, Hubert was appointed treasurer, while Reinach became its president. The *Année sociologique* was well represented, as both Antoine Meillet and Durkheim were on its board of directors. Mauss was also involved.

Hubert was still working with Mauss at the École pratique des hautes études, and together they trained a new generation of researchers, including Czarnowski, Davy, Jeanmaire, Lenoir, Maunier, Jean Marx and Pryzykuski. Several of them would subsequently contribute to the *Année sociologique*. Czarnowksi was working on a study of St Patrick ('Ireland's national hero'), which was subsequently published in the 'Travaux de *l'Année sociologique*' collection.[37]

Robert Hertz, who was close to both Mauss and Hubert, was writing a 'short monograph' on the cult of St Besse in the Val d'Aosta (Italy). 'What does it mean to the faithful to be there every year?' asked Hertz, who hoped that his monograph would be 'the starting point for more extensive research'. He wanted to find out if his hypothesis could be extended to other myths, and especially those of classical Antiquity. His research resulted in publications of folklore and comparative mythologies, but it was only in July 1914 that the planned book began to near completion. It was, said Durkheim a 'study full of insights and clever ideas'.

François Simiand was still working as a librarian, but had moved in 1906 from the ministry of trade to the ministry of labour, where he established a library and organized surveys of working-class living conditions and of the situation of the rural population. From 1910 onwards, he was a temporary replacement for A. Landry, who taught the historical and philological sciences at the École pratique des hautes études, and taught the course on the history of economic doctrines. In 1912, he published *La*

Méthode positive en science économique (the title was borrowed from that of his article of 1908), which appeared in Alcan's 'Bibliothèque de philosophie contemporaine'. He also applied for a chair at the Collège de France, but failed to be elected by one vote (Gillard and Rosier 1996).[38]

In Toulouse, Paul Fauconnet was teaching a course entitled 'Elementary notions of sociology', as well as giving tutorials and lecture on pedagogy and morality. He saw his role (which he considered to be 'essential and indispensable') as that of 'popularizer and teacher who spreads, corrects and compares ideas', adding that 'personally, my sole ambition is to popularize ideas that I did not discover'.[39]

Paul Lapie, who had been teaching at Bordeaux since 1903, carried out a study of young delinquents in 1909, and established an experimental psychology laboratory for the study of young people in 1910. He was very highly thought of ('the best and most devoted of teachers', said his superiors), and was appointed rector of the Académie de Toulouse. This was the beginning of a fine career in educational administration.

The New-Style *Année*

The decision had finally been taken: 'With this volume we inaugurate the new series of *L'Année sociologique*' (Durkheim 1980 [1911]: 55). The team had recoiled 'from the responsibility of suspending a publication which has rendered, and still may, services which no one, we are happy to affirm, dreams of denying' (Durkheim 1971[1908]: 2). They had often discussed the new formula, which introduced two major changes: the *Année* would now appear every three years, and could no longer publish original articles. What would have been articles would now appear in book form in the 'Travaux de L'Année sociologique' collection published by Alcan.

In order to justify the change, Durkheim first invoked the need for his collaborators to devote more time to their own work. They could no longer allow themselves to be almost fully absorbed by this bibliographic work. On the other hand, he had no regrets about the past: 'By a methodical grouping of the books and articles as we reported on them, we achieved a natural classification of natural phenomena, the first to be attempted in such conditions' (1971[1908]: 1–2). This had allowed sociology to cease being a purely dialectical form of literature and to win more respect from specialists from other disciplines. But when he founded the journal, he had, as he wrote in his prefatory note to Bouglé's *Essay on the Caste System*, always hoped that 'this procedure would be no more permanent than the circumstances which imposed it upon us in the first place' (ibid.: 2). It was now time to settle down to the task: 'The best way of advancing a science is not to outline its scope . . . but to confront . . . problems resolutely and attempt a solution.' He also noted that 'the proper format for an original sociological work is the book', rather than the article, because 'one must allow oneself some space if anything is to be achieved.' After 'ten years of collection and research . . . without excessive temerity', it was time for a change. The new series had 'no claim whatsoever to be an encyclopaedia, which anyhow we do not think to be a realistic aim at this time', but it would make it possible to raise 'particular questions bearing upon well-defined objects in the hope consequently of some precision in the result' (ibid.). While the new series would raise a wide variety of questions, it would also express a number of 'basic ideas'. Those ideas were the natural product of 10 years of collective work, though authors were free to express their own ideas and to take responsibility for them.

Durkheim was convinced that this change would allow 'some interesting improvements' to the journal. It would be easier to 'select from a greater number of the works that will be offered to us for review [and] retain for analysis only those that have genuine value'. It would now be possible to 'ask many questions that have so far escaped us', and to look at, for instance, 'so-called primitive societies.' He could not, however, conceal the fact that he was worried, and expressed the hope that 'our readers remain faithful and offer us their encouragement' (1980[1911]: 57).

'More room for the bibliography!' – this was the *Année*'s new slogan. Reviews and notices now took up almost 800 pages, as opposed to 500 in previous issues. The increased workload meant that new contributors had to be recruited, and the team was expanded to include Georges Davy (1883–1976), Jean Ray (1883–1943), Maxime David (1885–1914), Jean-Paul Laffitte (1881–?) and Louis Gernet (1882–1914). The name of Gaston Richard disappeared from the list of contributors. Jean-Paul Laffitte was the only newcomer to have had an atypical career: having first studied the natural sciences, he enrolled at the École pratique des hautes études (fifth section) in 1907 to study the history of religions, and then took a course in Sanskrit in the fourth section in 1908. He would eventually find a position with the International Labour Office (ILO).

Davy, Ray, David and Gernet were all graduates of the École normale supérieure, where the first three took the *agrégation de philosophie*, while Gernet was an *agrégé de grammaire*. Gernet was awarded his doctorate in 1917 for a thesis entitled 'The development of juridical and moral thought in Greece'; Davy and Ray did not obtain their doctorates until after the First World War (1922 and 1926 respectively). Some of the new recruits (David and Davy) attended Durkheim's lectures at the Sorbonne, while Gernet and Laffitte had studied under Mauss and Hubert at the École pratique. David had written his dissertation on group marriage in Australia under the supervision of Durkheim, and was now working on ethics in ancient Greece, with particular reference to the notions of honour and punishment (Mauss 1969[1925]: 490). Davy and David had followed in the footsteps of Robert Hertz, and had attended Frédéric Rauh's lectures at the École normale supérieure. They described him as 'one of their best teachers'.[40]

Georges Davy had studied both at the Sorbonne's faculty of letters (1904–5) and then at the faculty of Law (1906–7) before going on to the École normale supérieure (1905–8), taking his *agrégation de philosophie* in 1908. It is difficult to say precisely when he met Durkheim (he himself says that it was 'probably in 1903 or 1904') and, as he admitted to Lévy-Bruhl, Durkheim was somewhat reluctant to supervise 'a student from the École called Davy' for the *diplôme d'études supérieures* (Merllié 1989: 499). Davy was awarded a three-year grant by the Thiers foundation, and attended Mauss's lectures at the École pratique between 1909 and 1912. He then began his career teaching in a lycée in Chaumont before transferring to Saint-Omer. He also spent time abroad in Germany and England.[41]

Louis Gernet was born in Paris in 1882, and began his career teaching in a provincial secondary school (Saint-Omer) after taking his *agrégation* in 1906. In 1907, he entered the Thiers foundation and enrolled at the École pratique (fourth section) to study philology and Greek. He also took a law degree. His first major publication was *L'Approvisionnement d'Athènes en blé* (1909). A close friend of Paul Fauconnet, he was actively involved with *Les Cahiers du socialiste,* and published a pamphlet entitled 'Municipal socialism: the lessons from abroad' under the pseudonym Louis Garnier. As a philologist, a Hellenist and a jurist, Gerner adopted the 'sociological viewpoint', and 'effectively became Marcel Mauss's younger brother' and the disciple of Durkheim, for whom he had 'immense respect and great admiration'. He always saw the director of *L'Année sociologique* as a 'demanding editor, whose systematic rigour inspired a fearful respect, which his great personal kindness did not always dispel' (Davidovitch 1966).[42]

The general organization of the journal remained relatively unchanged. The 'criminal sociology and moral statistics' section (5 per cent of the total) was reinstated, and 'moral and juridic sociology' now took up only 19 per cent of the journal. Religious sociology (27 per cent) and economic sociology (25 per cent) were now the largest sections, while general sociology (7 per cent), social morphology (7 per cent) and miscellaneous (3 per cent) were still of secondary importance.

The few changes that were made included the introduction of a new rubric devoted to the sociological conditions of knowledge. This was, stated Durkheim and Bouglé (1910), a topic 'that has for a long time stood in the first rank of our preoccupations', as was apparent from the various studies published by the team: 'Now, since religion is essentially a social phenomenon, in order to seek what religious factors have entered into our representation of the world, we have rigorously attempted to determine some of the sociological conditions of knowledge.' They now proposed to deal with the issue of 'classification and categories', but to extend the debate beyond religion: 'Today we open a new chapter, which, we are quite sure, will not remain empty henceforth' (ibid.).

While there was still a division of labour, several rubrics were now organized on a more flexible basis and the contributors worked in teams. Durkheim oversaw the whole project, but also shared editorial responsibilities for several rubrics.[43]

Durkheim contributed fewer reviews (20) than in previous years. Several were on exogamy, the family and women (one was a review of Gaston Richard's *La Femme dans l'histoire*). He also discussed Bouglé's book on castes and a German study of suicide – 'the first comprehensive study that has appeared on suicide since the work we published in 1897'. His research interests – and especially the planned *Elementary Forms* – were often apparent: he frequently referred to totemism and, with Mauss, devoted a long review to Carl Strehlow's *Die Aranda- und Loritja-Stämme in Zentral-Australien* in the new 'totem system' rubric (Durkheim and Mauss 1969[1910]).

Durkheim and Mauss had awaited the publication of Strehlow's two fascicules with obvious impatience. They contained new information (on, for instance, mythology and ritual, and about whether or not there was any belief in a great God or in reincarnation) that sometimes confirmed and sometimes contradicted that supplied by Spencer and Gillen. They emphasized, not without a certain pride, that the new data 'confirmed' the hypotheses that had so often been advanced in the journal: (1) that the Arunta organization displayed specific features that were far from typical of primitive totemism, and that the idea of a male line of descent had replaced that of uterine descent; (2) that there were, as they had assumed, many totems. They avoided discussing certain of their interpretations at any length, as that would be the topic of a 'forthcoming book'. This was an obvious reference to *The Elementary Forms of Religious Life*: 'We will justify our stance in the book announced above.'[44]

The reorganization of the religious sociology section (which created a subsection on 'religious systems of inferior societies' and generated three further subsections) also reflected the argument of *Elementary Forms*. The purpose of the reorganization was to avoid forcing 'very disparate' religious systems into a single (and 'somewhat confused') rubric. As Mauss and Durkheim explained in a footnote, they wanted to differentiate between those religious that were 'truly and essentially totemic' and those in which totemism was 'giving birth to a new religious form', or between 'inferior religions with advanced totemism' and 'tribal religious systems'. The new nomenclature had the advantage of highlighting the intermediary forms that related totemism to more highly developed religious forms.[45] Their explicit aim was to clearly identify the stages: from clans to brotherhoods to tribes (societies that are not sufficiently developed to be called nations), leading to the emergence of national religious systems, and then the universalist religious systems (including Christianity). The classification was, the authors emphasized, 'provisional'.[46]

Ideals and Collective Enthusiasm

Durkheim showed little interest in international conferences, perhaps because he thought them a waste of time. He did not attend the first German sociology conference, which was held in Berlin in October 1910, but did briefly describe the papers presented (by Tönnies, Kantorowicz, Sombart, Troeltsch, Gothein, Simmel and Max Weber), without adding any critical commentary (Durkheim 1969[1913b]). He noted the 'suggestive subtlety' of Simmel's paper on the sociology of sociability. He had only one comment to make on Weber, who was behind the idea of undertaking surveys, publishing the results and organizing congresses: 'Max Weber indicates which subjects the society proposes to examine: the sociology of journals and the sociology of *Vereine*' (ibid.). He did, on the other hand, agree to go to Bologna for the International Philosophical Congress. This was one of his few official trips abroad.

Durkheim had written to Robert Michels the previous month to thank him for his invitation: 'I still intend to go to the Bologna conference, but I have no idea of which route I will take. If I travel via Turin, I would be delighted to accept your kind invitation.'[47] Michels (who had become professor of political economy at Turin in 1907), had sent his book *Zur Soziologie des Parteiwesens in der moderne Demokratie* to Durkheim, who passed it on to Célestin Bouglé . Published in Leipzig, the book dealt with political parties in Germany and introduced the idea of the famous 'iron law of oligarchy'. Bouglé summed up Michels's thesis in these terms: 'Wherever there is a mass to be moved, a minority will move it. An aristocracy is essential to the life of a democracy' (Bouglé 1913).[48] Even though he was associated with the *Revue internationale de sociologie* and attended the meetings of the Institut international de sociologie, Michels did make an attempt to 'have a chat with' Durkheim when he visited Paris in September 1910.[49] He was also in contact with some contributors to the *Année sociologique*, and especially Halbwachs, Bouglé and Georges Bourgin. He invited them to participate in the ambitious project for a sociology encyclopedia that he launched in 1913.[50]

The topic Durkheim submitted for discussion was 'Value judgments and judgments of reality' (Durkheim 1974[1911]). His paper was a great success. Xavier Léon reports that his audience was impressed by the force of his argument and by his natural authority: 'Those who were present . . . had the sight of a gathering that immediately fell under his sway and then spontaneously rose to its feet. They crowded around the platform, reaching out towards the orator as though they had been drawn to him' (cited in Davy 1919b: 194).

Durkheim had two aims: 'First, to show by specific example how sociology can help to resolve a problem of philosophy, and, secondly, to remove certain prejudices under which so-called positive sociology too often suffers' (1974[1911]: 80). The object of a judgement of reality or of existence is 'to define what is'; value judgements 'do not have for object the nature of things, but rather their worth in relation to persons'. Such judgements are not simply personal preferences, as they do correspond to 'some objective reality'. The problem is philosophical: what makes both forms of judgement possible? The usual answer is that value 'is intrinsic in some element of the thing judged' (ibid.: 84). That theory of value raises, however, a number of problems, as it overlooks the fact that 'value' can be economic, moral, religious, aesthetic or speculative.

And as can be seen from art and luxury goods (diamonds, pearls, furs, lace), the value of a thing is not reducible to its usefulness, either individual or social. 'All art is a luxury; aesthetic activity is not subordinated to any useful end' (1974[1911]: 85). Durkheim even goes so far as to accept that virtues such as philanthropy are irrational: 'There is virtue that is folly, and it is in its folly that its grandeur consists' (ibid.: 86). And the reason why luxury goods are so expensive is not, in sociological terms, that they are so rare, but that they are also the most esteemed:

> Life as man at all times has conceived it is not simply a precise arrangement of the budget of the individual or social organism . . . the careful balance between debit and credit. To live is above all to act, to act without counting the cost and for the pleasure of acting. If the evidence demands that we do not discount economy, as man must amass in order to expend, nevertheless that expenditure is his end, and to expend is to act. (Ibid.: 86)

Durkheim therefore clearly distances himself from social utilitarianism (and from any theory based upon a cost-benefit analysis): the value of clothing and adornment also has to do with the 'caprice of fashion'.

Value is not a property of things, and Durkheim gives other examples: to the extent that it is an object made of wood or stone, an idol is of no value. The flag for which soldiers die is nothing more than a piece of cloth. The fetishes that bring a faith to life are of no value in themselves. The same is true of the moral life: there is such a thing as the ideal of 'moral equality', and the fact that it exists is one of the differences between animals and men. If the thing itself is of no value, where does its value come from? Durkheim contends that it is in fact such ideals that give things a value. Then how are we to explain the existence of ideals (which vary from one human group to another)? In an attempt to answer that question, Durkheim analyses those periods of collective enthusiasm that give birth to a new kind of psychic life: 'This is a world not only more intense, but also qualitatively different' (1974[1911]: 91). Such situations can get out of control, with 'stupid destructive violence on the one hand, and acts of heroic folly on the other'. What Durkheim is trying to demonstrate is that the great ideals upon which civilizations are based are always established during these periods of enthusiasm. They are creative or innovatory periods characterized by an intense social life (frequent gatherings, more intense relationships, more active intellectual exchanges). He gives, in no particular order, the examples of the crisis within Christianity, the wave of enthusiasm that brought European students to Paris in the twelfth century, the Reformation and the Renaissance. At such times life becomes more intense. But, he points out, the illusion cannot be sustained because this mood of excitement is too exhausting. 'Once the critical moment had passed, the social life relaxes, intellectual and emotional intercourse is subdued, and individuals fall back to their ordinary level' (ibid.: 92). Everything goes 'back to normal', and the periods of 'fruitful torment' are subsequently marked by public festivals and ceremonies (which evoke memories and are 'minor versions of the great temporary movement').

Man has ideals because he is, according to Durkheim, a social being: it is society that forces him to 'rise above himself'. It involves him in a 'higher form of life'. The existence of such ideals demonstrates that 'to see society only as an organized body of vital functions is to diminish it, for this body has a soul which is the composition of collective ideals' (1974[1911]: 93).

Durkheim's thesis is that a value-judgement expresses 'the relation of a thing to an ideal'. The ideal is 'a symbol of the thing and makes it an object of understanding' (1974[1911]: 95). Those who criticize positive sociology for 'its fetish of facts and . . . systematic indifference to the ideal' are mistaken: 'Sociology moves from the beginning in the field of ideals . . . The ideal is in fact its peculiar field of study' (ibid.: 96). As Durkheim himself was to point out, the theme of the ideal is central to *The Elementary Forms of Religious Life*: 'I have so often been told that sociology cannot explain the ideal, that it is positivist and realist. I have shown that it is interested in the ideal because it is alive.' He was disappointed that, 'until now, no one has said anything to that effect', and that even Bouglé had 'not emphasized this' in his article.[51]

The Sexual Act: A 'Serious Act'

Durkheim was fully preoccupied with writing his book and preparing the *Année sociologique* for publication, and was making fewer public appearances. He did, however, take part in the Société française de philosophie's discussion of sex education in 1911 (Durkheim 1979[1911b]), and in the Union de la vérité's discussion of general culture and educational reform (or the 'New School', to be more specific) the following year (Durkheim 1979[1912]).[52] He also agreed to contribute to the *Nouveau Dictionnaire de pédagogie et d'instruction primaire* [New Dictionary of Teaching and Primary Education] that Ferdinand Buisson was planning.

On 28 February 1911, the Société française de philosophie met to discuss Dr Jacques-Amédée Doléris's report on sex education. Doléris was an obstetrician who was heavily involved in the campaign to halt the trend towards depopulation, which had been attributed to venereal disease. He had already addressed the issue of sex education at the recent International Congress on School Hygiene, and had been given a good reception (see Pederson 2007). Paul Bureau and Dominique Parodi, who were both familiar with these debates, were also involved in the discussion. In his speech, Durkheim noted that there was only one reference to free union in the whole of Doléris's report (which he summarized thus): 'By entering into a free union, one is laying oneself open to physical risks and even moral difficulties (illegitimate children, the resulting domestic upheavals and their repercussions)' (Durkheim 1979[1911b]:140). His aim was to defend sex education in order to improve the current state of affairs where sexual relations were concerned: the facts of life should be taught, simply and scientifically. Doléris noted with surprise that both public opinion and religious beliefs found that there was something 'mysterious' about the sexual act (ibid.: 141), and argued that this is 'a simple prejudice' and a 'relic' from a remote past. He recommended that sex education should be made available to both girls and boys, but that 'decency, prudence and simplicity' were required.

Durkheim did not dispute the need for sex education: 'No society has ever existed which has been totally without. Yet each civilization interprets it in its own way' (1979[1911b]: 140). He did not question 'the usefulness of the scientific education which would inform the two sexes about the physical nature of this act', provided that this was done discreetly. He was, on the other hand, annoyed by Doléris's suggestion that 'it is possible to legislate on morality in the name of hygiene'. The 'real issue' in Durkheim's view lay in discovering why self-restraint is a 'duty' and how the 'reasons for this duty can be expounded to the young man'. How, in other words, could the young man 'be made to understand that the state of marriage is justified in law and that extra-marital sexual intercourse is immoral' (ibid.: 140, 141)?

Durkheim also wished to correct Doléris's view that collective beliefs about sexuality are 'superstitions': even 'the crudest and most primitive religions are unanimous in regarding [the sexual act] as a grave, solemn and religious act'. Such ideas cannot result from a 'simple aberration or deception'; they correspond to something in reality, to 'some sentiment which men of all times have truly felt' (1979[1911b]: 141).

Given that it is impossible to embark upon an analysis of such a complex reality, Durkheim limits himself to 'a few pointers'. There is something 'mysterious' about the sexual act, which means that it cannot be 'grouped together with the acts of day-to-day life'. He is shocked to see Doléris suggesting that it is 'one of the ordinary acts of physical life', or 'the manifestation of a biological function, on a par with the digestion and the circulation' (1979[1911b]: 141, 143). Doléris was, by his own admission, not qualified to talk about history or ethology but remarked that in his particular field, which was biology, sexuality was 'fundamentally a biological act', and suggested that sociologists should try to discover 'why it had been shrouded in mystery'. In his view, such prejudices must 'originally have had social or economic causes' (ibid.: 143).

Going back to the 'mysterious nature of the sexual act', Durkheim remarks that it was revealed to him 'through historical and ethnographic research'. He criticizes his medical colleague for concentrating solely on 'the external gestures', which the psychologist studies, and for failing to take into consideration the sentiments, feelings and institutions which give these relations their specifically human form' (1979[1911b]: 144). The disturbing thing about the sexual act is that 'it necessarily seems immoral in one of its aspects, and, in another, profoundly moral' (ibid.: 145). This is not, he admits, a problem that can be resolved 'by a short discussion'. His concern, 'without resorting to any confessional postulate', is to make the young man 'understand the reasons for the singular, disturbing character of the sexual act . . . for it is only in these terms that he will not indulge in it lightly' (ibid.: 146).

There is, according to Durkheim, something about sexual relations that offends the moral sentiment: the fact that, as Kant says, 'one individual serves as an instrument of pleasure to another'. The 'moral anxiety' associated with the sexual act derives from a sentiment that lies at the root of our morality, namely 'the respect that man generates in his fellows'. This explains 'why we keep our distance from our fellows and why they keep their distance from us'. Hence the avoidance of intimacy and the need for modesty: 'We hide and isolate ourselves from others, and this isolation is at once the token and the consequence of the sacred character which has been vested in us' (1979[1911b]: 146).

Durkheim discusses sexuality in terms of desecration and sacrilege. There are boundaries that must be respected, and limits that must not be overstepped: 'We do not intrude without due cause on other people.' The sexual act is therefore 'a profanation [that] reaches an exceptionally high intensity, since each of the two personalities in contact is engulfed by the other'. This explains the 'basic immorality' that is implicit in the sexual act. But there are two facets to 'this curiously complex act . . . This desecration also produces a communion, and a communion of the most intimate kind possible between two conscious beings' (1979[1911b]: 147). Durkheim speaks of the emergence of a 'new personality . . . enveloping and embracing the other two'. However, he adds the proviso that the two individuals who have become one must separate again. If they do not, the profanation 'remains complete and irredeemable'. Durkheim concludes that because it binds together the persons it brings into contact, 'the sexual act is serious and solemn'. 'This is why morality cries out against free union, quite apart from the repercussions that it can have on domestic harmony' (ibid.: 147).

Is this a defence of bourgeois values, or of a scientific position? When Doléris remarks that Durkheim's attitude inevitably prevents him from considering the sexual act 'in all its simplicity', he protests: 'When I spoke of the necessarily mysterious nature of the sexual act, I was not doing so as a man, but on the contrary exclusively as a sociologist. I am quite aware that it is not to education that I owe the sentiment I endeavoured to analyse briefly' (1979[1911]:143–4). The mysterious nature of the sexual act was revealed to him 'through historical and ethnographic research': 'I even know the exact moment when I was struck by the extremely general nature of the fact and how wide its implications were' (ibid.: 144).

The Methodical Socialization of the Next Generation

The *Dictionnaire de pédagogie et d'instruction primaire* was now more than 30 years old. Ferdinand Buisson was planning a new edition and asked Durkheim, who had succeeded him at the Sorbonne, to contribute. The book was published by Hachette in 1911. Durkheim contributed three entries: 'Childhood' (with Buisson; see Durkheim 1979[1911a]); 'Education: its nature and role' (Durkheim 1956[1911]); and 'Pedagogy and sociology' (Durkheim 1956[1903]). Buisson and Durkheim begin by asking how the period of childhood is to be defined and refer to the word's etymology (from the Latin *in-fans*, not speaking) before turning to popular usage, as defined by dictionaries. They make a distinction between two very different periods: 'early childhood' (the first three to four years), to which the new child psychology devotes its attention, and the 'second period of childhood', or 'childhood in the more usual and general sense of the word', which refers to 'the normal period of education and instruction'. Their study is restricted to this 'second period', and the normal definition of childhood is their starting point. They then attempt to answer the question: 'What are the characteristics of childhood and the natural laws of that period of life?' Its characteristics are biological, and not social. This is 'a period of *growth*' and it is negatively characterized by weakness in both physical terms (the child is 'the puniest of beings, a small body'), mental terms (the child is 'weak and fragile . . . endowed with . . . limited faculties') and moral terms (weakness of will, little ability to distinguish between good and evil). Its positive characteristic is its mobility, and Durkheim and Buisson speak of the wonder of the child's intellectual and moral development: 'This diminutive *conscience* is a veritable kaleidoscope' (Durkheim 1979[1911a]: 149–51).

The entry on 'Education' is some 30 pages long and is divided into sections on the definition of education, the social nature of education and the role of the state. Durkheim begins by discussing two types of definition: Kant's (the goal of education is 'to develop in each individual all the perfection of which he is capable') and that of utilitarians like Mill ('to make the individual an instrument for himself and for his fellows'). Both definitions display, according to Durkheim, the same weakness in that there is no such thing as an 'ideal or perfect' education, 'which applies to all men indiscriminately': one had only to look at history to see that 'education has varied infinitely in time and place'. The examples of Athens, Rome, the Middle Ages and the Renaissance demonstrate how varied conceptions of education can be. Education can mean either subordinating the individual to the collectivity or shaping autonomous personalities, and can be seen in either religious or secular terms, but 'there are . . . ineluctable necessities that it is impossible to disregard' (1956[1911]: 61–4).

Durkheim therefore restates his belief that 'each society, considered at a given stage of development, has a system of education which exercises an irresistible influence on individuals'. It is therefore idle to believe that we can bring up our children as we wish: 'there are customs to which we are obliged to conform' (1956[1911]: 65). There are customs and ideas, and they are the product of 'a common life' and, usually, the 'work of preceding generations'. We therefore cannot sweep away the past and build whatever we want. The individual is not 'confronted with a *tabula rasa* on which he can write what he wants, but with existing realities which he cannot create, or destroy, or transform at will' (ibid.: 66).

If we wish to influence these realities, there is only one thing that we can do. We must 'learn to understand them' in the same way that the physicist learns to understand inanimate matter and the biologist learns to understand living bodies: we must begin by observing them. The same is true when it comes to determining the goals of education: 'But what is it that allows us to say that education has certain ends rather than others?' (1956[1911]: 67). It is not enough to say that its object is the training of children. Durkheim's proposed definition of education tries to identify the characteristics of past and present educational systems; he concludes:

> Education is the influence exercised by adult generations on those that are not yet ready for social life. Its object is to arouse and to develop in the child a number of physical, intellectual and moral states which are demanded of him both by the political society as a whole and the special milieu for which he is specifically destined. (Ibid.: 71)

'The political society' and the 'special milieu' – there are two aspects to any educational system. There are as many forms of education as there are social milieus, as we can see from the Indian caste system, modern social classes and the professions. All civilized countries are, according to Durkheim, characterized by their great diversity and specialization: every profession is a milieu *sui generis* that demands particular skills and special forms of knowledge. Hence the need for specialized forms of education. An educational system is also unitary because, while they are specialized, these different forms of education usually have a 'common basis'. Every society has a 'system of ideas, sentiments and practices', and they are inculcated into children because they are its 'social being'. In Durkheim's view, the social dimension of education is essential: 'Education means the methodical socialization of the next generation.' He restates the basic thesis that there are two distinct beings in all of us: an individual being and a social being (with a set of collective ideas, feelings and habits). The goal of education is to transform the individual being into a social being. Sociality is not an element in man's primitive constitution, and nor is it the product of some spontaneous development: submitting to a political authority, respecting a moral discipline, devoting ourselves, sacrificing ourselves and serving gods are not part of our 'congenital nature'. Heredity is a matter of 'vague and uncertain tendencies'. 'The child, on entering life, brings to it only his nature as an individual . . . To the egoistic and asocial being that has just been born [society] must . . . add another, capable of leading a moral and social life.' Such is the work of education: 'It creates in man a new being' (1956[1911]: 72). And in Durkheim's view, 'this creative virtue' is a 'special prerogative of human education'.

While education is essentially a response to 'social needs', the form it takes varies from one society to another. Durkheim gives the example of the great store that is set by a good intellectual culture, science or critical thinking: '[Man] has known the thirst for knowledge only when society has awakened it in him; any society has done this only when it has felt the need of it' (1956[1911]: 74). Society must therefore become more complex before science and reflective thought can emerge. So long as the social organization is simple, largely unchanging and constant, blind tradition is all that is required, in the sense that animals require only their instincts. In such societies, thought and free enquiry are useless and seem dangerous because they pose a threat to tradition.

Durkheim is well aware that there will be objections to this sociological view. If society does shape individuals in this way, should we not be talking about its 'insupportable tyranny' (1956[1911]: 75)? No, because it is in their interest to be shaped in this way: 'the new being that collective influence, through education, thus builds up in each of us, represents what is best in us. Man is man, in fact, only because he lives in society' (ibid.: 76). The same is true of morality:

> It is society, indeed, that draws us out of ourselves, that obliges us to reckon with interests other than our own, it is society that has taught us to control our passions, our instincts, to prescribe law for them, to restrain ourselves, to deprive ourselves, to sacrifice ourselves, to subordinate our personal ends to higher ends. As for the whole system of representation which maintains in us the idea and the sentiment of rule, of discipline, internal as well as external – it is society that has established it in our consciences. (Ibid.)

This also applies to intellectual and scientific life. Durkheim is announcing the thesis of *The Elementary Forms of Religious Life*: 'Science is the heir to religion. And a religion is a social institution.' He also demonstrates that all the cardinal notions that dominate our intellectual life (the notions of cause, law, space, number, body, life, consciousness, society, and so on) and that science elaborates are constantly evolving. Science itself is a 'collective work', as it presupposes 'a vast cooperation of all scientists, not only of the same time, but of all the successive epochs of history'. The same is true of language, which is, Durkheim reminds us, 'a social thing' (1956[1911]: 77).

Armed with this sociological conception of education, Durkheim can now turn with confidence to the highly controversial issue of the right and duties of the state with respect to education. The first question to arise is that of the rights of the family. If the child is essentially the property of its parents, it is their responsibility to direct, as they understand it, his intellectual and moral development. According to this view, education is essentially a private and domestic affair, and state intervention should be minimal. Durkheim does not share that view: if the function of education is essentially collective, society cannot be uninterested. It is up to society to remind teachers of the ideas and sentiments that must be inculcated into the child if it is to be able to live in harmony with its future environment. If schools fail to do that, they inevitably promote 'private beliefs', and there is then a danger that the whole nation will be divided and will break down into 'an incoherent multitude of little fragments in conflict with one another' (1956[1911]: 79). For Durkheim, it is all very simple: 'If one attaches some value to the existence of society – and we have just seen what it means to us – education must assure, among the citizens, a sufficient community of ideas and sentiments, without which any society is impossible' (ibid.: 80). The conclusion is obvious: the school system cannot be completely abandoned to 'the arbitrariness of private individuals'. Durkheim raises the issue of whether or not the state should have a 'monopoly' on education, but does not answer it for the moment because he does not wish to discuss such a complex question 'in passing'. His own view is that 'scholastic progress is easier and quicker where a certain margin is left for individual initiative; for the individual makes innovations more readily than the state' (ibid.). But such decentralization must not leave the state 'indifferent' to what happens in schools. On the contrary, it must exercise some control. One thing is certain: 'The principle of intervention could not be disputed' (ibid.).

Durkheim deplores the 'state of division' that he observes in France: there is no moral unity. The school must not be 'the thing of one party', and the teacher is remiss in his duties 'when he uses the authority at his disposal to influence his pupils in accordance with his own preconceived opinions' (1956[1911]: 81). It is up to society, and not the state, to outline 'this community of ideas and sentiments'. The majority must not, on the other hand, be allowed to impose their idea on the children of the minority. This is not an easy problem to resolve, especially when there are so many divergent views. The sociologist observes, however, that our civilization is based on 'a certain number of principles which, implicitly or explicitly, are common to all'. These are respect for reason, science, and the ideas and feelings that are basic to democratic morality. The role of the state is therefore to ensure that they are taught in schools.

Durkheim ends his article on education with some remarks on 'the powers of education and the means of influence'. Some take the view that education is all-powerful, and even that it can be a source of inequality. According to others, it has too little influence because innate dispositions and congenital tendencies are very difficult to overcome: the future of an individual may, in other words, be 'fixed in advance' (1956[1911]: 82). For his own part, Durkheim takes the view that one of man's characteristics is that 'his innate predispositions are very general and very vague'.[53] It might be argued that a child can inherit a very strong tendency towards given acts such as suicide, theft or murder, but Durkheim contends that 'these assertions are not at all in accord with the facts' (ibid.: 83). The same is true of occupational aptitudes, which some consider to be hereditary: 'the son of a great traveller can, at school, be surpassed in geography by the son of a miner' (ibid.: 84). He does, on the other hand, recognize the importance of family influences: children do receive from their parents what he calls very general faculties, for example strength of thought, a certain amount of perseverance, a sound judgment, imagination. But these faculties can be expressed in very different ways, depending on the circumstances and the way they are influenced: the child may become a painter, a poet, an inventive engineer, or a fearless financer. 'There is therefore a considerable difference between natural qualities and the special forms that they must take to be utilized in life. This means that the future is not strictly determined by our congenital constitution' (ibid.: 84). A vast field is open to the influence of education.

In order to demonstrate the power of educational influence, Durkheim uses the common argument that likens education to hypnosis, and compares the teacher to a hypnotizer: 'Far from being discouraged by our impotence, we might well, rather, be frightened by the scope of our power.' Parents and teachers have immense influence over children because 'nothing can happen in the child's presence which does not leave some trace in him'. Durkheim is thinking here of the 'thousands of little unconscious influences that take place at every moment and to which we pay no attention because of their apparent insignificance' (1956[1911]: 86). The effectiveness of education is, however, purely relative, when it works in fits and starts, and great when it is 'patient and continuous.' Authority obviously has a major role to play and, according to Durkheim, education is 'essentially a matter of authority'. It is also, he adds, a matter of effort. Durkheim firmly rejects the epicurean conception of education, which takes the view that the attractions of pleasure are the only spur that man needs, and that we can learn by playing. Life is 'serious and important', and 'education, which prepares for life, must share this seriousness ' (ibid.: 87). Certain goals must be established and must force the child to 'exercise a high degree of self-control'. The child must, in other words, learn to contain his natural egoism, subordinate himself to higher goals, and bring his desires under the control of his will. And there are, according to Durkheim, only two reasons for forcing ourselves in this way: physical necessity or a sense of moral duty. The sense of duty is the 'stimulus *par excellence* of effort' (ibid.: 88), for both children and adults, and it is much more powerful than necessity.

But how can a child understand what duty is? In Durkheim's view, only teachers or parents can teach him that. 'Moral authority is, in other words, the educator's dominant quality.' That moral authority does not derive from his power to reward and punish, but from his moral ascendancy: it comes from his inner faith, and to that extent he has something in common with the priest: 'He too is the agent of a great moral person who surpasses him: it is society. Just as the priest is the interpreter of his god, the teacher is the interpreter of the great moral ideas of his time and of his country' (1956[1911]: 89).

There is therefore no conflict between freedom and authority: 'Liberty is the daughter of authority properly understood. For to be free is not to do what one pleases; it is to be master of oneself, it is to know how to act with reason and to do one's duty' (1956[1911]: 89–90).

Pedagogy: A Practical Theory

Having defined education, Durkheim moves on to the notion of 'pedagogy'. Education can be described as 'the influence exerted on children by parents and teachers', but what is pedagogy? Unlike education, it consists 'not of actions, but of theories. These theories are ways of conceiving of education, not ways of practising it' (Durkheim 1956[1911]: 91). The pedagogies of Rabelais, Rousseau or Pestalozzi, for example, are different ways of 'reflecting on the phenomena of education' (ibid.: 92).

Is pedagogy a science? Durkheim had often asked the same question of sociology. Before a set of theories can be called a science, three conditions must, he argues, be met: the discipline must have its own purpose, and must deal with 'verified, selected, observed facts'; 'these facts must have within themselves a sufficient homogeneity to be classed in the same category'; and, finally, the science in question must study 'these facts to know them, and only to know them, in an absolutely disinterested fashion' (1956[1911]: 92–3). Durkheim is here defending the view that 'science begins at the point where knowledge, whatever it may be, is sought for itself'. That does not prevent the scientist from knowing that 'his discoveries will very probably be usable', but:

> so far as he devotes himself to scientific investigation, he is disinterested in practical consequences. He says what is; he establishes that things are, and he stops there. He does not concern himself with knowing if the truths that he discovers will be agreeable or disconcerting . . . His role is to express reality, not to judge it. (ibid.: 93–4).

Durkheim sees no reason why education should not become the object of a science that meets all these conditions. Educational practices and customs are, in his view, as real as any other social phenomenon, or 'real social institutions' which act upon us with 'imperative force': 'they can, therefore, serve as the object of one and the same science, which would be the science of education' (1956[1911]: 95).

For the moment, Durkheim opens two fields of study to 'scientific speculation' (1956[1911]: 98). The first is the past: various types of education corresponding to different types of society can be identified by using the comparative-historical method. Once they have been established, they can be 'explained' (by analysing their causes): 'One would thus obtain the laws which govern the evolution of systems of education'. Turning to the present, Durkheim then suggests that 'one could investigate how they function, that is to say, what results they produce and what are the conditions that make these results vary'. Hence the need for 'a good set of scholastic statistics' showing, for instance, data concerning 'scholastic offences' and how they vary according to region, age group and family status (ibid.: 98).

The origins and the workings of educational systems form two groups of problems 'the purely scientific character of which cannot be disputed' (1956[1911]: 99). The same cannot be said of 'the theories that are called pedagogical'. Durkheim makes a distinction between the science of education and pedagogy: 'Pedagogy is something other than the science of education. What is it then? . . . Shall we say that it is an art?' (1956[1911]: 100). As he demonstrates, there is indeed a difference between the experience acquired by a teacher in the exercise of his profession, and pedagogy: 'One can be a fine teacher and yet be quite unsuited for the speculations of pedagogy.' Conversely, the speculative pedagogue may lack all practical ability: 'We would have entrusted a class neither to Rousseau nor to Montaigne.' The same is true of politics and medicine: 'the best theorists on medical matters are not the best clinicians, by far' (1956b[1911]: 101).

Durkheim suggests that the term 'art' should be reserved for 'everything that is pure practice without theory', and gives the example of the art of the soldier, of the lawyer and of the teacher. 'An art is a system of ways of doing which are oriented to special ends and which are the product of either a traditional experience communicated by education, or of the personal experience of the individual' (1956[1911]: 101). It is not that there is no reflection involved at all, merely that it is of secondary importance. 'Between art so defined and science properly speaking, there is therefore 'a place for an intermediate mental attitude' (ibid.). That attitude gives rise to reflections about processes of action, and they may take the form of theories. Examples include theories of medicine, politics and strategy, which might be called 'practical theories'. Durkheim concludes that pedagogy is a practical theory of the same type: 'It does not study systems of education scientifically, but it reflects on them in order to provide the activity of the educator with ideas to guide it' (ibid.: 102).

Durkheim is, however, aware that 'a practical theory is possible and legitimate when it can rest upon an established and undisputed science, of which it is only the application . . . Now, on what sciences can pedagogy rest?' (1956[1911]: 102). The science of education, on which it should rest, 'hardly exists except in embryonic form'. Two other disciples could aid pedagogy: sociology and psychology. The situation is, on the other hand, far from ideal in that sociology is 'only a new science' and in that psychology, although established earlier, is 'the object of all sorts of controversies'. Pedagogic speculation is therefore not based upon any solid data. It might therefore be 'prudent and methodical to wait until these sciences . . . have made progress' (ibid.: 103).

We cannot wait for that to happen because 'our traditional system of education is no longer in harmony with our ideas and our needs'. There are therefore only two alternatives: 'either try to preserve the practices that the past has left to us, even though they no longer answer the exigencies of the situation, or to undertake resolutely to re-establish the disturbed harmony by finding out what the necessary modifications are' (1956[1911]: 103). The first solution is impractical and would come to nothing: 'Nothing is so fruitless as these attempts to give an artificial life and apparent authority to obsolete and discredited institutions' (ibid.: 103–4). The second alternative was the only realistic one: to inquire into the changes which are indicated, and realize them 'even though we do not have at our disposal all the elements that would be desirable for resolving the problem' (ibid.: 104). Durkheim is dismissive of the 'scientific puritanism which, under the pretext that science is not fully established, counsels abstention'. This is the 'sophism of ignorance', but the 'sophism of science' is just as dangerous: 'No doubt, to act under these conditions, one runs risks. But action never proceeds without risks; science, as advanced as it may be, would not know how to eliminate them' (ibid.).

It is not only in periods of crisis that pedagogy has its uses: it has become 'an indispensable auxiliary of education'. While it is true that the art of the educator consists mainly in 'instincts and almost instinctive practices . . . it could not do without reflections' for two reasons. The new imperative to train 'the individual personality' has become 'an essential element of the intellectual and moral culture of humanity', and the educator must therefore try to adapt his methods to 'the germ of individuality that is in each child.' Education must also respond to 'incessant changes': 'New needs and new ideas arise constantly . . . education itself must change' (1956b[1911]: 105).

Durkheim therefore rejects both the 'yoke of habit' and 'automatism', and the only way to avoid both these obstacles is to keep education adaptable by reflection: 'Reflection is the force *par excellence* antagonistic to routine, and routine is the obstacle to necessary progress.' He is convinced that, even if it is 'intermittent', pedagogy and pedagogical reflection will become 'a continuing function of social life' (1956b[1911]: 106). We must respond to change, in both our individual and our collective lives.

23

The Origins of Religious Life

There were now new developments for Durkheim. A Russian translation of *Suicide* appeared in 1912,[1] as did a Spanish translation of *The Rules of Sociological Method*. Alcan published *The Elementary Forms of Religious Life*, which Durkheim had completed the previous year, in a print-run of 1,500 (plus 100 copies over). The *Année sociologique*'s new formula gave both him and his collaborators some respite and allowed them to 'complete' research projects which, in many cases, they had begun several years earlier.

The 'Totemist School'

The first decade of the twentieth century marked the apotheosis of religious studies. 'Minds have rarely been more concerned with religious thought than they have been over the last ten years', remarked Gustave Belot (1913: 22). What had been of interest only to philosophers and theologians was becoming, as James H. Leuba (1913: 323) commented in the United States, 'an active element in the work of psychologists, ethnographers and sociologists'. The debates, which could be very heated, revolved around a few big questions. Could people exist without religion? What was the relationship between religion and magic? Was it possible to speak of a primitive monotheism? The question of the origins of totemism, which the evolutionist anthropologists had been studying since the end of the nineteenth century, was being widely discussed, but often in inadequate terms, as American anthropologist and professor at the University of Columbia, Alexander Goldenweiser, pointed out (1912: 600). Arnold Van Gennep went so far as to speak of an 'exogamous and totemic' sport that was becoming too popular on the other side of the English Channel: in 1905, Andrew Lang – a sworn enemy of Durkheim's – had published his major work *The Secret of the Totem*, and had subsequently 'given himself a lot of trouble' – too much so, according to some, given that he died in 1912 (Van Gennep 1912: 368). His English colleague James Frazer had just published *Totemism and Exogamy* (1911), which gave a sort of picture of totemism on different continents, and he was now working on the third edition of *The Golden Bough*. His goal was to 'give an overall view of all those peoples amongst whom totemism is, to a greater or lesser extent, to be observed'. There was a good deal of interest in totemism in France too. Salomon Reinach, who was closely connected to the *Année*, devoted a lot of space in his writings to totemism, which he described as 'a hypertrophy of the social instinct'. His *Orpheus* (1909) also focused on the issue of totem and taboo. He saw religions as a set of scruples that hampered human activity: the scruples were taboos. Van Gennep, founder of the *Revue des études ethnographiques et sociologiques*, had made a special study of totemism, and would later collect the articles he had written on the subject under the title *L'État actuel du problème totémique* (1920). He was somewhat sceptical about the idea of developing a general theory of exogamy and religion solely on the basis of 'Australian facts', which were, in his view, 'not simple or primitive phenomena but phenomena that were highly developed, and therefore very complex'. His relations with Durkheim and his collaborators were complex. In terms of their fields of interest and use of the comparative method, they were close, but he also kept his critical distance.

The interest in totemism was so great that there was even talk of a 'totemist school'. The expression was coined by the Egyptologist Georges Foucart, who had just published a new edition of his *Histoire des religions et méthode comparative* (1912). He attacked a 'certain ethnology' and its 'few fanatical and clumsy representatives' who made up a (French) school that was, in his view, neither 'real' nor 'serious', but which exercised an 'imperious intellectual dominance' that has done 'a lot of damage'. It was a kind of sect that was trying to convert the public to its 'faith in totems, taboos, collective sacrifice, and agrarian rituals'. The main targets of his criticisms were Durkheim, Henri Hubert and Marcel Mauss, as well as Salomon Reinach and Arnold Van Gennep, who were all supposedly members of the same 'school'. Georges Davy wondered what this 'totemist school' was all about (1913: 83); he was astonished to see Foucart, who was so ill-informed about developments in ethnology and sociology, 'declaring war, with such violence, on a school that does not exist'.

Georges Foucart was so intent upon provocation that he offered the anthropologists a 'peace treaty' based upon three principles: (1) ethnology should simply complement history and leave the task of establishing the structure of religious evolution to historians; (2) it should stop trying to construct a picture of the primitive religions of savages; (3) it should give up its claim to be able to explain subsequent development in religions purely on the basis of its own resources. Was this really a peace treaty? The Egyptologist's strategy was to discredit the 'totemist school', and to make Egyptian religion, rather than the totemism of Australian tribes, the sole standard and point of reference for all comparative research.

When the Fourth International Congress on the History of Religions opened in Leyden in 1912, Comte Goblet d'Alviella – a contributor to the *Revue de l'histoire des religions* – also defended the idea of an 'alliance' between the historical and ethnological methods. Was it therefore true to say that 'the day of manifestos' was over, and that there were now 'neither accusers nor apologists' (Alphandéry 1912: 233–4).

The Conflict between Morality and Religion

As Gustave Belot observed (1913: 331), it was not easy to 'reconcile science and belief' when it came to 'religious phenomena'. Virulent attacks were being made on the objectivist studies of morality and religion, and especially on the sociology of Durkheim and his collaborators. Even Gaston Richard, who had once contributed to the *Année* and who had succeeded Durkheim in Bordeaux, had become 'implacably hostile' to his doctrine and to its flagship *L'Année sociologique*. In Richard's view, the great weakness of Durkheim and his collaborators was their desire both to elaborate a science and to pursue a speculative metaphysical attempt to resolve the general problems of morality, religious philosophy and the theory of knowledge. In his view, these were two different – and contradictory – things. Durkheim's attempts to do both were all the more perilous and dangerous in that the science he invoked was a science that was still in gestation, still in the making.[2] Observers of the philosophical scene found the polemic between Durkheim and his former collaborator amusing.[3]

The conflict between morality and sociology was far from resolved. The expression even became the title of a book published by the Institut supérieur de philosophie in Louvain in 1911. Its author was Simon Deploige, a priest who would later become a Monsignor. Deploige was one of those who, in their attempts to pinpoint Durkheim's contradictions, had no qualms about recruiting former associates like Richard. He was also one of those who pinned the label 'Made in Germany' on Durkheim. 'When we have finished examining it, what is "French" about M. Durkheim's sociology? Not a lot, to be sure. The German input is overwhelming.' Deploige also discovered that 'behind the renowned sociologist there is a fervent moralist and a bold reformer' (Deploige 1927[1911]: 128). He devoted several chapters of his book to Durkheim, including one entitled 'Social realism'. He had many criticisms: Durkheim's thought was 'elusive and difficult to grasp'; he 'breaks the rules of his own method', and he has 'no sense of nuances'. Deploige also detected a tendency to worship society, which indicated a propensity for 'social mysticism' and came close to being a real 'sociolatry' (a doctrine which might, he claimed, usually be compared to sun-worship). He also established a parallel between Durkheim's project and that of Saint-Simon.

Simon Deploige's reaction had been triggered by the publication of Lucien Lévy-Bruhl's *La Morale et la science des mœurs* in 1903. Deploige saw the book as 'the veritable manifesto of a school' and as a 'brilliant expansion of the ideas that are preached by M. Durkheim and that are accepted by his collaborators'. He thought that there was an 'urgent need for a reaction': his goal was to respond to the 'active group of publicists' who were arguing in France that there was a conflict between ethics and sociology. Durkheim and the *Année sociologique* team were obviously part of that group: 'For almost 20 years, Durkheim, who is M. Lévy-Bruhl's colleague at the Sorbonne, has been arguing that the science of morality must be imbued with a new spirit' (Deploige 1927[1911]: 5). 'How has ethics come to be so discredited? What do the sociologists have against ethics?'

The fact that the third edition of *Le Conflit de la morale et de la sociologie* was prefaced by Jacques Maritain shows that Simon Deploige's stance was part of an attempt to defend the 'Thomist edifice' against the 'powerful attacks' of the sociologists. The 'edifice' was sturdy and hospitable enough to give shelter to sociology, provided that sociology could 'usefully collaborate' with moral philosophy: 'Only ignorance can argue that the two are in conflict' (Deploige 1927[1911]: 350–1). Deploige was looking for a third way between the individualism of a false liberal metaphysics and a false sociological science. His book was, according to Maritain, 'the most accurate and detailed historical and critical study of contemporary sociology' (in Deploige 1927[1911]: xviii).

Having come under direct attack, Durkheim felt obliged to reply. He indignantly denounced Deploige's book as 'an apologetic pamphlet' designed to discredit 'our ideas, by all means possible, for the greater glory of the doctrine of Saint Thomas' (Durkheim 1980[1913b]: 159). His response to the renewed accusation that he was a Germanophile was that he had been influenced by many non-German writers, including Comte and Renouvier in France, and by the English and American science of religions, as well as by American, and especially English, ethnology (Robertson Smith). Deploige's attack was simply intended to 'divert the thrust of French sociology', and Durkheim accused him of resorting to '*a conscious alteration of the texts*' and using 'incorrect quotations' (ibid.: 160).

In Durkheim's view, the debate was closed, and he refused to spend any more time discussing a book which concluded that 'a return to the social philosophy of Saint Thomas [is] necessary' (1980[1913]: 161). 'There is not, in our view, and there cannot be, any conflict between morality and sociology . . . We ask simply that the moral art be preceded by a science of morality, more methodical in approach than the usual speculations of so-called theoretical morality' (ibid.: 160). It was, in other words, time to look at the facts. Durkheim was not alone in criticizing Deploige so harshly: the *Revue de métaphysique et de morale* attacked him for his 'lack of accuracy', and for wrongly accusing Durkheim of confusing morality and normality, and immorality with the pathological.[4]

Simon Deploige was unhappy with Durkheim's response, and argued that he did not want to 'open a new debate, but simply to sum things up'. 'Durkheim has been no more successful at proving that sociology is "French" than he was in the past.' As for the conflict between sociology and morality, it was 'limited, but real. If we wish to put an end to this conflict, we must go back to the social philosophy of Saint Thomas' (Deploige 1927[1911]: 375–8).

A Primitive Mentality?

Lucien Lévy-Bruhl published his *Fonctions mentales dans les sociétés infé-rieures* in 1910. Like *La Morale et les science des moeurs*, which had been published seven years earlier, it was a great success, going through several editions (the second appeared in 1912), and was translated into several languages. When it was published, Durkheim discussed the pertinence of the title with his colleague. He took the view that although the word 'primitive' should not be dropped – that would be 'over-purist' – it should not appear in the title, so as not to 'define the form of mentality you are studying in purely chronological terms'. Lévy-Bruhl was presumably not setting out 'to study primitive mentality in its entirety . . . but only one aspect of it'. Durkheim asked where there was such a thing as a 'prelogical mentality'; he answered his own question: 'There is no mentality before logical mentality.' In the absence of 'any positive terms that could be used to express your idea of that mentality, without any need to define it in rela-tion to the logical mentality', the term 'prelogical mentality' seemed to him to be 'the least bad'.[5]

Although he was close to the Durkheim group, Lévy-Bruhl had never contributed to the *Année sociologique*, but the two colleagues shared the same interests and held very similar views. Lévy-Bruhl's intention was to study collective representations, and he accepted that they were socially determined. He supported the view that human mentality varied: every type of society had a corresponding type of mentality. His goal was, however, not so much to study their social determination as to study their logical specificity. According to Lévy-Bruhl, the characteristic features of the lower mentality were that it was essentially religious or mystical, and that it took no heed of experimental proofs. The way in which the primi-tive mind connected ideas to one another was based upon a notion of 'par-ticipation' (which is quite different from the principle of contradiction that typifies our mentality). It is therefore a 'prelogical mentality', and there are corresponding linguistic, computational and institutional features.

When the book appeared, Durkheim had just written the sections of *The Elementary Forms of Religious Life* that deal with the principle of participation. He decided to 'publish them in their original form without any changes but confine myself to adding certain explanations that indi-cate where I differ from Lévy-Bruhl in the evaluation of the evidence' (Durkheim 1995[1912]: 216 n58). Durkheim wrote a brief review of Lévy-Bruhl's book for the *Année sociologique*, pointing out that the author's aim was to define the type of mentality characteristic of 'lower' societies. Vastly different societies were grouped together under this heading, but this was inevitable given 'the present conditions of research' (Durkheim 1994[1913]: 169). 'The only thing to do is to make a start on some rough preliminary work.'

Durkheim admitted that he and his colleague were asking questions that were 'closely related' (1994[1913]: 170) because 'it is obviously not possible to understand the lower forms of religion without studying the mentality of the peoples practising them'. He also accepted that he and Lévy-Bruhl held 'the same fundamental principles': 'Like him, we believe that various types of mentality have succeeded each other in the course of history. Similarly we claim – and we have tried to establish this by analysing the facts – that the primitive mentality is essentially religious' (ibid.: 170–1).

He insisted, however, that his own point of view was somewhat different from that of Lévy-Bruhl. The latter's attempts to differentiate between the primitive mentality and our own took the form of a 'positive antithesis': religious and primitive thought on the one hand, scientific and modern thought on the other. Durkheim himself took the view that 'these two forms of human mentality, however different they may seem, are mistakenly thought to have originated from different sources: they grew out of each other and represent two stages in the same process of evolution' (1994[1913]: 171). He then took issue with Lévy-Bruhl: 'Even some of the contrasts that have been pointed out ought to be qualified' (ibid.: 172). The primitive mind tends to confuse things, but it is 'just as inclined to striking contrasts, and often applies the principle of contradiction to an exaggerated degree'. Conversely, he argues the law of participation is not peculiar to the primitive mind: 'Our ideas, now as formerly, participate in each other. It is the very condition of all logical activity' (ibid.: 173).

'Lévy-Bruhl definitely goes too far', wrote the American anthropologist Goldenweiser (1910). To say that he had his reservations would be an understatement. He too criticized Lévi-Bruhl for drawing too sharp a contrast between the prelogical nature of the primitive mentality and the logical nature of our mentality. This was, in his view, an untenable position, and one that was not based upon an objective study of the facts. In *The Mind of Primitive Man* (1911), Franz Boas also took the view that the differences between the primitive and civilized mentalities were not essential, but were differences of degree: the mental process was always the same. It was based upon judgement, and consisted in associating what we perceived with what we already knew.

In his review of Boas's study, Durkheim (1969[1913a]: 675–7) stated that he was in agreement with his American colleague over one essential point:

I too believe that there are no essential differences between primitive thought and the thought of civilized man. All the essential mechanisms of judgement and rationality are imminent within even the most rudimentary civilization, but only in an embryonic form. It is culture that makes them a reality.

We have then a process of evolution, and even of 'creation': 'In one sense, we can say that man had always used the experimental method, but experimental rationality in the true sense comes into existence only with the experimental sciences.' There is a 'great distance' between the two, and it is the weight of 'centuries of culture' that created predispositions; it therefore cannot be said that 'all races and all peoples have the same innate aptitude for all possible forms of mentality'. Durkheim does, however, qualify his statement: 'It is of course quite possible that some races, in particular, are probably wrongly despised; this is very likely to be true of American blacks.'[6]

Lucien Lévy-Bruhl was 'hurt and upset' by the violence and unfairness of Durkheim's criticisms, but did not defend himself and 'suffered in silence' (Albert Rivaud, cited in Merllié 1989).[7] He also turned down Théodule Ribot's invitation to review Durkheim's book for the *Revue philosophique*. It was reviewed by Gustave Belot, who detected a 'rather instructive little scholastic dispute' between Lévy-Bruhl and Durkheim.

Freud on Totem and Taboo

In *The Elementary Forms of Religious Life*, Durkheim uses notions such as 'dream', 'transference' and 'delirium', which are usually associated with the study of psychic phenomena, to analyse the social world. He also speaks of the collective mind and the unconscious. As Lévi-Strauss (1973[1962]: 69) puts it, 'The vogue of hysteria, and that of totemism were contemporary, arising from the same cultural conditions.'[8]

Freud's *Totem and Taboo* was published in 1913, and is subtitled 'Some points of agreement between the mental lives of savages and neurotics'.[9] Freud takes his inspiration from Darwin and Robertson Smith, and speculates that the primitive Oedipus complex and the murder of the father are to be found in all human societies and lie at the origin of all religions. The establishment of the totem prefigures religion, and that of taboo the transition from the savage horde to the organized clan. Totemism, exogamy and the prohibition of incest provide the model for all religions, including monotheism.[10]

In *Totem and Taboo*, Freud deals for the first time with a topic that forces him to rely upon the work of ethnologists, linguists and folklorists. He sets out to analyse totemism, which he describes as 'a religio-social institution which has long been abandoned as an actuality and replaced by newer forms. It has left only the slightest traces behind it in the religions, manners and customs of the civilized peoples of today'. His ambition is to 'deduce the original meaning of totemism from the vestiges remaining of it in childhood – from the hints of it which emerge in the course of the growth of our own children' (Freud 1989[1913]: xxix). He attempts, in other words, to establish a link between the psychopathology of the neuroses of 'civilized' man, primitive cultures and the psychic development of the child. Freud is, however, wary of drawing conclusions that go too far: 'Nor must we let ourselves be influenced too far in our judgement of primitive men by the analogy of neurotics. There are distinctions, too, which must be borne in mind.' Unlike neurotics, 'primitive men are *uninhibited*: thought passes directly into action.' He concludes 'that "In the beginning was the Deed"' (ibid.: 2000).

There are similarities between *Totem and Taboo* and *The Elementary*

Forms of Religious Life. Freud discusses the themes that Durkheim deals with at various points in his work: the prohibition of incest, totemism and exogamy, group marriage, the mother-in-law taboo, animism and magic, the moral consciousness, and religion – and refers to the same authors: Frazer, Lang, MacLennan, Fison, Gillen and Spencer, Morgan, Robertson Smith, Tylor, Westermarck and Wundt. The thesis that totemism is 'a religio-social institution' could have been put forward by Durkheim. Like Durkheim, Freud chooses to study, from a comparative perspective, tribes that have been described by social anthropologists as being 'the most backward and miserable of savages', namely 'the aborigines of Australia, the youngest continent, in whose fauna, too, we can still observe much that is archaic and that has perished elsewhere' (Freud 1989[1913]: 4).

Totem and Taboo contains references to the work of French researchers such as Salomon Reinach, Émile Durkheim, Henri Hubert and Marcel Mauss. Freud sums up Durkheim's main thesis in just a few words: 'The totem, he argues, is the visible representative of social religion amongst the races concerned; it embodies the community, which is the true object of their worship' (Freud 1989[1913]: 141).[11] Yet while Freud, like Durkheim, makes great use of the work of anthropologists, he knows little about sociology. The first reference to sociology to be found in his work comes in his 1913 essay 'The claims of psychoanalysis to scientific interest': in his view, the study of societies is synonymous with the study of civilization, and especially of the origins of myths and religions. Freud therefore makes sociology synonymous with, on the one hand, the study of primitive societies and, on the other, with group psychology, and even speculates about the existence of a 'group soul' which is the seat of the same processes that can be observed in the individual soul.

Totemism As Elementary Religion

The Elementary Forms of Religious Life is subtitled 'Totemism in Australia'. It is a contribution to the contemporary debates about religion, morality and knowledge. Those debates involved the disciplines of anthropology, sociology, the history of religions, psychology and philosophy. The book is also a synthesis of the work that Durkheim and several of his collaborators had been working on for some years, and he described it as 'an attempt to make certain fragmentary contributions to that science', while 'that science' is described as 'a complex one . . . which can advance only slowly and by collective labour' (Durkheim 1995[1912]: 18). 'I am expecting a fine book from Durkheim', Paul Fauconnet wrote to Marcel Mauss, 'and I admire the regularity of his output. I saw the beginning [*sic*]. He borrowed your subject and, to a certain extent, the comparative method. That is proof of how far our influence has spread. I think that he has been rather too clever about describing the method as his own.'[12] 'We will never know', wrote Maurice Leenhardt, 'if it was the uncle or the nephew who first thought about the elementary forms of religion' (Leenhardt 1950: 20).[13] Durkheim was aware of the collective nature of his research, and often cites the work of Hubert and Mauss, as well as that of Robert Hertz. He also attaches great importance to the notion of *mana* (the totemic principle) because of the major role it plays in the development of religious ideas.

The Elementary Forms of Religious Life was 'a book of considerable theoretical importance', but it was, argued Marcel Granet (1930), 'essentially a study of the facts' and 'a model monograph'. The book was ambitious, as it was about the sociology of religions, the theory of knowledge and the general theory of society. And the questions it raised concerned everyone: 'Can we speak of the end of religion?'; 'Is Christianity a thing of the past?'. Durkheim felt that 'the great things of the past that excited our fathers no longer arouse the same zeal along us'. Past ideals 'no longer suit our aspirations', but nothing has taken their place. The period he was living through was, as he said so often, 'a period of transit and moral mediocrity' and was characterized by 'a state of uncertainty and confused anxiety' (Durkheim 1995[1912]: 429). *Elementary Forms* obviously deals with religion (and not just primitive religions), but it also discusses politics and the mode of organization of all societies and groups of assembled individuals.

Durkheim was trying, first of all, to 'discover the causes that allowed religious sentiment to develop in human beings'. He wanted to demonstrate that certain Christian conceptions – such as those pertaining to the soul – were 'as old as religious thought'. His study was part of a vast research programme dealing with 'the human mentality'. It therefore went beyond the limits of the sociology of religion and also dealt with the theory of knowledge. 'Having started out from philosophy, I am trying to get back to philosophy; or rather, I quite naturally went back to philosophy because of the nature of the questions I encountered on my travels.'[14] Those questions, which all philosophers had been asking since the days of Aristotle, concerned the categories of the understanding – in other words, the 'essential notions' of all our intellectual life.

The book is divided into three main sections: 'Preliminary questions', 'Elementary beliefs' and 'Principal ritual attitudes'. The first section is a reworking of the earlier 'Concerning the definition of religious phenomena' (Durkheim 1994[1899]) and 'Examen critique des systèmes classiques sur les origines de la pensée religieuse' (Durkheim 1909).[15] The introduction ('Subject of the study: religious sociology and the theory of knowledge') attempts to define religion, gives a critical account of the two main conceptions of religion (animism and naturism), and attempts to justify, finally, the decision to study Australian totemism as elementary religion. In order to help the reader find his way around, an ethnographic map of Australia is included, with italicized capitals giving the names of some 30 tribes.

Durkheim begins by giving the reader some advice: 'We must begin by freeing our minds of all preconceived ideas'; we must, he repeats, set aside 'our preconceptions, passions or habits' (1995[1912]: 21, 22). This is a study, we are reminded, of all religious systems, 'the most primitive and simple as well as the most modern and refined' (ibid.: 22). All religions will, in other words, be discussed on equal terms. The way the book is organized around two main sections is, he explains, in keeping with his definition of religion as 'a unified system of beliefs and practices relative to sacred things . . . beliefs and practices which unite into a single moral community called a Church, all those who adhere to them' (ibid.: 44). Representations and ritual practices are the constituent elements of all religious life. But although the two are closely intertwined, they are 'different orders of facts', and must therefore be studied separately.

Durkheim begins with beliefs. Book Two is devoted to totemic beliefs in the true sense of the word, and to their origins. Durkheim deliberately restricts the discussion to the 'elementary notions' that are basic to any religion, and places special emphasis on totemic beliefs. He then turns to rituals. Book Three is devoted mainly to the twofold aspect of cults, which are at once negative and positive. Durkheim is therefore not attempting to provide a complete description of primitive cults or to reconstruct all ritual gestures, but to 'choose from the extremely diverse practices the most characteristic that the primitive follows in the celebration of his cult' (1995[1912]: 303). He also ignores oral rituals, which were to have been studied in a separate volume in the *Année sociologique* collection (it was to have been written by Marcel Mauss), but pays particular attention to initiatory rites and to marriage, which involve a major 'change of status.'

Questions of method

Questions of method were always of central importance to Durkheim. He obviously has to justify his decision to study a determinate group of societies, namely the tribes of central Australia, and energetically defends his decision to restrict the discussion to 'a solitary fact' that can 'shed light on a law': 'a multitude of vague and imprecise observations can only lead to confusion. In every kind of science, the scientist would be submerged by the facts that present themselves if he did not make a choice among them' (1995[1912]: 92). 'A single well-made experiment' can, on the other hand, prove a law and can demonstrate that it is 'universally valid' (ibid.: 418).

Although Australia is 'the main object of my research', Durkheim adds that it will be useful to study other societies, such as those of America. He does not propose to study American totemism in its own right, as doing so would require a 'whole set of specific investigations'. He adds in a footnote: 'I will depart from that circle of facts [the Australian data] quite rarely, when a particularly instructive comparison seems essential' (1995[1912]: 95).

Durkheim is often critical of the ethnocentrism that substitutes European ideas for primitive man's ideas about the world and society, and warns against the danger of attributing to primitive man ideas that are beyond his intellectual capabilities. He also raises the issue of whether or not we can believe what the natives say, and is often critical of ethnographers, who are usually happy with the answers they get to the questions they ask.[16]

Durkheim's study is based mainly on his in-depth knowledge of the ethnographic literature (which he discusses in chronological order[17]) but, given that none of this work describes the workings of a totemic religion in its entirety, he pays more attention to more recent research, and especially to that of Walter Baldwin Spencer and Francis James Gillen, which he describes as 'remarkable' on the grounds that their *Native Tribes of Central Australia* (1899) and *The Northern Tribes of Central Australia* (1904) have 'given new life to the study of totemism' (1995[1912]: 88). He also pays a lot of attention to the work of the German missionary Carl Strehlow, who had been living in Australia since 1892 and who had recently published his first observations in four fascicules dealing with the Aranta and Loritja tribes. Their discoveries had given rise to 'an abundant literature' (ibid.). In Durkheim's view, Australia is therefore 'the most favourable terrain for the study of totemism' (ibid.: 90).

In order to develop his argument, Durkheim is anxious to distance himself from both those who deny the religious nature of totemism and those who explain it as deriving from an earlier religion or describe it as a particular form of ancestor worship (Tylor, Wilken). He is also critical of attempts to explain the complex in terms of the simple, and of attempts to reduce clan or collective totemism to individual totemism (Frazer, Boas, Miss Fletcher, Hill-Tout). Such theses fly in the face of the facts: Australian tribes are more 'backward' and are therefore 'the most favourable terrain' because that is where we find the most primitive totemism known to us.

James Frazer is one of Durkheim's main interlocutors: he admires his 'fertile genius' and congratulates him on having adopted, in his later work, an 'intentionally sociological' method. He also has serious criticisms to make of his English colleague: there are significant gaps in his work, and it does not contain any study of mythology. He also criticizes his 'new' theory of totemism, or the claim that it is nothing more than a particular example of the belief in miraculous births, or the belief that women are impregnated by the spirits of the animals or plants surrounding them.

In the review he and Mauss wrote of his own *Elementary Forms of Religious Life*, Durkheim stresses the difference between himself and James Frazer. Durkheim is interested in studying a restricted group of societies (Australia), whereas Frazer wishes to make 'a comprehensive survey' of 'all the peoples among whom totemism is to be found' (Durkheim and Mauss 1994[1913]: 178). For Durkheim, totemism is 'a religion in the true sense of the word'.[18] For Frazer, it is 'a disorganized accumulation of magical superstitions': Frazer fails to recognize the 'social character' of totemism. Durkheim throws its social character into relief, as we can see from his analysis of the 'genuine state of ecstasy' into which the group of individuals enters. 'It is a fact that society produces sacred things at will and then stamps on them the characteristics of religion' (ibid.: 179).

For Durkheim, totemism is therefore a religion because totemic beliefs make 'a distinction between the sacred and the profane' (Durkheim and Mauss 1994[1913]: 178). It is also more complex than it might seem: it refers to the sacred by making use of three categories of things (the totemic emblem, the plant or animal, and the clan members). Totemism is not a collection of fragmentary beliefs, but a system of ideas that offers a 'total representation' of the world, or a conception of the universe. Turning to the notions of 'genus' and 'class', Durkheim then reiterates the conclusions he reached at the end of *Primitive Classification* (Durkheim and Mauss 1963[1903]).

Durkheim's argument can be summarized by what seems to be a simple equation: totemism = sacred things = religion. The origins or basis of religion are to not to be found in distinct beings, but in 'anonymous and impersonal forces' that are identifiable in certain animals, men or images but that cannot be identified with any of them. 'Taking the word "god" in a very broad sense, one could say that it is the god that each totemic cult worships. But it is an impersonal god, without name, without history, immanent in the world, diffused in a numberless multitude of things' (1995[1912]: 191). This 'quasi-divine entity' is truly ubiquitous and resides in 'force'. When he speaks of 'forces', Durkheim is referring to actual forces 'that bring about physical effects mechanically'. These impersonal and anonymous forces are like the physical forces studied by the natural sciences, and he likens the 'shock' felt by an individual who comes into contact with them to 'the effect of an electrical charge' (ibid.: 192). They can also be seen as 'fluids' that play the role of the life-principle.

Summing up his own book, Durkheim writes: 'If the moral force which is the soul of religion is divested of its material symbols, what remains is collective power. This is why, in so many lower religions, the power worshipped by the members of the cult is known in an anonymous and impersonal form: it is the Melanesian and Polynesian *mana*, the *waken* of the Sioux, etc' (Durkheim and Mauss 1994[1913]: 179). The notion of *mana* plays a vital role in both the development of religious ideas and in the history of scientific thought: 'It is the notion of force in its earliest form' (1995[1912]: 205).

The central thesis of *Elementary Forms* is that there exists a moral force, that it is the source of religion, and that this moral force is 'the collective force'. It is an 'anonymous force' that is made up of ideas and sentiments, and 'it can only live and act in and through particular *consciences.* Accordingly, it permeates them, and in doing so assumes individual characteristics' (Durkheim and Mauss 1994[1913]: 179). This is how the idea of a soul comes into being, and then the idea of 'the personality'. 'From souls to spirits there is but a single step.' There then emerges 'a group of rites which play a leading rite in the social life of these peoples, namely, initiation rites' (ibid.: 180). Religion is therefore above all 'a system of actions aimed at making and perpetually remaking the soul of the collectivity and of the individual'. Durkheim does not deny that religion has a 'speculative part to play', but insists that its principal function is 'dynamogenic:

It gives the individual the strength which enables him to surpass himself, to rise about his nature and to control it. The only moral forces superior to those which the individual *qua* individual has at his command are those issuing from individuals in association. That is why religious forces are and can only be collective forces. (Durkheim and Mauss 1994[1913]: 180)[19]

Elementary beliefs

In totemic religions, the most important beliefs 'naturally' concern the totem (meaning the clan's totem). At the basis of nearly all Australian tribes, there is one group that plays a dominant role: the clan. The main characteristics of the clan are as follows: (1) its members are united by ties of kinship simply because they have the same name; (2) the objects that designate the clan collectively, and which usually belong to the animal (kangaroo, crow) or vegetable kingdoms, are known as *totems* (1995[1912]: 100). Totemism therefore must be discussed in relation to the totemic clan's family role and Durkheim has to explain the rules. In the tribes he is studying, the child takes the totem of its mother, 'by birth' (ibid.: 104). He then recalls the distinctions that must be made between clan, phratry (a group of clans united by fraternal ties) and tribe (usually with two phratries). He also identifies another secondary group, namely the matrimonial class (sometimes two and sometimes four per phratry) (ibid.: 104–7).

The totem is an emblem or 'coat of arms' rather than a name, and it holds 'an important place' in the social life of primitives' (1995[1912]: 114). Totemic emblems are even found on the bodies of men (totemic tattoos). The totem is a 'collective label', and it also has a religious character. Durkheim dwells at some length on the instruments used in totemic rites. *Churinga*, for example, are engraved with a design representing the totem, and they are 'pre-eminently sacred things'. It is often believed that *churinga* 'serve as the residence of an ancestor's soul' (ibid.: 118, 121), but according to Durkheim, it is because they bear the totemic mark that they are sacred. Why, then, does the Australian 'feel a strong inclination to represent his totem'? Durkheim's explanation is that 'he simply feels the need to represent the idea which he has of it by means of an outward and physical sign, no matter what that sign may be' (ibid.: 126).

Durkheim now turns from images to the 'real beings' that are associated with the totemic object. These are totemic animals and plants, and they too are surrounded by rituals. Animals and plants normally play the 'profane role' of providing food, but if it is forbidden to eat them, they become 'sacred things'. The prohibition may take the form of a ban on eating, killing, gathering or, in some cases, touching. But whatever the nature of the prohibition, the figures representing the totem are accorded more respect than the things themselves. Durkheim therefore concludes that in totemic religion, in other words, it is not the totemic animal that is 'pre-eminently sacred' but the pictorial representation of it, 'because this symbol is the emblem or flag of the clan' (Durkheim and Mauss 1994[1913b]: 178).

What, asks Durkheim, is the place of man in the scheme of religious things? A man is regarded as a 'profane being' in everyday usage, but in the totemic system, 'every member of the clan is invested with a sacredness'. Every member of the clan is 'a man in the usual sense of the word and an animal or plant of the totemic species' (1995[1912]: 133). This duality, 'which to us is so strange', may occasion a 'logical shock' (ibid.: 134). Some organs are 'especially identified' with sacredness, 'most of all the blood and the hair', because 'the human body contains in its depths a sacred principle (ibid.: 136, 137). The clan member bears the name of the plant or animal of the totemic species because 'identity in name is presumed to entail an identity in nature' (1995[1912]: 134). There is something sacred about both the emblem – an animal or plant – and the clan member.

Collective Totemism and Individual Totemism

Durkheim now pursues his analysis. While the 'active ferment' of the religious life can be found within the clan, 'which enjoys very great autonomy' (1995[1912]: 156) and whose members are united by a single principle (the totem), the tribe cannot be ignored: the totemic religion is a 'complex system formed by . . . the union of all the particular cults addressed to the different divinities'. There is therefore a certain similarity between totemic religion (with its many totems) and Greek religion (with its different divinities). The segmentation of the tribe into clans and sub-clans poses no threat to its unity, as the individual cults are at once autonomous and bound up with one another. Totemic religion must, therefore, 'result from a sort of consensus among all the members of the tribe, without distinction' (ibid.: 156).

Totemism is a 'public institution' and it would appear that the individual has a part in it 'only as a member of a group', but Durkheim also points out that 'there is no religion without an individual aspect'. The same is true of totemism: 'There are totems that belong to each individual, that express his personality, and whose cult he celebrates privately' (1995[1912]: 157). Such totems are acquired, and not given. Durkheim now identifies 'sexual totemism' which is found in both male and female 'sexual corporations', and which appears to be intermediate between individual and collective totemism (ibid.: 166). And given that there are two sorts of totemism – that of the individual and that of the clan – 'it is appropriate to ask whether the one is not derived from the other and, if the answer is yes, to ask which is the more primitive' (1995[1912]: 174).

Even when they make no reference to spirits or god, all these beliefs are, in Durkheim's view, religious because they imply that things are classified as either sacred or profane. There is obviously something mysterious about this relationship between men and animals. What are the origins of these beliefs? Durkheim asks what causes the rise of the religious sentiment, before going on to refute theories – such as those of Tylor and Willen – that argue that totemism derives from an earlier religion, from the 'cult of the ancestors' or, like Jevons, that link it to a nature-cult. Durkheim rejects the view that religion originates in 'a well-considered act of will' (1995[1912]: 174): religions are 'complex things' and 'the needs they satisfy are too numerous and obscure' for that to be the case.' He is also critical of authors such as Frazer and Boas, who attempt to explain the complex by the simple. Such theories are 'ingenious intellectual constructs without empirical support' (1995[1912]: 177). It cannot be argued that religion is born in the consciousness of the individual, or that it is a response to individual aspirations.

The idea of force. Mana

'Totemism is the religion . . . of a kind of anonymous and impersonal force', of 'an impersonal god, without name, without history, immanent in the world'. Does this mean that it is the religion of a 'quasi-divine entity' (1995[1912]: 191)? Durkheim uses that expression on several occasions. In order to represent this 'diffuse energy' or 'force', the imagination uses images borrowed from the animal or vegetable kingdoms. These are, he adds 'veritable forces', 'even material forces', that have 'physical effects'. They also have a moral character and a moral power: 'The totem is a source of the clan's moral life' (ibid.: 192). Religions prove to be a 'means enabling men to face the world with greater confidence', and Durkheim gives the example of Christianity and the idea that God the Father is 'the guardian of the physical order as well as the legislator and judge of human conduct (ibid.: 193).

This might mean 'imputing ideas to the primitive that are beyond his intellect' (1995[1912]: 193), and in order to defend himself against the charge of being 'reckless' (ibid.: 197), Durkheim draws a comparison between the native religions of Samoa and those of various American tribes such as the Sioux and the Iroquois. They all have words to describe this immaterial force. The Sioux speak of *waken*, the Iroquois of *orenda,* and the Melanesians of *mana*. Gods, demons, genii and gods are, according to Durkheim, nothing more that the various concrete forms taken by this energy or force. The origins of religion lie not in determinate beings or objects, but in 'indefinite powers and anonymous forces' (ibid.: 202), and their impersonality is strictly comparable to that of the physical forces studied by the natural sciences. The origins of the notion of force are religious, but the notion also has 'a secular aspect that gives it relevance for the history of scientific thought as well . . . The idea of force is of religious origin. From religion, philosophy first and then the sciences borrowed it.' This had already been foreseen by Comte who 'made metaphysics the heir of "theology"'(ibid.: 202, 206).

'A Sort of Electricity'

How did men come up with this idea? asks Durkheim as he attempts to pursue his analysis and to explain the origins of the notion of *mana*. The totem is, above all, a symbol, a 'material expression of something else'. This thing is the outward and visible form of both 'the totemic principle or god', and that of a society, namely the clan. 'Thus, if the totem is symbol of both the god and the society, is this not because the god and the society are one and the same?' Durkheim therefore advances the hypothesis that: 'Thus, the god of the clan, the totemic principle, can be none other than the clan itself, but the clan transfigured and imagined in the physical form of the plant or animal that serves as totem' (ibid.: 208).

Well aware that his hypothesis will lead to an outcry, Durkheim raises the issue of the origins of this 'apotheosis'. It is clear, he argues, that a society 'has all that is required to arouse the sensation of the divine. A society is to its members what a god is to its faithful' (1995[1912]: 208). It fosters in us the 'sense of perpetual dependence', submits us to rules of conduct and thought (which may be contrary to our inclinations), 'categorically demands our cooperation', and subjects us to 'sacrifice'. This is not a matter of 'utilitarian calculation' (as a cost-benefit analysis would have it), but of 'respect': 'That intensity is what we call moral influence' (ibid.: 209). This is why even short commands leave no place for hesitation. The same might be said of 'the state of opinion, eminently a social thing', which is a 'source of authority' (ibid.: 210). Even science, which is often described as the antagonist of opinion, derives its authority from opinion; 'All the scientific demonstrations in the world would have no influence if a people had no faith in science' (ibid.). Durkheim expresses the hope that his analysis will put an end to 'erroneous interpretations of my ideas' and the impression that he considers 'physical constraint to be the entire essence of social life' (ibid.: 210 n6). Sociology is primarily interested in moral authority: the distinctive characteristic of sociological phenomena is 'social pressure'. What is more, the action of 'collective force' is not external: 'because society can exist only in and by means of individual minds . . . that force thus becomes an integral part of our being and, by the same stroke, uplifts and brings it to maturity' (ibid.: 211). The 'stimulating and invigorating effect of society' is especially obvious in certain circumstances, as 'in the midst of an assembly that becomes worked up' (ibid.: 211–12). In such circumstances, individuals become susceptible to doing and feeling things that they would never otherwise do or feel.

Durkheim gives several examples of the 'general exaltation' that results from revolutionary or creative epochs in which there is a 'general stimulation of individual forces' (1995[1912]: 213). He mentions the Crusades, Joan of Arc (who heard voices), and the French Revolution (when 'the harmless bourgeois is transformed into either a hero or an executioner'). The same phenomena can be observed in the periodical meetings that are organized by parties (political, economic or confessional): they allow their member to 'revivify their common faith by manifesting it in common', and to strengthen sentiments which 'if left to themselves, would soon weaken'. When a man starts to speak, he provokes a feeling that returns to him, but 'enlarged and amplified': 'It is then no longer a mere individual who speaks but a group incarnated and personified' (ibid.: 212). Such situations generate the general enthusiasm that is characteristic of revolutionary and creative epochs. Such hyperactivity results in 'a general stimulation of individual forces'. Under the influence of this general exaltation, passions are intensified and violence may result.

In Durkheim's view, the origins of religion lie in all these mental processes. What is true of exceptional circumstances is also true of everyday life: the affection of others gives us a feeling of comfort, and expressions of gratitude improve our self-esteem. Being in moral harmony with our fellows gives us confidence and courage. It produces 'a perpetual sustenance for our moral nature'. It provides a 'moral support': this is the 'moral conscience'. The social environment in which we live is alive with forces: some are free, but others are fixed in the methods and traditions that we employ – for example, language, rights and the 'treasury of knowledge' that is transmitted from one generation to the next. These are what Durkheim calls the 'benefits of civilization': 'Man is man only because he is civilized.' The society in which we live is 'at once demanding and helpful, majestic and kind' (1995[1912]: 214).

Two 'distinct and separate states' form in our consciousness, and give us the impression that we are dealing with 'two distinct sorts of reality' separated by a sharply drawn line of demarcation: the world of sacred things on the one hand, and the world of profane things on the other. Society is constantly creating sacred things and, for instance, conferring majesty upon sovereigns and politicians. This is due to public opinion: we keep ourselves at a distance from high personages, approach them with precaution and use a different language when we speak to them. Society also consecrates ideas, such as the idea of progress or free examination. The best example of society's 'aptitude for setting itself up as a god' is, according to Durkheim, the French Revolution and, more specifically, the first years of the Revolution: public opinion transformed the ideas of fatherland, liberty and reason into sacred things that became the object of a 'veritable cult (1995[1912]: 216).

Durkheim takes these examples from Western societies to demonstrate to his readers how the clan can suggest the idea of social forces to its members, and then ceases to speak in general terms in order to show how collective action can also give the clan a sense of the sacred. He then goes back to Australian societies and, like Mauss in his study of Eskimo societies, analyses the different phases that characterize their lives. Their lives are divided between a period of dispersal in which the population lives in small groups and in which economic activity predominates, and periods of concentration marked by collective gatherings or religious ceremonies. Such gatherings are characterized by 'transports of enthusiasm', with 'chaotic movements, shouting, screaming, gathering dust and throwing it in all directions' (1995[1912]: 217). People behave like madmen. Citing Spencer and Gillen, Durkheim describes these ceremonies, which usually take place at night, as a scene of 'truly wild frenzy' (ibid.: 219). Gestures and cries give way to songs and dances. The commotion is regulated, but 'a regulated commotion is still a commotion' (ibid.: 218). Wearing decorations and masks, it seems to the individual that 'he has become a 'new being'. In order to describe the effects these gatherings have on their participants, Durkheim speaks of 'a sort of electricity' which quickly transports them to an extraordinary height of exaltation (ibid.: 217). This effervescence finds expression in an 'intense hyper-excitement of physical and mental life as a whole', extraordinary actions and passions of such impetuosity that individuals are 'above and beyond ordinary morality': men exchange wives and, sometimes, incestuous unions are contracted (ibid. 218).

The life of these people oscillates between periods of utter colourlessness and periods of high excitement. The former is that of the profane world, the latter that of sacred things, and the two are mutually incomparable. Durkheim's hypothesis is that religion is a product of these moments of hyper-excitement or effervescence: 'Indeed, we may well ask whether this starkness of contrast may have been necessary to release the experience of the sacred in its first form.' Because it is compressed into limited periods, collective life attains a maximum intensity and power, 'thereby giving man a more vivid sense of the twofold existence he leads and the twofold nature in which he participates' (1995[1912]: 221).

It might seem surprising that the external forces which dominate the members of the clan should be thought of under the forms of totems. In order to explain this, Durkheim invokes what he calls the 'well-known law that the feelings a thing arouses in us are spontaneously transmitted to the symbol that represents it' (1995[1912]: 221). Black is the symbol of mourning, and the flag is the emblem of the fatherland. Similarly, the totem is the flag of the clan: there is 'a transfer of feelings' (ibid.). This is especially true of primitive peoples: 'the clan is too complex a reality for such unformed minds to be able to bring its concrete unity into clear focus' (ibid.: 222). This allows Durkheim to understand 'all that is essential' in totemic beliefs: 'religious force is none other than the collective and anonymous force of the clan'; the totemic emblem 'is, so to speak, the visible body of the god', and therefore 'holds first place in the series of sacred things'. The clan, like every other form of society, 'can only live in and by means of the individual consciousnesses of which it is made' (ibid.: 223). The force that transports the individual into the world of sacred things is inherent in him, but also comes to him from the outside.

Durkheim also brings out the ambiguity of these religious forces: they are at once physical and human, moral and material. They reside in men, but they are also the 'vital energy' of things. Their double nature is in his view a central explanatory principle: 'Because of its double nature, religion was able to be the womb in which the principal seeds of human civilization have developed' (1995[1912]: 224–55). Everything springs from religion: the techniques that serve the moral life (law, morality, the arts) and those that serve material life (the natural and technical sciences).

Illusion or delirium?

The earliest religious conceptions have often been attributed to feelings of weakness, and to man's fear and weakness on coming into contact with the world; men are, that is, victims of the nightmares of which they are themselves the creators. They are, it has been claimed, 'fantasmatic images' or dream-like 'aberrations'. Durkheim rejects that thesis and attempts to demonstrate that, far from being an 'inexplicable hallucination', religion gains 'a foothold in reality': 'That power exists, it is society.' Behind these figures, there is a concrete and living reality. The Australian is not 'the dupe of an illusion', and religion is not a 'fabric of errors'. Not only does religion provide a representation of the physical world: 'It is a system of ideas by means of which individuals imagine the society of which they are members.' Religion has 'a sense and a reasonableness that the most militant rationalist cannot fail to recognize' (1995[1912]: 226, 227).

Religion has been described as the product of a 'certain delusion', and it is quite true that religious life cannot attain any degree of intensity 'and not carry with it a psychic exaltation that is connected to delirium' (1995[1912]: 228). Prophets, founders of religions and great saints have an exceptionally sensitive religious consciousness, and 'often show symptoms of an excitability that is extreme and even pathological'. But while religion is not without a certain delirium, that delirium is *well-founded*: these images are not pure illusions, and 'correspond to something real' (ibid.). Similarly, every collective representation is in a sense delirious because it projects feelings on to things: 'The whole social world seems populated with forces that in reality exist only in our minds' (ibid.). Durkheim gives the examples of the flag (which is only a piece of cloth), human blood (which is only an organic fluid) and the postage stamp (which, when franked, may be worth a fortune): 'From the most commonplace objects, [collective representations] can make a sacred and very powerful being' (ibid.: 229). There is therefore something very specific about the social realm: 'There, far more than anywhere else, the idea creates the reality' (ibid.). Durkheim is even critical of the materialist theories on which he once relied and which, like the geographical realism of the German geographer Ratzen, 'derive all of social life from its material substrate (either economic or territorial)' and forget that 'ideas are realities – forces' (ibid.: 230 n41).

Any collective representation works on the basis of a pseudo-delirium, but Durkheim insists that this is not a delusion in the strict sense of that term, as the ideas that are objectified are grounded in reality – in other words, the nature of society. Objectification always requires an object – it doesn't matter what object – that becomes sacred. 'Nowhere can a collective feeling become conscious of itself without fixing upon a tangible object' (1995[1912]: 238). This is a general law: 'without symbols, moreover, social feeling could have only an unstable existence' (ibid.: 232). It follows that 'in all its aspects and at every moment of its history, social life is only possible thanks to a vast symbolism' (ibid.: 233). When the assembly has ended, the passions it aroused are extinguished, and those who were present feel a need to mark their bodies as a reminder of their common experience. Tattooing is one example: the tattoo is a kind of emblem that inscribes a distinctive mark on the body and expresses 'a communion of minds'. It was practised by both primitive people and the earlier Christians, and is still practised by sailors, soldiers and prisoners (ibid.: 234).

Religious Evolution and Logical Evolution

'Logical evolution is closely interconnected with religious evolution and, like religious evolution, depends upon social conditions', writes Durkheim (1995[1912]: 236). It is true that primitive logic seems 'crude' and 'unsettling', but Durkheim insists that 'we must be careful not to depreciate it', as it 'was a momentous contribution to the intellectual development of humanity'. It provided 'the first explanation of the world'. Indeed, religions rendered 'a great service' by constructing a first representation of what the relations of kinship between things might be. By suggesting that there may be internal connections between things, they opened up the way for science and philosophy. In order to create a 'world of ideals', a 'hyperexcitation of intellectual forces' was required, and that is possible 'only in and through society' (ibid.: 237, 239). In other words, collective thought was required. Durkheim therefore concludes that this 'mentality is far from being unrelated to our own. Our own logic was born in that logic.' The explanations offered by contemporary society are 'more certain, being objective' because they are based upon rigorously controlled observations, 'but they are not different in nature from those that satisfy primitive thought' (ibid.: 240).

The differences between Durkheim and Lévy-Bruhl are obvious. The latter holds that violation of 'the principle of contradiction' is the defining feature of the mentality of 'inferior' societies, which are therefore characterized by a certain 'one-sidedness'. Durkheim, in contrast, insists that there is no gulf between the logic of religious thought and that of scientific thought: 'Both are made up of the same essential elements, although those elements are unequally and differently developed' (1995[1912]: 241).

The dualism of body and soul

The idea of the soul is vague and variable: 'If we asked our contemporaries how they imagine the soul . . . the responses we would get would not have much greater coherence and precision [than those of the Australian]' (1995[1912]: 243). Durkheim's hypothesis is that the idea of a soul is not specific to the 'more advanced' religions: it is 'contemporaneous with humanity' (ibid.: 242). The work of the more advanced religious has been confined to refining it. Durkheim uses the ethnographic data to raise a whole series of questions that were once a matter for theology. Do women have a soul? Is there a hell beneath the earth and a heaven above the sky? Does the fate of souls depend upon the way they behaved on earth? What about reincarnation? Is sexual intercourse a necessary prelude to reproduction? Is the soul immortal?

The soul is essentially inconsistent and indeterminate, immaterial and independent of the body. When it is freed from the body, its goes to the land of souls. On the one hand, the soul, and on the other, the body. What led men into thinking that there are two beings within them? Durkheim's study of primitive myths leads him to the conclusion that: 'in a general way, the soul is none other than the totemic principle incarnated in each individual.' This comes as no surprise: 'Just as society exists through individuals, the totemic principle lives only in and through the individual consciousnesses whose coming together forms the clan' (1995[1912]: 251, 252).

The question of the individual and his identity is therefore far from being of secondary importance to Durkheim's analysis, which also deals with the doctrine of reincarnation (of which the Arunta apparently know nothing). There is such a thing as a religious principle. It emanates from an ancestor, is the essence of every individual, and is inevitably individualized. The ancestral soul, the totemic being and the individual soul are 'made of the same matter and substance' (1995[1912]: 257). The soul is something sacred (unlike the body, which is profane) and contains a particle of divinity. This is not, Durkheim insists, an illusion: 'There truly is a parcel of divinity in us because there is in us a parcel of the great ideals that are the goal of humanity.' The individual soul is 'only a portion of the group's collective soul . . . it is *mana* individualized' (ibid.: 267).

What of the belief in immortality, or the belief that the soul lives on after death? The primitive generally accepts the idea of death with a sort of indifference: 'accustomed to endangering his life continually, he easily lets go of it' (1995[1912]: 270). Could the conception of a posthumous life come to us from our experience of dreams? 'Our dead relatives and friends reappear to us in dreams: we see them acting and hear them speaking; it is natural to draw the conclusion that they still exist' (ibid.: 270–1). Durkheim finds this explanation inadequate. The belief in immortality is a sign of the 'perpetuity of the group's life. The individuals die, but the clan survives' (ibid.: 271).

Durkheim closes this section with an analysis of the idea of 'personality'. One element in the personality is impersonal or collective, while the other is individual or specific to the singular subject or individual. The 'individuating factor' is, he contends, the body. On the one hand, the organism (and the impressions and representations we derive from it); on the other, the ideas and sentiments which come from and express society (such as the ideas, beliefs and feelings that supply the basis of our moral life). This relatively independent 'world of representations' is therefore superimposed upon its 'material substrate', and this gives the actor the impression of both determinism and freedom: 'the only means we have of liberating ourselves from physical forces is to oppose them with collective forces' (1995[1912]: 274).[20]

Religious evolution is, according to Durkheim, characterized by two tendencies: on the one hand, 'the idea of spirit marks an important advance of the individuation of religious forces'; on the other, the emergence of 'higher-order mythical personalities' (1995[1912]: 286) leads to a 'religious internationalism'. Religious beliefs have a natural 'tendency' for going beyond boundaries and for 'spreading and becoming internationalized' (ibid.: 292). Societies constantly exchange ideas and the internationalization of totems (those of phratries) leads to the emergence of one god who, being immortal and eternal, is 'creator of the world, legislator of the moral order'. The notion of one god derives from 'the awareness of tribe': 'the various cults peculiar to each clan come together and complement one another in such a way as to form a unified whole' (ibid.: 299). Is this idea 'a European importation' or an indigenous notion? Durkheim is convinced that ideas relating to the existence of a high god are 'indigenous' and he rejects the idea of 'a mysterious revelation' that is so dear to Christianity (ibid.: 293).

Rites

At the end of Book Two, Durkheim argues that it is impossible to restrict the discussion to representations alone: belief and cults are indeed inter-dependent, but while it is true to say that a cult is dependent upon beliefs, the converse is also true. The idea that rites are a constituent part of religious life reflects, we can assume, the young Durkheim's own experience of Talmudic Judaism, which attaches great importance to rituals and to a whole set of regulations and multiple prohibitions. The Bible, for example, 'commands the woman to live in isolation for a definite period each month' (1995[1912]: 32).[21] Such remarks also reflect, however, the methodological perspective developed by Sylvain Lévi under the influence of his teacher Abel Berdaigne. The same perspective is central to Mauss and Hubert's study of sacrifice, which looked at two religions: Hinduism and Judaism (see Strenski 1997).

When he turns to the study of rites, Durkheim outlines an initial classification based on the distinction between negative and positive rites. He begins by discussing negative cults. They involve abstentions and privations, and consist in observing prohibitions, rather as though we could not detach ourselves from the profane world that is 'the natural theatre of our activity' without doing 'violence to our nature'. Pain is one of the negative cult's conditions of existence, and the belief that pain has a 'sanctifying power' is common to both the most primitive and 'the most recent and idealistic' religions (1995[1912]: 317).

In Durkheim's view, 'asceticism serves more than religious ends. Here, as elsewhere, religious interests are only social and moral interests in symbolic form' (1995[1912]: 321). Society is only possible at this price: 'of necessity, it requires perpetual sacrifice [of individuals]', and does violence to our natural appetites. A certain asceticism is thus inherent in all social life and 'an integral part of all human culture' (ibid.). Prohibitions imply a distinction between the sacred and the profane. The sacred and profane worlds use different languages, different gestures and involve different attitudes. There must therefore be an empty space between them because the sacred has an extraordinary 'contagiousness' that derives from 'the special nature' of religious things. Religious forces are transmitted in much the same way as heat or electricity: they are 'transfigured collective forces', made up of 'ideas and feelings that the spectacle of society awakens in us' (ibid.: 327). This is as true of the most primitive religions as it is of the most recent cults. Positive cults, on the other hand, uphold positive and bilateral relations with the sacred. Durkheim gives the example of sacrifice during the *intichiuma* initiation ceremony, which can be observed in all Australian societies. The cult was 'discovered' by the observations of Spencer and Gillen (subsequently confirmed by Strehlow), but it is 'closer to us than its apparent crudeness might have led us to believe' (ibid.: 343). While he relies upon Hubert and Mauss's work on sacrifice, Durkheim describes the most elementary form of the sacrificial institution (which involves a totemic meal or alimentary communion) in great detail, because it will become one of the foundations of higher religions. There is therefore something universal about this cult. All this is, of course, hypothetical, but its existence 'can no longer be disputed' (ibid.: 344).

It is, Durkheim insists, belief that gives ritual objects their sacred character: 'The sacred things are sacred only because they are imagined as sacred . . . the gods are in [a] state of dependence on the thought of man' (1995[1912]: 349–50). He also speaks of 'a mutually reinforcing exchange of good deeds between the deity and his worshippers . . . No doubt, the men could not live without the gods; but on the other hand, the gods would die if they were not worshipped.' Sacred beings are 'superior to men, but they can only live in human consciousnesses' (ibid.: 350, 351).

Social life is like a circle: on the one hand, 'the individual gets the best part of himself from society' – intellectual and moral culture, language, the arts, the sciences, and beliefs. If he did not, he would 'fall to the rank of animality'. On the other hand, 'society exists and lives only in and through individuals'. Durkheim is clearly proud of this insight: 'Here we touch upon the solid rock on which all the cults are built' (1995[1912]: 351). The function of religious ceremonies is to set the group in motion, to bring individuals together, to multiply relations between them, and to change the content of their consciousness. This is obvious from the difference between 'ordinary' days and feast days: on the one hand, utilitarian and individual preoccupations and, on the other, feasts, collective beliefs, reminders of tradition and the memory of great ancestors. On the one hand, private interests and, on the other, public – and therefore social – interests.

The positive cult 'naturally' takes periodic forms: there is a cycle of feasts that return at regular intervals. All this promotes a 'collective renewal', and every individual benefits from it: 'the individual soul is regenerated'. The same applies to the rhythms of religious and social life: 'Society is able to revivify the sentiment of itself only by assembling.' But society cannot be assembled all the time and cannot remain in congregation indefinitely. Hence the cyclical nature of feasts, which are often associated with the seasons. Durkheim endorses the conclusions of Marcel Mauss's essay on seasonal variations amongst the Eskimos. He also observes that 'The more societies develop, the less they seem to allow of too great intermittences' (1995[1912]: 354).

Durkheim now goes on to discuss mimetic rites in which the calls and movements of totemic animals are imitated; he describes them in detail. 'Though bizarre and grotesque in appearance', these jumps, cries and movements have in reality 'a meaning that is profound and human'. The participants actually believe that they are animals or plants, and 'they bear witness to one another that they are members of the same moral community' (1995[1912]: 362). Such rites make and remake kinship, 'for it exists only insofar as it is believed, and the effect of all these collective demonstrations is to keep alive the beliefs on which it is founded' (ibid.). All these ceremonies are 'salutary' in that they allow the worshippers to 'remake their moral being': 'The power of the rite over minds, which is real, [makes] them believe in its power over things, which is imaginary' (ibid.: 364). What applies to Australians also applies to the followers of more advanced religions: 'For both, this is a means of communicating with the sacred, that is, with the collective ideal that the sacred symbolizes' (ibid.: 362).

Turning to the function of rites, Durkheim argues that they are 'means by which the social group reaffirms itself periodically' (1995[1912]: 390). We can see this quite clearly from the totemic cult, which is the 'earliest form of cult': 'men who feel united – in part by ties of blood but even more by common interests and traditions – assemble and become conscious of their moral unity . . . they conceive this unity as a very special kind of con-substantiality. They regard themselves as all participating in the nature of a certain animal' (ibid.: 391).

> [These] childish games, naive and gauche gestures [and] crude modes of representation express and nurture a feeling of pride, confidence and rev-erence that is entirely comparable to the feeling expressed by the faith-ful of the most idealist religion when, gathered together, they proclaim themselves to be the children of the all-powerful God. (Ibid.)

Durkheim uses Spencer's and Gillen's descriptions of the ceremonies of the Warramunga to demonstrate that they do not serve any utilitarian purpose: they are a way of awakening feelings, and of relating the past to the present, and the individual to the community. They are, in other words, designed 'to revitalize the most essential elements of the collective consciousness and conscience' (1995[1912]: 379). He describes these com-memorative rites as performances or 'dramatic representations': 'the cele-brant is not playing the ancestral personage . . . he is that very personage' (ibid.: 378). The similarity with a dramatic performance is in fact obvious:

these rites serve no utilitarian purpose. They make men 'forget the real world so as to transport them into another where their imagination is more at home; they entertain' (ibid.: 384). This is, according to Durkheim a well-known fact: games and the principal forms of art seem to have been born in religion, and 'to have long retained their religious character'. Durkheim thus brings out an important aspect of religion, namely its aesthetic side: 'Although religious thought is something other than a system of fictions, the realities to which it corresponds can gain religious expression only if imagination transfigures them.' This is why religious thought lends itself to the 'free creations of the mind'. Durkheim regards works of art as a 'surplus' that finds expression in 'supplementary and superfluous works of luxury'. Jumping, whirling, dancing, shouting and singing serve no purpose; 'they merely satisfy the worshippers' need to act, move and gesticulate'. It is difficult to subordinate this exuberance to specific goals: these are 'games'. Games and art help to refresh 'a spirit worn down by all that is overburdening in day to day labour' (ibid.: 385).

There is obviously more to religion that this: 'When a rite serves only as entertainment, it is no longer a rite'. A rite is not just a game: 'It belongs to the serious side of life' (1995[1912]: 386). While the 'imaginary element' is not essential, it does not follow that it is negligible. It is what gives religion its 'appeal'. Religious ceremonies are closely associated with festivals, and vice versa. The cries, the songs and music 'carry men outside themselves'. Durkheim cites the examples of the secular feasts which 'put the masses into motion' and induce states of effervescence that border on the delirious, and of the popular feasts that break down the barriers between the licit and the illicit.[22]

Sad celebrations

The final chapter of the book is devoted to 'piacular rites' and to the ambiguity of the notion of the sacred.[23] Positive rites are performed in a state of confidence, happiness and enthusiasm: they are 'joyful feasts'. Then there are the sad celebrations that Durkheim describes as 'piacular'. These are ways of dealing with misfortune, with anything that bodes ill and anything that inspires sorrow or fear. The first example he gives is that of mourning and the abstentions that are associated with it: the name of the dead must not be pronounced, there must be no communication with strangers, and the ordinary occupations of life are suspended. 'The deceased man is a sacred being.' Women must cut their hair, remain silent throughout the period of mourning, and weep. Durkheim gives a long description of Australian 'final rites' (1995[1912]: 399). These mark the end of the period of mourning, and are characterized by extreme effervescence and bloodletting. The women wail, throw themselves to the ground, strike themselves and slash themselves with stones: 'In mourning, people hurt themselves in order to prove that they are in the grip of suffering' (ibid.: 400). The death of one of its members stirs up the emotions of the group. It experiences a kind of anger and exasperation. Its emotions are mixed: anguished sorrow and mutual piety: 'The dead man is not mourned because he is feared; he is feared because he is mourned' (ibid.: 405).

One initial fact remains constant: 'Mourning is not the spontaneous expression of individual emotions.' It is not 'the natural response of a private sensibility that is wounded by a cruel loss; it is an obligation imposed by the group.' The pain is certainly real, but there is no connection between these feelings and the gestures of those who perform the rite. They are expressions of a ritual attitude that is obligatory and sanctioned by punishment. Feelings become intensified because they are expressed collectively: 'something like a panic of sadness ensues' (1995[1912], 400, 404).

How are we to explain this cruelty? Durkheim sets aside mythical explanations in order to 'confront the reality they translate but distort'. These are 'collective rites', and they induce a 'state of effervescence' in those who take part in them. Durkheim gives the examples of fasting during Lent and on the anniversary of the fall of Jerusalem. If the believer is sad, 'it is first and foremost because he forces himself to be and disciplines himself to be; and he disciplines himself in order to affirm his faith' (1995[1912]: 403). The same is true of the Australian who, when he weeps and groans, is not merely expressing a personal sadness; he is also fulfilling a duty.

The death of one of its members enfeebles the group. It feels diminished, unites and gathers together to revive its strength. The 'sensation of renewed strength' counteracts the original enfeeblement: 'One comes out of mourning, and one comes out of it thanks to mourning itself' (1995[1912]: 405). This is the main point that Durkheim wishes to make: 'When social feeling suffers a painful shock, it reacts with greater force than usual.' Dejection and agony give way to confidence and a feeling of security. Mourning ceremonies are necessary to produce the relief that follows, as Robert Hertz demonstrated in his study of collective representations of death; 'it takes time for those effects to be neutralized' (ibid.: 405 n35).[24]

According to Durkheim, religious life always derives from the same 'state of mind': 'In all its forms, its object is to lift man above himself and to make him live a higher life than he would if he observed only his individual impulses. The beliefs express this life in terms of representation; the rites organize and regulate its functioning' (1995[1912]: 417).

It is, he argues, easy to understand this state of mind (he also speaks of a 'ritual mentality') because we can observe it in 'the most civilized milieu around us'. It leads to ritualism: even those believers who doubt the efficacy that dogmas attributed to various rites continue to observe them. The real justification for religious practices therefore has less to do with the goals that men appear to pursue than with the 'invisible action' that they exercise on minds. Preachers play not so much on our reason ('systematic evidence') as on our feelings ('moral support'). It is this 'predisposition towards believing' that saves, and it is 'impervious to experience' (1995[1912]: 364, 365). The same is true of science. Scientists are reluctant to reject a law based upon the authority of numerous and varied experiments simply because one fact appears to contradict it. The believer is resistant to the lessons of experience, and relies on other experience to prove himself right: 'The researcher does this more methodically but acts no differently' (1995[1912]: 366).

A Sociological Theory of Knowledge

Durkheim pursues his analysis still further in order to deal with one aspect of the theory of knowledge: namely, the categories of understanding and, in particular, causality. In the first part of his book, he clearly demonstrates that totemism, like any religion, supplies a 'total representation' of the world and that this cosmology is a 'product of social factors'. He reiterates the conclusions that he and Mauss reached at the end of their study of primitive classification: the idea that the beings of the universe could be gathered together in groups would have been inconceivable without the example of human groups (1995[1912]: 148). We can see this from the idea of genera: these are 'a tool of thought', and the model is supplied by human groupings, which are characterized by the idea of hierarchy, which is 'exclusively a social thing' (ibid.: 147). When, for instance, a classification consists of only two genera, it takes a dichotomous form (peace/war; water/land), and the contrast between the two elements reproduces a sort of social conflict. Before we can think, we need to see the spectacle of collective life: 'Society furnished the canvas on which logical thought has worked' (ibid.: 149). This does not, Durkheim is at pains to point out, mean that the individual consciousness has no role to play (ibid.: 372).

Turning to the notion of causality, Durkheim proposes what he himself calls nothing less than a 'sociological theory' of causality, and disputes his philosopher-colleagues' view that it is only an arbitrary construction of the imagination (1995[1912]: 372). He sets out to demonstrate that the conception of causality that dominates primitive thought 'has social causes' (ibid.: 367): groups elaborated the notion of causality for collective purposes. Durkheim's argument relies upon two 'equations'. He first equates 'cause' with 'force', taking the notion of *mana* as his prototype. He once more argues that collective forces are both psychic (objectified ideas and feelings) and impersonal (to the extent that they are products of cooperation). He then equates 'force' with 'power': the idea of force implies that of power and is thus synonymous with domination (and therefore dependency and subordination), adding: 'The relations that these ideas express are eminently social.' It is society that confers upon superior beings the property that makes their commands efficacious: 'The first powers the human mind conceived are those that societies instituted as they became organized' (ibid.: 370).

Durkheim is wary of his own conclusions, and is reluctant to describe his observations as 'a complete theory of the concept of causality': 'That issue is too complex to be resolved in this way.' The views he has set forth 'must be regarded only as indicative; they will have to be tested and fleshed out' (1995[1912]: 373).

At the very end of his book, Durkheim returns to the 'complex problem' of categories ('the permanent framework of mental life'). If categories are 'social things', how are we to explain the fact that 'the very things they express are social' (1995[1912]: 441)? He restates his thesis that categories correspond to various aspects of social life. The category of a genus corresponds to that of a human group, and that of time to that of the rhythm of social life. The category of space corresponds to that of society's occupation of space, and that of causality to that of collective forces ('the prototype for the concept of effective forces'). The same is true of the notion of the 'whole', which is basic to all classification: 'the concept of totality is but the concept of society in abstract form' (ibid.: 443).[25]

The individual lives within time and at a determinate point in space, and has a sense of similarity and of a certain regularity. Time must therefore be divided up or differentiated; a 'common time' must be established (to allow men to be summoned to ceremonies, to hunting or military expeditions). The idea of a means–end relationship must be established, and there must be a notion of collective causality if individuals are to cooperate with a common goal in view. 'Society presupposes a conscious organization of itself that is nothing other than a classification' (1995[1912]: 444). Hence the conclusion that 'society is by no means the illogical or alogical, inconsistent, and changeable being that people too often like to imagine.' Far from abandoning the notion of the collective consciousness, Durkheim describes it as 'the highest form of the psychic life, for it is the consciousness of consciousnesses' (ibid.: 445).

'But what could have made social life such an important source of logical life' (1995[1912]: 433)? Durkheim is aware that he may be being 'reckless', but is unwilling to leave such an 'important' question unanswered: 'We must make an effort.' He pursues his analysis by studying what 'makes up' logical thought ('the basic material of logical thought is concepts'), and tries to understand how society 'can have taken part in the formation of concepts'. There is, he argues, a close relationship between language and thought: 'The system of concepts with which we think in everyday life is the one the vocabulary of our mother tongue expresses, for each word translates a concept.' Indeed, 'conversation and all intellectual dealings among men consist in an exchange of concepts' (ibid.: 435). 'Common to all men', a concept is therefore 'the work of the community'. All concepts are 'collective representations', and they are the products of a long history: 'Each civilization has its own ordered system of concepts' (ibid.: 437).

The role of a concept is 'to ensure not only agreement among minds, but also, and even more, their agreement with the nature of things' (1995[1912]: 438). This raises the issue of the objective value of concepts. Durkheim does not dismiss the idea of objectivity, but he does demonstrate that, even today, concepts often derive from ordinary language and from common experience, and that, 'to be believed, it is not enough that they be true', even in science. Concepts must 'be in harmony with other beliefs and other opinions'. If they are not, 'they will be denied'. 'If bearing the seal of science is usually enough today to gain a sort of privileged credibility, that is because we have faith in science' (ibid.: 439). And our faith in science is basically no different from religious faith. Science too rests upon opinion: 'Everything in social life rests upon opinion, including science itself. We can make opinion the object of study and create a science of it; that is what sociology principally consists in' (ibid.: 439).

Durkheim is trying to convince and reassure his readers: when he states that the origins of logical thought are social, he is not denying its value. It is society (which is 'something universal') that opens the way to 'stable, impersonal and ordered thought' (1995[1912]: 445). Every society is 'an individuality' and has its 'idiosyncrasies', and a 'new kind of social life' is beginning to emerge. This international life will universalize religious beliefs, and 'as that international life broadens, so does the collective horizon'. This facilitates 'a truly and peculiarly human thought' that will become universal. This is, however, 'an ideal limit to which we come ever closer but in all probability will never attain' (ibid.: 446).

Idealization: a 'singular privilege'

It might be objected that the religions studied by Durkheim do not contain any great ideas and do not display the main ritual attitudes that are basic to the most advanced religions. It could be argued that the distinction between the profane and the sacred, the notions of a soul, spirits and a mythical personality, of a national or even international divinity, negative cults with ascetic practices, rites of oblation and communion, and mimetic, commemorative and piacular rites are all specific to totemism. Durkheim once more has to admit that 'a single religion' might seem to be 'a narrow basis' for his inductions, but he also insists that 'when a law has been proved by a single well-made experiment, this proof is universally valid' (1995[1912]: 418). He therefore sees no reason not to extend the most general findings of his research to other religions.

Durkheim argues against the so-called theoreticians who, in their attempts to analyse religion in rational terms, see it only as a system of ideas. Surely the first article of faith is the belief in salvation through faith? A mere idea, he retorts, has little efficacy; a religion is also a cult, a set of ritual acts. Thought alone is not enough: we must also enter the sphere of action, act, and repeat our acts on a regular basis. 'Anyone who has truly practised a religion knows very well that it is the cult that stimulates the feelings of joy, of inner peace, of serenity, and enthusiasm that, for the faithful, stand as experimental proof of their beliefs.' The cult is therefore 'the sum total of means by which that faith is created and recreated periodically'. It is always the cult that is efficacious (1995[1912]: 420).

Although he describes him as 'a recent apologist of faith', Durkheim states that he agrees with the American philosopher William James as to certain points ('religious belief rests upon a definite experience . . . "a tree is known by its fruits"'), though he also disagrees with him because the 'reality' which grounds it does not necessarily conform objectively with the idea the believers have of it. Religious conceptions are to the sociologist what the sensations of heat and light are to the scientist: the 'senses' representation of the world' must give way to one that is 'scientific and conceptual' (1995[1912]: 420).

One of the main conclusions of *The Elementary Forms of Religious Life* – and Durkheim restates it very clearly – is that behind mythologies and behind the sensations that are the basis for religious experience, we find society: 'This is the reality that makes [man], for what makes man is that set of intellectual goods which is civilization, and civilization is the work of society' (1995[1912]: 421). The cult plays a pre-eminent role in any religion:

> This is so because society cannot make its influence felt unless it is in action, and it is in action only if the individuals who comprise it are assembled and acting in common. It is through common action that society becomes conscious of and affirms itself; society is above all else an active cooperation . . . Thus it is action that dominates religious life, for the very reason that society is its source. (Ibid.: 421).

His study allows Durkheim to conclude that 'nearly all the great social institutions were religious in origin'. There is, he adds in a footnote, only one form of social activity that has not yet been 'explicitly linked to religion: economic activity' (ibid.: 421 n4). Even so, he believes that there is a link between economic value and religious value: 'it is evident that religious life must necessarily have been the eminent form and, as it were, the epitome of collective life' (ibid.)

Society is therefore the 'substrate' of all religious life. But to which society is Durkheim referring? He raises this question in order to forestall objections to his theory. Is he talking about real society or about a perfect society? His answer is that religion is both realistic and idealist: 'Far from ignoring and disregarding the real society, religion is its image, reflecting all its features, even the most vulgar and repellent' (1995[1912]: 423). 'Persistent idealization' is, in Durkheim's view, 'a fundamental feature of religions' (ibid.: 424). But is this idealization a natural human faculty or a mysterious virtue? 'Man alone has the capacity to conceive of the ideal and add it to the real.' This is a 'remarkable distinction'; it is a product of collective life which 'awakens religious thought when it rises to a certain intensity . . . because it brings about a state of effervescence that alters the conditions of psychic activity' (ibid.). An 'ideal world' that exists only in thought, and is attributed great dignity, is superimposed upon the real world of profane thought. It is obvious to the sociologist that this ideal is a 'natural product' of society because society 'must assemble and concentrate itself': 'A society can neither create itself nor recreate itself without creating some kind of ideal by the same stroke.' Durkheim therefore does not contrast real society and the ideal society: 'A society is not constituted simply by the mass of individuals who comprise it . . . but above all by the idea it has of itself' (ibid.: 425).

This capacity for idealization is not, however, an innate power. There is nothing mysterious about it, and it is not 'a sort of luxury'. It is a condition of man's existence. Ideals are obviously embodied in individuals and so tend to be individualized, but they depend upon social conditions. Personal ideals derive from social ideals. Durkheim is well aware that this sociological perspective may lead to misunderstandings, and therefore warns his readers that his theory is not 'merely a refurbishment of historical materialism'. He rejects the reflection theory on the grounds that 'collective consciousness is something more than a mere epiphenomenon of its morphological basis, just as individual consciousness is something other than a mere product of the nervous system'. The collective consciousness must, rather, be regarded as 'a *sui generis* synthesis of individual consciousnesses'. This synthesis has the effect of creating a whole world of sentiments, ideas and images which 'once born', follow their own laws. And that world enjoys great 'independence' (1995[1912]: 426).

Individual religion/universal religion

Durkheim raises a further two possible objections to his theory. If religion is the product of social causes, 'how can the individual cult and the universalistic character of certain religions be explained?' (1995[1912]: 426). While Durkheim does not deny that individual cults exist, he does reject the 'radical individualism that is intent on making religion out to be a purely individual thing' because 'it misconceives the fundamental conditions of religious life'. Such a theory is 'unrealizable in fact': 'the beliefs are at work when they are shared' (ibid.: 427).

It is, Durkheim argues, the same with religious universalism. Universalism is not 'exclusively the trait of a few very great religions' (1995[1912]: 427). He finds in the Australian system a cult that is, in a sense, international. All sorts of circumstances combine to make it international: trade between neighbouring tribes, travel, marriage. Borrowings are therefore common: 'There is no national life that is not under the sway of an international collective life' (ibid.: 428). And as life crosses frontiers, even the gods change and become 'great international gods'. As history progresses, international religious groupings become more important, and this explains why the 'universalistic tendency' becomes more pronounced.

The End of Religion?

There was no avoiding the question of the 'end of religion' in the early years of the twentieth century, and one might have expected Durkheim to follow the example of other scholars and intellectuals in predicting the death of religions. And yet he quite simply states that 'there is something eternal in religion' (1995[1912]: 429). And this is because 'there can be no society that does not experience the need at regular intervals to maintain and strengthen the collective feelings and ideas that provide its coherence and its distinct individuality.' He describes its 'remaking' through meetings, assemblies and congregations, adding that there is, in his view, no essential difference between a congregation of Christians, Jews remembering the exodus from Egypt and a gathering of citizens.

Durkheim was writing at a time of 'uncertainty and confused anxiety'. What, he asks, will be the 'feasts and ceremonies of the future'? Will it be Christianity or the French Revolution that provides the model? Neither seems to supply principles to which we can be passionately attached. Christianity defended an idea of equality and fraternity that left too large a place for unjust inequalities. The Revolution ended in failure, and revolutionary faith 'lasted only briefly' (1995[1912]: 430). But although the cycle of celebrations that it established 'quickly perished', everything leads him to believe that 'the work will sooner or later be taken up again'. 'The former gods are growing old or dying, and others have not been born' (1995[1912]: 429), but Durkheim predicts: 'A day will come when our societies once again will know hours of creative effervescence during which new ideals will again spring forth and new formulae emerge to guide humanity for a time.' As to what that new faith will be, 'that is a question that exceeds human faculties of prediction' (ibid.: 430).

Durkheim qualifies his answer by recalling the distinction he makes between religion as a 'system of ideas' or cosmology, and religion as a system of practices (rituals and feast). One is turned towards thought, and the other towards action. His thesis is that, while the system of practices meets universal needs, the same cannot be said of religion as a system of ideas. The primitive religion he has been studying is 'most unsettling to reason' (1995[1912]: 430). Everything about it seems 'full of mystery'. It presents a pronounced contrast between faith and reason. But appearances are deceptive; we have only to 'pull aside the veil' to see that there is a similarity between religious speculation and the reflections of scientists. They deal with the same realities, namely nature, man and society, and 'both attempt to connect things to one another . . . classify them and systematize them' (ibid.: 431).

While he once more asserts that 'the essential notions of scientific logic are of religious origin', Durkheim accepts that, to the extent that it 'reworks' them, science is 'more perfected': it 'brings to all its efforts a critical spirit', and keeps passions, prejudices and all subjective influences at bay. It therefore seems 'natural' that 'religion should lose ground as science becomes better at performing its task . . . science tends to replace religion in everything that involved the cognitive and intellectual functions' (1995[1912]: 431). He cites the example of Christianity, which has abandoned the 'realm of physical phenomena' to science. The resistance is gradually being overcome, but not without difficult: the idea submitting the psychic life to science is still repugnant to many. Durkheim believes, however, that 'this last barrier will give way in the end, and . . . science will establish herself as master even in this preserve' (ibid.: 432).

Science and religion do come into conflict, but 'religion exists; it is a system of given facts; in short, it is a reality' (1995[1912]: 432). It would appear that religion will be transformed and play another role in future. It will also 'borrow from' the sciences (the social sciences, psychology and the natural sciences) in order to justify its existence. And it is also true that 'science is fragmentary and incomplete; it advances but slowly and is never finished; but life cannot wait' (ibid.).

Durkheim returns, finally, to the famous antimony of science and religion (and morality) and makes the inevitable allusion to Kant, for whom practical reason and speculative reason are both aspects of the same faculty: both are oriented towards the universal. But while both science and morality imply that 'the individual is capable of lifting himself above his own point of view and participating in an impersonal life' (1995[1912]: 446), Kant cannot explain the 'sort of contradiction' between two antagonistic worlds: the world of matter and sense on the one hand, and the world of pure and impersonal reason on the other. Durkheim argues that 'impersonal reason is but collective thought by another name', and that 'there is something impersonal in us because there is something social in us' (ibid.: 447). So great is the distance between 'the world of senses and appetites on the one hand, and the world of reason and morality on the other' that 'it seems the second could have been added to the first only by an act of creation'. And it is society – 'the most powerful collection of physical and moral forces that we can observe in nature' – that has this creative power. Although we appear to be faced with an alternative – either to relate the higher faculties to lower forms of being (reason to sense, mind to matter) or to connect them with 'some reality above experience' – Durkheim suggests a 'third way'. It is opened up by sociology: we must recognize that society is a 'system of active forces' that exists 'above the individual': 'What must be done is to try out the hypothesis and test it against the facts as methodically as possible' (ibid.: 448).

'The New Sorbonne's Theology': Some Strong Objections

The publication of *The Elementary Forms of Religious Life* was initially greeted with silence. In July, Durkheim wrote to his nephew Marcel to tell him how he was feeling: 'So far, everything is going well as regards my book: no one is talking to me about it. The people I have sent it to all tell me the same thing: they are taking it on holiday with them. That's fine. All I ask is to be left in peace.'[26] When Henri Hubert was sent Durkheim's book, his first – and quite spontaneous – reaction was to write to Mauss: 'I've received Durkheim's book. Perhaps you should have signed it, because there is a lot of you in it. I'll talk to you about it soon.'[27] Célestin Bouglé was the first of Durkheim's close collaborators to review *Elementary Forms*: 'This time, you are well ahead of the rest',

Durkheim wrote to him. 'There have been no reviews of my book so far. Your article is very lively. I am sure it will arouse some curiosity.' He was especially touched by the speed of his collaborator's response: 'You are one of those people who are motivated by friendship.' But he felt a 'great need for peace', and asked for only one thing: 'Just leave me in my corner. I'm afraid of polemics, and that is probably a sign of senility.'[28] He then left, as planned, for a few days' holiday in Meudon.

Afraid of polemics? Durkheim sensed that his book would be heavily criticized. As was to be expected, the philosophers were more than dubious about it. They certainly saw *Elementary Forms* as a 'fine book' and 'a work that is rich in facts and ideas', and were prepared to accept that 'there is probably a lot of truth in this ingenious theory [of religion]', and that the sociological explanation for religious phenomena was timely and 'filled in some gaps'. But they also had a number of criticisms to make, as can be seen from the *Revue de métaphysique et de morale*, even though it was sympathetic to Durkheim. He was criticized, first of all, for not restricting himself to defending a purely sociological or positively theological position, but for having 'loftier ambitions' and trying to 'revolutionize' the theory of knowledge by relating it to a theory of religion. Then came the verdict, and it was harsh: 'We hope we will be forgiven for describing as somewhat summary his argument in favour of the social origins of intellectual categories, and indeed the social origin of ideas in general.' The journal also found it hard to understand how 'science and faith came be so radically different if they share the same impetus'. It had 'express reservations' about Durkheim's desire to 'extend the [sociological explanation] to include the psychological theory of knowledge'.[29]

That there should be 'very strong objections' to this 'new theory or religion' came as no surprise to Gustave Belot, who wrote a 'long and very incomplete' study of Durkheim's book for the *Revue philosophique*. It was, he exclaimed, 'a magisterial contribution to the general theory of religion, and one of the most important' (Belot 1913: 333). He admired Durkheim for 'his vigorous and systematic thought, which is often ingenious and even profound', 'his remarkably firm and precise language, which is an adequate instrument for a firm doctrine and strong convictions', and his 'scientific loyalty'. On the other hand, he challenged the thesis that the primordial functions of thought (ideals, science, art, morality and law) were religious in origin. In his view, Durkheim should have been looking at 'more humble and less dazzling' aspects of human activity.[30]

The Société française de philosophie discussed *Les Formes élémentaires de la vie religieuse* in February 1913. The subject of the debate was 'The religious problem and the duality of human nature'. In his contribution, Durkheim (1975[1913]) began by attempting to clarify the main theses of his book: a religion is not just a system of ideas. A religion mobilizes forces that 'raise up' the individual and allow him to live a higher and more intense existence. These moral forces (which are greater than those of the individual) are 'collective forces', or the product of the coming together of individual forces. He then turned to a question that dominated both philosophical speculation and religious thought, namely the 'duality of man'. The basic idea is that there are two beings within man, and that they are very often in conflict. Contradiction is 'one of the distinctive features of our nature', and we suffer as a result.[31]

Dismissing the various philosophical explanations (empiricism, utilitarianism, etc.), Durkheim looks to sociology to provide what he calls a 'third solution': 'Man is double simply because he is social.' The duality of human nature thus comes down to the 'antithesis between what is individual and what is social', and the mystery is dispelled: everything comes from society. This does not mean that the individual can be relegated to the background: 'Society can come into being only in and through individuals, as it is nothing more than an organized set of individuals.' He adds: 'Society needs individuals in order to exist. On the other hand, the individual needs society' (1975[1913]: 35).

Durkheim emphasizes, finally that the 'essential characteristic' of religion has to do with its 'dynamogenic power': a religion is not just a system of representations. It is also a system of forces that 'allow us to act, and to act in a special way': the main function of beliefs is to 'provoke actions'. On the one hand, thought and, on the other, action. Anyone who believes in 'the religious state' is in thrall to forces that both dominate and support him: he can therefore do more. The input of life leads to greater vitality, confidence and enthusiasm.[32]

Durkheim also takes the opportunity to reply to some objections and criticisms; he begins by restating some methodological rules: 'This explanation has been criticized on the ground that it is systematic. Some have expressed surprise that a single principle can be so supple as to explain a considerable number of facts . . . They forget that the whole of religion is dominated by one idea: that of the sacred.' And his answer to those who are surprised by the fact that loss of religious faith should coincide with a period of decadence is: 'It is inevitable that the gods should lie when the gods are nothing more than peoples in symbolic form . . . The faith of the individual can only be strong if it is shared by all' (1975[1913]: 29–30).[33] Durkheim ends his presentation by expressing surprise at the new 'classic' prejudice that prefers philosophy to the science of religion, which supplies philosophical reflection with 'less rich' material: 'Religion is the work of the complete man . . . No other viewpoint gives us a better view of the complexity of human nature' (ibid.: 36).

Those colleagues in the Société de philosophie who joined in the debate – Henri Delacroix, Alphonse Darlu, Jules Lachelier and Edouard Le Roy[34] – made no secret of their admiration for him, and complimented him. 'I am aware of all the power and beauty of the new and important book that Durkheim has given us', remarked Darlu. The ensuing debate, however, was stormy, and Durkheim came in for a lot of criticism.

It was the question of dualism that interested Delacroix: 'The psychological conditions that make social life possible and fruitful pre-exist it.' He scoffed at what he called 'the miracle of society exalting and transforming the individual consciousness'. In reply, Durkheim could not stop himself from expressing one regret: the debate had not addressed the book's central thesis, which should have been of interest to philosophers: the dynamogenic character of religion. 'I expected a serious debate about something that I regard as a fundamental proposition.' He nevertheless agreed to go along with his interlocutor and to reply to his questions. *Question*: is the social necessarily religious? *Answer*: no, because 'group states are relatively exceptional and short-lived, precisely because they are so intense'. *Question*: does the individual bear within him a full idea of what religion is? *Answer*: no, because although the social life is based upon individual consciousness, it does not emerge from it as a result of some spontaneous development.'

Durkheim made no secret of the fact that he had 'serious reservations' about the position his colleague was defending. Individual consciousnesses did have the 'predispositions that make social life possible', but these were preconditions and not causes.' His thesis did not, he said, imply 'miracles'. It had to be recognized that 'collective life does violence to the individual's basic instincts and penchants'. He concluded: 'We cannot live our collective life without making a major effort to control ourselves' (1975[1913]: 41–4).

Although he argued that individual creativity did have a role to play, Alphonse Darlu said that he agreed with one of Durkheim's central ideas and that religious, moral and even logical concepts were social in origin. This was, he claimed, an idea that was 'widely accepted'. His claim astonished Durkheim: 'I admit to finding the news of this unanimous agreement charming, but it does surprise me somewhat.' One of Durkheim's other arguments, on the other hand, seemed to Darlu to be 'outrageous' because it offended 'all our intellectual habits'. He could not accept, in other words, that religious conceptions were 'originally and essentially social things, or conceptions modelled on social things'. Although he professed to know little about totemism, Darlu was challenging the theory outlined by Durkheim and was sceptical about the 'hypostatized clan' thesis. He noted, finally, that there was a 'sort of contradiction' between the basic ideas behind his colleague's argument: were religious conceptions products of individual consciousnesses, or were they shaped by collective thought?

Durkheim was unmoved by Darlu's comment that he was offending 'our intellectual habits': 'The role of science was not to comment upon or paraphrase common-sense opinions, but to replace vulgar knowledge with a different type of knowledge', especially, he added, 'in the case of a new science' which, like sociology, was 'a new perspective on man, and a new instrument for analysing human nature'. 'It inevitably upsets received ideas.' To provide a full answer to Darlu's question, he would have to summarize the whole of his book. He therefore referred his interlocutor to his conclusion, and said that he was prepared to respond to any observations or objections that he might have. Durkheim did not think that he was 'guilty' of any contradiction: 'I said that religion is the collective force that penetrated individual consciousness . . . These collective states have a determinate influence on individuals, and it is at once stimulating and imperative. But they are not the work of individuals' (1975[1913]: 48–9).

Time was running out. Edouard Le Roy, for his part, simply went over a few points from Durkheim's 'programme', and asked him to clarify one methodological issue: 'I am not challenging his right to study the lower religions, but I do challenge his right to use them to define religion as such.' The essential thing about religion was not, he argued, to be found in its 'most rudimentary forms', but in its evolution and in long-term developments. Durkheim was quite 'at a loss' as to how to reply to this. He was obviously annoyed that those involved in the debate had not got to grips with the facts and arguments he was expounding, and that 'all too often the objections took the form of impressions, personal feelings, mental habits, or in other words prejudices and even acts of faith that did not lend themselves to discussion' (1975[1913]: 54).

Durkheim found it difficult to argue with Jules Lachelier because he reduced religion to 'a lonely, individual striving for freedom', to an 'attempt at self-perfection' and 'involvement in a higher life'. What he saw as the characteristics of 'true religion' had nothing to do with barbarous religions. 'I believe', he admitted, 'that Christianity had done a lot to enhance the human mind's idea of spiritual perfection.' Durkheim replied that (1) solitude was not a distinctive characteristic of religious life, and that (2) the notion that perfection means the pursuit of a supra-individual ideal was 'an essential and constant element in all religions'. But the main criticism he addressed to his colleague was that he regarded religion as a purely individual matter, and that he had the same notion of religion as did certain 'refined souls' or elite believers. The gods that interested him as a sociologist were 'the gods of the crossroads', 'the gods who have always helped, consoled and supported men'. 'The religion that interests me . . . is the religion that has allowed most of humanity to put up with life.'

The thing that annoyed Durkheim about this debate was that the participants often had a 'very impoverished idea' of society. We think of the judges, policemen and civil servants who are responsible for preserving the rule of law. Society was, he reminded his listeners, 'something very different': 'It is a new synthesis . . . because it is a synthesis of minds and it gives birth to a new kind of spirit or mentality.' And it was the sociologists who have made us aware of this by discovering 'a new realm'. The science of man had opened up 'unknown horizons' by discovering mental effervescence and the communion of consciousnesses. He concluded that society was, as the great thinkers had sensed, 'a sort of wonderful being that is higher than nature, a sort of god and what Hobbes called a mortal god' (1975[1913]: 55–7).[35]

Like the philosophers, the anthropologists and historians of religion had 'many serious reservations' (Van Gennep 1916: 338) about *Elementary Forms*. Alfred Loisy (1913) was sharply critical of that he called Durkheim's misuse of language, ambiguities and conjectures: 'The totem is no more a god than the men of the clan are gods . . . the purpose of all these ceremonies is of no more than utilitarian interest.' Durkheim was able to state that totemism was a religion only because he accepted a priori that the social and the religions were one and the same. Others described Durkheim's theory as 'the theology of the New Sorbonne' (Goblet d'Alviella 1913).[36]

The criticisms of Comte Goblet d'Alviella were more moderate in tone but just as negative. The Belgian scholar recognized the originality and 'growing importance' of Durkheim's work on the history of religions, but his criticisms were many and varied. His criticisms of competing theories were largely unfounded and incomplete. A kind of sociological mysticism led him to see society as a higher and autonomous organism. But the real points of disagreement between d'Alviella and Durkheim had to do with the role of individual activities and the individual consciousness. Whereas Durkheim speculated that 'the consciousness of society had preceded, along with the individual, any consciousness of personality', d'Alviella tended to think that 'social consciousness and individual consciousness developed in parallel because they act upon one another', and that society cannot have any 'real existence' outside its members. 'It makes its action felt in and through individuals.' Even though he refused to predict that 'something of the views of Durkheim and his disciples will last', d'Alviella said he was convinced that 'one thing is worth preserving: the assertion that the influence of society has coloured, oriented and coordinated the beliefs of individuals from the very beginning, and especially at the beginning.' It was therefore our duty to study religious facts (which are social facts) 'sociologically'.

The anthropologists were mainly interested in the question of totemism. Elementary taboos, the rule of exogamy, the hereditary nature of the totem and initiation rites were all topics for discussion. Salomon Reinach, who was on leave in Geneva in the early summer of 1912, described Durkheim's latest book as a 'masterpiece'. He made no secret of his admiration for Durkheim and shared some of his ideas, even though he was sorry that he did not describe religion as 'a system of scruples and prohibitions'.[37] Arnold Van Gennep had just published his *Essais d'ethnographie et de linguistique* (1913), and was in the process of publishing a long series of articles on 'the history of ethnographic method' in the *Revue de l'histoire des religions*. He later tried to reopen the debate on 'the totemic problem' with another long series of articles in the same journal. In them, he classified in chronological order all the theories of totemism from MacLennan and Spencer to Durkheim (whose theory he described as emblematic and collectivist – sociological) to Boas. He was somewhat harsh on his colleague, and had no qualms about stating that 'most of his first proposals are inaccurate' (the reference is to the thesis that lower societies are simple and homogeneous), that his theory was not new, and that his interpretation of the data would only be 'forced'. He certainly admired 'the ingenuity of the construct which, in terms of its breadth and simplicity, is worthy of the best constructs of Hindu metaphysicians, Muslim commentators and Catholic schoolmen'. But he refused to grant it any 'scientific veracity', and used the same facts and the same documents to elaborate a separate theory and reach a different conclusion: 'For my own part, I insist on regarding the belief in paternity as a basic psychological element' (Van Gennep 1916: 335).[38]

Speaking on behalf of the Le Playsians, Paul Descamps (1912) apologized for the fact that social science (or their version of it) had so far ignored Australia's Aborigines, even though a lot of work had been devoted to various schools of anthropology and ethnology. As he was not well informed about the social state of the Australians, Descamps refrained from discussing Durkheim's theses 'in detail' and restricted himself to a few comments. He was annoyed by Durkheim's analysis of those religious manifestations that turned into orgies and suspended the incest taboo: 'Let us not make [religion] responsible for these monstrous syntheses.' His main criticisms were as follows: simplicity was confused with primitiveness. Durkheim was too preoccupied with the issue of the genesis of religious feelings, and overstated the importance of religion to savages, whose actions were motivated 'not so much by metaphysical ideas as by the need to live, and to have something to eat and drink'. While he congratulated Durkheim on 'regarding ideas as facts', he also criticized him, for there were also 'material facts', including places, work, property and the means of existence. His conclusion was clear: 'The influence of the economic facts is preponderant.' Hence the need to begin by studying 'the facts of material life, the means of existence'.

The Foreign Reception. 'The End of a Controversy'

The Elementary Forms of Religious Life was more widely reviewed outside France than Durkheim's earlier works. Most of the reviews appeared in England and the United States, but the book was also reviewed in Italy and Germany. In England, E. Sidney Hartland, who was very familiar with Durkheim's work, described his French colleague's 'brilliant volume' for readers of the journal *Man*: 'It opens a new chapter in the discussion of religion, and must for many a day be the starting point of controversy' (Hartland 1913). He did, however, have some reservations, especially about the universality of totemism, but added: 'We in England have perhaps hitherto made too little of the influence of society in the genesis of religion [and] have attributed it too exclusively to the influence of external nature and the experience of individual life upon what is assumed, rightly or wrongly, to be the constitution of the human mind.' On the other hand, he criticized the French sociological school not for going to 'the opposite extreme', but for ignoring 'the part actually played by the individual'.

Alfred Radcliffe-Brown (born 1881) was the most 'Durkheimian' of English anthropologists and was, he said with some pride, the first to have introduced Durkheim's sociology to an English audience in the sociology lecture he gave in Cambridge in 1910 and at London University in 1909–10. As he wrote to Marcel Mauss (who spent two months in England during the summer of 1912), he was 'disappointed' by Durkheim's latest book.[39] He accepted Durkheim's general thesis about the social origins of religion, but had two main criticisms: (1) Durkheim did not fully understand 'the true nature' of Australian social organization, and especially of its classificatory system (phratries and classes were only a part of it); (2) he overstated the importance of the 'emblem-clan', which, although sacred, was not always associated with totemism. His own study of Australia had led him to conclude that symbolism was independent of totemism. Radcliffe-Brown took the opportunity to say how much he owed to Mauss: 'I can say that I completely agree with the conception of sociology put forward by the *Année sociologique*.' Realizing that Durkheim's views were 'either unknown or badly understood' in England, he expressed the hope that the new book would do something to change that, even though it contained, he reiterated, a 'misinterpretation of the real facts'.[40]

The Americans were also interested in the work being done on religion by the 'distinguished director' of the *Année sociologique* and his close collaborators. A review of Durkheim's 'remarkable recent essay' on the definition of religion appeared in the *American Journal of Sociology* in 1913 (Leuba 1913), but the essay James Leuba referred to was the article 'on totemism' (Durkheim 1985[1902]) and not *The Elementary Forms of Religious Life*. Leuba praised Durkheim for his 'vigorous' defence of the objective method, which was 'all too often neglected', admired his 'undeniably original work', and agreed that it was the sacred and not the divine that was the basic characteristic of religion; but he disagreed with him over several points, and especially his distinction between religion and magic and his psychology/sociology dichotomy. The position Durkheim had adopted on this issue in *Rules of Sociological Method* had left Leuba 'puzzled', and he was pleased to see that he had made 'concessions to psychology' in the second edition, even though he thought them inadequate. Leuba himself believed that the introspective psychological method did have a role to play in the study of social life, and rejected the idea of a social or collective consciousness: 'There is no such thing as a collective soul or collective feelings, but simply a collection of souls and feelings shared by all members of the group.'[41]

As soon as *Elementary Forms* was published, another review appeared in the *American Journal of Sociology*. It was by the University of Nebraska's Hutton Webster (1913). Webster began by describing the earlier work of Durkheim and his collaborators on the incest taboo, totemism and the matrimonial system, which he described as a contribution to social anthropology. Durkheim's most original contribution was, in Webster's view, his theory of collective representations. He did, on the other hand, identify certain weaknesses in *Elementary Forms*: the author overstated the importance of totemism in primitive societies and attached too much importance to the notion of *mana*.

In 1914, two fragments of *Elementary Forms* were translated into Russian as 'Sociology and the theory of knowledge'. The translator Pitirim Sorokin published three articles on Durkheim in 1913 and 1914: 'Symbols of social life', 'A sociological theory of religion', and 'Émile Durkheim on religion'. Sorokin was intellectually close to Durkheim and admired his erudition; he was also fascinated by his brilliant comparisons. He agreed with Durkheim that religion should be defined in terms of the sacred and accepted the idea that 'the prototype for the divinity was the community, and that the prototype for the divinity's properties were the social group's properties'.

The English translation of Durkheim's book appeared in 1915, as *The Elementary Forms of Religious Life: A Study in Religious Sociology*: 'Swain has finished the translation of my *Religion*: it has been printed, and he is preparing an index.'[42] *Elementary Forms* was the only one of Durkheim's books to be translated into English during his lifetime, and the *American Journal of Sociology* published another review of it. It was shorter and harsher (Weatherley 1917). Its author, Ulysses G. Weatherly, a professor at the University of Indiana, was sorry that Durkheim had not avoided the pitfalls that lay in wait for any study of the social origins of religion: he looked into the minds of savages in order to find the abstract mental processes of a scholar, and he based his generalizations on facts that were heterogeneous and often contradictory. The sacred/profane dichotomy was certainly 'useful', but only to the extent that it was not considered to be 'primordial'. Weatherley was astonished to find researchers like Frazer, Lang and Durkheim reaching such different conclusions on the basis of the same material; this proved, in his view, not only that the subject was difficult but also that 'our knowledge is imperfect'. But he congratulated Durkheim for his 'consistency': 'He is conscious that his theories do not cover all the facts of totemism as found among the American Indians.'

'A scientific event', exclaimed Bronislaw Malinowski when he hailed the appearance of the leader of the French group's 'important new book' in the journal *Folk-Lore* (Malinowski 1913). He had already identified with the Durkheimians and had even acknowledged his debt in *The Family Among the Australian Aborigines* (1913), which he described as 'his most Durkheimian work' (Young 2004: 238). He described Durkheim as 'one of the acutest and most brilliant living sociologists'; he also praised the work of the group of scholars who worked on the *Année*, and described Hubert, Mauss and Hertz as having 'successfully' worked on primitive religion. He recalled the stance Durkheim had adopted in the *Rules of Sociological Method*, where he had contended that social facts should be studied as things, and that there was no place in sociology for psychological explanations. That postulate seemed to some to be 'rather artificial', he noted, and difficult to apply, especially for British anthropologists who tended to look for psychological explanations for the origins of religion. The publication of *Elementary Forms* provided an opportunity to 'judge how successful his method was'.

Malinowski also had many serious objections. First, he did not think it possible to draw conclusions based almost entirely on just one tribe (the Aruntas). He queried the idea that the profane/sacred dichotomy was universal and also the assumption that totemism was an elementary form of religion. Finally, he rejected the idea that religion's origin lay in crowd phenomena and that mental effervescence was religion's only source. In conclusion, Malinowski went back to the *Rules* and demonstrated that Durkheim's theory of origins was in no sense 'a product of his objective method'. He did not, in other words, hide the fact that he was 'a little disappointed': 'Durkheim's points of view have some basic inconsistencies.' But even though he frequently attacked Durkheim's theory of religion ('Durkheim's theory is itself a somewhat mystical act of faith': Malinowski 1935: 236), he also recognized that it was 'one of the fullest and the most inspiring systems of sociology' (Malinowski 1944: 19).

Alexander Goldenweiser, an anthropologist and professor at Columbia University, had a 'deep interest' in totemism. He had devoted his doctoral thesis to the subject and had published an article entitled 'Totemism: an analytic study' in the *Journal of American Folk-Lore* in 1910. In it, he outlined a 'new conception of totemism' based on studies carried out in Australia and on the west coast of North America. He was still, as he put it, trying to 'keep up with and analyse' as best he could an ever-expanding mass of facts. He was very familiar with the work of Durkheim, and regarded his latest book as 'a brilliant treatise, but not a convincing one'.

When *Elementary Forms* was published, Goldenweiser, who was exasperated with all the confusion, the lack of understanding and the many 'pointless controversies' over totemism, wrote to Father Schmidt, who edited the journal *Anthropos* ('probably the most cosmopolitan of all ethnographic periodicals') to suggest that a sort of symposium should be organized to take stock of the 'totemic problem'.[43]

Goldenweiser reviewed Durkheim's book in the journal *American Anthropologist* (1915), noting: 'A contribution by Émile Durkheim always commands attention.' He emphasized that Durkheim's earlier work had had a great influence on sociological theory – and was, he noted, still read – and congratulated Durkheim and his collaborators Hubert and Mauss on their 'methodical and extensive survey' of sociological and anthropological literature in the *Année*. Goldenweiser gave a detailed analysis on what he called his French colleague's 'cardinal' doctrines by discussing the five theories outlined in his book: the theory of religion, the theory of totemism, the theory of social control, the theory of ritual and the theory of knowledge. Impressed by Durkheim's brilliant argument, he recognized the originality of his thesis, which saw religion as a symbol of social control. 'No one else before him has, to my knowledge, ever gone so far, nor has the author himself, in his former writings, ever gone so far in his social interpretation of psychic phenomena'.

He also had a lot of criticisms, many of them harsh and applicable to all Durkheim's arguments: (1) the choice of Australia as an almost exclusive source of information was unfortunate (it was not a typical case, and could not be used as a basis for generalization); (2) the theory of religion was inadequate, and did not pay enough attention to the individual and subjective dimension; (3) the theory of totemism did not take sufficient account of the ethnological point of view, which regards that institution as 'highly complex' in historical terms; (4) the theory of social control had to be rejected because it both overestimated and underestimated the social element, and failed to recognize the relationship between the individual and society (which is presented as a 'sublimated crowd'); the theory of ritual supplied a real insight – it was the most 'suggestive' and 'satisfactory' of the theories outlined in the book – but was too behaviourist and rationalist; and (5) the theory of knowledge suffered from an exclusive insistence on socio-religious experience as a source of mental categories. Goldenweiser concluded that *The Elementary Forms of Religious Life* contained errors, and that its central theses were 'unproven'.

Everyone agreed that Durkheim's book was a highly ingenious study but one that left 'an impression of unease'. They all had much the same criticisms to make: neither a general theory of religion nor a theory of totemism could be based solely upon Australian data, as Australian 'primitiveness' was very relative.

Was this the end of an era? The debate about totemism certainly went on. Franz Boas published an article in *American Anthropologist* using the title of his 1910 article, 'The origin of totemism', in which he discussed with Alice C. Fletcher and Charles Hill-Tout what had come to be known as the 'American theory' of totemism (because it was based on studies of the Kwakiutl of British Columbia) (Boas 1916).[44] But when *The Elementary Forms of Religious Life* appeared, totemism was no longer the central concern of anthropology. As became obvious at the International Congress of the History of Religions (in Leyden in 1912), the polemic had lost its edge and the tone was changing. 'The age of manifestoes is over. There are neither accusers nor apologists' (Alphandéry 1912: 230). Anthropologists were turning away from philosophical speculation, abandoning their literary pretensions and turning resolutely to fieldwork. They were more interested in analysing the social organization and specific cultures of local populations than in studying the origins of religion. In 1913, Malinowski published *The Family Among the Australian Aborigines*, and W. H. R. Rivers's *Kinship and Social Organization* appeared the following year. The history of religions was giving way to anthropology. The three new characteristics of anthropology in both Britain and the United States were 'dehistoricization, ethnographicization, and professionalization' (Stocking 1995: 232).

24

A Lecture Course, the Last Année *and the End of an Era*

Pragmatism

'The *Année* is coming along nicely', Durkheim told his nephew at the beginning of the summer of 1912, adding with some pride: 'As you can see, we have not been idle.'[1] Mauss still found publishing the *Année* a burden: 'I spend almost the whole year working on the *Année*. It really is poison – worse than the 'flu.'[2] The family in Épinal described the publication of every volume of the *Année* as a 'bout of 'flu' and 'a sociological disease'.

Durkheim spent June in Paris, as his son André was taking his final examinations in philosophy. He was somewhat worried: 'I am not expecting very brilliant results. I have the impression that his essays were not a great success. Perhaps he will make up for that in the oral.'[3] There was, as André put it, 'some friction' with Célestin Bouglé during the oral: 'He's a strange examiner.'[4] In the event, André did quite well in his exams, and was awarded *mention bien*: 'above average'. Durkheim was also worried about his own health. At the beginning of the summer, he had to ask for leave for the academic year 1912–13,[5] but was still teaching his course at the École normale supérieure, 'The formation and development of secondary education in France'. As he wrote to Célestin Bouglé, he felt that he was in the position of having to 'put up with feeling knocked out . . . I have to admit, on the other hand, that I am getting used to the idea of life as someone who has been demoted.' Being on sick leave really did make him feel that he had been demoted. His other classes, which amounted to two hours a week, were covered by Bouglé, a *chargé de cours*, and Henri Delacroix, *maître de conférences*. 'I hope', Durkheim told Bouglé, 'that the fact that I am on leave will have the merit of giving you a year of success and praise.'[6]

Durkheim had thought of going away on holiday, but had to consult his doctor first. His doctor did not foresee 'any obstacles to that'. There was, on the other hand, still the problem of the next *Année*. 'If enough books arrive on time, we may be able to go away without any delay.' Durkheim sent large numbers of books on to his collaborators. Émile and his wife spent a few days in Meudon: 'It's nice, except that I have to go to Paris too often.' At the end of July, he went on holiday to Waldhaus-Flims with his wife and children. 'Very beautiful countryside. Unfortunately, the weather is as unfavourable as it could be.'[7] He had not forgotten the *Année sociologique*: 'We have a lot of work ahead of us', he wrote to his nephew Marcel. 'I'm forced to think about it.' He intended to 'get down to work in September', and hoped to have 'got on with, but not finished' his share of the work inside the space of two months'. All this was preying on his mind: 'There are nights when the idea of all that work stops me sleeping.'[8] For the whole of August, he 'systematically lounged about'. The family then went back to Meudon, stayed there until 15 October and spent five 'excellent' weeks on holiday. 'I have never seen such beautiful autumn evenings in the countryside.' He added that 'It's enough to make anyone listless and become dreamy. Despite that, I have done some work. My contribution is coming along.'[9]

More than ever, Durkheim hoped that he would 'be given a hand' by various people', but, as always, he was worried all the same. He had the *Année sociologique* collection to edit, as well as the next volume of the journal.[10] His nephew's delays were an obvious cause for concern. 'I beg you to think of the *Année*. It will be a heavy task', he wrote to Marcel in England. He reminded him of their deadline: 'It must be published at the usual time', and advised him to get down to work 'without any delay and with enthusiasm', and to write drafts (which he promised to 'clean up').

Between his failure to be elected to the Collège de France in 1909 and the outbreak of the First World War, Mauss was preoccupied with his work on prayer. What had become of his thesis? In the summer of 1912, he went on a scientific mission to Belgium, Germany and England. His goal was to consult documents on the Australian tribes, and specially Strehlow's documentation (which was also of interest to Durkheim), to visit various institutions devoted to ethnography, and to make contact with professional ethnographers in all three countries. Closer contacts would, he hoped, 'serve to advance these studies, especially in France'.[11] Although he had not lost interest in the history of religions, he was increasingly drawn to ethnography, or 'the description of so-called primitive peoples'. Developments in that discipline in France were a long way behind those in the English-speaking countries and Germany, though some of his students were beginning to catch up.[12]

During the two months he spent in England, Mauss worked in the British Museum almost every day. And he discovered what he called 'an enthusiastic branch' of the *Année sociologique*. 'Marcel will tell you that one of the findings of his trip to England confirms that our work is of use, thankless as we may all find it.'[13] On his return to France, Mauss published an article entitled 'Ethnography in France and other countries' in the *Revue de Paris*. In it, he sounded the alarm: given the way this area of study was stagnating in France (where it looked 'thin and weak'), something had to be done. More resources had to be devoted to teaching and research, a new museum should be opened and a bureau of anthropology should be established (as in the United States). This was, he argued, a matter of urgency, as the facts that could be observed and the objects that could be collected were disappearing. And what was more, a country like France, which had a responsibility for its subjects' spiritual welfare, could not go on 'administering' peoples it did not understand. Henri Hubert, for his part, was trying to combine ethnology with the history of religion, philology and archaeology. In 1913, he published a series of articles on the hero cult, and used them for his introduction to Stefan Czarnowski's book on St Patrick. Durkheim, in the meantime, was developing an interest in folklore, and presented a project for a survey of folklore to the Comité des travaux historiques et scientifiques (of which he was a member), arguing that 'so many important elements have disappeared' even though they were 'of such importance to our history'. He added: 'Documents of real value may be lost.'[14]

Although he was on leave, Durkheim still attended the meetings of the university council, but declined to take on further responsibilities. When Rector Liard asked him to serve as '*rapporteur*' for the year, Durkheim pleaded 'serious health reasons'. He then went back to work and 'did what had to be done', as he put it.

One Last *Année*

Durkheim relied upon several new 'recruits', whom he had contacted through Mauss and Hubert, for volume XII of the *Année*. They were Jean Demangeon, Henri Jeanmaire, Pierre Roussel, Edmond Doutté, Edmond Laskine and Jean Marx. Paul Lapie, Dominique Parodi and Jean-Paul Lafitte did not contribute. Paul Lapie had been appointed rector of the Académie de Toulouse in June 1911. This marked the beginning of a long and productive administrative career, as he later became director of primary education (1914–25) and then rector of the *Académie de Paris* (1915–27).

Émile Durkheim was 55 when the next volume of the *Année* appeared in 1913. Most of the earliest contributors, including Mauss, Hubert, Bouglé and Simiand, were in their early 40s. The 'second generation' (including Hertz, Felice, Davy and Gernet) were in their early 30s. In 1898, the average age of contributors had been 29.5 years; in 1913, it was 35.5 years (excluding Edmond Doutté). The age of the new recruits varied. Roussel, Jeanmaire, Marx and Edmond Laskine had been the youngest contributors in 1911; Laskine was only 23.[15] They had all attended Mauss and Hubert's lectures at the École pratique des hautes études between 1907 and 1912. The first three were all *agrégés*. The older collaborators were delighted to have this influx of 'new blood', as we can see when Robert Herz's friend Robert Roussel agreed to contribute:

> Your place on the *Année* is assured, and I am sure that Durkheim will be delighted to have you as a collaborator. You must see him and have a chat with him as soon as you get back: he will be very interested in your ideas. And his conversation is always stimulating and suggestive. You will find here the atmosphere of sympathy and shared interests that are indispensable to all of us.[16]

Albert Demangeon was one of the older recruits, and a friend of Henri Hubert, whom he had known at the École normale supérieure.[17] He became a professor at the Sorbonne in 1911. Together with Durkheim and Jeanmaire, he now took editorial responsibility for the 'geographical basis of social life' rubric. Edmond Doutté (1867–1926) was in an unusual position as he was neither a *normalien* nor an *agrégé*. He chose what was at the time an 'adventurous' career as an administrator in Algeria before being appointed to a post at the University of Algiers in the 1900s. He was, according to Mauss, one of 'best Arabists in the world' and 'one of the great explorers of Morocco' (Mauss 1969[1927]: 520–1). He became co-editor of the *Année*'s 'universalist religious systems' and 'dogmas' rubrics.

The manuscript for the next volume of the *Année* was still not ready at the beginning of May 1913. An exasperated Durkheim laid the blame at Mauss's door: 'You are giving me a rough time, and wasting my time – as though I had a lot of time left . . . We have to get it finished. Things cannot go on like this . . . Let's get it finished. Let's get it finished.' It seemed that it was only when he was at his uncle's that Mauss could get anything done. 'So you will have to come to work here for a few days, and work all day if we want to get this finished.'[18]

There were no major changes to the way the *Année* was organized, except that the 'moral and juridic sociology' section (27 per cent of all reviews) was now almost as lengthy as 'religious sociology' (29 per cent) and 'economic sociology' (24 per cent). It is true that this section, which was edited by Durkheim and Mauss, now included several rubrics of 'primitive' societies and societies based on totemic clans. The other sections were once more much smaller: 'general sociology (8.7 per cent), 'social morphology' (3.5 per cent), 'criminal sociology and moral statistics' (2 per cent) and 'miscellaneous' (2 per cent). Some new subsections were also introduced: 'economic classes', for instance, now included 'working women.'

A few notes were added to explain how the various sections were organized and what line their editors intended to take; these included Hubert Bourgin on 'monographs of trade and industry', Antoine Meillet on 'language', and Durkheim and Mauss on 'tribal juridical systems' and 'the notion of civilization.' Durkheim and Mauss opened a new research area with the notion of 'civilization'. In their introductory note (Durkheim and Mauss 1969[1913]: 681–5), they recall that one of the *Année*'s rules is that social phenomena must be studied, not by 'leaving them up in the air', but by relating them to a definite substrate, named human groups occupying a specific portion of space that can be defined in geographical terms. Those groups are political society, the tribe, the nation, the *polis* and the modern state. The life of the nation is the highest form of group. But there are, they admit, structures that cross political frontiers and extend over wider spaces; there are also social phenomena which, like technology, aesthetics, language and religion, extend over areas that transcend national territories. These facts are not 'independent of one another' but form a 'complex and interlocking system', as each element implies the presence of every other element.

Durkheim and Mauss decided to call these systems, which have a unity of their own, 'civilizations': 'A civilization is a sort of moral environment in which a certain number of nations have their roots; each national culture is no more than a particular form of a civilization.'[19] They then made it clear that it is impossible to speak of 'civilization' without making reference to 'human civilization'. But, as can be seen from Auguste Comte's studies of 'the progress of civilization', the idea of human civilization is no more than an intellectual construct if it ignores the existence of national individualities: there is no such thing as 'civilization', but there are such things as geographically defined civilizations. This was a new field of research, and it opened up questions that had been overlooked until that time. Durkheim and Mauss outlined a hypothetical 'unequal coefficient of expansion and internationalization'. There are, on the one hand, things that are bound up with a people (political and juridical institutions, phenomena pertaining to social morphology) and, on the other, 'all the things that travel and that are borrowed' (myths, money, trade, the arts, technologies, tools, language, scientific knowledge, literary forms). The study of 'international life' is, Durkheim and Mauss, conclude, part of sociology because 'we must discover the collective interactions that give rise to that life'.

Volume XII also carried Durkheim's long review of Wilhelm Wundt's *Elemente der Völkerpsychologie*, which took as its subject-matter (human) civilization in its entirety, examining both its diversity and its history (Durkheim 1969[1913d]: 685–691). It was, noted Durkheim, a major book and expressed some 'suggestive views', but it did contain some errors and inaccuracies. Worse still, it overlooked the complex nature of the universal history of humanity: 'Different social species must be considered separately, and we must attempt to discover the laws that govern the many ways in which they interact in both time and space.' The new rubric dealing with 'civilization and types of civilization' was edited by Durkheim, Mauss and Hubert. In his introductory note to the 'language' section, Antoine Meillet (1913: 850–1) made a similar point, and argued the need to get away from pure linguistics and to look at how historical events and social conditions influenced linguistic phenomena. The 'external circumstances' must, in other words, be taken into account.

Other collaborators discussed the anthropological work of Boas, Frazer, Goldenweiser, Seligmann, Strehlow and Van Gennep. Volume XII also carried reviews of works by German (or German-born) sociologists, including Robert Michels, Werner Sombart[20] and Joseph Schumpeter.[21] As always, the *Année* also paid some attention to the work of its collaborators and associates, including Hubert Bourgin (*L'Industrie de la boucherie à Paris* and *Le Socialisme et la concentration urbaine*), Henri Lévy-Bruhl (*Le Témoignage instrumentaire en droit romain*)[22] and Lucien Lévy-Bruhl (*Les Fonctions mentales*). Mention was also made of Gaston Richard, a former collaborator who had just published his *Sociologie générale et les lois sociologiques*.

Durkheim's recent *Elementary Forms of Religious Life* was reviewed in both the 'general sociology' and 'religious sociology' sections. Both reviews were by Durkheim himself and began with discussions of other works, namely Lévy-Bruhl's *Les Fonctions mentales dans les sociétés inférieures* (see Durkheim 1994[1913]) and Frazer's *Totemism and Exogamy* (the latter review was co-authored by Mauss: see Durkheim and Mauss 1994[1913]).

Most of Durkheim's 30 reviews dealt with the religion, social organization or family organization of 'primitive' societies. One of them was of his English colleague Sidney Hartland's *Primitive Paternity* (Durkheim 1969[1913c]). Like Durkheim 15 years earlier, Hartland argued that the uterine theory of descent predated the agnatic theory. A mother's right was, he argued, a 'natural fact', whereas paternal power was a 'social convention'. But Durkheim had 'serious objections' to Hartland's conception of paternity and maternity in primitive societies. Such societies, like 'more advanced religions', did not believe that 'sexual relations are enough to explain the fact of generation', and held that all births were the products of an encounter between body and soul. Hartland's mistake was to overlook this 'duality of causes'. In some exceptional circumstance, Durkheim noted, only the spiritual factor (the soul) was taken into account. Examples included the 'immaculate conception' and the birth of certain heroes and gods.

A Bust and a Promotion. Official Recognition

Durkheim's mandate to the university council, which had run its course, was renewed at the beginning of 1913, together with those of the other members. The faculty of letters was still represented by Durkheim and Gustave Lanson (who was now appointed secretary). The vice-presidency went to M. Cauwès, who had been re-elected as the dean of the law faculty. 'Current affairs' were still the council's main preoccupation: the budget, various repairs, requests for funding for two high-voltage meters, disciplinary matters, grants, *cours libres* (Berthelot in philosophy and Worms in law, amongst others). Durkheim was in charge of the programme for grants to study at foreign universities (Fondation David-Weill). These grants of 3,000 francs were made available to some 10 *agrégés* and lycée teachers (including four women). Developing foreign contacts was still a major preoccupation: there were teacher exchanges, and a dinner was held in honour of Harvard's Lawrence Lowell in July. Two major building projects were also under way: a laboratory for the study of the evolution of inorganic beings was under construction in the faculty of sciences, and, in the faculty of letters, work had begun on the Institut de géographie thanks to an endowment of 500,000 francs from the Marquise Arconati-Visconti (née Peyrat), who thus became the university's 'great benefactor'. The plans were drawn up by the architect Nénot.

In the faculty of letters, life went on as normal. Alfred Croiset was re-elected as dean. Deaths and new appointments resulted in some changes.

Georges Rodier died prematurely, and his old chair became a chair in experimental psychology. It went to *chargé de cours* Georges Dumas. Charles Victor Langlois became director of the Archives nationales. Ferdinand Brunot, who had been put in charge of the new 'Archives de la parole' department, launched a project that used phonographs to record dialects and patois from around France before they died out – a 'considerable task'.[23]

Durkheim's eldest daughter Marie Bella was married in February 1913. She was 25. In accordance with her father's wishes, it was a civil wedding celebrated at the *mairie* of the 14th arrondissement. The decision was not to the liking of Durkheim's sister Rosine (Mauss's mother) who, remaining true to her principles, took offence and refused to attend the ceremony. 'I have received a nice letter from Émile, who understands that, while he must remain true to his principles – or the ideas he professes – and abstain from a religious ceremony, we too must be consistent with our traditional ideas.'[24] This was not the first time that Émile's attitude to religion had been a source of annoyance to his sister. He normally went to Épinal for religious festivals, and even that was not unproblematic. Rosine wrote to her son:

> I have to admit that I insist on celebrating Passover in the way that I have always celebrated it. The trouble is that I would like Émile to be there, but do not know how to reconcile the demands of his stomach with our ritual obligations. He does not want to be confined to his room to eat bread, but I could never sit down to eat with bread on the table.[25]

Émile and his wife contributed shares and debentures to their daughter's dowry.[26] Her husband Jacques Halphen (1880–1964) was 33. He was the son of Julien Halphen, a candle merchant from Metz who later became a registered broker and departmental head on the Paris stock exchange. Jacques had studied at the Conservatoire des arts et manufactures in Paris, and was 'in oil', as the family put it. He worked, that is, for the Compagnie industrielle des pétroles, and later became its director. The couple, who were very well off, set up home at 4 rue Anatole-de-la-Forge.

For Maurice Halbwachs, 1913 was a busy year. Within the space of a few days in May, he remarried and defended his second doctoral thesis (letters), entitled 'The working class and standards of living. Studies in the hierarchy of needs in contemporary industrial societies' (it was later published in the 'Travaux de l'*Année Sociologique*' collection).[27] His complementary thesis was called 'Theory of the average man. An Essay on Quételet and morality' (it too was published by Alcan as *Essai sur Quételet et les statistiques générales*). Halbwachs was close to François Simiand and argued in his main thesis that 'behaviours depend upon their agents' representations of market transactions and of the behaviours of other people'. Arguing against those whom he called 'German socialists', he attempted to show that the notion of social class referred neither to occupation nor to wealth, but to standards of living and levels of consumption. 'We should not be looking at what people earn, but at what they spend.' His research, which was based on French and German studies, was on rents and family budgets (see Steiner 2005).

The jury consisted of Célestin Bouglé, Charles Seignobos and Lucien Lévy-Bruhl. Bouglé described Halbwachs's thesis as 'a piece of work that should serve as an example to future generations', but both he and his colleagues still had 'some reservations'. The thesis made for difficult reading and the ideas expressed were unclear. There were some unfortunate turns of phrase, and Halbwachs was too quick to generalize on the basis of a survey of 200 families. The thesis also raised several questions, including the distinction between class and class consciousness, the need for comparisons with other countries, and the paradox of the 'desocialization' of the working class. Halbwachs was well aware that his conclusions might 'hurt people's feelings': 'When you are doing science, you are often obliged to offend received opinions.'[28] When a *maître de conférences* position fell vacant in Lille, Maurice Halbwachs, who had been teaching philosophy at the lycée in Tours since 1910, applied for it. Durkheim was quick to lend his support to a man who had been working with him on the *Année sociologique* for 10 years or so. Referring to the thesis Halbwachs had just defended, he described him as 'interested in new developments, and the method he has chosen indicates that he is capable of a sustained and persistent work over a long period'. He added: 'I think that he has all the qualifications required to make him a philosophy teacher who can effectively influence minds. His studies mean that he is well qualified to teach the course on pedagogy that, I believe, a *maître de conferences* at Lille would be required to teach.' But given that Halbwachs was already 36, Durkheim also had to add a few words of explanation: 'He became a *docteur ès lettres* at a relatively advanced age because his thesis topic required a long period of research, and because he thought he should first qualify as a doctor of law.'[29] Durkheim's support proved not to be enough. Halbwachs remained in Tours, where he became so bored that he accepted a position at the lycée in Nancy the following year.

In 1913 Durkheim was 55. He had now been teaching in the higher education sector for 25 years. His friends and collaborators on the *Année* organized a party for him in April 1913, and Célestin Bouglé commissioned the sculptor Paul Landowski to carve a bust of the professor to mark the occasion. Landowski, who won the Prix de Rome in 1900, was one of the Third Republic's official sculptors. He was also responsible for the Reformation Monument in Geneva (better known as 'Le Mur des réformateurs'), which was unveiled in 1909 to mark the 400th anniversary of the birth of Calvin. The statues of Calvin in Geneva and the bust of the stern and austere Durkheim were so similar that one could have been the model for the other.

Henri Hubert was not very enthusiastic about this initiative: 'Bouglé's bust is a hollow mask', he wrote to Mauss. 'I told Simiand that something else would be better.' Hubert was thinking of 'some kind of event' to go along with the work of art. It would punctuate things. He added:

'If nothing takes place, people would probably not be wrong to say that the blame lies with the bust.' He ceased to raise objections when he saw how pleased Durkheim was. 'If it makes Dk [Durkheim] happy, we could not hope to do better.'[30] 'What a very fine bust!' exclaimed Durkheim. It was, Davy later said, a bust in which the sculptor 'brilliantly brought to life the face of a meditative seer'. He also underlined the fact that this was the first time the 'entire little community' had gathered around its leader to show its affection for him. It was, he added, a 'small spiritual family' united by a 'shared method and a shared admiration for its leader' (1919b: 195).

Celebrations were the order of the day. In 1912, Davy published a long article entitled 'The sociology of Émile Durkheim' in the *Revue philosophique*; the following year, his anthology *Durkheim. Étude du système sociologique* was published with Michaud, much to the satisfaction of its subject: 'Sympathy such as yours makes me singularly indifferent to the attacks of certain publicity-seekers.' The young Davy, who was very close to Durkheim and his family, dreamed of marrying his teacher's daughter Marie. He had begun to write his thesis on *La Foi jurée*, but did not submit it until after the war.[31]

At the end of the academic year, the council of the University of Paris met to discuss a proposal to turn the chair in educational science into a chair in the sociology and science of education. The proposal came from the faculty of letters, which had already voted in its favour, but the decision had to be ratified by the council. When Rector Liard addressed the meeting, he asked Durkheim if he agreed that 'science of education' should remain, as it always had been, part of the chair's description. Durkheim had no objections. The council then accepted the rector's proposal that the chair be designated 'educational science and sociology.'[32] Sociology was now officially recognized by the Sorbonne, although 'educational science' still had priority.

The Fashion for Pragmatism

Durkheim's 1913–14 lecture course at the Sorbonne was on pragmatism. His goal, in Mauss's words (1969[1925]: 476), was to 'familiarize students with what was still a new form of philosophical thought' and to 'fill a gap in the education of those young people'. The lectures were addressed primarily to a 'few good minds' but made a 'great impression' on a very wide audience. They were also addressed to Durkheim's son André, who was now one of his students. The course, which began on 9 December 1913 and ended on 14 May 1914, comprised 20 lectures. The manuscript has, as Mauss put it, 'unfortunately' been lost. Georges Davy reconstructed it on the basis of notes taken by students, which provided what he called 'an echo of Durkheim's very words' and his style of teaching (repetition of points already made, frequent summaries).

Why pragmatism? Because 'pragmatist tendencies' were, as Célestin

Bouglé put it, 'fashionable' in Paris. Inevitably, there was a critical reaction. 'At the moment, this anti-pragmatist reaction is probably not without its uses' (Bouglé 1910). Durkheim also recognized its 'contemporary' relevance: 'Pragmatism is almost the only current theory of truth' (Durkheim 1983[1955]: 1). He rapidly traces the history of this 'slow, underground movement' which spread only gradually beyond the 'circle of private conversations' in America between 1895 and 1900 (ibid.: 8). In *The Elementary Forms of Religious Life*, Durkheim cites two works by William James, including *The Varieties of Religious Experience* (1903; the French translation appeared in 1906). When he discussed his book with an audience of philosophers, he acknowledged that he and James did have something in common, but he did so only so as to highlight more clearly their differences: 'The gulf that lies between myself and pragmatism is the gulf that separates rationalism from mystical empiricism. It is impossible to confuse the two' (Durkheim 1975[1913]).

While remarking that the movement had crossed the Atlantic 'very early', reaching first England and then Italy and France, he also noted with some irony that 'the pragmatists find it quite easy to recruit thinkers who are far from subscribing to all their theses'.[33] He was thinking here of Henri Bergson, to whom he devoted part of his last lecture on pragmatism. Durkheim knew Bergson well but had, it was said, an undying hatred for his fellow *normalien*. Durkheim, who had been rejected by the Collège de France, was teaching at the Sorbonne, while Bergson, who had been 'ostracized' by the Sorbonne, was at the Collège on the other side of the rue Saint-Jacques. They were in competition. Some young people, like Henri Massis and Alfred de Tarde ('Agathon') had displayed their preference for Bergson in an article published in *L'Opinion* in 1910. Furthermore, Alfred's father Gabriel Tarde had taken the side of Bergson and reviewed *Les Données immediates* in sympathetic terms.[34] In the 1910s, everything combined to make Bergsonism a philosophy for the young. Henri Bergson was *the* fashionable philosopher, and had elaborated 'a new philosophy'.[35] Now that several books had been published on Bergson, there was talk of a 'Bergsonian movement' or 'Bergsonism'. His name was synonymous with anti-intellectualism or even irrationalism: analysis was opposed in the name of synthesis, and reason in the name of intuition. 'The era of rationalist superstition is over. It is dead', proclaimed Le Roy (1900). On 10 January 1914, Bergson was elected president of the Académie des sciences morales et politiques; a month later, he was elected to the Académie française. His fame had reached its peak. Such fame, and the infatuation it brought, inevitably inspired criticism and even hatred. Julien Benda attacked Bergson in a series of articles on 'the success of Bergsonism' in the *Mercure de France*. An advocate of rationalism and clear thinking, Benda had declared war on the philosopher's doctrines, which he described as 'pathetic' (Azouvi 2007: 206).

Bergson's critique of intellectualism means that his doctrine was identified with the pragmatist movement (Berthelot 1913). Bergson was close to James, describing himself as one of his earliest admirers, and he was pleased to see that the philosophical trends they were defending on either side of the Atlantic were converging.[36] They had been corresponding since 1902, and had quickly become friendly. Although Bergson had turned down an invitation to preface the French translation of *A Pluralistic Universe* a few years earlier, that was because he did not want to introduce a book that devoted 'so much space' to his own work and described it in such 'favourable terms'.[37] He did, on the other hand, accept Gustave Le Bon's invitation to write a preface for the French translation of *Pragmatism*, which appeared in Flammarion's 'Bibliothèque de philosophie scientifique' in 1911. It is true that the pragmatist thesis of the heterogeneity of the conceptual and the real did borrow arguments from Bergson. Durkheim had more than one reason to be irritated by the Parisian fashion for pragmatism. But he made no secret of the fact that he took great interest in this philosophical trend, and found in it the 'same feeling for life and action' that he found in sociology: 'Both tendencies are daughters of the same period.' He detected a close kinship between pragmatism and sociology: both saw man and reason as 'products of history'. There were similarities between the two, but there were also differences, as was obvious from the criticism of James's study of religious experience made in *The Elementary Forms*: James's great weakness was his failure to look at rites, institutions and churches, or, in other words, anything to do with collective religion.[38]

Mauss had written a detailed review of *The Varieties of Religious Experience* for *L'Année sociologique* (Mauss 1969[1904b]), demonstrating that the American philosopher's introspective psychological analysis was incompatible with 'our science of sociology'. 'There is some uncertainty throughout M. James's book', he wrote. 'What does he mean by "experience"? And by "religious experience" in particular?'

Durkheim also had great admiration for John Dewey, even though he found that he was 'often heavy', that his arguments was 'laborious' and his thought 'not always clear'. As his nephew later put it, Durkheim regarded Dewey as a logician and 'a rigorous thinker'. Mauss met the American philosopher in 1926, when he visited the United States at the invitation of the Laura Spelman Rockefeller Foundation. The two men met again in Paris in 1930, when Dewey came to read a paper to the Société française de philosophie. 'Of all the moralists and philosophers, it is definitely Professor Dewey who is closest to the sociologists. And Durkheim rated him as by far the best of American philosophers.' He went on: 'Allow me to say that we are, to a certain extent, in agreement, and have been for a long time, with the form of rationalist pragmatism whose best representative is Professor J. Dewey, and that this positive account of moral facts meets with our approval' (Mauss 1969[1930]: 500).

Durkheim realized that pragmatism had a great fascination: it took as its starting point everyone's 'experience', established connections between thought and life, and had a 'very keen sense of the diversity of minds and of the way in which thought experiences temporal variations.' It was as different from rationalism as plasticity (change and contingency) was from stability (reassurance and rest). The social world was, according to the pragmatists, both unitary and disjointed, and made up of a great number of groups and social worlds – in other words, networks. It was, in a sense, a 'federal republic', as opposed to a monarchy. It contrasted 'untidiness' with 'rigidity' (and bureaucracy). The world certainly had its unity, but this unity was 'supple, flexible and multiform'. Durkheim also detected similarities between these arguments and those of Bergson: both were sensitive to the mobility of things, and with all that is fluid and obscure. Both Durkheim and the pragmatists tended to subordinate clarity of thought to murkiness and the 'confused complexities' of the real.

Durkheim was not, however, a fan of pragmatism, and said that he had 'distanced' himself from it because of the 'armed struggle' it was waging against Reason. 'That is a serious problem', he opined. Indeed, he was worried because he saw it as a twofold threat. At the national level, 'a complete refutation of rationalism . . . would turn the whole of French culture upside down.' 'If the form of irrationalism that pragmatism represents were to be accepted, the entire French spirit would be transformed.' And on the intellectual level, the fashion for pragmatism might reverse the philosophical tradition itself, given what he called that tradition's 'rationalist tendencies'.

Durkheim's relationship with pragmatism might be described as 'instrumental', as he attempted to use it to 'renew' traditional rationalism and to rouse philosophical thought from its 'dogmatic sleep'. His ambition was to find 'a formula that preserved the most important feature of rationalism while responding to pragmatism's justified criticisms of it.' His lectures on pragmatism were, according to Marcel Mauss, 'the crowning achievement of all Durkheim's work on philosophy' (Mauss 1969[1925]).

Pragmatism and Sociology

The first part of Durkheim's course on pragmatism is devoted entirely to the origins of this philosophical current, which are Anglo-American and not, as some liked to think, German (Nietzsche). Its founding fathers were Peirce (who was the first to use the word 'pragmatism') and William James, and its major spokesmen included Dewey and Schiller. There is, Durkheim notes, no general exposition or definite system. Pragmatism is, rather, a 'movement, an impetus'. Durkheim attempts to identify its 'essential theses'. In general terms, he is quite harsh on pragmatism: the doctrine is at once 'unitary and diverse', its arguments are abstract, there is no attempt at empirical verification, and there are some blatant contradictions. He obviously does not accept pragmatism's critique of rationalism (namely that its great weakness is its 'contemplative' nature, far removed from real life and human interests). But the 'doctrine' had a great fascination for him. He spends a lot of time expounding its 'positive theses', which deal with the problem of truth and, in one case, the relationship between thought and the real. There is more to life than instinct, routine and habit;

there are situations that make us uneasy, uncertain and worried. The function of thought is therefore not, in pragmatist terms, purely contemplative or speculative: 'it is primarily practical'. 'All action means the pursuit of some human interest.' There is therefore no divorce between existence and knowledge.

Necessity and determination are not everything. There is also a 'current of freedom or indeterminacy' within pragmatism. And while the world is 'chaos', men organize that chaos into categories (space, time, causality) in order to meet the needs of practical life. 'We are . . . genuine makers of reality.' Durkheim cites James: 'We are creators' (1983[1955]: 54). William James has a 'taste for danger', a 'need for adventure', and a preference for a world that is 'uncertain and malleable'. The American philosopher felt a need to make the truth 'more supple' and 'less stiff' so as to make it something that can be 'analysed and explained'.

Relativism

To Durkheim's regret, pragmatism has few or no moral applications: *'there is no such thing as a pragmatist morality'* (1983[1955]: 60). Religion, however, he is happy to note, is the object of a more far-reaching description. His lecture of 3 March 1914 was devoted to 'Pragmatism and Religion'. It is, however, clear that James and Durkheim have their differences. Whilst James does speak of the convergence of minds and a consensus of opinion, pragmatism restricts discussion to the individual, to psychology, and makes no distinction between the collective and the individual. But for Durkheim, 'the social' always has greater dignity than 'the individual. Truth, reason, morality and religion are all 'products of history and therefore of becoming . . . Everything in man has been made by man in the course of time' (ibid.: 67). Everything, including the 'august thing' known as truth, can be an object for sociology. And sociology is synonymous with *relativism*. Nothing is static or unique: the family evolves, there is no such thing as a single morality, and so on. There is therefore room for diversity, in both time and space. And if anything is typical of modern society, it is the diversity and tolerance that go with it.

Sociology therefore conveys a sense of the extreme variability of all that is human. Durkheim finds the same idea of variability in pragmatism, but complains that it has only one answer to the problem: *'practical utility'*. The notion of utility, which he had always rejected, seems to him to be confused. What about non-practical truths, useless beliefs and myths? For a long time, mythologies were an expression of the intellectual life of societies, and satisfied 'an intellectual need to understand' rather than a practical need. The same is true of science. As we can see from the example of alchemy, speculation and practice were originally intermingled, and 'in that sense it could be said that in origin the sciences are pragmatic': 'In all research there is no doubt a point of departure, an optimistic act of faith in the utility of research.' That, however, is no more than a transitory stage: the scientist is not concerned with the practical consequence of his discoveries (1983[1955]: 76–8).

Thought and Action

The central thesis of pragmatism is that knowledge exists only through action. Durkheim discusses Dewey's arguments, and demonstrates that there is a contradiction between thought and action. Consciousness can hamper action rather than facilitating it – as happens when a pianist thinks about the notes he is playing (1983[1955]: 79) – and action can paralyse thought. According to Durkheim, action and the act of thinking are in fact antagonistic: 'In order to think deeply it is necessary to abstain from all movement' (ibid.: 80). Durkheim draws a contrast between two very different types of men: the intellectual and the man of action. On the one hand, unlimited time for thinking, and hesitation, and, on the other, general sensations that are acute and strong, and action without any deliberation. On the one hand, internalization and hyper-concentration on the part of consciousness; on the other, externalization and release. Durkheim therefore rejects the pragmatist argument that there is a 'natural kinship' between thought and action.

Durkheim now extends the argument to all forms of knowledge, including the most refined (concepts). The pragmatists' mistake is, in his view, their failure to see that knowledge has its own nature, but they do ask the right question: 'How is the notion of truth to be elaborated?' All this is, in Durkheim's view, a matter of belief: 'Ideas . . . do not originate with individuals. They are collective representations' (1983[1955]: 84). He takes as an example two historical types of truth: mythological truths and scientific truths. The former are bodies of truth that are accepted without any examination, and the latter are always subject to verification or truth. There can, in his view, be no collective life without shared ideas or intellectual unanimity. These collective representations are not, he insists, 'pure fantasy', and they are not unrelated to the behaviours of individuals.

The idea of belief is of central importance to Durkheim, who makes no distinction between truth as belief, and the acceptance of a belief as true. The origins of belief, including scientific belief, are social, and its authority comes from society. No matter whether we are talking about science or religion, theoretical certainties or practical certainties, it is always the same: certainty means faith – in other words, a belief in being in possession of the truth. It is a 'disposition to act in conformity with a representation' (1983[1955]: 99). Durkheim then adds: 'It could well be that certainty is essentially something collective' (ibid.: 102). It relies upon the authority of tradition and the power of opinion, but it also involves communication: 'We are only certain when we are certain that we are not the only ones who are certain' (ibid.).

In order to demonstrate the utility of science, Durkheim turns to Ancient Greece, where the role of science was to 'synthesize individual judgements'. Thanks to science, disagreements cease, particularisms disappear, and minds turn to impersonal truths that are, it might be added, universal. According to Durkheim, collective truths are therefore the basis for a 'common consciousness'. Scientific representations too are collective representations, and scientific truth reinforces the social consciousness.

What is the role of sociology in all this? Durkheim admits that social science is still in a rudimentary state, and that it is a domain in which there is no possibility of experimentation. He certainly still claims to be a disciple of positivism but he is at pains to point out that, unlike Comte, he does not believe that sociology can guide the collective consciousness; it can, at best, put forward 'fragmentary hypotheses' (which have little influence on the popular consciousness). Does this mean, he asks, that we must 'take refuge in doubt', which may be a form of, or even a kind of, wisdom? What applies to the social world does not, he replies, apply to the physical world:

> We have to act and live, and in order to live we need something other than doubt. Society cannot wait for its problems to be solved scientifically. It has to make decisions about what action to take, and in order to make these decisions it has to have an idea of what it is. (Ibid.: 90)

Durkheim takes the examples of democracy, progress and the class struggle. In his view, these are 'formulae' or ideologies which, although not religious, might now be described as dogmas. These truths take a secular form, he goes on, but they have a mythological and religious foundation: 'For a long time to come, there will be two tendencies in any society: a tendency towards objective scientific truth and a tendency towards subjectively perceived truth, towards mythological truth' (1983[1955]: 91). This is, he believes, 'one of the great obstacles which obstruct the development of sociology.'

Durkheim gave his last lecture on 19 May: 'Are thought and the real heteronomous?' Durkheim's interlocutor here is Bergson. He contests his colleague's thesis that, in its primal state, life is undivided, and that life itself is 'an undivided force' (1983[1955]: 95). Durkheim argues that life began not with heterogeneity but in a state of confusion: the primal state is one of indeterminacy, as we can see from religious life: all forms of thought are there, but it is difficult to separate them. Myths and beliefs are embryonic forms of science, and poetry and rituals contain embryonic forms of morality, law and the arts. Evolution consists in the gradual separating out or differentiation of all these functions: secular and scientific thought become divorced from mythical and religious thought, art becomes divorced from religion, and morality and law from ritual.

In conclusion, Durkheim goes back to the question of truth. Truth, he contends, is at once a 'social thing' and a 'human thing': 'Even the collective element in it exists only through the consciousness of individuals, and truth is only ever achieved by individuals' (1983[1955]: 97). He reiterates the conclusion of *Elementary Forms*: 'Concepts are . . . modelled on realities, and in particular the realities of social life.' Truth therefore has an authority: '*Truth is a norm for thought in the same way that the moral ideal is a norm for conduct*' (1983[1955]: 98).

Bergsonism versus Sociologism. 'Creative Synthesis'

Durkheim was not finished with Bergsonism. At the beginning of January 1914, he took part in a discussion on 'A new way on posing the moral problem', organized by the Société française de philosophie. It was a 'confrontation between Bergsonism and sociologism' over the issue of 'moral progress and social dynamics'. The main speaker was Joseph Wilbois, a Bergsonian and Catholic whose *Devoir et durée. Essai de morale sociale* had been published in 1912.[39] He had been inspired by Bergson and Le Play to develop what he called a 'metasociology' designed to 'discover, beneath the interlacing of social laws themselves, the claims of freedom, and to renew humanity's trust in the creative impulses that are the sinews of the moral life'. He wished, in other words, to 'reconcile the new [Bergsonian] philosophy of freedom with the findings of the social sciences. The discussion was opened by Célestin Bouglé.

The discussion between Wilbois and Durkheim began with a methodological issue. Wilbois, who had written a 'very modest' monograph on an agrarian brotherhood in Vozdvijensk in Russia, used his experience to attack the 'documents on index cards' method: we cannot understand things from the outside. He added that 'It is very obvious that one cannot write the history of Christianity if one is not a believer, the sociology of the Hurons if one has never gone beyond New York, or musical criticism if one was born deaf.'

Sensing that he was under attack, Durkheim tried to 'clear up some misunderstandings' and, as he often did in discussions – and especially when he had no 'full knowledge' of his interlocutor's theory – he asked Wilbois to explain his approach more clearly, and to say why he distrusted the word 'explain', which had, he claimed, 20 different meanings in the social sciences. He had argued that 'no social fact can be explained'. His stance was diametrically opposed to that of Durkheim, who told him politely but firmly: 'It will be difficult for us to reach agreement, but I will not make an issue of it.'

When the issue of humanity's moral progress was raised, Durkheim tried to clarify his own position: (1) development is complex and never goes in a straight line; (2) the idea of development did not mean that the ethics of so-called inferior peoples should be viewed as 'inferior to ours'. They were at once similar (they shared the idea of sacrifice, oblation and self-sacrifice) and different: 'Every type of society has its own morality.'

When, finally, Wilbois (who claimed to be very familiar with the work of Durkheim and his close collaborators) criticized him for his almost exclusive emphasis on the 'static point of view', Durkheim was 'surprised' by the 'misunderstanding', arguing that he had, on the contrary, tried to devote at least some effort to studying 'creative syntheses'. 'New life can emanate only from living beings that associate and cooperate with one another, and they must therefore be contemporaries.' He immediately added that 'the new things that the society created in this way are added to a stock of things that it has not created, and which it has received. The new things are its fruits, because they derive from that which already exists.' Wilbois became belligerent and clumsily made new attacks of what he saw as the *Année sociologique*'s static methodology, claiming at the same time to follow Bergson, the *Année* and *La Science sociale*. Durkheim was in no hurry to continue the debate.

Religion and Free Thought. 'The Future Depends on Us'

There was no escaping the issue of religion. On 18 January, Durkheim defended his 'social conception of religion' during a debate organized by the Union des libres penseurs et des croyants libres pour la culture morale (Durkheim 1994[1914]). This was one of a series of 'conservations' about 'religious feeling today' organized by the union during the winter of 1913–14. The association was chaired jointly by Émile Faguet and Ferdinand Buisson, and brought together secularists and believers. The purpose of the 'conversations' was, as its secretary F. Abauzit put it, to 'determine the value of religious beliefs and the efficacy of a godless morality': 'A large number of enlightened minds and publicists are talking of a religious revival. Some see it as a mere illusion, and others denounce it as a serious threat. What is the truth of the matter?' (see Filloux 1970: 301–4). Gustave Belot also spoke during the discussion.

Durkheim, who was rather pleased to have been invited to take part – albeit at the last moment – was addressing two clearly defined groups made up, respectively, of free thinkers and free believers. He improvised; but he made it quite clear that there was nothing improvised about this way of thinking. He wanted to talk about the book he had published 'two years ago' on 'certain forms of religious life'; he also wanted to describe the 'spirit' in which he hoped the book would be studied and then discussed' (1994[1914]: 181).

He began by addressing the free thinkers, 'those who keep a completely open mind in the face of all dogmas'. The free thinker was a 'man who methodically sets himself the task of expressing religion in terms of natural causes, without introducing any kind of notion not borrowed from our ordinary discursive faculties' (1994[1914]: 182). He wanted to convince the free thinkers in the audience that religion was not just a system of representations (with 'something disconcerting about them . . . a sort of mysterious character that disturbs us') but a system of 'very special forces' (which are not physical but moral and which 'in the words of a well-known phrase . . . move mountains'). This was, he explained, the basic thesis of his study. Because it causes 'exceptionally intense forces to arise', 'religion has a 'dynamogenic influence' on consciousness. For the benefit of those who had not read his book, he made it clear that this was not 'an abstract

Morality and Religion

and purely philosophical hypothesis', but a 'particular piece of research' based upon an analysis of the facts and historical observation that had been 'subjected to the test of experience; and has 'so proved its validity' (1994[1914]: 183, 184).

Durkheim then turned to the free believers. What was he to say to them? He respectfully described the free believer as a 'man who while having a religion, who while even adhering to a denominational formula', nevertheless brings to the examination of this formula an openness of mind which he strives to keep as complete as possible. He spoke a different language from that of the free believers in his audience. He asked them to bear with him because agreement was impossible with anyone who valued 'a denominational formula in an exclusive and uncompromising way' or held 'the truth about religion in its definitive form', and 'my presence here' would have no meaning. Dialogue was possible only if 'we practise a sort of Cartesian doubt', and he invited them to forget their beliefs for the moment. He hoped that his listeners would not perpetrate 'the error and injustice into which certain believers have fallen who have called my ways of interpreting religion as basically irreligious'. 'There cannot be a rational interpretation of religion which is fundamentally irreligious: an irreligious interpretation of religion would be an interpretation which denied the phenomenon it was trying to explain' (1994[1914]: 185). 'Nothing', he concluded, 'could be more contrary to scientific method.' Religion was not a set of dogmas, but a totality of ideals:

> Above and beyond all the dogmas and all the denominations, there exists a source of religious life as old as humanity and which can never run dry: it is the one which results from the fusion of *consciences*, of their communion in a common set of ideas, of the morally invigorating and stimulating influence that every community of men imposes on its members. (Ibid.)

There was therefore no need to fear for the future of religion: 'There is no need to fear that the heavens will ever become finally depopulated, for we ourselves populate them' (ibid.: 186).

Was it possible to imagine 'a religion of the future, that is to say, a religion more conscious of its social origins'? Durkheim was unsure how to answer the question and recommended 'caution'. Calmly, and without any regrets, he observed that 'today our religious life is languishing' because 'our power for creating ideals has weakened' (1994[1914]: 186), and because 'our societies are going through a phase of profound agitation'. The period of equilibrium was over. The old ideals and divinities were dying, and the new ideals were not yet born. France and all the countries of Europe were experiencing a period of coldness. But despite the 'moral coldness which prevails on the surface of our collective life', Durkheim sensed that 'in the depths of society an intense life is developing . . . seeking outlets and . . . will ultimately find them' (ibid.). There were new aspirations, such as 'a higher justice', and, while they were disturbing, they were also 'sources of warmth'. Durkheim was even so bold as to predict that 'these new forces' were to be found 'among the working classes' (ibid.: 187).

The humanity Durkheim was thinking of was a humanity without a god: 'humanity is left on this earth to its own devices and can only count on itself to direct its destiny' (1994[1914]: 187). Such an idea might well 'disturb' anyone who believed in 'superhuman forces', but it was gaining ground. Durkheim found it 'highly comforting'.[40]

Dualism: The Grandeur and Wretchedness of Man

Durkheim was surprised to see that no review of his *Elementary Forms of Religious Life* had noted that the 'principle' on which his study was based was that of the constitutional 'dualism of human nature' (Durkheim 1964[1914]: 326). In 1914, he published an article called 'The dualism of human nature and its social conditions' in the journal *Scientia*.[41] The dualism he wished to discuss, and which he saw as characteristic of human nature, referred to the universal belief that we have both a body and a soul. Durkheim establishes a whole series of homologies: sensations and sensory tendencies, conceptual thought and moral activity, egotistic appetites and impersonal ends. This is the old formula of *homo duplex* (corresponding to Pascal's formula 'angel and beast'): 'individuality and . . . everything in us that expresses something other than ourselves' (ibid.: 328).

It is obvious that these groups of states of consciousness are not simply 'different': 'there is a true antagonism between them' (1964[1914]: 328).[42] 'We are never completely in accord with ourselves.' This is the source of both our misery and our grandeur. We are wretched because we are doomed to suffer, and great because it is this division that distinguishes us from animals: 'man alone is normally obliged to make a place for suffering in his life' (ibid.: 329). The body/soul antithesis is therefore not a 'vain mythological concept that is without foundation in reality. It is true that we are double . . . each of us is, to quote another of Pascal's phrases, "a monster of contradictions"' (ibid.: 330). Durkheim is convinced that man has at all times been malcontent and divided against himself. In all societies and all civilizations, beliefs and practices have been invoked to give a meaning to these divisions and to 'make them more bearable (ibid.: 331). This is a state of universal and chronic malaise and, far from diminishing as we move from lower societies (whose cults 'breathe forth and inspire a joyful confidence') to higher societies, it increases as the great religions of modern man 'continue to depict us as tormented and suffering' (ibid.: 332). Even if we assume that these discords are 'only superficial and apparent', it is still necessary to find an explanation for this antithesis, and there can be only one answer to the problem. The duality of soul ('something sacred . . . a bit of divinity') and body relates to the higher/lower contradiction and to the dichotomy of the sacred and the profane. There is 'something august' about the dignity of morality, duty and the moral imperative:

'sacred things are simply collective ideals that have fixed themselves on material objects' (ibid.: 335). The explanation lies in the operation 'by which a plurality of individual consciousnesses enter into communion and are fused into a common consciousness' (ibid.).

Durkheim endorses the theory of incarnation (which is found in Christianity), and describes it as a 'singularly creative and fertile psychic operation' (1964b[1914]: 336). Before collective representations can emerge, they must, that is, be embodied in material objects such as the figure, movements, symbols or words that symbolize them. These things are separated out and become sacred. This is not a purely imaginary or hallucinatory system of conceptions: 'the moral forces that these things awaken in us are quite real' (ibid.). Religions have therefore always had a dynamogenic influence. Durkheim now reiterates the argument put forward in *The Elementary Forms of Religious Life*: we alternate between periods of creative effervescence and periods of lower intensity. And it is during the latter periods, or when the group has dissolved, that 'these various ideals are themselves individualized': 'Each of us puts his own mark on them; and this accounts for the fact that each person has his own particular way of thinking about the beliefs of his church, the rules of common morality, and the fundamental notions that serve as the framework of conceptual thought' (ibid.: 337).

'It is not without reason, therefore, that man feels himself to be double', concludes Durkheim: 'He actually is double' (1973[1914]: 157). There are within him 'two classes of states of consciousness', one is purely individual and is rooted in our organism, the other is social and nothing but an extension of society. The latter are impersonal, and orient us towards ends that are held in common with others. We can therefore speak of 'two beings, which, although they are closely associated, are composed of very different elements and orient us in opposite directions' (1973[1914: 162). How are we to explain this dualism (which might be described as a duplication of the personality, or as schizophrenia)? It corresponds, according to Durkheim, to the 'double existence' that we lead: the one purely individual and the other social. Passions and egoistic tendencies derive from our individual constitutions, while our rational activity – logical and conceptual thought – is dependent upon social causes.

This explanation allows us to understand 'the painful character' of the dualism of human nature: society is not 'the natural and spontaneous development of the individual', and has 'its own nature'. It cannot emerge and cannot be maintained 'without our being required to make perpetual and costly sacrifices'. Because society 'surpasses us', it 'obliges us to surpass ourselves . . . a departure that does not take place without causing more or less painful tensions' (1973[1914]: 163). Living in society means, in other words, doing violence to certain of our strongest inclinations. As the 'role of the social being' becomes more important, it is highly improbable 'that there will ever be an era in which man is required to resist himself to a lesser degree . . . and live a life that is easier and less full of tension' (ibid.). To the contrary, 'all evidence compels us to expect our effort in the struggle between the two beings within us to increase with the growth of civilization' (ibid.).

'I Am a Grandfather'

A number of happy events took place in 1914: François Simiand got married, and Henri Hubert had his first son, who was called Marcel. The family moved into a large house overlooking the Seine at Chatou. And on 21 June 1914, Marie Durkheim gave birth to her first child, Claude.[43] 'So I am a grandfather!' Durkheim wrote to his nephew Marcel. 'It's a boy. Everything went well. I have just left Marie's, and I found her as well as could be expected.' The new grandfather noted the precise time at which the 'event' occurred: 9.50 a.m. He added: 'The young Louison looks just like Claude.'[44]

The university council met a few days later on 24 June 1914. Durkheim was not present at the meeting. One of the questions on the agenda was the appointment of a new director for the École normale supérieure, which came under the authority of the council. The names of Ernest Lavisse and Émile Durkheim were put forward as first- and second-line candidate respectively. Of the 13 votes cast, 13 were for Lavisse, 12 for Durkheim. Therefore, Durkheim, who was already a member of the university council was 'in line' for the post of director.

Part VI

The Great War

25

Unjustified Aggression

In 1911 French forces occupied Fès. The German response was to dispatch a gunboat to protect its interests, and this led to the so-called 'Agadir incident'. France then established a protectorate in Morocco, with Lyautey as *résident général*. President Caillaux decided to negotiate – though some called it 'haggling' – rather than use force and ceded part of the French Congo to Germany. The decision was unpopular and reawakened anti-German feelings. War seemed likely. Poincaré, who became head of government in 1912 and president of the republic in 1913, extended military service to three years in an attempt to build up the army. There was talk of 'armaments madness', but life went on and artists went on creating. Schönberg's *Pierrot Lunaire* was premiered in 1912, and Stravinsky's *Rite of Spring* received its first performance at the Salle Pleyel in 1913. Proust's *Du Côté de chez Swann* (the first volume of *À la Recherche du temps perdu*, which he had been writing since 1906) appeared that same year.

The slogan of the Socialist International was 'Make war on war', and Jean Jaurès was definitely committed to peace. In academic circles, the activist and jurist Théodore Ruyssens, who chaired the Association de la paix par le droit, was arguing the case for Franco-German reconciliation. In January 1912, a committee was established, 'Pour mieux se connaître' ['To know each other better'], to promote a 'rapprochement' between Germany and France. Charles Gide, Victor Marguerite and Émile Durkheim were all members of the honorary committee (Halls 2000).

The immediate pre-war period was marked by the rise of militarism. Marcel Mauss published an article entitled 'Contre l'affolement militaire' in *L'Humanité*. The decision to extend military service to three years led to widespread protests in 1913. The socialists organized demonstrations and meetings. Young trade unionists and students tried to turn the fight against three years of military service into a campaign to resist general mobilization (see Cohen 1989). The intellectuals who had been active during the Dreyfus affair returned to the fray. The first petition appeared in *L'Humanité* on 3 March 1913: the signatories expressed their horror at 'the prospect of such a serious measure being passed in a panic, as it would change military law with unprecedented haste'. There were fears that it would damage the economic and intellectual life of the country, or even that it would force French civilization into retreat. In-depth discussions were called for. The first to sign the petition was the novelist Anatole France. His name was followed by those of seven professors at the Collège de France (including Antoine Meillet and Sylvain Lévi) seven at the Sorbonne, including Charles Seignobos, Charles Andler, Léon Brunschvicg, Émile Durkheim and Célestin Bouglé. The petition was also signed by Marcel Mauss, Lucien Herr, Dominique Parodi, Hubert Bourgin, Émile Chartier ('Alain') and Félicien Challaye. A second list of names, including those of Lucien Lévy-Bruhl and François Simiand, was published on 16 March. It was Mauss's involvement that mobilized the *Année* network. He was now more active then ever, publishing articles, chairing a meeting in the 'Panthéon' riding school based on the theme 'The entire left against nationalist reaction', and drafting a petition 'For national dignity; against military panic'. In the issue of *Cahiers de la quinzaine* dated 27 April 1913, Charles Péguy violently denounced this 'sudden and underhand campaign' against the extension of military service to three years. He was harshly critical of the group of 'dear professors' who, by setting themselves up as 'the guardians of intellectual interests' and as 'the conservatory of French thought', were playing a double game and encouraging anarchy (see Sirinelli 1990: 42–5).

In the years leading up to the war, the decline of France and, more generally, of French civilization was once more the main topic of debate. 'Is France decadent?' asked Dominique Parodi (1914). As Robert Hertz had argued only a few years earlier, one had only to compare France's military might, industrial output, immigration or birth rate with those of other European countries to set the alarm bells ringing: 'The most obvious effect of depopulation is to put France in a position of inferiority with respect to other states, and especially Germany . . . The moral standing of a country depends largely upon its numerical size' (Hertz 1910: 11).

The situation was very worrying. As Jaurès put it, peace and democracy were as inseparable as reaction and war. 'We are playing dangerous games', wrote Mauss (1997[1914]), who refused to make any predictions because everything was so uncertain. He claimed to be optimistic, but the situation was, in his view, explosive.

Unjustified Aggression

On June 28, the heir to the throne of the Austro-Hungarian Empire, Archduke Franz-Ferdinand, and his wife were assassinated by Serb terrorists in Sarajevo. Marcel Mauss no more imagined that this would lead to war than did the other socialists. Durkheim also believed that 'while it is abominable, this murder guarantees peace in Europe'.[1] At the begin of July, he made a short trip to Amsterdam, where he was received by Jean-Jacques Selverda de Grave, professor of philology at the University of Groningen. He also took the opportunity to 'go to see a few Rembrandts:

his *Night Watch* is one of the most admirable things I have seen in my life'.
But 'due to the heat', he was 'so tired' that he could not stay in Holland for
as long as he would have liked.

In July, Austria issued an ultimatum and declared war on Serbia; this
event 'awakened Europe from its dreams of peace' (Durkheim 1975[1917]:
446). The military machine had been set in motion: partial mobilization in
St Petersburg, mobilization in Austro-Hungary, and France began to take
military measures. Jean Jaurès tried with irrepressible energy to keep the
peace. On the evening of 23 July, he was shot in the head as he dined with
his comrades from *L'Humanité*. Consternation ensued. The same three
words were on everyone's lips: 'He is dead . . . He is dead . . .'. Mauss, who
was on holiday in Chamonix, had lost both a friend and his hero (Mauss
1997[1921]).[2]

On 1 August both Berlin and Paris ordered a general mobilization.
Germany declared war on Russia on 1 August, and on France the following day. The former anti-militarists followed the example of the socialists,
abandoned their pacifist stance and became, as one of the characters in
Roger Martin du Gard's novel *Les Thibault* put it, 'the most eager' to
respond to the call and to 'get the war going'. In 1910, the *député* Marcel
Sembat had written a pacifist tract entitled 'Faites un roi, sinon faites la
paix' ['Make a king; otherwise, make peace'].[3] Together with Jules Guesde
and Albert Thomas, he now sided with the majority in the Socialist Party
(led by *L'Humanité*'s editor Pierre Renaudel) in calling for a fight for
victory. On 27 August, both he and Guesde agreed to serve in René
Viviani's government. Sembat was made minister for public works. This
was an important position in wartime, as the organization of transport
was vital if the army was to be supplied with weapons and food, if economic life was to continue and if the population's need for coal and other
supplies was to be met. His principal private secretary was Léon Blum, a
former socialist activist and journalist on *L'Humanité*.

The French army suffered so many setbacks that it was forced to retreat.
The enemy was drawing closer to Paris, and German planes were bombing
the capital. This worried Durkheim: 'The Germans are bypassing Paris
and moving south-east, and that worries me. What are they trying to do?'[4]
A few days later, he wrote: 'We have seen a terrible few days! It seems to
me that there really were times when people thought the Germans were
going to enter the city and that it was inevitable. I was even told that we
would have had to give up the attempt to defend the city.'[5] At the request
of the military, the government moved to Bordeaux in September.

Durkheim asked himself about the reasons for what was becoming a
real 'cataclysm': 'Who wanted war, and why?' It was clear to him that 'the
double murder [of Franz-Ferdinand and his wife] was the starting point
for the war', and that Austria was largely responsible: its 'warmongering'
ultimatum had been 'deliberately unacceptable'. But the real villain was
Germany. He and his colleague Ernest Denis wrote a full indictment, and
there was no shortage of proof: Germany had not made a single gesture
towards peace: it had all been empty talk: 'It was Germany that declared

war on Russia and France, using lies to justify both declarations of war' (Durkheim and Denis 1915: 59).

Many saw the fight against Germany as a war between 'civilization and barbarism'. Germany's brutality, cynicism and complete contempt for justice were, according to Henri Bergson, clear proof that the country had 'regressed to the state of savagery'.[6] How could the French not hate Germany? At the very beginning of the war, Maurice Halbwachs admitted to his wife: 'I cannot renounce the things I once admired. I owe too much to German thinkers', and he expressed the hope that the war would 'serve to promote the democratic ideal'.[7] Robert Hertz was equally reluctant 'to let my brain be addled and to use the war as an excuse for hating everything German, and for loathing Wagner and Nietzsche'.[8]

One of the first to be mobilized was André Durkheim, on 5 August. He had done one's year's military service in Lille before going to the École normale supérieure. A brilliant student, he had been awarded the *Diplôme d'études supérieures* for what his father called a 'very highly regarded' dissertation on 'Leibniz's notion of phenomenon'. He had just been declared eligible to take the oral part of the *agrégation* and was, as his father put it, 'taking his orals' when war broke out. It was with great emotion that he learned that his son had been mobilized: 'Until then, fortune had smiled upon me. Life had been good to me. I now had a definite feeling that this was the beginning of a new life for me.' André was preparing himself for 'the new duties that awaited him', and was trying to play down what looked liked an inevitable separation. 'He had never shown his affection and natural tenderness with greater charm; we had never felt that he was so completely ours' (Durkheim 1975[1917]: 448). Durkheim knew that his son had been overwrought when he took his *agrégation* and it was not 'without worry' that he saw him leave: 'André has gone. Durkheim is in a pitiful state', Mauss told Henri Hubert. Everything seemed 'very empty' to Émile and his wife. 'His bedroom was opposite ours and my study; that way, he was most closely involved in our lives. We could feel that he was by our side all through the morning, and all through the night.'[9] André often wrote to his family to let them know where he was. On 6 August, his regiment crossed the Belgian frontier and received an enthusiastic welcome from a population who greeted them as liberators. 'We experienced some unforgettable scenes', André wrote to his father.

Durkheim was in Paris in mid-August and had every intention of staying there 'at least until the situation becomes clearer'. He had rented a country house in Montmorency, but he and his family could obviously not go away 'until the war has moved away from the frontier'. André was 'very close to the Germans' in either Belgium or Luxembourg. He had yet to see any 'action', but was, Durkheim told Hubert, 'very close to the front'. He added: 'It goes without saying that this makes us twice as worried.' 'Let us hope we can rid Germany of Prussia, and Prussia of its military caste: that is our real war aim.'[10]

By 15 August, nearly four million men had been mobilized. This was, as Philippe de Félice put it, 'a storm that is scattering our lives in all directions'.[11] Several of the *Année sociologique*'s young collaborators, including Hertz, were among the first to be mobilized. Sergeant Robert Hertz was 33, and left his 'beloved' wife Alice and his 'little Antoine' in Paris. Maxime David, Antoine Bianconi, Jean Reynier and R. Gelly were also called up, as was Félice, who volunteered to serve as a chaplain: 'That's just about all I am fit for.' Some of Durkheim's friends and relatives were declared unfit for active service: amongst these were his nephew Henri and Mauss's student Raymond Lenoir as well as Célestin Bouglé and Maurice Halbwachs. Ignoring the express wishes of the director of higher education, the 'deeply patriotic' Bouglé would not contemplate staying in his position as a teacher; he wanted to be directly involved in the defence of the nation. Although unfit for active service, he volunteered and served as a medical orderly in Vichy and Riom, and then at a rehabilitation centre in Clermont; he then put in a request for a transfer to the military zone, where he remained until spring 1917. Halbwachs bitterly regretted having been declared unfit for service; he had hoped to be mobilized: 'I will regret not having seen action for the rest of my life.'[12]

Meanwhile, Marcel Mauss was declared fit for service on 17 August and, on 3 September, volunteered for the duration. He was 42, but considered himself 'strong enough to make a good soldier'. His decision to enlist worried those who were close to him, and especially his mother. And when he expressed a desire to be sent to the front, his uncle disapproved: 'Why go to such lengths? You did your duty by volunteering . . . I wouldn't send you to the front if I was in the government. You can serve the cause better without getting yourself riddled with bullets. Think about it. You've done everything.'[13] In December, Marcel became an interpreter attached to the British 27th Division.

Émile was anxious to have news 'from our soldiers'. By 'our soldiers', he meant André, Marcel and his son-in-law Jacques. He corresponded with his nephew (whose 'life is closely bound up with my own'[14]) on a regular basis, writing to him at least once a week, and sometimes more often. He talked about what he was doing and gave him family news about his daughter Marie, his grandson Claude, his sisters Céline and Rosine, telling him about their illnesses, travels and so on. He and his wife also had to look after 'their' soldiers by sending them postal orders, money and parcels of food and clothing (including woollen socks and flannel shirts for the winter). They also sent books, brochures and newspapers. In addition, they had commitments in Paris, such as keeping an eye on Mauss's apartment.

Durkheim obviously also talked about the war. In the early days of September 1914, he rejoiced at France's first victories: 'For the first time, we can at last feel that the iron monster has been wounded.' He also hoped that something positive would come out of the war:

> The kingdoms of Prussia and Austria are unnatural aggregates that were created by force and that are held together by force. They have not succeeded in gradually replacing forced and enforced dependency with a

consensual union. An empire that was shaped in that way cannot last. The geography of Europe will be redrawn on a rational and moral basis.[15]

The Battle of the Marne (6–13 September) marked the victory of the French and British forces which, under the leadership of Joffre, halted the German invasion. This 'prodigious' victory was greeted with enthusiasm by Robert Hertz: 'I am unshakeably optimistic, and I believe that a rejuvenated and rehabilitated France will have its place in the new Europe.'[16] Durkheim, for his part, was not 'over-optimistic': 'Our pain and suffering are not yet over.'[17] He believed that the war would go on until the effects of Germany's economic weakness and food shortages made themselves felt. France should not, he wrote to his friend Xavier Léon, 'be under any illusion'.[18] A few days later, he told Léon: 'Fostering illusions would be a bad thing . . . This terrible, interminable battle will not be decided quickly.'[19] The only prospect was that of a 'life of anxiety'. But he was impressed by the population's attitude during these 'painful moments'. People remained 'calm, and confident without being boastful . . . No screams, no gangs running through the streets. Everyone is serious, and prepared to do their duty.'[20]

Durkheim watched what was 'going on' with nervous attention, and read the 'war news' with great care. He regularly shared his impressions with his nephew in his letters, and sometimes even made predictions: 'It seems more and more likely that the denouement will come somewhere in the Balkans. That would be a triumph for logic: the fire that was started in the Balkans will be put out in the Balkans. But what is going on? That is the great mystery.' At other times, he refused to make any predictions: 'I do not know much, and I do not want to know anything, at least where day-to-day events are concerned.' He claimed to have 'absolutely no data to tell me what is going on', but added, a few days later: 'I have some definite news about the Russians: they are becoming dangerously short of rifles.' He was convinced of only one thing: 'We must be self-reliant.'[21]

Nor was his nephew under any illusion as to how long the war might go on: 'They think it will be a short war, but I think it will be a long campaign', he wrote to Henri Hubert. 'Millions of men will have to be worn down; it is a horrible task and it will take time. We will all see action, my dear chap.'[22] Maurice Halbwachs thought the same: 'All this will go on for a very long time, and we will suffer defeats even if we do win.' And while he did not wish to be too pessimistic, and hoped that 'a new Europe and a new society' would emerge from the ordeal, Sylvain Lévi was worried: 'The worst of all fears comes when you fear for the future of the country', he wrote to Henri Hubert.[23] Lévi did not believe that the war would soon be over: 'At the rate things are going, there seems to be no end in sight . . . But we all know that patience is one of victory's weapons.'[24]

At the beginning of September. André Durkheim was evacuated to Nevers as he was suffering from double exhaustion: first, his *agrégation*; then, since 5 August, at the front. Émile thought of going to see his son at the time; he was 'comfortably settled' in Guéthary (Basses-Pyrénnées) with his wife Louise. The situation worried him: 'We are well, even though no one can feel well anywhere. And the prospect of staying here, perhaps for months, frightens me somewhat.' The German advance on Paris had forced the government and President Poincaré to retreat to Bordeaux on 2 September, where they were beyond the reach of the German armies. They remained there until the second week in December.

Émile was very concerned about a 'possible return' to Paris. 'I must be in Paris for October. It goes without saying that academic life will start again. I have to be there.'[25] 'Not being at his post' was out of the question for the professor. 'I cannot be paid for doing nothing.' Not doing anything preyed upon his mind: 'I can't tell you how much it makes me feel like a deserter.'[26] A few days later, he wrote again to Mauss: 'The endless stampede of this war means that I am in a painful situation. I cannot stay here doing nothing. I can't wait to get away.' He was still in Guéthary at the beginning of October: 'I'm fretting . . . I can't wait to get back to Paris, even if I do have to go on my own. I can't stand being almost on holiday like this.'[27]

The University in a Difficult Position

On 8 September, the university council met for the first time since the outbreak of war. Durkheim was not present. The academic community was preoccupied with two questions: university finances and staff salaries. The University of Paris's financial situation had, Rector Louis Liard told the meeting, 'been prosperous; the war has suddenly made it disastrous'. He therefore asked the deans to freeze all expenditure that was not 'absolutely indispensable.' Given the likely fall in income from fees, various temporary measures would also have to be taken: laboratories and institutes would have to be closed, chairs would have to be frozen and some lectures cancelled, and grant programmes, scientific field trips and personal research would either have to be cancelled or postponed.[28] Various problems immediately arose, including that of the upkeep of the botanical garden. The rector's view about the payment of salaries in wartime was that they should go on being paid and that this was to do with 'the rights of individuals'. Staff salaries must therefore not be cut and payment must not be suspended. 'Fortunately, we have not yet reached that point', he told the next meeting, but he was sad to announce that there would be no promotions in 1915: 'In the present circumstances, paying everyone's salary will be difficult enough.' There was no freeze on promotions, but they were postponed.

The Sorbonne reopened. 'Academic life is about to start again!' Durkheim wrote to Xavier Léon. 'Neither we nor our students will be able to take much interest in it. And besides, I don't know what students we will have.'[29] As always, the council's attention was focused on 'current issues' such as heating, the state of the roof and the problem of the car belonging to the Nice observatory. But the war had created a new situation for the university: teaching had to go on and students had to be prepared to study for degrees and examinations (including the *agrégation*) even though so many teachers and students were in the armed forces. There also had to be plans for 'special exams to be taken after the war by students who are in the forces'. The ever-pragmatic Rector Liard recognized that 'the difficulties are real but not insurmountable'. The council expressed the wish that 'when hostilities are over, special measures will be taken to make up for the disruption to the classes of 1914, 1915 and 1916'.[30]

The University's financial position meant that it had much less room for manoeuvre than usual. When the proposed budget was analysed at the end of December 1915, Croiset found himself in the sad position of 'having to let go a distinguished teacher who had, over the past eight years, won the respect and sympathy of his colleagues', because the university would not fund his salary of 8,000 francs. The colleague in question was Célestin Bouglé. Émile Durkheim intervened to endorse the dean's remarks and to regret not only the departure of his colleague and close collaborator, but also the cancellation, albeit on a temporary basis, of a course on the history of social economics that had 'introduced something new into the faculty's teaching'. 'Even so,' the dean pointed out, 'M. Bouglé is not a victim . . . Although the lack of funding means that his secondment will come to an end, he will still have his position in Toulouse.' At the end of the discussion, Durkheim once more intervened to make his position clear: 'The faculty of letters has never dreamed of asking the university to establish a chair for M. Bouglé.' Louis Liard thanked his colleagues Croiset and Durkheim for 'not making proposals he would have had to reject'.[31]

There was no funding, and teaching conditions were deteriorating. 'Teaching has never been as exhausting as it is in the present circumstances', Dean Croiset said on behalf of his colleagues. 'We never get the same audience for two lectures in a row.' Durkheim agreed with him and asked that, because of the circumstances, the Shrove Tuesday and mid-Lent breaks not be cancelled: 'This year, the first semester is already so long that the teaching staff will be really exhausted. They are already beginning to look tired. A two-day break would do them a lot of good.' He added: 'The idea of a holiday does necessarily imply the idea of festivities.' The rector agreed with his colleagues in the faculty of letters, but suggested that they meet halfway – they could have two days for Shrove Tuesday but no break in mid-Lent – because he wanted, 'in the circumstances', to 'rule out any idea of festivities'.[32]

Intellectual and scientific activity slowed down as many young colleagues left for the front. What would happen to the learned journals? Several, including the *Année sociologique* and the *Année philosophique*, ceased publication. Others, like the *Revue de métaphysique et de morale*, just managed to survive. René Worms had recently resigned as editor of the *Revue internationale de sociologie*, which continued to appear throughout the war, and had handed the editorship over to none other than Gaston Richard, who was also secretary to the Institut international de sociologie. He recruited the Bourgin brothers, Roger Bastide and André Lalande, with Robert Michels and Pitirim Sorokin as foreign correspondents. This was beginning to look like a form of trench warfare.

What could the university do now that the country was at war and the younger generations were in the armed forces? The academic community could not remain passive, and tried to influence public opinion as best it could using its weapons of the spoken and written word. The big public lectures organized by the Société des amis de l'Université de Paris from the winter of 1915 onwards dealt with contemporary issues. Ernest Lavisse spoke on 'Prussia' and Charles Andler on 'Military sociology in nineteenth-century Germany'. At the École des hautes études sociales, 'the military situation' was on the syllabus, and a 'political week' was organized, with debates on domestic and foreign policy involving Marcel Cachin and Marcel Sembat. Most of the lectures announced for 1915 at the Collège libre des sciences sociales also dealt with the war: 'Wartime finance', 'The public spirit and the war', 'War and public health' and 'War orphans'. Ferdinand Buisson also gave a series of lectures on 'Social and moral action after the war'. Academics were already thinking about what would happen when the war ended.

There was also the problem of relations with German colleagues. Should what were often close relationships be broken off? In 1913, the sociologist Robert Michels left the University of Turin to pursue his career in Basel. His plans for the future included a great *Sociological Encyclopedia* that would include contributions from famous intellectuals – economists, historians and philosophers – as well as German, French and Italian sociologists. His network of contacts, the number of people he knew and his organizational abilities were such that no one was better qualified for such an undertaking. He had contributed to various German, Italian and French journals, and had attended the international congresses of 1909 and 1910. Durkheim and his close collaborators Bouglé and Halbwachs agreed to contribute to his encyclopedia project. Durkheim laid down only one condition: his article had to have a coauthor, whom he described as a former student and someone 'very distinguished' and who would 'support him very well'.[33] Maurice Halbwachs eagerly indicated which entries – themes and authors – he would like to write and which he believed himself 'competent' to write: they covered more than 50 authors and themes.[34]

In September, Durkheim, who was in the Basses-Pyrénnées to 'keep the women and children [in the family] safe from any threatened attack', told Michels that he had 'doubts' about contributing to a encyclopedia written in German for publication in Germany: 'The contributors would be paid in German currency.' In his view, there could be no question of a French author contributing to such a project. 'I cannot agree to make any gesture of solidarity towards a people that dishonoured itself by committing crimes that the entire civilized world condemns.' And to avoid all misunderstandings, he added: 'I am by no means a nationalist. But in my view, that makes the moral failings I have just described all the more serious.'[35]

Durkheim did not, however, rule out the possibility of accepting Michels's invitation 'when the war is over' and 'when peace has been re-established'. Knowing that Michels also wrote for the German-Swiss press, he also asked him for 'a favour for a cause for which he had been good enough to show some sympathy': 'Would you be willing to talk about [our] work?' By 'our work', he was referring to a series of pamphlets on 'the main questions raised by the war'. They were, he added, 'serious, scientific studies'.

A Response to the 'Manifesto of German Intellectuals'

When a group of 93 German intellectuals and academics published a manifesto and sent it to universities in neutral countries, French academics were somewhat more than annoyed. Even Durkheim's close collaborator Maurice Halbwachs, who was an admirer of all things German, was disillusioned: 'The manifesto of the German intellectuals is hard [to swallow]. These people are being deceived – and more than deceived – by their government.'[36] The member of the University of Paris's council planned to make an immediate reply. Durkheim was present for the discussion, and spontaneously expressed his agreement: 'The university cannot refrain from commenting . . . Rightly or wrongly, public opinion expects France to protest.' He recalled the toast that the secretary of the Berlin Academy of Sciences had made at the banquet given in his honour when he was in Amsterdam in July:

> At the time, the impertinent and tactless language of the man, who seemed to think the whole world depended on Germany, made me smile. I am now in a better position to realize that he was simply expressing, in a ridiculous way, the megalomaniac dreams of today's Germans. They feel an unhealthy need to rule the world.[37]

Rector Liard was not really convinced that such protests would have any effect, but thought that the university should protest in order to satisfy sections of French public opinion. He accepted Durkheim's arguments and concluded that 'something must be done'. The plan for a manifesto was supported by most council members. A manifesto of French intellectuals, on the other hand, was out of the question. How could anyone draw up such a list? 'We would have 500 or 600 signatories, perhaps even 1,000. It would be a crush, and it would end in failure.' A manifesto signed only by members of the university council was also out of the question. An attempt should be made to have it 'signed collectively' by every university in France.

The manifesto, which was dated 3 November 1914 and 'signed by every university in France' (with the exception of Lille) was simply entitled: 'The universities of France speak to universities in neutral countries.' It opened with a whole series of questions. 'Who wanted war?' 'Who, during the brief space of time Europe had for deliberation, had tried to find a formula for reconciliation?' 'Who, in contrast, had refused every proposal made by Britain, Russia, France and Italy?' 'Who triggered a war just when the conflict seemed to be dying down, as though it had been waiting for the opportune moment?' 'Who had guaranteed Belgian neutrality, and then violated it?' 'In what conditions had the University of Louvain been destroyed?' 'In what conditions had Reims cathedral been set on fire?' 'In what conditions had incendiary bombs been dropped on Notre-Dame in Paris?'

The 'facts alone' supplied the answer to all these questions. The French universities went on to denounce their German counterparts for betraying German thought and the German tradition of Leibniz, Kant and Goethe, and surrendering to Prussian militarism and its claim to 'world domination'. There was no shortage of proof. A teacher at the University of Leipzig had recently written: 'The future fate of European culture rests upon our shoulders.' Despite this narrow nationalism, French universities continued to believe that 'civilization is not the creation of one people, but that of all peoples, and that the intellectual and moral wealth of humanity was created by the natural variety and necessary independence of all national spirits'. What was at stake was clear: 'Like the allied armies [the universities] are, for their part, defending the freedom of the world.'[38]

Attracting Foreign Students

Given its prestige and the influence of its teaching staff, the university was in a position to play a major role in defending the universal dimension of scientific knowledge and also intellectual freedom by mobilizing its many networks in other countries. Exchanges between the University of Paris and American universities, and especially Harvard and Columbia, went ahead as planned. Ernest Lichtenberger, a professor of German language and literature, visited New York in the spring of 1915, and Gustave Lanson followed in his footsteps the following year. Their mission was to gather information about the attitude of Americans towards the war between France and Germany, and to influence American public opinion. The university was, in other words, one element in the strategy of a country that was at war.

The issue of foreign students quickly came up. This question had preoccupied the University of Paris for many years and was regularly discussed in council. Some worried about 'the constant increase in the number of foreign students who come to Paris simply to improve the standard of their spoken French', while others saw the influx of foreign students as 'one of the best ways of expanding French influence' – in other words, demonstrating that Paris was, above all, 'a centre for work and an intellectual focus'.[39] In late April 1915, Rector Liard told the members of council of his fears for the future 'After the war, there will be a fall in the number of students, and therefore a fall in income.' The university thus had to 'attract foreign students'. Hence the need for a committee to discuss the issue. The decision to form a committee was taken at the meeting of 7 February 1916, and Durkheim agreed to chair it. The committee set to work immediately and held its first meeting on 15 March; it then met for several hours a week until the Easter vacation. Durkheim's working method was to canvass or consult people who knew the United States well, as well as famous Americans who were 'known for their sympathetic attitude to France, and to the University of Paris in particular'.[40]

Durkheim presented the committee's report to council on 29 May. He began by paying tribute to the 'devotion' shown by everyone to whom the 'appeal' had been addressed. He then recalled that a committee should, as a matter of urgency, be set up to 'look into ways of keeping foreign students in Paris, and of guaranteeing that their material and extra-curricular living conditions were in keeping with their tastes and habits'. The goal of the commission was not, to his regret, 'very clearly defined. Was it meant to be looking at students of all nationalities?' The first exchanges made it clear that the committee would have to 'restrict itself to American students, given the extreme complexity of the questions, even when defined in this limited sense'. What was at stake was obvious: American students who intended to go to Germany had to be attracted to Paris. 'With a few rare exceptions, students who want to complete their education go to Germany . . . The main reason being that every American university has one or more adviser from German higher education who advises young people to go there, sings the praises of Germany's universities, hands out brochures, and so on.' The committee believed, however, that 'we can expect large numbers of students to come to Paris in order to demonstrate their sympathy for France and dislike of German culture'.[41]

But how many students could come to Paris? Durkheim believed that they 'might come in large numbers', given how many students there were in American universities and colleges. But if the scheme was to be successful – and here his informants agreed with him – they had to 'act, and act immediately'. There had to be an organized response, and the various problems should be dealt with 'resolutely'. The stakes were all the higher in that 'the solution we adopt may have repercussions on our academic life': 'We have an opportunity to reform certain customs, and we must seize it.' The problems or questions identified by the committee were as follows: (1) propaganda; (2) the question of degrees; (3) the moral and material organization of students' lives.

First objective: propaganda

It is all the more necessary to make ourselves known in America in that everyone agrees that we are either unknown or badly known there. Americans are well aware that there are a lot of great scholars in France, but they are usually unaware of the fact that there are centres of high culture in France, that academic life here is highly developed and that it bears comparison with that in Germany.

Hence the need for propaganda, 'but with a discretion that is in keeping with our French character'. The commission recommended the following methods: (1) publishing articles and interviews with senior academic figures in the American press; (2) writing a book on higher education in France (with photographs) and distributing it as widely as possible in the United States; (3) publishing and distributing a more academic book addressed especially to students and providing information on the courses on offer in Paris (this should include 'everything that can introduce American students to university life in Paris before they come here'); (4) organize courses in every American university to ensure that students interested in 'things French' have an adequate knowledge of the French language, which is 'poorly understood in the USA (with the help of the Alliance française d'Amérique and the funding of 10 or so grants for students who wish to spend two years in France and who intend to pursue an academic career); (5) establish a Franco-American Committee for propaganda purposes.

Second objective: degrees

It was clear to Durkheim that even when American students' interests and sympathies were aroused, they quickly encountered in the French system 'obstacles that might discourage them or put them off'. The rules were 'very difficult', admission requirements were very different, and some of them would have to pay fees.

Rector Liard thought that it would be possible to 'simplify' the rules and procedures, but Durkheim argued that this would still leave one problem intact: the nature of the academic qualifications awarded to foreign students. 'American students want, essentially, to be sure that their studies in France give them degrees whose authority cannot be questioned.' The difficulty arose because of the 'very peculiar' relationship between French universities and the state: in effect, the state was the degree-awarding authority, and a degree was a passport to employment in the public services. While the state awarded these degrees, there were also 'purely academic degrees that did not confer any rights on the holder'. This policy meant that there were two kinds of qualifications, and they did not have the same value; it was quite obvious to foreign students that purely academic degrees were 'of lower value'. The solution might, he thought, be to organize things around the more flexible system used for the science degree: a combination of three certificates of higher education were equivalent to a degree, and while some combinations were also equivalent to a teaching certificate, others were not. The degrees were 'the same in nominal terms, but not in terms of the rights they conferred'.

Third objective: organizing material and morale life

On arriving in Paris, students should find 'an organization that meets their needs.' Foreign students are, by definition, shy and there is therefore a danger that they will find themselves in the state of disorientation that even young French students experience. We must avoid that danger.' The publication of a general handbook and yearly booklets would, it was to hoped, help to prepare students for the new life that awaited them. It was also suggested that candidates for the *agrégation* in English should be recruited at the beginning of the academic year to help the new arrivals from America. These were only 'suggestions'. All these proposals would, Durkheim suggested, have to be looked at in more detail. He also pointed out that the teaching staff should not be forgotten, as they could play a 'major role': 'It is essential that students feel that they are supported by, guided by and in contact with their teachers.'

Turning to the more concrete issues affecting the lives of American students, the committee suggested, amongst other things, establishing a Franco-American university club to act as 'the centre of the lives of American students in Paris'.[42] Attention then turned to the question of accommodation for American students, who preferred to live with families. 'Such arrangements would be more in keeping with American ideas and customs.' Durkheim insisted that this statement required some qualification: 'Not all American students need to live with a family.' One thing was, however, clear: they all 'needed some comfort'; most would like a two-room apartment with a bathroom in a new house. The resources available to American students meant that they could afford such accommodation. This did, on the other hand, raise a lot of 'technical' questions: a supply of accommodation had to be created by advertising in the press, and there had to be quality controls.

Ultimately, Durkheim concluded, the important thing was that 'as soon as they arrive, and throughout their stay, students must feel that they are being looked after and supported'. Attempts therefore had to be made to 'create in France something resembling the tutorial and family-based system that means so much to English-speaking people'. This meant more contact between students and teachers, and between French and American students. There were all sorts of ways of promoting these contacts: friendship meetings, geographical and archaeological walks, organized visits to museums, tours of Paris, etc.

The most 'immediately urgent' of all these tasks was, in Durkheim's view, propaganda, and they had to begin without delay. He suggested setting up a standing committee similar to the one that had been responsible for the preliminary studies, made up of representatives from the various faculties and university institutions. It should take responsibility for outlining a general plan and ensuring its implementation. It should also have the power to modify it in the light of the lessons it learned day by day.

The committee had done its work well, concluded the rector as he warmly thanked Durkheim and its other members. He took the view that the propaganda work should begin before the American students arrived. The faculties and other institutions should therefore come to an agreement as a matter of urgency. But was that possible? Durkheim had good reason to be pessimistic, because 'we tried to reach such an agreement 25 years ago, and we failed to do so'.

The Propaganda Effort: 'Who Wanted War?'

Durkheim found the lack of activity and the waiting difficult, and wanted 'the authorities to find some way of making use of us in Paris'. Early in October 1914, Jacques Hadamard went to see him in Guéthary to discuss plans. Durkheim knew Hadamard well, as he had taught mathematics in Bordeaux (1893–7) and at the Sorbonne (1897–1909) before being elected to the Collège de France as professor of mechanics in 1909. A Jewish Dreyfusard (he was the cousin of Captain Dreyfus's wife), he was also a member of the Ligue des droits de l'homme.

The two colleagues discussed Hadamard's proposal to 'give lectures in neutral countries in order to fight German influence and its effects on public opinion'. Hadamard had recently submitted his proposal to Marcel Sembat through Léon Blum, and Sembat has passed it on to Théophile Delcassé, the radical *député* who was minister for foreign affairs. At the time, Blum was principal parliamentary secretary to the socialist Sembat, who had just been appointed minister for transport. Durkheim could not refuse Hadamard his support, but wanted 'to talk to the appropriate person in Bordeaux so as to ensure that the goal of the plan and the means for its implementation are described properly'.[43]

When he got back to Paris, Durkheim reworked the proposal into a 'pamphlet project', and his suggestion was approved by the ministry for foreign affairs at the end of October. The plan was for a series of 'Studies and documents on the war', to be published by the Librairie Armand Colin. The editorial committee was chaired by Ernest Lavisse from the Académie française.[44] Durkheim agreed to act as secretary to the committee, and all correspondence was sent to him at his home address. He immediately set to work on the first pamphlet by analysing a mass of documents and putting everything on index cards. His aim was to 'show what had led the Kaiser to rush things by declaring war on Russia': 'That the responsibility lies with Germany is beyond any doubt, and there are no serious criticisms to be made of Russia . . . I have proof.' He also wanted to reply to the German intellectuals. 'It keeps me busy, and it is fascinating', he told his nephew.[45]

At the end of October, Durkheim went to Bordeaux 'to talk to all those of our statesmen who have been involved in these events'. His first discussions were with the ministers Sembat and Jean-Baptiste Bienvenu-Martin, Berthelot from foreign affairs, and Russia's ambassador in Paris Aleksander P. Iswolski, with whom he had 'an interesting conversation'.

He also asked to meet President Raymond Poincaré, who agreed to speak to him at the beginning of January 1915. 'I spent an hour with him. I submitted all the delicate questions to him, and we found ourselves in agreement. The difference between him and the professional diplomats is that he is familiar with the texts, and not just with what he has been told about them.'[46]

All this activity was not, however, enough to 'distract [him] as much as [he] would have liked from the way the war was going'. 'It is diffi- cult to work on days when the news has been poor. But you get on with it all the same, once you get over the immediate shock, the tugs at the heartstrings and the melancholy.'[47] Durkheim made no secret of the fact that he was afraid, and the 'tenacity' of the Germans both frightened and disturbed him. He was writing his first pamphlets: 'I am working like I haven't worked for 30 years. It is unusual for me to leave my study before 10.30 or 11.' Fortunately, his 'tract' was 'finished' by mid-December. He wanted to keep it short: no more than 60 printed pages. But he also wanted to re-read it 'to make the exposition a little less dense'. He believed that he had 'irrefutable proof'.[48]

Now that his pamphlet was written. Durkheim was afraid that his life would be 'empty'. But in his capacity as secretary to the Comité de pub- lication des études et documents de la guerre, he found that he had 'quite a lot of correspondence and all sorts of worries'. 'I don't have a moment to myself', he wrote. And at the beginning of February, he again wrote: 'I am still a busy man.' He scarcely had time for 'the walk I should be having between 5 and 6'. He had in fact to 'be a Jack of all trades': he corrected the proofs of other pamphlets, including that by Joseph Bédier,[49] made sure that 'the publications are ready and that there will be no delays', oversaw their translation (into five or six languages with the help of a team of translators), made sure that they were distributed as 'widely as pos- sible', signed contracts with foreign publishers, and wrote many letters. Even though he had a 'great deal of help' (from, for instance, Max Leclerc at Éditions Armand Colin), it was a lot of work: 'I'm playing at being a journalist, organizing propaganda, outlining a proposal for my own pamphlet, and I have my classes. Of course I can put up with all that. But a bit of rest would be welcome.'[50] He also had to write an article for the *New York Tribune*. But that was 'a good business deal: This is the fourth reprint. Four print runs of three thousand copies . . . Everyone realizes that our propaganda is inaugurating a new genre.'

In terms of distribution, one of Durkheim's goals was to 'reach the socialist groups' in France (through Pierre Renaudel and Jean Longuet), in the neutral countries, and in Germany (through Milhaud, who was living in Switzerland). Renaudel, the editor of *L'Humanité*, was a friend of Marcel Mauss's; he was elected as a Socialist *député* in 1914. Longuet, also a Socialist *député* and a contributor to *L'Humanité*, was the leading light in the minority pacifist current in the Socialist Party. He was cooperative and agreed to meet Durkheim at the paper, but he did not turn up, leaving Durkheim 'hanging about for three-quarters of an hour'. Durkheim found

L'Humanité's attitude to him 'incomprehensible', as the paper would give him 'no hint as to how to contact socialist groups and personalities . . . I cannot explain *L'Humanité*'s attitude . . . I don't think I have said or done anything to hurt them.'[51]

Durkheim was harshly critical of *L'Humanité* and argued that its belief that 'it is possible [to rebuild on] the ruins of the socialism of the past' was 'based on a fantasy'. 'I don't believe a word of it', he retorted and gave at least two good reasons why he was sceptical. Being German in origin, Marxism was unlikely to enjoy any popularity in France, and Marxist slogans such as 'Workers of the world, unite' were, in the present circumstances, empty. There was no doubt in his mind: 'We have to reformulate what we mean by internationalism, especially as the old formula is deplorable and damages the cause of true socialism. International society transcends fatherlands. It is not a fatherland.'[52] Durkheim made his views clear in another letter to his nephew a few days later:

> The point is not to create a nationalist socialism, but to get away from the Marxist confusion that has damaged socialism, and that will damage it even more in future. It consists in seeing the workers' international society as a fatherland, and it is not a fatherland. Like every other form of international life, it complements the fatherland, but the workers are part of the fatherland just like everyone else. That is what we have to recognize. 'Workers of the world . . .' was a slogan for war. It has had its day, and it has done a lot of harm, except to the Germans, who have always interpreted it in their own way. Putting internationalism in its place is not the same thing as denying its existence. It complements national life, and is superior in one way and inferior in another. You cannot do anything to change what is blindingly obvious: there are as many forms of socialism as there are fatherlands.[53]

The first pamphlet to appear under Durkheim's name was coauthored with his colleague Ernest Denis, and was entitled *Qui a voulu la guerre? Les origines de la guerre d'après les documents diplomatiques* [*Who wanted war? The origins of the war according to diplomatic sources*]. It set out to provide objective proof that the German government was guilty. Durkheim and Denis were aware that they were biased and acting as 'both judge and jury': 'Our fatherland is at stake.' But they hoped to 'resist the possible influence of any nationalist prejudice, respectable as it might be' and to provide 'a full and objective account of events'. As with any other historical event, the origins of the war lay in 'distant and underlying causes' that were at once demographic, economic, ethnic, and so on. But 'impersonal causes' had no effect unless 'human desires can be turned into actions'. Before war could break out, in other words, 'the desire for peace must falter': a state had to want to go to war (Durkheim and Denis 1915: 3–4).

In order to answer the question 'Who wanted war?', Durkheim and Denis put together a collection of diplomatic statements from the Russian, French, Belgian and German governments, but they had no access to chancellery 'secrets'. Their goal was 'to trace step by step the series of exchanges that had filled the harrowing week during which the fate of Europe was decided'. All they had to do to reveal the truth was, they believed, to 'relate the facts, simply, honestly, and in order'. In other words, follow the course of political history and political actors. Having 'listed' the facts,[54] Durkheim and Denis drew up 'the moral balance sheet of the various actors in the tragedy, and apportioned their respective responsibilities'. The world was divided into two camps: those who wanted peace (Russia, Britain and France) and who, while they were prepared to defend their own interests, had supported all attempts at reconciliation, and the 'warmongers' (Austria and Germany). Denis and Durkheim argued that French foreign policy had always been 'irreproachable'. Of course, France had not forgotten Alsace and Lorraine – 'Who would dare to say that remaining true to the religion of memory is a crime?' – but had never wanted war, and had 'fought to the end, and with all its strength, to keep the peace' (Durkheim and Denis 1915: 54). As Célestin Bouglé also argued (1914),[55] France had gone to war primarily to defend moral goals such as justice, democracy, law and peace between peoples.

The charges against Germany, on the other hand, were damning: 'It was Germany that . . .', 'It was Germany . . . .' This was a new version of Émile Zola's 'J'accuse'. Durkheim and Denis criticized Germany for saying one thing and adopting a policy that meant another, and German diplomacy for its lack of 'psychological sense': 'It cannot see what goes on in the souls of individuals and nations, and does not understand the reasons why they act, especially when those reasons are complex and delicate' (Durkheim and Denis 1915: 56). Hence the 'misunderstandings' and the 'unfounded accusations'. They then analysed the character and behaviour of Kaiser Wilhelm, and concluded that they had changed: 'We forget that men change over time and as circumstances change.' He had undergone a 'moral revolution': a man of peace had become a warmonger.[56] His need to 'increase his prestige by doing something spectacular', his sense of honour, and the favourable situation were all so many facts that urged Germany 'not to miss' the opportunity that had come along. There was only one conclusion: Germany was guilty. When Robert Hertz, who was at the front, read Denis and Durkheim's study, he was somewhat disappointed: 'Durkheim's pamphlet is sober, vigorous and persuasive but, useful as it may be, it does not get us very far. But it is good that he has proved, coldly and scientifically, that the German government has been telling a pack of clumsy, crude and careless lies. And that is a relief for everyone!' (Hertz 2002: 196).

'The Monster': *Deutschland über alles*

Now that he had finished his first pamphlet, Durkheim was thinking of 'writing another tract on German imperialism': 'It was reading Treitschke that gave me the idea; he outlines a conception of the state that underpins what they are doing: contempt for international law, for neutrals, for small countries, and so on. It is a monstrous theory.'[57] He was trying to understand the mentality that could inspire such behaviour: 'We have here a real collective sickness, a sort of morbid hypertrophy of the will.'[58]

Durkheim was feeling 'a little tired': 'I am worn out with work and emotion . . . I am going to spend some time in bed over the next few days, and that will help me get over it', he told his nephew Marcel. But he was working – with interest – on his next pamphlet. 'I am still up to my ears in work', he wrote in April. 'Our propaganda industry is expanding by the day. I no longer have any time to myself. I haven't worked this hard since 1895–7.'[59] A few days later, he wrote: 'This very busy life would suit me very well if only my pamphlet was finished. I have had to restrict the subject in order to finish it.' His second pamphlet was entitled *L'Allemagne au-dessus de tout: la mentalité allemande et la guerre* [*Germany above all: German mentality and the war*]. 'An aggressive mood', 'a desire for war', 'contempt for international law', 'systematic inhumanity', 'cruelty as standard': how, asked Durkheim, could the Germans, who once belonged to 'the family of civilized peoples', have become such 'barbaric, aggressive and unscrupulous beings'? His hypothesis was that the origins of such actions were to be found in a 'set of ideas and feelings', and a 'mental and moral system' that served as a sort of 'backdrop to the country's consciousness'. There therefore was such a thing as a German 'mentality' or 'soul'. 'We knew of its existence, and we were to some extent aware of the threat it posed', said Durkheim who, as a young man, had so admired Germany.

Durkheim's study was largely based on the work of Heinrich von Treitschke, whom he described as 'one of those who educated contemporary Germany' and whom he regarded as 'an eminently representative figure'. Very much 'a man of his times', Treitschke was a friend of Bismarck's, an admirer of Wilhelm II, a professor at the University of Berlin, a journalist and a member of parliament, and he expressed 'the mentality of his milieu'. Hence the 'impersonal' nature of his work, in which 'all the principles of German diplomacy were outlined with a bold clarity'. That was, he concluded, more than enough to justify his choice (Durkheim 1915: 6).

What were these principles? They can be summed up in three points: (1) the state is sovereign, and above international law; (2) the state is above morality; (3) the state is above civil society. The system could be summed up as: 'The state is might.' The state described by Treitschke was a proud creature that could rescind international agreements and refuse to obey any international court; it waged war (a 'holy and moral' undertaking), demanded sacrifice and heroism of its people, and raised an army that was 'the physical strength of the nation'; and then it acted. The state was not 'an academy of the arts', and it was 'made to act, not think'. Great states were therefore preferable to small states because only a great state could develop a truly national pride.

Treitschke also rehabilitated Machiavellianism: the end justified the means. And while morality was usually seen as something that transcended the state, he elevated the state above all morality. Politics was therefore a 'dirty business', and no one could keep their hands clean. Hence the diplomatic ruses and the corrupt means used to subvert other states. The state's only duty was to be strong. The individual had to sacrifice himself to the community to which he belonged. In Durkheim's view, such a conception of the state was a 'historical and moral scandal': it marked a return to 'pagan morality' or 'tribal morality'. 'In our view – and when I say "our" I am referring to all civilized peoples and to everyone brought up in the school of Christianity – the primary goal of morality is to make humanity a reality' (Durkheim 1915: 24).

In a democratic society, the state and the people were 'two aspects of the same reality', but Treitksche argued that the relationship between state and what he called civil society (the family, trade, industry, religion, science, art) was antagonistic, even contradictory. He saw civil society as a 'mosaic of individuals and groups' without any natural unity in which there were conflicts, and as a 'confused tangle of all the interests one would imagine'. Civil society was a 'living kaleidoscope', and the state therefore had to be united, organized and stable. Relations between state and individual were also contradictory. Only the state had 'any sense of the common interest' and dictated laws that reflected that interest: citizens had a duty to obey. The world of politics was inevitably a harsh world. The ideal statesman was ambitious and intelligent, but he had the intelligence of a realist, an unbending will, and indomitable, unscrupulous energy.

Durkheim demonstrated that the acts (of war) committed by Germany were 'the logical application of this mentality'. Germany had violated Belgian neutrality and the Hague conventions, threatened small states that looked like 'real historical anachronisms', violated the law of nationalities (a principle recognized by 'civilized nations') and committed many acts of inhuman barbarity. These atrocities were not, he argued, individual crimes as they were all part of the sequence: from conception of the state, through rules of action (laid down by the army), to action (committed through the intermediary of individuals). They were expressions of a 'full organized system whose roots lay in the German public mentality and which functioned automatically' (Durkheim 1915: 39).

In conclusion, Durkheim described what he called the 'morbid nature' of the system of ideas known as the German mentality. Germany's soldiers, leaders and ministers were 'honest men', but in wartime, when public life was 'at its most intense', the mental system 'took over the conscience of individuals' and became the 'master of their wills'. They then became apologists for war, which thus became a school for abnegation and sacrifice. There was 'something abnormal and harmful' about this mystical idealism that made it 'a threat to humanity as a whole' (Durkheim 1915: 42). As pan-Germanism demonstrated, the will to absolute independence always turned the state into a 'superman' (*dixit* Nietzsche) and made universal hegemony an 'ideal limit'.

Durkheim analyses the formation of the pan-Germanist mythology that had helped to make Germany 'the highest earthly incarnation of divine might'. This was, in his view, 'a clear and typical case of social pathology'. He had no qualms about speaking of 'delirium' and 'megalomania', and diagnosed 'a morbid hypertrophy of the will, a sort of maniacal wanting'. This will, which aspired to 'wrench itself free from the action of natural forces', is, according to Durkheim, sick. When, by contrast, it accepted 'natural dependency', the will was 'normal and healthy'. Life was therefore based upon constraints: on the one hand, there was the physical world, with its 'natural forces', and, on the other, there was the social world', with its 'moral forces'. No one defied that law with impunity. This had two implications for the political life of both states and peoples: 'No state is powerful enough to rule for ever, to deny the will of its subjects, or to use external constraints to make them bend to its will.' And: 'A state cannot survive when it has humanity ranged against it' (Durkheim 1915: 45).

Durkheim likened the will for power to the major neuroses in which forces (those of the patient) sometimes become 'over-excited'. In the case of neuroses, the hyper-excitation was 'only temporary', and 'nature soon takes its revenge'. Not surprisingly, the same was true of the current war: Germany had been able to build 'a monstrous war machine', but it was impossible for Germany to rule the world. 'No one can tame the world', remarked Durkheim, adding: 'the monster's élan has already been halted.' His conclusion was deliberately optimistic: 'Life will not remain in chains for ever . . . it always begins to flow again, and throws the obstacles that block its freedom of movement up on to the river bank' (Durkheim 1915: 47).

Even though some colleagues and friends agreed with his analysis, Durkheim was slightly disappointed with the outcome of all his work: 'I was short of time, and simply took Treitschke as a representative example of a certain German mentality, and I had every justification for doing so. I found in his work the mental system I describe, and it explains all the actions of modern Germany. I tried to describe that mentality.'[60] Now that he had finished his second pamphlet, Durkheim took a few days of rest: 'As always when I have given birth to something, I needed a short break. Ten days were enough, and I'm feeling fine now.'[61]

Another 'well-documented' pamphlet appeared at the same time as Durkheim's. *Le Pangermanisme. Ses projets en cours* was by Charles Andler, professor of German language and literature in the Paris faculty of letters. A Dreyfusard and socialist activist, Andler was an ardent patriot and a prolific author who published four studies of pan-Germanism between 1915 and 1917. Durkheim tended to be quite critical of his colleague: 'I had no idea that Andler was so bad at saying what he thinks and had such difficulty in mastering his subject. I have not read a lot of his work.'[62]

Were there two Germanys, or one? Émile Boutroux (1915) supported the 'two Germanys' thesis: one was highly cultivated, and the other was barbaric. In his view, the war was a modern crusade, and a fully mobilized 'war literature' was needed to fight an enemy nation that had to be defeated both on the battlefield and in the intellectual sphere. Henri

Bergson also believed that there were two Germanys: the Germany of Hegel and that of Kant, a predator nation and a nation in love with moral beauty. He saw the war with Germany as 'civilization's war on barbarism' (see Azouvi 2007: 231).[63]

The propaganda campaign mobilized a number of academics. Philosophers, sociologists and historians became lecturers or essayists and used their skills in the interests of the nation. A few, like Élie Halévy, refused to lose their 'intellectual self-respect' by becoming propagandists. Halévy himself opted to serve as an orderly in a military hospital in Savoie: 'I would rather dress wounds than talk nonsense.'[64] Those journals that still appeared, like the *Revue internationale de la sociologie*, regularly published articles on the war. Flammarion published a series of books in its 'Bibliothèque de philosophie scientifique' collection, including its editor Gustave Le Bon's highly successful *Enseignements psychologiques de la guerre européenne* (1915) and *Premières conséquences de la guerre. Transformations mentales des peuples* (1916).

Bergson was one of the 'most mobilized' of all the philosophers: 'At the moment, I find it difficult to concentrate on anything other than the war. I am constantly preoccupied with it', he told a friend. He was one of the many who, being unable to serve on the front line, 'felt guilty about living in perfect safety' (see Prochasson and Rasmussen 1996: 194). Bergson enjoyed great fame. The Vatican blacklisted his work, but in January 1914 he was elected to the Académie des sciences morales et politiques. A month later, he was elected to the Académie française. He became one of French culture's most active spokesmen, and even agreed to go on lecture tours, first to Spain and then to the United States. The first of his four visits to the United States took place in January 1917. He met President Wilson in a bid to convince him to enter the war on the side of the Allies.

Other colleagues and contributors to the *Année* were also motivated by a 'desire to serve the national cause well' and were just as active. Lucien Lévy-Bruhl, Antoine Meillet, together with a number of other teachers, contributed anonymously to the *Bulletin de l'Alliance française*. The alliance was a national organization set up to promote the French language, and its *Bulletin* was designed to counter the 'enemy's cleverly organized' publicity campaign. While it obviously defended 'the cause of France', it also defended 'eternal justice, civilization, the sanctity of treaties and the freedom of all peoples'. The *Bulletin* began publication on 1 November 1914; from April 1915, it was also published in translation (in German, English, Spanish and Italian).

Lucien Lévy-Bruhl was also publishing propaganda, including a pamphlet entitled *La Conflagration européenne* (1915) and an article on the same theme: the economic and political causes of the European conflagration. His article appeared in the January 1915 issue of *Scientia*, an international journal published in Italy, which had asked representatives of various countries – some belligerent and others neutral – for their views on the war. The purpose of the 'survey' was to identify 'objectively, serenely and, in a word, scientifically' the factors and causes that had led to war.

In his reply, Lévy-Bruhl made no attempt to evaluate the personal role of individuals; in his view, actors were, especially at times of crisis, 'the individual organs of the collective will'. He did, on the other hand, attempt to identify the political, economic and even psychological causes of the war, and explained that there was a sort of structural misunderstanding between Germany and its neighbours: 'A feeling of hostility, in which we believed when it was not real, became real because we believed in it.'

When he read this article by his friend and colleague, Durkheim reacted immediately by sending him, at the end of February, his congratulations: 'The article on the war is of a high standard, and I readily agree with your main ideas and your conclusion.' He could not, on the other hand, accept the idea that the war was 'necessary'. 'I am not sure that there is such a thing as a necessary war, in the scientific sense of the term. Some wars are useful, and therefore likely to break out. But there are no causes that imply war in the sense of physical necessity.' He saw the war, rather, as a 'contingent event' in the sense that falling down the stairs or catching an illness was a contingent event. In his view, it was 'in our interests to believe that' because it made 'Germany's responsibility all the greater'.[65]

A Letter to Americans

'I am', he complained, 'caught up in all sorts of committees and commissions . . . I don't think I have worked this hard for 20 years.'[66] He was involved in a wide variety of committees and 'other little things of the kind':[67] the Ligue républicaine d'Alsace-Lorraine, the Comité français d'information auprès des Juifs des pays neutres (ministry of the interior), the Commission des étudiants américains (University of Paris), the Commission de révision des permis de séjour (ministry of the interior and préfecture de Paris), Pupilles de l'état (children in care). Even though he had 'a lot of work' on his hands, he also agreed to write an article for the *New York Tribune* 'about our propaganda, as opposed to that of the Germans'. The article appeared on 18 April 1915 under the lengthy title: 'French rebut Germany's bad faith accusations: committee of French scholars exposes Dr Dernburg's polemical method and substitutes one founded upon statements of events in their chronological order.' The article was short and unsigned, but made explicit reference to 'one of our books', meaning Durkheim and Denis's *Qui veut la guerre?* It was, according to the committee, a response to Germany's 'unofficial' ambassador to America Dr Dernburg, who had made some methodological errors in a recent article:

> The French authors having to treat a question of history simply followed the historical method, careful always to observe exactly chronological order and noting day by day, and even in certain moments, hour by hour, what every nation did for or against peace. In this fashion they ran no risk of arranging the facts too clearly in a manner most favourable

to their cause. The recital showed that not a day elapsed since the crisis broke upon this world without some effort being made to prevent war.

Very different was the method followed by Dr Dernburg. He did not apply himself to retrace the facts in their natural succession, but began by setting forth a thesis, which is: Russia had wanted war from the beginning, and England has not fought this aggressive disposition, but has rather encouraged it, either by duplicity or imbecility.[68]

As for the way hostilities were going, Durkheim was under the impression that German boasting had now given way to anger and panic; he was prepared to believe that the enemy would be 'crushed' but also admitted that the German temperament was 'sturdy'. He therefore refused to make any predictions: 'One has the impression that the two armies are standing opposite one another like two walls.' His attitude to those who were 'over-optimistic' was one of mistrust: 'I am as wary of encouraging rumours as I am of all the rest of them.' That did not prevent him from rejoicing: 'People realize that it is we who stopped the German flood, and that we have put the monster in check for the first time. And so they regard us as a people of heroes!' He was quite optimistic: 'Unless we experience a sudden collapse, there are a lot of things that we can count upon.' 'And he concluded: 'I have never heard of a war like this one: it raises a moral problem for the conscience of the whole world.'[69]

Defending French Science

There was more propaganda work. Durkheim agreed to contribute to a book 'on France's role in developments in the various sciences'. It was designed to 'tell San Francisco about France's role in their emergence and development'. What he called this 'punishment exercise' was set by the ministry in the run-up to the World International Fair due to be held in San Francisco in 1915. 'It means I have no time to myself', Durkheim complained.[70]

The two-volume *La Science française* was published by Larousse in association with the minister of public education, religion and the arts. It was an obvious promotional – not to say propagandist – campaign in the form of a library of France's greatest masterpieces, and its main architect was Lucien Poincaré, who had been director of higher education since 1914.[71] The great representatives of all the disciplines were invited to contribute: Bergson (philosophy), Durkheim (sociology), Charles Gide (economics), Le Dantec (biology), Appell (mathematics), Lanson (literature), and Emmanuel de Martonne (geography). Each contributor was asked to evaluate France's role in the evolution of his discipline. The book opened with Bergson's contribution: 'France has been a major initiator . . . The uninterrupted continuity of original philosophical work has been greater in France than in any other country' (Bergson 1915b: 15).

Durkheim's short contribution was entitled simply 'Sociology'. It appeared in the first volume of *La Science française* and was designed to 'set forth the role which belongs to France in the establishment and development of sociology'. France has, he insisted from the outset, played an important role as sociology was 'born among us . . . and remains an essentially French science' (1964[1914]: 376). Was Durkheim becoming a national chauvinist now that France was at war? His argument that it was only in eighteenth-century France and thanks to the *Encyclopédistes* that conditions were ripe for the emergence of sociology when the 'idea of determinism', which had been established in the physical and natural science, was extended to the social order.

Durkheim rapidly outlines three periods in the history of sociology: (1) the age of the precursors (Montesquieu and Condorcet); (2) the era of the founding fathers (Saint-Simon and especially August Comte); and (3), the era of specialization. In the era of specialization, sociology finally went beyond 'philosophical generalities' (1964[1914]: 379). After the war of 1870, the 'revival' of sociological thought came about thanks to the organization of a real division of labour and the defence of positive science. 'The author of the present note' identifies the 'specialists' as 'a whole group of workers to have joined their efforts with us', and who have studied 'three groups of facts': religious, moral and legal, and economic. He describes the 'reform' he introduced by founding the *Année sociologique*: it brought sociology and 'other special techniques' closer together, and gleaned from other areas of study 'facts that appear to be of particular interest to sociologists' (ibid.: 381).

Durkheim also discusses the work of Gabriel Tarde and Frédéric Le Play, describing it as important. Bibliographical references are provided for 25 books and journals. Some 10 of these works – including his own *Division of Labour in Society* and *Suicide* and Hubert and Mauss's *Mélanges d'histoire des religions* – were on exhibition in the 'Library of French science' display. Durkheim ends by remarking that over the past 25 years 'an intellectual movement' of great intensity had developed in France. France was 'predestined' to play that role because it satisfied a 'double condition': traditionalism had lost is domain and there was a veritable faith in reason. 'In other words, we are and shall remain the country of Descartes; we have a passion for clear ideas' (1964[1915]: 383).[72]

The (Russian) Jewish Question

The editorials that appeared in the *Archives israélites* at the very beginning of the hostilities carried headlines like 'A war for what is right', 'War and peace' and 'Religion and fatherland'. Jews had two homelands: the countries in which they were born or had grown up, and France, generous and emancipatory, where rights and justice were promoted. Their reaction to Germany's aggression was immediate and their response was unanimous: 'The French stand united' (Prague 1914: 253).

One of the issues that preoccupied Jewish communities in both Europe and America was the fate of the Jews of Eastern Europe, and especially those of Russia, where anti-Semitism was rife. Since the autumn of 1915, the Alliance israélite internationale was 'anxiously' following the measures being taken by the Russian government and trying to 'guarantee the equal rights of our co-religionists'.[73] Sylvain Lévi was an active member of the alliance's central committee:

> Jewish organizations here would not or could not do it. It seems to me to be impossible to let the Russians commit these atrocities without protest. They must be made to understand that there is a human conscience that protests and that is revolted by their actions ... Russia is becoming aware of freedom, and must be encouraged and supported. Unless there is a revolution – either legal or violent – the country will collapse.[74]

Lévi was also a professor at the Collège de France. Inspired by a 'deep sympathy for anything that seems likely to serve and honour the cause of Judaism', he became French Judaism's official wartime spokesman on the Zionist question – a question that divided the French Jewish community.

The Jewish community was mobilizing. January 1916 saw the establishment of a Ligue pour la défense des juifs opprimés and a Société d'aide aux juifs victimes de la guerre en Russie, and in February, that of a Société d'aide aux volontaires juifs. A new bimonthly bulletin entitled *L'Émancipation juive* began publication. Its first issue carried a report on Jews in Russia and Romania: 'I know', stated Sorbonne professor Gabriel Séailles, 'that for the Jews, Russia is the great land of suffering.'[75]

The Alliance israélite was planning to submit a memorandum to the minister for foreign affairs asking him to intervene in order to ensure an end to the sufferings of the Jewish population. Baron Edmond de Rothschild also intervened to ask a Russian minister to ask the Tsar's Russian government to guarantee Jews the legal right to equality. And when, in April 1916, two members of the Russian Parliament visited Paris, Rothschild, accompanied by Émile Durkheim and Sylvain Lévi, met them to discuss the Jewish question. This gave Durkheim the opportunity to 'meet' the baron, who was on the board of the Rothschild Bank and a director of the Chemin de fer de l'Est. 'A nice enough chap, but very narrow-minded', thought Durkheim.[76] In the course of their meeting, they described American Jews' 'hostile' feelings towards the Russians. They had only one demand, they explained: repeal the emergency legislation that oppressed Russia's Jews.

Durkheim, who had so far been indifferent to Judaism, was discovering that there was indeed a 'Jewish question'. He publicly reproached himself for his 'past indifference to his brothers of origin who suffered simply because they were Jews'.[77] In his view, the only solution to the Jewish question was the emancipation and assimilation of Jews, and he believed in 1917 that, thanks to the Russian Revolution, the emancipation of Russia's Jews, which had been greeted with 'joy and happiness' by all French Israelites, was an accomplished fact. In a letter published together with one from Chief Rabbi Lévy in the Moscow *Jewish Week*, he wrote:

The Russian Revolution seems to me to have done away with the Jewish question. The Jews are now sure to be assimilated into the other religious confessions; they will enjoy the same rights, and their martyrdom is over. Before this could be reversed, there would have to be a Tsarist reaction. But the past can never be restored, except in a temporary and artificial sense. Experience has shown that its roots are not in fact as deep as they seem to be. Unless serious mistakes are made, and there is nothing to suggest that they will be, we can therefore assume that the past has been abolished for ever. Russian Jews will at last have a fatherland, and they will love in it the same ways that French Jews love theirs.[78]

Was he being blind or hopelessly optimistic? Durkheim was becoming sensitized to the Jewish question and began to be involved in other activities with Sylvain Lévi. In the autumn of 1915, for example, he joined a committee (Office de propagande) that was trying to 'influence American Jews'. As Lévi put it: 'The question of the Russian Jews obviously dominates everything, and we cannot resolve it; but it is good that its importance has finally been recognized here and that parliamentarians . . . can no longer go on pretending to know nothing about it.' As his friend noted, Durkheim seemed to have 'taken things to heart' and 'brought a real zeal' to the committee's discussions. Lévi was planning similar campaigns in France, Britain and Italy: 'I'm working on it, and I can succeed.'[79] Lévi and Durkheim were inspired by the same feelings and the same conviction: patriotism.

Durkheim was also a member of the commission established by minister of the interior Louis Malvy on 26 December 1915 to examine the issue of residents' permits. He was charged with drawing up a report on the situation of the Russians in Paris, most of whom were Jewish. The role of the commission was, as Léon Trotsky put it, to 'care for Russian refugees'.[80] It was set up after 'a campaign against foreigners of Russian nationality', and especially the Jews who made up 95 per cent of the 'colony'. This anti-Semitic campaign, which had begun before the war, had some supporters on Paris's municipal council.

Why were Jews coming under attack? Some cited their distinctive language and customs, while others blamed them for spreading epidemics. They were also accused of fomenting public disorder. When war broke out, a 'new accusation' was made against them, to which public opinion was 'more sensitive':[81] it was claimed that they 'systematically refused to fulfil their duties towards both their country of origin and the country in which they were living'. This was supposedly a 'culpable' and 'general' abstention, and not 'the doing of isolated individuals'. Such criticisms caused great indignation within the Jewish community, which protested against the dilemma into which Russian Israelites had been forced by the authorities: they could either enlist in the Légion d'honneur or return to their countries of origin.

The Commission's mandate was to 'investigate how far this complaint was justified'.[82] When it began its work, the police inquiry was investigating the cases of almost 4,000 Russian nationals aged between 19 and 43 living in Paris's 10 police districts. This alone, together with summonses and interviews involved, caused 'real panic' in the Russian colony in Paris: several thousand refugees decided to 'leave in all haste' for either America or Spain. As its members admitted, the establishment of the commission caused 'more turmoil', and there was talk of more 'anti-Semitic persecution'. Its effects were quickly felt in other countries, and especially the United States, where people were becoming 'greatly over-excited by anything to do with the Jewish question'.[83] There was a danger that France's image would be tarnished at the very time it had to win 'American sympathies' (in order to negotiate a loan).

The report, which was submitted a year later in February 1916, was not actually signed by Durkheim, but the published extracts from minutes of its meetings do appear to indicate that he was its author. 'I have never before been so Jewish', he wrote to his nephew. 'If this goes on, I will become adviser to and guardian of exotic Judaism. And it has to be admitted that there are all kinds of wretchedness. I have just received a letter from a poor Russian Jew who really does seem to be being persecuted by the police and whose life is going to be ruined. So much misery!'[84] He estimated that he devoted one and a half days a week to the commission. He liked the group. 'The mood is usually good. It's a very friendly environment. I like it.' But it was, he admitted, 'a painful task': 'Deciding the fate of people on the basis of written reports without seeing the parties involved leaves the door so wide open to mistakes that it makes me shudder. We are working with living flesh, and that is a trade that does not suit me.' But he was quite satisfied when he submitted his report: 'My report does not mince its words.'[85]

The commission demonstrated that the grievance was groundless, and it had the documents and the figures to prove it. The call to immigrant Jews ('Do your duty: vive la France!') had not gone unheeded: many Russians had volunteered. More than 3,500 had enlisted in the Légion d'honneur since the outbreak of hostilities, and many more had been rejected as unfit for military service. The situation of the volunteers' families – and most of the volunteers were poor workers – was often deplorable, and they were described as being in a 'state of abject misery'. One thing was immediately obvious: far from having displayed the 'collective indifference' of which it was accused, the 'Russian colony' had, on the whole, 'done its duty'. When war broke out, there had been an 'impressive wave of enthusiasm', but the fervour of the early days had not lasted. The Russians certainly had good health and family reasons for losing their 'enthusiasm to enlist': they were not paid the same as French soldiers. The pressures brought to bear on the Russian colony had also forced many to flee the country. The commission did not have the resources to investigate these complaints in any detail, and simply examined some first-hand accounts. It was also obvious that the authorities had made a serious error by issuing summonses and investigating a population that was the only one to have been 'harassed'. The measures taken had dubious results, and, the commission found, unfortunate effects: there was a danger that the attempt to bring 'moral pressure' to bear on the Russians would expose France to 'suspicions and accusations' and that it would 'lose sympathy'. 'Starting again' (with more summonses and interviews) was, according to the commission, 'out of the question'.

This did not mean that 'nothing of use' could be done, and the commission put forward a number of proposals. One was that the Russian government should 'agree to an amnesty for political refugees' in exchange for new undertakings from France. It was obvious to the commission's members that there was an 'international aspect' to the refugee question, and that it was a matter for the ministry of foreign affairs as well as the police. Durkheim's role on the commission was exposed by Léon Trotsky, the 'dangerous enemy' and 'undesirable alien' who had found refuge in Paris and who was on the point of being deported.[86] He claimed that Émile had informed the Russian refugees' representative in Paris that the newspaper *Nache Slovo* was about to be banned and its editors deported. When he learned in August 1916 that the British government was going to introduce 'measures to force Russians to either enlist in the British army or go back to Russia', Durkheim immediately warned the president of the Comité de Londres against the effects of such measures. His intervention had the desired effect; 'Basically, we have won our case.'[87]

26

'Thinking of the Same Thing Day and Night'

'Dreadful News'

There was a lot of 'bad news'. It began to arrive in the autumn of 1914, when the *Année*'s young collaborator Maxime David was shot dead while leading a platoon of infantry. He was 'the first of our group to fall', as Mauss (1969[1925]: 490) put it. There was more sad news for the *Année* team on 16 March 1915: 'Bianconi was killed when he was hit in the chest in the Perthes Forest', Durkheim wrote to his nephew.[1] He made no comment. Antoine Bianconi was only 32.

When he heard of Antoine's death, Robert Hertz wrote to his wife from the front: 'I still have an appetite for a more complete devotion.' His exalted patriotism led him to see France as a 'chosen people' whose history had a 'biblical grandeur'; he wanted to 'march to where the devotion and the danger are greatest'. He was one of those men who gave the impression that 'they will never give enough for the internal and external deliverance of France'.[2]

Hertz felt that he was 'living through some great moments' and believed that France would be victorious. France's victory would be 'the victory of spirit over mass, of a generous impulse over brutal discipline, and of freedom over suffocating domination'. When he heard that Charles Péguy was dead, Hertz said that he was 'overawed': 'His end justifies his whole life, sanctifies it.'[3] Some of his friends saw Hertz as a 'fanatic'. In his letters to his wife, he denied this and tried to explain that his attitude was 'the result of long inner deliberations'.[4] He later wrote to her:

As a Jew, I feel that the time has come to give *a little more* than I owe . . . If I can get true naturalization papers for my son that would, I think, be the best present I could ever give him.

As a socialist, I have always maintained that the desire to serve the community can be just as powerful a motivation as the desire for profit or individual self-interest. . . . Some at least must *go beyond* what is asked of them.

As a sociologist and rationalist, I have also believed that the idea of the salvation of all is in itself enough to inspire and sustain individual sacrifices, including complete self-sacrifice, if need be. The moment has come for me to test my faith. It is now or never.[5]

Hertz described war as a 'fantastic experience of collectivism' and 'of cheerful service', but Durkheim had little time for such lyricism, and advised caution. When, for example, his nephew Marcel expressed a desire to go to the front, Émile told him:

> Be careful, now . . . There are ways of doing all you have to do – and more – and of being careful. The problem is that you must learn to be careful. You have to learn to take care of yourself now by observing what others do, asking them questions and learning from their experience.[6]

Georges Davy, who was teaching at the lycée in Saint-Omer, was called up in February 1915. He was ill but refused to 'give in'. Durkheim worried about him: 'I hope he does resign himself to "giving in". Otherwise, who knows what might happen!'[7] Jean Reynier, another contributor to the *Année*, was, as Mauss later put it (1969[1925]: 495), 'facing the same dangers as his friends' but he died 'for the fatherland' as the result of an accident involving a trench compacter in 1915. He was 32. The next to die was Robert Hertz. He had already suffered a minor wound but died in battle as the 330rd Regiment counter-attacked on 13 April 1915. The 'dreadful news' shook Durkheim, who told his nephew:

> I cannot tell you what effect this has had on me. My nerves are shot. I don't know why but, when I heard the news, I felt that you and André were more exposed then you were. So far, death has only taken people who, like Maxime David and Bianconi, were somewhat marginal to me. This time it is someone who was dear to me.[8]

Durkheim went to see Alice Hertz, who read passages from her husband's letters to her. He admired her 'stoicism' but thought it 'perhaps excessive'. But when he read Hertz's letters, he could not conceal the fact that he had mixed feelings:

> The poor boy left half-convinced that he would never come back. She read me some letters with an exaggerated detachment. You can do your duty – all your duty – without submitting to your fate before you have to. He wanted to redeem all the sins of Israel (in the true sense of the word). These letters reveal a great deal of nobility, an exceptionally noble soul and a singular state of mind. We will talk about it one day.[9]

In the autumn, Durkheim suggested to Alice Hertz that he should write an obituary of her husband for the yearbook of the Association des anciens élèves de l'École normale supérieure. She gave him the letters. Durkheim got down to writing the obituary in December, and read through them in order to paint a portrait of his former student. He was astonished by what he read:

> He was definitely a very noble soul, but his idealism was a little woolly-minded. Many passages in these letters to his wife are truly inspired, but it is impossible for me to say anything specific about them. There are some passages about the regeneration of France that sound like Barrès. He talks about Barrès with all the usual reservations, but with some sympathy.

When he learned of the death of Hertz, Barrès wrote a eulogy of the 'young hero' for *L'Echo de Paris*. His friends and teachers remembered 'the serene soul of a scholar who became a hero with such simplicity' (Alphandéry 1919: 339).

André's Campaign; or, Self-Abnegation

André Durkheim went back to the front in January 1915. Émile had hoped to see him before he left: 'It really pains my heart . . . It is a big disappointment'.[10] Two months later, André was evacuated to the hospital in Bar-Le-Duc, near Metz, with a high fever (the diagnosis was 'moderate typhoid'). Émile and his wife immediately went to visit him, and returned home 'as reassured as we can be when dealing with such a treacherous disease'.[11] Louise went back to visit her son to 'help him get through those interminable days in hospital'. When he began to feel better, André asked his father to come and see him. Durkheim described him as a 'big baby who needs his mummy and daddy', but readily agreed to go even though he did not have 'a lot of time to spare': 'It's true that getting away for 24 hours will do me no harm, even though, basically, I'm feeling fine.'[12]

Durkheim's grandson Claude was one of his great comforts even though, now that he was a big boy, he would run up and down the apartment and 'took up a lot of his grandfather's time'. 'Claude is a little darling'; 'Claude is a joy to me'; 'A ray of sunshine in the apartment', he wrote to Marcel. The man who had described himself as 'an old father' now found himself to be a young grandfather, and he was happy to be one: 'I had forgotten how wonderful little children are.'[13]

At his own request, André was now 'dispatched' to Cognac, where he was cared for 'almost maternally' by the wife of the primary school inspector. 'One gets the feeling that he is very satisfied'; 'He's living the life of Riley down there . . . He's putting a bit of flesh on his bones', remarked his father as he described his son's convalescence to his nephew.

André Durkheim had recovered by June 1915, and his morale was 'good'. He was initially sent to Brest, where his father visited him for a few days. He went alone, as his wife could not accompany him and felt that she would be 'of more use' in Paris. It was a tiring journey: 'Two nights on a train to get two nights in a bed.' Durkheim was sleeping very badly and, when he got home, he felt more shaken up 'than ever'. 'I am tired, but I've come back looking very well. We had splendid weather. When I left André, his morale was excellent and he is in good physical condition.'[14] André then passed through Paris 'on his way to the front'.

In mid-June, Durkheim, who normally planned his holidays in advance, still had no idea of what he was going to do during the 'hot days'. He thought of going to the seaside with his wife, his daughter Marie and 'little Claude', but could not make up his mind: 'I feel that, in principle, it is impossible for me not to be here, unless I am so physically tired that it becomes necessary to stop working. I loathe the idea of systematic rest and of holidays that are planned in advance.'[15] He was thinking – at most – of renting a house near Paris for the month of September.

Durkheim certainly had commitments, some of them of an educational nature – 'I'm up to my eyes with exams', he complained in July – but his main concern was for the three men in the family who were at the front: his son, his nephew and his son-in-law. At the end of June, André was 'very, very lightly wounded'. Émile immediately told his nephew and tried to reassure him that it was 'nothing very serious'. But he also added: 'He has had a narrow escape.' He had indeed. 'A bullet went through his kepi and left him with a parting a few centimetres long.'[16] He was hospitalized in Neufchâteau, where his mother and then his father went to visit him. André was then granted a month's sick leave. Durkheim arranged for his wife Louise and his children André and Marie to spend the month of August by the sea in Saint-Valéry-en-Caux (Seine-Inférieure). Durkheim, who was 'happy to wear an overcoat at high noon', liked the climate there. 'Saint-Valéry is not a fashionable resort, and nor is it a particularly picturesque resort. But it has an excellent climate. It is always cool, and often very cool. That is its main attraction.' 'My stay there has done me good', he wrote to Mauss.[17]

When his son went back to Brest, Durkheim moved to Sèvres. The weather in September was magnificent, and the temperature was perfect. 'The weather is soft enough to deaden your sensations, and you do not have the same feeling of being at war. At the same time, the war itself is, for the moment, less frightening. We have to be prepared for a harsh winter.'[18] He was very busy; his list of things to do included: (1) 'a pamphlet about Germany's lies'; (2) 'our foreign propaganda, which is always raising questions'; (3) 'our domestic propaganda, which is being organized'; (4) 'the children in care project'. 'That is enough to occupy the life of a man who has no talent for writing letters in a hurry.'[19] All this meant that he had to go to Paris on an almost daily basis, and that he often had to go to what he called [the ministry for] 'war'.

His main concern was the new 'plan for domestic moral supplies'. The idea had been 'promptly' accepted and approved by the council of ministers, he told his nephew. 'This is a big project, and it will not be up and running until the end of September.' Armand Colin first had to supply an estimate for the costs. 'Then we can do something.' The idea was to produce leaflets; in an ideal world they would be ready for the beginning of the new academic year in late September. 'School teachers are our main target. I'm resting at the moment, but I am also thinking about the first pamphlet I've been asked to write. It's a general outline for the series, and explains why we need it.'[20] 'I think we will start with the primary school teachers. We have to stir them into action, and provide them with the means to do something.' He was thinking of producing about 10 different pamphlets. This would, he thought, be a 'good action' that might 'get something done'. Durkheim had all the assistance he could ask for, but complained that his helpers were not 'very active'. Fortunately, he could reply upon Paul Lapie, who was now director of primary education and a supporter of the idea of a just war against barbarism, in which he believed primary school teachers had a vital role to play.[21]

There was a rumour that Henri Hubert had been 'sent to the front'. 'Is this true?' Mauss asked Hubert. 'If you do not go, I will be very happy for you. The important thing is to make oneself useful and do one's duty.'[22] At the beginning of March, Hubert was mobilized as a sergeant in an infantry regiment. As he was not strong enough to serve at the front, he was posted, on Colonel Cordier's orders, to the second bureau of the under-secretary for artillery (soon to become the ministry for armaments), which controlled road transport. When, in May, Albert Thomas was appointed under-secretary of state for artillery and military equipment, Hubert found himself alongside Thomas's closest collaborators François Simiand and Mario Roques.[23] He was also working with Hubert Bourgin, the head of the information service, who established the Comité de propagande socialiste pour la défense nationale in 1916 (it became the Comité socialiste pour la paix de droit in 1917).[24] The so-called 'Thomas network' had been very active since the beginning of the war. It included several socialist *normaliens* who were prepared stubbornly to defend the fatherland and promote the work of the ministry when Thomas was promoted to ministerial rank (with the same portfolio) in Briand's government. Now that he was a minister, Thomas kept his team together, and they went on working day and night, even on Sundays and public holidays. Maurice Halbwachs, a member of the moderate socialists' network, was 'drafted in' to work for the minister for armaments in Thomas's private office: this was 'office work as war service'. There was so many of Durkheim's associates in Thomas's ministry that it was said that the *Année* had 'taken over'. This rather alarmed its editor for all sorts of reasons: 'The weight of responsibility and the incompetence of those in charge terrifies me', he admitted to his nephew.[25]

In mid-October 1915, the 45th Regiment was billeted in Toulon while it waited for embarkation at Marseille, to the 'great joy' of Émile and Louise, who went there to see André. They found him 'in an excellent state of morale and very cheerful', and 'greatly looking forward to a voyage that would teach him something'. André was 'joyful, confident, full of enthusiasm, and even curious about the new life that lay in store for him'. They both felt much 'calmer' and left Toulouse with the memory of his 'sweet, smiling face' – the best of memories (Durkheim 1975[1917]: 450).

André was leaving for Serbia. Émile and his wife found the prospect of being separated from him 'painful, very painful': 'We've had some very bad days.' Émile tried to make himself see reason: 'Life must go on, and we have to get used to it.'[26]

André finally sailed for Salonica on 30 October 1915. He was delighted: 'I've always dreamed of going on a cruise', he wrote to his father, who was finding this new separation difficult and who was worried about the coming campaign's 'unknowns'. 'We are being as brave as we can be.' As soon as he landed, André was sent up to 'the lines of fire'. At first, it seemed that the campaign would not be too hard but, as Durkheim himself noted after the events, the situation rapidly became 'serious': fighting, forced marches, fatigue. It was obvious from his letters, however, that André's morale was still 'excellent' (Durkheim 1975[1917]: 450).

Émile Durkheim gave a public lecture early in November, but teaching did not begin until December. 'All that feels very remote to me!' At the beginning of the academic year, he complained: 'It's so exhausting. My days as a teacher will soon be over.'[27] He went on: 'My classes have started again. God knows it all feels remote. I don't think I'll be doing this job for much longer, always assuming that the war does not ruin us. It's unbearable.' He did not like the situation in which he found himself: 'Basically, I am living a life that could not be less suited to my tastes: I am doing lots of things, and I am only happy when I have just one thing to do! When am I going to get back to my natural life?'[28] He explained to his uncomprehending nephew: 'You don't really understand what I told you about my teaching. I don't devote much time to it. It's actually giving the lectures that wears me out. I feel tired even when I've prepared them badly. . . . I was very tired after the first few. It is not so bad now, but I still feel very tired, and it is all so pointless.'[29]

The war went on but the failure of the Allied advances resulted in heavy losses. The German counter-offensives met with little more success. The dead were now counted in their hundreds of thousands. 'Too much fear, too much bad news, too much mourning, too many massacres of the best of us, of a whole generation that should have taken our place. Too much grief', cried Lucien Herr.[30] By the end of December, Durkheim, who had had no news from his son, was worried: 'Time is passing so slowly! I am living in fear . . . The uncertainty that surrounds this whole expedition does nothing to dispel the fear I feel, and I cannot stop myself from feeling afraid.' By common consent, he and his wife avoided 'talking about that'.

André was badly wounded on the Bulgarian front on 11 December, and died from his wounds on 17 December. That very day, Émile, who had still had no news, wrote to his nephew to say 'it's been a long time'. At the end of December, he again complained: 'Time seems to be passing very slowly.' It was only on 2 January 1916 that the family learned that André had been listed as missing since 11 or 12 December. Durkheim was still busy with his teaching and commissions but had no enthusiasm for his work: 'You suffer and you live, and everything suggests that life will triumph.' These were 'difficult moments'. And whatever he did, there was always 'something else' on his mind. His depression, as he himself put it, was 'active', even though he refused to give in to it. By mid-February, he was completely disillusioned: 'There are fewer and fewer reasons to hope as the days pass. I will get used to it in time, but it hurts!'[31]

On 24 February, they received confirmation that André was dead. Durkheim told his nephew the news the following day: 'I am going to cause you a lot of grief. We cannot go on deluding ourselves. André was wounded, and has died from his wounds. He has been buried in the village of Davidovo.' He added: 'It is the images that hurt me.' He then wrote in a postscript: 'Your aunt has not been too badly affected in the physical sense. I am suffering only the mental effects of this.'[32] Marcel Mauss made no secret of his grief: 'Last night, a note from my uncle told me of the misfortune that has struck us. It was not unexpected but it was – it is – a blow.'[33] He told Henri Hubert how much he loved his cousin: 'André was the most charming of boys, and the very incarnation of tenderness and enthusiasm. He was both a brother and a pal to me. And I was his old man.'[34] 'Such sorrow', sighed Hubert. 'Poor child! I was very fond of him', exclaimed Paul Fauconnet, who had been to see Durkheim shortly before he received news of his son's death. Even though 'the letter announcing his death was calm', Fauconnet was worried: '[Durkheim] is a man who will let grief gnaw away at him without letting it show. And I am not sure how strong your aunt is.'[35]

This was a severe loss for the *Année sociologique* team: André would have become 'one the best'. 'Durkheim educated him, and made him his son in both senses of the word' (Maunier 1927). André 'would soon have been working with me', admitted Durkheim, who now forced himself to do his 'pious and sad duty' by writing the obituary of the son he had loved so much and by taking on the 'cruel but sweet task of describing his short life and his physiognomy': childhood, studies, success at school, mobilization, etc. He described, in as much detail as he could, André's campaign and especially 'what happened' in his last weeks and days: another Bulgarian attack, a retreat in complete silence, thick mist, a serious wound, hospitalization in Davidovo, death, burial in the village cemetery.

Durkheim recalled that his son had a 'sense of self-abnegation that naturally and painlessly prepared him to make sacrifices. He knew the value of life, but he felt that over-reflexive caution, especially on the part of a leader, was morally ugly. And so, he quite simply did the things that put an end to his life.' He also recalled that Second Lieutenant Durkheim had been mentioned for his 'outstanding service, and especially the initiative that had cost him his life'. One letter suggests that André had foreseen his own death: he asked his family and friends 'not to mourn him too much' and to 'think [of him] sometimes'. 'May [his friends and family] keep a little place for him in their memories, and may they think kindly of him from time to time. That is how he would have liked to be mourned' (Durkheim 1975[1917]: 452).

Think kindly of him? At first, Durkheim asked his friends not to come to see him. Henri Hubert was afraid to do so: 'Durkheim is steeling himself, the poor, poor man. Those who would like to see him would be so grateful to him if he would weep with them.'[36] Sylvain Lévi was another who could not bring himself to go to see Durkheim or write to him:

> Ever since the death of André, which is so menacing, I have been struck to see how Durkheim has somehow summoned up the strength to put his duty and its demands before his own pain. This inflexible attitude commands respect and admiration, but it also seems to demand silence. Spoken or written condolences can often offend someone who is suffering so bravely. I have heard nothing from him or Madame Durkheim since the news was made official.[37]

He then began to visit Émile frequently: 'His stoicism is admirable; mourning has simply strengthened his determination to serve his country and the common interest. We are going to see a lot of each other now, and I know that the man is worthy of the thinker.'[38]

Louise was also bearing up well. 'If your aunt is well in physical terms, she will also be well in terms of morale', wrote the husband who, for his part, spent the first few days 'moderating and analysing [his] sorrow' before realizing that he had chosen the 'wrong path'. He went back to work, with the satisfaction of knowing that 'there is hope'. That, he believed, would be his 'salvation'. He was thinking of giving up teaching – he found preparing his lectures 'insipid'[39] – and of 'abandoning this very active life and spending [his days] working quietly'. He also thought: 'I have so little to say that is new that I cannot go on much longer. I do not want to go on saying the same things for ever, and if I start doing something new in my lectures, I will never finish the other things I have to do.'[40] Should he, he wondered, 'get used to a life of peaceful and melancholic work'? The idea appealed to him. It would, he believed, allow him to 'get closer to the children without leaving the neighbourhood': 'One can live out one's days like that. I'll give it a go. I will try, and let experience be my guide.'

Durkheim was trying to cling to a philosophy that would help him find 'a moral equilibrium'. It was articulated around two principles (which he believed to be 'true'). The first was 'the principle that life triumphs over death, or in other words that beings in which there is some life react: life gets a new grip on them and supports them. And they can do nothing to stop it from flowing and manifesting itself.' He had gone back to work, and had completely rewritten Admiral Degouy's contribution to *Lettres à tous les Français*. But he had to admit that he was getting nowhere because he could not forget what had happened. 'In my circumstances, my own worst enemy is my ability to go on thinking about the same thing day and night for 50 years.' He hoped that work would allow him to forget by giving him something else to think about. This was not always easy: 'I have my moments of weakness. Moments when I can think of nothing but that poor child. I can tell you that, when I am neither working nor busy, there is not a moment when my thoughts are not with him. But I usually make sure that it does not get a stranglehold on me.'[41]

His second principle was: 'Life is flexible, even at the age of 58, and we can make what we wish of it in lots of ways.' He added: 'All the egotistic side to my life has gone.' He had the joy of knowing that his son André would benefit from what he was doing. He now had a duty to lead a disinterested, even ascetic life: 'In fact, I feel detached from all worldly interests. But that too is a joy. It is the joy of the ascetic who feels that he has risen above everything. It is a stern, melancholic joy; to the extent that we can predict the future, melancholy will in future be my way of life.' Admitting that he had 'a natural penchant for melancholy', he concluded: 'I do not know if I will ever laugh a lot, but I cannot do without laughter. And it seems very likely that my life is heading in that direction. You have no idea of the impression of joy that comes from the feeling of detachment that results from having no more worldly interests.'[42]

Émile was, as he himself said, 'very busy': he had his lectures at the Sorbonne, the *Lettres à tous les Français* to complete, and his work on the Russian commission. Indeed, he was still 'fascinated' with his work. But in the evening, when the day's work was done, and especially on days when he felt depressed, he lapsed back into his 'meditations'. 'I come home exhausted . . . So I do nothing in the evening.' Immediately after dinner, he took a pill – Dr Boulloche allowed him to a take heavy dose – and went to bed. But if he woke up during the night, he needed, he admitted to his nephew, to 'have something on [his] mind other than you know what'.

Lettres aux Français

In his capacity as secretary to the publication committee, Durkheim was involved in writing *Lettres à tous les Français*.[43] Originally published as unbound sheets, these pamphlets had a print run of three million copies, and most were distributed through a network of primary school teachers. 'These men and women', said the authors, 'are our best propaganda auxiliaries.' Durkheim was deeply involved with the committee's work, and there was even talk of him undertaking 'a lecture tour of the provinces with the English'. The goal of the *Lettres* was to 'improve the morale of the public mind' and to counter the effects of the daily reports that concentrated on various events and incidents and stirred up people's emotions, wore them down and got them too over-excited to look at their 'permanent causes'. It was hoped that, by giving an overall picture, they would give their readers 'reasons to be more optimistic'.

The 12 pamphlets were reprinted in book form by Armand Colin in May 1916. Durkheim himself made four contributions, and the project brought together a very heterogeneous group, including colleagues from the Sorbonne (Ernest Lavisse and Ernest Denis), a professor from the Collège de France (Antoine Meillet) and two military men (General Pierre Malleterre and Admiral Jean-Baptiste Degouy).[44] The first letter, which served as an introduction, was entitled 'Patience, effort and confidence', and was signed by Durkheim. He began by showing that this war was unlike any previous war: it was a war between two opposing coalitions of unparalleled size that could mobilize not only professional armies but whole nations, and that was being waged on an unprecedented geographical scale. In these conditions, time played a vital role and the emphasis had to be on a steady approach rather than on glorious feats of action. Victory would therefore be 'a long drawn-out, patient task' (1986[1916]: 220) that demanded an 'unshakeable will, ever remaining steadfast, in order to continue the struggle for as long as is necessary'. 'Don't lose your nerve'; 'Keep your self-control'; 'Save your strength'; 'Use all your energy to pursue the goal': these were the slogans Durkheim devised in a bid to ward off impatience, blind faith and depression – attitudes that had to be avoided.

The state of the people's morale and its willpower were vitally important. 'A people's willpower is made up of the willpower of each individual' (1986[1916]: 220). All this was, he added, a matter of mutual aid, and everyone, including civilians, had to make a contribution. 'Giving and receiving in turn, each of us is stronger and more resolute because he shares in the strength and resolution of all of us' (ibid.). He was speaking as a sociologist when he praised the 'instinctive wisdom' of France (which had 'been able to exercise self-control in every kind of circumstance') and recalled the importance of collective action and individual self-belief. Non-combatants also had 'battles to undergo': struggling against their nerves, showing their stamina, and putting up with the suffering and fears of wartime. Durkheim knew all this from personal experience. But there was also something else: France needed weapons and munitions, and it therefore needed money. Production had to be stepped up and spending had to be reduced. 'We are all bound to participate actively in the war, each in his own way . . . Faith is only sustained by action' (ibid.: 221). These were the words of a man who had made a specialist study of collective beliefs. He went on: 'In order to act energetically we must believe in the successful outcome of our action. Doubt casts down and paralyses; confidence gives strength. Victory is only possible when one hopes for victory' (ibid.: 222).

And while everyone is 'entitled to feel some reassurance and pride . . . it is dangerous to abandon oneself unresistingly and unreservedly to that sentiment' (1986[1916]: 223); rather than being hypnotized by the spectacle of military events, the French should be looking at the 'deeper causes' that would allow them to predict the outcome of the war. Durkheim's thesis, and the underlying theme of this series of pamphlets, was: 'We – our allies and ourselves – are in a better condition than our enemies to sustain a long drawn-out war, for our forces are still destined to grow, while Germany and Austria are close to exhausting their effort.' There was only one conclusion: 'Let us last out and we shall conquer' (ibid.).

The 'wearing down' of both French and German forces was obviously a major concern for the publications committee. According to its chairman Ernest Lavisse, a comparison of their strength was 'an invincible force': 'Our people have faith in the immortality of France' (Lavisse 1916). The committee began by studying 'Germany and her allies' (Austro-Hungary), and then the 'Quadruple Entente of Russia, Britain, Italy and France'. Durkheim himself agreed to make a study of the balance of power in various regions: (1) the East; (2) Belgium, Serbia and Montenegro; and (3) France.

The pamphlet on Germany's allies in the East was short, and dealt with Turkey and Bulgaria (Durkheim 1992[1916a]). Durkheim could not remain indifferent to what was going on there given that his son André had died in the Dardanelles. The 'eastern theatre', which had once seemed to be independent and of secondary importance, could no longer escape the 'principle of the single front', which had become 'an axiomatic part of both our strategy and our diplomacy'. Things had changed completely in only a few months: at the end of 1915, the situation had favoured the central powers, but all that had been reversed. It was true that the Turkish army had been reorganized and that the Bulgarian army was large, well-equipped and brave, but it was clear to Durkheim that 'neither Turkey nor Bulgaria can help Germany to make up for her losses'. In a word, Germany would have to rely upon her own resources for new forces. The pamphlet on Italy, Belgium, Serbia and Montenegro was in two parts (Durkheim 1992[1916b]). Antoine Meillet wrote the section on Italy, and Durkheim that on the other three countries. He argued that mention had to be made of 'the little states that have thrown their lot in with ours'. Not only were they still making a contribution to the war effort; the three countries had set an example without any historical precedent. Although they had been occupied, they were still sovereign states and still had autonomous governments. Their example should, argued Durkheim, give France a 'powerful stimulant'. 'Although they have been devastated and are in ruins, these little states are still a force: they symbolize one whole aspect of the ideal we are fighting for.'

Turning to France, in his final pamphlet Durkheim described his country's victories (1992[1916c]). He began by describing the battles of the Marne and the Yser, and then described the ongoing battle of Verdun. Verdun was a real hell, and although France emerged victorious, it cost the enormous collective sacrifice of 360,000 dead and wounded. This was proof, he was convinced, of the French army's defensive capacities, and of the 'tenacity of our resistance' in the face of such 'exceptional might'.

Regarding the offensive side of the war, Durkheim had to admit that France had not succeeded in 'breaking through' the enemy's front, but insisted that 'real progress' had been made. The three French assaults of February, May and September 1915 had inflicted heavy losses on the enemy. He produced statistical evidence to show that the explanation for this 'constant progress' was both technological (improved weaponry: machine guns, rifles, cannon) and economic (France's financial situation, as compared with that of Germany). He concluded: 'Everything is under way: the machine has been set up, and it is beginning to work harder.'

It takes money to go on fighting a war. 'The country whose financial might can endure longest will resist the longest.' Durkheim relied on two indicators to analyse the financial situation: the issue of paper money and loans. France increasingly had the advantage here, as it could raise loans from the great New York market and had the powerful financial support of Britain. What was needed was quite clear: on the one hand, an ongoing offensive and growth in the war industries and, on the other, the availability of financial resources. Nevertheless, Durkheim had to admit that he did not have the data to calculate 'how many men we are losing': there were no figures for French losses. He was, however, still optimistic because Italy – and especially Russia – still had huge reserves of manpower. The conclusion was obvious: against this 'powerfully organized' enemy with its 'incommensurable pride' and 'stubborn tenacity', there was only one thing to be done: 'tirelessly continue with our effort'.

Force of arms and the power of money were not the only things that decided 'the fate of battles'; it was also determined, Durkheim insisted, by 'moral force', and this included 'world opinion'. The Germans understood that, and had established a 'vast and clever news system' in a bid to win the support of neutral countries. As the situation changed, what was really at stake gradually became clearer: the security of international relations, the right of peoples to self-determination, and the rights of humanity. There was therefore a 'heightened sense of human consciousness', and that was 'an obstacle for our enemies, and a support for us'. 'We must place our trust in it for the future.' Ernest Lavisse reached the same conclusions at the very end of *Lettres*: 'So let us have faith in our future.'

The analysis made by the contributors to *Lettres* was anything but fatalistic. None of them overlooked the specifically military or economic dimensions of the situation, but they all attached great importance to its moral or cultural dimension. It was also a matter of faith, self-confidence and willpower, and public opinion was of vital importance when it came to the issues of sovereignty and human rights. The Caillaux affair had revealed both the importance of public opinion and the role of the so-called popular press.

The Insult

On 23 March 1916, Adrien Gaudin de Villaine, a former *député* (1885–9), who had been the senator for the Manche *département* since 1906, made a speech in the Senate about 'German espionage in France, and in Paris in particular'. He attacked the commission examining residents' permits and noted that 'certain French citizens of foreign descent, including M. Durkheim, who is a professor at our Sorbonne, are probably working for the German *Kriegsministerium* – or so it has been claimed'. Could Durkheim have been a spy? Was this the start of a new Dreyfus affair?

Durkheim's friends immediately approached the senator, who was astonished to learn that the name of the 'honourable professor' had figured in reports of his speech. On 25 March, the commission sent a letter of protest to the minister, and its president M. Brelet went to ask Gaudin de Villaine for 'an immediate retraction'. The Jewish press denounced the senator as a 'hot-headed anti-Semite', but also expressed its indignation at 'the Israelite senators and *députés* who had heard their coreligionist being insulted and suspected without a murmur of protest'.[45]

Durkheim himself claimed to be 'quite unaffected by this absurd insult; and said: 'I am above all that.' His only real feeling was one of 'real sadness' that a man should make 'such an odious accusation against a compatriot without any investigation, and purely on the basis of wild rumours in the press'. The next day, he expressed his views in a long telegram to the senator. He left him to apologize as he saw fit. 'I have lost interest', he told his nephew Marcel. He expressly asked the senator for only one thing: any retraction must make no mention of the name or memory of his son, who had died on the field of honour in Serbia.

> If you do not believe that I have devoted the whole of my life to serving science and my country and that all that I have done over the past 20 months to defend the national cause is not an adequate guarantee of my civic virtues, then remain silent. I do not wish the death [of André] to disarm my enemies, and I do not wish his blood to redeem me in some abominable fashion.[46]

These were 'eminently respectable sentiments', admitted the senator, who thanked Durkheim for his 'courteous words'. Negotiations continued: Gaudin was willing to retract, on condition that Durkheim agreed to have a conversation with him 'in the presence of a third party'. Durkheim refused: 'Regardless of what I do, it is up to you to decide where your duty lies, and what your loyalty tells you to do. That is why I reject your offer of a conversation.'

On Sunday 27 March, it was the turn of Louis Liard, the rector of the University of Paris, to enter the fray. Because of his 'great friendship' for his colleague, he agreed to organize a campaign in the senate: 'This is shameful!' He wrote 'in great anger' to the minister of public education and the arts to ask him to intervene:

> You know Monsieur Durkheim . . . You know that he is a man with a scrupulous and lofty conscience; you know that he is amongst those who, ever since the war began, has worked hardest to promote French propaganda in the neutral countries . . . For those who know the things that you know, the words cited above are shameful words. But no protest has been forthcoming from the government benches. As a result, many will believe that they are true.

He concluded that: 'The honour of Monsieur Durkheim, the honour of the whole University and, if I may be allowed to say so, the honour of the minister for public education, requires the government to repudiate such an odious accusation.' He expressed the wish that the minister would bring pressure to bear to persuade Gaudin de Villaine 'to appear at the senate's next sitting and to amend the minutes of the debate'. He also suggested that the minister should 'add a few words to give Monsieur Durkheim . . . the public expression of respect and sympathy that he deserves'.[47]

Durkheim himself describes how, in the session on 30 March, the minister Paul Painlevé addressed the house 'to protest indignantly against the language used by Gaudin de Villaine during the previous session'. The senator himself was not present: he had pleaded illness. He himself described the incident as 'odious and wretched'. It was odious because he could not be there to defend himself, and it was wretched because certain parties had seen fit 'to base the discussion on facts that never existed, or that no longer existed'. As Durkheim himself emphasizes, the minister was 'very zealous'. The incident was handled well. Senators, who were often not present for the beginning of debates, were urged to attend, and there was sustained applause. 'The impression was unanimous. The right applauded.'[48] Durkheim was quite satisfied: 'Everyone made an effort to ensure that the apology was as public as possible.'[49]

An outraged Gaudin de Villaine demanded: 'Why all this *ministerial and Talmudic* (!) fuss about a purely personal matter that is being courteously settled between the interested parties?'[50] Rather than apologizing, the senator defended himself by claiming that a mistake had been made in the transcript of his speech. In the 4 April issue of *La Libre parole*, a nationalist paper that had become notorious for its anti-Semitic comments during the Dreyfus affair, the senator attempted to describe to his 'old and faithful readers the incident, which might be of documentary interest to [you].' All could be explained, according to him, by 'the inevitable presence of a few errors' in the record of his speech published in *Le Journal officiel*. One such error was '[the stenographer's] inclusion of a phrase from [his] supplementary notes that had not been used in the speech'. The error was all the more regrettable in that 'it introduced into the debate the name of someone who had nothing to do with it'. He mentioned Durkheim by name, describing him as a professor at the Sorbonne whose 'absolutely materialist teachings could obviously not be further removed from my personal convictions, but which certainly do not raise any doubts as to his patriotic loyalty as an individual'. Gaudin de Villaine entitled his article 'My duty!' because he had been doing his duty as a patriot and a Frenchman by raising the issue of German espionage in France.

Durkheim, for his part, considered the incident 'closed' and got back to work. He had to turn the *Lettres* into a book, and he also had various commissions to deal with. He had, to his regret, 'many different things to do' and these provided a distraction. He was constantly being approached. Arthur Huc, for example, asked him to contribute to *La Dépêche de Toulouse* 'on a regular basis'.[51] Durkheim declined that invitation, but did not rule out the possibility of 'sending him something' if he thought it 'useful'. 'I haven't said no', he told Mauss.[52]

Durkheim felt in real need of a 'rest cure' and left for Biarritz in mid-April. The peace and quiet would, he hoped, be 'good for his health'. 'The main thing is to stop the pain from taking me over completely and spoiling everything. I think that the pain is now focused on his image. I now have to veil that place with a melancholy gauze.' He ended his letter to Mauss with these words: 'Basically, I have to convince myself that what has happened is real, so as to ensure that I do not go on seeing two contradictory images that are in conflict with one another.' He told his nephew that he had had a 'physical rest' and was 'in better shape'. His fortnight of 'isolation and rest' had also done his morale some good.

> The organism – by which I mean the moral organ – is healthy; it has not been invaded by the pain. I cannot stop it from finding somewhere to bleed. But the wound is localized; it is clean and I am keeping an eye on it. What comes out of it is fresh blood, and it bleeds all the time. It opens up 10 or 20 times a day – I can't really say how many times – and bleeds a little. That is a good description of my position.[53]

There had been no visible changes at home. 'We do not laugh much; I am incapable of laughing. But we do smile a lot, especially over Claude, who is a delightful child . . . We have adopted a rule: life goes on as before.' When his grandson was not there, the house was 'a little melancholy'. 'In a word, we are coming to terms with it.'

Durkheim was astonished to find that 'the therapy for pain is still what Epicurus said it was. To my knowledge, there have been no new developments since then. It is unimaginable to think that this is the greatest evil that besets men, and that almost nothing has been done to remedy it.' He went on:

> I am well aware that the religions were there, and that their practices are rich in unconscious experience and cumulative wisdom. But this wealth of crude, empirical wisdom, and nothing resembling any ritual practice, has not done me any good; nothing seems to have any effect. It all remains to be done.[54]

'Rest' did not, however, mean 'pure contemplation'. 'I have work to do', Durkheim told his friend Xavier Léon. He felt 'quite ready to get back to active life'. There was his teaching (which took up two and a half days a week), the *Lettres aux Français*, the commission on foreign students, a new commission to deal with the distribution of American funds, and a commission on the Jewish question. There was, in other words, enough to 'fill [his days] and even [his] evenings'. If he went on writing letters after 8 p.m., his wife would remind him of his promises, and he would obey her. He was, however, afraid that, once the *Lettres* had been reprinted in book form and once some of the commissions had finished their work, he would 'have nothing to do and no long-term projects to deal with'. 'That must not happen.' Perhaps he could try to write for *La Dépêche*. He obviously had a lot of different things to do but, to his regret, nothing was 'urgent'. 'I'd like to have something that fascinates me and makes more demands of me.'[55]

Teaching did make demands of him, especially now that fewer teachers were available to act as examiners. Dumas, Brunschvicg, Bouglé and Delacroix were in the army, and Lucien Lévy-Bruhl had a 'cushy number in the ministry for munitions'. Delbos was very ill, and about to die of pneumonia. 'Not even five of us left.' As there were 1,900 students sitting the *baccalauréat,* this meant a lot of work. 'All I am doing is exams, and it never ends. It's sickening.'[56]

Durkheim tried to free himself from his propaganda work to 'take care of Fauconnet and his thesis. I haven't forgotten them. But I have to get on with the task in hand.' A few months later, at the end of August 1915, when Paul Fauconnet told him that he was ready to have his thesis printed and to correct his proofs, Durkheim felt that he had been 'caught off guard'. 'I don't think it's ready for the printer in its present state. I was expecting to be able to look at it at the beginning of the academic year.'[57] Paul Fauconnet had finished his thesis on 'Responsibility', but did not submit it until after the war in 1920. He refused to revise it and, with one or two exceptions, to cite any of the books that had appeared in the meantime. 'I owe everything I know about sociology to Durkheim. Anything that is any good in this book comes, either directly or indirectly, from him.' He dedicated his book to 'the memory of my teacher, Émile Durkheim'. 'We were going to revise it and improve it together. The war and his premature death made that impossible.'[58]

The Last Article: 'Tomorrow's Politics'

Durkheim finally accepted the invitation from the editor of the *Dépêche de Toulouse* to contribute to a symposium on 'The politics of tomorrow'. Respondents were asked to address two questions: (1) Were there likely to be far-reaching changes in post-war political thinking? (2) Could it be assumed that party political programmes would prioritize economic issues? Émile had contributed to many symposia in which politicians, intellectuals and academics were asked about their views on contemporary issues. His response was probably written in May or June, but it was not published until 1917 and was the last text to be published in his lifetime. Durkheim was described as an 'eminent sociologist' and one of 'the most acute observers of social questions today'. It was said that his studies put him 'in the forefront of those who have patiently and over a long period of time observed economic problems and thought about them; most of his theories have now been verified by the lessons of experience'.

As he had already told his nephew, Durkheim's intention was to show that the republican party had no future unless it was 'open to socialism', and he was trying to encourage it to take that line.[59] His response concentrated mainly on economic issues. He initially refused to give any diagnosis as to what 'the spirit of France' might be like after the war. In such a 'critical period', there would inevitably be a lot of 'trial and error', and developments would be 'contradictory'.

One thing, however, was certain: 'Economic activity must be organized on a social basis.' The days when France was 'a people of small-scale producers and small shopkeepers' were over! The 'age of mediocrity in which there were no risks and no glory was over!' Durkheim outlined a 'new ideal' for a 'great nation' that had become aware of its greatness: France must have a taste for 'great things', and that taste must leave its mark on everything France did. If there was one problem that was not new and that had dominated the entire history of the nineteenth century, it was that of organization. Durkheim repeated the critique of the classical economists that he had elaborated at the very beginning of his career, and rejected the thesis that 'individual spontaneities' and 'anarchic and discordant' trends were enough to 'miraculously' restore order and harmony. And he reiterated a principle that had been revealed by Saint-Simon and that was basic to all socialist doctrines: 'Economic activity is an eminently social thing: it pursues social ends and social interests, and must therefore be "socially organized".' This was a 'basic truth'.

Durkheim said he was convinced that this question would become 'more acute' and 'more urgent' once the war was over:

> For one of the outcomes of this war, for which there is no historical prec-edent, will be to sharpen the social senses, to make them more active, and to make citizens more accustomed to pool their efforts, to subordinate their own interests to the interests of society, in both the economic realm and in every other form of human activity. (1999[1917]: 10)

This applied even to Britain, the classic home of individualism: thousands of independent factories – railways, shipping companies and mines – were now under state control and were in the process of becoming 'real public services'. 'State interference' was also being felt in the consumer domain, which was now subject to stricter controls. Durkheim therefore concluded: 'Individual caprices can no longer be given a free rein.'

The old individual/state dichotomy was thus becoming an 'archaic conception'. The state was playing an ever more active role in the organization of economic activity. Nationalizations would be expected. Far from being 'a temporary and more or less accidental' product of the war, this tendency would become more pronounced 'under the pressure of events'. 'The war has ripened it.' This was not a 'vision of social things' that would vanish once the war was over. It had once been only sociologists who had any sense of this reality. Now, everyone could sense it.

Durkheim was not, however, looking for 'the solution that is destined to triumph' (1999[1917]: 11). He was simply trying to indicate the terms in which the economic question would be posed. He had never been closer to socialism. But his socialism was not just any socialism. 'There will be no salvation', he told Xavier Léon in March 1915, 'unless socialism abandons its outdated formulae, or unless a new socialism emerges and perpetuates the French tradition. I have such a clear vision of what this might be.'[60]

'The Moral Greatness of France'

In January 1916, Durkheim took part in a symposium organized by the *Manuel general de l'instruction primaire*, which was a weekly paper for primary school teachers. Contributors were asked: 'What will the school of the future be and what ought it to be?' Durkheim's response was entitled 'The moral greatness of France and the school of the future' (1979[1916]). Before attempting to foretell the future, he suggested that it was necessary to 'consider the past', and began by contending that the moral climate in France was 'entirely without parallel'. Witness 'the heroism of her troops, and the calm, solemn patience with which she endures the appalling calamities of a war without historical precedent' (ibid.: 158).

The explanation lay, in his view, in 'our educational methods': schools had done their job creditably and had 'made men of the children entrusted to their care'. The terrible experience of the war 'now shows us which points should be the principal target of our endeavours'. On the eve of war, France had been 'burdened with a chaotic and mediocre public life': 'We desired nothing more than to live a calm, untroubled existence, fighting shy of long-term undertakings which were demanding and not without risks' (1979[1917]: 159–60). The war had triggered an 'upsurge of heroism' and awakened 'unsuspected strengths'. When faced with danger, the people of France had 'converged, and through the convergence of their action accomplished great things'. Durkheim even speaks of a 'miraculous rebirth', describing it as 'a psychological phenomenon of the simplest kind': the French had seen what needed to be done. He continued: 'If . . . we wish to avoid the pitfalls of the past, the wills of all individuals need to be directed, not only in time of crisis but in a normal, regular way, towards one single goal, transcending all religious symbols and party slogans.' And that goal was *'The moral greatness of France . . .* our duty as individuals to our country as well as our duty to humanity' (ibid.: 159).

Durkheim's thesis was that both individuals and collectivities must rise above themselves: 'A great people should have ambitions to match its inherent moral strengths. It must have the ambition to create a lasting work and to leave its mark upon history.' A strong personality could not express itself just by acts that were expressive of it. There was 'something morbid' about Germany's 'passion for the colossal' and 'inordinate taste for mediocrity' which was not 'worthy of a great nation'. But while he praised France for its 'spirit of self-sacrifice and self-denial', he regretted the fact that 'we did not possess the spirit of discipline in like measure'. While he was certainly not suggesting that France should subscribe to 'the blind, mass discipline practised by Germany', the fact remained that *'respect for rules* is the condition of all corporate action' (1979[1917]: 160).

There was no doubt that this feeling had weakened in France: 'the very idea of moral authority . . . has come under strong attack' (1979[1917]: 160). To make his point, Durkheim cited the example of 'one of our best educationalists', who had argued that the aim of democracy was to foster personal autonomy, which he contrasted with the notion of authority, of obligation and of the rule that is respected because it commands. This was, in Durkheim's view, a serious mistake:

> Respect for legitimate authority, which is to say moral authority, will have to be reawakened and the religion of the rule will have to be inculcated in the child. He will have to be taught the joy of acting in conjunction with others, according to the dictates of an impersonal law, common to everyone. (Ibid.: 161)

He was thinking here of school discipline, which 'must appear to children as something good and sacred – the condition of their happiness and moral well-being'. School discipline would then evolve into a 'social discipline'. Durkheim ended by earnestly advocating improvements, but made it quite clear that 'under no circumstances is there any question of a revolution' (ibid.).

Academic Propaganda in America

The commission dealing with American students wished to publish a book on 'higher education for the American market'. 'Most of the book will be down to me. I am writing a lot of it (four long – and difficult – chapters) and coordinating the rest, which will be written by the deans or directors of the relevant schools.' The work was not, he admitted to his nephew Marcel, 'gripping' and it was therefore 'going rather slowly'.[61]

Durkheim also agreed to make what he described as a 'sentimental' speech to a gathering of 50 ladies from the American community to explain 'our work with the Fraternité américaine' on behalf of the minister. He was more than happy to do this because 'certain good souls in the United States are spreading all sorts of rumours to the effect that we are dechristianizing our children and saying that the money is not reaching those it is intended for'. He liked to say that it was the 'feeling that [I] can be of some use' that gave him the strength to carry on with this kind of work: 'I admit to feeling that very strongly. The very fact that I no longer have any worldly interests frees me of all minor considerations, makes me more active and, I think, more effective.'[62]

By mid-August, Durkheim had 'almost completed [his] programme of work'. Together with his wife, his daughter and his grandson Claude, he went on holiday to Cabourg (Calvados), renting the villa des Tobys, which had a view of the sea. 'Absolute peace.' He was doing a little work: he had an 'enormous' and 'boring' thesis on the question of generations to read, the book on the University of Paris to write, and correspondence to catch up with. It was the conclusion to the book that worried him: he was trying to describe 'French high culture' without actually boasting about it. 'Nothing could be simpler' when it came to the historical and philological disciplines, but what could he say about the natural sciences?

I do not know much about them, and the specialists have come up with no suggestions. But I do think that the way we see the relationship between theory and its application must be specifically French. I have the impression that the two things are divorced in Germany: abstract, almost metaphysical, theory, empirical utilitarianism. For us, there has to be some connection between the two.

But he still had no more than 'a very vague' idea of what this might mean.[63]
His daily timetable was highly organized. The morning was spent on the beach with Claude and 'his lot'. He took a siesta after lunch, and then read the newspapers. He worked between 3 p.m. and 6 p.m., dined at 7.30 and went for a walk along the sea wall in the evening. A lot of his Jewish acquaintances were, he noted, on holiday in Cabourg: 'I know more than 30 Semites of both sexes in Cabourg, and not a single Indo-European!'[64] His state of 'semi-non-activity' soon began to prey on his nerves. 'I'm bored of being here, so far away from everything . . . I long to be in Paris.' A few days later, he added: 'I'm not unhappy here, and I might even be happy if it wasn't that the feeling that I am doing so little makes me miserable.'[65] He was quite happy to have had a holiday: 'Cabourg has done me good. We are sleeping better than we have done for a long time. At the same time, I have enough to do to make the time fly by.' He also felt that 'given the times we are living through, one feels ashamed at taking too much rest'.[66]

He went back to Paris on 19 September: 'I am working half-heartedly.' The book on the university was progressing slowly – some of the contributors were behind schedule. 'I do not like these periods of active relaxation: they are not good for me.'[67] He also had the 'Mante affair' to worry about. In June, Théodore Mante, a shipowner from Marseille, had been fined 20,000 francs and deprived of his civic and civil rights for a period of 10 years because he had, in the 1900s, set up a company that was nothing more than a front for its German parent company. His appeal was rejected, and the sentence was confirmed on 24 November. Durkheim took a special interest in the case because Mante was the chairman of the board of the Compagnie industrielle de pétrole, and his son-in-law Jacques Halphen was its director. His reading of all the documentation (the charges, the statements to the court, and the judge's summing up) had convinced him that 'the sentence is abominable': 'This kind of legal execution of a man is unheard-of.' And he concluded: 'This is worse than the Dreyfus affair.'[68]

At the end of October, Durkheim was once more 'very tied up with [his] academic propaganda for America': 'This is no small job.' He had to rework all the contributions. 'It all has to be knocked into shape. That is how I am spending my time.'[69] A few days later, he complained: 'I don't have a moment to call my own.' There was the *baccalauréat*, which was 'too much' and even 'harder and harder to put up with', university council meetings, and university receptions. 'I don't think I can go on doing this job for much longer. I've had enough. I need to get my life back.'[70]

He put the final touches to what he called his 'American propaganda' at the beginning of November. He then went back to teaching, but without any great enthusiasm: 'I could happily do without these classes. I really think I need a break.' Some 50 students had enrolled for the degree course. Fortunately, he also had plans to teach a course called 'An introduction to ethics'. 'That does interest me. It means that I can start cutting my book down to size'. But he also feared that this course would take too much out of him.

It was not until 1918 that Librairie Armand Colin published *La Vie universitaire à Paris*. It was designed to highlight 'all the great work that has been done in France over the past four years or so, and especially at the University of Paris and in our institutes of high culture.' It also attempted to 'predict something of the university's future by pointing to future improvements in its organization, and to the new conditions in which the university will find itself when the war is over.'

The book was addressed primarily to foreign students, and 'provided a useful introduction to life at the University of Paris and a full account of the intellectual resources available to them here'. As Durkheim remarked in his preface, it was intended to help foreign students, who often felt 'lost' when they came to Paris because the educational system was so complex. It was, in other words, meant to spare them some 'pointless experiences' (Durkheim et al. 1918: 1).

The book concentrated on the public higher education system, first because it was 'much bigger' and, second, because, despite its apparent diversity, it did have its 'historical, intellectual and moral unity'.[71] The spirit that 'inspired France's young students' was, Durkheim insisted, 'the same throughout'. The sector was made up of two kinds of institution: the University of Paris, with its faculties, schools, institutes and laboratories; and institutes of high culture that 'are outside the University but serve the same function and cooperate to the same ends'. They were the Collège de France, the Muséum d'histoire naturelle, the École nationale des chartes, and the École du Louvre.

The book respected this division and comprised two parts. Part I dealt with the University of Paris and its faculties and schools, each described by a dean, a director or a professor. The University of Paris was, in Durkheim's words, 'the first beacon of scientific life to have been lit, not only in France but in Europe, since the fall of the Roman Empire'. It was 'the mother of universities, *mater universitatum*', and it had, he added, 'even today . . . a population that is unequalled by any other university in the world' (Durkheim et al. 1918: 3).

The university was an institution that had not been 'built in a day'. Relying on the research he had done for his lectures on the history of secondary education in France, Durkheim divided its history into four great periods: the Middle Ages, the Renaissance, the revolutionary and Napoleonic period, and the Third Republic. He traced the origins of the university back to the Middle Ages, with the metropolitan school of Paris (Notre-Dame), the teachings of Abelard in the twelfth century, the emergence of corporations of masters and students, the establishment of the faculties (liberal arts, law, medicine and theology) and, finally, the emergence of colleges (including the Collège des Quatre-Nations) in the twelfth century. The Renaissance ushered in a period of 'mediocre and listless life' as the university became decadent, came under the control of the Jesuits, and ceased to play any part in scientific life. The faculties became professional schools that had no 'lofty ideals'. The Revolution did give birth to Condorcet's ambitious project, but it led nowhere. The number of specialist 'higher' schools increased: the Muséum, the École polytechnique, the École normale supérieure, the École des langues orientales, the École de Santé, and so on. The nineteenth century had its great and eloquent professors who honoured French thought (Cousin, Guizot, Villemain, and then Fustel de Coulanges and Paul Janet) and saw the emergence of a 'great scientific movement', but there was no 'highly organized higher education system'.

It was not until the Third Republic that the universities were 'restored'. The architects of their restoration were, in political terms, Victor Duruy, Jules Ferry and René Goblet and, in administrative terms, Albert Dumont and Louis Liard. The big idea was to bring disciplines and areas of knowledge closer together. 'Intellectual life cannot be intense if it is not concentrated. For intellectual life, dispersal means death.' An attempt was therefore made to 'bring the special schools together and, in order to wrest them away from their specialization, to make them parts of a whole, parts of a truly encyclopaedic school'. That encyclopaedic school had to be a university, concluded Durkheim as he paid tribute to Louis Liard, rector of the University of Paris: 'It was Louis Liard who finally organized the reconstituted universities . . . The result is a great achievement that will be the republican government's crowning glory' (Durkheim et al. 1918: 18).

In the second chapter, Durkheim gives a general description of the organization of the university, beginning with its sites and buildings, and going on to describe its constitution (faculties and schools with their deans or directors, the university council, its prerogatives and its members), its teaching staff and students and, finally, the degrees it awarded.

Durkheim's description of the University of Paris leads him to analyse the main transformations it had undergone since the 1880s. The teaching staff had been 'very rapidly' expanded, and the number of courses taught had increased at the same rate. Student numbers had risen considerably, especially in the faculties of letters and sciences.[72] The number of foreign students and women had also risen. Turning to the number of women students of French nationality, which was rising by the year, Durkheim pointed out:

These young women do not just attend lectures; they sit the same examinations and take the same degrees as the young men. They are awarded degrees, the *agrégation,* and doctorates. These figures reflect a major and welcome change in our customs: the barriers that kept the sexes apart, especially in the Latin countries, are coming down, and decency is none the worse for it.

This was a 'major revolution' and it was not restricted to the student body. The teaching staff had also been affected. He gave the example of Marie Curie, the widow of the 'famous' Curie, who was a tenured professor in the faculty of sciences.

The model Durkheim was defending, and which was exemplified by the new University of Paris, was that of an institution of higher education whose 'basic role' was 'the promotion of a disinterested scientific culture rather than the practical applications of science'.[73] While some of its faculties were, like the faculties of law and medicine, vocational schools, they were training students for professions that demanded a 'high level of scientific culture'. The university was, in a word, 'primarily a centre of speculative life'. And it was not what it had been in the Middle Ages, a closed corporation that was jealous of its privileges; it was a 'state institution, an organ of public life, but it was still in control of its own intellectual destiny'. He concluded: '[The University of Paris] combines the glory of its past with the vigour of its youth' (Durkheim et al. 1918: 30–1).

'A Last Burst of Energy and a Last Response to the Call of Duty': 'Introduction to Ethics'

'The war is now in its third year, and there is still no end in sight.'[74] As his friend Xavier Léon observed, Durkheim was now devoting himself to 'the cause' and 'taking no rest and no breaks'. He was writing a lot, but he also understood the power of the spoken word and attended many meetings to discuss 'important questions'. It was after one of these meetings early in November 1916 that Durkheim, who had just made an impassioned speech, suffered what Léon called 'the first onset of illness' (Léon 1917: 750). He asked his dean, Alfred Croiset, for '10 days leave on health grounds'. Dr Boulloche, who was treating him, ordered him not to work. He went for long walks, usually with his grandson Claude in the morning and with his wife in the afternoon. 'I am leading, as best I can, a vegetative life', he wrote to his nephew, without giving him any details as to his state of health (the letter was actually written by his wife). In a letter to Xavier Léon, he expressed the hope that be would be 'really back on [his] feet in a fortnight or so'. He asked his friends not to come to see him. 'I want to avoid conversations that might make me think of certain things, as I already find it difficult to keep my mind off them.'[75] His sisters Rosine and Céline were very worried. 'Émile is suffering from no longer having anything to do, and his voice is husky.' They thought that this was because he was 'in a highly nervous state'.[76] His friend Sylvain Lévi was anxious not to bother him: 'I've not seen Durkheim for a good month. I don't want to disturb his rest: he needs it.'[77] He didn't allow himself to visit until the beginning of February, and the hour he spent with his friend brought him 'great joy', as he told Mauss: 'I am deeply attached to him and I have learned that, beneath the somewhat stern, sour-faced mask there is an ardent, generous soul that is also very real.' He concluded: 'He really is a typical Jew. Like it or not, you do not find his like anywhere else.'[78]

Durkheim, who was still 'ill', applied for a period of leave from 1 January 1917 to 31 March 'on health grounds'. He was suffering from insomnia and headaches, especially 'after conversations with third parties who are neither relatives nor close friends'. He had therefore been ordered not to work: 'I am living a vegetative life.' All he could do was write a few letters and think about his book on ethics: 'I am still thinking about my book. But so long as you don't have a pen in your hand, it is no more than a game.'[79] When Mauss asked him about the war, he replied: 'I think about it as little as possible. The Russian enigma is becoming more and more indecipherable.' He had stopped reading the newspapers, and now refused to make 'any prognosis about the war'. As the war went on, life became more uncomfortable – it was 8 °C in his study – and he was finding that difficult. 'Hope it will eventually warm up. The shortage of coal worries me . . . We will have to ration ourselves and organize things so as to save on fuel.'

Even though he was on sick leave, Durkheim took on new responsibilities, and agreed to chair the historical commission on documents relating to the history of France's Jews during the war. He had, it was said, agreed to sponsor a study that would 'reveal the merits of Jews'.[80] Established in mid-January 1917 and sponsored by the Société d'études juives, the new commission was tasked with collecting data (statistics) and documents (biographies, bibliographies, iconography) to 'record how French citizens of Jewish origin had behaved during the war'. Its role was 'confined to collective highly reliable source material that had been subjected to the strictest controls' – in other words, to carry out its investigations 'in a purely scientific spirit equidistant from the prejudice of apologists and detractors alike'. There was, for the moment, no suggestion that any 'conclusions' should be drawn.

That there was a political side to this study was clear: 'It will obviously be interesting to know how those French citizens of Jewish origin who have never embraced any other religion behaved during the war, which called upon all the country's resources.' There was a desire to prove, should circumstances require it, that the Jews, who were 'French, just like other French citizens', had wanted to do only one thing in the struggle being waged by their fatherland: like 'all French citizens', they wanted to 'serve France'.[81] The death of Lucien Lazard, who had come up with the idea for the project, delayed its implementation.

Durkheim's state of health appeared to be improving, and his doctors now gave him permission to work. He wrote two short comments on articles from the *Vocabulaire technique et critique de la philosophie*, an enormous work in progress by his former student (and now colleague) André Lalande, which would be published to considerable acclaim after the war (Lalande 1968[1926]). Durkheim's two articles were on 'Society' and 'The sacred'. In his remarks on society, he noted that 'the great difference between animal societies and human societies is that in the former, the individual creature is governed exclusively from *within itself,* by the instincts' and that in human societies, their ways of acting 'are imposed, or are at least suggested *from outside* the individual' (1982[1917]: 248). The example Durkheim gives is that of language. Language and other 'institutions' 'take on substance as individuals succeed each other without this succession destroying their continuity'. Their presence is, he concludes, 'the distinctive characteristic of human societies, and the proper subject of sociology' (ibid.: 248).

Turning to the notion of 'the sacred', Durkheim (1917) notes that it is meaningful only insofar as it is distinct from 'the profane': '"Sacred" and "profane" are correlative terms . . . They form an essential framework for thought.' In an attempt to define the specific nature of the sacred, he examines criteria such as 'superiority' and 'prohibitions' (on, for example, touching). And in order to emphasize the difference between sacred things and profane things, he demonstrates that the two can only come into contact when there are definite rituals, and even then there are limitations.

In February, at the time when Durkheim's doctor told him that he could work, he began to write the book he had been planning on ethics. He wrote some 30 pages. In his introductory note, Mauss (1979[1920]: 77) remarked that this was 'just the start', and that Durkheim had begun 'even though he knew that he would not be able to see it through'. This was 'a final burst of energy and a last response to the call of duty'. The handwriting was 'neater than ever, albeit shaky' and, even though this was 'a final copy', 'the end of words are missing here and there. It is plainly apparent . . . that the author was ailing' (ibid.). Some sections had paragraphs that had been revised.

'Introduction to Ethics' was to have been the first volume of *La Morale*, and Durkheim had a full outline plan. He was not, he told Georges Davy, convinced that he would be able to finish it (see Davy 1960b: 12) and spoke to his nephew about abridging his *La Morale* or of turning it into an 'introduction' so he could devote himself instead to a study of the family. He wanted to spend what was left of his life writing 'a natural and comparative history of marriage up to the present day (Mauss 1969[1925]: 480–1). Durkheim knew that this task was 'too much for one man', and had thought of asking his nephew to 'help him': 'We planned to devote several years of our lives to it.'

On his desk, Durkheim kept a folder containing summaries of the lectures on which he intended to base his book, most of them dating from the course on ethics that he had taught before the war.[82] This material was, Mauss tells us, 'to serve as the basis for the following chapters, along lines that had already been tried and tested'. The titles, 'which spoke for themselves', were 'Critique of traditional ethics', 'Critique of the wholly subjective view of morality', 'Critique of the theory of Tarde', 'The problem of the Kantian solution', and 'Critique of Kantian ethics'. Durkheim made short work of anything that was not essential to his ideas or that did not satisfy him in terms of proof or system, but one thing was clear: 'his greatest wish was to publish his *Ethics* and *The Family*' (Mauss 1969[1925]: 488).

In the first lines of his 'Introduction to ethics', Durkheim once more asks the question: 'What is ethics or morality [*la morale*]?' Do not kill, steal, or rape; brotherly love, respect for children and remaining true to your promises: these are usually regarded as 'self-evident truths, immediately perceptible to the conscience at the level of intuition' (Durkheim 1979[1920]: 84). Morality therefore appears to be 'the same for everyone', notes Durkheim, picking up on the distinction he had made in his lectures at the Sorbonne between, on the one hand, practical morality and, on the other, theoretical morality. In the ordinary or practical sense of the word, morality is 'used to mean all judgments, be they individual or collective, which men pass with respect to their own actions or the actions of others, so as to single them out by ascribing a special value to them'. We speak of the moral consciousness even though 'man's reaction, when confronted with a moral or immoral action, is spontaneous, even unconscious, apparently stemming from the very depths of his nature' (ibid.: 79). But the term is also used 'to mean all systematic, methodical speculation on moral data [*les choses de la morale*]'. Alongside rules of ordinary morality, we also have 'doctrines' that are 'applied to the rules themselves, which they judge' (ibid.: 80). Moralists, or men of doctrine – Durkheim gives the example of Kant and the theorists of socialism – may not be in agreement with their contemporaries or with current notions.

The morality to which men subscribe at each moment of history has an 'ideal' that is embodied in institutions, traditions and precepts. This moral ideal is not 'immutable': 'it is alive, constantly changing and evolving' (1979[1920]: 81). New aspirations may emerge and may either 'modify or even revolutionize existing morality'. There are 'morally inventive' periods when the many currents that run through society are divided, attain awareness and are given conscious expression, rather as if 'only those periods which are divided over morality are morally inventive' (ibid.).

Durkheim's stance is therefore relativist: man is the product of history, and the moral ideal 'varies according to time and place' (1979[1920]: 83). There are differences between Greece, Rome, the Middle Ages and contemporary France. This diversity 'does not stem from a sort of deep-seated aberration . . . it is rooted in the nature of things' (ibid.: 84). 'The morality which a nation subscribes to expresses its temperament, its mentality and the conditions in which it lives.' While all civilizations have a common basis, they also have their own particular character, and 'the same may be said of morality'. Durkheim defends the idea of change: 'All life is richly endowed with seeds which are infinite in number and variety. Some of these have already sprung into being . . . Yet many are dormant, potential and unused for the present, though perhaps soon with the advent of new circumstances, they will spring into existence.' All life is change and is alien to that which is static: 'fixedness is the negation of life'. This is even more true of human nature: 'a man who is static is no longer a man at all' (ibid.: 86). Primitive men do not conceive of time, strength or causality in the same way as modern men, and there are differences between the Roman's 'sense of personality' and our own: morality is one of the essential elements of civilization, and civilization is 'an essentially chang-ing phenomenon' (ibid.). In a marginal note, Durkheim adds: 'There is such a thing as man in general. But this is not man in his entirety. Man is always alike, always identical, yet always different' (ibid.: 96 n10). How, then, can moralists define and determine goals? As always, Durkheim is critical of both those who adopt the introspective method, and those who look to psychology and turn morality into a practical application of psy-chology. But psychology is a discipline that studies 'a permanent being who belongs to no specific country or epoch' (ibid.: 85), and no moral end can be deduced from it. Durkheim therefore concludes that: 'The method generally employed by moralists therefore requires drastic revision' (ibid.: 91).

How could this be done? Unlike those who take the view that morality is 'founded upon an elementary self-evident notion', Durkheim takes the sci-entific view that 'there is no such thing as self-evident reality' (1979[1920]: 87–8), and that, in order to discover it, the scientist first looks at the 'exter-nal signs' that most clearly reveal it in order to 'discover the innermost properties of the thing'. Just like the scientists who study light or electricity, the moralist must proceed to 'a deeper analysis'. The approach required by the scientific method means that we must admit that 'we know nothing about it, nor could we know anything. We are in complete ignorance of what makes man a moral being.' If we wish to construct the notion of morality, we must carry out further research in order to make a scientific study of moral facts. While he accepts that 'morality exists as an observ-able fact', Durkheim also has to admit that 'we do not yet know what make up moral facts . . . which are distinguished from all other human phenomena by clearly defined and uniform characteristics' (ibid.: 88, 89). The art of morality and the construction of the moral ideal thus presup-pose 'an entire science which is positive and inductive and encompasses all the details of moral fact' (ibid.: 90), including the family, the professions and civic life. This science is, he admits, 'still in its infancy' (ibid.: 92), 'but there scarcely exists a more urgent task'.

Are we talking about a science of moral facts or a science of morality? Durkheim accepts that the notion of morality is ambiguous: in any given period, it is embodied in social norms (*moeurs*), though in a degraded form and reduced to the level of human mediocrity, as though it applied to 'the average man's' way of applying the rule of morality (*la morale*), and he never applies them without compromise or reservation (1979[1920]: 92). In a marginal note, he adds: 'opposition between *moeurs* and *morale*' (ibid.: 96 n9).

The goal of Durkheim's first volume is to provide a full account of the state of what he calls the 'science of moral facts', which must, like any science, be based upon the observation of reality, 'whether in the present or in the past'. 'As for speculations about the future, they are only applied science.' If we are to establish a science of moral facts, we have to 'explain to the best of our knowledge the principal facts of moral life, and to draw from these theoretical studies the practical conclusions implicit in them'

(1979[1920]: 92). Durkheim admits in the conclusion to his introduction that several questions remain unanswered: (1) moral facts are phenomena which relate to consciousness, but 'do they relate to the individual or collective consciousness?'; (2) moral facts are essentially social, but how are we to distinguish them from other social facts, and what is their place in the collective life as a whole? (3) what scientific method should be adopted to deal with them, and what 'practical conclusions may be deduced from these theoretical, scientific studies?' (ibid.: 93). The very way he formulates his questions is an indication of the scope of Durkheim's proposed study, which brings together the two great preoccupations of his scientific life: the (sociological) study of moral facts and the development of a secular morality.

'Better Die Than Live Like This'

March saw a recurrence of the problems Durkheim had experienced in November. He found this depressing: 'This prevents me from hoping that I can easily recover the ability to work, even to a limited extent, and that bothers me. What would there be left to fill my life? Such an existence is no life.'[83] He still followed current events carefully in the hope of learning something new. The situation in Russia worried him: 'The information I have received from Russia . . . is not cheering. There is a huge bureaucratic plot against the Tsar, who has the support of the army and the nobility. Who will win? No one knows.'[84] A few days later, he wrote: 'The darkness that is gathering over Russia frightens me. Nicolas will be bumped off one of these days, and that would not surprise me at all. Such an uncertain situation does not make us any the stronger.'[85] The 'events in Russia . . . bother me a lot', as he put it.[86]

The following month, Durkheim requested another period of leave, from 1 April to 30 September 1917.[87] By the beginning of May, he was feeling 'a little tired', and in order to write letters, he once more had to employ his wife as a secretary: 'It is not as though it was completely impossible for me to write but . . . my handwriting is not what it used to be, so there is little point in making an effort that would be wasted.'[88] He did, however, admit that his state of health was 'not very satisfactory'. Acting on the advice of his usual doctor, he now consulted Dr Dupré for a second opinion and was strongly advised to take 'a long rest'. So he was 'completely out to fallow until November'. His new doctor's advice was that he should then have a period of 'quiet and moderate work'.[89] 'I just need some rest', he kept on saying, as though in an attempt to reassure himself. He planned to go to Barbizon in June, and to spend three or four months there, but in fact rented a house in Fontainebleau for the months of June, July, August and September. Being told to seriously cut down on work was 'a pain', but he had little choice: 'You just have to come to terms with it.' In July, the minister Albert Thomas invited him 'to have a chat', but Durkheim had to decline the invitation because of his 'state of fatigue' and asked Henri Hubert to act as his 'faithful intermediary' and to follow Maurice Halbwachs's example by coming to see him: 'We will be able to talk at our leisure, and even write down the conclusions we reach.' He was not happy with this solution, as he would have liked to have accepted the minister's invitation: 'I find the idleness to which I am condemned especially painful at a time when one feels a need and a duty to make oneself as useful as possible.'[90]

When he visited him at the beginning of July, Marcel Mauss had a 'better impression' of his uncle, but also noted that 'he still gets tired just as easily'. 'Basically', he added, 'he is afraid rather than ill. But fear can make you ill too.'[91] His morale was still low, and even though it was 'not quite impossible to write', Émile refrained from doing so because 'I get tired very quickly and it is wise to avoid that'.[92] He knew how weak he was and kept 'the worried eye of a neurotic' on the alarming state of his heart: he knew that his life was in danger, and his natural inclination was to overstate the threat rather than to refuse to recognize it. He was, as his friend Xavier Léon remarked (1917: 750), 'obsessed with the threat hanging over him, as it already restricted what he could do, and might one day compromise the integrity of his brain'. Durkheim was a man who 'could not consent to his own decline'. He was, on the other hand, still serene.

Durkheim's student Georges Davy visited him regularly.[93] He was impressed by Durkheim's 'implacable stoicism':

> His ascetic thinness was more pronounced than ever, his eyes were more hollow and sparkled more brightly, and his gestures were more febrile. He was also less steady on his feet. A few months ago, this made it apparent to attentively tender onlookers that a body that was too weak could no longer meet the demands of a soul that was too great and too tense.

Davy knew perfectly well that the austere looks concealed an 'extreme sensitivity' and what he called 'a tender heart and an unquiet soul.' He also knew that, by taking his son away from him, the war had 'opened a wound in the depths of his heart, and that he wanted to keep it secret so as not to diminish the exceptional forces that he wanted, more than ever, to devote to science and the fatherland' (Davy 1919b: 181; see also Davy 1973: 17). Durkheim bravely revealed nothing of this. When Davy told him about his fiancée's health problems, Durkheim was at once ironic and sympathetic: '[His] love affairs are always very tragic . . . You can tell that the poor boy is very unhappy. I have to admit that the omens for this marriage are a little gloomy.'[94]

Louis Liard died in post in mid-September 1917. 'Emperors do not retire, and he was the emperor of the university', observed Émile Durkheim, who made no secret of how sad this made him. 'So poor Liard has passed away . . . We are really going to feel the void his loss has created. We really have very few men, because those who have left us are so irreplaceable.'[95] Durkheim was unable to attend the meeting of the university council on 22 October, and sent his apologies. Lucien Poincaré, the vice-rector, told the meeting that the loss of Louis Liard, who had been 'its leader, guide and father', had plunged the university into 'deep mourning'. Referring to the 'unjust aggression', Poincaré (who succeeded Liard as rector) added: 'Thanks to him, the university was allowed to go its own way, and adapted to the needs of the war.' But this had been a 'crushing burden' for him: 'This great heart could not withstand the patriotic fears he felt so acutely.'[96]

In October, Durkheim applied for a new period of leave for the whole of the 1917–18 academic year. Bouglé was appointed to teach the 'Ethics and sociology' course in his place. When Marcel Mauss told his friend Henri Hubert that 'Durkheim was not very well', Émile took offence:

> You know nothing about me, and you have heard nothing from me; I am therefore an unreliable witness. So you know nothing. That is one reason not to say anything. What is the point of spreading rumours about my health when they are based on nothing but my impressions, which are always very uncertain and naturally pessimistic?[97]

His nephew, who was on leave, visited his uncle again in mid-October, and Durkheim tried to reassure him: 'I have no difficulty in guessing that you were upset by the state in which you left me, but, basically, nothing major has happened since you left. So there is no reason for you not to stay in the good humour you need to be in.'[98] In his letters to Mauss, Durkheim kept him well informed about the state of his health and about what was happening in the family. He had few or no comments to make on the progress of the war. 'What a mess!', he wrote at the beginning of November. What did he think of the Bolsheviks' seizure or power? Did he believe, like his collaborator Maurice Halbwachs, that 'Russia had to come through this crisis'?[99]

Durkheim was tiring quickly. When he returned to Paris, he once more found himself unable to write and had to rely upon the 'good offices' of his wife. He was suffering from insomnia, but he was also having nervous spasms. It was increasingly clear that his problems were 'nervous in origin', but he was forced to admit that 'we still do not know what is causing this nervous illness'. As Fontainebleau had not had the desired effects, Dr Dupré once more advised 'rest'. Even though he found travelling difficult, there was talking of 'wintering' in the Midi, probably in Pau. His voice sounded 'husky' from time to time, and his handwriting was 'spidery and almost unreadable'. His doctor therefore advised him to revert to non-italic handwriting, and he sent a sample to his nephew. 'Can I do it?' he wondered. 'I have my doubts. I'm a bad scholar. But I will try.' All this 'infuriated' Durkheim, who concluded: 'Better to die than to live like this . . . I can't see myself writing another book, not even a short one, if this goes on. This is torture.'[100]

Davy came to visit him at the end of October before going to Lyon to take up his position at the lycée there. Durkheim told him that he was 'seeing men and things with eyes that seem already to have left life behind'. But he had lost none of his determination, and had resolved to defeat nature. His resolve was 'silent, almost savage'. 'Don't think I haven't cried', he told Davy. He went on: 'My son . . . I think I can talk to you about him today.' But, as his friend Xavier Léon noted, the 'sombre, silent sorrow' was eating away at him, and made everyone observe 'a frightening silence that was as cold as death'. Durkheim still refused to 'collapse into sterile lamentations' and wanted to 'be active and redouble his efforts to serve the cause'. Although weak and worn down by grief, he was still trying to do everything at once and devoted himself 'thoroughly' to all the patriotic commitments he had taken on, 'unsparingly', as though he were 'incapable of saving his strength'. His friends knew that Durkheim's health was 'naturally delicate' and could see that he was killing himself. 'It really was too much. We could feel it. We were afraid' (Davy 1919b: 183). It was, as someone later put it, an 'incurable wound'.[101] Émile Durkheim died at home at 4 avenue d'Orléans at 2 p.m. on 15 November 1917. He was 59. His daughter Marie sent a telegram to her cousin Marcel that same day: 'Papa passed away this morning. There was no pain.' Marcel was also immediately told by Henri Hubert that his uncle had died: 'Durkheim died suddenly at about midday.'

This was a 'great misfortune' for his 'very sad nephew': 'Not only do I feel the emptiness that not being able to correspond with Durkheim has left in my thinking; it also leaves an emptiness in the only moments when I could, albeit cautiously, pour out my feelings.'[102] Like his family and friends, Marcel saw a direct link between the death of the son and that of the father: 'The death [of André] affected him both as a father and as an intellectual; it was this that brought about the death of Durkheim.' Xavier Léon said: 'He died because his son died . . . He died of the nervous strain of devoting his whole heart and his whole mind to the struggle in which the very existence of France was at stake' (1917: 750). Writing in the *Dépêche de Toulouse* on 15 November 1917, Gabriel Séailles reached the same conclusion: 'Monsieur Émile Durckheim [*sic*] has just died. The death of his son, who was killed during the tough retreat from Salonica, left him inconsolable.' 'Cruelly wounded by the heroic death of a son who died for his country, Durkheim was also the victim of abominable calumnies', remarked Rector Poincaré.[103]

'Although he died far from the battlefields, he was, alas, a victim of the war', said Georges Davy as he wept for the teacher, scholar and friend who had died 'so prematurely'.[104] Everyone mourned the fact that the 'pain' that had worn Durkheim out had 'almost suddenly' carried him off when he was 'still in his intellectual prime and when we could still have expected a lot from him'.[105] Some, like Antoine Meillet, tried, however, to rationalize things: '[Émile] did very well to die quickly rather than falling to pieces. He did not feel the great pain of losing his powers. So much of the past had died with him. He was a centre and a leader. His death leaves us with a great void.'[106]

Durkheim was buried in the vault belonging to his wife's family in the Jewish section of the Montparnasse cemetery. In accordance with the wishes of the deceased, there was no pomp and no speeches (Worms 1917: 568). The funeral was attended by family friends, contributors to the *Année sociologique* and colleagues from the Sorbonne. Maurice Halbwachs came up from Toulouse to be present: 'Durkheim now stands behind us like a solemn, massive monument by the roadside.'[107] The following words were inscribed in Hebrew on the tombstone: 'TEHI NAFSHO SERURAH BISROR HAHAYYIM', meaning 'Let the soul of my Lord be bound in the bundle of life.'[108]

'In Memoriam'

On 16 November, the day after Durkheim's death, the minister of education wrote, via his director of higher education, conveying his 'deep sympathy' to the family: 'His great scientific and moral value, his teaching, and his work, whose methods and findings are widely accepted as authoritative in the field of sociology, Monsieur Durkheim has brought great honour to the University of Paris and to French science.'[109] The rector of the University of Paris, for his part, described Durkheim as 'A thinker, the head of a school and an admirable teacher', adding that Durkheim had been a 'good servant of French influence and of the University of Paris . . . his work and his memory will not be forgotten'.[110] 'Since his enrolment as a student at the École normale supérieure on 1 November 1879, Durkheim had served 38 years by November 1917.'[111]

'Émile Durckheim [*sic*] has just died', wrote Gabriel Séailles in the *Dépêche de Toulouse*. He described him as 'one of the great masters [*maîtres*]' of the French university system, 'sociology's most authoritative representative' in France and throughout the world, 'the founder and apostle of a doctrine', 'the founder of a school with far-reaching influence'. Such was the image of Durkheim that prevailed in French intellectual and academic circles immediately after his death.

Xavier Léon (1917: 751) ended his tribute to his friend with the following words: 'The task of those who remain is a heavy one, but it is essential. Let us care for the heritage of our dead: let us work.' The *Revue philosophique* also wished to commemorate the premature death of a close collaborator and announced that, after the war, it would be publishing a study of 'The doctrine of Émile Durkheim' (see Halbwachs 1918). Lucien Lévy-Bruhl had taken over as editor following the death of Théodule Ribot in January 1917, and this made the *Revue de métaphysique et de morale* fear that it had a new and dangerous competitor. 'You now have an adversary who is worthy of you', Élie Halévy wrote to Xavier Léon.

It was probably Lévy-Bruhl who wrote the eulogy of Durkheim for the *Revue philosophique*. He described him as 'the leader of a school in the strongest sense of that term', but added that 'his unchallenged authority religiously respected his collaborators' freedom of opinion'. He viewed the *Année sociologique* as 'a collection of facts and ideas, and a unique tool' that was all the more valuable in that it allowed very different minds to work together and to develop 'the various provinces of the new science'. Durkheim was 'one of France's masters of philosophy' and 'a powerful thinker who will long remain one of the great glories of contemporary French thought'. The philosophers, in other words, claimed Durkheim as one of their own: 'French philosophy and science could not have suffered a more cruel loss.'[112]

Émile Durkheim was praised for being not only 'the eminent scholar who gave France international fame' but also 'the good scholar who never lost interest in public affairs'. His old colleague Gabriel Séailles (1917) portrayed him as a man who, 'in his concern for what would happen after the war, felt the need, which had never been greater, to organize our democracy by giving it a sense of order in the service of freedom'. He concluded that 'social science led him to politics in the same way that theory led him to its applications'.

Even his adversaries praised him. The *Revue internationale de sociologie* (which had been edited by Gaston Richard since 1917) called him 'an authoritative sociologist'. René Worms, who wrote the tribute (1917: 568), recalled the similarities and differences between himself and Durkheim. They were alike in that they both wanted to 'make sociology a science in the true sense of the word, and not a work of literature' and to 'strive after objectivity'. But they also had their differences. Durkheim attached too much importance to objectivism, made a radical distinction between the collective and the individual, and rejected all value judgements. Although he was critical of his rigidity of thought and his dogmatic, intransigent and aggressive attitude, Worms acknowledged the 'importance' of Durkheim's role in 'our science', praised the 'considerable amount of work' he did, the dignity of his characters, and his services to science, justice (at the time of the Dreyfus affair) and the fatherland. He concluded: 'At least allow a somewhat suspect voice to say that even those sociologists who did not agree with him mourn his premature death.'

The *Univers israélite* also published an obituary. It began by describing the brilliant academic and professional career of a man it regarded as 'the leader of the French sociological school' who had 'such great influence of some of our young university students'. It went on to describe his 'firm, upright character, scrupulous strictness and inflexible probity', and praised the 'tireless zeal he devoted to patriotic propaganda'. He was, in a word, 'a man who served and honoured science and the fatherland'. The obituary ended on a sorrowful note: 'It pains us to think that this son of a rabbi knew nothing of the religion of his ancestors, that the sociologist had no sense of the social nature of Judaism, and that a scholar and pedagogic scholar of Jewish origin has without doubt driven away more than one Jewish intellectual from Judaism.'[113] The *Archives israélites* was more indulgent towards him; 'Although he did not practise Judaism, he remained a Jew at heart, and his oppressed brothers could count upon his devoted assistance.'[114] One could say of Durkheim what Marc Bloch said of himself: 'I was born Jewish', 'I am a republican', and 'I will die, as I have lived, as a good French citizen'. Because of the almost symbolic links between these three statements, his words could have been the motto of any French Jew of his day.[115]

Epilogue

On 16 December 1917 Célestin Bouglé was appointed to teach the course on ethics and sociology, and on 22 December he was appointed to teach on sociology of educational science at the Sorbonne for the academic year 1917–18. In February 1919, he was appointed professor of the history of social economics, and on 7 December the faculty of letters accepted a proposal to transform the chair in sociology and educational science, which had been left vacant after the death of Durkheim, into a chair in the history of social economics. When the proposal was laid before council at the end of the month, only Rector Poincaré expressed his sorrow at seeing the chair of sociology and educational science disappear, but he did not oppose the proposal. The vote was unanimous.

One of Durkheim's wishes was that a grant be awarded to a student from the University of Paris every year on the recommendation of a committee of philosophy professors. Anxious to make her husband's wish a reality, Louise Durkheim established the Fondation Émile et André Durkheim at the end of October 1917, and endowed the University of Paris with an income of 1,500 francs.[1] The council, most of whose members had worked with Durkheim, agreed to accept the endowment on a provisional basis. They were all faithful to the memory of the late professor. Speaking of his aunt, Marcel Mauss said: 'She remains calm and strong in the face of her misfortunes.' She was to become the 'fair executor' of her husband's wishes and 'the faithful archivist and copyist of his manuscripts', being one of the very few people who could decipher them (Mauss 1969[1925]: 524).[2]

Lucien Lévy-Bruhl, who was now editor of the *Revue philosophique*, was anxious to honour the memory of his colleague and asked Maurice Halbwachs to write an article summarizing Durkheim's work for the journal. This was 'an honour' that he could not refuse:

It may be a lowly task, but it does give me the opportunity to demonstrate that I am 'a philosopher'. Basically, it annoys me that I cannot devote myself completely to the sciences . . . I will not be critical. But I will – or plan to – write, a few heterodox remarks that occurred to me as I grappled with the master's thought . . . I have never felt closer to the centre of his 'doctrine' than I do now. It is very beautiful, but there are gaps and it shows some lack of understanding. It is in any case a superb linear thrust, and if I am not very much mistaken, it will outlast Bergson by a long way.[3]

The long article was entitled 'La doctrine d'Émile Durkheim' (Halbwachs 1918). Halbwachs knew that Durkheim's doctrine had been misunderstood and often seemed to be 'narrow, mechanistic and simplistic'. 'I would like to emphasize how complex [Durkheim's] method is.' At his best, Durkheim was not so much dogmatic as dialectical: 'Durkheim discusses things.' 'Ideas must be judged on the basis of their productivity', Halbwachs wrote (1918: 407). In 1925, he published a 'summary that is as accurate and literal as possible' of *The Elementary Forms of Religious Life*, praising it for both its breadth and its richness. In the early 1930s, he re-examined Durkheim's study of suicide in the light of a more sophisticated methodology: the result was *The Causes of Suicide* (Halbwachs 1978[1930]).

Georges Davy published a long study in the *Revue de métaphysique et de morale*: 'Durkheim: l'homme' (1919). When he became a professor at the Sorbonne, Paul Fauconnet devoted his inaugural lecture to 'The pedagogic work of Émile Durkheim'. In August 1924, Célestin Bouglé, who had already published a *Guide de l'étudiant en sociologie* (1921), published an article entitled 'The spiritualism of Émile Durkheim' in the *Revue bleue*. He was also preparing to publish six of the master's articles under the title *Sociologie et philosophie* (Bouglé 1974[1924]).

News does not always spread rapidly, especially in wartime and in post-war periods. It is usually not until the war is over that obituaries begin to appear in the foreign press. Victor Branford's obituary of Durkheim, for example, did not appear in the *Sociological Review* until 1918. Alfred Radcliffe-Brown, who was the most 'French' of the English anthropologists, was working in Pretoria in South Africa, and only learnt in 1921, 'with great sorrow', that Durkheim was dead. 'As you know,' he wrote to Marcel Mauss, 'I have great admiration for your work, and for that of Durkheim. They were a source of inspiration to me.'[4]

'In memoriams', many of them coauthored, begin to appear after the 52 months of war, during which 'our country' had made 'a superhuman effort, a bloody effort'. Writing in the *Revue des l'histoire des religions*, Paul Alphandéry (1919) wrote:

We now write the names of those who are missing quite automatically. Several of them died with weapons in their hands, and many were gradually worn down by the fears and the pain caused by that terrible epoch. The scourge killed them from afar. Both those who died at the front and those who died in their homes during those four years all make up the 'war dead' and, in this hour of austere victory, we gladly salute all of them with the same piety.

One of the 'war dead' was Émile Durkheim who 'in the prime of life, but sorely tried by the war, died after a short illness'. The journal stated that it would discuss 'in detail and with the praise it deserves, the work of a philosopher who was a pioneer in our field and a master whose many followers preserve his doctrines and draw out its many implications'.

As Marcel Mauss pointed out, few groups of researchers suffered 'so atrociously' during the war as the Durkheimians: 'We lost a whole generation of our best and most vigorous collaborators.' He went on: 'We will see that, if it had not been for the war, sociology, science and our country would have had a body of work that few studies have produced.' Everything remains to be (re)done. Mauss felt that he had a 'duty to the conscience of [his] uncle' to defend and promote his work. He hoped that this would be a way of 'fully appreciating a body of thought . . . whose influence and reputation is spreading and will continue to spread for a long time'. The *Revue philosophique* and the *Revue de métaphysique et de morale* quickly published a series of articles based on Durkheim's lecture notes: 'Rousseau's *Social Contract*' (1975[1919]), 'Rousseau on educational theory (1979[1919]), 'Introduction to ethics' (1979[1920]), 'The conjugal family' (1978[1892]), while parts of the lectures on socialism were collected and introduced by Mauss as *Le Socialisme* (Durkheim 1971[1928]).

Only a handful of the team survived the war: 'Our group is like peas in a devastated area where a few old trees that have been riddled with shrapnel go on trying for a few years to put up shoots', explained Mauss; 'it is going to take a lot of courage.'[5] The plan was to relaunch the *Année*, which meant finding financial backers, a publisher and contributors, including all the 'old hands' (Marcel Mauss, Henri Hubert, Célestin Bouglé, François Simiand, Paul Fauconnet and Maurice Halbwachs). The Institut français de sociologie was founded, with Mauss as president, and the *Année sociologique* was relaunched, using the old formula of articles and bibliographies. The first issue of the new series appeared in 1925, and included Mauss's 'In memoriam' and his classic 'Essai sur le don' ['Essay on the gift']. Durkheim's legacy was safe. Three of the official university chairs in sociology were held by Durkheimians, with Halbwachs in Strasbourg, and Fauconnet and Halbwachs at the Sorbonne, while the former Durkheimian Gaston Richard held the chair in Bordeaux. Paul Lapie had now left teaching to become director of primary education and saw to it that sociology became part of the degree syllabus in philosophy. This development, which the Durkheimians followed very carefully as study sessions for headteachers were organized and as a syllabus was drawn up, proved to be highly controversial (see Geiger 1979).

Two years later, the *Année* team succeeded in publishing a second volume, but not without difficulty. There would be no follow-up, and the second volume was the last in the new series. It was a failure. Everyone was overworked, and the team had little unity, as everyone retreated into their own domain or speciality. The team had also been undermined by deaths and other trials. Henri Hubert died in 1927, and Paul Fauconnet, François Simiand and Antoine Meillet in the 1930s. There was, however, also something of a revival and the French school of sociology was reborn. The Institut d'ethnologie de Paris was founded in 1925, and Marcel Mauss was elected to the Collège de France in 1930. The first fascicule of *Annales sociologiques* (series A: 'General sociology') was published in 1934. This was not just a revival; it was a form of revenge. 'Dame sociology' had finally been admitted to the Collège de France, and Mauss's tenured chair was indeed in sociology.

Then came the rise of fascism and a new war. What would Durkheim have thought of all this? When Svend Ranulf, who had been his student at the École pratique, asked that question, Mauss replied that while fascism might look like 'a salvation from individualism', Durkheim would have found it 'unacceptable'. He then explained to his Danish correspondent that the 'return to the primitive' they were witnessing in Europe was something they had not expected. The hyper-excitement, the way the community was taking priority over individuals was, he concluded, leading not to the development of civilization, but to 'social regression'. This was 'too clear a proof of things that we predicted, and proof that we should have waited for them to be verified by evil and not by good'.[6]

'In those times of clashes, tactics, diametrically opposed political systems, radical institutions, revolutions and equally savage reactions', sociology's continued success in the faculties still gave rise to reactions that could be violent, recalled Célestin Bouglé (1938: 37): 'There were appeals to socialism, and to religion. Political passions and pedagogic trends combined to create uproar.' 'In death, Durkheim has finally completed the task of bourgeois preservation that he began in life', screamed a furious Paul Nizan in his *Les Chiens de garde* (1981[1932]: 98). This was, as Mauss put it so well, a time of conflict. We must not, he went on, keep Durkheim's views on the problems facing Europe to ourselves and, referring to his uncle's remarks on professional ethics, he stated that he was convinced that Durkheim's 'clear intuition' had long ago allowed him to propose a better solution that anyone else: the 'right and practical solution was ethical, juridical and economic' (Mauss 1969[1937]: 504). He also took advantage of the platform offered him by the Collège de France to pay tribute to his uncle by devoting his lectures of 1931–2 to 'An exposition of Durkheim's doctrine on civic and professional ethics'.

During the Occupation, the Gestapo requisitioned the house at 9 avenue Jules Janin in the 16th *arrondissement*, where Émile and Louise's daughter, Marie Halphen, was living, and promptly threw all the documents – manuscripts, letters – left by Durkheim and carefully filed in a big cupboard, out of the window. Hundreds and hundreds of sheets of paper swirled around in the wind, and a memory was blown away. The traces of an immense body of work were erased, the secrets of a lifetime were lost.

The Spirit of the Times

Durkheim said of his writings on pedagogy that they were not so much 'models to be imitated' as 'documents about the spirit of the times' (see Debesse 1922: 6). While his work is still highly controversial, no one can deny that his articles and books are indeed 'models to be imitated' – classics. Just like Karl Marx and Max Weber, Durkheim was the founding father of a discipline; he has even been described as 'the sociologist *par excellence*' (Simon 1991: 319).

But does his work reflect the spirit of his times? As I have tried to demonstrate throughout this study, Durkheim was certainly a man of his time. We can see him sitting on a pebble beach, wearing a jacket, a tie and a hat and holding a newspaper in August 1915. The photograph was taken at Saint-Valéry-en-Caux. The image it projects is that of a stern professor who is conscious of his authority, function and status. Émile was a man with a sense of discipline and duty, unstinting in his efforts and always ready to make sacrifices. He led an austere life that was completely devoted to his academic work of preparing lectures, meeting students, writing articles and books, editing a journal and corresponding with colleagues.

He was also, it must immediately be said, a 'New Sorbonne' professor. He was not just a teacher but also a researcher, who sought distinction not for his bookish erudition, dialectical skills and flights of oratory, but for his scientific attitude, his systematization of data and his ability to stay in contact with things. In a word, he preferred rigour to brilliance. This was the scientific *habitus* he sought to inculcate into his students and collaborators. That much is obvious from the painstaking work that went into writing so many reviews for the *Année sociologique* – a task that required both a great capacity for synthesis and a sharp critical mind (when it came to sources, etc.). He did not see research as an individual task for one man: it was a form of teamwork involving both exchanges and interdependence, arguments over ideas, and the collection of data. For this *fin-de-siècle* scholar, the art – and the difficulty – lay in the encounter between yesterday's philosopher and the scientists of the future. The tension between the two is central to all Durkheim's work.

The photograph of Durkheim on the beach shows him surrounded by his family: his wife Louise, his son André (in uniform and smoking a cigarette), his niece Juliette (Cahen) and his two daughters. Was he the head of a family, a patriarch? Durkheim enjoyed a close relationship with his family: they attended the same festivals, and exchanged visits, letters and services. Yet, in his view, kinship no longer had the integrative function it once had, now that society was making the transition from the extended family to the conjugal family. Émile and Louise were the perfect example: they were a couple with two children, and they showered them with affection. Émile took a very romantic view of the couple-relationship: it was a form of 'fusion'.

As we have seen, the study of domestic life was one of Durkheim's constant preoccupations: he studied sexual relations, the division of sexual labour, marriage, family and divorce. His stance towards the family was the same as his stance towards society as a whole. It was relativistic: every society has its own way of life, its own customs and its own morality. And when society changes, we have to change with it. This was obviously true of the French society Durkheim observed, not without some fears for the future. Were its traditions a thing of the past? Durkheim was always cautious and tried to find a balance: he was opposed to all forms of traditionalism, but did not reject all traditions and customs. He was open to change and even legal reforms (of the divorce laws, for instance). Yet the values he defended can seem 'conservative'. He defended marriage and criticized those who spoke up for free love, and his criticism of divorce by mutual consent led some feminists to include him in the long list of the defenders of patriarchy. He by no means objected to young people being taught about sexology, but refused to allow sexology to reduce sexual relations (which were, in his view, something mysterious) to some 'reproductive' function.

The positions defended by Durkheim were not meant to be purely ideological: they were, as he constantly reminded his readers, scientifically based on either his own research or that of others. The horror of blood, the prohibition and exogamy were all well documented in the anthropological literature. The organization of domestic life was highly regulated. But Durkheim also observed that so-called primitive societies observed some curious practices: during festivals and in moments of effervescence, all kinds of transgression took place – the rules of exogamy were broken and sexual licence was common. The fascination this exoticism held for the researcher was obviously great, and might even be described as excessive, if not obsessive. But as we can see from the books and periodicals of the day, this reflected 'the spirit of the times': the West was discovering the *Other*. As Gauguin remarked when he left for Tahiti in 1895, 'the future belongs to the painter who can paint the tropics'.

The spirit of the times obviously also meant republicanism, and it would be a very puritanical republicanism: 'Being a republican is not enough', Jules Simon liked to say, 'if one does not observe the austerity of republican customs' (cited in Horne 2002: 50). Attempts were being made to turn education (which was, as we have seen, under the thumb of Protestant administrators) into an apprenticeship in self-government, and to make every citizen into an individual with a capacity to develop his personal autonomy and to acquire new habits (such as hygiene, looking to the future and saving). Civic education was thus a central issue for the new educational structures that were designed to promote secularism and to make individualism the central value of the Republic. Make way for human rights and the cult of the individual!

Émile Durkheim spoke out about the Dreyfus affair and the separation of church and state, criticized trade unionism in the public services, and defended occupational associations, socialism and patriotism. He was, in a word, an intellectual steeped in the spirit of the Third Republic. This was *la république des professeurs* and its credo centred on the words 'democracy', 'secularism' and 'science'. The republican ethos, as defined by the Montesquieu to whom Durkheim had devoted his Latin thesis, was: love of the laws and the fatherland, the democratic and egalitarian ideal (equal rights), recognition of the 'power' of education, defence of the public interest as opposed to individual self-interest, and the feeling of an immense debt towards a society that promoted altruism as opposed to egotism. The power of institutions was preferable to that of individuals, and the marshal's sword should give way to the law. Jules Ferry was the law made man, and the Third Republic was the embodiment of the Enlightenment dream of the rule of law.

Durkheim's three great books were on the division of labour in society, suicide and the elementary forms of religious life. If we also take his teaching into account, it becomes obvious that his main fields of interest were education and pedagogy, morals and law, marriage and the family, and ethics and religion. It was force of circumstances that made him take an interest in education, and he did so almost despite himself: sociology entered the university via the 'side door' of education. According to Durkheim, institutions, morals and law were sociology's true objects of study. It was as though social life was essentially a 'legal life' with rules and sanctions. It was therefore the embodiment of social science, which is why the *Année sociologique* attached so much importance to moral and juridical sociology, and almost as much to the sociology of religion, and advocated the study and understanding of the law. Durkheim's studies of marriage and the family, which range from his study of the prohibition of incest to the study of totemism and exogamy in Australia to the planned book on marriage, the family and kinship, are, perhaps, less well known, but, as Georges Davy put it (1931: 106), that does not detract from their importance. Religion, it might be said, is the 'root' of all Durkheim's work. Social life is by its very nature religious, and every religion is by its very nature social. Durkheim has often been seen as a Jewish prophet.

Son of a rabbi, Jewish prophet: even as he kept his distance from Judaism (and claimed to have rejected it) and described himself as a free thinker, his contemporaries often described him as a Jew and identified him with the Judaism of his parents. This became obvious when Senator Gaudin de Villaine insultingly accused of him of making a 'Talmudic fuss' in the senate and the government. It was not always said in so many words, but he was at times a victim of anti-Semitism. Some found it offensive that a non-Christian should attempt to study a Christianity he could never hope to understand, and others, like Simon Deploige, accused him of betraying his country by importing ideas that had been 'made in Germany'. In the context of the Dreyfus affair, such attacks on a Jew strongly implied a form of anti-Semitism.

Durkheim's relationship with Judaism was complex. He came from a Jewish background and family, but was not a practising Jew. Should his interest in religions, and especially primitive religions, be seen as an instance of the return of the repressed? Could it be an expression of a nostalgia for a lost and idealized primitive community such as Ancient Israel (Tiryakian 1979: 112)? While the thesis is credible, it should also be recalled that Durkheim was highly critical of Ancient Israel, describing it as a lower or even backward civilization, while he admired other religions, and especially Christianity, which had, in his view, made obvious contributions to the progress of civilization (including the cult of the individual). Durkheim analysed as a scientist the passionate relationship between societies and religion, and discovered that a whole world of knowledge, beliefs and emotions were religious in origin.

His personal trajectory, the development of knowledge and the transformations of society were all products of a combination of factors. Durkheim's life and work are characterized by the tensions of his times, and by those of modernity. The tension was between religion and reason, to use the title of the article Émile Boutroux published in 1914. Like everyone else, Durkheim was trying to reconcile the two – or at least to reduce the tension between them, even though his collaborators saw him as 'a rationalist empiricist'.

From the Durkheimian perspective, it takes two 'motors' to get a society 'going': integration and regulation. On the one hand, we have institutions, social environments and ideals; on the other we have rules, both formal and informal. The family, the community, religions, political society and, to an increasing degree, the world of work are our environments. But which word or expression could be used to describe the society that was emerging at the turn of the twentieth century, which the first great industrial war threatened to destroy? Was it an industrial society, a capitalist society, a democratic society or a modern society?

Neither Durkheim nor his collaborators denied that there was an 'industrial' and capitalist side to the contemporary economy, which had once been a national economy but which was now becoming international thanks to the almost boundless expansion of markets, the increase in the number of big companies and capitalist speculation. This was obviously a democratic society in one sense, but the very nature of parliamentary and representative democracy was problematic. When Durkheim described the new society that was emerging from the old and becoming differentiated from it, he spoke, rather, of the social processes of differentiation and specialization that helped to make modern society so complicated – in the sense that Halbwachs speaks of social complication – and so organized. The society they describe is an 'organized society', which suggests that the societies of the past were either unorganized or not so highly organized.

Durkheim's main preoccupation, if not obsession, was society's 'moral discontent': European societies were going through a 'moral crisis'. Anomie was not a temporary problem caused by an over-rapid economic transition; it was something deeper, and a characteristic feature of modern society. How could it survive this moral crisis? And if the preconditions for its survival were, as Durkheim believed, the separation of church and state, the gradual release of morality from the grip of religion and the development of a science of moral facts, what would the society he wanted to see look like? There was only one answer to that question: it would be a secular society.

Durkheim was well aware that there are 'currents' in any society, and that in its depths there are subterranean forces that might explode at any moment. But he also believed in the power of reason and in the contribution of sociology as a bulwark to hold back the forces of irrationalism. The passions that were unleashed (with first the Dreyfus affair and then the First World War) in what everyone believed to be a civilized Europe destroyed many of his illusions. Hence the moral and then the physical repercussions of the death of his son André.

Does that tragedy represent a challenge to Durkheim's sociological theory and his analyses? In one sense it does, as his work is a product of his era and society, and reflects the spirit of his times. But while it was a product of its context, Durkheim's vision of sociology (which he regards as a science) allows society and its members to look at themselves objectively and to relativize things in such a way as to reach a conclusion that is universally valid: today's societies, like those of the past, all work on the basis of belief and ritual.[7] The work of Émile Durkheim is beginning to show its age and yet, 150 years after his birth, it has lost none of its contemporary relevance or its acuity.

Notes

Introduction

1 See Rawls 2004; Jones 2001. See also Robert Prus's paper 'Émile Durkheim reconstructs the pragmatist divide', which was read to the Annual Congress of the American Sociological Association, Philadelphia, August 2005.
2 See Alpert 1939; Clark 1968a; LaCapra 1972.
3 Alexander 1988: Alexander and Smith 2005; Besnard 1987; Jones 1984; Lacroix 1981; Leroux 1998; Mergy 2001; Meštrović 1988; Mucchielli 1998; Paoletti 2005; Pickering 1994; Schmauss 2001; Steiner 1994; Strenski 1997; Tiryakian 1979; Turner 1993.
4 There are several hypotheses. According to some, including Lukes (1985[1972]) and Lacroix (1981), Durkheim's 'early' texts are those written between 1885 and 1887 (1887 was the year Durkheim's career began in Bordeaux). According to others (Nye), *The Rules of Sociological Method* (1894) and *Suicide* (1897) can be included in this category. Others (Giddens 1971; Hawkins 1980), finally, suggest a different and apparently more precise periodization and argue that Durkheim's 'early works' are those written between 1883 (or 1885) and 1983. The argument is as follows: the 'young Durkheim' period, between 1883 or 1885 and 1893 – just before the publication of the *Rules* – is a period during which he published reviews, two major studies '(Introduction à la sociologie de la famille' and 'Suicide et natalité: étude de statistique sociale') and wrote both his theses, *Quid Secundatus Politicae Scientiae Instituendae Contulerit* (1892) and *The Division of Labour in Society* (1893).
5 Bernard Lacroix, for his part (1981) emphasizes that Émile's father Moïse Durkheim died in 1896. His interpretation of that event is socio-psychoanalytic: the death of his father was the condition or possibility for an objective and sociological study of religion, but the transgression was so great as to trigger a profound feeling of guilt in the son.
6 The French *professeur* is a much more general term than the English 'professor'. A teacher working in the primary sector is an *instituteur* (fem.: *institutrice*). A teacher in the secondary or higher sector is addressed as *professeur*. [Translator's note]

1 A Jewish Education

1 The 'line' went back to Leib Elsass, a rabbi in Muntzig. The office was therefore not always handed down from father to son, but also from father-in-law to son-in-law.
2 Marcel Mauss, 'Notes': 1; Marcel Durkheim family archives. This is a three-page typescript, apparently written by Marcel Mauss in the early 1940s to demonstrate that 'the various lines from which [he] was descended had lived in the area for a long time.'
3 Letter from unknown correspondent to O. Worms de Romilly, 11 August 1831; Consistoire de Paris, Archives du consistoire de Paris, 3G2.
4 Certificate provided for Moïse Durkheim by Baruch Guggenheim, chief rabbi of Nancy,

13 May 1833; Archives du consistoire de Paris, 3G2. At this time, Moïse Durkheim lived at 17 rue du Moulin-en-Ville.

5 Moïse Durkheim, who was described at the time as a 'doctor of theology and aspiring rabbi', was in fact a member of the commission established by the Consistoire de Nancy in December 1833 to study the problem of marriages. Moïse replaced one of its members, Rabbi Cain from Verdun, who was not always able to attend meetings as expected. See Simon Schwarzfuchs, 'Le rabbin Moïse Durkheim' manuscript; forthcoming.

6 Minutes of 26 May 1834, Consistoire israélite de la circonscription de Nancy; Archives du consistoire de Paris, 3G2.

7 In order to become a rabbi, Moïse Durkheim had, in accordance with the rules, to have the support of three chief rabbis who had to award his 'certificates of ability'. He turned to the chief rabbi of Frankfurt; his other two referees were Aaron Wolff (Metz) and Baruch Guggenheim (Nancy). As the chief rabbi of Frankfurt was not French, he had to turn to the chief rabbis of Paris and Strasbourg, and obtained their signatures in May 1835.

8 Certificate dated 13 May 1835 and signed by Baruch Guggenheim, chief rabbi of Nancy; Archives du Consistoire de Paris, 3G2.

9 Letter from the chief rabbi of Paris to the Consistoire central des Israélites de France, 28 May 1835; Archives du Consistoire de Paris, 3G2.

10 Under the terms of a law passed by the July Monarchy in 1831, ministers of the Jewish religion were paid by the public revenue department on the same basis as Catholic and Protestant priests.

11 The Marx family took the name Marx-Isidor in 1808.

12 Letter from the sous-préfet of Mirecourt, 3 June 1834; Archives départementales des Vosges, 88/7.V.25.

13 Marriage contract between Moïse Durkheim and Mélanie Isidor, 16 August 1837; Archives départementales des Vosges, 5 E 22/289

14 Émile Durkheim, letter to Marcel Mauss, June–July 1808; Durkheim 1998: 148.

15 The population increased steadily, to 23,223 in 1897, and to 28,080 in 1901.

16 The Jews of the Vosges and Haute-Marne *départements* numbered 1,902, and their needs were catered for by the Épinal rabbinate; Archives départementales des Vosge, 88/7 V 12.

17 An account of the opening of Épinal's synagogue was published in the weekly *Archives Israélites* on 15 July 1864.

18 Postmortem inventory, 7 April 1896; Archives départementales des Vosges, 5E 26/141.

19 Marcel Mauss, 'Notes': 2.

20 Personal communication from Henri Durkheim; Greenberg 1976: 626. See also Derczansky 1990: 158; Strenski 1997.

21 Marcel Mauss, 'Notes': 2. As well as ritual prayers, it contained a miscellany of sacred poetry, texts on rabbinical law and aphorisms from Rabbi Yeheil of Paris. The various texts included in the collection were written in the Ashkenazi script; Rabbi Simon Schwarzfuchs, 'Le rabbin Moïse Durkheim', manuscript, 2008.

22 *Archives Israélites*, 15 August 1864: 692.

23 Gilles Grivel, biographical note of Kiener (Chrétien Henry, known as *Christian*, 1807–96), sénateur des Vosges (1882–96), forthcoming.

24 Sylvain Lévi, letter to Marcel Mauss, 17 February 1917; Fonds Hubert-Mauss, IMEC-Caen.

25 This is Steven Lukes' hypothesis (1985[1973]), while Pickering (1994: 36n1) suggests that there was a rabbinical school in Metz. There is in fact no proof that the young Durkheim attended such a school.

26 Archives départementales des Vosges, 88/7V25. Steven Lukes (1985[1973]: 39) cites a sum of 2,500 francs, but does not say in which year.

27 Moïse Durkheim, letter from Épinal to members of the Consistoire de Paris, 16 October; Archives du Consistoire de Paris, 3G2. Moïse Durkheim's request had the support of the members of the Consistoire israélite de Nancy.

28 Letter from the Consistoire de Nancy to the Préfet des Vosges, 15 May 1857; Archives départementales des Vosge 7V 22.
29 Prefect's letter to Consistoire de Nancy, 11 June 1857.
30 Rapport du commissaire de police des Rambvillers au préfet des Vosges, 1975; Archives départementales de Vosge, 8bis M 18.
31 Collège d'Épinal, Rapports hebdomadaires; Archives départementales des Vosges, 13T14. Cf Davy 1960b.
32 A national competition in which the best pupils competed for various prizes. [Translator's note]
33 Letter to O.Worms de Romilly, president of the Consistoire central, 11 August 1831, Strasbourg; Archives du Consistoire de Paris, 3G2. The author of the letter goes on to say that Moïse Durkheim's behaviour in Frankfurt had gained him 'access to the Rothschilds' house in Paris'. There is no record of Moïse Durkheim spending any time in Paris.
34 Letter to Marcel Mauss, June 1905; Durkheim 1998: 358.
35 Durkheim letter, 12 November 1878, Paris; Archives nationales, F_{17} 22850, Dossier Durkheim.

2 École Normale Supérieure

1 Rabbi Durkheim asked the chief rabbi of France, Senator Émile Georges and *député* Eugène Jeanmaire to support his request. Chief Rabbi Isidore was the cousin of Émile's mother Mélanie (née Isidore). Eugène Jeanmaire (1808–86) was the left-wing *député* for the Vosges from 1876 to 1881.
2 Born in Paris in 1859, Henri-Louis Bergson was the son of Michel Bergson, a Jew of Polish origin, and Katherine Levinson, the daughter of a doctor of English origin. Michel Bergson was a pianist and composer who trained in Germany and then travelled in Italy before settling in Paris. In 1863, he accepted the post of director at the Conservatoire de Genève and then returned to France before going to London, where he made a living by giving private lessons. With seven children, the family's financial situation was more than precarious. It was the chief rabbi of Geneva, Joseph Wertheimer, who, impressed with the young Henri's intellectual abilities, paid for him to stay at the Institut Springer in Paris, a private Jewish boarding school, while he attended the Lycée Bonaparte (now Condorcet). Greenberg (1976) compares the trajectories of the fathers of Henri Bergson and Émile Durkheim: 'The same destiny: that of two Jews who were born a generation too soon.'
3 Janet went on to study medicine and was elected to a chair in experimental psychology at the Collège de France in 1902; Casanova was elected to a chair in Arabic language and literature at the Collège de France in 1909; Goblot taught the history of philosophy and the sciences in Lyon; Doumic was elected perpetual secretary of the Académie Française; Le Breton went on to teach at the Lycée de Bordeaux in 1885, and then at the faculty of letters in Bordeaux from 1893 onwards; Picard became a teacher at the Collège Rolin. Holleaux was appointed senior lecturer in the faculty of letters in Bordeaux in 1886, before becoming a *chargé de cours* [junior lecturer] there in 1888; in 1904 he became director of the École Française in Athens, and lectured on Greek institutions at the Sorbonne before being elected professor of Greek epigraphy at the Collège de France in 1927.
4 *Normalien* is the name given to pupils and ex-pupils of an École normale supérieure. [Translator's note]
5 *Le Centenaire de l'École normale supérieure*, 1895, p. 560.
6 This unsigned obituary is, in all probability, by Xavier Léon, editorial director of the *Revue de métaphysique et de morale*.
7 Report of M. Perreur to M. le Recteur, faculty of letters, Paris, 11 March 1893.
8 Born in La Pouèze (Maine-et-Loire) in 1836, Alfred Fouillée took the *agrégation* as a relatively mature student. When the family firm went bankrupt, he decided not to prepare for the École normale supérieure's entrance examination, and taught at a college

in Ernée before going to Paris, where be tried to make a living by writing and doing some coaching. On the advice of a teacher at Louis-le-Grand, he sat the *agrégation* in 1872, and was ranked first. He subsequently taught at lycées in Douai, Montpellier and Bordeaux, and at the faculty of letters at Bordeaux. He submitted his doctoral thesis, 'Freedom and Determinism', in 1872, and the public *soutenance* [oral examination] was something of a political and social event. He was then appointed *maître de conférences* at the École normale supérieure, but he retired on health grounds in 1879 and went to live near Meudon, where he continued to write. His wife Augustine was the author of *Le Tour de la France par deux enfants*. Published under the pseudonym 'G. Bruno', the book, which found a very wide audience, became a sort of 'republican catechism' highlighting the issue of ethics, the value of education and patriotism.

9 Fustel de Coulanges, letter, 14 October 1882; 'Dossier Durkheim', Archives nationales, F$_{17}$ 25768. Cf Lukes 1985[1973]: 64n94.

10 Ollé-Laprune (1839–1898) taught in secondary schools until 1875 and then became *maître de conférences* at the École normale supérieure. His *La Certitude morale* was published in 1880; he was a constant critic of the growing influence of science on philosophy (Fabiani 1998: 95).

11 Émile was a hard-working student who read widely. As a young man, he read works by historians (Champollion's *L'Egypte sous les Pharaons*), literary writers and specialists (Goethe's *Conversations with Eckermann*, Sainte-Beuve's *Portraits littéraires*) and, obviously, philosophers (Victor Cousin's *Du Vrai, du beau et du bien* and *Fragments philosophiques*; Leibniz's *Letter and Opuscules*).

12 In 1904, Gabriel Monod was appointed to a chair at the faculty of letters, Paris (in the history of medieval civilization) before being appointed to a temporary chair in history at the Collège de France in 1906.

13 Fustel de Coulanges joined the staff of the École as a *maître de conférences* in 1870, before being appointed professor of ancient history (1875–8); Charle 1985, 76–7.

14 Born in Montrouge in 1845, Émile Boutroux (1845–1921) studied at the Lycée Henri IV and won first prize for philosophy in the *concours général*. He attended the École normale supérieure (1866), taking the *agrégation de philosophie* in 1868. He received a grant to study in Germany (1869). As a *docteur ès lettres*, he began his career in Caen, and was then appointed *chargé de cours* and professor of philosophy at the Faculties of Letters in Montpellier and then Nancy before 'going home' to the École normale supérieure as *maître de conférences* in 1877. The following year, he married Aline Poincaré, the daughter of Dr Poincaré, professor in the faculty of medicine at Nancy, and sister of the mathematician Henri Poincaré (1854–1912), professor in the faculty of science in Paris and member of the Académie des sciences; Charle 1985: 34–6.

15 Renouvier is the author of *Essais de critique générale* (1854–64), *Introduction à la philosophie analytique de l'histoire* (1864), *Les Principes de la morale* (1864), *La Science de la morale* (2 vols, 1874), *Traité de logique générale et de logique formelle* (3 vols, 1875) and *Traité de psychologie rationnelle* (3 vols, 1875). At this time, he was preparing a voluminous two-volume *Esquisse d'une classification systématique des doctrines philosophiques* for publication in 1886.

16 Renouvier published a book entitled *Le Personalisme* in 1903.

17 *Bulletin administratif du ministère de l'instruction publique*, 31 October 1881; cited in Paoletti 1992: 17.

18 Archives nationales, F$_{17}$ 710939. See Cherval 1993, Annexe 6. 'Les deux copies de Durkheim à l'agrégation de philosophie de 1882.'

19 Fustel de Coulanges, letter, 14 October 1882.

20 The student graduating in first place. [Translator's note]

3 'Schopen' at the Lycée

1 *L'Union de l'Yonne*, 4 November 1882, p. 2.

2 Letter to Célestin Bouglé, 23 August 1897; Durkheim 1975: ii/405.

3 Letter to Célestin Bouglé, 23 August 1897; Durkheim 1975: ii/405.

4 Report by M. Thomas Chappius, rector of the Académie de Dijon for the year 1882–3, II, June 1883; Dossier Durkheim, Archives nationales, F_{17} 25768. See also Lalande 1960: 22. Thomas Chappuis (1822–97) was an *agrégé de philosophie* and rector of the Académie de Dijon from 1880 to 1894.

5 Report by M. Thomas Chappius, rector of the Académie de Dijon for the year 1882–3, II, June 1883; Dossier Durkheim, Archives nationales, F_{17} 25768.

6 No. d'ordre 8069, library book, 1882–3, Lycée Stéphane-Mallarmé de Sens; Archives régionales d'Auxerre.

7 Émile Durkheim, *Cours de philosophie fait au lycée de Sens en 1883–1884* (Paris: Bibliothèque de la Sorbonne, MS 2351). An English translation of these lecture notes has been published (see Durkheim 2004). The manuscript of more than 400 pages was discovered by Neil Gross, a graduate student at the University of Wisconsin in 1995. A selection appeared in *Durkheimian Studies/Études durkheimienne* 2 (1996): 5–30. The text is based on notes taken by André Lalande (1867–1962). As a new pupil at the lycée in Sens, Lalande copied the notes of a student who had followed Durkheim's lectures the previous year (Gross 1996a; 1996b). On the authenticity of the notes, see Gross's 'Introduction' to Durkheim 2004.

8 It was Malebranche who denigrated the imagination as a *folle du logis*, an expression that found its way into the language. An English equivalent might be 'the madwoman in the attic'. [Translator's note]

9 It was, according to Jean-Claude Filloux (1977: 18n23), this book that introduced Durkheim to Schopenhauer.

10 'As for pessimism, it has no effect on education. Schopenhauer, it is true, is quite fashionable, and is widely quoted. But as for his pessimistic doctrine itself, I do not know of any teacher who has been inspired by it. It is, on the other hand, very popular with students, who happily combine pessimism with Wagnerism, which, it seems, is simply pessimism set to music' (Durkheim 1975[1887b]: 454–5).

11 Brunetière is thinking of the period when the German philosopher was fashionable. He took advantage of the French translation of *Welt als Wille und Vorstellung* (*The World as Will and Representation*) to come to his defence.

12 The thesis that Schopenhauer's notion of the will and philosophy of pessimism do more to explain Durkheim's sociology than any other theory of human action is defended by Stjepan Meštrvić (1988). In order to prove his case, Meštrvić goes all over the place in search of indirect influences: Ribot, Nietzsche, James, Levy-Bruhl and even Henri Bergson (Meštrvić 1992: 32–3). The influence of the German philosopher affects, he claims, not only Durkheim but also several of his collaborators, who 'use Schopenhauer's vocabulary'. The same thesis is taken up by Hans Joas: 'Schopenhauer and not Hobbes . . . must be seen not only as the source of specific assumptions in, for example, the study of suicide, on the dangers of the anarchy of the individual's instinctual life, but also for the presuppositions of Durkheim's "rationalism" which from the outset was never a simple rationalism' (Joas 1996: 52). There have been some rather surprising attempts to compare Comte with Schopenhauer (Marcuse 1937).

13 I therefore cannot go along with Meštrvić (1992: 30) when he claims that 'Durkheim never criticizes Schopenhauer, either directly or by implication.'

14 When it comes to the moral sciences, Durkheim identifies four kinds of science: philosophical, social, philological and historical. He is not referring to sociology, but to the social sciences, and the social sciences, in his view, comprise three disciplines: politics, law and political economy. Politics is the 'science of society', and its explicitly normative aim is 'to determine the best form for human society to take' (2004: 215). Durkheim attaches great importance to the historical sciences, devoting a whole lecture to them.

15 This is a very un-Schopenhauerian conception of the great man. According to Schopenhauer's *World as Will and Representation* (1958), 'genius' means the ability to act in purely contemplative fashion.

16 His annual salary was 4,100 francs (plus 250 francs for teaching a course at the girls' school).

17 Report of the rector of the Académie de Douai, 21 April 1885; Dossier Durkheim, Archives nationales F_{17} 25768.

18 See the annual reports by the rector of the Académie de Douai, M.D. Rollen, 10 June 1884, 21 April 1885, 10 June 1885; Dossier Durkheim, Archives nationales $F_{17}25768$.

19 Report of 11 April 1885; report by M. Evellen, 4 July 188; Dossier Durkheim, Archives nationales $F_{17}24768$.

20 Ribot's text appeared originally in English in the British journal *Mind* 2: 366–82.

21 This analysis is based upon the list of philosophy teachers in university faculties between 1893 and 1895; 'La philosophie dans les facultés de France', *Revue de métaphysique et de morale* (1893): 98–100. There are two notable absences: Émile Boutroux (Paris) and Octave Hamelin (Bordeaux).

22 As well as Théodule Ribot's articles on 'The affective foundations of the personality' and Charles Richet on 'Mental suggestion and probability calculation', the journal published H. Beaumis' 'Experimentation en sycomore par le somnambulisme provoqué', Dr Sikorski's 'The psychical evolution of children', Alfred Binet's 'Sensation and movement' and Charles Ferré's on 'Hypnotism in hysterics'. The journal reported the activities of the Société de psychologie physiologique, including the meetings it devoted to hashish (spring 1885), and reviewed many publications, including *Brain*, *Mind*, *The Journal of Mental Science* and the *Archives de neurologie*

23 Gustave Le Bon was born in Nogent-le-Rotrou (Eure-et-Loir) in 1841. His career was atypical in that he was both self-taught and an outsider. The son of a junior customs official, he did poorly at secondary school – he did not take his *baccalauréat* – and followed his father into the customs service. He then began to write articles and books on medicine and hygiene and moved to Paris to study medicine. In 1866, he began to call himself 'Doctor' and his friends affectionately called him by that title. During the war of 1870–1, he joined the health service for the army of Paris. A member of several learned societies, including the Société d'anthropologie and the Société de géographie, he developed an interest in historical and ethnographic studies in the late 1870s and early 1880s. In 1881, J. Rothschild published his *L'Homme et les sociétés. Leur origine et leur histoire*. In 1885–6, he explored India and Nepal. He never wrote a doctoral thesis. See Marpeau 2000.

24 Born in Sarlat (Dordogne) in 1843, Gabriel Tarde had a degree in history from the University of Toulouse, and returned to Sarlat as a magistrate. Between 1863 and 1893, he held various positions in the region's courts. In 1894, he was appointed Directeur de la statistique judiciaire at the Ministry of Justice.

25 They were also quite friendly. The reviews of Le Bon's *La Civlisation des Arabes* (1884) and *La Civilisation de l'Inde* (1887), for example, were written by Ribot himself.

26 Tarde defends the idea of regulation because the need for legislation appears to be 'a need that may well be socialist, but also eminently social.' There was, he claimed, a danger that the state would become not only a warrior state, but also a manufacturing, usurious and trading state, as well as an educational state, with all the advantages (and disadvantages) that implied.

27 Tarde's other article is entitled 'Natural Darwinism and Social Darwinism'.

28 In the preface to the fifth (1910) edition of his book, Fouillée is very clear about the similarities between his views and those of Durkheim (society as a 'set of collective representations and impulses') and their differences ('his conception of social constraints is, in my view, far too mechanistic').

29 *Politique expérimentale* was the title of a book published in 1885 by the engineer Léon Donnat (1832–93); 'Études de politique scientifique' was the subtitle of Albert Régnard's *L'État, ses origines, sa nature et son but* (1885). Durkheim reviewed both for the *Revue philosophique*. See Favre 1989: 62–4.

30 According to Durkheim (1970[1886]: 211): 'Revolutions and sudden creations no more occur in the world of science than they do in the world of things.' It was all a matter of evolution: [sociology] has 'always existed in a latent and diffuse state'.

4 Travels in Germany

1 Émile Durkheim, letter to Monsieur le directeur (Louis Liard, 10 August 1886), Épinal; Dossier Durkheim, Archives nationales $F_{17}25768$.

2 'Nécrologie [obituary]. Louis Liard', *Revue philosophique* 94 (October 1917): 471. Louis Liard was the author of *Descartes* (1882), and of *Logiciens anglais contemporains* [Contemporary English logicians] (1878) and *La Science positive et la métaphysique* 'Positive science and metaphysics' (1879). He also wrote a history of higher education in France.

3 The expression 'new psychology' is used by Alfred Fouillée (1891: 814). See Silverman 1989: ch. 5.

4 Alfred Binet, letter of 3 October 1895 to Gaston Paris (cited in Clark 1973: 49).

5 Mauss 1969[1928]: 29. On Nieglick, see Durkheim 1975[1887b].

6 Letter to Célestin Bouglé, 16 May 1896, Bordeaux; Durkheim 1975: ii/392.

7 Letter to Marcel Mauss, 4 May 1898, Bordeaux; Durkheim 1998: 133.

8 Durkheim was struck by 'the great number of lectures dealing with the same questions and that seem to do double duty'. That certainly had one advantage: 'philosophy thrives on discussion' – but Durkheim also saw it as 'a real waste of strength' (Durkheim 1975[1887b]: 439–41).

9 The teaching of ethics would, in Durkheim's view, teach students 'what sympathy and sociability are' and would give them some 'idea of what a law is'. What applied to (future) citizens also applied to (future) politicians: the latter might acquire some 'idea of what law, customs, manners and religions are, and of the role of and relationship between the various functions of the social organ' (1975[1887b]: 485).

10 Even though Wundt accepts that 'collective phenomena do not exist outside the consciousness of individuals', he is critical of attempts to explain them in terms of calculation or will power. He had discovered – 'by inference', adds Durkheim – that 'we act without knowing why we act. The reasons we give ourselves are not the real reasons' (1975[1887d]: 326).

11 Jhering supplies what Durkheim describes as a 'highly ingenious' theory of fashion: 'The real reason [for fashion] is social: it arises from the upper classes' need to find external signs that distinguish them from the lower classes. As the latter always tend to imitate the former, fashion spreads through contagion. But as it loses all its value once it has been adopted by everyone, it must, by its very nature, constantly reinvent itself' (Durkheim 1975[1887d]: 296).

12 Within a few years, Durkheim would qualify this statement: 'I certainly have a debt to Germany, but I owe much more to its historians than to its economists' (Durkheim 1982[1907]: 260).

13 'Renseignements confidentiels (1886–7)'; Dossier Durkheim, Archives nationales $F_{17}25768$.

5 The Bordeaux Years: Pedagogy and the Social Sciences

1 'Renseignements confidentiels (année 1887)', Dossier Durkheim; Archives nationales $F_{17}25768$.

2 In the case of Paris, it would, in Durkheim's view, have been preferable to adopt a 'radical and rational plan', to sweep away all traces of the past, and to 'build the restored university outside the city walls, in the countryside and in the centre of a vast park'. 'Respectable traditions' won the day: 'This whole *quartier* had already been known for years as the land of study, *le pays latin*, as they used to say, and it seems impossible to dispossess it without being unfair' (Durkheim 1918: 467).

3 Bordeaux was ranked second in law, second in the arts and third in the sciences (Weisz 1983: 39).

4 Figures from a census of the Jewish population of the Bordeaux district, which had four synagogues (in Bordeaux, Libourne, Arcahon and Nantes) and covered several *départements*. Minutes of the meeting of 22 march 1897, Consistoire israélite de Bordeaux, Délibérations 1896–1914: 30–1; Archives municipales de Bordeaux, 22C5. Bordeaux's Jewish population seems therefore to have fallen since 1861 when, at 3,000 people, it represented 3.13% of the total population (Nahon 2003: 225).

5 Chief Rabbi Israël Lévi, *La Petite Gironde*, 2 November 1889, Consistoire israélite de Bordeaux; Archives départementale de la Gironde 2C12).

6 Chief rabbi Zador Kahn, *La Petite Gironde*, 16 March 1889, Consistoire israélite de Bordeaux; Archives départementales de la Gironde, 2C12.

7 They represented just under 10% of the total number of students (1,389) enrolled in the Académie de Bordeaux. The number of students in the faculty of letters gradually rose to 263 in 1892–3. Some 30 were studying philosophy (17 degree candidates and 17 candidates for the *agrégation*).

8 A *normalien* and *agrégé de philosophie*, Henri Marion (1846–96) was awarded his doctorate for his thesis on 'Moral Solidarity' (1880). Appointed chargé de course in 'educational science' at the Paris faculty of letters in 1883, Marion was the author of books on that topic (*Leçons de psychologie appliquée à l'éducation* and *Rapport sur l'enseignement secondaires des filles*, 1881). He was very active in this area, and was largely responsible for the establishment of the Écoles normales that were established in Saint-Cloud and Fontenay.

9 At this time, the term was used only in institutions, both state and private, that trained primary schoolteachers, and in private institutions such as the École libre des hautes études scientifiques et littéraires (Gautherin 1987: 12).

10 As Charle (1984: 47) notes: 'Durkheim's maternal grandfather was, like his father-in-law, a boiler-maker and had lived in Paris towards the end of the Second Empire. He may therefore have had business contacts with – or even been employed by – the Dreyfus firm.'

11 'Renseignements confidentiels (1889), Dossier Durkheim; Archives nationales F$_{17}$25768.

12 M. Stapfer, in *Comptes-rendus des travaux des facultés de droit, de médicine, des sciences et des lettres*, Année académique 1891–2; Bordeaux 1892: 60.

13 On relations between Duguit and Durkheim, see Pisier-Kouchner 1977.

14 One of Saint-Marc's first articles, 'Law and sociology', was published in the *Revue critique de législation et de jurisprudence* in 1888; later, he would publish 'The domain of sociology' in the *Revue d'économie politique*. He was listed as a contributor to the *Revue internationale de sociologie*, but did not publish any of his own articles there, using the journal simply to advertise his papers.

15 *Cours libre*: an open public lecture, not associated with any degree course. [Translator's note]

16 Source: Lukes 1985[1973]: 617–18.

17 Gautherin 1987: 11–13.

18 'Nécrologie [Obituary]. Georges Rodier (1864–1913)', *Revue de métaphysique et de morale*, supplement, May 1913: 1.

19 He asks the same question in his first lecture on the sociology of the conjugal family (Durkheim 1978[1888b].

20 'Renseignements confidentiels', 1888–9, Académie de Bordeaux; Archives départementales de la Gironde, TV111–143.

21 Report by Inspector-General J. Zeller, 'Renseignements confidentiels', 1888. Dossier Durkheim; Archives nationales F$_{17}$25768. The inspector had one more criticism to make of Durkheim: 'It seems to me that his theories and his formulations about social *solidarity* are somewhat lacking in practical historical knowledge.'

22 Rector's report, 12 June 1888, 'Renseignements confidentiels', Dossier Durkheim; Archives nationales F$_{17}$25768

23 Rector's report, 22 May 1889, 'Renseignements confidentiels', Dossier Durkheim; Archives nationales F$_{17}$25768.

24 Cf 'Cours et conférences, Université de Bordeaux' (notes taken by Marcel Mauss); Fonds Hubert-Mauss, IMEC-Caen.

25 Albert Léon was a case apart. Born in Bordeaux in 1879, and a Jew, he was afflicted by blindness in early childhood. He nonetheless pursued his studies successfully, and in 1898 obtained a degree for his memoir, 'Extension in Malebranche and Spinoza', written under the supervision of M. Rodier. Awarded his philsophy *agrégation* in 1900, he spent his career as a teacher in the lycée in La Roche-sur-Yon.

26 Born in Paimpol in 1869, Marcel Cachin studied in Bordeaux, and was awarded his *licence ès lettres* in 1893. He was then awarded a two-year grant to study for the philosophy *agrégation*, but did not enter for the examination. Enrolled as a non-degree

student in 1896–7, he eventually abandoned his studies in order to 'make socialism', as he himself put it in his personal file. (Dossier no 1369, Archives de l'université Michel-de-Montaigne, Bordeaux-3.) Marcel Cachin became one of the leaders in the future French Communist Party.

27 Alfred ('Franck') Alengry (1865–1946) was born in Saint-Tropez, where his father was a tax collector in the 'indirect contribution' department. Because of his 'difficult situation' (his mother had been widowed), he was awarded a grant to study for a degree in Bordeaux, where he attended lectures by Espinas, Hamelin and Durkheim, and prepared for the philosophy *agrégation* (he was ranked eight in 1892). In 1900, he defended his doctoral thesis, 'A Historical and critical study of sociology in Auguste Comte', at the Sorbonne. In 1902, he also submitted a doctoral thesis on law at the University of Toulouse; it was on Condorcet, a theoretician of constitutional law and precursor of the social sciences. After a short career in secondary teaching, he worked in school administration, first as an inspector and then as a university rector in Chambéry and then Besançon. He published a three-volume *Psychology of Education* (1906–7) (Condette 2006: 41–2).

28 Durkheim's book was not translated into Russian until 1900. Roussanov thought it a 'remarkable work' that bore the hallmark of a 'great talent'. Its translator P.S. Lunkvitch was critical of it, and contrasted the Durkheimian utopia with the Marxist utopia.

29 Born in Périgeux in 1877, Charles Lalo was educated at the lycée in Bordeaux and at the Lycée Louis-le-Grand in Paris. He returned to Bordeaux on a student grant and obtained his *licence ès lettres* in 1898 and prepared for the *agrégation* in 1899. He began his teaching career at the lycée in Bayonne in 1903.

30 Paul Hourticq was born in Brossac (Charente), where his father was a licensed tobacconist. He was educated in Poitiers, where he passed his *baccalauréat ès lettres* in 1894. He was then awarded a grant to study for the *agrégation,* finally passing it in 1899, after three referrals.

31 Born in 1870, Abel Aubin began his studies at the teacher training college [*école normale supérieure d'instituteurs*] in Angoulême and then taught in a college in Cognac. After doing his military service, he returned to study in Poitiers, where he was awarded a degree. Having been awarded a grant, he then decided to study for the *agrégation* in Bordeaux. He deferred his studies for two years, applied again in July 1898, and was eventually awarded the *agrégation* at his third attempt.

32 An anonymous translation of the book as *The Non-Religion of the Future* was published by Heinemann in 1897. [Translator's note]

33 Jean-Marie Guyau also published poems and wrote on the theory of education. He died at the age of 33 in 1888. In 1889, Alcan published two of his other books posthumously: *Education et hérédité. Étude sociologique* (with a short introduction by Alfred Fouillée) and *L'Art au point de vue sociologique.* Guyau was the son of Augustine Guyau, who became famous with her *Le Tour de France par deux enfants.* She lived with the philosopher Alfred Fouillée, who adopted Jean-Marie as his son.

34 Letter to Célestin Bouglé, Bordeaux, 14 May 1900; repr. in *Revue française de sociologie* 15 (1976): 170.

35 In the biographical note he wrote on Victor Hommay, Durkheim (1975[1887a]) describes the accident in detail and paints a picture of his friend as a somewhat melancholy man who, cooped up in a provincial secondary school, had led a rather sad and lonely life.

36 Edmond Villey was professor of political economy in the law faculty in Caen, and a member of the editorial committee of the *Revue d'économie politique.*

37 Émile Cheysson (1836–1910), an engineer and economist, became a member of the Leyplayist movement, and had been defending political economy for the previous 20 years. One of the first group of teachers at the faculty of law in Caen, he was appointed to a tenured chair in political economy at the École des mines (Paris) in 1884.

38 Born in 1851 and originally a doctor, Jacques Bertillon was the son of Louis Adolphe Bertillon (who died in 1883). In 1872, he became a member of the Commission permanente de statistique and of the Société de statistique de la ville de Paris. In 1882, he became the editorial director of the *Annales de démographie internationale* and then

replaced his father at the École d'anthropologie and the Ville de Paris's statistical bureau when the latter died. Jacques Bertillon was one of the founders of the Alliance nationale pour l'accroissement de la natalité française [National alliance for an increase in the birth rate in France] (1896).

39 Chirac had already published an article on sociometrics in the *Revue socialiste* in 1887.

40 He then qualified this statement, arguing that, 'when the birth rate rises beyond a level which is too high, it once again becomes a cause of of suicides' (1992[1888]: 192). He extends the analysis by taking into account other factors such as population density (town/countryside), occupation (agriculture/industry and trade/liberal professions) and marital status (single/married).

41 Born in 1843, Paul Leroy-Beaulieu was a jurist with an interest in the social sciences. In 1872, he taught a course on financial history at the École libre de sciences politiques (its director was his brother Anatole); in 1880, he was elected to the Collège de France, where he took the chair left vacant by his father-in-law, the economist Michel Chevalier.

42 Le Comité de rédaction, 'Notre programme', *Revue d'économie politique* 1 (1887): 2.

43 Not all contributors to the journal shared this view. In response to Schäffle's work, the *Revue* published an article entitled 'Economic science and national politics'. Its author, Charles Turgeon, taught in the faculty of law in Rouen, and was quite hostile to the professorial socialists: 'We trust in the omniscience and omnipotence of God; the professorial socialists trust only in the omniscience and omnipotence of the state.'

44 The other was a review of the German philosopher W. Lutoslawski's *Erhaltung und Untergang des Staatsverfassungen nach Platon, Aristoteles und Macchiavelli* (Durkheim 1986[1889]: 83–6).

45 The notes – more than 100 pages of them – that Marcel Mauss took during his uncle's lectures of 1893 give an accurate picture of just how much importance he attached to Hobbes. The lecture plan includes 'Biography and bibliography, The role of politics in natural laws and ethics, Genesis and nature of the state, The [illegible] and the state. Natural societies, slavery, the family, religious society. Natural and civil laws. Conclusion'. He is obviously referring to *Leviathan*, but also to other works in either their English (*The Elements of Law, Human Nature*) or Latin (*De Corpore politica*) versions. One of the conclusions Durkheim drew from these lectures was that 'Social facts should be dealt with as though they were natural things, and they should be studied in the same way that we study other things: we must rid ourselves of received ideas, prejudices and the feelings they inspire in us if we are to understand them for what they are' (Durkheim, "Hobbes", notes taken by Marcel Mauss, 1893; Fonds-Hubert-Mauss, IMEC-Caen).

46 He also discussed the doctrines of the realists and the encyclopaedists (the leading figure was the little-known Comenius), and went on to discuss Rousseau, Condorcet, Pestalozzi and finally Herbart, who was also under-appreciated. Mauss also mentions Froebel, to whom Durkheim may have devoted some lectures.

47 The letter probably dates from June 1897.

48 As Xavier Léon notes in his editorial note to Durkheim's 'La Pédagogie de Rousseau' published in 1919 in *Revue de métaphysique et de morale*; see Durkheim 1973[1919]: 371.

49 As Xavier Léon remarks in his 'editorial note' (in Durkheim 1973[1919]: 371), Durkheim writes *sentimentaliste* and not *sentimental*: 'The word does not appear in Littré's dictionary, but Durkheim had no qualms about inventing words to express his meaning.'

50 An *étudiant libre* is registered with the university, but not aiming for any formal qualification. [Translator's note]

51 Émile Durkheim, letter to Marcel Mauss, 1899; Durkheim 1998.

52 Mauss, 'Lettre de province. Impression sur l'enquête en Russie' (1920); Mauss 1997: 1.

6 The Individual and Society: The Social Bond

1 'Renseignements confidentiels, année académique 1891–1982'; Archives départementales de la Gironde TV-111-143.

2 See Davy 1960[1953]. The Latin text was translated into French by A. Cuvillier, and

served as the basis for Ralf Mannheim's first English translation in 1960. A later English translation by W. Watts Miller and Emma Griffiths was published by the Durkheim Press (Oxford) in 1997.

3 As Besnard et al. point out (2003: 3), the title of the English translation –*The Division of Labour in Society* – captures Durkheim's meaning very well.

4 Durkheim cites nine texts by Spencer, but relies mainly on the first four books of the monumental *Principles of Sociology*, which were translated into French between 1878 and 1887 (Besnard et al. 2003: 68).

5 Letter to Marcel Mauss, 18 June 1894, Bordeaux; Durkheim 1998: 36.

6 Report of M. Perreur to the rector, 11 March 1893; Dossier Durkheim: 1.

7 Paul Janet (1823–99) was a moralist and political scientist. A former pupil and collaborator of Victor Cousin, he was a close associate of Émile Boutmy at the time when he established the École libre des sciences politiques. Charles Waddington (1819–99) was a professor of the history of ancient philosophy, and was on the point of retirement. Gabriel Séailles (1852–1922) had been a *maître de conférences* since 1886, and had just been appointed *directeur des conférences* in philosophy; he worked with Janet on *L'Histoire de la philosophie* (1887). One of his areas of interest was the philosophy of art; his doctoral thesis was *Essai sur le génie en art* (1883), and his most recent publication was *Léonard de Vinci, l'artiste et le savant* (1892). Victor Brochard (1848–1907) had published editions of Descartes's *Discours de la méthode* and *Principes de philosophie*; *chargé de cours* in ancient philosophy since 1892, he was appointed as a professor in 1894. Henri Maron (1846–96) had been a professor of educational science since 1887; his doctoral thesis of 1880 was entitled *La Solidarité sociale* (the fourth, expanded edition was published in 1893). He was also the author of *Leçons de morale* (1882) and *Le Mouvement des idées pédagogiques en France depuis 1870* (1889). See Charle 1985.

8 Dean's report, 8 March 1893; Dossier personnel d'Émile Durkheim, Archives nationals-CARAN, F_{17}: 4; peport of M. Perreur to the rector.

9 Résumé of Durkheim's oral examination, summarized by Muhlfeld (1893: 440–3; in Durkheim 1975: ii/288–91).

10 Dean's report. As later readers would point out, the thesis does have its weaknesses: Durkheim makes no attempt to go into the history of ideas in any detail, or to situate the author in terms of the political context of the *Ancien Régime*. There are no, or few, references to Montesquieu's other works. See Watts Miller 1997; Richter 1969: 156; Lukes 1985[1973]: 279.

11 Resumé by L. Muhlfeld; Durkheim 1975: ii/289–90.

12 Resumé by L. Muhlfeld; Durkheim 1975: ii/290.

13 Report of M. Perreur.

14 Report of M. Perreur.

15 Report of M. Perreur.

16 Cited in Muhlfeld's résumé; Durkheim 1975: ii/289–90.

17 'Émile Durkheim, Renseignements confidentiels'; Archives départementales de la Gironde, TV111–143.

18 Born in 1848, Émile Egger studied at the École normale supérieure and was ranked first in the *agrégation* in 1872. He began his academic career at the faculty of letters in Bordeaux (*maître de conferences* 1877) before being transferred to the faculty of letters in Nancy in 1882. His doctoral thesis of 1881 was entitled *La Parole intérieure*. He also took an interest in psychology and the medical sciences, and he published *Science ancienne et science moderne* in 1890. In 1893, he was appointed *chargé de cours* in philosophy at the faculty of letters in Paris.

19 Émile Durkheim, letter to the director of higher education (Louis Liard, 5 December 1893), Bordeaux; Dossier Durkheim, Archives nationales, F_{17}25768.

20 In a note appended to the second edition, Durkheim remarks: 'We have confined ourselves to eliminating from the original Introduction some thirty pages, which now appear to us to be of no value' (1984[1893: lvii]). Those pages do not appear in the English translation. [Translator's note].

21 Célestin Bouglé in *Les Pages libres*, October 1897; cited in Lukes 1985[1973]: 300.

22 Durkheim, letter to Marcel Mauss, 28 May 1894, Bordeaux; Durkheim 1998: 33.

23 CARAN-F$_{17}$ 13424; Durkheim 2003: 147.

24 Born in Paris into a modest family of shopkeepers, Lévy-Bruhl (1857–1939) studied at the École normale supérieure and was an *agrégé de philosophie* (1879). He began his career as a teacher of philosophy at the lycée in Poitiers (1879), before moving to Amiens in 1879, and finally to Louis-le-Grand in Paris in 1885. In 1884, he was awarded his *doctorat ès lettres* for his thesis entitled 'The idea of responsibility', and in January 1889 he was appointed *maître de conférences* in philosophy at the faculty of letters in Paris. He made a 'good marriage' by combining his intellectual resources with the economic capital of a much wealthier family – the Bruhls. When they were married, he added the name of his wife Louise to his own. The author of a study of the development of national consciousness in Germany (*L'Allemagne depuis Leibniz*, 1890), Lucien Lévy-Bruhl was also a professor of the history of political ideas in Germany at the École libre des sciences politiques. Close to Jaurès and a man with socialist sympathies, he, like Durkheim, did not join the socialist party, apparently for fear of wasting his time and becoming involved in petty squabbles (see Mauss 1997[1939]; Merllié 1989).

25 René Worms quickly reviewed the thesis and attempted to show that Durkheim was more of a Spencerian than he thought (Worms 1893).

26 Fouillée was struck by the correlation between degeneracy and urban life, and his review is a summary of Durkheim's book. Being convinced that neurosis posed a threat to the nation as well as to individuals, he feared that the nation's moral vigour, courage and firmness of purpose – and these were, in his view, the qualities that created the life force – would be sapped. This was the 'evil' brought about by intellectual over-excitement: Fouillée's proposed remedy was better physical hygiene and a return to rural values.

27 Durkheim's book did not escape the notice of the British psychological and philosophical journal *Mind* ('Book review of Émile Durkheim, *De la division du travail social*,' *Mind*, new series 5 (January) 1893: 397–400).

28 Schmoller 1894, cited in Schmid 2003: 234. Ferdinand Tönnies (1896 – cited in Schmid 2003) criticized Durkheim on the grounds that his analysis of the division of labour was 'scholastic' and 'uncritical', and that, when he applied it, he failed to take into account the genesis of the development of capitalism and the wage-system.

29 Barth 1895, cited in Schmid 2003: 235. Bouglé replied to Barth's criticisms of Durkheim in his review of the former's *Die Philosophie der Geschichte also Sociologie* (Bouglé 1898a).

30 Undated letter to Marcel Mauss; Durkheim 1998.

31 The debate over the definition of socialism was pursued by the philosophers. In the new *Revue de métaphysique et de morale*, it was Paul Lapie, a future contributor to *L'Année sociologique* who criticized Durkheim's approach: he placed too much emphasis on centralization and gave the state, which he saw as a central system or even brain, too great a role. Unlike Durkheim, Lapie refused to reduce socialism to the socialization of economic forces; it is primarily a matter of human relations. In more general terms, Lapie wondered if Durkheim made too great an allowance for preconceived ideas because he was unable to remain true to the historical method he was defending. He criticized him, first, for his 'systematic use of biological expressions' (such as 'function' and 'organ'). He then added that the famous 'new method' that *The Division of Labour in Society* seemed to proclaim promised an insight into 'the special nature of the social organism . . . We must therefore find a special method for sociology, rather than confusing it with biology' (Lapie 1894: 203).

7 An Object, a Method and Some Rules

1 Reports of M. Perreur to the rector, 11 March 1893: 4.

2 'Renseignements confidentiels', 1 July 1893.

3 Archives nationales, AJ$_{16}$2560: 478–479; cited in Weisz 1979: 96.

4 Maurice Hauriou, a professor of administrative law in Toulouse who also taught a *cours libre* on sociology, took an active part in the debate. He described sociology as the 'most dangerous' of the sciences because it studied society and could therefore have serious

practical implications that might lead not only to social reforms, but also, he predicted, to insurrections or assassinations (Hauriou, *Les Faculté de droit et de sociologie* (1893), cited in Weisz 1979: 91). Greatly influenced by Gabriel Tarde, Hauriou suggested that, before sociology was taught, it had to demonstrate that its findings did not offend 'the old moral and juridical traditions (Hauriou 1894: 393). Hauriou published his major work, *La Science sociale traditionnelle*, in 1894. It was dedicated to Gabriel Tarde.

5 Archives nationals $AJ_{16}2560$, pp. 478–479; cited in Weisz 1979: 97.

6 Émile Durkheim, letter to Ernest Lavisse, 1 December 1984; Durkheim 1975: ii/486.

7 Émile Durkheim, letter to Marcel Mauss, 10 December 1893, Bordeaux; Durkheim 1998: 25.

8 Émile Durkheim, letter to Ernest Lavisse, 1 December 1894; Durkheim 1975a: ii/486.

9 Émile Durkheim, letter to Marcel Mauss, 15 May 1894, Bordeaux; Durkheim 1998: 32.

10 Dick May, letter of 3 April 1894 to Ernest Lavisse; cited in Weisz 1979: 99.

11 'Rapport mensuel', cited in Weisz 1979: 100.

12 Émile Durkheim, letter to Marcel Mauss,18 June 1894, Bordeaux; Durkheim 1998: 36.

13 M. Coat, 29 June 1895; 'Émile Durkheim, Renseignements personnels'.

14 Émile Durkheim, letter to Marcel Mauss, 18 June 1894, Bordeaux; Durkheim 1998: 36.

15 See his comments during L. Glocker's *oral examination*; Durkheim 1975[1905d]: 358. Herbart (1776–1841), who was born in Oldenbourg and died in Göttingen, studied with Fichte and is regarded as the founder of pedagogy as a scientific and academic field. He also defended the idea that psychology can be an experimentally based science.

16 Letter to Marcel Mauss, 10 December 1894, Bordeaux; Durkheim 1998: 26.

17 Letter to Marcel Mauss, 19 February 1894, Bordeaux; Durkheim 1998: 27.

18 Émile Durkheim, undated letter to Marcel Mauss, February or March 1894; Durkheim 1998: 30.

19 Edgar Milhaud, letter to Marcel Mauss, 24 June 1932, Geneva; Fonds Hubert-Mauss, IMEC-Caen.

20 Émile Durkheim, to Marcel Mauss, 18 June 1894, Bordeaux; Durkheim 1998: 35

21 Letter to Marcel Mauss, 19 February 1894, Bordeaux; Durkheim 1998: 28.

22 René Worms (1867–1926) trained as both a lawyer and a philosopher, and had two careers. His father, Émile Worms, was a professor of political economy in the faculty of law in Rennes. René was a magistrate (*conseiller d'État*), a *normalien* (1887) and an *agrégé de philosophie* (1888). In 1891, he submitted a thesis to the faculty of law entitled 'De la volonté unilatérale considérée comme source d'obligations ['On unilateral will as a source of obligations]', and wrote a dissertation, 'La morale de Spinoza, Examen de ses principes et de l'influence qu'elle a exercée dans les temps modernes' ['The ethics of Spinoza: An examination of his principles and contemporary influence']. The latter was published in 1892, and was awarded a prize by the Institut de Paris. The same year saw the publication of his *Précis de philosophie* and *Eléments de philosophie scientifique et de philosophie sociale*. Worms defended his doctoral thesis at the Sorbonne in February 1896. His Latin thesis was entitled 'De natura et methodo sociologiae', and his principal thesis *Organisme et société*. Worms later took another doctorate in the sciences. See Ouy (1926) and Clark (1968b).

23 Letter to Marcel Mauss, June 1894 ; Durkiem 1998: 35–6.

24 Review of René Worms, 'Organisme et société', *Revue de métaphysique et de morale* 4 (1896): 9–10. The members of the jury were Paul Janet, Émile Boutroux, Alfred Espinas, M. Himly, M. Egger and G. Séailles.

25 *Revue de métaphysique et de morale* 2 (January 1894 supplement): 3.

26 The organizing committees for the first congresses included Tarde, A. Fouillée, A. Espinas, C. Letourneau and E. Levasseur (France), and, from abroad, E. Ferri, A. Schäffle, F. Galton, L. Gumplowicz, A. Marshall, F. Tönnies, G. Simmel, H. Giddings, L. Ward, A. Wagner and E. Tylor.

27 Born in 1861, Lydie Martial (whose real name was Anna Carnaud) was the wife of Maximilien Carnaud, a *deputé* for Marseille. She published several books at the beginning of the century: *L'Éducation humaine* (1901), *La Femme intégrale* (1902) and *Vers la vie* (1904). She gave two lectures to the Société de sociologie de Paris: 'Le rôle sociale de

la femme' and La sociologie et la morale'. Lydie Martial founded a journal and established the Union de la pensée féminine (1902) and the École de la pensée (1903).

28 Xavier Léon was a member of the Jewish Parisian bourgeoisie which, while it was assimilated, still upheld the traditions: Léon received a religious education, and Zadoc Kahn,
the chief rabbi of Paris, officiated at his bar-mitzvah. His father, who was descended
from a family of butchers from the Vosges, had inherited a fortune derived from trade.
Although he held a degree from the Sorbonne and was admissible to the *agrégation*,
Léon did not sit the oral examinations. It has been said of him that he was a 'social
philosopher': he held a salon which aspired to being what he himself called an 'intellectual free-for-all'. It was of course attended by academics and philosophers, but also by
musicians, including Darius Milhaud, the cousin of his wife Gabrielle Bloch-Larocque.
Georges Sorel, who contributed to the journal, was a regular visitor.

29 Léon Brunschvicg and Élie Halévy were from different social backgrounds. Born in
Paris in 1869, Brunschvicg was from a modest Jewish family, and his father was a
dealer in soft-furnishings from Alsace. He began his career in secondary education,
teaching in Lorient (1891), Tours (1893) and Rouen (1895) before returning to Paris,
where he taught at the Lycée Condorcet and then Henri-IV. Of Jewish (on his father's
side) and Protestant (on his mother's side) descent, Élie Halévy was from an intellectual and cosmopolitan bourgeois family. His father Ludovic Halévy was a famous
librettist, and his mother, who was descended from an important Protestant family of
watchmakers, was a woman of considerable moral authority and had a great influence
on her children, Élie (1870–1937) and Daniel (1872–1962). Élie was the scholar in the
family, and Daniel the artist. Fascinated by England, Élie devoted most of his work
to English culture. Aside from his *La Formation du radicalisme philosophique*, his great
project was a *Histoire du peuple anglais*, the first volumes of which appeared in 1912
and 1913 respectively.

30 Élie Halévy, letter to Xavier Léon, 21 October 1892; Halévy 1996: 77.

31 *Revue de métaphysique et de morale* 1 (1893).

32 Gabriel Tarde, letter Xavier Léon, 13 September 1893; Bibliothèque Victor Cousin,
Université Sorbonne-Paris 1, Ms 366.

33 Editorial, 'Enseignement', *Revue de métaphysique et de morale* 3 (1895): 232.

34 Élie Halévy, letter to Célestin Bouglé, September or October 1892; Halévy 1996: 70.

35 Dominique Parodi, undated letter to Célestin Bouglé, 28 September 1892(?); Halévy
1996: 69.

36 Parodi (1870–1959) was born in Genoa. His father Alexandre Parodi was Italian, and
sought exile in France shortly after the birth of his son: he had great success with his
historical drama *Rome vaincue*, which starred Sarah Bernhardt.

37 Paul Lapie, letter to Xavier Léon, May 1894; cited in Besnard 1979: 9. Born on 4
September 1869 in Montfort (Marne), Lapie was the son and grandson of primary
school teachers from the Champagne area. He prepared for the *concours* to the École
normale supérieure at the Lycée Henri-IV as a 'deserving scholarship boy' [*boursier
de mérite*]. After failing the *concours,* he obtained a grant to study for a degree, and
attended lectures by Boutroux and Séailles at the Sorbonne. Having qualified as a very
young *agrégé de philosophie* (1893), he was appointed to a teaching post at the lycée
in Tunis (and remained there until 1896). Lapie devoted his life to education, first as
a teacher and then as an administrator (rector, director of primary education, deputy-
rector of the University of Paris).

38 Paul Lapie, letter to Célestin Bouglé, 13 December 1893, Tunis; *Revue française de sociologie* 20/1 (January/March 1979): 33.

39 Célestin Bouglé, undated letter to Élie Halévy (1894), cited in Besnard 1979: 14. The
decision to publish the article should not, however, be seen as proof that the *Revue*
was taking a stance on the debates that divided the sociologists. Halévy himself was
critical of Simmel, whom he met in Berlin in April 1895. He found the German sociologist 'interesting but enigmatic' (letter of 2 February 1894 to Xavier Léon; Halévy 1996
499).

40 Georg Simmel, letter to C. Bouglé, 27 November 1895; Simmel Archives, University of
Bielefeld. The text also appeared in English in the *Annals of the American Academy of*

Political and Social Science (and was reprinted by Albion Small in the first issue of the *American Journal of Sociology* in 1896) and, in Italian translation, in *La riforma sociale* in 1899.

41 Simmel's 'Influence du nombre des unités sociales sur le caractère des sociétés' appeared in the *Annales de l'Institut international de sociologie* in 1894/1895.

42 Célestin Bouglé, undated letter to Élie Halévy; cited in Besnard 1979: 14.

43 Élie Halévy, letter to Célestin Bouglé, 16 March 1895; Halévy 1996: 47.

44 Célestin Bouglé, letter to Xavier Léon, 9 May 1894; cited in Besnard 1979: 9.

45 A fairly laudatory review of Bouglé's 'little book' appeared in the *American Journal of Sociology* 2 (1897): 131–2.

46 Émile Durkheim, letter to Célestin Bouglé, 14 December 1895, Bordeaux; *Revue française de sociologie* (1976): 166.

47 Lucien Febvre, letter to Marc Bloch, 10 May 1933; Bloch and Febvre 1994: 373.

48 Georges Sorel is something of an enigma, in terms of both his social and intellectual trajectory. Born in Cherbourg in 1847 into a Catholic bourgeois family faced with material difficulties, he was initially educated at the École polytechnique and began his career as a civil engineer with the Ponts et chausées [Highways and bridges department] in 1867. He then took leave of absence, moved to Paris and joined the editorial committee of *Le Devenir social*. He became its most active contributor, publishing over one third of all the articles it printed between 1895 and 1897, and emerging as a heterodox Marxist (Sand 1996).

49 James H. Tuft was professor of psychology at the University of Chicago. He also published a summary of the *Rules* in the May, July and November 1895 issues of the *Psychological Review*. He describes his 'recent sociological tendencies' from the point of view of psychology and the history of ideas. His article deals mainly with Tarde's books (*Les Transformations du droit* and *La Logique sociale*) and Durkheim's article on the 'rules' in the *Revue philosophique*. The position defended by Tufts is as follows: there is no such thing as an individual who is not influenced by social forces, just as there can be no social or collective feeling without the support of an individual consciousness. The differences between Durkheim and Tarde were also emphasized in a short report of the debate about sociology and democracy between Bouglé and Andler ('Sociology and democracy', *American Journal of Sociology* 1 (1896): 797–8).

50 Émile Durkheim, letter to Gabriel Tarde, 25 March 1895; cited in Borlandi 1994b.

51 Émile Durkheim, letter to Gabriel Tarde, 25 March 1895; cited in Borlandi 1994b.

52 Émile Durkheim, letter to Lucien-Lévy-Bruhl, 24 June 1895, Bordeaux; cited in Merllié 1989: 510.

53 See also Bernès 1895b. Bernès's initial description of Durkheim is friendly: 'A sociologist who has already proved his worth, and also a very lucid philosopher of mind and a very vigorous logician.' Annoyed by Durkheim's 'marvellous dialectical suppleness', which allows him to regard, with some puzzlement, crime as 'a sign of social health', he then goes on to the offensive, criticizing him both for his objectivism and his overfrequent borrowings from biology (the distinction between the normal and the pathological), attacks him for his 'over-exaggerated' realism and describes his sociology as 'realist'.

54 CARAN-F₁₇ 13424 in *Émile Durkheim, L'Evaluation en comité* (Oxford: Durkheim Press, 2003), p. 148.

55 Bernès's lecture notes were published in instalments in the *Revue internationale de sociologie* in 1895 and 1896.

8 1895: The Revelation

1 Many new initiatives were taken in various European countries. Italy saw the launch of journals such as *La Riforma sociale* in 1895 and *La Rivista di sociologia* in 1896. In Spain. M. Azcarate opened the École des hautes études in 1896 with an inaugural lecture on an 'An Introduction to Sociology'. In Belgium, Simon Deploige became the editor of the new *Revue sociale catholique*, which devoted a lot of space to sociology. On the

other side of the Atlantic, a group of professors at the University of Chicago founded the *American Journal of Sociology*.

2 Josef Breuer and Sigmund Freud's *Studies in Hysteria* was published in 1895. Written in a novelistic style and quite devoid of technical jargon, it describes the case histories of eight women who, according to the authors, were all cured of their neuroses. Freud subsequently became the 'thinker of the dark enlightenment' who demonstrated that 'the ego is not master in its own house'.

3 In his very strange thesis, Izoulet suggested that society and the state could be refounded on a new philosophical basis in accordance with the biosocial hypothesis and presented analyses of countless subjects: the relative advances of the elite and the mob, social selection, hierarchy, respect for the law, sovereignty, and so on. The candidate was keen to spell out the difference between Durkheim and himself, and criticized the latter's 'more optimistic and less strictly scientific interpretation of the same truths'. Durkheim had, he argued, shown that the division of labour worked to the advantage of the elite, and that the masses were doomed to poverty and pauperization.

4 Run by economists (A. Leroy-Beaulieu, E. Gasson and G. Picot), the Comité's role was to study 'the causes of social ills and to define the moral and material preconditions for any social progress by making a distinction between feasible reforms and sterile utopias'. Its goal was to combine the spirit of freedom and solidarity in order to defeat socialism. An awareness of 'the need to be educated about social questions' would, it was hoped, promote 'the spirit of wisdom that must preside over any wise and sane evolution.'

5 Born in 1851, Léon Bourgeois had a doctorate in law and began his career as a civil servant in 1876 as a lawyer in the legal department of the ministry of public works, before becoming a *sous-préfet*, a *préfet*, director of the ministry of the interior and finally a chief constable [*préfet de police*]. He then embarked upon a political career as the Republican *député* for La Marne in 1888. He held ministerial office on several occasions (education and justice). Bourgeois was for a long time the president of the Ligue de l'enseignement. In his capacity as minister for public education, he helped to reorganize the universities by grouping them into faculties, and to organize a 'modern' system of secondary education. The acknowledged leader of the Parti radical, he became Président du conseil in 1895.

6 Picot published a number of pamphlets, including *Socialisme, radicalisme, anarchie* (1895) and *La Lutte contre le socialisme révolutionnaire* (1896).

7 Renseignements confidentiels, 15 June 1894, 24 June 1895 and 29 May 1896, Bordeaux; Archives nationales, Dossier Durkheim F$_{17}$25768.

8 The texts were republished in book form as *Pour et contre l'enseignement philosophique* (Alcan, 1894).

9 When they met on 13 June 1896, Durkheim submitted a 'lengthy, detailed and well-argued' report on the *agrégation* to his colleagues in the faculty of letters at Bordeaux. After some discussion, his proposals were adopted (*Comptes-rendus de travaux des facultés de droit, de médecine, des sciences et des lettres*, année académique 1894–5, Bordeaux).

10 On this controversy, see Fabiani 1993.

11 Editorial note, 'Une Rectification de M. Durkheim', *Revue de métaphysique et de morale* (1895): 352–3. The following year, the Conseil supérieur de l'instruction publique modified the *agrégation* examination: one of the dissertations on philosophy had to deal with a topic relating to an area of philosophy (psychology, logic, ethics, education or metaphysics), and the dissertation on the history of philosophy had to deal with specified periods. The *Revue de métaphysique et de morale* took the view that this reform was 'neither desirable nor opportune': it would have preferred one of the dissertations to be on practical philosophy or on a set topic such as logic, mathematics, physiological psychology, or the philosophy of sociology; 'Agrégation de philosophie. Réforme de l'examen', *Revue de métaphysique et de morale* 4 (September 1896 supplement): 12–15.

12 Lapie discussed Gabriel Tarde's *La Logique sociale* (1895) in his overview of 'the year in sociology'. Tarde describes the religious phenomenon as a social phenomenon, and filial piety as the first form of religion. The theme of religion was very present in philosophy journals. The *Revue de métaphysique et de morale*, for example, published Henri Havard on 'Religion and evolutionist science', Ellis MacTaggart on 'The basis of belief.

Preliminary Notes for a study of theology', and Spir's 'Essay on the foundations of religion and ethics'.

13 Born in 1857, Alfred Loisy was the son of a peasant, and was ordained in 1879. He was forced to resign from his teaching post because of his writings on the religion of Israel and the Gospel, and had been accused of 'modernism'. He was then excommunicated by Pope Pius X: his 'sin' was wanting to apply scientific freedom to the study of Catholicism.

14 The École pratique des hautes études was founded in 1868 by Victor Duruy, the minister for public education who, as Durkheim himself recalled (1975[1918b]: 482), undertook to 'reform our system of higher education'. He established a school where young people could learn to 'study the scientific discipline of their choice on a practical basis.' The École pratique had close contacts with the faculties of sciences and letters, but was not part of either and was originally organized around four disciplines: mathematics, physics and chemistry, natural history and physiology, and historical sciences and philology. The emphasis was on erudition and research.

15 Here, Durkheim is distancing himself from the work of his colleague Alfred Espinas on animal societies: he refuses to accept that marriage is something 'inherited from lower animal species'.

16 Émile Durkheim, letter to Cesare Lombroso, 16 May 1895, Bordeaux; *Durkheimian Studies/Études durkheimiennes* 5 (1999): 23.

17 Mauss himself describes how much work he did: 'Quantitative method: classification of 26,000 suicides recorded in 75 boxes of individual index cards'; Mauss 1979[1930]: 210.

18 Émile Durkheim, undated letter to Marcel Mauss; Durkheim 1998: 43.

19 *Comptes-rendus des travaux des facultés de droit, de médicine, des sciences et des lettres,* année académique 1894–5. Bordeaux: 177.

20 Émile Durkheim, letter to Cesare Lombroso, 28 January 1895, Bordeaux; cited in Bosc 1999: 21.

21 Émile Durkheim, letter to Gabriel Tarde, 28 March 1895, Bordeaux; *Durkheimian Studies/Études durkheimiennes* 6 (1994). See Borlandi 1994b.

22 Émile Durkheim, letter to Gabriel Tarde, 31 March 1895, Bordeaux; *Durkheimian Studies/Études durkheimiennes* 6 (1994): 11.

23 At Clermont-Ferrand, E. Joyau, for example, was discussing 'The principles of social science: an examination of the basic theses of individualism and socialism', while Charles Adams was lecturing on 'Moral and social solidarity in philosophy' at Dijon. Alfred Espinas's lectures at the Sorbonne in 1896 were on Babeuf, Saint-Simon and Fourier. At the Sorbonne, theses for the *doctorat ès lettres* were being written on the history of socialism, with André Lichtenberger writing on 'Socialism in the eighteenth century', and Sébastien Charléty on 'The history of Saint-Simonism.'

24 *Revue internationale de sociologie* 7 (July 1896): 575.

25 'Renseignements confidentiels,' année 1895–6.

26 Émile Durkheim, letter to Célestin Bouglé, 16 May 1898; Durkheim 1975: ii/392.

27 Durkheim's lecture notes for the period November 1898 to June 1900 were published in 1950 with a foreword by Hüseyin Nail Kubali and an introduction by Georges Davy (see Durkheim 1957[1950]).

28 Émile Durkheim, letter to Célestin Bouglé, 24 March 1896, Bordeaux; Durkheim 1975: ii/390–1.

29 Ibid.

30 As Bouglé notes, Andler's defence of democracy leads him to reject sociology as a whole.

31 Élie Halévy, letter to Célestin Bouglé, 11 May 1896, Sucy-en-Brie; Halévy 1996: 179.

32 Émile Durkheim, letter to Célestin Bouglé, 16 May 1896, Bordeaux; Durkheim 1975: ii/392.

33 Émile Durkheim, letter to Xavier Léon, 26 May 1896, Bordeaux; Durkheim 1975: ii/462

34 Émile Durkheim, 'Correspondance', *Revue de métaphysiqe et de morale* 4 (July 1896 supplement): 20.

35 'Enseignement de la morale au Collège de France,' *Revue de métaphysique et de morale* 4 (May 1896 supplement): 10.

36 *L'Univers israélite* 51/20 (7 February 1896).

37 Moïse Durkheim and Mélanie Isidor had married with a communal estate settlement. Rabbi Durkheim left his wife, his three children (Rosine, Céline and Émile) and his grandson Henri (Félix's son) more than 400,000 francs, in addition to the house. He left Russian and Egyptian bonds, and bonds issued by the Crédit foncier de France bank and the City of Paris. There were also a lot of shares, mainly in railways; Inventaire après-décès, 7 April 1896, Archives départementales des Vosges, 5 E 26/141.

38 This text was communicated to the author by Rabbi Schuhl's great-granddaughter Mme Eliane Roos Schuhl. See also Schuhl 1995.

39 Sylvain Lévi, letter to Marcel Mauss, 26 July 1896.

40 This is the hypothesis put forward in Bernard Lacroix's psychoanalytic study of Durkheim's trajectory (Lacroix 1981).

41 See Philippe Besnard's very convincing critique of Lacroix's hypothesis (Besnard 1981: 130f.).

42 Émile Durkheim, letter to Célestin Bouglé, 16 May 1896, Bordeaux; Durkheim 1975: ii/392.

9 Converts: From Suicide to *L'Année sociologique*

1 Letter to Célestin Bouglé, 16 May 1896, Bordeaux; Durkheim 1975: ii/392–3.

2 Undated letter to Marcel Mauss (July 1896); Durkheim 1998: 45–6.

3 Undated letter to Marcel Mauss (late November or early December 1896); Durkheim 1998: 48.

4 Undated letter to Marcel Mauss (late November or early December 1896); Durkheim 1998: 45–6.

5 Undated letter to Marcel Mauss, July 1896; Durkheim 1998: 45.

6 Cf. his undated letter to Marcel Mauss (late November or early December 1896); Durkheim 1998: 47: 'Punishment lies at the origin of a different kind of sacrifice: penal sacrifice or expiation is a different form of communion but the two do have something in common in that the victim of penal sacrifice is a living being or a thing.'

7 Undated letter to Marcel Mauss (late November or early December 1896); Durkheim 1998: 47.

8 Letter to Marcel Mauss, Sunday morning, June 1897: Durkheim 1998: 72–3.

9 Gabriel Tarde, undated visiting card sent to Marcel Mauss, Fonds Hubert-Mauss, IMEC-Caen.

10 Born in Saint-Nicolas-de-Port in Lorraine, Marcel Drouin (1871–1943), after taking his *agrégation* in 1895, went to Germany to improve his understanding of German culture. He began his career teaching philosophy in Alençon. In 1897, he married Jeanne Rondeaux, and thus became the brother-in-law of André Gide, who was already a close friend. From 1900 onwards, he was a contributor to the *Revue blanche*, writing articles on foreign literature under the pseudonym 'Michel Arnauld' (Bourrelier 2007: 899–900).

11 Sylvain Lévi, letter to Marcel Mauss, 27 June 1927, Tokyo; Fonds Hubert-Mauss, IMEC-Caen.

12 Marcel Mauss, 'Henri Hubert', undated (1927); Fonds Hubert-Mauss, IMEC-Caen.

13 Undated letter to Marcel Mauss, July 1896; Durkheim 1998: 45.

14 *L'Univers israélite*, 51/54 (31 July 1986): 569.

15 Undated letter to Marcel Mauss (February 1897); Durkheim 1998: 51.

16 Undated letter to Marcel Mauss (February 1897); Durkheim 1998: 51.

17 See, for instance, Lapouge (1895: 1018). Lapouge was the librarian of the faculty of law in Rennes. In January 1897, he published a memoir entitled 'Depopulation in France' in the *Revue d'anthropologie*. The causes he invoked in order to explain depopulation are not only sociocultural (the high cost of living, debauchery, the clergy's declining influence on families), but also psychophysiological (neurasthenia) and anthropobiological (racial interbreeding).

18 Durkheim defines the main characteristic of ordinary action as a stable relationship with both the physical environment and the social environment: 'Living means responding

appropriately to outer stimuli and this harmonious correspondence can be established only by time and custom.' We therefore cannot reconstruct everything 'every time there is necessity for action'. Because he is always taken by surprise by circumstance, the neuropath 'has to invent new forms of conduct' but his improvised contrivances 'usually fail' (Durkheim 2002[1897]: 14, 15, 16).

19 Dr Collington's *L'Indice céphalique de la population française* (1890) and George Vacher de Lapouge's *Anthropologie de la France* (1894) and *Les Sélections sociales* (1895) were well known, as was the work of the English statistician Francis Galton.

20 Durkheim also takes into account the 'artificial lighting' which, in European cities, 'restricts darkness more than elsewhere' (2002[1897]: 72).

21 Durkheim gives the example of the mass suicide of Jews during the war against the Romans. This was the result of 'a collective resolve, a genuine social consensus': during the assault on Jerusalem 'some of the besieged community committed suicide with their own hand . . . Forty Jews, having taken refuge underground, decided to choose death and killed one another' (Durkheim 2002[1897]: 82).

22 The case of England puzzles Durkheim: how is it that 'the classic land of individual freedom' (Durkheim 2002[1897]: 115) has a lower suicide rate than other Protestant countries? The country is, he argues, less 'free' than one might think: there is a high number of 'common obligatory beliefs and practices', a powerfully integrated Church, great respect for tradition, a hierarchical clergy. Religion is, in other words, 'more strongly constituted (ibid.: 116]).

23 Durkheim in fact identifies three types of altruistic suicide. When the idea of duty is involved, we have obligatory altruistic society. When the obligation is less powerful and when there is no question of renunciation or abnegation, the suicide appears to be more spontaneous, and can therefore be described as 'optional'. There is also, finally a third type of altruistic suicide, described by Durkheim as acute altruistic suicide, which, as we can see from Brahmanism and Hinduism, is characterized by 'the joy of sacrifice (Durkheim 2002[1897]: 181). There is an element of melancholy in this type of suicide, but it is not the melancholy of the egoist, with his 'feeling of incurable weariness and sad depression'. It springs from hope, and 'even implies enthusiasm and the spur of a faith eagerly seeking satisfaction' (ibid.:184).

24 Compared with man, woman is also less susceptible to what Durkheim calls sexual anomie: during the period of greatest sexual activity (20–40 years) suicide rates for unmarried people rise less rapidly amongst women than amongst men. This once more demonstrates that women are less interested than men in sex.

25 Durkheim's alarmist viewpoint notwithstanding, suicide rates in most European countries ceased to rise, and actually began to fall from 1920–30 onwards (Baudelot and Establet (2008[2006]): 45). See also Baudelot and Establet (1999).

26 Rector, 8 June 1898; Renseignements confidentiels, 1897–8.

27 Undated letter to Marcel Mauss (late November or early December 1897); Durkheim 1998: 48.

28 Letter to Célestin Bouglé, 9 July 1897, *Revue française de sociologie* 20/1 (January–March 1979): 40.

29 Émile Durkheim, letter to Célestin Bouglé, 6 July 1897; Durkheim 1975: ii/401.

30 Dominique Parodi, letter to Célestin Bouglé, 6 July 1897; *Revue française de sociologie* 20/1 (January–March 1979): 43.

31 Paul Lapie, letter to Célestin Bouglé, 9 July 1897; *Revue française de sociologie* 20/1 (January–March 1979): 40.

32 Émile Durkheim, letter to Célestin Bouglé, 20 June 1897; Durkheim 1975: ii/399

33 Émile Durkheim, letter to Célestin Bouglé, 6 July 1897; Durkheim 1975: ii/401.

34 Émile Durkheim, letter to Célestin Bouglé, 25 July 1897, Bordeaux; Durkheim 1975: ii/403.

35 Born in Saint-Denis in 1874, Paul Fauconnet was a friend of Marcel Mauss. They met when they were both taking the philosophy *agrégation*.

36 Anon. *Revue de métaphysique et de morale* 3 (September 1897 supplement). The anonymous reviewer may have been the journal's director Xavier Léon.

37 Outside France, a brief review appeared in the *Journal of Mental Science* in 1898.

38 Émile Durkheim, letter to Célestin Bouglé, 23 August 1897; Durkheim 1975: ii/405.
39 CARAN-F$_{17}$, cited in Émile Durkheim 2003: 149.
40 Émile Durkheim, letter to Xavier Léon, March 1898; Durkheim 1975: ii/464.
41 At the beginning of the letter he wrote to his colleague in July 1897, Durkheim tells him about the marks his son Paul would be getting in his exams: 'I am thinking of giving him 13 or even 14 [out of 20].' (Letter to Gabriel Tarde, 16 July 1897, Bordeaux; *Durkheim Studies/Études durkheimiennes* (Autumn 1994): 12). Durkheim expected Tarde to be critical of his book: 'I find it quite natural that you should reply to me, and I can only be honoured that you do.' He told him that he had no intention of 'replying. Not directly at least . . . Henceforth, my method will be judged by the way I have applied it . . . when my teaching commitments leave me the leisure I need to publish the findings I have obtained.'
42 There was no English translation of *Suicide* until 1912.
43 Renseignements confidentiels (1897–8); Dossier Durkheim, Archives nationales F$_{17}$25768.

10 *L'Année sociologique:* Birth of a Team

1 The first of Dr O. Thon's three articles on 'The present status of sociology in Germany' appeared in May 1897, and C.W.A. Veditz's 'Sociological instruction in France' was published in July of the same year. It was said of France that 'Paris has long been a center in social sciences'.
2 *Revue de métaphysique et de morale* 4 (September 1896 supplement): 4–6.
3 Célestin Bouglé, letter to Élie Halévy, 13 January 1936; cited in Besnard 1979: 8.
4 Émile Durkheim, letter to Célestin Bouglé, 16 May 1896, Bordeaux; *Revue française de sociologie* 20/1 (January–March 1979): 392.
5 Émile Durkheim, letter to Célestin Bouglé, 16 May 1896, Bordeaux; *Revue française de sociologie* 20/1 (January–March 1979): 392.
6 Paul Lapie, letter to Célestin Bouglé, 20 November 1896, Pau; *Revue française de sociologie* 20/2 (January–March 1976): 36.
7 Born in Paris in 1860, Richard was two years younger than Émile, but their educational and professional careers were similar. Gaston studied at the École normale supérieure (1880–3), where he came under the influence of Fustel de Coulanges. He passed his *agrégation de philosophie* in 1885, and then taught philosophy at lycées in Vendôme (1889–91), Constance (1889–91) and Le Havre (1891–1902). He submitted his thesis on 'The origins of law' in 1892, one year before Durkheim, but Durkheim was appointed to a university post long before his colleague. See Pickering 1979.
8 Undated letter to Marcel Mauss, February 1897; Durkheim 1998: 52.
9 Undated letter to Marcel Mauss, July 1896; Durkheim 1998: 49.
10 Letter to Célestin Bouglé, December 1896, Bordeaux; Durkheim 1975: ii/393.
11 Undated letter to Marcel Mauss, February 1897; Durkheim 1998. François Simiand was born in 1873 in Gières (Isère). His father was a primary schoolteacher. He was educated at the lycée in Grenoble (1883–90) and the *classe préparatoire* at the Lycée Henri-IV in Paris, where he was taught by Henri Bergson. Admitted to the École normale supérieure in 1892, he took a *licence ès lettres* in 1892, and the *agrégation de philosophie* in 1896. He also studied under Bergson. From 1896 to 1899, he was a boarder at the Fondation Thiers and worked as a librarian at the ministry for trade from 1901 onwards. In 1896, he published an article entitle 'Sur quelques relations de la pensée théorique avec les intérêts particuliers' in the *Revue de métaphysique et de morale*. In his capacity as the editor of the 'Année sociologique' column, he also published reviews, including one on Durkheim's *Suicide* and one on *L'Année sociologique*. He also contributed 'lecture notes' on taxation and its foundations, exchange and money to the *Manuel général de l'instruction primaire*. See the bibliography in Gillard and Rosier 1996: 277–305.
12 Paul Lapie, letter to Célestin Bouglé, 14 March 1897, Pau; *Revue française de sociologie* 20/1 (January–March 1976): 37.

13 Paul Lapie, letter to Célestin Bouglé, 7 May 1897, Bordeaux; *Revue française de sociologie* 20/1 (January–March 1979): 39.
14 Paul Lapie, letter to Célestin Bouglé, 24 March 1897, Pau; *Revue française de sociologie* 20/1 (January–March 1979): 39.
15 Letter to Célestin Bouglé, 6 July 1897, Bordeaux; Durkheim 1975: ii/401.
16 Letter to Célestin Bouglé, 25 September 1897, Bordeaux; Durkheim 1975: ii/413.
17 Undated letter to Célestin Bouglé, December 1986; Durkheim 1975: ii/394
18 Letter to Marcel Mauss, June 1897; Durkheim 1998: 72.
19 Letter to Marcel Mauss, Monday morning, June 1897; Durkheim 1998: 67.
20 Letter to Célestin Bouglé, 6 July 1897, Bordeaux; Durkheim 1975: ii/402.
21 Letter to Célestin Bouglé 20 June 1897; Durkheim 1975: ii/398.
22 Letter to Marcel Mauss, June 1897; Durkheim 1998: 89.
23 Letter to Célestin Bouglé, 20 June 1897, Bordeaux; Durkheim 1975: ii/398.
24 Letter to Marcel Mauss, June 1897; Durkheim 1998: 65.
25 Letter to Émile Durkheim, June 1897; Durkheim 1998: 70. Durkheim gave Célestin Bouglé the same advice. 'Basically, it is the residue of either things or ideas – and its extent may vary – that should determine the length of the analysis . . . We must, don't you think, abandon the current critical practice of concentrating on the author at the expense of the book and of rating talents rather than noting the findings and their importance. When it comes to science, shouldn't rating authors be less important than rating the things (opinions or documents) we owe them?' (Letter to Célestin Bouglé, 20 June 1987, Bordeaux; Durkheim 1975: ii/398.)
26 Letter to Célestin Bouglé, 25 July 1897, Bordeaux; Durkheim 1975: ii/403.
27 Letter to Marcel Mauss, Saturday, 10 April 1897, Bordeaux; Durkheim 1998: 52.
28 Letter to Célestin Bouglé, 20 June 1897, Bordeaux; Durkheim 1998: ii/406.
29 Letter to Marcel Mauss, 15 July 1897; Durkheim 1998: 78.
30 Letter to Marcel Mauss, December 1897; Durkheim 1998: 91.
31 Letter to Marcel Mauss, June 1987; Durkheim 1988: 72.
32 Letter to Marcel Mauss, Sunday, n.d., 1897; Durkheim 1998.
33 Letter to Marcel Mauss, 3 July 1897; Durkheim 1998: 75–6.
34 Letter to Marcel Mauss, 15 July 1897; Durkheim 1998: 79.
35 Letter to Louis Liard, 14 July 1897, Bordeaux; *Durkheimian Studies/Études durkheimiennes* 2 (June 1978): 2.
36 Letter to Marcel Mauss, 1897; Durkheim 1998: 84.
37 Letter to Marcel Mauss, July 1897; Durkheim 1998: 81.
38 Letter to Marcel Mauss, July 1987; Durkheim 1998: 81.
39 Letter to Marcel Mauss, July 15 1897; Durkheim 1998: 81.
40 Paul Lapie, letter to Célestin Bouglé, 9 July 1897; *Revue française de sociologie* 20/1 (January–March 1979): 40.
41 Letter to Célestin Bouglé, 23 August 1897, Adelboden, Switzerland; Durkheim 1975: ii/406.
42 Letter to Célestin Bouglé, 16 October 1897, Bordeaux; *Revue française de sociologie* 17/2 (April–June 1976): 168.
43 Letter to Célestin Bouglé, 3 April 1897, Bordeaux; *Revue française de sociologie* 17/2 (April–June 1976): 169.
44 In January 1897, Albert Milhaud published an article entitled 'The class struggle in medieval Flanders: artisans vs merchants' in the *Revue internationale de sociologie.*
45 Letter to Marcel Mauss, 10 November 1897, Bordeaux; Durkheim 1998: 86.
46 Letter to Marcel Mauss, 22 December 1897, Bordeaux; Durkheim 1998: 97.
47 Letter to Marcel Mauss, early January 1898; Durkheim 1998: 100.
48 Letter to Henri Hubert, 10 December 1897, Bordeaux; *Revue française de sociologie* vol. 28/3 (1987).
49 Martonne spent the years 1896–7 in Germany. On his return to France, he worked as a tutor at the École normale supérieure, and then as a *chargé de cours* (meteorology) at the Paris faculty of sciences' laboratory for physical geography. In 1899, he was appointed *chargé de cours de géographie* at the faculty of letters in Rennes. He defended his thesis on Walachia in 1902. In December 1900, he married Joséphine, the daughter of Vidal de

la Bache, professor of geography at the Paris faculty of letters. The author of a popular *Traité de géographie physique* (1908), from 1909 onwards Martonne pursued his career in the same faculty.

50 Undated letter to Henri Hubert, March 1897; *Revue française de sociologie* 28/3 (1987): 494.

51 Letter to Marcel Mauss, April 1898; Durkheim 1998: 131.

52 Undated letter to Henri Hubert, March 1987; *Revue française de sociologie*, 28/3 (1987): 495.

53 Henri Hubert, letter to Marcel Mauss, Paris; Fonds Hubert-Mauss; IMEC-Caen.

54 Letter to Marcel Mauss, 14 January 1898, Bordeaux; Durkheim 1998: 105.

55 See Durkheim 1969[1898]. This was a review of the critical study of Steinmetz's book on 'religion and the origin of penal law' published by Mauss in the *Revue de l'histoire des religions* in 1897.

56 Adopting an evolutionist perspective, Richard also outlines a history of suicide based on the following sequence: first, primitive suicide, which is altruistic, then religious suicide (suicide as a way of prolonging religious ecstasy) and suicide amongst soldiers, and finally modern suicide, which allows the unstable and neurasthenics to 'resolve the difficulties of life'.

57 Bouglé edited the 'General sociology' section, and he outlines a vast domain that included biological sociology, with the proviso that social science must 'get away from biological analogies and look directly at the phenomena that are within its own remit'.

58 Salomon Reinach tended to admire Durkheim, praised the quality of his writing, and described him as a 'profound thinker'. On the whole, he agreed with his analysis, which related the horror of incest to the principle of exogamy, and recognized exogamy to be the product of a prohibition. 'Durkheim is perfectly right', wrote Reinach, but he also criticized his colleague for justifying the horror of blood on moral grounds, or even what he called 'contemporary moral grounds'. He also challenged the view that the kinship/sexual relations dichotomy related to the duty/pleasure (love) dichotomy. 'The reasons invoked by Durkheim are very weak', he wrote. He concluded that, despite the 'admirable logic' of his article, Durkheim had not succeeded in explaining the phenomenon of exogamy, and suggested that he should pursue his research by 'looking at things more closely'. *L'Année*'s contacts with Reinach (1858–1932) were made through Henri Hubert, who was closely involved with the Musée Saint-Germain. Reinach was also close to Sylvain Lévi, whom he met at the Alliance israélite universele in 1887. In 1898, he became the Alliance's vice-president. Together with his brother Joseph, he then became involved in the Dreyfus affair.

59 *Folk-Lore*, 9/111 (September 1898): 251–4.

60 Albion W. Small, review of *L'Année sociologique*, *American Journal of Sociology* 4 (1898): 700. Small was just as harsh when the second volume appeared: the bibliography seemed to him to be 'far from complete'; in his view, two-thirds of the books reviewed should just have been listed. 'Critical attention' could rather have been focused on the rest; *American Journal of Sociology* 5 (1900): 124. Five years later, he repeated the same criticisms: 'We must repeat our former judgements, however, that the reviews leave much to be desired'; *American Journal of Sociology* 8 (1903): 277–8. Lester Ward, who contributed to the *Journal*, was a member of the Institut international de sociologie and regularly attended its conferences.

61 Letter to Henri Hubert, 10 May 1898; *Revue française de sociologie* (1987): 496.

62 Letter to Célestin Bouglé, 30 May 1899; Durkheim 1975: ii/433.

63 Letter to Célestin Bouglé, 22 March 1898, Bordeaux; Durkheim 1973: ii/424.

64 Henri Hubert, undated letter to Marcel Mauss (1898); Fond Hubert-Mauss, IMEC-Caen.

65 Letter to Henri Hubert, March 1898; *Revue française de sociologie* (1987): 490.

11 The Dreyfus Affair and the Defence of Human Rights

1 Letter to Marcel Mauss, Sunday (February 1898); Durkheim 1998: 110.

2 *Le Nouvelliste*, 29 May 1895; see Larre 1998.

3 Consistoire israélite de Bordeaux, Minutes, 6 June 1899; Archives de la ville de Bordeaux, 20C4.

4 Rosine Mauss, letter to Marcel Mauss, 20 February 1898, Épinal.

5 Rosine Mauss, letter to Marcel Mauss, 23 January 1898, Épinal.

6 Élie Halévy, letter to Célestin Bouglé, Tuesday,16 November 1897; Halévy 1996: 202. 'I bear a Jewish name and I am a Protestant. Am I the victim of a caste illusion?' he wondered.

7 Élie Halévy, letter to Célestin Bouglé, 18 November 1897; Halévy 1996: 205.

8 Undated letter to Henri Hubert; Fonds Hubert-Mauss, IMEC-Caen.

9 Letter to Marcel Mauss, Sunday, February 1898; Durkheim 1998: 110.

10 Letter to Paul Lapie, 22 September 1898; *Revue française de sociologie* 20/1 (1979): 120.

11 Maurice Halbwachs, *Carnet de notes* (1), 15 February 1897; IMEC-Caen.

12 Élie Halévy, letter to Célestin Bouglé; Halévy 1996: 210.

13 Paul Lapie, letter to Élie Halévy, 22 November 1897; Halévy 1996: 211.

14 Octave Hamelin, letter to Marcel Mauss, 7 September 1898; Fonds Hubert-Mauss, IMEC-Caen.

15 Élie Halévy, letter to Célestin Bouglé, Tuesday evening, 15 February 1898; Halévy 1996: 215.

16 Sylvain Lévi, letter to Marcel Mauss, 3 April 1899; Fonds Hubert-Mauss, IMEC-Caen.

17 Élie Halévy, letter to Célestin Bouglé, 7 February 1899; Halévy 1996: 261.

18 Letter to Henri Hubert, 22 February 1898; *Revue française de sociologie* 28/3 (1987): 488.

19 Letter to Célestin Bouglé, 18 March 1898, Bordeaux; Durkheim 1975: ii/417.

20 Élie Halévy, letter to Célestin Bouglé, 10 March 1898, Paris; Halévy 1996: 235.

21 Undated letter to Henri Hubert (late February 1898); *Revue française de sociologie* (1987): 489.

22 Undated letter to Marcel Mauss, February 1898; Durkheim 1998: 113.

23 Letter to Célestin Bouglé, 18 March 1898, Bordeaux; Durkheim 1975: ii/417.

24 Letter to Célestin Bouglé, Bordeaux, 22 March 1898; Durkheim 1975: ii/423.

25 Letter to Marcel Mauss, Sunday, February 1898; Durkheim 1998: 109.

26 Letter to Marcel Mauss, Sunday, February 1898; Durkheim 1998: 109.

27 Octave Hamelin, Émile Durkheim and George Rodier, letter to 'Monsieur le Directeur', 3 February 1898, Bordeaux; *Durkheim Studies/Études durkheimiennes* 8 (2002): 4.

28 Letter to Marcel Mauss, 19 March 1898; Durkheim 1998: 117.

29 Marcel Mauss, letter to Henri Hubert, 1898, Leyden; Fonds Hubert-Mauss, IMEC-Caen.

30 Letter to Marcel Mauss, 19 March 1898; Durkheim 1998: 117. Paul Foucart (1836–1926) was a *normalien* and *agrégé de lettres* who held the chair of epigraphy and antiquities at the Collège de France. His son Georges, who was born in 1965, had just obtained his *doctorat ès lettres* in 1897. He was to become head of oriental antiquities at the Bordeaux faculty of letters.

31 Letter to Célestin Bouglé, 3 April 1898, Paris; *Revue française de sociologie* (1976): 169.

32 Letter to Henri Hubert, 5 June 1898; *Revue française de sociologie* (1987): 497.

33 Letter to 'Monsieur le Directeur', Bordeaux, 26 July 1898, *Durkheim Studies/Études durkheimiennes* 8/n.s. (2002): 5. Both *Le Temps* and *Le Nouvelliste* published the letter.

34 Letter to the director, *Le Temps*, 28 July 1898.

35 Letter to Marcel Mauss, July 1898; Durkheim 1998: 164.

36 Note signed by M. Bizot, 29 May 1899; Dossier Durkheim, Archives départementales de la Gironde, TV 111–143.

37 Letter to Camille Jullian, 24 October 1898, Bordeaux; *Durkheim Studies/Études durkheimiennes* 7 (1982): 2. Durkheim's emphasis.

38 Letter to Marcel Mauss, 4 August 1898, Villars-sur-Ollon; Durkheim 1998: 169–70.

39 The journal was edited by the academic Arsène Darmesteter and the literary critic Louis Ganderax. When Darmesteter died, Ernest Lavisse, professor of modern history at the Sorbonne, took over as co-editor. The journal enjoyed the financial support of Calmann-Lévy, at the time the most important publisher in France. The writers it published included Maurice Barrès, Paul Bourget, Anatole France, Alphonse Daudet, and

some of the Russian novelists (Tolstoy, Chekov). Its pages were also open to young academics such as Georges Séailles, Célestin Bouglé and Charles Andler.

40 Letter to Marcel Mauss, 19 March 1898, Bordeaux; Durkheim 1998: 115.

41 Olivier Dumoulin, 'Ernest Lavisse', in Julliard and Winock 1996: 682–3.

42 Letter to Célestin Bouglé, 22 March 1898, Bordeaux; Durkheim 1975: ii/423. 'Do you see any other alternative?' he went on. 'Oh, if only *Le Temps* would take it! But there is no possibility of that.' He had also thought of *Le Siècle*, but concluded that doing so would be a waste of time because 'those who read it are already convinced, and the rest don't read it'.

43 When his 'little collection' of lectures was published, Bouglé sent a copy to Brunetière, whom he had met in the library at the École normale supérieure: 'If you read it, you will see that I disagree as strongly as could be with some of your ideas or methods. You will also see that there is a different side to it and that I am, within my little circle, continuing the struggles that you once waged.' The points over which they were in agreement were the critique of anti-Semitism and socio-anthropology, Bouglé even suggested to Brunetière that he should write an article on 'the general vanity of the ambitions of socio-anthropology' for the *Revue des Deux Mondes*. (Célestin Bouglé, undated letter to Ferdinand Brunetière, 1902, Montpellier; Papiers Brunetière, in Terry N. Clark, Papers, Department of Special Collections, University of Chicago)

44 Marcel Mauss, undated letter to Henri Hubert (1898).

45 Letter to Marcel Mauss, 11 August 1898, Vilars-sur-Ollon: Durkheim 1998: 171.

46 Letter to Marcel Mauss, July 1898: Durkheim 1998: 155.

47 Letter to Célestin Bouglé, 28 November 1898, Bordeaux; Durkheim; 1975: ii/425.

48 Letter to Célestin Bouglé, 28 November 1898, Bordeaux; Durkheim 1975: ii/425–6.

49 Émile Zola, letter to Eugène Fasquelle, 20 October 1898; cited in Mitterrand 2002: 547.

50 Marcel Mauss, undated letter to Henri Hubert, 2000; Fonds Hubert-Mauss, IMEC-Caen.

51 Maurice Halbwachs, *Carnets*, HBW2.B1-01.4, IMEC-Caen.

52 Letter to Marcel Mauss, February 1898; Durkheim 1998: 112–13.

53 Letter to Marcel Mauss, February 1898; Durkheim 1998: 113.

54 Letter to Célestin Bouglé, 13 March 1899, Bordeaux; Durkheim 1975: ii/438.

55 Undated letter to Marcel Mauss, December; Durkheim 1998: 182.

56 Dossier Durkheim, Bordeaux; cited in Lukes 1985[1973]: 359 n2.

57 Letter to Célestin Bouglé, 13 March 1899, Bordeaux; Durkheim 1975: ii/438. Durkheim mentions that F. Rauh was one of the colleagues who signed the petition.

58 Letter to Célestin Bouglé, 17 April 1899, Bordeaux; Durkheim 1975: ii/429.

59 See Dagan's 1901 article, 'Le prolétariat juif mondial'; cf. Bourrélier 2007: 698–9.

60 The scholars who replied included the demographer Émile Levasseur; Charles Letourneau, professor at the École d'anthropologie; Achille Loria, professor at the University of Padua; Georges Renard, professor at the University of Lausanne, Edmond Picard, professor at the new university in Brussels, Albert Réville, professor at the Collège de France, M. de Molinari, editor-in-chief of the *Journal des economistes*; Louis Manouvier, professor at the École d'anthropologie; and Émile Duclaux of the Académie des sciences.

61 Paul Fauconnet, who was a Dreyfusard, developed the scapegoat thesis in his doctoral thesis, which was supervised by Durkheim. 'This is what happens during an epidemic of "treasonitis". A whole crowd, army or people thinks that it has been betrayed. The agitators and the press need someone to blame. There are no traitors, because there has not really been any treason.' They need a scapegoat: 'Society fools itself' (Fauconnet 1928[1920]).

12 A Failure?

1 Letter to Marcel Mauss, February 1898, Bordeaux; Durkheim 1998: 108.

2 Letter to Marcel Mauss, Bordeaux, Sunday, February 1898; Durkheim 1998: 112.

3 Letter to Marcel Mauss, late March 1898; Durkheim 1998: 122

4 Letter to Marcel Mauss, late March 1898; Durkheim 1998: 122.
5 Letter to Marcel Mauss, late March 1898; Durkheim 1998: 121.
6 Letter to Henri Hubert, 30 March 1898, Fonds Hubert-Mauss, IMEC-Caen.
7 Letter to Marcel Mauss, 4 May 1898, Bordeaux; Durkheim 1998: 136.
8 Letter to Marcel Mauss, Sunday, February 1898, Bordeaux; Durkheim 1998: 108.
9 Letter to Henri Hubert, 5 June 1898; *Revue française de sociologie* (1987): 497.
10 Letter to Marcel Mauss, 19 March 1898, Bordeaux; Durkheim 1998: 118.
11 Letter to Henri Hubert, 5 June 1898, *Revue française de sociologie* (1987): 497.
12 Henri Hubert, undated letter to Marcel Mauss, 1898; Fonds Hubert-Mauss, IMEC-Caen.
13 Henri Hubert, undated letter to Marcel Mauss, 1898; Fonds Hubert-Mauss, IMEC-Caen.
14 Letter to Marcel Mauss, Wednesday, early April 1898; Durkheim 1998: 124.
15 Letter to Marcel Mauss, 27 February 1898, Bordeaux; Durkheim 1998: 200.
16 Letter to Marcel Mauss, Wednesday, early April 1898; Durkheim 1998: 124. Durkheim took advantage of a visit to Épinal to have 'a serious talk' with his sister Rosine, who was Marcel's mother. He had little difficulty in convincing her that Marcel should not take a post in a lycée that year: he should devote the next two years to his thesis, and to writing something on the anthropological school. For her part, Rosine said that she was 'prepared to make more sacrifices for two years' to allow her son to 'develop normally' and 'get rid of his thesis'. She had not forgotten that it had taken her brother Émile a long time to complete his thesis (Rosine Mauss, letter to Marcel Mauss, Épinal, 20 June 1898).
17 Letter to Marcel Mauss, 15 June 1898, Bordeaux; Durkheim 1998: 145–6.
18 Letter to Marcel Mauss, July 1988; Durkheim 1998: 151.
19 Letter to Marcel Mauss, July 1898; Durkheim 1998: 151.
20 Letter to Marcel Mauss, July 1898; Durkheim 1998: 165.
21 Marcel Mauss, undated letter to Henri Hubert, June 1898; Fonds Hubert-Mauss, IMEC-Caen.
22 Henri Hubert, undated letter to Émile Durkheim, 1898.
23 Letter to Marcel Mauss, early 1898; Durkheim 1998: 166–7.
24 Letter to Marcel Mauss, 11 August 1898; Durkheim 1998: 171.
25 Letter to Marcel Mauss, August 1898; Durkheim 1998: 173.
26 Letter to Marcel Mauss, August 1898; Durkheim 1998: 174.
27 Undated letter to Henri Hubert, November or December 1898; *Revue française de sociologie* (1987): 499.
28 Letter to Marcel Mauss, 28 November 1898; Durkheim 1998: 179–80. Durkheim also sent his congratulations to Henri Hubert via his nephew.
29 'Robert Javelet on Durkheim' (1975), in *Durkheimian Studies/Études durkheimiennes* 9 (2003): 8.
30 Letter to Célestin Bouglé, 4 December 1898, Bordeaux; *Revue française de sociologie* (1979): 389.
31 Letter to Marcel Mauss, December 1898; Durkheim 1998: 187.
32 Letter to Marcel Mauss, 9 April 1898; Durkheim 1998: 131.
33 Letter to Henri Hubert, 8 February 1899; *Revue française de sociologie* (1987): 500.
34 Letter to Henri Hubert, 8 February 1899; *Revue française de sociologie* (1987): 501.
35 Undated letter to Marcel Mauss, March 1899; Durkheim 1998: 204.
36 Isidore Lévy (1871–1959) was an *agrégé d'histoire* who had studied the history of religions of the École pratique des hautes études, where he met Marcel Mauss. Following a two-year (1897–9) stay with the Institut français d'archéologie orientale in Cairo, he was asked to teach a *cours libre* on the northern Semites in the school's fifth section.
37 Isolating statistics or giving it priority was, on the other hand, out of the question. In Durkheim's view, statistics did not constitute a scientific discipline in its own right but a tool that the social sciences had to use.
38 Letter to Gaston Richard, 11 May 1899; Durkheim 1975: ii/9–10.
39 Richard 1975[1928]. Richard's article includes an extract from Durkheim's letter to him.

40 Undated letter to Marcel Mauss, April–May 1899; Durkheim 1998: 213.
41 Undated letter to Marcel Mauss, April–May 1899; Durkheim 1998: 215.
42 Dominique Parodi, undated letter to Célestin Bouglé, 1897; *Revue française de sociologie* 20/1 (January–March 1979): 43.
43 Letter to Célestin Bouglé, 30 May 1899; 1975: ii/431.
44 Mauss (1969[1899]) had, it is true, been harsh on C.P. Tiele's *Elements of the Science of Religion*. The Dutch scholar was highly respected in France, but Mauss had described his book as 'non-scientific' and based upon theological assumptions. Basically, it was 'an edifying book'. In 1907, the Durkheimians persuaded the budgetary commission of the Chambre des députés not to release the funds that would have allowed a chair in the 'psychology of religious phenomena' to be established at the Collège de France. The chair was intended for Raoul Allier, a Protestant contributor to the *Revue de l'histoire des religions*. The journal (to which both Mauss and Hubert contributed) subsequently changed its line, and gradually came to attach greater importance to the religions of so-called 'non-civilized' peoples.
45 Michel (1857–1904) had been taught by Renouvier, and was one of his disciples. His *L'Idée de l'état* (1890) was a defence of a basic individualist liberalism, but did not entirely rule out state intervention. Michel was a Dreyfusard, and had a dual career as a teacher and a journalist on *Le Temps*. Jewish by birth, he became an agnostic and later turned to Protestantism.
46 *Revue de métaphysique et de morale* 8 (January 1900 supplement).
47 Letter to Célestin Bouglé, 13 March 1899, Bordeaux; Durkheim 1975: ii/427.
48 Letter to Célestin Bouglé, 9 May 1899, Bordeaux; Durkheim 1975: ii/431.
49 Letter to Célestin Bouglé, 17 April 1899, Bordeaux; Durkheim 1975: ii/429.
50 In his *L'Idée de l'état, essai critique sur l'histoire des théories politiques et sociales*, Michel (1896) outlines a position that is at once republican and individualist, and attempts to reconcile the ideals of freedom and equality. Michel does not reject scientific research as such, but is critical of the drift towards the positivist and scientistic view that sees society as a whole that has to be organized. In his view, any ideal is an expression of an ethical desire, and it is pointless to draw whatever conclusions we like from our observations of social reality and historical developments (see Spitz 2005: ch. 11).
51 Letter to Célestin Bouglé, 17 April 1899, Bordeaux; Durkheim 1975: ii/429.
52 There was also a review in the *Revue de métaphysique et de morale*, which was edited by Parodi's friend Halévy: '[Bouglé] has not written the first chapter of a science of society; he has added a chapter to the metaphysics of mind.'
53 Letter to Henri Hubert, 18 June 1900; *Revue française de sociologie* (1987): 508.
54 Undated letter to Marcel Mauss, April–May 1899; Durkheim 1998: 214.
55 Undated letter to Marcel Mauss, April–May 189); Durkheim 1998: 216
56 Letter to Célestin Bouglé, 13 March 1899, Bordeaux; Durkheim 1975: ii/428.
57 Letter to Marcel Mauss, Wednesday, February 1899; Durkheim 1998: 253.
58 Born in Geneva in 1874, but of American nationality, Joe T. Stickney was the son of Austin Stickney, a Harvard graduate (1852) and professor of Latin at Trinity College, and Harrier Champion, a descendant of sometime governor of Connecticut Jonathan Trumble. He studied at Harvard (honors in classics, 1895) before going to Paris to study under Sylvain Lévi at the École pratique des hautes études, where he wrote a dissertation. It was there that he met Marcel Mauss and Henri Hubert. His great passion was his 'love of literature'; he was a poet, but lived long enough only to publish one slim volume, *Dramatic Verses* (Boston 1902). He remained in France until 1903, when he was awarded his *doctorat ès lettres* at the Sorbonne for his thesis, *Les Sentences dans la poésie grecque*. His Latin thesis was entitled *De Hermolia Barbari Vita et Ingenio*. Durkheim was present when he defended it in public. That same year, he left France and his friends Hubert and Mauss – not without some regrets – and went back to the United States, where he took up, without any great enthusiasm, a position as instructor in Greek language and literature in the department of classics at Harvard. Stickney died of a brain tumour in 1904. He was 30 (see Rand 1904).
59 Undated letter to Marcel Mauss, June 1899; Durkheim 1998: 219
60 Undated letter to Marcel Mauss, June 1899; Durkheim 1998: 221.

61 Undated letter to Marcel Mauss, December 1899; Durkheim 1998: 233.
62 Letter to Marcel Mauss, 27 December 1899; Durkheim 1998: 237.
63 Letter to Célestin Bouglé, 13 June 1900, Bordeaux; *Revue française de sociologie* (1976): 173.
64 Undated letter to Marcel Mauss, January 1900; Durkheim 1998: 250.
65 Letter to Célestin Bouglé, 13 June 1900; *Revue française de sociologie* (1976): 173.
66 This section, which was once more edited by Henri Muffang, carried only four reviews; one of them of Muffang's own article, 'Schoolchildren and students of Liverpool' (Muffang 1899). His observations dealt with age, profession of parents, place of birth, height, eye colour, shape of nose, maximum breadth and length of head (cephalic index). Muffang was a great admirer of Lapouge, and wanted to draw the reader's attention to England's relative homogeneity in terms of the anthropological make-up of the population (as measured by the cephalic index), compared with that of other European countries.
67 Letter to Henri Hubert, 2 May 1899; *Revue française de sociologie* (1987): 511.
68 On aesthetic sociology's role in the *Année*, see Fournier 1987.
69 So-called 'fourth branch' societies, namely the United States and European societies, have reached the lower stage. They will reach the 'average' stage of culture only when all men are well fed and well housed, when war is universally condemned, when liberal education is available to all, and when crime and punishment are unusual. As for 'higher culture', it is so far removed from us – by one or two millennia – that it cannot be described.
70 Undated letter to Henri Hubert, November or December 1898; *Revue française de sociologie* (1987): 498.
71 Undated letter to Marcel Mauss; Durkheim 1998: 315. Durkheim published a harsh review of Steinmetz's *Das Verhältnis von Eltern und Kindern bei dem Landvolk in Deutschland* in the same volume of *L'Année* (Durkheim 1900)
72 Letter to Marcel Mauss, 10 July 1899, Bordeaux; Durkheim 1998: 249.
73 Bochard said only a few words about the reviews, and concentrated on three of the articles, which he criticized harshly. Being a follower of Tarde, he believed that invention was the basis of all intellectual life, and that the development of new ideas was the result of individual initiatives.
74 Letter to Marcel Mauss, 10 July 1899; Durkheim 1998: 223.
75 Letter to Marcel Mauss, 7 November 1899; Durkheim 1998: 228.
76 Letter to Xavier Léon, 7 February 1900, Bordeaux; Durkheim 1973: ii/464.
77 The text was published in the *Archives d'anthropologie criminelle* in 1900. It describes the evolution of professional, ecclesiastical and military groups, which become more liberal, and therefore less exclusive, as they develop. Durkheim gave it a short review in the *Année*, and concluded: 'This evolution does not signify, however, that corporate feeling is destined to disappear, because it is inseparable from the association' (Durkheim 1980[1900]: 105).
78 Although he admired Bergson, Parodi criticized him for his 'occasional lack of decisiveness' and demanded 'clarifications', especially about the origins and social nature of laughter.
79 'Nécrologie [obituary]: Georges Sorel (1847–1922)', *Revue de métaphysique et de morale* (October–November 1922 supplement).
80 Assemblée des professeurs, 7 January 1900; Collège de France. Archives du Collège de France, C-XIII. Bergson.
81 Letter to Marcel Mauss, Wednesday, January 1900, Bordeaux; Durkheim 1998: 242.
82 Tarde's inaugural lecture 'Leçon d'ouverture d'un cours sur la philosophie moderne' was published in the *Revue internationale de sociologie* 8/3 (March 1900).
83 'Informations', *Revue internationale de sociologie* 8/3 (March 1900): 238.
84 Richard also criticizes Tarde for several things, and especially the way in which he 'psychiatrizes' the social: he made society look like 'an asylum for madmen and hysterics', and made 'the relationship between the hypnotized and the hypnotizer' the prototype and origin of 'inter-mental' relations.

13 Summed Up in One Word: Solidarity

1 Dreyfus was retried at Rennes after being brought back from imprisonment in Guyana. On 9 September 1900, he was again found guilty, but 10 days later his entire punishment was remitted. The amnesty law did not apply to treason, and the verdict on Dreyfus was finally overturned only in 1906. [Translator's note]

2 Bergson's *Le Rire* was published in 1900. The following year, he delivered a lecture on dreams to the Institut général psychologique. Freud's *Interpretation of Dreams* had just been published. Psychology's main task for the coming century was, according to Bergson, to explore the unconscious and to study, using the appropriate methods, the subterranean world of the mind. It would, he believed, be possible to make discoveries as significant as those made in previous centuries by the physical and natural sciences. Deborah Silverman (1989: 307–10) explores the similarities between Rodin's *art nouveau* and the work of Georg Simmel and Sigmund Freud.

3 Letter to Xavier Léon, 7 February 1900, Bordeaux; Durkheim 1975: ii/464.

4 The German sociologist Georg Simmel was supposed to speak during the session on 'Creative synthesis', which was chaired by Henri Bergson. Simmel was unable to attend in person but asked Élie Halévy to summarize his paper, which provoked a lively discussion. Simmel suggested that his 'formalist' conception should be applied to the problem of religion and that religiosity should be defined as a sort of category of sentiment.

5 The object of the congress was to describe the current state of teaching at all levels in various countries, including France, Germany, Belgium, Switzerland, Austria, England and the United States. It also discussed the issue of popular social education and the possibility of putting it on an international basis. The other papers on France were from Charles Gide (professor in the faculty of law at Montpellier and *chargé de cours* at the Paris law faculty) on the teaching of the social sciences in universities, and Marcel Bernès (Lycée Louis-le-Grand) on the social ethics in secondary schools. Henri Hauser (University of Clermont-Ferrand) chaired a session on popular social education; a few years later, he published a book called *L'Enseignement des sciences sociales*. The American delegation included the sociologists James Mark Baldwin and Lester Ward, while Russia was represented by the sociologists Eugène de Roberty and Maxim Kovalevsky. The congress was chaired by Dick May, Secretary General of the École des hautes études sociales, and concluded that the teaching of the social sciences went hand in hand with democracy. There was a lot of interest in adult education, and calls for a more active pedagogical strategy. See May 1900. The proceedings were published in 1901 as *Congrès de l'enseignement des sciences sociales*.

6 *Premier Congrès national et international des coopératives socialistes tenu à Paris*, 7, 8, 9 and 10 July 1900; Société nouvelle de librairie et d'édition, p. 164. For Mauss's account, see Mauss 1900a.

7 *Congrès international d'éducation sociale, 26–30 septembre 1900*, Paris: Alcan, 1901: ix–xi.

8 Ferdinand Buisson said of radicalism that it was 'a rational and daring application of solidarism'. In his *La Politique radicale* (1908), Buisson traces the 'luminous' history of the Radical Party. He identifies the main elements of its programme as the emancipation of the individual from intellectual servitude and economic slavery, the separation of church and state, fair distribution of the tax burden, far-reaching reforms in the legal and juridical system, and emancipation of education from all religious credos. This political programme did not mean that socialism was the implacable enemy, but it did reject socialist utopianism: some great public services should be socialized, but private property rights must be defended. Léon Bourgeois wrote a preface to the book.

9 See Dominique Parodi's criticisms (1904a, 1905). These were, he notes, 'lofty, generous and seductive ideas', but they were also vague: the idea of a debt to the community was so vague that its extent was impossible to calculate, and the sociological aspect of the problem had not been taken into consideration.

10 Durkheim makes a distinction between science and art; he also contrasts the world of knowledge with the world of action: knowledge demands time, whereas action is always a matter or urgency and brooks no delay; knowledge demands proofs whereas action

relies upon passion and prejudice; knowledge takes all possible precautions, whereas action is influenced by irrational suggestions. Durkheim had never before placed such emphasis on the necessary dissociation between theory and practice. That dissociation is, in his view, a product of civilization: it implies the existence of a 'relatively advanced mentality' (Durkheim 1973[1900]: 5).

11 La Rédaction, 'Déclaration', *Le Mouvement socialiste*, 1 (January 1899): 1.

12 Letter to Marcel Mauss, 5 December 1899?; Durkheim 1998: 229.

13 Undated letter to Marcel Mauss, July 1899; Durkheim 1998: 225.

14 Undated letter to Marcel Mauss, July 1899; Durkheim 1998: 226.

15 Letter from the rector of the University of Bordeaux to minister for education, 16 July 1899.

16 Evaluation of 5 March 1900; Dossier Émile Durkheim, Renseignements personnels, 1899–1900.

17 M. Bizos, note, 5 May 1900; Dossier Émile Durkheim, Renseignements personnels, 1899–1900.

18 M. Bizos, note, 20 April 1901; Dossier Émile Durkheim, Renseignements personnels, 1900–1901.

19 Undated letter to Marcel Mauss, July 1899; Durkheim 1998: 226.

20 François Simiand, letter to Marcel Mauss, 2 January 1899.

21 See also Lazard 1939; Mauss 1997[1935].

22 These rubrics for Section I are from issue 36 (June 1904).

23 The contributors for 1904 included Arnold Van Gennep, a contemporary of Mauss's at the École pratique whose relationship with contributors to the *Année* was always difficult.

24 Simmel's thesis, as summarized by Durkheim, is that money, defined as both an instrument of measurement and a pure symbol, is an abstract expression of abstract relations, and that the abstract nature of money, or its role as a means to any end, appeals to the speculative faculties of the mind at the expense of sensitivity, the heart and the imagination. It therefore 'drains life of colour'.

25 Durkheim may have published other reviews in *Notes critiques* in 1905, but numbers 49 and 50 are missing from the holdings in French libraries and the major public collections. Between 1901 and 1903, Henri Hubert and Marcel Mauss contributed, respectively, 18 and 15 reviews.

26 Bauer was a philosophy teacher who described himself as a moralist and sociologist, and a contributor to both the *Revue philosophique* and the *Revue internationale de sociologie*. His book was published in the 'Bibliothèque sociologique internationale' collection, which René Worms edited for Editions Giard & Brière.

27 Édouard Herriot, n.d. 'Un républicain', in *Célestin Bouglé, 1870–1940* (Dossier Célestin Bouglé, AJ/16/5885, Archives nationales).

28 Letter to Célestin Bouglé, 29 October 1901; Halévy 1996 : 311.

29 Both Basch and Bouglé taught at the Paris faculty of letters (where Basch became a *chargé de cours* in German language and literature in 1906) and were members of the central committee of the Ligue des droits de l'homme. Bouglé joined in 1909, and became its vice-president in 1911.

30 Richard had great admiration for British society, which had 'succeeded in guaranteeing the fullest possible social development while avoiding revolutionary crises'. He establishes a correlation between political doctrines and religions: 'The aversion to altruism is to Protestantism what the school of sociality (and obedience) is to Catholicism. That does not, however, make it the defender of liberalism, which is in its eyes nothing more than a confused mixture of ideology and historical empiricism.'

31 Lapie defends the (Durkheimian) idea that societies have made the transition from the rule of violence to the rule of law, and from the era of force to that of contracts and arbitration. He believed that arbitration (between civil parties) could bring about political peace at both the national and international levels. While he feared that vested interests, prejudices and passions would militate against that solution, he still wondered if this was a dream 'that had to be dreamed'. When he left Bordeaux for Rennes, Paul Lapie published a book entitled *La Justice par l'état* (1899a). It was subtitled 'Étude de morale sociale'.

32 In Richard's view (1900b), the central question was that of justice. Society had to make the transition from penal justice to social justice, or in other words a justice that strove to improve the living conditions of the indigent (those who had no family and no regular employment, those who had been abandoned in childhood, tramps, alcoholics, etc.) and to re-establish social bonds: the dissolution of social bonds led to criminality.

33 Durkheim's answer to the classical economists who regard the corporative system as a 'kind of rather tyrannous militarization' is that this is 'not a matter of coordinating any changes outwardly and mechanically, but of bringing men's minds into mutual understanding . . . [I]t is not on economic grounds that the guild or corporation seems to me to be essential but for moral reasons. It is only through the corporative system that the moral standard of economic life can be raised' (1957[1950]: 29).

34 'Every citizen nowadays is obliged to be attached to a *commune* (parish). Why then should the same principle not apply to the profession or calling? All the more, since in fact the reform we are discussing would in the end result in the professional association taking the place of the jurisidictional area as a political unit of the region.' Durkheim immediately adds that the corporative organization (which would be made up of both employers and employed) would have to be 'attached to the central organ, that is, to the state', which has responsibility for a range of functions, including the settling of industrial conflicts (1957 [1950]: 39).

35 This text is based upon the lecture notes taken by Armand Cuvillier at the Sorbonne in the academic year 1908–9.

14 *L'Année* in Crisis

1 Undated letter to Marcel Mauss, January 1900; Durkheim 1998: 250.
2 Undated letter to Marcel Mauss, February 1900; Durkheim 1998: 254.
3 Letter to Marcel Mauss, Monday, 5 February 1900; Durkheim 1998: 253
4 Undated letter to Marcel Mauss, February 1900; Durkheim 1998: 251.
5 Undated letter to Marcel Mauss, February 1900; Durkheim 1998: 253.
6 Letter to Marcel Mauss, Friday, February 1900, Bordeaux; Durkheim 1998: 255.
7 Paul Lapie, letter to Célestin Bouglé, 18 February 1900; *Revue française de sociologie* 20/1 (1979): 41.
8 Letter to Marcel Mauss, Friday, February 1900, Bordeaux; Durkheim 1998: 255.
9 Letter to Marcel Mauss, Monday, 5 February 1900; Durkheim 1998: 253.
10 Letter to Henri Hubert, 10 March 1900; Durkheim 1998: 506.
11 Letter to Henri Hubert, 10 June 1900; Durkheim 1998: 506.
12 Letter to Henri Hubert, 18 June 1900; Durkheim 1998: 508.
13 Letter to Marcel Mauss, 3 August 1900; Durkheim 1998: 268.
14 Letter to Marcel Mauss, 8 August 1900, villa des Rosiers, Houlgate; Durkheim 1998: 269.
15 Paul Lapie, letter to Célestin Bouglé, 11 July 1900, Rennes; *Revue française de sociologie* 10/1 (January–March 1979): 42.
16 Undated letter to Marcel Mauss, Tuesday, April or May 1900; Durkheim 1998: 262.
17 Undated letter to Marcel Mauss, November or December 1900; Durkheim 1998: 275.
18 Marcel Mauss, undated letter to Henri Hubert; Fonds Hubert-Mauss, IMEC-CAEN.
19 Undated letter to Marcel Mauss, Wednesday, May 1900; Durkheim 1998: 265.
20 Letter to Henri Hubert, July 1900; *Revue française de sociologie* (1987): 511.
21 Letter to Henri Hubert, 10 July 1900; *Revue française de sociologie* (1987): 511.
22 Letter to Henri Hubert, July 1900; *Revue française de sociologie* (1987): 511.
23 Letter to Henri Hubert, June 1900; *Revue française de sociologie* (1987): 509.
24 Undated letter to Henri Hubert, April or May 1901; *Revue française de sociologie* (1987): 517. Cf. Durkheim's letter of 11 May 1899 to Gaston Richard (Durkheim 1975: ii/9–10): 'Society sees its own life and the objects to which it relates as sacred. It colours them with religiosity. Why? It would take a long time to discuss that!' And he concludes: 'There are

certain elementary notions (I am not saying that they are simple in logical terms) that dominate the whole of humanity's moral evolution.'

25 Letter to Marcel Mauss, 24 January 1900; Durkheim 1998: 248.
26 Undated letter to Marcel Mauss, January 1900; Durkheim 1998: 249.
27 Undated letter to Marcel Mauss, January 1900; Durkheim 1998: 250.
28 Letter to Marcel Mauss, Monday 5 February 1900; Durkheim 1998: 251.
29 Undated letter to Marcel Mauss, November or December 1900; Durkheim 1998: 274–5.
30 M. Bizos, 21 April 1902, Bordeaux; 'Renseignements confidentiels, 1901–2. Dossier Durkheim.
31 In 1901, the *Revue Philosophique* published articles by Alfred Espinas (1901), Marcel Bernès (1901), Gabriel Tarde (1901) and Palante (1901).
32 Letter to Célestin Bouglé, 14 May 1900; *Revue française de sociologie* (1976): 170. The first two articles in the series were by M. Loria and A. Asturaro.
33 Undated letter to Marcel Mauss, Friday, April 1900; Durkheim 1998: 257–8.
34 Undated letter to Marcel Mauss, May 1900; Durkheim 1998: 263.
35 Letter to Marcel Mauss, 4 June 1900; Durkheim 1998: 266.
36 Undated letter to Marcel Mauss, November 1900; Durkheim 1998: 174.
37 Richard explicitly rejects economic determinism and accepts that 'far from establishing societies with a view to production, humanity owes its productive power to social culture and social discipline.'
38 Undated letter to Marcel Mauss, November 1900; Durkheim 1998: 274.
39 Marcel Mauss, undated letter to Henri Hubert, 1900; Fond Hubert-Mauss, IMEC-Caen. Cf. Fournier 2007[1994]: 110–12.
40 Letter to Célestin Bouglé, 13 June 1900, Bordeaux; *Revue française de sociologie* (1976): 174.
41 Letter to François Simiand, February 1902; Durkheim 1975: ii/443.
42 Letter to Célestin Bouglé, 14 May 1900, Bordeaux; *Revue française de sociologie* (1976): 171.
43 Review of *L'Année sociologique*, *Revue de métaphysique et de morale* 9 (November 1901 supplement): 8.
44 Letter to Célestin Bouglé, 6 July 1900; *Revue française de sociologie* (1976): 176.
45 The 'Miscellaneous' section now included rubrics on 'Technology' (Hubert) and 'Aesthetics' (Hubert and Parodi).
46 Durkheim draws upon Fritz Roeder's study of the Anglo-Saxon family (*Die Familie bei den Angelsachsen*) to identify the causes that improves the position of women during the Middle Ages and amongst modern peoples: 'The woman owes this respect of which she has become the object to the absolutely special position she has assumed in the life of luxury, of art, of the imagination. Now, this sort of life can only be developed in comfortable surroundings. That, no doubt, is why the enhancement of feminine dignity began in the upper classes of society and spread to the others only later on and very slowly' (1980[1901]: 254).
47 Review of *L'Année philosophique*, *Revue de métaphysique et de morale* 9 (1901).
48 Letter to Célestin Bouglé, 13 August 1901, Plombières, Vosges; *Revue française de sociologie* (1976): 178.
49 Undated letter to Marcel Mauss, February or March 1901; Durkheim 1998: 276.
50 Undated letter to Marcel Mauss, March 1901; Durkheim 1998: 278.
51 Undated letter to Marcel Mauss, February or March 1901; Durkheim 1998: 277.
52 Undated letter to Marcel Mauss, March 1901; Durkheim; 1998: 278.
53 Letter to Henri Hubert, January 1901; *Revue française de sociologie* (1987): 512.
54 Letter to Henri Hubert, 14 January 1901; *Revue française de sociologie* (1987): 513–14.
55 Letter to Henri Hubert, 6 February 1901; *Revue française de sociologie* (1987): 516.
56 Undated letter to Marcel Mauss, February or March 1902; Durkheim 1998: 276.
57 Undated letter to Marcel Mauss, March 1901; Durkheim 1998: 279.
58 Undated letter to Marcel Mauss, April or May 1901; Durkheim 1998: 286, 287.
59 Undated letter to Marcel Mauss, May 1901; Durkheim 1998: 287.
60 Letter to Henri Hubert, 14 November 1901; *Revue française de sociologie* (1987): 520.
61 Undated letter to Marcel Mauss, December 1901; Durkheim 1998: 302.

62 Undated letter to Marcel Mauss, December 1901; Durkheim 1998: 302.
63 Undated letter to Marcel Mauss, January 1902; Durkheim 1998: 308.
64 Undated letter to Marcel Mauss, February 1902; Durkheim 1998: 314.
65 Undated letter to Marcel Mauss, February or March 1902; Durkheim 1998: 320.
66 Undated letter to Marcel Mauss, February 1902; Durkheim 1998: 317.
67 Letter to Henri Hubert, 5 February 1902; *Revue française de sociologie* (1987): 521. Durkheim told Alcan that he was prepared to accept a reduction in his fees and to cover the cost of corrections (over 20% of all costs).
68 Paul-Louis Huvelin (1873–1924) held a doctorate in law (1897) and *agrégation de droit* (1899) and was a *chargé de cours* in the Aix-en-Provence law faculty (as of 1898). He then transferred to the Lyon Law Faculty in 1899, and was appointed professor in 1903. A future contributor to the *Année* (vols. 6–12), he published a brochure entitled *Les Tablettes magiques et le droit romain* in 1901; see Audren 2001.
69 Letter to François Simiand, February 1902; Durkheim 1975: ii/443–4.
70 Letter to François Simiand, 15 February 1902, Bordeaux; Durkheim 1975: ii/443–4.
71 Undated letter to Henri Hubert, December 1902; *Revue française de sociologie* (1987): 522.
72 Letter to François Simiand, 2 January 1902, Bordeaux; Durkheim 1975: ii/445.
73 Letter to Henri Hubert, 10 March 1902; *Revue française de sociologie* (1987): 524.
74 Undated letter to Marcel Mauss, February 1902; Durkheim 1998: 319.
75 Undated letter to Marcel Mauss, 9 or 10 March 1902; Durkheim 1998: 319.
76 Undated letter to Marcel Mauss, December 1901 or January 1901; Durkheim 1998: 306.
77 Marcel Mauss, undated letter to Henri Hubert, Fonds Hubert-Mauss, IMEC-Caen.
78 Undated letter to Marcel Mauss, April 1902; Durkheim 1998: 325.
79 Undated letter to Marcel Mauss, February or March 1901; Durkheim 1998: 277.
80 Undated letter to Henri Hubert, late June 1901; *Revue française de sociologie* (1987): 518.
81 Letter to Octave Hamelin, 29 June 1901, Épinal; Durkheim 1975: ii/452.
82 Rabbi Moïse Schuhl, 'Mélanie Durkheim', June 1901. The handwritten text of this eulogy (4 pages) was communicated to the author by the rabbi's great-granddaughter Éliane Roos Schuhl.
83 Henri Durkheim, cited in Jean-Claude Filloux, 'Présentation. L'Homme', in Durkheim 1970: 301.
84 Letter to Octave Hamelin, 2 July 1901, Épinal; Durkheim 1975: ii/454.
85 Formule de déclaration de mutation après décès, no. 118, 27 December 1901; Archives du département des Vosges, 3Q15/1188
86 Copy of letter to 'Mon cher ami' (April 1901).
87 Letter to Henri Hubert, June 1901; *Revue française de sociologie* 28/1 (1987): 519.
88 Letter to Marcel Mauss, November 1901; Durkheim 1998: 289–90, 293.
89 Albert Réville, letter to Marcel Mauss, 4 November 1901; Fonds Hubert-Mauss, IMEC-Caen.
90 Letter to Marcel Mauss, November 1901; Durkheim 1998: 292.
91 Copy of Durkheim's letter to Brochard, enclosed in letter to Marcel Mauss, November 1901; Durkheim 1998: 295.
92 Letter to Marcel Mauss, March 1901; Durkheim 1998: 280.
93 Letter to Marcel Mauss, November 1901; Durkheim 1998: 297.
94 Letter to Marcel Mauss, December 1901; Durkheim 1998: 298.
95 Letter to Marcel Mauss, January 1902; Durkheim 1998: 310.
96 Born in Moulins in 1866, Antoine Meillet was an *agrégé de grammaire* (1889) and *docteur ès lettres* (1897). Between 1898 and 1904, he carried out research on the comparative syntax of Armenian, travelling to the Caucasus in 1890 and to Armenia in 1901. See Vendryes (1937) and Mauss (1969[1936]).
97 'Let us hope,' he wrote, 'that we can turn political ethology into a science rather than a literary genre (portraits, random individual observation). It should become a science that discovers the faculties of a people's mind beneath its institutions.' This political ethology was part of what he called a 'concrete sociology' (as opposed to an abstract sociology): it would, he hope, help to develop a 'science of social beings' (which is as

essential as a science of social facts), and should have a political 'practical interest' that would make it possible to educate the people (Lapie 1902a).
98 Letter to François Simiand, 29 November 1901, Bordeaux; Durkheim 1975: ii/440.
99 Letter to François Simiand, 18 December 1901, Bordeaux; Durkheim 1975: ii/441.
100 Letter to François Simiand, February 1902; Durkheim 1975: ii/443.
101 Lucien Herr expressed the same view in *Notes critiques* (May 1901) in his description of the *Année*'s goals and achievements.
102 Letter to Xavier Léon, 21 September 1902, Paris; Durkheim 1975: ii/465.
103 Letter to Xavier Léon, 27 September 1902, Épinal; Durkheim 1975: ii/466.
104 Durkheim reprinted his review in vol. VII of *L'Année sociologique*.

15 At the Sorbonne

1 The collection included books by such prestigious figures as William James, Henri Pirenne and Roberto Michels. Le Bon's great project was to invite all the major figures in the university to write a 'philosophical synthesis of the various sciences' for an educated but non-specialist readership. See Marpeau (2000: 178).
2 Ideological differences probably had something to do with this. Le Bon had kept very quiet during the Dreyfus affair (his silence masked a refusal to support Dreyfus). He had made openly anti-Semitic remarks on a number of occasions, describing Semites as a 'middling race' living in state of semi-barbarism, and he vocally denounced the immorality of Jews. He was also openly hostile to socialism.
3 Political economy or social economics was taught at the École nationale des mines (E. Cheysson), the École nationale des ponts et chaussées (Charles Gide), the Institut national agronomique (M. Chevallier) and the Conservatoire national des arts et métiers (E. Lévesque, E. Lévasseur and P. Beauregard).
4 The École d'anthropologie de Paris offered free public lectures on the various topics covered by that discipline: prehistoric anthropology, biological anthropology, zoological anthropology, physical anthropology (L. Manouvrier), ethnology (G. Hervé), ethnography and linguistics (A. Lefèvre) and ethnographic technology (A. de Mortillet). The only lectures dealing specifically with sociology were taught by Charles Letourneau, and were subtitled 'History of civilizations'. A doctor of medicine and the holder of a doctorate, Letourneau (born 1831) had been associated with the École d'anthropologie since 1886. His lectures on the history of civilizations were based upon evolutionist theory. A 'tireless researcher', his many publications represented a real 'sociological encyclopedia' (see Verneau 1902). Letourneau had been a member of the Société d'anthropologie de Paris since 1865; he was elected president and served as its secretary-general until his death. His works include *L'Évolution du mariage et de la famille*, *L'Évolution de la propriété*, *L'Évolution politique*, *L'Évolution juridique*, *L'Évolution religieuse*, *l'Évolution littéraire* and *L'Évolution de l'éducation*.
5 The École libre des sciences politiques was the only one of these institutions to award diplomas. It was divided into sections: economics and finance, economics and social studies, diplomacy, and a general section offering teaching in public law and history. Teachers included Gabriel Tarde, Lucien Lévy-Bruhl, Élie Halévy and Émile Cheysson.
6 Until then, the Collège libre des sciences sociales was simply a study group offering evening classes on human geography (J. Brunhes), demography (Dr J. Bertillon), the history of the French labour movement (Hubert Lagardelle) and 'feminology' (Mme Soulez-Darque).
7 Born in 1852 into an old aristocratic family, Henri de Tourville was described by Paul Bureau as 'the founder of social science, together with and after Frédéric Le Play'. His close associates had great admiration for him; Bureau spoke of his 'magnificent body of work' and described him as a 'scholar of great stature'. When Tourville died in 1903, Edmond Demolins went on with his work, 'which had begun so well'. He wanted to turn *La Science sociale* into a 'sort of social encyclopedia that would always be up to date and in order'.
8 Born in Marseille, Edmond Demolins (1852–1907) was the son of a doctor and historian

(his father trained at the École des chartes). He rapidly became one of the most active members of Le Play's Société d'économie sociale and wrote several monographs. His *À quoi tient la supériorité des Anglo-Saxons?* gave rise to lively discussion. Demolins's close friend Paul des Rousiers (1857–1934) was originally from Confolantais, where he was a rural landowner. He studied law at the Institut catholique de Paris and was active in the Union de la paix sociale, which he founded in about 1880. He was the author of studies of England and the United States: *La Vie américaine* (1892), *La Question ouvrière en Angleterre* (1895), and *Les Industries monopolisées aux Etats-Unis* (1898). His *Les Grands Ports de France* was completed in 1909. See Kalaora and Savoye (1989).

9 Born in 1859 in Algeria, where her father Michel Aaron Weill (born in Moselle and trained at the rabbinical school in Metz) was chief rabbi in the Consistoire d'Algérie. Jeanne Weill initially embarked upon a literary career, published novels and contributed to the *Revue blanche*. Her younger brother Georges became a brilliant historian of socialism.

10 Sociéte de sociologie de Paris, minutes of the meeting of 12 February 1908; *Revue internationale de sociologie* 16 (1908): 197–8.

11 Letter to Marcel Mauss, April 1902; Durkheim 1998: 326.

12 Letter to Célestin Bouglé, 1902; Durkheim 1975: ii/434.

13 Undated letter to Marcel Mauss, 1902; Durkheim 1998: 327.

14 Undated draft of a letter from Marcel Mauss to Émile Durkheim, 1902; Fonds Hubert-Mauss, IMEC-Caen. In 1901, Mauss and Dr V. Kasimir jointly undertook to guarantee the Boulangerie's loan of 40,000 francs from the Grands Moulins de Corbeil. The loan produced no income. In June 1902, Kasimir and Mauss agreed 'not to require the Coopérative socialiste to repay the loan except in the form of debentures issued by the said Cooperative'.

15 Undated letter to Marcel Mauss, 1902; Durkheim 1998: 330.

16 Undated letter to Marcel Mauss, 1902; Durkheim 1998: 335.

17 Henri Delacroix, undated letter to Marcel Mauss, 1902; Fonds Hubert-Mauss, IMEC-Caen.

18 Letter to Marcel Mauss, 8 June 1902; Durkheim 1998: 337.

19 Letter to Célestin Bouglé, 8 June 1902, Bordeaux; Durkheim 1975: ii/436.

20 Letter to Marcel Mauss, June 1902; Durkheim 1998: 340.

21 Letter to Marcel Mauss, April or May 1899; Durkheim 1998: 215.

22 Letter to Célestin Bouglé, 21 July 1900; *Revue française de socology* (1976): 177–8.

23 Letter to Célestin Bouglé, 19 June 1902; Durkheim 1975: ii/437.

24 Letter to Camille Jullian, 28 June 1902; *Durkheimian Studies/Études durkheimiennes* 7 (June 1982): 2–3.

25 Letter to Marcel Mauss, June 19020; Durkheim 1998: 343. Alphonse Aulard (1849–1928) was an *agrégé de letters* (1871) and a *docteur ès lettres* (1887), and had taught history at the Sorbonne since 1886. He was the author of *Histoire politique de la Révolution française*. A Dreyfusard and a republican, he was a supporter of secularism.

26 Letter from Alfred Croiset to Monsieur le Recteur (Gréard), 26 June 1902; Archives nationales, Dossier Durkheim, AJ16 214. Alfred Croiset had been dean of the faculty of letters since 1898, and remained in post until 1919. Octave Gréard (1828–1904), an *agrégé de lettres* and *docteur ès lettres*, was approaching the end of his term of office, having served as deputy rector of the Académie de Paris for 20 years. He had been the 'eminence grise' behind every minister, and had played an active role in the reform of secondary education in 1899 and 1902. See Condette (2006: 204–6)

27 Rosine Mauss, letter to Marcel Mauss, Épinal, 29 June 1902.

28 Letter to Marcel Mauss, June 1902; Durkheim 1998: 343.

29 Letter to François Simiand, 28 June 1902, Bordeaux; Durkheim 1975: ii/450.

30 Letter to Camille Jullian, 28 June 1902; Durkheim 1975: ii/3

31 Letter to Octave Hamelin, 30 July 1902; 1975: ii/455. At the beginning of August 1903, Durkheim asked Hamelin what he intended to do, but did not want to give the impression that he was pressurizing him: 'I fear that my reasons for wanting you to be in Paris are too personal, and that I am taking too little account of your interests and happiness' (letter to Octave Hamelin, 2 August 1903, Gérardmer; Durkheim 1975: ii/457–8). In

Durkheim's view, Hamelin had almost a 'duty' to come to Paris. 'I am convinced that, once you have got over this difficult period, you will like this change of existence' (letter to Octave Hamelin; Durkheim 1975: ii/458).

32 Letter to Marcel Mauss, July 1902; Durkheim 1998: 345.

33 Letter to François Simiand, 28 June 1902, Bordeaux; Durkheim 1975: ii/450.

34 Letter to Octave Hamelin, 21 October 1902, Paris; Durkheim 1975: ii/456.

35 Charle's study of the staff appointed between 1879 and 1908 also shows that many of them (70%) were from middle-class provincial backgrounds. Two were the sons of pastors, but Émile was the only one whose father was a rabbi. Protestants and Jews were in the minority: during the period 1809 and 1908, they made up, respectively, 13% and 4.5% of the teaching staff of the faculty of letters. This variable must, however, be approached with some caution, as spiritual-religious beliefs were becoming complex, especially at the turn of the century: many teachers were beginning to distance themselves from religion and to describe themselves as non-practising, free-thinkers, rationalists or anti-clerical.

36 Durkheim's portrait of his friend and colleague (which might almost be a self-portrait) describes him as 'both an apostle and a thoughtful man', 'a mixture of concentration and enthusiasm who led an intense life', 'a man of passion who was only passionate about great and noble causes'. 'He was a tender, sensitive man with a loving heart.' 'Life was sometimes harsh for someone with such delicate sensibilities that the slightest contact could upset him badly.' Morality and psychology were his special areas of study.

37 See René Worms, letter to *L'Univers israélite* 58/26 (February 1903).

38 The 30 or so Dreyfusards also included Ferdinand Buisson, Ernest Denis, Alfred Espinas, Charles Langlois, Gustave Lanson, Gabriel Monod and Charles Seignobos. At least 10 of the staff were anti-Dreyfusards, including Léon Crouslé, Charles Dejob, Edmond Dubois, Émile Faguet, Jules Girard, Alfred Mézières, Louis Petit de Julleville and Aimé Puech.

39 See, for instance, Durkheim 1901.

40 Letter to Célestin Bouglé, 13 August 1901, villa des Marronniers, Plombières (Vosges); *Revue française de sociologie* (1976): 178.

41 Durkheim cites Puvis de Chavannes' comments on his work in his history of the University of Paris 1975[1918]: 20 n1): 'The Sorbonne sits on a block of marble in a clearing in a sacred wood; at her sides, there are two genii carrying palms; a spring gushes from the ground at her feet. To her right, Eloquence stands, while Poetry is represented by the Muses, who sprawl in various attitudes on the grass. History and Archaeology excavate the entrails of the past; Philosophy discusses the mystery of life and death. The Sciences stand to her left. Geology, Physiology, Botany and Chemistry are symbolized by their attributes. Physics parts her veils before a swarm of students, who present her with an electrical flame in the shade of a bower as a token of their work to come. Geometry meditates upon a problem.'

42 Conseil de l'Université de Paris: minutes of the meeting of 10 November 1902; Archives nationales AJ/16/2587.

43 A postgraduate diploma [*diplôme d'études supérieures*] was introduced in 1907–8.

44 In 1901–2, Alfred Espinas taught a course entitled 'Studies of the major psychosociological problems', and in 1902–3, Victor Egger taught a course on general psychology. The Sorbonne had a 'physiological psychology laboratory' run by Alfred Binet, the founder of *L'Année psychologique* and an unsuccessful candidate for a chair at the Collège de France (he was defeated by Georges Dumas). Dumas (1866–1946) was an *agrégé de philosophie*, a doctor of medicine and was awarded a *doctorat ès lettres* for his thesis 'Sadness and joy'. Binet said of him that he was the 'only man in France to have done any experimental psychology' but 'was self-taught and acknowledged no master'. He did not, to general regret, have a doctorate. Minutes of the Conseil de l'Université de Paris, 5 May 1902; Archives nationales, AJ$_{16}$ 2587.

45 Review of *L'Année sociologique* (1903), *Revue de métaphysique et de morale* 11 (November 1903 supplement): 10.

46 Evaluation du Recteur, 23 April 1903. Renseignements confidentiels. Dossier Richard, 1902–3; Académie de Bordeaux, Archives départementales de la Gironde, TVIII–230.

47 Letter to Octave Hamelin, 22 August 1903; Durkheim 1975: ii/458.

48 Georges Radet, Report presented to the Conseil de l'Université; University of Bordeaux: 141.

49 The lecture was originally published as 'Pédagogie et sociologie', *Revue de métaphysique et de morale* 1 (1903): 37–54.

50 Marcel Mauss, undated letter to Rosine Mauss, 1902; Archives familiales de Pierre Mauss.

51 'Notes and Abstracts. Pedagogy and Sociology', *American Journal of Sociology* 8 (1903): 712–13.

52 Review of *L'Année sociologique* (1903), *Revue de métaphysique et de morale* 11 (November 1903 supplement): 10.

53 Letter to Octave Hamelin, 21 October 1902; Durkheim 1975: ii/456. According to information supplied by Marcel Mauss, Durkheim also taught a course entitled 'Physiology of law and morals' (the first part dealt with 'Social Morality').

54 Letter to Octave Hamelin, 21 October 1902; Durkheim 1975: ii/456.

55 Marcel Mauss, undated letter to Henri Hubert, 1902; Fonds Hubert-Mauss, IMEC-Caen.

56 Marcel Mauss, letter to Henri Hubert, 2 December 1902; Fonds Hubert-Mauss, IMEC-Caen.

57 Sources: *Le Livret de l'étudiant de Paris*, Université de Paris, 1902–17; 'Université de Paris', in *Rapport présenté au ministre de l'instruction publique sur la situation de l'enseignement supérieur, 1902–1915*. This list of lectures differs slightly from the list drawn up by Steven Lukes (1985[1973]: Appendix A) on the basis of the supplements to the *Revue de métaphysique et de morale* and information supplied by Marcel Mauss. This is because Durkheim repeated his lectures on 'The physiology of law and manners' when he began teaching in Paris, and that they became, as Mauss puts it, 'lectures on morality and even practical morality or, rather, moral organization'. Mauss concludes that 'All Durkheim's work on morality, and especially that done in Paris, is of a piece'. According to information supplied by Mauss, Durkheim also lectured on the following topics at the Sorbonne: 1902–3: Physiology of law and morals. Part I: Social morality. Domestic organization; 1903–4: Physiology of law and morals. Part II: Morality of special groups in society, the family, professional groups, etc.; 1904–5: Morality (including civic and professional morality); 1905–6: The family; 1907–8: Physiology of law and morals. Part I: Morality in society. 1910–11: The family; 1915–16: Civic and professional morality. The lecture 'Theoretical morality' to which Mauss refers was probably that on 'Morality' described in the *Livret de l'étudiant de Paris* for the academic year 1914–15.

58 *Livret de l'étudiant à Paris, 1912–1913*. Melun: Université de Paris, 1912.

59 According to the *Livret de l'étudiant de Paris* for 1915–16, Durkheim's lectures were on Saint-Simon, and not Auguste Comte, as Lukes has it. According to the *Livret*, Durkheim was scheduled to give a series of lectures entitled 'An introduction to morality' and 'Intellectual education' and to take tutorials for degree candidates in 1916–17.

60 Gabriel Séailles, 'Émile Durckheim' (*sic*), *La Dépêche de Toulouse*, 15 November 1917.

61 Reports on subscription requests were read 'in committee' and then discussed by members. Their observations and comments provided the basis for the *rapporteur*'s decision to grant or reject the request for a subscription. The reports were then sent to the ministry.

62 Durkheim reviewed Lévy-Bruhl's book in *L'Année sociologique* 7 (1904).

16 Le Grand Manitou and the Totem-Taboo Clan

1 Tarde's book was also reviewed by Gaston Richard (Richard 1902a). The review was at the same time laudatory and critical: Richard criticized Tarde for his 'psychiatrization' of social issues, and claimed that he made society look like 'an insane asylum or a hospital for hysterics.'

2 See Worms (1903b). Ferdinand Tönnies, a member of the Institut, was not present but contributed a paper to be read on his behalf. That year, he also published a long essay

on Germany in the 'Mouvement social' section of the *Revue internationale de sociologie*. It was a detailed account of the last 10 years of the nineteenth century (1890–1900).

3　'Gabriel Tarde (1841–1904)', *Revue philosophique* 29/57 (January–June 1904): 685.

4　'Nécrologie. Gabriel Tarde', *Revue internationale de sociologie* (1904).

5　Letter to Marcel Mauss, April 1902; Durkheim 1998: 325.

6　Durkheim and Fauconnet criticize Ward and Tarde by pointing to 'the untenable position of this conception of the social science' (Durkheim 1983[1903]: 184); they take as their object the simplest of social relations and prioritize certain social phenomena rather than others on purely a priori grounds.

7　The texts were published in Galton et al. 1905. 'Notes and Abstracts' on 'The relation of sociology to social sciences and to philosophy' also appeared in the *American Journal of Sociology* 10 (1905): 134–7, 257–71. For an account of the meeting, see Becquemont 1995.

8　Charles Seignobos (1850–1942), an *agrégé d'histoire*, was a few years younger than Durkheim and had been teaching at the Sorbonne since the early 1880s, lecturing on the role of pedagogy in the historical sciences and modern history. The author of a major *Histoire politique de l'Europe contemporaine* (190897), he had recently become editor of *L'Européen*. Charles-Victor Langlois (1863–1929) was an *agrégé d'histoire* and a *docteur ès lettres*. He too taught at the Paris faculty of letters, where he lectured on the history of the Middle Ages. He was also director of the Musée pédagogique.

9　Charles Péguy, 'Pour moi', cited in Azouvi 2007: 125. In 1904, Péguy gave a series of three lectures at the École des hautes études sociales; their general title was 'De l'anarchisme politique. Essai d'une méthode pour commencer à travailler dans les sciences sociales'. The method he defended was the antithesis of that used by Durkheim and his colleagues.

10　Simiand did criticize Mantoux for clinging to some of the habits of the 'pure historian' (anecdotes, the importance given to individual actions, chronology, a failure to distinguish between the search for origins and the search for causes), but he also detected in his work methods revealing a 'new spirit . . . of a sociological nature'.

11　Célestin Bouglé, undated letter to Daniel Halévy, cited in Besnard 1979: 24.

12　Personal communication from Mme Kennedy (Durkheim's great-niece); see Lukes 1985[1973]: 372 n32.

13　Élie Halévy, letter to Célestin Bouglé, 11 July 1903; Halévy 1996: 341.

14　Born in Cambrai in 1869, Charles Fossey was another graduate of the École pratique des hautes études, where he studied Greek epigraphy and Byzantine philology. He later became a member of the École française d'Athènes (1894–7), and then of the Institut français d'archéologie orientale in Cairo (1897–9).

15　A lawyer at the Paris bar, Paul Huvelin also studied the history of canon law at the École pratique des hautes études (fifth section) in 1897–8, and wrote a dissertation on 'Magic and individual rights'. A *chargé de conférence* at the Paris faculty of law in 1897, he was appointed *chargé de cours* in Aix the following year. He taught a course on the history of French law and public law.

16　Durkheim reviewed two books dealing with the status of women in different historical and geographical contexts: William Rullkoeter's *The Legal Protection of Women among the Ancient Germans* (Durkheim 1980[1903e]), and Maurice Courant's *En Chine. Moeurs et institutions* (Durkheim 1975[1903b]). It was the question of the separation of the sexes and of sexual taboos that interested him: 'It is not impossible that, because it surrounds women with mystery the complete separation of the sexes stimulates the sexual sense and goes some way to explaining China's refined sensuality.'

17　Durkheim adds (1980[1903a]: 262–3): 'It remains, it is true, to explain how the popular imagination was able to impute so easily to the gods the acts which were forbidden to men. But it is precisely because the gods are not men.'

18　In Durkheim's view, mixed marriages represent a 'breakdown of the traditional moral equilibrium' because the cultural differences between the partners are so great. This instability 'quite naturally opens the door to the divorce court (1980[1903c]: 423).

19　Letter to François Simiand, 15 February 1902; cited in Clark (1973: 183).

20　Ribot gave his interviewees a list of 13 words – dog, animal, colour, form, justice, kindness, virtue, law, force, time, relation, cause, infinity – and asked them to tell him 'immediately, and without thinking, if the word evoke anything and, if so what'. Their answers allowed him to identify three types of thought; concrete, visual-typographic and auditory.

21 Lapie's study looked at 29 students aged between 16 and 18, They were given sentences (such as 'The return of a comet was expected in 1902') and asked what ideas it suggested.

22 Undated letter to Marcel Mauss, February 1902; Durkheim 1998: 319.

23 Undated letter to Marcel Mauss, February or March 1902; Durkheim 1998: 320.

24 Review of *L'Année sociologique* (1903), *Revue de métaphysique et de morale* (November 1903 supplement): 9–13.

25 Here, Bouglé reaches the same conclusions as Durkheim, The division of labour has the positive effect of promoting harmony and equality, provided that (1) functions are adapted to a variety of faculties, and are freely chosen (which implies the 'equalization of 'economic situations'; (2) contracts must be freely negotiated; (3) professional groups are so organized as to ensure that their members respect their obligations; (4) there is a 'moral atmosphere' (hence the important role of education in ensuring that consciousnesses are 'socialized').

26 Bouglé's article is reprinted in his work entitled *Qu'est-ce que la sociologie?* (1925: 63–94).

27 The article is a review of several works: Alfred Coste, *L'Expérience des peuples*, Achille Loria, *La Sociologia*, Émile Faguet, *Problèmes politiques du temps présent* and Émile Boutmy, *Essai de psychologie politique du peuple anglais.*

28 Paul Lapie, letter to Célestin Bouglé, 4 March 1903, Aix; *Revue française de sociologie* 10/1 (January–March 1979): 42.

17 The Next Generation

1 *Pour la raison* was a collection of Lapie's lectures to students, primary teachers and workers

2 Lévy-Bruhl was a *normalien* and *agrégé de philosophie*, and had written his doctoral thesis on 'The idea of God in Seneca'. As Mauss remarked, he led a double life for more than 20 years: by day, he was a philosopher with a university chair; by night, at home and with other people, he was one of the 'most productive and popular of the authors of books on sociology in France'.

3 Lévy-Bruhl's conclusions were rejected not only by Durkheim's enemies, but also by some of his close associates, including Frédéric Rauh, once a fellow student at the École normale superior. Rauh was now back in Paris, where he had replaced Henri Bergson at the École normale supérieure in 1900. His main areas of interest were morality and psychology (*De la méthode dans la psychologie des sentiments*, *Psychologie appliquée à la morale et à l'éducation*). In his *L'Expérience morale* (1903), Rauh identifies the inadequacies and objectivist prejudices in Lévy-Bruhl's book, and criticizes what he terms the 'illusions of the devotees of nature'. Rejecting the idea that morality is nothing more than a cog in the social machine, he defends that of individual spontaneity: 'A moral judgement is not an observation, but a form of consent on the part of an individual consciousness.'

The Durkheimian Gaston Richard also struck a discordant note when he argued that 'society does not act *uno tenore.*' In his article on the conflict between sociology and moral philosophy (1905), he wrote: 'No matter what we do, collective morality will never be the collective behaviour of an undifferentiated mass within which qualitative differences between personal wills emerge.' In his view, social norms had to be assimilated by the individual conscience, and were very unevenly reflected in the behaviour of different individuals.

4 Durkheim's discussion of the problem of violence moves easily between society and school and back again: the threat of despotism is always there: 'When two populations, two groups of people having unequal cultures, come into continuous contact with one another, certain feelings develop that prompt the more cultivated group – or that which

deems itself such – to do violence to the other' (1961[1925]: 192–3). Both relations between colonizer and colonized and 'hazing' are characterized by 'a veritable intoxication, an excessive exaltation of self, a sort of megalomania'; the same might, with some qualification, be said of the teacher–pupil relationship: 'Is there not at the core of pedantry . . . a hint of megalomania?' (ibid.: 193, 194).

5 Durkheim advises his students to consider the use of collective rewards and punishments.

6 Durkheim accepts that art can have a moral function because a love of art does imply 'a certain disinterestedness'. He therefore concludes (1961[1925]: 273–4) that 'it would be well to give all children an aesthetic education'. Yet while he accepts that an interest in art can be a leisure activity, he remains very suspicious of it: 'Art is a game. Morality, on the contrary, is life in earnest' (ibid.: 273).

7 Marcel Mauss, 'Notes de cours sur la magie en Mélanésie' (1901–2); Fonds Hubert-Mauss, IMEC-Caen.

8 Henri Hubert, letter to Marcel Mauss, 1905; Fonds Hubert-Mauss, IMEC-Caen.

9 *Revue de métaphysique et de morale* (1904): 12–15.

10 Marcel Mauss, undated letter to Henri Hubert; Fonds Hubert-Mauss, IMEC-Caen. The second more important section was 'moral and juridic sociology', with more than 140 pages (27%), followed by 'economic sociology' (18%), and 'criminal sociology and moral statistics' (6.5%). The 'social morphology' section remained marginal (3.5%), as did the seventh and final 'miscellaneous' section (3%).

11 Mauss also reviewed the book in *L'Année sociologique* 8 (1905).

12 Réville accepted that 'religious facts are social facts', but criticized Hubert for overlooking 'individualities' and, in a word, being seduced by the 'exaggerations of the sociologists, who have become so obsessed with looking at the trees that they can no longer see the wood'.

13 The article was reviewed in *L'Année sociologique* 10 (1907).

14 Henri Berr, letter to Marcel Mauss, 10 May 1906; Fonds Hubert-Mauss, IMEC-Caen.

15 Lucien Herr, letter to Marcel Mauss, 8 September 1906; Fonds Hubert-Mauss, IMEC-Caen.

16 Letter to Marcel Mauss, August 1904; Durkheim 1998: 353.

17 Letter to Octave Hamelin, 11 September 1904, Versailles; Durkheim 1975: ii/459.

18 Simiand's thesis was published by the Société nouvelle de librairie et d'édition in 1904, but the book did not go on sale. The definitive edition appeared in 1909, with the subtitle 'Contribution à la théorie économique du salaire'; see Steiner 2005: 129–38.

19 Letter to the rector, 14 March 1903; Dossier Paul Fauconnet, Archives nationales AJ 16 1066.

20 Robert Potter (an architect) and his wife were friends of Joe Stickney. Henri Hubert met them during their visits to France.

21 Letter to Marcel Mauss (1903?); Durkheim 1998: 132.

22 Rosine Mauss, letter to Marcel Mauss, 21 May 1904; Archives familiales, Pierre Mauss.

23 Letter to Octave Hamelin, Versailles, 11 September 1904; Durkheim 1975: ii/460.

24 Paul Lapie, letter to Xavier Léon, 12 January 1904; *Bulletin d'études durkheimiennes*: 3.

25 Élie Halévy, letter to Célestin Bouglé, 12 January 1905; Halévy 1996: 359.

26 Letter to Henri Hubert, 16 April 1905; *Revue française de sociologie* (1987): 528.

27 Letter to Octave Hamelin, 11 September 1904, Versailles; Durkheim 1975: ii/459.

28 Letter to Marcel Mauss, 6 July 1905; Durkheim 1998: 361.

29 Robert Hertz, letter to Pierre Roussel, 27 April 1907, Paris; *Durkheimian Studies/Études durkheimiennes* 5 (1999): 52.

30 Letter to Marcel Mauss, June 1905; Durkheim 1998: 359.

31 There was little change in the relative size of the other sections. 'General sociology' and 'economic sociology' were slightly expanded (15% and 20% of all pages devoted to reviews). The introduction of rubrics dealing with 'the individual and society', 'group psychology and collective ethology' and 'civilizations' changed the nature of 'general sociology' somewhat. The miscellaneous section was still marginal (2%), and now contained only three sections: 'aesthetic sociology' (Hubert), 'technology' (Hubert and Mauss) and 'language' (Meillet).

32 J. Ch. review of Hubert Bourgin, 'Essai sur une forme d'industrie', *Revue de synthèse historique* 15/4 (1907).

18 *The Evolution of Educational Thought*; or, Triadic Culture

1 Alfred Croiset, 'Rapport de la faculté des lettres', in Université de Paris, *Rapport présenté au ministre de l'instruction publique sur la situation de l'enseignement supérieur*. Melun: Imprimerie administrative, 1904–5, p. xxviii.
2 Lapie was advocating nothing short of a 'radical' or even utopian revolution in the schools and universities, with the creation of real *cités universitaires* with offices, apartments and houses for the staff. Academic life would revolve around the library, a real 'temple of free work.' He was arguing the case for a general culture that, without being encyclopaedic, was 'balanced', gave students greater freedom of choice and promoted a 'liberal discipline'
3 This lecture was published the following year in the *Revue bleue* as 'L'Évolution et le rôle de l'enseignement secondaire en France' (see Durkheim 1956[1906]).
4 Marcel Mauss, undated letter to Rosine Mauss, 1905; Archives personnelles, Pierre Mauss.
5 Marcel Mauss, letter to Henri Hubert, 12 December 1904; Fonds Hubert-Mauss, IMEC-Caen.
6 Durkheim mentions only one great event: the creation of the University of France in 1808; this merged all educational agencies into a single organism directly dependent upon the central power (1973[1938]: 306).

19 Church, State and Fatherland

1 The Union pour la vérité was the successor to the Union pour l'action morale, founded in 1892 by the philosopher Jules Lagneau and 15 or so friends, including Gabriel Monod and Paul Desjardins. The goal of the original Union was to strengthen the social bond.
2 Desjardin's *Catholicisme et critique: refléxions d'un profane sur l'affaire Loisy* caused great annoyance in Catholic circles. A very active man, Desjardins organized lectures all over France, including one at the Abbaye de Pontigny, which is where he died. See Pickering 2006: 8–9.
3 Durkheim's lecture has been lost; see Pickering (2003a). Ferdinand Buisson and Dominique Parodi were involved with the École de la paix in subsequent years; it appears to have closed in 1912.
4 'Religion and Morality' was first published in *Philosophical Review* 15 (1906): 255–7. The text is a summary 'written from memory' by André Lalande, who admitted that he may have 'misremembered' certain details. Lalande was a *normalien*, an *agrégé de philosophie* and a *docteur ès lettres*. Durkheim taught Lalande at the lycée in Sens.
5 In a footnote, Durkheim wonders if the scientist's devotion to science can be moral: even though the search for the truth is not really or truly moral, the abnegation of the scientist who is passionate about sciences is 'in some way similar to moral abnegation'.
6 Élie Halévy, letter to Célestin Bouglé, 16 February 1906; Halévy 1996: 374.
7 See Alfred Valensi's *L'Application de la loi du divorce en France*, which Durkheim reviewed in volume 9 of *L'Année sociologique* (see Durkheim 1980[1906d]). He criticizes Valensi for his superficial analysis of the 'obvious connection' between divorce and suicide: 'It is the sufferings of the individual, caused by the sickness of a social and fundamental institution, that are coming to be translated into the yearly total of suicides' (ibid.: 431).
8 Letter to Marcel Mauss, June 1905; Durkheim 1998: 359.
9 Letter to Marcel Mauss, 6 July 1905; Durkheim 1998: 361.
10 Letter to Octave Hamelin, 16 September 1905, Versailles; Durkheim 1975: ii/460.
11 Letter to Marcel Mauss, June 1905, Épinal; Durkheim 1998: 357.
12 Letter to Marcel Mauss, June 1905?, Épinal; Durkheim 1998: 356.

13 Letter to Marcel Mauss, 28 July 1905, Paris; Durkheim 1998: 365. The letter ends with the usual '*Je t'embrasse*' ['With my love'].
14 Letter to Marcel Mauss, 28 July 1905, Paris; Durkheim 1998: 365.
15 Letter to Marcel Mauss, August 1905, Épinal; Durkheim 1998: 368.
16 Letter to Marcel Mauss, 11 March 1906?; Durkheim 1998: 376.
17 Letter to Henri Hubert, May 1906; *Revue française de sociologie* (1987): 529.
18 Émile Durkheim's advice to his young associate was: 'Take good care of your physical and moral health.' Letter to Henri Hubert, May 1906; *Revue française de sociologie* (1987): 529.
19 Letter to Marcel Mauss, May–June 1906?; Durkheim 1998: 377.
20 Letter to Henri Hubert, May–June 1906, *Revue française de sociologie* (1987): 530.
21 Élie Halévy, letter to Célestin Bouglé, 11 December 1905; Halévy 1996: 373.
22 Élie Halévy, letter to Célestin Bouglé, 26 December 1905; Halévy 1996: 382.
23 Letter to Marcel Mauss, 25 July 1905; Durkheim 1998: 364.
24 Letter to Marcel Mauss, Klosters, 13 August 1905; Durkheim 1998: 367.
25 Lucien Herr, letter to Marcel Mauss, 8 September 1906; Fonds Hubert-Mauss, IMEC-Caen.
26 Undated letter to Marcel Mauss, September 1906; Durkheim 1998: 378–9.
27 Undated letter to Marcel Mauss (1904–6?); Durkheim 1998: 380.
28 Letter to Octave Hamelin, 28 August 1906; Durkheim 1975: ii/461.
29 Letter to Marcel Mauss, 1906; Durkheim 1998: 378–9.
30 Paul Fauconnet, letter to Marcel Mauss, 15 September 1906); Fonds Hubert-Mauss, IMEC-Caen.
31 Letter to Henri Hubert, May or June 1906; *Revue française de sociologie* (1987): 530.
32 The 'general sociology' (8%) was smaller than before, as was 'criminal sociology and moral statistics' (4%), which now took up less space than 'social morphology' (43%). The marginal 'miscellaneous' section (2.5%) still consisted of the 'aesthetic sociology', 'technology' and 'language' rubrics.
33 Henri Hubert, letter to Marcel Mauss, 1906; Fonds Hubert-Mauss, IMEC-Caen. He also had some help from the Danish ethno-linguist William Thalbitzer, who attended Mauss's lecture during the winter of 1905. Thalbitzer had recently published a major study of the Inuit language. See Saladin d'Anglure 2004.
34 Bouglé received 20 votes, and Malapert 5; minutes of the meeting of 16 June 1906, Board of the faculty of letters, Paris; Archives nationales AJ 16 4759: 195–6. See Pickering 2003b.

20 A Tenth Anniversary

1 Like several of his colleagues – Louis Liard, Henri Bergson, Émile Boutroux, Victor Brochard and Théodule Ribot – Durkheim agreed in July 1904 to subscribe to the fund that was being raised to erect a monument to the memory of Charles Renouvier. Bouglé and Lapie, from the *Année*, also contributed.
2 Xavier Léon, letter to Élie Halévy, 27 June 1908; cited in Paoletti (1997).
3 While Bergson destructured time and saw duration as an infinitely varied stream of consciousness, Hubert saw the properties of the 'time environment' as a framework structured by the rules that allowed rituals to function. See Isambert (1979: 195) and Mauss (1969[1907]).
4 He borrowed, for instance, the idea that members of a given society see their society as the transcendent being they call God; see Aubin 1910.
5 Maunier's *L'Économie politique et la sociologie* was published in the Bibliothèque socio-logique internationale in 1910, and he attended François Simiand's lectures at the École pratique in 1911. His relationship with the Durkheim group was therefore complex, being both close and distant (see Mahé 1998). It was only in the inter-war period that Maunier really became closely associated with the group; at this time, the group had tried to relaunch the *Année sociologique* and adopted the *Annales sociologiques* formula. It was then that he published his study of ritual exchange in North Africa. Alcan pub-lished his *Mélanges de sociologie nord-africaine* in 1930.

6 In the early 1910s, the main impetus behind the Société internationale de science sociale came from Paul Descamps, Paul des Rousiers and Paul Bureau. Paul Bureau, a doctor of law and a professor at the Institut catholique de Paris, was one of the first associates of Tourville and Demolins. The school's international nature was signalled by its many foreign members. Several of its French members came from various regions of the country. Its members included several abbots and aristocrats, as well as some 15 or so women, including the marquise de Lisle.

7 See Gérin 1912. The article included a critique of Durkheim's methodology. Gérin, a Canadian (1864–1951), trained as a lawyer, and worked as a translator in the Chambre des communes, Ottawa. He was the author of several monographs on peasant families in Québec.

8 Bureau later published *La Science des moeurs*, subtitled 'Introduction to sociological method' (Paris: Bloud et Gay, 1926; 2nd edn.).

9 Arnold Van Gennep was born to Dutch parents in 1873, but was brought up in France. His educational and intellectual career was unusual. He graduated from the École des langues orientales in 1896, spoke several languages (Arabic, the Slavic languages, Finnish and Hungarian) and had written on numismatics. Van Gennep never held an academic position. From 1901 to 1908, he was head of translation in the information department of the ministry for agriculture. When he failed in his attempt to obtain a chair at the Collège de France, he sold his library and went to live in Florence. 'There is no position in Paris for me', he told Mauss (letter of 14 February 1909; Fonds Hubert-Mauss, IMEC-Caen). He was eventually appointed to a chair in ethnography at the University of Neuchâtel in Switzerland (1912–15). See Belmont 1974.

10 He translated his study of totemism into French in 1898.

11 Antoine Meillet, 'Présentation de la candidature d'Arnold Van Gennep en second ligne', Procès-verbal de l'assemblée du 17 février 1907, Collège de France; Archives du Collège de France. G-IV-g 32L. Van Gennep, letter to 'Monsieur 'Administrateur', 19 February 1907.

12 Meillet was an *agrégé de grammaire* and *maître de conférences* at the École Pratique des hautes études. He was elected to the chair formerly held by Michel Bréal (a professor at the Collège from 1899 to 1900), winning all but one of the votes of the Collège de France and the Académie des inscriptions et des belles-lettres in the first round. For Charles Fossey (1869–1900), an *agrégé de lettres* (1894) who taught a course on Babylonian religion at the École pratique des hautes études, it was a different story. Fossey was elected in exceptional circumstances after the controversy surrounding the election of his rival Father Scheil, a 'secularized Dominican', who had been denounced as 'either an impostor or an ignoramus'. Following the intervention of Bienvenu-Martin, who exercised his right as a minister not to appoint the first-choice candidate, Fossey, the second-choice candidate, was eventually elected.

13 Rosine Mauss, letter to Marcel Mauss, Friday, February 1907; Archives familiales, Pierre Mauss. The other candidates were Georges Foucart, Arnold Van Gennep and Maurice Vernes.

14 Henri Hauser wrote to the dean of the faculty of letters to inform him that he intended to apply for the position, admitting that 'it may seem strange for a historian to ask to replace a philosopher'. His suggestion was that the course, which was on the history of economic doctrines, with the 'history of actual economic facts', and he listed his various contributions to economic history: *Ouvriers du temps passé XV–XVIe siècle* (1899), *L'Enseignement des sciences sociales in France* (1901), *L'Impérialisme américain (1903*, 'Les Origines du capitalisme moderne' (*Revue d'économie politique*) and *Le Compagnage d'arts et métiers à Dijon* (1907). See 'Lettre de Henri Hauser au doyen Alfred Croiset', Dijon, 3 November 1907, in Dossier Bouglé, Archives nationales, AJ/16/5885.

15 When he learned that Ernest Lichtenberger (born in Strasbourg 1847, *agrégé d'allemand* in 1873, *docteur ès lettres* 1878), was taking a period of leave, Durkheim thought of 'bringing in Basch'. Born in Hungary in 1873 and an *agrégé d'allemand*, Basch wrote his doctoral thesis on Kant's aesthetics (1897). He was a very active Dreyfusard.

16 Letter to the director (Charles Bayet), 4 December 1907; *Revue française de sociologie* 10/1 (January–March 1979): 116. The Belgian-born Charles Bayet was an *agrégé*

d'histoire and a medieval specialist. He had taught at the faculty of letters at Lyon, where he also became dean, before becoming rector of the Académie de Lille and then director of primary education. In September 1902, he replaced Louis Liard as director of higher education. It was Bayet who oversaw the incorporation of the École normale supérieure into the Sorbonne in 1904.

17 Letter to the director, *Revue française de sociologie* 10/1 (January–March 1979): 116.

18 Lapie studied the files of more than 100 young people (92 boys and 10 girls) aged over 18 who had been brought before the courts between December 1908 and January 1910. He demonstrated that school was in fact a 'temporary refuge' for several children who 'entered the school system with a propensity for crime because of their family heritage'. The study was published in *L'École et les écoliers* (1923).

19 Durkheim examined Louis-Germain Lévy, 'The family in ancient Israel' in 1905–6; G. Aslan, 'The ethics of Guyau' in July 1906; Gabriel Revault d'Allonnes, 'The psychology of a religion' in March 1908. In 1909, he examined four theses: E. Cramaussel's 'The first intellectual awakening of the child'; Francis Mangé's 'Systematization in the sciences'; M. Pradines's 'The principles of every philosophy of action'; and M. Mendousse's 'From animal training to education'. (See Lukes 1985[1973]: 621–654.)

20 'Totemism is a form so constant among primitive religions that, when one finds traces such as those you indicate yourself, there is a strong presumption in favour of a totemic origin' (Durkheim 1985 [1973]: 628). Lévy (1860–1937), a philosopher and rabbi, was a tireless advocate for the critical and exegetical study of Judaism. He began his career by studying the history of religions at the École pratique des hautes études, and later founded the Union libérale israélite, which defended a modernist or reformist vision of Judaism. In 1904, he helped to found the Copernicus non-consistorial synagogue. In *Une Religion rationnelle et laïque*, Lévy contended that the religion of the twentieth century would be born of fusion between prophetism and science. Judaism was not, in his view, a stable or immutable religion, but was open to progress and change. He saw it as one version of a universal religion.

21 *Les Documents du progrès* was published monthly in Berlin, Paris and London; its French publisher was Alcan. Most of the articles it published were very short. Contributors to the symposium included Durkheim, Worms, Simmel, Tönnies, Galton, Branford, Giddings, Ward and Small. Broca contributed an account of current trends in sociology in France and America.

22 Lalande was a *maître de conférences* (logic and scientific method) at the Sorbonne, and had recently published *Précis raisonné de morale pratique* (1907). He was one of the founders of the Société française de philosophie and served as its secretary-general from 1901 to 1937. Gustave Bloch (the father of Marc) was a professor of Roman history at the Sorbonne, and author of *La Gaule indépendante et la Gaule romaine* (1900). Paul Lacombe wrote two major books: *De l'histoire considérée comme science* (1894) and *Introduction à l'histoire littéraire*. He had recently published *La Psychologie des individus et des sciences chez Taine* (1906); his *Taine, historien et sociologue* was published in 1909. A friend of André Berr and contributor to the *Revue de synthèse historique*, he defended the idea of history-as-science and was in favour of synthetic science: a synthesis of the general and the particular, of the 'evental' [*événementielle*] and the institutional, and of contingency and necessity. His project for a general theory of human behaviour took into account both the individual and the institutional dimension, and relied heavily upon psychology. When he spoke of 'psychology', Lacombe meant 'collective psychology'. He wanted to be close to those he called '*sociologistes*'.

23 Letter to Marcel Mauss, 28 December 1906; Durkheim 1998: 381.

24 Letter to Marcel Mauss, 12 April 1907; Durkheim 1998: 383.

25 Paul Fauconnet, letter to Célestin Bouglé, 26 February 1907, Cherbourg; *Revue française de sociologie* 10/1 (January–March 1979): 44.

26 Célestin Bouglé, undated letter to Élie Halévy, 1907. The librarian was Simiand, the 'home-nurse' was Fauconnet, and the 'fanatic' was Mauss. See Besnard 1979; 24

27 Élie Halévy, letter to Célestin Bouglé, 26 November 1907; Halévy 1996: 393.

28 Marcel Mauss, letter to Célestin Bouglé, 23 July 1907; *Revue française de sociologie* 10/1 (January–March 1979): 48.

29 Émile Durkheim, letter to Marcel Mauss, 1 October 1907; Durkheim 1998: 387.
30 Célestin Bouglé, undated letter to Élie Halévy, 1907; cited in Besnard 1979: 24.
31 Isaac Althaus Loos was a professor at the State University of Iowa.
32 Their agents have similar characteristics, the rites are similar, and the representations are identical. The reference to the occult and the illicit appears to be the only difference between magic and religion. Huvelin asks whether we have to look at the goals of magical rites, or take account of the interests they represent. Not necessarily, as all technologies (music, the arts, medicine, mathematics, etc.) were once associated with magical practices. Huvelin was interested in private tort and what he called collective conventions (agreements between two or more individuals with a view to a legally binding contract, and especially obligations).
33 The same review also deals with Adolphe Landry's *Principes de morale rationnelle*, but Durkheim pays little attention to it because the discussion is 'not purely methodological' and because the author attempts to demonstrate that 'our whole doctrine is derived from utilitarian premises' (1980[1907b]: 138).
34 Durkheim is surprised to find that Westermarck's argument (that moral facts are rooted in elementary emotions such as anger, indignation and sympathy) has been 'constructed in a somewhat sketchy manner' and that the reader finds himself in 'the midst of a world of abstractions, and of abstractions constructed without much method' (1980[1907e]: 156).
35 According to Simmel, fashion answers the need for both conformism and separatism, and thus returns to the basic dualisms of human nature: rest–movement, union–separation, universal–individual. For the first time, Bouglé spoke of his German colleague in ironic terms: 'M.S [Simmel] plays with his usual ingenuity in the midst of these subtle distinctions and fleeting reflections' (Bouglé 1907c: 197).
36 Halbwachs criticizes Vilfredo Pareto for his failure to present any observations or series of facts, or to do anything more than use merely 'analyses of ideas and abstract notations', and a series of 'dense arguments about political economy'. Halbwachs was puzzled by what was 'no doubt original' work, and called it 'a curious mixture of abstract imaginings and very fanciful scholarship' (Halbwachs 1907).
37 Paul Fauconnet, letter to Marcel Mauss, 1908; Fonds Hubert-Mauss, IMEC-Caen.
38 Letter to Marcel Mauss, 10 August 1907, Kandersteg; Durkheim 1998: 385.
39 Marcel Mauss, undated letter to Henri Hubert, September 1907; Fonds Hubert-Mauss. IMEC-Caen
40 Simon Deploige, letter, 12 November 1907; Deploige 1927[1911]: 363–72. The third edition of Deploige's book was prefaced by Jacques Maritain. Deploige's specialism was the philosophy of Thomas Aquinas, about whom he wrote two books: *La Théorie thomiste de la proprieté* and *Saint Thomas et la question juive.*
41 Letter to the rector (Louis Liard), 7 January 1907; Dossier Durkheim, Archives nationales, AJ16 214.
42 Dossier Émile Durkheim, Légion d'honneur, Archives nationales, LH 874.
43 According to Lukes (1985[1973]: 378 n61), the philosopher in question was F. Evellin.
44 Paul Fauconnet, letter to Célestin Bouglé, 26 February 1907, Cherbourg; *Revue française de sociologie* 10/1 (January–March 1979): 44.
45 Report from the council of the University of Paris, meeting of 26 July 1909; Archives nationales, AJ 16584
46 Durkheim disagreed with his colleague Paul Lapie, who also took part in the debate. In Lapie's view, the problem with the *agrégation* was that it was tightly regulated and allowed students no freedom. Durkheim in fact again accepted that students should 'be taught to 'understand scientific method by putting it into practice'.

21 'Change the World'

1 Robert Hertz, letter to Pierre Roussel, 22 June 1907; *Durkheimian Studies/Études durkheimiennes* 5 (1999): 54–5.
2 Robert Hertz, letter to Marcel Mauss, 11 February 1908; Fonds Hubert-Mauss, IMEC-Caen.

3 Paul Fauconnet, letter to Marcel Mauss, 1908; Fonds Hubert-Mauss; IMEC-Caen.
4 Robert Hertz, letter to Albert Thomas, 6 February 1908; cited in Prochasson 1996: 4.
5 'One of the best economic publications of recent years', wrote J. Chevalier in the *Revue de synthèse historique*, emphasizing its methodological importance. The same issue of the journal contained another review of Simiand's 'fine work'. It was by Paul Fauconnet (1908). Looking exclusively at the methodological dimension, Fauconnet showed that, while the analysis of the data was the work of an economic historian, Simiand's interpretation of it was 'truly sociological': human action takes place within an institutional framework, and it is not the work of individuals or of *homo economicus* but of groups. He also demonstrated that while Simiand's economic sociology might well be speculative and complex, it was not unrelated to the 'problems of practice': the data presented was of immediate practical relevance. It was a way of showing that sociology could 'be a guide to action and could shed light upon it'.
6 Born in 1847, Renard attended the École normale supérieure (class of 1867), but did not take the *agrégation*. He was elected to a chair in labour history at the Collège de France. He had three careers: as a professor, a journalist and a socialist activist. Now the editor of the *Revue socialiste*, he was once *La Petite République*'s literary critic. He met Simiand at the Conservatoire des arts et métiers, where he taught labour history from 1901 onwards. He also published *Le Régime socialiste* (Alcan, 1907).
7 *Bulletin du Groupe d'études socialistes*, *Rapport sur l'année 1910*, undated, May 1910; Fonds Hubert-Mauss, IMEC-Caen.
8 Other members included Edgar Milhaud, Ernest Poisson, Alfred Bonnet, Jacques Ferdinand Dreyfus and Albert Thomas. Two members – André Lebey and Albert Thomas – entered parliament.
9 Brochure de la Librairie du Parti socialiste; *Les Cahiers du socialiste*, no. 3, Paris, 1908 (32 pp).
10 Georges Weill (1910) described it as 'an essay in social psychology that is of some considerable interest', but added that it would not convince historians: 'Like M. Hubert Bourgin and M. Simiand, M. Halbwachs is one of a group of workers who do their utmost to eliminate individuals in favour of the collective, and to discover the permanent social element that lies beneath changing historical phenomena.' As Halbwachs demonstrated (1910: 657), land speculation also had to do with representations inspired by public opinion.
11 Gaston Hervé and his newspaper *La Guerre sociale* (which sold up to 50,000 copies) were successfully waging antipatriotic campaigns at this time.
12 Marcel Mauss, letter to 'Monsieur' (unnamed), 20 October 1904; Fonds Hubert-Mauss, IMEC-Caen.
13 Édouard Toulouse was the editor of several journals (including the *Revue scientifique* and *Demain*) and collections, including the ambitious *Encyclopédie scientifique*, which included a 'Bibliothèque de sociologie'. He also published books for the general public, including *Les Conflits intersexuels et sociaux* (1904) and *La Question sexuelle et la femme* (1918). See Huteau 2002; Berrebi-Hoffmann and Lallement 2007.
14 As far Richard's distinction between 'society' and 'community', which roughly corresponds to that between organic and mechanical solidarity, Durkheim ironically remarks that 'the author . . . is very anxious to refuse any joint responsibility for the ideas from which we draw our inspiration' (1980[1913c]: 85).
15 Letter to Xavier Léon, 24 July 1908, 260 rue Saint-Jacques; Durkheim 1975: ii/466–48)
16 Letter to Léon Xavier, 22 August 1908, 2 rue Sadi-Carnot, Épinal; Durkheim 1975: ii/468.
17 Émile Boutroux, former professor of the history of philosophy at the Sorbonne, had just retired and was now an emeritus professor. His *Science et religions dans la philosophie contemporaine* was published in 1908. Boutroux described himself as an 'ancient Christian'. In his view there was no conflict between science and religion, as they had different objects: science sides with facts, and religion with action –this is 'the ferment of life'. Édouard Le Roy (1870–1954) was an *agrégé de mathématiques* (1895) and held doctorates in both science (1898) and letters (1906). Since October 1909, he had taught special mathematics at the Lycée Saint-Louis. A practising and militant Catholic, he

published his first book (*Études de philosophie et de critique religieuse. Dogme et critique*) in 1907). Édouard Le Roy was appointed to the Collège de France, first as a replacement for Bergson (1914–20) and then as professor of philosophy (1921–41). His *Une Philosophie nouvelle: Henri Bergson* was published in 1913.

18 Marcel Mauss, letter to Henri Hubert, 16 August 1908; Fonds Hubert-Mauss, IMEC-Caen.

19 The rest of the text has been lost.

20 Henri Hubert, undated letter to Marcel Mauss, 1898; Fonds-Hubert Mauss, IMEC-Caen.

21 Undated letter to Marcel Mauss, November 1908; Durkheim 1998: 389.

22 Undated letter to Marcel Mauss, 1909; Durkheim 1998: 392.

23 Letter to Marcel Mauss; Durkheim 1998: 390.

24 Paul Fauconnet, undated letter to Marcel Mauss, 1909; Fonds-Hubert-Mauss, IMEC-Caen.

25 Paul Fauconnet, undated letter to Marcel Mauss, 1909; Fonds Hubert-Mauss, IMEC-Caen. The consternation was all the greater in that, in the second round of voting, Mauss was defeated by his colleague Jules Toutain (whom he regarded as a 'reactionary candidate' and 'an imbecile').

26 Abel Rey, letter to Marcel Mauss, 3 February 1909; Fonds Hubert-Mauss, IMEC-Caen. Born in 1873, Abel Rey was an *agrégé de philosophie* and had recently defended his doctoral thesis on 'contemporary physicists on the theory of physics'. A former Dreyfusard, he was appointed as *chargé de cours* (philosophy) at the Dijon faculty of letters in 1908, and founded a laboratory for experimental psychology there. He was also the author of *Leçons de psychologie et de philosophie* (1903), *Eléments de philosophie scientfique et morale* (1903), and *La Philosophie moderne* (1908).

27 When it comes to educational techniques, Rousseau recommends that, rather than using exhortations or appeals to the 'idea to shine', children should simply be taught to imitate the acts. The love of imitation is, in his view, natural: 'One act which itself summons forth another' (Durkheim 1979[1919] 191).

28 It is possible to get some idea of its content from the notes taken by two students: Georges Davy (a contributor to the *Année*) and Armand Cuvillier. They contain several abbreviations, some illegible words and a few inaccuracies. The lecture notes were given to Steven Lukes, who transcribed them for his doctoral thesis (Lukes 1969). Cuvillier (1887–1973) was educated at the École normale supérieure (class of 1908). He taught in many lycées, including Louis-le-Grand, before becoming a professor at the Sorbonne (1945–53).

29 Durkheim devoted a whole section of his course to respect for life. The explanation lies, he argued, in the sacred nature of life: homicide was, like sacrilege, a crime against a sacred principle because it 'violates the prohibitions that protect the soul'. This, he contended, explained the origins of the disapproval of homicide: 'There is within us a religious force or a soul that is dispersed throughout our bodies.'

30 These obligations include military service, 'a debt which must be paid'.

31 The schoolteacher's task, Durkheim strongly asserts, is to have the pupil acquire 'the sense of the social', making him discover that 'the [social] world is made up of social forces, mental phenomena, states of opinion, states of the public or collective consciousness'. Statistical data show that, in a society, it is as if 'individuals act by virtue of concerted agreement'. 'Opinion is the only possible foundation of all social life.' And 'there could never have been anything but governments of opinion'. The same holds for science, whose authority comes from 'the authority with which opinion endows the scientific spirit'.

32 Durkheim reasserts his belief that sociology is of practical use: just as it is impossible to act on things without understanding them, we cannot act upon institutions, states of mind or representations unless we understand them. It is perfectly clear to him that the 'science of customs' or 'the genetic study of moral standards' is 'the indispensable base of all moral art that would be rational . . . We have no other lever in hand' (1980[1907a]: 148).

33 The rest of the discussion, in which Parodi again took part, was specifically about 'the

rationality of inequalities'. Durkheim could not accept that 'the universal inequalities of caste and class, as they existed in the past, were less rational than our current inequalities' (1979[1910]: 67). 'Our present inequalities are founded on the nature of our present societies, as those of India are founded upon the nature of Hindu societies.' What of 'the relative equality towards which we are moving today'? It has to be recognized that 'we are unequal. We have neither the same physical force, nor the same intellectual power, nor the same energy of will.' Such inequalities appear to be 'founded in the nature of our societies' and do not result from 'blind tradition', but morality demands that we be treated as equals. We therefore have to explain how this 'transfiguration' takes place (ibid.: 72). For similar reasons, inequalities of caste and class could not have 'become established and been maintained by artifice and ruse', but 'necessarily resulted from conditions of communal life' (ibid.: 71). Such inequalities 'would not have persisted if they had not been founded in the nature of things'. He then adds: 'Traditional justifications often have more value than people believe . . . the justifications are often very close to the facts and determine rational justification.' He takes the example of the feudal regime in the organization of medieval societies to demonstrate that: 'At that time the feudal system was rational, just as it was to lose that rationality later' (1979[1910]: 75, 76).

22 Regent of the Sorbonne

1 Students from the law faculty, opposed to the renewal of Dean Lyon-Caen's mandate, held demonstrations. Chairs were broken, piled up and set on fire in the inner courtyard. There were further disturbances over the next few days, and they became more serious. The dean had the buildings evacuated by the police and asked the council to close the faculty.

There were more demonstrations two years later in February 1911 when students tried to prevent Professor Wahl from giving his lectures. They accused him of not speaking loudly enough and complained that he was a harsh examiner. There was an uproar in his classroom, with shouts of 'Resign! Resign! Down with Wahl!' as the trouble reached its peak. The new dean, M. Cauwès was so alarmed that he asked the police to evacuate the premises. Disowning Wahl was out of the question. The university council suspended second-year classes until the end of the first semester.

2 Gaston Bonnier, 'Actes du Conseil de l'Université et principaux faits intéressant à l'Université', *Rapport annuel* (1909–10): 38.

3 Minutes of the Conseil de l'Université de Paris, 6 May 190; Archives nationales AJ16 2588.

4 Speech by Louis Liard, 20 September 1913 (meeting of 6 October 1913); minutes of the Conseil de l'Université de Paris; Archives nationales AJ16 8458.

5 Actes du Conseil de l'Université, *Rapport annuel 1909–1910*, pp. 32–3.

6 Alfred Croiset, 'Discours prononcé à l'ouverture des conférences de la faculté des lettres de Paris', November 1909; *Revue internationale de l'enseignement* 56 (1909): 396–7.

7 Gustave Lanson, 'Faculté des lettres', in Université de Paris, *Rapports annuels 1912–1913*, Paris: Imprimerie et librairie nationales des chemins de fer, 1914, pp. 38–39.

8 Agathon, 'L'Esprit de la nouvelle Sorbonne', *Mercure de France*, 1911, pp. 204–5.

9 Rauh was buried in the Montparnasse cemetery on 22 February 1909. Durkheim spoke on behalf of his friends, and addressed a 'last farewell' to 'a friend, a very old friend' to whom he had been 'tenderly attached'. In intellectual terms, Frédéric Rauh had, he recognized, certainly abandoned metaphysics in order to come 'into contact with facts' and had become 'infinitely curious', but he was always 'a philosopher at heart' (Durkheim 2006[1909]).

10 *Agrégé de philosophie* (1894) and *docteur ès lettres*, Delacroix (1873–1937) had been a *maître de conférences* in Montpellier before becoming professor of philosophy at Caen. He was the author of *Les Grands Mystiques chrétiens* (1908) but, while retaining an interest in religion, had also developed an interest in psychology. In 1912–13, he taught the course on the application of psychology to education. Léon Brunschvicg joined the faculty when Gabriel Séailles took a period of leave. Born in 1869, a gradu-

ate of the École normale supérieure, an *agrégé de philosophie* and a *docteur ès lettres*, Brunschvicg was a regular contributor to the *Revue de métaphysique et de morale* and one of the driving forces behind the recently founded Société française de philosophie. He was coeditor, with Pierre Boutroux, of Pascal's *Oeuvres complètes* and author of *Les Étapes de la philosophie mathématique* (1912). He was married to Cécile Kahn, a very active defender of women's rights and a member of the Conseil national des femmes françaises. In 1936, she became the first under-secretary of state for women in Léon Blum's government.

11 The problem was that the capital endowment of 110,000 francs would be exhausted by January 1916 and the chair would lapse. The annual sum of 5,000 francs received by the university was not in fact enough to pay the professor's salary, and had to be topped up from other sources.

12 Minutes of the meeting of the Conseil de l'Université de Paris, 27 November 1911; Archives nationales AJ$_{16}$ 2589. See also Dossier Célestin Bouglé, Archives nationales AJ$_{16}$ 5885. Bouglé's salary was set at 8,000 francs, plus a possible allowance of 2,000 francs.

13 Paul Fauconnet, letter to Marcel Mauss, 29 December 1911, Toulouse; Fonds-Hubert-Mauss, IMEC-Caen.

14 Gaston Richard had been promoted to the rank of professor at Bordeaux. His sociology lectures were entitled 'Public opinion' (1912–13) and 'Social and political differentiation' (1913–14).

15 The group now had a presence in the faculties of letters in Paris (Bouglé), Bordeaux (Lapie) and Toulouse (Fauconnet). Although they were not specialists, two other teachers in provincial universities were discussing issues related to sociology. In Lyon, A. Bertrand was teaching a course called 'The stages and rhythm of social progress' in Lyon, and Jean Delvolvé was teaching 'Social factors in moral education' in Montpellier. Delvolvé's presence at the Second International Congress on Moral Education at The Hague in 1912 was testimony to his interest in moral education.

16 'On dit . . . on dit', *La Vie parisienne*, 20 July 1912; cited in Azouvi 2007: 14.

17 In 1904, Gustave Lanson published an article on 'literary history and sociology' in the *Revue de métaphysique et de morale*. That sociology was of interest to literary historians is evident from Marius-Ary Leblond's lengthy *La Société française sous la Troisième République d'après les romanciers français* (Alcan 1905). Leblond argues that the novelist, who is intimately involved in life, is the ideal witness to his times, and may even be more insightful than the historian or the specialist who is confined to his study. The novelist may, in other words, be better than the sociologist at observing society. Writers themselves were discovering sociology and, like Paul Bourget (*Littérature et sociologie*, Paris: Plon, 1906), declared themselves to be disciples of Auguste Comte and ardent believers in the positivist method. Their new political philosophy was what Bourget called 'traditionalism through positivism'. Bourget also wrote: 'Social facts are a reality, just as physiological facts are medical realities.' He believed that societies have their traditions and habits, and that they are residues or vestiges of the past. Dominique Parodi was not the only one to be surprised by Bourget's position: The so-called right-wing positivists tend to agree with the authentic left-wing positivists. They have succeeded in appropriating positivist relativism to justify their moral and political doctrines' (Parodi 1906). See Lepenies 1990.

18 The authors also remark in a footnote: 'In his lecture of morality, Durkheim teaches his students that a historical culture is a precondition for the acquisition of any philosophical culture.' He confuses historical culture with philosophical culture. This, they conclude, is the new Sorbonne's 'basic axiom'.

19 Péguy admitted that he had once dreamed of acquiring the great distinction, sophistication and elegance of Marcel Mauss, with his 'fine profile, noble look, flowery language, functional (but sober) dress, well-trimmed curly beard, long sociological trousers, republican cuffs, his excellent German, his lily-and-roses complexion, and a waistcoat that was at once chaste and voluptuous' (Péguy 1910: 49–50).

20 Émile Faguet was born in 1847. A *normalien* and *agrégé de lettres*, he was author of a two-volume *Histoire de la littérature française* (1900). He was also a member of the

Académie française. An anti-Dreyfusard and a nationalist, he was a member of the Ligue de la patrie française (Charle 1985: 73–4).

21 Marcel Mauss, '*Les Jeunes Gens d'aujourd'hui* et Agathon', undated manuscript (1910) signed 'Criton'; Fonds Hubert-Mauss, IMEC-Caen.

22 It should be recalled that the *Revue internationale de sociologie* also published Guillaume de Tarde's 'L'Évolution sociale' (Guillaume was Gabriel Tarde's other son). The paper was read to the Société de sociologie de Paris in March 1911.

23 Gustave Lanson (1857–1934) was one year older than Durkheim. An *agrégé de lettres* (1877), he was author of a popular *Histoire de la littérature française* (first published in 1895, it was reprinted many times) and had joined the faculty as *maître de conférences* in French language and literature in 1900 after a long career in secondary education. In 1894–5 and 1896–1900 he replaced Brunetière at the École normale supérieure. A secular republican, Dreyfusard and teacher at the École des hautes études sociales, he was a very active figure in the academic world. He acted as secretary to the university council, and as assessor for the dean of the faculty of letters from 1910 to 1913. After the First World War, he became director of the École normale supérieure.

24 The rector's official title was 'deputy rector'; in keeping with an 'old tradition', the minister for public instruction was regarded as the rector of the University of Paris, even though he had no rectoral role.

25 Académie de Paris, *Rapport au ministre de l'instruction publique sur la situation de l'enseignement supérieur, 1905–1906*. Melun: Édition administrative, 1907, p. xxxiii.

26 René Worms's lecture course, 'The individual social sciences and general sociology', at the faculty of law was a case in point. As was usual in such cases, it wasn't Worms's authorization to teach that was discussed by the council, and Durkheim never raised any objections.

27 The council read the charges, called in and interviewed the student who had been charged, and then discussed the case. Durkheim intervened during a disciplinary hearing in which a medical student was accused of stealing a microscope. The student claimed that he had 'acted without thinking'. Durkheim asked him how many days had lapsed between the theft and its discovery. 'One day', replied the student, who pointed out that he had confessed to his crime the day after it was discovered. The council ruled that he should be excluded from all the university's schools and faculties for a period of two years (minutes of a meeting of 28 February 1911; Conseil de l'Université de Paris, Archives nationales, AJ/16/2589).

28 Minutes of a meeting of 11 July 1910; Conseil de l'Université de Paris, Archives nationales, AF16 2588. One of the 19 grants of 3,000 francs (three of which went to women) was awarded to his collaborator Maurice Halbwachs, who was teaching philosophy at the lycée in Toulouse.

29 Minutes of a meeting of 22 December 1911; Conseil de l'Université de Paris, Archives nationales AJ 16 2589.

30 A graduate of the École normale supérieure and an *agrégé de philosophie*, Victor Delbos (1862–1916) taught at Henri-IV and Louis-le-Grand before becoming a *maître de conférences* at the Sorbonne in 1902. He became a professor of philosophy and psychology in 1909. His doctoral thesis was on the development of Kant's practical philosophy. He became a Spinoza specialist: *Le Spinozisme*, his lecture notes, were published in 1916.

31 Paul Fauconnet, letter to Marcel Mauss, 19 December 1911; Fond Hubert-Mauss, IMEC-Caen.

32 Marcel Mauss, letter to Henri Hubert, 15 October 1912; Fonds Hubert-Mauss, IMEC-Caen.

33 Rosine Mauss, letter to Marcel Mauss, December 1912, Épinal.

34 She inherited 701,747 francs on 31 March 1911, and 194,571 francs on 18 May. Most of this money was invested in stocks and shares: Banque française pour le commerce et l'industrie, Usines métallurigiques de la Basse-Loire, Compagnie des chemins de fer andalous, Compagnie des chemins de fer du Sud de l'Espagne, and Beers Consolidated Mines Limited, etc.

35 It was only late in the day that Hubert told his friend Marcel that he was marrying Alma Schierenberg (1880–1924), a young woman from Wiesbaden in Germany: 'I have always

wanted to get married . . . I can't forgive myself for waiting so long to tell you. Blame *L'Année sociologique.*' He said nothing to Durkheim. The latter remarked [to Mauss]: 'It is only thanks to you that I hear that Hubert is getting married. It was the same when he became engaged. I don't even know the date of the wedding' (letter to Marcel Mauss, 20 August 1910, Hôtel du Mont-Blanc; Durkheim 1998: 392).

36 René Verneau (b. 1852) was a doctor who studied under Broca and Quatrefages. In 1909, he became professor of anthropology at the Musée d'histoire naturelle.

37 Durkheim met the young man, who made a 'good impression' on him. He was pleased to hear that the manuscript was already with the typesetter, and suggested that it should be entitled *Contribution à l'étude de la mythologie héroïque* or *Recherche sur les conditions sociales d'un mythe héroïque*; letter to Henri Hubert, *Revue française de sociologie* (1987): 532. The book was not published until 1919, and was finally entitled *Le Culte des héros et ses conditions sociales. Saint Patrick, héro national de l'Irlande*, with a major preface by Hubert.

38 In 1932, François Simiand was elected to the Collège de France, where he succeeded his old friend Georges Renard as professor of labour history.

39 Paul Fauconnet, letter to Dominique Parodi, 2 January 1911, Toulouse; *Bulletin d'études durkheimiennes*: 2.

40 When Gustave Belot gave Rauh's work a somewhat poor rating, David, Davy and Hertz (together with H. Daudin, R. Hubert, R. Le Senne and H. Wallon) wrote to the director of the *Revue philosophique* (vol. 74, October 1912: 319) to challenge his assessment, point out that Rauh had the ability to stimulate his students' intellectual curiosity, to give them a taste for research and to encourage their interest in ideas.

41 Davy taught at the Institut français in London in 191–14. His university career began in Dijon in 1919, and he later became dean of the faculty of letters there. That was the beginning of a distinguished administrative career: Rector of the Académie de Rennes (1930), Inspecteur Général de l'Instruction publique dans l'enseignement secondaire, rector of the Académie de Lyon (1944). He ended his career as professor of sociology and dean of the faculty of letters in Paris (Condette 2006: 133–4).

42 After the First World War, Gernet began his university career in Algiers, where he was appointed *chargé de cours* in 1921. In 1938, he became dean of the faculty of letters, and in 1946 he was appointed director of the EPHE's sixth section.

43 He coedited 'sociological conditions of knowledge' with Bouglé; 'the totem system' with Mauss; 'juridical systems in societies that are not differentiated on the basis of totem clans' and 'domestic and matrimonial organization' with Bouglé and Davy; 'organization of secondary groups' (castes, districts and urban groups) with Reynier; 'procedure' with Fauconnet; 'international morality' with Bouglé; 'criminality by country' with Ray; and 'suicide' with Davy.

44 When more fascicules were published in 1912, Mauss reviewed them on his own (Mauss 1969[1913]). He thanked the author for 'making available what is already a considerable amount of documentation', and especially the 'precious collection of 1500 verses that make up a sort of Australian Rig Veda'.

45 'Systèmes religieux des sociétés inférieures', *L'Année sociologique* 10 (1910): 75–6. This short text is unsigned.

46 In the next volume of the *Année* Durkheim and Mauss introduced a new subsection – 'Systèmes religieux primitifs décomposés' [breakdown of primitive religious systems] to take account of the specificity of 'decayed religions' and 'degenerate societies'. It is useful to study these states of degeneracy in themselves and for themselves. The introduction of a new rubric seemed all the more essential in that 'religious systems that are decaying have sometimes been seen as primitive and simply systems'. A special rubric devoted to the legal systems of decayed societies was then introduced. Hence the new interest in the process of 'social regression.'

47 Letter to Robert Michels, 9 March 1911; *Durkheimian Studies/Études durkheimiennes* 11 (November 1985): 6.

48 Bouglé found it unfortunate that the many anecdotes to be found in Michels's book were all borrowed from *Sozialdemokratie*, which thus became 'a scapegoat'. Hence the 'rather narrow' focus. He is more interested in a 'psychology of the German people

rather than in a sociology of parties'. Bouglé was not convinced that Michels's conclusions also applied to other countries, and found his book 'incomplete'.

49 Émile Durkheim, letter to Robert Michels, 27 September 1910; *Durkheimian Studies/ Études durkheimiennes* 11 (November 1985): 6.

50 Michels was born in Cologne in 1876, and had an academic background. He had studied at the universities of Leipzig, Munich and Paris. His doctorate in history (1900) was on Louis XIV's invasion of Holland. His political ideas meant that he could not find a position in a German university: between 1903 and 1907, he was active in the Italian Socialist Party, the SPD and the Socialist International. His French friends included Hubert Lagardelle, with whom he attended the 1911 Stuttgart Congress (according to Célestin Bouglé, who 'truly thought' that he had glimpsed him' there). Bouglé, letter to Robert Michels, 23 January 1911; *Durkheimian Studies/Études durkheimiennes* 11 (November 1985): 10.

51 Letter to Célestin Bouglé, 13 October 1912; Durkheim 1975: ii/438.

52 There were in fact two separate discussions. The first was chaired by Paul Desjardins, who argued that there was a need for new schools because 'the modern French family is unfitted to the task of bringing up its children'. Durkheim replied that it was 'an exaggeration to speak of the modern family in such terms'. He was 'the first to deplore the fact that the notion of authority has become more lax in the family and at school'. He concluded: 'It should not be forgotten that in the older generation discipline was excessively harsh . . . There is no proof that the family is appreciably inferior to what it was formerly. It is merely different' (Durkheim 1979[1912]: 156).

The second discussion was about boarding schools. Desjardins was of the opinion that education should be removed from 'the hectic bustle of towns'. He was presumably thinking of the example set by the École des roches. He was, on the other hand, unsure as to how the new boarding schools should be organized: should they be 'family' or 'scholastic' groupings? Durkheim replied to his 'friend' that it would appear that France was unable to do without boarding schools (1979[1912]: 156). Moving them to the country, on the other hand, was not a viable solution: 'It is well known what boarding schools in the country cost. They are accessible to only a minority of well-to-do children.' That could not be a general solution. Durkheim was not in favour of 'great boarding schools' on the grounds that they were 'unnatural'. A compromise solution should be found, 'but perhaps this is impossible' (ibid.).

53 Durkheim gives the example of the instinct of preservation, maternal instinct, paternal instinct and even the sexual instinct. 'These are drives in a given direction; but the means by which these drives are expressed vary from one individual to another, from one occasion to another. A large area remains reserved, then, for trial and error, for personal accommodations' (1956[1911]: 83). The movements we make when our life is in danger are not invariable: 'We adapt them to circumstances.'

23 The Origins of Religious Life

1 Durkheim's Russian translator was A.N. Ilyynski, and his editor was V.A. Bazarov – the pseudonym of Vladimir Rudnev (1874–1939), a philosopher and economist who started out as a Bolshevik but then took the side of the 'revisionists'. Bazarov thought highly of the work of Durkheim, who was already known to the Russian public as 'one of today's most eminent sociologists'. He was praised for his talent and his enormous erudition. In 1898, Nikolaï Russanov, who had studied with Durkheim in Bordeaux, had reviewed *Suicide* in the 'Lettres de France' column he wrote for the journal *Rousskoie bogatstvo*. Although Russanov was critical of Durkheim's suggested remedy for the anomie of modern society (giving occupational groups a bigger role), his very detailed review was, on the whole, positive. The Russian edition of *Suicide* is in Lenin's personal library, now in the Kremlin. See Manicke-Gyöngyosi 1984.

2 In June 1911, Gaston Richard published a series of articles entitled 'Sociologie et métaphysique' in the Protestant journal *Foi et vie*. Twenty years later, he published an article on 'Durkheim's pathology' (Richard 1930). In a letter to an unidentified correspondent,

Richard called into question the intellectual honesty of Durkheim and his collaborators: 'In the course of my study of the religious ideas of the Greek tragedians, I discovered that Durkheim & Co simply appropriated the Englishman Marett's thesis about *mana*. That is a way of winning glory without too much difficulty' (Gaston Richard, letter to 'Cher collègue et ami', 21 October 1934; Dossier Gaston Richard, vol. 111–230, Archives départementales de la Gironde).

3 In the *Revue philosophique*, G.-L. Duprat (1912), congratulated Gaston Richard, whom he described as an 'eminent sociologist', on developing a sociology that 'respected the rights of other sciences', that had 'a limited field with well defined laws', and that tried to 'reconcile a tolerant idealism with an honest positivism'.

4 *Revue de métaphysique et de morale* (September supplement 1911): 11.

5 Letter to Lucien Lévy-Bruhl, 18 August 1909; cited in Davy 1973: 319–20.

6 Boas described primitive mentality as displaying little power to inhibit, little capacity for attention, a lack of originality and a lower standard of spoken language. His conclusion astonished Durkheim, who pointed to the inhibiting function of taboos, the complexity of the organization of primitive societies and the originality of their myths. He found his American colleague's analysis 'summary and unsatisfactory': 'Deduction and dialectics take up more room than the observation of the facts.'

7 Rivaud also claims that Lévy-Bruhl 'never changed his opinions, which were much more nuanced and sophisticated that those of the orthodox Durkheimians'.

8 On the parallels between Freud and Durkheim, see Friedland 2005.

9 The French subtitle is 'Interprétation par la psychanalyse de la vie sociale des peuples primitifs'.

10 See Roudinesco 2000. Freud had great admiration for Robertson Smith who, in his *Religion of the Semites*, puts forward the hypothesis that the curious ceremony known as the totemic meal was, from the very beginning, an integral part of the totemic system.

11 Freud also refers to Hubert and Mauss's 'Esquisse d'une théorie générale de la magie'; he likes the idea that magic has to do with 'technique' rather than 'pure speculative curiosity' (1989[1913]: 97).

12 Paul Fauconnet, undated letter to Marcel Mauss; Fonds Hubert-Mauss, IMEC-Caen.

13 When Durkheim tackled the question of relations between the family and religion, which was 'quite difficult at the time', Mauss built some cubes for him: 'each side situated the kinsman or relative by marriage in terms of their position in matrimonial law. The cubes thus represented exchanges and reciprocal relations between the groups.'

14 Letter to Georges Davy, 13 September 1991; in Davy 1973: 301.

15 The first chapter ('Definition of religious phenomena and of religion') is a 'new version' of the paper published in the *Année sociologique*. Durkheim introduces various modifications concerning the definition of religion, but adds that 'they do not, however, involve any fundamental change in the conceptualization of the facts' (1995[1912]: 21 n1).

16 When, on the other hand, the natives were asked by Strehlow to explain the point of their ceremonies, they replied that 'the ancestors have so instituted things', a response that convinced Durkheim (Durkheim 1995[1912]: 375).

17 He refers to the work of Lang (1791), MacLennan (1869), Lewis Morgan (1877), Fison and Howitt 91880), Powell, Smith and Dorsey (Bureau of American Ethnology), Frazer (1887 and 1890) and Robertson Smith, not forgetting that of other American researchers such as Boas, Cushing Krause and Stevenson.

18 Durkheim's answer to the question 'which comes first, magic or religion?' is very different from Frazer's. According to Frazer, magic is 'a primary datum', of which 'religion is a derivative'; Durkheim holds that, on the contrary, 'the faith men have in magic is only a special case of religious belief in general' and 'the product, or at least the indirect product, of a collective effervescence'. Durkheim is at pains to point out that the results of his analysis 'strongly resemble and confirm those attained by MM. Hubert and Mauss'. Behind what appears to be a 'crude industry, based on crude science', they bring to light 'a whole background of religious conceptions . . . a whole world of forces, the idea of which magic took from religion' (1995[1912]: 366–7).

19 Durkheim discusses the 'exogamy' section of Frazer's book separately, but is just as

critical because he rejects the widespread view that there is a link between exogamy and totemism.

20 Durkheim returns to the importance of the individual factor in a footnote: 'Even if the essential element of personality is that which is social in us from another standpoint, there can be no social life unless distinct individuals are associated within it, and the more numerous and different they are, the richer it is' (1995[1912]: 275 n128).

21 Durkheim adds that 'such restrictions are not peculiar to the Hebrews: in various forms, they are found in numerous religions' (1995[1912]: 32).

22 'Notably in sexual matters', Durkheim adds in a footnote (1995[1912]: 386 n82). The state of effervescence, the frenzy and the sexual licence are all signs of our nervous over-excitement, but should not be seen as having any specific ritual meaning. They are 'merely discharges of activity' and 'simply arise from the state of overexcitement provoked by the ceremony'.

23 The ambiguity arises, according to Durkheim, because there are both benevolent religious forces (which inspire respect, love and gratitude) and evil and impure forces (which inspire fear) that invoke the idea of impurity. The whole of religious life thus gravitates around two very different poles: pure and impure, holy and sacrilegious, the divine and the diabolical. But although opposite to one another, these two aspects of religious life are also closely akin: 'A simple change in external circumstances' can change everything: 'The pure is made from the impure, and vice versa' (1995[1912]: 415). The sacred is ambiguous because 'the two poles of the religious life correspond to the two opposite states through which all social life passes'. Extreme dejection gives way to high-spiritedness, painful anger to ecstatic enthusiasm. The propitiously sacred and the unpropitiously sacred are what collective well-being is to ill-being (ibid.: 417).

24 Durkheim analyses the other occasions men have for 'wailing and lamentation' (1995[1912]: 406), such as the loss of a 'religious treasure' (the *Churinga* of the Arantas), the distress in which society finds itself after an inadequate harvest, or events that seem to threaten the existence of the group (the southern lights). The group reacts with groans, cries, mutilations, great excitement, and a real state of frenzy or even sexual licence. Such things are, remarks Durkheim, 'instructive': the rites are efficacious because they are collective and 'raise the vital tone' (ibid.: 408).

25 In a footnote, Durkheim adds: 'In all probability, the concepts of totality, society and deity are at bottom merely different aspects of the same notion' (1995[1912]: 443 n18).

26 Undated letter to Marcel Mauss, July 1912; Archives Pierre Mauss.

27 Henri Hubert, letter to Marcel Mauss, 4 July 1912; Fonds Hubert-Mauss, IMEC-Caen.

28 Letter to Célestin Bouglé, 20 July 1912; *Revue française de sociologie* 17 (1976): 179–80. Bouglé introduced some qualifications. Referring to 'the exalting meetings in which collective enthusiasms are forged', he noted that, in *The Elementary Forms*, Durkheim had indicated that their day was surely not over and that they still had a role to play when societies felt the need to buckle down to some major reorganization. He went on: '[Durkheim] is obviously thinking of socialism as a regenerative faith.' The fact that Durkheim described socialism as a faith, and not as a science or as a fully fledged social science would, he noted, 'annoy certain believers in historical materialism who discover in that doctrine the complete, perfect sociological system' (Bouglé 1938: 34).

29 Review of *Les Formes Élémentaires de la vie religieuse*, *Revue de métaphysique et de morale* (March 1903 supplement): 1–3.

30 In Belot's view, the activities that may have given birth to science included hunting, cookery and various technical and commercial activities.

31 We can, so to speak, be said to be 'schizophrenic': 'We can never agree with ourselves.' We are condemned to 'live divided against ourselves', 'all sorts of friction and conflict', 'a contradictory monster that can never be quite satisfied with itself' (Durkheim 1975[1913]: 32). This antagonism is, Durkheim points out, no more than one instance of the dichotomy that is basic to both religious thought and practice: soul/body, senses/reason, selfish appetites/moral will, profane/sacred, etc.

32 As the function of religious forces is to act upon minds, they must emanate from consciousnesses: 'Only consciousnesses can act upon consciousnesses . . . And the only consciousnesses that are greater than the consciousness of the individual are those of

groups.' He continues: 'Society is therefore the pre-eminent source of the moral life that sustains the moral life of individuals', and it is society that has the dynamogenic action of religion (1975[1913]: 28).

33 Respect for his own methodological rules means that Durkheim must (1) regard religions as historical phenomena, or as 'human institutions' that are born, that mature and that die, and (2) refuse to restrict the argument to the way believers perceive their religion: 'Any science must be based upon the rationality of the things it sets out to study.'

34 Delacroix (1872–1937) was an *agrégé de philosophie* and a colleague of Durkheim's at the Sorbonne. He had an interest in psychology, but later published a book entitled *La Religion et la foi* (1922). Alphonse Darlu (1849–1921) taught in Périgueux, Angoulême and Bordeaux before being appointed a professor of philosophy at the Lycée Condorcet, where he taught, amongst others, Xavier Léon, Élie Halévy and Leon Brunschwicg. He also taught at the École normale supérieure in Fontenay-aux-Roses, and became inspector-general of public education. Jules Lachelier (1832–1918) was an *agrégé de philosophie* and *maître de conférences* at the École normale supérieure (1879–1900) and an inspector-general of education in the Seine *département*; he is regarded as one of those responsible for the reform of philosophy teaching. Édouard Le Roy (1870–1954), *agrégé de mathématiques*, *docteur ès sciences* and *docteur ès lettres*, taught mathematics in several lycées, including at Versailles and Saint-Louis. He was Henri Bergon's replacement at the Collège de France in 1914; his *La Philosophie nouvelle* (1913) is a study of Bergson. He took an interest in the question of religion, publishing *Études de philosophie et de critique religieuse. Dogme et critique* in 1907. He returned to the same subject in *Le Problème de Dieu* (1929). He was said to be a practising and militant Catholic.

35 It was only after the debate that Durkheim received comments from Laberthonnière, who refused to accept that primitive religions were religions in the true sense of the word. Durkheim feared that be had not made himself understood: the 'real explanation' for primitive cults lay not in physical coercion (which 'is purely imaginary') but in moral goals. The sacred is all-important. If there was a difference between Christians and primitive peoples, it was that the former had a 'clear awareness' of the moral role of religion, and the latter 'a more obscure sense' of it.

Durkheim's analysis of the individual's 'spontaneous gift' of himself to the group (in, for instance, great outbursts of collective enthusiasm) was, in Laberthonnière's view, 'very contemptuous'. Durkheim replied: 'They are not to be despised. It is to them that we owe the great collective ideals by which humanity lives.' He added: 'These are joyful outbursts.' Laberthonnière was not wrong to say that the individuals who were carried away by these moments of effervescence were 'intoxicated'. Taken in themselves 'these psychic states are 'truly pathological or very close to being pathological states'. But none of this was 'humiliating for religion', as religious life, like social life, 'does violence when it is intense'.

36 Goblet d'Alviella was a contributor to the *Revue d'histoire des religions.* While he acknowledged pointing out that Durkheim had been interested in the sociology of religion for more than 25 years, d'Alviella described him as 'the unchallenged leader, or at least the instigator', of the neo-sociological school, which some described as 'the theology of the New Sorbonne', and emphasized the collective nature of his 'undertaking'.

37 Henri Hubert, who was 'touched' by Reinach's admiration for Durkheim, still argued that Durkheim was right and that Reinach, who was his superior, was wrong (Hubert 1913: 80–81).

38 He described his own theory as 'classificatory and kinship-based, territorialist and therefore social'.

39 Colleagues say that the only books he took with him on his field trip to the Andaman Islands in 1906–8 were his volumes of the *Année sociologique*. See Stocking 1995: 307.

40 Alfred Radcliffe-Brown, letter to Marcel Mauss, 6 August 1912, Birmingham; *Durkheimian Studies/Études durkheimiennes* 4 (December 1979): 2–7. At the time, Radliffe-Brown was writing what was to have been a book on the pre-totemic civilization of the Andaman islanders, in which he planned to adopt an evolutionist perspective.

He never completed it. Twenty years later, he once more explained why he disagreed with Durkheim: 'I found his deduction of tribal religion from clan religion too rigid' (Letter to Marcel Mauss, 14 February 1930; *Durkheimian Studies/Études durkheimiennes* 10 (October 1984): 9.

41 James Leuba was a professor at Bryn Mawr College and had just published *A Psychologist Study of Religion*. An extract appeared in the *Revue philosophique* in October 1912 under the title 'La Religion comme type de conduite rationnelle'; the book was later translated into French.

42 Letter to Marcel Mauss, 9 May 1915; Durkheim 1998: 461. The book was published in London (Allen and Unwin) and New York (Macmillan).

43 Alexander Goldenweiser, letter addressed to 'Dear Sir' (P.W. Schmidt), 31 December 1912, New York; cited in Van Gennep 1916: 298. The plan was to ask scholars who were 'interested in totemism' and who were 'at the moment involved in totemic research' to set out in fairly brief articles (1) their interpretation of totemism, and (2) their conception of the totemic problem. The French scholars identified by Goldenweiser were Durkheim, Hubert, Mauss and Van Gennep. Schmidt, who was very much in favour of this, said that he was 'available for the project' and sent a circular letter (dated 20 February 1913) to several possible contributors. For France and Belgium, he added the names of Foucart, Le Roy and Trilles to the list. The other scholars approached were J.W. Frazer, N.W. Thomas and Sir Laurence Gomme (Britain), F. Graebner, R. Thurnwald, P. Ehrenreich (Germany) and Hill-Tout and J.N.E. Hewitt (United States).

44 The 1910 article appeared in the *Journal of American Folk-Lore*. In 1918, Alexander Goldenweiser published his reply to his colleague Boas in the *American Anthropologist* ('Form and content in totemism').

24 A Lecture Course, the Last *Année* and the End of an Era: Pragmatism.

1   Undated letter to Marcel Mauss, July or August 1912; Durkheim 1998: 394.

2   Marcel Mauss, letter to Henri Hubert, 15 October 1912; Fonds Hubert-Mauss, IMEC-Caen.

3   Undated letter to Marcel Mauss, July or August 1912; Durkheim 1998: 394.

4   André Durkheim, letter to Marcel Mauss, 7 July 1912; Fonds Hubert-Mauss, IMEC-Caen.

5   Decree of 10 July 1912, signed by director of higher education Bayet; Dossier Durkheim AJ_{16} 214, Archives nationales.

6   Letter to Célestin Bouglé, 13 October 1912; Durkheim 1975: ii/438.

7   Letter to Marcel Mauss, August 1912; Durkheim 1998: 396

8   Undated letter to Marcel Mauss, August 1912, Hôtel Segnes, Waldhaus-Flims, Grisons; Durkheim 1998: 531

9   Letter to Célestin Bouglé, 13 October 1912; Durkheim 1975: ii/438.

10 As the editor of the *Année sociologique* collection (Alcan), Durkheim had to oversee the books it published. He was very surprised to learn that Stefan Czarnowski's *Le Culte des héros et ses conditions sociales. Saint Patrick, héros national de l'Irlande* had been printed even though the publisher had given him no warning. 'Lisbonne should have spoken to me before printing it; that is what our contract stipulates.' Durkheim had received proofs from Henri Hubert, but he had 'not yet had time' to read them. If there was one thing that worried him, it was the title: 'I'd thought of something like *Contribution à l'étude de la mythologique héroïque* or *Recherche sur les conditions sociales d'un mythe héroïque*, or something along those lines.' Hubert, who was on holiday at his parents-in-laws' in Wiesbaden, suggested *Recherches sur les conditions sociales du culte des héros. Saint Patrick héros national de l'Irlande*, which seemed 'very good' to Durkheim.

11 Marcel Mauss, *Rapport de mission au ministre* n.d. (1913); Fonds Hubert-Mauss, IMEC-Caen.

12 They included Marius Barbeau in Canada, Claude Maître in Indonesia, and René Maunier in Egypt. His pupil Henri Beuchat, together with the New Zealander Diamond Jenness, was a member of the first great scientific expedition to the Arctic, which was

led by N.U. Stefanson. Beuchat's role was to study the language, customs and religious beliefs of the Eskimo populations. During the early stages of the expedition, the trawler 'Karkluck' was shipwrecked, and Beuchat died of cold and hunger on an island. Marius Barbeau had just completed his Oxford thesis, entitled 'The totemic system of north western tribes of North America' (1910) under the supervision on R.R. Marett. While he pursued his studies in Oxford, he went to Paris to attend Mauss's lectures. On his return to Canada, he became one of the first members of the anthropological team headed by Edward Sapir.

13 Émile Durkheim, letter to Henri Hubert, 16 September 1912, Meudon; *Revue française de sociologie* (1987): 531. Mauss met Rivers and Haddon in Cambridge, Marett in Oxford and Seligman in London. Haddon, Rives and Seligman had all been members of the famous Cambridge Torres Straits Expedition.

14 Durkheim chaired the session of 17 June 1914 in his capacity as vice-chairman of the committee. The question was also raised the following year (*Bulletin du Comité des travaux historiques et scientifiques*, 1913–1914–1915, É. Le Roux, p. 60).

15 Roussel (1881–1945) was born in Nancy and was educated at the lycée there and at Henri-IV before studying at the faculty of letters in Nancy and taking a *licence ès lettres*. He then attended the École normale supérieure and became an *agrégé ès lettres* (1904) before becoming a member of the École française d'Athènes in 1905. Between 1906 and 1912, he was involved in archaeological excavations at Delos, and edited *Inscriptiones Graecae* in 1913. After being awarded his doctorate for *Les Cultes égyptiens à Delos* in 1918, he taught Greek language and literature at the faculty of letters in Bordeaux.

Henri Jeanmaire (1884–1960) was born in Paris and was an *agrégé d'histoire* (1909). He taught history in a secondary school in Besançon. In 1911, he made a study trip to Leipzig and in 1913, was preparing to submit a dissertation of Greek philology at the École pratique. His field of study was Greek religion, and involved comparisons with so-called primitive societies in Black Africa.

Jean Marx (1884–1974) had recently passed the *agrégation* (in law), in 1912. After the war, he pursued an academic career in that subject. Edmond Laskine (1890–1943) was born in Paris, and was educated at the Lycée Condorcet before attending the École Normale Supérieure (1908). He passed the philosophy *agrégation* in 1911.

16 Robert Hertz, letter to Pierre Roussel, 4 June 1910, Paris; *Durkheimian Studies/Études durkheimiennes* 5 (1999): 56. Hertz and Roussel were both socialists and had frequented the Société nouvelle de librairie.

17 Demangeon (1872–1940) was a *normalien* (1892) and *agrégé d'histoire*. He began his career teaching in secondary schools, defended his doctoral thesis on *La Picardie et les régions voisines* in 1905, and began his university career in Lille. He was coauthor of a *Dictionnaire de géographie* (1907).

18 Undated letter to Marcel Mauss, 13 May 1913; Durkheim 1998: 397.

19 Durkheim and Mauss give several examples of civilizations that transcend political frontiers: Christian, Mediterranean, North-American (the Tlinkit, the Tsimshian and the Haida).

20 Maurice Halbwachs wrote at length on Sombart's *Die Juden und das Wirtschaftsleben* (1911), describing it as a major book that brought together 'an abundant collection of detailed and suggestive facts', and dealt with the important subject of the economic role played by Jews over the previous 300 years (Halbwachs 1913b). Halbwachs summed up Sombart's central argument that historical conditions had made them the 'true creators of capitalism'. Those conditions obviously included the diaspora, their status as outsiders, their loss of rights and also their religious beliefs. Halbwachs's answer to the question 'Is religion alone enough to explain the "mental nature" of the Jew?' was: 'There are no grounds for asserting that their religion, as opposed to the economic conditions in which they found themselves, explains their role as the creators of the capitalist system.'

21 Halbwachs (1913a) was critical of Schumpeter's *Theorie der wirtschaftlichen Entwicklung* (1912). He attacked the author for placing all the emphasis on economic factors, and for adopting an abstract and ahistorical perspective based upon a conception of 'a static society that was in equilibrium.' In 1914, Schumpeter published a critical review of Simiand's *La Méthode positive en sciences économiques.* He began by praising the work

of 'the group of sociologists in Paris' who, gathered around the *Année sociologique*, had produced 'so many excellent things', but he went on to criticize what he saw as their errors: a 'rather puerile narrow-mindedness' that led them to regard their method as the only possible method, and their 'total lack of even an elementary knowledge' of anything outside their own field of research (Schumpeter 1996[1914]).

22 Henri was the son of Lucien.

23 Langlois's dream was to assemble a collection of 50,000 phonographic recordings of the dialects spoken in more than 10,000 villages. The first 'trial' was to begin in the Ardennes, with the financial support of the university. Short speeches by professors at the university, including Durkheim, were also being recorded

24 Rosine Mauss, letter to Marcel Mauss, 16 February 1913, Épinal; Archives personnelles Pierre Mauss.

25 Rosine Mauss, letter to Marcel Mauss, 2 March 1904; Archives personnelles Pierre Mauss. Marcel Mauss, like his uncle, had little patience with family and ritual obligations. 'There is not much point to this whole system', he told his friend Hubert (undated letter). His attitude annoyed his mother: 'I prefer to admit that I do not like having you here for the festivals. I do not wish to be offended or embarrassed because I want to keep to our old traditions . . . I cling to them mainly because I am too old to change, but also because you have no suggestions as to what should replace them' (letter to Marcel Mauss, 3 March 1899, Épinal).

26 The shares and debentures were worth more than 50,000 francs, and were in the Gouvernement d'Indochine, Société foncière, Ateliers et chantiers de la Loire, Chemins de fer fédéraux de Suisse and other companies; Formule de déclaration de mutation par décès, département de la Seine, 1er bureau des successions, no. 118, 17 May 1918.

27 Halbwachs had been divorced for some years, and remarried on 18 May 1913. His wife Yvonne (born 1889) was the daughter of Victor Basch, an *agrégé d'allemand*, *docteur ès lettres* and professor of German language and literature at the Sorbonne. The politically active Basch (a militant Dreyfusard, founding member of the Ligue des droits de l'homme and member of the Socialist Party) had recently published two books: *La Philosophie allemande au XIXe siècle* (with Charles Andler and Célestin Bouglé) and *Neutralité et monopole de l'enseignement* (with Léon Blum, Alfred Croiset, Gustave Lanson, Dominique Parodi and Salomon Reinach). Halbwachs and his wife had two children: Francis (born in Tours in 1914) and Pierre (born in Paris in 1916).

28 'Thèses de doctorat', *Revue de métaphysique et de morale* (September 1913 supplement): 19–23. See Topolov 1999.

29 Letter to Monsieur le Directeur (Charles Bayet), 13 June 1913; *Revue française de sociologie* 20 (1997): 116.

30 Henri Hubert, letter to Marcel Mauss, 13 May 1913; Fonds Hubert-Mauss, IMEC-Caen.

31 Émile Durkheim, letter to Georges Davy, 27 April 1913; Davy 1973: 303. Davy was appointed to teach philosophy at the lycée in Chaumont in 1909, but did not take up his post until 1912. Between 1909 and 1912, he was an intern at the Fondation Thiers, and made several visits to Germany

32 Minutes of the meeting of 30 June 1913, Conseil de l'Université de Paris; Archives nationales, AJ/16/2589.

33 James's *A Pluralistic Universe, Pragmatism* and *The Meaning of Truth* were translated into French in 1910, 1911 and 1913 respectively. Durkheim noted that the title *A Pluralistic Universe* was 'somewhat inappropriately' translated as *Philosophie de l'expérience*.

34 When Tarde died in 1904, Henri Bergson was elected to his chair at the Collège de France. It was Bergson who unveiled the monument to Tarde in Sarlat; in his address, he described him as a thinker who had succeeded in transcending disciplinary boundaries, and who had elaborated both a truly psychological sociology and a sociology that was capable of ripening into a psychology.

35 This was the title of the study Édouard Le Roy published with Alcan in 1912. In 1912–13, Le Roy replaced Bergson at the Collège de France.

36 Henri Bergson, letter to William James, 15 February 1905; cited in Azouvi 2007: 148.

37 Bergson added: 'Allow me to say that the book really does not need a preface by me. James's fame is universal': letter to Gustave Le Bon, 31 August 1908; cited in Marpeau 2000: 208. The sixth section of James's book is devoted to Bergson and his critique of intellectualism.

38 As he explained in his lectures on pragmatism, Durkheim liked James's notion that religion suggests that there is something greater than us, that there is a force that transcends us. He also appreciated him because 'James tries to prove, not that God exists, but that belief in the divine can be reconciled with "the results of natural science"' (1983[1955]: 62). He also gave him credit for refusing to prove the existence of God and recognizing that a belief in God was incompatible with the scientific data.

39 A graduate of École normale supérieure (sciences section), Joseph Wilbois was the son-in-law of Edmond Demolins, and author of a monograph entitled *L'Avenir de l'église russe* (2nd edition 1907). Bouglé reviewed his *Devoir et durée* in volume XI of the *Année sociologique*. He congratulated Wilbois on having avoided 'Tarde's indeterminism' and on arguing that inventiveness should be seen as a 'collective project that is within sociology's remit'. He was, on the other hand, astonished to see Wilbois describing the *Année*'s collaborators as 'spiritualist psychologists'. 'The criticism should be qualified, as it is novel.'

40 A number of questions were submitted to Durkheim, and he gave written replies that were published in the collective *Le Sentiment religieux à l'heure actuelle* (Paris: Vrin 1919). Was it legitimate to seek the essential elements of religious life in its most rudimentary forms? Was it possible to find in the collective consciousness all the elements of the religious consciousness of the great initiators of that time, for example Jesus? Would it not be desirable to study the social phenomena caused by the action of an allegedly superior religion like Christianity on the collective consciousness of a pagan tribe or people? Durkheim referred his questioners to his book for a justification of his research methods (the decision to study a very simple religion, and to study Australians). He also recognized the importance and interest of extending the sociology of religion to include the study of 'great religious personalities' ('a problem which has never been methodically studied') and of the impact of the great religions.

41 Durkheim makes it clear from the outset that sociology 'cannot, in reality, deal with . . . human groups without eventually touching on the individual who is the basic element of which these groups are composed' (1964[1914]: 325). In order to make himself quite clear, he adds: 'Society can exist only if it penetrates the consciousness of individuals and fashions it in "its image and resemblance".'

42 Durkheim sums up this thesis in the following terms: 'The ego cannot be completely other than itself, for, if it were, it would vanish – this is what happens in ecstasy. On the other hand, however, the ego cannot be entirely and exclusively itself, for, if it were, it would be emptied of all content' (1960[1914]: 328).

43 Marie Durkheim and Jacques Halphen went on to have two more children: Étienne (born 1919) and Maurice (born 1923). Claude went on to study law, and Étienne studied business at the École supérieure de commerce de Paris.

44 Undated letter to Marcel Mauss, 21 June 1914; Durkheim 1998: 397. Louison was named after his grandmother Louise.

25 Unjustified Aggression

1 Letter to Jean-Jacques Salverda de Grave, 7 November 1914; *Durkheimian Studies/ Études durkheimiennes* 9 (November 1983): 2.

2 Durkheim said of Jaurès that 'He was not a thinker, but a force of nature with no sense of his own importance.' Recalling discussions with him, he went on: 'The strange thing is that, when you were talking to him about doctrines and ideas, he was judicious and showed a lot of common sense. That is what made him so charming to talk to' (letter to Marcel Mauss, 20 May 1916; Durkheim 1998: 524). Durkheim reacted badly to Lucien Lévy-Bruhl's obituary of Jaurès in the *Annuaire de l'École normale supérieure*, complaining that it was 'astonishingly dry, even if it is a little long' and that it said nothing about

the man himself. 'The subject [Jaurès] was difficult but a fine man. [Lévy-Bruhl] wanted to find in him a thinker who never existed.' When a Société des amis de Jaurès was established in June 1916, Émile Durkheim was invited to join the board. But when Lévy-Bruhl informed him that Jean Longuet was a member, he declined the invitation and, following a discussion with Renaudel, 'resigned himself to doing nothing' and said that he would not attend the meeting. 'It was the least I could do' (letter to Marcel Mauss, 7 June 196; Durkheim 1998: 525).

3 Marcel Sembat (1862–1922), a brilliant lawyer and a journalist on *L'Humanité*, was a socialist *député*. He had been a vocal critic of 'ministerialism' and had strongly opposed Millerand's decision to accept a post in Waldeck-Rousseau's government. Sembat was close to Marcel Mauss (who had also known Blum since his days on the Société nouvelle de librairie et d'édition), and had never made any secret of his admiration for the work of the *Année sociologique*'s collaborators (Henri Hubert, letter to Marcel Mauss, March 1916; Fonds Hubert-Maus, IMEC-Caen). See also Mauss 1997[1922].

4 Letter to Marcel Mauss, 6 September 1914, Guéthary; Durkheim 1998: 408.

5 Letter to Marcel Mauss, September 1914, Guéthary; Durkheim 1998: 410–11.

6 Bergson, speech of 8 August 1914 to the Académie des sciences morales et politiques; Bergson 1972: 1102.

7 Maurice Halwachs, letters to Yvonne Halwachs, 12 August 1914; Tours, 19 August 1914; Fonds Hubert-Mauss, IMEC-Caen.

8 Robert Hertz, letter to Alice Hertz, 28 November 1914. See also Hertz's letter of 5 December 1914 to P. Roussel (*Durkheimian Studies/Études durkheimiennes* 5 (1999): 57–8).

9 Émile Durkheim, letter to Rosine Mauss, 5 May 1915; Archives personnelles, Pierre Mauss.

10 Letter to Henri Hubert, 17 August 1914; *Revue française de sociologie* 28/3 (1987): 533.

11 Philippe de Felice to Henri Hubret, 10 March 1915; Fonds Hubert-Mauss, IMEC-Caen.

12 Letter to Yvonne Halbwachs, 11–12 August 1914; cited in Becker 2003: 39.

13 Letter to Marcel Mauss; Durkheim 1998: 423.

14 Émile Durkheim, letter to Jean-Jacques Salverda de Grave, 17 June 1915; *Durkheimian Studies/Études durkheimiennes* (November 1983): 6.

15 Letter to Xavier Léon, 15 September 1914; Durkheim 1975: ii/472.

16 Robert Hertz, letter to Maurice Halbwachs, 5 December 1914; Fonds Halbwachs-Mauss, IMEC-Caen.

17 Letter to Marcel Mauss, 18 September 1914, Guéthary; Durkheim 1998: 415.

18 Letter to Xavier Léon, 15 September 1914; Durkheim 1975: ii/470.

19 Letter to Xavier Léon, 2 October 1914: Durkheim 1975: ii/471.

20 Letter to Jean-Jacques Salverda de Grave, 4 November 1914; *Durkheimian Studies/Études durkheimiennes* 9 (November 1983): 2.

21 Letter to Marcel Mauss, 10 December 1915, Guéthary; Durkheim 1998: 494.

22 Marcel Mauss, undated letter to Henri Hubert; Fonds Hubert-Mauss, IMEC-Caen.

23 Sylvain Lévi, letter to Henri Hubert, 10 August 1914, Paris; Fond Hubert-Mauss, IMEC-Caen.

24 Letter from Sylvain and Daniel Lévi to Marcel Mauss, 31 December 1914; Fonds Hubert-Maus, IMEC-Caen.

25 Letter to Marcel Mauss, 17 September 1914, Guéthary; Durkheim 1998: 414.

26 Letter to Marcel Mauss, 26 September, Guéthary; Durkheim 1998: 418.

27 Letter to Marcel Mauss, 2 October 1914, Guéthary; Durkheim 1998: 420–1.

28 The cancellation of some courses created problems. In the autumn of 1915, for instance, it was proposed that the course of Hungarian language and literature be cancelled. At its meeting of 25 October, the council voted to cancel for the duration of the war for financial reasons. At the next meeting, Durkheim told his colleagues: 'If I had been in possession of the information I have since received on this issue, I would have cast my vote differently.' The council agreed to re-examine the issue at its next meeting. Durkheim then explained his position. He had believed that cancelling the course would save the university money, but this proved not to be the case. He had also believed that

the decision would not be prejudicial to the interests of Louis Eisenmann, who taught the course. That proved not to be the case: 'On the contrary, the decision would damage his interests as it would break his continuity of service. It is in M. Eisermann's interest to teach, or go on teaching, in higher education.' Why should his interests not be taken into account, given that he had done nothing blameworthy? The council voted to run the course, and Rector Liard concluded that 'the interests of M. Eisenmann coincide with the general interest' (minutes of the meeting of 11 December 1915, Conseil de l'Université de Paris, Archives nationales AJ$_{16}$2589). Born in Hagenau (Bas-Rhin) in 1867, Louis Eisenmann was Jewish, and an *agrégé en histoire* (1892) with a doctorate in law (1904). He had been teaching Hungarian language and literature in the faculty of letters since 1913 (Charle 1985: 75–6).

29 Letter to Xavier Léon, 30 October 1914; Durkheim 1975: ii/474.

30 The issue of special examinations for candidates in the class of 1916 (who could expect to be called up in April) was raised at the meeting of 18 December 1914. Some members of Council wanted 'overall measures' to be taken after the war, both in the public interest and out of concern for justice, while others refused to take hasty measures and argued that each 'class of conscripts' should be dealt with on a case-by-case basis. Durkheim pointed out that there were degree candidates in the class of 1916 who had, of their own free will, spent two years preparing for their exams and who were therefore in their second year of study. Could not liberal measures be introduced for all those who, referred or not, could prove that they had been in regular attendance for one year? (minutes of the meeting of 18 December 1914, Conseil de l'Université de Paris, Archives nationales, AJ$_{16}$2589).

31 Minutes of the meeting of 20 December 1915, Conseil de l'Université de Paris; Archives nationales, AJ$_{16}$ 2589.

32 Minutes of the meeting of 7 February 1916, Conseil de l'Université de Paris; Archives nationales, AJ$_{16}$2589.

33 Letter to Robert Michels, 9 January 1914; *Durkheimian Studies/Études durkheimiennes* 11 (November 1985): 6–7; See Borlandi's introduction: 'Letters from Durkheim, Halbwachs, Bouglé, G. Bourgin to Robert Michels (1909–1917)'.

34 The themes chosen by Halbwachs included democracy, demography, ethics, eugenics, *homo economicus* and class. His long and varied list of authors included Bergson, Bouglé, Boutroux, Comte, Espinas, Le Play, Jaurès, Lévy-Bruhl, Taine and, of course, Durkheim. He felt obliged to justify his decision to write on both Bergson and Durkheim: 'I know Bergson very well (he taught me for four years at my lycée and then at the École normale supérieure), and I obviously know Durkheim' (letter to Robert Michels, 5 December 1913, Tours; *Durkheimian Studies/Études durkheimiennes* 11 (November 1985): 9–19). Georges Bourgin, who knew Michels's work well and who went on to translate his *Le Prolétariat et la bourgeoisie dans le movement socialiste européen*, also agreed to contribute (letter to Robert Michels, 5 February 1914).

35 Letter to Robert Michels, 26 September 1914, Tours; *Durkheimian Studies/Études durkheimiennes* 11 (November 1985): 7. Durkheim also asked his colleague to tell him which of his colleagues in Paris 'did not have the same doubts', as he wanted to talk to them so as to 'explore their reasons', which he hoped, 'believe me', to find 'justified'.

36 Maurice Halbwachs, letter to Yvonne Halbwachs, 15 October 1914; Fonds Hubert-Halbwachs, IMEC-Caen.

37 Letter to Jean-Jacques Salverda de Grave, 7 November 1914; *Durkheimian Studies/Études durkheimiennes* 9 (November 1983): 2.

38 Minutes of a meeting of 28 October 1914, Conseil de l'Université de Paris; Archives nationales, AJ$_{16}$2589. The manifesto was signed by the following universities: Paris, Aix-Marseille, Algiers, Besançon, Bordeaux, Caen, Clermont, Dijon, Grenoble, Lyon, Montpellier, Nancy, Poitiers, Rennes and Toulouse. The University of Lille could not be consulted.

39 Gaston Bonnier, 'Actes du Conseil de l'Université et principaux événements intéressants à l'Université', *Rapport annuel 1909–10*: 41.

40 Minutes of the meeting of 26 April 1915, Conseil de l'Université de Paris; Archives nationales AJ[16] 2589. Durkheim also wrote to James Hyde, Morton Fullerton, Barnard

(president of the Harvard Club), Walter Berry and M. Gibbons (former professor at Princeton).

41 Durkheim's comments were based on a letter from Mr Wigmore, dean of the faculty of law at the University of Wisconsin, who had recently urged some of his colleagues to 'combine their efforts to give French science and French education the position it deserves in American public opinion'.

42 As well as organizing 'friendship meetings' for French and American students and teachers, the club could also provide accommodation for visiting teachers and students.

43 Letter to Marcel Mauss, 2 October 1914, Guéthary; Durkheim 1998: 419.

44 The membership included Jacques Hadamard, Émile Boutroux (Académie française), two professors from the Collège de France (Joseph Bédier and Henri Bergson) and several of Durkheim's colleagues at the Université de Paris: Charles Andler, Ernest Denis, Gustave Lanson and Charles Seignobos.

45 Letter to Marcel Mauss, 2 October 1914, Guéthary; Durkheim 1998: 420–1.

46 Letter to Marcel Mauss, 6 January 1915; Durkheim 1998: 428.

47 Letter to Marcel Mauss, 12 November 1914, Guéthary; Durkheim 1998: 422.

48 Letter to Marcel Mauss, 11 December 1914, Paris; Durkheim 1998: 424.

49 Joseph Bédier wrote two pamphlets (*Les Crimes allemands, d'après des témoignages allemands* and *Comment l'Allemagne essaie de justifier ses crimes*) and André Weiss wrote one entitled *La Violation de la neutralité belge et luxembourgeoise par l'Allemagne*. They were published by Armand Colin in 1915. Durkheim was very annoyed when he learned that the German press had found 'five or six inaccuracies' in Bédier's text: 'That gives the critics a toehold. They are saying that he forged the documents' (letter to Marcel Mauss, 16 March 1915, Paris; Durkheim 1998: 445).

50 Letter to Marcel Mauss, 21 February 1915, Paris; Durkheim 1998: 438.

51 Letter to Marcel Mauss, 16 March 1915, Paris; Durkheim 1998: 446.

52 Letter to Marcel Mauss, 28 March 1915; Durkheim 1998: 446.

53 Letter to Marcel Mauss, 5 April 1915, Paris; Durkheim 1998: 450.

54 The sequence of events, dates and times established by Denis and Durkheim was as follows: the Austrian ultimatum and the Serb response (23–25 July), the breaking off of diplomatic relations and the declaration of war on Serbia (25–28 July), Germany's first ultimatum to Russia (19–30 July), and the declaration of war on Russia and France (31 July – 3 August).

55 See also Bergson 1915a: 14ff.

56 Denis and Durkheim identified a number of reasons for his change of character: (1) the failure of imperial policy in Morocco; (2) the enhanced reputation of the Crown Prince; (3) the threat of disintegration of the Austro-Hungarian Empire; (4) the spirit of vengeance: the Archduke had been a personal friend; (5) the apparent weakness of other countries: the threat of civil war in Britain, the fact that Russia had been paralysed by major strikes, nationalist agitation and internal divisions in France.

57 Letter to Marcel Mauss, 13 January 1915, Paris; Durkheim 1998: 430. Heinrich von Treitschke was a historian, theoretician of pan-Germanism and the author of a major history of Germany in the nineteenth century.

58 Letter to Jean-Jacques Salverda de Grave, 31 March 1915; *Durkheimian Studies/Études durkheimiennes* 9 (November 1983): 5

59 Letter to Marcel Mauss, 17 April 1915; Durkheim 1998: 453.

60 Letter to Marcel Mauss, 17 June 1915; Durkheim 1998: 466.

61 Letter to Marcel Mauss, 17 June 1915; Durkheim 1998: 465.

62 Letter to Marcel Mauss, 17 June 1915; Durkheim 1998: 465. Charles Andler (1866–1933) was born in Alsace, and was the founder of the Ligue républicaine d'Alsace-Lorraine, which was charged with promoting French legislation in the annexed territories. He had the support of a number of academics from Alsace and Lorraine, including Sylvain Lévi, Lucien Lévy-Bruhl, Émile Durkheim and Marcel Mauss. In 1918, he helped the Ligue to published the monthly journal *L'Alsace républicaine*, and participated in the reorganization of the University of Strasbourg.

63 On the wartime mobilization of intellectuals, see Hanna 1994; Soulez (1989).

64 Élie Halévy, letter to Xavier Léon, 12 December 1918; cited in Prochasson and Rasmussen 1996: 185–6.
65 Letter to Lucien Lévy-Bruhl, 22 February 1915; see Merllié 1989. The other 18 'representatives' who responded included Wilhelm Wundt, Vilfredo Pareto and Lujo Brentano.
66 Letter to Xavier Léon; cited in Merllié 1989: 476.
67 Letter to Marcel Mauss, 11 April 1916; Durkheim 1998: 515.
68 *New York Tribune*, Sunday, 18 April 1915: 1.
69 Letter to Marcel Mauss, 24 March 1915; Durkheim 1998: 448.
70 Letter to Marcel Mauss, 100 February 1915; Durkheim 1998: 435.
71 Lucien Poincaré (1862–1920) was an *agrégé* (physics, 1887) and held a doctorate in the physical sciences (1890). He was the brother of president of the republic Raymond Poincaré and the first cousin of the world-famous mathematician Henri Poincaré. Appointed *chargé de cours* in physics at the Sorbonne in 1895, he soon took on administrative responsibilities as rector of the Académie de Chambéry and director of secondary education. He became vice-rector of the Académie de Paris in 1917.
72 Durkheim also cites the work of Mauss, Hubert, Bouglé, Simiand and Halbwachs. He briefly mentions that of Lévy-Bruhl, Letourneau, Dumont and Lapouge.
73 Letter from the Alliance israélite universelle to Cyrus Adler, American Jewish Committee, 16 September 1915; cited in Chouraqui 1965: 217.
74 Sylvain Lévi, letter to Marcel Mauss, 22 August 1915; Fonds Hubert-Mauss, IMEC-Caen.
75 Gabriel Séailles, speech to the Société d'aide aux volontaires juifs, *Archives israélites* 98/81 (16 January 1916): 35. Ferdinand Buisson, Charles Seignobos, Antoine Meillet and Eugène Gley were all members of the society. Born in Épinal in 1857, Gley was a doctor of medicine. A member of the Académie de médecine, he became professor of general biology at the Collège de France in 1908.
76 Letter to Marcel Mauss, 11 April 1916; Durkheim 1998: 515.
77 The point was made in an obituary published in *L'Univers israélite* 73/12 (30 November 1917): 294–5.
78 *L'Univers israélite* ('Journal des principes conservateurs du judaïsme'), 72/40 (29 June 1917): 367. The letters from Rabbi Lévy and Durkheim were passed on for publication in the paper by M.I. Biélinski, a journalist for *Semaine juive de Moscou*. Lévy also sang the praises of the Russian Revolution, the 'natural outcome' of which was 'the emancipation of my dear coreligionists in Russia'.
79 Sylvain Lévi, letter to Marcel Mauss, 9 November 1915, Paris; Fonds Hubert-Mauss, IMEC-Caen.
80 Léon Trotsky, letter to 'Monsieur le ministre' (Jules Guesde), 11 October 1916; cited in Mergy 2001: appendix K.
81 Public opinion was all the more 'sensitive' because seven Russian soldiers had been condemned to death and executed. They were part of a group of 27 volunteers who had joined the Légion d'honneur. They had requested a transfer to regular regiments but, after 'a vulgar incident', had refused to obey orders and had been brought before a court martial. The commission did not want them to be cleared of 'obviously illegal actions', but had to admit that 'unfortunately, the damage has been done'. They were 'clearly guilty' in that the 'mutiny' had led to the murder of a French officer. The incident led to the deportation of some Russian refugees, and Trotsky, who was in Paris at the time, described it as 'an act of provocation'.
82 'Rapport sur la situation des Russes du département de la Seine, February 1916', *Genèses* 2 (December 1990): 169.
83 'Rapport sur la situation des Russes du département de la Seine, February 1916', *Genèses* 2 (December 1990): 173.
84 Letter to Marcel Mauss, 15 February 1916; Durkheim 1998: 499.
85 Letter to Marcel Mauss, 12 March 1916; Durkheim 1998: 506.
86 The exiled revolutionary leader was rather proud of having linked his fate to that of the French opposition and of having been one of the French government's 'first victims'; he wrote a letter to minister of state Jules Guesde on 11 October 1916: 'Deported by you, I

leave France with the deep conviction that we will prevail . . . Without you and against you, long live socialist France!' (cited in Mergy 2001: appendix K).
87 Letter to Marcel Mauss, 8 August 1916; Durkheim 1998: 541.

26 'Thinking of the Same Thing Day and Night'

1 Letter to Marcel Mauss, 12 March 1915, Paris; Durkheim 1998: 444.
2 Robert Hertz, letter to Alice Hertz, 5 December 1915; Hertz 2002: 139.
3 Robert Hertz, letter to Alice Hertz, 16 September 1914; Hertz 2002: 55.
4 Letter to Alice Hertz, 16 September; Hertz 2002: 139. During the early months of the war, Hertz went on working as an anthropologist and interviewed his comrades, who were peasants from Mayenne and Brittany, about their folklore and popular traditions. His findings were published in the *Revue des traditions populaires* in 1917.
5 Robert Hertz, letter to Alice Hertz, 3 November 1914; Hertz 2002: 98.
6 Letter to Marcel Mauss, 20 December 1914; Durkheim 1998: 426.
7 Letter to Marcel Mauss, 24 March 1915; Durkheim 1998: 447.
8 Letter to Marcel Mauss, 1915; Durkheim 1998: 454.
9 Letter to Marcel Mauss, 1915; Durkheim 1998: 454.
10 Letter to Marcel Mauss, 13 January 1915; Durkheim 1998: 430.
11 Letter to Marcel Mauss, 27 February 1915, Paris; Durkheim 1998: 440.
12 Letter to Marcel Mauss, 12 March 1915, Paris; Durkheim 1998: 444.
13 Letter to Xavier Léon, 10 March 1915; Durkheim 1975: ii/476.
14 Letter to Marcel Mauss, 1 June 1915; Durkheim 1998: 461.
15 Letter to Marcel Mauss, 15 June 1915; Durkheim 1998: 466.
16 Letter to Marcel Mauss, 14 December 1915; Durkheim 1998: 495.
17 Letter to Marcel Mauss, 29 August 1915; Durkheim 1998: 475.
18 Letter to Marcel Mauss, 15 September 1915, Sèvres; Durkheim 1998: 480.
19 Letter to Marcel Mauss, 1 September 1915, Sèvres; Durkheim 1998: 477.
20 Letter to Marcel Mauss, 15 August 1915, Saint-Valéry-en-Caux; Durkheim 1998: 473.
21 Paul Lapie published statistics on the number of school teachers, *normaliens de classe* and inspectors who had been mobilized. In his view, the wartime task of teachers was to introduce some order and justice into what might otherwise become an arbitrary requisition system. This would allow them to exercise a 'real moral influence' (Lapie 1915: 11).
22 Marcel Mauss, letter to Henri Hubert, 11 May 1915; fonds Hubert-Mauss, IMEC-Caen.
23 A *normalien* and *agrégé* (grammar), Mario Roque (1875–1961) was director of studies (romance philology) at the École pratique des hautes études. He enlisted in 1914, and was sent to Serbia and Romania on a fact-finding mission that lasted for 27 months.
24 Hubert Bourgin was the author of many pamphlets, including *Les Origines diplomatiques de la guerre*, *Pourquoi la France fait la guerre?*, *Pourquoi l'Allemagne veut la Belgique?* and *Militarisme allemand*.
25 Letter to Marcel Mauss, 15 August 1915; Durkheim 1998: 473.
26 Letter to Marcel Mauss, 20 October 1915; Durkheim 1998: 486.
27 Letter to Marcel Mauss, 1 December 1915; Durkheim 1998: 491.
28 Letter to Marcel Mauss, 6 December 1915; Durkheim 1998: 492.
29 Letter to Marcel Mauss, 14 December 1915; Durkheim 1998: 494.
30 Lucien Herr, letter to Marcel Mauss, 15 July 1915; Fonds Hubert-Mauss, IMEC-Caen.
31 Letter to Marcel Mauss, mid-February 1916; Durkheim 1998: 501.
32 Letter to Marcel Mauss, 25 February 1916; Durkheim 1998: 501.
33 Marcel Mauss, letter to Rosine Mauss, 29 February 1916.
34 Marcel Mauss, letter to Henri Hubert, February 1916; Fonds Hubert-Mauss, IMEC-Caen.
35 Paul Fauconnet, letter to Marcel Mauss, Tuesday 26 February 1916; Fonds Hubert-Mauss, IMEC-Caen.
36 Henri Hubert, letter to Marcel Mauss, 28 February 1917; Fonds Hubert-Mauss, IMEC-Caen.

37 Sylvain Lévi, letter to Marcel Mauss, 8 March 1916; Fonds Hubert-Mauss, IMEC-Caen.
38 Sylvain Lévi, letter to Marcel Mauss, 1 April 1916; Fonds Hubert-Mauss, IMEC-Caen.
39 Letter to Marcel Mauss, 8 March 1916; Durkheim 1998: 504.
40 Letter to Marcel Mauss, 30 March 1916; Durkheim 1998: 510.
41 Letter to Marcel Mauss, 30 March 1916; Durkheim 1998: 509.
42 Letter to Marcel Mauss, 30 March 1916; Durkheim 1998: 508.
43 The committee that published *Lettres à tous les Français* was chaired by Ernest Lavisse, and its treasurer was Max Leclerc from the Paris chamber of commerce. Its members included Charles Andler, Émile Boutroux, Henri Bergson, Jacques Hadamard, Gustave Lanson, Charles Seignobos and André Weiss.
44 Durkheim had 'serious problems' with General Malleterre, who submitted an essay called 'The decline of Germany'. 'This cannot possibly be published', wrote Durkheim. 'The tone is not right. Not a single fact. Impassioned and tumultuous' (letter to Marcel Mauss, 19 September 1915; Durkheim 1998: 493). Although he was meant to write four pamphlets, Malleterre wrote only one: 'Wearing down the Austro-Hungarian forces'.
45 *Archives israélites*, 30 March 1916.
46 Letter to Marcel Mauss, 10 April 1916; Durkheim 1998: 513.
47 Letter from the vice-rector of the university of Paris to the minister of public education, religion and the arts, 27 March 1916, Paris; Dossier Durkheim, Archives nationales, F/17/25768.
48 Letter to Marcel Mauss, 3 or 9 April 1916; Durkheim 1998: 512.
49 Letter to Marcel Mauss, 11 April 1916; Durkheim 1998: 514.
50 Gaudin de Villaine, 'Mon devoir!' *La Libre Parole*, 4 April 1916: 1; emphasis in the original.
51 The paper was founded in 1870 and described itself as 'the newspaper of democracy'. Its editors were Huc, an anti-clerical free thinker and freemason, and Maurice Sarraut, a radical-socialist senator. It was a regional paper, but enjoyed a good reputation both locally and nationally for being 'a true oracle of radical thought'. A number of politicians and intellectuals wrote for it, including Célestin Bouglé.
52 Letter to Marcel Mauss, 18 April 1916, Biarritz; Durkheim 1998: 515.
53 Letter to Marcel Mauss, 9 May 1916; Durkheim 1998: 520.
54 Letter to Xavier Léon, Biarritz, 10 April 1916; Durkheim 1975: ii/480.
55 Letter to Marcel Mauss, 11 May 1916: Durkheim 1998: 522.
56 Letter to Marcel Mauss, 8 July 1916; Durkheim 1998; 531. Victor Delbos (1862–1916) was an *agrégé de philosophie* and a doctor of law who taught philosophy and the history of philosophy at the Sorbonne. 'A very good colleague . . . a good, upright mind. We will find it hard to replace him', said Durkheim.
57 Letter to Marcel Mauss, 20 August 1915; Durkheim 1998: 474.
58 Fauconnet also thanked his friend Mauss: 'I owe a great debt to the advice given me by Marcel Mauss . . . who agreed to read my manuscript (Fauconnet 1928[1920]: iii). The question of responsibility, seen through the prism of a theory of sanctions, was central to the Durkheimian programme: the rules of responsibility are an integral part of the system of the facts that are described as 'sanctions' and the concept of responsibility, defined as a social fact, is part of the system of collective representations.
59 Letter to Marcel Mauss, 22 April 1916; Durkheim 1998: 518.
60 Letter to Xavier Léon, 30 March 1915; Durkheim 1975: ii/478.
61 Letter to Marcel Mauss, 12 July 1916, Cabourg; Durkheim 1998: 532. Durkheim wrote the preface, chapters 1 and 2 of Part I and the introduction to Part II.
62 Letter to Marcel Mauss, 26 July 1916; Durkheim 1998: 537.
63 Letter to Marcel Mauss, 12 August 1916, Cabourg; Durkheim 1998: 542–3.
64 Letter to Marcel Mauss, 19 August 1916, Cabourg; Durkheim 1998: 544.
65 Letter to Marcel Mauss, 26 August 1916, Cabourg; Durkheim 1998: 547.
66 Letter to Jean-Jacques Salverda de Grave, 9 October 1916, Cabourg; *Durkheimian Studies/Études durkheimiennes* 9 (November 1983): 7.
67 Letter to Marcel Mauss, 9 October 1916; Durkheim 1998: 552.
68 Letter to Marcel Mauss, 27 September 1916; Durkheim 1998: 550.

69 Letter to Marcel Mauss, 20 October 1916; Durkheim 1998: 555.
70 Letter to Marcel Mauss, 31 October 1916; Durkheim 1998: 556.
71 The sector also included private institutions founded by individuals or associations; these were outside the state sector. Durkheim gives the example of the Institut Catholique de Paris, which he describes as a 'real university'. Others had a 'more unusual profile': the École libre de sciences politiques, the École d'anthropologie, the Institut Pasteur.
72 The figures given by Durkheim are as follows: teaching staff (all grades) = 353; total staff = some 700 (including all those involved in scientific work in any fashion). Students = 17,308. The figures are for 1914.
73 When Louis Havet described the École pratique des hautes études as the 'sanctuary of pure, disinterested science' and the university as a purely 'didactic' institution, Durkheim replied: 'This was not an accurate picture of what is taught in our faculties. The practice of science, by which I mean pure science, is, on the contrary, of vital importance.' Of course the university trained teachers with a talent for didactics, but they also had to have 'a taste for science'. 'A teacher who has no personal knowledge of scientific methods cannot be a fully-rounded teacher . . . A school of higher education that did not teach the method and practice of science would not be worthy of the name' (Letter to Louis Havet, 10 October 1916; Durkheim 1975b).
74 Letter to Jean-Jacques Salverda de Grave, 9 October 1969; *Durkheimian Studies/Études durkheimiennes* 9 (November 1983): 7. Salverda de Grave (1863–1947) acted as a middleman and helped to distribute the *Lettres à tous les Francais* in Holland. He been a student of Gaston Paris in France, was a linguist and a philologist; in 1913 he published *L'influence de la langue française en Hollande*.
75 Letter to Xavier Léon, 28 November 1916; Durkheim 1975: ii/479.
76 Rosine Mauss, letter to Marcel Mauss, 4 November 1916.
77 Sylvain Lévi, letter to Marcel Mauss, 27 December 1916; Fonds Hubert-Mauss, IMEC-Caen.
78 Sylvain Lévi, letter to Marcel Mauss, 17 February 1917; Fonds Hubert-Mauss, IMEC-Caen.
79 Letter to Marcel Mauss, 30 January 1916; Durkheim 1998: 566.
80 *Archives israélites* 73/47 (22 November 1917): 188. The commissions' board also included Sylvain Lévi and Israël Lévi (vice-presidents). Lucien Lazard (archivist) and Albert Manual (deputy secretary).
81 'Une publication, une réimpression, une commission', *L'Univers israélite* 73/10 (16 November 1917). The commission's membership included two professors from the Collège de France (Henri Bergson and Jacques Hadamard) and several of Durkheim's colleagues at the Sorbonne (Gustave Bloch, Gustave Glotz, Lucien Lévy-Bruhl, M. Lyon-Caen, Gaston Milhaud and Albert Wahl). Salomon Reinach (Institut de France) and Henri Hauser (University of Dijon) were also members. The population studied was described as follows: 'Current usage regards as Jewish all those whose ancestors were officially of the Jewish confession, irrespective of whether or not they are believers or sceptics, practising or indifferent.'
82 The titles were 'Value judgement and ideal', 'The individual moral conscience and objective morality', 'Objective and subjective viewpoint (sentiment of justice; notion of justice', 'Collective and average type', 'Unity of the two elements (ideal and duty)', and 'How can we attach ourselves to society?'
83 Letter to Marcel Mauss, 28 March 1917; Durkheim 1998: 575.
84 Letter to Marcel Mauss, 1 March 1917; Durkheim 1998: 572.
85 Letter to Marcel Mauss, 15 March 1917; Durkheim 1998: 573.
86 Letter to Marcel Mauss, 15 (May) 1917; Durkheim 1998: 577.
87 Decree from the minister of public education, religion and the arts, signed by the director of higher education Théodore Steeg, 24 April 1917; Dossier Durkheim, Archives nationales, AJ$_{16}$214. Durkheim received half his salary while undergoing treatment.
88 Letter to Marcel Mauss, 5 May 1917; Durkheim 1998: 576.
89 Letter to Marcel Mauss, 15 (May) 1917; Durkheim 1998: 577.
90 Letter to Henri Hubert, 3 July 1917; *Revue française de sociologie* (1987): 534.
91 Marcel Mauss, letter to Rosine Mauss, 17 July 1917.

92 Letter to Marcel Mauss, 18 August 1917, 1 av. d'Orléans; Durkheim 1998.
93 Georges Davy attended Durkheim's lectures at the Sorbonne, and Mauss's lectures at the École pratique between 1909 and 1914, together with Chaillié, Gelly, Jeanmaire, Lenoir and Maunier. He began to write a thesis on *La Foi jurée* under the supervision of Durkheim. The topic was in line with the preoccupations of Mauss, whose lectures of this period covered the question of oaths and archaic forms of contract, with specific reference to the north-western American custom of *potlatch*. Davy did not submit his thesis until after the war (1922) and then turned it into a book (subtitled *Étude sociologique du problème du contrat. La formation du lien contractuel*) which was published in the 'Travaux de l'Année sociologique' collection. He dedicated it to the memory of Émile Durkheim and Lucien Lévy-Bruhl, 'with heartfelt and respectful gratitude'. Davy's thesis led to a polemic within the Durkheimian group. Mauss did not attend the oral examination and the thesis was harshly criticized by Marcel Granet (see Besnard 1985).
94 Letter to Marcel Mauss, 4 November 1917; Durkheim 1998: 584. Georges Davy was appointed as a professor of philosophy at the lycée in Lyon in October 1917; he married Marie Vial in May 1918. In May 1919, he was appointed *chargé de cours de philosophie* at the Dijon faculty of letters.
95 Letter to Célestin Bouglé, 18 September 1917, Fontainebleau; Durkheim 1975: ii/439.
96 Minutes of the meeting of 22 October 1917, Conseil de l'Université de Paris; Archives nationale, AJ$_{16}$25890.
97 Letter to Marcel Mauss, 1 October 1917; Durkheim 1998: 581.
98 Letter to Marcel Mauss, 2 November 1917; Durkheim 1998: 583.
99 Maurice Halbwachs, letter to Yvonne Halbwachs, Nancy, 13 May 1917; Fonds Halbwachs, IMEC-Caen. In Bouglé's view, Bolshevism was doomed to failure because it made 'socialism from below' impossible (Bouglé 1998[1918]: 50ff). After the war, Mauss wrote a long sociological study (Mauss 1997[1924]) of the various mistakes made by the Bolsheviks: a minority had taken action against a majority, had resorted to violence and had rejected the market.
100 Letter to Marcel Mauss, November 1917; Durkheim 1998: 585.
101 'Nécrologie: Émile Durkheim', *Revue philosophique* 85 (January–June 1918): 95.
102 Marcel Mauss, letter to Henri Hubert, 11 December 1917: Fonds Hubert-Mauss, IMEC-Caen.
103 Minutes of the meeting of 26 November 1917, Conseil de l'Université de Paris; Archives nationales, AJ$_{16}$2589.
104 Association amicable des anciens élèves de l'École normale supérieure, 1919: 60–5.
105 Minutes of the meeting of 26 November 1917, Conseil de l'Université de Paris; Archives nationales, AJ$_{16}$2589.
106 Antoine Meillet, letter to Henri Hubert, 10 November (1917); Archives familiales Gérard Hubert.
107 Maurice Halbwachs, letter to Yvonne Halbwachs: IMEC-Caen: HBW2 A1-02-3.
108 In keeping with the Ashkenazi rite, the same inscription can be read on most of the tombs, and is taken from the passage from the Bible in which Abigail predicts that David will enjoy a long life (I Samuel 25: 29). The inscription is something of an enigma, as only the first five letters are legible (Pickering 1994: 35; see Lutzky 1998).
109 Letter from Daniel Vincent, director of higher education, to Alfred Croiset, dean of the faculty of letters, 16 November 1917; Dossier Durkheim, Archives nationales, AJ$_{16}$214.
110 The rector also recalled Durkheim's services to the university, especially in his capacity as a member of council: 'Monsieur Durkheim was one of those who best understood the role of the university and its need to expand its activities abroad.' This eulogy was unanimously approved by members of council; minutes of the meeting of 26 November 1917, Conseil de l'Université de Paris; Archives nationales, AJ$_{16}$22589.
111 État des services de M. Durkheim, David Émile; University of Paris, faculty of letters, 28 January 1918. Over the previous six years, Durkheim's annual salary had averaged 12,000 francs. His pension started at 6,000 francs, one-third of which was payable to his widow Louise Durkheim. According to the 'Form of declaration: transfer by death' dated 17 May 1918 (Bureau des successions de Paris, Départment de la Seine), David

Émile Durkheim's estate comprised (1) from Mme Durkheim, 1,404,021 francs, of which half was inherited from her uncle Moïse; (2) estate of M. Durkheim, 97,745 francs, including the sum of 60,644 francs left him by his mother; (3) community of property, 156, 520 francs. The community of property comprised dividends, share and debentures. There was no will. Émile Durkheim's sole heir was his daughter Marie.

112 'Nécrologie. Émile Durkheim', *Revue philosophique* 25 (January–June 1918): 91–2.
113 'Émile Durkheim', *L'Univers israélite*, 73/12 (30 November 1917): 294–5.
114 'Nouvelles diverses', *Archives israélites* 78/46 (22 November 1917): 188.
115 These words are from the 'Testament de Marc Bloch' (1941) and 'Pourquoi je suis républicain' (1943), repr. in Bloch 1999[1946]. (See Milner 2006: 13.)

Epilogue

1 Minutes of Conseil d'administration de l'Université de Paris, 27 October 1919; Archives nationales.
2 Louise Dreyfus was not yet 60 when a 'horrible illness' carried her off.
3 Maurice Halbwachs, letter to Yvonne Halbwachs, 14, 20 and 24 January 1918; IMEC-Caen, HBW2 A1-02-3.
4 Alfred Radcliffe-Brown, letter to Marcel Mauss, 24 May 1921, Pretoria; Fonds Hubert-Mauss, IMEC-Caen.
5 Marcel Mauss, letter to Henri Hubert, 27 September 1917; Fonds Hubert-Mauss, IMEC-Caen.
6 Marcel Mauss, letter to Svend Ranulf, November 1936; Mauss 1997: 764–5.
7 There is an element of functionalism in Durkheim's work, but the expression is not his. And while functionalism does look at the functions of various institutions and at how they all help to preserves society's cohesion, it also attempts to analyse their causes. The main anthropological advocates of functionalism were Malinowski and Radcliffe-Brown. As we have seen, Radcliffe-Brown was close to the Durkheimians and advocated a form of structural-functionalism (see Radcliffe-Brown 1952).

References

Abbott, Andrew. 1999. *Department & Discipline. Chicago Sociology at One Hundred*. Chicago: University of Chicago Press.

Abitbol, Michel. 1989. *Les Deux Terres promises. Les Juifs en France et le sionisme, 1897–1945*. Paris: Olivier Orban.

Agathon. 1911. 'L'Esprit de la nouvelle Sorbonne', *Mercure de France*.

Agathon. 1995[1913]. *Les Jeunes Gens d'aujourd'hui*, ed. Jean-Jacques Becker. Paris: Imprimerie nationale.

Alexander, Jeffrey C. 1982. *Theoretical Logic in Sociology*. Vol. 2: *The Antinomies of Classical Thought: Marx and Durkheim*. Berkeley: University of California Press.

Alexander, Jeffrey C., ed. 1988. *Durkheimian Sociology: Cultural Studies*. Cambridge: Cambridge University Press.

Alexander, Jeffrey C. and Smith, Philip, eds. 2005. *The Cambridge Companion to Durkheim*. Cambridge: Cambridge University Press.

Alpert, Harry. 1939. *Émile Durkheim and His Sociology*. New York, Russell & Russell, 1961.

Alphandéry, Paul. 1912. 'Le IVe congrès international d'histoire des religions à Leyde', *Revue de l'histoire des religions* 33/66.

Alphandéry, Paul. 1919. 'In memoriam, 1914–1918', *Revue de l'histoire des religions* 79.

Andler, Charles. 1896. 'Sociologie et démocratie', *Revue de métaphysique et de morale* 4/2: 243–256.

Andler, Charles. 1977[1932].*Vie de Lucien Herr, 1864–1926*. Paris: F. Maspero.

Aron, Raymond. 2003. *Mémoires*. Paris: R. Laffont, 2003.

Assouline, Pierre. 1997. *Le Dernier des Camondo*. Paris: Gallimard.

Aubin, Abel. 1903. Review of Célestin Bouglé, 'Le procès de la sociologie biologique', and of Gabriel Tarde, 'La réalité sociale', *L'Année sociologique* 6.

Aubin, Abel. 1910. Review of René Worms, *Philosophie des sciences sociales*, *L'Année sociologique* 11: 20–21.

Audren, Frédéric. 2001. 'Paul Huvelin, juriste et durkheimien', *Revue d'histoire des sciences humaines* 4: 117–130.

Azouvi, François. 2007. *La Gloire de Bergson*. Paris: Gallimard.

Barrès, Maurice. 1898. 'La protestation des intellectuels', *Le Journal. Quotidien littéraire, artistique et politique* (1 February).

Barth, P. 1895. Review of É. Durkheim, *De la division du travail social*, *Vierteljahresscrift für wissenschaftliche Philosophie* 19: 101–108.

Basch, Victor. n.d. 'Bouglé, citoyen', in Édouard Herriot, *Célestin Bouglé, 1870–1940*. Dossier Célestin Bouglé, AJ/16/5885, Archives nationales.

Baudelot, Christian and Establet, Roger. 1999. *Durkheim et le suicide*. Paris: PUF.

Baudelot, Christian and Establet, Roger. 2008[2006]. *Suicide. The Hidden Side of Modernity*, trans. David Macey. Cambridge: Polity.

Becker, Annette. 2003. *Maurice Halbwachs, un intellectuel en guerres mondiales 1914–1945*. Paris: Agnès Viénot.

Becker, Jean-Jacques. 1995. 'Présentation', Henri Massis et Alfred de Tarde, *Les Jeunes Gens d'aujourd'hui*. Paris: Imprimerie nationale.

Becquemont, Daniel. 1995. 'Durkheim en Angleterre: un débat à la Sociological Society en 1904', in Massimo Borlandi and Laurent Mucchielli, eds., *La Sociologie et sa methode. Les règles de Durkheim un siècle après*. Paris: L'Harmattan, pp. 285–296.

Belmont, Nicole. 1974. *Arnold Van Gennep, créateur de l'ethnographie française*. Paris: Payot.

Belot, Gustave. 1893. 'Sur la définition du socialisme', *Revue philosophique* 35.

Belot, Gustave. 1894. 'L'utilitarisme et ses nouveaux critiques', *Revue de métaphysique et de morale* 2.

Belot, Gustave. 1898. Review of *L'Année sociologique* 1, *Revue philosophique* 45.

Belot, Gustave. 1901. Review of *L'Année sociologique* 3 and 4, *Revue philosophique* 52.

Belot, Gustave. 1903. Review of *L'Année sociologique* 5, *Revue philosophique* 55.

Belot, Gustave. 1905. Review of *L'Année sociologique* (1904), *Revue philosophique* 54.

Belot, Gustave. 1913. 'Une théorie nouvelle de la religion', *Revue philosophique* 85.

Ben-David, E. 1864. 'Chronique israélite de la quinzaine', *Archives israélites*, 25th year, no. 14, 18 July.

Ben David, Joseph and Collins, Randall. 1966. 'Scandal factors in the origins of a new science: the case of psychology', *American Sociological Review* 31/4: 451–465.

Bénard, Charles. 1899. *Histoire des expositions de Bordeaux*. Bordeaux: G. Gounouilhon.

Bergson, Henri. 1910[1889]. *Time and Free Will: An Essay on the Immediate Data of Consciousness*, trans. F.L. Pogson. New York: Macmillan.

Bergson, Henri. 1911[1896]. *Matter and Memory*, trans. N.M. Paul and W. Scott Palmer. New York: Macmillan.

Bergson, Henri. 1915a. 'La guerre et la littérature de demain. Hier et demain', *Revue bleue* 53 (8–15 May).

Bergson, Henri. 1915b. 'La philosophie', in *La Science française*. Paris: Ministère de l'instruction publique et des beaux-arts.

Bergson, Henri. 1963[1932]. *The Two Sources of Morality and Religion*. Notre Dame: University of Notre Dame Press.

Bergson, Henri. 1972. *Mélanges*, ed. André Robinet. Paris: PUF.

Berkovitz, Jay R. 1989. *The Shaping of Jewish Identity in Nineteenth Century France*. Detroit: Wayne State University Press.

Bernès, Marcel. 1894. 'Les deux directions de la sociologie contemporaine', *Revue de l'économie politique* 8.

Bernès, Marcel. 1895a. 'La philosophie au lycée et à l'agrégation', *Revue philosophique* 39: 605–625.

Bernès, Marcel. 1895b. Review of Émile Durkheim, *Les Règles de la méthodes sociologique*, *Revue de l'économie politique*.

Bernès, Marcel. 1895c. 'La sociologie. Ses conditions d'existence. Son importance scientifique et philosophique', *Revue de métaphysique et de morale* 3.

Bernès, Marcel. 1895d. 'Sur la méthode en sociologie', *Revue philosophique* 39.

Bernès, Marcel. 1900. 'La sociologie dans l'enseignement secondaire', *Revue internationale de sociologie* 8/1 (January).

Bernès, Marcel. 1901. 'Individu et société', *Revue philosophique* 51.

Berr, Henri. 1900. 'Sur notre programme', *Revue de synthèse historique* 1/1 (July).

Berr, Henri. 1906. 'Les progrès de la sociologie religieuse', *Revue de synthèse historique* 12/1 (February): 16–43.

Berrebi-Hoffmann, Isabelle and Lallement, Michel. 2007. *La Femme comme énigme sociologique. Les durkheimiens face à la question feminine*. Les documents de travail du LISE, CNRS-CNAM 23.

Berthelot, Jean-Michel. 1995. *1895. Durkheim. L'avènement de la sociologie scientifique*. Toulouse: Presses universitaires du Mirail.

Berthelot, Marcellin. 1895. 'La science et la morale', *Revue de Paris* (February).

Berthelot, René. 1913. *Le Pragmatisme de Bergson*. Paris: Alcan.

Besnard, Joséphine. 2000. 'La référence aliéniste de Durkheim: Alexande Brierre de Boismont', in Massimo Borlandi and Mohamed Cherkaoui, eds., *Le Suicide, un siècle après Durkheim*. Paris: PUF, pp. 47–63.

Besnard, Philippe. 1979. 'La formation de l'équipe de *L'Année sociologique*', *Revue française de sociologie* 20/1: 7–31.

Besnard, Philippe. 1985. 'Un conflit au sein du groupe durkheimien, la polémique autour de la *Foi jurée*', *Revue française de sociologie* 26/2: 247–257.

Besnard, Philippe. 1987. *L'Anomie, ses usages et ses fonctions dans la discipline sociologique depuis Durkheim*. Paris: PUF.

Besnard, Philippe. 1993. 'De quand date l'éducation morale?', *Durkheimian Studies/ Études durkheimiennes* 7 (Autumn): 8–10.

Besnard, Philippe. 2000. 'La destinée du *Suicide*', in Massimo Borlandi and Mohamed Cherkaoui, eds., *Le Suicide, un siècle après Durkheim*. Paris: PUF.

Besnard, Philippe, Borlandi, Massimo and Vogt, Paul, eds. 2003. *Division du travail et lien social. La thèse de Durkheim un siècle après*. Paris: PUF.

Birnbaum, Pierre. 1971. 'Préface', in Émile Durkheim, *Le Socialisme*, ed. Marcel Mauss. Paris: PUF.

Bloch, Marc. 1999[1946]. *Strange Defeat. A Statement of Evidence Written in 1940*, trans. Gerard Hopkins. New York: Norton.

Bloch, Marc and Febvre, Lucien. 1994. *Correspondance*, vol. I. Paris: Fayard.

Blum, Léon. 1982[1935]. *Souvenirs sur l'Affaire*. Paris: Gallimard.

Boas, Franz. 1916. 'The origin of totemism', *American Anthropologist* 18: 319–326.

Bochard, A. 1899. Review of *L'Année sociologique* 2, *Revue internationale de sociologie* 7/7 (July).

Bochard, A. 1900. Review of *L'Année sociologique* 3, *Revue internationale de sociologie* 8/12 (December).

Borlandi, Massimo. 1994a. 'Les deux éditions de 1893 et la véritable date d'achèvement de la *Division du travail social*', *Durkheimian Studies/Études durkheimiennes* 6: 3–4.

Borlandi, Massimo. 1994b. 'Informations sur la rédaction du *Suicide* et sur l'état du conflit entre Durkheim et Tarde de 1895 à 1897', *Durkheimian Studies/Études durkheimiennes* 6: 4–13.

Borlandi, Massimo. 2000. 'Lire ce que Durkheim a lu', in Massimo Borlandi and Mohamed Cherkaoui, eds., *Le Suicide, un siècle après Durkheim*. Paris: PUF.

Borlandi, Massimo and Cherkaoui, Mohamed, eds. 2000. *Le Suicide, un siècle après Durkheim*. Paris: PUF.

Bosc, Olivier. 1999. 'L'invitation à l'Exposition. Une correspondance inédite d'Émile Durkheim à Cesare Lombroso en 1895', *Durkheimian Studies/Études durkheimiennes* 5.

Bosco, Augusto. 1897. Review of Émile Durkheim, *Le Suicide*, *Rivista italiana di sociologia* 1/3: 376–383.

Bossu, Jean. 1976–84. 'Émile Durkheim, un professeur, un savant, un homme d'une grande conscience', in *Chronique des rues d'Épinal*, 3 vols. Épinal: Jeune chambre économique.

Boucher, Joseph. 1900. 'Le congrès international des étudiants et anciens étudiants socialistes', *Le Mouvement socialiste* 47 (December).

Bouglé, Célestin. 1894a. 'Les sciences sociales en Allemagne. G. Simmel', *Revue de métaphysique et de morale* 2.

Bouglé, Célestin. 1894b. 'Les sciences sociales en Allemagne. A. Wagner', *Revue de métaphysique et de morale* 2.

Bouglé, Célestin. 1895. 'Les sciences sociales en Allemagne. R. von Jhering', *Revue de métaphysique et de morale* 3.

Bouglé, Célestin. 1896a. 'Sociologie et démocratie', *Revue de métaphysique et de morale* 4: 118–128.

Bouglé, Célestin. 1896b. 'Sociologie, psychologie et histoire', *Revue de métaphysique et de morale* 4: 362–371.

Bouglé, Célestin. 1898a. Review of P. Barth, *Die Philosophie der Geschichte als Sociologie*, *L'Année sociologique* I: 116–123.

Bouglé, Célestin. 1898b. Review of G. Simmel, 'Superiority and subordination as subject-matter of sociology', *L'Année sociologique* 1: 153.

Bouglé, Célestin. 1899a. *Les Idées égalitaires*. Paris: Alcan.

Bouglé, Célestin. 1899b. 'Philosophie de l'antisémitisme (l'idée de race)', *La Grande Revue* (1 January).

Bouglé, Célestin. 1899c. Review of Émile Durkheim, 'Représentations individuelles et représentations collectives', *L'Année sociologique* 2.

Bouglé, Célestin. 1900a. *Pour la démocratie française*. Conférences populaires. Paris: Édouard Cornély.

Bouglé, Célestin. 1900b. Review of Émile Durkheim, 'La sociologie en France', *L'Année sociologique* 3.

Bouglé, Célestin. 1901. 'Le procès de la sociologie biologique', *Revue philosophique* 51.

Bouglé, Célestin. 1902a. 'La crise du libéralisme', *Revue de métaphysique et de morale* 10/5 (September): 635–652.

Bouglé, Célestin. 1902b. Review of P. Fauconnet and M. Mauss, 'Sociologie', *L'Année sociologique* 5.

Bouglé, Célestin. 1903. 'Revue générale des théories récentes sur la division du travail', *L'Année sociologique* 6: 73–133.

Bouglé, Célestin. 1905a. Review of H. Berr, 'Le problème des idées dans la synthèse historique', *L'Année sociologique* 8.

Bouglé, Célestin. 1905b. '*Une doctrine idéaliste de la démocratie*: Henry Michel', *Revue politique et parlementaire* 43: 562–577.

Bouglé, Célestin. 1907a. 'Note sur le droit et la caste en Inde', *L'Année sociologique* 10: 138–168.

Bouglé, Célestin. 1907b. Review of *Revue internationale de sociologie*, June 1905– June 1906, *L'Année sociologique* 10.

Bouglé, Célestin. 1907c. Review of G. Simmel, *Philosophie et mode*, *L'Année sociologique* 10.

Bouglé, Célestin. 1910. Review of E. de Roberty, *Sociologie de l'action* (1908), in *L'Année sociologique* 9: 46–47.

Bouglé, Célestin. 1912. *Sociologie de Proudhon*. Paris: Armand Colin.

Bouglé, Célestin. 1912[1896]. *Les Sciences sociales en Allemagne: le conflit des méthodes*. Paris: Librairie Félix Alcan.

Bouglé, Célestin. 1913. Review of Robert Michels, *Zur Soziologie des Parteiwesens in der moderne Demokratie*, *L'Année sociologique* 12: 477–479.

Bouglé, Célestin. 1914. 'Remarques sur le polytélisme', *Revue de morale et de métaphysique* 22/5 (September).

Bouglé, Célestin. 1923[1904]. *La Démocratie devant la science. Études critiques sur l'hérédité, la concurrence et la différenciation*, 3rd edn. Paris: Alcan.

Bouglé, Célestin. 1925. *Qu'est-ce que la sociologie?* Paris: Alcan.

Bouglé, Célestin. 1925[1897]. 'Qu'est-ce que la sociologie?', in Bouglé, *Qu'est-ce que la sociologie?* Paris: Alcan, pp. 3–32.

Bouglé, Célestin. 1925[1899]. 'La sociologie populaire et l'histoire', in Bouglé, *Qu'est-ce que la sociologie?* Paris: Alcan, pp. 33–56.

Bouglé, Célestin. 1930a. 'E. Durkheim', in *Encyclopedia of the Social Sciences*, vol. 5. New York: Macmillan.

Bouglé, Célestin. 1930b. 'L'œuvre sociologique d'Émile Durkheim', *Europe* 22.

Bouglé, Célestin. 1932[1904]. *La Démocratie contre la science*. Paris: Alcan.

Bouglé, Célestin. 1935. *Bilan de la sociologie française contemporaine*. Paris: Alcan.

Bouglé, Célestin. 1936. 'La méthodologie de François Simiand et la sociologie', *Annales sociologiques* A/2: 5–28.

Bouglé, Célestin. 1938. *Humanisme, sociologie, philosophie. Remarques sur la conception française de la culture générale*. Paris: Hermann & Cie.

Bouglé, Célestin. 1974[1924]. 'Preface', in Émile Durkheim, *Sociology and Philosophy*, trans. D.F. Pocock. New York: Routledge & Kegan Paul.

Bouglé, Célestin. 1998[1918]. *Qu'est-ce que le bolchevisme?*, in *Cahiers Anatole Leroy-Beaulieu*. Paris: FNSP.

Bourdieu, Pierre. 1980. 'Le Nord et le Midi. Contribution à l'analyse de l'effet Montesquieu', *Actes de la recherche en sciences sociales* 35 (November): 21–25.

Bourdieu, Pierre. 1990. *Contre-feux*. Paris: Liber/Raison d'agir editions.

Bourdieu, Pierre. 1998. *Acts of Resistance: Against the New Myths of Our Time*, trans. Richard Nice. Cambridge: Polity.

Bourgeois, Léon. 1902. *Essai d'une philosophie de la solidarité*. Paris: Alcan.

Bourgeois, Léon. 1906[1900]. 'La solidarité et la liberté', in Bourgeois, *Solidarité*. Paris: A. Colin.

Bourgin, Georges. 1913. 'De la fausse sociologie en histoire', *Revue du mois* (10 March).

Bourgin, Hubert. 1905. 'Essai sur une forme d'industrie. L'industrie de la boucherie à Paris au XIXe siècle', *L'Année sociologique* 8.

Bourgin, Hubert. 1938. *L'École normale et la politique. De Jaurès à Léon Blum*. Paris: Fayard.

Bourrelier, Paul-Henri. 2007. *La Revue blanche. Une génération dans l'engagement 1890–1905*. Paris: Fayard.

Boutroux, Émile. 1874. *De la contingence des lois de la nature*. Paris: Baillière.

Boutroux, Émile. 1908. 'La philosophie en France depuis 1867', *Revue de métaphysique et de morale* 16: 683–716.

Boutroux, Émile. 1915. 'L'Allemagne et la guerre', letter to the editor, *Revue des deux mondes* (30 March).

Branford, Victor. 1918. 'Durkheim: a brief memoir', *Sociological Review* 10: 7–8.

Bredin, Jean-Denis. 1983. *L'affaire*. Paris: Julliard.

Brierre de Boismont, Alexandre. 1865. *Du Suicide et de la folie suicide*. Paris: G. Baillière.

Broca, Paul. 1876. *Le Programme de l'anthropologie*. Paris: Masson.

Brochard, Victor. 1901. 'La morale ancienne et la morale moderne', *Revue philosophique* 26/51 (January).

Brooks, John I. 1993. 'Philosophy and psychology at the Sorbonne, 1885–1913', *Journal of the History of Behaviorial Sciences* 29: 123–145.

Brunetière, Ferdinand, 1890. 'La philosophie de Schopenhauer et les conséquences du pessimisme', *Revue des Deux Mondes* (1 November).

Brunetière, Ferdinand. 1895. 'Après une visite au Vatican', *Revue des Deux Mondes* (1 January): 97–118.

Brunschvicg, Léon and Halévy, Élie. 1896. 'L'année philosophique 1893', *Revue de métaphysique et de morale* 2.

Buisson, Ferdinand. 1908. *La Politique radicale*. Paris: Giard et Brière.

Burnouf, Émile. 1886. *La Vie et la pensée. Éléments réels de philosophie*. Paris: Reinwald.

Cabanel, Patrick. 1994. 'L'institutionnalisation des sciences religieuses en France (1879–1908). Une entreprise protestante', *Bull. Soc. Prot. Fr.* (January–March): 33–80.

Cahen, Isidore. 1892. 'Du suicide chez les Juifs', *Archives israélites* 52 (29 December).

Cantecor, Georges. 1904. 'La science positive de la morale', *Revue philosophique* 29/57 (January–June).

Cavignac, Jean. 1991. *Les Israélites bordelais de 1780 à 1850. Autour de l'émancipation*. Paris: Éditions Publisud.

Charle, Christophe. 1984. 'Le beau mariage d'Émile Durkheim', *Actes de la recherche en sciences sociales* 55.

Charle, Christophe. 1985. *Les Professeurs de la faculté des lettres de Paris. Dictionnaire biographique 1809–1908*, vol. I. Paris: Institut national de recherche pédagogique: Éditions du CNRS.

Charle, Christophe. 1990. *Naissance des 'intellectuels', 1880–1900*. Paris: Éditions de Minuit.

Charle, Christophe. 1994. *La République des universitaires, 1870–1940*. Paris: Éditions du Seuil.

Charle, Christophe. 1995. 'Les normaliens et le socialisme (1867–1914)', in Madeleine Rebérioux and Gilles Candar, eds., *Jaurès et les intellectuels*. Paris: Éditions ouvrières.

Charle, Christophe. 2004. *Le Siècle de la presse (1830–1939)*. Paris: Seuil.

Cherval, André. 1993. *Histoire de l'agrégation*. Paris: Éditions Kline.

Cheysson, Émile. 1889. 'L'économie sociale à l'Exposition de 1889', *La Réforme sociale* 2: 1–19.

Chirac, Auguste. 1905. *Introduction à la sociométrie*. Paris: Giard et Brière.

Chouraqui, André. 1965. *L'Alliance israélite universelle et la renaissance juive contemporaine. Cent ans d'histoire (1860–1960)*. Paris: PUF.

Cladis, M. 1992. *A Communitarian Defense of Liberalism*. Stanford: Stanford University Press.

Clark, Terry N. 1968a. 'Émile Durkheim and the institutionalization of sociology in the French university system', *European Journal of Sociology* 9: 27–71.

Clark, Terry N. 1968b. 'René Worms', *International Encyclopedia of the Social Sciences*. New York: Macmillan and Free Press.

Clark, Terry N. 1968c. 'The structure and functions of a research institute: The *Année sociologique*', *European Journal of Sociology* 9: 72–91.

Clark, Terry N. 1973. *Prophets and Patrons: The French University and the Emergence of the Social Sciences*. Cambridge: Harvard University Press.

Cohen, Yolande. 1989. *Les Jeunes, le socialisme et la guerre*. Paris: L'Harmattan.

Condette, Jean-François. 2006. *Les Recteurs d'académie en France de 1808 à 1940*, vol. 2. Dictionnaire biographique. Lyon: INRP.

Coser, L.A. 1960. 'Durkheim's conservatism and its implication for his sociological theory', in K.H. Wolff, ed., *Durkheim, 1858–1917: A Collection of Essays*. New York: Harper Torchbook, pp. 211–232.

Coste, Adolphe. 1900. *Impressions de l'Exposition universelle de 1900*. Paris: Giard.

Coulanges, Fustel de. 1879. 'Leçon d'ouverture. Des transformations de la propriété foncière en France du IIe au Xe siècle', *RCL* 16.

Coulanges, Fustel de. 1888. *Histoire des institutions politiques de l'ancienne France. La monarchie française*. Paris: Hachette.

Coulanges, Fustel de. 1889. *L'Alleu et le domaine rural pendant la période mérovingienne*. Paris: Hachette.

Croiset, Alfred. 1906. 'Rapport du doyen de la faculté des lettres', in Université de Paris, *Rapport présenté au Ministre de l'Instruction publique sur la situation de l'enseignement supérieur*, 1903–1904. Melun: Imprimerie administrative.

Croiset, Alfred. 1918. 'La faculté des lettres', in Émile Durkheim et al., *La Vie universitaire à Paris*. Paris: Librairie Armand Colin.

Dagan, Henri. 1899. *Enquête sur l'antisémitisme*. Paris: Stock.

d'Alviella, Goblet. 1913. 'La sociologie de M. Durkheim et l'histoire des religions', *Revue de l'histoire des religions* 33/73: 192–220.

Danziner, K. 1990. *Constructing the Subject*. Cambridge: Cambridge University Press.

Darlu, Alphonse. 1895. 'Réflexions d'un philosophe sur la question du jour. Science, morale et religion', *Revue de métaphysique et de morale* 3.

Davidovitch, André. 1966. 'Louis Gernet et *L'Année sociologique*', in *Hommage à Louis Gernet*, Collège de France (16 February).

Davy, Georges. 1913. Review of Georges Foucart, *Histoire des religions et méthode comparative*, *L'Année sociologique* 12.

Davy, Georges. 1919a. 'Émile Durkheim', in *Annuaire de l'Association amicale des anciens élèves de l'École normale supérieure*.

Davy, Georges. 1919b. 'Émile Durkheim: l'homme', *Revue de métaphysique et de morale* 26: 181–198

Davy, Georges. 1931. 'La famille et la parenté selon Durkheim', in *Sociologues d'hier et d'aujourd'hui*. Paris: Félix Alcan, pp. 103–157.

Davy, Georges. 1960[1953]. 'Introductory note', in Émile Durkheim, *Montesquieu and Rousseau: Forerunners of Sociology*, trans. Ralf Mannheim. Ann Arbor, MI: University of Michigan Press.

Davy, Georges. 1960a. 'Allocution pour la commémoration du centenaire de la mort de Durkheim', *Annales de l'université de Paris*, 1.

Davy, Georges. 1960b. 'Centenaire de la naissance de Durkheim', *Annales de l'université de Paris* 1.

Davy, Georges. 1973. *L'Homme, le fait social et le fait politique*. Paris: Mouton.

Davy, Georges. 1973[1960a]. 'Durkheim, voie nouvelle ouverte à la science de l'homme', in Davy, *L'Homme, le fait social et le fait politique*. Paris: Mouton.

Davy, Georges. 1973[1960b]. 'L'homme comme "être dans le groupe"', in Davy, *L'Homme, le fait social et le fait politique*. Paris: Mouton.

Debesse, Maurice. 1922. 'Préface', in Émile Durkheim, *Éducation et sociologie*. Paris: Alcan.

Deloire, P. 1897. Review of Émile Durkheim, *Le Suicide*, *La Revue socialiste* 26/155: 635–636.

Delprat, G. 1900. 'L'enseignement sociologique à l'université de Bordeaux', *Revue philomatique de Bordeaux et du Sud-Ouest* (August).

Deploige, Simon. 1927[1911]. *Le Conflit de la morale et de la sociologie*, 3rd edn. Paris: Nouvelle Librairie nationale.

Derczansky, Alexandre. 1990. 'Note sur la judéité de Durkheim', *Archives des sciences sociales des religions* 35/69.

Descamps, Paul. 1912. 'Le totémisme chez les indigènes de l'Australie', *Bulletin de la Société internationale de science sociale* 96 (September): 105–110.

Deshairs, Léon. 1900. 'L'art à l'Exposition', *Le Mouvement socialiste* 2.

Didry, Claude. 1990. 'De l'état aux groupes professionnels. Les itinéraires croisés de L. Duguit et É. Durkheim au tournant du siècle (1880–1900)', *Genèses* 2 (December).

Du Bos, C. 1946. *Journal 1921–1925*. Paris: Corréa.

Duguit, Louis. 1893. 'Un séminaire de sociologie', *Revue internationale de sociologi* 1/5–6: 201–208.

Dumesnil, Georges. 1888. 'Les cours de science de l'éducation', *Revue internationale de l'enseignement*.

Duprat, G.-L. 1912. Review of Gaston Richard, *La Sociologie générale et les lois sociologiques* (1912), *Revue philosophique* 74: 512–516.

Durkheim, Émile. 1888. 'Suicide et natalité: étude de statistique morale', *Revue philosophique* 26: 446–463.

Durkheim, Émile. 1899. 'La sociologie dans l'enseignement secondaire', *Revue internationale de sociologie* 7/10 (October).

Durkheim, Émile. 1900. Review of R. Steinmetz, *Das Verhältnis von Eltern und Kindern bei dem Landvolk in Deutschland*, *L'Année sociologique* 3.

Durkheim, Émile. 1901. Review of Adna Ferrin Weber, *The Growth of Cities in the Nineteenth Century*, *L'Année sociologique* 4: 577–582.

Durkheim, Émile. 1902. Review of Georges Palante, *Précis de sociologie*. *Revue de synthèse historique* 4: 114–115.

Durkheim, Émile. 1907. Review of Andrew Lang, *The Secret of the Totem*, *L'Année sociologique* 10: 400–409.

Durkheim, Émile. 1909. 'Examen critique des systèmes classiques sur les origines de la pensée religieuse' *Revue philosophique* 67: 1–28, 142–162.

Durkheim, Émile. 1915. *L'Allemagne au-dessus de tout. La mentalité allemande et la guerre*. Paris: Librairie Armand Colin.

Durkheim, Émile. 1917. 'La définition du sacré et du profane', *Bulletin de la Société française de philosophie* 15: 1–2.

Durkheim, Émile. 1956. *Education and Sociology*, ed. P. Fauconnet, trans. Sherwood D. Fox. Glencoe, IL: Free Press of Glencoe.

Durkheim, Émile. 1956[1903]. 'Pedagogy and sociology', in *Education and Sociology*, ed. Paul Fauconnet; trans. Sherwood D. Fox. Glencoe, IL: Free Press of Glencoe, pp. 113–134.

Durkheim, Émile. 1956[1906]. 'The Evolution and the role of secondary education in France', in *Education and Sociology*, ed. Paul Fauconnet; trans. Sherwood D. Fox. Glencoe, IL: Free Press of Glencoe, pp. 135–154.

Durkheim, Émile. 1956[1911]. 'Education: its nature and role', in *Education and Sociology*, ed. Paul Fauconnet; trans. Sherwood D. Fox. Glencoe, IL: Free Press of Glencoe, pp. 61–89.

Durkheim, Émile. 1957[1894]. *Professional Ethics and Civic Morals*. Preface by H. N. Kubali; Introduction by G. Davy. New York: Routledge.

Durkheim, Émile. 1960[1892]. *Quid Secundatus Politicae Scientiae Instituendae Contulerit*, trans. A. Mannheim, in Durkheim, *Montesquieu and Rousseau: Forerunners of Sociology*. Ann Arbor, MI: University of Michigan Press.

Durkheim, Émile. 1960[1918]. 'Rousseau's *Social Contract*', trans. R. Manheim, in Durkheim, ed., *Montesquieu and Rousseau: Forerunners of Sociology*. Ann Arbor, MI: University of Michigan Press, pp. 65–138.

Durkheim, Émile. 1961[1925]. *Moral Education*, ed. Everett K. Wilson. New York: The Free Press of Glencoe.

Durkheim, Émile. 1962[1928]. *Socialism*, trans. Charlotte Sattler, ed. Alvin W. Gouldner. New York: Collier Books.

Durkheim, Émile. 1963[1898]. *Incest: The Nature and Origin of the Taboo*, trans. Edward Sagarin. New York: Lyle Stuart.

Durkheim, Émile. 1964[1914]. 'The dualism of human nature and its social conditions', in K.H. Wolff, ed., *Essays on Sociology and Philosophy*. New York: Harper Torchbook.

Durkheim, Émile. 1969. *Journal sociologique*. Paris: PUF.

Durkheim, Émile. 1969[1898]. Review of Marcel Mauss, 'La religion et les origines du droit pénal', in Durkheim, *Journal sociologique*. Paris: PUF.

Durkheim, Émile. 1969[1899]. Review of Friedrich Ratzel, *Politische Geographie*, in Durkheim, *Journal sociologique*. Paris: PUF.

Durkheim, Émile. 1969[1900a]. Review of Arsène Dumont, *Natalité et démocratie*, in Durkheim, *Journal sociologique*. Paris: PUF.

Durkheim, Émile. 1969[1900b] Review of F. Ratzel. *Anthropogeographie, Erster Theil: Grundzüge der Anwendung der Erdkunde auf die Geschichte* (*Anthropogéographie*, première partie: 'Principes de l'application de la géographie à l'histoire'), in Durkheim, *Journal sociologique*. Paris: PUF.

Durkheim, Émile. 1969[1900c]. Review of B. Spencer and F.J. Gillen, *The Native Tribes of Central Australia*, in Durkheim, *Journal sociologique*, Paris: PUF.

Durkheim, Émile. 1969[1901]. Review of Adna Ferrin Weber, *The Growth of Cities in the Nineteenth Century*, in Durkheim, *Journal sociologique*. Paris: PUF.

Durkheim, Émile. 1969[1902a]. Review of J. Kohler, *Rechte der deutschen Schutzgebiete*, in Durkheim, *Journal sociologique*. Paris: PUF.

Durkheim, Émile. 1969[1902b]. 'Sur le totémisme', in Durkheim, *Journal sociologique*. Paris: PUF.

Durkheim, Émile. 1969[1904a]. Review of Georg Simmel, *The Number of Members as Determining the Sociological Form of the Group*, in Durkheim, *Journal sociologique*. Paris: PUF.

Durkheim, Émile. 1969[1904b]. Review of Georg Simmel, *Über räumliche Projektionen sozialer Formen*, in Durkheim, *Journal sociologique*. Paris: PUF.

Durkheim, Émile. 1969[1905]. 'Sur l'organisation matrimoniale des sociétés australiennes', in Durkheim, *Journal sociologique*. Paris: PUF.

Durkheim, Émile. 1969[1913a]. Review of Franz Boas, *The Mind of the Primitive Man*, in Durkheim, *Journal sociologique*. Paris: PUF.

Durkheim, Émile. 1969[1913b]. Review of the first German sociology conference [*Premier congrès allemand de sociologie* (1910)], in Durkheim, *Journal sociologique*. Paris: PUF.

Durkheim, Émile. 1969[1913c]. Review of E. Sidney Hartland, *Primitive Paternity* (1909), in Durkheim, *Journal sociologique*. Paris: PUF, pp. 716–720.

Durkheim, Émile. 1969[1913d]. Review of Wilhelm Wundt, *Elemente der Voelkerpsychologie* (1912), in Durkheim, *Journal sociologique*. Paris: PUF, pp. 685–691.

Durkheim, Émile. 1970. *La Science sociale et l'action*. Paris: PUF.

Durkheim, Émile. 1970[1884]. Review of Alfred Fouillée, *La Propriété sociale et la démocratie*, in Durkheim, *La Science sociale et l'action*. Paris: PUF.

Durkheim, Émile. 1970[1886]. 'Les études de sciences sociales', in Durkheim, *La Science sociale et l'action*. Paris: PUF.

Durkheim, Émile. 1970[1906]. 'Internationalisme et lutte des classes', in Durkheim, *La Science sociale et l'action*. Paris: PUF.

Durkheim, Émile. 1971[1908]. 'To the Readers of the *Année Sociologique*', in

C. Bouglé, ed., *Essays on the Caste System*, trans. D. F. Pocock. Cambridge: Cambridge University Press.

Durkheim, Émile. 1971[1928]. *Le Socialisme*, ed. Marcel Mauss. Paris: PUF.

Durkheim, Émile. 1973[1890]. 'The principles of 1789 and sociology', in *Émile Durkheim: On Morality and Society*, ed. Robert N. Bellah, trans. Mark Traugott. Chicago and London: University of Chicago Press.

Durkheim, Émile. 1973[1898]. 'Individualism and the intellectuals', in *Émile Durkheim: On Morality and Society*, ed. Robert N. Bellah, trans. Mark Traugott. Chicago and London: University of Chicago Press.

Durkheim, Émile. 1973[1900]. 'Sociology in France in the nineteenth century', in *Émile Durkheim: On Morality and Society*, ed. Robert N. Bellah, trans. Mark Traugott. Chicago and London: University of Chicago Press.

Durkheim, Émile. 1973[1904]. 'The intellectual elite and democracy', in *Émile Durkheim: On Morality and Society*, ed. Robert N. Bellah, trans. Mark Traugott. Chicago and London: University of Chicago Press.

Durkheim, Émile. 1973[1908]. 'Pacifism and Patriotism', *Sociological Inquiry* 43/2: 101–103.

Durkheim, Émile. 1973[1914]. 'The dualism of human nature and its social conditions', in *Émile Durkheim: On Morality and Society*, ed. Robert N. Bellah, trans. Mark Traugott. Chicago and London: University of Chicago Press.

Durkheim, Émile. 1974[1898]. 'Individual and collective representations', in Durkheim, *Sociology and Philosophy*, trans. D.F. Pocock. New York: Routledge & Kegan Paul.

Durkheim, Émile. 1974[1906a]. 'The determination of moral facts', in Durkheim, *Sociology and Philosophy*, trans. D.F. Pocock. New York: Routledge & Kegan Paul, pp. 35–62.

Durkheim, Émile. 1974[1906b]. 'Replies to objections', in Durkheim, *Sociology and Philosophy*, trans. D.F. Pocock. New York: Routledge & Kegan Paul, pp. 63–79.

Durkheim, Émile. 1974[1911]. 'Value judgments and judgments of reality', in Durkheim, *Sociology and Philosophy*, trans. D.F. Pocock. New York: Routledge & Kegan Paul.

Durkheim, Émile. 1975. *Textes*, ed. V. Karady. Paris: Éditions de Minuit.

Durkheim, Émile. 1975[1883]. 'Le rôle des grands hommes dans l'histoire', in Durkheim, *Textes*, vol. 1, ed. V. Karady. Paris: Éditions de Minuit.

Durkheim, Émile. 1975[1885]. 'Gumplowicz, Ludwig, *Grundriss der Soziologie*', in Durkheim, *Textes*, vol. 1, ed. V. Karady. Paris: Éditions de Minuit.

Durkheim, Émile. 1975[1886]. Review of Guillaume De Greef, *Introduction à la sociologie*, in Durkheim, *Textes*, vol. 1, ed. V. Karady. Paris: Éditions de Minuit.

Durkheim, Émile. 1975[1887a]. 'Notice biographique de Victor Hommay', Annuaire de l'Association amicale des anciens élèves de l'École normale supérieure, in Durkheim, *Textes*, vol. 1, ed. V. Karady. Paris: Éditions de Minuit.

Durkheim, Émile. 1975[1887b]. 'La philosophie dans les universités allemandes', in Durkheim, *Textes*, vol. 3, ed. V. Karady. Paris: Éditions de Minuit.

Durkheim, Émile. 1975[1887c] Review of M. Guyau, *L'Irréligion de l'avenir*, in Durkheim, *Textes*, vol. 2, ed. V. Karady. Paris: Éditions de Minuit.

Durkheim, Émile. 1975[1887d]. 'La science positive de la morale en Allemagne', in Durkheim, *Textes*, vol. 1, ed. V. Karady. Paris: Éditions de Minuit.

Durkheim, Émile. 1975[1888]. Le programme économique de M. Schaeffle', *Revue d'économie politique*, in Durkheim, *Textes*, vol. 2, ed. V. Karady. Paris: Éditions de Minuit.

Durkheim, Émile. 1975[1893a] 'Introduction' to *De la division du travail social*, in Durkheim, *Textes*, vol. 2, ed. V. Karady. Paris: Éditions de Minuit.

Durkheim, Émile. 1975[1893b]. Review of Gaston Richard, *Essai sur l'évolution de l'idée de droit*, in Durkheim, *Textes*, vol. 1, ed. V. Karady. Paris: Éditions de Minuit.

Durkheim, Émile. 1975[1895a]. 'L'enseignement de la philosophie et l'agrégation de philosophie', in Durkheim, *Textes*, vol. 3, ed. V. Karady. Paris: Éditions de Minuit.

Durkheim, Émile. 1975[1895b]. 'Lo stato attuale degli studi sociologici in Francia', *La riforma sociale* 3: 607–622, 691–707; trans. as 'L'état actuel des études sociologiques en France', in Durkheim, *Textes*, vol. 1, ed. V. Karady. Paris: Éditions de Minuit.

Durkheim, Émile. 1975[1895c]. 'L'origine du mariage dans l'espèce humaine d'après Westermarck', in Durkheim, *Textes*, vol. 3, ed. V. Karady. Paris: Éditions de Minuit.

Durkheim, Émile. 1975[1897] Contribution to 'Enquête sur l'œuvre de H. Taine', in Durkheim, *Textes*, vol. 1, ed. V. Karady. Paris: Éditions de Minuit.

Durkheim, Émile. 1975[1899]. 'Contribution à Henri Dagan. *Enquête sur l'antisémitisme*', in Durkheim, *Textes*, vol. 2, ed. V. Karady. Paris: Éditions de Minuit.

Durkheim, Émile. 1975[1902]. Contribution to 'Enquête sur l'influence allemande', in Durkheim, *Textes*, vol. 1, ed. V. Karady. Paris: Éditions de Minuit.

Durkheim, Émile. 1975[1903a]. Intervention à la soutenance de la thèse de Ch. Ribéry, Essai sur les classifications et le caractère', in Durkheim, *Textes*, vol. 3, ed. V. Karady. Paris: Éditions de Minuit, pp. 349–351).

Durkheim, Émile. 1975[1903b] Review of Maurice Courant, *En Chine. Moeurs et institutions*, in Durkheim, *Textes*, vol. 3, ed. V. Karady. Paris: Éditions de Minuit.

Durkheim, Émile. 1975[1903c]. Review of Ernest Crawley, *The Mystic Rose: A Study of Primitive Marriage*, in Durkheim, *Textes*, vol. 3, ed. V. Karady. Paris: Éditions de Minuit.

Durkheim, Émile. 1975[1903d]. Review of M. Lang, *Social Origins*, in Durkheim, *Textes*, vol. 2, ed. V. Karady. Paris: Éditions de Minuit, pp. 123–128.

Durkheim, Émile. 1975[1904–5]. 'Intervention à la discussion sur "La séparation des Églises et de l'État" aux séances des 12 mars et 7 mai 1905 de l'Union pour l'action morale', in Durkheim, *Textes*, vol. 2, ed. V. Karady. Paris: Éditions de Minuit, pp. 165–169.

Durkheim, Émile. 1975[1904a]. 'Intervention à la soutenance de la thèse de G. Glotz', *La Solidarité de la famille dans le droit criminel en Grèce* (1904), in Durkheim, *Textes*, vol. 1, ed. V. Karady. Paris: Éditions de Minuit, pp. 241–243.

Durkheim, Émile. 1975[1904b]. 'Réponse à M. Lang', in Durkheim, *Textes*, vol. 2, ed. V. Karady. Paris: Éditions de Minuit, pp. 128–129.

Durkheim, Émile. 1975[1904c]. Review of Maurice Gaudefroy-Demombynes, *Les*

Cérémonies du mariage chez les indigènes d'Algérie, in Durkheim, *Textes*, vol. 3, ed. V. Karady. Paris: Éditions de Minuit.

Durkheim, Émile. 1975[1904d]. Review of Charles Letourneau, *La Condition des femmes dans les diverses races et civilisations*, in Durkheim, *Textes*, vol. 3, ed. V. Karady. Paris: Éditions de Minuit.

Durkheim, Émile. 1975[1904e] 'La sociologie et les sciences sociales', in Durkheim, *Textes*, vol. 1, ed. V. Karady. Paris: Éditions de Minuit.

Durkheim, Émile. 1975[1905a]. 'Contribution à "La morale sans dieu, essai de solution collective"', in Durkheim, *Textes*, vol. 2, ed. V. Karady. Paris: Éditions de Minuit.

Durkheim, Émile. 1975[1905b]. 'Intervention dans le débat "Sur l'internationalisme"', in Durkheim, *Textes*, vol. 2, ed. V. Karady. Paris: Éditions de Minuit, pp. 178–186.

Durkheim, Émile. 1975[1905c]. 'Intervention à la soutenance de la thèse de H. Bourgin: *Fourier, contribution à l'étude du socialisme français*', in Émile Durkheim, *Textes*, vol. 1, ed. V. Karady. Paris: Éditions de Minuit, pp. 183–184.

Durkheim, Émile. 1975[1905d]. Review of L. Gockler, *La Pédagogie de Herbart*, in Durkheim, *Textes*, vol. 3, ed. V. Karady. Paris: Éditions de Minuit.

Durkheim, Émile. 1975[1906a]. '[Religion and morality]', in Durkheim, *Textes*, vol. 2, ed. V. Karady. Paris: Éditions de Minuit.

Durkheim, Émile. 1975[1906b]. 'Sur l'internationalisme', in Durkheim, *Textes*, vol. 3, ed. V. Karady. Paris: Éditions de Minuit.

Durkheim, Émile. 1975[1907a] Contribution to a debate of the Union pour la vérité, 'Sur la réforme des institutions judiciaires: l'enseignement du droit', in Durkheim, *Textes*, vol. 1, ed. V. Karady. Paris: Éditions de Minuit.

Durkheim, Émile. 1975[1907b]. Contribution to an international inquiry on 'La question religieuse', in Durkheim, *Textes*, vol. 2, ed. V. Karady. Paris: Éditions de Minuit.

Durkheim, Émile. 1975[1907c]. Obituary of Octave Hamelin, in *Le Temps* (September 18), in Durkheim, *Textes*, vol. 1, ed. V. Karady. Paris: Éditions de Minuit.

Durkheim, Émile. 1975[1907d]. 'Religion: les origines', in Durkheim, *Textes*, vol. 2, ed. V. Karady. Paris: Éditions de Minuit.

Durkheim, Émile. 1975[1908a]. Contribution to 'Enquête sur l'impuissance parlementaire', in Durkheim, *Textes*, vol. 3, ed. V. Karady. Paris: Éditions de Minuit.

Durkheim, Émile. 1975[1908b]. Participation in the debate 'Le fonctionnaire citoyen', in Durkheim, *Textes*, vol. 3, ed. V. Karady. Paris: Éditions de Minuit.

Durkheim, Émile. 1975[1908c]. Participation in the debate 'Science et religion', in Durkheim, *Textes*, vol. 3, ed. V. Karady. Paris: Éditions de Minuit.

Durkheim, Émile. 1975[1909a]. 'Débat sur le mariage et le divorce', in Durkheim, *Textes*, vol. 2, ed. V. Karady. Paris: Éditions de Minuit.

Durkheim, Émile. 1975[1909b] 'Morale civique et patrie', in Durkheim, *Textes*, vol. 3, ed. V. Karady. Paris: Éditions de Minuit.

Durkheim, Émile. 1975[1909c]. 'Morale professionnelle et corporation', in Durkheim, *Textes*, vol. 2, ed. V. Karady. Paris: Éditions de Minuit.

Durkheim, Émile. 1975[1909d]. 'Note sur la spécialisation de l'agrégation de la philosophie', in Durkheim, *Textes*, vol. 2, ed. V. Karady. Paris: Éditions de Minuit.

Durkheim, Émile. 1975[1909e]. 'Leçon sur la morale', in Durkheim, *Textes*, vol. 2, ed. V. Karady. Paris: Éditions de Minuit.

Durkheim, Émile. 1975[1910a]. 'Intervention à la soutenance de Maurice Pradines', in Durkheim, *Textes*, vol. 2, ed. V. Karady. Paris: Éditions de Minuit.

Durkheim, Émile. 1975[1910b]. 'Intervention au débat à la soutenance de thèse de Joseph Second, *La Prière, étude de psychologie religieuse*', in Durkheim, *Textes*, vol. 2, ed. V. Karady. Paris: Éditions de Minuit.

Durkheim, Émile. 1975[1911]. 'Préface' in Octave Hamelin, ed., *Le Système de Descartes*, in Durkheim, *Textes*, vol. 1, ed. V. Karady. Paris: Éditions de Minuit.

Durkheim, Émile. 1975[1912]. 'Intervention au débat à la soutenance de thèse de E. Terraillon, *L'Honneur, sentiment et principe moral*', Durkheim, *Textes*, vol. 2, ed. V. Karady. Paris: Éditions de Minuit.

Durkheim, Émile. 1975[1913]. 'Le problème religieux et la dualité de la nature humaine', in Durkheim, *Textes*, vol. 2, ed. V. Karady. Paris: Éditions de Minuit; trans. in Henrika Kucklick and Elizabeth Long, eds., *Knowledge and Society: Studies in the Sociology of Culture, Past and Present*. Greenwich, CT: JAI Press, pp. 1–62.

Durkheim, Émile. 1975[1916]. 'Hertz Robert', in Durkheim, *Textes*, vol. 3, ed. V. Karady. Paris: Éditions de Minuit.

Durkheim, Émile. 1975[1917]. 'Durkheim, André-Armand (1892–1917)', in Durkheim, *Textes*, vol. 3, ed. V. Karady. Paris: Éditions de Minuit.

Durkheim, Émile. 1975[1918a]. 'L'histoire de l'université', *La Vie universitaire à Paris*, in Durkheim, *Textes*, vol. 1, ed. V. Karady. Paris: Éditions de Minuit.

Durkheim, Émile. 1975[1918b]. 'Organisation générale de l'université de Paris', *La Vie universitaire à Paris*, in Durkheim, *Textes*, vol. 1, ed. V. Karady. Paris: Éditions de Minuit.

Durkheim, Émile. 1975[1919]. 'La "pédagogie" de Rousseau', in Durkheim, *Textes*, vol. 3, ed. V. Karady. Paris: Éditions de Minuit.

Durkheim, Émile. 1976[1900]. 'Rôle des universités dans l'éducation sociale du pays', *Revue française de sociologie* 17/2.

Durkheim, Émile. 1977[1938]. *The Evolution of Educational Thought: Lectures on the Formation and Development of Secondary Education in France*, trans Peter Collins, intro. Maurice Halbwachs. London and Boston: Routledge & Kegan Paul.

Durkheim, Émile. 1978[1885]. Review of A. Schaeffle, *Bau und Leben des sozialen Körpers: Erster Band*, in *Émile Durkheim on Institutional Analysis*, ed. and trans. Mark Traugott. Chicago: University of Chicago Press, pp. 93–114.

Durkheim, Émile. 1978[1888a]. 'Course in sociology: opening lecture', in *Émile Durkheim on Institutional Analysis*, ed. and trans. Mark Traugott. Chicago: University of Chicago Press, pp. 43–70.

Durkheim, Émile. 1978[1888b]. 'Introduction to the sociology of the family', in *Émile Durkheim on Institutional Analysis*, ed. and trans. Mark Traugott. Chicago: University of Chicago Press, pp. 205–228.

Durkheim, Émile. 1978[1889]. Review of F. Tönnies, *Gemeinschaft und Gesellschaft*, in *Émile Durkheim on Institutional Analysis*, ed. and trans. Mark Traugott. Chicago: University of Chicago Press, pp. 115–122.

Durkheim, Émile. 1978[1892]. 'The conjugal family', in *Émile Durkheim on Institutional Analysis*, ed. and trans. Mark Traugott. Chicago: University of Chicago Press, pp. 229–239.

Durkheim, Émile. 1978[1895]. 'Crime and social health', in *Émile Durkheim on Institutional Analysis*, ed. and trans. Mark Traugott. Chicago: University of Chicago Press, 181–190.

Durkheim, Émile. 1978[1901]. 'Two laws of penal evolution', in *Émile Durkheim on Institutional Analysis*, ed. and trans. Mark Traugott. Chicago: University of Chicago Press, 153–180.

Durkheim, Émile. 1978[1906]. 'Divorce by mutual consent', in *Émile Durkheim on Institutional Analysis*, ed. and trans. Mark Traugott. Chicago: University of Chicago Press, pp. 240–252.

Durkheim, Émile. 1978[1909]. 'Sociology and the social sciences', in *Émile Durkheim on Institutional Analysis*, ed. and trans. Mark Traugott. Chicago: University of Chicago Press, pp. 71–87.

Durkheim, Émile. 1979[1904]. Review of Émile Durkheim, 'Pédagogie et sociologie', in *Durkheim: Essays on Morals and Education*, ed. W.F.S. Pickering. London: Routledge, pp. 126–129.

Durkheim, Émile. 1979[1908] 'A discussion on positive morality: the issue of rationality in ethics', in *Durkheim: Essays on Morals and Education*, ed. W.F.S. Pickering. London: Routledg, pp. 52–65.

Durkheim, Émile. 1979[1909]. A discussion on the effectiveness of moral doctrines', in *Durkheim: Essays on Morals and Education*, ed. W.F.S. Pickering. London: Routledge, pp. 129–140.

Durkheim, Émile. 1979[1910]. 'A discussion on the notion of social equality', in *Durkheim: Essays on Morals and Education*, ed. W.F.S. Pickering. London: Routledge, pp. 65–76.

Durkheim, Émile. 1979[1911a]. 'Childhood', in *Durkheim: Essays on Morals and Education*, ed. W.F.S. Pickering. London: Routledge, pp. 149–154.

Durkheim, Émile. 1979[1911b]. 'A discussion on sex education', in *Durkheim: Essays on Morals and Education*, ed. W.F.S. Pickering. London: Routledge, pp. 140–148.

Durkheim, Émile. 1979[1912]. 'A discussion on the boarding school and the New School', in *Durkheim: Essays on Morals and Education*, ed. W.F.S. Pickering. London: Routledge, pp. 155–157.

Durkheim, Émile. 1979[1916]. 'The moral greatness of France and the school of the future', in *Durkheim: Essays on Morals and Education*, ed. W.F.S. Pickering. London: Routledge, pp. 158–161.

Durkheim, Émile. 1979[1919]. 'Rousseau on educational theory', in *Durkheim: Essays on Morals and Education*, ed. W.F.S. Pickering. London: Routledge, pp. 162–194.

Durkheim, Émile. 1979[1920]. 'Introduction to ethics', in *Durkheim: Essays on Morals and Education*, ed. W.F.S. Pickering. London: Routledge, pp. 77–96.

Durkheim, Émile. 1980[1898–9]. 'Prefaces to *L'Année sociologique*', in Yash Nandan, ed., *Émile Durkheim: Contributions to* L'Année sociologique. New York: Free Press

Durkheim, Émile. 1980[1900]. Review of G. Tarde, 'L'esprit de groupe', in Yash

Nandan, ed., *Émile Durkheim: Contributions to l'*Année Sociologique. New York: The Free Press.

Durkheim, Émile. 1980[1901/2]. Review of G. Simmel, *Philosophie des Geldes [Philosophy of Money]*, in Yash Nandan, ed., *Émile Durkheim: Contributions to L'Année Sociologique*. New York: The Free Press

Durkheim, Émile. 1980[1901a]. 'General concepts. Reviews', in Yash Nandan, ed., *Émile Durkheim: Contributions to L'Année Sociologique*. New York: The Free Press.

Durkheim, Émile. 1980[1901b]. Review of Alfred Fouillée, *La France au point de vue moral*, in Yash Nandan, ed., *Émile Durkheim: Contributions to L'Année Sociologique*. New York: The Free Press.

Durkheim, Émile. 1980[1901c]. Review of Charles Lefebvre, *Leçons d'introduction générale à l'histoire du droit familial français*, in Yash Nandan, ed., *Émile Durkheim: Contributions to L'Année Sociologique*. New York: The Free Press.

Durkheim, Émile. 1980[1902]. Review of Charles Seignobos, *La Méthode historique appliquée aux sciences sociales*, in Yash Nandan, ed., *Émile Durkheim: Contributions to l'*Année Sociologique. New York: The Free Press.

Durkheim, Émile. 1980[1903a] Review of A. Esmein, 'Les coutumes primitives dans les écrits des mythologues grecs et romains', in Yash Nandan, ed., *Émile Durkheim: Contributions to L'Année Sociologique*. New York: The Free Press.

Durkheim, Émile. 1980[1903b]. Review of Abel Pouzol, *La Recherche de la paternité*, in Yash Nandan, ed., *Émile Durkheim: Contributions to L'Année Sociologique*. New York: The Free Press.

Durkheim, Émile. 1980[1903c]. Review of Friedrich Prinzing, *Die Ehescheidungen in Berlin und anderwärts*, in Yash Nandan, ed., *Émile Durkheim: Contributions to L'Année Sociologique*. New York: The Free Press.

Durkheim, Émile. 1980[1903d] Review of *Rivista italiana di sociologia*, in Yash Nandan, ed., *Émile Durkheim: Contributions to L'Année Sociologique*. New York: The Free Press.

Durkheim, Émile. 1980[1903e]. Review of William Rullkoeter, *The Legal Protection of Woman among the Ancient Germans*, in Yash Nandan, ed., *Émile Durkheim: Contributions to L'Année Sociologique*. New York: The Free Press.

Durkheim, Émile. 1980[1903f] Review of S.R. Steintmetz, 'Der erbliche Rassen- und Volkscharakter', in Yash Nandan, ed., *Émile Durkheim: Contributions to L'Année Sociologique*. New York: The Free Press.

Durkheim, Émile. 1980[1904a]. Review of Bauer, *Das Geschlechtsleben in der deutschen Vergangenheit*, in Yash Nandan, ed., *Émile Durkheim: Contributions to L'Année Sociologique*. New York: The Free Press.

Durkheim, Émile. 1980[1904b]. Review of E. Glasson, *Histoire du droit et des institutions de la France*, in Yash Nandan, ed., *Émile Durkheim: Contributions to L'Année Sociologique*. New York: The Free Press.

Durkheim, Émile. 1980[1904c]. Review of Lucien Lévy-Bruhl, *La Morale et la science des moeurs*, in Yash Nandan, ed., *Émile Durkheim: Contributions to L'Année Sociologique*. New York: The Free Press.

Durkheim, Émile. 1980[1905]. Review of M. Mielziner, *The Jewish Law of Marriage and Divorce*, in Yash Nandan, ed., *Émile Durkheim: Contributions to L'Année Sociologique*. New York: The Free Press, pp. 269–271.

Durkheim, Émile. 1980[1906a]. Review of Albert Bayet, *La Morale scientifique'*, in Yash Nandan, ed., *Émile Durkheim: Contributions to* L'Année Sociologique. New York: The Free Press, pp. 135–137.

Durkheim, Émile. 1980[1906b]. Review of Théodule Ribot, *La Logique des sentiments*, in Yash Nandan, ed., *Émile Durkheim: Contributions to* L'Année Sociologique. New York: The Free Press, pp. 103–104.

Durkheim, Émile. 1980[1906c]. Review of Gabriel Tarde, 'L'interpsychologie', in Yash Nandan, ed., *Émile Durkheim: Contributions to* L'Année Sociologique. New York: The Free Press, pp. 72–73.

Durkheim, Émile. 1980[1906d]. Review of Alfred Valensi, *L'Application de la loi du divorce en France*, in Yash Nandan, ed., *Émile Durkheim: Contributions to* L'Année Sociologique. New York: The Free Press, pp. 427–432.

Durkheim, Émile. 1980[1907a] Review of Gustave Belot, 'En quête de la morale positive', in Yash Nandan, ed., *Émile Durkheim: Contributions to* L'Année Sociologique. New York: The Free Press.

Durkheim, Émile. 1980[1907b]. Review of Alfred Fouillée, *Les Éléments sociologiques de la morale*, in Yash Nandan, ed., *Émile Durkheim: Contributions to* L'Année Sociologique. New York: The Free Press.

Durkheim, Émile. 1980[1907c]. Review of G. Richard, 'Les lois de la solidarité sociale', in Yash Nandan, ed., *Émile Durkheim: Contributions to* L'Année Sociologique. New York: The Free Press.

Durkheim, Émile. 1980[1907d]. Review of Auguste Rol, *L'Évolution du divorce*, in Yash Nandan, ed., *Émile Durkheim: Contributions to* L'Année Sociologique. New York: The Free Press.

Durkheim, Émile. 1980[1907e]. Review of Edward Westermarck, *The Origin and Development of the Moral Ideas*, in Yash Nandan, ed., *Émile Durkheim: Contributions to* L'Année Sociologique. New York: The Free Press.

Durkheim, Émile. 1980[1910a]. Review of Gaston Richard, *Les Femmes dans l'Histoire*, in Yash Nandan, ed., *Émile Durkheim: Contributions to* L'Année Sociologique. New York: The Free Press.

Durkheim, Émile. 1980[1910b]. Review of Marianne Weber, *Ehefrau, und Mutter in der Rechtsentwicklung*, in Yash Nandan, ed., *Émile Durkheim: Contributions to* L'Année Sociologique. New York: The Free Press.

Durkheim, Émile. 1980[1911]. 'Preface to *L'Année Sociologue*', in Yash Nandan, ed., *Émile Durkheim: Contributions to* L'Année Sociologique. New York: The Free Press.

Durkheim, Émile. 1980[1913a]. Review of Henri Berr, *La Synthèse en histoire: Essai critique et théorique*, in Yash Nandan, ed., *Émile Durkheim: Contributions to* L'Année Sociologique. New York: The Free Press.

Durkheim, Émile. 1980[1913b]. Review of Simon Deploige, *Le Conflit de la morale et de la sociologie*, in Yash Nandan, ed., *Émile Durkheim: Contributions to* L'Année Sociologique. New York: The Free Press.

Durkheim, Émile. 1980[1913c]. Review of Gaston Richard, *La Sociologie générale et les lois sociologiques*, in Yash Nandan, ed., *Émile Durkheim: Contributions to* L'Année Sociologique. New York: The Free Press.

Durkheim, Émile. 1981[1900]. 'The realm of sociology as science', trans. Everett K. Wilson, *Social Forces* 59/4 (June): 1054–1070.

Durkheim, Émile. 1982[1895] *The Rules of Sociological Method*, in Durkheim, *The Rules of Sociological Method and Selected Texts on Sociology and its Method*, ed. Steven Lukes, trans. W. D. Halls. New York: Free Press.

Durkheim, Émile. 1982[1898]. 'Letter to the editor of the *American Journal of Sociology*', in Durkheim, *The Rules of Sociological Method and Selected Texts on Sociology and its Method*, ed. Steven Lukes, trans. W. D. Halls. New York: Free Press.

Durkheim, Émile. 1982[1899]. 'Social morphology', in Durkheim, *The Rules of Sociological Method and Selected Texts on Sociology and its Method*, ed. Steven Lukes, trans. W. D. Halls. New York: Free Press.

Durkheim, Émile. 1982[1900] 'Preface to the second edition', *The Rules of Sociological Method*, in Durkheim, *The Rules of Sociological Method and Selected Texts on Sociology and its Method*, ed. Steven Lukes, trans. W. D. Halls. New York: Free Press, pp. 34–47.

Durkheim, Émile. 1982[1901]. 'The psychological conception of society', in Durkheim, *The Rules of Sociological Method and Selected Texts on Sociology and its Method*, ed. Steven Lukes, trans. W. D. Halls. New York: Free Press.

Durkheim, Émile. 1982[1903] (with Paul Fauconnet). 'Sociology and the social sciences', in Durkheim, *The Rules of Sociological Method and Selected Texts on Sociology and its Method*, ed. Steven Lukes, trans. W. D. Halls. New York: Free Press.

Durkheim, Émile. 1982[1907]. 'Letter to the director of *Revue néo-scolastique*', in Durkheim, *The Rules of Sociological Method and Selected Texts on Sociology and its Method*, ed. Steven Lukes, trans. W. D. Halls. New York: Free Press.

Durkheim, Émile. 1982[1909]. 'The contribution of sociology to psychology and philosophy', in Durkheim, *The Rules of Sociological Method and Selected Texts on Sociology and its Method*, ed. Steven Lukes, trans. W. D. Halls. New York: Free Press.

Durkheim, Émile. 1982[1917]. 'Society', in Durkheim, *The Rules of Sociological Method and Selected Texts on Sociology and its Method*, ed. Steven Lukes, trans. W. D. Halls. New York: Free Press.

Durkheim, Émile. 1983[1955]. *Pragmatism and Sociology*, ed. John, B. Allcock, trans. J. C. Whitehouse. Cambridge: Cambridge University Press.

Durkheim, Émile. 1984[1893]. *Division of Labour in Society*, trans. W. D. Halls. Basingstoke: Macmillan.

Durkheim, Émile. 1985[1902]. 'On totemism', *History of Sociology* 5/2: 79–121.

Durkheim, Émile. 1986[1889]. Review of W. Lutoslawski's *Erhaltung und Untergang des Staatsverfassungen nach Platon, Aristoteles und Macchiavelli*, in *Durkheim on Politics and the State*, trans. W. D. Halls, ed. A. Giddens. Stanford: Stanford University Press, pp. 83–86.

Durkheim, Émile. 1986[1893]. 'Note on the definition of socialism', in *Durkheim on Politics and the State*, trans. W. D. Halls, ed. A. Giddens. Stanford: Stanford University Press.

Durkheim, Émile. 1986[1899]. 'Réponse à l'enquête sur la guerre et le militarism', in *Durkheim on Politics and the State*, trans. W. D. Halls, ed. A. Giddens. Stanford: Stanford University Press.

Durkheim, Émile. 1986[1906]. 'Intervention dans le débat sur "Patriotisme et internationalisme des classes sociales"', in *Durkheim on Politics and the State*, trans. W. D. Halls, ed. A. Giddens. Stanford: Stanford University Press.

Durkheim, Émile. 1986[1916]. 'Patriotism and militarism', in *Durkheim on Politics and the State*, trans. W. D. Halls, ed. A. Giddens. Stanford: Stanford University Press, pp. 194–233.

Durkheim, Émile. 1988[1902]. Review of Arthur Bauer, *Les Classes sociales. Analyse de la vie sociale, Notes critiques* 3/19: 256–257; repr. in *Durkheimian Studies/Études durkheimiennes* 4: 5–7.

Durkheim, Émile. 1992[1888]. 'Suicide and fertility: a study of moral statistics', *European Journal of Population* 8/3: 175–197.

Durkheim, Émile. 1992[1916a]. 'Les alliés de l'Allemagne en Orient: Turquie, Bulgarie', in Ernest Lavisse, ed., *Lettres à tous les Français*. Paris: Armand Colin, pp. 83–94.

Durkheim, Émile. 1992[1916b]. 'Les forces italiennes: la Belgique, la Serbie, le Monténégro', in Ernest Lavisse, ed., *Lettres à tous les Français*. Paris: Armand Colin, pp. 162–165.

Durkheim, Émile. 1992[1916c]. 'Les forces françaises', in Ernest Lavisse, ed., *Lettres à tous les Français*. Paris: Armand Colin, pp. 167–182.

Durkheim, Émile. 1994[1899]. 'Concerning the definition of religious phenomena', in *Durkheim on Religion: A Selection of Readings with Bibliographies*, ed. W.S.F. Pickering, trans. J. Redding. London: Routledge & Kegan Paul.

Durkheim, Émile. 1994[1913]. Review of L. Lévy-Bruhl, *Les Fonctions mentales dans les sociétés inférieures*, in *Durkheim on Religion: A Selection of Readings with Bibliographies*, ed. W.S.F. Pickering, trans. J. Redding. London: Routledge & Kegan Paul.

Durkheim, Émile. 1994[1914]. 'The social conception of religion', in *Durkheim on Religion: A Selection of Readings with Bibliographies*, ed. W.S.F. Pickering, trans. J. Redding. London: Routledge & Kegan Paul.

Durkheim, Émile. 1995[1912]. *The Elementary Forms of Religious Life*, trans. Karen E. Fields. New York: Free Press.

Durkheim, Émile. 1998. *Lettres à Marcel Mauss*, ed. Philippe Besnard et Marcel Fournier. Paris: PUF.

Durkheim, Émile. 1999[1917]. 'La politique de demain', *Durkheimian Studies/ Études durkheimiennes* 5.

Durkheim, Émile. 2002[1897]. *Suicide*, trans. John A. Spaulding and George Simpson. London: Routledge.

Durkheim, Émile. 2003. *L'Évaluation en comité*, ed. Stéphane Baciocchi and Jennifer Mergy. Oxford: Durkheim Press.

Durkheim, Émile. 2004. *Durkheim's Philosophy Lectures; Notes from the Lycée de Sens Course, 1883–1884*, trans. Neil Gross and Robert Alun Jones. Cambridge: Cambridge University Press.

Durkheim, Émile. 2006[1909]. 'Frédéric Rauh', in *Durkheimian Studies/Études durkheimiennes* 12(1).

Durkheim, Émile and Bouglé, Célestin. 1910. 'Les conditions sociologiques de la connaissance', *L'Année sociologique* 11: 41–42.

Durkheim, Émile and Denis, Ernest. 1915. *Qui a voulu la guerre? Les origines de la guerre d'après les documents diplomatiques*. Paris: Librairie Armand Colin.

Durkheim, Émile and Mauss, Marcel. 1963[1903]. *Primitive Classification*, trans. and ed. Rodney Needham. Chicago: University of Chicago Press.

Durkheim, Émile and Mauss, Marcel. 1969[1910]. Review of C. Strehlow, *Die Aranda und Loritja-Staemme in Zentral-Australien*, in Durkheim, *Journal sociologique*. Paris: PUF.

Durkheim, Émile and Mauss, Marcel. 1969[1913]. Note sur la notion de civilisation', *L'Année sociologique*, 12, 1913, in Durkheim, *Journal sociologique*. Paris: PUF.

Durkheim, Émile and Mauss, Marcel. 1994[1913]. Review of J. Frazer, *Totemism and Exogamy* (1911), and Émile Durkheim, *Les Formes élémentaires de la vie religieuse*, in *Durkheim on Religion: A Selection of Readings with Bibliographies*, ed. W.S.F. Pickering, trans. J. Redding. London: Routledge & Kegan Paul.

Durkheim, Émile, et al. 1918. *La Vie universitaire à Paris*. Paris: Librairie Armand Colin.

Espinas, Alfred. 1878. *Des Sociétés animals*, 2nd edn. Paris: Librairie Germer Baillière et Cie.

Espinas, Alfred. 1882. 'Les études sociologiques en France', *Revue philosophique* 14.

Espinas, Alfred. 1888. 'Rapport annuel de la faculté des lettres', in Académie de Bordeaux, *Comptes-rendus des travaux de la faculté de droit, de médecine, des sciences et des lettres*, année académique 1887–8. Bordeaux.

Espinas, Alfred. 1891. *Histoire des doctrines économiques*. Paris: Armand Colin.

Espinas, Alfred. 1901. 'Être ou ne pas être ou du postulat de la sociologie', *Revue philosophique* 51.

Essetier, D. 1930. 'M. Gaston Richard', *Foi et vie* 6.

Fabiani, Jean-Louis. 1993. 'Métaphysique, morale, sociologie, Durkheim et le retour à la philosophie', *Revue de métaphysique et de morale* 98/1–2 (January–June): 175–193.

Fabiani, Jean-Louis. 1998. *Les Philosophies de la république*. Paris: Éditions de Minuit.

Fabiani, Jean-Louis. 2003. 'Clore enfin l'ère des généralités', in Émile Durkheim, *L'Évaluation en comité*, ed. Stéphane Baciocchi and Jennifer Mergy. Oxford: Durkheim Press, pp. 151–200.

Faguet, Émile. 1907[1898] 'Sur *Le Suicide*', *Revue bleue* (20 April), in Faguet, *Propos littéraires*, 4th series. Paris: Société française d'imprimerie et de librairie, pp. 321–334.

Fauconnet, Paul. 1898. Review of Émile Durkheim, *Le Suicide*, *Revue philosophique* 45 (April).

Fauconnet, Paul. 1904. Review of Lucien Lévy-Bruhl, *La Morale et la sciences des mœurs* (1903), *Revue philosophique* 29/57 (January–June).

Fauconnet, Paul. 1908. 'La méthode sociologique appliquée à l'étude des faits économiques', *Revue de synthèse historique* 16/48 (June): 180–187.

Fauconnet, Paul. 1928[1920]. *La Responsabilité. Étude de sociologie*, 2nd edn. Paris: Librairie Félix Alcan.

Fauconnet, Paul. 1956[1922] 'Introduction: Durkheim's pedagogical work', in *Education and Sociology*, ed. P. Fauconnet, trans. Sherwood D. Fox. Glencoe, IL: Free Press of Glencoe.

Fauconnet, Paul and Mauss, Marcel. 1901. 'Sociologie: objet et méthode', in *La Grande Encylcopédie*, vol. 30, pp. 165–175.

Favre, Pierre. 1989. *Naissance de la science politique en France, 1870–1914*. Paris: Fayard.

Ferneuil, Thomas. 1889. 'Individualisme et socialisme', *Revue d'économie politique* 3.

Feydeau, Ernest. 1873. *Mémoires d'un coulissier*. Paris: Librairie nouvelle.

Filloux, Jean-Claude. 1970. 'Présentation. L'homme', in Émile Durkheim, *La Science sociale et l'action*. Paris: PUF.

Filloux, Jean-Claude. 1977. *Durkheim et le socialisme*. Genève: Librairie Droz.

Fouillée, Alfred. 1881. 'La morale contemporaine en Allemagne', *Revue des Deux Mondes* (1 March).

Fouillée, Alfred. 1891. 'Les grandes conclusions de la psychologie contemporaines – la conscience et ses transformations', *Revue des Deux Mondes* 107.

Fouillée, Alfred. 1894. 'L'enseignement philosophique et la démocratie française', in *Pour et contre l'enseignement philosophique*. Paris: Alcan.

Fouillée, Alfred. 1895a. 'Dégénérescence. Le passé et le présent de notre nation', *Revue des Deux Mondes* 131: 793–824.

Fouillée, Alfred. 1895b. 'La psychologie des peuples et l'anthropologie', *Revue des Deux Mondes* 128: 365–396.

Fouillée. Alfred. 1899. 'La sociologie dans l'enseignement secondaire', *Revue internationale de sociologie* 7/10 (October).

Fouillée. Alfred. 1922[1880]. *La Science sociale contemporaine*. Paris: Librairie Hachette.

Fournier, Marcel. 1987. 'Durkheim, *L'Année sociologique* et l'art', *Durkheimian Studies/Études durkheimiennes* 12 (January): 1–11.

Fournier, Marcel. 2007[1994]. *Marcel Mauss: A Biography*, trans. Jane Marie Todd. Princeton: Princeton University Press.

Fournier de Flaix, E. 1890. 'L'économie sociale, sa méthode, ses progrès', *Revue de l'économie politique* 4: 414–430.

Frazer, James. 1910. *Totemism and Exogamy*, 4 vols. London: Macmillan.

Freddy, Raphaël and Weyl, Robert. 1977. *L'Imagerie juive en Alsace*. Toulouse: Privat.

Freud, Sigmund. 1989. *Totem and Taboo*, trans. J. Strachey; intro. P. Gay. London: Routledge; orig. German 1913.

Friedland, Roger. 2005. 'Drag kings at the totem ball: the erotics of collective representation in Durkheim and Sigmund Freud', in J.C. Alexander and P. Smith, eds., *The Cambridge Companion to Durkheim*. Cambridge: Cambridge University Press.

Galton, Francis, et al. 1905. *Sociological Papers*. London: Macmillan.

Gane, Mike. 1992. *The Radical Sociology of Durkheim and Mauss*. London: Routledge.

Gautherin, Jacqueline. 1987. 'Note sur Durkheim et la pédagogie à Bordeaux', *Durkheimian Studies/Études durkheimiennes* 12 (January).

Gautier, Émile. 1880. *Le Darwinisme social*. Paris: Derveaux.

Geiger, Roger. 1979. 'La sociologie dans les écoles normales primaires', *Revue française de sociologie* 10/1 (January–March): 257–268.

Gérard, O. 1893. 'Introduction', in H. R. Nénot, *Monographie de la nouvelle Sorbonne*. Paris: Imprimerie nationale.

Gérin, Léon. 1912. 'Aperçu d'un enseignement de la science sociale', *Bulletin de la Société internationale de science sociale*, part I (April), part II (July–August).

Giddens, Anthony. 1971. 'Durkheim's early works', in Giddens, *Capitalism and Modern Social Theory*. Cambridge: Cambridge University Press, pp. 65–81.

Gide, Charles. 1887. 'Chronique, 1870–1887', *Revue d'économie politique* 1.

Gide, Charles. 1894. 'Le néo-collectivisme', *Revue de l'économie politique* 8: 420–440.

Gide, Charles. 1903. 'L'économie sociale à l'Exposition universelle de 1900', *Revue internationale de sociologie* 11/4 (April).

Gillard, Lucien and Rosier, Michel (eds.). 1996. *François Simiand (1873–1935). Sociologie-Histoire-Économie*. Amsterdam: Éditions des archives contemporaines.

Giovanni Paoletti, 1995. 'La réception des *Règles* en France', in Massimo Borlandi and Laurent Mucchielli, eds., *La Sociologie et sa methode. Les règles de Durkheim un siècle après*. Paris: L'Harmattan.

Goblot, Edmond. 1900. Review of *L'Année sociologique* 3, *Revue de synthèse historique* 1/3 (December): 245–252.

Goblot, Edmond. 1902. Review of *L'Année sociologique* 4, *Revue de synthèse historique* 4/2: 239–240.

Goblot, Edmond. 1903. 'Notes critiques sur *L'Année sociologique* 5, *Revue de synthèse historique* 6/16.

Goblot, Edmond. 1904. Review of *L'Année sociologique* 6, *Revue de synthèse historique* 7/23 (April).

Goldenweiser, Alexander. 1911. Review of Lucien Lévy-Bruhl, *Les Fonctions mentales dans les sociétés inférieures* (1910), *American Anthropologist* 13: 121–130.

Goldenweiser, Alexander. 1912. 'The origin of totemism', *American Antrhopologist* 14.

Goldenweiser, Alexander. 1915. Review of Émile Durkheim, *Les Formes élémentaires de la vie religieuse*, *American Anthropologist* 17: 719–735.

Goldstein, J. 1987. *Console and Classify. The French Psychiatric Profession in the Nineteenth Century*. Cambridge: Cambridge University Press.

Granet, Marcel. 1930. 'La sociologie religieuse de Durkheim', *Europe* 86: 287–292.

Greenberg, Louis M. 1976. 'Bergson and Durkheim as sons and assimilators: the early years', *French Historical Studies* 9/4.

Grivel, Gilles. 1997. 'Le Parti républicain dans les Vosges, de 1870 à 1914'. Doctoral thesis, University of Nancy-II, 2 vols.

Grivel, Gilles. 2005. 'Histoire de la communauté juive d'Épinal', *Annales de la société d'émulation du département des Vosges* 16.

Gross, Neil. 1996a. 'Durkheim's lectures at Sens', *Durkheimian Studies/Études durkheimiennes* 2.

Gross, Neil. 1996b. 'A Note on the sociological eye and the discovery of a new Durkheim text', *Journal of the History of the Behavioral Sciences* 32.

Guirard, Paul. 1895. 'Fustel de Coulanges', in *Le Centenaire de l'École normale supérieure*.

Halbwachs, Maurice. 1907. Review of Vilfredo Pareto, *Manuel di economia politica*, *L'Année sociologique* 10: 527–528.

Halbwachs, Maurice. 1910. Review of *Les Expropriations et les prix des terrains en France*, *L'Année sociologique* 11.

Halbwachs, Maurice. 1913a. Review of Joseph Schumpeter, *Theorie der wirtschaftlichen Entwicklung* (1912), *L'Année sociologique* 12: 594–598.

Halbwachs, Maurice. 1913b. Review of Werner Sombart, *Die Juden und das Wirtschaftsleben* (1911), *L'Année sociologique* 12: 623–629.

Halbwachs, Maurice. 1918. 'La doctrine d'Émile Durkheim', *Revue philosophique* 85.

Halbwachs, Maurice. 1925. *Les Origines du sentiment religieux*. Paris: Librairie Stock.

Halbwachs, Maurice. 1928[1907]. *Leibniz*, 2nd exp. edn. Paris: Mellottée.

Halbwachs, Maurice. 1941. 'Célestin Bouglé, soliologue', *Revue de métaphysique et de morale* 48/1.

Halbwachs, Maurice. 1977[1938]. 'Introduction', in Émile Durkheim, *The Evolution of Educational Thought: Lectures on the Formation and Development of Secondary Education in France*, trans Peter Collins. London and Boston: Routledge & Kegan Paul.

Halbwachs, Maurice. 1978[1930]. *The Causes of Suicide*, trans. Harold Goldblatt. New York: Free Press.

Halévy, Daniel. 1932. *Pays parisiens*. Paris: Gallimard.

Halévy, Élie. 1996. *Correspondance, 1891–1937*. Paris: Éditions de Fallois.

Halley, André. 1901. *En flânant. À travers l'Exposition de 1900*. Paris: Perrin.

Halls, W.D. 2000. 'Durkheim and pacifism: contemporary political issues, 1900–1914', *Durkheimian Studies/Études durkheimiennes* 6: 5–14.

Halphen, Étienne. 1987. 'Préface', in *Durkheim, cent ans de sociologie à Bordeaux*. Bordeaux: Socio-Diffusion.

Halphen, Étienne. 1998. *Hommages à Émile Durkheim*. Oxford: Société des amis d'Émile Durkheim.

Hamon, A. and Hamon, D. 1905. 'The political situation in France', *American Journal of Sociology* 11/1 (July).

Hanna, Martha. 1994. *The Mobilization of the Intellect. French Scholars and Writers during the Great War*. Cambridge: Cambridge University Press.

Hanotaux, Gabriel. 1908. *Histoire de la France contemporaine, 1871–1900*. Vol. 4: *La République parlementaire*. Paris: Ancienne Librairie Furne-Société d'édition contemporaine.

Harris, Joseph. 1995. *The Tallest Tower: Eiffel and the Belle Époque*. Boston: Houghton Mifflin.

Hartland, Sidney E. 1899. Review of Baldwin Spencer and F.J. Gillen, *The Native Tribes of Central Australia*, *Folk-Lore* 10.

Hartland, Sidney E. 1900. Review of *L'Année sociologique* 2, *Folk-Lore* 11 (December): 92–96.

Hartland, Sidney E. 1903. Review of *L'Année sociologique* 6, *Folk-Lore* 14 (December): 432–435.

Hartland, Sidney E. 1904. Review of *L'Année sociologique* 7, *Folk-Lore* 15 (September): 359–365.

Hartland, Sidney E. 1907. Review of *L'Année sociologique* 9, *Folk-Lore* 27 (March).

Hartland, Sidney E. 1913. Review of Durkheim, *The Elementary Forms of Religious Life*, *Man* 13/6: 91–96.

Hauriou, Maurice. 1894. 'Réponse à "un docteur en droit" sur la sociologie', *Revue internationale de sociologie*.

Hawkins, M.J. 1980. 'Traditionalism and organicism in Durkheim's early writings, 1885–1893', *Journal for the History of the Behavioral Sciences* 16: 31–44.

Hawkins, M.J. 1995. 'Durkheim and republican citizenship', in K. Thompson, ed., *Durkheim, Europe and Democracy*. Oxford: British Centre for Durkheimian Studies, 1995, pp. 12–41; repr. in W.S.F. Pickering, ed., *Émile Durkheim. Critical Assessments of Leading Sociologists*, vol. 3. London and New York: Routledge, 2001, pp. 295–316.

Hemmer, Abbé. 1905. 'Réflexions sur la situation de l'Église de France au début du XXe siècle', *La Quinzaine* (1 May).

Herr, Lucien. 1893. Review of Émile Durkheim, *De la division du travail social*, *Revue universitaire* 2/1.

Herr, Lucien. 1894. Review of Durkheim, *Revue universitaire* 3/2.

Herr, Lucien. 1898. 'À M. Maurice Barrès', *Revue blanche* (15 February).

Herriot, Édouard. n.d. 'Un républicain', in *Célestin Bouglé, 1870–1940* (Dossier Célestin Bouglé, AJ/16/5885, Archives nationales).

Hertz, Robert. 1905. Review of E. Demolins, R. Pinot et P. de Rousiers, *La Méthode sociale*, in *L'Année sociologique* 8.

Hertz, Robert. 1907. 'Contribution à une étude sur la représentation collective de la mort', *L'Année sociologique* 10.

Hertz, Robert. 1909. Review of Henri Hubert and Marcel Mauss, *Mélanges d'histoire des religions*, *Revue de l'histoire des religions* 60.

Hertz, Robert. 1910. *Socialisme et depopulation*. Paris: Les Cahiers du socialiste 10.

Hertz, Robert. 2002. *Un Ethnologue dans les tranchées. Lettres de Robert Hertz à sa femme Alice*, ed. Alexander Riley and Philippe Besnard. Paris: CNRS éditions.

Hertzog-Cachin, Marcel. 1980. *Regards sur la vie de Marcel Cachin*. Paris: Éditions sociales.

Horne, Janet R. 2002. *A Social Laboratory for Modern France. The Musée Social and the Rise of the Welfare State*. Durham, NC, and London: Duke University Press.

Hubert, Henri. 1901. 'Étude critique sur un ouvrage d'histoire réligieuse. J.G. Frazer, *Golden Bough*', *Revue de synthèse historique* 2–3: 276–282.

Hubert, Henri. 1902. Review of B. Spencer and F.J. Gillen, *The Native Tribes of Central Australia*, *Revue de l'histoire des religions* 23/45.

Hubert, Henri. 1904a. 'Introduction', in P.-D. Chantepie de Saussaye, *Manuel d'histoire des religions*. Paris: Alcan.

Hubert, Henri. 1904b. Review of J.T. Stickney, *Les Sentences dans la poésie grecque d'Homère à Euripide*, *L'Année sociologique* 7: 671.

Hubert, Henri. 1905. 'J.T. Stickney', *Revue archéologique* 1: 130–131.

Hubert, Henri. 1907. Review of Marcel Mauss, *L'Origine des pouvoirs magiques dans les sociétés australiennes*, *L'Année sociologique* 10.

Hubert, Henri. 1913. Review of S. Reinach, *Cultes, mythes et religions* (1912), *L'Année sociologique* 12.

Hubert, Henri and Mauss, Marcel. 1964[1899]. *Sacrifice: Its Nature and Function*, trans. W.D. Halls; foreword by E.E. Evans-Pritchard. Chicago: University of Chicago Press.

Hubert, Henri and Mauss, Marcel. 1969[1906]. 'Introduction à l'analyse de quelques phénomènes religieux', in Marcel Mauss, *Œuvres*, vol. 1. Paris: Éditions de Minuit.

Huteau, M. 2002. *Psychologie, psychiatrie et société sous la Troisième République. La biocratie d'Édouard Toulouse.* Paris: L'Harmattan.

Huvelin, Paul. 1907. 'Magie et droit individuel', *L'Année sociologique* 10.

Isambert, François-André. 1979. 'Henri Hubert et la sociologie du temps', *Revue française de sociologie* 10.

James, Tony. 1995. *Dream, Creativity, and Madness in Nineteenth-Century France.* Oxford: Clarendon Press.

Janet, Paul. 1865. *La Crise philosophique.* Paris: Germer-Baillière.

Janet, Pierre. 1889. *L'Automatisme psychologique. Essai de psychologie expérimentale sur les formes inférieures de l'activité humaine.* Paris: Alcan.

Jankelevitch, S. 1902. 'Nature et société', *Revue philosophique* 7/53 (January–June).

Jankélévitch, S. 1905. 'Sciences des mœurs et expériences morales. À propos d'ouvrages récents', *Revue de synthèse historique* 10: 38–49.

Jarrassé, Dominique. 2002. 'Les synagogues de Bordeaux', in *La Synagogue de Bordeaux.* Bordeaux: Éditions le bord de l'eau – consistoire israélite de Bordeaux, pp. 15–47.

Jaurès, Jean. 1969[1911]. *L'Armée nouvelle.* Paris: Éditions sociales.

Javalet, Robert. 1969. *Épinal à la Belle Époque.* Mulhouse-Dornach: Presses des Établissements Braun et Cie.

Joas, Hans. 1996. *The Creativity of Action.* Chicago: The University of Chicago Press.

Jones, Robert Alun. 1984. *Émile Durkheim: An Introduction to Four Major Works.* Beverly Hills, CA: Sage.

Jones, Robert Alun. 2003. 'La science positive de la morale en France: les sources allemandes de la *Division du travail social*', in Philippe Besnard, Massimo Borlandi and Paul Vogt, eds., *Division du travail et lien social. La thèse de Durkheim un siècle après.* Paris: PUF, pp. 11–43.

Jones, Susan Stedman. 2001. *Durkheim Reconsidered.* Cambridge: Polity.

Julliard, Jacques and Winock, Michel, eds. 1996. *Dictionnaire des intellectuels français.* Paris: Seuil.

Kalaora, B. and Savoye, A. 1989. *Les Inventeurs oubliés. Le Play et ses continuateurs aux origines des sciences sociales.* Seyssel: Champ Vallon.

Karady, Victor. 1979. 'Stratégies de réussite et modes de faire-valoir de la sociologie chez les durkheimiens', *Revue française de sociologie* XX/1: 49–82.

Karsenti, Bruno. 2006. *La Société en personnes. Études durkheimiennes.* Paris: Economica.

Kopp, Robert. 2005. '"Les limbes insondés de la tristesse". Figures de la mélancolie romantique de Chateaubriand à Sartre', in Jean Clair, ed., *Mélancolie. Génie et folie en Occident.* Paris: Gallimard/Réunion des musées nationaux, pp. 328–340.

LaCapra, Dominick. 1972. *Émile Durkheim: Sociologist and Philosopher.* Ithaca, NY: Cornell University Press.

Lacroix, Bernard. 1981. *Durkheim et le politique*. Paris: Fondation des sciences politiques; Montréal: Presses de l'université de Montréal.

Lacroze, René, 1960–1. 'Émile Durkheim à Bordeaux (1887–1902)', *Actes de l'Académie nationale des sciences, belles-lettres et arts de Bordeaux*, 4th series, vol. 17.

Lagardelle, Hubert. 1899. 'Le socialisme et l'affaire Dreyfus', *Le Mouvement socialiste* 1.

Lagardelle, Hubert. 1900. 'La leçon de la conférence Guesde-Jaurès', *Le Mouvement socialiste*, 15: 705–707.

Lalande, André. 1900. 'Le Congrès international de philosophie', *Revue de métaphysique et de morale*.

Lalande, André. 1960. 'Commémoration du centenaire de la naissance d'Émile Durkheim', *Annales de l'université de Paris* 30: 22–25.

Lalande, André. 1968[1926]. *Vocabulaire technique et critique de la philosophie*. Paris: PUF.

Lang, Andrew. 1904. 'Correspondence. Dr. Durkheim on *Social Origins*', *Folk-Lore* 15/1 (March): 100–102.

Langlois, Charles Victor. 1900. 'La question de l'enseignement secondaire en France et à l'étranger. Pour sauver l'enseignement classique. Les modes d'organisation de l'enseignement secondaire', *Revue de Paris* 1.

Langlois, Charles Victor and Seignobos, Charles. 1898. *Introduction aux méthodes historiques*. Paris: Hachette.

Lapie, Paul. 1894. 'La définition du socialisme', *Revue de métaphysique et de morale* 2.

Lapie, Paul. 1895. 'L'année sociologique 1894', *Revue de métaphysique et de morale* 3.

Lapie, Paul. 1898a. Review of Antonio Labriola, 'Essais sur la conception materialiste de l'histoire', *L'Année Sociologique* 1: 270–277.

Lapie, Paul. 1898b. 'Questions pratiques. La justice pénale', *Revue de métaphysique et de morale* (March).

Lapie, Paul. 1899a. *La Justice par l'état: étude de morale sociale*. Paris: Alcan.

Lapie, Paul. 1899b. 'Questions pratiques. L'arbitrage politique', *Revue de métaphysique et de morale* 7: 102–6.

Lapie, Paul. 1901. 'La réforme de l'éducation universitaire', *Revue de métaphysique et de morale* 9.

Lapie, Paul. 1902a. 'Études critiques. Éthologie politique', *Revue de morale et de métaphysique*: 514–515.

Lapie, Paul. 1902b. *Pour la raison*. Paris: E. Cornély.

Lapie, Paul. 1904. 'Expériences sur l'activité intellectuelle', *Revue philosophique* 29/57 (January–June): 168–192.

Lapie, Paul. 1905. Review of Gaston Richard, *Notions élémentaires de sociologie*, *L'Année sociologique* 8: 171–175.

Lapie, Paul. 1908. *La Femme dans la famille*. Paris: O. Doin.

Lapie, Paul. 1915. *L'Instituteur et la guerre*. Paris: H. Didier.

Lapie, Paul. 1927. 'L'éducation morale dans les écoles françaises', *Enseignement public* XC: 103–112.

Lapouge, G. de. 1895. 'Recherches anthropologiques sur le problème de la dépopulation', *Revue d'économie politique* 9.

Larre, Élodie. 1998. 'Les juifs et l'opinion bordelaise de 1890 à 1902'. Master's thesis, University of Bordeaux.

Lavisse, Ernest. 1992[1916]. 'La paix que les Allemands voudraient faire', in Lavisse, ed., *Lettres à tous les Français*, Paris: Armand Colin, pp. 35–46.

Lazard, Max. 1939. 'François Simiand, 1873–1935', *Bulletin de l'Association française pour le progrès social* 238–9: 4–8.

Le Roy, Édouard. 1900. 'Science et philosophie. IV, *Revue de métaphysique et de morale* 8: 37–72.

Leenhardt, Maurice. 1950. 'Marcel Mauss', *Annuaire de l'École pratique des hautes études*. Section des sciences religieuses, Meulon.

Lehman, N.J. 1993. *Deconstructing Durkheim: A Post-Post-Structuralist Critique*. London: Routledge.

Lemaître, Jules. 1895. L'esprit normalien', in *Le Centenaire de l'École normale supérieure*.

Lenoir, Raymond. 1930. 'L'œuvre sociologique d'Émile Durkheim', *Europe* 13.

Lenoir, Rémi. 2003. *Généalogie de la morale familiale*. Paris: Éditions du Seuil.

Léon, Xavier. 1893. 'Introduction', *Revue de métaphysique et de morale* 1.

Léon, Xavier. 1917. 'Nécrologie [Obituary]. Émile Durkheim', *Revue de métaphysique et de morale* (July).

Léon, Xavier. 1921. 'Nécrologie [Obituary], Émile Boutroux (1845–1921)', *Revue de métaphysique et de morale*, October–December supplement.

Léon, Xavier and Halévie, Élie. 1993. 'Correspondance (1891/1898)', *Revue de métaphysique et de morale* 98 (January–June).

Lepenies, Wolf. 1990. *Les Trois Cultures. Entre science et littérature, l'avènement de la sociologie*. Paris: Éditions de la Maison des sciences de l'homme.

Leroux, Robert. 1998. *Histoire et sociologie en France. De l'histoire-science à la sociologie durkheimienne*. Paris: PUF.

Leroy, Géraldi. 1981. *Péguy. Entre l'ordre et la revolution*. Paris: Presses de la Fondation nationale des sciences politiques.

Leuba, James H. 1913. 'Sociology and psychology. The conception of religion and magic and the place of psychology in sociological studies: a discussion of the views of Durkheim and of Hubert and Mauss', *American Journal of Sociology* 19: 323–342.

Levasseur, Émile. 1894. 'L'histoire de la démographie', *Revue de l'économie politique* 7.

Lévi-Strauss, Claude. 1973[1962]. *Totemism*, trans. Rodney Needham. Harmondsworth: Penguin Books.

Lévi, Sylvain. 1932. 'Discours prononcé aux obsèques de Paul Alphandéry', *Revue de l'histoire des religions* 105.

Lévy-Bruhl, Lucien. 1895. 'Questions sociologiques', *La Revue bleue*, 4th series, 111/5 (22 June): 776–782.

Lévy-Bruhl, Lucien. 1903. *La Morale et la science des mœurs*. Paris: Alcan.

Liard, Louis. 1890. *Universités et facultés*. Paris: A. Colin.

Littré, Émile. 1879. 'De la théologie considérée comme science positive et sa place dans l'enseignement laïque par Maurice Vernes', *Revue de philosophie positive* (May–June): 365–374.

Logue, William. 2003. 'Sociologie et politique: le libéralisme de Célestin Bouglé', in

Philippe Besnard, Massimo Borlandi and Paul Vogt, eds., *Division du travail et lien social. La thèse de Durkheim un siècle après*. Paris: PUF.

Loisy, Alfred. 1909. Review of Henri Hubert and Marcel Mauss, *Mélanges d'histoire des religions*, in *Revue critique d'histoire et de littérature religieuses* (May).

Loisy, Alfred. 1913. 'Sociologie et religion', *Revue d'histoire et de littérature religieuses*: 45–76.

Loisy, Alfred. 1932. *Mémoires pour servir à l'histoire religieuse de notre temps*, vol. 2. Paris: Émile Noury.

Lukes, Steven. 1969. *Émile Durkheim: An Intellectual Biography*, 2 vols. University of Oxford: Faculty of Social Studies.

Lukes, Steven. 1982. *Durkheim: The Rules of Sociological Method and Selected Texts on Sociology and its Method*, trans. W. D. Halls. New York: Free Press.

Lukes, Steven. 1985[1973]. *Émile Durkheim. His Life and Work*. Stanford: Stanford University Press.

Lutzky, Harriet. 1998. 'On Durkheim's tombstone', *Durkheimian Studies/Études durkheimiennes* 2: 38–41.

Mahé, Alain. 1998. 'Un disciple inconnu de Marcel Mauss: René Maunier', in René Maunier, *Recherche sur les échanges rituels en Afrique du Nord*. Paris: Bouchène.

Maire, Gilbert. 1935. *Bergson, mon maître*. Paris: B. Grasset.

Malinowski, Bronislaw. 1913. Review of Émile Durkheim, *Les Formes élémentaires de la vie religieuse*, *Folk-Lore* 44/4 (December): 525–526.

Malinowski, Bronislaw. 1935. *Coral Gardens and Their Magic*, vol. 2. London: Allen and Unwin.

Malinowski, Bronislaw. 1944. *A Scientific Theory of Culture and Other Essays*. Boston: Beacon Press.

Mänicke-Gyöngyosi, K. 1984. 'The reception of Durkheim in Russia and Soviet Union', *Durkheimian Studies/Études durkheimiennes* 10: 13–76.

Mantoux, Paul. 1903. 'Histoire et sociologie', *Revue de synthèse historique* 7 (October): 121–140.

Marcuse, Alexander. 1937. 'La philosophie de l'Aufklaerung au temps du romantisme, Auguste Comte et Arthur Schopenhauer', *Revue de synthèse* 14/2: 149–159.

Marillier, Léon. 1901. 'Le folk-Lore et la science des religions', *Revue de l'histoire des religions* 41.

Marpeau, Benoît. 2000. *Gustave Le Bon. Parcours d'un intellectuel, 1841–1931*. Paris: Éditions CNRS.

Marrus, Michael R. 1971. *The Politics of Assimilation. A Study of the French Jewish Community in the Time of the Dreyfus Affair*. Oxford: Oxford University Press.

Maublanc, René. 1930. Contribution to 'L'œuvre sociologique d'Émile Durkheim', *Europe* 23: 287–300.

Maunier, René. 1927. Review of *L'Année sociologique*, new series, *Revue philosophique* (July–August): 303–307.

Mauss, Marcel. 1898. 'L'Année sociologique', *Internationales Archiv für Ethnographie* 11.

Mauss, Marcel. 1900a. 'Le congrès international des coopératives socialistes', *Le Mouvement socialiste* (15 October): 494–502.

Mauss, Marcel. 1900b. 'La guerre du Transvaal', *Le Mouvement socialiste* (1 June).

Mauss, Marcel. 1900c. 'Le jugement de la Haute Cour et la propagande socialiste', *Le Mouvement socialiste* (1 February).

Mauss, Marcel. 1903. Review of C. Letourneau, *La Psychologie ethnique*. *L'Année sociologique* 6.

Mauss, Marcel. 1904. Review of P.-D. Chantepie de la Saussaye, *Manuel d'histoire des religions*, *Notes critiques* (5 June).

Mauss, Marcel. 1962[1928]. 'Preface', in Émile Durkheim, *Socialism*, trans. Charlotte Sattler, ed. Alvin W. Gouldner. New York: Collier Books.

Mauss, Marcel. 1969. *Œuvres*. Paris: Éditions de Minuit, 1969.

Mauss, Marcel. 1969[1897]. 'La religion et les origines du droit pénal d'après un livre récent', in Mauss, *Œuvres*, vol. 2, Paris: Éditions de Minuit, pp. 651–698.

Mauss, Marcel. 1969[1899]. Review of C.P. Tiele, *Elements of the Science of Religion*, in Mauss, *Œuvres*, vol. 1, Paris: Éditions de Minuit.

Mauss, Marcel. 1969[1900]. Review of B. Spencer and F.J. Gillen, *The Native Tribes of Central Australia*, in Mauss, *Œuvres*, vol. 2, Paris: Éditions de Minuit, pp. 413–422.

Mauss, Marcel. 1969[1902]. 'L'enseignement de l'histoire des religions des peuples non civilisés', in Mauss, *Œuvres*, vol. 3. Paris: Éditions de Minuit.

Mauss, Marcel. 1969[1904a]. 'Philosophie religieuse, conceptions générales', in Mauss, *Œuvres*, vol. 1, Paris: Éditions de Minuit.

Mauss, Marcel. 1969[1904b]. Review of W. James, *The Varieties of Religious Experience*, in Mauss, *Œuvres*, vol. 1, Paris: Éditions de Minuit, pp. 58–65.

Mauss, Marcel. 1969[1905]. 'Notes sur le totémisme', in Mauss, *Œuvres*, vol. 1. Paris: Éditions de Minuit.

Mauss, Marcel. 1969[1907]. Review of Henri Hubert, 'La représentation du temps dans la religion', in Mauss, *Œuvres*, vol. 1. Paris: Éditions de Minuit.

Mauss, Marcel. 1969[1908]. 'L'art et le mythe d'après Wundt', in Mauss, *Œuvres*, vol. 2, Paris: Éditions de Minuit.

Mauss, Marcel. 1969[1909]. *La Prière*, in Mauss, *Œuvres*, vol. 1, Paris: Éditions de Minuit.

Mauss, Marcel. 1969[1910]. Review of Arnold Van Gennep, *Les Rites de passage*, in Mauss, *Œuvres*, vol. 2, Paris: Éditions de Minuit.

Mauss, Marcel. 1969[1913]. Review of C. Strehlow, *Die Aranda und Loritja-Staemme in Zentral-Australien*, III, in Mauss, *Œuvres*, vol. 2. Paris: Éditions de Minuit.

Mauss, Marcel. 1969[1925]. 'In memoriam. L'œuvre inédite de Durkheim et de ses collaborateurs', in Mauss, *Œuvres*, vol. 3. Paris: Éditions de Minuit, pp. 473–499.

Mauss, Marcel. 1969[1927]. 'Notices biographiques', in Mauss, *Œuvres*, vol. 3. Paris: Éditions de Minuit.

Mauss, Marcel. 1969[1930] 'Intervention à la suite d'une intervention de J. Dewey', *Bulletin de la Société française de philosophie* (1930), in, Mauss, *Œuvres*, vol. 3. Paris: Éditions de Minuit.

Mauss, Marcel. 1969[1933]. 'La sociologie en France depuis 1914', in Mauss, *Œuvres*, vol. 3. Paris: Éditions de Minuit.

Mauss, Marcel. 1969[1935]. 'Sylvain Lévi', in Mauss, *Œuvres*, vol. 3, Paris: Éditions de Minuit.

Mauss, Marcel. 1969[1936]. 'In memoriam: Antoine Meillet', in Mauss, *Œuvre*s, vol. 3, Paris: Éditions de Minuit.

Mauss, Marcel. 1969[1937]. 'Introduction à la morale professionnelle d'Émile Durkheim', in Mauss, *Œuvres*, vol. 3. Paris: Éditions de Minuit, pp. 500–505.

Mauss, Marcel. 1969[1939]. 'Théodule Ribot et les sociologues', in Marcel Mauss, *Œuvres*, vol. 3. Paris: Éditions de Minuit.

Mauss, Marcel. 1979[1920]. 'Introductory note', in Émile Durkheim, 'Introduction to ethics', in *Durkheim: Essays on Morals and Education*, ed. W.F.S. Pickering. London: Routledge, pp. 77–96.

Mauss, Marcel. 1979[1930]. 'L'œuvre de Mauss par lui-même', *Revue française de sociologie* 10/1: 209–220.

Mauss, Marcel. 1997. *Écrits politiques*, ed. Marcel Fournier. Paris: Fayard.

Mauss, Marcel. 1997[1899]. 'L'action socialiste', in *Écrits politiques*, ed. Marcel Fournier. Paris: Fayard, pp. 72–82.

Mauss, Marcel. 1997[1904]. 'La coopération socialiste', in *Écrits politiques*, ed. Marcel Fournier. Paris: Fayard, pp. 142–147.

Mauss, Marcel. 1997[1914]. 'La situation extérieure. Roulements de tambours', in *Écrits politiques*, ed. Marcel Fournier. Paris: Fayard, pp. 222–225.

Mauss, Marcel. 1997[1921]. 'Souvenirs. Conseils de Jean Jaurès pour une révolution russe', in *Écrits politiques*, ed. Marcel Fournier. Paris: Fayard, pp. 434–437.

Mauss, Marcel. 1997[1922]. 'Marcel Sembat. Souvenirs', in *Écrits politiques*, ed. Marcel Fournier. Paris: Fayard.

Mauss, Marcel. 1997[1924] 'Appréciation sociologique du bolchevisme', in *Écrits politiques*, ed. Marcel Fournier. Paris: Fayard.

Mauss, Marcel. 1997[1928]. 'Portraits', in Mauss, *Écrits politiques*, ed. Marcel Fournier. Paris: Fayard.

Mauss, Marcel. 1997[1935]. 'François Simiand', in Mauss, *Écrits politiques*, ed. Marcel Fournier. Paris: Fayard, pp. 754–757.

Mauss, Marcel. 1997[1938]. 'Fait social et formation du caractère', *L'Ethnographie* 93/1–2: 9–14.

Mauss, Marcel. 1997[1939] 'Lucien Lévy-Bruhl (1857–1939)', in Mauss, *Écrits politiques*, ed. Marcel Fournier. Paris: Fayard.

Mauss, Marcel. 2001[1904]. *A General Theory of Magic.* London: Routledge.

Mauss, Marcel and Beuchat, Henri. 1906. 'Essai sur les variations saisonnières des sociétés eskimos', *L'Année sociologique* 9; repr. in *Seasonal Variations of the Eskimo: A Study in Social Morphology*, trans. J.J. Fox. New York: Routledge, 1990.

Mauss, Marcel and Hubert, Henri. 1903. 'Représentations religieuses d'êtres et de phénomènes naturels', *L'Année sociologique* 6.

May, Dick. 1900. 'Le congrès international de l'Enseignement des sciences sociales', *Revue de métaphysique et de morale*.

Mazade, Ch. de. 1880. 'Chronique de la quinzaine', *Revue des deux mondes* 39 (15 June).

Meillet, Antoine. 1903. 'Linguistique', *L'Année sociologique* 6.

Meillet, Antoine. 1906. 'Comment les mots changent de sens', *L'Année sociologique* 9.

Meillet, Antoine. 1913. 'Le langage', *L'Année sociologique* 12.

Mergy, Jennifer. 1998. 'On Durkheim and *Notes critiques*', *Durkheimian Studies/ Études durkheimiennes* 4: 1–7.

Mergy, Jennifer. 2001. 'Nations et nationalismes: Durkheim et les durkheimiens. De la question de l'Alsace-Lorraine à la Société des Nations'. Doctoral thesis, University of Paris-IX Dauphine.

Merllié, Dominique. 1989. 'Lévy-Bruhl et Durkheim. Notes biographiques en marge d'une correspondance', *Revue philosophique* 4: 493–514.

Meštrović, Stjepan G. 1992. *Durkheim and the Postmodern Culture*. New York: Aldine de Gruyter.

Meštrović, Stjepan G. 1988. *Émile Durkheim and the Reformation of Sociology*. Totowa, NJ: Rowman & Littlefield.

Michel, Henry. 2003[1890]. *L'Idée de l'État*. Paris: Fayard. Corpus des œuvres de philosophie en langue française.

Milhaud, Gérard. 1937. 'La pédagogie', in *Les Sciences sociales en France. Enseignement et recherché* (preface by Célestin Bougé). Paris: Centre d'études de politique étrangère.

Milner, Jean-Claude. 2006. *Le Juif de savoir*. Paris: Grasset.

Mitterand, Henri. 2002. *Zola*. Vol. 3: *L'Honneur*. Paris: Fayard.

Montesquieu, 1989[1748]. *The Spirit of the Laws*, trans. and ed. Anne M. Cohler, Basia Carolyn Miller and Harold Samuel Stone. Cambridge: Cambridge University Press.

Mortillet, Gabriel de. 1998[1884] 'Programme', in Laurent Mucchielli, *La Découverte du social. Naissance de la sociologie en France*. Paris: La Découverte.

Mucchielli, Laurent. 1994. 'Durkheim et la révolution des sciences humaines', *La Recherche* 25/268 (Sept): 896–902

Mucchielli, Laurent. 1998. *La Découverte du social. Naissance de la sociologie en France*. Paris: La Découverte.

Muffang, Henri. 1898. 'Histoire d'une idée. L'anthroposociologie', *Revue internationale de sociologie*: 13–14.

Nahon, Gérard. 2003. *Juifs et judaïsme à Bordeaux*. Bordeaux: Molat.

Nandan, Yash. 1980. 'Introduction', in Nandan, ed., *Émile Durkheim: Contributions to L'Année sociologique*. New York: Free Press.

Némedi, D. and Pickering, W.S.F. 1995. 'Durkheim's friendship with the philosopher Octave Hamelin', *British Journal of Sociology* 46/1 (March): 107–125.

Netter, Nathan. 1938. *Vingt siècles d'histoire d'une communauté juive. Metz et son grand passé*. Paris: Librairie Lipschutz.

Nisbet, R.A. 1967. *The Sociological Tradition*. London: Heinemann.

Nizan, Paul. 1981[1932]. *Les Chiens de garde*. Paris: François Maspero.

Nye, R.A. 1983. 'Heredity, pathology and psychoneurosis in Durkheim's early work', *Knowledge and Society: Studies in the Sociology of Culture Past and Present* 4: 102–142.

Ouy, A. 1926. 'René Worms (1869–1926)', *Revue internationale de sociologie*.

Paicheler, Geneviève. 1992. *L'Invention de la psychologie modern*. Paris: L'Harmattan.

Palante, Georges. 1901. 'Les dogmatismes sociaux', *Revue philosophique* 51.

Paoletti, Giovanni. 1992. 'Durkheim à l'École normale supérieure: lectures de jeunesse', *Durkheimian Studies/Études durkheimiennes* 4 (Autumn): 9–21.

Paoletti, Giovanni. 1997. '*L'Année sociologique* et les philosophes: histoire d'un débat (1898–1913), MS (September).

Paoletti, Giovanni. 2005. 'Durkheim, historien de la philosophie', *Revue philosophique* 195/3: 275–301.

Pareto, Vilfredo. 1898. Review of Émile Durkheim, *Le Suicide, Zeitchrift für Sozialwissenschaft* 1: 78–80; repr. in Vilfredo Pareto, *Mythes et ideologies.* Genève-Paris: Droz, 1966, pp. 122–124.

Parodi, Dominique. 1900. Review of Célestin Bouglé, *Les Idées égalitaires: étude sociologique, Revue philosophique* 49: 544–552.

Parodi, Dominique. 1901. Review of Henri Bergson, *Le Rire, Revue de métaphysique et de morale* 9.

Parodi, Dominique. 1902. 'Liberté et égalité', *Revue de métaphysique et de morale* 10.

Parodi, Dominique. 1904a. Review of *Essai sur la solidarité, L'Année sociologique* 7: 386–398.

Parodi, Dominique. 1904b. Review of Gaston Richard, *L'Idée d'évolution dans la nature et l'histoire, L'Année sociologique* 7: 161–166.

Parodi, Dominique. 1905. Review of *Applications sociales de la solidarité, L'Année sociologique* 8: 373–374.

Parodi, Dominique. 1906. Traditionalisme et positivisme', *Revue de synthèse historique* 39 (December): 265–289.

Parodi, Dominique. 1914. 'Sur la défense de l'esprit français. Vl. La France est-elle en décadence?', *Libres Entretiens*, Union pour la vérité 21/8 (July–August): 616–617.

Pederson, Jean Elizabeth. 2007. 'Éducation sexuelle et morale laïque chez Durkheim', in Florence Rochefort ed., *Le Pouvoir du genre. Laïcité et religion 1905–2005.* Toulouse: Presses Universitaires du Mirail, pp. 11–127.

Péguy, Charles. 1902. 'Les récentes œuvres de Zola', *Le Mouvement socialiste* 3.

Péguy, Charles. 1910. 'Victor-Marie, comte Hugo', in Péguy, *Œuvres choisies, 1900–1910.* Paris: Bernard Grasset.

Pénin, M. 1996. 'La *Revue d'économie politique*, ou l'essor d'une grande devancière (1887–1936)', in L. Marco, ed., *Les Revues d'économie en France (1751–1994).* Paris: L'Harmattan.

Pickering, W.S.F. 1979. 'Gaston Richard: collaborateur et adversaire', *Revue française de sociologie* 20/1: 163–182.

Pickering, W.S.F. 1994. 'The enigma of Durkheim's Jewishness', in W.S.F. Pickering and H. Martins, eds., *Debating Durkheim.* London: Routledge.

Pickering, W.S.F. 2003a. 'A lost lecture on honour', *Durkheimian Studies/Études durkheimiennes* 9/1: 5–6.

Pickering, W.S.F. 2003b. 'Durkheim's 1906 election to a chair at the Sorbonne', *Durkheimian Studies/Études durkheimiennes* 9: 3–4.

Pickering, W.S.F. 2006. 'Durkheim's contribution to the debate on the separation of Church and State in 1905', *Durkheimian Studies/Études durkheimiennes* 12.

Pickering, W.S.F. and Martins, H. 1994. *Debating Durkheim.* New York: Routledge.

Pisier-Kouchner, E. (1977). 'La sociologie durkheimienne dans l'œuvre de Duguit', *L'Année sociologique*, 3rd series, 28: 95–114.

Prague, H. 1914. 'La guerre pour le droit', *Archives israélites* 32–34 (27August).

Prochasson, Christophe. 1996. 'Le socialisme', in Lucien Gillard and Rosier (eds.), *François Simiand (1873–1935). Sociologie-Histoire-Économie.* Amsterdam: Éditions des archives contemporaines.

Prochasson, Christophe. 1999. *Paris 1900: Essai d'histoire culturelle.* Paris: Calmann-Lévy.

Prochasson, Christophe and Rasmussen, Anne. 1996. *Au Nom de la patrie. Les intellectuels et la Première Guerre mondiale (1910–1919).* Paris: La Découverte.

Radcliffe-Brown, A.R. 1952. *Structure and Function in Primitive Society.* New York: Free Press.

Rand, E.K. 1904. 'Joseph Trumbull Stickney', *Harvard Graduate Magazine.*

Raphaël, Freddy and Weyl, Robert. 1980. *Regards nouveaux sur les juifs d'Alsace.* Strasbourg: Éditions d'Alsace.

Rappoport, Charles. 1991. *Une Vie de révolutionnaire, 1883–1940.* Paris: Éditions de la Maison des sciences de l'homme.

Ratzel, Friedrich. 1900. 'Le sol, la société et l'état', *L'Année sociologique* 3.

Rauh, Frédéric. 1903. *L'Expérience morale.* Paris: Alcan.

Rauh, Frédéric. 1904. Review of Gaston Richard, *Notions élémentaires de sociologie, Revue de synthèse historique* 9/25 (April).

Rawls, Ann Warfield. 2004. *Epistemology and Practice: Durkheim's The Elementary Forms of Religious Life.* Cambridge: Cambridge University Press.

Reinach, Salomon. 1899. 'La prohibition de l'inceste et ses origines', *L'Anthropologie* 10: 61–69.

Reinach, Salomon. 1903a. Review of Émile Durkheim, 'Sur le totémisme', *L'Anthropologie* 13.

Reinach, Salomon. 1903b. Review of É. Durkheim et M. Mauss, 'De quelques formes primitives de classification', *L'Anthropologie* 13: 601–603.

Relle, O. 1910. Review of Henri Hubert and Marcel Mauss, *Mélanges d'histoire des religions,* in *Le Mois littéraire et pittoresque* (June).

Renan, Ernest. 1990[1882]. 'What is a nation?', trans. Martin Thom in *Nation and Narration,* ed. Homi K. Bhabha. London: Routledge.

Renouvier, Charles. 1874. 'La psychologie de l'homme primitif', *Critique philosophique* 2.

Renouvier, Charles. 1875a. 'Les races ethniques. Les premières conditions du progrès', *Critique philosophique* 2.

Renouvier, Charles. 1875b. 'La religion', *Critique philosophique* 1.

Renouvier, Charles. 1879. 'Les idées primitives et l'origine des religions selon Herbert Spencer', *Critique philosophique* 1.

Renouvier, Charles. 1908. *Science de la morale,* vol. 2, bk 4, rev. edn. Paris: Alcan; orig. pub. 1869.

Renouvier, Charles. 1981[1848] *Manuel républicain de l'homme et du citoyen.* Paris: Garnier Frères.

Réville, Jean. 1905. Review of P.-D. Chantepie de la Saussaye, *Manuel d'histoire des religions, Revue de l'histoire des religions* 51.

Réville, Jean. 1909. *Les Phases successives de l'histoire des religions.* Paris: Leroux.

Reybel, 1904. 'Le socialisme et la question d'Alsace-Lorraine', *La Revue socialiste* 229 (January): 88.

Ribot, Théodule. 1879. *La Psychologie allemande contemporaine.* Paris, Alcan.

Ribot, Théodule. 1897. *L'Évolution des idées generals*. Paris: Alcan.

Ribot, Théodule. 2000[1877]. 'Philosophie et psychologie en France', *Revue d'histoire des sciences humaines* 2: 107–123.

Richard, Gaston. 1895. Review of Enrico Ferri, *L'Omicidio nell'antropologia criminale*, *Revue philosophique* 40: 642–643.

Richard, Gaston. 1898a. 'Avertissement', *L'Année sociologique* I: 392–394.

Richard, Gaston. 1898b. Review of Émile Durkheim, *Le Suicide*, *L'Année sociologique* I: 404–405.

Richard, Gaston. 1900a. 'Les crises sociales et les conditions de la criminalité', *L'Année sociologique* 3.

Richard, Gaston. 1900b. 'La responsabilité et la peine', *L'Année sociologique* 3: 409–411.

Richard, Gaston. 1901a. 'Revue générale. Philosophie du droit et droit économique', *Revue philosophique* 26/52 (February).

Richard, Gaston. 1901b. 'Revue générale. Travaux sociologiques sur le droit de punir', *Revue philosophique* 26/52 (May).

Richard, Gaston. 1902a. Review of Gabriel Tarde, *Psychologie économique*, *Revue philosophique* 54: 640–648.

Richard, Gaston. 1902b. 'Sociologie et science politique', *Revue philosophique* 27/53 (January–June): 300–317, 405–424.

Richard, Gaston. 1905. 'Le conflit de la sociologie et de la morale philosophique', *Revue philosophique* (January).

Richard, Gaston. 1909. *La Femme dans l'histoire. Étude de l'évolution de la condition sociale de la femme*. Paris: O. Doin.

Richard, Gaston. 1930. 'La pathologie sociale de Durkheim', *Revue internationale de sociologie* 38/3–4 (March–April): 114–127.

Richard, Gaston. 1975[1928]. 'L'enseignement de la sociologie à l'École normale primaire', *L'Educateur protestant*, in Émile Durkheim, *Textes*, vol. 1, ed. V. Karady. Paris: Éditions de Minuit, p. 9.

Richter, Melvin. 1960. 'Durkheim's politics and political theory', in K.H. Wolff, ed., *Durkheim, 1858–1917: A Collection of Essays*. New York: Harper Torchbook.

Richter, Melvin. 1969. 'Comparative political analysis in Montesquieu and Tocqueville', *Comparative Politics* 1.

Rose, N. 1985. *The Psychological Complex*. London: Routledge & Kegan Paul.

Roudinesco, Élisabeth. 1986. *Histoire de la psychanalyse en France*, vol. 1. Paris: Le Seuil.

Roudinesco, Élisabeth. 2000. *Dictionnaire de la psychanalyse*. Paris: Fayard.

Saint-Marc, H. 1893. Review of É. Durkheim, *De la division du travail social*, *Revue d'économie politique* 2: 861–870.

Saladin d'Anglure, Bernard. 2004. 'Mauss et l'anthropologie des Inuit', *Sociologie et Sociétés* 36/2 (Autumn): 91–131.

Sand, Shlomo. 1996. 'Georges Sorel', in Jacques Julliard and Michel Winock, eds., *Dictionnaire des intellectuels français*. Paris: Seuil, pp. 1072–1073.

Saunier, Charles. 1923. *Bordeaux*. Paris: Librairie Renouard, H. Laurens.

Schmauss, Warren. 1994. *Durkheim's Philosophy of Science and the Sociology of Knowledge*. Chicago: University of Chicago Press.

Schmauss, Warren. 2001. 'Durkheim's early views on philosophy, hypotheses, and sociology', *Durkheimian Studies/Études durkheimiennes* 7: 9–20.

Schmid, Michael. 2003. 'La réception dans la sociologie allemande', in Philippe Besnard, Massimo Borlandi and Paul Vogt, eds., *Division du travail et lien social. La thèse de Durkheim un siècle après*. Paris: PUF.

Schmoller, Gustav von. 1889. 'La division du travail étudiée du point de vue historique', *Revue d'économie politique* 3.

Schmoller, Gustav von. 1894. Review of É. Durkheim, *De la division du travail social, Jahrbuch für Gesetzgebung* 18: 286–289.

Schopenhauer, Arthur. 1958. *The World as Will and Representation*. Colorado: Falcon Wing.

Schroeder-Gudehus, Brigitte and Rasmussen, Anne. 1993. *Les Fastes du progrès. Le guide des Expositions universelles*. Paris: Flammarion.

Schuhl, Éliane Roos. 1995. *'Patrie et religion'. Le grand rabbin Moïse Schuhl (1845–1922)*. Paris: École pratique des hautes études, section des sciences religieuses.

Schumpeter, J.A. 1996[1914] 'La méthode positive en économie politique', in Lucien Gillard and Rosier, eds., *François Simiand (1873–1935). Sociologie-Histoire-Économie*. Amsterdam: Éditions des archives contemporaines, pp. 137–142.

Séailles, Gabriel. 1917. 'Émile Durckheim', *La Dépêche de Toulouse* (15 December).

Seidman, S. 1983. *Liberalism and the Origins of European Social Theory*. Oxford: Blackwell.

Seigel, Jerrold. 1987. 'Autonomy and personality in Durkheim: an essay on content and method', *Journal of the History of Ideas*: 483–507.

Silverman, Debora. 1977. 'The Paris Exhibition of 1889: architecture and the crisis of individualism', *Oppositions* 8 (spring): 71–91.

Silverman, Debora 1989. *Art Nouveau in Fin-de-siècle France. Politics, Psychology, and Style*. Berkeley: University of California Press.

Simiand, François. 1898. 'L'année sociologique 1897', *Revue de métaphysique et de morale* 6.

Simiand, François. 1902. 'Essai sur le prix du charbon en France et au xixᵉ siècle', *L'Année sociologique* 5: 1–81.

Simiand, François. 1903a. 'Méthode historique et science sociale', *Revue de synthèse historique* 6/16 (February): 1–22.

Simiand, François. 1903b. Review of Gabriel Tarde, *Psychologie économique*, *L'Année sociologique* 6.

Simiand, François. 1907. Review of Paul Mantoux, *La Révolution industrielle au XVIIIe siècle, L'Année sociologique* 10.

Simmel, Georg. 1894. 'Le problème de la sociologie', *Revue de métaphysique et de morale* 2.

Simmel, Georg. 1898. 'Comment les formes sociales se maintiennent', *L'Année sociologique* I.

Simmel, Georg. 1912. 'L'œuvre de Rodin comme expression de l'esprit moderne', in Simmel, *Mélanges de philosophie rélativiste*. Paris: Alcan.

Simon, Pierre-Henri. 1991. *Histoire de la sociologie*. Paris: PUF.

Sirinelli, Jean-François. 1990. *Intellectuels et passions françaises*. Paris: Fayard.

Small, Albion W. 1902. Review of Émile Durkheim, *De la division du travail social*, and of Gabriel Tarde, *Psychologie économique, American Journal of Sociology* 1.

Small, Albion W. 1906. Review of *L'Année sociologique* 8, *American Journal of Sociology* 11.

Sorel, Georges. 1895a. 'Les théories de M. Durkheim', *Le Devenir social* 1: 1–26, 179–180.

Sorel, Georges. 1895b. 'Théories pénales de MM. Durkheim et Tarde', *Archivio di psichiatria, scienze penali ed antropologia criminale* 16: 219.

Sorel, Georges. 1907. '*L'Évolution créatrice*', *Le Mouvement socialiste* (15 October): 257–282.

Sorel, Georges. 1999[1906]. *Reflections on Violence*, ed. Jeremy Jennings. Cambridge: Cambridge University Press.

Soulez, Philippe. 1989. *Bergson politique*. Paris: PUF.

Spencer, Baldwin and Gillen, F.J. 1899. *The Native Tribes of Central Australia*. London: Macmillan & Co.

Spitz, Jean-Fabien. 2005. *Le Moment républicain en France*. Paris: Gallimard.

Stapfer, M. 1887. 'Rapport du doyen de la faculté des lettres', in Académie de Bordeaux, *Comptes-rendus des travaux des facultés de droit, de médecine, des sciences et des lettres*, année académique 1887–8. Bordeaux.

Stapfer, M. 1894. 'Rapport de la faculté des lettres', in Académie de Bordeaux, *Comptes-rendus des travaux des facultés de droit, de médecine, des sciences et des lettres*, année académique 1893–4. Bordeaux.

Steiner, Philippe. 1994. *La Sociologie de Durkheim*. Paris: La Découverte.

Steiner, Philippe. 2005. *L'École durkheimienne et l'économie*. Geneva-Paris: Librairie Droz.

Steinmetz, S.R. 1900. 'Classification des types sociaux et catalogue des peuples', *L'Année sociologique* 3: 43–149.

Stocking, George W. Jr. 1995. *After Tylor. British Social Anthropology, 1888–1951*. Madison: University of Wisconsin Press.

Strenski, Ivan.1997. *Durkheim and the Jews of France*. Chicago: University of Chicago Press.

Tarde, Gabriel. 1884. 'Études sur le socialisme contemporain', *Revue philosophique* 18 (August).

Tarde, Gabriel. 1895[1893]. 'Questions sociales', *Revue philosophique* 35; repr. in Tarde, *Essais et mélanges sociologiques*. Lyon: Storck.

Tarde, Gabriel. 1895a. *Essais et mélanges sociologiques*. Lyon: Storck; Paris: Masson.

Tarde, Gabriel. 1895b. 'Criminalité et santé sociale », *Revue philosophique* 39: 148–162.

Tarde, Gabriel. 1895c. *La Logique sociale*. Paris: Alcan.

Tarde, Gabriel. 1899. 'La sociologie dans l'enseignement secondaire', *Revue internationale de sociologie* 7/10 (October).

Tarde, Gabriel. 1900. 'Leçon d'ouverture d'un cours sur la philosophie moderne', *Revue internationale de sociologie* 8/3 (March).

Tarde, Gabriel. 1901a. 'L'action des faits futurs', *Revue de métaphysique et de morale* 9.

Tarde, Gabriel. 1901b. 'La réalité sociale', *Revue philosophique* 51.

Tarde, Gabriel. 1975[2004]. 'Sociologie et sciences sociales', *Revue internationale de sociologie*, 1904, in Émile Durkheim, *Textes*, vol. 1, ed. V. Karady. Paris: Éditions de Minuit.

Tarde, Gabriel. 2000. 'Contre Durkheim à propos de son *Suicide*', in Massimo Borlandi et Mohamed Cherkaoui (eds.), *Le Suicide, un siècle après Durkheim*. Paris: PUF, pp. 219–255.

Thirard, J. 1976. 'La fondation de la *Revue philosophique*', *Revue philosophique* 166: 401–413.

Tillier, Bertrand. 2004. *Émile Gallé. Le verrier dreyfusard*. Paris: Éditions de l'Amateur.

Tiryakian, A. Edward. 1979. 'L'école durkheimienne à la recherche de la société perdue', *Cahiers internationaux de sociologie* 66: 97–114.

Tönnies, Ferdinand. 1903. 'Mouvement social. L'Allemagne', *Revue internationale de sociologie* 11/8–9 (August–September).

Topolov, Christian. 1999. 'Les faits et les preuves dans les thèses de Maurice Halbwachs', *Revue d'histoire des sciences humaines* (Septembre): 11–47.

Tosti, C. 1898a 'The delusions of Durkheim's sociological objectivism', *The American Journal of Sociology* 4/1: 171–178.

Tosti, C. 1898b. Review of Émile Durkheim, *Le Suicide*, *Psychological Review* 4.

Tosti, C. 1898c. 'Suicide in the light of recent studies', *The American Journal of Sociology* 3/4: 464–471.

Traugott, Mark, ed. 1978. *Émile Durkheim on Institutional Analysis*. Chicago: University of Chicago Press.

Turner, S., ed. 1993. *Émile Durkheim: Sociologist and Moralist*. New York: Routledge, 1993.

Unger, Gérard. 2005. *Aristide Briand. Le ferme conciliateur*. Paris: Fayard.

Van Gennep, Arnold. 1912. 'Andrew Lang, folklorist and critic', *Folk-Lore* 33/3 (September): 366–369.

Van Gennep, Arnold. 1916. 'L'état actuel du problème totémique', *Revue de l'histoire des religions* 38/75.

Vendryes, J. 1937. 'A. Meillet (1866–1936)', *Bulletin de la société de linguistique* 38/112.

Verneau, R.S. 1900. Review of H. Hubert and M. Mauss, 'Essai sur la nature et la fonction du sacrifice', *L'Anthropologie* 2: 106–107.

Verneau, R.S. 1902. 'Nécrologie [Obituary]. Le Dr. Charles Letourneau', *L'Anthropologie* 13: 295–297.

Verneau, René. 1911. 'L'Institut français d'anthropologie', *L'Anthropologie* 22.

Villey, Edmond. 1888. 'Le rapport sur l'administration de la justice criminelle pendant l'année 1886 et la progression de la criminalité', *Revue d'économie politique* 2: 332–333.

Vogüe, Melchior de. 1889. 'À travers l'exposition', *Revue des Deux Mondes* 94.

Watts Miller, W. 1993. 'Durkheim's Montesquieu', *British Journal of Sociology* 44: 693–712.

Watts Miller, W. 1997. 'Durkheim et Montesquieu', *in* Émile Durkheim, *Montesquieu/Quid Secundatus Politicae Scientiae Instituendae Contulerit*. Durkheim Press: Oxford.

Weatherly, Ulysses G. 1917. Review of É. Durkheim, *The Elementary Forms of Religious Life* (1916), *American Journal of Sociology* 22 (May–July): 561–562.

Webster, Hutton. 1913. Review of *Formes élémentaires de la vie religieuse*, *American Journal of Sociology* 18 (May–July): 843–845.

Weil, Francis. 1898. 'La famille Durkheim', *Revue du Cercle de généalogie juive* 46 (Summer).

Weill, Georges. 1910. Review of Maurice Halbwachs, *Les Expropriations et le prix des terrains à Paris*, *Revue de synthèse historique* 20 (August).

Weisz, George. 1976. 'Introductory Note' to 'Émile Durkheim on the French Universities', *Minerva* 14/3 (Autumn): 377–379.

Weisz, George. 1979. 'L'idéologie républicaine et les sciences sociales', *Revue française de sociologie* 10.

Weisz, George. 1983. *The Emergence of Modern Universities in France, 1863–1914*. Princeton: Princeton University Press.

Worms, René. 1893. Review of Émile Durkheim, *La Division du travail social*, *Revue internationale de sociologie* 1.

Worms, René. 1903–7. *Philosophie des sciences sociales*, 3 vols. Paris: M. Giard and E. Brière.

Worms, René. 1903a. 'Après dix ans', *Revue internationale de sociologie* 11 (January).

Worms, René. 1903b. 'Le cinquième congrès de l'Institut international de sociologie', *Revue internationale de sociologie*, 11/8–9 (August–September).

Worms, René. 1917. 'Émile Durkheim', *Revue internationale de sociologie* 25/11–12.

Young, Michael W. 2004. *Malinowski. Odyssey of an Anthropologist, 1884–1920.* New Haven: Yale University Press.

Index